CU00926091

THE BUILDINGS OF SCOTLAND

FOUNDING EDITORS:
NIKOLAUS PEVSNER & COLIN McWILLIAM

BORDERS

KITTY CRUFT, JOHN DUNBAR AND RICHARD FAWCETT

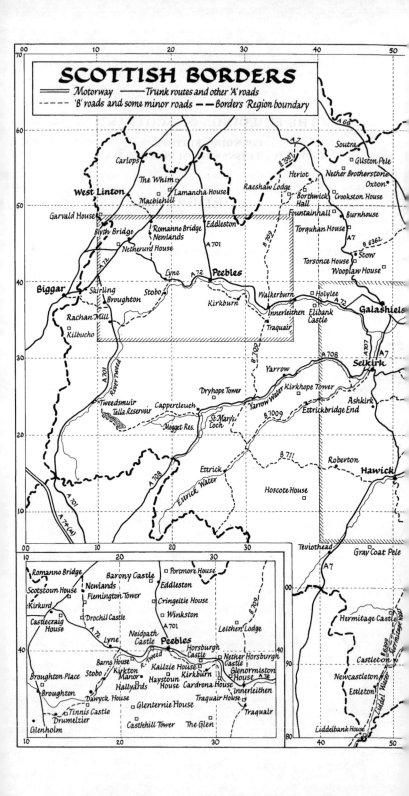

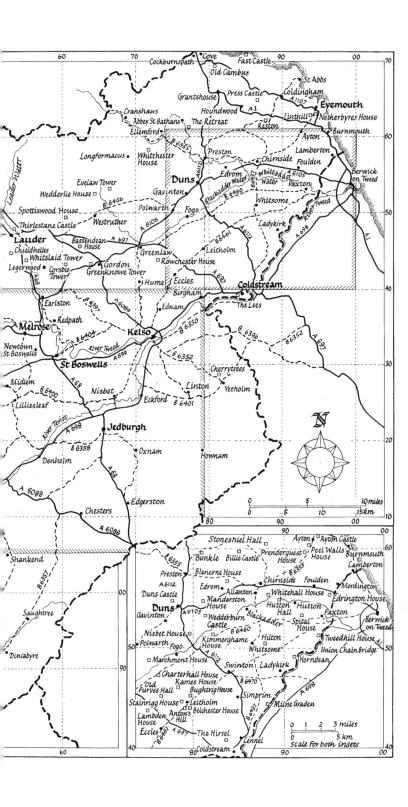

Main map (top):

Cockburnspath Cove Fast Castle
Old Cambus
Grantshouse Press Castle St Abbs Coldingham
Cranshaws Houndwood A1 Eyemouth
Abbey St Bathans The Retreat Reston Linthill Netherbyres House
Ellimford A6112 Ayton Burnmouth
B6355 Preston
Longformacus Whitchester Chirnside Lamberton Foulden
House Duns Edrom Whitadder Water A6105 Berwick on Tweed
Evelaw Tower Gavinton Blackadder Water Paxton
Wedderlie House A6456 Polwarth Fogo B6460 Whitsome River Tweed A698 A1
Spottiswood House B6105 Westruther Ladykirk B6461 A6112
Thirlestane Castle A697
Lauder Bassendean Greenlaw Leitholm
Childhelles House Rowchester House
Whitslaid Tower Gordon Hume Eccles A69
Legerwood A68 Corsbie Greenknowe Tower Birgham Coldstream
Tower
Earlston B6397 A6089 Ednam The Lees B6396 B6352 A697
Melrose Redpath B6404 Kelso B6350
Newtown river Tweed A699 B6352
St Boswells St Boswells Cherrytrees
Midlem B6400 Nisbet Linton Yetholm
Lilliesleaf Eckford B6401
River Teviot A698 Jedburgh
B6358 Oxnam Hownam
Denholm A68
A6088
Chesters Edgerston
A6088
Shankend B6357 Saughtree Dinlabyre

10 miles
5
0 5 10 15 km

Inset map (bottom):

Stoneshiel Hall Ayton Ayton Castle
Prenderguest Peel Walls Burnmouth
Bunkle Billie Castle House House Lamberton
B6355 Blanerne House B6355
Preston Chirnside Foulden Mordington
A6112 Edrom Allanton Whitehall House Edrington House
Duns Castle Manderston Hutton Hutton Paxton
Duns House Hall Berwick
Gavinton A6105 Wedderburn Blackadder Spital on Tweed
Castle B6460 House
Nisbet House Kimmerghame Hilton Tweedhill House
Polwarth Fogo House Whitsome Union Chain Bridge
Marchmont House A6112 Swinton Ladykirk Horndean
Charterhall House Kames House B6470
Old Bughtrig House Simprim A698
Purves Hall Leitholm Milne Graden B6437
Stainrigg House Anton's Belchester House
Lambden Hill B6437
House A697 The Hirsel
Eccles Lennel
Coldstream

0 1 2 3 miles
0 5 km
scale for both insets

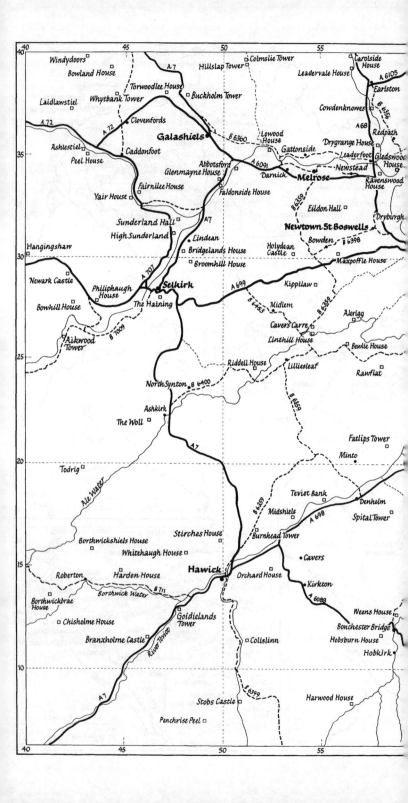

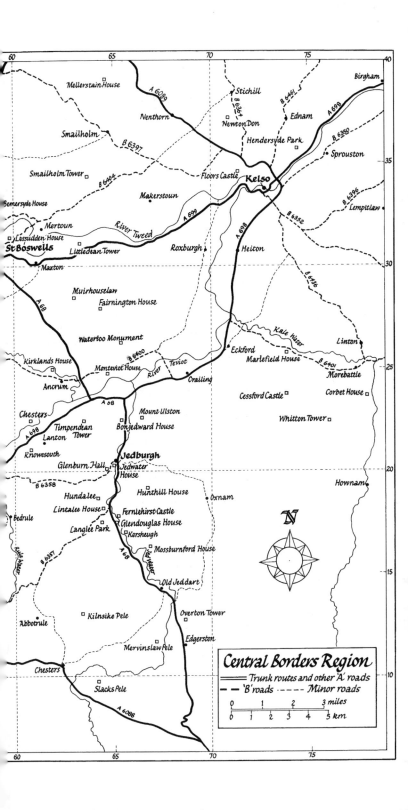

Borders

BY

KITTY CRUFT

JOHN DUNBAR

AND

RICHARD FAWCETT

WITH CONTRIBUTIONS FROM

SABINA STRACHAN

JOHN GIFFORD

AND

IAN GOW

THE BUILDINGS OF SCOTLAND

YALE UNIVERSITY PRESS
NEW HAVEN AND LONDON

YALE UNIVERSITY PRESS
NEW HAVEN AND LONDON
302 Temple Street, New Haven CT 06511
47 Bedford Square, London WC1B 3DP
www.pevsner.co.uk
www.yalebooks.co.uk
www.yalebooks.com

Published by Yale University Press 2006
Reprinted with corrections, 2008
2 4 6 8 10 9 7 5 3

ISBN 0 300 10702 1
ISBN-13 978 0 300 10702 9

Copyright © Kitty Cruft, John Dunbar and
Richard Fawcett 2006

Printed in China
through World Print
Set in Monotype Plantin

For Borderers,
past and present

ACCESS TO BUILDINGS

Many of the buildings described in this book are public places, and in some obvious cases their interiors (at least the public sections of them) can be seen without formality. But it must be emphasised that the mention of buildings or lands does not imply any rights of public access to them, or the existence of any arrangements for visiting them.

Some churches are open within regular hours, and it is usually possible to see the interiors of others by arrangement with the minister or church officer. Particulars of admission to Ancient Monuments and other buildings in the care of Scottish Ministers (free to the Friends of Historic Scotland) are available from Historic Scotland, Longmore House, Salisbury Place, Edinburgh EH9 ISH or its website, www.historic-scotland.gov.uk. Details of access to properties of the National Trust for Scotland are available from the Trust's head office at 5 Charlotte Square, Edinburgh EH2 4DU or via its website, www.nts.org.uk. Admission is free to members, on whose subscriptions and donations the Trust's work depends.

Scotland's Gardens Scheme, 22 Rutland Square, Edinburgh, EH1 2BB, provides a list of gardens open to visitors, also available on the National Gardens Scheme website, www.ngs.org.uk. Scotland's Churches Scheme, Dunedin, Holehouse Road, Eaglesham, Glasgow G76 0JF, publishes an annual directory of churches open to visitors while *Hudson's Historic Houses, Castles and Gardens Open to the Public* includes many private houses.

Local Tourist Offices can advise the visitor on what properties in each area are open to the public and will usually give helpful directions as to how to get to them.

CONTENTS

LIST OF TEXT FIGURES AND MAPS

MAPS

MAP REFERENCES

The numbers printed in the margin against the place names in the gazetteer indicate the position of the place in question on the area map (pages ii–v), which are divided into sections by the 10-kilometre reference lines of the National Grid. The reference given here omits the two initial letters (formerly numbers), which in a full grid reference refer to the 100-kilometre squares into which the county is divided. The first two numbers indicate the western boundary, and the last two the southern boundary, of the 10-kilometre square in which the place is situated. For example, Coldstream, reference 8030, will be found in the 10-kilometre square bounded by grid lines 80 (on the *west*) and 90, and 30 (on the *south*) and 40; Bowhill House, reference 4020, in the square bounded by grid lines 40 (on the *west*) and 50, and 20 (on the *south*) and 30.

ACKNOWLEDGEMENTS
FOR THE PLATES

Royal Commission on the Ancient and Historical Monuments of Scotland The authors are deeply indebted to the photographers of the Royal Commission on the Ancient and Historical Monuments of Scotland (RCAHMS) who took the majority of the colour photos specially for this volume. Photographs are copyright of the RCAHMS with the exception of the following:

Country Life: 50
John Haddington: 60
Historic Scotland: 1, 3, 5, 6, 7, 8, 9, 41
Tony Kersting: 40, 49, 61, 63
Courtesy of Lord Palmer: 77
Scottish Borders Council: 4
Thames and Hudson: 2

The plates are indexed in the indexes of names and places, and references to them are given by numbers in the margin of the text.

FOREWORD

Borders is the ninth volume of the Buildings of Scotland series, covering the former counties of Berwickshire, Peeblesshire, Roxburghshire and Selkirkshire. The authors have divided responsibility for the gazetteer mainly along subject lines, Richard Fawcett having dealt with the majority of churches and other ecclesiastical monuments, John Dunbar with castles and other secular buildings earlier than *c.* 1700 and Kitty Cruft with later secular buildings, including country houses. However, in some western parts of the region, notably around West Linton, Broughton and Tweedsmuir, John Dunbar has covered most buildings other than churches. Richard Fawcett wrote the entries for the villages of Abbey St Bathans and Cranshaws, and also The Retreat. The entries for the burghs of Galashiels, Hawick, Jedburgh and Selkirk have been contributed by Sabina Strachan, and for the burghs of Coldstream, Duns and Eyemouth by John Gifford, The Building of Scotland Trust's Head of Research. Ian Gow has written the Abbotsford entry. To all three the authors are deeply grateful, as also to Stratford Halliday, who contributed the accounts of prehistoric and Roman monuments to the gazetteer, together with the associated section of the introduction, and to Andrew McMillan who provided the accounts of topography, geology and building stones for the introduction. In compiling the remainder of the introduction the authors have adopted a similar division of labour as for the gazetteer. The account of the textile industry in the industrial buildings section, however, has been contributed by Sabina Strachan. So there has been a great deal of collaboration, and in nearly every case authors and contributors have taken the opportunity to comment upon one another's drafts – always to mutual benefit. In addition the entire text has been read by Mary Cosh and John Gifford, whose kindly but searching gaze has enabled many mistakes and inconsistencies to be corrected. Inevitably, some errors and omissions will remain and the authors would be grateful to be notified of these.

For the series as a whole John Gifford extracted some thirty years ago all Scottish references from C19 and C20 architectural periodicals. Arrangement of these notes by individual buildings grouped within parishes was undertaken for this volume by Yvonne Hillyard, who also greatly supplemented these notes with information extracted from such sources as the various Statistical Accounts of Scotland, C19 gazetteers, local histories and guidebooks. Otherwise the authors and contributors have for the most part conducted their own research, a task that would have been quite impossible without the support of the staffs of numerous institutions both national and local, notably Edinburgh

Central Public Library, Edinburgh University Library, HBOS, Historic Scotland, the C.E. Kempe Society, the National Archives of Scotland, the National Library of Scotland, the National Museums of Scotland, the RIBA Drawings Collection, the Royal Bank of Scotland and Scottish Power. At the Royal Commission on the Ancient and Historical Monuments of Scotland particular thanks are due to Angus Lamb and his fellow photographers for the many colour photographs taken specially for this volume, as also to Diane Watters and her colleagues in the National Monuments Record of Scotland for processing this material and supplementing it with other illustrations from the Commission's collections. Within Scottish Borders Region a great deal of help has been forthcoming from the Council's Department of Economic Development and Environmental Planning (Archaeology and Countryside Section) and Department of Education and Lifelong Learning (Public Libraries at Duns, Kelso, Melrose and Peebles, Scottish Borders Archives, Selkirk, and Borders Regional Council Museum Service). The Arts and Humanities Research Board kindly provided funding for the period of research leave during which Richard Fawcett's accounts of churches were largely prepared. Special thanks are due to Historic Scotland and The Buildings of Scotland Trust for funding Sabina Strachan's contributions to this volume. The authors are grateful to The Buildings of Scotland Trust for meeting their travelling costs.

Information on individual buildings has been provided by Scottish Borders planning and building control staff and by numerous architects, including Andrew Davey, Tony Dixon, William Grime, Neil Hynd, Philip Mercer, the late Frank Scott, James Simpson, David Warren and Crichton Wood. Many archaeologists, archivists and historians have also given freely of their time and expertise, including David Breeze, Iain Brown, Neil Brown, Piers Dixon, Margaret Fox, Donald Gordon, Alastair Maxwell-Irving, Audrey Mitchell, Susan Oakes, Miles Oglethorpe, the late Isabelle Paterson, Ted Ruddock, Bill Scott, David Walker and Mark Watson. But the authors' greatest debt must be to the owners, occupiers and custodians of the hundreds of buildings visited during the course of survey. Too numerous to name individually, they invariably offered a courteous welcome, understanding and freedom of access, even to those parts that other visitors seldom reach. Not infrequently they also came up with valuable new information or suggestions as to other building in the locality that might be worth visiting. In some cases they also went out of their way to provide special facilities or offer access to private papers not otherwise available for research, special thanks in these respects being due to the Duke of Buccleuch, the Earl Haig, the Earl of Home, Catherine and Flora Maxwell-Stuart, Lady Brigid McEwen and the Administrator of the Sue Ryder Foundation, Marchmont House, Lord Polwarth and the late Duke of Sutherland.

At Penguin Books, where the series was originally undertaken, the editors were Elizabeth Williamson and Bridget Cherry, while since 2001 the volume has been edited for Yale University Press by Charles O'Brien. All have shown tact, patience and good humour in master-minding what proved to be an unexpectedly lengthy production process. Bernard Dod has acted as Copy Editor and Pat Taylor Chalmers as Proof Reader. Among the Yale team the coordination of the text has been undertaken by Emily Winter, Managing Editor. Illustrations were commissioned and co-ordinated by Emily Rawlinson and her successor Emily Lees, general area maps were drawn up by Reg and Marjorie Piggott and town plans and plans of buildings by Alan Fagan. The index of Artists was prepared by John Gifford and the indexes of Patrons and Places by Judith Wardman.

In Scottish Borders, as in preceding volumes in the series, certain general policies have been adopted. The format remains that established by Sir Nikolaus Pevsner in *The Buildings of England*, but with some Scottish quirks. Almost all churches and public buildings are included as a matter of course, as are buildings, especially in towns and villages, which, whatever their architectural quality, are too conspicuous to be entirely ignored. With some minor buildings, such as late Georgian farmhouses, those which are in or immediately next to a village have been mentioned but isolated examples have been left out. The more important rural buildings such as castles and country houses have individual entries in the gazetteer. An entry in brackets shows that the building has not, for whatever reason, been personally visited. The inclusion of archaeological sites has had to be selective.

INTRODUCTION

It was Sir Walter Scott, more than anyone else, who shaped the identity of the Borders. Before his day the region was viewed, at least by outsiders, chiefly as a frontier zone. Through it, in medieval times, English armies marched N to Stirling and Edinburgh, followed during the C18 by tourists interested only in discovering the Highlands. Southwards, in 1603, James VI hurried by on his way to claim the English throne, followed down the years by an increasing number of Scotsmen seeking fame and fortune in London. Scott perceived, what its inhabitants had always known, that the region had a will and character of its own and that on most issues Borderers, whether Scots or English, had more in common with one another than with policy makers in Edinburgh or London.

The commonality of history and culture that Scott stressed in writings such as *Minstrelsy of the Scottish Border* (1802–3) and *Border Antiquities* (1814) extends in some measure both to landscape and to architecture. Scottish Borders, like Northumberland, has a varied topography embracing wide expanses of windswept upland as well as wooded valleys and stretches of fertile river plain. But the absence of any city or large town, coupled with the low density of population (today about 107,000 inhabitants in about 1820 sq. miles), gives the region a predominantly rural quality to which architecture must respond. This it has successfully done, at least until the later C20, thanks partly to the use of local building materials and partly to successive generations of improving proprietors who created an ideal landscape for the realisation of Scott's vision. Today, as this volume seeks to demonstrate, the Borders contain an impressive array of interesting and significant buildings of many kinds and of all periods up to the present. But what rightly attract the visitor first and foremost are the ruined abbeys and castles, historic churches, baronial mansions and traditional rural buildings that Scott made his own.

TOPOGRAPHY, GEOLOGY AND BUILDING STONES
by Andrew A. McMillan

The landscape of the Scottish Borders is a richly varied one from the turf-covered, steep-sided hills and wide valley floors of the Southern Uplands and Cheviot Hills to the expansive, undulating, low-lying ground of the Berwickshire Merse. The spectacular cliff scenery of the Berwickshire coast forms the eastern

Geological System	Age in millions of years	General distribution	Quarries and pits	Typical Scottish building stone types
QUATERNARY	2 to present	Alluvial and glacial deposits in the valleys	Clays worked for brick and tiles at Linthill, Berwickshire and Carlops, Peeblesshire	Various glacially-derived materials, both of local and far-travelled origin
TERTIARY	65–2	Scattered Tertiary dykes		Basaltic andesite
TRIASSIC	250–200	Annan Basin	Corsehill	Red fluvial sandstone
PERMIAN	300–250	Dumfries Basin Thornhill Basin Lochmaben Basin	Locharbriggs Gatelawbridge, Closeburn Corncockle	Red desert dune sandstone
CARBONIFEROUS	360–300	Berwickshire	Swinton, Whitsome Newton Formerly worked at Sprouston, Hendersyde, Mellendean Deepsykehead	Ballagan Formation Sandstone, thin limestone, mudstone
		Peeblesshire		Lower Limestone Formation (Midland Valley)
		Kelso district	Local crags worked (e.g. Smailholm)	Kelso Volcanic Formation: Basalt lavas volcanic vent rocks including trachytes and agglomerates
		Melrose	Chiefswood	
DEVONIAN	415–360	Roxburghshire, Lauderdale	Ancient workings of Ploughlands, Hundalee, Ferniehirst, Ulston Moor	Variably coloured, pink, buff and yellow sandstone; thinly bedded material used for paving and roofing
		Peeblesshire	Blyth Muir Broomieleas	
		St Abbs and the Cheviot Hills		Andesite lavas and other igneous rocks generally poor sources of building stone
SILURIAN	443–415	Ettrick Forest, Moffat,	Interleithen, Stobo ('slate' quarries)	Greywacke ('whin') used extensively as rubble, siltstone locally used as stone 'slate'
ORDOVICIAN	490–443	Moorfoot and Lammermuir Hills of the Southern Uplands		

Geological timescale and distribution
of rock types used in the Borders as building stone

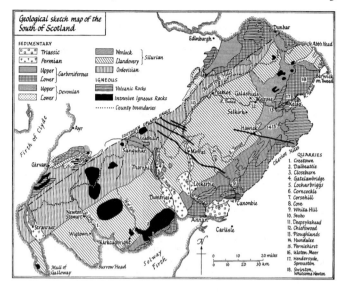

boundary of the district – an abrupt challenge to the easterly-derived storms of the North Sea. The Borders form the eastern extension of the Southern Uplands; that part stretching NE from Hart Fell, White Coomb (822 m.), Broad Law (840 m.) and Dollar Law (817 m.), N of Moffat (Dumfries and Galloway), to the coast, comprises rounded hills of rough pasture and glaciated U-shaped valleys. The Moorfoot Hills (Windlestraw Law, 659 m.) and Lammermuir Hills (Meikle Says Law, 535 m.) form the northern border of the region, while the southern boundary is dominated by the Cheviot uplands, the eroded remnants of a major 400-million-year-old volcanic centre. In the SW, the tortuous boundary with Dumfries and Galloway extends SE from the Moffat area over the high ground of Eskdalemuir Forest into Liddesdale and the English border. Much of this ground is currently afforested. The River Tweed rises in Tweedsmuir to the N of Moffat and flows NNE to Peebles then ESE to Melrose and Kelso before turning NE to Berwick. Southern tributaries include the Yarrow Water, which rises from St Mary's Loch and flows through Selkirk, and the River Teviot, which rises SW of Hawick and joins the Tweed at Kelso. Northerly tributaries include the Gala Water, which rises in the Moorfoot Hills and flows southwards to meet the Tweed at Galashiels, and the Leader Water, which rises in the Lammermuir Hills and flows southwards through Lauder and Earlston to the Tweed near Melrose. E of Kelso the River Tweed flows through the fertile cultivated lowlands of the Merse and is fed E of Coldstream by the Northumbrian River Till. Near

Berwick the Tweed is joined by the Whiteadder Water, which
drains the northern part of the Merse from Greenlaw, Duns and
Chirnside. The principal villages and towns of the Borders developed on the valley floors of the Tweed and its tributaries. In the
upland areas isolated farms, towers and historical buildings form
an integral part of this varied and attractive landscape. As in other
parts of Scotland, the building materials and architecture of the
villages and towns of the Scottish Borders are strongly influenced
by the local geology and the natural landscape.

Geology

The oldest rocks of the eastern Southern Uplands of the
Scottish Borders were formed from sediments deposited on
the floor of the long-vanished Iapetus Ocean. They belong to the
ORDOVICIAN and SILURIAN periods of the sub-era known as
the Early Palaeozoic (490–415 million years ago). The continents
surrounding the ocean started to collide around 440 million
years ago, and the rocks were compressed, tightly folded, faulted
and stacked against each other. Out of this collision a new landmass, the Southern Uplands, was formed. In the Southern
Uplands the folded strata mainly lie vertical or at steeply dipping
angles, and the spectacular cliffs around Fast Castle on the coast
give a good impression of the scale of folding of these rocks. The
principal rock type is greywacke, a form of compact, hard, dark
grey sandstone composed of mineral and rock fragments.

The succeeding period of time is known as the DEVONIAN
(415–360 million years ago). During Early Devonian time a significant period of land uplift and erosion resulted in the deposition of coarse-grained river gravel deposits, remnants of which
are now seen in the form of conglomerates, which in the Borders
are referred to as the 'Great Conglomerate' and occupy large
tracts of ground (*c.* 200 sq. km.) in Lauderdale, in particular the
Leader Water Valley around Lauder and Earlston. Contemporary
volcanic activity generated the predominantly andesitic lavas of
St Abb's Head and the Cheviot Hills, where an intrusive body of
granite beneath the lavas forced the landmass into a dome. Following a further period of erosion, Late Devonian red sandstones
were laid down, and at Siccar Point on the coast and at Jedburgh
we now see the angular unconformity between the hard, vertically bedded greywackes and the softer, near-horizontally bedded
red sandstones. These world-famous localities were discovered by
James Hutton (1726–97), who realised the significance of the
unconformity in terms of the immense periods of time during
which the geological cycle of sedimentation, burial and folding,
land uplift and erosion was repeated.

The transition between the Devonian strata and those of the
succeeding CARBONIFEROUS (360–300 million years ago) is best
seen at Pease Bay, N of Siccar Point, where the red beds pass
upwards imperceptibly and without a break from one geological
system to the next. However, at Cove the succession changes
upwards, and the presence of mudstones and thin limestones
with marine fossils heralds a change. S of the Lammermuir Hills
and particularly well developed in the Merse district is a

sequence of rocks, now referred to as the Ballagan Formation, comprising thin impure limestones (dolomites), interbedded with siltstones and sandstones. Higher in the succession thick pale-coloured fluvial sandstones are developed in the form of the Fell Sandstone Formation, especially in the Newcastleton area over the Larriston Fells. Younger Carboniferous strata are of marine origin, as indicated by some of the limestone-dominated sequences well exposed on the coast around Berwick.

All of the Carboniferous rocks in Berwickshire and Rox-burghshire lie on the northern margin of a regionally significant basin, the Northumberland Trough, which had started to develop in response to a major period of fault rifting. Early in this fault-ing episode, extensive basaltic lavas were extruded onto the land surface. These basalts are referred to as the Kelso Volcanic For-mation and, further W, as the Birrenswark Volcanic Formation. Numerous volcanic vents of a range of rock compositions are attributed to this period and these now form prominent small hills such as the Eildon Hills (trachytes and felsites), Smailholm (dolerite), Dirrington Laws (felsite), Dunion Hill and Rubers Law (dolerite). The Minto Hills are formed of vent agglomerates which are also well seen at the Chiefswood quarries, a source of building stone for nearby Melrose.

The present-day landscape was formed in the period between the Carboniferous and the Quaternary Ice Age, which com-menced some two million years ago. Late Carboniferous rocks are not present in the Borders, nor are the bright red sandstones formed in the arid, desert conditions of the Permian period (300–250 million years ago) or the red fluvial sandstones of the Triassic period (250–200 million years ago) which occur in Dum-friesshire. A few dykes (thin elongate bodies of igneous rock injected when molten into the Earth's upper crust) of Tertiary age are representatives of the major volcanic episode which was responsible for the formation of the igneous centres of western Scotland such as the islands of Arran, Mull, Rum and Skye. During the Quaternary period, the development of the present drainage system was affected by glacial processes which left their legacy in deposits of glacial tills and glaciofluvial sands and gravels and lake clays, particularly within the major valleys. In places, dry valleys are seen, the product of erosion by meltwater channels as the ice sheets dispersed. In post-glacial times (post-12,000 years ago) peat developed on hillsides and lower flats and alluvial gravels accumulated on the river floodplains.

Building stones

Before the C19, the principal building material, apart from timber, was STONE. This was extracted from the most easily exploited sites. Much of this material was used with little if any further dressing to form random rubble walls. Stone gathered manually from the land as part of field clearance work during the late C18 and early C19 was set aside to make for easier use of ploughs and other equipment. In the Lowlands, early C18 buildings used these glacially rounded, weathered sandstones and igneous rocks with thick mortar beds and pinnings to course the wall's construction. In the Southern Uplands mainly hard greywacke sandstones were used. Their irregular fracture, resulting in variable shape and size, demanded skilled mason work.

In areas where suitable rock cropped out, small quarries were developed and stone became established as the local building material. Local stone was extracted not only for domestic and farm use but also for larger buildings, such as castles. The relatively small dimensions of locally available stones dictated that walls were mainly constructed with small openings, a feature suited for the purpose of defence, with large blocks of dressed stone often imported for use as lintels and corbels to span wider window and door openings. The form, colour and design of a building were therefore determined by the use of geologically different stones. Stones used for tombstones and slabs, crosses and effigies also utilised local stone of sedimentary origin, such as sandstones that could be easily worked and sculpted. As the needs of man increased and villages and towns grew from early settlements so the requirement for building materials increased. In the centuries before mechanised transport it was costly to transport large quantities of building materials over large distances. Many local sources, however, yielded abundant, good-quality stone. Typically in towns and villages along the course of the River Tweed, local greywacke was used with softer, more easily worked pale yellow sandstones as quoins and sills. Good-quality sandstone suitable for these purposes is present within the Devonian and Carboniferous strata of the eastern Borders.

With the development of the canal and railway networks, stone from further afield was used. Towards the end of the C19 and especially with the expansion of the railway network, red sandstone from Dumfriesshire and Lanarkshire became very popular. The opening of the railways (Peebles–Edinburgh, 1855; Peebles–Glasgow, 1864) also enabled exploitation of sources of good-quality pale-coloured Carboniferous sandstone from the Midland Valley of Scotland. As local supplies became depleted, stone began to be imported from northern England. The use of natural stone declined after the First World War as brick and concrete started to gain the ascendancy. In the last thirty years this decline has, to some extent, been reversed with the recognition that, used appropriately, the natural product is not only aesthetically more pleasing but also more durable, and enables architects to build on the unique character of each town.

Greywackes, often locally and colloquially referred to as WHINSTONE or whin (a term which has also in the past been employed geologically for hard rocks of igneous origin) are typically hard, grey to grey-brown sandstones composed of rock and mineral grains. Hard to work and to dress, and possessing a characteristic irregular fracture, typically they were used as roughly hewn blocks as rubblework for many Borders towns, villages and farms. For example, two quarries, known as the 'Town' and 'Gentlemen's' quarries, supplied Selkirk's needs in the mid C19. As the main indigenous material they were extensively employed for stone dykes in many parts of the district.

In Peeblesshire, Early Devonian red SANDSTONE was available from a number of sources. The old quarries at Blyth Muir may have supplied stone for the principal buildings of the Roman Antonine fort at Lyne, and similar stone was quarried from Broomlee Hill, where the late C18 *Statistical Account of Scotland* records that 'Broomieleas' supplied all Tweeddale with red free-stone for pavement slabs. Quarrying at Broomieleas probably extended back to the C16 and its red sandstone may have been used at Drochil Castle.

Late Devonian sandstones, found in Liddesdale and in the Jed-burgh and the Melrose districts, have a range of colours from pinkish grey to red brown, and are composed predominantly of quartz grains. They have been used to good effect in these areas including the abbeys at Melrose, Dryburgh and Jedburgh. Quar-ries at Ploughlands, 1 km. SE of Melrose, are said by several authorities to have supplied stone for both Melrose and Dry-burgh abbeys. At Ploughlands today exposures reveal bright red, pink and purplish, cross-bedded and massive sandstone, partly flaggy (thin-bedded). At Dryburgh a pale pinkish grey, cross-bedded sandstone predominates. Numerous local quarries sup-plied Jedburgh Abbey including Hundalee, Tudhope, Ferniehirst and Ulston Moor. A range of yellow, buff and dark red sand-stones has been used. The quarries at Ancrum and Ferniehirst supplied both red and white sandstone freestone in the district, and Ferniehirst was used in Jedburgh Castle. Denholmhill, near Hawick, supplied white sandstone for the former Melrose Railway Station. Red sandstone was used from Cairba Hill, New-castleton, for the Free Church there. Devonian sandstones are seen to good effect in the village of Earlston where buff colours predominate. Pink sandstone is also seen in window surrounds to its greywacke-constructed library (1856). Late Devonian sand-stones of Eastern Berwickshire were also used as a prime build-ing source. Coldingham Priory, restored in the 1850s, beautifully displays pale pink and yellow cross-bedded sandstones of local provenance.

Early Carboniferous rocks form an important resource of building stone in Berwickshire and in the Langholm district of neighbouring Dumfriesshire. Generally softer than greywackes, both the Devonian and Carboniferous rocks are more amenable to being worked and dressed. Thick, massive beds, used in con-junction with harder rubble stone in a building, were a prime source of freestone and were most frequently used as dressed blocks for quoins and for windows and lintels. Over many years quarries around Swinton and Whitsome Newton have supplied good-quality sandstones of the Ballagan Formation (earliest Car-boniferous). The stone is of varying hue and has been widely used in local buildings, as well as being exported to cities such as Edin-burgh. Local sandstones of the Ballagan Formation were also used in Coldstream and Kelso. Stone was also worked from this formation at several quarries for local purposes, including Eccles, Lees and Lennel near Coldstream. Sprouston Quarry supplied the pale grey to buff and yellowish sandstone for Kelso Abbey and Kelso Bridge. The abbey may also have been supplied by the local quarries of Hendersyde and Mellendean, stone from which was also used with sandstone from Longannet (Stirlingshire) at Thirlestane Castle. Pink sandstone dressings for Thirlestane came from Dean Brae quarry (Late Devonian) at Bassendean.

Pale yellow colours predominate in buildings of The Hirsel and in the older town houses of Coldstream.

Within the Ballagan Formation a notable source of white brecciated dolomitic LIMESTONE known as Carham Stone was extensively quarried S of the River Tweed just E of Kelso. This stone and other associated limestones were used extensively in the district both as a construction material and as a source of lime. Clarabad Quarry, near Paxton, supplied sandstone for Hutton Church. At Duns, both yellow and bright red sandstones of the Ballagan Formation have been employed in town houses and churches. At Langholm, the off-white to pale orange Whita Sandstone of the Ballagan Formation was quarried at several localities for local use, and was used for the construction of the Episcopal Church in Hawick in 1858. It was also used as a monumental stone, for example in the monument to James Hogg (1860) on the shore of St Mary's Loch (Cappercleuch). Stratigraphically higher sandstones of the Fell Sandstone Formation were also extensively used. On the Scottish side of the Border quarries worked sandstones in the Larriston district. In Northumberland, sandstone quarries at Doddington and Otterburn also supplied the Scottish Borders with Carboniferous sandstone. Pinkish Doddington stone was used at Kelso Abbey for the Roxburghe Memorial Cloister. N of the Southern Upland Fault in the West Linton district, both limestone and sandstone of Early Carboniferous age were extensively quarried between Whitfield and Deepsykehead. Similar strata were worked near Spitalhaugh. By the 1850s Deepsykehead was the largest freestone quarry in Peeblesshire, supplying dressed white sandstone throughout the county. The Glen, S of Traquair, was built of this stone.

The influence of PERMIAN RED SANDSTONES is also seen in the district. These sandstones are distinctive in their bright red colour, coarse grain and bedding. During the late C19 they became popular sources of stone, particularly from the Dumfriesshire basins of Lochmaben (Corncockle Quarry), Dumfries (Locharbriggs Quarry) and Thornhill (Gatelawbridge and Closeburn quarries). The stone was often used as dressing in both quoins and windows in greywacke constructions. Throughout the Borders many towns (e.g. Peebles, Galashiels) display the use of greywacke with red sandstone dressings. Cranshaws Church (reconstructed 1898) is an example where the hard grey greywacke is enlivened by red sandstone of presumed Dumfriesshire origin for arches and windows. Red sandstones have often been used for entire buildings, such as some of the more prestigious buildings in the market towns. The fine-grained red to red-brown sandstone of Corsehill, Annan, was also employed in the Borders district.

IGNEOUS ROCKS tended not to make good dressable building stone; the Cheviot igneous rocks seem to have been unsuitable because of their close jointing. A notable exception is the use of pitchstone andesite from Thomson's Walls (just across the Border) in the building of Yetholm Church. The Eildon Hills are remnants of Early Carboniferous trachyte and felsite intrusions. The Chiefswood Vent is an associated, but slightly later volcanic feature, c. 2.3 km. across and forming a grassy hill SW of Melrose.

The Chiefswood Quarry exposes tuff and agglomerate composed of very poorly sorted blocks (up to 25 cm.) and smaller fragments of mainly greywacke with some trachyte fragments. As the tuff consolidated in a volcanic vent it acquired a good near-vertical jointing and as a consequence it was worked extensively for use in both Melrose Abbey and other buildings in and around Melrose. Early buildings at the abbey (e.g. the C12 cloister) employed orange or greenish-grey, variably weathered agglomerate. Agglomerate also forms the foundations just w of the nave to the main abbey and also the early C13 expansion (e.g. the N part of the cellarium, which also employs red sandstone and red trachyte). Around Kelso, there are extensive tracts of Late Devonian/Early Carboniferous basalt lavas (the Kelso Volcanic Formation), which tend to weather badly, although hard-weathering dolerites have been employed locally to very good effect. Examples include Smailholm Tower, constructed of black intrusive basalt with red sandstone window and door dressings. Like nearby Hume Castle, Smailholm stands on a basaltic plug, which because of its resistance to erosion forms the high ground and provides a strong building material. Many of the buildings in the main street of the village of Gordon are constructed of squared rubble of black basalt. Exotic igneous rocks were often employed for C19 and C20 tombstones. Notable examples include the use of pink Peterhead (Aberdeenshire) Granite for the tomb of Sir Walter Scott in Dryburgh Abbey. Today foreign crystalline igneous and metamorphic rocks make their incongruous appearance in most sizeable towns in the form of polished cladding on commercial buildings.

Most early buildings would have had roofs of different types of thatch (straw, reed, heather, turf, etc.) and this was still in use into the early C19. Kirk Yetholm church was thatched in 1836, reputedly the last of its kind in Scotland, and now rare domestic examples survive in the town and at Polwarth and Earlston. Shales of Lower Palaeozoic age (interbedded with greywacke) are capable of being cleaved and provided buildings of the C17 and C18 with a form of stone 'SLATE'. Quarries at Stobo and Grieston in Peeblesshire were once cited as 'the best sources of slate and scaillie' in Tweeddale, and Stobo Quarry was probably working before the C18. The shale 'slates' are of Ordovician age and of blue-black hue. A fine example of their use is at Altarstone Farm, below the quarry, where courses are laid in diminishing size up the roof. Grieston Hill Quarry was opened up in the C17 to produce grey-green shale 'slates' of Silurian age, and provided the slatework at Traquair House, Nether Horsburgh Castle and the churches of Traquair and Innerleithen. This indigenous industry was effectively killed off in the C19, when the development of the railway network saw large quantities of true slate imported from northern England and Wales. Selkirkshire, in particular, used Welsh blue slates.

From the end of the C18 pantiles provided an alternative roofing material, and became popular in Berwickshire and East Lothian especially for cottages, barns, byres and mills. These were made from abundant sources of CLAY from glacial tills and lake sediments accumulated during and following deglaciation. This clay was also suitable for BRICKS, and throughout Berwickshire and Roxburghshire many chimneys were built or rebuilt of brick. Yet there appear to be very few documented brick and tile works in Berwickshire. A brick and tile works was recorded at Linthill on the banks of the Ale Water and on either side of the Whiteadder Water, near the site of Edrington Castle, E of Paxton. Here a fine reddish lake clay was used. A number of small commercial brickworks operated in the region during the C19 and early C20. In Peeblesshire clay was dug at brick and tile works at Upper Whitfield during the early C19 and at Paxton can be seen the remains of continuous 'Newcastle' kilns of the 1880s.

QUARRYING, and other extractive industries, have left little in the way of standing buildings. The freestone quarries at Deepsykehead, near Carlops, retain an early C19 manager's house and some fragments of workshops. COAL AND LIMESTONE were mined in the same area and several limekilns survive, including a double kiln of C19 date situated within sight of the Deepsykehead quarries.

PREHISTORIC AND ROMAN BORDERS
by Stratford Halliday

The earliest recognisable architectural monuments in the Border landscape were constructed about six thousand years ago, erected by the first farming communities during the NEOLITHIC period. These are by no means the earliest traces of man in the Southern Uplands, but this was the first occasion upon which communities expressed their identity with large public monuments, most of them apparently bound up with funerary rituals and religion. The most enduring aspect of Neolithic settlement throughout the British Isles has proved to be the earthen BARROWS or stone CAIRNS that were raised over communal burial chambers. In the western and northern parts of Scotland these chambers are constructed of large upright slabs and drystone masonry, with massive capstones or corbelled roofs, and narrow passages approaching from outside the mound, often from a monumental façade. This formal stone architecture is rarely encountered in the E of the country, where the majority of the tombs that have been recorded are simply long mounds of earth or stones. At least six are known in the Borders, the most striking being the Mutiny Stones (Longformacus). Largely preserved from stone-robbing by its remote location deep in the Lammermuirs, the cairn measures c. 80 m. in length by up to 2 m. in height, and displays all the typical features of these monuments, lying roughly E and W and tapering W from its broad E end. Not all the cairns were of this size, and a small example on Broughton Knowe is only 20 m. in length. While these monuments appear to be of relatively simple design, excavation elsewhere (e.g. Lochhill, Dumfries and Galloway) has revealed that their construction often involved a complex series of stages, initiated by the erection of a timber chamber or mortuary structure, in some cases opening off a timber façade. The main structural timbers were usually of considerable size, and elements of these monuments may have stood 4 m. or more high.

In the Borders, the surviving long barrows and cairns stand in isolation, mainly in the uplands around the fringes of the Tweed Basin, and there are only hints that they were once incorporated into CEREMONIAL COMPLEXES. The best example is in the vicinity of a pair of standing stones on Sherriffmuir (Lyne). Standing only 1.1 m. and 1.25 m. in height, neither is in itself an imposing stone, but they are now the sole visible elements of a concentration of monuments recorded in antiquarian accounts and from aerial photographs. In the late C18, several smaller stones extended E from the standing stones, and there were also two cairns nearby (*The Statistical Account of Scotland* (1792), 326). Cropmarks on aerial photographs have revealed other features of the complex, including two pairs of opposed ditch segments, perhaps flanking a small long barrow, some 80 m. to the W of the standing stones. On the opposite bank of the Lyne Water the terrace W of Meldon Bridge is enclosed by a line of pits, and an 'avenue' of pits approaches the perimeter on the WNW. Excavation has shown that the pits were the sockets for large timbers measuring between 0.4 m. and 0.6 m. in diameter, and probably standing 4 m. in height. Dating from the second half of the third millennium B.C. (Late Neolithic to Early Bronze Age), the enclosure also contained other settings of timbers, in most cases closely associated with cremation deposits.

Timber was evidently an important structural component of these complexes in the Borders, although the architectural dimension is virtually lost to us today. The architecture of both Meldon Bridge (Lyne) and another large pit-defined enclosure in Lauderdale was probably one in which the massive posts formed a monumental façade of free-standing uprights, possibly spanned with lintels. Small interval posts may indicate the presence of a light wattle screen between the main uprights. The 'avenue' was equally monumental, but whether it really approached an entrance into the enclosure is not known. Other recorded examples appear to have been free-standing structures.

Other timber monuments have been discovered during excavation of STONE CIRCLES, although none of the handful of stone circles recorded in the Borders has been excavated. The largest is on Borrowston Rig, in the hills E of Lauder, where about thirty small stones form an oval setting measuring *c*. 41 m. by 36 m. This circle is also accompanied by at least two circular burial cairns, one of which appears to have contained some form of megalithic setting. A distinctive feature that is only known from southern Scotland is best seen at Ninestone Rig (*see* Newcastleton) where an oval setting of low stones *c*. 7 m. in maximum diameter has two larger stones set up eccentrically in the SW arc. A similar feature may have been present on Burgh Hill, Hawick, although this circle is much larger, measuring *c*. 16 m. by 13 m.

The final blocking of many Neolithic chambered tombs often dates from the second half of the third millennium B.C., a millennium or more after they were first constructed. Frequently incorporated into the blocking are sherds of a new style of pottery – Beaker Pottery. This was a crucial period of change, the beginning of the BRONZE AGE, when metal tools first made their appearance in the British Isles, at first cast in copper, and later bronze. Some ceremonial monuments seem to have spanned this

period, as at Meldon Bridge (Lyne), but new funerary practices
emerged, largely focused on individual burials.

New practices are also manifested in the architecture of
FUNERARY MONUMENTS, the most striking of which are large
circular cairns occupying skylines that dominate huge tracts of
country. Amongst the most spectacular examples are the three
set in a row on the summit of Dirrington Great Law, high above
the moorland to the s of Longformacus. Of the three, the central
one measures only 7.5 m. in diameter and 0.5 m. in height, but
the other two are over 1.8 m. high, the eastern 15.5 m. in diameter, and the western 17 m. within a ditch 2.5 m. in breadth. On
Dirrington Little Law, a lower hill on the parish boundary to the
sw, there is an even larger cairn, c. 20 m. in diameter by 2 m. in
height. Others are not in quite such spectacular positions, but
are equally impressive monuments, such as the Upper and
Nether Cairns on North Muir, near West Linton. The Upper
Cairn, which is the northeasterly, has been extensively quarried,
but it still forms a substantial mound of stones over 4 m. in
height. The Nether Cairn, however, is undisturbed, and is one of
the best-preserved cairns in the Border counties, displaying a
conical profile 3.5 m. in height, and a low platform of cairn material encircling its base, a rare feature anywhere in Scotland. The
typical cairn may cover a primary central burial, often a crouched
inhumation in a cist or box of stone slabs, and sometimes accompanied by grave-goods. The richer grave groups may have a
Beaker, or a type of vessel known as a Food Vessel, and other
grave-goods include jet buttons and necklaces. Satellite burials
may have been interred beneath the cairn at the same time, or
let into the body of the mound at a later date. These may also be
in cists, but include cremations deposited in various forms of
Cinerary Urn. In addition to burials beneath cairns or barrows,
numerous unmarked cists and urns have been ploughed up in
the lowlands, occurring both singly and in cemeteries. As with
so many of the Neolithic monuments, Bronze Age burial cairns
and flat cemeteries remained in use long after the initial inter-
ments were made.

The later Bronze Age and Pre-Roman Iron Age

The first firm evidence for domestic architecture is provided by
strings of circular house-platforms dug into the hillsides in the
headwaters of the Tweed, which are likely to have been first occupied in the Early Bronze Age. Four platforms have been excavated at Green Knowe (Lyne), in the Meldon Valley, revealing
that in most cases two or three timber ROUND-HOUSES had
stood successively on each platform. These round-houses ranged
from 8 to 10 m. in diameter and were built to a fairly uniform
design. The walls were probably of wattle, woven through upright
stakes set or driven into shallow foundation trenches, and the
roof was supported on a ring of more substantial timbers lying
about one third of the radius within the line of the wall. The
entrances were furnished with shallow porches and usually lay in
the southern arc. Within the interior there was usually a hearth
in a shallow pit close to the post-ring. Research has suggested

that walls would have stood at least 1 m. high, and were presumably weather-proofed with daub, sheltered beneath the eaves
of a thatched roof. Steeply pitched, with its rafters rising at an
angle of at least 45 degrees, the roof formed a rigid cone. This
was supported with a ring-beam on the top of the internal post-
ring. Round-houses between 8 m. and 10 m. in diameter have
floor areas from 50 to 78 sq. m., and the apex of the roof would
have stood at least 5 m. above the floor.

Shortly after 1000 B.C. new forms of settlement appear. This
was a time when bronzesmiths added a wide range of new tools
and weapons to their repertoire, amongst them the first true
swords. These and earlier types of weapon – particularly daggers,
rapiers and spearheads – hint at a darker aspect of life during the
Bronze Age, one that is also manifested in the construction of
the first FORTIFICATIONS. The largest of these fortifications in
the Borders encloses c. 16 ha. on the northern of the three
summits of the Eildon Hills above Melrose. The excavation
demonstrated that some of the five hundred platforms within the
interior were occupied in the Late Bronze Age. The defences,
however, were not dated, but several other extensive fortifications
are known to have been occupied at this time, including Traprain
Law (Lothian), and Burnswark (Dumfries and Galloway). Typically they crown commanding topographical features, not only
dominating the surrounding landscape, but also forming prominent landmarks in the countryside, characteristics shared with
several other forts, notably Hownam Law (4 ha.) on the northern fringe of the Cheviots, and White Meldon (3.2 ha.; Lyne).

By the end of the Bronze Age, about 700 B.C., the architecture
of some of the round-houses had assumed monumental proportions, measuring up to 15 m. in diameter, the walls formed of
upright timbers set in continuous bedding trenches. The interiors were divided into annular zones, a layout betrayed by shallow
grooves and ring ditches that are often still visible in the turf
today. Many of these larger RING-DITCH HOUSES enclosed 177
sq. m. and their roofs soared c. 10 m. above the floor. In some
cases there was an inner post-ring, possibly supporting an upper
floor or half-loft. These imposing structures occurred in settlements comprising anything up to a dozen or more buildings. For
the first time, many of the settlements were enclosed, some by
substantial defences built of timber, earth and stone. Indeed, it
is from this period that the evolution of the SMALL FORTIFICA-
TIONS that dominate the settlement record of the middle centuries of the first millennium B.C. can be traced. Even in their
weathered and eroded state, some of these Iron Age forts are
impressive, projecting an image of power and authority. Less
spectacular are the settlements where today the perimeter is
defined by little more than a shallow groove c. 1 m. in breadth.
Excavation has shown that these grooves mark foundation
trenches for upright timbers. Still visible some two millennia
later, these remains are unique to the Borders. Particularly good
examples can be seen on the Gray Coat, near Hawick, Woden
Law, near Hownam, and on South Hill Head in the Meldons
(Lyne). Both Gray Coat and South Hill Head enclose a single
ring-ditch house, the former with two close-set concentric
trenches, the latter with two eccentric trenches. In both cases the

depth of the trenches indicates that they held substantial timbers. Typically, palisade trenches increase in breadth to either side of the entrance, implying that the wall was highest here, almost certainly presenting a façade that was designed to enhance the monumental character of the houses within the interior. At the Gray Coat, the trenches link and return at the entrance, forming a box-like structure that may well have supported some form of raised walkway fronted by a parapet.

The palisades cited above were relatively small enclosures from 25 m. to 45 m. across, but larger timber-built defences evidently preceded many of the forts. Such an example was first revealed by excavation at Hownam Rings, but free-standing enclosures of this sort have been recorded on Stanshiel Hill, near Hownam, and on White Hill, near Broughton. Hownam Rings, with at least three concentric circuits of banks and ditches, typifies many of the forts found in the Borders. The apparently earthen ramparts probably hide stone or timber faces, which in their original form would have stood at least 3–4 m. in height, and many probably incorporated a substantial timber framework, forming a box-like structure comparable to that of the twin palisades on Gray Coat. This timber component is now invisible, but its presence can be inferred at Tinnis Castle, where the timberwork evidently caught fire, and stones of the rampart became molten and fused in the ensuing conflagration.

The defences of these MULTIVALLATE FORTS usually evolved over a long period, and sometimes display evidence of progressively more elaborate schemes. This elaboration is usually most evident at the entrances, with the provision of additional ramparts, or inturns designed to expose the flanks of any attacking force. Achieving tactical advantage, however, was not necessarily the primary role of the defences, which in many instances appear to have been designed simply to project an image of the power and status of the occupants. At Kip Knowe (Morebattle), for instance, in the Bowmont Valley, the obvious line of approach is confronted by a massive belt of defences, and yet the rear of the fort is apparently undefended, simply dropping away into the valley below. Many forts utilising natural promontories exhibit this same weakness and must surely have fallen to any determined assault. This desire to impress is presumably enshrined in the erection of belts of upright stones – *chevaux de frise* – on Dreva Craig (Broughton) and Cademuir (Kirkton Manor). Designed to break up a mounted attack, the tactical positioning of the *chevaux de frise* at Cademuir can hardly be faulted, hidden in a shallow gully where it would be invisible until the riders breasted the crest of the slope. However, the idea of a mounted assault on the massive stone wall of the fort, which at this point of the circuit may have stood 5 m. high, is frankly preposterous.

By the final centuries of the first millennium B.C. a massive expansion of settlement and agriculture was underway, and a host of small settlements bounded by walls, banks and ditches appeared throughout the Borders. Typically these settlements contain levelled platforms for round-houses at the rear, and scooped yards at the front. In some cases they overlie the abandoned defences of earlier forts, a pattern that can be seen at Hownam Rings. The typical round-house was now much smaller and more specialised in its use. Often occurring in pairs, the various activities of life – living, sleeping, food preparation, cooking, crop processing, craft-work and manufacture – were separated into one or the other. In the eastern Borders the use of timber for the walls had given way to stone. Recurring features include a stone threshold, a raised plinth at the rear, and a central hearth.

The Roman Iron Age

Several of the larger fortified enclosures, such as that on Eildon Hill (Melrose), may have been occupied at the time of the Roman invasion *c.* 79 A.D. Life in the small settlements appears to have continued undisturbed, and scraps of pottery and other artefacts recovered from them certainly show that the native population had access to Roman goods. So much so, that it is often suggested that the Votadini, the tribal grouping occupying much of Roxburghshire and Berwickshire, had allied themselves with the Romans.

The organisation of the tribal lands is not fully understood, but a few minor centres can probably be recognised in the handful of BROCHS and DUNS known in the Borders. Circular in plan, and standing anything up to 9 m. in height, the architecture of brochs is best observed in northern Scotland. Nevertheless, the two recorded in the Borders – Edinshall (Abbey St 3 Bathans) and Torwoodlee (Galashiels) – display all the familiar features, from the chambers constructed within the thickness of the massive walls, to a checked entrance flanked by a guard cell, and a stair leading to the wall-head. Now reduced to stumps, it will never be known if they ever rivalled the height of some of their northern counterparts, but, transplanted into southern Scotland, these towers or ring forts are a spectacular manifestation of the wealth and status of their occupants. In both these cases they overlie earlier forts, at Edinshall lying at the core of a cluster of yards and stone-walled round-houses. Excavation has shown that southern brochs were occupied during the C1 and C2 A.D. The small dun at Stanhope (Drumelzier) is altogether cruder in its construction, but it too is of this date.

These are not the only exotic styles of architecture to make their appearance at about this time. In addition to the brochs and duns, souterrains – underground chambers – have been discovered at Newstead and at Broomhouse Mains, near Preston. One of the two Newstead examples incorporated stones robbed from the nearby Roman fort of Trimontium, thus placing its construction no earlier than the end of the C2 A.D.

The key to successive Roman strategies to hold southern Scotland was a powerful garrison of cavalry and infantry based in the FORT at Newstead, standing astride the principal routeways through the Borders, whose site has been revealed in the fields on the S side of the Tweed between the village of Newstead and the Leaderfoot viaduct. Rebuilt on at least three occasions, the initial fort enclosed about 4.2 ha. (10.3 acres) and displayed a remarkable design in which the quadrants of the thick turf rampart were staggered around the perimeter, in such a way as to place each of the four entrances in a re-entrant. Despite the apparent ease with which the Romans achieved military supremacy, the chain of forts established along the face of the Highlands had been abandoned by 87 A.D. Nevertheless, Newstead was rebuilt, suggesting that there was no intention to withdraw from southern Scotland altogether. The new fort was roughly square, enclosing about 5.3 ha., and its turf rampart was now some 13.7 m. in thickness and may have stood up to 8.5 m. in height. Ultimately this too was abandoned, and Roman forces withdrew to a line between Newcastle and Carlisle until the beginning of the 140s A.D., when a new frontier system – the Antonine Wall – was constructed across the Forth–Clyde isthmus. Newstead was again rebuilt, this time in stone, but the new frontier proved equally temporary, only lasting about twenty years. Once again, however, the refurbishment of the defences of Newstead reveals Roman strategic ambition in the Borders, and its garrison remained in occupation until the late C2.

With the exception of a shallow hollow marking the site of a small amphitheatre to the NE, little of the fort at Newstead is 4 visible at ground level. At Lyne, however, a well-preserved Antonine fort can be seen to the W of the church, displaying the typical playing-card shape of Roman forts and enclosing an area of 2.2 ha. The thick turf rampart still stands up to 2.5 m. in height externally at the NE corner and along the W side, but annexes to the N and S of the fort are only known as cropmarks on aerial photographs. These have also recorded what is assumed to be a slightly later Antonine fortlet to the N, and an earlier Flavian fort on the opposite side of the Lyne Water at Easter Haprew.

Forts also provided secure staging posts for forces on the march, who often erected temporary fortifications along their route. At Pennymuir (Oxnam), in the foothills of the Cheviots, there is a remarkably well-preserved TEMPORARY CAMP adjacent to Dere Street, the main road leading N from York. The rampart, which still stands up to 1.2 m. in height, encloses 17.5 ha., and each of the six entrances is covered by an outlying length of rampart known as a traverse, a device to prevent hostile forces from rushing the gap. The SE corner has been incorporated into a later camp, and elements of at least two more have been recorded nearby. Most of the other temporary camps in the Borders are known only as cropmarks, occuring at intervals along Dere Street and the road leading westwards up the Tweed. To the N of Pennymuir, the next cluster of camps occurred around a small fort at Cappuck, near Jedburgh, while at Newstead, the hub of the communications network, there are numerous camps, large and small. Continuing up Lauderdale, others occur at St Leonard's Hill and Channelkirk.

The withdrawal from the Antonine Wall was by no means the last occasion on which Roman armies ventured into Scotland in strength. Conflicts with the tribes persisted, and the Emperor Severus campaigned against the Maeatae and Caledonii in A.D. 209–11. Although no longer in occupation, the Romans appear to have felt secure enough in the Borders to use Newstead as a marshalling point on the line of advance, and a series of enormous (6–7 ha.) camps at Newstead, St Leonard's Hill and Channelkirk have been attributed to these campaigns. Quite what

impact this had in the Borders is not clear. It was apparently followed by a century of peace on the northern frontier, but the
character of this peace is more difficult to define. In the Borders,
for instance, there is little evidence to show that the C1 and C2
settlements were still occupied in the C3 and C4, and material of
this period is very rare. A single C5 brooch, recovered from the
floor of a round-house at Crock Cleugh (Morebattle) in the
Bowmont Valley, may be the result of casual loss long after the
abandonment of the site, rather than evidence that this style of
architecture outlived the Roman province. With the possible
exceptions of the three souterrains, and a fort incorporating
Roman masonry on the summit of Rubers Law (Bonchester
Bridge), the people that populated the landscape virtually disappear from view for the rest of the millennium.

THE EARLY CHURCH IN THE BORDERS

There are no visible structural remains of the early Church within
the Scottish Borders, but a combination of documents, archaeology and carved stones gives some idea of the growing importance of Christianity perhaps as early as the C5. Among the first
pointers is an inscribed stone at Yarrow of the C5 or C6, recording the burial of two men described as princes in a way that suggests they were Christian. A related stone of around the C6 found
at Manor Water, and now in the museum at Peebles, has an enigmatic inscription with a cross before the name. Another stone of
early date, from Over Kirkhope, near Ettrick, and now in the
National Museum of Scotland, shows a small figure with hands
raised in prayer and a cross on his chest.

From the C7, we begin to hear of MONASTIC COMMUNITIES.
At Old Melrose, where a satellite of Iona was founded by St
Aidan between 635 and 651, St Cuthbert, the future bishop of
Lindisfarne, first became a monk. At this stage SE Scotland was
coming increasingly under the control of the Anglians of Berni-
cia, and their influence is seen both in new religious foundations
and in the works of art produced to enhance worship. Old
Melrose was within a loop of the Tweed that could be cut off by
a short earthwork bank and palisade, and promontory sites were
also sometimes selected for these foundations. Between 661 and
664 St Aebbe, a step-daughter of King Aethelfrith of Northumbria, set up a monastery for both men and women at a place
named as Colodaesburg (or Urbs Coludi), which is thought to
have been on the headland of Kirk Hill, s of St Abbs Head, probably within earlier fortifications.

These monasteries were presumably expected to minister to
the spiritual needs of local layfolk, and the principal administrative sites of the Anglian leaders are also likely to have contained
churches serving the laity. At Whitmuirhaugh Farm, near Sprouston, in the late C6 or C7 the incoming Anglians evidently reoccupied an existing defensible enclosure, and at a corner of a large
cemetery adjacent to the site there is evidence for a timber-
framed chapel. Elsewhere, minsters staffed by groups of clergy
may have served as mother churches, with dependent chapels

serving outlying areas. Among candidates as minster sites are Eccles, Stobo and Mow. Other churches were founded by prelates, and Bishop Ecgred of Lindisfarne is said to have built a church at Gedwearde (Jedworth or Jedburgh) after granting the site to Lindisfarne *c*. 830.

There must have been an important church at Jedburgh even before the time of Ecgred, however, because two fragments of a mid-C8 stone shrine or sarcophagus have been found there, with a third fragment located at Ancrum. Its superb carved decoration, with birds and beasts among stylised foliage trails, and bands of interlace to the borders, is related to other important Anglian works of art, including the Ruthwell Cross (Dumfries and Galloway). The design of these stones shows clear awareness of eastern Mediterranean art, a reminder of the wide range of contacts of Scottish patrons. Other CARVED STONES probably date from the C9 and C10. These include a cross-shaft base at Mary Queen of Scots' House in Jedburgh, part of a possible cross-slab found at Gattonside and now in the National Museum of Scotland, and a cross-shaft fragment at Innerleithen Church. The Jedburgh cross base has single or paired animals with some interlaced foliage on all four faces, while the Gattonside fragment has interlace patterns on one side and key patterns on another. The Innerleithen shaft, the most unusual of this group, has pecked cup marks linked in linear groupings.

The years when the earlier stones were carved were evidently turbulent. King Kenneth mac Alpin (†858) is said to have burned the monastery at Old Melrose, as he extended control over his kingdom. Soon afterwards, *c*. 870 and during one of the first waves of Scandinavian attacks, the nunnery at St Abbs Head was destroyed by the Danes. Nevertheless, the continuing production of carved stones suggests that spiritual needs were still being addressed. The chief artistic evidence of the Scandinavian impact is seen in several HOGBACK stones, as at Ancrum, Bedrule, Lempitlaw, Nisbet, Old Cambus and Stobo. Their form is derived from house-shaped shrines and memorials, and characteristically their double-pitched 'roofs' are carved with a tile pattern. The type probably originated in north Yorkshire in the C10, when that area was dominated by Norse-Irish settlers, though none in the Borders are thought to be earlier than the C11, and some may be of the C12.

One of the most important archaeological finds for the early Church in the Borders was at The Hirsel, where a small square church with rounded corners may have been first built in the C9 or C10 for the household and dependants of the landowner. In the course of the Middle Ages it was periodically extended or adapted, a valuable indicator that the sacred character of sites used for worship might lead to long continuity of use. Indeed, even after the Reformation, when church buildings were no longer considered inherently sacred, there could be great loyalty 14 to both sites and buildings. The C12 church at Stobo, for example, which is still in use for worship, is probably on the site of an earlier minster. In that case the church is clearly essentially medieval, but many churches of early C19 appearance must embody parts of the buildings that occupied the site in the Middle Ages.

THE MEDIEVAL CHURCH (1100–1560)

In common with the wider European Church, the Scottish Church underwent an organisational transformation and spiritual renewal at the turn of the c11 and c12. Much of this was achieved in the reigns of the three sons who succeeded Malcolm III and St Margaret to the throne, of whom David I (1124–53) was especially active. He had spent his formative years at the English court of his brother-in-law, Henry I, where he closely observed the ecclesiastical and monastic reforms then taking place across England and Western Europe. Under his leadership the pattern of Scottish dioceses and parishes began to take on its definitive later medieval form, and many religious houses were established. Nevertheless, the medieval Church was never static, and new parishes continued to be formed and others suppressed, while more recent forms of religious life were periodically introduced. One significant change in the later Middle Ages was a move towards more personal forms of devotion, with a shift in the loyalties of layfolk towards the churches in which they worshipped at the expense of the older monastic and cathedral institutions.

There was no cathedral in the Borders, the area being divided between the dioceses (later the archdioceses) of St Andrews and Glasgow. The part belonging to St Andrews was in its archdeaconry of Lothian, and was mainly within the deanery of Merse, with some outliers in the deanery of Haddington. The part belonging to Glasgow was divided between the archdeaconries of Glasgow and Teviotdale; the deanery of Peebles was within the former, and the deanery of Teviotdale within the archdeaconry of the same name. By c. 1300 there were about eighty-seven parishes within the Borders, together with a number of dependent chapels, some of which later achieved parochial status. However, 57 of the parish churches were eventually appropriated to some religious institution, which meant that the principal teinds (tithes) went to that institution, with a chaplain or vicar being instituted in most cases.

The area was particularly well endowed with religious houses, several being foundations of magnificent scale; a number have substantial remains, though only parts of the priory church at Coldingham and of the nunnery church at Abbey St Bathans continue in use for worship. The Borders abbeys are one of the most impressive groups of monastic churches in Europe. Their concentration in this area was doubtlessly part of David I's vision of how he wished Scotland to be viewed from the neighbouring kingdom (though their location became disadvantageous following the outbreak of the wars with England from the 1290s). David's wish for the Scottish Church to be at the vanguard of the movement for spiritual renewal is particularly evident in the fact that the Tironensian house at Selkirk, founded as early as c. 1113, was the first 'reformed' monastery anywhere in Britain. But religious life remained accessible to new ideas throughout the Middle Ages, and the latest community established in the area, for Observant Franciscans at Jedburgh, came less than half a century before the Reformation. By that time there were: Benedictines at Coldingham; Tironensians at Fogo and Kelso (the latter originally at Selkirk); Cistercians at Melrose; Augustinians at Jedburgh; Premonstratensians at Dryburgh; Trinitarians at Peebles; Franciscans at Roxburgh and Jedburgh; and Cistercian nuns at Coldstream, Eccles and St Bathans. In addition, there was a collegiate foundation at Peebles, and at least twenty-nine hospitals of various kinds.

The Monasteries

Much of what we know of Scottish ecclesiastical history comes from monastic chroniclers, and the contribution of the monks and canons presumably lost nothing in the telling. Nevertheless, it is certain that in the C12 and C13 the monasteries were at the cutting edge of religious reform. They were also regarded as a civilising influence and as an effective tool for establishing greater control over the surrounding population. All of these factors would have underlain David I's establishment of so many great abbeys along the Border, and, where the king gave such a positive lead, his greater subjects followed. Patronage of the religious orders was a demonstration of the prestige of those subjects who could afford the costs, and it also provided them with dynastic mausolea where prayers could be offered for their dead. The great campaign of major church building, instigated across Scotland from the early C12 onwards, required large numbers of master masons and other craftsmen who had to be brought from elsewhere. In the Lowland areas this usually meant importing craftsmen from England, where the king and many of the greater nobility had close connections, and the architectural implications of this infusion of creative talent are nowhere more clear than in the Borders ABBEYS.

The earliest major church we know to have been started is the one found through excavation below the later choir of Coldingham, which was probably built for King Edgar *c.* 1100. It had an elongated aisle-less choir with an E apse and a small tower W of the choir, but we have no idea if a distinct nave was planned. In the layout of the other abbeys some decades later we find a wide range of designs, demonstrating the awareness of Scottish patrons of what was happening in many parts of England. At
8 Jedburgh, started *c.* 1138, the E parts of the church had a square-ended aisle-less presbytery, an aisled choir of two bays, and transepts each with an E apse, W of which was an aisled nave. This is a development on a plan type of which one of the earliest known examples was at Southwell Minster (Nottinghamshire), of *c.* 1100. As laid out in the later C12, Dryburgh
9 had a related plan, albeit with aisles rather than apses on the E side of the transepts, but in this case the immediate inspiration was probably the abbey's own mother house of Alnwick (Northumberland).

Melrose, started *c.* 1136, had more specialised needs; the early Cistercians demanded an austere setting for their worship, with separate choirs for monks and lay brethren, and only limited access for layfolk. Excavation has exposed a first plan of a type developed only a short time earlier in the order's original home of Burgundy, but that had been slightly adapted for Melrose's

mother house at Rievaulx (Yorkshire). A short rectangular presbytery flanked by transepts with three rectangular chapels on the
E side of each extended into a long aisled nave with space for two
choirs; the refinement copied from Rievaulx was that the two
chapels flanking the presbytery stepped forward from the outer
chapels. The most extraordinary plan for any of the abbeys was
at Kelso, where two sets of transepts formed a double-cross plan. 5
The details of the E end are only partly understood, but the nave
was aisled, with the central vessel continuing W of the W transepts
to form a full-height vestibule. The ultimate inspiration for this
plan was presumably the great Carolingian and Ottonian Imperial abbeys, and again we are reminded how cosmopolitan were
Scotland's contacts. The more immediate source of the plan,
however, was perhaps one of the abbeys with W transepts in the
English eastern counties, such as Bury St Edmunds (Suffolk) or
Ely (Cambridgeshire).

The smaller monastic houses had simpler requirements. The
Trinitarian priory of Peebles, first built in the second half of the
C13, had an elongated rectangular church, to which a W tower
porch was added in the C15. A similar rectangular plan was probably employed in the mid-C12 for the Cistercian nunnery at
Eccles, and in the early C16 for the Observant Franciscan friary
at Jedburgh.

Most monastic churches underwent later modifications. At
Jedburgh the E end was rebuilt to a slightly extended plan as early
as the last decades of the C12. Coldingham was altogether rebuilt 10
around the same time, with an extended aisle-less rectangular
choir, transepts with E chapel aisles, and apparently an aisled
nave. But the most extensive rebuildings were of the later Middle
Ages, and were frequently necessitated by damage in the wars
with England. At Melrose the English devastation of 1385 6,7
prompted the start of work on a large new church which was
never finished; most unusually, a plan very similar to the original was adopted, though in the course of building an outer row
of nave chapels was added on the side away from the cloister.
Major repairs were also needed at Dryburgh after 1385; the nave
was extensively rebuilt in the process, possibly initially with the
thought of making it shorter than its predecessor. The reconstruction that left the most visible impact at Jedburgh was to the
N transept, which was extended in the mid C15 to provide space
for additional altars and burial places.

In the abbey church INTERIORS, we are again reminded of the
lengths to which the patrons went in obtaining the best master
masons. The most unusual design is the choir of Jedburgh. It may
have been started as a two-storey composition, with the cylindrical arcade piers rising through two storeys and the gallery
seemingly suspended within the arcades. The closest surviving
parallel for this is at Romsey Abbey (Hampshire), where David
I's aunt was a nun, though possibly earlier variants may have
existed at Reading (Berkshire) and Tewkesbury (Gloucestershire). At Kelso the E parts have been lost, and the upper storeys 5
of the remaining parts were only completed late in the C12. The
distinctive feature here is the treatment of the upper storeys as
two independent rows of small arches in front of mural passages.
This has some parallels at the collegiate church of St John at

22   INTRODUCTION

Chester, though Kelso's disregard of bay division in the middle
storey is unusual.

On a smaller scale, the main impact of the aisle-less late C12
10 choir at Coldingham Priory is created by the delicately detailed
arcading in front of the wall passage at the level of the windows.
This type of design has roots in the original nave of the collegiate church of Ripon (Yorkshire), and was further developed at
Nun Monkton Priory (Yorkshire) and St Bees Priory (Cumberland). The rebuilt E end of Jedburgh was perhaps of a related
8 design. The nave of Jedburgh was also under construction at this
time, and it reminds us of the particularly close architectural links
between lowland Scotland and northern England. The basic
formula of arcades carried on clustered-shaft piers, a tall gallery
subdivided by two inner arches, and a clearstorey with an arcaded
passage probably looks back to St Andrews Cathedral (Fife),
started soon after 1160, which itself possibly took inspiration
from the cathedral then under construction at York. This type of
design was further developed at Arbroath Abbey (Angus), and at
the priories of Hexham (Northumberland) and Lanercost (Cumberland) around the same time as at Jedburgh.

The last major new design to be started was at Melrose, after
6,7 the English attack of 1385. The two-storey elevation, with traceried balustrades to the clearstorey passage, shows awareness of
slightly earlier designs in Yorkshire, such as the choirs of Selby
Abbey and Howden Collegiate Church. However, the net vault
over the presbytery, which has no close parallels elsewhere in
Scotland, could look to earlier experiments in the English West
Country, as at Gloucester Cathedral and Tewkesbury Abbey.

One of the best indicators of late medieval architectural attitudes is WINDOW TRACERY, and there is a fascinating group at
Melrose. In the phases soon after 1385, we have the most impressive group of English-inspired rectilinear tracery in Scotland. In
the next phase curvilinear forms were introduced, combined with
'spherical' figures, and it seems certain from an inscription
recording the presence of the Paris-born mason John Morow that
French models were being reflected. In this we see one of the
earliest indicators of a rejection of English architectural guidance
after many decades of hostility.

In the windows along the S nave chapels of Melrose, we find
Scottish masons working out a fresh approach to tracery design,
developing curvilinear forms that display awareness of current
Continental fashions but that represent an essentially Scottish
synthesis. We are also made aware of the contacts between the
abbeys of the area, because the design in the fifth chapel from
the E is repeated in the N transept at Jedburgh. Contacts between
the abbeys are further evident in the use of similar rose windows
in the W nave gable of Jedburgh and the W refectory gable at Dryburgh. Another tendency occasionally found in the later Middle
Ages, that of looking back to earlier Scottish designs, is also seen
at Jedburgh Abbey, where the S choir chapel has a window with
a large quatrefoil that has a rather mid-C13 appearance on first
sight.

We know varying amounts about the CONVENTUAL BUILD-
INGS at Coldingham Priory, Dryburgh Abbey, Eccles Nunnery,
Jedburgh Abbey, Jedburgh Friary, Kelso Abbey, Melrose Abbey

and Peebles Priory. In most cases that knowledge is limited to
the main core of buildings around the cloister, though occasionally we also have information on outlying buildings. The preferred location for the cloister was s of the nave. At Jedburgh
Friary, Melrose and Peebles, however, it was N of the nave and,
most unusually, at Coldingham it was s of the choir. At Melrose
and Peebles the location of the water supply was the most likely
explanation for the position of the cloister. At Jedburgh Friary,
on a restricted urban site, the reason was perhaps the need to
have easy access for the church from the street, while giving a
more secluded position to the domestic buildings. At Coldingham the first monastic buildings had presumably been placed
against the church when it was no more than an extended rectangle with an E apse and a W tower, and it was perhaps considered unnecessary to relocate them when a nave was eventually
built.

Where we have sufficient evidence to understand the planning,
the arrangement of spaces around the cloister was relatively stan-
dardised, with even the Trinitarians at Peebles and the Franciscans at Jedburgh adopting an interrelationship of spaces initially
developed for the older orders. In this the refectory was on the
opposite side of the cloister from the church, while the E range
usually contained the sacristy, parlour, chapter house and
warming room below the first-floor dormitory. The use of the W
range was the most variable. At Dryburgh there was initially no
range on that side, whereas at Melrose there was progressive construction of a complex and extensive series of ranges towards the
abbey's outer courtyard, where the activities of the lay brethren
would least disturb the life of the monks. At Kelso we have no
more than the W range parlour, and at Eccles there are only fragments of the E range. At Peebles no more than the lower walls of
the sacristy and the excavated footings of the other buildings
survive, while at Jedburgh Friary we have excavated partial
footings.

The most complete conventual range is at Dryburgh Abbey, 9
where it was probably built before the existing church. Below the
dormitory, from N to s, are the sacristy and library, followed by
the parlour, chapter house, day stair to the dormitory, warming
room, slype and day room; the latrine block must have been at
the outer end of the range, over the water channel. The dormitory shows evidence of later adaptations, including the unique
addition of a third storey, all of which may be associated with a
less communal late medieval approach to monastic life. This part
was later adapted as a residence for the commendators. At
Melrose, where the buildings are reduced to excavated footings
or lower walls, the latrine block projected at right angles from the
E side of the E range, while in its final form the refectory projected at right angles from the N range, as became common at
Cistercian houses. Many of the earliest buildings at Melrose were
rebuilt in response to the rapid early expansion of the community, and both the E and N ranges appear to have been largely C13
in their definitive form, while the cloister was expanded to the W
by absorbing an earlier lane between the quarters of the lay
brethren and the cloister. Excavations at Jedburgh Abbey have
revealed a comparable picture of rebuilding and enlargement,

with the cloister being extended to both s and w, apparently resulting in the refectory projecting over the s walk.

For buildings beyond the main claustral rectangle, the evidence is fragmentary. As already said, Melrose had extensive ranges w of the cloister for the domestic, agricultural and industrial needs of the lay brethren. Also at Melrose, N of the main core the foundations of an abbot's hall and chamber have been found, which were later supplemented or replaced by the commendator's house to its w. A vaulted chamber, E of the cloister, could be part of the infirmary, while it may be suspected that a guest house is embodied within a later house in what would have been the abbey's outer courtyard to the w. At Jedburgh a C13 abbot's residence was presumably within a range parallel to the refectory, though this function is thought to have been later served by a building w of the cloister. Of the other essential buildings, fragments of a large C12 infirmary have been found at Kelso, E of the cloister, while at Dryburgh there is a small gatehouse at the outer edge of a bridge over the water channel s of the cloister.

Medieval Parish Churches

The Scottish parochial system was largely a creation of the C12 and C13. At Ednam, *c.* 1105, there was an early case of a landowner erecting a church on lands granted under the newly introduced system of feudal tenure, at the start of the process that was to provide the majority of settlements with their own church. Most churches were, of course, periodically remodelled in response to demographic needs or new architectural and liturgical tastes; but regrettably few have survived in completely medieval form, though it is certain that more medieval fabric remains beneath the post-Reformation veneer of many churches than was once thought.

During the C12 great efforts were made to build parish churches of high architectural quality, even if of small scale. Fine
15 chancel arches at Legerwood and Old Cambus (now gone), a
13 unique carved tympanum at Linton, and doorways at Chirnside,
11 Edrom and Stobo indicate the level of enrichment that might be achieved, as do fragments at Hobkirk, Minto, St Boswells and Yetholm. The majority of C12 churches were probably of two rectangular compartments, a smaller E part for the chancel and a larger w compartment for the nave, as was evidently the case at
15 Legerwood, Old Cambus, Simprim and Smailholm. There might
14 also be a w tower, as at Stobo and Southdean, though both those were perhaps additions. There might also be a semicircular apse at the E end, though the only remaining parochial C12 example in the area is at Bunkle. Some churches had stone barrel vaulting over part; Old Cambus seems to have been vaulted throughout, while Bunkle has a half-dome over the apse.

It seems that, as elsewhere in Scotland, from the C13 the majority of new parish churches were of rectangular plan, with no architectural differentiation between chancel and nave. Although all were greatly modified after the Reformation, the plans of Bassendean, Cockburnspath, Longformacus and Newlands Churches, amongst many others, are likely to perpetuate the form of their medieval predecessors. The survival of a traceried window head at Cockburnspath suggests a mid-C13 date for that church, but there is little to indicate the dates of the others.

Several churches were at least partly rebuilt in the later Middle Ages. At Linton, Lord Somerville is said to have rebuilt the chancel in the 1420s, while at Southdean the excavated chancel was evidently a late medieval structure of fine masonry, with traceried windows and elaborate liturgical furnishings. At the former, amongst other more practical motives, Somerville was presumably seeking to earn merit through good works, and he would expect prayers to be offered for his soul in due course. At Edrom, Archbishop Robert Blackadder of Glasgow added a chantry chapel off the s side of the nave c. 1499 where prayers could be said for him in perpetuity; this survives in modified form as a laird's aisle, and it is likely that some other lairds' aisles similarly originated as medieval chantries. At Peebles Church a chapel N of the nave was probably built by John Geddes of Rachan c. 1427. At that church, in 1541 a college of priests was also founded jointly by the burgh and John Hay of Yester, with a duty to pray for the salvation of their founders and benefactors. The finest single act of patronage at a church of parochial scale in the area was the building of the church of Ladykirk. There, apparently in thanksgiving for being saved from drowning, in the years c. 1500 James IV commissioned a fully vaulted church, with polygonal apses to its choir and transeptal chapels. It was an exceptional building, but a reminder of what may have been lost at other churches.

The Reformation took a massive toll of the FIXTURES AND FURNISHINGS associated with the old forms of worship. Altars, the most important focus of worship, have left very little evidence, though the locations of many are evident. A particularly precious survival is a stone inscribed with five crosses that was probably from the *mensa* (top slab) of the altar of Southdean Church (Chesters), and which may have sealed relics set into that altar; it is now re-set into the communion table in the C19 church. Other examples have been discovered at Coldingham Priory and Jedburgh Friary.

Aumbries (wall cupboards) have survived at a number of churches. One that may have served as a sacrament house for the reservation of the consecrated host is on the N side of the chancel at Swinton Church, while the two aumbries in the E presbytery wall at Melrose Abbey were perhaps relic lockers. A more frequently surviving fixture is the piscina, where the chalice and patten used at Mass were cleansed. A C12 example survives in the SW transept of Kelso Abbey, within an arched recess, and it is possible a basin in the top of a small shaft and cushion cap at Hobkirk Church was a C12 pillar piscina. The most impressive C14 and C15 piscinae are at Melrose Abbey, the later ones being particularly lavishly detailed. Some carved fragments at Southdean Church are assumed to have been from liturgical furnishings; as well as a piscina, there may have been canopied sedilia where the priest and his assistants sat at certain points of the Mass.

One of the greatest known losses of furnishings is the timber

choir stalls that were imported from Bruges for Melrose Abbey,
though we can see the stumps of the walls between the choir piers
against which they stood, and we also have the solid stone pulpitum or choir screen that closed off the W end of the choir from
the nave. It is possible the cross-wall inserted in Peebles Priory
in 1656 to create a smaller church for the parish incorporates part
of the screen wall between choir and nave there.

Of the nave furnishings, the only one to have survived in
any numbers is the font. The earliest may be at Linton, which
looks something like a large scalloped capital. Simpler fonts
survive at Bassendean, Lilliesleaf, Lyne, Polwarth, Southdean
and West Linton. A hollowed-out stone of uncertain use, but
sometimes mistakenly described as a font, is in the parlour at
Dryburgh Abbey; it has relief carvings and intertwining mythical
beasts and foliage on its faces, and must be of late C12 or early
C13 date.

There is very little medieval STAINED AND PAINTED
WINDOW GLASS since, apart from its inherent fragility, it was a
natural first target of the reformers when religious imagery was
depicted. Nevertheless, many churches must have had decorated
glass. At Ednam, c. 1330, Coldingham Priory paid for a glazier
named *William* to place glass in six windows, while at Ladykirk
in 1504 the glazier *Thomas Peebles* installed windows for the king.
The best physical evidence for medieval glazing comes from
Jedburgh Abbey and Coldingham Priory, where fragments have
shown that some windows had figurative scenes executed in a full
gamut of colours, while others had decorative grisaille patterns
in a more limited range of colours.

Ceramic TILE FLOORS were probably laid in many of the more
important churches. They might be plain, like examples from
Peebles Priory, inlaid with patterns of different colours or set out
to form larger geometrical or mosaic designs, as at Melrose
Abbey. Melrose also has tiles unique in Scotland in having
inscriptions. The best tiles to remain in place are within the
chapter house at Melrose, though they are now sadly weathered.
The patterns include spoked intersecting hexagonal groupings,
and combinations of square and diagonally aligned shapes creating an illusion of stepping cubes. Some of the same designs
have been found at Melrose's daughter house at Newbattle,
suggesting a shared workforce; there may have been a tile kiln
not far from Melrose at Tilehouse, where fragments have been
found.

There is little MONUMENTAL SCULPTURE in the area. One
of the most important finds has been parts of a possible early C13
canopied tomb-shrine at Melrose, which perhaps housed the
remains of St Waltheof. There are also slight indications of what
was possibly a C13 canopied shrine in the S nave wall at Peebles
Priory. Otherwise the only remains of memorials of architectural
character are a number of tomb recesses. Melrose Abbey has
arched recesses in the presbytery flanks which were presumably
intended for burials. There is a tomb recess in the N chancel wall
of Stobo Church which has been moved W of its original position, and there are traces of a similar recess in the chancel of
Southdean Church (Chesters). In this position a tomb could be
used as an Easter Sepulchre, where a representation of the cru-

cified Christ and a consecrated host were ritually entombed between Good Friday and Easter Sunday. One other tomb recess is in the N transept gable wall at Jedburgh Abbey, which was later adapted for a monument to Lord Jedburgh (†1631).

Few EFFIGIES have survived, and the rarest is of a late medieval prioress at Abbey St Bathans. Swinton has a crudely carved effigy of Sir Alan Swinton, and there are effigies of Patrick Home and his wife in the Blackadder vault at Edrom. The smallest surviving effigy is at Bedrule. Some monument fragments in the museum at Melrose Abbey give a better idea of the quality that could be achieved, including the lion footrest of an effigy.

The most common medieval memorials were RECUMBENT SLABS. At Jedburgh there is a C12 stone with a cross flanked by plaits on the upper face and interlace decoration round the deep flanks. At Fogo there is part of a C13 slab with a cross embellished with fine stiff-leaf foliage. Many burials would have been marked by incised LEDGER SLABS, and a fragment from Peebles Priory (now in the Chambers Institution) is of relatively high quality. But not all were so competently worked, and a charmingly naïve representation of a knightly figure at Stobo Church is at the lower end of the artistic gamut. Another slab at Stobo commemorates one of its vicars, Robert Vessy (†1473); apart from a perimeter inscription, the only image is a chalice. Another favoured form for monuments was a coped slab of polygonal profile, sometimes with rolls sunk into the angles; one at Ancrum appears to have an incised chalice on its upper face.

The most widespread type of incised slab had a cross on a stepped base as its principal feature, which might be accompanied by a sword or a symbol of the status or trade of the person commemorated. The cross-heads varied from simple Latin forms, as on an example at Coldingham Priory, to complex foliate patterns, as on an example in the museum at Melrose Abbey. In a variant found on several examples, the cross ends finish on a diagonal line.

POST-REFORMATION CHURCHES

The watershed in the process of the Reformation was parliament's repudiation of the Pope and the abolition of the Mass in 1560, though for over a century there was lively debate both on how the Church should be governed, and on forms of worship. The role of bishops was a particularly thorny issue, and from the 1570s the pressure increased for the Church to be governed by a Presbyterian system of church courts. Nevertheless, bishops were only finally removed from the state Church in 1689, and for much of this period there was a pragmatic coexistence of bishop and presbytery, with a general consensus that preaching should be at the centre of worship.

By the Reformation each parish had its own church, and there were outlying chapels within many of those parishes; unfortunately, all of the greater churches in the Borders, and many of the smaller ones, had been badly damaged in the recent wars with

England. The difficulties the reformed Church had in wresting control of ecclesiastical finances from existing benefice holders meant there was little prospect of initiating major campaigns of repair or new church building, and the majority of medieval churches remained in use for many years, with only such modifications being made as were strictly necessary. This was also the case at the great monastic churches, where various parts of the buildings continued to meet the congregations' changed and more limited needs for many years.

The main post-Reformation requirement was to adapt the churches for worship in which, although regular communion was still seen as desirable, preaching predominated. An altar at the E end was usually replaced by a pulpit against one of the long walls as the chief focus, with galleries and various forms of seating grouped around it. Aesthetic considerations were a luxury that could seldom be afforded, and even at such an architecturally imposing church as that created in the early C17 within the monastic choir of Melrose Abbey, accounts of visitors indicate that the largely unregulated provision of seating had resulted in haphazard arrangements. Pews, lofts or galleries might be installed by the principal families, the burgesses, the trade guilds and the schools, which sometimes rose to considerable heights, while other seating of various kinds was provided by others wherever space could be found.

The wish of the lairds to accommodate both themselves and their deceased forebears with suitable dignity could take several forms, especially with increased enforcement of the regulations against burial within church walls. Following financial provisions set in place in 1633, the principal heritors (landowners) received the parochial teinds (tithes), and also took over financial responsibility for the church and minister, except in the burghs, where this responsibility passed to the council. Some heritors chose to adapt the chancel as a location for a pew or loft, and also as a burial place which it could be claimed was outside the church walls. Thus, where a laird's 'aisle' is at the E end of a church, as at Swinton or Ettrick, it is possible it is on the site of a medieval chancel. Elsewhere, as at the C12 churches of Stobo and Legerwood, what had been an architecturally distinct chancel in the medieval building was eventually walled off as a burial vault. At some churches the laird had an inherited interest in a medieval chantry chapel projecting from one flank of the church, and this could also be adapted as a laird's 'aisle', as happened to the Blackadder Aisle at Edrom, where a burial vault was inserted at the lower level and a gallery constructed above.

Like their medieval predecessors, the majority of post-Reformation CHURCHES BEFORE THE EARLY C19 were of rectangular plan, or had a rectangle at the core of an augmented plan. In many cases this is because a medieval structure had been retained, with only minimal adaptation. Indeed, where the core of a church is rectangular, and it is known to occupy a medieval site, it may be suspected that at least part of the medieval structure has survived, however transformed that structure may have been. This is particularly likely when that rectangular core is relatively elongated since, for post-Reformation churches, plans that were wider in relation to their length were generally preferred, as

at the chapel next to Ferniehirst Castle of before 1621. The protracted efforts that might be made to repair and adapt an existing church are clear at Greenlaw, which underwent major repairs   21
in 1675, was extended westwards *c.* 1712 to connect with a newly
constructed court house and tower, while a N lateral 'aisle' was
added in 1855. As a result, little medieval fabric can be positively
identified, and yet it was the medieval structure that conditioned
much that was done.

As at Greenlaw, a favoured method of augmenting a rectangular church was to add a laterally projecting 'aisle' to one flank,
giving it a T-shape. This meant there were three arms directed
towards a pulpit set at the middle of the remaining long (usually
S) wall. The 'aisle' at Yarrow could be as early as 1640, and by
the time Polwarth was remodelled in 1703 T-plans were common.
In some cases, as at the old church at Stow, or at Bowden and   20
Eckford, the added 'aisle' was relatively small, being solely for the
laird and his household. Elsewhere, the 'aisle' was for congregational use and was given similar proportions to the existing parts
of the church (e.g. Fogo of *c.* 1683). T-plan churches remained
in favour well into the C19, though where they were built on new
sites, as at Castleton in 1808, the three arms tended to be wider
in relation to their length, thus bringing the congregation closer
to the pulpit.

Other layouts were also explored. At Lauder, in 1673, the Duke   18
of Lauderdale built a church of Greek-cross plan, though this
was perhaps essentially an augmented T-shape, since the E arm
originally contained the communion table and was perhaps not
regarded as an integral part of the church. Another form of centralised plan is seen at Kelso, of 1771, which has an octagonal   23
plan with galleries initially around all eight sides. Some churches
have an almost square plan, as at Jedburgh Trinity, of 1818, and
Leitholm, of 1833.

Into the C17 there was still some sense of architectural continuity with the medieval Church, since most churches were still
of medieval origin. There was also a view that simplified Gothic
forms were appropriate, as seen in the traceried windows at Lyne,
Ayton, Stow, Lauder and in the Scott of Gala Aisle at Galashiels.   19
By the later C17, however, a simplified classical vocabulary was
increasingly preferred, with external architectural emphasis
placed on one of the long walls, and most commonly the S
face. The quiet dignity of many of these churches can be highly
attractive.

The symmetrical arrangement of doorways and windows to the
main face was greatly favoured, though doorways might be relegated to the end walls. At Polwarth, as remodelled in 1703, three
square-headed doorways alternated with two round-headed
windows, with five large inscribed tablets above the doorways and
at each end of the wall; a bell-tower abutted the W gable. Greenlaw, as remodelled in about 1712, had two doorways and a
plethora of windows between and above them, and with the tall
tower (designed for the court house) at the W end. At Greenlaw
the internal location of galleries was marked by two storeys of
windows at each end of the front, and this arrangement is a   21
common pointer to the existence of galleries, even where they
have since been removed. The S wall at Roxburgh as remodelled

in 1752 has four windows at the centre, and a lower window at each end below the galleries, whereas at Oxnam, as remodelled in 1738, it is wider areas of blank wall at each end that hint at the possibility of galleries. In some cases it was perhaps felt that two tiers of windows for the galleries would mar the harmony of the principal front, and they were confined to the rear elevation, as at Bunkle church of 1820, where the N elevation used to have a tall central rectangular window, with a pair of superimposed rectangular windows on each side.

BELL-TOWERS with handsome classical detailing, set against one of the gable walls, were built at Eccles (1774), Coldstream (1795) and Eyemouth (1811). In the latter two cases the towers were so fine that they survived later rebuilding. An alternative was to build an elaborated bellcote above a buttress-like turret at the centre of the main front, as at Whitsome (1803) and Makerstoun (1808). At Newcastleton South Church an unusual hybrid was built from 1838, with a slender five-stage tower at the centre of the S front, developing out of what was little more than a turret. But it was always more common to have a birdcage BELLCOTE on one of the gables, with four rectangular piers or balusters supporting a solid roof of ogee or pyramidal profile.

Of CHURCH FURNISHINGS, little C17 work has survived, the main exceptions being the pulpit and modified laird's pew at Lyne Church of 1644, and the ambitious Ker of Cavers Loft at Bowden of 1661, none of which are in their intended positions. By the late C18, as a corollary of the search for architectural forms to express the ideals of reformed worship, more seemly furnishings began to be provided. It became common to have uniform sets of pews, with or without doors, galleries at the same levels as each other and with panelled fronts of uniform design, all looking towards a pulpit capped by a substantial tester, albeit sometimes with a rival focus in a laird's loft.

In new churches such homogeneity was attainable from the start, and the rectangular or square churches of Channelkirk, of 1817, and Jedburgh Trinity, of 1818, have a regular horseshoe arrangement of galleries. At new T-plan churches such as Ettrick, of 1824, or Newlands, of 1838, galleries were provided in all three arms. Where existing churches were being reordered a similar degree of uniformity might be introduced, as at Maxton as refurnished in 1812, which has similar galleries at the two ends. At Fogo, however, although the galleries in the two main arms are broadly alike, close examination reveals differences resulting from the fact that they were built for different families. Pulpits that deserve particular mention include those at Makerstoun of 1808, Fogo of 1817, Ettrick of 1824 and Newlands of 1838. Few lairds' lofts have survived unmodified, but the remodelled laird's loft at Eckford of 1724 is noteworthy. Reworked fragments at Legerwood and Ashkirk (the latter dated 1702) are also assumed to be from lofts, and at Polwarth a rail of turned balusters from the laird's pew has been re-set as a communion rail.

The first half of the C19 was a period of dramatic developments for the Scottish churches. In these decades, two OTHER DENOMINATIONS (besides the Church of Scotland and its offshoots) began to play an increasingly prominent role. In 1792 legislation allowed members of the Episcopal Church to worship freely and they began building churches in the major towns, especially from the second quarter of the C19 onwards, including *William Burn*'s church at Peebles (1830). At the same time, liberty began to be allowed to the Roman Catholic Church, following on from the Catholic Relief Act of 1793 and the Catholic Emancipation Act of 1829; the hierarchy was re-established in 1878.

The Church of Scotland itself underwent dramatic change in 1843 when, in response to profound concerns about secular and state controls, a third of its ministers left it to form the Free Church of Scotland. As a consequence, a high proportion of parishes was divided. The Church had already suffered secessions in the C18 and early C19, most notably in 1733, 1761 and 1839, and convictions tended to be held so firmly in the seceding churches that they had themselves been prone to further divisions. But the Disruption of 1843 split the Church completely. A further significant grouping was created when the United Secession and the Relief Churches (the principal secessionist groupings) came together to form the United Presbyterian Church in 1847. As a result of all these developments, new churches were required to an extent unparalleled since the C12, though the first churches built for new congregations after the Disruption tended to be very utilitarian in character. In parallel with these changes, a new sense of missionary zeal had been emerging from the turn of the C18 and C19, one aspect of which was that the poor condition of many existing churches resulted in their being deemed unsuitable for their exalted role, and they were remodelled, rebuilt, or even relocated.

From the late C18, the spirit of Romanticism had allowed medieval architecture to be viewed in a light largely free of confessional associations, and the Gothic style came to be increasingly regarded as appropriate for places of worship. A precociously early example of the GOTHIC REVIVAL may be the E gable of Foulden Church, which was given a follified embattled wall-head perhaps as early as 1786. The reintroduction of Gothic forms is initially seen in a gradual application of individual motifs to churches otherwise of essentially unmedieval appearance. This is seen in the window tracery, crowsteps and tabernacle-like bellcote of *James Gillespie Graham*'s Channelkirk Church of 1817, or the square window labels of *John & Thomas Smith*'s churches at Ettrick, of 1824, and Yarrow, of 1826. However, attempts to reflect both the massing and the detailing of medieval architecture soon began to be attempted, as in *W. H. Playfair*'s Minto Church, of 1830, or *Robert Brown Jun.*'s Yetholm, of 1836, though the results might be more charming than convincing. The Norham-inspired Romanesque vocabulary of *Ignatius Bonomi* at Hutton in 1835 was more scholarly, though the attempt to reconcile medieval architectural forms with preaching halls was to trouble architects for some time.

At this time, the architectural world s of the Border was undergoing a major change in its attitude to churches. The OXFORD MOVEMENT, established in 1833, called for correct Gothic, based on scholarly analysis of English architecture as the only acceptable style for churches. A principal channel for bringing these ideas to Scotland was the Episcopal Church, which was increasingly influenced by the Church of England, though the

Roman Catholic Church was also providing increased architectural opportunities. Changing attitudes are well illustrated in the
two parts of the Episcopalian church at Peebles. *William Burn*'s
nave of 1830 is a simple, brightly lit hall in token Gothic, which
could have served any denomination equally well; the choir of
1882, however, by *Hay & Henderson*, was designed in a spirit of
earnest medievalism. The introduction of the new ideas is best
seen in two landmark Episcopalian churches designed by English
architects: *John Hayward*'s St John the Evangelist at Jedburgh of
1843–4 (to which *William Butterfield* probably made a significant
contribution), and *G. Gilbert Scott*'s St Cuthbert at Hawick of 1855,
built under the patronage of the Marchioness of Lothian and
Duke of Buccleuch respectively. Where the Episcopal Church
had led, the Catholic Church soon followed, with the small but
carefully detailed church at Kelso of 1857, and a highly ambitious
church at Galashiels of 1856, both by *W. W. Wardell* of London.

However, while medieval planning and Gothic architectural
forms were well suited to the more ritualistic services of the Episcopal and Catholic churches, they did not fit so well with the
requirements of the Church of Scotland at this time. One
straightforward solution was to make the church itself look like
a nave, with a chancel-like vestry at one end. This was done at
David Rhind's Roberton Church in 1863, and at Saughtree in
1872, and occasionally there was a laird's loft in a tower, as at
Hobkirk of 1862. At other times an imposing Gothic show front
might be placed in front of a preaching hall, as at *William Young*'s
24 Old Parish Church, Peebles (1885–7). But the great master in
gothicising Presbyterian requirements was *J. M. Wardrop* of *Brown
& Wardrop* and later of *Wardrop & Reid*. At Langton (Gavinton)
and Kirkton Manor, both of 1872, he did little more than make
a vestry look like a chancel (an apse in the latter case). Yet, when
given the resources, he could create assuredly asymmetrical
arrangements with apparent groupings of chancel, nave, aisles,
transepts and tower masking a T-plan arrangement. The best
26 examples of this are Ayton (1864), and Stow (1873), though
Heatherlie Church, Selkirk, of 1874 (largely demolished), was
also a creditable essay.

It is likely, however, that most congregations saw 'correct'
Gothic architecture as a distraction best left to the Episcopalians
and Catholics, and to the great landed patrons. In most cases
what was needed was as much Gothic as would create a seemly
appearance, but which still allowed the basic form of the under-
lying church to be a lofty and spacious preaching hall. The results
of this approach are seen in *J. McKissack & W. G. Rowan*'s
Ladhope Free Church (later St Andrew), Galashiels, of 1884, and
Hardy & Wight's Earlston Parish Church of 1891, both of which
are elongated halls with galleries around three sides, focused on
a massive pulpit against an end wall, and by this date the pulpit
could be almost swallowed up by an enormous organ. Externally
these hall churches were often given groupings of gables along
the flanks. But the great emphasis was on the entrance front,
which was usually a tripartite composition with a high central
gable-wall pierced by a doorway below a large traceried window,
and with a tower to one side and a lower block to the other side;
there were generally stairs to the galleries in both side elements.

This basic formula is found repeated in many of the larger churches of the Borders, including *Robert Baldie*'s Selkirk Parish Church of 1878. Such tripartite grouping of elements at the entrance front could also be introduced when an existing church was remodelled, as seen in the enlargement of Broughton Church by *R. A. Bryden* of 1885. Nevertheless, there were architects producing highly individual work, and it may be noted that the Free and United Presbyterian Churches were now increasingly willing to foster architectural creativity. Perhaps the most astonishing personal contribution was that of *F. T. Pilkington*, who developed a delightful version of Gothic in which complex massing, rich detailing and a unique counterpoint between superimposed wall planes created an exotic synthesis. His work is to be seen at Innerleithen Parish Church (externally) and Kelso North Free Church, both of 1865, and at Morebattle Free Church of 1866. A less eccentric, but still markedly individual approach, is seen in the buildings of *John Starforth*. His best church in the Borders is Kelso U.P. of 1885, which demonstrates his skill in building up large-scale three-dimensionally-massed elements which seem almost to have been hewn from the living rock.

The idea of the church as an auditorium remained paramount within the Church of the Scotland for most of the C19, but in the last decades a body of opinion emerged which laid new stress on the beauty of worship. From 1886 a number of Ecclesiological Societies were formed, which were influenced by the Oxford Movement, but which sought Scottish solutions and were not tied to Gothic as the only acceptable style. Under their influence, in many cases a pulpit against one of the long walls was superseded as the main focus by a communion table placed at the end of the long axis, and preferably in an architecturally distinct chancel, with the pulpit repositioned to one side and a font at the other. This often necessitated the removal of galleries at one or both ends. At the same time, greater encouragement was given to the ecclesiastical crafts, including stained glass, carpentry and embroidery, leading to a remarkable raising of standards. Despite being largely limited to the 'high' wing of the Church, the ECCLESIOLOGICAL REVIVAL was to be widely influential, and its impact is seen even in many churches where the pulpit continued to reign supreme. Within the Borders the architects who played a particularly prominent role in reordering churches to meet these new requirements included *J. P. Alison* of Hawick, *P. Macgregor Chalmers* of Glasgow and *George Fortune* of Duns.

A prime requirement for ecclesiological reordering might be finding some way to create a chancel. At Stichill in 1905 and at Sprouston in 1911, *Alison* and *Chalmers* respectively simply added a small chamber at one end of the building, and this was always the most common approach, even though a small chancel could look out of proportion against a large preaching hall. But there were other possibilities. At Legerwood in 1898 *Hardy & Wight* reopened an existing chancel that had previously been converted for use as a burial vault, while at Linton in 1910 *Chalmers* created a chancel on old foundations that had been adapted as a laird's aisle in a truncated form. Another alternative was to cut a slice off one end of a church and frame it by an arch, though there were always difficulties with proportions in such cases, and it is 12 hard to deem *Fortune*'s chancel at Bunkle of 1905 a total success. There might also be difficulties in reconciling other features with the new chancel, and several laird's pews were left facing a blank wall once the pulpit had been removed, as at Eckford after *Sydney Mitchell & Wilson*'s remodelling of 1898, and at Longformacus after *George Fortune*'s addition of an eastern apse in 1892. Nevertheless, when reordering extended to the whole church, some striking interiors were created, perhaps most notably as a result of *Chalmers*' work at Crailing of 1892 and *Alison*'s work in a Renaissance idiom at Stichill of 1905. It might be added that chancels could be added to T-plan churches, as done by *A.N. Paterson* at Yarrow in 1906, or to large-scale aisled churches, as *Alison* did at Wilton Church, Hawick, in 1908.

Fashions in CHURCH FURNISHINGS in the late C19 and C20 ran in parallel with architectural taste, with the greatest single factor being the growing strength of the Gothic Revival. As the Episcopal Church, in particular, took on board the ideas of the Oxford Movement, at Jedburgh, St John (1843–4), by *John Hayward* (and possibly *William Butterfield*), and at Kelso, St Andrew (1867–9) by *R. Rowand Anderson*, interiors were created which attempted to replicate those of the Middle Ages. But for most Presbyterian congregations medievalising altars, prayer desks, screens, and pews were alien to their forms of worship, and in general it was felt most appropriate simply to ensure that the furnishings were well proportioned and constructed, while making their decorative detailing Gothic where possible, as may
25 be seen in *Wardrop & Reid*'s remodelling of Duns Parish Church (1880). As with the churches themselves, however, much changed with the new emphasis on craftsmanship brought in with the Ecclesiological Revival, and architects such as *J.P. Alison* and *Robert S. Lorimer* found they were able to develop their ideas on furnishings as much within Presbyterian as Episcopalian contexts, while being no longer limited to a purely Gothic idiom. The former's refurnishing of Stichill (1905), in particular, has Arts and Crafts detailing of a high order.

An important development in the mid C19 was the emerging acceptability of figurative STAINED GLASS. At 'advanced' centres such as Glasgow Cathedral this possibility had been tentatively aired as early as the 1830s, though it was only in the 1850s that it began to be installed there. In the Borders it was perhaps again the Episcopalians who took some of the earlier steps, as with a series of windows in the chancel of Jedburgh by *Ward & Nixon*. But by the last quarter of the century many Presbyterian congregations were also happily installing stained glass, either as individual windows, or as more complex iconographic schemes, such as that at Duns Parish Church of 1880 by *David Small*. The company which established the strongest hold on the market was that of *Ballantine* of Edinburgh (in various combinations of family members), though many other companies found ample work, including *J.H. Baguley* of Newcastle, *Clayton & Bell*, *C.E. Kempe* of London and *James Powell & Sons* of London. Amongst a plethora of slightly saccharine Good Shepherds, Good Samaritans, and Sowers of the Seed, much good glass was produced, especially as the Ecclesiological Revival encouraged higher standards. Amongst more recent glaziers who have produced note-

worthy windows, mention must be made of *Herbert Hendrie* (at
Caddonfoot and Selkirk St John the Evangelist), *Marjorie Kemp*
(at Longformacus and Drumelzier), *Sadie McLellan* (at West
Linton), *Douglas Strachan* (at Linton, Galashiels and Yarrow,
amongst others) and *William Wilson* (at Roxburgh, Eyemouth St
Ebba, Melrose Holy Trinity, Stow and Lilliesleaf).

Churches since 1914

Relatively few churches have been built in the Borders since the
First World War, though many have been reordered in response
to changing views on worship. The greatest expansion has been
amongst the evangelical denominations, and their prime requirement has generally not been architectural excellence, as witnessed by the Eyemouth Free Baptist Church of 1987, though
the corrugated iron hall occupied by the Evangelistic Gospel
Mission at Yetholm since 1931 has some charm. There has also
been some expansion in the Roman Catholic Church but, again,
few new buildings have been raised: the use of a prefabricated
Territorial Army hall at Earlston since 1949, and the adaptation
of a boat-building shed at Eyemouth in 1961 have characterised
that Church's generally utilitarian approach. The two finest
modern buildings raised for Catholic use are both by *Reginald
Fairlie*: his convent chapel of 1914 at Hawick, and the church and
hall at Jedburgh of 1937, the latter an L-shaped grouping in a
simplified rendered Gothic style.

Two modern structures for the Church of Scotland which
must be singled out were both raised to serve new housing
schemes. The church of 1953–5 by *J.P. Alison & Hobkirk* on the
Burnfoot scheme on the NE edge of Hawick is a prominently
located harled structure, with Arts and Crafts nuances in the
great arch that frames the entrance. The church of 1971 by
Wheeler & Sproson for the Langlee estate to the E of Galashiels
is one of the most distinguished C20 churches to have been built
in Scotland. Replacing a C19 church in the centre of the town
built for a Free congregation, it extends out from the hillside
amidst a development which leaves no doubts on the convictions
of the Nordic modernists who planned it.

The Churches in Scotland are facing difficult times. The divisions and secessions of the C18 and C19 left many parishes architecturally overprovided, and declining congregations have more
recently placed in doubt the future of many churches. The problems of overprovision had been highlighted by the unions in 1900
(of the Free and United Presbyterian Churches to form the
United Free Church) and 1929 (of the United Free Church and
the Church of Scotland), and many buildings have already been
demolished while others have been put to a variety of alternative
uses from arts centres to garages, some of which have proved to
be short-lived. Even while this book has been in preparation
churches have continued to be lost, including some of architectural significance, such as Wilton South Church in Hawick and
St Mary's West Old Parish Church in Selkirk. We are facing
unprecedented losses of buildings that are major contributors to
our landscapes and townscapes, as well as an important part of
our cultural history.

MAUSOLEA, MONUMENTS AND STATUES

The restraint on burials within churches after the Reformation
was in response to a decree of the reformed Church which led,
by the end of the C17, to monuments previously inside being
erected in churchyards and burial grounds by noble and wealthy
families. But a certain sense of democracy in death brought innovation, in the right of every man to be buried in his own acquired
plot (or lair). CARVED GRAVESTONES, often with moralising
inscriptions, became a feature in many churchyards in Lowland
Scotland and are particularly rich in the Scottish Borders. These
form a fascinating collection of headstones or wall monuments,
with table tombs and obelisks for those who required something
more assertive, and enclosures or roofed aisles for those who
wished to remain apart from their fellows in death. Such memorials were the principal outlet for the artistic activities of several
generations of masons, and they provide particularly important
evidence for local sculptural styles as well as for family history
and for the attitudes of those who commissioned them. Unfortunately, as a result of natural processes of decay, as well as
neglect and vandalism, many of them are now in a sadly deteri-
orating state.

On memorials of all kinds, reminders of death are a common
theme through the C17 and well into the C18. The universal
admonition of 'memento mori', is accompanied by reliefs of
skeletons, skulls, bones, coffins, sextons' spades and hourglasses.
There might also be references to human transience, as on the
stone of James Hunter (†1765) at Roxburgh, which urged: 'Stop
traveller as you go by,/ I once had life and breath;/ But falling
from a steeple high / I swiftly passed through death.' Winged
angel heads could be a pointer to the joys of heaven for the elect,
though the bones that some of them brandish were perhaps less
heartening. Further reminders of the person commemorated
might be provided by symbols of his or her trade. On some stones
there was a portrait of the deceased, either looking directly outwards or in profile, and possibly reading the scriptures or con-
27 templating a skull as at Linton parish church. Some of the best
stones were made by masons for members of their own families;
29 the touchingly portrayed affection between James Blakie (†1739?)
and his wife at Birselees (St Boswells) could be because a mason
relative had carved their stone. Even more moving is a stone at
28 Stobo of three sisters of the Thomson family who died in 1723
at the ages of twenty-one, nineteen and twelve, and who are
shown comforting each other.

Many stones have a simple architectural frame carved in relief,
with pilasters supporting a pediment. As the C18 progressed,
architectural detail tended to become more 'correct', though it
was often pattern-book based and might thus be misinterpreted,
as on a monument at Heriot, where the eggs of an egg-and-dart
border are hollowed. Baroque swags were also popular, though
few achieved the prodigies of complexity of a monument of 1751
30 at Bowden, nor the grandeur of John Ker's memorial at Legerwood. Towards the end of the C18 taste increasingly demanded
a more austere approach to the design of memorials. Nevertheless, delightful personal touches were still introduced, as on an

uninscribed memorial to a musician at Melrose, which has a portrait profile and a crossed violin and flute.

For those with greater funds there was the option of a family
BURIAL ENCLOSURE with high walls to separate them from the
other occupants of the churchyard, and perhaps with Tuscan
pilasters giving prominence to the entrance front and doorway,
as at the Mackay of Scotston enclosure of post-1798 at Newlands.
In the C19 the vocabulary of the façade might be Gothic, as in
the Makdougall enclosure at Makerstoun. In that case the enclosure occupies the site of the church that had been moved to a
new site in 1807–8, and the abandonment or relocation of
churches frequently provided the opportunity for the old church
to be adapted as burial enclosures. At Preston, which had been
linked with Bunkle by 1718, the old church was progressively
divided by local families into three enclosures.

In the course of the later C18 and C19 there was perhaps less
scope for artistic expression than before, and many headstones
were given little greater individuality than a simple blocked pediment at the head. Nevertheless, a visit to many churchyards
reveals that there were still creative masons, as seen for example
at Castleton. There, several table tombs appear to show the hand
of one mason, while in the mid C19 the Douglas family commissioned a related series of headstones decorated with reliefs of
draped urns flanked by upturned torches. There is also an attractive triple-pinnacled headstone of Rococo Gothic design for
Isabel Veitch (†1809). But the most striking monument there is
a large Greek Doric ciborium for Eliza Scott (†1847), from which
a slightly unexpected dome emerges. Imposing free-standing
monuments of this last kind are relatively uncommon, though
others that might be mentioned include a Tuscan ciborium tomb
at Cockburnspath for the Rev. Andrew Baird (post-1843), and a
Gothic canopied tomb at Jedburgh Abbey, probably of 1837, for
John Rutherfurd. Personal tragedies could still be remembered
by evocative carving as that in Holy Trinity graveyard, Melrose,
to James Walker Fairholme RN, lost in the Arctic with Sir John
Franklin, 1845–6.

At the turn of the C19 and C20 the craft revival encouraged
production of a number of more creative memorials. At Chirnside, the remodelling of the church by *Sydney Mitchell & Wilson*
in memory of Lady Tweedmouth (†1904) included a small external burial atrium at the w end, with a relief representation of her
by *Waldo Story* internally. Another form of burial atrium was
created for the Duke of Roxburghe at Kelso Abbey by *Reginald
Fairlie* in 1933–4; in this case it took the form of an L-shaped pair
of vaulted cloister walks on the site of the west claustral range.
Extensions to graveyards in the C20 assumed a cemetery-like
appearance with rows of stereotypical headstones. It was left to
sculptors and artists to produce works of quality. At Holy Trinity,
Melrose, *Eric Gill* lettered the Middleton stone, *c.* 1928, and
carved a male figure. The same church's Dundas Cross, based on
the Kildalton Cross, continues the long tradition of carved stone
crosses, also much used as memorials to the dead of the First
World War (*see* below). At Caddonfoot the memorial for Lord
Craigmyle (†1944) is given prominence by two high-relief
carvings of ships' prows. More recently, occasional pieces of

creativity are to be found, such as the split boulder with low-relief decoration commemorating Francis Cowan (†1996) at Edrom. But in general, the design of memorials into the C21 has been poor, and the current prevalence of polished granite with gilded vignettes of praying hands or figures departing into the sunset is deeply depressing.

There are a few notable private family MAUSOLEA. The earliest, buried in the trees at Mellerstain, a classical temple built by *James Runciman* in 1736, celebrates the life of George and Lady Grisell Baillie. At Macbiehill, the square mausoleum with a pyramidal vaulted roof by *Robert Somerville*, mason, 1769, contains memorials of the Montgomery and Beresford families, and at Springwood Park, Kelso, *James Gillespie Graham* designed a Neoclassical temple, c. 1822, for the Scott Douglas family. Dramatically exposed on Gersit Law is *Peddie & Kinnear*'s Monteath Douglas Monument, 1864, near Ancrum, a large domed Byzantine-style mausoleum with lions guarding the entrance, built for General Monteath Douglas of Stonebyres.

COMMEMORATIVE ARCHITECTURAL MONUMENTS are usually prominently sited and the most striking in the Borders is the hilltop Waterloo Monument by *Archibald Elliot*, 1817–24, for William Kerr, sixth Marquess of Lothian, comprising a cylindrical column supporting a viewing platform and spire, giving glorious views of the countryside and aerial views of Iron Age hill forts below. Early C19 monuments to individuals are also classical in style, such as the tall (24 m. high), Neoclassical column of 1834 at Coldstream for Charles Marjoribanks, MP, of The Lees, which acknowledges his 'amiable qualities and political principles'. It supports a figure of Marjoribanks, a replacement of 1874 after the original was destroyed by lightning.

The patronage of a single individual occasionally produced curious bodies of work, none more so than the eccentric eleventh Earl of Buchan who commissioned the boldly carved, warlike, but rather jolly figure of William Wallace at Dryburgh of 1814. *John Smith* represents him as the Guardian of Scotland, holding a saltire shield and double-handed sword. Buchan had already erected an obelisk to Hugh de Morville at Dryburgh Abbey in 1794 and was also responsible for the attractive Gothic memorial archway at Orchard Gate, Dryburgh, conceived as a robust tribute to his parents, c. 1820, with piers like small turrets carved with Baronial details. In an entirely different vein is the nearby Ionic circular Temple of the Muses dedicated by Buchan to the poet James Thomson, author of *The Seasons*, who also has an obelisk at Ednam by *John Smith*. This tradition of monuments to poets and writers became a Borders speciality in the C19, but often with very different solutions. John Leyden, poet, orientalist and linguist, is the subject not only of the impressive Leyden Monument at Denholm, in the form of a handsome Gothic spire supported by red Aberdeen granite columns, designed by *Hector H. Orrock* and sculpted by *A. Handyside Ritchie*, 1861, but also an obelisk by *Robert Robinson* of 1895 at nearby Henlawshiel. Similarly commemorated is James Hogg, the celebrated 'Ettrick Shepherd' whose Neoclassical obelisk by *A. G. Heiton*, 1898, marks the site of his birthplace at Ettrick, with portrait medallion by *W. Hubert Paton*. This is a superior work to *Andrew Currie*'s isolated

monument to Hogg erected in 1860 by St Mary's Loch, Cappercleuch, which shows the poet clad in shepherd's plaid with his
dog, Hector, at his feet. This has been overpainted in white, a
sad fate which has befallen other stone STATUES, including
Currie's 1859 statue at Selkirk of Mungo Park, surgeon, explorer
and writer and, also at Selkirk, that of Sir Walter Scott by *A.
Handyside Ritchie*, 1839, which shows Scott seated in Sheriff's
dress in front of the Old Court House. Scott is the figure who
commanded respect more than any other figures of his day and
small monuments to him appear in several places throughout the
Borders. Some of his glory is granted also to George Meikle
Kemp, sculptor of the Scott Memorial in Edinburgh, who has his
own memorial at Redscarshead (Eddleston) erected in the 1930s.

Commemorative monuments erected to family members take
several forms including the memorial gateway with paired Tuscan
columns and carved armorials at Shedden Park, Kelso, 1861,
which commemorates Robert Shedden, who perished searching
for Sir John Franklin's expedition. A good contrast of styles over
an interval of several generations can be seen at The Hirsel,
where, hidden away by the Leet Water, is an obelisk (6.1 m. high)
erected by the ninth Earl of Home in memory of his son William,
Lord Dunglass, killed at the Battle of Guildford in 1781 during
the American War of Independence. Of more recent date is the
neat bronze statue of Lord Home of The Hirsel (Sir Alec
Douglas-Home, 1903–95) by *Bill Scott*, forming the centrepiece
of a ring of sculptured stones and seats, which celebrate his
statesmanship and interest in country pursuits.

Monuments after 1900 reflect developing trends in public
sculpture. Particularly notable are the bronze African figures and
pictorial panels added to Mungo Park's monument in Selkirk in
1906 and 1912 by *Thomas J. Clapperton*, who in the latter year
also designed the splendid bronze figure of 'Fletcher' bearing
aloft a captured English banner, which commemorates Selkirk
men killed at Flodden in 1513. An equestrian statue at Hawick,
'The Horse' by *William F. & Thomas Beattie*, celebrates the four
hundredth anniversary of a skirmish in 1514, when the callants
(youths) defeated the English marauders. In Duns, the medieval
friar and theologian John Duns Scotus is honoured with a half-
length bronze by *F. D. Seitschler*, 1966, while of the same decade
is a pylon with a clock and model racing car at Chirnside, a
poignant reminder of the racing driver Jim Clark, killed in 1968.

There are a large number of War Memorials in the Borders;
most parishes had one, and often two. Always rare are Boer War
memorials, but good examples are the tall obelisk Wauchope
Monument, Yetholm, by *Thomas Marwick*, executed by *Waldie &
Son*, 1902, in memory of Major General Wauchope, and the
Patriotic Monument at Hawick, 1903, by *J. N. Scott & A. Lorne
Campbell*, with a figure of a soldier by *Thomas D. Rhind*. The
majority of First World War memorials are representations of a
carved Celtic cross, sometimes with a double-handed sword
upon the shaft, and simple crosses on a base. At Melrose, *Robert
S. Lorimer* designed a Greek cross, 1921, and at Kelso his mercat
cross style memorial incorporates a statue of St George with a
lance, by *C. & O. Pilkington Jackson*, and at Skirling (1920) his
square shaft is topped by a cross. Figures of soldiers are partic-

ularly poignant, with notable examples at Walkerburn by *James B. Dunn*, 1923, with a great-coated 'Tommy' by *Alexander Carrick* set within a concrete and white granite enclosure. At Minto, the soldier stands guard on a boulder base, by *Thomas J. Clapperton*, 1925; Newcastleton's soldier, on a granite base, has a fixed
115 bayonet. Hawick's memorial is a cenotaph, 1921, by *James B. Dunn*, with a bronze winged statue of the 'Spirit of Youth Tri-
94 umphing over Evil' by *Alexander Leslie*; a grander composition is *Robert S. Lorimer's* clock tower and memorial at Galashiels, 1924–7, which is fronted by a sturdy equestrian statue of a Border Reiver (mosstrooper) by *Thomas J. Clapperton*. Sprouston's tall cairn of *c.* 1920 tapers to a rock, a lion astride the top by *J. S. Rhind*. In the courtyard of the Chambers Institution, Peebles, is the finest memorial as a work of art. The domed hexagonal shrine
33 by *B. N. H. Orphoot*, 1922, shelters a Celtic cross decorated with Byzantine mosaic work by *G. Malranga*, carving by *Thomas Beattie* and bronze panels by the *Bromsgrove Guild*.

MOTTES, CASTLES AND TOWER HOUSES

The Borders form the southern part of the historic province of Lothian, comprising the medieval sheriffdoms of Berwick, Roxburgh, Selkirk and Peebles (originally Traquair), all of which were in existence by the early C13. A number of factors ensured that the region was well stocked with CASTLES. In the first place much of it was attractive for settlement, containing not only some of the best agricultural land in Scotland but also considerable areas of royal demesne, as well as six early burghs, all but one of them royal. Secondly, a large part of the region lay less than thirty miles from the English border, the rich, cereal-producing lands of the Berwickshire Merse actually looking directly across the River Tweed into Northumberland. In consequence, throughout the period of the Anglo-Scottish wars, i.e. from the late C13 to the late C16, the Borders counties were subject to intermittent incursions by English armies, the southern part of the area at times being under direct English occupation. To meet this threat the government secured the royal castles as and when it could and in general (but not invariably) encouraged the building and strengthening of private castles in the region. During the latter part of the period, in particular, there was also endemic feuding between different kinship groups along, and on either side of, the Border. In such circumstances those who could afford to do so took steps to provide themselves with defensible houses in order to protect themselves, their families, goods and livestock.

Castles, then, were erected for residential and administrative, as well as for strategic and defensive purposes, and in the Borders, more than in some other parts of Scotland, castle building continued up to the time of the Union of the Crowns in 1603 and beyond. The earliest record of such activities occurs *c.* 1100, when one of King Edgar's English barons, a certain Robert fitz Godwin, tried to build a castle on his estate near the English border but was prevented from doing so by followers of the Bishop of Durham. By the time of the late C13 First Wars of Inde-

pendence there were about a dozen major castles in the region –
about the same density as in other parts of lowland Scotland –
together with at least fifteen or sixteen lesser ones. Numbers
increased markedly in the later Middle Ages and it can be esti-
mated that during the C16 and early C17, by which time even
lesser landholders were generally building in stone, there were at
least two hundred and seventy castles, towers and defensible
houses and probably considerably more. During the later Middle
Ages the region, with adjacent parts of northern England, was
administered under the Laws of the Marches by wardens
appointed on each side of the Border. The Scottish East March
took in most of Berwickshire, while the Middle March comprised
the sheriffdoms of Peebles, Roxburgh and Selkirk.

Robert fitz Godwin's castle has not been identified, but may
well have been either a motte or a ringwork (i.e. an earthen platform surrounded by a bank and ditch), for it is known that several
of the Anglo-Norman and Breton barons who colonised the
region during the C12 and C13 erected structures of these types.
MOTTE CASTLES were also favoured by the Kings of Scots to
serve as local administrative headquarters and to foster developing trading centres. David I built mottes at Selkirk, Peebles,
probably Jedburgh and possibly Roxburgh, where extensive
earthworks survive. Most, if not all, of the mottes were formed
by modifying natural mounds.

Among EARTHWORK CASTLES erected by the greater barons
the most important were Lauder, Liddel and Hermitage. Lauder
and Liddel were the *capita* of the powerful families of de Morville
and de Soules, both established in extensive lordships by David
I. In each case a naturally strong position overlooking a river
valley, at Lauder a ridge and at Liddel (Castleton) a promontory,
was adapted to enhance its defensive capability. At Lauder, where
the site is now partly overlain by Thirlestane Castle, these modifications produced what might loosely be described as a motte-
and-bailey castle, while Liddel looks more like a ringwork with
an adjacent, but slightly smaller, bailey. Hermitage Castle
replaced Liddel Castle as the principal castle of Liddesdale at
about the beginning of the C14, but the impressive earthworks
there, recently identified as a massive ringwork with associated
bailey, are likely to have been constructed during the 1240s. The
lesser baronial castles include mottes at Hawick and Riddell, both
probably in existence by the middle of the C12, and ringworks at
Bunkle and Smailholm. At Peebles excavation on the summit of
the motte revealed traces of two C12 timber structures, while at
Selkirk, as refurbished by Edward I, the buildings included a
timber tower on the summit of the motte and a timber palisade
enclosing the bailey; the principal gateway, however, was of stone.
Some Anglo-Norman barons may have lived in now vanished
timber halls, while others may have inhabited what can be
described as MOATED SITES, which, it is currently assumed, date
from the C12 to the mid C14. About half a dozen have so far been
identified within the Borders. Among the best-preserved are
Dykehead (Bonchester Bridge) and Muirhouselaw (Maxton), the
former possibly a residence of the Turnbull family.

In contrast to the English side of the frontier, only a few fragmentary remains of C12 and C13 STONE CASTLES can now be

seen in the Borders. In part this is explained by the loss of a number of major castles through destruction or decay, but it also has to be remembered that a number of the English examples, including the royal castle of Berwick upon Tweed, were, in fact, founded by the Kings of Scots and their followers during those periods when parts of Cumbria and Northumberland lay under
39   Scottish rule. The baronial castles of Hume and Bedrule deserve mention here on account of their plan forms, for neither retains much in the way of standing masonry. If Hume Castle did, indeed, originate in the C13 its large size (40.6 m. by 39.4 m. externally), simple rectangular plan and the apparent absence of mural towers and gatehouse, link it to a group of three royal castles (Kincardine (Kincardineshire), Kinclaven (Perth and Kinross) and Tarbert (Argyll and Bute)), all probably erected during the reign of Alexander II (1214–49). To judge from its overall size (c. 61 m. by 40 m.), the Comyn castle of Bedrule, too, was an establishment of the front rank. In this case the plan appears to be that of a developed castle of enclosure, complete with gatehouse and mural towers, suggesting a date of erection about the turn of the C13 and C14.

The existing remains of stone castles of the C14 and C15 are again scanty. It is difficult to appreciate that Roxburgh Castle, as reconstructed by the English Royal Works following its recapture by Edward III, was one of the finest castles of the Anglo-Scottish border. The centrepiece of the late medieval castle was an inner bailey having a donjon at one corner and curtain walls strengthened by intermediate towers. The main approach seems to have been from the E, and on this side the curtain incorporated three towers each 50 ft (15.2 m.) high, the central one being a gatehouse having a first-floor hall as well as a barbican. The chief architect of the reconstruction, carried out at very high cost mainly during the 1380s and 1390s, was *John Lewyn*, one of the leading English master masons of the day. Lewyn's name has also
40   been linked with the first stone castle of Hermitage, apparently erected c. 1355–70 by Hugh Dacre, a Cumbrian baron, in what was then English-occupied Liddesdale, but as yet the attribution remains unproven. Surprisingly, in view of its frontier position, Dacre's castle seems to been a lightly defended manor house of quite modest size, and one wonders whether it was intended primarily as a hunting box. Only the lowest storey now survives, but the house seems to have comprised two residential blocks flanking a tiny oblong courtyard of which the other two sides were enclosed with screen walls. Close parallels are hard to find on either side of the Border, although there are similarities with the arrangements seen at the roughly contemporary castles of Millom (Cumberland), and Danby (Yorkshire); neither of these, however, is as compact as Hermitage.

Fragments of two late medieval CASTLES OF ENCLOSURE can be seen at Fast and Cowdenknowes, their plans in each case being determined largely by the natural configuration of the site. At Fast Castle, where the curtain wall stands on the edge of the sea cliffs, there were two courtyards at different levels, the upper one containing a hall and chamber block with an associated kitchen and the lower a single-storey service range. At Cowdenknowes there was a single courtyard. As developed during the early and middle decades of the c16, this seems to have comprised a curtain wall with two or more corner towers, together with a service range and what was probably either a hall and chamber block or a tower house; this last was replaced by a Renaissance mansion in 1574 (*see* below, p. 53).

Tower Houses

In the Borders, as in many other parts of Scotland, the great majority of castles built during the later Middle Ages were so-called TOWER HOUSES, the term used here to describe a castle of which the principal component was a defensible residential tower designed primarily for occupation by the lord and his immediate household. Although present appearances may sometimes argue otherwise, the tower did not stand alone, but was grouped with other elements, such as hall, kitchen and stable, the whole complex being linked by an outer wall to form a defensive enclosure known as a barmkin.

It seems that tower houses began to be erected in the region during the last two or three decades of the c14, i.e. at about the same time as in other parts of Scotland, but perhaps a quarter of a century later than in Northumberland and Cumbria. In marked contrast to Northumberland only a handful of substantial tower houses are known to have been built in the Borders before the middle of the c15 and probably not more than about thirty in all before the death of James IV in 1513. The most important survivors comprise a group of five very large towers (average base area 338 sq.m.) built by the Crown and noble, or near noble, families. Much the biggest was Hermitage Castle, reared on the 40 stump of the earlier manor house during the late c14 and early c15. The tower house was unusual in having rectangular turrets at each corner, an arrangement found also in the somewhat earlier towers of Dacre Castle and Langley Castle on the English side of the Border. Some of the architectural detail was also decidedly northern English in character, suggesting that the Douglas earls, like their Dacre predecessors, brought masons in from Northumberland or Cumbria.

Neidpath Castle (*c.* 1375–1400?) and Cessford Castle (*c.* 1425– *p. 161* 50?) were massive L-plan towers, vaulted at two or more levels *37, 38* and with their bulky walls honeycombed with ancillary chambers. Duns Castle (*c.* 1460–90?), of which only the lowest portion survives, was also built on an L-plan, while the royal tower of Newark Castle, here ascribed to *c.* 1465–90, was a simple oblong, well equipped with mural chambers, but vaulted only at first-floor level. The tower, constructed within an earlier barmkin containing a great hall and other buildings, seems to have been designed primarily as a private lodging for the King. At first-floor level was the King's hall with a kitchen at its lower end, while above were superimposed suites, each consisting of an outer and inner chamber plus closets. At Neidpath the barmkin was quite small and the principal hall seems to have been contained within *p. 44,* the tower, where it occupied the whole of the middle tier of the *579* main block, with an associated kitchen in the wing. Above was the lord's hall and chamber, plus closets, with perhaps a similar *37*

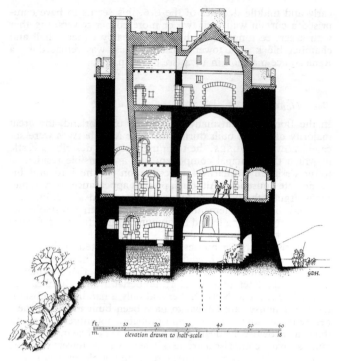

ft.   10   20   30   40   50   60
m.   elevation drawn to half-scale   18

Neidpath Castle. Reconstuction of interior.

38 suite for his wife directly above that. The arrangements at Cess-
40 ford may have been similar, although the very large barmkin
    could easily have accommodated a hall. At Hermitage Castle
    greater emphasis was placed upon the castle's military role, the
    upper floors, including what seems to have been a great hall, evi-
    dently capable of accommodating a good-sized garrison. The lord
    and his family were housed in the largest of the angle turrets,
    which contained a stack of well-appointed chambers on three
    levels, as well as a kitchen.

    In addition to this group of very large tower houses, there are
    about a dozen examples of more modest size (average base area
    103 sq.m.) which can be attributed to the late c15 and early c16.
    These were built mostly by established landholding families of
    middling rank, such as the Haigs, Swintons, Lauders and
    Pringles. All were of simple, oblong plan with walls usually
    between 1 m. and 2 m. thick rising to a height of three or four
    storeys. The ground floor was invariably vaulted, sometimes with
    an entresol floor within the vault, and in some cases, e.g. at
    Corsbie and Castlehill Towers, there were vaults at an upper level
    as well. Most of these towers have lost their upperworks, but
    Cranshaws Tower retains its original open wall-walks. Smailholm
41 is the only tower in this group to retain a barmkin, which in its

initial phase appears to have contained a single-storey hall with associated chamber, together with a kitchen.

So far as we can judge from the very slender evidence now available, the planning arrangements adopted in this group of tower houses were scaled-down versions of those found in the larger towers. In cases such as Smailholm Tower, where the barmkin contained a hall and chamber(s), the tower presumably functioned mainly as a private lodging. Where there was little or no separate residential accommodation we must assume that the laird's seigneurial duties were normally performed within the tower, with the hall – usually a spacious room occupying the whole of the first floor – serving as guest chamber, estate office, court room and banqueting hall as and when required. At Bemersyde and Cranshaws Tower there was a kitchen at the lower end of the hall, but elsewhere cooking is likely to have been carried out within the barmkin. There were usually at least two floors above the hall to house the laird and his family, but how these were arranged is hard to say. In most of the towers of this group each of the upper floors seems to have comprised a single chamber only, but these may have been subdivided by timber partitions. Like their grander counterparts, most of these towers were fitted with mural latrines served by internal discharge shafts. Furnishings were probably scanty, with items often being moved from one chamber to another to ensure the most flexible use of space. When John Lowis of Manor was summoned to deliver up his tower of Castlehill in June 1555, the only furniture forthcoming was a table, two benches, four hanging doors without locks and 'ane hart horn (chandelier) hingand in the hall'.

The hundred years or so after the Battle of Flodden (1513) saw a progressive increase in the number of tower houses erected in the region, with building activity apparently peaking during the last decades of the C16 and the early years of the C17. Several factors combined to bring this about. One of the most important was the widespread feuing of Crown and Church lands from the reign of James IV onwards. Feu-ferm tenure gave the feuar security of possession, and because his annual feu-duty was fixed at the outset he also benefited from contemporary price inflation. Encouraged by a government keen to promote rural improvement, many feuars marked their new-found status by erecting stone-built houses, mostly in the form of towers. Another factor which could create conditions favourable to building was the forcible transfer of wealth through Border warfare. For much of the time the government also encouraged the construction of tower houses in the interests of security and as a means of defence against foreign or other enemies. The licence for the erection of Ayton Tower (1471), situated only 6km. from the Border, specifically mentions its proposed role in resisting English attack. In an Act of Parliament of 1535 entitled 'For Bigging of Strenthis on the Bordouris', landholders having rentals worth £100 or more were required to build a barmkin of stone and lime 60ft (18.3m.) square with walls 0.9m. thick and 5.6m. high in order to safeguard their tenants and their goods in time of trouble, 'with ane toure in the samin for him self gif he thinkis it expedient'. Lesser landholders were to build 'pelis and gret strenthis' for the same purpose. It is clear from official reports of the English raids of the 1540s that considerable numbers of towers and barmkins were in existence at that time. These raids, and other major incursions in 1522–3 and 1570, laid waste the most populous areas of the East and Middle Marches, devastating towns, villages and monasteries, as well as towers and peles. Not all affected buildings were completely destroyed, however, for stone-built tower houses, even when gutted 'both roof and walls', could be made habitable again. Only when the attackers resorted to gunpowder, as at Branxholm Castle in 1570, was it necessary to carry out a major reconstruction.

In contrast to the previous period, the century following the death of James IV (†1513) saw a greater volume of tower house building on the Scottish, than on the English, side of the Border. As before, the builders were drawn mainly from established landowning families, such as the Scotts, Douglases and Riddells, but now with a sprinkling of substantial feu-ferm and kindly tenants and one or two professional men and burgesses. Their distribution was governed mainly by the availability of good agricultural land, and they stood mostly in the valleys below an altitude of *c.* 240 m. In some areas, such as the lordship of Melrose, where feus were often quite small in extent, towers lay thick upon
47 the ground. Several towers, including Aikwood, Buckholm Tower and Greenknowe Tower, were built to replace older buildings on the same, or an adjacent, site, while in other cases, such as Traquair House, an earlier fabric was remodelled and enlarged.
52 Of the three dozen or so tower houses described here about a quarter can be attributed to *c.* 1513–70 and the remainder to the late C16 and early C17. In general they are smaller than their predecessors (average base area 75 sq.m.), those of the early and middle decades of the C16 being characterised by their simple rectangular plans, thicker walls (*c.* 1–1.8 m.) and open wall-walks.

From about the middle of the C16 onwards the L-plan returned to favour and about a dozen tower houses of that period are of this type. Oblong towers continued to be built, however, and other layouts are occasionally found. At Darnick Tower a T-plan was adopted, while Old Thirlestane Castle, originally oblong, was converted to a T by the addition of a stair-turret. The early tower at Traquair House, as reconstructed in about the second quarter of the C16, seems to have had a residential wing on one side and there are traces of similar wings, contemporary or near contemporary with the tower, at Greenknowe Tower and Nether Horsburgh Castle.

All these towers are likely to have had associated BARMKINS, the most interesting of the few surviving examples being at Whytbank, where recent site clearance has revealed, in addition to the tower house, a two-storey range incorporating a kitchen and a first-floor hall and chamber, as well as two other ranges containing what may have been a granary, a barn and a brewhouse. At Holydean Castle one range of the barmkin survives, containing a kitchen or bakehouse, and good examples of barmkin gateways can be seen there and at Buckholm. At both Buckholm and Whytbank the barmkin appears to have been constructed mainly with clay mortar rather than lime mortar.

In some respects these later tower houses were less well equipped for DEFENCE than their predecessors. Certainly their

thinner walls (usually less than 1.2 m.) and larger, and more
numerous, window openings made them vulnerable to siege
operations, while some of them seem to have been roofed with
thatch rather than slate. From the 1580s onwards – e.g. at Greenknowe Tower and Hillslap Tower – parapeted wall-walks and open
angle rounds began to give way to oversailing roofs and pepper-   42
pot turrets, and where traditional features of this kind were
retained, as at Kirkhope Tower and Evelaw Tower, they seem to
have been valued as much as badges of rank as for any military
purpose. But the main threat at this period came not from siege
armies, but from swift-moving and lightly armed raiding parties,
whether from across the Border or across the hill. The most effective means of defence against such attack was the hand firearm,
and as these weapons came into common use from about the
1540s onwards, so tower houses and barmkins were increasingly
provided with gunloops (also known as gunports and shot-holes).
Apart from the huge loops inserted into the late C14 tower house
of Hermitage Castle c. 1540, and evidently intended for cannon,
the earliest dated examples of this type of defence in the region   40
occur at Winkston (1545). Thereafter, the great majority of tower
houses were equipped with gunloops of one kind or another,
although some of the loops found in the later towers, such as
Aikwood (1602), look more decorative than functional. Another
vital aid to security was the yett, a heavy, grated door of wrought
iron hung immediately behind the outer, wooden entrance door
and secured by a bolt or drawbar. In Scottish Borders examples
survive at Barns, Greenknowe and Smailholm.

So far as DOMESTIC PLANNING is concerned, the main developments traceable at this period are the increase in the number
of chambers – despite a general reduction in base area – and
improvements in staircase design. Progress in both these respects
was greatly facilitated by the adoption of the L-plan, which also
made it convenient to place the principal entrance close to the
inner, or re-entrant, angle. In several cases, e.g. at Greenknowe
Tower and Hillslap Tower, the lowest flight of the stair occupied
the wing, while the upper flights were housed in a small turret
thrust out in the re-entrant angle, an arrangement which left the
upper floors of the wing free to contain additional chambers. In
other cases, as at Cardrona Tower and Darnick Tower (1569), the
stair rose vertically within the wing, occupying almost the entire
area at each level. In a number of towers, such as Timpendean,
the first floor contained both hall and kitchen, while a few towers
of the late C16 and early C17, including Aikwood Tower and
Lessudden House, had a hall-and-chamber arrangement at this   47
level. It is on the upper floors, however, that the increase in the
number of chambers is most noticeable. L-plan tower houses,
such as Greenknowe Tower, sometimes contained three chambers on each floor at these levels, the uppermost ones also being
equipped with closets or studies contained in angle-turrets.
Oblong tower houses usually contained only a single chamber at
each level, as before, but at Colmslie Tower and Aikwood Tower
the second floor incorporated a two-room suite which probably
served as the laird's private quarters. One domestic innovation
which must have made life more agreeable for the occupants was
the introduction of the soil-box latrine (also known as the stool

of ease, close stool or dry closet) in place of the open, shafted latrine. While some towers, such as Barns Tower, continued to be equipped with shafted latrines, the portable variety became increasingly popular from the third quarter of the C16 onwards. A number of tower houses of this period also bear witness to the more widespread use of window glass. At Greenknowe Tower many of the windows were part glazed, the upper part of the opening containing small panels of glass set within lead frames, while the lower part was fitted with timber shutters.

Peles and Bastles

Only the upper ranks of Border society could generally afford to build tower houses. Men of lesser substance, such as portioners and smaller tenant farmers, as well as the more prosperous merchants and tradesmen in the burghs, sought comfort and security in defensible residences of more modest kinds. Contemporary sources make it clear that considerable numbers of such buildings, known by various names, including PELES and BASTLES, existed in the region during the C16. In this volume, following the terminology employed by RCAHMS, peles denote small, barn-like, stone buildings built with clay mortar and usually unvaulted, while bastles denote larger houses built with lime mortar and usually with vaulted ground floors.* During the C13 and C14 the term pele (from the Latin *palus*, a stake) was used to describe a defensible enclosure equipped with a palisade, like the one at Selkirk Castle. The peles that lesser landholders in the Borders were enjoined to build by the Act of 1535 were probably mostly of this type, but by then the term was also being used to denote defensible houses of timber and clay of a kind now known only from contemporary documents. During the C16 we hear of peles and pele houses of stone and in more recent times Border tower houses in general have come to be known as pele towers.

Although at one time probably more numerous than tower houses, peles and bastles were more vulnerable to change and few now survive within Scottish Borders – or indeed elsewhere in Scotland. The PELES are small, oblong structures of two storeys and a garret having external proportions of between 1:1.2 and 1:1.7 and overall base areas of between 50 sq. m. and 88 sq. m. Constructed of local rubble bound with clay, these buildings were ceiled with timber joists and their gable-ended roofs were probably covered with turf and thatch. There were separate entrances to ground and first floors, the lower doorway usually being placed in an end wall and the upper one, which must have been reached from a forestair, in a side wall. In most cases there seems to have been no internal communication between these two levels other than by ladder. The ground-floor chamber, invariably poorly lit, probably housed a horse or two as well as cattle, while the upper floors contained living quarters for the farmer and his family. There were no stone-built chimneys, but the upper floors were probably heated by canopied fireplaces of clay and wattle. These houses did not stand alone, but

---

* This classification differs from that used in *The Buildings of England: Northumberland* (1989).

formed part of farmsteads incorporating outbuildings and enclosures which today survive only as turf-grown footings. Of the four
peles of this kind described in this volume, three (Kilnsike,
Mervinslaw, Slacks Pele) belong to a group of about a dozen in
the uplands of the Jed Water, immediately to the N of the
Anglo–Scottish frontier. One or two have been noted elsewhere
in the region, e.g. Gray Coat Pele in Upper Teviotdale, and many
more are to be found just across the Border in the Northumbrian
and Cumbrian uplands. Most of the Scottish examples were
probably built by small tenant farmers during the late C16 and
early C17.

Sharing some of the characteristics of the pele is the BASTLE,
a term (from the French *bastille*, a small fortification) used during
the late C15 and C16 to describe various kinds of defensible house
and other lightly fortified places. In the Borders the term seems
to have been current mainly in the East and Middle Marches,
where mention was made not only of individual bastles, but of
groups of two or more. Thus, three bastle houses were said to
have been captured at Bughtrig, near Eccles, in 1544, while the
village of Lessudden was reported to contain no fewer than
sixteen bastles at that time. Later writers, prompted by Sir Walter
Scott, equated bastles with the numerous towers that are
known to have existed in Border towns, such as Hawick and
Jedburgh.

The bastles are mostly of elongated oblong plan, with external
proportions in the range of 1:1.6 to 1:2.4 and overall base areas
of between 75 sq. m. and 122 sq. m. They were thus, for the most
part, both larger and longer than peles and some of them, at least,
contained two rooms on the first floor – perhaps hall and
chamber – and were equipped with stone-built chimneys. Old
Gala House, Galashiels which is unusual in being unvaulted, had
a heated chamber on the ground floor as well, but in most cases
this floor was probably occupied by a stable and byre. Bastles
were more architecturally sophisticated than peles. Windydoors
incorporated a moulded entrance doorway, Old Gala House was
embellished with an armorial panel, while Fisher's Tower,
Darnick, was equipped with gunloops.

Of the few surviving bastles most are found in towns and villages or stand isolated in good agricultural land, but Windydoors
has an upland location. Rather more information about their
dates of erection and the identity and status of their builders is
available than for the peles. The core of Fairnington House may
be the 'bastell house' burnt by the English in 1544 and afterwards
rebuilt, while Littledean Tower probably incorporates part of the
'stone house' that escaped destruction in the same year. Littledean belonged to a cadet branch of the Kerrs of Cessford, while
Fisher's Tower, Darnick, was probably erected *c.* 1570 by John
Fisher, a substantial tenant of the lordship of Melrose. The bastle
that forms part of the present Old Gala House was built as a secondary residence by Andrew Pringle of Smailholm, a wealthy
laird, in 1583.

Artillery forts, town defences and later defensive works

Apart from improvements made to Lochmaben Castle (Dumfries and Galloway), in the West March, there was little building

activity at the royal castles in the Borders during the reigns of James IV and V (1488–1542). All this changed during the early years of Mary's reign, when Henry VIII invaded Scotland in an attempt to enforce the betrothal of the young queen to his son Prince Edward. Because it was Henry who took the initiative, and because his commanders decided that the best way to subdue southern Scotland was to install sizeable garrisons at strategic points, much of this building was carried out by the English government. In the Borders military engineers of the English Royal Works erected ARTILLERY FORTS at Eyemouth and Lauder (Thirlestane Castle) during the late 1540s, using the latest techniques of Continental fortification. Indeed, Eyemouth *p. 270* Fort (1548) appears to have been the first *trace italienne* fort to have been built in the British Isles. These forts were primarily earthwork defences designed to resist cannon fire. They comprised broad ditches and low, immensely thick curtain walls punctuated by near triangular bastions flanked by gun emplacements providing crossfire. Similar principles were applied to the design of the fort erected within the former inner bailey of Roxburgh Castle, which also incorporated two raised gun platforms for outward defence. Works undertaken by the Franco–Scottish alliance in opposition to English forces included the strengthening of Hume Castle in 1545 and the reconstruction of Eyemouth Fort in 1558. Here the central bastion of the original fort was retained and a second curtain was constructed outside it, having a large bastion at each end.

Provision for TOWN DEFENCES varied considerably over time and from one burgh to another. In some cases reliance was placed simply upon a ditch and bank, each burgess being required to build a turf dyke at the rear of his property to connect with that of his neighbour, thus forming a complete circuit of the burgh. Gateways, known as ports, were constructed at the main points of entry to control access. At Selkirk, Jedburgh and Hawick defences of this kind seem to have been in use throughout the medieval period, although each burgh also contained a number of stone-built residential towers or bastles which provided an additional level of personal security for the wealthier inhabitants. At Berwick (Northumberland), however, where strategic considerations encouraged both the English and Scottish governments to lay out large sums on defence, Edward I supplemented the original palisaded embankment with stone walls which were afterwards heightened by the Scots. At Roxburgh a stone wall was added in the early C14 and at Peebles as late as the 1570s. The surviving portion of this latter wall, including a blockhouse equipped for firearm defence, constitutes the only substantial fragment of early town defences now visible in the Borders.

Later defensive works are more miscellaneous in character. Although the Borders saw a good deal of military activity during the Civil Wars – Hume Castle, for example, was largely demolished following its surrender to Cromwell's army in 1651 – the only surviving remains of any consequence are the Covenanters' redoubt on Duns Law. This is a bastioned earthwork erected as a temporary base for General Leslie's forces *c.* 1639. A number of C20 DEFENCE WORKS also survive, although many have been dismantled during recent decades. Stobs Camp, which operated as a military training base for more than fifty years, preserves interesting remains of a practice trench system, while *Rennie*'s splendid Kelso Bridge of 1801–4 is guarded by a Second World War pill-box whose loopholes pierce the original parapet. Other Second World War works include the Drone Hill radar station (*see* Grantshouse), Charterhall Airfield (commissioned during the First World War) and a munitions factory at Charlesfield (*see* St Boswells) which produced many of the incendiary bombs dropped by the RAF on Germany in 1943–5.

MANSIONS AND COUNTRY HOUSES

Although tower houses remained popular up to the end of the c16 and beyond, some of the greater lairds had already begun to build larger houses of a rather different kind. First appearing in the Borders in about the 1570s, these EARLY MANSIONS were no less lofty than tower houses, but their elongated plan form gave them a more horizontal emphasis which reflected their distinctive accommodation arrangements. Some of them, such as Traquair House and Hutton Hall (1573), incorporated earlier tower houses, while others, like Branxholme Castle (1572–6) and 52 Ferniehirst Castle (1598), embodied a prominent tower at one 44 end, as if to reaffirm their castellated status. All of them contained an impressive suite of reception rooms laid out horizontally and served by separate public and private stairs – an arrangement probably borrowed from the royal palaces of James IV and James V. The reception suite, normally comprising a hall, outer chamber and inner chamber, was usually set directly over a vaulted cellarage, the principal entrance to the house being placed at the foot of a stair-tower situated at or near one end of the range. The upper floors might contain a separate suite of chambers for family use, as well as additional chambers and perhaps a gallery. Sometimes, as at Drochil Castle (1578) and Thirlestane Castle (*c.* 1587–90), the principal accommodation was contained within a single main block, but courtyard layouts were also popular, residential and service wings being grouped round two or three sides of a rectangular court or barmkin, with the principal gateway placed in one of the remaining sides.

These mansions were erected by wealthy lairds, many of them of noble or near-noble rank. Drochil Castle was a secondary residence of the Earl of Morton, Regent of Scotland, while Thirlestane was built by Sir John Maitland, James VI's Secretary 49 and Chancellor. Court connections also assisted the rise of the Stewarts of Traquair, the Kerrs of Ferniehirst and the Homes of Hutton Hall and Cowdenknowes. About a dozen of these mansions now survive in whole or part, together with several smaller ones, no less advanced in their planning and decoration, built by lesser lairds like the Lumsdens of Blanerne and the Pringles of Torwoodlee. Like contemporary tower houses, these mansions were defensible against Border raids, but were not designed to resist full-scale assault. Their thick stone walls and vaulted and sparsely lit ground floors gave them some protection against fire, while gunloops, iron yetts and window bars discouraged all but

the most determined intruder. In one or two cases more substantial defences were employed. At Cowdenknowes (1574) the
mansion was built inside an earlier barmkin, while at Branxholme
Castle, whose builder had seen his earlier residence blown up by
an English army only two years previously, a comprehensive
system of firearm defence was installed. Even as late as *c.* 1609
Nisbet House was equipped with no fewer than two dozen gunloops, while others were installed at Traquair House in the 1640s.
In most of these houses the roofs descended sheer to the wall-
head, but Branxholme Castle may have had an open wall-walk
at one end, while Thirlestane Castle seems to have incorporated
oversailing parapet-walks. Angle turrets were invariably roofed
and the fact that contemporaries often referred to them as
'studies' suggests that their primary function was recreational.

Another link between these mansions and contemporary tower
houses was a shared vocabulary of surface decoration. Characteristically this comprised a mixture of quasi-classical elements –
moulded string and eaves courses, entablatures, pilaster-framed
doorways and windows etc. – with revived Romanesque and
Gothic motifs such as chequered billets, nailhead, dogtooth and
chevron. Prominently displayed armorial panels were also
popular and some of the grander houses, such as Branxholme
Castle and Cowdenknowes, incorporated elaborate inscriptions.
Stylistic links were mainly with Lothian which, with the Borders,
became the focus of a distinctive school of early Renaissance decoration. The elaborate Roman lettering found at Cowdenknowes
appears in contemporary inscriptions around Edinburgh and at
Luffness House (Lothian, 1584), while the chevron ornament at
Blanerne Castle is paralleled at Innerwick Castle (Lothian). Connections can also be traced with the Stirling school of masons,
as seen at Torwood Castle of 1566 (Stirling and Central Scotland). At Hillslap Tower (1585), Dr Philip Dixon has postulated
the presence of both Scottish and English masons, the work of
the latter being characterised by the use of label mouldings of a
kind frequently found in late C16 Northumberland and Cumbria.
Label and other mouldings of English type also occur at Branxholme, in Upper Teviotdale, while mullioned and transomed
windows of Cumbrian appearance are found at nearby Harden
House in the second quarter of the C17. It is probable, therefore,
that the style of early Renaissance decoration found in most parts
of the region was introduced from Edinburgh and Central Scotland, with Northumberland making its own contribution in one
or two cases. By the early C17, if not before, this style had been
assimilated by local masons, notably those belonging to the Mein
and Bunzie families of Newstead. In the more remote parts of
Teviotdale, however, as earlier in Liddesdale, Cumbrian influence seems to have predominated.

During the 1620s and 1630s a distinctive kind of Scottish
Renaissance decoration, characterised by Mannerist motifs, such
as strapwork and buckle quoins, made a limited incursion into
the Borders. Examples appear in the private chapel at Ferniehirst
Castle and at Sir Patrick Hume's mansion of Redbraes Castle
(Marchmont House). The presence of Edinburgh masons seems
likely in both cases. Earlier fashions were not easily displaced,
however, and as late as 1680 the entrance doorway of the new

wing at Wedderlie House was decorated with revived Gothic as well as classical ornament.

One of the earliest of these mansions was Cowdenknowes, which may have played a key role in the dissemination of new ideas of planning and decoration. Probably replacing an earlier tower house, the new mansion incorporated a fashionable three-room suite on the first floor and a near-symmetrical show front embellished with finely carved ornamental detail, elements of which reappeared in later Borders houses such as Ferniehirst Castle. Hutton Hall, a stylish L-plan mansion, now retains only a modified version of its first-floor suite, while at Branxholme Castle the bones of a probable hall, chamber and closet sequence survive in c19 guise. All these houses seem to have been completed during the mid 1570s and all formed part of courtyard layouts incorporating earlier buildings.

The two most remarkable mansions of this group were Drochil Castle and Thirlestane Castle. Drochil had an unconventional double-pile plan based on a central corridor giving direct access to the chambers on either side – single-chamber lodgings to the N and reception and family rooms to the S. Additional accommodation was contained in two large towers thrust out from diagonally opposite corners of the main block, while the top floor of the corridor may have housed a gallery. The very large number of lodgings could suggest that the mansion was built as a hunting seat, while the exotic plan may derive from French examples, such as Chenonceau (Indre-et-Loire), published in Androuet du Cerceau's *Les Plus Excellents Bastiments de France* (1576–9). Although apparently not by the same hand, the ornamental detail is similar in style to that seen at Morton's Fife residence, Aberdour Castle, and at Morton's Gateway, Edinburgh Castle.

43

44

p. 211

Drochil Castle.
Engraving by R.W. Billings, *c.* 1845.

Possible candidates as designer of Drochil include *John Roytell*,
49 the Regent's French master mason. Thirlestane, too, had an
unusual plan, in this case designed to provide an extended suite
of reception rooms on the *piano nobile*, housed within an elongated main block punctuated at each corner by a circular tower.
The elevations, symmetrical on both their long and short axes,
were no less striking, for they incorporated balustrated parapet-
walks and balconies – an early example of the viewing platforms
that soon became popular in lairds' houses. As at Drochil, elements of the design may have been taken from du Cerceau's
volumes of 1576–9, e.g. the description of Saint-Germain-en-Laye
(Yvelines). Other links between Drochil and Thirlestane include
the redented gunloops and the distinctive way in which the circular angle towers merge with the rectangular caphouses above.

At Ferniehirst Castle the processional character of the reception suite was taken a stage further with the creation of an
enfilade of no fewer than five chambers, including a charming
timber-lined closet in the SE angle tower. Only at the Palace of
Holyroodhouse (Edinburgh), among his Scottish residences, did
James VI and I enjoy as much public and private space as Sir
Andrew Kerr. Moreover, the approach at Ferniehirst to what
should perhaps now be called the state apartment was by way of
a handsome open-well staircase, apparently the first of its kind
in the Borders. The ornamental detail is rich and varied, but not
innovative.

51 Among the larger houses of the early C17, Nisbet House seems
decidedly old-fashioned. Not only was it unusually well equipped
for defence, but its plan showed no advance upon that of Cowdenknowes, built perhaps forty years previously. Roughly contemporary with Nisbet, but very much more up to date, was the
48 substantial wing of 1611 added to the earlier bastle at Old Gala
House. Here the ground-floor cellars and kitchen were unvaulted
while the principal stair seems to have been of scale-and-platt

Thirlestane Castle.
Engraving by John Slezer, 1693.

type. By taking in the earlier chambers in the bastle a four-room suite may have been contrived on the first floor, including a large hall. Redbraes Castle, as remodelled in the fashionable Jacobean style in about the second quarter of the century, must have been one of the most impressive houses of its day, but only fragments survive. Traquair House was enlarged in 1599 and 1642 in keeping with the rising fortunes of its Stewart lairds, while during the 1670s the Duke of Lauderdale called in *Sir William Bruce* to remodel Thirlstane Castle. Bruce made no attempt to disguise the building's castle-like appearance, but the near-axial approach that he created, with its progressive build-up in height and depth towards the centre, was wholly in keeping with contemporary taste. Internally the most important changes were the creation of a family apartment on the ground floor and the sumptuous refurbishment of the state apartment. 52 p. 54 49 p. 717

The SMALLER MANSIONS of the late C16 and early C17 are less numerous and more fragmentary. Corbet Tower (1572?) and Blanerne Castle embodied architectural detail of high quality in the local Scottish Renaissance style, and the same was true of Old Torwoodlee House (1601) and Old Fairnilee House. Enough survives of the two latter to show that they incorporated elongated main blocks containing centrally placed entrance doorways opening into straight staircases which divided the house into two parts of roughly equal size. Both houses seem to have contained three-room suites on the first floor, and in both the scale stair rose to the first floor only, the ascent thereafter continuing by means of a newel staircase. Old Fairnilee also had at least one unvaulted living room on the ground floor, whereas at Old Torwoodlee the ground floor was probably vaulted throughout. The adoption of a central scale stair, with the consequent detachment of the hall from the remainder of the first-floor suite, foreshadowed the compact symmetrical plans that became popular later in the C17. Although new to the Borders, similar designs had already appeared elsewhere, a possible model being Duntarvie Castle (Lothian) of 1589.

The placing of some, at least, of the family living rooms on the ground floor, seen most conspicuously at Thirlestane Castle during the 1670s, is also found in a number of other C17 houses. At Harden House, built in several phases from about 1600 onwards, none of the ground-floor rooms seems to have been vaulted, and by the end of the century the hall, dining room, and probably the laird's own bedchamber, were all at this level. At Wedderlie House, where a large L-plan wing was added to the original tower house in 1680, several family rooms, together with the kitchen, were placed on the ground floor; none of the ground-floor chambers of this period were vaulted. Linthill is an L-plan block of mid-C17 date with an extruded staircase in the re-entrant angle. Here, the unvaulted ground floor seems originally to have comprised kitchen and cellarage, the family living rooms being on the two main upper floors.

Several of these mansions and houses must once have contained schemes of contemporary INTERIOR DECORATION, but only at Traquair House and Thirlestane Castle do substantial elements remain. Many of the chambers at Traquair seem to have been lavishly decorated with tempera painting in or after

1599 and a particularly fine mural painting of birds and animals, framed by Scriptural texts, can be seen in an upper room. Fragments of tempera-painted ceilings of similar type also survive at Neidpath Castle, Old Gala House and Sparrow Hall, Cockburnspath, while at Nisbet House one of the principal rooms seems originally to have been covered with a joisted and boarded ceiling painted with imitation timber graining.

Ribbed plaster ceilings of English Jacobean type were introduced into Scotland in about the second decade of the C17, and an early example, decorated with medallion heads and running ornament in low relief, is preserved in one of the upper chambers at Thirlestane Castle. The splendid high-relief ceilings that now adorn the state apartment are the work of London plaster-
50 ers brought in by *Sir William Bruce* during the 1670s. A contemporary ceiling in simpler style by local craftsmen can be seen at Harden House. Both Thirlestane and Harden also contain interesting carved stone chimneypieces, those at Harden incorporating spirited renderings of the Classical orders executed by a Newstead mason *c.* 1680. A Newstead mason of an earlier generation was probably responsible for the huge armorial lintel at Old Gala House, all that now survives of what was evidently a most impressive hall chimneypiece. C17 carved woodwork is in short supply, but Thirlestane retains some tantalising fragments of Mannerist doorpieces, possibly brought up from Ham House (Surrey), during the 1670s, while Traquair houses a remarkable oak door transferred from the now demolished Terregles House (Dumfries and Galloway). Examples of plain pine panelling can be seen at Neidpath Castle and Wedderlie House.

Country houses in the LATE SEVENTEENTH CENTURY express a desire to impose symmetry on informally planned older houses, rather than a major rebuilding. A particularly important but unrealised scheme was proposed for Traquair House by *James Smith* in 1695. He was asked to remodel the house to a symmetrical design, but only executed the formal courtyard, flanked by service wings and linked by classical screen walls containing a principal gate, the details of which show Smith's familiarity with Italian architecture. The greatest influence on houses into the EARLY EIGHTEENTH CENTURY, however, was the designs of *Sir William Bruce*, whose own house at Balcaskie (Fife) of the 1660s still informed the remodelling, completed in 1715, of Barony Castle (Black Barony) where Sir Alexander Murray extended his C16 tower house to a symmetrical U-plan arrangement with four-storey square angle towers terminating in ogee roofs. Also completed at about this date, and also following the pattern of a house with angle towers of equal height, is Marlefield, erected (or possibly extended) for Sir William Bennet, who is known to have been a friend of Bruce. The Hirsel, built for the seventh Earl of Home soon after 1706, has a U-shaped plan with projecting two-
54 bay wings and single-bay closet towers projecting from the corners, the SW one incorporated in a later addition. Its W front, however, is topped by a chimneyed pediment. This was the general pattern in the late C17 and early C18, where owners satisfied themselves with improvements rather than rebuilding to achieve the appropriate external appearance and the desired level of comfort in planning. Even in lesser houses this could reveal

work of serious ambition, as at Lessudden House, remodelled in the late 1680s, where the first-floor principal chambers are reached by a stone and timber staircase of unusually grand design, perhaps modelled on Bruce's stair at the Palace of Holyroodhouse (Edinburgh). It reappears in similar form at Fairnington House. The desired symmetrical effect externally was achieved at Smailholm House, where the walls of the s wing were raised and regularised in 1707, the interior remodelled and given suites of panelled rooms on each floor connected by a handsome oak stair. Classical detail was also employed as at Old Gledswood in 1703 with a symmetrical crowstepped five-bay block, with cavetto-moulded skewputts, and a moulded doorpiece with entablature.

During the C18 many of the Borders families were linked to each other and to the Scottish aristocracy in general by marriage and patronage. Well-connected nobles and lairds enhanced the value of their estates by agricultural improvement but might also enjoy new sources of income in government positions or the employ of the East India Company. An enthusiastic interest in art, gardens and landscape, nurtured by a wider education and undertaking the Grand Tour, increased the ambition of many amongst the landed class to adopt English and Continental models of architecture and to integrate house, garden and landscape into a complete design. The introduction of the CLASSICAL MANSION HOUSE to Scotland is often attributed to *Sir William Bruce*, but his only work in this style in the Borders is Mertoun House, designed in 1703 for Sir William Scott of Harden, whose wife was a relation. Mertoun is a smaller version of Bruce's Kinross House (Perth and Kinross, 1685–93), complete with a double-pile plan and mezzanine rooms. It typifies the model of houses of the 1670s such as Moncreiffe and Dunkeld (both Perth and Kinross, and demolished), probably designed by Bruce on a compact rectangular plan with symmetrically composed elevations, of two principal storeys with formal emphasis on the *piano nobile* with a piended roof, sunk basement and attic and a tripartite plan. Only a few C18 houses in the Borders, however, show overt classical influences, but it is plainly obvious in the design of Edrom House, which although usually dated to the 1740s, has features, such as thick glazing bars and roof flashings with scalloped ornament, that must suggest an earlier C18 date. Edrom is slightly smaller than Renton House, dated 1715, which is also classical, but unusual in the use of vertical divisions defining the centre three bays, expressed as shallow pilasters on the main façade and as flush rustication on the s elevation. Renton also has two detached pavilions guarding the entrance. Rather more sophisticated is Edgerston House, built *c.* 1720, which displays the latest classical details with an accented pedimented centre on the front and full-height bow at the rear.

Confirmation of Classicism as the appropriate style for new houses after 1715 was made by *William Adam*. He may have been involved at Marlefield, by whose owner he was certainly recommended to John, first Duke of Roxburghe, Secretary of State for Scotland, for the remodelling of Floors Castle in 1721–6. This is Adam's first documented work as an architect. Here he incorporated an earlier tower house, which dictated the elongated

p. 562

Floors Castle, north front, by William Adam *c.* 1721

double-pile plan-form of the new house. The main block had an
enfilade of state apartments along the s front and was given pedimented corner towers, a distinctly Palladian feature, and a fash-
p. 284 ionable, low horizontal layout with flanking pavilons set forward
on either side of a forecourt. For George Baillie, at his new house
of Mellerstain, only Adam's pavilions, stabling in one and family
60 accommodation in the other, were built in 1725. Engravings of
the elevations and plans of the much-altered Broomlands, Kelso
(1719) and the undated Longformacus House were included in
Adam's *Vitruvius Scoticus*, which he began to compile in the
1720s. These, probably not by Adam himself, conform to regular,
compact plans but Adam's Minto House (*c.* 1738–43, demolished
1993) was designed to an interesting V-shaped plan with circular hall and octagonal garden room.

There was an upsurge in the building of large, medium and
small COUNTRY HOUSES AFTER 1750. During this period
English pattern books became popular, especially James Gibbs's
A Book of Architecture (1728), which was expressly intended as a
pattern book for gentlemen in remoter areas of the country, and
Gibbs's *Rules for Drawing the Several Parts of Architecture* (1732)
which enabled correct copying by masons and wrights of the
Orders and Baroque motifs.

56,57 The major houses were led by Paxton House, begun in 1758
to designs by *John Adam*, which developed the compact villa into
a fully realised Palladian scheme of a central block with tetrastyle
Doric portico and quadrant wings. Particularly influential in its
design appears to have been Isaac Ware's *A Complete Body of
Architecture* (1756–7). The masonry work here (by *James Nisbet*)
67 is impressive, which cannot be said for Marchmont House by
Thomas Gibson for the third Earl of Marchmont (1750–7), whose
rubble walling externally did not prepare the visitor for the spectacular interior decoration, with plasterwork by *Thomas Clayton*
that ranges from militaristic seriousness to lighthearted Rococo.
Although extensively remodelled in the C19 and early C20,
Marchmont was, as James Macaulay has noted, 'a model of
Burlingtonian Palladianism, with its broach work on the basement, unaccentuated centre and a Venetian window in each projecting end bay', showing a debt to Houghton Hall, and to the
Earl's enlightened London friends, Alexander Pope and the third
Earl of Burlington. Also derived from Palladio are the closed
quadrant links to pavilions.

Other country house owners concentrated on the interior
embellishment and refurbishment of existing houses, as at
53,55 Traquair House, where *c.* 1762 the fifth Earl of Traquair created

a series of superb painted interiors. From the 1770s signs of a shift in stylistic preference can be detected at Mellerstain, where 60 *c.* 1770 *Robert Adam* provided the house, to link the wings designed by his father in 1725 (*see* above), but dressed up its plain, essentially classical exterior with castellations, machico- lated corbel courses and Tudor hoodmoulds. Its matchless inte- riors are fascinating for their mixing of Neoclassical designs, 61 emphasising an interest in Roman antiquity, with a much rarer use of Gothic plasterwork. At Wedderburn Castle (1770–5), 62 Adam, as at Mellerstain, kept to an essentially classical rectan- gular symmetry but the work is a lapidary proclamation of lineage and landownership, making use of military features culled mostly from his favoured source, Diocletian's Palace at Spalatro. The developed Romanticism of Adam's Castle Style appears only in miniature at Stobs Castle, unfinished at his death in 1792 and altered in execution. A more fully realised example of the Castle Style is Stobo Castle of 1803–4 by *Archibald & James Elliot*, which is clearly indebted to Inveraray Castle in the use of a square plan with corner turrets, Gothic detailing and a central block rising above the height of a battlement which contains the principal staircase. Its silhouette takes full advantage of the picturesque site. Castellated Gothic found further enthusiasm in the domes- tic work of *James Gillespie Graham*, notably at Bowland House of *c.* 1813–15, an asymmetrical composition, and the fully fledged Picturesque Gothic style at Duns Castle, also by Gillespie 63 Graham, 1818–22 for William Hay, who, steeped in his lineage but not an antiquary, wanted a dramatic skyline creating a pic- turesque effect. For this Gillespie Graham borrowed the design of Robert Lugar's Tullichewan Castle (Stirling and Central Scot- land), and dressed it up. Dressing up on a grander scale in this period is shown by *W.H. Playfair's* remodelling of William Adam's Floors Castle, building 1838–49, which borrows from George Heriot's Hospital, Edinburgh, to achieve its fantastic 69 inventive skyline of turrets.

The Scottish Borders are well endowed with SMALLER COUNTRY HOUSES AND COUNTRY VILLAS in this period, which share some of the stylistic enthusiasms of their large counter- parts. From the mid C18 their designs followed symmetrical, rec- tangular tripartite plans, usually with pedimented frontispieces and classical doorpieces, and sometimes with wings or pavilions. Examples and variations of this house form, which became stan- dard not only for smaller mansion houses and lairds' houses but also for manses and farmhouses (*see* p. 81), were provided by a late C18 manual: *The Rudiments of Architecture or The Young Workman's Instructor* (1772) by *George Jameson*. Jameson had worked as a carver at Traquair House in the 1740s and also pro- duced one of the earliest Scottish architectural publications, *Thirty Three Designs with the Orders of Architecture* (1765). But his later publication was to prove most influential for the southern Scottish contractors, masons and wrights. These masons, who often referred to themselve as 'mason architects' in contracts, adapted Jameson's designs to suit their clients, who included smaller landowners, newly rich merchants, retired officers and government servants who had succeeded to or acquired small estates. They built small houses or 'villas' especially for the summer months, in which to enjoy rural solitude, walking, fishing and socialising. Their preferred taste was for a detached block set in a miniature landscape, in which a walled garden could be cultivated and treed walks laid out. As the c18 advanced, plan-forms appeared with bowed and semi-octagonal elevations, rep-resented internally by shaped rooms, while Tudor Gothic details reflected the growing appreciation of the Picturesque in the late c18.

This class of house is too numerous to mention more than a few outstanding examples. Among the largest are two, which in spite of their setting within or on the edge of towns, should be considered as country villas, rather than town houses. At Eye-
109 mouth, the Palladian-style Gunsgreen House, probably by *John and James Adam, c.* 1753, for John Nisbet, an Eyemouth mer-chant, has a proud position overlooking the harbour and was for-merly set within its own small estate. The source seems to be Isaac Ware's design for Chesterfield House, London (1748–9).
108 Ware seems also to have been the source for Ednam House, on the outskirts of Kelso, which *James Nisbet*, using all the skills he had acquired in building Paxton House, designed and built in
71 1761 for James Dickson, a local man who made his fortune in London. Dignified Barns House by *James Brown* (1773) has an urn-topped pediment at the front and full-height bow at the rear. It was built to replace a tower house, which terminates the vista
70 from the front door. The Kelso architect *William Elliot* designed The Yair (1788), with a full-height, parapeted, bowed entrance bay; Chesters House (1790), which has pavilions and a wide, arcaded Doric porch; and The Haining, Selkirk (1795), a classi-cal country villa with a canted bay, later turned back to front and transformed into a Roman villa by *Archibald Elliot (c.* 1818–23). The well-proportioned Crailing House (1803) has Giant Order rustic pilasters, and of the same year is Glenburn Hall, *William Elliot's* most sophisticated design, which sports a Roman Doric distyle porch, and hoodmoulded windows. Of the smaller
75 country villas built as retreats, Carolside is a perfect late c18 example, enhanced with bow-ended balustraded wings *c.* 1806.
72 It has features in common with the early c19 Regency-style Lead-ervale House which has a curved Ionic-columned portico, and bows on the side elevations. Also similar is Gledswood House,
73 built *c.* 1805, but with a semicircular Doric portico. Holylee by the notable Borders architect, *John Smith*, has a typical pedi-mented exterior but an interesting cross-corridor plan. The Greek Revival style became popular after the Napoleonic Wars with the patronage of Tory politicians, and is well represented by Neoclassical Newton Don by *Robert Smirke*, 1815, in his 'new square style', and by the severe Milne Graden House by *James Gillespie Graham*, 1822.

Just as the Grand Tour had suggested alternative sources for architectural styles, so it provided wealthy men with substantial art collections, deserving of rooms for proper display. Paxton
58 House stands out for the addition of a top-lit Picture Gallery in 1811, the first of its kind in Scotland, designed to hold the col-lection of paintings acquired by Patrick Home of Wedderburn and brought to Paxton by his nephew, George Home, to be shown in a setting of serious Neoclassicism by *Robert Reid*. But

the house as a setting for display was given new meaning in the EARLY NINETEENTH CENTURY by the building of Abbotsford House for Sir Walter Scott. Here was a client who was intensely interested in architecture and landscape, and with a strong antiquarian taste, shown in his collecting of pieces from historic buildings. Such was Scott's interest in all aspects of the creation of his house that inevitably it became one of the most famous houses in the land and the most visited. Its style owes as much to Scott's ideas and to a group of amateur designers as to the professional architects employed by him. Abbotsford's building ran concurrently with work at Bowhill House, for Scott's kinsman the Duke of Buccleuch, and involved the same architects, although with different results. At both houses *William Stark* was engaged at first, and succeeded after his death by *William Atkinson*, who designed classical symmetry for Bowhill but at Abbotsford a protype of the Scottish Baronial style which was to spread across the country from the mid C19 (*see* below). The third architect to link Bowhill and Abbotsford is *William Burn*, who in the 1830s considerably adapted Bowhill to provide the family with a country house in which zones of rooms for the family, for entertaining and guests, and for servants were carefully delineated. In the 1850s Burn designed a family wing at Abbotsford for Scott's successors, the Hope-Scotts, to give them much-needed privacy away from the prying eyes of tourists to this literary shrine. This was the essence of Burn's revolutionary contribution to C19 country house design – the development of plan-forms which increased the privacy of owners from servants and guests and which, as David Walker has observed, were 'assembled with the most compelling logic and economy in the sequence in which they were to be used'.* To this end, Burn remodelled and extended many of the larger houses in the Borders, but his most appealing works are found in smaller houses, particularly his 'cottage houses' often executed in a Cotswold Tudor style. Examples are Teviot Bank (1833) and Anton's Hill (1836). Dawyck House (1827) is a mixture of Baronial and Elizabethan motifs, whilst modest Scottish Jacobean was used at Cardrona House (1841) but with a hint of Scottish Baronial that suggests the hand of Burn's pupil and assistant *David Bryce*.

It was from the confines of William Burn's office that Bryce led his profession in the popularisation of the SCOTTISH BARONIAL style, by encouraging his own pupils, principally *C. G. H. Kinnear* (later of *Peddie & Kinnear*), *J. M. Wardrop* (*Brown & Wardrop* and *Wardrop & Reid*) and his chief clerk *James C. Walker*. Bryce had a strong sense of massing and design, and provided a plan convenient for all levels of the Victorian household, a hidden benefit of employing styles whose asymmetry made it possible to break with formal planning. The need for an appropriate publication was served by R.W. Billings's *The Baronial and Ecclesiastical Antiquities of Scotland* (1845–52), which was partly financed by William Burn, and became the source of authentic detail for patrons and architects. *James Gillespie Graham* used Billings's plates for many of his quirky details in the dramatic Scottish Baronial of his Ayton

64,65, 66

68

* David Walker, 'William Burn, the Country House in Transition', in *Seven Victorian Architects*, ed. J. Fawcett (1976).

Castle, a rare departure into the style for Graham towards the end
of his life. Details from Billings's plates were routinely used by
Bryce, Kinnear, Wardrop and Walker. The most frequent quota-
tions from C16 and C17 Scottish houses were from Pinkie House,
Winton House, the round towers of Fraser Castle and Huntly
Castle, and the unique gabled tower with its oriel window and
chimney cope at Maybole Castle (Ayrshire). Hartrigge in Jedburgh (1854; demolished), one of Bryce's first remodellings, had
p. 325 a tall Maybole-type entrance tower, a detail repeated at The Glen
76 (1854 and 1874), which also sports square-plan pepperpot turrets
of a type found at Pinkie House. At Portmore House (1850) the
square entrance is of the Winton type, as are the tall octagonal
chimneys on plinths, and Winton detail also appears at Sunderland Hall (1850), where Bryce designed an L-plan of public rooms
round a late C18 house. The motif of an aedicular window in a
chimneyed crowstep gable was also much used by Bryce, as at
Kimmerghame House (1851), and at Langlee Park in 1868,
together with the tower detailing. *C. G. H. Kinnear*'s great house
of Glenmayne (1866), an asymmetrical composition with a
Renaissance-detailed five-storey tower, owes much to Billings and
Bryce. A large Baronial addition to Dryburgh House (Dryburgh
Abbey Hotel; 1876) is in assertive red sandstone with a plethora
of Bryce features, while Drygrange (1889) mixes Scottish Renaissance and English Jacobean with a Castle Fraser entrance tower,
and a fine example of the Maybole Castle orieled gable. At Glenternie House (1867–8), *J. M. Wardrop* used many Bryce-derived
features; for the large and pretentious Stichill House (1866;
demolished) he borrowed the design of Charles Barry's entrance
tower at Dunrobin Castle, Sutherland.

In the late C19 and early C20 landed property was being
acquired increasingly for sporting activities and smart country
house entertaining. This change was accompanied by a waning
interest in Baronial and its succession by a Scottish Renaissance
style, perceived as more authentic in its re-creation of a 'national
style'. Splendid Leithen Lodge (1885–7) by *Sydney Mitchell &
Wilson*, built to resemble a mid-to-late C17 laird's house, skilfully
accommodates an early C19 house as part of a perfectly equipped
lodge for shooting and entertaining. *Thomas Leadbetter*'s The
Holmes, St Boswells (1894), is rather dull classical with some
Baroque, but of interest for the survival of the complete Victorian interior. Also at St Boswells is the incomparable, but eccentric, Braeheads House (1905–6) by *F. W. Deas*. Scottish Domestic,
the entrance modelled on ones from Huntly and Fyvie castles,
with an open loggia of a type used by Deas at his own house The
Murrel (Fife). Fairnilee House, 1904–6, is the best domestic
project of *John J. Burnet* – an integral concept of house, formal
garden, stables and cottages to house the gardener and staff,
designed in Scottish Renaissance style with some lavish Baroque
ornament. Burnet's remodelled Castlecraig House is classical but
the interior is lush Scottish Renaissance.

INTERIORS are a prominent feature of these, and other, larger
Borders houses of the late C19 and early C20. They reflect a
common desire for a more congenial domestic environment, contrived with Arts and Crafts care by Scottish craftsmen and
designers. *Scott Morton & Co.* and the plasterer *Leonard Grandi-*

son of Peebles became indispensable to *Robert S. Lorimer* and many other architects creating late C17 Scottish Renaissance style interiors. At Leithen Lodge, Grandison's plasterwork reflected the functions of the rooms, while at Peel House, 1899–1905, he created an opulent mix of Renaissance and classical decoration, complemented by woodwork supplied by Scott Morton. The survival of Grandison's plasterwork at The Holmes (*see* above) adds much to the sense of an untouched Victorian interior, and the continued existence of the Grandison firm ensured that the splendid 1880s plasterwork at Portmore could be re-created from the original moulds after a fire in the late C20. Lorimer employed *Thomas Beattie* for the reconstruction of the interior of Marchmont House in 1914–17 and earlier at The Glen, where ceiling patterns are derived from C17 originals at Lorimer's own home, Kellie Castle (Fife). Classicism also enjoyed a revival in the late C19 and the epitome of this and the social Edwardian country house is Manderston House, which was extensively remodelled   77 in 1902–5 by *John Kinross* for Sir James Miller. It has a magnificent interior, with decorative work mostly by *Grandison* and *Scott Morton & Co.* that explicitly evokes the Neoclassical interiors by Robert Adam at Kedleston, Lady Miller's ancestral home, combined with revival styles of the French C18. Such opulence also finds expression at Floors Castle, which was made over in the 1920s by the London decorators *Lenygon & Morant* for May, Duchess of Roxburghe, an American heiress.

Traditionalist Scottish architects slipped easily into the English ARTS AND CRAFTS MOVEMENT, but maintained their own personal style in introducing Scottish vernacular motifs. Lord and Lady Carmichael, active professionals in the Arts and Crafts Movement, found their practitioner in *Ramsay Traquair*, a pupil of Lorimer, who extended and adapted Skirling House (1908) embellishing it, inside and out, with lively and amusing decoration – the ironwork by *Thomas Hadden* is particularly outstanding. After the First World War, little of note was built until the 1930s. Broughton Place by *Basil Spence* shows his ability to adapt   78 his client's preference for a 'medieval keep' and provide a charming L-plan C17-style tower house. Three good houses are by *Leslie Grahame Thomson*, another of Lorimer's pupils: Srongarbh, West   79 Linton, designed in 1935 for his own occupation, Alerigg of 1936, with some quite witty Arts and Crafts detailing, combined with Lorimer-inspired details, and the similarly inspired Beckett's Field, Bowden, of 1939. The only house to plough a different furrow is Bewlie House of 1937–8 by *Guy Elwes*, which is Neo-Georgian but minimally detailed and built of concrete, suited to its bare landscape setting.

POST-WAR COUNTRY HOUSES are represented by two innovative small Modern Movement designs by *Peter Womersley* for single-storey, timber-framed dwellings, with rectangular plans laid out on Miesian principles. First was The Rig, Gattonside   *p. 320* (1956), designed for himself as a house and office, and followed by the larger High Sunderland (1957), for Bernat Klein, textile   80 designer, for whom Womersley then provided the dramatic   *p. 337* Design Studio and teaching premises, in brick, glass and concrete,   81 which is creatively set in trees, and linked to the house by bridge and walkway.

LANDSCAPE GARDENING. Daniel Defoe and John Macky
were surprised on their visits to the Borders in the early C18, to
see how many estates were treed, with the formation of enclosures and shelter belts and the creation of formal avenues. By the
mid C18, with political stablity established and the start of the
agricultural age, an appreciation of the Borders landscape had
developed and with it an enthusiasm for 'naturalistic' planting.
Of particular significance is the landscape at Dawyck House,
where exotic trees were introduced by the Veitch family in the
C17, and planting continued in the C18 by *James Naesmyth*, a
student of the Swedish botanist Carl Linnaeus, who established
an extensive landscape around the house. At Floors Castle from
1697 the fifth Earl of Roxburghe obtained seeds and trees not
only from the celebrated garden of James Johnston, Secretary of
State, at Orleans House, Twickenham, but also from Lord
Burlington's gardens at Chiswick, creating the large formal layout
shown on an estate plan of 1736. This vanished, however, from
the late C18 in favour of a more naturalistic arrangement with
views extending from the landscape to the Cheviot Hills. Mellerstain's landscape was laid out at the same time as *William Adam*'s
pavilions were being built (1725–6), perhaps to Adam's design,
with avenues of trees, a canal and exploitation of the natural features of the landscape. The pavilions were placed on a N–S axis
with a view N to Mellerstain Hill, and S to the turreted Gothic
silhouette of Adam's sham Gothic Hundy Mundy, acting as a terminal vista in the tradition of Sir William Bruce at his houses of
Kinross (Perth and Kinross) and Balcaskie (Fife). The small
landscape and garden around the new Paxton House was laid
out, *c.* 1758, by *Robert Robinson*, who planted the fields with strips
of trees, and naturalised the Linn Burn with a series of pools
linked by straight water between densely planted banks of trees.
   The Picturesque fashion, promoted by Sir Uvedule Price's
Essays on the Picturesque (1794–1801), was a profound and
ruinous influence on William Hay at Duns Castle, who had the
mid-C18 landscape redesigned in 1812 by *Thomas White Jun.* to
create an appropriately Romantic setting for his house. At
Bowhill House planting started seriously in 1760, but it was not
until *c.* 1832, when the fifth Duke of Buccleuch employed *W.S.
Gilpin*, that planting and landscape design were undertaken on
any scale, and the grounds laid out to a Picturesque scheme that
included the creation of two lochs. Sir Walter Scott started to
plant large swathes of trees at Abbotsford in 1812, but, although
enthusiastic in advising his friends on planting and improving,
he sought a middle way in his own territory, advocating a 'formal
informality' in the gardens he created round the house, composed of enclosed courts and narrow terraces linked by steep
grassy banks, with the river meadows designed as parkland.
   The most typical component of the Scottish estate is the
WALLED GARDEN, examples of which exist in the Borders in
large numbers, but now are mostly derelict, or in other use. Many
contained summerhouses and greenhouses, one of the best being
at Blackadder, which has a late C18 hexagonal classical pavilion,
its first floor with remains of a later decorative scheme and gilded
decoration, fronted by a mid-C19 greenhouse. A C20 counterpart,
85 by *Basil Spence*, can be seen at Broughton Place.

DOVECOTS are usually found in stables and farm steadings but some free-standing examples survive. A splendid beehive-type at Mertoun House, in red sandstone rubble, is dated 1576; Marchmont House's cylindrical cote by *James Williamson*, 1749, must 82 have been designed to terminate the main avenue, and Nisbet House has a pentagonal and battlemented cote. Lectern types are the most familiar, the crowstepped one at Kailzie dating from 83 1698. At Whitehall House is a C18 two-chambered cote; the beak skews have carved faces, and some climbing poles survive inside.

The principal fronts of STABLES COURTS were often architecturally grand, suitable to be viewed from the house or on the approach to it, and frequently adorned with a spire or tower over the entrance pend, e.g. the Scots crown over the pend at Duns Castle, 1818–22, by *James Gillespie Graham* and the octagonal spire of 1791–4, by *John Baxter Jun.* to its stable court. The well- 84 articulated pedimented late C18 front is topped by a high-domed octagonal clock tower at Newton Don. The magnificent classical elevation of The Whim's stables, by *John Henderson*, 1775, with a columned portico decorated with acanthus and flutes, distinctly outshines the mansion house. At The Haining by *John Smith*, *c.* 1823, there are two fronts, the N with a large Tuscan-columned arch flanked by niches with busts, and an impressive long balustraded crescent-shaped S front with an arcaded ground floor. The finest stables are those in Palladian style at Ladykirk House by *George Tattersall*, 1843, with an attached riding school by *H.S. Ridley*, *c.* 1850. They compete only with the stable courts executed in the grand manner at Manderston House, by *John Kinross*, 1895, where the finishing is lavish, and the craftsmanship superb. Most smaller country houses had stables courts, often combined with farm steadings, usually classical.

Designs for LODGES often have a stylistic affinity with the mansion house reflecting the privileged standing of the owner and none more so than at Duns Castle, *c.* 1820. The South Lodge, eccentric and asymmetrical, combines a round tower, a square turret and archway, the North Lodge has Gothick tracery and a flat pointed arch, while Pavilion Lodge by *John Baxter Jun.*, 1774–7, is Gothick with castellated towers. At Ayton Castle, *James Gillespie Graham*'s idiosyncratically detailed South Lodge used most of the Baronial details from the mansion house. Much calmer are the lodges at Paxton House, which are Palladian, with a classical screen, *c.* 1789, decorated with *Coade* stone urns and cherubs' heads, and recumbent lions. The impressive Lion 74 Gateway and Porter's Lodge of 1799 by *William Elliot* at Ladykirk House are based on Robert Adam's screen at Syon House, complete with the Percy lion. At Stobs Castle, *c.* 1817, Elliot provided a version of Adam's Moor Park screen. For smaller mansion houses single-storey lodges with canted bays or simple Tudor bracketed eaves and hoodmoulds were popular.

ROADS, RAILWAYS, HARBOURS AND LIGHTHOUSES

From the departure of the Roman armies in the C3 until the later C18 'made' roads in the Borders were rare outside the burghs, responsibility for their maintenance under the supervision of the local landowners acting as Justices of the Peace and Commissioners of Supply, empowered to exact 'statute labour' or money in lieu from the inhabitants of each parish. Some rivers were crossed by ferries. EARLY BRIDGES, however, did exist and some, though much remodelled can still be seen. Tweed Bridge, Peebles, retains late C15 work, while the C16 Canongate Bridge, Jedburgh, is a hump-backed bridge of three arches with triangular cutwaters and semi-hexagonal refuges. The mid-C17 Stow Pack (or Old) Bridge across the Gala Water comprises three arches of increasing size, while Leithen Old Bridge, Innerleithen, is a modest single span dating from 1701, the parapet splayed at each end, and Old Manor Bridge (*see* Kirkton Manor), a rubble hump-backed bridge, inscribed with the date 1702, informs visitors that it was erected by the Earl of March, fulfilling the intention of his father, *William, Duke of Queensberry*.

From the 1760s Acts of Parliament were passed for the construction of turnpike roads, and accompanying bridges, in the Borders by bodies of trustees able to borrow money for the purpose and to recoup their costs by levying tolls. Largely as a result, the region had acquired 246 km. of new roads and bridges by the 1790s. Most LATE EIGHTEENTH CENTURY AND NINETEENTH CENTURY BRIDGES follow a basic design, with corbelled-out parapets, V-shaped cutwaters and dressed voussoirs. Coldstream Bridge by *John Smeaton* was built together with a tollhouse in 1762. Its arches are all the same radius and in the spandrels are striking decorative ashlar rings, designed by *Robert Reid* of Haddington, filled with black rubble. The rubble-built Yair Bridge by *William Mylne* was probably built 1764, when the Act for building the road was passed, though Mylne designed it in 1759. Its triangular cutwaters extend upwards as refuges. Drygrange Old Bridge, Leaderfoot is a daring design by *Alexander Stevens Sen.*, 1778, with two side arches of 55 ft (16.7 m.) span and a middle arch of 105 ft (32 m.) with a 34 ft (10.3 m.) rise; it was also innovative for the use of French-style curved and pointed cutwaters, a feature also of Stevens's design (executed by *William Elliot* in 1794–5) for Teviot Bridge, Kelso, but there combined with pairs of columns to each pier. The inspiration for this must have been Robert Mylne's Blackfriars Bridge, London (1760–9) and reappears, in a larger context, in *John Rennie*'s Kelso Bridge, built in 1799 for the local road trustees, whom Rennie provided with a tollhouse at the bridge's N end. The Great Post Road N from London (A1) had become the main carriage route through Berwickshire from 1768. *David Henderson*'s remarkable Pease Bridge, built in 1783 near Cockburnspath, solved the biggest problem met by travellers in negotiating the steep descent and ascent across the Pease Burn, from which the middle pier of the bridge now rises 117 ft (35.7 m.). The heavy load of the crossing is reduced by the use of arched cylindrical voids, an innovation introduced by Henderson following his experience surveying the North Bridge, Edinburgh, after its collapse in 1769.

In the early C19 *John & Thomas Smith* erected numerous stone bridges in the area, notably North Bridge, Hawick, 1832. One of the most interesting is Low Peel Bridge, Ashiestiel (1847) with a

86
p. 173
89

span of 130 ft (40 m.), apparently the longest span for a rubble bridge at that time. Hewn stone is used only for corbels and copes. Also unusual is Mertoun Bridge by *James Slight* of Edinburgh, 1839–41, whose arches were constructed of three laminated rib-beams formed from half-logs of timber. The present masonry superstructure dates from 1887. In the late C19 and C20 many existing bridges were widened, and a number bypassed. A good unaltered example is Ellemford Bridge, erected *c.* 1886 by the Berwickshire Road Trustees, with three stately spans, the cutwaters bullet-shaped in plan, and with wide pilasters at the ends. Belonging to the early C20 are five identical bridges by *J. & A. Leslie & Reid*, 1928, in reinforced concrete with balustraded parapets, which cross the winding Jed Water: four survive in their original form, two at Jedburgh and two S of the town. At Leaderfoot the Drygrange Bridge by *Sir Alexander Gibb & Partners*, 1971–3, is a steel box-girder and reinforced concrete structure with a slight longitudinal curve over the river, bypassing its late C18 neighbour. Latest is Hunter Bridge, Kelso, by *Blyth & Blyth*, 1999, carrying the town's bypass over the River Tweed, its restrained design sympathetic to the setting of the historic town.

Several crossings in the Borders were at the forefront of new technology for building SUSPENSION BRIDGES. The earliest (and the first bridge in Britain to use iron chains) was at Dryburgh by *John & Thomas Smith*, 1817. Destroyed by violent winds in 1818, it was rebuilt at once to a revised design by the Smiths on a 'more elegant plan'. This was for pedestrians, and the oldest surviving vehicular suspension bridge in Britain is the Union Chain Bridge across the Tweed of 1819–20; designed and constructed by *Capt. Samuel Brown*, who provided the 'superior' wrought-chain links which made it the longest span bridge in the Western world (*c.* 1,580 ft; 486 m.). Brown was also responsible for another early surviving carriage bridge, Kalemouth suspension bridge (Eckford) over the River Teviot, 1830. This used wrought-iron rods and chains, with its deck strengthened by timber cross-braced side railings. Gattonside suspension footbridge, of 1826, is the oldest functioning example of the work of *Redpath, Brown & Co.*, who fabricated and erected the metalwork; the castellated masonry pylons and tollhouse are by *John Smith*. The graceful Priorsford Bridge, Peebles, of 1905 by *James Bell*, eschews masonry in favour of latticed steel pylons. 88 87

TOLL HOUSES are fairly common, but many have been badly altered. Typical is that at Eddleston, *c.* 1770, with a gabled porch. Classier is Castleloan Toll Bar, Greenlaw, dated 1831, with a full-height pedimented stone porch, canted bays and octagonal chimneys. The gabled Fountain Cottage, a former tollhouse at Ladykirk, with a bay window and stone slab hoods over doors and windows, dates from the first Ladykirk & Norham Bridge, 1838–9; a late C19 tollhouse with hoodmoulds and stone flat-roofed porch served the later bridge. An even rarer survival is at Allanton, where a former ferryman's cottage tucked between bridges crossing the Whiteadder and Blackadder Waters is a reminder of the earlier method of crossing the rivers.

RAILWAYS have almost entirely vanished from the Borders. The whole system closed, except for the East Coast main line, in the 1960s and not a single working station remains, although station houses survive, mostly converted to other use and usually to the detriment of their original character. Designs commonly reflect the 'house style' of the railway companies; deep overhanging bracketed eaves, sometimes gabled, and the platforms with simple bracketed canopies, the more important decorated with patterns of serrated fretted boarding. Much the most impressive architecturally is *John Miller*'s Melrose Station, opened in 1849 on the North British Railway's Edinburgh–Hawick line (the Waverley route, extended from Hawick to Carlisle after 1859), and intended as a gateway for travellers to Melrose Abbey, Abbotsford and the Scott country. It has two-storey Scottish Jacobean offices with a platform at an upper level, by *Blackie & Sons*, with cast-iron columns with lotus capitals. At Burnmouth, the 1849 North British Railway station house and offices have classical detailing and clock still *in situ*, while the Berwickshire branch to the larger station at Chirnside, 1863, which served the local village and provided goods traffic for Chirnside Paper Mill, has a cosy timber-clad waiting-room with sliding doors and a fireplace. Typical examples of small stations are at Innerleithen and Walkerburn, both of 1866 for the North British Railway's Peebles and Galashiels line. At Shankend is a gabled, quite picturesque group of cottages and station house, with a two-storey signal box, near to the impressive Shankend Viaduct which marches across the Langside valley for 1,200m. This carried the Border Union Railway's Hawick–Carlisle line of 1862, as did the four tall arches of the Stobs Viaduct (*see* Hawick). Earlier is the Roxburgh Viaduct by *G. Glennie*, 1850, for the St Boswell–Kelso line of the North British Railway over the River Teviot, which is built on a curve with skew arches and a notable low-level iron truss footbridge supported by extensions from the river piers. Of similar curved form is the sandstone Neidpath Viaduct (Kirkton Manor), constructed in 1864 to take the Caledonian Railway across the River Tweed through the South Park Tunnel before entering its terminus at Peebles. The breathtaking Leaderfoot Viaduct by *Charles Jopp, Wylie & Peddie*, 1865, took the Berwickshire railway from St Boswells to Duns across its nineteen brick arches which soar 115 ft (35.5m.) above the River Tweed.

It was with the improvement of HARBOURS and the introduction of larger fishing boats in the C19 that Berwickshire ports like Eyemouth and Burnmouth began to flourish. Eyemouth harbour incorporates works of several periods, from *John Smeaton*'s initial defences of *c.* 1770 at the mouth of the Eye Water to the deep-water basin of the late C20. Eyemouth also retains warehouses, smokehouses and other harbour buildings of C18 and later date. In the early 1830s three harbours were funded, partly by the Commissioners of the Herring Fishery and partly by public and private subscription. Burnmouth Harbour was founded in 1831, and improved in 1879 by *D. & T. Stevenson*; St Abbs' inner harbour was built by *Mitchell & Wilson* in 1831, improved in 1848–9, and extended from 1883 by *D. & T. Stevenson*. Cove, a natural harbour and landing place used since the C17, has a dramatic harbour approach, via timber steps and a rock-cut passage of 1831, enhancing the picturesque quality of the site.

In 1786 Parliament passed 'An Act for erecting certain LIGHT-HOUSES in the Northern parts of Great Britain' by which the

Commissioners of Northern Lighthouses became responsible for the erection and maintenance of lighthouses. Only one was built on the precipitous Berwickshire coast at St Abbs Head on a 300 ft (91.44 m.) cliff, by *D. & T. Stevenson* in 1862; a circular plan with a triangular-paned lantern. In 1876 St Abbs acquired the first siren fog signal in Scotland. M-gabled Keepers' Houses look down on the light and foghorn.

BURGH AND VILLAGE BUILDINGS

From the C12 until the late C17 the right to engage in foreign trade was restricted to the merchant burgesses of royal BURGHS, of which early examples are to be found at Jedburgh, Peebles and Selkirk. Burghs of barony were dependent on a lord other than the king, and although barred from foreign trade they were entitled to house incorporations of craftsmen and to hold regular fairs. More numerous than royal burghs, some like Kelso and Galashiels eventually developed into sizeable towns while others became estate villages or disappeared.

In the C18 and C19 VILLAGES were established or improved for the housing of rural craftsmen and landless labourers, others for workers in a particular industry. Carlops, 1784, was founded as a cotton-weaving centre, Newcastleton, 1793, for handloom weaving, and Gavinton to take the dwellers from the original village on the Langton estate. Late C18 Swinton was improved and enlarged for estate labourers, and carters, who introduced the farm machinery industry into Roxburghshire, and Morebattle was settled and developed in the mid C18 with small tenant farmers and labourers when the uplands were cleared for sheep farming. In the mid C18 the Earl of Marchmont produced a plan for new housing in Greenlaw strictly controlled by the feu conditions. All new housing was to be of two storeys and existing single storey cottages in poor condition raised to that height or rebuilt.

Public and Commercial buildings

The essential symbol of burgh status is the MARKET CROSS, where formal proclamations were made and criminals punished. Usually a shaft topped by a decorative capital sometimes with a finial; most have been restored or renewed and incorporate only fragments of their original parts. The Peebles cross has a C15 shaft and capital beneath a cubical sundial and added finial, topped by a weathervane, and a similar vane at Galashiels is dated 1695. The much-mutilated C16 Bowden Cross became a War Memorial *c.* 1920. Melrose, restored in the C19, incorporates a mid-C17 90 capital with a unicorn finial. Classical crosses at Duns, 1792, and Coldingham, 1815, replaced earlier ones.

The burgh's public affairs were transacted at the TOLBOOTH, known later as the Town House, which housed the burgh council chamber, court house and prison. C17 and early C18 tolbooths were usually dignified by steeples or towers. Lauder Town House, 93 although largely rebuilt, *c.* 1773, but to the original mid-C16 plan, survives as a good example, and Greenlaw's court house tower, 69 *c.* 1700, became the parish church tower, after its adjacent court house was demolished in 1830, and the church extended to embrace the tower. Peebles Town House, 1753, is a neat, more formal Georgian building, nestling into the streetscape, and Selkirk Town House, 1803–4, combines a town hall and court house with an elegant soaring spire, which replaced an early C16 92 building. Kelso's classical Town Hall smartened up The Square in 1816, but its genteel style was remodelled in Edwardian Baroque in 1904–6.

From the mid C19 a small amount of building was prompted by the 1833 Municipal Reform Act, which provided for the election of town councils in each of the burghs. These councils accrued a growing number of civic responsibilities through the course of the C19. Among purpose-built TOWN HOUSES the best examples are to be found in the expanding burghs, notably the sturdy vernacu- 94 lar style Burgh Chambers in Galashiels of 1867 by *Robert Hall & Co.*, greatly improved by *Robert S. Lorimer*'s Scottish Renaissance extension of 1923–7, and Hawick's Town Hall, by *James C. Walker*, 1884, a dominant Scottish Baronial building with a landmark clock tower. County councils were established in 1889 (and replaced in 1975 by regional and district councils, themselves replaced by unitary authorities in 1996. Peeblesshire erected its agreeable Neo-Baroque County Offices at Peebles by *Dick Peddie & Walker Todd* in 1932, incorporating part of the former poorhouse of 1856 into its rear elevation. In the C20 Newtown St Boswells became the administrative centre of Roxburghshire which took the bold step in 1961 of commissioning *Peter Womersley* to design the County Buildings. Though not fully completed when opened in 1968, it dominates the village by virtue of its scale and materials.

Before the establishment of county councils, each county (those in the Borders being Berwickshire, Peeblesshire, Rox- burghshire and Selkirkshire) was, more properly, a sheriffdom (the seat of a sheriff with wide legal and administrative respon- sibilities). The county towns housed SHERIFF COURTS which usually served also as meeting places for other local government bodies such as the Commissioners of Supply. A Greek Revival Sheriff Court for Roxburghshire was built at Jedburgh in 1812. The small burgh of Greenlaw, county town of Berwickshire from 1697, is dominated by its unusually grand (alas, deserted) Court House by *John Cunningham*, 1829–31. From 1853 Greenlaw had to share its status as the county town with the much larger burgh of Duns which duly acquired a Jacobean Sheriff Court, *c.* 1855. Also Jacobean was Peebles Sheriff Court of 1848, by *Thomas Brown Jun.* Legislation in 1860 established proper funding for the building of sheriff courts and in 1861–2 *David Rhind* consider- ably extended Jedburgh's Sheriff Court to provide a new court room. Much more expensive, at a cost of £10,152, was Rhind's 96 bold Baronial Sheriff Court of 1868–70 in Selkirk but the money was probably well spent. It also served as the County Buildings and housed a police station in its basement whence a passage leads under the road to the (former) jail (*see* below).

From the late C18 the growing interest in imprisonment as a reformative measure created a need for PRISONS that could provide more than lock-up cells in tolbooths. Jails were built at Peebles, *c.* 1780, Selkirk in 1803–4, and Newgate, Jedburgh, in

1756, the latter replaced by the commanding landmark of Jedburgh Castle Jail in 1820–3, designed by *Archibald Elliot* and built *p. 421* according to the principles of prison reform advanced by John Howard. In its crenellations, portcullis gate and boundary wall Elliot closely followed Robert Adam's advice that prisons should resemble fortifications. A General Board of Directors of Prisons in Scotland was established in 1839, and its architect, *Thomas Brown Jun.*, built the new Jacobean Peebles Sheriff Court and Prison in 1848 against the former jail, in which mullioned and transomed windows were inserted, and the interior remodelled by *Kinnear & Peddie* in 1892.

After 1856–7 each county was obliged to have a police force. Peebles Police Station was built in 1881 in a Baronial style, and thrifty Jacobean was used by *James Jerdan* in 1894 at Duns. The Police in rural areas were always well housed. The late C19 police house at Swinton provided a family home and a single-cell station; even smaller is the attractive early C20 square police house (Littledean) at Eckford.

Places for meetings were provided by PUBLIC HALLS, which might incorporate several functions under one roof. Victoria 97 Halls, Selkirk, designed by *Hippolyte J. Blanc* in 1895, a red sandstone Renaissance building set in its own grounds, contains two halls for meetings and concerts. Jedburgh's Public Hall is French Renaissance, built in 1900–1 by the prolific *J. P. Alison*, who also provided good, small rural halls for Bonchester Bridge, 1899, and Roberton, 1923. The Tait Hall, Kelso, by *J.P. Alison & Hobkirk*, 1934, is an innovative design verging towards the Beaux Arts. Such buildings were important components of community life in rural areas, often large enough to accommodate a hall, small meeting rooms and a hall-keeper. They are sometimes of surprising ambition, such as Stow's formidable Baronial hall, dated 1855, which was built incorporating a library and reading room. The splendid Village Hall at Bowden, designed in 1897 by *John* 99 *Wallace*, was his only significant work before his early death. In remote areas corrugated iron halls from catalogues were more common. A good example at Teviothead, 1907, has bargeboards and hoodmoulds. Some halls belonged to particular groups, such as Working Men's Institutes (Free Jacobean in Duns, 1877, by *David Duns*, and the Ballantyne Memorial Institute at Walkerburn, 1903, by *James B. Dunn*) or the Freemasons' halls: sturdy Scottish Baronial in Galashiels by *Hall & Murray*, 1876; turreted in Selkirk by *Hippolyte J. Blanc* in 1887. Examples of Volunteer Halls can be found in the Drill Hall, Chirnside, 1870, with a classical front, and at Duns with a Jacobean Renaissance gable, *c.* 1900.

LIBRARIES and READING ROOMS have a long history in the Borders. One of the earliest was in Paxton's first school, already equipped with a school library, which served as the Old Library from 1846 until the late C20. Such buildings were often in the gift of local benefactors, as at Earlston, where the attractive Reading Room and Library, founded in 1852 by the Hon. Robert Baillie, was provided with purpose-built rooms in 1856, and at Swinton where a late C18 house was remodelled in 1888, with accommodation for the librarian on the first floor. Buildings with an educational purpose were often adapted as in the case of *James*

Cunningham's Mechanics' Institute, Coldstream, built in 1861. By then burghs were allowed to finance PUBLIC LIBRARIES from the rates. The library at Galashiels, 1873, simple with classical details, was given more civic presence in 1889 by *George Henderson* with a crenellated double-height bay window. The best examples belong, however, to the period after *c.* 1890 when the Scottish-born American steel magnate Andrew Carnegie provided funds for new buildings. The best are those at Kelso (1905) and Jedburgh (1900) by *George Washington Browne*, architect of the Carnegie-funded Central Library, Edinburgh. Both are Scottish Renaissance with Jacobean detailing, that at Kelso being domestic in appearance, that at Jedburgh more freely detailed with a large semicircular window to the reading room. Hawick's
102 library (1904, by *J.N. Scott & A. Lorne Campbell*) is also Scottish Renaissance, set in a prominent position by North Bridge and with a tall octagonal tower demanding attention. Sometimes associated with libraries were small PUBLIC MUSEUMS. The building housing the Chambers Institution, Peebles, given to the town by Dr William Chambers, the publisher, was remodelled by *John Paris* in 1857–9 as a reading room, library and museum
115 in matching Baronial style. The Wilton Lodge Museum, Hawick, was converted from a country house to a public museum by *J.P. Alison* in 1910, with the Scott Art Gallery added by *Aitken & Turnbull* in 1975.

The Scottish educational system from the C17 to the late C19 was based on the parish and burgh. A distinctive feature was the provision of a school in every parish paid for by the heritors (landowners) of each parish, but they were not obliged to provide a schoolhouse for the master until *c.* 1803. In early SCHOOLS the schoolroom was a simple large room. At Ancrum the schoolrooms were built against the E gable of the parish church in 1762 but were converted for a stable and vestry in 1803. In the late C18 and early C19 parish schools were rebuilt or extended. Overhanging timber-bracketed eaves, plain and decorative bargeboards and gabled porches typify many of the schools erected in rural areas in the Borders in the C19, for example the Tudor-detailed Hutton Primary School by *James Cunningham*, 1844, and his Ladykirk School of 1859, with separate entrances for boys and girls either side of a well-lit classroom.

Paxton has four school buildings, mostly converted to other use, which illustrate the expansion of provision over the course of the C19, culminating in the school by *William J. Gray Jun.* of 1873, with a bellcote and tapering spire. This last was provided under the 1872 Education Act, which made elementary education compulsory for all children and laid down standards for buildings erected by newly established elected School Boards. The schools are characteristically symmetrical, with separate entrances for boys and girls, and rarely of more than a single storey in rural areas. A few are ambitious, notably at Gavinton, 1874, which has large mullioned and transomed windows, separate gabled porches and a large bellcote. The burgh schools tend to be more assertive: the former Kelso Public School by *A. Herbertson & Son*, 1878, in strong red sandstone, is typical. Historic styles vary, from the Neo-Jacobean design by *Hardy & Wight* for Jedburgh Grammar School in 1884 to the Neo-Georgian of the former Berwickshire High School (now Borders College), Duns, by *R. A. Bryden*, 1896, which incorporates a genuine late Georgian villa.

Hawick High School 1908, by *Joseph Blaikie*, was extensively 98 rebuilt and extended in the late 1920s after a fire but J.A. 100 Carfrae's work here, though attractively Scottish, is rooted in C19 tradition. Not so the work of *Reid & Forbes*, which from the 1930s provide particularly rich pickings for school buildings. The firm came to prominence in 1928 winning a competition for Leith Academy, Edinburgh, in an Art Deco style. Their earliest work in the Borders is at Morebattle, 1931, which demonstrates progressive approaches to planning with classrooms with glazed walls opening to a veranda and a strip of swivel-hinged windows, introducing the children to sunshine and fresh air. Its walls are plain but the streamlined extension to Jedburgh Grammar School is more truly indicative of the modern style of 1935. But the most exciting products of the firm's *œuvre* are two designs which exploit Art Deco influences: Kelso High School, 1936, has 103 an entrance tower clearly influenced by Frank Lloyd Wright, not least in the use of South American motifs for its jazzy detail. This tower feature is repeated with daring effect in the rural environs of Chirnside in 1937–8, where the prominent site makes the school a much-loved period piece. The firm continued into the post-war era with a design for Coldstream Primary School in 1956–7, which is far more traditional in composition.

Post-Second World War schools in the Borders sometimes superseded Victorian schools, as at Duns, where the High School was moved to a long, low building by *J. & F. Johnston* in 1953–8. Particularly in the larger burghs, most new building was for primary schools, built to serve new housing areas, as at Galashiels (including Balmoral Primary School of 1955 and the flat-roofed Langlee Primary School of 1954–8, by *Scott & McIntosh*) and Selkirk, where the Bannerfield Estate (*see* p. 679) required expansion of Selkirk Landward School (now Philiphaugh Community School) in plain Modernist style by *J. & J. Hall* of Galashiels, 1954–7. New secondary schools of the post-war period are rarer but occasionally distinguished, notably *Scott & McIntosh*'s Galashiels Academy of 1960–4, with blocks of mixed height, concrete-framed with tight grids of fenestration and brick infill.

By the 1970s different conventions of planning were being explored. Priorsford School, Peebles, by *G.R.M. Kennedy & Partners*, 1972, was one of the first open-plan designs in Scotland, much visited by educationalists from all over the world, with teaching areas (for infants and primary) clustered around a communal activity space. A tougher aesthetic was pursued at Broomlands Primary School, Kelso, by *Borders Regional Council* architect, *Glen McMurray*, 1980, enclosed by an industrial shell of glass and profiled metal roof with turned-down eaves, but which fits well into its leafy setting. By the same architect, but of 1995, is Newtown St Boswells Primary School, a large hangar with a vaulted glazed roof over a long communal corridor flanked by lower open classrooms. The concept of a mall running through the school, a type of plan emerging from the late 1980s across Britain, is also found in Kelso High School's Music Department 105 of 1994 by *Borders Regional Council*.

74 INTRODUCTION

Specialist TECHNICAL EDUCATION, to promote expertise in the textile industry, was centred on Galashiels, where a training school was founded in 1882 and expanded as the Scottish Woollens Technical College, 1908–9 by *John Hall Jun.** Its original buildings survive on Market Street, bold red sandstone Greek Revival with a figure of Industry. Its successor was built on a new campus in 1964–6 by *R. Forbes Hutchison and G. R. M. Kennedy* (now part of Heriot-Watt University), with workshops and teaching rooms under butterfly and monopitched roofs which project over whinstone and glazed walls. Attractively set into the hillside are the Students' Residences by *Walter Scott*, 1968–9.

Dispensaries, which began to appear at the end of the C18, were often the forerunners of provincial HOSPITALS. Such was the case in Kelso where the Cottage Hospital of 1909 by *Sydney Mitchell & Wilson* originated with the Kelso Dispensary (founded 1777). This was attended by a local physician and supported by voluntary subscriptions, but people who could not afford treatment were admitted without charge. Hot and cold water baths were added in 1818. Hawick Cottage Hospital is earlier, of 1885, by *John McLachlan*, in a Picturesque style with many gables. In the same mode is McLachlan's Coldstream Cottage Hospital of 1888. Galashiels Hospital, also a former Cottage Hospital, is by *John Wallace*, 1892, T-plan with a ward each side of an administrative block. Others grew out of former poorhouses, as at Kelso whose buildings of 1854 by *John Smith* were converted to hospital use by *J.P. Alison* in 1911 and extended in the same simple classical style. The suitably remote Melrose Infectious Diseases Hospital (Borders Primary Care) is at Newstead and has three small wards and an administrative block in red sandstone with brick dressings by *G. Monteith*, 1903. Dingleton Hospital, Melrose, was built as the Melrose District Asylum by *Brown & Wardrop*, 1869, with a single Italianate block, and expanded by *Sydney Mitchell & Wilson*, 1895–1904. Its landmark concrete Boiler House of 1977 is a late work by *Peter Womersley*, who in 1967 designed the excellent Edenside Health Centre, Kelso, with surgeries contained in drum-like volumes of white render, glass and slate. Borders hospital provision was centralised in 1976–87 with the building of the Borders General Hospital at Melrose by *Reiach & Hall*, set on a low-lying site at the foot of the Eildon Hills. In white concrete blockwork with contrasting pink bands, claimed to evoke the colour of the local earth, and tent-like entrance canopies.

Public recreation takes many forms. The burghs were well equipped with CINEMAS in the C20 and two are worth a mention. The Playhouse, Peebles, by the cinema specialist *Alister MacDonald*, was built in 1932, Kelso's former Relief Church was remodelled as The Roxy by *J. P. Alison & Hobkirk*, c. 1931, with Art Nouveau detailing. More surprising is the absence of THEATRES, a lack answered by *Richard Murphy Architects'* clever conversion of the former Free Church in Peebles for the Eastgate Arts Centre, 2003–4.

SPORT and LEISURE have provided some important landmarks for the Borders, notably the racecourse at Kelso, devel-

* Under threat 2005.

oped on land provided by the Duke of Roxburghe, whose stand
was built in 1822–3 to a design, by *John Carr* of York, supplied   p. 452
to the 'gentlemen of the County' in 1778, presumably for an
earlier racecourse outwith the town. It is remarkably unaltered,
outside and in, but hemmed in by later stands. Comparable but
of a different generation is the boldly sculptural grandstand in
shuttered concrete at Galashiels Football Club by *Peter Womersley*, 1967, with *Ove Arup & Partners*, engineers. Simple and effective designs for public swimming pools can be found set on
low-lying ground by the Tweed in Peebles by *Morris & Steedman*,
1983, and, of the same year, in the leafy surroundings of Scott
Park, Galashiels, by *Duncan Cameron & Associates*. Unavoidably
eyecatching is the stripy Postmodern façade of Teviotdale Leisure
Centre, Hawick, 1982 by *Faulkner Brown, Hendy & Stonor*.

Large POST OFFICES, serving a public and commercial function, date from the late C19 and early C20, built by *H.M. Office
of Works*. Galashiels Post Office, 1894, is large and assertive, a
version of Queen Anne, with flanking octagonal towers and projecting porch. 1902 is the date of the single-storey Renaissance
office in Melrose which, in scale, fits well into the streetscape, as
does *W. T. Oldrieve*'s understated Neo-Georgian in Kelso. Duns
Post Office is Scottish Jacobean, *c.* 1900, single-storey with a
balustraded wall-head clasped between crowstepped gables.

CORN EXCHANGES were required in several burghs and these
provided spaces for stalls once a week, and at other times were
available for social occasions. Many have gone but part preserved
is *J. T. Rochead*'s exchange in Hawick, of 1865, and two designs
by *David Cousin*, of 1855 at Kelso in Cotswold Tudor style and
Scottish Jacobean for Melrose, 1863. Earlston's Corn Exchange   95
of 1868 has an attractive pointed belfry and clock.

From the mid 1820s all the major BANKS, with the exception
of the Royal Bank of Scotland, undertook a programme of
branch bank building. A branch office usually consisted of a plain
two- or three-storey and basement building, three to five bays
wide, with a ground-floor telling room and on the upper floors
a house for the agent, who was often a local solicitor, accountant
or land agent. In Peebles, Bank House was remodelled for the
Union Bank by *William Railton c.* 1860 and altered and added to
in Italianate style by *David Rhind* in 1871 for the Commercial
Bank. The imposing Italianate British Linen Co. Bank by
Wardrop & Reid, 1887, has the agent's house above, while on the
other side of the street the Bank of Scotland displays a stripped
classical front by *J.D. Cairns*, 1934–5. The former British Linen
Bank (Industrial Bank) in Galashiels is Renaissance by *Wardrop
& Reid*, 1880, and the Royal Bank of Scotland was rebuilt by *J. R.
McKay* in 1946 and given a long symmetrical façade with an
advanced pedimented centre. The Bank of Scotland in Melrose,
by *George Washington Browne*, 1897, is in his Free Renaissance   101
style, a bold building topped by a sculptured cartouche and
obelisks. Hawick has a full complement of banks: the Italianate
Royal Bank of Scotland by *J. Dick Peddie*, 1857; Lloyds TSB (formerly Hawick Savings Bank) by *J.P. Alison*, 1914, in Italian
Renaissance fashion; the Bank of Scotland by *David Cousin*, 1863,
is Venetian with a long bracketed first-floor balcony, and the

imposing former Commercial Bank of 1852 acts as the terminal block at the s end of the High Street. Jedburgh has an Italian Renaissance Commercial Bank by *David Rhind*, 1868. In Duns the Royal Bank of Scotland is a Renaissance palazzo by *Peddie & Kinnear*, 1857, and the Bank of Scotland by *H.O. Tarbolton*, 1928, rather feeble Jacobean. The façade of the Bank of Scotland, Kelso, by *John Burnet*, 1860, is nicely detailed, and a rusticated gateway leads to the agent's house at the rear. Two rural banks of note are the late C19 Royal Bank of Scotland, Ayton; a classical house for the agent, with single-bay pavilions, one set back, the other forward. At Earlston, the two-storey classical agent's house has single-bay bank premises at one end.

The streets of many burghs and villages preserve original SHOPFRONTS. Particularly good examples, including late C19 cast-iron examples, survive in Kelso. Decorative work of *c.* 1900, where it survives, is often memorable, for example the figurative tiled panels of the former dairy in Innerleithen by *James Duncan Ltd* with Art Nouveau surround, a style still popular in the early 1930s, as shown by the shopfront in Eastgate, Peebles, by *J.D. Cairns*, 1931, fronting a shoe emporium. Larger COMMERCIAL BUILDINGS or stores are more unusual. An intriguing survival is the palazzo-style former offices (now Barclays Bank) in Woodmarket, Kelso, built in 1865 by *James W. Smith* for Stuart & Mein, nurserymen and seed merchants, and decorated with gardening motifs, flowers and fruit. Providing a good piece of Baronial townscape in Peebles High Street is Veitch's, Ladies' and Gentlemen's Outfitters, established in 1885 as a commercial development by Robert Veitch. Frequently among the most memorable and sometimes most imposing commercial developments are the Co-operative stores in the towns, built from the late 1870s. The best is that in Galashiels High Street built in 1888–90 by *J. & J. Hall*, but good designs also enliven the streets of Hawick, Jedburgh and Selkirk.

The main routes into Scotland from the s were well equipped with HOTELS and INNS from the C18. Many were simple vernacular buildings in villages and small burghs. Most have been altered: occasionally to their benefit, as with the remarkable Art Deco refitting by *James Taylor* of the Crook Inn, Tweedsmuir. Large hotels, for wealthier visitors, often included assembly rooms for the local population, and have some architectural style. Kelso acquired a number, the grandest of which is the Cross Keys Hotel, built by James Dickson of Ednam *c.* 1760. Originally a stage post, it had extensive stabling used by the Caledonian Hunt and Kelso Races. The pleasant classical Castle Inn, Greenlaw, rebuilt *c.* 1835 by *John Cunningham*, replaced a former mid-C18 inn. Some C18 stabling survives. Further up the A68 the late C18 Black Bull Hotel, a former coaching inn, welcomed visitors to Lauder. An early C19 Palladian windowed ballroom also made sure it was suitable for guests of the Earl of Lauderdale. New hotels were constructed and old inns enlarged to serve summer visitors and tourists. One such is the Traquair Arms, Innerleithen, its core a mid-C19 three-bay villa, acquired or built to accommodate summer visitors enjoying not only walking and fishing but also increasingly the waters at St Ronan's Wells, made famous by Walter Scott. Hydropathic treatment became popular during the later C19. The dramatically sited Peebles Hydro Hotel by *James Miller* of 1905 replaced a burnt-out French Renaissance hotel by *John Starforth*, 1878–81. Miller's Neo-Georgian design is similar to his earlier hotel at Turnberry, Ayrshire. The bright cream harling and rosemary-tiled roof make sure the hotel is visible from across the town. The Waverley Castle Hotel, Melrose, by *James C. Walker* (1871) was always more serious in dispensing its curative sessions, perhaps indicated by the unforgiving exterior, built in mass concrete, probably the first of its kind in Scotland. Public enthusiasm for such treatments revived in the late C20, expressed in the dazzling extensions for the spa at Stobo Castle by *R. D. Cameron Associates*, 1997–8.

BURGH AND VILLAGE HOUSING

Border towns were easily burned by border raiders as medieval houses were almost certainly timber-framed and stone structures were rare. There are, however, two early surviving examples of substantial TOWN LODGINGS. Drumlanrig Tower, Hawick, was erected in the mid C16 by the Douglases of Drumlanrig as a base for their administration of the barony of Hawick and is a defensible tower, similar in all respects to the rural tower houses of neighbouring lairds, but subsequently enlarged as a town house for the Duchess of Buccleuch and later incorporated into the High Street's frontage. Mary, Queen of Scots' House, Jedburgh, a modest T-plan residence of *c.* 1600, likewise has affini- 107 ties with the rural towers and mansions of the region, although its absence of defensive features and access from the street by means of a close emphasise its pacific history as a merchant's home.

TOWN HOUSES were erected by landowners in their local burghs as a base for business and, if large enough, for occupation during the winter 'season'. A few survive, albeit altered, including the Duke of Queensberry's town house in Peebles, now incorporated in the Chambers Institution, its wall thicknesses and a part-vaulted basement the only reminders of the former lodging. Also at Peebles, the main part of the Cross Keys Inn is the much-altered town house of the Williamsons of Cardrona, its C17 origin suggested by a dormer pediment dated 1693 and a late C17 stone chimneypiece. Nos. 5–7 Bridge Street, Kelso, 91 incorporates the house of the Ormistons of Hendersyde, revealed by restoration which exposed the late C17 front of a two-storey dwelling built over a large vaulted cellar. Also late C17 is Blackhill's Close, Castlegate, Jedburgh, which retains a notable Renaissance doorway and an elaborate sundial with tabular and bowl-shaped dials. C18 and early C19 town houses are rarer survivals, particularly important being the mid-C18 Chester House, Eyemouth, of two storeys with good classical detailing and well-preserved interior.

The main streets of most towns and large villages in the Borders were developed, or redeveloped, from the late C18 with TERRACED HOUSING, generally of two or three storeys. The architecture was not ambitious, but a pilastered doorpiece, a bracketed canopy, or tripartite windows with narrow sidelights became usual. Houses in the former royal burgh of Lauder, mostly dating from the late c18 and early c19, were built to a symmetrical pattern of two storeys and three bays with byres to the rear, a style repeated throughout the Borders in most agricultural small burghs and villages. Only when building was strictly controlled did the building pattern change. The Duke of Buccleuch's tenants in the grid-planned Newcastleton village were provided with long leases and two acres of land to build single-storey weavers' cottages along the gridded streets and lanes, and two-storey houses with four acres for the professionals in the main squares. Kelso exhibits a curiously un-Scottish layout in which all the principal streets converge upon a spacious granite-setted market square. The square was developed from the end of the c18, the housing having the appearance of Edinburgh town houses, but with shops integrated into the ground floors, many with pilastraded shopfronts which give a well-ordered impression. More two-storey late Georgian and early c19 Georgian survival terraced housing is also found at Coldstream, though on a much smaller scale, where fronts of polished ashlar, with channelled quoins, mutuled eaves cornices and flyover balustraded entrance stairs, give atmosphere to the main street.

ESTATE HOUSING in the Borders villages is often distinguished and replaced much poorer rural dwellings; good c19 examples can be found at Abbey St Bathans, Sprouston, Sinclairshill on the Kimmerghame estate and Foulden. Speculative developments of housing in the burghs are rarer, but particularly attractive are the picturesquely composed double cottages of 1863 that make up Maxwellheugh Terrace, Kelso, reputedly designed by *Lady Douglas* of Springwood.

A more dominant aspect of c19 Borders mill towns and villages is WORKERS' HOUSING. Much of it has disappeared from Selkirk and Galashiels but in Hawick several pockets of such housing survive, including skilled workers' housing in Slitrig Crescent, of *c.* 1800, and a mix of cottage-type houses and tenements in Wellogate, developed after 1888 by the Hawick Working Men's Building & Investment Co. Good provision of housing for industrial workers can be seen at Walkerburn, where the first mill was founded in 1850. Still surviving are not only plain, flatted dwellings of the 1850s and 1860s for mill workers, of four rooms on each floor, but also superior housing for artisans and managerial staff. In the same village the mill owner, Sir Henry Ballantyne, initiated a garden city scheme for cottage-style housing and flatted houses, built 1921–5 by *Dick Peddie & Walker Todd*, who employed the same style for council housing in Innerleithen, begun in 1920. Garden suburb-type housing can also be found in Peebles at Elliot's Park, laid out by *J.D. Cairns* in 1919–22 for the Scottish Veterans' Garden City Association.

Ballantyne also gave his name to the Royal Commission Report of 1917 that proposed state intervention to solve the working-class housing problem and ushered in an increased role for town and county councils in housing provision. This was most obvious in the larger burghs during the 1930s, which gained acres

of cottage dwellings and flats. Much of this is ordinary but individual schemes stand out, notably the housing (Cowdrait and
Ross) for Berwickshire County Council at Burnmouth of 1935
by *William H. Kininmonth* and *Basil Spence* of *Rowand Anderson
Paul & Partners*. Kininmonth went on to build further housing
here for fishermen's families in 1948.

An emerging body of domestic architecture in this period
emphasised traditional Scottish vernacular design and planning
designed to evoke a sense of community. A key proponent of this
was *Frank C. Mears*, who (in partnership with *C.D. Carus-Wilson*
after 1928) developed garden suburb type housing for the Association for the Preservation of Rural Scotland, *c*. 1935, in Connor
Street, Peebles, and produced the eyecatching, village-like setting   116
for the Lucy Sanderson Cottage Homes, Galashiels, designed as
dwellings for retired mill workers in 1930–3.

The POST-WAR PERIOD has produced a certain amount of
urban renewal and some large new communities. In Selkirk the   118
Burgh Council acquired a site for the Bannerfield estate by *Basil
Spence & Partners*, 1945–64. A strictly ordered development
with rows of terraced houses and three-storey flatted blocks
grouped around large grassy squares, four of them linked by a
tree-lined boulevard. The scheme was Spence's second post-
Second World War commission and was important in Scotland
for the introduction of the Radburn system of traffic segregation.
Large municipal housing schemes in the industrial centres of
Hawick and Galashiels were under way from the 1950s, the most
important in Galashiels where Easter Langlee was developed
from 1967 with Scandinavian-inspired social housing by *Wheeler
& Sproson*; Wester Langlee's housing was laid out in phases,
begun by the Town Council in the early 1950s and continued
1972–6, by the *Scottish Special Housing Association*, who also
carried out the initial phases of Tweedbank from 1973, an effort
(prompted by the 1968 Johnson–Marshall Plan for Central
Borders) to expand the population of this area by 25,000 and
support it with new industries, contained in an industrial estate.
In spite of some imaginative landscaping around the man-made
Gun Knowe Loch, the standard here was not maintained in later
phases.

In some of the burghs, efforts were made from the 1960s to
improve housing conditions in the old centres. In Selkirk the Old
Town Renewal by *Sir Frank Mears & Partners* was unduly ruth-
less in clearing away the old parts and replacing them with courts
and terraces off the main thoroughfares. In common with that
firm's work elsewhere at this date, the tone is strongly vernacular, but at Galashiels the Modernists offered a different solution
in the redevelopment of Church Square in the old town as a
formal composition of three-storey blocks by *Peter Womersley*,
after 1960, and his pupil *Duncan Cameron*, 1963–5. Later c20
redevelopments in the burghs made greater efforts to preserve
historic character: notably at Jedburgh, where the *Scottish Special
Housing Association* produced some imaginative restoration and
infill in the 1970s, and Kelso where *J. & F. Johnston & Partners'*
redevelopment, 1974–9, of the medieval streets of Woodmarket
and Horsemarket provide a similarly satisfying mix of old and
new. In Hawick, the restoration of Drumlanrig Tower, 1990–5,

for the Scottish Buildings Heritage Trust was accompanied by sensitive restoration of buildings in Towerdykeside, much enhancing the character of the medieval close.

SUBURBAN VILLAS, set in their own gardens and sometimes with stables and lodges, were built from the late C18. Good early examples survive in Kelso, including Edenside House (c. 1796), Woodside House, Ednam Road (c. 1800 for Jean Scott of Harden) and Tweedbank, Shedden Park Road (1806). All are classical. Slightly later is Orchard House, Bowmont Street, Kelso, which retains much of its interior, and Late Georgian classicism is also predominantly the character of Duns villadom, housing bankers, lawyers and architects, which lies s of the town in the vicinity of Station Road, including Maryfield with a full panoply of panelled giant pilasters.

The villa intended as a retreat to the attractive countryside, or to a social community on the outskirts of town, can be found to perfection in the Borders. An interesting collection is at Gattonside, where small villas were built from the early C19, almost all due to the motivation of Sir Walter Scott as friend or patron. Notable are two early simple classical villas by *John Smith*, Abbotsmeadow (1826) for a local lawyer, and Allerly (1823) for Scott's friend Dr David Brewster. Other outsiders also built country retreats at Gattonside, drawn by the attractions of fishing on the Tweed. Gattonside House was started c. 1808–11 as a classical villa but much extended for a Liverpool businessman, while Pavilion began as stables which were adapted and extended by the fourteenth Lord Somerville as a fishing lodge for use by his family or to rent out during the fishing season. On the outskirts of Kelso sites were advertised in the early C19 for building and were taken up with enthusiasm. The best is Walton Hall, Roxburgh Street (1820), built for Sir Walter Scott's publisher John Ballantyne in Regency style with a Veneto villa plan; opposite his brother Alexander built a *cottage orné*, The Elms, by *William Elliot*.

Large villas, sometimes approaching the scale of suburban mansions, appear from the mid C19, and in a variety of styles. Many were erected for the wealthier owners of local industries and placed within reach of their works, e.g. Thornfield House, Selkirk, of 1871 by *Peddie & Kinnear* for James Brown of Ettrick Mill. This is Italianate, but greater eclecticism of style characterises ambitious villas elsewhere by this date. At Walkerburn, the success of the Ballantynes' textile mills funded the erection of villas for several generations of the family. Tweedvale, built for Henry Ballantyne, is entirely traditional but has a lodge of 1868 by *F. T. Pilkington*, whose idiosyncratic style is fully expressed in the pair of villas for Ballantynes' sons: The Kirna (1867) and Stoneyhill (1868), the former in the rogue Gothic of Pilkington's churches, the latter in an exaggeratedly weird French Gothic. More conventional in style, but grander in scale, among Victorian villa-mansions are those found in the neighbourhood of Abbotsford Road, Galashiels. Scottish Baronial found particular favour among the magnates here, including two houses by *William Hay*: Kingsknowes, an aggressively red sandstone design of 1868–9, and Abbotshill of 1874. Both have fine conservatories by *Mackenzie & Moncur*. Among smaller villas, classical and Italianate styles endure into the second half of the C19, but from

1850 also exploit the historicist styles of the larger houses, such as the Scottish Domestic style of The Knoll, Duns, with its crow-stepped gables and gablets, and nearby Parkside, 1850, with its inventive display of idiosyncratic Jacobean detail.

Improvements in transport played an instrumental role in encouraging the building of villas in several places for holidays and retirement, notably at Melrose, where the Waverley line was opened in 1849 and provided access to Scott country and salmon fishing on the Tweed. At Peebles, served by the Caledonian Railway from 1864, the southern slopes of the Tweed are filled with excellently varied examples of Late Victorian and Edwardian villas and mansions, ranging from Dilkusha of 1897 with its fine panelled interior, to Reiverslaw, 1904, by *A. Hunter Crawford* and Arnsheen, a freely mixed composition of Baronial and Scottish Domestic motifs by *J. D. Cairns* for himself, 1914. Maplehurst, Abbotsford Road, Galashiels, a half-timbered industrialist's mansion by *J. & J. Hall*, has a good interior with Art Nouveau detailing. Arts and Crafts styling was popular before 1914 among smaller villas too, such as Norwood, Rosalee Brae, at Hawick of *c.* 1904, with mock Tudor half-timbering and a castellated tower. Villas after 1914 are a rarity, and designs showing awareness of the Modern Movement are without example in the Borders, until *Peter Womersley*'s small Modernist house, The Rig (1956) and *Duncan Cameron*'s Achnacairidh (1967), the most recent of the villa retreats to be erected at Gattonside.

RURAL BUILDINGS: MANSES, FARMHOUSES AND STEADINGS

Besides lairds' houses the most substantial dwelling in a parish was the minister's MANSE. After 1663 there was a legal obligation on the parish heritors (landowners) to provide a 'competent' manse for the incumbent, a responsibility that continued until 1925. Each minister was dependent on the produce from his glebe, as well as the tithe paid to him for his livelihood, and each manse was provided with a stable and steading. Early manses, with clay floors and thatched roofs, were in a dire state by the mid c18. Dating from this period of improvement is the substantial and remarkably unaltered Kilbucho Old Manse of 1751, where dated lintels record its earlier history. At Traquair Manse (Kirkbride House) the original house built by *William Hislop* and *John Wright*, 1694, was refronted in the late c18 with a three-bay façade, typical of manses from that date forward. Agricultural surveys of the Borders counties published in the late c18 and early c19 show that manses were built upon much the same plan as farmhouses: symmetrically planned, of two storeys and usually of three bays, and increasingly to standard dimensions (approximately 34–40 ft (10.3 m.–12.2 m.) by 19–22 ft (5.8 m.–6.7 m.) within the walls). Slate roofs also became the norm.

In the early c19 the size and comfort of manses increased, in particular by the addition of space for dining and drawing rooms, improvements which were frequently forced on the heritors by the Church Presbytery backed by the Court of Session. *James Gillespie Graham* and *Robert Wright* both served as Presbytery architects, rebuilding Greenlaw Manse (Mansefield) in 1817, to provide the comforts of an Edinburgh town house. Morebattle Manse (Wellgate) by *John Winchester* and *William Clark*, 1828–9, is a typical two-storey three-bay manse with a pilastered doorway, with two-storey whinstone bay windows added in 1852 which enlarged the principal rooms. A classical court of offices, 1856, housed the minister's gig. Numerous other C18 manses were improved, sometimes on several occasions, such as Foulden Manse, which was built in 1774–6, but extended and altered in 1813, 1841 and 1897. A number of manses were built at the expense of the principal heritor, or built by a wealthy minister for himself, much disapproved of by the Church authorities. Polwarth Manse, for the Rev. Robert Home, is a fine example by *James Cunningham*, 1836, with good classical detailing and full-height shallow bows. Free Church manses built after 1843 followed the same pattern as parish manses, and as later Free Churches exhibited a greater degree of wealth, their manses followed suit. At Swinton, for example the rebuilding of the church in 1859–60 was accompanied by the provision of impressive mutuled and finialled gatepiers with decorative iron gates forming a grand approach to the new manse.

The Borders contain some of the best arable and grazing land in Scotland, developed from the mid C18 by enlightened proprietors of large estates who invested directly in areas of enclosure, constructed drystone walls and planted hedges and thousands of trees. They also improved their tenants' farms, and provided decent housing for their servants, labourers and mechanics. As in most other parts of Scotland, these agricultural improvements swept away a pattern of rural settlement that had changed little since medieval times. Besides the defensible farmhouses of the late C16 (see p. 48), most rural dwellings were constructed of perishable materials – unmortared or clay-mortared stone, clay, turf, timber, wattle-and-daub and thatch – and do not survive.

Most early farmhouses were single-storey, with the cattle lodged either at one end of the dwelling or, in larger establishments, in a separate byre. Excavations at Springwood Park, Kelso, exposed the remains of a row of C13–C14 cruck-framed houses with clay walls on stone footings, thatched roofs and, apparently, open hearths. Comparable discoveries at Lilliesleaf revealed similar techniques of construction continuing into the C17, and clay walls were still to be seen in some parts of the region, e.g. Coldingham Moor, as late as the 1950s. Some of these early houses were evidently sizeable, and Charles Findlater, describing the 'better farm dwellings' of Peeblesshire as they had existed shortly before the period of improvement in his *General View of Agriculture* (1802), wrote of houses measuring about 50 by 20 ft (15 m. by 6 m.) overall, with walls 6 ft (1.8 m.) high. They contained three rooms separated only by partitions formed by box beds. In the middle was the kitchen, with its 'roundabout fire side', i.e. a central hearth with a lath and plaster chimney suspended above it. One of the end rooms would have been the private quarters of the farmer's family, while the other – a chamber seemingly not found in the majority of pre-improvement farmhouses – was perhaps a best room for the entertainment of guests.

The poorest dwellings belonged to cottars, ploughmen and shepherds, and as late as the 1790s the shepherds' cottages of Roxburghshire were described by the parish minister of Galashiels as 'miserable temporary hovels', having walls constructed of alternate layers of stone and turf, and roofs of slender timber covered with turf and rushes. The original Black Dwarf's Cottage (Kirkton Manor) of the early 1760s is known to have had walls of this type, but no examples survive of this or of cothouses – typically single-roomed dwellings with space at one end for a cow and a wicker-framed clay chimney suspended above an open hearth.

From the C18 onwards skilled tenants were able to improve their holdings through longer leases and allowances to improve or rebuild FARMHOUSES AND STEADINGS. In time, with mutual prosperity, this enabled the larger estates to develop formally planned Home Farms. The Act of 1770 'to encourage the Improvement of Lands in Scotland held under settlement of strict entail', accelerated development as landowners were permitted to charge their estates with three-quarters of the cost of improvements made. All of these building activities are detailed in the fascinating 'Registers of Improvement', which were lodged with the sheriff courts. Improvement of farmhouses and their steadings in the four counties of the Borders progressed at the same time, and in Peeblesshire alone about fifty new farmhouses had been built by 1800. New farm buildings frequently formed a rectangular court with the house usually on the s side, though gradually the farmhouse was sited further away from noxious farm odours. The rubble steadings were generally simple and utilitarian. Minimal decoration of the farmhouse was kept to classical doorpieces, but many became smarter from the early C19 with added wings, and tripartite and bowed windows. West Mains Farm, Castlecraig, a late C18 farmhouse 'of a more superior kind', has small single-storey wings; the adjacent pedimented stable range was built by *James & Alexander Noble* in 1809, fronting late C18 traditional rubble-built steadings. Mainside Farm (Hownam) is a good example of a 'new' farmhouse and steading built 1775 in place of a fermtoun of nine cottages. All farms on the Roxburghe estates were improved from the early C19, their elevations and plans recorded in 1843 in a remarkable farm book. The least-altered are the 'Roxburghe Farms' (Roxburgh) where the principal farm, Roxburgh Mains, built in 1835, was made 'superior' with an advanced centre bay and block pediment and corniced doorway with cavetto reveals. Its excellent contemporary farm offices include a still active threshing mill. The long w wing of the stylish farmhouse at Howford Farm, Traquair, 1839–40, was built to house farm servants, but mostly they were housed in separate FARM COTTAGES, usually sited at the approach to the farm. These also improved from the early C19 and rows of single-storey cottages, often with attic dormers, are obvious around the countryside. The most dramatic group is found at Sinclairshill on the Kimmerghame estate, where two rows of traditional dwellings were transformed into Cotswold Tudor style cottages in the mid-C19.

At Makerstoun, Manorhill Farm is a late C19 MODEL FARM with a typical Victorian gabled farmhouse and a good range of large cattle sheds, still serving their original purpose. But few examples can surpass the magnificence of the Buxley Model Farm and Dairy at Manderston, distinguished by opulent accommodation and impeccable craftsmanship. Designed by *John Kinross* from 1897, it pre-dates his work on the main house, and incorporates earlier farm buildings in a picturesque mix of Scottish Baronial, Gothic with Renaissance details, and a simpler C17 Scottish Domestic style with crowstepped gables. STEADINGS associated with large estates indicate the importance of the principal farm with commanding tall towers or spires. The arched opening into the U-plan court at Blackadder Mains Farm, 1785, is surmounted by a square tower with clock and bell, originally topped by a splendid lead-clad spire. At Ladykirk Home Farm, mid-C19 cottages flank a square dovecot tower with Diocletian openings, one with tiers of flight-holes, pedimented dormer openings on the wall-head, and a tall bellcast roof with a cock weathervane.

INDUSTRIAL BUILDINGS

Before the late C18 the Borders had a predominantly rural economy, with the bulk of the population living on the land. An essential local service was provided by GRAIN MILLS, of which some sixty water-powered examples are marked on Timothy Pont's late C16 maps of the region. No mills of this date appear to survive, but their late C18 and C19 successors are not uncommon, although few remain in working order. The mill built at Blyth Bridge by a firm of local masons has a carved panel recording the high price of grain in 1817, the year of its construction. Wind power was little used for industry in earlier times, the best-preserved of the few remaining windmills is at Eyemouth. Industries associated with livestock include bacon curing, represented by the mid-C19 farmhouse and steading at Rachan Mill, and poultry farming, whose most interesting architectural manifestation is at Romanno Bridge, where a C19 woollen mill was converted into an incubator house in the early C20. The business of farming, with the movement of stock for sale and buying and selling of agricultural implements, made AUCTION MARTS important. Two were provided close to railway stations. The mart at Newtown St Boswells, established by John Swan & Co., has its original, octagonal sale ring (designed for driving livestock in a circle) of 1872, with a shallow ventilator and decorative weathervane. Reston mart is early C20, on the site of an earlier mart, and has an octagonal timber sheep ring with a triangular ventilator, and tiered seating. Many Borders villages retained working SMITHIES until well into the second half of the C20, and one or two still remain, e.g. at Midlem and St Boswells. The tiny village of Clappers, near Mordington, has both blacksmith's house and smithy, the latter still containing its forge and tools.

The TEXTILE INDUSTRY and the manufacture of woollen goods came to dominate the economies of the Borders towns and villages during the C18, C19 and C20. The WEAVING industry, like other handcrafts such as leather working and tool making, was domestic in scale. Many cottage workshops survive in modified form, including some in planned villages such as Carlops and Newcastleton, both founded by local landowners in the late C18 to promote handloom weaving. The woollen industry of the Southern Uplands developed first from 'worsted' yarn (twisted from long, combed wool), woven into fabric and then finished in 'waulk' (fulling) mills or hand-knitted into coarse HOSIERY. There were three waulk mills in Galashiels by the 1580s, and a Board of Manufacturers was established there in 1727 to support the manufacture of blankets and coarse 'jerseys'. Hawick developed as a trading centre for wool, yarn and worsted goods in the mid-C18 because of its connections to Edinburgh, Carlisle and Newcastle. A fledgling carpet industry emerged there in 1752, but the burgh became a centre for hosiery manufacture in 1771 with the introduction of the faster 'hand-frame' for knitting. Baillie Hardie established the first 'stocking shop' in Hawick and others followed (about eighty in total by 1857, and many others in Denholm, Kelso, Melrose and Selkirk). One survivor is William Beck's Stocking Shop in Hawick of *c.* 1800, with a small square window for each stockinger and his frame. Denholm is particularly interesting, for not only were some of the houses surrounding the village green occupied by stockingers but Westside Mill was built in the late C18 to accommodate a small number of individual stocking frames, representing the transitional phase of the industry towards the fully mechanised textile trade that later concentrated in the burghs.

The ready availability of water from the rivers and their tributaries provided power for mills and, combined with innovations in technology, made it possible for local entrepreneurs to build larger MILLS, chiefly for spinning and carding, which increased in number in the second half of the C18, encouraged by Board of Trustees' grants for spinning. Surviving early spinning mills are small, such as Caerlee Mill, Innerleithen (*c.* 1788) and Botany Mill, Galashiels (1797). Although knitting and weaving remained predominantly cottage industries, the growth of the mechanised production of woven cloth is reflected in the establishment of the Galashiels Manufacturers' Corporation in 1777 and the building of a Cloth Hall there in 1791–2, which survives, although much altered. Woven cloth was first manufactured in Hawick in 1787, but it was the growing popularity of TWEED from *c.* 1830 that led to a boom in mill buildings for weaving. Examples from this time, such as the High Mill of Forest Mill, Selkirk (built in 1838), follow traditional patterns, typically of three storeys and an attic with regularly spaced fenestration over five or six bays. Notable later examples include *John & James Smith*'s 1850 extension to Ettrick Mill, Selkirk which created a tall, long 119 main façade with an elaborate pedimented centre and returned ends and the late C19 multi-gabled front block of Gala Mill, Galashiels.   120

Technological advances included the introduction of power looms, notably by the far-sighted John Laing & Sons in Wilton Mills, Hawick, who installed a steam engine in 1831 to supplement two water wheels. As communications improved, particularly with the opening of the railways to the burghs in 1849–62, coal became cheaper to fire steam-powered frames (first installed in the Borders at Wilton Mills in 1858). By the 1860s some mills had 'double-decked' attics that provided top-lit working area and storage. Further advances in spinning machinery came with 'mules' using vertical and horizontal shafts; such mills were typically multiples of five or six bays in length. Inside, most were arranged four bays deep, to accommodate two pairs of mules facing each other, and would be either one or two mules in length, with a stair-tower at one end or at the centre. An example is Tower Mill, Hawick, rebuilt in 1851 with power provided by a broad water wheel (later used to generate electricity). Cast-iron columns were increasingly used to support the floors of C19 mills, reducing the need for solid internal walls which would restrict vital operating space for mules. Timber floors were the norm however and few (if any) of the mills seem to have been built using costly fireproof construction of jack arches and cast-iron beams. An exception is part of Ettrick Mill, Selkirk. Ferro-concrete was used for the construction of Ladhope Mills, Galashiels, in 1914 (dem. 2003).

As the demand for stockings declined, manufacturers diversified into high-class woollen underwear using broad gauge frames, which lent themselves more readily to mechanisation and division of labour. This fostered centralisation of spinning and frame-knitting on a single site and is reflected in the expansion of the
121 mills into large factories by the later C19, as at Wilton Mills, Hawick which was extensively rebuilt after 1867. At its peak in the 1890s, Netherdale Mill in Galashiels had two mills, office, engine house, tall brick chimney and weaving sheds that covered thirty acres and employed 650 people. Complexes included elaborate engine houses with cast-iron water tanks such as those at Waverley Mills, Innerleithen, c. 1871 and Ettrick Mill, Selkirk, 1874, both by *Thomas Aimers* of Galashiels. The mills and offices also reflected the status of the firms, as shown by the French Renaissance exuberance of Mansfield Mills, 1880, and Eastfield Mills, 1882, in Hawick.

In the early C20 manufacturers diversified into KNITWEAR, famously creating the 'twinset' and Pringle diamond pattern. Small firms were also established at this time, such as the knitwear factory on Carnarvon Street, Hawick, by local architect
122 *Alex Inglis*, 1911. The growing importance of colour in knitwear of the C20 is reflected in the large dyehouses, usually low sheds with ridge ventilators.

As important to the textile industry as the mills and factories were WAREHOUSES for selling tweed and cloth. The largest of these, dating from 1885 and later, is Holland & Sherry's warehouse (originally Thorburn & Co.) in Peebles, which continues to operate. It comprises an office and warehouse with an interior of timber floors and cast-iron columns behind an impressive frontage, and was extended twice as the firm's business developed to serve international markets.

Two other industries dependent upon an abundant supply of water were papermaking and brewing. PAPERMAKING was established on the Eye and Whiteadder Waters, Berwickshire, by the end of the C18, being described in 1813 as 'the only manufacture of any importance' in that county (*General View of Agriculture*, p. 455). Carlops, too, made a minor contribution to the industry at that period, supplying woollen felts for the neighbouring paper mills at Penicuik, Midlothian. Today only the Chirnside Bridge Mill remains in operation, having been relocated from Broomhouse, a little higher up the Whiteadder Water, in 1842. The greater part of *David Cousin*'s building of that date survives, together with a fine brick chimneystack and a former manager's house with Italianate details. BREWING was concentrated in the towns from the C18. Each burgh supported at least one brewery but few have bequeathed any buildings of note, except at Coldstream, Chirnside and Melrose. Most interesting, however, is the domestic brewhouse at Traquair House, brought back into commission in the 1960s after a century's disuse, which displays a complete range of traditional brewing apparatus in its original setting.

As the principal Borders towns expanded during the C19 they developed their own WATER SUPPLIES, usually in the form of modest-sized local reservoirs. Remnants of the waterworks survive at Selkirk, of 1903, but the most notable building project, the Talla Waterworks, Tweedsmuir (1897–1905), was designed for the benefit of the citizens of Edinburgh. In addition to the reservoir itself, the works included a stylish and sumptuously equipped company headquarters and an aqueduct *c.* 55 km. in length, with a strongly architectural survey tower for calculating the alignment of the aqueduct on Harlaw Muir, near Deepsykehead (Carlops).

Commercial salmon FISHING was a major C19 industry carried on by netting from boats and by sportsmen who formed angling clubs and built shiels (shelters) which became relatively common on both banks of the eastern stretch of the River Tweed as far as Berwick. The mid-C19 Finchy Shiel, near Paxton, formed part of a larger fishing station, and the restored boathouse at Paxton was used for commercial fishing. Each site has a fish store built into a bank.

In the late C20 the search for renewable sources of energy led to the exploitation of WIND POWER. In 2000 the first of what looks likely to become a series of windfarms, powered by clusters of giant propeller-driven turbines, was constructed on Dun Law, Soutra, presenting the southbound traveller on the historic Edinburgh–Jedburgh road with a dramatic new gateway to the Borders.

GAZETTEER

ABBEY ST BATHANS

Charmingly isolated in a secluded valley framed by wooded slopes, near the Whiteadder and Monynut Waters, a setting that must have attracted the Cistercian nunnery, which was here by the early C13. There are two clusters of buildings: one next to the Parish Church; the other around Abbey St Bathans House. Both proclaim the guiding hand of the Turnbulls, an architecturally inclined family who were principal landowners from 1786.

Former FREE CHURCH, Bankhead. Now a house. 1870s, of timber with quarry-glazed windows.

KIRK of LAMMERMUIR (Parish Church). On the site of the nunnery, whose church probably served the parish from an early date and continued to do so post-Reformation. Repaired and remodelled on several occasions in the C17 and C18, when it was also truncated. Much now dates from those operations, and of the rectangular core, only the lower portion of the E wall and parts of the N wall are clearly medieval. The most prominent features are a SW porch and a NE laird's aisle capped by a tower and spire: these date from a restoration of 1867–8 by *John Lessels*, for John Turnbull. Whinstone rubble walls throughout with buff or red ashlar dressings. The E wall is probably medieval up to a sharp intake at the base of the gable. The central, two-light C13 plate-traceried window (partly renewed) gave the cue for the design of the other windows inserted in the 1860s. Blocked doorway and fragmentary tusking on the N side, and accounts of wall foundations to the E, suggest the claustral ranges were to the N and extended E of the church. The 1860s parts are richly detailed in Romanesque Revival style. The SW porch has a doorway with assertively red nook-shafts and the laird's aisle doorway, decorated with the Turnbull arms, is yet more lavish. Capping the tower above the aisle is a slated broach spire. Plain interior with a hammer-beam roof. – PAINTED TEXTS flank the E window. – STAINED GLASS, grisaille designs. – A survival of particular importance is the EFFIGY of a C15 prioress, found during restoration, now set in a niche created in the E wall. – LEDGER SLAB, re-set in S porch, Rev. George Home, †1705. – CHURCHYARD. C18, C19 and C20 memorials, including two table tombs. Turnbull enclosure, W of church, with Gothic centrepiece.

Former MANSE. On a hillside terrace S of the church. Two-storeyed three-bay core by *Sim* of Duns, 1822, of squared and snecked whin with ashlar dressings, between additions of 1845.

ABBEY FARMHOUSE. L-plan, originally rectangular, with a mid-C19 NE gabled wing and turret with conical roof in the re-entrant angle. Single-storey outbuildings and dairy to rear. Opposite is its quadrangular STEADING, unfortunately modified.

THE SQUARE, NE, is six mid-C19 estate cottages in two interlocking L-shaped groupings, with four houses to the W, and two to the E. Ingeniously picturesque with irregular faces N and E, the latter especially important since it was visible from the Turnbulls' house. The careful modulations of the planes and asymmetrical groupings of gables, gablets, dormers and chimneys show awareness of the latest publications on estate buildings.

ABBEY ST BATHANS HOUSE. Now subdivided. Built for the Turnbulls. It originated, probably in the early C19, as a thatched *cottage orné* (the datestone inscribed 1694 is unprovenanced), set at the base of a knoll with the ground falling away steeply N to the Whiteadder. This earlier core is identifiable at the centre of the SW entrance front as a two-bay section with first-floor dormers rising through the eaves, and with a salient gabled section at its N end terminating the NW range. Later extensions, especially in the 1870s, retain something of the original character (if not the scale) in the plethora of traceried bargeboards, dormers, and barley-sugar chimneystacks. The detailing of the NW front is more overtly Baronial, having a central tower-like pavilion with diagonally intaken flanks at the upper levels, a tall pyramidal roof, and a quadrant bartizan on its NE side; smaller full bartizan at the NE angle. Attractive interiors, particularly the stair with barley-sugar balusters and timber arcading. Many fittings were introduced in the 1880s by Dorothea Veitch from Bassendean House (q.v.). – Picturesque LODGE, STABLES and GROOM'S COTTAGE. W of the stables is an artfully composed Z-plan complex including GAMEKEEPER'S COTTAGE and KENNELS.

3   FORT and BROCH, Edinshall, 2 km. SE. Massively constructed broch measuring almost 17 m. in diameter within a wall from 5.2 m. to 6.4 m. in thickness and up to 1.5 m. in height. The entrance, flanked by two guard chambers, is on the SSE, and there are also three other chambers within the thickness of the wall, one of which contains a stair. The broch probably dates from the C1 or C2 A.D., and was inserted into the ruins of an earlier multivallate fort, which is also overlain by an undefended settlement of stone-walled round-houses.

THE RETREAT. *See* p. 646.

ABBOTRULE

Just the church and the site of Abbotrule House.

PARISH CHURCH. A possession of Jedburgh Abbey from perhaps the early C12, it was abandoned in 1777. E and W gables and part of the S wall, with a late medieval chamfered rectangular S doorway. Chamfered intake to the E gable; the birdcage bellcote on the W gable (which required the additional support of a buttress after the roof had been removed) is no earlier than C17. MEMORIAL of 1748 attached to W gable, segmental pediment supported by Tuscan pilasters; a skeleton holds a lance and hourglass. – CHURCHYARD, S, with a medieval coped stone with angle rolls, and a fallen headstone with a portrait bust.

ABBOTRULE HOUSE, the property of the Kerr family from the early C17 until 1818, was demolished in 1956 leaving only a w gable. – STABLES. Symmetrical courtyard range, first built *c*. 1810, with an arched entrance topped by a lead cupola, and flanking single-storey wings ending in pavilions. Derelict Gothic SUMMERHOUSE with a pointed-arched doorway, flanked by similar windows, and a pedestal fountain.*

ABBOTSFORD[†] 5030
3.2 km w of Melrose

Abbotsford, the home of Sir Walter Scott from 1811 until his death in 1832, is one of the most famous houses in the world; the archetype of a literary shrine and the crucial house in the popularisation of the Scottish Baronial Revival. A particular pleasure of a visit today depends on the almost miraculous and complete survival of Scott's collections, which remain *in situ*, more or less in the positions he planned for them.

As Sheriff-depute of Selkirkshire from 1799, Scott was obliged to reside in the county during the summer for the transaction of official business. From 1804 to 1811 he rented the old house of Ashiesteel (q.v.) from a kinsman, before purchasing the nearby farm called Clarty Hole from Dr Robert Douglas, minister of Galashiels, to form the nucleus of the present Abbotsford. Its command of a stretch of the River Tweed was a prime attraction and its new name was a historical allusion to Melrose Abbey, which was visible from the grounds. Scott wrote that he intended 'building a small cottage here for my summer abode, being obliged by law, as well as induced by inclination, to make this county my residence'. With the profits of his literary successes, he was soon able to create a small estate. In his son-in-law's words, 'twelve years afterwards the site was occupied not by a cottage but a castle'. In 1820 Scott was raised to a baronetcy by George IV. His worldwide celebrity and the press of visitors both before and after his death obliged his descendants to preserve Abbotsford as he had left it. In spite of successive enlargements, Scott's Abbotsford hardly strays beyond a generous suburban villa scale and the exterior is secondary to the importance of the internal plan.

Although modest in scale in comparison with ducal Bowhill[†] (q.v.), Abbotsford's BUILDING HISTORY is unusually challenging to unravel. Although Scott was firmly in control and his house is truly 'a Creature of the Poet's own fancy', he; some evolved and tested his ideas on a bewildering array of advisers professional but with a predilection for the amateur. In developing his ideas Scott relied on his friend James Skene of Rubis-

---

* A C17 vase, one of a pair from Marlfield (q.v.), was recorded here in the mid 1930s.
† The account of Abbotsford is by Ian Gow.
‡ Where work was being carried on simultaneously by the same architects.

Abbotsford in 1812, the farmhouse before extension.

law, the antiquarian and amateur artist, as well as Daniel Terry, an actor who had trained as an architect. To Scott they were better equipped to deliver the innovative originality that he craved in his house and grounds. Abbotsford evolved in three stages. Although Scott always intended to build anew, the layout of the existing farm set limitations and still underpins the planning of the extensive later buildings on its site. The original FARMHOUSE lay between its farmyard (SW) and walled garden (NE). *William Stark* supplied a design 'for an ornamental cottage in the style of the old English vicarage-house . . . But, before this could be done, Mr Stark died.' The farmhouse seems to have been developed into a *cottage orné* with a modish primitive pedimented portico of tree trunks.

The first addition, for a SW WING, was made in 1817–18, with *William Atkinson* as executant architect (builders, *Sanderson & Paterson* of Galashiels). This created a substantial dining room with a bay window commanding the Tweed view, suitable for the entertainment of the many admirers and tourists, with a kitchen immediately below and connected to the farmhouse by an armoury, essential for displaying Scott's fast-expanding antiquarian collections. The wing also provided Scott with a private study, at its far s end. Atkinson concealed the farmyard and domestic offices with a screen wall, behind which lay additional service rooms, creating a U-shaped courtyard that is still identifiable. The s façade of the new wing was screened by a fashionable conservatory, and the composition terminated by a miniature tower leading to a viewing platform. Scott was unhappy with its 'modern Gothic, a style I hold to be equally false and foolish', and invited *Edward Blore* 'to Scottify it' with detailing that quoted from old Scots precedents.

The taller, grander NE WING, and walled entrance court (*see below*), is of 1822–3, again by Atkinson, but with *John & Thomas Smith* of Darnick as builders. This wing replaced the cottage, although Scott 'was very reluctant to authorize the demolition of the rustic porch . . . with its luxuriant overgrowth of roses and jessamines until winter had robbed it of its beauties'. In its place is a Baronial porch, based on that at Linlithgow Palace. The two-storey whinstone and ashlar façades further strive to impart a Scotch accent, bristling with crowstepped gables and pepperpot turrets at the angles while the roof-line is elaborated into a picturesque, almost fairytale silhouette, with a phalanx of tall chimneys. Crosses on the gables make associations with Melrose Abbey, while the polished ashlar projecting SE stair turret is perhaps a deliberate historicist Scoticism.

The pronounced Scottish character of Abbotsford was achieved by several means. Scott's fame, combined with his attractive personality, meant that an endless succession of gifts showered down onto Abbotsford, and his architects were challenged to incorporate and display these tributes prominently to flatter their donors. This largesse included many original fragments of celebrated historic buildings in Edinburgh and elsewhere, most famously the door of Edinburgh's Tolbooth (dem. 1817), whose rather skittish placing was to so enrage Ruskin. Many of these fragments had become available because of the improving spirit that prevailed in the 'Modern Athens' of the time. The interior was fitted up with further examples culled from this collection of ancient fragments and was to be furnished with much old furniture. These original fragments were augmented by casts taken from such venerable Gothic shrines as nearby Melrose Abbey and Roslin Chapel. Many of these casts were taken by *George Bullock*, the sculptor turned cabinet-maker favoured by Scott, although where these gave out Atkinson recommended recourse to the collection of the plasterer, Bernasconi, 'who has the greatest collection of casts of Old Buildings of any person in the Kingdom'. These two sources of supply, ancient and modern, were harmonised through the detailing of the connecting new work, which was faithfully copied from similar historical precedents, and the whole was personalized through the decorative use of heraldry to create what might be dubbed a unique 'Scott's Baronial' style.

In 1853 the house was inherited by James and Charlotte Hope-Scott, who had to balance the family's private needs against the public demands of the many visitors. James Hope-Scott's solution to this challenge was to render Abbotsford unique in terms of country house planning: 'He added a new wing to the house, formed a terrace, and constructed an ingenious arrangement of access by which the tourists might be admitted to satisfy their curiosity while some sort of domestic

protection was afforded.'* *William Burn* was asked to graft a
suitably subordinate new private entrance for the family onto
the front of the office court, with a corridor skirting the court
(the new work is borne on steelwork, preserving Scott's original basement offices), and connecting to Scott's Entrance
Hall. To the l. of the new porch and also screening the court,
Burn provided Hope-Scott with a detached Library and Business Room and such was the skill that informed these changes
that the only casualty – although a grievous one in terms of
the Regency atmosphere of Abbotsford – was to be Scott's conservatory.† One of the unusual pleasures of visiting Abbotsford
today derives from the experience of being treated like a C19
tourist. One still follows the route established by Hope-Scott,
in which the public are brought in on foot by a SE gate and
conducted to the E wing's basement 'Tourist Entrance' through
a deep cutting, out of sight from the family. From the 'Waiting
Room', 'parties of ten or twelve' were led on guided tours.

Inside, Atkinson's spiral staircase, ascending from basement
to ground floor, perhaps rather deliberately recalls the circular
stairs of Scotch Baronial architecture and has spare wrought-
iron balusters enlivened with cusps. In a niche in the small stair
LOBBY is displayed a cast of the bust of Shakespeare, taken
from his tomb in Stratford-upon-Avon by *Bullock* and displayed on a pedestal of his own design.

Scott's reception rooms may be the best-preserved late
Georgian interiors in Scotland. The ENTRANCE HALL takes
the form of a miniature Gothic Baronial Hall, with a plaster
roof imitating heavy timber beams. In the centre of the ceiling
are shields, originally painted with Scott's family heraldry by
his decorator, *D.R. Hay* (but crudely repainted since), which
disappear into *trompe l'oeil* mists of time. The beams were
painted 'to appear somewhat weather beaten and faded' to
match the old oak panelling, ejected from Dunfermline Abbey
during its renovation; the curved cupboards are said to have
comprised the pulpit. Other panels obtained by Hay in
Edinburgh to eke out this first supply had a Romantic provenance, allegedly taken from the Palace of Holyroodhouse.
Niches in the E wall are elaborated with plaster casts, from
Melrose Abbey, to provide a setting for the two full suits of
armour, then a rarity in Scotland. The three plaster figures of
saints are also casts taken from Melrose. None of these antiquarian elements appear on Atkinson's more austere sections
of the room but were cobbled together on the spot by Scott's
joiner, *Joseph Shillinglaw* of Darnick. The Hall also had to serve
as an overflow from the adjacent Armoury. Atkinson's fireplace
takes its detail from the cloister of Melrose Abbey and his
drawing shows the antique grate in place, which was said to
have belonged to the murdered Archbishop Sharp. To the
upper walls Scott fixed two cuirasses, picked up by him, if not
actually purchased, on the battlefield of Waterloo in 1815. The
heraldic stained-glass windows were supplied by *Henry Brown*,

64

66

---

*Robert Ornsby, *Memoirs of Robert Hope-Scott of Abbotsford*, 1884.
†Its appearance is known from a view of 1845 published in Fox Talbot's *Sun
Pictures in Scotland*, a testimony to the contemporary fame of Abbotsford.

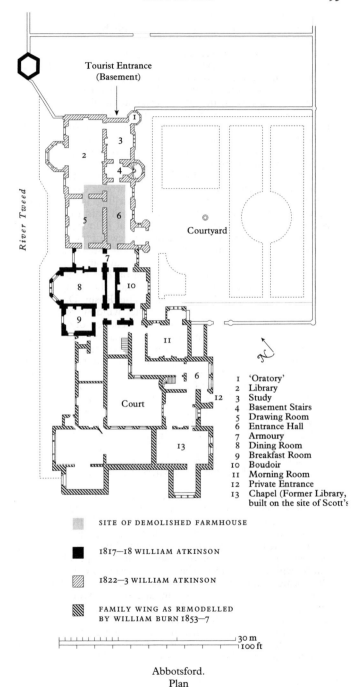

Tourist Entrance
(Basement)

River Tweed

Courtyard

1   'Oratory'
2   Library
3   Study
4   Basement Stairs
5   Drawing Room
6   Entrance Hall
7   Armoury
8   Dining Room
9   Breakfast Room
10 Boudoir
11 Morning Room
12 Private Entrance
13 Chapel (Former Library,
    built on the site of Scott's

Court

SITE OF DEMOLISHED FARMHOUSE

1817—18 WILLIAM ATKINSON

1822—3 WILLIAM ATKINSON

FAMILY WING AS REMODELLED
BY WILLIAM BURN 1853—7

30 m
100 ft

Abbotsford.
Plan

Potter and Glass Manufacturer, of Edinburgh in 1824. The
interior of the PORCH has a plaster vault by *William Baird*,
painted in imitation of ashlar by Hay.

E of the hall and basement staircase is Scott's modest and
less assertively Gothic STUDY, which was planned as his private
retreat; contemporary visitors dubbed it the 'Sanctum sancto-
rum'. Scott delighted in the 'philosophical novelties' of new
technology, and what may be an original gas fitting survives*
above his desk. Hay painted the window wall with imitation
panelling to harmonise with the fitted bookcases. A stair leads
to Scott's private dressing room above, via a cast-iron gallery
giving access to the upper bookcases, and then leading to a
spiral stair in the corner turret. The ground floor of this turret
was thus freed to be developed into an 'oratory' for particularly precious relics. It now enshrines a bronze cast of Scott's
death mask. Incorporated into its panelling is ornamental
carving with classicising Renaissance detail, said to be from a
bedstead used by Mary Queen of Scots at Jedburgh in 1566.

Along the N front, with commanding views of the Tweed, the
LIBRARY was the principal reception room, spacious enough
for a dance, with a generous canted bay large enough to
contain two sets of bookshelves. Atkinson had to develop his
initial design for the ceiling to incorporate the many casts of
medieval bosses from Roslin Chapel. The 'Roslin Drop' is the
central feature of the chapel-like oriel window recess with
Gothic sashes. This ceiling with its constellation of cast bosses
may be *William Baird*'s masterpiece. Atkinson's preliminary
design allowed for a gallery but the executed cedarwood cases
are single-storeyed. Hay suggested 'the painted imitation
drapery . . . in a sombre hue of green' to relieve the blank attic
zone above. At the E end in a position designed for Bullock's
plaster cast of Shakespeare (*see above*) is *Francis Chantrey*'s
marble bust of Scott, a present to Lady Scott by the sculptor
in 1820 and placed here on the day of Scott's funeral. The black
and gold decoration of the overmantel portrait harmonises
with the marble chimneypiece. Three 'Roman Lamps' are
among those supplied by *James Milne*. The Gothic library table
'was done entirely in the room where it now stands' by *Joseph
Shillinglaw*.

The character of the DRAWING ROOM was established by
the gift of the sumptuous green-ground scenic Chinese wallpaper, 'twelve feet high . . . enough to furnish the Drawing
Room, and two bedrooms', from Scott's relation, Captain
Hugh Scott of the East India Company. Atkinson's detailing,
however, remained resolutely Gothic and his purple marble
chimneypiece is the most elaborate of several he designed for
the E wing. Either side are little bronzed canopic vases on truss
brackets, survivors of the pneumatic bell system. Floor-to-
ceiling sash windows in modern Picturesque taste and a pier
glass designed by Atkinson and supplied from London by
Condor. *James Milne* supplied the seven-light gasolier lustre.

The ARMOURY comprises part of the 1817–18 W wing and
was designed with boarded walls for the display of Scott's fast-

---

* The gas house was replaced by Burn's additions.

growing collection of antiquarian relics. The N section retains Atkinson's plaster-vaulted ceiling while the S section, separated by Atkinson's original wheel-traceried dwarf gates, must have been largely rebuilt by Hope-Scott when Scott's adjacent conservatory had to be demolished. Clive Wainwright has suggested that the stained-glass windows may have been designed by Daniel Terry's wife, *Elizabeth Nasmyth*, daughter of portraitist Alexander Nasmyth.

The DINING ROOM remained in the private wing until 1954 and was fashionably modernised *c.* 1930, lightening Atkinson's antiquarian gloom. Enough survives of his astringent Gothic to show the contrast with the greater elaboration of the later 'Scott's Baronial' interiors. The ceiling design had to incorporate casts of Gothic detail taken by Bullock but a humble cabbage, above what would have been the Master's place in front of the sideboard, is surely a joke. The plain Gothic chimneypiece is in the red Mona marble from Anglesey favoured by Bullock. Gothic recess opposite the bay window, holding the sideboard designed by Atkinson, flanked by two niches for lamps with wine cupboards below. The dining tables were made by Bullock from ancient oaks recently felled in the park at Drumlanrig Castle.

W of the dining room lies Scott's original Study (later the BREAKFAST ROOM). Double Gothic sash window to the Tweed. A smaller sash window allowed supervision of the office court. A main circular stair continues to the first floor's spinal bedroom corridor connecting Scott's E and W wings. The BEDROOMS are plain and their decoration has been modernised with simple reeded cornices and unornamented flat timber Greek Revival chimneypieces. In the original KITCHEN beneath the Dining Room is the motto 'Waste not want not'.

Burn's additions after 1853 for the Hope-Scotts (not open to the public) constitute a separate house for the family to retreat into during the summer tourist season. Both houses only functioned together during the winter. The rooms were lightened and modernised by Lady (Louise) Maxwell-Scott after 1928. The ENTRANCE HALL and extensive corridors have Puginian Gothic Revival half-panelling. The principal sitting room (NE of the entrance hall) was designed to house the library of Scott's son-in-law and biographer, J.G. Lockhart, but was extended later with an additional NE-facing bay window to become the MORNING ROOM. Above this is the 'Family Bedchamber' with the Hope-Scotts' dressing rooms. On the site of Scott's conservatory is a smaller sitting room, called THE BOUDOIR. The original vaulted passage, which lay between the Conservatory and Dining Room, survives with a plethora of plaster casts from which it is known as the 'Religious Corridor'. SW of the entrance, the CHAPEL was created from the Library in 1857, when the Hope-Scotts converted to Catholicism. The fireplace now supports an altarpiece in the manner of Ghirlandaio; the carved altar frontal is Flemish late Gothic *c.* 1480, while the statues are Bavarian. Hope-Scott's BUSINESS ROOM has a rose window possibly salvaged from Scott's conservatory.

Burn greatly extended the services ranges around the inner

court of this wing and provided a large new kitchen at the NW
corner. Although the walls of the court appear to be largely
rebuilt, there remains a souvenir at basement level of the original farmhouse in the so-called 'Dr's Byre' with cobbled floor.
GARDENS and LANDSCAPE. Scott was an enthusiastic planter
and improver, and the sloping site and complex levels afforded
him picturesque opportunities. Abbotsford is also a crucial
house in the popularisation of a Scotch Baronial style of
gardening, re-creating a sense of enclosure redolent of old-
fashioned gardens, but here combined with an almost theatrical striving for effects and vistas.

The walled SOUTH COURTYARD was intended to read like
a cloister. Its SE wall had a trellised arcade of greenery attractively framing niches for fragments of ancient sculpture alternating with bas-relief panels, but only the sculpture has
survived. The roundels, from the Mercat Cross of Edinburgh
(dem. 1756), were presented in 1814 by Henry Raeburn, who
had originally incorporated them into his own property. These
alternate with antique sculptural elements from the Roman
fort at Old Penrith. The SW wall holds an eclectic collection of
antique and Indian statuary. On the exterior of the great
Gateway are fixed the iron 'jougs' – instruments of medieval
restraint and punishment – from Threave Castle (Dumfries
and Galloway), the ancient Border stronghold of the Douglases. – FOUNTAIN: said to be from the Mercat Cross of Edinburgh. – To the r. of the porch is a stone MOUNTING BLOCK,
sculpted by *John Smith* to represent Maida, the most famous
of all Scott's many pet dogs, who is entombed below. The Latin
epitaph was translated into English as:

> Beneath the sculptured form which late you wore,
> Sleep soundly, Maida, at your master's door.

The courtyard's sense of enclosure was maintained by
Hope-Scott, who used it to confine tourists while allowing
sight of the façade through lofty W gates of latticed timber, like
a portcullis. The NE wall of the court is conceived as an open
arcade, originally with cast-iron Gothic tracery, which frames
a dynamic view over the series of WALLED GARDENS.* Their
design is by *John & Thomas Smith*, working to Scott's programme, and the drama is heightened because they rise in terraces to a handsome Gothic greenhouse; the Gardener's House
tops a further eminence. In the central of the three gardens is
an unfinished statue of 'Morris asking mercy from Helen Macgregor' described in Scott's *Rob Roy*, carved by *John Greenshields* and placed here after Scott's death.

The garden's N TERRACES were created by Hope-Scott
during the 1850s with Burn's castellated Game Larder and Ice
House topped by a viewing platform. The ENTRANCE LODGE
is dated 1858. Scott recorded that the STABLES had been built
in 1812 'according to Stark's plan'. Although unworthily
altered later, they preserve an air of distinction with a handsome unifying stone belt.

---

* These were inaccessible to C19 vistors.

AIKWOOD TOWER

4020

3.5 km. NE of Ettrickbridge

A handsome early C17 tower house standing high above the E   47
bank of the Ettrick Water. When first erected it must have been
the focus of a cluster of ancillary buildings, and although none
of these now survive the adjacent steading of Oakwood Farm partially recreates the original setting.

The lands of Aikwood, formerly a stead (i.e. tenant's holding)
in the royal forest of Ettrick, were feued to Michael Scott in 1517.
A confirmation charter of 1541 states that Michael had by then
made a fine house, with a tower and other improvements, but the
existing tower house can hardly be as early as this and may rather
be ascribed to Michael's descendant, Robert Scott. His initials,
together with those of his wife, Elspeth Murray, and the date
1602, are re-set above a cellar doorway. In 1649 Aikwood, by then
the centre of an extensive barony of the Scotts of Harden, was
described as one of the principal houses in Selkirkshire, and in
1722 was still regarded as 'a very fine house with orchards and
planting, very pleasant'. It was probably not long after this that
the property, then usually termed Oakwood, became a tenanted
farm, and at some date before 1814 a substantial two-storeyed
wing was extended SE from the tower to serve as a farmhouse.
This, in turn, was converted into stables *c.* 1852, when a new
dwelling-house was erected nearby. Meanwhile, the tower house
had been adapted for agricultural use, undergoing a series of
minor alterations and repairs while still retaining much of its
original character. Restored as a private residence, with associated office and exhibition space by *Malcolm Hammond* of *William
A. Cadell Architects*, 1990–2.

The tower is stylishly built with liberal use of freestone dressings   47
and an extensive repertoire of carved detail. The planning is
more sophisticated than might be expected in a simple oblong
tower of this size (11.6 by 7.2 m. externally), the two principal
floors being subdivided to include both hall and chamber. All
four of these rooms were heated and each floor incorporated
a latrine furnished with a soil-box. In addition, there was
vaulted cellarage and an attic lit by dormers, making four
storeys in all; a fifth was squeezed in in 1990–2, perhaps replacing an original loft within the roof.

EXTERIOR. The masonry is of local rubble with dressings of
red and yellow sandstone. Except on the ground floor, where
additional doorways were inserted during the late C18 and C19,
most of the external openings appear to be original. If so, the
variety of mouldings that they exhibit must represent a conscious striving after effect, which in some cases is further
heightened by the alternation of differently coloured stones.
Edge-rolls predominate, but some of the windows have
rounded or chamfered arrises, while the round-headed
entrance doorway in the NW wall is wrought with a prominent
double roll and hollow. The original oak door has been skilfully repaired. There is no parapet, the roof being received
directly upon the wall-head, at diagonally opposite corners of
which there are gable-roofed caphouses, as at the contemporary houses of Whytbank Tower and Kirkhope Tower (qq.v.).

At Aikwood, however, the caphouses are set out on double corbel courses enriched with billet and chip-carved ornament. Similar detail appears upon two of the chimneys, and some of the dormer pediments are decorated with fleurs-de-lys. The gables are crowstepped with cavetto-moulded skewputts. There is a sprinkling of circular pistol-holes, but whether intended for defence, or simply for show, is hard to say. A couple of oval-mouthed gunloops, one near the entrance, the other in the rear (SE) wall, look more businesslike.

INTERIOR. The tower house is now generally entered via the SE wing, but in the original arrangement the cellarage was approached from a lobby opening off the entrance in the NW wall. The internal mouldings of the tower are again deliberately varied. The larger of the two cellars, now a kitchen, has a good-sized hatch in the vault (probably inserted in the C18 when a smaller one was blocked), while the vault of the other cellar contains a small, square aperture, perhaps a rudimentary speaking-tube like the one at Traquair House (q.v.). The entrance lobby also opens into a newel stair of freestone in the W corner of the tower, which serves all floors; only the lowest treads survive, the remainder having been rebuilt with a massive rubble newel, possibly in 1836, when repairs are known to have been made. The dominating feature of the first-floor HALL is the handsome chimneypiece with its joggle-jointed, arched lintel supported on corbels; the archaic late Gothic moulding of the jambs is closely paralleled in the barmkin hall at Whytbank Tower. The hall is well lit and plentifully furnished with mural cupboards; the double-leaf pine door is one of several originals to survive. The mural corbels are modern light-fittings, not original ceiling supports. The adjacent chamber, tiny as it is, has its own fireplace as well as a latrine; the elegant little coffered ceiling of pine was installed in 1990–2 (*Falconer Grieve*, joiner). The tiled floors of hall and chamber were probably laid some time during the C19, when the upper floors of the tower were used as a granary. The arrangement of the second floor, probably designed as the private quarters of the laird and his wife (and now once more serving that purpose), is similar to that below, but the latrine opens off the hall, or outer chamber. The original roof, which incorporated collar-beam trusses laid without purlins, was replaced in 1990–2.

The SE WING was remodelled in 1990–2 as an exhibition area, offices and library. – WALLED GARDEN and orchard, designed by *Louise Wall*, 1991.

5020   ALERIGG
              4.5 km. NE of Lilliesleaf

Accomplished Arts and Crafts Baronial by *Leslie Grahame Thomson*, 1936, showing a debt to his time in Robert S. Lorimer's office, e.g. dormers with curved Dutch gables and bellcast roofs sweeping over deep eaves. Symmetrical N front on a curved plan with a centre wall-head gable over a balcony, and S elevation with full-height central bow and half-shouldered chimneystack to its r. – a typical Lorimer feature. Curved w corner projecting over a loggia.

ALLANTON

8050

Allanton stands high above the junction of the Blackadder and Whiteadder waters, close to the gates to Blackadder (q.v.) estate.

Former FREE CHURCH, 1 km. s. Now stables. 1844. Closed for worship in 1956. T-plan of buff rubble, with a low vestry and porch to the s. Paired lancets and oculi in the gable walls are its only external ecclesiastical pretensions. Thinly constructed collar-beam roof with arched braces and kingposts, the rafters crossing diagonally over the junction of the arms. – MANSE. Mid-C19. Traditional. Hearse house and stables.

ALLANBRAE. By *John Lessels*, 1854, as a school for the daughters of senior staff on the Blackadder estate. Rebuilt in 1924 after a fire. Tudor-style with a square-plan arcaded porch with octagonal piers and a full-height canted bay to the r., carved with shields.

ALLANTON BRIDGE. Two spans over the Whiteadder Water. Dated 1841, by *Robert Stevenson & Sons*. Handsome, built entirely in red dressed sandstone, the voussoirs continued as splayed channelled masonry in the arches. Rounded cutwaters, with a pilaster above; broad pilasters at the ends.

BLACKADDER BRIDGE, over the Blackadder Water. Dated 1851. Two flat elliptical arches. Yellow sandstone with channelled ashlar dressings. Rounded cornice to the parapet and coping. Pointed cutwater. Tucked in a copse between the two bridges is an early C19 rubble FERRYMAN'S COTTAGE.

DESCRIPTION

Allanton is a single street, mostly lined with single-storey terraced cottages. The earliest were built in the early C19 with gardens, on feus granted by Steuart of Allanbank. From the s end, w side, is the mid-C19 SMIDDY HOUSE with Tudor-style hood-moulds and fishscale bands of green, red and grey slating – a decorative motif used extensively in Allanton and on the Black-adder estate, e.g. at the two-storey ARDSHIEL. Further along set into the wall is a Baroque-style cast-iron WATER FOUNTAIN with shell basin; the luxuriant upper surround has cherubs playing instruments, lots of foliage and a masked head. LYDD COTTAGE (South Lodge) and WESTSIDE COTTAGE (North Lodge) flanked the entrance to Blackadder House (q.v.). They are mid-C19 classical, in finely droved ashlar with a canted three-light bay to the centre. Cast-iron railings and pedestrian gates survive. SHEAF HOUSE has a pedimented doorpiece flanked by tripartite windows with projecting window margins, the lintels swept in below the eaves, above corbelled out to gabled dormers. BALDRICK and FERNBANK (The Old Schoolhouse) are mid-C19 with the former schoolhouse at the N end; the street frontage has Tudor hoodmoulds over all open-ings and bargeboards to the N gable. Next door is ALLANTON

VILLAGE HALL, the former schoolroom. Single-storey with a
fanlit doorway and latticed casements. At the bottom of the
hill is Allanbrae (*see* above).

Returning up the E side, a mid-C19 single-storey tailor's
premises (William Purvis & Co., originally one of three in the
village) has a pilastered and corniced doorway, and a
pilastraded and corniced shopfront. Projecting window to
the r. and carriage pend. Sawtooth-coped skews and scroll-
bracketed skewputts. The single-storey workroom at the rear
has rows of roof-lights. HOLMEKNOWE also includes a tailor's
shop and manufactory. Shopfront with tripartite segmental-
arched openings, the centre one originally the doorway. Single-
storey block to rear with loft space. The estate's CARTER'S
HOUSE is late-C19 picturesque with curvilinear-gabled stone
dormerheads with finials. Segmental-arched pend under a
channelled ashlar arch to the yard at rear. At the top of the
street the ALLANTON INN was two cottages joined together
c. 1835. Whinstone rubble with sandstone margins and deep-
set doorways. Attached is the dignified OLD FIRE STATION,
which was built as a stable and hay loft, probably for the inn.
Recessed archway with a raised entablature and ornamental
scrolls. Sadly its cast-iron dolphin-spouted water pump has
disappeared.

FARMS

ALLANBANK STEADING (Allanbank Courtyard), 1.1 km. W. U-
plan, begun *c.* 1780 by Sir Robert Steuart of Allanbank; N
range dated 1820. Round-arched pend, pedimented Venetian
window and urn finial.

BLACKADDER BANK FARM, 1.8 km. S. Neo-Jacobean of 1864.
BLACKADDER BANK COTTAGES, late C19, have lean-to
pigsties.

BLACKADDER MAINS, 2.7 km. SW. Dated 1785. Huge U-plan
court of one- and two-storey ranges, with curvilinear Jacobean-
style gables with arrowslits. E and W ranges terminate in T-plan
cottages.

BLACKADDER MOUNT FARM, 1.3 km. SW. Showy, symmetrical
S elevation, with a clock tower over a pend, originally with a
spire. Probably 1798, the date of the bell. Second court of 1877
with offices.

ANCRUM

Late C18 and C19 houses surround a triangular green once lined
with lime trees. Standing on rising ground immediately S of the
Ale Water, the village was formerly known as Nether Ancrum to
distinguish it from the now defunct settlement of Over Ancrum,
which lay on the N side of the river. Its origins evidently go back
to the Middle Ages, when the township and surrounding lands
formed part of the barony of Ancrum held in free regality by the
bishops of Glasgow, who had a residence nearby. Burnt by
English armies in 1513 and 1545, the village was afterwards

rebuilt on its present site and is shown on Pont's map of the late c16 as a single row of houses flanking each side of a street. An attempt in 1639 to have Ancrum made a burgh of barony was abandoned two years later.

OLD PARISH CHURCH. 1.6 km. w. The church was a possession of the bishops of Glasgow before 1170. The medieval building continued in use for worship after the Reformation, but was replaced by a new structure to its s by *John Blaikie* and *James Trotter* in 1761–2 (the latter date on a tablet on the w wall). A schoolroom against the E wall was in 1803 converted into a vestry, and there was further rebuilding by *John Smith* in 1831–2. Following construction of a new church in the village, in 1891 the c18 church was reduced to a Romantic ruin by *Easton* of Glasgow, for Sir William Scott of Ancrum. Scott had in 1872 built a burial enclosure at the E end of the church, which was then extended into the vestry, while the w end of the nave became a burial enclosure for the Ogilvies of Chesters House (q.v.).

Much of the s wall has gone; the N wall had few openings, but the low-set windows at each end (one now blocked), are a reminder that there were galleries. Birdcage bellcote on the w gable. The Scott burial enclosure at the E end has one- or two-light pointed windows in the s and E walls, the two-light windows having foliate hoodmould corbels. CARVED STONE, c12(?), with what may be a crudely carved Agnus Dei, re-set on a window jamb on the s side of church. – MEDIEVAL COPED GRAVESTONE in Scott enclosure, with an incised chalice(?). – CHURCHYARD. HOGBACK STONE, 0.2 km. s of the church, complete but damaged; early c12 with double ridge and tegulated decoration. – Some c18 headstones with relief portraits.

PARISH CHURCH. At the w end of the village, built to replace the old church. 1888–90 by *Hardy & Wight*, with walls of red rock-faced snecked sandstone from the Harrietsfield quarry. The gabled N main front has detailing not quite equal to the overall scale: two pairs of lancets at the lower level and two two-light Geometric-traceried windows above; at the apex of the gable is a small birdcage bellcote. Projecting from the E side of the front, a polygonal porch contains the gallery stair, the doorway set within a gabled salient. Cruciform in plan, with a sw vestry, and a second doorway at the SE corner; the flanks have two-light windows, while gables to E, w and s have three-light windows with Geometric tracery. Internally the communion table is at the s end. Narrow N gallery; scissor-braced roof. – COMMUNION TABLE, reduced Gothic, 1952. – STAINED GLASS. s end, Last Supper, *A. Ballantine & Son*, c. 1906. w transept, Abraham, Dorcas, St Paul, *James Benson* of Glasgow, c. 1906. w side, sower and reaper, *A. Ballantine & Gardiner*, 1900. N end, Venerable Bede, in bright Italian glass, 1958. – SUNDIAL, brought here from old church, said to have been dated 1747.

MANSE (now Glebe House). NW of the present church. Mainly mid c18, originally thatched but reroofed in slate in 1792, with c19 and late c20 extensions. From the previous manse are a re-set stone lintel dated 1649 with inscription in Hebrew;

'Jehovah is the portion of the sons of Levi'; lintel in the garden wall also dated 1649.

ALE BRIDGE, 0.4 km E. A rebuilding *c.* 1830 of an earlier bridge, indicated by a mixture of random and coursed rubble. Dressed stone arch supported by battered walls.

BRIDGE, built over the Ale Water E of church in the early C19 for parishioners on the other side of the river. Picturesque single-arched hump-back with small approach arches on either side and splayed cutwaters.

MARKET CROSS. Moved to the centre of the village green *c.* 1870. Late C16. Tall stone shaft with chamfered angles and floriated stops at the foot, set in a socket stone with carved foliaceous enrichment at each corner. The crosshead is missing. To the E, the War Memorial by *A.N. Paterson*, 1919, in the form of a market cross on a five-sided plinth with shields.

PRIMARY SCHOOL, Causewayend. Dated 1866. Neo-Tudor by *A. Herbertson & Son*. Red sandstone, single-storey with overhanging and bracketed eaves. Clock presented by John Paton of New York, 1886.

DESCRIPTION. Houses round the green are mostly C19. On the W side VICTORIA is pretty with white dressings, raised quoins and an Ionic-pilastered doorway. The CROSS KEYS on the N side is C19 with a carriage pend, but refaced in 1906 in red sandstone and ashlar with stone mullions. Of the same date, the etched glazing in the vestibule door and pine-panelled bar with fluted quasi-consoles. Completing the terrace, three cottages with flat bowed façades and pilastered doorways. At CAUSEWAYEND, SW of the Green, five late C18 two-storey houses, harled with exposed dressings. Good housing at SUNNY BRAE, E end of Main Street, of 1975 by *Borders Regional Council* (project architect, *James Thornton*). Single- and two-storey houses, formerly brightly coloured, are adapted to conform to the sloping site and character of the village. Opposite, THE KNOWE by *Wilson & Tait* for Roxburgh County Council, 1935, is twelve houses grouped in fours, with gables to the front and open porches.

ANCRUM HOUSE, 0.8 km. N. By *Wardrop & Reid*, 1875; demolished in the 1960s. It replaced an earlier house whose late C18 LODGES and GATEWAY (on the A68) survive. The lodge gables are covered by castellated screen walls, semicircular headed niches with drip-moulds and Gothic windows. Small castellated BRIDGE in the same mode.

MONUMENT, Lilliard's Edge, 4 km. N. Low, cope stone-walled rectangular enclosure, with inscriptions, supposedly containing the grave of the 'fair maiden Lilliard' who fell at the Battle of Ancrum Moor, 1545. The present, much repaired, monument, probably C19, may have replaced an earlier one.

OLD BRIDGE, Bridgend, 1.5 km. SE over the River Teviot. By *Alexander Stevens Sen.*, 1784 in local red sandstone. Three segmental arches with rusticated voussoirs, a smooth parapet supported on corbels, and triangular cutwaters carried above the parapet as pedestrian refuges; on the W side of the N cutwater is the shield of Douglas of Bonjedward. By-passed in 1939 by the NEW BRIDGE to the E, by *Blyth & Blyth*. Concrete faced with freestone.

MONTEATH DOUGLAS MONUMENT, Gersit Law, 3.2 km. NW.
Monumental Neo-Byzantine mausoleum of 1864 for General
Sir Thomas Monteath Douglas of Stonebyres (†1868.) By
Peddie & Kinnear. Excavated out of the rock with a basement
from which massive curved abutments reach out and support
two recumbent stone lions, one asleep, the other awake. The
mausoleum has semicircular pediments and Ionic pilasters to
each face, with corner piers of banded rustication and a dome
topped by a simple cross. Inside, an ashlar-lined chamber (4.9
sq.m. by 15.2 m. high) and the tomb flanked by carved angels.
A sense of mystery is invoked by the dome studded with glazed
stars – similar to Peddie's telling hall in the Royal Bank of Scotland (Dundas House), Edinburgh, 1857.
CHESTERS HOUSE. *See* p. 166.
KIRKLANDS HOUSE. *See* p. 472.
MONTEVIOT HOUSE. *See* p. 569.
WATERLOO MONUMENT. *See* p. 743.

ANTON'S HILL
0.5 km. S of Leitholm

3040

1836 by *William Burn* for General Sir Martin Hunter. Designed
to be built in stages, starting, unusually, with the service wing
and finishing with the principal elevation in 1853. In Burn's
Cotswold Tudor, of coursed cream sandstone with ashlar
margins. Kneelered gables and wall-head gabled windows,
with finials. The asymmetrical entrance front has a projecting
full-height gabled entrance bay to l. and a curvilinear pediment
to the doorcase containing a coat-of-arms. A square three-light
bay to r. and gabled office wing, formerly single-storey; heightened 1864. Full- and single-height canted bays on the S front,
a full-height square one on the W elevation and small projecting, turreted tower. On the S and W fronts, stone seats are
recessed into the chimney-breasts of the kitchen wing; a practical way of shielding the family from the servants' view.
Inserted in the S recess is the coat-of-arms of the Dicksons,
former owners of the estate, dated 1727. Inside, central well
stair with decorative iron balusters, and principal rooms with
marble chimneypieces. – LODGES. Mid-C19. – WALLED
GARDEN. Possibly early C19. A house was erected within its
walls in the 1990s. – STABLES of 1833–4, converted in the
1990s for a dwelling and courtyard infilled.

ASHIESTIEL
3 km. W of Caddonfoot

4030

A neat and rather secluded mansion of several periods, Ashiestiel
stands on a bluff above the River Tweed, completely obscured by
closely grown trees. Home of the Russell family from 1712 to the
1940s. Sir Walter Scott tenanted the house 1804–12, before
moving to Abbotsford (q.v.). It was here that he wrote *The Lay
of the Last Minstrel*, *Marmion*, and the first part of *Waverley*. In

his day the house was an irregular L-plan, with part of the s wing
said to date from 1660 and w wing of *c.* 1780. It is now a U-plan
created by several additions including an extension of the w wing
and the addition of an E wing in 1829–30 by *John & Thomas
Smith*. The Smiths remodelled the s front of the house in 1847,
when the entrance was moved and a new drive formed on this
side to Low Peel Bridge (*see* below).

Two storey and attic, and a basement at garden level on the N
side. Harled with red sandstone margins. The s front has
finialled, crowstepped gabled wings projecting to the s, a circular carved motif in each gable-head. As reworked in 1847,
the centre three-bay block was given crowstepped gables and
a stone wall-head balustrade pierced by three charming
Regency-style triangular-headed dormers with Gothic glazing.
Stone porch with a blocking course and small pediment, the
design repeated on the extensions to corridors (1829–30) in
front of the single-bay links to the wings. On the E elevation is
a SUNDIAL, *c.* 1830, by *J. Dunn*, Edinburgh, built into the sill
of the N window with copper dial and gnomon mounted on a
square block of stone; visible from inside the house. The w elevation has a projecting three-storey, single-bay flat-roofed
tower of unknown date, decorated with a crosslet, and small
round-headed windows. The N front comprises the centre
three bays, with the Smiths' extension at the E end, and three
bays at the w end which may incorporate earlier work.

   Rambling INTERIOR reflecting the various additions and
alterations. The C17 house was only one room wide. It is
entered through the s porch, which has tall niches each side,
straight into the HALL contrived from a stone lobby; to the w,
a storeroom and housekeeper's room. The N window has a
deep embrasure, the s window slightly less, which, together
with a roll-and-hollow moulded stone chimneypiece in the w
wall, appears to indicate a mid-C17 date. The stair at the rear
leads to the upper floor of the centre block. To the E of the hall
is a low square room known as the OLD DINING ROOM and
evidently used by Scott as a study. Each wing is accessed by
its own stair at the ends of the centre block. A first-floor room
at the N end of the w wing has a timber and gesso chimneypiece with urns and rosettes; at the s end, a bedroom with a
coved ceiling, *c.* 1780. The first floor of the E wing contains the
dining and drawing rooms. Honeysuckle and egg-and-dart
cornices, and Doric-columned marble chimneypieces, black in
the dining room, white in the drawing room. Attic rooms
above.

   LODGES. Mid C19, single-storey with piend roofs and
central chimneys. WEST LODGE, with canted bay windows
flanking a tall crowstepped gabled porch, is probably by *John
Smith*, 1847. Square gatepiers and cast-iron spearheaded gates.
– THE AISLE. A square, walled burial enclosure for former
owners with inscribed slabs.
LOW PEEL BRIDGE, 1.4 km. E. *John Smith*, 1847. The first effort
collapsed, much to Smith's distress, but reconstruction began
immediately. A wide single arch with a span of 40 m. in dark
grey whinstone rubble with deep voussoirs of long stone slabs

set on end and a shallow buttress at each end. Repaired and
strengthened in 1952.

ASHKIRK 4020

Just a church, manse and schools.

PARISH CHURCH. The church belonged to the bishops of
Glasgow by 1170. Attractively sited on sloping ground W of the
village, the present building is on the site of its predecessor.
Rebuilt 1790–1 by *James Trotter*, possibly following the
medieval plan, as a harled rectangle with an ogee-capped birdcage bellcote on its W gable. It was lit mainly by round-headed
windows, though later alterations have modified these. The S
aisle, perhaps added in the early C19, resulted in an unusual
L-plan. Internal remodellings in 1893 and 1962, the latter by
J. Wilson Paterson; the communion table and pulpit are now on
a diagonally set W platform. Two surviving galleries, at the E
end and in the aisle, have raised and fielded panels. The E
gallery has a fretted band below the cornice. – COMMUNION
TABLE, panelled and traceried. – PULPIT. Polygonal, with sunk
roundels to panels, presumably 1893. – WAINSCOT PANEL, on
N wall, with Ionic pilasters and armorial panel, dated 1702,
with initials of Sir Gilbert Elliot and his wife, Dame Jean Carre,
said to be from the Elliot pew at Minto. – STAINED GLASS. W
wall, etched glass with ruby acanthus border; N wall, armorial
panel for Charles Balfour Scott, †1838 (his grave is in the
enclosure outside the window); S wall, Faith, Hope and
Charity, *c.* 1912.
  MEMORIALS. Chiefly to the Cochran family along N side,
and to the Cree-Scott family along S side. Along the external
N wall are three C18 memorials to the Scott family – CHURCH-
YARD. A pleasing, if partly derelict, mixture of memorials and
enclosures. One early C18(?) group, probably by a single
mason, has *memento mori* flanked by Tuscan pilasters, with
winged angel heads in the shaped pediment. One stone has a
relief three-quarter portrait. Some robustly designed table
tombs, one group having volute supports. The Corse-Scott
enclosure has a keystone dated 1646, but rebuilt 1887. The
Ogilvie enclosure has a memorial to Adam Ogilvie, †1721 with
Corinthian pilasters.

HALKYN. Former manse of 1784 (five bays and one room deep)
with mid-C19 overhanging eaves, and a pilastered and corniced
doorway. N addition, with a canted bay, by *John Smith*, 1838.
He must have added the vaulted corridor along the rear, and
the spacious geometric staircase with decorative baluster.
Three timber and gesso chimneypieces, *c.* 1780, ornamented
with urns, swags and fruit (from No. 38 George Square,
Edinburgh, dem. 1964). A door lintel dated M.W.S. (for Mr
Walter Stewart, minister of Ashkirk) 1748, on a former
steading, probably indicates an earlier manse.

Former SCHOOL and SCHOOLHOUSE. By *John Smith*, 1836–7,
with neat ball-finialled bellcote. Mid-C19 gabled house to the
l., said to have been built for a schoolmistress.

NORTH SYNTON. *See* p. 601.
TODRIG. *See* p. 725.
THE WOLL. *See* p. 763.

9060   AYTON

Ayton was enclosed *c.* 1750, and a new village begun after 1765
with land feued by James Fordyce of Ayton Castle (*see* below) for
about thirty houses, mostly of three storeys and tiled, placed on
an attractive sloping bank. In the mid C19 the line of the great
London road (A1) was altered, feus were granted on a new building line and in a regular form. The old village, closer to the castle,
was largely demolished. Villas began to appear in the mid C19.

OLD PARISH CHURCH OF ST DIONYSIUS. An overgrown frag-
    ment (in the churchyard E of its successor) of a chapel depen-
    dent on Durham in the early C12, which became parochial after
    the Reformation. It remained in use until 1865. Extensive areas
    of cubical masonry show that a rectangular medieval church
    remained the basis for later development. A centrally placed N
    'aisle', with a small, attached N bell turret, augmented the
    church to a T-plan. A laird's 'aisle' was added at the E end of
    the S flank, presumably in the C17 on the evidence of the three-
    light S window; the memorial to Fordyce of Ayton, 1884, now
    blocks the opening into the church from that aisle.
        CHURCHYARD. Memorial stones from the C17 to the C20,
    together with burial enclosures for Alexander Skene (in the
    angle between the N aisle and chancel of the church) and for
    the families of Innes of Ayton and Whitehill, and of Hood.
26 PARISH CHURCH. A splendid estate church of buff coursed
    rock-faced masonry with ashlar dressings, its spire rising above
    the treetops of a wooded enclosure at the S end of the village.
    Designed by *J.M. Wardrop* (of *Brown & Wardrop*) in 1864 (the
    date on the vestry chimney) and opened 1865, three-quarters
    of the cost of about £5,000 being met by A.M. Innes of Ayton.
    It is a skilfully composed textbook essay in the English
    Decorated style with few externally obvious concessions to
    Presbyterian needs. The nave has a S aisle, with a tower porch
    at its W end, and there are asymmetrical transepts between the
    nave and the E arm, the latter terminating in an apse and with
    a N vestry. A timber N porch to the E arm covers the entrance
    from the castle side, and an angled vestibule between chancel
    and S transept provides a third entrance. The dominant 36 m.
    high tower, with its stone broached spire, has a full panoply of
    lucarnes and gargoyles. Fine external detailing throughout:
    especially to the windows, from the eight-petal rose of the W
    front and the curvilinear tracery of the transepts and apse, to
    the circular S clearstorey openings.
        Internally the ingenuity of planning becomes clear: three
    arms covered by arch-braced and panelled roofs were directed
    towards the pulpit in the shallow N transept; the castle pew was
    in the apse. The foliage capitals of the S arcade pier and
    responds merit inspection. A reordering in 1973 created a
    chancel for the communion table in the E arm and changed

the castle pew into a children's area. – COMMUNION TABLE. Memorial to dead of First World War. – FONT, octagonal panelled shaft with foliate bowl, 1856. – ORGAN, two towers of stencilled pipes flanking the N transept window, originally powered by the nearby Eye Water. – STAINED GLASS, a coordinated scheme by *James Ballantine & Son*. Apse, works of mercy; S transept, Nativity; N transept, Sermon on the Mount.

GLEBE HOUSE (former Manse), SW of the church. A late C19 refronting of an early C19 house by *James Stevenson* of Berwick. Pedimented doorcase flanked by tripartite windows. Sprock-etied eaves to the bellcast roof.

DESCRIPTION. One long wide street, of mostly two-storey, three-bay houses, some with integrated pends to rear stabling. Begin at the NW end of the HIGH STREET with on the r. a terrace of late C18 and early C19 houses built on steeply sloping ground with steeply accessed segmental-arched entrances to the basements. OAKLANDS at the top end is probably later, and is flatted with a side balcony entrance. SAWMILL HOUSE ends the terrace. Five bays, three bays to the l. for the house, the others probably for the office, which led through to the sawmill, mostly demolished except for a pantiled two-storey range with two segmental cart openings. To be noted further down is the RED LION HOTEL. Of eight bays, its segmental-arched pend and four bays to the l. are late C18 (indicated by a scrolled skewputt). ST MARGARET'S with angle quoins, has an attractive later piended porch. Next door the late C18 OLD SCHOOLHOUSE, with deep-set entrance, and behind it the mid-C19 OLD SCHOOL, a single-storey gabled T-plan, with bracketed eaves and mullions. Many of the houses on this side of the High Street retain original late C18 details but have been otherwise 'improved' in the C19 and C20. Nos. 7–9 retains a continuous pantiled roof with grey slate easing course. Its win-dowless rear elevation is unaltered. The next block, uphill, is similar, but with bands of plain and fish-scale slates instead of tiles. At the bottom of the High Street the red sandstone rubble MOFFAT HOUSE is more interesting. Three storeys with a tall corniced doorway, and small attic windows tucked under the eaves.

On the High Street's opposite side, from the top are later villas. The best is COLVILLE HOUSE, a three-bay classical villa with single-bay wings, and a consoled and corniced doorway. Inside, a stained-glass window records the death of Elezer Colville, an Edinburgh surgeon, †1853, who built the house in 1822. His son built COLVILLE LODGE, dated 1852; gabled with Tudor detailing. Arched porch with thin cast-iron columns, and large pointed wall-head windows. Further downhill is the prominent CLOCK TOWER HOUSE, dated 1880, with its square six-storey tower, with a corbelled and castellated parapet and square bartizan, attached to a two-storey range to the r.

OLD TOWN comes in from the l., with housing on one side only, much of it by the *Eildon Housing Association*, 1992, but includ-ing some traditional three-bay houses, rendered and painted.

The new housing is sympathetic and in scale, with pends to rear parking, but it is a pity that the former street line was not kept at the corner with High Street. At the top of Old Town is early C19 HILLSIDE, with a small wall-head pediment and round-arched doorway and fanlight. BEANBURN, on the opposite side of the High Street, has mostly C19 villas, with coped front walls and square gatepiers with pyramidal caps. On the l., the classical HEATHERBANK was built as the Royal Bank of Scotland in the late C19. Two-storey, of three bays with single-storey pavilions on each side. Piended and platformed roof with overhanging timber bracketed eaves. On the r., KIRK-LANDS was the manse of the Burgher church. Early to mid-C19 classical, with deep-set doorway with decorative frieze and consoled cornice. Single-storey and attic coachhouse to NW. At the top SUMMERHILL (formerly St Helen's), c. 1870, has Gothic and Tudor detailing. Stylised hoodmoulds, and moulded skewputts with engaged columns clasping the corners below. A bipartite window, above the entrance door, has a seg-mentally-arched hoodmould with a carved tympanum.

AYTON CASTLE
0.8 km NE

Scottish Baronial of 1845–51 by *James Gillespie Graham*. The early castle was forfeited after the 1715 Jacobite rebellion, and vested in the Crown until purchase in 1765 by James Fordyce, Commissioner for Lands, Woods and Forests of Scotland, who planted the estate and began the new village of Ayton (q.v.). In 1834 the property was dramatically destroyed by fire and bought in 1838 by William Mitchell-Innes, Director of the Royal Bank of Scotland, who commissioned its replacement. Extensions and alterations followed: first by *David Bryce*, master of the Baronial, in 1860–1, and then by *J.M. Wardrop* in 1864–7. In 1888 the castle and estate were sold to Henry Liddell of Middleton Hall, Northumberland, whose descendants are still in occupation.

Ayton is one of only two works by Gillespie Graham in the Baronial style. He extended Brodick Castle, Isle of Arran, in 1845, and writing to its owner, the tenth Duke of Hamilton, mentioned that he had just finished plans for Ayton, 'in which I have introduced a tower similar to that at Brodick but upon a much larger scale'. Details from Billing's *The Baronial and Ecclesiastical Antiquities of Scotland* (1845–52) are also much in evidence, although often used in an eccentric way. The contractor was *Alexander Rae* of Edinburgh.

The EXTERIOR is asymmetrical, of two to four storeys of square, coursed, tooled red sandstone rubble quarried at Chirnside. The entrance is finished in beautifully polished ashlar, which brings out the marbling in the stone. A deep battered base course, a characteristic feature of Gillespie Graham's work, continues round the whole building. Corbelled eaves with rope-moulded corbelling to the turrets, crenellated parapets with waterspouts, and crowstepped gables. The N elevation has a three-storey crowstepped entrance tower, with open corner turrets – a porte cochère was never built. Wide pilasters, with rope-moulded tops that meet over the doorway as a hood-mould and enclose a coat-of-arms, flank the basket-arched doorway. Small oriel window above (lighting the former smoking room) and, in the gable, a bipartite window with eaves corbelling arched over their tops as segmental heads. In the gable another armorial. A circular stair-tower in the re-entrant angle to the r. is corbelled out to a square, making an L-plan with the entrance tower. On the l. is a billiard room added by *Bryce*. Set back to the r. is another tower (*see* below) and the two-storey family wing to the w; its conical-capped turrets at each corner were heightened by Wardrop. E of the entrance is the crenellated and crowstepped servants' wing with open turrets. The service court at the E end of the N elevation juts forward, originally two storeys but heightened on this side in 1861 by *Bryce*, who also added the parapeted coach pend, with a row of prominent wall-head dormers, decorated with different motifs. A square bell-tower topped by pyramidal-capped belfry and bell, assembled the ground staff to meals. A high rampart wall extends N, then E and S, hiding the service court, with a tall arched entrance in the S side.

The principal feature in the S elevation is the four-storey and attic, two-bay 'great tower' with three conical-capped corner turrets, and an open one in the SE corner; a crowstepped cap-house on top. An oriel window, in the form of a garderobe, breaks the parapet corbel course. Another fanciful garderobe or machicolation, on the W face. To the E the two-storey, square-turreted drawing room with large two-storey bay added by *Bryce* and single-storey flat-roofed dining room extensions by *Wardrop*, effectively masking the original façade, with a single bay left open to admire a large Mitchell-Innes armorial in the gable-head. Servants' accommodation at the E end.

INTERIOR. The plan of the house was laid out by Gillespie Graham along a transverse E–W corridor, off which all the principal rooms open to the S, with the entrance hall and circular principal staircase on the N side. The W end of the corridor leads into the three-storey family wing and private staircase, at the E end is the service wing. The ENTRANCE HALL opens into the corridor (Gallery); the rich ochre marbling of its columns survives from the 1840s, the rest was redecorated in 1873–5 by *Bonnar & Carfrae* with heraldic painting on the compartmented ceiling. Devout conceits on the entrance hall ceiling, whose walls are decorated with *D.R. Hay*'s 'patent damask', imitation textile stencilled with a pattern, on a painted and varnished ground of stylised flowers, including the thistle and rose. The predominant colours are green and gold, and other walls were decorated with richly coloured wallpapers. The principal spiral staircase, opening off the corridor, ends in a strapwork balustrade, and the first-floor landing is barrel-vaulted, forming a suitable entrance to the former smoking room. The rooms along the S front from l. to r. are pure opulence. The DINING ROOM and DRAWING ROOM both have Scottish Renaissance plaster strapwork ceilings, while the Library has a more Scottish Jacobean feel with a compartmented ceiling, heavy with pendants and bosses. The smoking room at the E end by *J.M. Wardrop* is timber-panelled in Tudor style with a painted comb ceiling.

GARDENS. To the s, rampart walls enclose a terraced garden. Ornamented with circular corner turrets with crenellated parapets, pyramidal-capped newels and solid balustrades, and hooped iron gates to the linking stone steps. – WALLED GARDEN, NW of the castle on a steeply sloping site. Three wide tiered terraces, the steps linking the terraces with squat panelled balustrades. – A two-stage octagonal SUMMERHOUSE in the NE wall, with an arcaded elevation to the garden, and a tapering capped roof with banded fish-scale slating and finial. – STABLES to the NE, c. 1850. W elevation of seven bays with projecting gabled centre. Stalls with iron railings and ball-finialled newels survive. – DOVECOT, E, C16 beehive type in two stages of sandstone rubble, originally harled. Panel above the door inscribed TF EW 1745 probably celebrates a repair. A stone-slabbed, shallow-domed roof, the circular aperture containing a later octagonal cap with flight-holes. Inside, a timber potence and ladder on a fixed triangular frame survive.

NORTH LODGE. Late C19 with overhanging bracketed eaves and decorative roof finials. Square gatepiers with corniced pyramidal caps. Mid-C19 SOUTH LODGE (B6355), probably by *Gillespie Graham*. Scottish Baronial in red sandstone with a pend flanked by circular towers.

AYTON MAINS, 1 km. NE. c. 1870. An asymmetrical Tudor-gabled farmhouse, its farm cottages with hoodmould and canopied entrances.

WHITERIG FARMHOUSE, 2.8 km. S. Classical, of five bays, c. 1800.

PEELWALLS HOUSE. *See* p. 636.

PRENDERGUEST HOUSE. *See* p. 640.

2030

BARNS HOUSE
1.2 km. NW of Kirkton Manor

71 A pretty house built by James Burnet of Barns, 1773, to whom *James Brown* of Edinburgh was described as 'architect'; the contractor was *Michael Naesmyth*, with whom Brown worked on his development of George Square. Two storeys, basement and attic in harled rubble with yellow sandstone margins and rusticated angle quoins. Corbelled eaves course, and a piended roof with chimneystacks set on the transverse walls. The s (principal) elevation has three widely spaced bays, the centre advanced with a pediment and three gracious urns. A small stone label at the base of the pediment is dated 1773 in Roman numerals; space above was left for a shield 'if thought proper'. Later C18 Ionic portico and mostly plain window margins. The N elevation has a full-height central bow and at the W end two small oculi. W extension of 1998 by *Richard Murphy Architects* with a roof garden connected by a curved bridge to the main garden.

Inside, much good plasterwork by *James Whitehead*. In the grand, square, stone-flagged hall, a deep modillioned cornice, and ceiling rose, delicately framed by a radiating fan motif, within a circle of husks. A stone C17(?) chimneypiece, carved with a representation of Neptune and accompanying naiads, has a fireback illustrating Neidpath Castle and fish in the River Tweed by *Lord Charteris of Amisfield*, 1996. To the r. the drawing room, occupying the full depth of the house, with a deep classical frieze and dado rail. A marble chimneypiece with yellow insets has an urn on the frieze panel, and a cast-iron basket supplied by *Richard Foster*, *c*. 1792. The dining room ceiling has a centre roundel of fronds, rosettes and husks, corniced doors with fluted architraves. Late C18 timber and gesso chimneypiece, decorated with garlands of bows, rosettes and drops, imported from Gosford House (Lothian). The w end of the house has an inserted mezzanine between the ground and first floors and a narrow dog-legged stair with a solid newel serving all floors.

Large WALLED GARDEN, late C18(?), with high coped walls and arched openings, mostly blocked. – STABLES, 1770s. Octagonal tower, its fish-scale slating presumably Victorian and low flanking links, each with a niche, to slightly advanced two-storey pavilions with high, arched carriage openings. – LODGE, early C19 with later large piend-roofed addition. The porch with hoodmould and oculus was part of a tollhouse at Eddleston, brought here by the twelfth Earl of Wemyss in the late C20. – SW of the stables is a HOUSE and STEADING, perhaps mid-C18. A re-set lintel, inscribed 'James Burnet Esqr. 1764', may belong to the farmhouse, for which mid-C18 drawings exist, where Burnet is thought to have lived before the house was built.

BARNS TOWER, 1 km. SW, was the late C16 home of the Burnets and converted into accommodation for retired estate employees after the building of the new house. Sensitively restored for residential use by *Malcolm Hammond* of the *Pollock Hammond Partnership*, 2001–3. The tower is a simple oblong (8.5 by 6.0 m.) of three storeys and an attic built of local rubble masonry with dressings of red and buff-coloured sandstone; re-harled with pink finish in 2003. The larger windows have quarter-round arrises, quirked on their external margins, and some were originally barred and half-glazed. The walls have a pronounced external batter, and when the roof was repaired in the C18 the eaves were extended outwards to shed water more effectively. The uppermost courses of the walls may have been rebuilt at that time, but there is nothing to suggest that the tower originally incorporated an open wall-walk. The existence of tusking at the NW corner suggests that a barmkin was contemplated. The approach stair to the ground-floor doorway on the w side of the tower probably dates from the late C18, when the ground in this area seems to have been cut back to accommodate the drive to Barns House. The wrought-iron yett looks original, but is now hung outside the timber door rather than inside as was customary. The door lintel bears the incised dates 1488 and 1489, both evidently bogus. A more accurate indicator of the date of building is the lintel of the window directly above the doorway, which bears the initials of William Burnet, 4th of Barns, and his wife, Margaret Stewart, who were married in 1576.

The ground floor contains a barrel-vaulted chamber, now

subdivided. The first-floor hall is reached by a straight stone stair in the thickness of the N wall, while access to the upper floors seems originally to have been obtained by crossing the hall to a newel stair – again of stone – in the SW corner. This was superseded in the C18 by a more conveniently placed stair-case of pine, but the upper flight survives. When the tower was modified for estate use the hall was screened off from the new stair in the NE corner, a replacement fireplace was installed and the stone-flagged floor was renewed where necessary. Most of the original ceiling joists seem to have been retained, however, and these are unusual in that they rest upon individual stone corbels rather than upon runners. An original latrine in the NE corner of the tower was served by an open discharge chute. The collar-rafter roof has been altered and repaired, but many of the original oak timbers remain in use.

BARON'S FOLLY *see* FAIRNINGTON HOUSE

2040

BARONY CASTLE
0.6 km. W of Eddleston

Dignified mansion on the steep, wooded N bank of the Dean Burn (the Fairy Dean), at various times called Darnhall. Black Barony, a tower house, existed here in the C16 in the possession of John Murray. Considerably added to *c.* 1700–15 by Sir Alexander Murray, who remodelled the L-shaped tower house, and added a substantial and commodious range. This reflected the earlier prevailing taste, set down by Bruce and Mylne in the later C17, for a symmetrical flat-roofed range flanked by pro-jecting towers, but was old-fashioned by the early C18. By 1843 the house was in poor condition and, moving with the times, Alexander Oliphant Murray, ninth Lord Elibank, obtained designs for a new mansion house by *James Gillespie Graham* in a Neo-Jacobean style. This was unexecuted, and instead repairs and alterations to the house were commenced, *c.* 1847. Further embellishments were made in 1887. The house became a hotel in 1930 and is now a conference centre.

The principal (E) front is dominated by the early C18 house, a substantial rectangular block, with a symmetrical U-shaped façade of three storeys and attics, the middle five bays flanked by four-storey, square, single-bay angle towers, terminating in ogee roofs. Built of rubble and harled, with sandstone dress-ings. The towers have rusticated quoins, there is a moulded eaves course, and the windows have chamfered arrises. The central entrance doorway has a lugged and moulded surround, surmounted by an entablature. The timber frieze and pedi-ment, and a strapwork pediment containing a cartouche and the initials AOM and EMM (for Alexander Oliphant Murray and his wife, Emily Maria Montgomery) are mid-C19, probably by *Alexander Roos,* then at work on the gardens. He also may have added the roof balustrade and dormer windows with circular heads and decorative finials. The irregularly shaped NW wing incorporates the C16 tower house, with a newel stair on the N elevation which originally ascended through two storeys – the top probably by Roos. So many alterations have taken place that the original character of this L-shaped block has been obscured, but it probably incorporates work of more than one period. The early C18, three-storey and attic, crowstepped central part of the W front has four bays, with mid-C19 dormers to match those on the E front. Across the ground floor is a flat-roofed extension by *Lorimer & Matthew*, 1934; altered in 1999.

The two-storey, five-bay L-shaped family wing to the N was built *c.* 1855, probably by *Charles MacGibbon*. An uncompromising two-storey block of bedrooms was added to the E end of this block, along the high bank on the N side of the fore-court, by *Dick Peddie & McKay*, *c.* 1975, and extending W from this block, a large rendered crowstepped and gabled addition is built into the high N bank of the garden court, N side of two storeys, dropping to single storey at the front, with a circular stair-tower at the W end, 1999. Against the S gable of the main house, and linked by a single-bay stair-tower, is a two-storey crowstepped bachelors' wing, with a corner tower, added in 1877. Extending W, *Thomas Tod & Co.* added a single-storey, piend-roofed ballroom in 1933; pilasters divide the three round-headed glazed openings. Inside, the guts are lost. Only a C16 vaulted cellar remains in the N wing, and a roll-moulded doorway giving access to a smaller vaulted compartment adapted as a wine cellar. Painted decoration attributed to *Alexander Roos* was found in the Salon in 1984.

STABLES, NW, probably 1850s. – ICE HOUSE, NE, has an egg-shaped chamber with short entrance passage. The lintel of the outer door carries the date 1789. The large WALLED GARDEN and Gothic summerhouse by *Alexander Roos* were destroyed in 1999. The surviving single-storey GARDENER'S HOUSE is by *Charles MacGibbon*, 1855. A similar LODGE, also by MacGibbon, in coursed whinstone with polished dressings, has a moulded panel above the entrance doorway inscribed 'Black Barony'. The wrought-iron gates were made for Port-more House (q.v.) in the 1920s. Classical with lots of decora-tive foliage.

LANDSCAPE and PLEASURE GROUNDS, mostly 1850s, very eroded and not improving. The C18 lime avenue leading up to the E front survives, but is no longer an entrance. The 'ground and flower garden [was] designed by M Rous [sic] an Italian architect and landscape gardener'[*] who probably designed the few picturesque garden buildings. His designs seem to be based on J.C. Loudon's *Cottage, Farm and Villa Architecture* (1833). At the E end of the Yew Walk on the S side of the Dean Burn, which was enlarged in the mid C20 into an inappropri-ate pond, was a curved seat. Terminating the W end is a cir-cular GAZEBO, brick with stucco render and a domed roof covered in fish-scale slates. It is open on three sides, with round-headed niches in the rear wall, probably for statues or urns; below is a semicircular seat of planking covered in rustic

[*] C. McIntosh, *Book of the Garden*, 1853.

work. A circular mount (Moat Knowe) halfway along the walk
is a puzzle – either a viewing point, or for other pleasurable
use, or a natural promontory trimmed to shape by later gardeners. On elevated ground in the midst of trees, 0.3 km. SW,
is the derelict BELLEVUE TEMPLE. An octagonal Doric
gazebo on a rubble podium, with pointed swept roof, fish-scale
slates, and moulded eaves course. The central finial is repeated
round the wall-head. Chinese railing and gate.

DARNHALL MAINS, 1.3 km. N. Late C18 crowstepped gabled
farmhouse added to in the mid C19 and given a turreted tower.

6040   BASSENDEAN HOUSE
                          3 km NW of Gordon

Mansion expanded from a late C16 tower house, probably built
by William Home, with N extension c. 1690 and further additions in the C19 and C20. In 1830 the house was extensively
restored, described by the *New Statistical Account* (1834) as
'repaired and modernized in a handsome style' and apparently
given dormer windows, a flat-roofed, three-storey E porch and
two-storey N extension.

The remains of the tower (7.0 m by 5.2 m.) are at the S end
of the present house. Originally of three storeys, of random
rubble, with dressings of red sandstone from the celebrated
Bassendean quarries. A late C16 angle turret survives at the NW
corner, and an original slit-opening on the S side, but c. 1862
the rest was reduced almost to a single storey (although the NE
quoins survive almost to the wall-head) and used as the sub-
structure for a greenhouse. Upper storeys rebuilt in 1930 by
George Arthur & Son with an angle turret at the SE corner. A
sundial on the SW corner is dated 1690, possibly the date of
the three-storey N extension, which has chamfer-arrised
windows with relieving arches on the E elevation. A bolection-
moulded panel frame may indicate the position of the original
entrance. The W elevation, partly obscured, has a crowstepped
gablet with chimney. A projecting crowstepped gable and angle
turret were added in c. 1874 in place of the earlier porch and
the small two-storey N extension was extended for John Fer-
gusson-Home. Its crowstepped gable and two-storey canted
bay windows were apparently designed by his second wife,
Dorothea Veitch. Coursed grey ashlar. Finials of heraldic motifs,
of thistles, crescents etc. Crowstepped entrance porch of four
columns with acanthus capitals. Interior mostly of 1874 with
chunky plaster ceiling roses and cornices.

N are STABLES, a small court and steading, with a crowstepped stable added 1862. On the S gable is a dovecot with
three tiers of pigeonholes and, above, a Palladian-style arcaded
cupola. – WALLED GARDEN. Panel over entrance in W
wall dated '1863 JFH-DH' (for John Fergusson Home and
Dorothea Home). – Single-storey, Baronial LODGE with crowstepped gables, thistle finials and tall red sandstone chimneys
with splayed corners and moulded copes. Panel inscribed 'JH
18(62)' (for John Home). – GATEPIERS with deep, moulded

caps surmounted by lions' heads resting on cushions, originally from the piers of the s lodge (dem.).

BURIAL ENCLOSURE, 0.4km. SE. The old parish church, adapted after closure in 1649 as a burial enclosure for the Homes of Bassendean. Initially a chapel granted to Cold-stream Nunnery in the late C12, it became parochial before the Reformation. The remains are of a complete but un-roofed rubble-built rectangle; essentially a late medieval struc-ture. All openings are along the s flank: towards the w end a rectangular doorway with chamfered jambs; near the middle a rectangular window, and towards the e end a two-light rectangular mullioned window. Some of the window reveals were evidently reused from a larger window. Height-ening along the s and n walls presumably dates from regular-isation of the wall-head following adaptation. Inside is a small stoup recess e of the doorway, with a second larger recess further e. A small aumbry or piscina survives s of the site of the high altar, and a rebated recess in the n wall was presum-ably a sacrament house. FONT(?), an irregular circular basin lying on the floor. – GRAVE SLABS, one medieval with an incised cross with fleur-de-lys terminals, another with incised shears.

BEDRULE   5010

Fragments of hogback stones suggest Bedrule was a place of worship from the late C11, though little is known of its medieval history.

PARISH CHURCH. The church was presumably always on the present site, close to a steep slope down to the Rule Water on the w. It was rebuilt in 1804, and remodelled in 1877, and areas of uncoursed rubble on the n (in fact NW) side of the present nave, and in parts of the n transeptal aisle could date from those campaigns. But the existing structure dates largely from a rebuilding of 1914 (the date against the entrance) by *Thomas Leadbetter*, for Sir Robert and Lady Usher. It is cruci-form, and of buff or pink snecked rubble with red ashlar dress-ings: the main body runs e–w, with transeptal aisles off the e end of the flanks and a short narrow e chancel; the vestry is in the angle between chancel and n aisle. The squat three-storey w tower houses the main entrance. It has a stair-turret on its n side, and the belfry stage, with pairs of small lancets on two faces, is finished with a corbelled and crenellated parapet around a slated pyramidal roof. Most windows have intersect-ing or Y-tracery, but there is a triplet of lancets in the e wall. The interior has plaster ceilings of polygonal profile and there is a gallery within the tower. – STAINED GLASS. e window, First World War memorial, *Douglas Strachan*, 1922. s aisle, heraldic, post-1917. s side nave, shepherd and sower, 1992. w window, SS Andrew and Mungo, 1933. – PLAQUES. n aisle, Thomas Greenshields Leadbetter, †1931. w wall, Ellinor Elliot, †1834, elongated marble octagon with winged cherub above. – CARVED STONES, within w porch two fragments of hogback stone with tegulated decoration, C11 and C12. Small worn medieval relief effigy with sword at its side.

CHURCHYARD. Many stones with *memento mori* and symbols. S of church, an imposing headstone with swan-necked pediment for John Best †1822. N of nave, table tomb for James Borland †1713, arcaded sides to base with winged angel heads in arches. – Former MANSE dated 1794 but with a later gabled addition.

BEDRULE BRIDGE. Mid-C19. Elegant, high, arched single-span in polished ashlar.

BEDRULE FARM. Early C19, harled, with red sandstone margins, angle quoins and a fanlit doorway. Partly rebuilt in the mid C19.

CASTLE, 0.2 km. NW. Fragmentary remains of a major castle of enclosure built by the Comyns in the late C13. It appears to have comprised an oval courtyard (about 61 by 40 m.) enclosed by a curtain wall punctuated by projecting circular towers and entered through a gatehouse on the NW side.

Former SCHOOLHOUSE. Early C19, but remodelled by *Robert Falla*, 1851, with piended wall-head dormers.

WAR MEMORIAL. 1919, by *Leadbetter & Fairley*. A column, on a stepped base, with a circular head decorated with a St Andrew's Cross, crown and thistle.

WELLS LODGE. Late C18 former lodge to Wells House (dem. 1951).* Wrought-iron GATEWAY with delicate leaf decoration and William Elliot's monogram. Carved urns and heraldic beasts have been removed.

7040   BELCHESTER HOUSE
                         0.5 km. SE of Leitholm

Home of the Dickson family since the C14. The house developed over a long period, and is said to incorporate the remains of a tower house. It became U-plan, *c.* 1800, with the addition of two gabled wings, and in the 1830s the courtyard was enclosed, and the W elevation became the entrance front. Two storeys in harl-pointed sandstone. The entrance front is of four bays with a flat-roofed pilastered porch. The other elevations are simple, with finialed gables. Inside is an elliptical dome on pendentives over a panelled hall; chimneypiece with carved lovers' knots and duelling pistols. The Jacobethan timber stair has carved tread ends, twisted and plain balusters and balustrade to a first-floor balcony. Some good chimneypieces and decorative cornices. – STABLES, *c.* 1830, in squared and snecked cream sandstone and whin sandstone rubble. Pedimented, of seven bays, with square dovecot surmounting the central pend; a blind Diocletian opening contains a geometric pattern of pigeon holes. Similarly detailed flanking coachhouse wings. A much-worn panel inscribed GT 1743 GD. Renewed 181(9).

LODGE. Mid-C19 picturesque. – SUNDIAL, *c.* 1830. Octagonal base, with neatly engraved dial and gnomon inscribed 'Calculated for Berwickshire'.

---

*A remarkable armorial pediment of *c.* 1690 is preserved in Hawick Museum.

BEMERSYDE 5030

First contemplated as a township by James Haig of Bemersyde House (*see* below) in 1754.

DESCRIPTION. The few unaltered single-storey houses, built with slated roofs, probably date from *c.* 1820. On the N side of the road at the W end is the GARDENER'S COTTAGE and PINK COTTAGE (with later dormers). On the front of Gardener's Cottage several fragments of apparently medieval carved stone have been built into a wall, including a niche framed by saw-tooth ornament and topped by a human head, a piece of leaf ornament and part of a roll-and-hollow moulded door. They may come from the nearby ruins of Dryburgh Abbey (q.v.). Further up the hill THE SMIDDY has a single-storey workshop. Across the road the SHEPHERD'S HOUSE may date from the mid-C18 development. Originally a pair of single-storey cottages, it conforms to the original contract, which stipulated that each house should be 66 ft (20.1 m.) long and contain two dwellings.

BEMERSYDE HOUSE. A late medieval tower house enlarged during the late C18 by the erection of W and E wings. Since the C12 the residence of the Haigs, one of the oldest established Border families, with a building history to match. However, the first three centuries of occupation have left no visible trace and the earliest portion of the existing mansion is a tower apparently erected during the late C15 or early C16, perhaps by William Haig, 13th of Bemersyde, who was killed at the Battle of Flodden. Bemersyde, with neighbouring properties, was attacked by Hertford's troops in 1545, and it was possibly as a result of damage sustained that the upperworks of the tower were rebuilt, probably *c.* 1581. In 1760–1 James Haig added a W wing to the tower (by *Robert Mason* of Ridpath) and built, or rebuilt, a range of offices to the SW, while an E wing (perhaps by *James Pringle*) was added in 1795–6 to provide more public rooms and a new staircase. The W wing was remodelled, extended and in part heightened by *Peddie & Kinnear* in the 1860s, but reduced to its previous height in 1959–61 by *Ian G. Lindsay & Partners*, who also introduced a new principal staircase and removed the SW service wing.

EXTERIOR. Visually, the house has much greater unity than its complicated architectural history would lead one to expect, the mildly castellated style of the wings (the W one shorn of its crenellations in 1959–61) being very much in tune with the only half-convincing militarism of the tower. The W elevation of the W wing is in a crowstepped Scottish domestic style, while the S front is provided with large, tripartite windows with hoodmoulds. The tower house in the centre is of simple, oblong plan (11.3 by 8.7 m. over walls some 1.9 m. in thickness) and rises to a height of four storeys and an attic. The three lower storeys evidently belong to the original period of construction, the upper parts probably rebuilt *c.* 1581 on the evidence of a dated armorial panel now set over the entrance to the stable court, which bears the coat-of-arms and initials of Andrew Haig and his third wife, Elizabeth Macdougall. On the N and S sides of the tower the walls are crowned by an open 46 parapet-walk set out on an ovolo-moulded corbel course of two members interrupted by ornately carved gargoyles. The parapet is capped by a cable moulding which continues along the tops of the slender, open rounds which punctuate each corner of the tower. These, too, are decorated with a mixture of revived Romanesque and proto-classical detail in a style not unlike that employed contemporaneously at Cowdenknowes (q.v.). The rounds were not entirely ornamental, however, for some incorporate pistol-holes. The E chimneystack, with its chequered coping, evidently belongs to the same period, but the W one is probably a replacement of c. 1690, when Anthony Haig is said to have removed an upper vault and re-roofed the tower. The masonry is of sandstone rubble ranging in colour from buff to red, with quoins of similar material, all probably quarried in the immediate locality. The internal facework of the two upper floors, however, is said to incorporate large quantities of moulded stones removed from the nearby buildings of Dryburgh Abbey. The original windows of the tower have chamfered arrises, while some of the later ones have quirked edge-rolls and others have plain, rounded arrises; many of these openings were originally barred.

INTERIOR. The present ground-floor doorway in the S wall is of 1923, replacing an original one; the bolection-moulded surround incorporates the arms of Earl Haig. Within the doorway a passage leads to a newel stair in the SE corner of the tower. In the original scheme the GROUND FLOOR was occupied by a cellar, above which was an entresol floor ceiled with a slightly pointed barrel vault. In remodelling the tower c. 1690 Anthony Haig converted the cellar into a pair of bedchambers, but by 1796 these seem to have given way to a parlour, which in 1841 James Haig turned into a dining room and entrance lobby. The present arrangement dates largely from 1923 (by J.P. Alison), when the whole ground-floor area of the tower was refurbished as an entrance hall. As in the neighbouring and roughly contemporaneous tower of Smailholm Tower (q.v.), it is likely that the ENTRESOL FLOOR was originally approached by ladder from below. Anthony Haig turned the entresol chamber into a dining room, opening up a doorway from the newel stair and inserting, or enlarging, a pair of windows in the S wall. The moulded plaster string and centrepiece planted beneath the apex of the vault may have been inserted at the same time, but most of the fittings were probably installed in the 1840s or 1850s, when the chamber became a library; it is now a bedroom.

The SECOND FLOOR (counting the entresol floor as the first) has seen less alteration than the other levels of the tower and is still recognisable as a late medieval hall and kitchen. The hall (now Red Room) was lit by good-sized windows (since enlarged) in the side walls, some or all of which were originally equipped with bench seats. The odd-looking chimneypiece, with its curious mixture of classical and revived Gothic detail, probably dates from c. 1690 (the cornice, however, from 1923). The oak ceiling-joists, some evidently in secondary use, rest on individual stone corbels. The E wall is considerably thicker than its neighbours, and within the N portion is a sizeable chamber approached from a passage leading off the lower end of the hall. Prior to 1923 this chamber contained a large fireplace (now much reduced in size), together with a service hatch communicating directly with the hall, suggesting that this was a kitchen rather than a private chamber. Off the s side of the passage there opens what was probably a latrine. As rebuilt in the 1580s, each of the two UPPER FLOORS probably contained one or more chambers. In about 1690 each floor was adapted to contain two bedrooms, and in 1923 these were replaced by a single lofty chamber with a gallery at the w end giving access to the wall-walks on either side; oak panelling and timber wagon ceiling supported on individual stone corbels. As at Smailholm Tower, where the upperworks were reconstructed at about the same time, the wall-walks were entered from the uppermost chamber of the tower rather than directly from the main stair. The doorways opening onto the walks are unusual in being recessed for protection against the weather and greater ease of access. The watcher on the s walk was also provided with shelter in one, if not two, small chambers formed within the thickness of the gable walls. The main public rooms, with conventional Edinburgh New Town interiors of the 1860s, occupy the first floor of the w WING.

STABLES. Mid-C19, linked to the house on the E by an archway. The single-storey s range has a central pediment and chimneyhead as a finial; hayloft door in the pediment's centre. Similar N range, but heightened, probably in the 1920s. Screening the s wall of the stables from the gardens, a high pretty pink brick wall with pale sandstone cope, decorated with alternate blind oculi and niches with Gibbsian surrounds, all in pale sandstone; probably early C20. Handsome, sixteen-sided SUNDIAL inscribed 'Bemersyde 1691', supported on a baluster, the whole now standing upon a stepped pedestal base. Also originally on the lawn, but moved to the garden in 1863, is a STATUE said to portray Wattie Elliot of Hermitage, a hero of Border warfare. Clad in full armour and wearing a slightly bemused expression, he now stands guard over the parterre. The distinctive style of carving suggests the hand of *John Smith*, the sculptor of the nearby Wallace Statue at Dryburgh, *c.* 1814.

BEWLIE HOUSE 5020
2 km. E of Lilliesleaf

By *Guy Elwes*, 1937–8, in a Neo-Georgian style with Modernist detailing. Built in concrete, with nothing pretty about it, which probably suits the dramatic setting with its sweeping views s to the Cheviot Hills. Two-storey U-plan, with s projecting wings and NE service range. Inside is an octagonal N hall with a stair rising round its side to a landing and then dividing. Simple Neo-Georgian decoration throughout.

BEWLIE OLD FARM, s. C18 laird's house, extended *c.* 1800. Fine WALLED GARDEN with a handsome decorative cast-iron two-leaf gate with an overthrow, framing a view to Bewlie House between square piers with cast-iron urn finials.

8050

BILLIE CASTLE
3.5 km. NW of Chirnside

Fragmentary remains of a castle of the Rentons, attacked several
times in the C16. Probably abandoned as a residence in or
before the middle of the C18 and ruinous by 1834. The remains
comprise an oblong enclosure (41 m. by 31 m.) bounded on
three sides by a broad, flat-bottomed ditch. On the fourth (s),
side there are two ditches, which may have been flooded by
means of an earth dam constructed at either end. Within the
enclosure can be seen the turf-grown footings of several stone
buildings, including what was probably an oblong tower house
(15 m. by 11 m.) approached by a small gatehouse spanning the
adjacent section of the N ditch. Immediately to the E there are
another two enclosures, as well as a lime kiln. It is possible that
the castle was originally constructed as a lightly defended,
moated residence (cf. Dykehead, Bonchester Bridge) and that
the tower house and other stone buildings were added in the
C15 and C16 to give greater residential and defensive capability.

7030

BIRGHAM

A small village on the N side of the Tweed with splendid views
over Northumberland.

GRAVEYARD, S of the main street is the site of a chapel where the
Treaty of Birgham may have been negotiated in 1290; by this
it was agreed that Margaret, the Maid of Norway, should marry
Edward, Prince of Wales (later Edward II of England). The
subsequent death of Margaret led ultimately to a long period
of warfare between Scotland and England. Faint traces of a
rectangular structure survive.

MILLENNIUM CAIRN. By *George Fairley*, 2000.

DESCRIPTION. On the E side of the Eccles road are eight single-
storey ORLIT prefabricated houses built in 1950 in four blocks
of two using pre-cast concrete panels. On the opposite side of
the road is the OLD SCHOOLHOUSE, with gabled stone porch
carved with a pig's head. The attached schoolroom is now the
village hall.

DUB COTTAGE, 0.8 km. SW (A698). Late C19, gabled fishing
cottage with cast-iron columned veranda.

HOMEBANK FARM, 1 km. NE (A698). 1860s, with a rather extraordinary French pavilion roof. Stylised scrolled sills and hoodmoulds, and porch with high pointed-arched hoodmoulded
doorway.

SPRINGHILL HOUSE. *See* p. 694.

8050

BLACKADDER
1.5 km. W of Allanton

Blackadder House was built *c.* 1764, possibly incorporating the
remains of the medieval castle, was altered and added to in the
1780s and greatly extended in the 1850s by *John Lessels* for

Thomas Boswall. It was demolished *c*. 1925. NORTH LODGE, 1878. Carved bargeboards and stone mullioned and transomed windows. Bands of green fish-scale roof slates. – SOUTH LODGE (B6460). Two-storey lodges, much altered, flank a fine pair of late C18/early C19 ashlar gatepiers with round-arched niches, and decorative plinths supporting jolly, curly-maned lions *couchants*. Cast-iron gates. Of similar date, with lions on its parapet, is BLACKADDER COTTAGE (former North Lodge), in coursed stugged sandstone. Cast-iron pedimented porch and Venetian windows. *See* also Allanton

Two bridges over the Blackadder Water: BLACKADDER BRIDGE (Gold Nick) is picturesque, early C19 with a single arch flanked by engaged circular piers. Balustraded parapet. BLACKADDER BRIDGE, mid-C19. Wrought-iron girder with stugged ashlar piers, polished dressings and rusticated quoins. Latticed parapets. A similar bridge (destroyed 1947), further upstream, gave access to the walled garden.

WALLED GARDEN. Late C18 and later. Tall sandstone rubble coped walls, with handmade brick linings to N and E walls. Gatepiers, one still with a ball finial, and wrought-iron gates with decorative flanking panels with cresting. – GREEN-HOUSES, ranged along the N wall, by *Robert Knox*, a local wright, possibly mid-C19 and now ruinous. Later window mechanisms, hot water heating system etc. by *W. Richardson & Co.*, Darlington, survive. Rising behind the wall, with entry into the central glasshouse, a stylish hexagonal late C18 or early C19 two-storey SUMMERHOUSE in droved sandstone with polished recesses, flanked by symmetrical ranges of rubble out-buildings. Fluted timber doorpiece with narrow sidelights and radial fanlight. The first-floor room is domed with traces of a decorative scheme attributed to *Euphemia Boswall* (the *Gardeners' Chronicle*, 1880, described it as 'of great beauty depicting Chinese and Japanese subjects'). – GARDEN COTTAGE, NE of walled garden. Early C19.

BLACK BARONY *see* BARONY CASTLE

BLANERNE HOUSE   8050
0.5 km. NE of Edrom

Property of the Lumsdens, who were established here by the C14. By *William Burn*, *c*. 1830, seemingly repaired after a fire in 1895. Scottish Tudor with corbelled chimneyheads and mostly kneelered gables. Harl-pointed cream sandstone rubble. H-plan, with advanced gabled wings to front and back, those on the main front having kneelered gables with blind panels. Wide balustraded stone stair to a flat-roofed porch, with a central round-arched window; above is a corbelled apex stack to the gable. Doorcase with engaged columns on panelled plinths, a coat-of-arms in a panel above. The S elevation has a five-bay centrepiece with a round-arched window in a corbelled gable-head. Interior refurbished after 1895; a dog-leg timber stair with panelled newels and carved finials may date from the mid C19.

BLANERNE CASTLE, 0.1 km. SW, built earlier for the Lumsdens, seems to have occupied three sides of a courtyard. Only the stair-tower of an L-plan mansion at the NW corner and a kitchen or bakehouse occupying part of the E side survive. The character of the carved detail indicates a late C16 date, and some of the mouldings recall contemporary work at Cowdenknowes and Bemersyde House (qq.v.). The stair-tower is constructed of random rubble with dressings of buff-coloured sandstone; most of the openings have plain, round-arrised margins and there are oval-mouthed gunloops in the E and S sides. Square on plan, it rises to a height of two main storeys and finishes in an elegant, ovolo-moulded eaves cornice of two members. The lower storey evidently contained a newel stair rising to the first floor, while above the landing there seems to have been a small chamber. Over the entrance a bolection-moulded frame for an armorial panel above a broad band of chevron ornament. The kitchen evidently belongs to the same, or to a slightly later, period. It is an oblong building of two main storeys capped by crowstepped gables. A large fire-place occupies the lower (S) end of the ground floor, while above was a good-sized chamber, together with a smaller one squeezed in beside the chimney.

BLYTH BRIDGE

Small village by the crossing of the Tarth Water, much expanded in the late C20.

DESCRIPTION. The present BRIDGE, a segmental arch with red sandstone dressings, was probably built 1819 by *James & Alexander Noble*, masons for the BLYTH BRIDGE MILL. This is of 1817, L-plan and two storeys in the same red sandstone. Disused but retaining its breast-shot, timber-spoked wheel and a panel recording the high price of grain (2s. 6d. per peck) in the year of construction. Former SMITHY opposite and, tucked in behind the mill, ROBIN HILL in red sandstone, with gabled SE front; possibly the former manse of the Free Church (dem.).

SCOTSTON HOUSE. *See* p. 661.

BONCHESTER BRIDGE

5010

A village on the Rule Water.

BRIDGE. Early C19, widened in the late C20(?) in concrete but faced with reused masonry.

LAIDLAW MEMORIAL HALL. By *J.P. Alison*, 1899, in red stugged sandstone with confident, Tudor detailing. Tall, square, sparsely crenellated tower and large hall across the rear.

WAR MEMORIAL. Grey granite, with an inscribed base, sup-porting a pillar decorated with embossed carved sword, a cross on top, *c.* 1920.

HORSE AND HOUNDS INN. Began as a coaching inn in 1701, but the present building is probably early C19. Five bays, with the three-bay inn to the l., rendered and lined out as ashlar, and a former smithy(?) and stabling to the r.

DESCRIPTION. Two rows of COTTAGES were built by the Weens estate. One row has swept gabled dormers and matching door canopies, c. 1877, the other row has a heraldic panel dated 1897. Adjoining, a two-storey BLACKSMITH'S HOUSE, and two-bay SMITHY, with a wide but low doorway.

FORT, Rubers Law, 3.5 km. N. Walls enclosing the craggy summit and an annexe on the S incorporate numerous fragments of Roman masonry, and were therefore constructed after the Romans withdrew from SE Scotland. Another rampart, which contours lower down the slope, indicates that this was probably the site of an earlier tribal oppidum.

MOATED SITE, Dykehead, 4.7 km. S. A well-preserved medieval earthwork possibly associated with a residence of the Turnbull family. An approximately square enclosure (55 m. by 49 m.) with rounded corners bounded by a broad, flat-bottomed ditch. On either lip of the ditch is a bank, the outer one, now planted with trees, apparently of earth and the inner one at least partly of masonry. Entry was by means of a causeway crossing the ditch on the NE side.

WEENS HOUSE. *See* p. 749.

BONJEDWARD HOUSE
2 km N of Jedburgh

6020

Built for Archibald Jerdon of Bonjedward in the early C19, two-storey and attic, three-bay villa in sandstone rubble with cream margins. Long and short quoins, moulded eaves and piended and platformed roof. The W front centre bay slightly advanced with a pilastered and corniced doorcase, a tripartite window above, both with narrow sidelights. Interior with a central stair hall and drum cupola. Neoclassical plasterwork in the main rooms, and a Greek key frieze and pilastered buffet recess in the dining room. – WALLED GARDEN with coped rubble walls. Extended mid C19. – Early C19 STABLES and LODGE.

BONJEDWARD MILL. A former waulk mill, rebuilt as a grain mill c. 1870. The E range houses a cast-iron wheel with an arched culvert over the lade. Timber float boards and gearing.

BORTHWICK HALL*
0.5 km. SE of Heriot

3050

By *John Henderson*, 1852–3 for Sir Charles Lawson, eminent seedsman. Baronial, dominated by a three-storey square bartizaned tower, with corner stair-turret and crowstepped caphouse. The complex composition of bold crowstepped gables,

* Account based on that by Colin McWilliam in *The Buildings of Scotland: Lothian* (1978).

conical-roofed corbelled turrets, Tudor hoodmoulds and corbelled balconies is tied together with a rope-moulded string course which meanders round the house, even disappearing inside only to reappear. The entrance hall is effectively lofty. A rope-moulded corbelled stair-turret breaks into one corner, as do other turrets into bedrooms. One Jacobean compartmented ceiling remains. The other rooms on the ground floor were discreetly remodelled, *c.* 1930, for William Blair, an Edinburgh lawyer. In an alcove at the end of the now divided billiard room is a chimneypiece with armorial tiles by *G. H. Potts*, designed by *de Hoenische*. – Boldly crowstepped LODGE, probably by *Henderson*, between circular-capped gatepiers. Lawson planted a pinetum at Borthwick Hall, including seed of *Cupressus lawsoniana*, first purchased in 1855 from William Murray of San Francisco for the Lawson Seed and Nursery Co. of Edinburgh.

BORTHWICK WA'AS *see* BORTHWICKBRAE HOUSE

4010

BORTHWICKBRAE HOUSE
2.5 km. SW of Roberton

The estate was owned by the Elliot family from 1695 until *c.* 1891. The core of the present house must have been built shortly after the marriage in 1792 of William Elliot to an heiress, Marianne Lockhart of Cleghorn. The architect was probably *William Elliot*, a relative and son of the minister of Cavers. To this three-storey and attic, five-bay house, were added lower piend-roofed wings by *John Smith*, 1824, for Colonel William Lockhart. Harled rubble and sandstone margins, with channelled quoins, and a moulded eaves course on the earlier block, which takes in the window lintels. The wings have tripartite windows with narrow sidelights on the ground floor, Venetian ones above. A similarly detailed single-storey flat-roofed extension across the S front must be the 'new look' added by *J. P. Alison* for R. Noble, *c.* 1891. A later C19 three-storey addition connects with the N gable of the E wing. Geometric staircase, with decorative balusters, of 1824.

BURIAL GROUND, Borthwick Wa'as, 0.5 km. SE. The site of a chapel, which may have been built for Melrose Abbey. Amongst mainly C19 memorials are several earlier stones, some with *memento mori* and emblems, together with several decaying table tombs. William Crou, 'guner', †1671, emblems including gun, brace of birds and a dog.

4010

BORTHWICKSHIELS HOUSE
1.5 km. NE of Roberton

Harled C18 laird's house extensively remodelled in the C19 and C20.

The main block, of two storeys above a basement with a S front of three bays, was probably built by Alexander Scott of Galalaw soon after he acquired the property in 1731. Perhaps a little later a pavilion of one storey and a basement was added at the E end. The first major remodelling was carried out in 1837 by *John Smith* who dressed up the main block with giant angle pilasters, a pinnacled steep pediment at the centre of the wall-head, and a heavy porch. At the same time was added a W pavilion with the E pavilion altered to match, the front of each being given tripartite windows under a wall-head pediment, also pinnacled. Then in 1913, *J. P. Alison* removed the pediments from the pavilions, which were given mansard roofs fronted by Venetian-windowed dormers, removed the porch and pediment's pinnacles from the main block, and added a large NW wing with a Baroque Ionic porch. Yet more work was carried out *c.* 1950 when the main block's centre bay acquired thin pilaster strips and a bowed French window.

To the N a barrack-like bedroom block was tidied up and given some shape, *c.* 1950, by judicious demolition, and given a stone balustrade, the roof stepping down from the present entrance gable. Decorated stone vases on the front parapet are said to have come from Wells House (Bedrule), along with the stone balustrades on each side of the house. A small angled sundial on the SW corner has two faces and is inscribed WT (Turnbull?) 1742; a tiny carved head on top and the gnomons survive.

Alison gave the house a classical interior, except for an existing geometric stone staircase with moulded treads and slim, carved cast-iron balusters. A white marble chimneypiece with fluted jambs with thistle tops looks late C18 or early C19, and may be original.

WALLED GARDEN. Early–mid C19 with harled gardener's house, added to by *Alison.* – STABLES. Converted by *Alison* for a dwelling. – LODGE. Mid-C19 with decorative glazing.

BOWDEN

PARISH CHURCH. A highly rewarding building. The parish was one of the original endowments of Selkirk Abbey, *c.* 1113; although the present church is largely of the C17 and later, its rectangular core presumably perpetuates the medieval structure. At the E end is a higher portion (the Roxburghe Aisle), built as an 'aisle' and burial vault for the first Earl of Roxburghe in 1644 (dated and initialled above the upper doorway), with a forestair on the S side; it could be on the site of a medieval chancel. On the N side a transeptal projection was added for the Kers of Cavers in 1661 (dated and inscribed above the W doorway), with an inserted burial vault below. Major structural repairs were carried out by *Robert Spider* and *John Swanston* in 1794 (datestone on S wall); it was suggested in 1908 that this had included removal of a medieval barrel vault over the church, though this seems unlikely. Further repairs or alterations are recorded in 1799, 1813 and 1865. The greatest changes were made in 1908–9, however (the date over the rebuilt entrance to the Roxburghe Aisle), when *P. Macgregor Chalmers* created a more ecclesiologically correct arrangement.

An elevated chancel was created within the Roxburghe Aisle, and the timber Cavers loft was moved further E, away from the opening to the transeptal 'aisle' to which it belonged. A new external forestair was provided to the re-positioned loft, and a vestry was built on the N side of the chancel in 1911–12 by *R. & J. Grieve*.

20   The church is of whin rubble, with raised margins to the Roxburghe Aisle. As remodelled in 1794 it had rectangular windows along the S flank, but there are arched windows to the Roxburghe Aisle and an oculus in its E gable; a birdcage bellcote with pyramidal roof was placed over the W gable. *Chalmers* reformed most windows, giving arches to those along the S flank of the nave, except for a pair of large rectangular windows behind the pulpit. A shallow gabled porch was erected over the S doorway, and a second bellcote was eventually added over the E end of the N nave wall. To make the Roxburghe Aisle more seemly for use as a chancel he replaced the hipped W end of its roof by a gable over a new chancel arch; he also inserted Y-tracery in its windows and provided paired round-headed windows below the E oculus.

Inside, the early C20 chancel is demarcated by a pointed arch of two continuous chamfered orders and raised five steps above the retained burial vault. The eastward relocation of the Ker of Cavers Loft exposed the wide pointed arch into the upper part of the N 'aisle', which was adapted as an organ loft. The W gallery was rebuilt. Both chancel and nave have ribbed barrel ceilings, the former pointed and the latter of segmental section. – COMMUNION TABLE and CHOIR STALLS. In a Caroline style, 1909. – KER OF CAVERS LOFT. An outstanding piece of ecclesiastical woodwork (presumably contemporary with the Ker Aisle of 1661 since it bears the same initials). Carried on later fluted cast-iron columns, the front and flanks are arcaded, four arches on each side of a central rectangular panel along the front, and two on each flank; the arches are separated by hybrid Tuscan/Ionic columns capped by brackets below the bracketed cornice. At the centre of the front the rectangular panel has the painted arms and motto of the Ker family, and within the four arches on each side are painted stars and flowers. Above the loft is a canopy supported by Tuscan columns; it has triangular spandrels on each side below the cornice and a centrally placed pediment above. Within the pediment the initials of Sir Thomas Ker and Dame Grizel Halket, his wife. On the wall below the loft a board with painted moralising text. – STAINED GLASS. Nave, S wall from E to W, armorial and grisaille, 1872, re-set; St Andrew, 1909; Christ Carrying the Cross, *c.* 1908. N side in blocked doorway, Adoration of Magi, *M.I. Wood*, 1939. – PLAQUES. E end N wall, Sir Lauder Brunton, by *Robert S. Lorimer*, 1920. Middle N wall, Rev. J.M. Allardyce, †1893; S wall, Major Robert Baillie, *c.* 1888, and Lady Grizell Baillie, both by *Charles Sutherland* of Gala. Nave W wall, F.M.B. Blaikie, †1915, marble with portrait relief. – War Memorial, S nave wall, 1920, *P. Macgregor Chalmers*. – SUNDIAL, at SW angle, originally 1666; now 1989.

CHURCHYARD. First boundary wall built 1789; reconstructed 1819–20. Attractive concentration of headstones, table

tombs, piers, obelisks and crosses. Several good C18 headstones. Janet Liwd, †1712, pediment formed from wings and
green man. William Thorburn, †1733, angel holding bone and
skull. William Thomson, †1721, relief figure and symbols. Fine
lettering on pier monument capped by urn for John Harvey,
†1817, to s of church. Of several monuments built into church
wall, particularly notable is James Wright Lea, †1751, with
elaborate baroque cartouche and border. – CHURCHYARD
GATE, C17 with inserted wrought-iron screen of 1820, having
a ducal coronet in the overthrow.

MANSE to the w, built 1793, by *John Robertson*. Two-storey
and attics, of whinstone rubble, originally limewashed, harled
in 1815. N addition of 1801, entrance door and lobby of 1865.
The stables and byre are of 1793.

VILLAGE HALL, Main Street. 1897 by *John Wallace*, son of a well- 99
known village family, in the François Premier manner of Washington Browne's Edinburgh Central Library. A rectangular hall
with a row of dormer windows each side, the front to the s, a
steeply pedimented centrepiece clasped each side by two
octagonal buttresses with bands of different-coloured stone.

DESCRIPTION. Uphill from the church is the VILLAGE, where
late C18 and C19 houses line a long, triangular green at the w
end. Along the s side they were originally mostly single-storey
and thatched, now harled with dormers, and on the N side a
mixture of single- and two-storey houses, some of coursed
ashlar, others of rubble and harled. The WAR MEMORIAL, a
restoration *c.* 1920 of the market cross, stands in the centre of
the village. Mutilated C16 cross-head and octagonal stop-
chamfered base. Opposite is the SCHOOLHOUSE, converted to
a house and Post Office by *Dennis Rodwell*, 1987. Dated 1831,
designed by *John Smith* with mason work by *William Spaden*.
Single-storey, coursed square ashlar with sandstone dressings.
Pedimented gable to street and porch to Commonside. The
former SCHOOLMASTER'S HOUSE by the War Memorial is
probably contemporary. Two-storey with dressed sandstone
margins and doorcase with blocking course. A mid-C19 porch
incorporates sidelights with lying-panes and Gothic fanlight
above. In COMMONSIDE, the OLD SMIDDY is early C19, a
single storey of rubble with a steeply pitched roof. Restored
1975 by the National Trust for Scotland. Adjacent is an octagonal stone and slated WELL, dated 1861. Further E, HOLY-
ROOD COTTAGE on the N side, THOMAS AIRD'S COTTAGE
with centre gablet and timber-hung dormers; variations on this
theme can be seen elsewhere in Bowden.

BECKETT'S FIELD, s of Market Cross, on a ridge with superb
views towards the Cheviot Hills. Designed in 1939 by *Leslie
Grahame Thomson* and *Frank J. Connell*, for A. Hutcheson, livestock auctioneer. A combination of traditional and modern elements, e.g. steeply pitched slate roofs and central chimneys,
but also a deep base course of grey engineering brick, incorporating the sills of the ground-floor sash windows. The
entrance to the N has a round stair-tower with bell-shaped
turret and long narrow vertical window of a type favoured by
Thomson's master, Robert S. Lorimer. On the s elevation is a
large slate-hung bow with a flat roof serving as a canopied

balcony. Narrow balconies also project over the s-facing
terrace. Much original decoration, detailing and fittings
survive inside.

BOTHENDENE, E end of the village. Dated 1901. Scottish
Domestic with classical detailing. E-plan of whinstone rubble
with red sandstone dressings. Projecting s gables with moulded
eaves and canted bay windows on the ground floor, with Venetian windows above. Scots Renaissance style chimneypiece and
panelling in the dining room.

HOLYDEAN CASTLE. See p. 383.

MAXPOFFLE HOUSE. See p. 527.

4020   BOWHILL HOUSE
                       6.4 km. SW of Selkirk

68   Huge sprawling C19 late Georgian and Georgian survival
mansion constructed in rather piecemeal fashion for the Dukes
of Buccleuch as the principal seat of their extensive Borders
estates. Set between the Yarrow and Ettrick rivers and backed by
wooded hills, the site commands a long vista to the partly wooded
moors to the S and W.

The genesis of the house was an unpretentious small mansion
house built for John Murray, Lord Bowhill, c. 1708 during the
fifty-year period when the Bowhill estate was out of Buccleuch
ownership. This consisted of a s-facing two-storey and basement piend-roofed main block joined by short links to pavilions, which projected to the S. The estate was bought back by
the second Duke of Buccleuch in 1747 and in 1812 his great-
grandson, Charles, fourth Duke of Buccleuch, who had for
some years used Bowhill as an occasional summer residence,
commissioned *William Stark* to design a 'villa'; also of two
storeys and a basement, clamped onto the s front of the main
block of the early C18 house. This was completed in 1814,
William Atkinson acting as executant architect after Stark's
death the year before. Immediately on completion of the 'villa'
addition the Duke employed Atkinson to extend the house,
replacing the C18 pavilions by long lateral E and W wings, their
N elevations aligned with the back of the C18 house, their s
fronts set well back from the front of the 'villa'. The W wing
had been built but the E only begun in 1819 when work was
halted on the Duke's death and the succession as fifth Duke
of his thirteen-year old son, Walter Francis. It was not until
1831, after the fifth Duke's marriage to Lady Charlotte Anne
Thynne, that work resumed, now with *William Burn* as architect and *Thomas Kemp* as clerk of works. Burn added a full-
height pavilion (for nursery accommodation) at the W wing's
NW corner, completed the E wing but thickened it to the N and
gave it a NE pavilion. A much more drastic departure from
Atkinson's design was the decision to move the entrance from
the house's S side to its N, accompanied by a rebuilding of the
original early C18 house as a three-storey and basement block,
a raising of Stark's 'villa' to the same height and the erection
of a square tower-like lantern on the roof over this central

portion of the house. Then a final major extension, also for the fifth Duke, was carried out in 1875–7 by Burn's nephew and successor, *J. Macvicar Anderson*, who infilled the space between the E wing and the detached early C19 stables to the E with further additions including a smoking room, billiard room and chapel.

The EXTERIOR masonry, all of unrelieved dark whinstone in brick-sized blocks, is more evocative of institutional use than ducal splendour. Sandstone dressings, the wings and main block tied together by band and sill courses. Moulded architraves to most windows; wallhead finished with cornices and blocking courses.

At the N (entrance) front, the basement is sunk and screened by an urn-topped balustrade. Slightly set back at the front's centre is Burn's three-storey and basement rebuilding of the C18 house. Four bays, the centre two slightly advanced and with deep porch over the basement, its sides with tripartite windows, its front a pedimented Doric columned aedicule. Tripartite windows at the ground and first floors of the outer bays. Extending E and W from this, the six-bay fronts of the wings, the l. bay of the 1814–19 W wing minimally advanced, the whole front of the slightly longer 1830s E wing set further forward. At the W wing's end and projecting quite boldly is the 1830s NW pavilion. On its roof a louvred square belfry, presumably of the 1870s, its bell (rung from the basement) intended to announce services in Macvicar Anderson's chapel behind, the chapel's five windows clearly visible above the pavilion.

The S (garden) front, its basement exposed, makes a similar not altogether successful attempt at symmetry. The three-storey and basement, confidently advanced centrepiece is Stark's 'villa' of 1812–14, the top floor added by the 1830s, by Burn who was also responsible for its parapeted porch approached by a perron. In each outer bay, a ground floor tripartite window of 1812–14, with big consoles supporting its cornice. Flanking the centrepiece, the five-bay fronts of the two-storey and basement W and S wings added by Atkinson and Burn. At the W end and well recessed, the S elevation of the NW pavilion with one bay carried up as a three-storey and basement tower. Much more emphatic, although only of one storey and basement is Macvicar Anderson's SE addition of the 1870s, the billiard room's large bay window breaking forward from its front. E of this and set forward again is the S range of the early C19 STABLES, apparently by Atkinson. Two-storey front of five bays, the end bays' ground floor openings round-arched; small square windows at the upper floor.

In the centre, slightly advanced, was the pend to the court, now blocked; above is a bracketed pediment and on top a large louvred clock tower, the clock by *Robert Bryson & Sons*, 1861. The inner court has been adapted to housing and garaging; the outer N court was curtailed in the 1830s, with a new entrance by *John Smith*, 1837, consisting of a round-arched pend with panelled piers, and open bellcote. The dairy was adapted as the Bowhill Theatre in 1989 by *Law & Dunbar-Nasmith* (project architect, *Graham Law*).

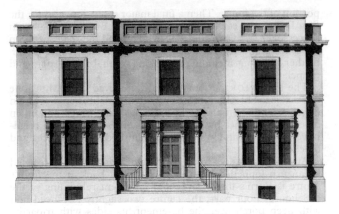

Bowhill. South elevation. Drawing by William Stark, *c.* 1812.

INTERIOR. The importance of Bowhill today is not so much the standard of the architecture, but the replanning of the interior by *William Burn*, with the family rooms in the w wing and NW pavilion, and the public rooms in the centre block and E wing. This became the setting for an outstanding collection of paintings and furniture by the leading artists and craftsmen of their day. Much was brought here in the mid to late C20, particularly from other family residences. The arrangement is as Burn left it in 1832, beginning with the outer and inner entrance halls created within the shell of the C18 house. This leads into the top-lit, full-height SALOON at the centre of the house. This has a gallery on three sides with a Jacobethan fret balustrade and plain newel posts, the soffits with lozenge-shaped panels. To the r. is the STAIRCASE HALL with simple panelled ceiling. All the rooms on the principal floor are linked by a long corridor which continues E and W of the staircase hall and saloon. In the SW corner of this block is the DRAWING ROOM of the early C19 house, which was enlarged to an L-plan by taking in Stark's entrance hall. Burn made it lavish with a Jacobethan fret ceiling (the plasterer was *Thomas Annan*), similar in spirit to the saloon balustrade, and a lush cornice, all gilded. White marble chimneypiece in Louis Revival style. In the W wing is the LIBRARY, whose more conventional panelled ceiling with inset rosettes is probably Atkinson's work. The early C18 chimneypiece came from Dalkeith House, Midlothian. The DUCHESS'S BOUDOIR in this wing has a gilded Jacobethan ceiling and a French chimneypiece, otherwise the rooms are simply decorated. E of the drawing room is the MORNING ROOM, the 1812–14 dining room but refitted by Burn, with a simple compartmented ceiling, a Louis Revival chimneypiece, and C17 handpainted Chinese wallpaper. In Burn's E wing is the DINING ROOM, with another compartmented ceiling, and a caryatid chimneypiece from Montagu

House, Whitehall.*The 1870s wing contains the former chapel (now Monmouth Room) and the billiard room (now Italian Room).

LANDSCAPE. Schemes were prepared by *W.S. Gilpin*, and the landscape was laid out with his advice, *c.* 1832. These included the making of the upper and lower lochs, and the magnificent series of terraces, described by Gilpin in his 'Improvements for Bowhill' as 'Terraces etc. under the house', and 'The Lake', and 'The Approach'. – WALLED GARDEN, SE. Mid-C19 with a fine range of restored late C19 greenhouses. – GARDEN COTTAGE. Single-storey with ancillary buildings, including segmental-arched cartsheds. – ICEHOUSE, E of the upper loch, mid-C19. An interesting example of a domed icehouse built into a large mound. Brick-lined. A door in the rubble frontage leads into a vestibule with two inner doors, the one into the egg-shaped chamber being tilted inwards so that it always stayed shut to keep out the warm air. In the roof a chute providing ventilation, and probably also for loading ice. In the bottom a sump for drainage. – Octagonal C19 rustic SUMMERHOUSE, NE of the house, with timber-boarded walls and pyramidal slated roof. Interior clad in split logs with panels containing geometric patterns. Renovated, with much new work, in the 1980s.

LODGES AND BRIDGES

EAST LODGE (General's Lodge), 0.6 km. NE of the mansion house. By *William Burn*, built *c.* 1832. A picturesquely situated gabled single-storey and attic whinstone lodge, with overhanging eaves, and bracketed timber square bays, and conventional canted bays. Later additions include an inserted sandstone porch. A sketch of the lodge appears in a planting scheme by Gilpin 'in association with Mr Burn'. It stands at the S end of the GENERAL'S BRIDGE over the Yarrow Water. The present high, single-arched bridge looks early C19. – The NORTH LODGE, 2.9 km. NW, is also by *Burn*. – NEWARK BRIDGE, by *John Smith*, 1827. – CARTERHAUGH LODGE, I.I km. SE is the same style as the East Lodge but with a gabled porch. – CARTERHAUGH BRIDGE. Single-arched early C19 bridge over the Ettrick Water. – FAULDSHOPE LODGE, 2.6 km. SW. Mid-C19. A pretty single-storey house with overhanging eaves and hoodmoulds, rendered and painted. – FAULDS-HOPE BRIDGE, also by *Smith*, 1834. Single-arched whinstone bridge, with graceful curved approaches, and a slight hump. – WEATHERHOUSE, I km. S. Mid-C19. The estate sawmill is here, but only some remnants of C19 steadings and a long single-storey building in whinstone, now used as the estate office, remain from the earlier mill. A cottage with overhanging eaves and gabled doorway matches the estate style. – GILLKEEKET, I.I km. SE. A U-plan symmetrical range of single-storey and attic gabled cottages built *c.* 1850, to accommodate married farm labourers.

* Built for the fifth Duke by *William Burn*, 1859–62 (dem. *c.* 1950).

4030
BOWLAND HOUSE*
4.9 km. s of Stow

A castellated Tudor Gothic mansion on a spectacular hilltop site, built *c.* 1813–15 for General Alexander Walker by *James Gillespie Graham*, with *John Smith* as superintending architect. The principal elevations are in dark whinstone cut into brick-sized blocks with sandstone dressings. The s front has a turreted porte cochère, and over it the frontal pretence of a square tower, in fact a heavily machicolated parapet concealing a large water tank. A small tower at the w end is balanced by two thin octagonal turrets to the E; the front is treated in a similar way to Gillespie Graham's Culdees Castle (Perth and Kinross; 1810) but is asymmetrical. An earlier house, adjoining to the N, was mostly removed for Neo-Tudor additions by *George Henderson*, 1890, for William Ramsay, and further extensions were made to the E by *Rowand Anderson & Paul*, 1926, including a three-storey gable with a square-plan oriel. Plaster rib-vaults in the entrance hall and over the staircase, which has a delicate Gothic cast-iron balustrade. A few early C19 chimneypieces survive, the character of the rest being late C19 with much panelling. Set in the arcades of a retaining wall to the rear of the house are three stone SCULPTED SLABS brought back from India by General Walker. – SUNDIAL. Cube, dated June 1708. – NORTH LODGE. Castellated Tudor, *c.* 1820, in coursed whinstone.

4010
BRANXHOLME CASTLE
5 km. SE of Hawick

Built 1572–6 as the principal seat of the Scotts of Buccleuch, who by that time had established themselves as one of the leading families in the Middle March. A mansion rather than a tower house, the building was nevertheless designed to be strongly defensible, as recent events had demonstrated it needed to be. As the Scotts continued to prosper they outgrew Branxholme, but the house has remained in their possession and, although much altered, still retains a good deal of its original character.

An earlier tower house at Branxholme survived an English attack in 1544, but was blown up with gunpowder by the Earl of Sussex in 1570. The building was described by its destroyers as 'a very stronge howse, and well sett; and very plesant gardens and orchards about ytt'. Sir Walter Scott rebuilt the house round a barmkin roughly 24 m. square, the main block being placed on the s side, directly overlooking the steep left bank of the River Teviot. No doubt the early castle occupied the same position, for the site is naturally strong, being protected not only by the Teviot, but also by a small burn that bounds its N and E sides. The main block was of Z-plan, comprising an elongated rectangle (23.2 m. from w to E by 8.5 m.

* Account based on that by Colin McWilliam, *The Buildings of Scotland: Lothian* (1978).

transversely) with square towers at the SW and NE corners. The
SW tower was equipped with gunloops providing both frontal
and flanking fire, while the NE tower contained the main staircase. Another range occupied the N side of the barmkin, which
must also have contained the entrance, while the W and E sides
were no doubt enclosed by screen walls. At the NE corner of
the barmkin there projected a square tower furnished with
gunloops on all sides. Between them the two fortified towers
would have flanked all four sides of the house, but it is possible that a third tower of similar type originally stood at the NW
corner of the barmkin.

Following the purchase of the Dalkeith estate (Lothian) by
the second Earl of Buccleuch in 1642, Branxholme ceased to
be a principal family residence and for more than a century
the house seems to have lain undisturbed. In 1757 the W gable
and part of the side walls of the main block were rebuilt, while
in 1765–9 a more extensive programme of alterations was
undertaken to adapt the house to become the residence of the
chamberlain of the Buccleuch estates. These works, directed
by *James Brown*, the Edinburgh wright-architect, included the
building of a new stair wing on the N side of the main block,
the reconstruction of the original stair in the NE tower, the
refurbishment of the interior and additions to the stables and
other offices. A second wing was added to the NE corner of the
main block in 1790. In 1837 the house was again enlarged by
William Burn and *John Smith*, when further additions, including a sizeable entrance hall, were made to the N side of the
main block and a new E courtyard wing was built to link the
main block with what remained of the original NE corner
tower.

EXTERIOR. The approach is from the N across what was formerly a free-flowing burn but is now a subterranean aqueduct.
Originally the burn was probably spanned by a bridge leading
to an entrance in the N barmkin wall, and the present arrangement appears to date from the second half of the C18, when
the N range and W screen wall of the courtyard must have been
removed and the ground levelled up. As it stands today, the N
FRONT of the house appears as a miscellaneous cluster of late
C18 and early C19 additions screening the main block of
1572–6, whose roof and upperworks can in part be glimpsed
at the rear. The late Gothic entrance porch of 1837 is wedged
between the large, three-storey wing of 1790 to the l. and the
smaller, two-storey staircase wing, probably of 1765, to the r.
To the r. again is a corridor (originally an open arcade) and a
conical-roofed angle turret of 1837. All this work is of the
plainest description, but the N wall of the 1790 wing incorporates some very showy features salvaged from the original
entrance of the early house, which probably stood close to the
re-entrant angle of the main block and NE stair-tower. The
doorway comprises a segmental-headed opening wrought on
jambs and lintel with a complex series of quirked, roll-and-
hollow mouldings which rise from high, bulbous bases. The
surround is framed by a prominent label mould, while above
the door is a black-letter inscription with the date 1571 and
lines marked by a rose and thistle. Above are two armorial

panels which evidently surmounted the original entrance. Neither is now fully legible though known, from C19 descriptions, to mark the dates of rebuilding begun by Sir Walter Scott on 24th March 1571 (i.e. 1572) and completed by his widow, Margaret Douglas, in October 1576. The form of these inscriptions (including the description of Branxholme as a hall), the style of lettering (black letter and Roman) and the nature of the mouldings are all more characteristic of Cumberland than Roxburghshire and it seems likely that the carver hailed from there. A third panel at second-floor level reads: 'THIS WING WAS REBUILT IN 1790'.

The S FRONT and SW ANGLE TOWER provide the main clues to the character of the early house. The former has a height of three storeys and the tower rises two storeys higher. The masonry is of harled rubble, the C16 dressings being of pink and buff-coloured sandstone. In their present form all the openings on the S front appear to be of C18 and C19 date, the second-floor windows, which have chamfered arrises, probably having being formed in the 1760s, when the fenestration appears to have been regularised. The large, corbelled bay windows lighting the *piano nobile* were inserted in 1837. The E gable of the main block is intaken at first-floor level, probably to accommodate what was once a large, stepped kitchen chimney. All four sides of the SW tower originally incorporated double-splayed gunloops at ground-floor level. It is noticeable that the dressed freestone quoins of the tower commence only at first-floor level. This peculiarity, taken in conjunction with the obvious irregularities of the tower walls, suggests that earlier masonry may survive on the ground floor; the gunloops, however, are almost certainly of 1572–6. The upper floors of the tower incorporate a number of original windows, some at least of which were formerly barred, while a number incorporate grooves for lead-framed glazing. Above second-floor level the wall of the tower is founded upon the W gable of the main block, the tower thus becoming L-shaped on plan. At third-floor level the walls project on an ornamental corbel course comprising alternate single and double members. The attic is gable-roofed with plain copings rising from moulded skew-putts. Much of the superstructure of the tower was probably renewed when the W gable of the main block was rebuilt in 1757, and prior to this there may have been an open wall-walk along one or more sides. The roof of the main block, however, probably descended directly to the wall-head, as now.

For the E COURTYARD WING of 1837 Burn adopted the same mild Baronial style employed in the additions to the N front. The wing is one and a half storeys in height, the upper floor being lit by pedimented dormers; the courtyard front incorporates a conical-roofed stair-turret. The W wall of the wing probably follows the line of the early barmkin wall, but C16 masonry survives only at the N end, where the wing abuts the ground-floor chamber of the original NE corner tower. This was equipped with gunloops on four sides, but all have been removed or partially blocked. These loops were of the same type as those in the SW tower of the main block, but the internal apertures were larger, measuring up to 0.18 m. in diameter, suggesting that they may have been intended for small cannon, rather than the usual handguns, and it is perhaps relevant to note that an early, breech-loading cannon was recorded at Branxholme in the late C19. The W wall of the tower shows the scar of the missing N range, which evidently comprised two or more storeys, the lower one vaulted. The corner tower itself must originally have been at least two storeys high, the lowest storey again being vaulted.

INTERIOR. The GROUND FLOOR of the early house seems originally to have contained a range of four barrel-vaulted cellars entered from a corridor to the N; the E cellar was evidently a kitchen. The vaults remain, but some of the original dividing walls have been removed or replaced, and the floor of the corridor has been raised to suit the level of the N additions. At the W end of the corridor a passage leads into the SW tower, both passage and chamber being vaulted. At the opposite end of the corridor, close to where the C16 entrance must have been, a door opens into the NE stair-tower, which is almost completely encased within the NE wing of 1790. In the original arrangement the stair probably rose to the first floor only, above which there would have been a smaller stair corbelled out in the re-entrant angle. The existing stair, which probably dates from 1765–9, serves all floors. The original layout of the FIRST FLOOR is uncertain, but it may have comprised a large hall occupying the E two-thirds of the main block, together with a chamber at the W end and a closet in the SW corner tower. The existing arrangement, in which a series of rooms opens off a corridor to the N, was probably introduced in 1765–9 and modified in 1837. Some of the rooms contain plain, marble chimneypieces belonging to the latter phase. An original newel stair in the SW corner tower commences at this level and gives access to the SECOND FLOOR of the main block and to all the upper floors of the tower. The second-floor layout of the main block is similar to that below. The chamber in the tower at this level contains what seems to be a latrine of the soil-box variety, apparently the only one now surviving in the early house. The roof of the main block appears to have been reconstructed in the second half of the C18 making some use of original timbers.

The present ENTRANCE HALL on the N side of the house leads into the stair wing of 1765–9, the timber staircase itself, however, evidently being a replacement of Burn's day. This rises to the first floor only, access to the second floor being provided by the NW turret stair of 1837 as well as by the two stairs in the early house. Burn also put in a service stair to the ground floor of the early house, which lies below the level of the entrance hall.

BRIDGELANDS HOUSE   4030
1.2 km. NE of Selkirk

A three-storey, three-bay classically detailed house of 1791, with a lower two-storey early C19 addition, remodelled 1842–51 by *John Smith* for George Rodger, factor for the Napier and

Thirlestane estates. Harled, with cream sandstone margins and long and short angle quoins. A corniced doorpiece is flanked by tall canted windows added by Smith, who remodelled the top floor and added the projecting gabled stair-tower with a large keystoned round-arched window at the rear. The early C19 wing was remodelled in 1900. The glazed vestibule screen to the hall and elegant geometric stair with decorative balusters are Smith's work, but the wide panelled doors in the hall and classical cornice in the drawing room are probably late C18. – STABLES, dated 1898. By *William G. Wilson* of Bloomsbury, London. A splendid Tudor-detailed complex with a hint of Art Nouveau. Base of red sandstone from Moat quarries, Northumberland; rendered upper floor and coved eaves. A trio of gables has Venetian-style windows, the gable-heads filled in with 'hand-placed spar'. – SUNDIAL in the centre gable with a smiling face, a bat and insect.

4020   BROOMHILL HOUSE
                    1.7 km. NE of Selkirk

Late C18 farmhouse, remodelled and extended by *John Smith* in 1824 to form an L-plan. Harled with red sandstone margins and an interior decorated in the latest Edinburgh fashion. Good plasterwork in the entrance hall with a scalloped ceiling rose, and Gothic motifs continued across the soffit of the stair arch. Curved stair with ornate cast-iron balusters. Wide curved panelled door from the vestibule to rooms beyond – a good solution in a tight space. In the principal rooms, three splendid Edinburgh-type timber and gesso chimneypieces, one with the Nelson Monument topping the jambs, lots of thistle and shell decoration; another, the 'Lady with Anchor' pattern, the jambs with back-to-back seahorses in urns on top, and the third with a victorious eagle in the centre. – WALLED GARDEN and restored rubble HORSEMILL with six piers supporting a slated conical roof.

1030   BROUGHTON

An attractive, architecturally diverse village in Upper Tweeddale. Although standing at a major crossing place and provided with a church by the C12, Broughton was slow to develop. Rebuilt *c.* 1770 'after the English fashion' – probably a reference to the regular arrangement of neat stone-built cottages with slate roofs SE of the old church. In the mid C19 the village still comprised only two short rows of houses, a mill and an inn. Expansion, when it came, involved a leap across the Biggar Water to Calzeat, *c.* 1 km. S, where a new church had been built fifty years earlier to serve the united parish of Broughton, Kilbucho and Glenholm. The coming of the railway in 1860–3 enabled professionals and businessmen to travel daily to Glasgow and Edinburgh and encouraged the development of Broughton with villas as a congenial retreat for holidays and retirement. In spite of continued expansion up to the present, the old and new villages remain visually distinct, while the tree-lined open spaces, well-tended gardens and surrounding fields maintain the rural character of the whole. The village is now best known for its association with the family of the author John Buchan, whose grandfather settled here in the 1850s.

FREE CHURCH, now the John Buchan Centre. 1843–4, a low T-plan harled rubble building with dressed margins and quoins. Gothicised in 1892 by *R. A. Bryden* of Glasgow, with a new E front and N porch in coursed rock-faced snecked red sandstone rubble, and with a large three-light rectilinear window as its centrepiece. Arch-braced roof, with decorative arcading between two levels of collars, beneath a plaster ceiling of polygonal profile; at the junction of the arms are diagonally crossed rafters. – STAINED GLASS. N end, Mary Anointing Christ's Feet, post-1895. S end, Good Samaritan, 1892, *A. Ballantine & Gardiner*; Simeon, 1896, *Ballantine & Gardiner*. Buchan's father was minister of the church for a brief period and the church now contains the Buchan Collection, which includes a fine Victorian marble chimneypiece from Bank House, High Street, Peebles (*see* p. 622). Just N stand the church SCHOOL AND SCHOOLHOUSES of 1845; on the opposite side of the road is the plain MANSE of 1849.

OLD PARISH CHURCH. Although a dependent chapel of Stobo was here by the late C12, the remains are largely of the C17 and 1726. Superseded 1803 by the church at Calzeat. Only the rubble-built E wall and stumps of the N and S walls remain. Excavation in 1922 located a N porch and vestry, and an asymmetrical laird's 'aisle' at the W end. The surviving gable has restored crowsteps and a bellcote. At the SE corner is the burial vault of George Haldane and Nicole Tweedie, built 1617 and repaired 1725 according to an armorial stone. Vault largely rebuilt by *James Grieve* in 1926, in belief that it was the cell of the C7 St Llolan. In the wall a panel commemorating Grieve (†1939), 'architect and builder'.

PARISH CHURCH, Calzeat. 1803–4 by *Thomas Brown*. Initially a harled rectangle with round-arched windows at the centre of the flanks and, from what survives at the E end, probably two tiers of windows at each end (the upper ones round-headed). The pulpit was against the N wall. Extended 1885–6 by *R. A. Bryden*, with harled transeptal projections at the W end to emphasise the relocated communion table and pulpit, and a red rock-faced sandstone entrance block at the E end. This latter has a central gabled section, a lower laterally gabled S section, and a tower to the N. At the centre is a round-arched doorway below a triplet of round-arched windows rising into the gable. The tower is square up to the base of the central gable, and then octagonal with angle broaches; a slated spire with round-arched lucarnes at its base has been removed. Internally the W transeptal projections are demarcated by pairs of arches on cylindrical piers with foliate caps; there is an E gallery. Arch-braced roof with collars. The present arrangement of communion table and pulpit dates from reorderings in 1937 and 1983. – COMMUNION TABLE, CHAIRS, PULPIT

and FONT. Simplified Gothic, 1937. – STAINED GLASS. Flanking communion table: Miracles of Christ, 1886. N transept,
Israelite Without Guile, Sower, Light of the World, 1886. s
transept, Paul teaching at Athens, 1907, *Edward Frampton* of
London. Nave N side, Good Samaritan, 1886. s side, Charity,
1886, *J. & W. Guthrie* of Glasgow. E end, Christ in Majesty,
Works of Mercy, 1886, *J. Jennings* of London. Roof-lights: E
end s side, 'Let there be light', N side, 'There was light'; w end
s side, Morning, N side, Evening, 1922, *James Grieve*.

BROUGHTON SCHOOL. *Reid & Forbes*, 1935–7. A welcoming,
long, low building with white-harled walls, grey-painted dressings and roofs of Westmorland slate. E-plan with tall, gabled
wings with overhanging eaves and a central porch with
moulded stone doorway. Behind is the school of 1875 (dated
on its gable). Single-storey schoolroom, with segmental-
headed windows, and former schoolmaster's house.

COMMUNITY HALL. By *John Hardie Glover* of *Basil Spence &
Partners*, 1955. Plain, white-harled with slated, gabled roofs and
a row of small square windows towards the street. Immediately
to the s is the earlier hall provided by Broughton estate in 1885;
gabled entrance porch with date panel above.

WAR MEMORIAL, in front of Broughton school. A plain whinstone obelisk quarried at Gameshope, near Tweedsmuir.
Unveiled by John Buchan in September 1920.

DESCRIPTION

Although the layout of the old village remains much as depicted
on late C18 and early C19 maps, most of the houses have been
altered or rebuilt. The gabled BEECHGROVE, at the N end, may
have been in existence in 1799, but its present appearance, with
overhanging eaves, probably owes much to Victorian refurbishment. The same is true of BROUGHTON GREEN, on the
w side of the main street, originally a farmhouse and inn,
worked in conjunction with the courtyard steading opposite.
Buchan's grandfather was tenant from 1851. Elsewhere there
are rows of mainly single-storey estate cottages of whinstone
rubble with attractively variegated dressings of red and buff
sandstone. One or two perhaps of early C19 date, but most of
them later – two dated in the early 1870s with the initials of
the then McQueen laird. At the corner of the Dreva road is a
two-storey row built, or rebuilt, by *James Grieve* in traditional
style in the 1920s, part of it occupying the site of the former
smithy. The road continues across the Broughton Water by a
bridge, also by *Grieve*, 1923, replacing the original ford.

Beyond the Biggar Water, in CALZEAT, a sprinkling of Victorian and Edwardian villas gives the s end of the village a quite
different character. GALA LODGE, on the Moffat road, is a
solid three-bay Scots house of whinstone with dressings of buff
sandstone. Another three-bay house, immediately s of the
Parish Church, is dated 1827, but its triple-gabled front and
spreading eaves look later. ARDBUCHO, reputedly built by *R.A.
Bryden* as a holiday home, seems to have been enlarged in
Tudor style from a modest single-storeyed house. Arts and
Crafts Tudor also found favour along the Kilbucho road, where
ST BEDE'S has timber oriels and a gabled front overlooking

the former railway. One at least of these Tudor villas appears
to be brick-built, reflecting the influence of the railway.

s of Calzeat more villas stand either side of the A701. Mainly
Arts and Crafts; the best, CHAPELGILL, lies about 0.3 km. s
up the Whitslade road on a superb site looking E over the
Tweed valley. 1897 by *R.A. Bryden* for George Deans Ritchie,
a gentleman farmer, cf. Bryden's houses at Quarrier's Homes,
Bridge of Weir, Renfrewshire. Buff-coloured sandstone with
dressings of the same material; presumably brought in from
Lanarkshire by railway. Contrasting with the solid masonry
below, prominent half-timbered Tudor gables cap the principal elevations, the larger one to the E carried on ornate brackets over bay windows. Above the entrance porch on the s is a
panel bearing the monogram initials of the builder. Inside, a
good pine staircase, and in the former drawing room, two
stained-glass windows depicting craft scenes. WHITSLADE,
about 0.1 km s, is plain late C18 or early C19 and traditional.
Beside it can be seen the vaulted ground floor of its predecessor, an L-plan C16 tower house.

EASTER CALZEAT, 0.8 km. SE. 1815. The former parish manse,
set on low-lying ground chosen by the minister, who subsequently beautified it with planting. Finished 'in a superior
style' at a cost of some £1,300, the house is a spreading hip-
roofed block of harled rubble with prominent quoins. Three-
bay front with projecting pedimented centrepiece, now masked
by a Victorian porch.

RACHAN LODGE, 1.8 km. s on the A701, belonged to Rachan
House of *c.* 1850 (dem. *c.* 1948). Mainly ashlar, with hipped
roofs (part gabled at the front), spreading eaves and circular
stone chimneys. Similar E lodge. The BRIDGE carrying the
main drive over the Holms Water has a sturdy cut-out stone
balustrade. Within the former policies are an ornamental
LAKE, a COURT of offices now adapted for residential use and
a brick-built WALLED GARDEN.

FORT and SETTLEMENT, Dreva Craig. 1.8 km. SE from old
village. The wall of the fort, which encloses an area *c.* 40 m.
across, is approximately 4 m. thick, but is more impressive for
the massive scree of rubble that has tumbled down the slope
below. An outer wall is set further down the slope, and a
chevaux de frise of upright stones has been erected on both the
SW and NE. On the NE, however, it has been largely obliterated by the construction of a small cluster of round-houses. A
more extensive Late Iron Age or Romano-British settlement,
comprising a series of walled courts and yards, occupies a
terrace below the fort on the NW.

FORT, White Hill, 6 km. WSW. Situated on the summit of a long
ridge, the defences of this pre-Roman fort, perhaps clad, comprise a low rampart with an external ditch enclosing at least
two concentric palisades. Two outlying earthworks are visible
downslope to the W. One may enhance the defences, but the
other encloses the whole of the crest of the ridge.

LONG CAIRN, Broughton Knowe, 2.5 km. NW, in the shallow
saddle between Broughton Knowe and Langlaw Hill.
Partly robbed, this small long cairn, perhaps of the third mil-
lenium B.C., is no more than 20 m. in length, tapering from E
to W.

BROUGHTON PLACE
0.8 km. NE of Broughton

78 The old house of Broughton was destroyed by fire in 1773, and the next owners of the estate, the McQueens of Braxfield, resided mainly in Lanarkshire. In 1936 Broughton Place was bought by Professor and Mrs Thomas Elliot, who immediately commissioned *Basil Spence* of *Rowand Anderson, Paul & Partners* to build a new house (completed 1937) on the site of the earlier one. They are said to have wanted a 'medieval keep', but what they got was a massive, post-medieval house in the Scottish Domestic style. As at Lorimer's Balmanno Castle (Perth and Kinross) and Formakin (Renfrewshire), to which Spence's design was probably indebted, the core of the house is a tall L-plan residential block with a stair-tower in the re-entrant angle, kitchen and offices being relegated to a separate wing. There is a lesser stair-tower at the NW corner of the main block and a much larger tower at the NE corner, all three being of circular plan with conical, slightly bellcast roofs. Between the two N towers stretches the austere entrance front with its small, irregularly placed windows and off-centre doorway, while to the S the house opens out onto the garden, the large, more or less symmetrically placed windows providing ample light to the principal rooms. The harled (brick cavity) walls, swept stone roofs punctuated by dormer windows and crow-stepped gables combine to give the house a sufficiently convincing C17 appearance. The dressings are mainly of pink sandstone, and some of the doors and windows have bolection mouldings. The principal entrance incorporates a massive, nail-studded oak door beneath an inscribed commemorative panel. Other Elliot family initials appear on the dormer pediments on the N and S sides of the house. All the carving, including the rather mischievous figure sculpture in the crowstepped gable on the N front, is by *Hew Lorimer*.

The INTERIOR was subdivided for flats in 1975 (by *Law & Dunbar-Nasmith*), and the ground floor, which is open to the public, now houses an art gallery. As first laid out, however, this floor provided a suite of spacious public rooms, served by a N corridor, while the three floors above (servants at the top) contained more than a dozen bedrooms, as well as bathrooms and dressing rooms. The kitchen and service accommodation in the W wing, which was no less generous, included a large servants' hall. The very large DRAWING ROOM on the E side has a panelled dado and stone bolection-moulded chimney-piece. The plain ceiling is supported on twin transverse beams which, like the cornice, are decorated with a running pattern of thistles in low relief plasterwork – all very much in the English Early Jacobean style. The LIBRARY (former sitting room) in the NE tower is a charming little room, panelled in walnut and with elaborately carved radiator grilles. The ribbed plaster ceiling has panels with low-relief sprays of thistles and roses. All the plasterwork is by *L. Grandison & Son* of Peebles and there is also good wrought ironwork by *Thomas Hadden*, including rails on the main turnpike stair incorporating rose and thistle designs.

The WALLED GARDEN to the S includes a sunk tennis court   85
overlooked by a delightful ogee-roofed summerhouse (originally also a dovecot). *c.* 0.15 km. to the NW of the house are
the former GARAGES, also by *Spence*, a U-plan block with
harled walls, slate roofs and plain coped gables. At the top of
the splendid approach avenue of beech and lime are
GATEPIERS capped with lions dormant, one grinning, the
other growling, both by *Hew Lorimer.* Halfway down the
avenue is BROUGHTON PLACE FARM, built in 1816 for Robert
Dundas McQueen for £1,127. Described in 1834 as the 'best
finished house in this vicinity'. Two-storey, gable-ended farmhouse of harled rubble with sandstone dressings; three-bay
front with later porch. Contemporary STEADING and WALLED
GARDEN.

BUCKHOLM TOWER   4030

2 km. N of Galashiels

The roofless shell of a late C16 tower house with attached
barmkin overlooking the N bank of the Gala Water. The Pringles
had a house here before the middle of the C16, but the tower
appears to have been erected by John Pringle of Buckholm in
1582.*

The TOWER rises to a height of three storeys and an attic and is
oblong on plan (9.1 m. by 6.7 m.) with a short stair wing (4.9
by 3.5 m.) projecting E from the NE corner. A two-storey wing
was added to the S gable about the end of the C18, when the
internal arrangements of the tower were modified and new
windows inserted on the two principal floors. The masonry is
of local whinstone rubble, the quoins formed of large blocks
of the same material. This is odd, because elsewhere in the
building lavish use is made of imported red and buff-coloured
sandstone (probably from the Melrose area) to create a varied
repertoire of mouldings. In this respect, as also in its planning,
Buckholm shows a close affinity with the neighbouring tower
of Hillslap (q.v.). Of the surviving C16 windows some have
plain, rounded arrises, others are roll-moulded, while several
have pilaster-framed surrounds either with or without drip-
moulds. In one case the flat, rectangular-section pilasters
return across the lintel in ogival curves to terminate in a fleur-
de-lys. The gabled roof descended directly to the wall-head
without a parapet, and the gables themselves were coped, not
crowstepped as usual. The entrance arrangements were also
unusual, for there were two external doorways, one on the
ground floor close to the re-entrant angle of main block and
stair wing, and the other opening directly into the E wall of the
wing at a higher level. This last was approached by means of
a stone bridge from the barmkin (*see* below), within which the
ground slopes steeply upwards on this side of the tower. The
space beneath the bridge gave access from the lower doorway

---

*A dated stone panel with Pringle's coat of arms, which was formerly placed over
the main entrance, is now at Torwoodlee House (q.v.).

to the N part of the barmkin, the adjacent corner of the wing being splayed off at this level to facilitate passage. Both door-ways were rebated for outer and inner doors, and the upper one, which has evidently been heightened, formerly incorpo-rated the carved panel mentioned above.

The lower doorway opened into the stair lobby from which an inner doorway gave access to a barrel-vaulted storeroom originally lit only by slits. The N end of the storeroom was orig-inally partitioned off, perhaps as a wine cellar; as at Hillslap Tower it had its own door to the stair. In the N wall is a double-splayed oval-mouthed gunloop which seems to have consti-tuted the only defensive provision for the tower. The upper floors are at present inaccessible.*

The tower stood largely outside, but was approached through, the BARMKIN. Part of its S wall survives, including a handsome semicircular-arched gateway wrought with a quirked edge-roll surmounted by a hoodmould. Above the gate was a bretasche or wall-walk carried on slab corbels. Parts of the S and E barmkin ranges can also be traced, while to the N there was probably an enclosing wall returning to join the N gable-wall of the tower. The masonry of the barmkin wall, except for the gateway, is bonded with clay mortar, as at Smail-holm Tower (q.v.). Footings of various other buildings, perhaps formerly comprising a farmtown, can be seen to the S.

7040   BUGHTRIG HOUSE
                  1 km E of Leitholm

Early C19 classical mansion of three bays, two storeys and basement, with a slightly advanced centre framed by giant pilasters. Coursed cream sandstone with a finely broached finish, also used for the shorter wings added c. 1840, probably for Archibald Dickson. The Doric-columned porch to the *piano nobile* was moved to its present position at basement level in the early C20. The STABLES, also remodelled in the early C20, appear to have been part of a much larger complex, including steadings etc. Late C19 or early C20 greenhouses in the WALLED GARDEN, probably by *Mackenzie & Moncur*; the central projecting conservatory has good cast-iron finials. – EAST LODGE. Early C19, classical, in coursed diagonally droved cream sandstone. Square gatepiers with shallow pyra-midal caps. – WEST LODGE. Early C20, classical, three-bay front with keystoned Venetian windows. Panelled gatepiers with ball-finialled caps.

8050   BUNKLE

BUNKLE AND PRESTON PARISH CHURCH. 1820, using materi-als from its predecessor. Initially a rectangle of coursed rubble

---

*RCAHMS suggests that each of these contained two heated chambers and that the upper flights of the stair were of timber.

and ashlar dressings, with a domed birdcage bellcote (dated) above a buttress at the centre of the w wall and a reused medieval pinnacle on the e wall. The lower w block for porch, vestry and gallery stair is of 1905 by *George Fortune* of Duns, part of a major remodelling in a Romanesque idiom. The original fenestration is best seen on the n side, where a tall narrow central window was flanked by two tiers of smaller single windows towards the outer ends; only one of the smaller windows is now open. The main (s) front has two pairs of Romanesque Revival windows towards the centre of the wall, and two larger single round-headed windows set uncomfortably close to the wall ends. The e front also has a pair of round-headed windows. The church is entered through a Romanesque Revival doorway in the s side of the w block.

INTERIOR. The remodelling of 1905 sliced off the e end to create a shallow raised 'chancel'. Central arch flanked by blind arcading, all with rather meagre detailing: more a proscenium than a chancel arch. The w gallery, carried on reeded cast-iron columns, has a front which, like the flat plastered ceiling, is largely of 1820. – COMMUNION TABLE, Romanesque detailing, 1900. – PULPIT, polygonal, probably of 1820, re-set on later base. – WAINSCOTTING, partly of 1820, re-set. – STAINED GLASS, e windows, two Maries at the tomb, *c.* 1922. – CHURCHYARD, several table and chest tombs. Some stones with *memento mori*, others with portraits of the deceased.

OLD CHURCH. The only relic of the medieval church is the early C12 semicircular e apse, a reminder of what must have been lost with the later rebuilding of so many churches of C12 foundation. Of squared rubble, with smaller stones to the semidomical vault, the latter now covered by late medieval stone flags above a cavetto-moulded cornice. Narrow windows with splayed rear arches opened to SE and NE, the latter now blocked, and a small aumbry on each side. Arch with jambs and round arch of rectangular profile; the impost blocks with a bottom chamfer. Repairs were made *c.* 1718. Following construction of the new church in 1820 the apse was retained as a burial place for the Home of Billie family.

KIRKSIDE HOUSE. Former manse. Two-storeyed, asymmetrical, with Neo-Tudor detailing by *William J. Gray Sen.*, 1846. Coursed cream sandstone to front, squared and snecked to rest. Gablet-coped skews, bracketed skewputts and ballfinialled gables, one with a dated shield. The COACH HOUSE and STABLES date from the previous manse.

BUNKLE CASTLE, 0.3 km. W. Fragmentary remains of a baronial castle of enclosure likely to have been founded by the Bonkle family in the C12. An account of an English raid in 1544 refers to the burning of the 'manour and church' of Boncle. The castle occupies a low knoll, trimmed to form a roughly circular earthwork up to 57 m. in diameter surrounded by a broad ditch and, at least in places, by an outer bank. Perhaps originally functioning as a ringwork of earth and timber, the castle was at some stage – probably not later than the C13 – enclosed by a stone curtain wall 1.6 m. thick. Part of this wall, together with a fragment of an internal building, survives on the NW side; the entrance appears to have been on the opposite (SE) side, overlooking the church.

5010   ## BURNHEAD TOWER
                         2.4 km. NE of Hawick

A much altered, but still inhabited, tower house probably erected by the Elliot family in about the third quarter of the C16. The design is similar to that of the nearby tower of Goldielands (q.v.). The tower may originally have been free-standing, but now forms the N wing of a small Victorian mansion. Oblong on plan (9.5 m. by 7.0 m.), it formerly contained three storeys and a garret, but today there are only two main storeys below the wall-head. The N end of the tower is capped by an open parapet-walk supported on individual corbels, but it is uncertain whether or not this originally extended round the other three sides. Random rubble masonry with sparing yellow sandstone dressings. The original windows have chamfer-arrised margins. A round-headed doorway in the E wall opens into a lobby leading to a roughly formed spiral stair in the tower's NE corner. Two vaulted cellars occupy the ground floor; the larger has a (blocked) oval-mouthed gunloop in the W wall. Good-sized first-floor hall and smaller, vaulted chamber formed partly within the tower's NW corner. A little above the level of the former entrance to the hall the stair contains a stone sink – an unusual feature, but one paralleled in the contemporary and neighbouring tower of Timpendean (q.v.).

4040   ## BURNHOUSE*
                         1 km. SE of Fountainhall

Small country house of c. 1820. Random whinstone rubble with droved sandstone margins. Five bays, the centre advanced and a pediment. Rear N wing, 1862, in similar style. – Early C19 circular DOVECOT of coursed rubble. – LODGE, c. 1820. Rustic Tudor, with lattice windows.

9060   ## BURNMOUTH

A fishing village divided between Lower Burnmouth, picturesquely situated by a harbour at the foot of a steep ravine, and Upper Burnmouth at the top.

PARISH CHURCH. Built in 1888 as a combined hall and place of worship for the Good Templars, it is precariously perched by the steep road down to the harbour. Severely plain box, partly pebbledashed and partly cement-rendered, with E porch and lower W office block. Refurbished in 1929, when a rudi-

---

* Account based on that by Colin McWilliam in *The Buildings of Scotland: Lothian* (1978).

mentary bellcote was added to the E gable and pews from Dunblane Cathedral installed.

HARBOUR. Founded in 1831, and greatly improved in 1879 by *D. & T. Stevenson*, with a new breakwater, pier extension and beacon. An inner basin was constructed in 1959.

DESCRIPTION. At the N end of LOWER BURNMOUTH is PARTANHALL, a row of simple single-storey fishermen's cottages hugging the waterside. Nos. 14–20 at the s-end are by *William H. Kininmonth* of *Sir Rowand Anderson, Kininmonth & Paul*, 1948. A terrace of seven two-bay houses, divided by giant-order pilasters, each differently coloured with cantilevered and railed concrete balconies. Two-storey with basements for fishermen's stores. Slightly N is COWDRAIT and ROSS, Berwickshire County Council housing of 1935 by *Rowand Anderson, Paul & Partners* (project architects, *William H. Kininmonth* and *Basil Spence*).

There were more fishermen's cottages at UPPER BURNMOUTH, in bad repair in the mid C19. The North British Railway came in 1849. Of that date is STATION HOUSE, converted for housing *c.* 1962. Single-storey coursed rubble T-plan with deep eaves. A few other houses were built in the late C19 but development mostly dates from the 1930s. BURNMOUTH PRIMARY SCHOOL at the top of the hill is mid-to-late C19, gabled with a canopied recessed porch.

CADDONFOOT

PARISH CHURCH. Built by *David Rhind* for outlying parts of the parishes of Selkirk, Galashiels, Stow, Innerleithen and Yarrow. Of squared snecked whinstone with red sandstone dressings. The first part, of 1860–1, was a rectangle with a porch towards the E end of the s side and a vestry diagonally opposite. In 1875 Rhind added a polygonal apsidal E extension, and new windows were cut through the N wall; later the porch was extended E, with the original doorway blocked and a new one cut through a window. The full panoply of Gothic detailing includes buttresses with square pinnacles at the angles of the original building, a gabled bellcote on the W gable, Y-traceried windows along the s flank and W wall (with a small rose above the pair in the latter), and a cornice with block corbels. The porch gable has angle buttresses and the relief of a Burning Bush (emblem of the Church of Scotland) above the outer doorway. The E apse has diagonal buttresses.

Internally, contrary to expectations, the communion table and pulpit are at the W end, not in the apse. Apart from the pews, much dates from an early C20 re-fitting in a Lorimerian idiom. Open-timber roof with arched braces to apse, presumably of 1875. Main body with later oak segmental barrel ceiling and vine-trail-decorated cornice; the transverse and longitudinal ceiling ribs have carved bosses at the intersections. – COMMUNION TABLE, traceried front and sides, 1911. – REREDOS, *A.N. Paterson*, with relief carving of resurrected Christ and Maries at the Tomb. – PULPIT, octagon with blind tracery. – FONT, timber octagon with carved panels; praying angel finial to lid. – LECTERN, rectangular with openwork tracery. – ORGAN CASE, N wall, *Alfred Greig*. – PLAQUES. Over original inner doorway giving details of first building; in extended porch to Robert Small, first minister of new parish, 1867–1909. – STAINED GLASS, W windows, SS Andrew and Christopher; Christ as Carpenter and as Teacher, *Herbert Hendrie*, 1933. – CHURCHYARD. First World War memorial to SE of church. Some interesting C19 and C20 memorials and enclosures. Mitchell enclosure to N has a large Celtic cross. 2nd Lord Craigmyle, †1944, W of church, two ships' prows in high relief flanking a central tablet.

   MANSE. Gothic of 1864, in whinstone with red sandstone dressings. Deep projecting eaves with scalloped bargeboarded gables, and mullioned and transomed windows, with Gothic tracery on the first floor.

PARISH HALL. 1929. The gift of Lady Anderson of Yair. Rendered and buttressed. Scottish Domestic front with a crow-stepped gable and a moulded doorway with a dressed stone surround.

CADDONFOOT HOUSE. In the style of Norman Shaw. Coursed whinstone with red sandstone dressings and deep eaves, with mock half-timbered gables and decorative ridge-crest. The chimney flues have hammer-dressed quoin stones. – Neat brick SUMMERHOUSE and GARDEN SHED in matching style with stained-glass windows. On a top terrace a FOLLY, probably intended as a prospect tower. In three stages with the square top corbelled out from the corners. LODGE and STABLE in the same style as the house.

ASHIESTIEL. *See* p. 105.

FAIRNILEE HOUSE. *See* p. 173.

PEEL HOUSE. *See* p. 635.

CAPPERCLEUCH

Former YARROW FREE CHURCH. Now a house. A charmingly diminutive rectangular box with N vestry, the side and back walls harled. The main (S) front is of whinstone with ashlar dressings and margins; an axial two-storey tower-porch (dated 1845) rises in front of the crowstepped gable, capped by a spirelet behind a crenellated parapet with obelisk pinnacles.

CHAPEL KNOWE, 1.1 km. NW at Henderland, on the summit of a wooded mound. Turf-covered foundations mark the site of the MEGGET CHAPEL, a dependency of Traquair. It was ruinous before 1603. Railed BURIAL ENCLOSURE of 1841 enclosing a late medieval GRAVE-SLAB on a masonry plinth, inscribed HERE LYES PERYS OF COKBURNE [AND HIS] WIFE MARIORY.

BURIAL ENCLOSURE, 1.2 km. NE, high above the N shore of St Mary's Loch. Possibly the site of the parish church of St Mary of the Lowes, which existed by the later C14 and possibly well before then, but was superseded by the church of Yarrow (q.v.) in 1640. Sole pointers to its location are mounds and masonry fragments at the N end of the enclosure. – MONUMENTS. Mainly C18 and C19, dominated by large early C19 enclosure to Bryden and Grieve families, with tall urn-capped piers at the angles. Interspersed with the more prominent monuments are rows of poignantly anonymous rough grave markers.

DESCRIPTION. Set upon a substantial plinth overlooking the isthmus separating St Mary's Loch from the Loch of the Lowes is the celebrated MONUMENT by *Andrew Currie* to James Hogg, 'The Ettrick Shepherd' (†1835), unveiled in 1860 (*see also* Ettrick). The poet is represented as a seated figure with his plaid and staff, his sheepdog Hector at his feet. In his left hand a tablet inscribed: 'He Taught The Wandering Winds To Sing'. The plinth, inscribed at base, rises to a cornice decorated with rams' heads and oakleaf tendrils. On the E face a cartouche containing a harp and garland above the commemorative inscription; additional inscriptions on the other three sides. Hewn stone, painted white over all. Just across the isthmus is TIBBIE SHIEL'S INN, scene of many of Hogg's convivial gatherings with contemporary *literati*. The original single-storey cottage built for Isabella 'Tibbie' Shiel in 1823 is readily identifiable, its thatched roof now replaced by one of slate. To the N a late C19 hip-roofed block of two storeys, its main front facing down St Mary's Loch. Later extensions.

MEGGET RESERVOIR, 5km. W. 1983. *Robert H. Cuthbertson & Partners*, engineers, *W.J. Cairns & Partners*, landscape architects.

DRYHOPE TOWER. *See* p. 228.

CARDRONA HOUSE 3030
1.5 km. SE of Kirkburn

A modest Scottish Jacobean mansion for Captain James Ker by *William Burn*, 1841, replacing a house for the Williamson family described as 'new' in 1715. The design and plan are remarkably similar to those of Bourhouse (Lothian), which was designed in Burn's office by *David Bryce* in 1835. Burn was in poor health in 1841, and it is more than possible that Bryce also carried out this job. Asymmetrical, almost U-plan, with the stairwell in the centre and lower service wing to the W. Two storeys of pale coursed sandstone with a broached finish. Crowstepped gables and canted and square-mullioned bay windows with ball-finialled parapets. The wall-head dormers have moulded pediments. There is a hint of Scottish Baronial in the projecting entrance, which is corbelled out from the round to a square and topped by a crowstepped gable, with a corbel course taken over the doorway as a hoodmould containing a raised panel. Reset stones of 1719 and 1686 were probably salvaged from the earlier house.

The interior retains a circular vestibule with a foliaceous cornice, and drawing room with ribbed ceiling and a liver-coloured French-type chimneypiece. Cast-iron balusters on the stair. – The WALLED GARDEN probably incorporates C18 work; its mid-C19(?) greenhouse has a central projecting conservatory with flanking wings. The mid-C18 rectangular DOVECOT is rubble-built with a string course; the stones in the front course are set at right angles to the wall. Crowstepped gables and skewputts. The estate has a good collection of mid-C19 buildings, but mostly altered and now severely compromised by infill housing.

CARDRONA TOWER, probably erected in the late C16 by the Govan family, stands high above the mansion to the W in a patch of cleared woodland. Now a roofless shell, L-shaped on plan, it comprises an oblong main block (10.2m. by 6.8m.) with a projecting stair-tower (2.4m. by 3.1m.). It contained a barrel-vaulted cellar, a first-floor hall and two upper floors containing three or four chambers between them. The masonry is of local rubble with dressings of dark red sandstone, most of which have been plundered. Defensive provision was minimal, but there are traces of what may have been a corbelled angle turret at the S corner; the walls seem too thin (1.1m.) to have carried a parapet-walk. The doorway opens directly into the foot of the stair, and above is a housing for an armorial panel. Fragmentary remains of a SW barmkin. The tower was probably abandoned soon after 1685, when the Williamsons acquired Cardrona and built their new house.

1050   CARLOPS

Founded as a cotton-weaving centre by a local laird, Robert Brown of Newhall (Lothian), in 1784. The site chosen was a short pass through the lower slopes of the Pentland Hills, which had carried a major N–S route since Roman times. The textile industry declined during the second half of the C19, but as it did so the village found a new role as a health resort for summer visitors who came to walk the surrounding hills and explore the scenery associated with Allan Ramsay's pastoral comedy, *The Gentle Shepherd.** Today Carlops remains a centre for day visitors and has also become a dormitory village for Edinburgh.

PARISH CHURCH, originally Free Church. Workmanlike preaching box of 1850 by *Charles Lawson*, builder and owner of the Deepsykehead quarries, from whose sandstone the oblong, gabled church is built. Entrance at the E end, directly off the village street, with a timber bellcote on a dated stone base perched on the gable above. A mix of round-headed and pointed-arch windows, all with lattice lead glazing. Session house at the W end (rebuilt 2005). The interior was refurbished and re-seated in 1897 by *Hardy & Wight*, of Edinburgh, who probably introduced the present pews. Most of the other fittings look original, including the mildly Gothic PULPIT at the W end. All very plain, apart from the luminous post-war STAINED GLASS panel in the N window and the handsome (replacement) Gothic ORGAN.

WELL, Main Street. Set within a semicircular-headed alcove flanked by swept, coped walls topped by finials. Incised date of 1860 and initials of the donor, Hugh Horatio Brown of Newhall.

VILLAGE HALL, Main Street. Timber-clad; low broad-eaved roof extending over porch. By *Fred Walker Associates*, 2004.

*First published in 1725.

DESCRIPTION

On either side of the main Biggar–Edinburgh road (A702) are rows of single-storey cottages, many of them originally occupied by handloom weavers, and some two-storey blocks. Constructed of random rubble (in some cases harled) with freestone dressings, all now have slated roofs, although some, at least, were originally pantiled. As first built many of the cottages comprised a kitchen and workroom flanking a through passage opening off the front door; both rooms would have been fitted with box beds.

At the s end of the village, on the l. side of the road, the OLD MANSE, erected 1861–2 for the minister of the then Free Church at a cost of £366 by *Robert Wilson*, of Dalkeith (*Charles Lawson*, builder, Deepsykehead). One and a half storeys with gabled roof, the main front incorporating a central gablet with fleur-de-lys finial; central window with shouldered lintel and bracketed sill. Further N, on the same side, a pair of cottages, now LYNBURN, the s one with a garden grotto built in 1823 by the then occupant, *Charles Wilson*, a plasterer and amateur sculptor. Small in size, but crowded with detail, this sports an Ionic doorway flanked by battlemented screen walls and pylons. Above the doorway a self-styled armorial achievement. Beyond is the CHURCH HALL of 1900, incorporating part of an earlier schoolhouse. Tiled ridge with finials. Prominent dormer windows incorporating donors' initials. At the narrowest point of the pass, where the flanking rock outcrops were cut back for road metal during the C19, is ROCK FARM, said to have been built as an inn. Three-bay front with pedimented doorway dated 1804. Gabled roof with roll-moulded skewputts. Nearby a two-storey BARN of similar date, perhaps originally partly residential. Beyond the church, on the l., the ALLAN RAMSAY INN, part of which may have originated as a wool store. Five-bay front with central pedimented doorway dated 1792. Four-bay addition with forestair.

PATIE'S MILL, off Mill Lane at N end of village, was originally equipped to produce woollen felts for the local paper mills, but subsequently adapted for use as a meal mill; converted for residential use 1964–5 by *Stuart Harris*, with garage extension on site of former drying kiln. Two-storey gable-roofed block with off-centre entrance; lintel dated 1800. On the w gable an overshot cast-iron wheel, replacing an earlier pitch-back wheel. In garden an early C18 obelisk SUNDIAL formerly at Prestonpans, Lothian. Segmental-arched access BRIDGE also c. 1800.

KITLEYKNOWE, 0.9 km. SE, is a late C18 former entrance lodge of Newhall House (Lothian), with handsome gatepiers.

DEEPSYKEHEAD, 2 km. SE. Extensive traces of former sandstone quarries, described in 1791 as supplying 'all Tweeddale' with white freestone. At their peak, about the middle of the C19, the operator, Charles Lawson, employed up to 100 men and maintained a yard in Peebles to supply local trade. Quarrying ceased in 1873. Fragmentary remains of stone-built WORKSHOPS, some formerly with pantiled roofs. The present FARMHOUSE of Deepsykehead, a well-built two-storey block of early C19 date with attached stable and offices, appears to have been erected for the quarry manager. A short distance upstream from the quarries a well-preserved early C19(?) double LIME KILN with inclined loading ramp; the chambers are brick-lined.

SURVEY TOWER, 2.3 km. SE. Standing in the middle of Harlaw Muir and looking at first sight like a derelict tower house, constructed in 1897–1905 in conjunction with the Talla Water Works, near Tweedsmuir (q.v.). The tower (about 4 m. square at base and 8 m. in height) encloses a tapering column of masonry upon which was mounted a telescopic instrument used to calculate the alignment of the aqueduct, which at this point flows some distance beneath the surface. Smaller columns that served a similar purpose can be seen elsewhere along the line of the aqueduct.

NORTH ESK RESERVOIR, 2 km. NW. Constructed in 1843–50 to regularise the supply of water serving mills and factories on the River Esk (*D. & T. Stevenson*, engineers, *William Middlemiss*, resident engineer). Earth and stone dam with keeper's house adjacent. Depth indicator pier and tunnel mouth in rock-faced ashlar, the latter with central inscription panel and swept flanking walls.

5030   CAROLSIDE
                          2.1 km. NW of Earlston

75   A serene late C18 Georgian mansion house set down on a plain in a sharp curve of the Leader Water. The circumstances of its erection are something of a puzzle, but it is possible that the central portion was built for James Hume, Lord Chief Justice of East Florida, who returned to Scotland in 1783 with a handsome pension from the British government.

This is of five bays and three storeys above a raised basement, with chimneystacks framing the piended roof. Windows on the ground and first floors have lugged architraves, with cornices over the lower ones, and alternate triangular and segmental heads over the upper ones. The design seems to be based on Isaac Ware's Chesterfield House, London, illustrated in his *Complete Body of Architecture* (1756). The walls are harled and lined out to resemble ashlar, with sandstone margins and narrow sandstone strips at the angles, including the E and W wings. These may have been constructed in 1806, when Hume is known to have added to the house for his retirement, and are of a single storey and basement with balustrades and bow-fronted side elevations. Each has a corniced three-light window on the s front and sides which are dignified by anta-mullions treated as columns, markedly similar to windows at Monreith House (Dumfries and Galloway), where *Alexander Stevens Jun.* was working 1790–4. Could Stevens have been the architect here? Jambs with panelled tops and bases continue down to frame the horizontal basement windows below, which have anta-pilastered mullions. The large entrance porch and the basement balustrade may be *c.* 1835, when a new drive was constructed and the ground in front of the house possibly raised. From the centre of the N elevation extends a W-facing three-storey harled block, dated 1936, with a full-height bowed projection to the l., and a Venetian window to the r. Conservatory added to the N in 1956. Single-storey with wide, recessed and fluted pilaster strips.

The interior of the central block, although much reconstructed (probably after a fire in 1936), has a screen of Composite columns in the hall which appear to be original (cf. Leadervale House, p. 489). The two principal rooms in the wings are identical in shape. The DINING ROOM (E) has key-patterned ribs on the ceiling, and two round-headed niches in the N wall. Timber and gesso chimneypiece with Gothic pilastered jambs, a delicately ornamented sub-frieze, thistle ornamentation, and central panel with eagles and alligators. Doors have matching thistle friezes, and slightly bowed and reeded jambs. In the DRAWING ROOM (W) a chimneypiece imported from Baronscourt, Co. Tyrone in the later C20; late C18 inlaid scagliola, reputedly by the elusive *Pietro Bossi* of Dublin (fl. 1785–98).

NW of the house is an oval rubble-built WALLED GARDEN, with a high straight wall along the N side for greenhouses. On the other side of the N wall are the STABLES with coachhouses and haylofts, partly converted for housing. They could be late C18, rubble with red sandstone dressings, weathered to a beautiful pink. Formerly symmetrical with a central round-arched pend, now infilled. Opposite the stables, former GARDEN BUILDINGS were given a symmetrical façade in the early C20 with a centre pediment over a keystoned arch. In the end bays are round-arched keystoned doorways, the bays marked by flush red sandstone quoins.

SW of the house, carrying the W drive from the former principal entrance, is a picturesque late C18 BRIDGE. Single span of sandstone rubble and ashlar dressings, with raised voussoirs beneath a continuous round-arched band. Prominent corbels beneath the parapets, which have attractive concave ramps where they step up to the central section; their detailing is a hallmark of *Alexander Stevens Sen.* (cf. Teviot Bridge, Kelso). The approach walls are stepped out to N and S with circular terminating piers. Mid-to-late C19 iron gatepiers and gate to the N. There are the remains of a single-storey, rubble-built Gothick structure (perhaps a GROTTO) to the r. of the approach from the N. All that is left is a rustic façade with pointed blind arches. – Late C18 Gothick WEST LODGE with bowed S front and pointed doorways each side of a wide window with Gothic glazing. V-jointed rusticated stone gatepier, with fluted frieze and corniced cap.

CASTLECRAIG HOUSE   1040
1 km. SE of Kirkurd

A sizeable country house (now nursing home) built in 1798 for Sir John Gibson Carmichael but extensively remodelled by *John J. Burnet* for James Mann, a Glasgow industrialist, in 1905.

The house is austere, of three storeys, basement, and attics beneath a piended platformed roof, with short straight links to two-storey pavilions. Seven-bay S front of regular-coursed grey ashlar, vertically broached, the centre three bays advanced beneath a triangular pediment containing the Carmichael armorial. The small flat-roofed Doric portico must be early C19; it is not shown in an engraving of 1808. The other elevations are of coursed buff sandstone. The N and S elevations of the pavilions have open pediments of 1905 when window openings on the second floor of the main house were raised, and a second set of chimneys built against the W and E flanks rising up like arched pylons. Burnet drastically altered the N façade by adding a continuous single-storey block along the whole elevation. Its principal entrance is set back behind four columns with a Venetian window above. Interesting ironwork, including wrought-iron door knockers: two on the S portico, and one by the door on the W elevation; two are said to be Italian, the third is probably early C20 and the work of *Thomas Hadden*, Carmichael's friend and collaborator (cf. Skirling House, p. 686).

INTERIOR. The ground floor was lavishly refitted by Burnet in a late-C17 Scottish Renaissance style. The present entrance from the N is into a small vestibule and l. through a rather insignificant door into a low vaulted hall with a central Composite column. Large Scottish Renaissance grey marble chimneypiece, with a deep frieze and panelled jambs; the frieze decorated with four small roundels, signed by *William Sherriff*, of a woman and children engaged in various games. A wide barrel-vaulted corridor runs through the centre of the house from W to E, opening out to a circular domed vestibule at the E end. Along the N side a screen of free-standing marble columns carries the hall cornice out as an entablature over the columns – one of Burnet's favourite features.

From the circular vestibule one reaches the appropriately panelled BUSINESS ROOM to the NW; the LIBRARY in the N end of the E pavilion has a barrel-vaulted ceiling. The BILLIARD ROOM (S) has a coved shallow vaulted ceiling, with plasterwork barley-sugar columns and lozenge decoration on the chimneypiece. Next W, a PARLOUR, oak-panelled with a Lorimer-type plaster ceiling with fruit and flowers, but also a C18 chimneypiece. Pine with fluted pilasters, composite capitals, urns and garlands; the decoration above the doors appears to have been made up from strips of C18 carving. Along the S front is the DRAWING ROOM created out of the outer hall and drawing room of the C18 house. Three-quarter panelling with a coved compartmented ceiling and semi-elliptical chimneypiece with lozenge decoration. The DINING ROOM next, from which an imported C16 Italian ceiling was removed to Skirling House (q.v.) *c.* 1905. Burnet's decoration includes chimneypieces with plump free-standing columns supporting semi-elliptical entablatures; the one in the library under the gallery is like an inglenook. The first and second floors are less disturbed and retain their original planning. Access to the attic floor is by a scale-and-platt stair in the NW corner. In 1905 three C18 pine chimneypieces were moved up to the first floor, one simple, with garlands and roundels, another grander and prettier with attractively curved console pilasters, a central urn, ribbons and drops. The third is a typical 'Edinburgh' type with fluted pilasters, acanthus capitals, shells, flowers and wheat.

SUNDIAL. A limestone baluster-shaft with winged cherubs' heads. The copper dial, dated 1725, has been removed. – Most of the C18 steadings and STABLES were partly rebuilt in 1892. Entry to the court is through cushioned gatepiers with square caps and ball finials. Opposite, a two-storey house of red sandstone with wall-head dormers and a central gablet with ball finials, defined on the elevation by flat pilasters. Adjacent to the NE the C18 WALLED GARDEN, rubble with a flat stone cope.

EAST LODGES, 0.3 km. NE (A72). The SE lodge may be C18, with bellcast roof and panelled chimneystack, but refronted in 1809 by *James & Alexander Noble*, to match the newly built NW lodge, with circular-headed recessed panels flanked by quatrefoils. Contemporary round gatepiers with conical tops are linked to the lodges by a low wall with some Arts and Crafts wrought-iron decoration of the 1890s on the railings, now mostly gone; the decorative gates have disappeared. – INK BOTTLE LODGE, 0.6 km. SE (A72), is probably of *c.* 1760, contemporary with an earlier mansion house. Three-bay square lodge of random rubble with central chimney, all thickly rendered.

KIRKURD OLD PARISH CHURCH lies outside the E garden wall of Castlecraig House. A possession of the bishops of Glasgow from before 1170; abandoned in 1766 when the policies of Castlecraig were being improved by John Carmichael of Skirling. The sole relic is a heavily overgrown square barrel-vaulted chamber without external facing, presumably the burial vault of a post-Reformation laird's aisle. S and E of the vault are a number of table tombs and headstones. – HEADSTONES include John Wood, †1728, with full-length portrait; family of Archibald Brown, †1741, with full-length female portrait.

CASTLECRAIG MILL (The Old Watermill), 0.35 km. S. Converted to a house. Late C18. Whinstone rubble with red sandstone dressings, the overshot wheel fed by a sluice from ponds to the S. The sluice gate is dated 1782.

CASTLEHILL TOWER   2030
3 km. SW of Kirkton Manor

A fragment of a late medieval tower house of the Lowis family of Manor, almost the only survivor of the ten or so towers that once existed in the Manor Valley. The land was acquired early in the C15 and the present tower probably erected late in that century or early in the next. The building was ruinous by 1775 and in spite of steps to repair and consolidate the fabric in 1884, it has since deteriorated further.

The site is a strong one, comprising a rocky knoll surrounded by a ditch on all but the steepest side. The tower occupies the W part of the summit, the remainder of which seems formerly to have been enclosed by a stone wall to form a small barmkin. The tower was oblong on plan, measuring *c.* 11.5 m. by 9.1 m. over walls *c.* 1.9 m. thick. It probably comprised four main storeys, but now stands to a maximum height of two full storeys on the w side, the other three sides being reduced to first-floor level. Local random rubble masonry with quoins of the same material; the doors and windows are formed with chamfer-arrised dressings of buff and yellow sandstone, some of which have been renewed. The entrance doorway in the E wall gave access to a lobby from which an inner, round-arched doorway led into the outer of two barrel-vaulted cellars that occupied the ground floor. From the lobby a stair rose within the thickness of the N wall to enter the lower end of the first-floor hall. This was evidently ceiled by a barrel vault, within the upper part of which there may have been an entresol floor of timber. The large, segmental-headed window in the w wall appears to have been reconstructed, but the position of the other windows and of the fireplace is uncertain. A newel stair in the NW corner of the tower ascended to the upper levels where, to judge from the existence of twin latrine chutes in the w wall, there were another two floors.

5090   CASTLETON

CHURCHYARD. Site of the church granted to Jedburgh Abbey *c.* 1150. MONUMENTS include: Eliza Scott, †1847, an ambitious Greek Doric ciborium with a slightly unexpected dome; John Armstrong, †1779, a Neoclassical obelisk; Isabel Veitch, †1809, Rococo Gothic triple headstone with plethora of pinnacles. Several early C19 table tombs are of related designs, and further evidence of the personal style of local masons is seen in large numbers of headstones. Those of the Douglas family, of the mid C19, have upper reliefs of draped urns flanked by wreathed inverted torches. – CROSS, 0.2 km. E, assumed to be the former market cross. Cross base with chamfered edges, in which fragments of the cross were set up in 1938.

PARISH CHURCH, 1.25 km. WSW of the churchyard. Disused. Relocated here in 1808 (the date above a doorway in the E arm), and remodelled 1885. First built with limewashed rubble walls and ashlar dressings, it was of a T-plan, with a small vestry at the S end. Initially the windows were probably all rectangular, as still along the S face, and there were galleries in the three arms. In 1885 *James Burnet* of Langholm inserted broad lancets in most parts, and added a new N frontispiece of buff stugged rubble, with a pointed-arched doorway, a triplet of lancets, a quatrefoil and a gabled bellcote in ascending order. A small vestibule was formed beneath the N gallery (the only gallery to be retained), and coved and ribbed plaster ceilings were inserted. An elevated trifoliate arch on the S wall marks the pulpit site.

LIDDEL CASTLE, immediately N of the churchyard. The impressive, earthwork remains of the C12 castle of the de Soules, lords of Liddesdale, the principal stronghold of the lordship until superseded by Hermitage Castle (q.v.) in the early C14. The

site is immensely strong, a steep-sided promontory lying
between the Liddel Water and the gorge of a tributary burn,
having been shut off to landward by two broad ditches dug
roughly parallel to one another from flank to flank. The oblong
area between the two ditches (72 m. by 24 m.) evidently formed
an outer bailey, which was further defended on its s side by a
rampart overlooking the outer ditch. The inner enclosure (56
m. by 45 m.), best described as a ringwork, is roughly triangular in shape and the ground surface is level enough to have
accommodated buildings. The outer bailey seems to have been
entered close to its sw corner, while the inner bailey may have
been approached by way of a timber bridge spanning the ditch.

CAVERS 5010

For many centuries an important estate centre and seat of the
hereditary sheriffs of Roxburghshire, with a baronial residence
and adjacent parish church. Cavers is today little more than a
desirable rural retreat on the outskirts of Hawick.

OLD PARISH CHURCH, within the policies of Cavers House (*see*
below). Abandoned for worship since 1822 and later used as
hall, school and agricultural store. Now derelict. At the E end
are substantial remains of an early C12 rectangular chancel,
with a chamfered base course, large areas of cubical masonry
up to two-thirds of the height of the wall, and a small arched
window on the N side. Parts of the elongated structure to the
w incorporate walling of the medieval nave, while a s 'aisle' for
the Gledstanes of Cocklaw (dem. mid C18) perhaps originated
as a late medieval chantry. But much of the building is of the
C17, the date 1662 on the w doorway indicating when some of
this was done. The walls were evidently heightened throughout, and several new windows inserted, including a large Y-
traceried and transomed E window, and an oculus with a saltire
cross of tracery in the w wall. A slated bellcote was constructed
on the w gable. The chancel was adapted for the Douglas of
Cavers family, with a loft above the burial place, reached by a
forestair to the s. Also in the C17, an 'aisle' was added against
the N side of the nave for the Elliotts of Stobs, which opened
into the church through a semicircular arch (now blocked); it
has an asymmetrical four-light intersecting-traceried N
window. The low height of the aisle walls may reflect the original height of the nave walls. The date 1730 on a re-set lintel
in an offshoot w of the Elliott aisle indicates when further work
was carried out. During yet further remodelling, pointed-
arched windows and N doorway were inserted, the doorway
having a fanlight of intersecting tracery. – CHURCHYARD.
Large numbers of C17, C18 and C19 memorials. C13 cross-
incised grave-slab.

PARISH CHURCH, 0.5 km. NW of its predecessor. 1822. A pretty
Gothick confection of snecked coursed rubble, with ample buff
ashlar dressings. The main body, of three bays, is aligned along
the contours of the sloping site; it has Y-traceried windows
and pinnacled buttresses at the angles and between the bays

(diagonal in the former case). The small buttressed tower at the centre of the SW front is intaken below mid-height, and a triplet of tabernacles adorns its leading face and the flanking church walls; the belfry stage has a gable over the lancet on each face and tall pinnacles at the angles. During alterations of 1928, two doorways flanking the tower were changed into windows, a porch was added to the SW front, and a vestry was thrown out at the NE end. The present internal arrangements also date from then, with a NE communion table platform and a gallery for the Elliott pew at the opposite end. Ceiling of depressed arched profile. – COMMUNION TABLE and PULPIT, simplified rectilinear Gothic, 1928. – STAINED GLASS, in oculus at E end, Christ with Children. – FUNERAL HATCH-MENT, Sir William Elliot, †1864.

Former MANSE (Caverslea). A plain two-storey, three-bay harled house of 1813, with red sandstone margins and flush angle quoins. Traditional U-plan steading and walled garden.

CAVERS HOUSE
0.2 km. SE of Cavers

The roofless shell of a mid- or late C15 tower house of the Douglas family, incorporating part of what may have been an earlier residence of the Balliols. During the 1540s Cavers was twice burnt by English troops, but the lower floors of the tower, at least, evidently survived these assaults. Extensive alterations were made during the C17 and C18, including the addition c. 1750–6 of a hip-roofed block on the N side of the tower, with a bow-fronted entrance facing E. In 1885–7 *Peddie & Kinnear* carried out a major scheme of enlargement and reconstruction, mainly in Scottish Renaissance style. During this phase the entrance was moved to the N side of the house. The mansion was unroofed and largely demolished in 1952.

The surviving fragment comprises the tower, which occupied the SE corner of the mansion, together with the adjacent portion of the later house to the N. The tower house measures about 15.3 m. by 8.8 m. over walls up to 2.6 m. thick, the SW corner being intaken in the form of a 90-degree re-entrant angle; latterly it rose to a height of five storeys and an attic. The masonry is mainly of random rubble with sandstone dressings, but the lower portion of the S wall is constructed of coursed sandstone blocks, and similar facework can be seen at this level at various places in the interior. Towards the E end of the internal S wall at first-floor level is a trefoil-headed niche containing a piscina and credence supported on moulded brackets; the detail indicates a date c. 1300. This niche, which appears to be *in situ*, was discovered when a vault was dismantled in 1885–7, and its presence suggests that the tower incorporates part of an older building, perhaps the chapel of the 'old manor place' mentioned in 1432. The middle storeys of the tower seem to have been rebuilt during the C17 and again remodelled when the upper storeys were renewed in 1885–7.

CAVERS CARRE

5020

3 km. NE of Lilliesleaf

Built *c.* 1775, extended and remodelled *c.* 1800.* Two storeys with a platformed, piended roof, and chimneystacks on the transverse walls. Rubble work using small stones, with sandstone margins. Three widely spaced bays on the S elevation, and a later porch. Extensive late C19(?) two-storey additions at the rear. Inserted above the ground-floor windows on the principal fronts are round-headed pediments, said to be early C18 marriage stones, inscribed with the arms and initials of various Carres and their wives. Tripartite plan inside; its simple decoration looks later than *c.* 1800. – Rubble-built lectern DOVECOT with crowstepped gables, two chambers and twenty-eight dove holes set in a long line along the roof ridge. Original stone nest boxes. Probably early C18. The sandstone panel dated 1532 must be a Victorian piece of humour.

CESSFORD CASTLE

7020

3 km. SW of Morebattle

The shell of a massive L-plan tower house and its outworks, 38 prominently sited on the summit of a flat-topped hill affording magnificent views of the valley of the Kale Water and Cheviot Hills. One of the major strongholds of the Middle March, the castle played an eventful part in late medieval Border warfare before being adapted to a more peaceful role as a domestic residence.

Although some of the architectural evidence could point to a slightly earlier date, the castle was probably largely erected during the second quarter of the C15, when Cessford came into the hands of the rising family of Ker of Altonburn. The same family, now represented by the Dukes of Roxburghe, has continued in possession up to the present day. Its proximity to the Anglo-Scottish frontier made Cessford a frequent target of English armies, and in 1519 the castle was reported to have been 'cast down'. Four years later it suffered a famous siege and eventual surrender to the Earl of Surrey, who reckoned it the strongest place in Scotland after the castles of Dunbar (Lothian) and Fast (q.v.). The account of this siege provides useful information about the defences, notably that the castle was 'vawmewred' (equipped with an outer bank of earth) and had a barbican, with another barbican within to defend the gate of the 'dongeon' (tower house). The castle was burnt during Hertford's invasion of 1544 and again in the following year, when the walls of the tower proved too thick to be undermined, and it seems likely that the damage inflicted on these occasions permanently reduced its defensive capability and left it at least partly ruinous. The upperworks of the tower house

---

*Foundations of an earlier house were found beneath a floor in the principal part of the house in the late C20.

were drastically remodelled *c.* 1600. The castle was abandoned as a Ker family residence in favour of Floors Castle (q.v.) in the mid C17.

The TOWER HOUSE is exceptionally strong, the external walls averaging 3.9 m. in width. The main N–S block measures 19.4 m. by 13.8 m. externally and the wing, some 11.0 m. in width, projects 6.7 m. E. The tower is thus a little larger than the broadly contemporary towers of Neidpath Castle (q.v.) and Dalhousie Castle (Lothian), with substantially thicker walls than both. As first built, the main block comprised a ground floor with vaulted entresol, a lofty vaulted hall and at least one further floor above. The wing contained four floors, three of them vaulted, within the height of the hall vault, together with two or more upper floors. A newel stair in the re-entrant angle gave access to all floors and probably also to a parapet-walk. The existing arrangement of the upperworks evidently dates from the reconstruction of *c.* 1600, when the N, W and S walls of the main block seem to have been reduced in height and re-roofed immediately above the hall vault. At the same time the upper floors of the wing were rebuilt and linked to earlier mural chambers in the remaining (E) wall of the main block. This conversion must have given the tower a very odd appearance, which was compounded by the arrangements adopted for roofing the wing. Here the comparatively slender walls of the rebuilt upper storeys were raised upon the inner portion of the much more massive walls below, making it necessary to construct lean-to roofs between the lower and upper wall faces on three sides.

The masonry is varied, mainly comprising roughly coursed blocks of red sandstone, but with a mixture of buff-coloured sandstone blocks and a coarser purplish stone in places. Some of the lower quoins are extraordinarily long. There is a splayed base plinth on all sides, except the N wall of the wing, as also a splayed intake-course at the level of the hall-vault and another at first-floor level on the E wall of the main block only. These are unusual features in a Scottish tower house, but not uncommon in Northumberland (e.g. Etal, Cocklaw). The existence of a prominent straight joint in the S wall, at the junction of main block and wing, coupled with the makeshift vaulting arrangements in relation to the mutual wall within, suggest that the upper floors of the wing were commenced some time before the corresponding levels of the main block. Here and there the walls show signs of extensive damage (much of it probably inflicted during the siege of 1523) and subsequent repair. All the windows are plain, lintelled openings, the original ones chamfered, those of *c.* 1600 roll-moulded. The reconstruction of this latter date evidently included the use of fashionable ornamental detail, as witness the survival of a fragment of billet carving at the wall-head of the wing.

The tower was entered by upper and lower doorways in the re-entrant angle, both rebated for outer and inner doors. Some time before the siege of 1523 additional protection was given to this area by the construction of what Surrey described as a 'false barbican', evidently no more than a screen wall, some

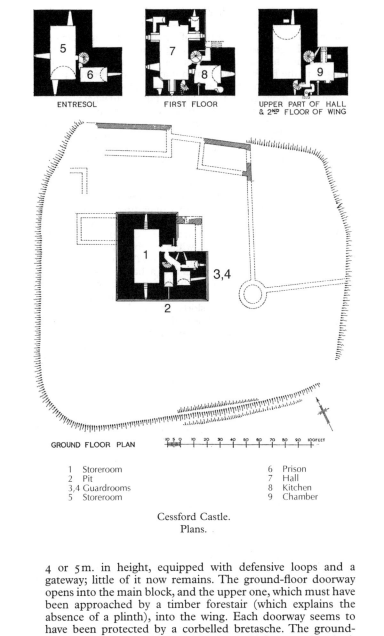

ENTRESOL   FIRST FLOOR   UPPER PART OF HALL & 2ND FLOOR OF WING

GROUND FLOOR PLAN

1 Storeroom
2 Pit
3,4 Guardrooms
5 Storeroom

6 Prison
7 Hall
8 Kitchen
9 Chamber

Cessford Castle.
Plans.

4 or 5 m. in height, equipped with defensive loops and a gateway; little of it now remains. The ground-floor doorway opens into the main block, and the upper one, which must have been approached by a timber forestair (which explains the absence of a plinth), into the wing. Each doorway seems to have been protected by a corbelled bretasche. The ground-floor entrance opens into a lobby from which a round-arched, chamfered doorway leads into the lowest floor of the main block, evidently a storeroom lit by slits to N and S. The entresol above, entered from the stair, was also a single compartment,

timber-floored and originally ceiled with a barrel vault. A door
on the s of the lobby gives access to a passage leading to the
stair and beyond that to two of the three tiny chambers that
occupy the ground floor of the wing. Two were probably guardrooms, the third an unlit pit-prison, formerly entered from a
hatch in the room above, which may also have been a prison.

The upper, and principal, entrance to the tower, placed
some 5 m. above ground, led via the stairwell to what was probably a great HALL; this occupied the full length of the main
block (12.2 m.) and rose some 6.1 m. to an open vault (now
collapsed). The hall was lit from four large windows on three
sides, all but one of them provided with bench seats. At the
centre of the N wall is a handsome, canopied chimneypiece
with moulded jambs and bases and carved foliaceous capitals;
on either side is a mural chamber, the E one evidently a latrine
and its neighbour perhaps a closet. Each was entered from an
adjacent window embrasure rather than directly from the hall,
so the occupants would have enjoyed a fair degree of privacy.
A third mural chamber, at the lower end of the hall, was
entered from the SW corner, while a doorway close to the SE
corner opened into a narrow spiral stair. At the level (or nearly
so) of the hall the wing contained a barrel-vaulted kitchen
which communicated with the hall both via the principal stair
and by means of a service hatch. The kitchen had its own fireplace and oven, as well as a slop-sink, but the only lighting was
from a deeply splayed window in the E wall. Above the kitchen,
and approached via the secondary stair at the SE corner of the
hall, was a well-appointed room in the wing with an en-suite
latrine. This was also provided with two good-sized windows,
one having bench seats and a cupboard in the embrasure, a
canopied fireplace (afterwards contracted) and a laver which
discharged through the s wall. The chamber also communicated directly with the main staircase and its position suggests
that, like the similarly placed room at Neidpath (q.v.), it may
have been allocated to the keeper of the castle.

The original layout of the upper floors of the tower is uncertain, but it is possible that the accommodation included a
second hall and associated chamber for the lord. As rebuilt *c.*
1600 the wing seems to have contained several superimposed
chambers, some equipped with latrine closets and roll-
moulded fireplaces. The unusual roofing arrangements must
have made it difficult to provide adequate lighting for these
rooms, and the two upper chambers seem to have been lit in
part from windows in the W wall, overlooking the re-roofed hall
vault, and in part by borrowed lights in the side walls (cf. Craig
Castle, Aberdeenshire). Additional accommodation was contrived by making use of two original chambers in the adjacent
(E) wall of the main block, which communicated with the wing
via the stairwell.

Little remains of the OUTBUILDINGS apart from two fragments of a two-storey range, on the N side of the tower, which
has a moulded window jamb of late C16 or early C17 appearance, suggesting that the N portion of the barmkin was
replaced by additional residential accommodation. Originally

the outworks seem to have formed an approximately rectangular enclosure measuring about 66 m. from N to S by 73 m. transversely, surrounded by an earthen bank and outer ditch, both now much reduced.

CHANNELKIRK *see* OXTON

CHARTERHALL HOUSE 7040
2.5 km. S of Fogo

1966 by *Cairns, Ford & Yuill* for Alexander R. Trotter. The present house replaced one of 1851 by *John Lessels* but incorporated its laundry, offices and a stone porch of 1857. Scottish Domestic with some Scottish Arts and Crafts detailing. Asymmetrical, two-storey and harled. On the S front a full-height porch and stair; to the l., the Trotter coat-of-arms carved by *David Kerr* for the earlier house. A large bow window on the S front.

SUNDIAL. Semi-cylindrical cross-shaped dial-stone with inscribed concave faces; ball-shaped finial with numerical inscriptions. – STABLES by *John Lessels* and *Balfour Balsillie*. Large court, a C20 groom's cottage at the entrance with bargeboarded gables. WEST LODGE by *John Smith*, 1842. Pretty Tudor. Cast-iron gates with spearheaded railings; a rose and buckled crest as decoration.

SOUTH LODGE by *Lessels*, 1865. Asymmetrical Tudor, well detailed with lead crockets, cast-iron cresting with flowers and fleur-de-lys. Ornamental cast-iron gates by *Robert McConnel & Co.*

CHERRYTREES 8020
1.3 km. NW of Yetholm

Small classical villa erected *c.* 1798, its design and date suggesting the hand of *William Elliot*.

Two-storey, basement and attic five-bay central block, the S front and side elevations of droved and polished ashlar, the rear elevation of rubble work on a rusticated basement. A metope and triglyph frieze, dentilled cornice and blocking course crown the wall-head, and in the centre is a pediment, originally decorated with three urn finials (one still on the garden wall) and an oval oculus. Spacious steps with curved stone balustrades terminate in stone piers linked to the low coped wall shielding the basement area. Doric-columned doorway with blocking course.

The single-storey and basement wings with canted bay windows were added by Adam Brack Boyd in 1852 to the design of *John Smith*; the stone supplied locally from 'Mr

Boyd's own quarry'.

Interior much altered in the 1960s with fittings imported from tenements in Edinburgh's New Town and St James Square, including beautifully executed enriched late C18 and early C19 timber and gesso chimneypieces with trademark details of seashells, fronds, thistles, roses and nautical references. On one, twin columns are banded together on the jambs and topped by Gothic niches with seashells; another has anchor motifs and lively fish.

The WALLED GARDEN, a rectangle of whinstone rubble with curved corners, was laid out and built by *Smith* in 1812. Of the C19 glasshouses along the N wall only the central conservatory survives. This has an inserted Gothic front, of semi-octagonal buttresses rising to chimney-like funnels, with pointed-arched openings and cusped glazing. The whole suggests some downtakings from a country house; there is a strong resemblance to the detailing on Inchrye Abbey (Fife) (1827; dem. from 1956). Immediately to the N of the house a mid-C19 square-plan WATER TOWER, linked to the reservoir.

STEADING to the NE. *c.* 1800 and later. Part demolished but formerly a substantial quadrangular group of courtyards. Converted to housing, a showroom and garages, 1997, by *Gibbon Lawson McKee*. In the centre of the largest court is a mid-C19 square two-stage dovecot and clock tower, now free-standing but originally attached to a range of buildings. The upper part is like a traditional tolbooth tower, with brackets cut at each corner above the lower stage, clock faces in hoodmoulded timber panels, a crenellated parapet with obelisk finials, and a slated pyramidal spire. The two-storey FARMHOUSE was converted *c.* 1838 to a threshing mill, with housing for the wheel attached. A fine range of eight segmental stone vaults (dated 1838) is built into the banked-up ground S of the reservoir and provides a large working platform above. – Good early C20 RIDING STABLES uphill from the steading. Timber boarding and rendered, with red round-edged roof tiles.

WEST LODGE, *c.* 1800. Ashlar and whinstone with a W bow. Sympathetic E addition of 1990 by *Povall Worthington*. Square gatepiers with cornice and caps, outer piers have urn finials and quadrant whinstone walls. – EAST LODGE (Garden Cottage). Late C19.

CHESTERS

Small agricultural village with a row of vernacular cottages, formerly a joiner's shop, blacksmith's house and smiddy.

CHESTERS CHURCH. The successor to the earlier church (*see* below), built in 1690 but itself threatening collapse by the early C18 and eventually superseded in 1874. Its principal remains are of the W gable, half of the S wall, and a short section of the N wall. The harled rubble W wall has two levels of rectangular windows, and at the gable apex is the stump of a bellcote. The S doorway with two orders of cavetto mouldings, and the jambs of the window to its E, together with the chamfered base course and areas of squared masonry along the s wall, are presumably from the old church. – MONUMENT, against internal w wall, Gothic red sandstone and polished granite memorial of Cunninghams of Abbotrule, first recorded death 1891. – CHURCHYARD. Good small headstones with *memento mori*, one with unusually realistic winged skull below winged angel head. Table tomb to s of church, the base having arcading with paired arches. Imposing Neoclassical aedicule for Rev. William Scott †1809. Some cast-iron memorials. Composite cast-iron Gothic 'headstone' with marble inset for John Scott †1854; table tomb for Rev. Thomas Thomson †1716 (struck by lightning after exorcising Wolflee House!), with replacement cast-iron plate of 1867; cast head plate for family of William Murray, erected 1871. – BURIAL ENCLOSURE of Elliots of Wolflee in sw corner of churchyard, channel-rusticated entrance.

SOUTHDEAN OLD PARISH CHURCH, Southdean. First recorded in the C13, though likely to have been a C12 foundation. Following the collapse of its roof in 1688, a new church was built at Chesters (*see* above), using much masonry from the old church. In 1910 the site was excavated and the exposed lower walls were consolidated, while the lower part of the tower was rebuilt to house the carved and moulded stones that had been found. (Traces were also found of what was thought to have been an earlier church a short distance to the N, though it is more likely to have been some ancillary building.) The church was a three-cell structure, like that at Stobo, with a rectangular chancel, a wider and longer rectangular nave to the w with two doorways in the side walls, and a w tower. From changes of detailing it was clearly the product of at least three building campaigns. The chancel had a two-stage chamfered base course and diagonal buttresses at the E corners, and was faced with high-quality ashlar, whereas the nave was unbuttressed and of rubble; the tower had a single chamfered base course and rubble walls. Fragments of architectural details and liturgical furnishings suggest the choir underwent sumptuous late medieval rebuilding, with canopied sedilia and piscina, at least one traceried window, and possibly even a ribbed vault. Still in place is the lower part of a tomb recess on the N side, and the projecting lower wall below the sedilia on the s side. – CHURCHYARD, now much trampled. Propped against the N nave wall, a small late medieval grave-slab with foliate cross head and sheep shears. Several C17 and C18 memorials.

SOUTHDEAN PARISH CHURCH. 1874–6 (former date above entrance) by *George Grant* of Glasgow. A buttressed rectangle of red rock-faced masonry, in the Early English style; there is a gabled w porch, a vestry on the E side, and a gabled bellcote on the N gable. Lit mainly by single lancets, but with small oculi on each side of the porch and vestry roofs, the s wall emphasised by a triplet of lancets. Roof with arch-braced collar-beams and upper scissor beams. – COMMUNION TABLE. Set into its upper surface is a small rectangular stone marked with five roughly incised crosses, found at the old church; it was presumably the seal stone for the relics set into the mensa of the high altar: an important survival (others have been found in the Borders at Coldingham Priory and Jedburgh Friary). – FONT, from the old church, octagonal with traces of a roll moulding to the upper edge. – STAINED GLASS, with one exception by *James Ballantine & Son*. S windows: Good Shepherd, David, St Paul. W windows, from S to N: Christ and Children, 'the glory of children are their fathers', Good Samaritan. E windows, from S to N: 'the bridegroom cometh', David, Christ Stilling the Waters (by *J.H. Baguley* of Newcastle). N windows: Moses, Joshua.

Former MANSE (Southdean House). *c.* 1795, with later canted bay windows and small gabled dormers. Traditional late C18 steading.

VILLAGE HALL. 1914. A large meeting room in harl-pointed rubble, with two extensions, and a flèche ventilator.

WAR MEMORIAL, *c.* 1920, a simple standing stone with carved cross.

KILNSIKE PELE. *See* p. 468.

MERVINSLAW PELE. *See* p. 565.

SLACKS PELE. *See* p. 687.

6020

CHESTERS HOUSE
2.7 km SW of Ancrum

Built for Thomas Ogilvie, second son of the laird of Hartwoodmyres, who returned home from India in 1786, purchased the Chesters estate in 1787, and commissioned *William Elliot* to build a new house, completed in 1790. Two storeys and attic, of seven bays with single-bay links, each with a corniced doorway, to low two-storey matching pavilions with Venetian windows. In coursed sandstone, with dressed surrounds and channelled quoins. A band course between ground and first floors and chimneystacks on the cross wall of the piended and platformed roof. Advanced centre defined by channelled pilasters supporting a pediment, formerly with urn-shaped finials. A bold Doric porch extends as an arcade in front of the adjacent bays, and the entrance doorway is lugged with moulded architrave. This feature, in grey sandstone, is probably later, perhaps by *John Smith* who was 'looking through the house' with William Ogilvie in 1831. Internally the plan is a central hall with staircase to the rear and one room in each corner. – STABLES. Quadrangular court, fronted in Palladian style with a keystoned arch pend and Diocletian opening above, linked to similarly detailed pavilions. – Mid-C19 gabled LODGE; plain bargeboards, a bracketed stone canopied doorway, and a stone-mullioned canted bay. Square obelisked gatepiers.

8050

CHIRNSIDE

Shown on Pont's map of *c.* 1590 as a cluster of houses on the N side of the church, the village seems to have assumed its present T-plan form well before the middle of the C18.

Main Street straggles along the exposed brow of Chirnside Hill, with Kirkgate descending s from Crosshill to the parish church. Housing in the late C18 and early C19 was confined principally to the s side of the e end of Main Street, now mostly altered, but one or two pantiled cottages remain. The rest of the street dates from the mid-to-late C19, with much infill in the mid-to-late C20.

CHURCHES

PARISH CHURCH, Kirkgate. Successive augmentations and remodellings have created an exuberant agglomeration of elements around an early C12 core. The rectangular plan of the medieval building is evident in the lower masonry of all four original walls. A later w tower is said to have been built, but was demolished c. 1750. A transeptal N 'aisle' was added after the Reformation, which may have been remodelled in 1705 (on the basis of a lost inscription) and again in the 1830s. Major restoration was carried out in 1878 by J. M. Wardrop, with much over-sized Romanesque Revival detail. This was upstaged by a restoration of 1907 by Sydney Mitchell & Wilson for the second Lord Tweedmouth in memory of his wife, Fanny (†1904), with major additions on the more visible w and N sides.

Externally, apart from the lower walls, the only survivor of the first church is a fine early C12 doorway, originally set within a salient towards the w end of the s face. Its slightly depressed chevron-decorated inner order is carried on engaged shafts with scalloped caps, while the outer order has a roll moulding carried on renewed disengaged shafts with cushion caps; it has a rubble tympanum above a lintel. The church is now dominated by the broad squat tower raised over the w end of the nave in the 1907 campaign. Capped by a saddleback roof behind a corbelled parapet, it is flanked and overtopped by a substantial N stair turret, with a spirelet and pinnacles; a porch projects w from its base. Also of 1907 are a hall and vestry N of the N 'aisle', with the screened Tweedmouth burial atrium in the space between tower, 'aisle' and hall. These, in a stylised Arts and Crafts version of Scottish Gothic, are what is seen when approaching from the village. Other additions of 1907 were a gabled open porch carried on cylindrical piers over the s doorway, and a small memorial 'aisle' for Fanny, Lady Tweedmouth in the angle between chancel and N 'aisle'.

Internally the restoration of 1907 left the liturgical arrangements little changed. The three arms are focused on the pulpit and communion table near the centre of the s wall, with galleries in all three arms. The scissor-braced roofs, pews and gallery fronts are also largely of 1878 and contrast markedly with the 1907 craft detailing within the w tower and the streamlined Gothic of the hall and vestry. Above the w gallery a vertiginous space rises to a flat panelled ceiling above an arcaded clearstorey passage within the tower. – COMMUNION TABLE, Romanesque arcading, W. & J. Jeffrey, 1911, more in the spirit of 1878 than 1907. – PULPIT, of same vintage and with similar Romanesque arcading; bobbin-turned balusters to stair. – RELIEF CARVING of Fanny, Lady Tweedmouth in N chapel by *Waldo Story*, dated 'Rome, 1896'. – INSCRIBED STONE, towards end of s internal wall, 'Helpe the Pvr 1573 VE'. – SUNDIAL, at SW angle, said to have been dated 1816.

CHURCHYARD, several good C18 memorials, including table tombs; Neoclassical obelisk to the Rev. Henry Erskine (†1696), father of two leaders of the Secession of 1732. – GATE, four-centred arch surmounted by crenellated wall, built 1910 to commemorate the second Lord Tweedmouth (†1909), by *Sydney Mitchell & Wilson*. – War Memorial in front of the church. A Celtic cross by *Robert Blackadder*, *c.* 1920.

Former FREE CHURCH, now Crosshill Community Centre. By *William J. Gray Jun.*, 1896–8. W entrance front of snecked buff rubble with echelon triplet of lancets above a lower triplet, and capped by octagonal spired bellcote. Flanked by polygonal lateral projections, that to the s containing the entrance.

PUBLIC BUILDINGS

CHIRNSIDE PRIMARY SCHOOL. *Reid & Forbes*, 1937–8. A striking Art Deco school prominently sited below a ridge and a landmark from miles around because of the tower above the entrance, which has a deeply recessed stylised doorway with engaged columns, a channelled cornice and polygonal finials. Above is a tall window with decorative glazing set in a deep niche, with a channelled apron, and a tiered and finialled canopy, and a channelled blocking course at the top with stylised South American motifs. Flat-roofed wings, that to the l. with a bowed end. Some Art Deco interior work survives, e.g. patterned granolithic flooring and the staircases, one with geometric-patterned iron uprights and consoled ends. Stepped quadrant walls flank the entrance steps to round-ended gatepiers with two-leaf wrought and cut sheet steel gates; the perfect entrance to this elegantly composed school.

CHIRNSIDE BRIDGE, 1 km. W. Built 1782 over the Whiteadder Water. Three segmental arches and a semicircular flood and access span in rubble work. Dentilled cornices to the parapet and pedestrian refuges carried up from triangular cutwaters.

CHIRNSIDE BRIDGE PAPER MILL, 1 km. W. Dated 1842, extended 1851 and 1897. Part demolished 1971–3. The original building, mostly of three storeys, with a tall brick stack to the rear, was designed by *David Cousin*. Sandstone with pink dressings to the front, and painted rubble and brick for the rest. Two piend-roofed blocks, the centre three bays gabled, each side of a two-storey three-bay gable-end. Stepped gables with finials. A plaque on the E gablehead is inscribed 'Y. Trotter & Son (limited) paper makers' and the dates of building. The excellent mid-C19 MANAGER'S HOUSE AND OFFICES is two-storey and basement with Italianate detailing. Broad eaves with timber ornamental brackets. On the W elevation the centre bay breaks the eaves, and has a pilastered doorway with narrow sidelights. Above, a pedestal with urn stands on a consoled block pediment. On the E elevation, the s window is in Gothic style with intersecting glazing bars, a hoodmould, and blind quatrefoil above, and below, a square-headed entrance for carts etc. Inside, some good plasterwork and a delicately finished

Gothic room, with much use of clustered columns, a white marble chimneypiece with carved ornament, and the cornice with cameo portraits in white and gold. Staircase with a cast-iron balustrade, and ball-finialled newels. – SUMMERHOUSE, octagonal with blind quatrefoil openings below a dentilled cornice, bracketed eaves and pyramidal roof.

CHIRNSIDE RAILWAY BRIDGE, NW of Chirnside Mill. 1863. Five-span round-arched viaduct, sandstone with channelled dressings and rock-faced piers. Disused.

CHIRNSIDE RAILWAY STATION, N of Chirnside Mill. Opened 1863 on the North British Railway's Berwickshire line. Former stationmaster's house and office, and timber-clad waiting room, with sliding timber doors and original fireplace.

JIM CLARK MEMORIAL, Crosshill. By *Ian Scott Watson*. A pylon incorporating a clock decorated with a model racing car, in the memory of racing driver Jim Clark, killed in Germany in 1968.

DESCRIPTION

There are some incidents along MAIN STREET from the E end. FIELD HOUSE, set back from the street on the N side, is possibly mid-to-late C18, with the upper windows tucked under the eaves, but remodelled in the mid C19. LOCHIEL on the N side before Crosshill, is a former United Presbyterian Manse of 1866. Gabled with Tudor detailing, and small single-storey wings. Its former church to the rear was replaced with housing by the *Kirk Care Housing Association*, 1984. Across the street a DRILL HALL with a projecting gabled front, its doorway flanked by engaged columns with composite caps, and inscribed in the gablehead '7th BBY [Borders Branch Yeomanry] 1870'. The hall has pointed-arched openings. At Crosshill is the former Free Church on the SE corner; the undistinguished buildings on the SW corner replaced a former school with a tall spire – its height and bulk much missed. The RED LION HOTEL on the N side apparently dates from the late C18 or early C19, but is now mostly mid-C19. Further W is CROFTS HOUSE, a former mid-C19 farmhouse with Jacobean curvilinear gables and dormerheads. At the W end ELM BANK was the former Ninewells School and Schoolhouse, an unendowed mixed school established by Miss Hume of Ninewells (*see* below). Dated 1851. Asymmetrical Neo-Tudor.

From Crosshill, KIRKGATE leads S, with THE OLD MANSE (former Glebe House) on the r. Built 1847 with later work by *James Stevenson*. Classical with an advanced pilastered doorpiece flanked by tripartite windows with narrow sidelights. At the foot of Kirkgate are the Parish Church and War Memorial (*see* above), and further E Chirnside Primary School (*see* above). BREWERY HOUSE on the W side is probably early C19, said to have been built by a wealthy publican, who erected 'large buildings for a brewery and malting, joined with a bakery'.* Two storeys, three bays, with a former stable and gig house to the rear. S elevation with a round-arched doorway,

---

* *New Statistical Account*, 1834.

the W with a bullseye window, repeated on the E elevation, and four-light canted oriel. The interior has decorative plasterwork, a dog-leg stair with capped newel posts and good fittings including shelved alcoves. To the NE is THE OLD BAKERY (Stob a Chion). Late C18. A three-bay house with a gabled addition. The N elevation of the four-bay, single-storey and attic bakery has a boarded opening with arched flight-holes, and projecting sandstone ledge above. Some early ovens inside, one inscribed '*James Cruikshank & Co*, Edinburgh', with fluted pilasters and segmental-arched pediment. On the opposite corner the early C19 WATERLOO ARMS HOTEL AND COTTAGE. L-shaped, and comprising a number of white-washed traditional blocks. Waterloo Cottage is harled with pink sandstone margins, and mullioned bipartite windows.

NINEWELLS HOUSE, the boyhood home, and later summer home, of the historian and philosopher, David Hume (1711–76), was rebuilt by *William Burn*, 1839–41, in a hand-some Tudor style, but demolished in 1954. Its C16 beehive DOVECOT survives N of the parish church in the garden of Auburn House. Red rubble sandstone with a continuous rat course, and a stone-slabbed, shallow-domed roof with a central opening, formerly protected with a finial of iron forked spikes. NINEWELLS WALLED GARDEN. S of village by the B6437. Early C19. Five-sided, with tall coped rubble walls, and some brick linings. The NORTH LODGE by *John Lessels*, 1852, stands on the A6105.

ROCK HOUSE (A6105). Marooned in trees by Chirnside Bridge. A picturesque oddity, perhaps intended as a lodge to Ninewells House. Only the front wall survives, of vitrified pieces of moss and other vegetation and partly built out of the solid rock. Pointed-arched windows on the ground floor, quatrefoil above. Formerly a weighty oak door opened to two rooms, occupied until the mid C20.

BILLIE CASTLE. *See* p. 122.

WHITEHALL HOUSE. *See* p. 759.

4010

CHISHOLME HOUSE

5.3 km. S of Roberton

High and remote on the moors above the S bank of the Borth-wick Water. Late C18, very likely by *William Elliot*, of three storeys and basement in harled rubble with sandstone dress-ings and channelled quoins. Three bays with Venetian windows flanking a central Tuscan tetrastyle portico, above which are two tiers of tripartite windows. Gabled early C20 rear exten-sion by *James Jerdan & Son*, with a conical roofed corbelled-out turret in the angle with the house. This has a decorative red sandstone feature in the gable-head and corbel motifs at the angles. Jerdan remodelled the interior with much use of timber panelling. Late C18 geometric stair. U-plan court of former stables and barn, with a two-storey house. Mid-C19, possibly with early C20 catslide wall-head dormers.

CLOVENFORDS   4030

A small village whose nucleus in the mid c18 was an inn and smithy, which served the carriage and coach trade after the new road between Galashiels and Peebles was opened in the early 1770s. The famous and profitable Tweed Vineries were founded 1869 but closed in 1959, and almost entirely cleared for housing in 1998. The pattern of the old village disappeared at the same time, when the crossroads became a large roundabout.

DESCRIPTION

In MILLBANK ROAD stands the former INN, described by Dorothy Wordsworth in 1803 as 'a simple stone house without a tree near or to be seen from it'. Remodelled c. 1980, with a simple late c18 appearance. Two-storeyed and harled. Four-bay s front with two doorways. To the N is SMITHY ROW, single-storey, harled cottages, attractively stepped to the slope, which appear to have been formed from the c18 former smithy. The two-storey CLOVENFORDS HOTEL, harled and lime-washed, was originally two early c19 three-bay villas with central doorways. In the W one the two flanking bays have had full-height bows added; wall-head dormers on the E one. In front of the hotel stands a pedestrian STATUE of Sir Walter Scott, looking suitably academic with scroll in one hand, the other resting on two books. His plinth is decorated with a shield, thistles and oak leaves. It dates from 1908, when it was first used in a cycle parade through Galashiels. The contemporary Galashiels press claimed that it was constructed with a metal frame, over which a set of clothes was draped, plastered and painted!

At the W end of Millbank Road is a late c18 hump-backed BRIDGE which carried the A72 over the Caddon Water. Quite shapely, rubble-built, with narrow whinstone voussoirs, and boulder coping. Further on is the surviving gable of the c18 school (the rest was demolished for road widening), known locally as 'The Luggie' and bearing a memorial tablet to John Leyden (†1811), antiquarian, physician, poet and Orientalist who taught here in 1792. Across its top is an inscription taken from Scott, 'A lamp so early quenched'.

At the E end of the village on the N side of the A72, the ground was feued in 1869 for the erection of three villas as summer residences. Two seem to have been erected, CRAIGVIEW, with two-storey canted bays, and the more interesting ROWAN-DEAN, which is gabled with overhanging bracketed eaves and has a small picturesque square bay with its own bracketed and slated roof. Down the Caddonfoot Road on the l. is WOOD-BURNSIDE, built c. 1870 for William Thomson, the owner of the Tweed Vineries. A tall two-storey and attic, three-bay, whin-stone house with a steeply pitched roof carrying two piended dormers. A timber porch with shaped bargeboards and finial. Round about is a collection of small industrial buildings associated with the vineries.

WHYTBANK TOWER. *See* p. 761.

7070   COCKBURNSPATH

James VI made Cockburnspath a free burgh of barony in 1612 with
the right to hold a weekly market and a yearly fair. It slumbered
until *c.* 1800, when the small village 'presented a most decayed and
miserable appearance'* and improvements were begun by Lady
Helen Hall of Dunglass (Lothian). These continued slowly until
the early C20, and since the 1960s the village has increased in size
with new housing on the w and se sides. Cockburnspath first
attracted 'The Glasgow Boys' in 1883, who spent their summers
painting the lush but dramatic landscape of gorges and cliffs.

Former FREE CHURCH, now church hall. By *William J. Gray
Jun.*, 1889–90; adapted as hall 1939. Rectangle of squared
whinstone with freestone dressings. Main (se) front with
central doorway flanked by lancets. Plate-traceried rose of
seven sexfoils; octagonal bellcote corbelled out at gable apex.
Arch-braced roof now largely concealed. – The OLD MANSE,
by *Stevenson & Son*, 1889–91, of two storeys, with a consoled
and corniced doorcase, and full-height canted bay.

PARISH CHURCH, The Square. Originally a chapel of Oldham-
stocks (Lothian), it became parochial *c.* 1610. In its late
medieval state it was of extended rectangular plan with walls
of pink sandstone rubble above a chamfered plinth course and
with diagonal buttresses at all four angles; much of this survives. The most striking survival is the head of a C13 traceried
window with a central quatrefoil between trefoiled light-heads,
re-set above the se doorway. Straddling the w wall is a unique
small circular tower, possibly of the later C16, to which an
upper stage with cruciform openings was added in 1827. The
other significant additions to the medieval plan were an e
burial chamber and a transeptal n 'aisle' which resulted in a
T-plan. The ashlar burial chamber has a barrel vault covered
by stone flags, and bore the date 1614 and the initials of
William Arnot. The n 'aisle' was perhaps first added in 1807
but has been much remodelled. The whole church has been
refenestrated with round-headed windows, while leaving traces
of earlier openings. It was restored and decorated by *William
Davidson* in 1925.

   Pulpit and communion table at the centre of the s wall. Galleries in the e and w arms have arcaded fronts, and are carried
on pairs of cast-iron columns. Ceilings of polygonal section,
following the profile of the rafters and collars. – PULPIT, with
intersecting arcading and arcaded backboard. – FONT, octagonal panelled bowl on quatrefoil pier, 1907. – STAINED GLASS,
central window in n aisle, Christ with Children, flanked by
simple foliate designs, *c.* 1906. – LEDGER SLAB in e vault, arms
and initials of Lady Jean Hay.

   CHURCHYARD, good range of C17 and C18 gravestones and
table tombs. John Miskin, †1732, winged angel with *memento
mori*; Thomas Lyal, †1768, rustic Baroque foliage. C19 predilection for obelisks culminates in the lavishly crocketed and finialled
memorial to James Aitchison (†1866). Prominent Tuscan ciborium monument to Rev. Andrew Baird, minister 1831–43.

* *New Statistical Account*, 1834.

OLD CAMBUS PARISH CHURCH OF ST HELEN, 2.5 km. E. The ruins of what must have been an unusually fine C12 church occupying a wind-swept site overlooking the North Sea. Two hogback stones suggest there was a church here from the C11, though the earliest parts of the existing structure are probably of the mid C12, when the church was a possession of Durham Cathedral. Following union with Cockburnspath (q.v.) c. 1610, the church fell into decline; masonry was removed c. 1861, and the E gable blown down in 1866.

Built of well-cut local red sandstone, the church was of two rectangular compartments. Remarkably, both parts were barrel-vaulted, and early views show that the chancel arch and window rear arches had chevron decoration and chip carving. Small rectangular recesses on each side of the chancel arch may have been associated with altars; more puzzling is a series of three seg-mental-arched recesses below the level of the S nave windows – were they inserted tomb recesses? Gaps in the masonry indicate the location of doorways on the two sides of the nave. The W wall, rebuilt probably in the C15, stands to a greater height than the rest. It has diagonal buttresses and a large number of putlog holes, and embodies much reused masonry.

CHURCHYARD. HOGBACK STONES, both probably C11. The first, by the E gable, has three panels with beasts on one side and three rows of tiling on the other; the second, less complete, is S of the chancel, and has a beast on one side and four rows of tiling on the other.

MARKET CROSS. Possibly C17. An irregularly stepped base supports a square shaft with splayed angles, swelling out at the top, the N and S faces carved with a thistle, the narrower faces with the Tudor rose.

OLD TOWER BRIDGE, 1.8 km. SE. A single-arched bridge spanning the Tower Burn. Probably built c. 1786.

PEASE BRIDGE, 0.8 km E of Old Tower Bridge. 1783, designed

Cockburnspath, Pease Bridge.
Engraving, after a drawing by Alexander Carse, c. 1790

by *David Henderson*, who was probably also the contractor. Built to avoid a dangerous pass over the Pease Dean, remarkable for its depth and picturesque scenery. At 130 ft (39 m.) high it was considered at the time to be the highest bridge in Europe, heralding the way for Thomas Telford's high viaducts. Four red sandstone arches. The middle pier rises from Pease Burn at the bottom of the gorge; the other two from the rocky sides. Each spandrel has an arched cylindrical void (2.7 m.).

PRIMARY SCHOOL. 1912 by *Gray & Boyd*. Single-storey, rendered with a whinstone base course. Gables and a bell-turret. Late C20 additions.

WAR MEMORIAL. 1920s. Celtic cross on a large inscribed base.

SPARROW HALL (Old Manor House), Causeway. A colourful group of buildings standing immediately SE of the Parish Church. The main components are two oblong blocks, possibly mid or late C16, founded at different levels and joined at one corner, where there is an extruded stair-turret. At one time the complex must have been a good deal larger, for there are traces of other buildings on the W side. The three-storey N block is constructed of local sandstone rubble with dressed margins and pantiled roof. Most of the window margins have quarter-round arrises, but some are chamfered. The ground floor comprises two barrel-vaulted cellars, one having an entrance door on the E side; this was blocked in the C18 or early C19 when a forestair was erected to give separate access to the first floor. A chamber at this level incorporated a boarded and joisted tempera-painted ceiling,* probably early C17, decorated with bunches of fruit and foliage, trophies and grotesque human heads; the predominant colours black and white touched with green and red. The S block, set obliquely to its neighbour, is constructed of similar materials, but is only two storeys high. The S wall contains a number of good-sized windows having surrounds wrought with edge-roll mouldings. Three closely spaced stone corbels of two members project from the W wall a little below the wall-head. It seems unlikely that these ever formed part of a continuous wall-walk, but it is possible that they originally supported a box-machicolation or, since there are no signs of a doorway below, a latrine serving an upper floor.

Any attempt at analysis must be speculative. Both blocks may formerly have been defensible and it is possible that they were originally erected as bastles by separate owners. Subsequently the complex seems to have become the principal residence, or manor house, of part of the Cockburnspath estate. To this phase may be attributed its enlargement and conversion to a single dwelling, as also the installation of the painted ceiling. The most likely owners at that period are the Arnott family of Edinburgh, merchants who had extensive interests in and around Cockburnspath prior to their enforced sale of the property in 1621.

DESCRIPTION

Most of the village's interest is found at THE SQUARE, which has in its centre the Market Cross (*see* above), and the Parish

*Discovered in 1987; now in the care of Historic Scotland.

Church (*see* above) set back on the E side. Its former MANSE is a spreading building of no particular architectural quality, connected with the graveyard by a garden door. Repaired 1791, 1808 and 1834, when most of what is seen was probably executed. The cobbled yard and stables were added *c.* 1880. On the S side of the church lane is an attractive Neo-Tudor former SCHOOL and schoolhouse by *Duncan Menzies*, 1870, with tall gables, and a wide stone-mullioned window in the N gable. Leading to the W is the CAUSEWAY: on the r. are late C18 pantiled cottages (repaired 1990), then Sparrow Hall (*see* above), and at the foot the OLD SMIDDY, which retains an L-shaped pantiled range. On the W side of the Square is the former WHITE SWAN, an inn, remodelled in the mid- to late C19. Deep eaves with exposed rafters, attractively shaped over wall-head dormers. Leaving the square to the N, on the l. are the former premises of GEORGE HAY & SONS, merchants, established in the C18 but closed in 1993 and awaiting restoration. Two-storey harled buildings, with a single-storey and pantiled block at each end, one a byre, the other a beer and wine store. Large windows on the ground floor, horizontal windows with deep reveals above, formerly with sliding sashes. Further along on the E side, HAWTHORN COTTAGE was the postmaster's house. Late C18, but on a garden wall is a cube SUNDIAL, with one gnomon remaining, inscribed IH – MV (John Home & Margaret Virtue). Home served as postmaster 1673–89.

FAST CASTLE. *See* p. 276.

COCKBURNSPATH TOWER
1.6 km. SE of Cockburnspath

Fragmentary remains of a C15 tower house and barmkin perched on the steep left bank of a tributary of the Pease Burn. The site is important strategically, for it lies immediately beside what must always have been the main E coast route into Scotland from the S. Possibly the early castle of Cockburnspath, belonging to the Earls of Dunbar and March, stood here, but the present one is more likely to have been built by the Humes, perhaps by Sir Patrick Hume of Fast Castle (q.v.), who was granted the lands of Cockburnspath, with its tower, in 1488.

The TOWER HOUSE, a simple oblong (10.7 by 8.8 m.), seems to have been almost entire, but roofless, when illustrated for Grose's *Antiquities of Scotland* in 1789. Since then the S half has been reduced to ground-floor level. The N half still rises in part to a height of three storeys, above which there may originally have been a fourth (not, however, shown by Grose). The masonry is of local red sandstone rubble with dressings of pink and white sandstone; the surviving margins have chamfered arrises. Much of the N wall is heavily buttressed, the masonry being strengthened by a series of splayed offset courses. A continuous, splayed string course also ran round the tower at second-floor level. An original entrance doorway, now blocked, is placed near the centre of the N wall; the opening, which is semicircular-headed, is rebated for an external door. Above it there seems to have been a slot-machicolation, manned from the first-floor window embrasure, but this was dispensed with when a single-storey extension was added to this side of the tower. The extension has since disappeared, but a chimney flue which was cut into the wall to serve it can still be seen. It is difficult to make much of the interior in its present tree-grown state, but the ground-floor chamber was evidently vaulted and the first- and second-floor chambers were lit by embrasured windows, some at least of which were equipped with bench seats. Grose's view shows a spiral stair in the SW angle of the tower.

The BARMKIN, or courtyard, occupied an oblong platform to the N and E of the tower. The W and E sides contained parallel ranges of offices, while the other two sides seem to have been filled by screen walls, that to the S incorporating the principal gateway to the castle. The E range is the earlier, probably dating from the latter part of the C16. It comprised three barrel-vaulted chambers, including what may have been a kitchen at the S end; above, there was presumably at least one other storey. One of the doorways opening into the barmkin formerly had a handsome roll-moulded and rusticated surround, fragments of which now lie scattered on the ground. In its present form the W range, one and a half storeys in height, may be as late as the C18. The binding mortar is mainly of clay and the masonry incorporates re-used fragments of earlier date.

9060

COLDINGHAM

Coldingham, set back from the sea, lies in a deep valley between two burns. By the late C18 the village mostly comprised crofts with roofs of turfs and divots, centred round Coldingham Priory and the Market Cross. Its development began in the late C18, when Coldingham Moor and other surrounding land was enclosed, and more profitable work enabled the thatched crofts to be rebuilt and slated, and new houses built. Progress must have been slow as by the mid C19 School Road (Crossgate) and Bogan were described as composed of 'inferior' houses. The village still retains much of its mid-C19 character, but in the early C21 new housing is becoming evident.

COLDINGHAM PRIORY

Coldingham has the only church of a religious house in the Borders of which a substantial part remains in use for worship; its monastic choir still serves as the parish church, though only the N and E walls now perpetuate the original design, the rest being chiefly of 1854–7. The partial preservation of the medieval church is particularly remarkable, since the priory had one of the most troubled later histories of any monastery in Scotland.

The predecessor of the priory was the double monastery of Urbs Coludi (see St Abbs), founded for both monks and nuns by St Aebbe before 661–4. The Benedictine priory originated c. 1098 in a grant by King Edgar to the cathedral priory of Durham. A church at Coldingham was dedicated c. 1100 in the presence of that king, though it probably did not become the home of a monastic community until the 1130s. This first church was replaced in the late C12 by the present building, work presumably being in progress when Prior Bertram of Durham encouraged donations towards the work (1189–1212). What remains of the church was completed in the early C13, perhaps delayed by an attack by King John in 1216. So far as later works are concerned, there are references to the highly esteemed English master mason *John Lewyn* being sent from Durham to Coldingham in 1364, but nothing remains identifiable of that date.

During the Wars of Independence, after 1296, the priory was frequently unsafe for the Durham monks, and after a long period of conflict Durham's claims over the house were eventually abandoned in 1478. Shortly before, James III attempted to have the priory refounded as a Chapel Royal, though the scheme foundered on the king's death in 1488. The priory suffered particularly badly during the later phases of the wars with England; it was burnt by the Earl of Hertford in 1542, again in 1544, and there was further destruction in Hertford's campaign of August 1545. There is nothing that can be linked with rebuilding after the onslaughts of the C16, though the excavated fragments of the chapter house may show fire damage. After the Reformation, the commendatorship was gained by Alexander Home, later first Earl of Home; the lands of Coldingham Priory and Jedburgh Abbey were together erected into a temporal lordship for him in 1606. The church was devastated by Cromwell's troops in 1648 but the choir was repaired for worship in 1661–2 by the mason *George Wilson Jun.*, of Canongate, Edinburgh, with the involvement of the royal master mason *John Mylne Jun.* Galleries were subsequently inserted. Views in Grose's *Antiquities of Scotland* (1789) show the rebuilt s and w walls, with heavily rusticated doorways, and shuttered windows possibly of Serlian type; there was also a tall bellcote rising from a buttress at the centre of the w wall. A major restoration of the choir was carried out in 1854–7 by *William J. Gray Sen.*, with *Balfour Balsillie* as mason. This involved reconstruction of the s and w walls, removal of the galleries and lowering of both internal and external ground levels. The work cost £2,200, of which £625 was contributed by the government. Gray's surviving drawings illustrate several alternative schemes, including proposals for a s transeptal 'aisle', an aisle running along much of the s flank, and a w vestibule, but a straightforward rectangular plan with a s porch was eventually adopted.

It is difficult to know when anything of THE CHURCH other than when the choir was built, since nothing remains of the aisled nave or N transept, while our understanding of the fragmentary s transept is vitiated by excessive rebuilding. However, it should be noted that construction of the chapels on the E side of the N transept must have involved modifications to work erected in the first building phase of the choir. This suggests that, on completion of the choir, there was a brief pause before work continued with the rest of the building, though resumption of work seems likely to have been within the first decades of the C13.

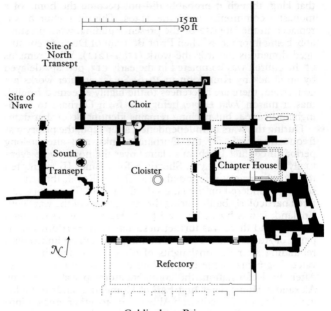

Coldingham Priory.
Plan.

PLAN. Excavations below the existing church in 1854–5 revealed what were probably the foundations of part of the church dedicated in 1100: an elongated aisle-less structure, only a little smaller than the later choir, with a semicircular E apse and a narrow square tower at its W end. Although possibly intended as a central tower, no evidence was found for a contemporary nave extending W, and it is possible that, although planned, no nave was built at that time. The late C12 church which replaced that first building had an aisle-less choir of eight tightly spaced bays, and this is now the only part to stand to full height. There may have been a sacristy of secondary construction against part of its N flank, and there were transepts with space for three chapels on the E side of each, those chapels slightly inset from the transept gables. Limited excavation has suggested that the aisled nave was about 39 m. long; some published plans show it as being of six bays. There are references to a tower rising to about 27.5 m. at the NW corner of the N transept and to an octagonal building having being located about 27.5 m. E of the church, but there can be no certainty about either.

EXTERIOR. The choir is constructed of finely jointed high-quality red sandstone ashlar, now crudely over-pointed. Its E wall is divided into three narrow bays by buttresses, and has square corner turrets of relatively wide projection with pronounced angle rolls. At the lower level of the façade each bay has decorative blind arcading, with two attenuated arches to each bay, rising from a quirked and chamfered string course, which is itself above a multi-chamfered base course. The detailing is notably refined, with the twin shafts at the centre of each pair of blind arches resting on a projection of the string course carried on a small corbel. The shaft caps are of waterleaf type and the round arches have two orders of chevron decoration. If the decoration of the lower storey is Transitional in character, at the upper level it is so pronouncedly early Gothic that it seems there could have been a slight pause between the two parts. The lancet windows piercing the upper stage, one to each bay, rise from a string course which steps up below each window. The window arches are framed by fine mouldings, with a keeled roll as the leading feature, which are carried on disengaged shafts with heavy shaft-rings at mid-height. The capitals of these shafts are of a variety of crocket and stiff-leaf forms, and most of the bases have pellet decoration. The pyramidal capping of the angle turrets and the coping of the low E gable date from the restoration of 1854–7.

The N wall of the choir is eight bays long, the wider W bay would have corresponded with the chapel aisle on the E side of the N transept. It resembles the E gable, but without chevron decoration to the wall arcading at the lower level. An inserted small arched recess in the third bay from the E (a piscina?) supports the suggestion that a sacristy was built against this flank. At the upper level of the W bay there is now a simple lancet in the E part, while at the lower level there are two pointed arches of blind arcading which clearly represent a later modification.

The choir's S and W elevations date entirely from the 1850s, albeit presumably incorporating masonry of the 1661 rebuilding. The S elevation has an enriched two-storey square porch W of centre, with a vestry on the upper floor; its gable is capped by a bellcote. Otherwise the S face is plain, with little more than a simple sequence of lancet windows above a stepped string course. The W elevation was rebuilt to closely follow the E elevation. W of this are the excavated remains of the W end of the choir and the tower of the earlier church. The base of the S respond shows that the W arch of that tower had jambs with a semicircular axial shaft attached to a rectangular core and flanked by smaller half-shafts.

INTERIOR. The finest feature of Coldingham is the design of the E and N walls of the choir interior. They belong within a northern English and Scottish tradition of aisle-less designs as seen at Ripon Minster, Nun Monkton Nunnery (Yorkshire) and St Bees Priory (Cumberland), and to which the rebuilt presbytery of Jedburgh Abbey (q.v.) may also have belonged. The leading features of this type are an unfenestrated lower wall, and an upper stage (or two upper stages in the case of Ripon nave and Jedburgh presbytery in its final phase) with windows, a mural passage and open arcading towards the interior.

At Coldingham the lower stage has a wall arcade of pointed 10 arches with keeled mouldings, between the heads of which are sunk foiled figures or vesicae; it was heavily restored in 1855, when the internal ground level was lowered by 1.4 m. and the bases rediscovered. The upper stage has an arcade of pointed arches on the inner face of the wall passage. Tall arches correspond to the windows while there are shorter arches in front of the unpierced sections of wall; the higher arches rise from engaged shafts resting on the abaci of the shorter arch capitals. Along the E wall there is a simple alternation of one short arch between each tall arch, with the stumps of what appear to have been sub-arches within the lower arches. Along the N wall there are two shorter arches between each of the higher ones, except at the W end, where there are three shorter arches. There is no correspondence of rhythm between the lower and upper stages.

The capitals of the upper arcading, all with square abaci, represent one of the most important groupings of early Gothic foliage types in Scotland, being of comparable significance with the N nave aisle wall arcade capitals of Holyrood Abbey (Edinburgh) of *c.* 1195. The combination of waterleaf, crocket and stiff-leaf forms of varying degrees of complexity, and in no obvious chronological sequence, richly deserves fuller study. The larger piers have clusters of five engaged shafts with the leading one keeled; those between the pairs of shorter arches have paired shafts separated by a spur. The bases are of water-holding form.

Of the arcading which once ran along the S wall, only the upper E shafts survived to the rebuilding in the 1850s. The reconstructed W wall has a simplified version of the two levels of arcading of the E and N walls, albeit without the wall passage. Also dating from the 1850s is the flat-ribbed ceiling, with arched braces at the junction of the transverse ribs with the side walls.

Reordering of the interior by *Gordon & Dey* in 1955 focused worship on the communion table at the E end, rather than the pulpit against the S wall. Bland furnishings. – STAINED GLASS. Fragments of medieval glass are in the National Museum of Scotland in Edinburgh and in Eyemouth Museum; most are grisaille of the first half of the C13, but among later pieces is a fragment depicting a human face. Within the CHOIR – E WALL: N, Nativity *c.* 1876; central, Crucifixion *c.* 1903; S, Ascension *c.* 1890, all *Nathaniel Bryson* of Edinburgh. – N WALL: third from E, War Memorial window, 1921 (a knight offered a martyr's crown), *G. Baguley & Son* of Newcastle; then from r. to l.: St Luke and Visiting the Sick *c.* 1959; heraldic, *Robert Home* of Edinburgh; heraldic *c.* 1895; Consider the Lilies *c.* 1898, *G. J. Baguley* of Newcastle. – PORCH: E window, abstract design, *Joanna Scott*. – MONUMENTS. W of the church, within the earlier crossing, simple inscribed tombstones to Priors Radulf (*c.* 1203) and Ernald (*c.* 1207–11). Set vertically along the external W wall of the S transept several cross-inscribed gravestones, and a medley of architectural and sepulchral fragments.

THE TRANSEPTS. The only other part of the church to have upstanding remains is the S TRANSEPT, and what survives of that has been extensively rebuilt. The piers opening into the three-bay chapel aisle, of which only stumps survive, were unusual in their elongation along the E–W axis: towards the transept itself was a spaced pair of round shafts, while there was a triplet of round shafts to N and S supporting the arcade arches; on the E side of the piers was a cluster of five closely spaced shafts to support the vault ribs over the chapels. The surviving arch into the transept from the s nave aisle has a round arch carried on responds with triplets of shafts, and with an order of dogtooth towards the transept. Internally, the s and w walls of the transept had pointed decorative arcading at the lower level, carried on single engaged shafts, the one surviving capital of waterleaf type. Nothing remains of the upper parts of the transept. At the SE corner excavation revealed a stair-turret of unusually generous proportions. A displaced cushion capital in the s transept presumably comes from structures associated with the early church.

The N TRANSEPT has entirely disappeared, apart from the s arches of the decorative arcading of its SE chapel where it ran along the outer face of the W bay of the choir. The way this arcading overlays the plinth and arcading of the choir as first built, and the pronounced filleting rather than keeling of the main element of the arches, indicate that these chapels involved a change of design. A drawing of 1851 appears to show the arcade arches rising no higher than the decorative arcading against the choir wall, with rectangular piers and responds with angle rolls. There was an arch into each chapel, separated by a lower blind arch.

The remains of the CONVENTUAL BUILDINGS are insub-stantial; they were first excavated in 1890–1 and on several occasions in the C20. They flanked the s side of the choir rather than the nave, a most unusual arrangement, but one that has parallels, e.g. at Rochester. At Coldingham their location was perhaps because they perpetuated the site of earlier conventual buildings against the choir of the first church. The undercroft of the REFECTORY, known traditionally as 'Edgar's Walls', was first excavated in 1890–1. On the s side of the cloister, it was a structure of seven by two bays with rubble walls, but evi-dently with ashlar quoins and plinths to the buttresses along the sides away from the cloister. The undercroft vaulting, in square compartments, was carried on single shafts along the walls (except at the angles, where it was corbelled), and by a central row of piers. The shaft bases, with two superimposed rolls, suggest an early C13 date. The remains of the E range are even less complete and much has been covered over since exca-vation. Abutting the SE turret of the choir were the lower walls of a slype of two square compartments defined by wall-shafts. To its s are the remains of the CHAPTER HOUSE. The provi-sion of stepped seats in the E portion (now obscured) and of heavy single wall-shafts in the W portion suggest the space was divided into vestibule and chapter house proper. Foundations located s of the chapter house, which project to its E on an irregular alignment, may have been of the reredorter under-croft. Within the cloister garth, footings have been located of the inner walls of the walks along the E and s sides.

CHURCHES AND PUBLIC BUILDINGS

Former UNITED PRESBYTERIAN CHURCH. Now semi-derelict. 1870, by *William J. Gray Jun.* on the site of a church of 1793; secularised 1952. A T-plan structure with porches in the SE and SW angles, the former originally capped by a low spire. The principal S and E faces are of pink stugged ashlar, the others of rubble; triplets of lancets predominate. Large garage doors have been cut through the E and W walls, and little but the E gallery and an arch-braced roof survive within. The hall to the SW, built to commemorate the Rev. Andrew Brodie Robertson (†1899), remains in use.

COLDINGHAM PRIMARY SCHOOL, School Road. Board School, dated 1893, single-storey, with a coursed rock-faced sandstone front, and moulded eaves. Central curvilinear gable, with Tudor-detailed pedimented niche framing a datestone, supporting a bellcote and weathervane. Round-arched tripartite windows in the flanking stepped gables. Late C20 flat-roofed brick-built classrooms at the rear.

MARKET CROSS, School Road. Dated 1815, said to occupy the site of an earlier cross. A classical column, supported on a circular base, and surmounted by a square stone block carved with the Home crest on one side. On each of the other three sides was a sundial, mostly worn away. An urn-shaped finial on top.

PUBLIC HALL. Late C19. Coursed cream sandstone front with a finialled gable and gableted skewputts. Inside, a hammer-beam roof with decorative springers and carved pendants.

WAR MEMORIAL, corner of High Street and School Road, in a small garden. 1923, signed *J. Wood & Sons* of Coldingham. Classically detailed with an inscribed face and carved wreath above. On top is a square sundial.

DESCRIPTION

Most of the late C18 and early C19 houses were remodelled in the mid- to late C19. Starting from the NE at the foot of FISHER'S BRAE is BURNBANK on the r. An early C19 three-bay house, with brick relieving arches, and a single-storey C18 pantiled cottage attached. TEVIOT HOUSE on the l., a pantiled, two-storey and attic house set into the hillside, is probably late C18. Sandstone rubble with brick relieving arches over the ground-floor windows. One or two traditional single-storey pantiled cottages remain, mostly rather altered, otherwise there has been some demolition and late C20 infill. On the r. is CHRISTISON'S BRAE, leading to BOGAN: a row of late C18 and early C19 cottages said to have been built for weavers. Originally mostly single-storey, with gardens back and front. Most have been raised a storey and given wall-head dormer windows. GRACEHURST, on the l. of the brae, is set on a steeply sloping site. Two storeys and attic, *c.* 1800, with a steeply pitched pantiled roof and battered basement.

HIGH STREET continues uphill from Fisher's Brae. Mostly mid-to-late C19, some conveniently dated. At the top on the l. is FERN NEUK. A harled two-storey, three-bay house closing in the end of a terrace, with a quirky gabled porch with squat, square bulbous columns on a solid balustrade, with engaged columns behind. Curved stone wall-head dormers above. Canted windows to the side elevations with tiled roofs, and lying-pane glazing. On the r. the War Memorial (*see* above).

Part of the centre of Coldingham has been destroyed by the building of a large garage. SCHOOL ROAD (formerly Crossgate) leads uphill to the W. On the r. is a short terrace of three houses, basically late C18, with later alterations. BARRIE HOUSE retains its depressed-arched cart opening; BROMLEY HOUSE has a steeply pitched roof with scrolled skewputts, and the early C19 ANCHOR INN has lightly rock-faced render. Across the road, and not set off to its advantage, is CROSSGATE HOUSE, the best C18 survival. It is tall with a steeply pitched pantiled roof, and crowstepped gables with moulded skewputts, one on the rear with a carved head.

Next on the l. are OLD SUNNYBANK and THE BARN. The first is pantiled, two storeys, and harled, with pink sandstone dressings with wide chamfered margins. Its door lintel is inscribed 'RC MY 1724'. The Barn, part of a late C20 conversion of three pantiled cottages, bears a similar lintel inscribed 'RC MY 1738'. Was this a piece of early development, perhaps for Robert Cossar, a local inhabitant? Both houses have capped gatepiers. COURTBURN HOUSE, a former school, is basically late C18, with additions and alterations. Two storeys and three bays, with a single-storey wing set back to the l., and a later two-storey wing set back to the r. Flanking single-storey additions have crenellated parapets. Harl-pointed rubble to the main block, with pink sandstone dressings. The rear elevation with a circular first-floor window fronts School Road. Late C20 housing on the r. before the Primary School, and the entrance to Bogangreen House (*see* below).

BRIDGE STREET leads S from the cross. In the mid-C19 this was the shopping street, with an inn, Post Office, and draper's and grocer's shops. First on the l., the NEW INN. Perhaps early C19. Two-storey, three-bay L-plan block, with a tall, two-bay stable and hay loft to l., and a curved corner to the NE. The POST OFFICE is late C18, two storeys, and formerly a three-bay house with scrolled skewputts. Its projecting three-bay classically detailed shopfront is C19, with large windows flanking a centre door, framed by pilastered quoins and a continuous bracketed cornice. Opposite the Post Office, GLENCOURT COTTAGE lies back from Bridge Street. This was a former dame's school. Two storeys and three bays, four on the ground floor. Its steeply pitched roof and scrolled skewputts suggest a late C18 date. Later alterations. Further on the r. is the richly ornamented ABBEY COTTAGE, dated 1840, with Neo-Jacobean strapwork decoration. Its porch has decorative carving round an oval date panel, a thistle and fleur-de-lys motifs above, in a stepped and scrolled gable with an urn-shaped finial. The angles of the front have corbelled concave niches with foliate stops beneath polygonal angle shafts. Four-light canted bays each side of the entrance with decorative waterspouts below parapets that have foliate and floral friezes.

Off to the l. from Bridge Street is THE ROW, leading to the Priory (*see* above). BURNLEA by the S entrance to the Priory is early C19. Two storeys, three bays, and a single-storey piend-roofed pantiled earlier wing. Narrow quoin strips. At the end of The Row are the pyramidal-capped gatepiers to the MANSE (Benedict House). Built 1801, when it faced the graveyard. Repaired

1828, and perhaps extended at this date for dining room, drawing room and new stair. Though much remodelled and added to from 1849 by *John Lessels* and *William Waddell*, the dining room retains good plasterwork.

BOGANGREEN HOUSE, West Loch Road. Smart late C18 farmhouse. Pedimented doorway formerly flanked by Venetian windows. Its steading and walled garden survive. Pyramidal-capped gatepiers, hooped-iron gate and quadrant walls.

BONARDUB, Eyemouth Road. Asymmetrical Arts and Crafts seaside villa of 1901 for Miss E.B. Simpson. Harled and whitewashed with pantiled roof, and overhanging timber bracketed eaves and bargeboards. Veranda under a swept roof.

MELVILLE HOUSE, Eyemouth Road. *c.* 1900, with Scottish-Renaissance detailing.

HALLYDOWN FARM, 2.8 km. SE. Late C18, classical; the refined details rare in a simple Berwickshire farmhouse of this date. Perron stair with a good iron balustrade. Tall round-headed keystoned stair window at the rear.

PRESS CASTLE. *See* p. 640.

8030

COLDSTREAM*

Small town which probably began as a settlement next to the Cistercian nunnery beside a ford across the River Tweed which had been founded by Gospatrick, Earl of Dunbar, in the mid C12. In 1621 Coldstream became a burgh of barony under the superiority of Sir John Hamilton of Trabroun, the former commendator and now feudal baron of the priory lands. The present town was probably laid out soon after around a market square, and in 1705 the site of the parish church was moved to Coldstream from Lennel 2 km. to the NE. Following an act of Parliament in 1762 a turnpike road was formed from a new bridge over the Tweed downstream of the town and passed along the town's N side to a second new bridge over the Leet Water and thence towards Edinburgh. Building feus were offered for sale along this road in 1771 and Coldstream's present High Street developed soon after. Much of the older part of the town was rebuilt in the C19 but with only a modicum of industrial development. C20 expansion has been to the N.

CHURCHES

Former COLDSTREAM FREE CHURCH, Victoria Street. Now a bar. First built in 1846 as a simple rectangular structure, and greatly enlarged in 1891; secularised after 1950. The principal 1891 addition was a frontispiece of buff stugged masonry, with a four-storey tower at the NW corner. That tower has windows of two, three, one and two lights from bottom to top, each face being capped by a gable framing a clock face, with a high weathervane behind. The centre of the front is gabled, with a three-light traceried window; arched doorway below now con-

---

* The account of Coldstream, except for the churches, is by John Gifford

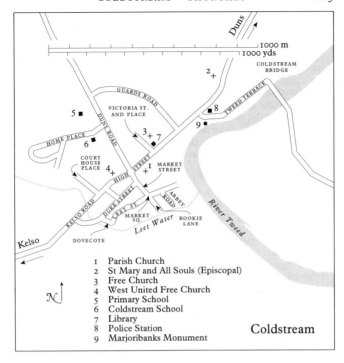

1000 m
1000 yds

COLDSTREAM
BRIDGE

2 +

GUARDS ROAD

VICTORIA ST.
AND PLACE

5 ■

DUNS ROAD

8 ■

TWEED TERRACE

HOME PLACE

6 ■

3 + 7

9 ●

COURT
HOUSE
PLACE

4 +

1 +

HIGH STREET

MARKET
STREET

KELSO ROAD

DUKE STREET

LEET ST.

ABBEY ROAD

MARKET
SQ.

BOOKIE
LANE

Leet Water

River Tweed

Kelso

DOVECOTE

N

1 Parish Church
2 St Mary and All Souls (Episcopal)
3 Free Church
4 West United Free Church
5 Primary School
6 Coldstream School
7 Library
8 Police Station
9 Marjoribanks Monument

Coldstream

cealed by a bland insert made when the church was used as a cinema. s of the front is a lower gabled section with a single lancet.

Former COLDSTREAM WEST UNITED FREE CHURCH, High Street. Now St Cuthbert's Church Centre. Built in 1907 by *George Reavell Jun.*, secularised 1963. English Perpendicular style, with attractive Arts and Crafts nuances; the walls of pink snecked rock-faced rubble with polished dressings. Basically T-shaped, with transeptal projections at the NW end, and with offices to the W and N. The main SE front has a salient gabled section with a squat six-light window within a depressed two-centred arch, above a deep-set doorway with chamfered jambs and a moulded segmental arch. Most prominent is the heavily buttressed tower at the S angle, which dominates the western approaches to the town. Above rubble lower walls, the tower's belfry stage has pairs of two-light traceried windows continued up into blind panelling, above which is a deep crenellated parapet framed by stocky pilasters, the upper part being pierced. – STAINED GLASS, by *Percy Bacon & Bros* of London and *Ballantine* of Edinburgh.

PARISH CHURCH. High Street. A church of 1795 by *Alexander Gilkie* was rebuilt in 1906–8 by *J.M. Dick Peddie*, incorporating the late C18 W tower. It is a slightly forbidding structure of buff rock-faced snecked rubble with polished ashlar dressings and parapet. The five-bay nave has its main front facing N, with a porch in the second bay from the E; a short chancel of one bay is to the E. Round-headed windows, except for the oculus above the porch, have lugged architraves with keystones on the more visible N and W sides. The W wall has shaped semi-gables on each side of the tower. The latter's lower storeys, which incorporate an entrance, were re-cased in ashlar with emphasised block quoins; the clock stage has recessed Tuscan columns at the angles, and the top stage is octagonal with a low stone spire. Internally, arcades of Tuscan columns rise from octagonal plinths; the aisles and chancel have groined plaster ceilings and the nave a barrel ceiling. – PULPIT, stone, 1906. – STAINED GLASS, E window, First World War memorial; windows in S aisle of 1934 and 1951.

St MARY AND ALL SOULS (Episcopal), at the far NE end of the town. Of pink Doddington rubble with polished dressings, it was built in 1913–14 by *Charles T. Ewing* of Crieff. An Early English buttressed rectangle, aligned from N to S, its walls running without break into a semicircular N apse. Timber porch against the S bay of the E flank, and vestry and schoolroom against the W flank; gabled bellcote above the bargeboarded S gable. The windows are mainly single or paired lancets without hoodmoulds, but there is a triplet in the chancel bay, and another in the S wall. Internally, the open-timber roof combines scissor-braces and arch braces. Around the apse, painted decoration by *Mrs Ellington* consists of rose trails, lilies and sacred monograms. – RETABLE, oak, with painted Virgin and Child, St Catherine and St Andrew. – PULPIT, octagonal with openwork tracery, 1926. – FONT, small stone octagon on polished shaft, 1900. – STAINED GLASS, apse, Crucifixion and Noli Me Tangere; E side choir, Good Shepherd; schoolroom, trefoil with Dove (relocated from earlier church).

PUBLIC BUILDINGS

COLDSTREAM BRIDGE, 0.7 km. NE. A very fine bridge with five segmental arches, each of 18 m. span and smaller segmental land arches at each end; constructed 1763–6. Designed by *John Smeaton* for the Tweed Bridge Trustees, borrowing the architectural devices – triple projecting keystones to the main arches, modillions under a plain cornice at the parapet base and, in each spandrel, a blackened blind-eye decoration surrounded by a masonry ring with projecting keystones on its horizontal and vertical diameters – from an earlier design by *Robert Reid* of Haddington, who became resident engineer for the work. Smeaton used these devices on his later bridges at Perth and Banff in Scotland and at Hexham in Northumberland. Downstream cauld (weir) added *c.* 1784. The bridge's foundations were protected with concrete in 1922 and the bridge was strengthened with concrete relieving arches and widened by cantilevered footpaths in 1960–1.

COLDSTREAM COTTAGE HOSPITAL, Kelso Road. By *John McLachlan*, 1888. Single-storey, built of stugged masonry. Display of gables and gablets at the broad-eaved roof.

COLDSTREAM HEALTH CENTRE, Kelso Road. Built in 1976. Single-storey T, with harled walls and concrete tiled roofs.

COLDSTREAM LIBRARY, High Street. Originally Mechanics' Institute. By *James Cunningham*, 1861–3. Tall and narrow two-storey, three-bay temple front of stugged ashlar, with polished ashlar pilasters and overall pediment. Cornices and vestigial block pediments skied over the ground-floor windows. Longer s side elevation to Victoria Street but also of three bays with three-light ground-floor windows and Venetian windows above.

COLDSTREAM PRIMARY SCHOOL, Home Place. By *Reid & Forbes*, 1956–7. Traditional in general composition, a long two-storey pitch-roofed block with a steeply gabled advanced centrepiece, but the windows form almost continuous horizontal bands.

COLDSTREAM SCHOOL, Home Place. Now in other use. The first part, at the rear, was built in 1858. Broad-eaved school with hoodmoulded windows and an empty bellcote on the s gable; schoolhouse on its e side. w extension by *George Duns*, 1899–1900, a tall single storey with a broad, gabled centrepiece to the w front; bracketed eaves.

MARJORIBANKS MONUMENT, Tweed Terrace. By *John Hay* of Liverpool, 1834. Over 24 m. high, consisting of a corniced ashlar pedestal on which stands a tall fluted Doric column surmounted by a drum topped by a statue of the striding figure of Charles Marjoribanks, M.P. for Berwickshire. The original statue by *A. Handyside Ritchie* was destroyed by lightning in 1873, its replacement of 1874 carved by *Andrew Currie*.

POLICE STATION, High Street and Tweed Terrace. Dated 1868. Villa-like, with mullioned windows and bargeboarded gables. Two-storey rectangular bay window to the e, its upper floor projected on continuous corbelling and covered with a slabbed roof.

DESCRIPTION

KELSO ROAD, the entry from the sw, begins with the Coldstream Cottage Hospital and Coldstream Health Centre (*see* Public Buildings, above). Then, on the r., the harled LADIESFIELD of 1953. Neo-Georgian, the main block with a pedimented doorpiece, a three-light window in the r. bay of the first floor and a tall window in the l. bay. It is followed by a lodge to The Hirsel on the l. of the road and the lodge and gateway to The Lees (qq.v.). Just N of these, on the l., LEES FARM COTTAGES, an early c19 piend-roofed rubble-built row of three cottages, the l. door now a window. Immediately to their w, at a lower level beside the Leet Water, LEES FARM, a late Georgian piend-roofed courtyard steading, the two-storey ranges with segmental-arched cartshed openings and small first-floor windows. The courtyard is now filled with a utilitarian shed. To the e of the road, a path leads to the stables of The Lees (q.v.).

The town proper begins N of the Leet Water. e of the main road and overlooking the river, Nos. 1–3 DOVECOTE, a rubble-built (partly harled) cottage terrace of *c.* 1800 dressed up as an asymmetrically composed eyecatcher with Gothic ground-floor windows and doors, battlemented screen walls at the end gables, and a couple of battlemented towers, one with a quatre-foil window at the upper floor, the other's square upper window under a huge crosslet dummy arrowslit. The terrace fills the space between the s ends of DUKE STREET and LEET STREET. In both, C19 Georgian and Georgian survival vernacular domestic architecture but also housing by *R.A.C. Simpson* of *Oldfield, Simpson & Saul*, 1961. This is a determined evocation of C17 Scotland, the walls harled or of hungrily pointed rubble, the roofs pantiled and with scrolled skewputts. Pulvinated friezes at the corniced doors of Nos. 16–20 Duke Street. Forestairs at Nos. 33–4 Duke Street and Nos. 18–19 Leet Street.

HIGH STREET carries the main road N of the Leet Water. Its w side starts with the early C19 two-storey Nos. 1–3, originally a single house with a bowed s end containing Venetian windows. Scrolled skewputts to the main block, whose E front was originally of three bays. On the house's division into two in the late C19 an additional door was inserted and a two-storey, very shallow rectangular bay window added. One house is now pebbledashed, the other covered with render imitating bullnosed masonry. The street's norm is two-storey late Georgian and C19 Georgian survival terraced housing. At No. 10, of the early C19, a consoled cornice to the door. The three-storey CASTLE HOTEL is of *c.* 1800 with club skewputts at the gables and central gablet. At the top of COURT HOUSE PLACE to its N, COURT HOUSE LODGE, the former burgh court house and lock-up of *c.* 1800 and now rather altered. It is a square pavilion-roofed building of two storeys, the ground floor's stonework rock-faced; round-headed windows (some dummies) to the first floor.

At Nos 16–20 High Street, on the E side, more housing of *c.* 1960, also by *R.A.C. Simpson*, like that in Duke Street and Leet Street. Harled and pantiled, with scrolled skewputts and a ball finial at the projecting gabled centrepiece; pulvinated friezes at the corniced doorpieces. Nos 15–19 High Street on the w side form an early C19 two-storey and basement terrace, the first floor marked off by a string course. Ashlar front (partly painted) of seven bays, with channelled quoins and a mutuled eaves cornice. Heavy pilastered and corniced doorpiece to No. 17 at the slightly advanced centre. At No. 15, a quite delicate console-corniced doorpiece. Consoled cornice but much heavier and looking like a replacement of the later C19. Scrolled iron balustrades to the flyover stairs to the entrances. Then, No. 19, its door with a blocky consoled cornice, of the earlier C19. At No. 25 of *c.* 1800, a consoled pediment over the entrance and a moulded eaves cornice. This house is muscled into by the early C19 No. 27, whose front is of ashlar, polished and with square-jointed rustication at the basement, polished at the ground floor and broached at the first; heavy pilastered and corniced doorpiece. The flyover entrance stair has balustrades of the same design as those of Nos. 15–19. Then, the burgh's WAR MEMORIAL, by *George Washington Browne*, 1922–3. Polished ashlar segmental screen

wall with ball-finialled gatepiers (to Home Park) at the ends
and a cenotaph in the centre. It stands beside the former Coldstream West United Free Church (*see* Churches, above).
Further N, on the S corner of Duns Road, No. 37 High Street
of the mid or later C18. Ashlar front with rusticated quoins, the
ground floor now with a Georgian survival shopfront of the
mid or later C19 and a late C19 two-light window. Between
the windows of the first floor and the moulded eaves cornice,
four panels, the centre two oblong, the outer two oval.

In DUNS ROAD, on the corner of Home Place, THE MANSE
(originally Coldstream Free Church Manse), a substantial
Georgian survival villa of *c.* 1860. Three-bay front, the door
flanked by two-light ground-floor windows. In HOME PLACE,
the former Coldstream School and Coldstream Primary
School (*see* Public Buildings, above).

On High Street's S corner with Market Street, the NEWCASTLE
ARMS HOTEL. The main part is an early C19 piend-roofed
square block of three bays by three. The W front's doorpiece
has a consoled segmental pediment. At the N elevation, a
Venetian ground-floor window. Mid-C19 S wing with elliptical-
arched coach house openings.

In MARKET STREET, C19 Georgian and Georgian survival vernacular. More of the same in the irregularly shaped MARKET
SQUARE. Rising above its surroundings is the three-storey
CHEVIOT HOUSE (Nos. 27–8 Market Square) of *c.* 1870.
Ashlar front with Jacobean Renaissance detail. Original
shopfront and an Artisan Mannerist door. Lugged architraves
to the elliptical-arched first-floor windows. The second-floor
windows rising through the eaves are set in Corinthianish
pedimented aedicules. The pend under No. 24 Market Square
gives access to WHITHOUSE SPRINGHILL, a mid-C19 store
converted to a house by *Tom Pyemont*, 1996. Rubble-built main
block of two storeys, the upper floor at the E end added in
1996. At the W gable, a first-floor entrance, the line of its
missing forestair visible in the masonry. Single-storey SE jamb,
its timber-clad W wall of 1996. Inside, the drawing room occupies the whole of the jamb, the original roof structure retained
and exposed. In BOOKIE LANE, remains of the Late Georgian
rubble-built COLDSTREAM BREWERY. At the SE end of
ABBEY ROAD, the early C19 ABBEY HOUSE with a wrought-
iron Regency porch at the SE front and a Venetian window in
the NE gable.

In HIGH STREET N of Duns Road and Market Street, Coldstream Parish Church (*see* Churches, above) on the E. Set back
from the street immediately to its S, a rubble-built two-storey
grain mill of *c.* 1890. On High Street's W side, the early C19
Nos. 51–3, the ground floor with square-jointed rustication
and a consoled cornice to the door; mansard roof, probably
provided *c.* 1900. No. 59, perhaps of Late Georgian origin, was
given a new front *c.* 1900. This is stripped Jacobean with a
steeply pitched gablet and crown-spired buttresses. It is followed by an early C19 two-storey, basement and attic terrace
(Nos. 61–71), most of the ashlar façades now painted. Aprons
under the first-floor windows; bowed N corner. Late C19
shopfront with polished granite columns at No. 61.

The narrow site between Nursery Lane and Victoria Street is filled by VICTORIA LODGE, a mid-C19 villa, its broad eaves supported on stone brackets. Three-bay ashlar front with pilastered porch in the centre. At the slightly advanced and gabled r. bay, a two-storey canted bay window. On the N corner of VICTORIA STREET, Coldstream Library and, behind it, the former Coldstream Free Church (*see* Churches and Public Buildings, above). Opposite the Library, No. 84 High Street of *c.* 1800 with a Roman Doric columned doorpiece; the canted bay shop windows were added *c.* 1900. Consoled cornices over the doors of No. 86. Then, the BANK OF SCOTLAND (originally British Linen Co. Bank), by *Kinnear & Peddie*, 1891, its symmetrical Jacobean Renaissance a little pompous. VICTORIA HOUSE, set back from the W side of High Street, is late C18, its tiny horizontal second-floor windows squeezed under the eaves of the roof (now covered with concrete pantiles). Opposite, a small car park fronts the entrance to HENDERSON PARK, a municipal garden opened in 1961. At its E end, a battlemented octagonal two-storey GAZEBO, perhaps of the late C18, overlooking the River Tweed. To the N, Nos. 100–100C High Street form a piend-roofed double house, the five-bay front of broached ashlar. The r. three bays (No. 100C) seem to have been the first part built, probably at the beginning of the C19, with delicate fluted consoles to the corniced doorpiece. The two l. bays (No. 100) have stone of a different colour and a plain doorpiece. At the N end, No. 100A, a flat-roofed addition of the later C19. It is also of two storeys but lower and faced with polished ashlar. Narrow three-bay front with pilastered corners and a wall-head cornice and parapet; parapeted porch at the slightly advanced centre. Immediately N of this and set slightly back from the street, SAFFRON QUARTER, by *Michael Rasmussen*, 1999, attempts to evoke Voysey but is curiously inappropriate in this urban context. Harled, with a high piended roof; a low round tower beside the round-headed entrance.

In GUARDS ROAD, TRAFALGAR HOUSE, built as Coldstream Parish Manse in 1830–2. *Thomas Hamilton* was the architect. Large-scale two-storey villa immaculately dressed in polished ashlar, the broad-eaved piended roof's central platform surrounded by a parapet of chimneys. E front of three bays, the ground- and first-floor openings combining to read as tall verticals despite the interruption of cornices over the ground-floor windows and a first-floor sill course. The door and its sidelights are set in a very broad pilastered and corniced surround. Five-bay N elevation, the first-floor windows with aprons. The other sides have been overlaid by late C20 extensions.

In High Street N of Guards Road, CHEVIOT VIEW on the E is a rubble-built house of the early C19 with a heavy pilastered and corniced doorpiece; low second-floor windows (now blocked) immediately under the eaves. It is followed by villas of the late C19 and the Police Station (*see* Public Buildings, above) on the corner of High Street's junction with Tweed Terrace. In High Street's N continuation, St Mary and All Souls Episcopal Church (*see* Churches, above). On the SE side of TWEED TERRACE, the Marjoribanks Monument (*see* Public Buildings, above). This road leads out to Coldstream Bridge (*see* Public

Buildings, above). At the bridge's w end, THE OLD MAR-RIAGE HOUSE, a C18 house restored in 1957. It is rubble-built with a pantiled roof. Single-storey to the road but with two floors below exposed in the fall of the ground at the back. The main block's front is of three bays, the slightly advanced centre of polished ashlar and containing a door flanked by large side-lights. Stone brackets under the eaves. Pilaster at the E end abutting a lower piend-roofed lateral wing. The house's w end abuts one of the corniced and ball-finialled Late Georgian gatepiers at the end of the drive to Lennel House (q.v.).

THE MOUNT, Castlelaw, 3.5 km. NW. A well-preserved motte probably constructed by a member of the Darnchester family sometime during the C12 or C13. It appears to be almost entirely of artificial construction and comprises a truncated cone up to 16 m. in height with a flat summit about 20 m. in diameter. Towards the end of the C19 the motte was planted with trees and turned into a garden mount by William Waite, who rebuilt the nearby mansion of Castlelaw (of which a frag-ment still stands). Two causeways crossing the SW and SE sec-tions of the surrounding ditch were possibly constructed at the same time. A marker stone beside the SE causeway bears a Gothic inscription ST MARGARET'S WALK.

THE HIRSEL. *See* p. 379.
THE LEES. *See* p. 490.
LENNEL HOUSE. *See* p. 494.
MILNE GRADEN HOUSE. *See* p. 567.

COLISLINN 5010
4.8 km s of Hawick

A small C17-style tower house of the early C20 by *J. P. Alison* for Walter Haddon, Hawick solicitor and bank agent. Two and three storeys, harled white with red sandstone margins. Round, conical-capped towers, one containing the entrance, and a crowstepped tower house with machicolated parapet, angle bartizan and corner tower corbelled out at first floor.

COLMSLIE TOWER 5030
4.3 km. NE of Galashiels

The oldest of three fortified houses standing within a short dis-tance of one another in the valley of the Allan Water. Like the neighbouring tower of Hillslap (q.v.), Colmslie belonged to a branch of the Cairncross family, and the architectural evidence suggests that its builder was the William Cairncross who is recorded during the second quarter of the C16. What may be his initials appear on a lintel from the tower now built into the neigh-bouring farmhouse. The building was ruinous by 1821, when a drawing showed a cottage attached to the w gable of the tower.

Now a shell, the building is oblong on plan measuring 12.6 m. by 8.5 m. over walls 1.5 m. thick. It originally comprised at least three main storeys and a garret, but little of the fabric now survives above second-floor level. The masonry is of local random rubble with dressings of red sandstone. The ground floor is now full of debris and its vault, if any, has collapsed. The first floor contains two chambers, the larger one to the W a well-lit hall with big gable fireplace and two recesses for furniture. The adjacent chamber, evidently a kitchen, also has a gable fireplace, in this case equipped with an oven and slop-sink. The entrance seems to have opened directly into the N wall of the hall and must have been approached by a forestair. A newel stair in the NE corner gave access to the upper floors and presumably also to the ground-floor chamber, to which there seems to have been no separate external entry. The arrangement of the second floor is uncertain, but there were probably outer and inner chambers, as at Newark (q.v.). Most of the larger windows at this level were equipped with bench seats, while between the two in the S wall were a mural chamber and a latrine with a mural discharge chute. This was probably the laird's private suite and one of these rooms is likely to be 'the upper chamber (*cenabulum*) of the place of Comislie' in which a legal transaction involving William Cairncross took place in 1551.

7020

CORBET HOUSE
1.8 km. SE of Morebattle

A shooting lodge built for A. Sholto Douglas of Chesterhouse and Gateshaw by *Hardy & Wight*, 1896. Asymmetrical composition of two storeys and attics, in coursed rubble and sandstone dressings with standard Scottish Baronial features derived from David Bryce, e.g. projecting crowstepped gables with flanking corbelled-out turrets and a corner turret corbelled out from a canted bay. The turrets have fish-scale slates, the mullioned windows on the first floor have segmental pediments. In the centre, however, is a square French Gothic entrance tower with a high pointed turret carried on machicolations. Double-height staircase hall with a gallery and Neo-Tudor decoration of a ribbed ceiling with a rose motif. The suite of public rooms along the N and E sides includes a dining room with buffet and a classical timber chimneypiece. From here a floor pedal by the door summoned the servants from the kitchen. The W guest wing has an elegant stone stair. Single-storey kitchen offices.

CORBET TOWER. Looking a little lost in the garden is a much-altered four-storey tower of 1572. Although free-standing, the building is too small (6.8 m. by 5.0 m. externally) to have been a tower house and is unlikely, because of its situation, to have been a corner tower of a barmkin. More probably it was a corner tower of a sizeable mansion of L- or Z-plan, such as Cowdenknowes or Branxholme Castle (qq.v.), which was built to replace an earlier tower burnt by the English in 1544. The parent house was probably removed *c.* 1815 when the tower was drastically remodelled as a belvedere. Of this date are the N wall, adjacent sections of the side walls and most of the upperworks, including the crowsteps and gable finials;

the internal fittings, including the stair, belong to a *c*. 1900 refurbishment.

The original masonry is of local whin rubble with red sandstone dressings, but the early C19 masons reused red sandstone as rubble, employing grey sandstone for their own dressings. These include Gothic windows and ornamental crosslet loops in the N wall. There are genuine oval-mouthed gunloops (as well as a few early C19 replicas) in the E, S and W walls, which suggests that the main block of the vanished house ran W from behind the present N wall of the tower, probably also taking in part of the W wall. The blocked first-floor doorway in this wall seems to be a relic of the belvedere, but the well-preserved ground-floor doorway in the same wall was probably the original entrance of the early house. This has roll-moulded margins and an inscribed lintel incorporating the sacred monogram IHS, flanked by the date 1572(?) and two sets of damaged initials, probably IK and BK, for James Carr, or Kerr, of Corbethouse, who succeeded to the property *c*. 1566, and his wife (Eliza)beth Kerr.

To the NW is the late C18(?) WALLED GARDEN and STABLES, very likely a remodelling of 1896. Picturesque with gables and central pend. Completely preserved fittings by *Musgrave & Co.* of London and Belfast; chutes dispensed hay and oats from the floor above. Gabled LODGE to the SE.

CORSBIE TOWER
6040

2 km. E of Legerwood

A prominent fragment of the oblong tower house (12.2 m. by 8.2 m.) of the Cranstouns of Corsbie, probably dating from the end of the C15. Its strong site overlooks and is partly surrounded by the former Corsbie Loch. The tower incorporated a vaulted ground floor, a first-floor hall with a large fireplace, another hall or large chamber in the vaulted entresol and at least one more floor above that, the top one showing signs of secondary use as a dovecot. Only two walls survive, but these show the unusual character of the masonry, which comprises facework of mixed basalt and sandstone rubble combined with neatly rounded corners of sandstone ashlar. Newel stair in one corner with an adjacent series of superimposed mural latrines with chutes. There are traces of other buildings in the vicinity, as also of an outer bank, which has evidently enclosed the whole and may have originated as a ringwork associated with the early Stewart holdings in Legerwood parish.

COVE
7070

Cliff-top settlement built in 1809 by the Halls of Dunglass (Lothian) to house the families of the fishermen and farmworkers on their estate. Ten single-storey cottages were built first, fronting on to a cultivated area, with further cottages added later at the W end. Two-storey harled and gabled coastguard houses and a look-out post appeared *c*. 1911 (now housing).

COVE HARBOUR. A natural harbour and a landing place by at least the early C17: attempts were made to build breakwaters from 1740 but all were destroyed by storms. In 1830–1 Sir John Hall built the present harbour with funding from the Commissioners of the Herring Fishery. Two PIERS, one almost straight, the other with an angled head.

DESCRIPTION. A dramatic approach to the harbour is made by timber steps leading down from the cliff top to a winding track, from where a long sloping TUNNEL (55.7 m. long with a fall of 6.1 m.) bores through the promontory rock. This was cut through in 1751–4 to gain access to the shore. Its N entrance has splayed walls, and there is excavated cellarage to the W, perhaps enlarged from natural caves. A range of four well-equipped cellars may date from the mid C18, and was no doubt useful for purposes other than fishing.* HARBOUR COTTAGES, a pair of early C19, or earlier, single-storey rubble cottages, are set on a sloping site, built off the bedrock, and linked by a square piended bay. Stores since 1946, the S cottage has a cellar which may have been used for salt panning.

<h1 style="text-align:center">COWDENKNOWES</h1>

5030

1.5 km. S of Earlston

43 An important and complex Renaissance house, in a prominent position above the E bank of the Leader Water, the late C16 phase of which evidently proved highly influential in the spread of architectural fashions in the Borders.

Although there may have been an earlier residence here, the oldest portion of the existing complex was probably erected either by John Home of Whiterigs, a younger brother of the second Lord Home, or by his son Mungo, some time between the acquisition of Earlston (q.v.) in 1489 and 1506, when the fortalice and manor of 'Coldaneknollis' are mentioned in a confirmation charter. This fortalice was evidently a sizeable establishment, probably comprising an enclosed, rectangular courtyard, or barmkin (occupying roughly the area of the present lawn), embodying one or more corner towers as well as (presumably) a tower house or residential block. In 1546 a small English force made an unsuccessful attempt to destroy the house with gunpowder, and it may have been as a result of damage sustained that further building operations were undertaken, perhaps in 1554, when a two-and-a-half-storey range was erected on the E side of the barmkin with an integral four-storey tower at the NE corner. Another major building project was implemented in 1574, when the N side of the barmkin was partly occupied by a new mansion, probably replacing an earlier residence in a similar position. This new house, erected by Sir James Home, Warden of the East Marches and a prominent figure at court, was of notably innovative design, incorporating a near-symmetrical front and an eyecatching array of Renaissance detail in a style

* They were recorded in 1963 and blocked up by Borders Regional Council in 1981.

subsequently employed elsewhere, e.g. at Greenknowe Tower, Bemersyde House and Ferniehirst Castle (qq.v.)

Some time between 1784, when Professor Francis Horne purchased the estate, and *c.* 1808, when drawings of the house were made by the Rev. John Sime, a major scheme of reconstruction was carried out. The upper floors of the late-C16 mansion were partly rebuilt while the E barmkin range was demolished, apart from the NE tower, which was remodelled. In 1866–7 *Brown & Wardrop* provided a large scheme to baronialise the house for Robert Cotesworth, of which only a simplified version was realised, and in 1883 *John Watherston & Sons* linked the NE tower to the late-C16 house so that it could serve as the entrance, approached by a new drive on that side. In 1997–8 the house was repaired and refurbished by *Andrew Davey* of *Simpson & Brown*.

The original BARMKIN is now represented mainly by an oblong tower (*c.* 11.6 m. by 7.9 m.) of *c.* 1500 at the SW corner, overlooking the Leader Water. The ground floor has two vaulted chambers and what seems to be a third now infilled with rubble. A hatch in the floor of the NW chamber gives access to a prison. The upper portion of the tower has been largely removed and the first floor converted into a balustraded viewing platform opening off the lawn. There are no traces of the S side of the barmkin, but footings of a heavily buttressed wall along the W side, where a mid-C19 engraving shows what appears to be a length of crenellated curtain wall, may be of medieval origin.

The roof raggles and blocked doorways of the former E barmkin range are visible in the S wall of the NE TOWER, built *c.* 1554; also a small carved figure, probably of medieval date. The upperworks of the tower seem to have been reconstructed *c.* 1800, in an antiquarian style, and Sime's drawings show it much as now. Continuous three-member corbel course supporting a rudimentary classical frieze with paterae in the metopes; also a sprinkling of quatrefoil gunloops like those in the late-C16 house. The parapet and gables incorporate three pilaster-framed window surrounds evidently in reuse (they have glazing grooves and bar sockets), which may have been removed from the second floor of the 1574 mansion during alterations. A fourth blank window, dated 1554 within an ogival pediment, probably derives from the demolished E range. In 1883 Watherston pushed a big, new Neo-Jacobean entrance through the E wall of the tower at first-floor level and added a two-storey link to the house on the W.

Although considerably enlarged and rebuilt, the LATE-C16 43 HOUSE incorporates more original work than at first appears. Doubts about the authenticity of the carved detail are dispelled by Sime's drawings, although clearly much of the facework has been renewed or re-dressed. The house seems to have comprised a three-storey U-plan block, of which the larger (SW) wing probably incorporated part of an earlier building, as evidenced by the splayed base plinth on the W side. The N wall is thicker than the remainder, at least on the ground floor, and this suggests that the central and E portions of the house were built against the inner face of the early barmkin wall. The house measures about 26.5 m. on its E–W axis, while the main block has a width of 6.5 m. The SW wing (7.3 m. by 6.1 m.) contains an extruded stair-turret in the re-entrant angle, while Sime's drawings show that the smaller SE wing (4.3 m. by 2.7 m.) formerly contained a spacious newel stair rising to the first floor only. Both stairs have showy entrances, the former bearing the initials of Sir James Home and his wife, Katherine Home, of the Blackadder family, with the date 1574, and the latter what are perhaps the monogram initials of James's father, Sir John (who may have begun the house) and his wife Margaret Kerr. Both also incorporate one or more quatrefoil gunloops. Running round the first-floor corbel course of the SE wing is an incomplete inscription beautifully cut in ornate Roman letters: FEIR GOD FLIE FROM SINN AND MAK FOR YE LYFE EVERLISTYNG THE HIER TH–; an almost identical inscription occurs at Holydean Castle (q.v.). The very rich architectural detail is a mixture of revived Romanesque (mostly billet, cable and chip-carved); French Renaissance (as in the SE entrance, where the mouldings and entablature resemble those at Torwood Castle (Stirling and Central Scotland)), and Scottish Renaissance. This last is best represented by the pilaster-framed windows lighting the *piano nobile*, their sills being integral with the *cyma reversa* stringcourse that returns across the S front. The openings look too big to be original, but the half-glazing grooves and bar sockets argue otherwise. Other mouldings include the edge-roll and single and double cavetto.

The ground-floor windows of the S front seem to have been renewed with hoodmoulds c. 1800, and the present second-floor windows are likely to date from the same period. The roofs have probably always fallen sheer to the wall-head, without parapets, as now. The alterations of c. 1800 also saw the upper levels of the SW wing remodelled to provide a new first-floor drawing room. At the same time the tops of the SW stair-turret and SE wing were rebuilt with Venetian windows (now replaced) and crowstepped gabled roofs. The W elevation, extended by *John Smith*, 1820, has an oriel at first-floor level. Brown & Wardrop's alterations of 1866–7 principally involved the addition of a second storey to the SW wing (probably restoring it to its original height), with corbelled-out conical turrets and pediments above the windows. A large octagonal turret was angled out from the SW corner, adding panoramic views to the drawing room.

INTERIOR. The present entrance to the house is through the NE tower, remodelled for that purpose in 1883. It has a single chamber at each level, the lowest one inaccessible, that at first floor refurbished as the entrance vestibule. The interiors are mainly of the 1880s, but the second-floor chamber has a pretty mid-C18 chimneypiece. An original (i.e. mid-C16) newel stair in the SW corner rises from this level to the wall-walk. At that time communication between the lower floors was presumably provided by a stair in the adjacent E barmkin range, and when this was demolished a forestair was constructed on the E side of the tower. Beyond the vestibule, an entrance hall in the link building opens into a long corridor laid along the N side of the late-C16 house probably c. 1820. The library and adjacent half-turn timber staircase at the W end of the corridor are contemporary.

The ground floor of the late-C16 house contains three vaulted storerooms, the middle one formerly entered from a doorway in the S wall; there was no corridor in the original arrangement. Both wings are also vaulted, the SW one probably incorporating an early kitchen; the vault in the SE wing was presumably inserted when the stair was removed, perhaps in the 1860s. In 1574 this stair probably gave access from what must have been the principal entrance to a large hall occupying the greater part of the main block; beyond this there would have been an outer chamber together with an inner chamber in the SW wing, each served independently by the secondary stair in the re-entrant angle. The layout of the first floor was modified c. 1800 to take account of the new drawing room in the SW wing, and again in the 1860s, when a new dining room was formed at the E end. The interior decoration of 1883 by *Charles W. Swanson* was carried out by *Scott Morton & Co.* and includes timber panelling, particularly in the entrance hall and dining room. The contemporary oak chimneypiece in the E wall of the drawing room replaces an earlier one of white marble in the W wall. A Gothic-style chimneypiece of red sandstone from the demolished Minto House (q.v.) was installed in the library in 1997–8.

A FERNERY to the NW of the house was once part of a conservatory. What remains is the iron door, decorated with pieces of cork to resemble bark, and the rockwork inside. It may have been glazed over but is now open to the sky. – STABLES. A monumental Baronial design by *John Watherston & Sons*, dated 1884, with a large court. An array of carved pediments over the windows and ogee-shaped hoodmoulds over the segmental-headed archways. Nicely detailed lantern-shaped louvres on the roof ridges. – The GARDENER'S HOUSE stands high up in the NE corner of the walled and hedged pleasure grounds. Probably c. 1820. Coursed grey whinstone with red sandstone dressings. Gothic windows with hoodmoulds. Later attics. – LODGE on the approach from the E. Probably by *John Smith*, c. 1820. Pretty with bracketed gables and mullioned windows.

CRAILING 6020

PARISH CHURCH. At Kirkmains, NW of the village. A rectangular harled building of c. 1775 with several additions. Against the W (in fact SW) gable is a gabled porch; against the N flank is an early C19 laird's 'aisle'. At the E end is a slightly discordant rubble-built apse of 1892–3 by *P. Macgregor Chalmers* (who also carried out works in 1907). The S front has four arched windows, that towards the W end having a transom corresponding to the internal loft floor; there are tablet memorials between some of the windows. Above the W gable is a rectangular birdcage bellcote.

Internally there is some discomfort in the contrast between the original building and Chalmers' attempt to create a more medieval space. The thicker walling at the two ends of the s flank indicates there were lofts at each end, with the elevated loft of the N laird's 'aisle' (the space below now treated as a vestry) on the third side. Only the W and laird's lofts survived the 1892–3 remodelling. The truncated W loft retains a re-set C18 front with squat Composite pilasters alternating with raised and fielded panels, though the Arts and Crafts supporting pillars betray Chalmers' hand. The main body of the church has a segmental plaster ceiling, through which project two braced tie-beams, with kingposts rising up to a ridge-beam. The apse is entered through a wide semicircular arch with chamfered arrises and with a diminutive screen wall in its lower part. It has an open-timber roof. The curved wall of the apse is painted maroon with masonry lining, and with fleur-de-lys and IHS stencils; at the upper level is an acanthus frieze with inscriptions. – COMMUNION TABLE, PULPIT and FONT. The first two of oak and the third of stone, all in Chalmers' Romanesque style. – LECTERN. Base with central core surrounded by three spiral-decorated shafts capped with mythical beasts, in the style of *Robert J. Lorimer*. – STAINED GLASS. Apse, Christ the True Vine and Bread of Life; Humility and Charity. s wall nave, W end, Christ Anointed and Woman Taken in Adultery, 1892. – CHURCHYARD. Mainly C19 and C20 memorials. Narrow three-sided burial enclosure for Paton family, uncomfortably close to s front.

Former CRAILING UNITED FREE CHURCH, now Lothian Hall. Correctly detailed red rock-faced sandstone essay in Early English, of 1900–1; in use as the village hall since 1931. Aligned from SE to NW, the main emphasis is on the SE gable and SW flank, the former having a triplet of lancets with a full array of nook-shafts, shaft-rings and moulded arches. Along the SW side is a carefully grouped combination of porch, 'aisle', and hall and vestry block.

NISBET CHURCHYARD. 1.8 km. NW. A chapel was granted to Jedburgh Abbey in the time of David I. It was demolished after 1754, its site now a hollow rectangle at the centre of the churchyard, with the Rutherford burial enclosure at its E end. Some C18 stones have *memento mori*. – HOGBACK MONUMENTS. Three small undecorated fragments of a possible hogback stone with a coped upper part, of uncertain date, are within the churchyard. A second hogback of early C12 date, found *c.* 1890, is in Hawick Museum. – Wrought-iron GATES erected by Adam Young of Eskbank, 1919.

CRAILING BRIDGE, 1833. Two-span bridge over Oxnam Water, with corbelled cornice and battlemented parapet.

CRAILING PRIMARY SCHOOL (Crailing Old School). T-plan former Board School by *A. Herbertson & Son*, 1887. Rock-faced sandstone, broad eaves and tripartite windows. Adjacent gabled schoolmaster's house.

MANSE (Greenloaning). Mid-C19, three bays, the harled walls enlivened with red sandstone margins and flush quoins. Projecting full-height gabled porch, the first floor on a continuous corbel.

War Memorial, *c.* 1920. A high plinth supporting an inscribed panel, topped by a broken pediment with an embossed cross.

Crailing House. A well-proportioned Regency-style mansion of 1803 by *William Elliot* for James Paton of the East India Company. His family owned the estate from 1802 until 1948 when it was bought by the twelfth Marquess of Lothian. Two storeys, basement and attic under a shallow piended and plat-formed roof with a distinctive bellcast carried well over the wall-head. Five-bay front with advanced centre fronted by four giant pilasters supporting a raking pediment with blind oculus. The entrance is round-arched with an elliptical fanlight. Unusually, there are balustraded bows to the side elevations, rising two storeys from the basement. Interior altered by *Reginald Fairlie*, 1952. Graceful geometric stair at the rear. –

Stables, a large court with a Palladian front. Central pend (blocked) surmounted by a cupola and weathervane and links to corner pavilions. – West Lodge. Mid-C19, apparently a rebuilding of an early C19 thatched cottage with rusticated quoins. Early C19 rusticated gatepiers with carved urns. – Mid-C19 East Lodge, of three bays with lying-pane windows. Ball-finialled gatepiers. – Summerhouse, 0.4 km. E along the Oxnam Water. Mid-to-late C19, with a pointed roof thatched with twigs, timber-slatted walls and arcaded front. A tree-trunk balustrade to lean on. Timber-boarded inner walls and semi-circular seat.

In the grounds are the fragmentary remains of a chapel granted to Jedburgh Abbey in the early C12. There are traces of a W offshoot but only the NW corner stands to any height. In the churchyard the earliest stones are late C17, two with standing figures.

CRANSHAWS

A small but dispersed settlement in the valley of the Whiteadder Water.

Old Parish Church, 0.7 km SW. A church here by the C13 was demolished and replaced on a new site in 1739 (*see* below). The site was partly excavated and tidied up in 1889; the lower walls are still visible, the E gable wall rising to 4 m.

Parish Church, in a walled churchyard. The building of 1899, partly incorporating its predecessor of 1739 (dates on a tablet above the entrance), is an essay in Romanesque Revival by *George Fortune* of Duns. Of whinstone rubble with red sand-stone dressings, the main body is a five-bay aisle-less rectan-gle with an E apse. A porch covers the entrance in the W bay of the S flank, and towards the E end of the windowless N wall are a laird's 'aisle' and vestry. The crowstepped gables have prominent finials, except at the W end, where there is a cor-belled-out birdcage bellcote. The lavish external detail includes nook-shafts and chevron to the windows, a porch arch with two orders of engaged nook-shafts and a continuous cable-moulded inner order, and an eight-light rose above a bipartite window in the W wall. The inventive enrichments include an impish figure of Time holding a sundial (the latter dated 1731) at the SW corner.

Wagon ceiling with major transverse and minor diagonal ribs rising from head corbels. Arches carried on heavy three-quarter shafts open into the apse and the elevated laird's 'aisle', the former having chevron and *paterae* to the arch, and the latter with an arcaded parapet. Amongst noteworthy internal carvings is an angel between the lights of the w window. – COMMUNION TABLE, PULPIT and CHAIRS, all Romanesque; the pulpit has a bracket for the baptismal basin. – STAINED GLASS: apse, Crucifixion; w window, Nativity and Ascension; porch, windows given by *Fortune*. – TABLETS above s porch arch and above s door, commemorating 1899 rebuilding. – Carved ROYAL ARMS, above vestry doorway, from the old church, without top element of tressure and therefore presumably carved according to Act of 1471.

MANSE. T-plan, of rubble with droved dressings. Possibly incorporating a building of 1711, but largely of the early and mid C19. The main (s) front of three bays and two storeys has a central gabled porch and a slated roof within skewed gables.

Former SCHOOLHOUSE and SCHOOL, at N end of village. Substantial early C19 house, with harled walls and painted margins. Central gabled porch. A single-storey offshoot to the s balances the larger schoolroom to the N.

SMIDDYHILL BRIDGE, 1 km. SE, over the Whiteadder Water. Two unequal segmental arches of whin rubble, with buff ashlar arches and dressings. Dated 1887; repaired 1997.

BROOMBANK. 2.5 km SE. Built for the Whitchester (q.v.) gamekeeper, a good example of later C19 estate building. Walls of whin rubble and buff ashlar dressings with bipartite windows rising into triangular gables.

CRANSHAWS TOWER

1 km. w

During the later Middle Ages Cranshaws belonged to the Swintons of that Ilk, one of the oldest established baronial families in Berwickshire, who had received a grant of the property from Archibald, fourth Earl of Douglas, in 1401. There was probably a residence at Cranshaws at that time, but the existing tower is likely to have been erected during the late C15 or early C16, possibly by Sir John Swinton, seventeenth of Swinton (†*c*. 1520). It is unusual among Border tower houses in having been occupied almost continuously since its erection without substantial enlargement. In consequence, the exterior retains much of its medieval character while the interior shows evidence of successive alteration and refurbishment, the latest by *Ian Begg* in the 1970s.

The tower is oblong on plan, measuring 12.2 m. from N to s (in fact NW to SE) by 7.9 m. transversely over walls up to 1.8 m. thick at base. The masonry is of (renewed) harled rubble with sandstone dressings and rounded corners, as at the contemporary tower of Corsbie (q.v.). Originally the lowest division was probably vaulted, comprising a ground-floor cellar with an entresol floor in the vault (cf. Smailholm Tower), but the vault must have been removed in or before the C19. Above was a hall and another full upper storey, as well as a garret rising within an open wall-walk carried on individual stone corbels. The crenellated parapet was rebuilt 1831–4 by *John Henderson*, builder, for Charles Watson, when the roof was also renewed at a slightly lower level than the original. The gables are crowstepped and one of the bottom steps carries a sundial bearing the initials PD and the date 1770. The original windows, which survive mainly at second-floor level, have broad-chamfered margins, while the later windows, many of them apparently enlargements or insertions of the 1830s, have narrow-chamfered or round-arrised margins. The surrounds of the garret windows are rebated for external shutters. The bolection-moulded doorway in the W wall is probably of the 1890s, part of a major scheme of restoration for Andrew Smith of Whitchester (q.v.), and occupies the position of the original entrance. The doorway in the E wall is a C19 insertion, while the wide-mouthed gunloop in the N wall was fashioned in the 1970s to disguise a vent. Although the tower now stands in isolation, it must originally have had associated outbuildings and perhaps a barmkin.

Inside, the entrance opens directly into the main ground-floor chamber. While the present ground-floor layout of dining room and kitchen dates from the 1970s, it probably reflects the original division of the cellarage. An adjacent opening leads into a newel stair in the NW corner. This rises to the full height of the building and probably originally terminated in a cap-house. The staircase intrudes into the interior in such a way as to facilitate the construction of a small chamber in the NE corner of the tower at each level. On the entresol floor, where the present three-room layout is mainly of the 1890s and 1970s, the existence of an original NE chamber is evidenced by the survival of its deeply splayed window. At the level of the hall the NE chamber seems to have been entered directly from the staircase, the ghost of its blocked doorway visible alongside the wide-chamfered doorway of the hall itself. This chamber, which is ceiled at a lower level than the hall, may originally have been an intercommunicating kitchen, as at Newark Castle (q.v.). The medieval hall was a lofty and well-appointed chamber, ceiled at a slightly higher level than today. Flanking a fireplace in the S wall was a pair of high-level windows, while the side walls contained larger windows furnished with aumbries in their embrasures. A latrine equipped with a mural discharge-chute opened off the NW corner. The existing chimneypiece, inserted by Andrew Smith in 1895, has a roll-moulded surround and segmental-arched head carved with the armorial bearings of the successive owners of Cranshaws. The panelling, some of it recently re-set, is of the same period, while the ceiling by *Albert Cram*, with its modelled cranes (for Cranshaws), was added in 1979. There seems to have been a small NE chamber at an intermediate level, entered directly from the stair, and another on the second floor itself. Originally, the main chamber at this level was probably an upper hall; one of the window embrasures retains an aumbry like those below.

CRANSHAWS FARM, grouped with the tower, has a T-plan FARMHOUSE of c. 1800. The rectangular STEADING has a round-arched GATE at its N corner, capped by a steeply pointed pediment, bearing the arms and initials of Andrew Smith and his wife; a cryptic inscription refers to the coronation of Edward VII in 1902.

CRINGLETIE HOUSE
3 km. s of Eddleston

A pleasing small Baronial mansion, now a hotel, standing on a wooded plateau to the w of Eddleston Water. The house appears to be a remodelling c. 1861 by *David Bryce* of an earlier house built by Sir Alexander Murray of Blackbarony in 1663–6. Although this house was described by the family chronicler as 'destroyed by rats' and said to have been pulled down in 1861 by James Wolfe Murray, Bryce seems instead to have refaced the walls with stugged red sandstone. The general appearance of the s range certainly suggests he was working to an existing ground plan, as does the treatment of the double crowstepped gables on the s elevation, whose chimneys are linked by a corbelled-out parapeted screen hiding a valley gutter. The N gable is also crowstepped, but cuts into an existing gable. The w, or garden elevation, is the show front, with the three-storey and attic s block descending to a two-storey, three-bay crow-stepped range, symmetrically composed with two-storey para-peted canted bays; above are pedimented wall-head dormers, and in the roof small timber pedimented ones. The lower, crowstepped block has hoodmoulds over two of the first-floor windows, and a Brycean canted bay window, corbelled out to a rectangle at first-floor level. The hoodmoulds and form suggest a mid-c19 date for this range. At the end is the simple windowless façade of the stables, probably erected in the 1850s.

The s front has bulgy conical-roofed corner turrets with fish-scale slates and finials, and a panel inscribed: WHATEVER ME BEFAL THANKS THE LORD OF ALL. There is an odd assort-ment of windows on this elevation, where Bryce would surely have made more of the s view down the valley to Peebles. A string course defines the ground and first floor, another runs over windows, panel and turrets at eaves level. The E, or entrance, elevation has a projecting three-storey and attic wing, crowstepped with a two-storey conical-roofed stair-turret cor-belled out from its SE corner, with fish-scale slates and a weath-ervane, and tall stone-mullioned window. A small sturdy basket-arched porch invites entry. A wall-head dormer and roof dormers match those on the w side. A single-storey kitchen wing, against the N gable and E side of the earlier house, links to the crowstepped gabled stable court. A number of mid-c19 heraldic panels record the baronial ancestry and marriages of the family, and one of these, dated 1666, may be a replica of a datestone on the early house. Another, carved with a column, the date 1861 and the monogram initials DB, provides evidence of Bryce's association with the building (cf. The Glen). An extension by *Simpson & Brown*, 2003, has a red sandstone screen wall and slit windows to the drive, glazed walls to the garden, and a flat sedum-planted roof.

INTERIOR. The plan is not a rational Bryce one of an L-shaped sequence of public rooms with the entrance at the end of the L and the stair off the main corridor: another reason for believing he remodelled an existing house. Instead the principal entrance opens into a vestibule with a short flight of steps to the staircase hall. Apart from the vestibule, which is characteristically Brycean, the appearance of the other rooms is early C20 Neo-Georgian, probably done for Sir George Sutherland, who married Elizabeth Wolfe Murray in 1904. The timber staircase has twisted balusters and panelled newel posts and most of the rooms are panelled, with marble or timber chimneypieces. The full treatment was reserved for the first-floor drawing room (possibly contrived from two rooms), which has panelled walls and a garlanded timber chimneypiece with pedimented overmantel. The painted ceiling has a large central roundel with a surround of wreaths of leaves and a classical scene of a male figure, with lots of winged cherubs, all sitting on clouds. Two cartouches are monogrammed GES for George and Elizabeth Sutherland. The painted ceiling panel over the N end of the room shows a balcony scene, with drapes and urns on the balustrade, flowers and parrots.

WALLED GARDEN N of the house. Rubble walls, lower along the S side, and greenhouses. Mid-C19 SUNDIAL. Octagonal baluster, carved decoration round the top, with copper plate and gnomon. – DOVECOT, 0.2 km. SW. C18. Square greywacke rubble with sandstone quoins, slate roof. Probably adapted to its present use as there is no string course and no nest holes. Four dove holes in the S wall, set in dressed red sandstone, cut across an earlier circular opening, above a segmental arched entrance. – LODGE. Dated 1857 WM, for James Wolfe Murray, over a blocked entrance door. Harled with corner pilaster strips. Wide bay window and bracketed eaves. – N LODGE. Early C19, single-storey, gabled with bracketed eaves. Much altered.

CROOKSTON HOUSE*   4050
1.5 km. NE of Fountainhall

The house of 1816–17, of five bays and two storeys on a basement, in grey whinstone with sandstone dressings, can still be seen on the S and E fronts. In 1860–4 it was heavily Jacobeanised by *Brown & Wardrop* for John Borthwick of Crookston, using the same materials. They added a new roof above the old one, with curly gabled dormered attics and a balustrade between, corner bartizan turrets (originally with ogee roofs) and a large S porch. A big classical conservatory, attached to the house, was demolished late C20, the site forming a terrace to the W. Some Georgian interiors survive. The staircase was recast with Jacobean woodwork and an

* Account based on that by Colin McWilliam, *The Buildings of Scotland: Lothian* (1978).

armorial window of 1873. A modest Roman Doric chimney-piece was reused in the large drawing room, which has a curious hybrid ceiling: heavy square compartments (with tiny pendants) at the corners only, the deep members not crossing the whole span. The ballroom is quite classical, compart-mented and coved. Built into the rear wall are two fragments of an early cross shaft with interlaced carving: said to have come from the parish church of Borthwick (Lothian). There is also a stone inscribed IESUS FOR MY PORTIOUN, AS AL SUFI-CIENT TO CONTENT 161(?). – NORTH LODGE, 1870, by *Brown & Wardrop*. In grey whinstone, with T-braced finialled gables, deep overhanging eaves, and arcaded porch with square columns, the roof continuing over it as a lean-to canopy. – SOUTH LODGE. Probably early C19, but remodelled *c.* 1870. – GATEWAY (Angel Gates). Dated 1871. Tall, square rusticated piers surmounted by pedestalled carved angels, each carrying a heraldic shield inscribed JB (John Borthwick) and EP (Eliz-abeth Pringle). Excellent decorative iron gates. A family coat-of-arms over the gate has been removed to the house.

BORTHWICK MEMORIAL. Dressed stone pyramid on an inscribed pedestal, erected *c.* 1810 in memory of William Borthwick (†1809) by his father John, 12th of Crookston.

OLD CROOKSTON HOUSE, 0.5 km. N, is a charming C17 laird's house possibly incorporating part of an earlier tower and with C19 additions in scale with the original work. The Borthwicks' principal previous residence. T-plan, comprising an oblong main block with a wing projecting from the centre of the s side; three storeys, the uppermost one lit largely by dormers. The wing is mainly of *c.* 1860, but encases a square stair-turret with C17 entrance doorway at its foot. Harled rubble masonry, the early windows, most of which have chamfer-arrised margins, having dressings of pink- and buff-coloured sandstone. An earlier tower is thought to occupy the E portion of the house, where the upper part of the N wall has at some time been rebuilt at a reduced thickness, giving the crowstepped gable at this end a decidedly lopsided appearance. The ground-floor chamber within was formerly barrel-vaulted and may originally have belonged to a small, free-standing tower house (*c.* 7.9 m. by 6.8 m.). In its C17 form, at least, the house seems to have had three main rooms at each level, the central one on the ground floor having been a kitchen. The w room at this level was refurbished in the early C18, possibly as a parlour, and con-tains fielded panelling of that period. The principal rooms have always been on the first floor, to which the C17 turnpike stone stair still provides the only access.

DARNICK

Originally a bustling township occupied by tenants of Melrose Abbey, the mid-C18 village was little more than an irregular group of thatched cottages clustered around Darnick Tower. From the early to mid C19 most of the cottages were improved or rebuilt and smart villas appeared to fill the gaps, no doubt greatly influenced by Sir Walter Scott, owner of the neighbouring Abbotsford estate, and the residence in the village of the mason/architect family of John Smith Sen. and his sons John and Thomas. From *c.* 1859, the sculptor Andrew Currie had his workshop in the grounds of Darnick Tower.

Of the five defensible towers that once stood in the village, DARNICK TOWER is the only one to survive more or less intact. Built in 1569 by Andrew Heiton. John Heiton sold most of the land to Sir Walter Scott *c.* 1820, but restored the tower for his own occupation, and *c.* 1823–7 seems to have added a two-storeyed E wing, possibly by *John & Thomas Smith.* Heiton's son had tower and wing remodelled in 1860–1 by *John Smith*, and, taking a leaf out of Scott's book, turned the tower into something approaching an antiquarian museum. Further alterations were made by Andrew Heiton Jun., who continued to add to the antiquarian collections.

The T-plan C16 tower comprises an oblong main block (11.2 m. by 6.4 m.) with a rectangular stair-turret (93.1 m. by 2.2 m.) projecting midway along the S side. Three storeys and a garret, with the turret rising higher to finish in a gabled caphouse surmounted by a cross finial. Random rubble masonry with dressings of local red and buff sandstone. The slate roof is received on crowstepped gables. The main block rises to an open wallwalk and prominent, crenellated parapet carried on individual corbels, while the caphouse is set out upon a double corbel course, the lower member being continuous. The thicker W gable, containing the chimney flues, encroaches on the wallwalk. In order to minimise this obstruction the outer face of the gable has been made convex (cf. Littledean Tower). Since it is known that prior to the restoration of *c.* 1823–7 the roof was thatched and the parapet uncrenellated, it may well be that the entire superstructure of the tower, including the garret and caphouse (which lacks crowsteps), was renewed at that time. A single, oval-mouthed gunloop is placed high up in the S wall to command the S approach.

The entrance doorway at the foot of the stair-turret is equipped with outer and inner doors: the outer door is an iron yett from Doune Castle (Stirling and Central). The lintel bears the sacred monogram IHS between the initals of Andrew Heiton and his son, John, on one side and the date 1569 and the initials KF, probably for Katherine Fisher, on the other (the date, now barely decipherable, has also been read as 1595). About halfway up the S wall of the stair-turret is a C19 panel charged with a Heiton bull's head. It looks as if a single-storeyed wing at one time ran S from the stair-turret. The early C19 E wing is of two main storeys, the entrance placed within a turret on the N side; above the door is a panel bearing the Heiton arms.

As refitted in Victorian times, the interior of the house (inaccessible at the date of visit) must have resembled a miniature Abbotsford, home to a growing collection of Scottish antiquities and *objets d'art.* Originally the tower seems to have contained a single main room on each floor, the lowest one being a vaulted kitchen. The vault is said to have fallen *c.* 1780, following which the room was subdivided, the W division becoming a dining room. The first-floor room, originally the hall, was panelled throughout, with a compartmented ceiling; elaborate Gothic chimneypiece in W wall evidently replacing an earlier one. Beside the entrance from the staircase an apparently original stone laver equipped with a mural discharge-spout. The second floor contains two bedrooms, while the garret, entered from the E wall-walk, has been fitted out as an armoury. The main newel stair terminates in a vault at this level, a smaller newel stair continuing upwards to the cap-house, which is also vaulted. Above both vaults there are perches for pigeons. Most of these features probably replicate earlier ones, but some may have been introduced or enhanced during the restoration of the upperworks c. 1823–7.

In the GARDEN lies the canopied head of a late Gothic TOMB or niche, probably brought from Melrose Abbey (q.v.) Other medieval CARVED STONES possibly emanating from the same source include fragments of dogtooth ornament built into the parapet-walk of the tower and part of a nook-shaft now supporting a C17 sundial on the S wall of the wing.

FISHER'S TOWER, c. 50 m. S, is the ruinous and roofless shell of a second defensible house of a more modest kind, perhaps better described as a bastle. Probably erected by John Fisher, who is on record c. 1555–75, the house probably dates from the latter part of this period. Oblong on plan, the building (12.1 m. by 6.8 m.) may originally have contained three full storeys, but as remodelled in the early C18, when the W half was built, or rebuilt, it comprised two storeys and an attic. Masonry of local rubble with red sandstone dressings. The original windows have roll-moulded margins and the later ones chamfered margins. Above the ground-floor entrance in the N wall is the sacred monogram IHS, which is said to have been accompanied by the initials JF, now no longer visible. The E gable incorporates two wide-mouthed gunloops, one on the ground floor and the other on the floor above. In the original arrangement the first floor seems to have contained a hall heated by a large fireplace in the E gable, but subsequently heating was provided for the ground floor also, the gunloop embrasure being converted into a fireplace. The attic probably contained two rooms, one at least of which was heated. The staircase arrangements are uncertain and there is nothing to show whether or not the ground floor was vaulted.

DESCRIPTION. At the junction of ABBOTSFORD ROAD and Smiths Road is THE GABLES, attributed to *John Smith*, c. 1840. A single-storey and attic, three-bay house with panelled and reeded entablatures to the entrance and windows. On the E side of Abbotsford Road the SMITH MEMORIAL HALL, dated and inscribed *In Memoriam* JS (John Smith) 1869; bellcote dated 1891. Plate-traceried window and doorway, both with hoodmoulds with foliaged stops. Attractive catslide ventilators along the roof ridge. Down Fishers Lane to the E is Darnick Tower (*see* above), while continuing along Abbotsford Road leads to Fisher's Tower (*see* above). Further on is the entrance drive to TOWER COTTAGE, built for John Heiton by *John Smith*, c. 1860. Single-storey, enlarged to a T-plan in the early C20. Tall octagonal stacks on rectangular plinths frame the broad-eaved piended roof. Abbotsford Road continues to the N, and on the l. is the park surrounding John Smith's home, Darnlee (*see* p. 559). At the S end of SMITHS ROAD is DARNICK DAIRIES, an early C19 single-storey range; the W part has moulded eaves course and catslide ventilators along the ridge. Converted to housing *c.* 1997.

DAWYCK HOUSE 1030
3.3 km. SW of Stobo

A spread-out Scottish Jacobean mansion superbly set within mature trees on low ground on the River Tweed's S bank. Built for Sir John Naesmyth by *William Burn*, 1832–7, to replace a tower house (dem. 1830). Burn's house was nearly doubled in size in 1898 by *John A. Campbell* for Mrs Alexander Balfour, with N and S additions in matching style. The planning is typical of Burn's smaller 'cottage house' designs, providing a block of two public rooms to the garden, vestibule and staircase hall, a small L-plan private wing at the W end and N service wing (minor extensions in 1909 by *Robert S. Lorimer*). Dawyck repeats on the garden (S) front its architectural treatment of the double crowstepped gable and central dormer of the entrance front, from Burn's Tyninghame House (Lothian),* but shows his style developing, in the use of corbelling from the round to the square, crowstepped gables, turreted towers with tall pointed caps, typical Scottish wall-head dormers and canted and square bay windows. Particularly pleasing are Jacobean diagonally set chimneys, and curly dormerheads. Campbell's additions extended the house E of the entrance, concluding on the N side with a two-storey canted bay window fronting a three-storey crowstepped double gable, and on the garden side with a double gable and arcaded veranda. Inside, oak panelling and discreet Gothic decoration. Wide oak-panelled circular stair. In the billiard room, part of Campbell's extension, a Gothic lincrusta paper ceiling by *Leonard Grandison*. Some of the bedroom doors are finished with panels of yew, presented in 1934 to Colonel F.R.S. Balfour by the Prince of Wales.

The CHAPEL, SW of the house, was built in 1837 by *Burn*, on the site of an earlier chapel. Early English, L-shaped on plan in coursed whinstone with sandstone dressings. Red tiled roof of 1898, replacing stone slabs, and a belfry with a double tier of shaped balusters. Late medieval FONT on a later pedestal. – STAINED GLASS. Three-light N window to E.R. Balfour, †1897, by *Christopher Whall*. – GARDENS. The S TERRACES, with stone walls, steps and richly carved faceted globe finials, were built *c.* 1820 by Italian landscape gardeners, who built similar terraces at Chartwell, Kent for the Colquhouns (related by marriage to the Naesmyths).

* David Walker, 'William Burn', in *Seven Victorian Architects*, ed. Jane Fawcett (1976).

The Dawyck policies, including the ARBORETUM up the Scrape Glen, are now in the care of the Royal Botanic Garden, Edinburgh. Until 1691 the lands of Dawyck belonged to the Veitch family who first introduced exotic trees. The Naesmyths continued the tradition of planting, in particular *James Naesmyth* (succeeded 1721), who studied under the Swedish botanist Carl Linnaeus and established the overall plan of the present landscape. Between 1800 and 1930 successive owners supported plant-hunting expeditions. NE of the house is an understated group of VISITOR CENTRE and OFFICES. Ridge-roofed.

NORTH LODGE. Late C19, picturesque with a timber-gabled entrance porch supported by dumpy red sandstone columns. Decorative gunloops. – W along the B712 are BELLSPOOL COTTAGES, a picturesque row dated 1800; reconstructed 1909 with Arts and Crafts detailing. – The former STABLES (now dwelling) are probably 1863, converted for motor cars *c.* 1909, when the central gabled pend was given a moulded red brick arch with a monogrammed keystone and bargeboarded gables added.

DAWYCK MILL FARM, 1.5km. NE by the Drove Road from Tweedsmuir to Peebles. Farmhouse dated 1876 and bow-ended corn mill of 1807.

WESTER DAWICK, 0.5km. SW. Built by Sir James Naesmyth *c.* 1819, extended late C19. Picturesque cottage, of 1875, with latticed windows and diagonally set chimneys.

5010   DENHOLM

A pleasant village, associated particularly with the stocking-weaving industry, laid out in the late C18 and early C19 around a green.

PARISH CHURCH, Kirkside. Free Church of 1844–5, built following the Disruption; it became the parish church in 1929. A small rectangular building with a main (SW) front of buff snecked rubble with ashlar dressings and raised margins; corbelled skews to the gable. Through this gable rises a salient with a pointed arch framing the entrance; the salient steps inwards to support a small belvedere-like tower with two pointed arches to each face, a pyramidal roof and a ball finial. Clock face dated 1885. Flanking the entrance are single, broad, pointed windows, with three similar windows along the rubble flanks. At the NE end is a brick hall dated 1892 and designed by a joiner, *Furness*. Inside, the SW gallery was originally intended as a schoolroom. – On the Hawick road is the former MANSE (Beachlands) of 1849 with a bracketed and corniced doorway under a finialled gable. Later addition to the r. with a wall-head dormer.

DENHOLM BRIDGE, Minto Road, over the River Teviot. Dated 1864. A fine rubble bridge of three arches with rock-faced voussoirs and rounded cutwaters.

WAR MEMORIAL, Westgate. Simple shaft with an incised cross on a high plinth, *c.* 1920.

LEYDEN MONUMENT, in the centre of the green. Erected in 32
memory of Dr John Leyden, antiquarian, physician and poet,
who was born at Denholm. A striking Decorated Gothic spire
in Swinton stone, raised on two tiers of squat red Aberdeen
granite columns with foliated capitals. By *Hector H. Orrock*,
sculpted by *A. Handyside Ritchie*, 1861.

DESCRIPTION

The cottages in MAIN STREET, on the s side of the green, are
all two-storey and harled with painted margins. A range of two-
storey late C18 houses, formerly thatched, including the CROSS
KEYS HOTEL, and KIRKVIEW and MINTLAW, has round-
arched door surrounds, but Kirkview is more sophisticated,
with a block-modillioned eaves course. Next along, the TEXT
HOUSE, probably *c.* 1900, aptly named for the two diamond-
shaped panels that read 'Tak tent in Time – All was others' and
'Ere Time be Tint – All well be others'. It has a canted bay
topped by a pediment and jettied out over an arched, recessed
doorway. Each side are wide pilasters embellished with stylised
capitals. Quite out of character with the village, its crudity has
charm. At the corner of WESTGATE are the War Memorial (*see*
above) and WESTGATE HALL, a C17 house of two storeys and
garret, formerly harled. The entrance doorway has a quirked,
edge-roll moulding, the lintel dated 1663. The w skewputt is
carved with the Douglas heart, the others are scrolled. The
interior has been modernised except for a large fireplace with
a massive lintel, recessed at each end, bearing the initials and
armorials of Sir Archibald Douglas of Cavers and Dame
Rachael Skene.
WESTSIDE has some rebuilding; Mill Wynd to the l. leads to the
remnants of DENHOLM MILL, a three-storey rubble building
now gutted and used as a garage. Of most interest is the late
C18 former WESTSIDE MILL, now a dwelling, at the rear of
Greenview. Three-storey with two rows of small, regularly
spaced and deeply recessed square windows, each for an individual stocking frame: a good example of early industrialisation of rural stocking-making before the development of C19
factory production in the towns. Dovecot in the roof, entered
from the gable, is now blocked.
The N side of the green has an unexciting but practical PRIMARY
SCHOOL of the 1960s on the l., followed by the late C19 OLD
SCHOOLHOUSE with tripartite windows flanking a doorway
with narrow sidelights, fronted by a square parapeted porch.
A single-storey schoolroom to the l. with large hoodmoulded
windows. It replaced an earlier school in a two-storey house
which was sited in the middle of the green. SUNNYSIDE, built
of ashlar, has five bays, with band courses, moulded cornice
and parapet, and a pend to the rear courtyard where there are
steps to the first floor. Flanked by five-bay blocks in pink sandstone, with entries to the upper floors. These blocks, probably
mid-C19, may have replaced earlier rows, as did the late C19
DENHOLM HOUSE, which is set back in its garden.
LEYDEN ROAD has a row of three C18 thatched cottages; the
centre one, LEYDEN COTTAGE, was the birthplace of Dr John

Leyden in 1775. 'Restored by the Edinburgh Border Counties Association, 1896'. Single-storey with a loft, harled with painted margins and a thatched catslide dormer. KIRKSIDE, on the E side of the green, has the church (*see* above) and some thoughtful infill by the *Eildon Housing Association*, 1989. Less sympathetically restored is ELM HOUSE at the SE corner, whose panel on the S gable relates that in '1800 W. Little build'.

HENLAWSHIEL OBELISK, 4 km. SW. Granite obelisk by *Robert Robinson* of Hawick, 1895, marking the site of the cottage where Dr John Leyden spent his boyhood.

SPITAL TOWER. *See* p. 693.

TEVIOT BANK. *See* p. 715.

5090

DINLABYRE

BURIAL ENCLOSURE for the Olivers of Dinlabyre, hidden in woodland on a terrace above the B6357. Carefully composed classical façades. The splendid three-bay entrance front has rusticated pilaster strips with chamfered block quoins at the angles and an arched entrance, with block-rusticated surround, capped by a pediment with an acanthus-leaf cartouche, dated 1749. Blind arches in the side bays have commemorative panels; the tympanum of the entrance arch (now on the ground) has similar inscriptions. In the narrower central bay of the NW side is a marble memorial to William Oliver, †1830. Inside, at the centre of the NE wall, is a swan-neck-pedimented tablet with a winged angel head and *memento mori*.

1040

DROCHIL CASTLE
5 km. NW of Lyne

Overlooking the Lyne and Tarth waters, the castle's fragmentary upperworks, glimpsed above surrounding trees, give no hint that this was one of the most remarkable Renaissance mansions in Scotland. Begun by James Douglas, fourth Earl of Morton, while Regent of Scotland (1572–8), the building was probably incomplete at the time of his execution in 1581 for his part in the murder of Henry, Lord Darnley. The castle appears to have been occupied, at least in part, during the C17, and c. 1680 was described as 'a great bulk of a House, five large stories high the one half without a roof and unfinished', but Adam de Cardonnel's drawing of 1789 shows it already in decay.

The PLAN, unique among Scottish castles of the period, took the form of an oblong block (25.6 m. by 21.1 m.) having rooms grouped in tenements on either side of a central corridor which traversed the building on its long axis. The main block rose to a height of four storeys and a garret. Lean-to roofs of the N and S tenements were received upon the corridor walls, which

p. 53   were carried a storey higher and contained most of the chimney flues. Large circular towers projected from the SW and NE corners of the main block, while smaller turrets were corbelled out at the tops of the other two corners. The corner towers seem to have contained five storeys and a garret, the two uppermost ones being corbelled to a square slightly smaller than the diameter of the tower below – a mannerism seen also at Thirlestane Castle (q.v.). From the ground-floor entrance at the W end of the corridor, a wide newel stair rose to the full height of the main block, giving access, either directly or by means of the corridor, to the rooms on either side, as also to those on the first and fourth floors of the corner towers, which were reached from supplementary transverse corridors. The remaining floors of the towers were approached p. 53 by newel stairs corbelled out in their re-entrant angles. There appears, however, to have been no means of access between the ground-floor kitchen and cellars and first floor other than via the principal stair. The principal reception rooms occupied the S side of the main block's first floor, and the family rooms probably occupied the second floor of the S tenement, but it is uncertain to what extent the upper floors on this side of the building were ever completed.

The castle is built of local whinstone rubble with dressings of dark red sandstone probably quarried at Broomlee Hill to the N. Nothing remains of the S tenement above the first floor. Some use is made of simply moulded stringcourses and corbel courses, while the upper member of the corbelling that supports the re-entrant stair-turret of the SW corner tower is decorated with chequer and sawtooth ornament. Most of the

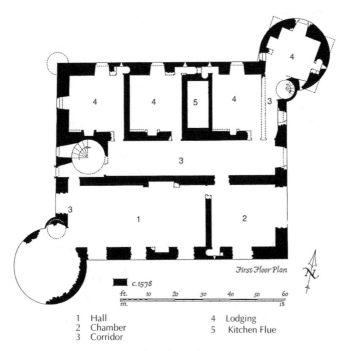

First Floor Plan

c.1578

| ft. | 10 | 20 | 30 | 40 | 50 | 60 |
| m. | | | | | | 18 |

1	Hall	4	Lodging
2	Chamber	5	Kitchen Flue
3	Corridor		

Drochil Castle.
Plan of first floor.

windows have plain rounded arrises, but some are wrought with quirked edge-rolls; many appear to have been fully glazed within protective iron grilles. The wall-head of the main block seems to have been surmounted by a blocking course, which was pierced at intervals by the dormer windows that lit the third floor. Little remains of the w entrance, but to judge from the small window that survives immediately above it the doorway was richly decorated. The window takes the form of a robustly carved aedicule incorporating Morton's initials and armorial devices of fetterlock, heart and mullets. The home-spun classical detail has similarities with that seen in other buildings associated with Morton. The main defensive provision comprised a series of gunloops on the two lower floors of the corner towers, some of those on the ground floor having redented ingoes (to deflect incoming shot) similar to those at Thirlestane.

The first-floor reception rooms in the s tenement comprised a large hall (c. 13.8 m. by 6.11 m.), with a smaller intercommunicating chamber to the E. The N wall of the hall evidently incorporated a splendid chimneypiece with spiral-shafted jambs, while the opposite wall may have contained a buffet for the display of plate. The function of the chamber in the sw tower is uncertain, although its position at the lower end of the hall suggests that it may have been an ante-room; alternatively it could have been an inner chamber, sited to command the views up the Tarth Water. In the N tenement the kitchen occupied the E end of the ground floor, its enormous chimney placed unexpectedly within the body of the house, which it must have helped to heat. The first and upper floors in this tenement seem to have contained up to seventeen lodgings, most of them with their own heating and sanitation. In addition the vertical space between the first- and fourth-floor transverse corridors giving access to the NE tower contained two small, superimposed chambers, perhaps servants' rooms. The top floor of the central corridor may have been a long gallery, lit both from a window at the E end and from dormers; it appears to have had a flat boarded ceiling.

A range of vernacular steadings, tucked into the hillside to the sw, bears a stone, possibly from the castle entrance, bearing Morton's initials and the date 1578.

DRUMELZIER

PARISH CHURCH. Parts of a medieval chapel dependent on Stobo, which later became parochial, survive within the existing building, though its present appearance dates largely from c. 1800 and a restoration of 1872, by *John Mitchell*. A harled rectangle with red sandstone dressings. Two gabled porches project towards the ends of its s flank, with a pair of Y-traceried windows between. Towards the E end is a round-arched entrance to the Tweedie Vault of 1617, above which is a replica armorial plaque for James Tweedie (†1612), and l. of the vault doorway is a c13 lancet head. On the w gable is a square bell-cote with a pyramidal cap, pinnacles and a ball finial. Inter-

nally, within what was the medieval chancel, the barrel-vaulted
TWEEDIE VAULT has a trefoil-headed C13 piscina at the E end
of its s wall, and there are traces of the rear arch of the lancet
window noted externally. Polygonal plaster ceiling, and the
floor slopes down towards the pulpit at the w end; there is a
gallery and retiring room over the Tweedie Vault. The loft stairs
are lit by the lancet window head, whose wide splay and chamfered rear arch confirm a C13 date. – FONT. Octagonal, grey
marble, late C19(?) – Early C19 PULPIT, between w windows,
semi-octagonal front, stairs on each side with cast-iron balusters. – STAINED GLASS, windows flanking pulpit, inscriptions
and lozenges in clear glass by *Marjorie Kemp*, 1926.
MANSE (Tinnis House). 1787. Much altered with mid-to-late C19
extensions. The late C18 steading survives.
PARISH HALL. Arts and Crafts inspired, by *Frank C. Mears*,
1939. Horizontal timber boarding on a low whinstone base,
with recessed windows lighting the main hall. A wide s gable,
the windows arranged in Voyseyesque fashion.
DRUMELZIER CASTLE, 1.3 km. sw. Residence of the Tweedie
family and then of the Hays. Depicted by Grose in 1791 as a
tower house of modified L-plan 'much out of repair'; only the
lower portions of its walls now survive.
NORMAN'S CASTLE, 5.5 km. ssw, high above the floor of the
Tweed near Stanhope. A small DUN with enclosing rampart
and ditch. The interior measures *c.* 7.5 by 4.5 m. within a wall
from 3.6 m. to 4.5 m. thick and up to 1.2 m. high. The entrance
is on the sw. Excavations in 1959 recovered a penannular, or
open-ring, bronze brooch dating from the late C1 or C2 A.D.
TINNIS CASTLE. *See* p. 724.

DRYBURGH   5030

Dryburgh is known for its Abbey, and in the mid C19 was
described as a small hamlet consisting of about half a dozen cottages, all single-storey and thatched, with small gardens. From
the late C18 the village was improved, often eccentrically, by
David Stuart Erskine, eleventh Earl of Buchan, who acquired the
Abbey and its estate in 1786.

THE ABBEY

Widely considered the most beautiful of the Border abbeys,   9
Dryburgh is set within a delightfully wooded loop of the Tweed,
with ruined buildings that compose themselves wonderfully picturesquely. It offers the fascination of the evocation of the aspirations and tensions of religious life as recorded in the writings
of the abbey's most famous leader, Adam of Dryburgh (1184–*c.*
1188). But for many the abbey's most compelling associations are
with the romanticism and antiquarian pursuits of Sir Walter Scott
(†1832) and of the eleventh Earl of Buchan (†1829), both of
whom are buried within its walls.

Traditionally, St Modan, a particularly shadowy C7 saint, is said
to have based his missionary activity here, but the present

buildings are the remains of probably the first Premonstraten-
sian abbey in Scotland. Founded, according to the *Melrose
Chronicle*, in 1150 by Hugh de Morville, Constable of Scotland
and friend of King David I, by whom extensive lands were
granted. The first canons came from Alnwick in 1152, presumably once temporary first buildings had been erected.
There are possible traces of earlier structures at the junction
of the E face of the E conventual range and the S side of the
adjoining parts of the church.

Construction of permanent buildings probably started in the
late C12 with the E conventual range and the lower walls of the
adjacent transepts and presbytery, the two latter being completed around the mid C13. The costs of building evidently
impoverished the abbey, a state exacerbated by the profligacy
of Abbot John (1240–*c*. 1255). There is mention of debts
in 1242 and in 1255, when the bishop of St Andrews and
the abbot of Jedburgh were mandated to collect the revenues,
part to pay off the house's debts, and part to support the
community.

The wars with England created further difficulties. In 1322
Edward II fired the abbey; it was again burnt by Richard II in
1385 and there was another devastating fire in 1461. Yet more
English attacks took place in the C16: one in 1523 necessitated
extensive repairs, while a raid of 1544 damaged the conventual
buildings but not the church, and there was possibly even
greater damage in 1545. From 1506 the abbey had been led by
secular commendators rather than abbots, and in 1539 Thomas
Erskine became the first of a succession of members of that
family to hold the office.*

In 1604 the abbey became part of the temporal lordship of
Cardross, held by John Erskine, Earl of Mar, along with Cambuskenneth Abbey and Inchmahome Priory (Stirling and
Central Scotland). Ownership of the abbey's estates later
passed successively to the Scotts of Ancrum, the Haliburtons
of Newmains and the family of Tod. The abbey was bought in
1786 by the eleventh Earl of Buchan (himself the inheritor of
the title of Lord Cardross), an antiquarian of wide interests
and a founder of the Society of Antiquaries of Scotland in
1780. He lavished close attention on the remains, which were
visible from his residence of Dryburgh Abbey House (*see*
below) to the S E. As well as investigating and landscaping its
ruins, he placed several eyecatchers within it, including a now
lost statue of the architect Inigo Jones in the cloister. He was
buried within the sacristy and library in 1829. Sir Walter Scott
was buried in the N choir chapel in 1832. The abbey was
acquired in 1918 by Lord Glenconner, who gave it to the nation
in 1919, and the site was subjected to clearance excavations in
the 1920s.

---

*The E conventual range, already adapted to meet changed patterns of monastic
life before the Reformation, was extensively modified for occupation as a commendator's residence.

THE ABBEY CHURCH

The PLAN of the church consisted of an aisle-less PRESBYTERY
of three short bays, an aisled CHOIR of two bays, TRANSEPTS
with E chapel aisles, and a crossing with a TOWER. The aisled
NAVE in its final form was of six irregularly spaced bays, the
third bay from the E being particularly long, while the two W
bays are significantly narrower. A screen wall crossed the nave
and aisles on the line of the second piers W of the crossing
piers, enclosing the canons' choir. The most complete remains
are the N side of the choir, the adjoining E side of the N transept
and the S wall of the S transept; there are also reduced sections
of walling around the three sides of the presbytery, the E side

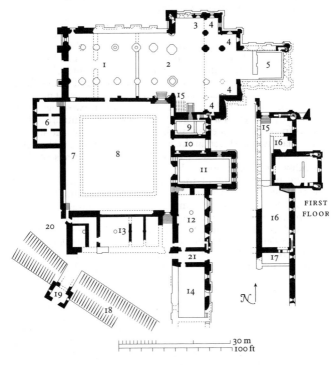

30 m
100 ft

1	Nave	12	Warming Room
2	Canons' Choir	13	Undercroft, Refectory over
3	North Transept	14	Novices' Day Room
4	Chapels	15	Night Stair
5	Earlier Presbytery	16	Canons' Dormitory
6	Cellars	17	Treasury
7	Cloister Walk	18	Water Channel
8	Cloister Garth	19	Gatehouse
9	Library and Sacristy	20	Site of Kitchens
10	Parlour	21	Slype
11	Chapter House		

Dryburgh Abbey.
Plan.

of the s transept, the N side of the N transept, and along the s
and w sides of the nave.

EASTERN PARTS. The walls of the unaisled PRESBYTERY are
largely reduced to the level below the windows, and there are
few coherent remains on the s side. Nevertheless, the base
course around the eastern parts has tiers of chamfered courses
below a keeled roll, like that of the E range of the conventual
buildings, suggesting they were laid out together as part of the
first substantive campaign. (However, the lower walling of the
s transept chapel appears to have had no base course, and may
be a relic of an earlier structure.)

Within the presbytery there are slight remains of decorative
wall arcading around the lower walls, which are clearest at the
SE corner. The pattern of buttressing points to an E triplet of
windows. On the N side there survives a single jamb of the w
window, which shows that the presbytery lancet windows corresponded in height to both the arcade and middle storeys of
the adjoining choir, above which was the clearstorey. Internally
and externally the lancets in both presbytery and choir were
framed by an outer order carried on disengaged nook-shafts,
with moulded capitals and waterholding bases. The taller
windows of the presbytery had nook-shafts in two stages, separated by a single shaft-ring. The glazing seems initially to have
been in timber frames set within rebates towards the interior
(the glass now restored in the choir and transept chapels). After
the E side of the transept aisle, the hoodmouldings of these
windows also have dogtooth decoration.

The bay divisions of the CHOIR and TRANSEPT CHAPEL
AISLES were initially marked by keeled triplet shafts. The shafts
at the SE corner of the transept chapel start above the string
running below the windows, to allow space for a piscina, which
flanked the altar there. The E responds of the choir arcade had
axial triplets of shafts (the leading one keeled) flanked by disengaged nook-shafts. The N transept chapel's N respond has a
more elaborate version of this arrangement; but in the s
transept the respond – which is probably earlier – had a keeled
triplet against a broad pilaster. So far as the piers are concerned, the NE crossing pier was of bundled-shaft type, with
triplets on the cardinal axes (the leading shafts being keeled),
which are separated by pairs of keeled shafts. The intermediate piers, however, had filleted shafts to the cardinal axes, and
half-shafts to the diagonal axes, the various elements being separated by right-angled salients. This is a type which has some
analogies with the weak piers of Glasgow Cathedral crypt and
the nave arcade piers at Inchmahome Priory, both probably of
the 1240s.

The N choir and transept chapel aisles have quadripartite
vaulting. The wall shafts at the junction of the two aisles are
set back from the angle, which created difficulties in constructing the vault over this bay, hence the sharp intake of wall
and the additional arch of connecting ribs. Two bays of vaulting have bosses with stiff-leaf decoration, while the central bay
has a depiction of Christ in Majesty. Traces of painted decoration have been identified on some ribs, arch mouldings and

bosses, mostly geometrical, but of foliage patterns on the inner side of the N transept arch; little is now visible.

Above arcade level, the bays are divided by filleted triplets of wall-shafts rising from between the arcade arches to the wall-head, and the stages are marked by string courses. The form of the middle stage is unusual in having the wall pierced by a foiled circlet recessed within a pointed segmental arch. It is hard to find parallels, although Westminster Abbey and Hereford Cathedral N transept, both of the 1240s, have windows in the outer wall of the middle storey with foiled circles. At clearstorey level, the E bay on the N side has an arcade of five arches on the inner face of the wall passage, carried on cylindrical shafts; the wider central arch corresponds to the single lancet window on the outer face of the wall. The W bay of the choir clearstorey has an inner arcade of only three cusped arches. The rectangular opening through the outer wall of the E bay is later, and above this externally are corbels – possibly for a bellcote.

The two-bay E elevation of the N transept generally resembles that of the choir, but here the inner arcade to each clearstorey bay is of three arches, carried on small piers with rolls and segmental hollows. They are similar to that in the W bay of the choir, but without the cusping. These arcades reveal a new finesse of detailing, seen in elements such as a rounded stock rising from the abaci of the piers which dies vertically into the arch soffits. This detail, which is also seen in the lancets of the N transept N gable wall, has parallels in the post-1270 work at Elgin Cathedral. Externally these N gable windows have an inner order of continuous mouldings, with an outer order carried on triplets of shafts separated by a band of dogtooth. A new type of string course is introduced below these windows. At the NW corner the base course also changes, to a roll at the base of a deep chamfer (its upper parts are lost).

The lower S wall of the S transept was built along with the adjacent E claustral range, and must be the earliest part of the church to have been built to any height. Very little survives of 9 the choir and transept aisles on the S side, but they appear to have been broadly similar to those on the N. Three doorways open off the S transept. One within the aisle gives onto a stair leading both down to the sacristy and up to the higher parts of the transept; a second (much modified) also leads to the sacristy. A third elevated doorway in the SW corner is at mid-height of the night stair to the dormitory. On the adjacent W window hoodmould is a delightful corbel with a bat, which must have looked down on many generations of canons wearily descending the night stair.

The upper S wall of the transept has a five-light window in which all lights reach up to the containing arch; a stepped base accommodated the double-pitched roof of the adjacent dormitory. Like all the other windows, it was originally provided with internal rebates for glazing frames, though later glazing chases start at the level of the dormitory roof apex, suggesting that the lower part of the windows was blocked by that stage. Of the six-bay NAVE, there is little more than the S aisle wall, parts of the W front, and fragments of a number of arcade piers. Regrettably, we know nothing about the design of the nave above the arcade level, and it is not even known if it had a three-storey elevation. Two later building phases may be represented in what survives, in addition to the original work. The SE PROCESSIONAL DOORWAY from the nave to the cloister is perhaps of *c.* 1200. (Its inner orders were removed to Newton Don, near Kelso, but rebuilt in their original position in 1894, albeit with extensive restoration.) It is round-arched and of four orders: an inner order with bands of massive dogtooth, and three other orders carried on disengaged shafts set against angled faces. The E jamb has caps of chastely simple form, with crockets at the angles; the W jamb has more luxuriant foliage, some of stiff-leaf type, others with seven or nine leaves to each sprig.

The two E bays of the nave and aisles were divided from the rest by the choir screen. The position of an altar in front of the screen is indicated by a piscina in the S nave wall. On the N side, the second pier W of the crossing was encased within the screen and thus partly protected from destruction. It had filleted shafts on the cardinal axes, half-round shafts on the diagonal axes, and quadrant hollows between. The nave piers are raised on high bases with a concave intake above the sub-bases (cf. Glasgow Cathedral and Inchmahome Priory). This pier type appears to have continued down the nave, but in at least two cases the bases themselves are of a later type, suggesting either remodelling or late completion.

The attack of 1385 clearly necessitated extensive rebuilding in the nave. Perhaps at this stage there was a thought of reducing the nave to four bays, since within the S wall there is a section of base course of late type, running through the wall thickness. Immediately to its E there is also a doorway to the cloister, seeming to confirm that the nave was to have extended no further W. However, it was then decided that the nave should be longer, with a new doorway into the cloister further W, facing towards the W walk. A base course of the same form as that incorporated in the S wall was used (or relocated?) for the rebuilt W front. The most impressive surviving feature of the rebuilt nave is the W DOORWAY, which has four continuous orders of mouldings, with two bands of square flower between, the mouldings rising from bases with four simple bands of moulding.

MONUMENTS and WORKED STONES. PRESBYTERY, several memorials in E wall, some re-set from elsewhere, and some probably inserted by the eleventh Earl of Buchan. N CHOIR AISLE, Sir Walter Scott, †1832, and his wife, red polished granite double tomb-chest; set into E wall, memorial of Scott's ancestor, John Haliburton, †1640; to E of Scott's tomb, grave of John Gibson Lockhart, †1854, Scott's son-in-law and biographer, red polished granite with bronze portrait medallion by *John Steell*. N TRANSEPT, memorial of Field Marshal Earl Haig, †1928, to same design as that of his soldiers. S TRANSEPT, re-set in S wall of S chapel, floor slab of Adam Robson of Gledswood, an incised cross, with inscription around border. NAVE, set in masonry of N wall, a reused stone on which are markings for a game of merelles or nine men's morris.

THE MONASTIC BUILDINGS

The CLOISTER is s of the nave and, because of the slope of the land, is lower than the floor level of the church. The slope also called for progressive downward stepping of the rooms within the E conventual range. Initially it seems that only ranges along its E and S sides were built, though a prominent string course along the W wall could have been intended as the seating for the barrel vault of a W range. A short W range was eventually added. The evidence of the surviving structures is invaluably supplemented by John Slezer's views of 1693.

The E CONVENTUAL RANGE is one of the most complete examples of a monastic building to survive in Scotland, and in its primary form probably dates substantially from the late C12, albeit possibly incorporating earlier fragments at the N end of its E wall. The EXTERIOR will be considered first, starting with the outer E face, the only structure to break the line of which is the outer part of the CHAPTER HOUSE, its E gable having a stepped triplet of lancets separated by buttresses; a stepping string course continues around the windows as a hoodmoulding. The two salient flanks of the chapter house have single lancets. Above the chapter house there is evidence of much rebuilding and heightening when this part of the range was remodelled, both before and after the Reformation. Between the s transept and chapter house, the SACRISTY is lit by a pair of round-headed windows with a vesica between their heads (a markedly Cistercian motif), while the PARLOUR originally had a round-arched doorway, which was infilled in the early C19 when the Erskine vault was formed within (see below), and a pair of round-headed openings formed in the blocking wall. A string course extends round the heads of the sacristy windows and parlour doorway as a hoodmoulding; a second string course steps up to run below the dormitory windows, the surrounding stonework of which has here been robbed.

s of the chapter house the E face of the range was articulated with broad pilaster-buttresses, weathered back at the string below the dormitory windows. In the s bay of the WARMING ROOM is an original small round-headed window; the two N bays have (post-1385?) large and steeply pointed Y-traceried windows with transoms. A late small doorway (now blocked) connected through a curved passage to a doorway in the s flank of the chapter house. Immediately next to the chapter house, but well above ground level, is another late doorway, inserted when a stair running eastwards replaced the night stair; there are traces of a lean-to roof above it. s of the warming room, the slype doorway is round-headed with a simple chamfer, above which is a small window to a mezzanine chamber. The room s of the slype was lit by large round-headed windows with sawtooth-decorated hoodmoulds (like that in the s transept chapel). On the upper floor of the range, s of the chapter house, there were at least six round-headed windows

to the dormitory, all of which have been partly infilled (probably after 1385), to form small ogee-headed openings.

The W FACE of the E range survives only within the area of
the cloister, extending from the SE corner of the transept to
the E gable of the refectory. At the N end, recessed into the wall
of the S transept, is a segmental-arched book press with a
rebate for a door frame and slots for shelves. S of this, a round-
headed doorway of two continuous chamfered orders and a
chamfered hoodmould opens into the LIBRARY and SAC-
RISTY. Next S off the E walk, the entrance to the PARLOUR was
originally a plain round-headed opening with a chamfered
hoodmoulding, but a smaller arched doorway was inserted
when it was made into the Erskine burial aisle in the early C19,
and the arms of a branch of the Erskine family set between the
two arches.

The CHAPTER HOUSE entrance, as might be expected, is
the grandest feature towards the cloister. Its round-headed
doorway resembles the SE processional doorway into the nave,
though possibly slightly earlier. It has a continuous dogtooth-
decorated inner order framed by three orders with disengaged
shafts; these shafts have elegantly attenuated waterleaf capitals
and waterholding bases. Flanking the doorway on each side is
a round-headed arch; they enclose deeply set pairs of pointed
arches on three pairs of shafts with chalice capitals. Below the
N window is an inscription 'Hic jacet Archibaldus', assumed to
be one of the Earl of Buchan's more confusing contributions
and it was perhaps part of his – mercifully abandoned – scheme
to make the chapter house part of a Temple of Caledonian
Fame. S of the chapter house is a round-headed archway with
a door rebate near the middle of the wall, opening onto the
day stair to the dormitory.

At regular intervals along this wall are vault springings, indicating an abortive proposal to have stone vaulting over the E
walk. However, as built the walk had a timber lean-to roof,
with corbels for the wall-plate and pockets for the half-collars.
Only part of one DORMITORY window remains on this side,
framed by two orders of continuous chamfers. The wall-head
above is indicated by a short stretch of corbel table embodied
within the masonry at the SW corner of the transept. In his
views of the abbey of 1693, John Slezer shows a row of eight
windows at first-floor level, extending from the church to the
chapter house, with smaller windows beyond. However, Slezer
also shows an upper tier of windows, with yet more windows
between their heads; he also shows the range rising to the
height of the adjacent transept. Nothing survives of this upper
storey, if it ever existed. If it *was* built it was perhaps intended
to provide individual, rather than communal accommodation
for the canons, with later modifications for the commendators.

The INTERIOR of the E RANGE begins with a narrow barrel-
vaulted space for the SACRISTY and LIBRARY, which were
presumably separated by a timber partition. The sacristy was
entered by the spiral stair from the S transept aisle. (There is
also a doorway into it at the centre of the transept, down a
straight flight of steps, but this is heavily modified.) The inte-

rior is now occupied by memorials to the family of the Earls of Buchan. On the central axis, table tomb of eleventh Earl of Buchan, †1829 (death mask(?) and astrological markings below cursive Latin inscription). Against E wall, memorial (using medieval altar as base and elevated two steps above the floor level) of Margaret Fraser, wife of eleventh Earl of Buchan, †1819 (portrait medallions of Earl and Countess set in front of altar, and obelisk above, supporting marble urn); in SW corner, memorial of second wife of twelfth Earl of Buchan, †1838 (plinth supporting urn); various grave-slabs in floor; against N wall, heroic bust by *William Reid*, 1804; against S wall, bust of eleventh Earl at age of 69. There is an arched piscina in the S wall with a floor drain below it. Traces of painted decoration, with black, red and blue lines, survive in the SE corner on the string course running below the vault.

The adjacent PARLOUR is barrel-vaulted, with a chamfered string course at vault springing level. The outer ends of the passage were modified, as already described, when it became a burial place for the Erskine family in the early C19. Memorial to several generations of family below E window. There are two aumbries in the S wall. The parlour now contains a small display of carved stones, including a late C12/early C13 basin (or shaft base?), each face with relief carvings of intertwining dragons biting their spiralling tails, from which foliage develops; vaulting boss with figure of St Andrew; another boss with *Agnus Dei*; another with stiff-leaf decoration; a post-Reformation gravestone depicting Adam and Eve, the figures unusually depicted as fully naked.

The CHAPTER HOUSE is an impressive barrel-vaulted room, entered (by a modern timber stair) from a dramatically high point because of the terracing of the cloister above the level of much of the E range. The E wall has three lancet windows, though the vault has slightly eclipsed their rear-arch apices. A bench runs around all four walls. Along the E wall, where the abbey's dignitaries had their seats, there is intersecting arcading carried on disengaged shafts, with simply moulded caps and waterholding bases. This, probably the earliest complete chapter house in Scotland, is additionally valuable for its early decorative PAINTING. Along the E part of the N wall are traces of *trompe-l'oeil* arcading, reflecting the real arcading of the E wall, and within the arches of both real and painted arcading are painted patterns. (There appears to have been later timber arcading along the N and S walls.) Elsewhere, above the general limewash of the walls, was imitation ashlar jointing, while string courses, windows and vaults were emphasised by geometrically patterned bands.

The WARMING ROOM could be entered either from a doorway at the foot of a stair from the cloister at the E end of the refectory, or from the slype adjoining the S end. It had two piers along the N–S axis, which once supported six compartments of quadripartite vaulting; the piers were of basically octagonal form, with deeply cut re-entrants at the angles. The wall ribs of the vaulting survive along the E, W and S walls, and rise from triplet wall-shafts carried on foliate corbels above the string course which ran below the original windows; the shafts have foliate or simply blocked-out capitals. The fireplace was originally at the centre of the E wall, but it was blocked after 1385 when a new one, with a projecting canopy, was built at the centre of the W wall; at that time the two N windows of the E wall were greatly enlarged. At the N end of the chamber are the two arches which carried the day stair from the cloister to the dormitory. There used to be an early-C19 polygonal enclosure at the NE corner, housing a corridor from the chapter house to the area E of the range, with a doorway also into the warming house.

The SLYPE is a barrel-vaulted corridor, with a round-headed W arch with straight jambs, and a rebated E doorway; doorways within vault intersections opened onto the chambers on each side of the corridor. The slope of the land and low height of the slype left space for a mezzanine between its vault and dormitory floor. The full extent of the range S of the slype is unknown; what survives is the partial shell of a room of similar proportions as the warming room. This had six compartments of quadripartite vaulting carried on two piers. The surviving (reconstructed) pier is of the same type as that in the warming room, and has a waterholding base and waterleaf capital.

The two principal means of access to the first-floor DORMITORY were by the night stair from the church, and by the day stair from the cloister; but there was also a doorway reached from the spiral stair at the SE corner of the transept. Access to a later upper floor above the chapter house was by spiral stairs in the turrets flanking the rebuilt E gable. The shoulder-lintelled doorway onto the NE of these latter stairways indicates possible dates after the attacks of either 1322 or 1385. Access to the wall-head parapet on the W side of the range, and to the upper parts of the main body of the heightened E range (if Slezer's depiction was accurate), was off the spiral stair in the SW corner of the S transept. A mural stair in the E wall of the dormitory led down to the mezzanine chamber over the slype. The dormitory itself has been extensively remodelled and subdivided, evidently on several occasions.

The S CONVENTUAL RANGE was almost entirely occupied by the REFECTORY, elevated above cloister ground level over an undercroft. In the E wall are two shallow pockets, possibly associated with a canopy over the dais at that end. The W gable was rebuilt in the C15, when a twelve-petal rose window was inserted, of a similar design to that in the W gable at Jedburgh Abbey. Little remains of the N and S walls, and nothing of the refectory entrance, but close to its likely site, towards the S end of the W cloister wall, is a segmental-arched lavatory recess. W of the refectory, above a small doorway opening onto a stair down to the kitchen basement, is a pastoral staff and shield with the arms of James Stewart, to whom the abbey was granted in 1523. Slezer indicates that the S arcade of the cloister may have survived in the late C17, though his details are unreliable.

At the NW corner of the refectory a doorway presumably led through to KITCHENS to the W. A horizontal moulding above the outer side of this doorway suggests there was once a lobby between refectory and kitchen, though later marks of a double-pitch roof, which cut through this moulding, show that the kitchen range eventually abutted the refectory. The basement below the refectory was of two compartments, of two and four bays. Initially it was covered by quadripartite vaulting carried on a central row of octagonal piers of the same type as in the E range; this was later replaced by barrel vaults, of which the two bays in the W compartment survive. Below the refectory dais, at the E end, was a stair from the cloister to the area beyond the S range. The round-headed doorway to the cloister at the head of the stair is framed by three unbroken orders of arches, the innermost chamfered.

Initially the W CONVENTUAL RANGE appears to have been left unbuilt perhaps because of financial difficulties. A block with a basement of three barrel-vaulted chambers, one with a fireplace, was built at a late stage, probably in the C16. The range was entered by a segmental-headed doorway cut through the W cloister wall at its N end. The vaults now contain a selection of carved and moulded stones from the abbey, including parts of an elaborately traceried window.

On the outer bank of the lade, across a bridge SW of the refectory, are the remains of a two-storey GATEHOUSE, of which the most complete part is the N wall. On the N gable kneelers are the arms of Greenlaw and Kerr. SW of the gatehouse is an OBELISK erected by the eleventh Earl of Buchan in 1794 to commemorate Hugh de Morville, represented in low relief on the side towards the abbey. In deeper relief are figures of James I and James II, possibly later additions. An inscription says the figures were carved by *George Burnet* and lettering cut by *D. Forson*, for Sir David Erskine (the illegitimate son of the Earl of Buchan who inherited the Dryburgh Abbey estate).

Small GRAVEYARD, N of the church. Particularly worthy of mention is a small group of C17 and C18 headstones and memorials to tenants and staff of the Dryburgh estate, with portrait figures (mostly half-length) reading books, and most with pediments in the form of winged angels' heads; one, †1756, has a full-length figure; Peter Stirling, tenant, †1847, with a draped female figure pointing heavenwards (possibly carved by his son, *Edwin Stirling*, a sculptor patronised by Sir David Erskine and trained by John Smith); a cadaver-shaped upright memorial to James Hood, †1799.

OTHER BUILDINGS

DRYBURGH SUSPENSION BRIDGE. The first chain bridge in Britain; its span is 261 ft (79.6 m.), built in 1817 by *John & Thomas Smith*, with a wooden platform suspended from iron chains. Twice reconstructed, first after a gale in 1818 'on a new and more elegant plan' by the Smiths and again in 1872, when firm posts were placed along the walkway, with a strong wire rope attached to each post and fixed in the centre of the bridge.

DRYBURGH ABBEY HOTEL (Dryburgh House), S of the Abbey. Solid red sandstone Baronial remodelling of an existing early C19 house by *C.G.H. Kinnear* of *Peddie & Kinnear* for Lord Jerviswood, 1876. Converted for a hotel *c.* 1931 by the Scottish

Motor Traction Company who realised the importance in the Borders of tourism by road. Kinnear gave the s elevation of the Georgian house two crowstepped gables, defined by a string course round three projecting bays, and a tall square crow-stepped tower house with a square conical-roofed turret on a circular corbelled-out base. The tower's w elevation has a chimney gable with a corbelled-out wall-walk with square open turrets, and to the l. a crowstepped gable broken by a crenel-lated balcony. Attached to the N is a ballroom added in 1937 with a castellated front pierced by a large window with astra-gals. Other additions of this period are in matching style and materials. Extensions of 1997–8 by *Architectural Ltd.* are in arti-ficial stone of matching colour. Three storeys with small pedi-ments and two-storey canted bays. Much-altered interior, but the decorative cast-iron balustrade of the early C19 staircase sur-vives. The hotel offices occupy a remnant of an earlier tower house* (destroyed in the early C19 rebuilding): a single, barrel-vaulted chamber with a doorway with a roll-and-hollow mould-ing. Rooms on the first floor still retain opulent late C19 cornices and friezes. – STABLES. Early C19, extended 1876. Good timber flèche ventilators, and a central pedimented entrance. – The crowstepped LODGE, with a wide gabled porch and Tudorish arched entrance, must be by *John Smith, c.* 1840.

DRYBURGH ABBEY HOUSE. SE of the Abbey. A tower house was built here in 1572 for George Haliburton of Mertoun. Later added to. David Erskine, eleventh Earl of Buchan, demolished the tower in 1784, then repaired and extended the remaining parts.† His house was largely destroyed by fire in 1892 and reconstructed by *Henry F. Kerr* for Oswald Erskine. The ridge-roofed entrance block (N) appears to be the earliest part, and was perhaps there in 1784. If so, the arrangement of windows, and lack of them, suggests that this was originally the rear ele-vation, the entrance front now concealed by a matching s block, possibly added by the eleventh Earl of Buchan. This has a two-storey octagonal E bay and a two-storey bow against the w gable, both added by *John Smith*, who was discussing a new house for Lady Buchan in 1839. Kerr's embellishments are Scottish Renaissance, e.g. circular corner bartizans, linked by a solid wall-head balustrade, which is continued, with decora-tive machicolations, across the E gable. The entrance has Ionic colonettes, a frieze of triglyphs, obelisk finials and pediment containing the Erskine crest. The interior of the house was totally renewed in 1892 in a mixture of Scottish Renaissance and classical decoration.

DOVECOT, SW, dated 1828. A cylinder of reused rubble stone with pink harling. Corbelled-out wall-head with a domed slated roof. – Adjacent SUNDIAL on a small knoll, comprising a large square stone base with an inscription and circular dial by *Adam Simson* of Lessudden. – Tunnel-type ICE HOUSE, NE of the house. – Gothic STABLES by *John Smith*. A courtyard

* This was the seat of the Erskines of Shieldfield and afterwards of the Riddells of Muserig.
† The appearance of the tower is known from a panel uncovered in the hall of the present house.

block with a central pend, the w front with a crenellated wall-head, topped by a large Erskine crest; the end bays have tall blind arches, crenellated gables and crosslets. The walling between is decorated with blind arcading. Late C19 fittings by the *Carron Co.* include jolly horse-head finials to the newel posts.

The reconstructed remains of the medieval abbey's CORN MILL were converted to a fishing house. Two-storey, rubble-built, with droved corner stones, and a reused cusped window similar to one in the s wall of the N transept of the Abbey; copied on the E façade. Traces of a large arch over the lade (culverted in 1892). GATEWAYS on the drive to the stables have a rustic stone arch (w), and cannon spouts (E). – The LODGE and GATEPIERS appear to incorporate what remains of the Lower Lodge to the Abbey, dating from c. 1817, and the Porter's Lodge, a single-storey octagon re-roofed c. 1840 when a two-storey E addition was made with bracketed overhanging eaves, probably by Smith. The square gatepiers are original, but the crosses on top of the piers are now missing.

DESCRIPTION

On a mound N of Dryburgh Suspension Bridge, at the w end of the village, is the Neo-Grecian TEMPLE OF THE MUSES, built by the eleventh Earl of Buchan and dedicated to the poet James Thomson, author of *The Seasons*. Circular with nine Ionic columns carrying a shallow domed roof with a finial of a lyre carrying a bust of Thomson (a replacement of the original). The Temple contained originally a *Coade* stone statue of the Apollo Belvedere on a circular pedestal showing nine Muses with laurel wreaths modelled 'in the die'. Now missing. Bronze figures of the Four Seasons by *Siobhan O'Hehir* were installed in 2002.

DRYBURGH MAINS, by the Temple, is a late C18 two-storey, three-bay farmhouse of squared ashlar, with a single-storey addition to the E, *c.* 1820. To the E are two-storey cottages, harled with painted bands, heightened from single-storey thatched cottages *c.* 1820. Later timber dormerheads. STIRLING COTTAGE at the E end is named after the sculptor, Edwin Stirling, who lived here and was patronised by Sir David Erskine, illegitimate son of the eleventh Earl. It has a crenellated corner tower, corbel course and turret roof. Small decorative niches at second floor.

Further up the road to the l. is ORCHARD GATE, the principal entrance into Orchard Field. Pink sandstone Gothic arch of *c.* 1820, flanked by round turret-like piers with incised crosses, corbelled-out cornices, crenellations with projecting cannon spouts, wreathed with a rope device, and topped by obelisks with small ball finials. Inscribed across the arch the words HOC POMARIUM SUA MANU SATUM PARENTIBUS SUIS OPTIMIS SAC D S BUCHANAE COMES. ('D[avid] S[tuart], Earl of Buchan, dedicated this orchard, planted with his own hands, to the best of parents'.) Fine early C20 wrought-iron gates presented by Lord Glenconner, their design based on the Bear Gates at Traquair House (q.v.). Overthrow with a central shield and decoration of tulips and rosettes. The double gates have a thistle motif and spreading branches, each side decorated with flowers, leaves and seed heads. The wall on the S side of the field has circular corner turrets, projecting copes and water-spouts.

Opposite the gate is TWEED COTTAGE built *c.* 1960 in red sandstone and incorporating the C18 Quarry Cottage. Coursed rubble and sandstone dressings, single-storey with bracketed overhanging timber eaves. Bargeboards decorated with scrolls. *John Laidlaw & Sons* added to the E end in the same style, *c.* 1990. Stylish summer house by *Nigel Bridges*, 1990, in Yorkshire oak. Built using medieval joinery techniques and its lead roof embossed by hand. Inside, the ceiling illustrates the history of joinery since pre-Roman times.

NEWMAINS, at the N end of the village, on a steep site. Colonial-style bungalow with a veranda with decorative cast-iron railings. By *L. Ingleby Wood*, 1900, extended by *Lorne Brown Associate*s, 1998, in matching materials. Under the veranda is a passage leading to storage chambers (for fish?) accessed by doors from the garden. Good oak Neo-Tudor stair and C18 chimneypiece imported from Edinburgh New Town, with centre panel of a shepherd boy with crook.

WALLACE STATUE, Clint Hill, 0.7 km. N. A colossal red sandstone statue by *John Smith* of the 'Great Patriot Hero', erected in 1814 by the eleventh Earl of Buchan at his most eccentric. Wallace stands with saltire shield and a double-handed sword on an appropriately large base. Repaired by *Bob Heath* and *Graciela Ainsworth*, 1991. Contemporary 'cinerary' urn, with a burning flame. Smith also designed a lodge (dem.) for the monument keeper. The gatepiers survive; railings renewed in 1992.

GLEDSWOOD HOUSE. *See* p. 323.

5030

DRYGRANGE HOUSE
4.1 km. NE of Melrose

Drygrange takes its name from a medieval grange belonging to Melrose Abbey. The imposing house is picturesquely situated on the banks of the Leader Water. By *C. G. H. Kinnear* of *Kinnear & Peddie*, 1889, for Edward Sprot of Riddell.*

Scottish-Renaissance mixed with English Jacobean, and even Queen Anne features. The N entrance front is crowded with eclectic detail: mullioned and transomed windows, conical-roofed round turrets, decorated dormerheads, and aedicules above the bay windows fronted by stone balustrades. Elements of the design are archaeological and scholarly. In the re-entrant angle of the L-plan is a four-storey circular entrance tower of Castle Fraser type, with a heavily stepped corbel course, and a three-storey turret, corbelled out at second-floor level over a squinch arch. Its stone balustrade was replaced in 1910 by

---

* His brother, Lt. General Sprot, supervised the work and had the plan compressed after the foundations had been laid, *Pers. Comm.*

crenellations. At its base is an elaborately detailed columned doorcase with classical frieze. Above the cornice a sculptured heraldic panel (with woolsack), flanked by obelisk finials, erected for Thomas Roberts, a Selkirk woollen mill owner, *c.* 1905. The w wing consists of a plainer crowstepped and turreted 'tower house', containing business room with private circular stair-tower. Its N elevation is based on Maybole Castle, Ayrshire. A two-storey and attic projection also extends N from the E end of the main block with a Maybole-type chimneystack grouped with a circular tower. The S elevation is more relaxed, nearly symmetrical, with well-detailed bay windows and pediments, excellently crafted by its builders, *A. Herbertson & Son.*

Additions were made after 1958 for St Andrew's College, beginning with a timber-boarded chapel to the SW, with a row of windows along the wall-heads. Extending from the E end of the S front is a wing (Convent of the Sisters of Mercy) by *Charles W. Gray* of *Reginald Fairlie & Partners*; traditional, with pinky-red brick toning in well. Two-storey end bays and a stone base course. Similarly traditional N wing of 1967 for library and theatre.

Much of Kinnear's INTERIOR survives, including the circular entrance hall which has a Jacobean strapwork frieze and swan-necked pedimented chimneypiece. Hat pegs line the top of the wainscot panelling. White marble steps rise to the principal floor, which has wainscotted rooms with two-tier chimneypieces with broken pediments. The dining room chimneypiece has half-fluted Doric columns below, coupled fluted Corinthian columns above, flanking shell niches. The ceilings are ribbed into compartments, with decoration of thistles, fleurs-de-lys and roses. The drawing room was either unfinished or changed, *c.* 1905, for Thomas Roberts, who put in the Rococo plaster ceiling. Of that date the timber lining and Lorimer-type ceiling of the boudoir and business room; the latter with trailing vine leaves and bunches of grapes, and a monumental grey stone bolection-moulded chimneypiece with dentilled cornice and swags of fruit across the frieze; the boudoir has a smaller one of the same type.

The grounds were completed by Roberts, who laid out the S terrace and garden in 1904. – SUMMER HOUSE of pink sandstone rubble, said to have been brought from the nearby Roman fort at Newstead. A pillar which occupied a niche at the centre of the front gable has been removed but the interior incorporates various carved fragments, including the head of a late Gothic niche and a massive vaulting corbel, both probably from Melrose Abbey (q.v.). A panel bears the initials VL, perhaps for William Lithgow (†1571), whose family leased the lands of Drygrange from the abbey for several generations. – WALLED GARDEN. Grand Neo-Jacobean entrance, originally to a conservatory, 1906 by *Peddie & Washington Browne*, who also remodelled S LODGE, in C17 Scottish style, 1905. Tall panelled gatepiers with egg-and-dart enrichment and decorative urn finials of 1889; the fine scrolled wrought-iron gates and screen walls are 1906. – N LODGE, former factor's house, by *C. G. H. Kinnear*, 1889; broad eaves and plain bargeboards. Gatepiers with decorative obelisk finials. – STEADING, N of the house. *c.* 1800, altered *c.* 1840 and the roof raised by *Kinnear*, 1889 for a central clock tower with ogee roof. Converted for offices by *Cameron Associates, c.* 1993.

DRYHOPE TOWER

2020

4 km. E of Cappercleuch

The shell of a four-storey tower house associated with the Scotts of Dryhope, probably erected about the middle or third quarter of the C16, but partially dismantled in 1592, when the government ordered its destruction. A carved sandstone panel now incorporated in the steading at Dryhope Farm, and bearing the initials of Philip and Mary Scott with the date 1613, may commemorate the renovation of the tower in that year, but it had ceased to be a laird's residence by the late C17.

The oblong tower (10.1 m. by 6.9 m.) originally comprised a vaulted cellar, a first-floor hall with vaulted entresol, and another floor, now incomplete, above that. The upperworks have disappeared, but there was probably an open walk on two or more sides. Local whinstone rubble masonry with dressings of cream-coloured sandstone, nearly all now robbed. There is evidence of extensive repairs to the fabric within the past century or so, including the rebuilding of the ground-floor entrance in the NW wall. This opens into a lobby with a stair on one side and the cellar doorway beyond. There are no windows in the cellar, but some light must have been admitted through three double-splayed gunloops, one in each wall except that containing the entrance. The gunloops have square-cut, wide-mouthed apertures, but two are now blocked; their throats are U-shaped, the only known example of this type in the eastern Borders. The hall was lit on three sides, the SE and NE windows having bench seats; it was also equipped with two mural cupboards and a sink. But there were apparently no latrine cubicles either here or elsewhere in the tower. In the NW wall is the scar of a big fireplace, placed unusually close to the door from the stair. Rows of rough stone corbels on the two long sides supported the runners of a timber ceiling. The entresol chamber was lit mainly from a NE window, with two supplementary lights cut into the haunch of the vault. The BARMKIN evidently contained several buildings, with others lying outside.

DUNS*

7050

The county town of Berwickshire from 1661 to 1696 and again from 1903 until the county's abolition in 1975, Duns is the successor of a burgh of barony erected in 1490 which stood on the NW side of Duns Law *c.* 1 km. N of the present town. The buildings of that burgh were burned during the English invasions of

*The account of Duns, except for the churches, is by John Gifford.

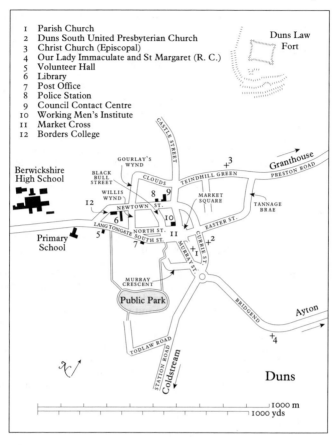

1 Parish Church
2 Duns South United Presbyterian Church
3 Christ Church (Episcopal)
4 Our Lady Immaculate and St Margaret (R. C.)
5 Volunteer Hall
6 Library
7 Post Office
8 Police Station
9 Council Contact Centre
10 Working Men's Institute
11 Market Cross
12 Borders College

Duns

the mid C16 and a new town of Duns laid out on the present site
c. 1590. That town seems to have consisted principally of a long
street (Langtongate, its line briefly divided into North Street and
South Street, and Easter Street) with the large space of Market
Square at its centre and the Parish Church just to its s. In the
late C17 or early C18, perhaps linked to the confirmation of the
burgh's legal status in 1670, Newtown Street was formed to the
N. Considerable redevelopment of the town followed in the mid
and later C18 and continued into the C19, when it was accompanied by the construction of a disproportionately numerous
array of villas to the s to house the town's bankers, lawyers and
architects, who served the surrounding area. In 1853 Duns
became the site of a Sheriff Court. Industry has never been of
much importance here and the town has retained its market town
image into the C21.

CHRIST CHURCH (Episcopal), Teindhill Green. 1853–4, built
under the direction of *William Hay* of Duns Castle, with
Messrs *Duns* as contractors, in a stripped-down Romanesque

idiom. Walls of cream-coloured snecked masonry and a slated roof of alternating fish-scale and horizontal bands. The aisle-less rectangular chancel, with a N sacristy, has a three-light traceried E window as its main focus. The four-bay aisled nave has a tower-porch towards the W end of the S aisle, the tower capped by a slated broached spire above a robust corbel table; the doorway is modelled on that at Chirnside Parish Church. A hall range projects N at the W end of the nave. The chancel ceiling has horizontal crested bands and stencilling. Nave arcades of monolithic cylindrical piers with scalloped caps; the clearstorey has simple rectangular windows and the roof is arch-braced. There is a W gallery. – STAINED GLASS. E window, Crucifixion, c. 1906; S flank chancel, first from E, St Margaret, by *R. Francini* of Florence, 1895; third from E, Sacred Monogram, c. 1876; S nave aisle, first from E, a Knight, c. 1944; second from E, St Cuthbert, c. 1894; fourth from E, St Alban, c. 1900; N nave aisle, first from E, Virgin and Child, c. 1913; second from E, St Ninian.

Former DUNS SOUTH UNITED PRESBYTERIAN CHURCH, Currie Street. Now a showroom. First built 1763, and rebuilt 1851, according to an inscription; secularised in 1976. A rectangle with rubble flanks pierced by tall timber-traceried windows; the main face, of stugged ashlar with octagonal buttresses and pinnacles at the angles, is capped by a square corbelled bellcote flanked by diminutive crenellation to the gable. The four-centred arched doorway is within a salient crenellated frontispiece framed by octagonal buttresses; on each side of an axial four-centred-arched three-light window with intersecting tracery are tall timber-traceried windows. Internally the U-shaped galleries are carried on cast-iron columns. The pulpit and communion table are centred between two traceried lancets.

OUR LADY IMMACULATE AND ST MARGARET (R.C.), Bridgend. 1881–2 by *Archibald Macpherson* of Edinburgh. Red rock-faced coursed sandstone, pierced by single or paired lancets on the N and W faces; the rest harled in the expectation of adding a chancel and S aisle. N porch in W bay. Internally, the blocked three-bay S arcade, on cylindrial columns, together with an arch in the E wall, await the planned extensions. Simple hammerbeam roof. – ALTARPIECE, a startlingly opulent Baroque *tour de force*, with Corinthian pilasters and Solomonic columns carrying a broken segmental pediment and central cartouche; originally a fireplace at Langton House (Gavinton), acquired 1925. – Red granite ALTAR, 1969–72. – STAINED GLASS oculus above altar, Virgin and Child with Duns Scotus.

PARISH CHURCH, Church Square. The last vestiges of the medieval church, which belonged first to Duns Hospital and then to Dunbar Collegiate Church, were demolished in 1874. The later history is summarised on a tablet on the tower 'Erected 1790. Destroyed by fire 1879. Restored 1880'. The existing church, largely the work of *Wardrop & Reid* in 1880, is commandingly placed on the N side of a spacious churchyard. It is a T-plan structure, with many offshoots to sides and rear for porches and a hall. The (S) show front is of buff droved ashlar with polished quoins and dressings; at its centre is the handsome tower, still largely of 1790, but a little small for the remodelled church. The tower has a pedimented doorcase and inscribed tablet to the lower stages, above which is a slightly inset storey with blind oculi, finished with consoled pediments and urn finials; at the summit is an octagon with round-headed windows capped by a stone spire. On each side of the tower a round-headed window has timber tracery with two arched lights and an oculus. Each of the outer bays has a blocked pedimented doorcase below a round-arched bipartite window to the gallery. The symmetry of this façade has been compromised by two memorials: a classical one in the E doorway for the Hay family; the other, a Gothic aedicule between the doorway and window W of the tower, for the Rev. William Menzie (†1881). The side and rear elevations are of rubble, with two storeys of round-headed windows arranged singly, in pairs, or, at the upper level of the N aisle, as a triplet.

Internally a three-sided arrangement of galleries is carried on cast-iron columns, facing the pulpit, communion table and organ against the S wall. The roof is of ceiled hammerbeam form, with a central roof-light. – COMMUNION TABLE, with traceried front, 1909. – ORGAN with stencilled pipes. – STAINED GLASS. Flanking the communion table, Nativity and Baptism to E, Sermon on Mount, and Ascension to W; W wall, lower level, Ruth, 1895; E wall, lower level, 1880, 'Noli Me Tangere', 1880; N wall, lower level, Parable of Talents, Good Shepherd, 1881; Martha and Mary, Christ and Children, 1880; E wall, upper level, Good Samaritan and Sower, Christ Healing, the majority by D. Small of Edinburgh. – CHURCHYARD, mainly C18 and C19 memorials, some with slate panels and well-preserved fine lettering. Home of Wedderburn BURIAL ENCLOSURE, erected 1875, reuses stones from the aisle formerly attached to the medieval parish church. One is dated 1608; the other records repairs carried out in 1763.

WILLIS WYND CHAPEL. Tiny box of c. 1825. Rubble flanks, main front of stugged ashlar, largely obscured by later vestibule, above which is a blocked round-headed window and an inscribed tablet in a raised section of wall.

PUBLIC PARK
Station Road

The land was given in 1891. Entrance GATEWAY with channelled ashlar gatepiers, their cornices supported on simple moulded corbels. On the gates, the coats-of-arms of Andrew Smith of Whitchester who gave the land for the park and Sir James Miller of Manderston who paid for its landscaping, gates and railings. Immediately inside the entrance, a War Memorial, a tall obelisk of c. 1920. Just to its S, a MONUMENT to John Duns Scotus, by F. D. Seitschler, 1966, a giant bronze half-length of the medieval friar and theologian, its expressionism verging on the kitsch. S of that, a polished granite MONUMENT of 1981 to Polish soldiers stationed at Duns and killed in the Second World War. A Maltese cross on a tapered pedestal.

PUBLIC BUILDINGS

BERWICKSHIRE HIGH SCHOOL, Langtongate. By *J. & F. Johnston*, 1953–8. Long, low and lightweight-looking. Rendered walls and flat roofs.

BORDERS COLLEGE, Newtown Street. Originally Berwickshire High School. The tall main block at the s is by *R. A. Bryden*, 1896. Lumpish Neo-Georgian, faced with stugged ashlar. It incorporates and overlays a late Georgian villa (Ivy Lodge) whose w end is still visible, with a ground-floor Venetian window in its s front. Plain harled N addition by *R. A. Bryden & Robertson*, 1910.

BOSTON FREE CHURCH SCHOOL *see* Description, below.

COUNCIL CONTACT CENTRE, Newtown Street. Built as the Sheriff Court House, *c.* 1855. Jacobean, of two storeys and an attic, the masonry of squared rubble, the roof covered with fish-scale slating. Front of three bays, all with gables whose bottoms are stepped, the centre slightly recessed and with a smaller gable. Hoodmoulded door and three-light windows at the ground floor. Above, mullioned and transomed windows surmounted by a string course which forms hoodmoulds over the outer windows and jumps up over a shield (uncarved) above the centre window. Hoodmoulded and louvred attic openings at the outer bays. E addition of *c.* 1970.

DUNS PRIMARY SCHOOL, Langtongate. By *A. Herbertson & Son*, 1880. A single tall storey of hammer-dressed ashlar, with bracketed broad eaves. U-plan front with hoodmoulded windows in the advanced and gabled ends; broad gablet containing a dummy oculus at the centre. Low rear additions of the later C20.

THE KNOLL HOSPITAL, Station Road, *see* Description, below.

LIBRARY, Newtown Street. Built in 1939 but barely conscious of the C20. Harled Jacobean front gable.

MARKET CROSS, Market Square. Executed by *George Wilson*, with carved work by *William Smeaton*, 1792, and originally erected near this site, it was taken down *c.* 1820. Re-erected in the Public Park in 1897, it was moved back to Market Square in 1994. Of red sandstone ashlar. Corniced pedestal, the N face carved with a cross, the s with the coat-of-arms of the burgh of Duns. This supports a pot-bellied column surmounted by an entablature, its underside enriched with guttae. On top, a cubic sundial, its w face bearing the goat's-head crest of the Hays of Duns Castle. Acorn finial, apparently a replacement of 1897.

POLICE STATION, Newtown Street. Thrifty Jacobean, by *James Jerdan*, 1894–6. Two-storey front of polished ashlar. At the first floor, steep triangular pediments over the mullioned two-light outer windows, a semicircular pediment to the centre window. Horribly plain w addition of *c.* 1970.

Former POST OFFICE, South Street. Scottish Jacobean of *c.* 1900. One tall storey, with a balustraded wall-head between crowstepped gables.

Former SHERIFF COURT HOUSE, Newtown Street, *see* Council Contact Centre, above.

VOLUNTEER HALL, Langtongate. Built *c.* 1900. Utilitarian

rubble hall behind a two-storey office block with a Jacobean Renaissance broad gable front.

WORKING MEN'S INSTITUTE, Market Square. Free Jacobean by *David Duns*, 1877. Two-storey and attic, the four-bay front of stugged buff-coloured ashlar. Two-bay centrepiece marked off at the first floor by columns supported on heavy moulded corbels and carrying a balcony-like parapet in front of a shaped gable.

DESCRIPTION

STATION ROAD carries the A6112 in from the S. At its S end, preluding the town, is CHEEKLAW HOUSE, its piend-roofed W block built in the early C19 and given a bay window in the mid C19 when the E wing was added or remodelled with simple Jacobean detail. Behind, CHEEKLAW FARM, the harled house of the early C19, the rubble-built courtyard steading of the mid C19. Plain Victorian row of farm workers' cottages on the E side of the road. A little to the N and set back in the DUNS INDUSTRIAL ESTATE E of Station Road, an early or mid-C19 three-storey rubble-built GRANARY of seven bays by three, with elliptically arched windows and hoist openings at the centre of the long sides. The piended roof (now covered with corrugated iron) is surmounted by an off-centre gabled ventilator.

Set back on Station Road's W side, THE KNOLL, a late C19 villa with crowstepped gables and gablets and a bay window. Single-storey rear additions of *c.* 1980 and 2003 for the house's present use as a hospital. This is the first of a string of late Georgian and Victorian villas and is followed by NORHAM LODGE, a late Victorian lumpy Jacobean villa. Then, the larger mid-C19 SOUTHFIELD LODGE, stodgy classical, built of stugged ashlar. Slightly advanced centre with a Roman Doric portico and a scrolly low parapet; shallow canted bay windows at the outer bays. Giant anta-pilasters at the corners of the house. On the N side of TODLAW ROAD to the W, PARKSIDE, built as the Boston Free Church Manse in 1850. Not large but luxuriating in an inventive display of idiosyncratic Jacobean detail. At the outer bays, two-light windows, those of the ground floor corniced. Above the first-floor windows and placed just behind the eaves are ball-finialled shaped stone dormerheads. Shaped chimney gablet over the centre from which projects a two-storey canted bay, its ground floor a loggia porch with round-headed arches carried on fluted columns; over the upper floor, a ball-finialled parapet pierced by round-headed arcading. Horizontal-patterned glazing to the windows.

On the E side of Station Road, the piend-roofed two-storey TODLAW of *c.* 1825, a high garden wall pierced by a Tudorish gateway hiding its S front. This is of three bays, the centre door-piece's bundle-shafted columns with capitals of upright foliage and surmounted by a cornice supported on heavy blocks. Plain two-storey mid-C19 E addition, its windows with horizontal panes. Horizontal-paned windows also at the Jacobean THE HERMITAGE of *c.* 1840 on the N corner of Todlaw Road and Station Road. To its N, two-storey sheltered housing (BOSTON

COURT) by *Bain, Swan Architects,* 1987. Pseudo-vernacular, in buff and red reconstituted stone. N of this, the Public Park (*see* above). It is overlooked by WELLNAGE, set high above the E side of Station Road. Built *c.* 1800, this was originally a two-storey piend-roofed villa with a full-height canted bay project-ing from the centre of its W side. In the mid C19 it was extended N by one bay and a porch was added to the E front. To its N, a small STABLES courtyard built in several stages in the mid and later C19, the ball-and-spike finialled S gable containing the depressed arch entrance; ogee-roofed stone cupola on the W range's N end. N of this, BLYTHBANK, also of *c.* 1800 and piend-roofed. Two-storey and basement, three-bay ashlar front with a Roman Doric columned surround to the fanlit entrance at the slightly advanced and pedimented centre. First-floor sill course, rusticated quoins and a mutuled cornice. Then, on the corner of Station Road and Bridgend, MORELANDS of the earlier C19. Again, a three-bay ashlar front with a first-floor sill course and slightly advanced centre, but its doorpiece consists of paired anta-pilasters and its first-floor window is of three lights; broad vestigial pilasters at the outer corners. To its E, on the S side of BRIDGEND, the early C19 HAYMOUNT. Piend-roofed, with a pilastered doorpiece, but shallow canted bay windows were added in the mid C19. E of this, the drive to TRINITY HOUSE. Georgian survival of the earlier C19. Three-light first-floor window above the parapeted porch at the centre bay of the droved ashlar front.

CURRIE STREET leads N from Station Road past the E side of the parish churchyard. On the street's E side, the early C19 two-storey HAWTHORN COTTAGE. Three-bay front, with a pilastered door surround at the central porch; three-light ground-floor windows at the outer bays. Further up, No. 9 Currie Street, also of two storeys. It is probably of C18 origin but the ground floor was altered in the earlier C19 when it acquired three-light windows and a console-corniced door. Further up, the former Duns South United Presbyterian Church (*see* Churches, above).

EASTER STREET crosses the top end of Currie Street. At its E end is MANSEFIELD, a late C18 house built of squared rubble, with rusticated quoins and club skewputts. Pedimented door-piece with a lugged architrave and pulvinated frieze. The single-storey E wing is an addition of the early C19.

MURRAY STREET continues Station Road to the NW. On its NE side, the churchyard of Duns Parish Church (*see* Churches, above). On the SW, more villas. At the SW corner, MARY-FIELD, another piend-roofed late Georgian villa, the centre of its S front slightly advanced, with a Roman Doric columned and corniced surround to the segmentally fanlit door. Broad panelled giant pilasters at the corners; blocking course which rises to form parapets over the end pilasters and the centre bay. Immediately to its N, BARNIKEN HOUSE of *c.* 1840, like a smaller version of Maryfield but with shallow canted bay windows. N of this, on the N side of MURRAY CRESCENT, a mid-C19 Elizabethan double house (Nos. 14–16 Murray Street), built of stugged ashlar, with a two-storey canted bay window to the S front. The S entrance is contained in a single-storey gabled porch, the E in a full-height gabled projection. Horizontal-paned windows. N of this, Murray Street becomes C19 and C20 rag-bag urban, but fronting a lane on the SW side is No. 6, a former stable of the earlier C19 with Gothic doors (two now windows) at the ground floor. The first-floor windows rise into gablets, the stone-canopied narrow centre window's gablet broader than the others.

MARKET SQUARE at the top end of Murray Street is a sizeable but irregularly shaped space. Roughly in the centre, the Market Cross (*see* Public Buildings, above). The surrounding buildings are an architectural medley. On the S side, E of the corner with Murray Street, Nos. 1–3, a commercial block of the earlier C20. Only two storeys and an attic but the very high ground floor and giant pilasters give it a bullying scale. To its E, the three-storey but much lower No. 5 of *c.* 1800, with rusticated quoins; its corniced shopfront may be a mid-C19 insertion. At the S end of the E side and slipping out of the square towards the back of Duns Parish Church (*see* Churches, above), No. 6, also of three storeys and with rusticated quoins but mid-C19 in its present form with a hoodmoulded entrance. Its scale is continued by Nos. 7–8. Early C19, with tall first-floor windows and a mutuled eaves cornice; pilastered and corniced doorpiece at the r. bay. No. 9 is infill of 1978 attempting a quiet Georgian manner. More assertive the BANK OF SCOTLAND (originally, British Linen Co. Bank) at No. 10 on the corner of Easter Street. Stripped Jacobean Renaissance of a sort, by *H. O. Tarbolton*, 1928. Two-storey E extension by *Walter Duns*, 1966.

On Market Square's N side, at the E end, the ROYAL BANK OF SCOTLAND (Nos. 11–12) by *Peddie & Kinnear*, 1857. This is a Renaissance palazzo, the three-storey front of polished ashlar. Ground-floor windows with shouldered arches and rope-moulded jambs and lintels set in architraves, their lugs decorated with rosettes. A frieze of Vitruvian scroll and a cornice-like sill course mark off the first floor whose round-headed windows are framed by corniced architraves; in the spandrels, carved foliage enclosing the Royal Bank's initials. Another but simpler frieze-and-cornice sill course under the small second-floor windows, again with shouldered arches and architraves, the spandrels decorated with rosettes. Very broad bracketed eaves to the shallow-pitched piended roof. Beside the bank and set slightly back is the much less formal harled WHIP AND SADDLE INN of 1824, its SW corner canted at the bottom and splayed to a right angle above. Bellcast-eaved roof, piended at the SW corner, its gabled wooden dormers Victorian additions. Rear wing (No. 16 Market Square) stretching back to form the S end of Castle Street's E side.

CASTLE STREET as far N as Newtown Street is partly filled with late C20 housing designed in a sort of Neo-vernacular manner enlivened by occasional Postmodern touches. On the E, No. 18, a plain and altered building of the later C18, was the Burgh Court House. Inside, the ground-floor back room (now divided in two) was the court room. Its N end has an attached screen of fluted Ionic columns with rosetted capitals. The paired columns at the centre frame an alcove for the baron bailie's seat; pulvinated frieze enriched with foliage. The egg-and-dart cornice extends round the room (cut across by the partition wall). Wall panelling survives in the present N room. On the W side, two houses, also of the later C18, both with rendered fronts. At No. 13, a segmental pediment over the door. Ionic columned and corniced doorpiece at No. 15, whose ground-floor windows have been altered.

On Market Square's N side, W of Castle Street, the Working Men's Institute (*see* Public Buildings, above). Beside it, Nos. 23–27, much altered but probably C18 in origin, a small blocked window visible at the l. of the first floor; simplified brackets under the eaves cornice. Taller rendered block, also of three storeys but of the earlier C19, at No. 28, the first-floor windows architraved and corniced. The scale drops to two storeys at the early C19 Nos. 29–30, the broached ashlar front now painted. At the NW corner of Market Square, the WHITE SWAN HOTEL, its blocks forming an L. The N block is probably early C19 and originally plain but a late C19 canted bay window has been added to the centre of the front. W block of *c.* 1800. Three-bay E front with three-light first-floor windows at the outer bays and a pedimented gablet (some of the detail lost) over the centre bay; round-headed attic window in the S gable.

BLACK BULL STREET runs uphill behind the White Swan Hotel. Set back on the W, its gable fronting the street, No. 9, a surviving C18 cottage. The rendered two-storey façade of No. 11 is mid-C19, its shopfront's entablature supported by Corinthian columns and pilasters. Also on the W side, the early C19 three-storey BLACK BULL HOTEL, its ground floor altered but the crude Doric columned doorpiece surviving; tall windows to the first floor.

On Market Square's W side, an island block. Its W end is occupied by Nos. 36–37 (the former Commercial Bank of Scotland), a two-storey palazzo of *c.* 1900 but without panache. E of this, the late C19 Nos. 38–45, plain except for buckle quoins. At the E end of the block, a pair of three-storey buildings facing the square. The N (Nos. 40–41) is late C19 and minimally Jacobean. The S (TOLBOOTH HOUSE, Nos. 42–43) is early C19. E gable of three bays, with round-headed windows and doors at the rusticated ground floor. Above, giant corner pilasters and, in the top of the gable, a clock erected in 1976. Anta-pilastered doorpiece at the S elevation. Behind this island block is GOLDEN SQUARE. At its SW corner, a mid-C19 Georgian survival L-plan block (Nos. 2–3 Golden Square). SE of this, at the E end of South Street, a former temperance hotel (No. 1 Golden Square and No. 46 Market Square) of *c.* 1900, the corners with channelled pilaster strips and ball finials. Opposite, No. 47 Market Square, an early C19 town house, its front built of broached ashlar (now painted). Heavy pilastered doorpiece, fluted aprons under the first-floor windows and a mutuled eaves cornice. On its E side, Nos. 48–49 Market Square, also early C19, with architraved first-floor windows and rusticated quoins; shopfront at the ground floor. Then, Nos. 50–51, the ground floor also now occupied by a shop. Above, rubble walling and an open pedimented gable. It may be late C18. After a small single-storey block of the late C20 (Nos.

53–54), Nos. 56–57 Market Square on the w corner of Murray
Street, a large gently Italianate block of *c.* 1870.

NORTH STREET and SOUTH STREET leading w from Market
Square form two sides of a triangle. Both are predominantly
two-storey C19 vernacular with some late C20 infill, the block
at Nos. 18–28 North Street covered in lumpy harling, Nos.
9–11 South Street Postmodern. On South Street's s side, the
former Post Office (*see* Public Buildings, above). Further w,
No. 45 South Street, late Georgian with broad channelled
pilaster strips at the corners. At the harled and much-altered
No. 47 South Street, the door lintel is inscribed DG. MM.
1714. At the junction of the two streets, WILLIS WYND climbs
uphill to the N. For Willis Wynd Chapel, *see* Churches, above.

LANGTONGATE, the exit from the town to the sw, is again largely
C19 vernacular but the harled No. 7 is C18 with a five-bay s
front facing away from the street. Beside it, TURNBULL
COURT, inoffensive late C20 housing but ignoring the street-
line. Aloof behind front gardens on the N, the mid-C19 double
house of Nos. 16–18. Bay-windowed Jacobean U-plan front,
the doors surmounted by consoled stone balconies with
pierced parapets; central chimney with diagonally set square
stacks. Further w, on the s side, the bulk of the Volunteer Hall
(*see* Public Buildings, above). Immediately to its w, on the
other side of Earlsmeadow, No. 11 Langtongate, a curiosity of
c. 1900. Two-storey front of polished red ashlar, the ground-
floor windows set between freely treated Corinthianish
pilasters, the capitals of the broad end pilasters with lions'
heads between the volutes, the fluted central pilasters with
cherubs' heads. They support an egg-and-dart cornice-sill
course under the upper floor's windows. The multi-gabled No.
13 Langtongate is a cottage of the later C19 with a canted bay
window, its upper part corbelled out to the square, bracketed
broad eaves and horizontal-pane glazing. For Duns Primary
School to the w, *see* Public Buildings, above. At the w end of
the town, the early C19 SUNNYSIDE. L-plan, with open pediments to the gables of the front block. The South Lodge of
Duns Castle (q.v.) and Berwickshire High School (*see* Public
Buildings, above) are isolated outliers to the town.

NEWTOWN STREET, running SW-NE, is the main N street of the
town centre. At its w end, Borders College (*see* Public Buildings, above) on the s side. No. 46 opposite is more appealing,
a detached house of *c.* 1800. Rubble front, the windows of its
five-bay ground floor and three-bay first floor symmetrically
disposed. No. 44 (WESTWOOD) is set behind a front garden.
Piend-roofed early C19 villa, the ashlar stonework of the front
droved at the outer bays but broached at the slightly advanced
centre. Panelled giant pilasters at the corners support a
mutuled eaves cornice surmounted by a blocking course which
rises into a parapet at the centre; pilastered doorpiece. At the
house's w end, a piend-roofed stable, also pilastered and parapeted. Low E addition of 1875. E of this, the street establishes
an architectural norm of C18 and C19 terraced vernacular.
Breaking the norm is the Library (*see* Public Buildings, above)
on the s. On the N, the crowstep-gabled late Georgian but
altered Nos. 36–40.

GOURLAYS WYND to the N contains more C19 vernacular, Nos. 10–12 with pantiled roofs. It leads up to CLOUDS, a street of villas enjoying views over the town. Near the W end, the early C19 ST ALBANS, its main block with open-pedimented gables and a three-bay S front. The piend-roofed ROSEBANK to its E is also early C19. Originally approached by a driveway from Newtown Street, it faces S, the front with Venetian windows at the ground floor flanking a corniced doorpiece.

On Newtown Street's S side facing up Gourlays Wynd is No. 43 (BOSTON HOUSE), built in 1846 as the Boston Free Church School and School of Industry. Jacobean, of two storeys and an attic. Plenty of carved detail including shells topped by human heads over the doors and the Burning Bush emblem of the Free Church of Scotland. No. 24 Newtown Street, on the N side, built as the British Linen Co. Bank, is by *William Waddell*, 1846. Two-storey piend-roofed main block, its front of polished ashlar, the ground-floor entrance and windows set in overarches carried on broad pilasters, the first-floor windows segmental-headed. A parallel late Georgian rear block, also piend-roofed, projects for one bay to the W where it displays broached ashlar walling with a broad corner pilaster, first-floor band course and a parapet. At its W, a contemporary screen wall pierced by an elliptical-headed arch. Another former bank (Bank of Scotland) at No. 14. By *James Smith* of Edinburgh, 1850–2, it is like a large and prosperous piend-roofed villa. Polished ashlar front with a Roman Doric portico, sill courses under the windows and a mutuled eaves cornice. For the Police Station and Council Contact Centre, *see* Public Buildings, above.

CASTLE STREET N of Newtown Street contains harled two-storey housing of the early and mid C19 on the W (Nos. 29–39). On the E, the sturdy corniced and ball-finialled Late Georgian gatepiers and office range of the demolished Duns Parish Manse. More C19 vernacular housing in the street's N stretch N of Clouds. At the corner with TEINDHILL GREEN, No. 1 Teindhill Green and No. 62 Castle Street, an early C19 two-storey and attic block, built of whinstone with sandstone dressings. Piend-roofed three-bay S end, the centre slightly advanced under an open pediment, a dummy oculus in the tympanum; rusticated quoins. E of this, on the N side of Teindhill Green, are mid- and late C19 villas. Plain Jacobean at No. 6. Georgian survival at No. 7. The late Victorian No. 15 has bargeboarded dormerheads, a jerkin-head roof and a small conservatory, its octagonal cupola surmounted by an elaborate wrought-iron finial. After Christ Church (*see* Churches, above), MOUNT VIEW, a plutocratic Jacobean villa of *c.* 1850, its entrance contained in a tower finished with a lead-covered ogee roof. Then, KIRKWELL HOUSE (the former Christ Church Rectory), by *Hay & Henderson*, 1880. Baronial, with crowstepped gables and a conical-roofed fat turret; stone balcony corbelled out above the entrance.

TANNAGE BRAE descends the hill to the S. At its foot, the single-storey WELLFIELD LODGE of the later C19, with a semi-octagonal Roman Doric portico and stone canopies over the flanking two-light windows. It stands at the beginning of a drive to WELLFIELD HOUSE, whose present principal approach is from PRESTON ROAD. This is a harled early C19 villa. Entrance front facing NW. Two-storey main block with rusticated quoins and a Roman Doric portico, its frieze with rosettes and triglyphs. Lateral wings, originally single-storey but heightened by *J.P. Alison* in 1903, the first-floor windows with pedimented dormerheads. At each wing, a bowed and Venetian-windowed projection, its battlement moved here from the back of the wing in 1903. Garden elevation with a basement fully exposed in the steep fall of the ground. At the centre, a single-storey and basement balustraded projection, its basement containing a door, its ground floor a Venetian window. The other ground-floor windows are tall and formerly had balconies. The wings again have Venetian-windowed projecting bows. Their first-floor Venetian windows and Dutch gables date from their heightening in 1903. (Eclectic but lavish interior by *J.P. Alison*, 1903.)

FORT, Duns Law, 0.8 km. N. Overlooking the town is Duns Law, where General Alexander Leslie unfurled the standard of the Covenanting army at the start of the Bishops' Wars in 1639. The summit is crowned by the denuded ramparts of a prehistoric fort within which can be seen the earth and boulder footings of a square redoubt (67 by 67 m.) having a small square bastion at each corner. This probably dates from the time of Leslie's campaign. An inscribed 'COVENANTERS' STONE' marks the traditional site of the raising of the standard. 0.2 km. to the NW, standing upon a stretch of sloping ground overlooking Duns Castle (q.v.), another INSCRIBED STONE commemorates the site of the old town of Duns, abandoned following its destruction by English armies during the C16 Border wars.

KIMMERGHAME HOUSE. *See* p. 469.
MANDERSTON HOUSE. *See* p. 514.
NISBET HOUSE. *See* p. 597.
WEDDERBURN CASTLE. *See* p. 744.

DUNS CASTLE   7050
0.8 km. NW of Duns

An enlarged tower house set in mature parkland. The early C19 Gothic additions and remodelling convey a fine sense of picturesque massing, preserving the essential nature of the medieval stronghold without accepting its form or details.

Duns was acquired by the Dunbar Earls of March *c.* 1320, and they seem to have had a residence here from that date. The present house, however, is an immense castellated Gothic remodelling of a later castle by *James Gillespie Graham*, 1818–22 for William Hay. The house that he inherited in 1807 comprised a massive L-plan tower house, probably built in the late C15 by George Home of Ayton and/or his son John, to whom jointly James III had granted the town and lands of Duns. Purchased in 1696 by William Hay of Drumelzier, the house was upgraded in the mid C18 and is shown in a drawing of the 1790s, with the altered tower house at the E end, a narrow five-bay range, and a low two-storey crenellated addition at the W end. Attempts to make more gracious this plain, harled group were undertaken shortly after by *John Baxter Jun.*, with the addition of a fashionable three-storeyed bowed section on the N front, attached to the W side of the tower house. As the result 'had nothing either curious or picturesque about it', William Hay determined to create an asymmetrical Gothic castle, with a suitably dramatic skyline in which antiquarian correctness was of little interest so long as unrestrained visual effect was achieved. By 1817 he had commissioned *Richard Crichton* to remodel the old tower. Crichton's plan for a wide turreted porch was unrealised by his death in the same year, and Hay turned to Gillespie Graham to contrive his ambitious scheme. The freedom of expression at Duns came probably from Hay, who considered himself an amateur architect. He contracted *William Waddell* to carry out his intentions based on working drawings, principally of Gothic ceilings, niches and chimneypieces, not normally supplied by Gillespie Graham. Most of Gillespie Graham's 'picturesque effects' at Duns Castle appear to have been borrowed from Tullichewan Castle, West Dunbartonshire by Robert Lugar, 1808;[*] published in his *Plans & Views of Buildings* in 1811. For details, Thomas Rickman's *An Attempt to Discriminate the Styles of English Architecture*, 1817, and A.C. Pugin's *Specimens of Gothic Architecture*, 1821, were also available.[†] Duns was Gillespie Graham's masterpiece, but after this success he returned, at Dunninald (Angus), to the well-tried formula of a turreted mansion with a large circular tower. Hay's passion for the Picturesque, inspired by Sir Uvedale Price, extended to the cultivation of a setting for the castle amongst overgrown shrubs, trees and lawns and, ultimately, to bankruptcy of the estate by 1829.

EXTERIOR. The main bulk of the original TOWER HOUSE can still be identified at the E end of the mansion. Constructed largely of pink sandstone, this was an L-plan of four or five storeys, comprising a main block (*c.* 15.2 m. by 10.7 m.) running W and E, together with a N wing (*c.* 9.1 m. by 9.1 m.); much of the fabric survives up to second-floor level, the original external walls measuring up to 2.4 m. in thickness. The rest is Gillespie Graham uniting the disparate elements behind a refacing of buff sandstone quarried on the estate. There are machicolated parapets, windows with square and pointed hoodmoulds, their label stops carved with grotesque heads and crouching figures, mostly by *John Anderson*, who carved the prominent gargoyles. They are said to represent Scottish worthies, including the Scottish fiddler Neil Gow. A battered base course continues round most of the building, a typical feature of Gillespie Graham's work.

63   The principal (S) elevation has a crenellated entrance bay with four-stage octagonal corner towers. In front is the porch, a smaller version of the design recommended by Richard Crichton; it has corner piers to match the flanking towers, each

[*]Dem. 1954, *see* John Gifford and Frank Arneil Walker, *The Buildings of Scotland: Stirling and Central Scotland* (2002), pp. 786–7.
[†]James Macaulay, *The Gothic Revival* (1975), p. 242.

with quatrefoil detailing on the entablature, and carved eagles perched on top. There is some Hay heraldry in the centre of the arch. Above the porch a large hoodmoulded tripartite window and above that a corbelled-out oriel. The bays to the E of the entrance incorporate the main block of the tower house, with large traceried windows (note the differing heights) at the first floor, which have balconies supported by moulded brackets. In the upper floors, and on the W side, the windows are more regular. The fourth bay on the W is set forward, and has a recessed crowstepped gable behind a parapet with a fleur-de-lys finial. This elevation is finished at each end by square towers, that to the W with a very deep parapet, that to the E of four stages, with wide chamfered corners, and pointed slit windows with trefoil tracery. A Gothic niche projects from the SW corner with a carved figure, probably late C19.

The E elevation of the tower has a large square oriel window, mullioned and transomed with a crenellated parapet. Graham added a machicolated crowstepped gable at the top to match a mid-C18 gable; behind rises a bold group of chimneys with star-shaped copes. The N wall of the tower incorporates glazed openings, perhaps of former garderobes, one above the other. Over the doorway in the re-entrant angle (probably the position of the original entrance to the tower) is a C19 panel inscribed: BUILT 1320 (the approximate date at which the Earls of March acquired Duns). Above is another Gothic niche with a carved figure said to be St John, probably added in the late C19. The central feature on the N elevation, the large crenellated three-storey bow, is a remodelling of John Baxter Jun.'s bow-ended addition of the 1790s. A four-stage octagonal tower projects from the NE corner, between these two features is a traceried window with a bracketed balcony. The W façade has another three-storey bow in the centre.

Attached to the SW corner of the house, a crenellated screen wall, with buttresses defining the eleven bays, terminates in a round tower. In the centre a square pend to the service court, with pretty ornamental machicolations to the parapet, and on top a stone arcaded lantern with a finialled Gothic open-crown roof, very like a miniature C15 English market cross. 84

INTERIOR. Apart from the lower flights of a newel staircase rising from the doorway in the NE re-entrant angle, little remains of the early arrangements. The early C19 replanning was achieved by Gillespie Graham's addition to the entrance tower pushed into the centre of the building, which also improved circulation, with corridors between the principal rooms in the older E part and the family accommodation at the W end. The decoration was completely remodelled in a Perpendicular Gothic style by Gillespie Graham, with notably excellent plasterwork by *Anderson & Ramage,* contemporary with their work in the Palace of Holyrood House, Edinburgh, and the sculptor *John Steell,* who evidently worked here as an apprentice to his father. Beautiful ribbed and fan vaulting, four-centred arches and Perpendicular panelling set the scene.

From the porch one enters an impressive three-storey HALL, flooded by light from the large S window, whose walls retain

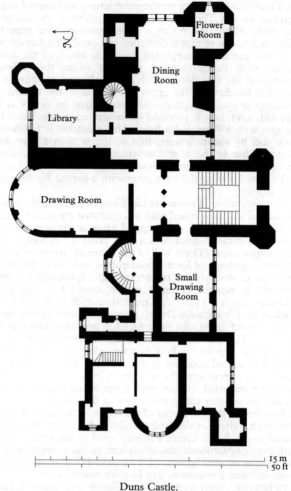

Duns Castle.
First-floor plan.

the original plaster lined out in imitation of ashlar. From the
ground floor an Imperial stair, with cast-iron Gothic balusters,
rises to the first floor. On the E and W walls canopied Gothic
niches. At the N end of the hall, two tiers of stone-arcaded
screens with clustered columns, set diagonally, open to the
lower and upper corridors: both have rib-arched vaulting, the
lower with decorative bosses. But the glory of the hall is its
ceiling, divided in two by transverse ribs ending in highly decorated corbels, a riot of playful figures with details from Hay
heraldry. A fan vault with a central inverted-cone pendant boss
over the staircase, and the expanse of decorated ribbed panels
over the hall, convey a feeling of movement, best apprehended

from the upper corridor, like series of undulating waves disappearing into the landscape.

The three principal rooms lead off the hall through the N and E corridors, beginning with the wide Gothic doors into the DRAWING ROOM, contained within Baxter's addition. Quite sparsely decorated, relying on a low oak dado, Gothic doors and window shutters decorated with thistle and vine themes, and a lierne-vaulted ceiling; in the centre a circular panel containing the Hay arms. A mini-version of the ceiling decorates the bowed window recess. Grey stone chimneypiece with Gothic pilaster jambs. At the N end of the E corridor is the LIBRARY (study) with a beautiful fan-vaulted ceiling. Tucked into the wall between the library and the dining room is a newel stair, a rebuilt version of the one that originally served the upper levels of the tower house. The DINING ROOM evidently occupies the site of the early hall, and the present strongroom in the N wall is probably an original mural chamber. The decoration here was changed after William Hay, 5th of Duns, succeeded his father in 1876. The walls were panelled in oak, and a Gothic cusped ceiling inserted. Majestic chimneypiece, created from an older overmantel, carved with scenes from the life of George, fifth Lord Seton (an ancestor of the Hays), said to be by *Steell*, supported on fantastic Chinese dragons acquired in 1886. In the first landing in the W wing is the D-shaped principal stair with another cast-iron Gothic balustrade, a ribbed vault in the lower corridor, a prettier one on the first floor. Off this landing is the SMALL DRAWING ROOM (former morning room), which appears to have an inserted ceiling perhaps of the 1960s. Pretty built-in bookcases with vine decoration across shelves, and on the doors. Identical grey stone chimneypiece to the one in the library.

The rooms of the upper floors are more simply treated, although one, W of the entrance tower, has a coved ceiling and a pretty fretwork cornice. At the top of the entrance tower, the BILLIARD ROOM (above the hall), reached by the newel stair. Oriel recess with Gothic plasterwork, Gothic doors and a foliage frieze.

SUNDIAL. In front of the S elevation. A C19 octagonal pedestal with quatrefoil detailing, supporting a copper dial by *John Adie*. – The STABLES, W of the house, were built by *John Baxter Jun.*, 1791–4. Two-storey courtyard block of eleven by fifteen bays. E elevation of droved ashlar, with a pointed-arched pend to the court. Above this an octagonal spire with blind roundels in each face of its base, and clocks on the E and W sides, a simplified version of a spire Baxter built later at Bellie Kirk, Fochabers (Moray). Flanking pavilions with overarched openings. A curved screen wall, by *Gillespie Graham*, links the stable block to the NW corner of the house. In the centre a square crenellated tower housed the dairy. A similar tower, but smaller, in the centre of the N section was a privy, and another tower to the l. contained a larder. – NORTH LODGE, c. 1820. Single-storey Tudor lodge, adjoining a Tudor-arched gateway spanning the road, flanked by square gatepiers with Gothic cusped panels. – SOUTH LODGE, c. 1820, is a random combination of lodge and round-arched gateway topped by a miniature bellcote-shaped finialled gable. A round capped tower to the l., a smaller ogee-roofed square tower to the r., and long screen walls to the road terminating in small turrets. An amateur sketch suggests *William Hay* as the author. – PAVILION LODGE. By *John Baxter Jun.*, 1791. Gothic with two towers, and crenellated pointed archway between. – WALLED GARDEN, probably 1802–7.

William Hay employed *Thomas White Jun.* in 1812 to create the park, and redesign the C18 LANDSCAPE. White's plan is represented by the present pattern of woodland and clumps of trees, although Hay amended the layout towards a more Picturesque arrangement, so that his castle should stand in 'meadows cut out of woodland'.

5030   EARLSTON

A large village, a former burgh of barony, of interest historically for its association with the memory of Thomas the Rhymer, the C13 poet and seer. In the late C18 most inhabitants were employed in linen weaving and by the mid C19 there were two manufacturers, one producing the well-known 'Earlston gingham'. The remainder of the population was engaged in agriculture.

CHURCHES

PARISH CHURCH, Church Street. 1891–2, by *Hardy & Wight*. Located at the far E end of the village, and set so far back that it only registers on the approaches from the E, it is a large building to which the detailing is not quite equal. Red rock-faced snecked rubble with ashlar dressings in a C13 style. The main (S) front has a tower at the SE angle and a lower porch block to the SW. The central gabled section has the main doorway flanked by buttresses, with a two-light window on each side; at the upper level is a three-light window with quatrefoils set within an intersecting matrix. The four-storeyed tower is capped by an open arcaded parapet with a weathervane on a pinnacle at the SW corner. Along each flank are three gables pierced by two tiers of windows: triplets of lancets below, with three lights reaching up to the window arch above. Organ chamber and vestry project to N. Internally, galleries run around three sides (with a vestibule and modern offices below the S gallery); they are carried on square piers, with slender columns supporting the lateral roofs. The massive pulpit, communion table and organ are at the N end. – COMMUNION TABLE, 1920. – Medieval CROSS SLAB, with Maltese Cross. – MEMORIALS, re-set into SE corner of church. A stone records successors of Thomas the Rhymer, 'Auld Rymr[s] race'. C17 and C18 memorials to Brown of Park family, with double gablet. – CHURCHYARD. C18 and C19 table tombs, obelisks and headstones. Notable pier-type memorial to the family of William Wilton (†1724), with urn finial and agricultural symbols.

Former EAST UNITED PRESBYTERIAN CHURCH, High Street. 1872 by *A. Herbertson & Son* of Galashiels; demolished 1985. All that remains is the hall, dated 1904, in rock-faced buff snecked stone with harled flanks.

Former WEST UNITED PRESBYTERIAN CHURCH, High Street. 1881, heavily altered and disused. Low w vestry block and louvred dormers in the roof.

PUBLIC BUILDINGS

CORN EXCHANGE, The Square. Partly demolished and altered. Dated 1868 in a panel framed by a stepped hoodmould. Whinstone with pink dressings. Central crowstepped gable, clock and pointed-roofed belfry.

EARLSTON PRIMARY SCHOOL, High Street. The former Board School by *A. Herbertson & Son,* 1872. Plain, single-storey with overhanging eaves. Late C20 accretions.

LIBRARY and READING ROOM, The Square. Erected 1856. Two storeys, three bays, of greywacke with pink sandstone dressings and a pilastered doorpiece. Enlarged 1897; tall crowstepped dormers with finials. A panel with thistle decoration reads 'Reading Room & Library Inst. 1852 [founded] by the Hon. Robt. Baillie'.

WAR MEMORIAL, The Green. *Thomas J. Clapperton,* 1925. A Celtic cross on a boulder base.

DESCRIPTION

HIGH STREET runs E–W. Ground was first feued for speculative building in 1796, attracting feuars who wished to build their own houses; a condition imposed was to build to a height of three storeys. Some are still recognisable, e.g. ROSEMILL on the s side with its back to the street, and a small attic window in each gable. Most of the housing along High Street, however, is mid-C19 and later, in the local vernacular of two storeys and three bays, mostly in dark whinstone rubble. A number, expensively, use brick-sized whinstone blocks. Pilastered and corniced doorcases in various forms, one with a cable-moulded hoodmould with scrolled label stops. Some nicely detailed and integrated pilastered shopfronts, e.g. the Post Office (N side), probably date from the later C19. Towards High Street's E end is the Parish Church (*see* above), then at East Green is Earlston Primary School (*see* above) on the l., followed by housing on both sides. Set back, on the l., in South Park is the derelict FLUTHER'S COTTAGE, a mid-C19, small, two-roomed rubble cottage with its original thatched roof beneath corrugated iron, a unique survival. A-frame adzed couples have been reinforced by timber couples. Further down High Street, on the s side, the ROYAL BANK OF SCOTLAND was built as the Commercial Bank. Additions and alterations by *David Rhind,* 1864 and 1878. Two-storey, three-bay classical house with single bay for the bank to the r., entered through a classical stone porch. A tripartite window on the first floor lit the manager's drawing room or business room.

High Street opens out to THE SQUARE on the r. The RED LION
HOTEL is mid-C19 in dark whinstone. Two storeys, three bays
and a pilastered and corniced doorpiece. After a gap is the
remnant of the Corn Exchange (*see* above), followed by the
Library (*see* above) and Hanover Close, part of a late C20 sheltered housing complex. On High Street's s side is THE GREEN
with the War Memorial (*see* above) in the middle. At its NW
corner the WHITE SWAN is a two-storey, mid-C19 house, rendered and lined out to simulate ashlar, later acquiring the
early-C19 coaching inn to the r. On the s side of The Green a
terrace of three houses, probably early C19, two with pilastered
doorcases, one with fluting on the pilasters and frieze of swags
with urns, the other with panelled pilasters and applied stars
in the frieze.

At High Street's w end, set back to the s, THE MANSE sits in a
large glebe. Built in 1814, two storeys and attic, three bays, in
whinstone with some red sandstone. Raised angle quoins;
pilastered and corniced doorway, and a small attic window in
each gable. Large rubble-walled garden, and a contemporary
U-plan steading with red sandstone margins; later decorative
ventilators.

On the opposite side of High Street is THE THORN. Built on a
plot feued in 1825 by John Spence W.S., and described (in
1834) in the *New Statistical Account* as 'lately erected by a gentleman of the law, whose correct taste has thus given an ornament to the town'. Cream sandstone with long and short
quoins, band courses, a deep cornice and blocking course
under a piend roof. Built into a slope, the front is single-storey
and basement, with steps and cast-iron balustrade to a
pilastered doorcase, flanked by tripartite windows. The w elevation is two-storey with an architrave and cornice to the doorpiece. Inside, a central well stair has cast-iron balusters;
decorative plasterwork and marble chimneypieces. Segmental-
arched carriage gateway and pedestrian gateway with spearheaded iron gate. Set in the wall is a marble drinking fountain
to 'John Young, Doctor in Earlston 1884–1934'. Single-storey
stable block and washhouse. The remainder of THORN
STREET is composed of traditional two-storey, three-bay
houses. No. 5 has an advanced centre bay with a block pediment, a pilastered doorcase and tripartite window above; No.
8 has distinctive round-arched hoodmoulds over the ground-
floor windows. Across the A68 are the remains of the THOMAS
THE RHYMER'S TOWER. Traditionally associated with
Thomas of Ercildoune (Earlston), †c. 1297, but in fact a
fragment of a late medieval tower house, possibly that mentioned in the late C16 as belonging to the Homes of Cowdenknowes. Only the sw corner and parts of the two adjacent walls
survive, of local rubble masonry with dressings of dark red
sandstone; the walls measure about 1.2 m. thick and rise to two
storeys. The ground-floor chamber, originally barrel-vaulted,
evidently incorporated a timber entresol floor supported on
corbels.

CAROLSIDE. *See* p. 152.
COWDENKNOWES. *See* p. 194.
LEADERVALE HOUSE. *See* p. 489.

ECCLES

Mid-C19 Eccles was a small village with a row of single-storey thatched cottages. Remodelled by the Eccles estate in the late C19 and early C20. Some single-storey cottages remain on the N side of Main Street, now slated, one or two with lying panes and stone-canopied doorways.

Former FREE CHURCH (Village Hall). 1844. T-plan with a lateral N 'aisle' and a lower E hall and vestry. Regularly spaced lancets. Adapted in 1939 with new entrance through the N aisle.

PARISH CHURCH. A notable work of rural classicism constructed in 1774 (the date inscribed within the porch). Local tradition asserts that a burial enclosure N of the present church is the relic of an earlier church, though it is perhaps more likely that the priory church (see below) served the parish. A large rectangle of droved squared rubble with ashlar dressings, margins and gable skews. The slender E tower-porch rises two ashlar-built storeys above the church, the upper storey having arched belfry openings below a modillioned cornice; a pyramidal concave-sided cap is topped by a prominent finial. On each side of the tower were two windows, the lower rectangular and the upper arched. The symmetry of this front was marred by a low, gabled vestry block N of the tower, of 1862, by *I. Noble*. At the centre of the S front are three tall, widely spaced arched windows, the central one having had a doorway at its base; at each end is a circlet window above a doorway adapted as a window. Most of the arched windows have intersecting glazing bars at their head, while the circlet windows have rose patterns. The N front has a simple succession of three arched windows, with a modern rectangular window towards the W end. The W face has a central rectangular doorway flanked by rectangular windows, with three arched upper windows and a small circlet within the gable.

The interior was remodelled by *Williamson* in 1930. The pulpit and communion table were relocated to the W end, the N gallery removed and the W gallery subsumed within a hall, with vestries below. Only the modified E gallery survives, with a raised and fielded panelled front supported by Tuscan columns. A shallow recess framed by the W gallery columns re-set *in antis* was created for the communion table. – COMMUNION TABLE and CHAIRS, 1930. – STAINED GLASS. S side, centre, War Memorial, 1948 by *Douglas McLundie* of the *Abbey Studio*; oculus above communion table, *Agnus Dei*. – BURIAL ENCLOSURE, N of church, possibly C17, now collapsing and overgrown. – CHURCHYARD. Attractive mixture of mainly C19 headstones and table tombs, but some earlier. Imposing polished red granite obelisk to Logan family. Several more ambitious memorials and enclosures at W end of churchyard; Greig of Eccles enclosure with rusticated quoins and doorway with lugged architrave abuts the remains of the priory.

PRIORY. Founded for Cistercian nuns *c.* 1156, probably by Gospatrick, Earl of Dunbar and his wife Derdere.

Only enigmatic fragments remain. A wall running E–W, and forming a boundary between the narrower W part of the

churchyard and Eccles House (*see* below), has stretches of mid-
C12 cubical masonry embodying the blocked rear arch of a
doorway and a double-chamfered string course with alternating billet decoration. This was perhaps the s wall of the
church. Seen from the garden of Eccles House this wall has a
corresponding stretch of string course, while the blocked
doorway can be seen to have a continuous quirked angle roll
likely to represent a late medieval remodelling. The w extension of this wall is of C19 date, belonging to the outbuildings
associated with the house.

A second wall, at right angles to this, may have been part of
the E conventual range. Immediately next to the first wall are
two barrel-vaulted compartments entered through widely
arched openings, with a curving stair leading to an upper floor.
At that upper level, above the s side of these two compartments, the wall appears to have the lower parts of window
ingoes below the apex of the ground-floor vault. Further s,
more work of apparently mid-C12 date may be seen: after a
short length of wall with cubical masonry and a string course,
the w wall of the range steps forward as a broad pilaster-
buttress. A truncated wall running E behind this point (now
partly masked) is ashlar-faced and has what appears to be a
bench at its base and a pavement to its s, suggesting this was
the chapter house.

The junction of the E and s sides of the cloister could be
indicated by an arch springing some distance s of the structures already discussed, while the internal wall articulation of
a passage through the s conventual range may be preserved in
a series of decorated pilasters s of that arch. Is it also possible
that a well to the sw had served the lavatorium at the entrance
to the refectory, and that the approximate position of the sw
corner of the cloister is thus indicated? A number of FRAG-
MENTS of C12 and C13 date are located around the gardens in
the vicinity of the priory remains. These include a capital that
appears to be of scalloped form, a nook-shaft capital of waterleaf type, and what appears to be a corbel fragment with spear-
shaped leaves.

CROSSHALL CROSS, 1 km. N. A late medieval disc-headed cross
over 4 m. high, set in a massive cubical base. The tapering shaft
has a male figure and a hound on one face and a Latin cross
on the other; one of the sides has a cross and the other a sword.
Shields with unidentified arms are carved on one face and one
side, just below the cross-head.

ECCLES LEITHOLM PRIMARY SCHOOL. Early 1960s by
Berwickshire County Council. Neat, in pinkish red brick. Glazed
w elevation, monopitched block to rear. Timber fascias.

ECCLES HOUSE. By *Leadbetter & Fairley*, 1898. Scottish Renaissance, mostly with painted harling and cream ashlar dressings
above a rock-faced sandstone base course. – SUMMERHOUSE.
Square, in harled rubble, with a gabled and columned porch
and Venetian window. Red tiled pyramidal roof. – NORTH
LODGE (B6461). Mid-C19, but remodelled, possibly late C19.

GLEBE HOUSE, 0.8 km. E. Originally Eccles Parish Manse. By
William Elliot; built by *Alexander Gilkie*, 1813.

LAMBDEN HOUSE. *See* p. 481.

ECKFORD

ECKFORD PARISH CHURCH. On the site of a church granted to Jedburgh Abbey by the early C13, the rectangular main body of the present church probably perpetuates the plan of its medieval predecessor. Largely rebuilt in 1665–8, but with later additions that included a substantial N laird's 'aisle' of 1722–4 (resulting in a T-plan) and a W porch. In a restoration of 1848 by *John & Thomas Smith* the roof was renewed, a birdcage bellcote added to the W gable, new S windows formed and the interior re-furnished. Further restoration and reordering by *Sydney Mitchell & Wilson* in 1898 moved the focus of worship to the E end.

The main W entrance is covered by a wide porch with a crenellated wall-head. The S front has a pair of tall arched windows rising into ashlar gables on each side of the central axis, probably of 1848, and a small rectangular window towards its W end below the surviving gallery. The E wall has a large Venetian window of 1898. The laird's 'aisle' is entered through an elevated E doorway with a lugged architrave and dentilled cornice. Its windows have moulded arrises, and on the N face is an arched recess with block rustication, and a painted inscription commemorating 'Dominus Gulielmus Bennet' (Sir William Bennet of Grubet) and the date 1724. (Flanking the arch are small arched vents to the burial vault at the lower level of the 'aisle'.) Above this is a tablet flanked at its lower level by the two halves of a split swan-necked pediment with the date 172[4]. The gable has volute skewputts and an axial chimney with raised margins.

Internally, the reordering of 1898 created a wainscot-lined E chancel. The W gallery has a panelled front and is carried on cast-iron columns; it is reached by a stair within the porch with barley-sugar balusters. The elevated Bennet loft, with a panelled front framed by pilasters, used to face across to the pulpit when it was between the two S windows before 1898. – SUNDIAL. At E end of S wall. – JOUGS, 1718, hanging on S wall, towards E end.

CHURCHYARD. The older part, around the church, has several good memorials, both upright stones and table tombs. One stone has a seated figure reading a book, others have *memento mori*. Enclosure at E end of church, with crudely carved medieval cross-slab and some wall memorials to ministers. Amongst more recent memorials, large Ionic aedicule for David McDougall, †1883, with portrait bust and Rococo cartouche. Humphrey Scott Plummer, †1991, W of laird's aisle; good lettering. – The WATCH HOUSE, at the old entrance to churchyard, is small and circular with a crenellated parapet.

KALEMOUTH SUSPENSION BRIDGE over the River Teviot, 0.4 km. NE. 1830. One of the earliest surviving carriage suspension bridges. Designed by *Captain Samuel Brown, R.N.*, iron chain manufacturer (*see* also Union Chain Bridge, p. 739), erected by *William Mather* of Kalemouth, at the expense of William Mein of Ormiston. The oak timber deck (54 m. long by 5 m. wide), strengthened with strong timber cross-braced side railings to counter the effect of strong winds, is suspended from iron

rods and chains that are supported by masonry pylons, two at
each end. Discreetly repaired in 1988 by *Peter Jackson*, Chief
Engineer for *Borders Regional Council*, who renewed the oak
deck and handrails in Canadian Douglas fir, and replaced
wrought-iron bracing and fixings in steel. The contemporary
TOLL COTTAGE is single-storey, extended in stone but marred
by unsympathetic additions.

DESCRIPTION. Near the Parish Church is KIRK COTTAGE,
1828, the Beadle's house and stables, much altered. Wall-head
dormers with brick infill to the pediments added in 1891. E-
plan stables for the parishioners built 1841. At the churchyard's
S gate a WAR MEMORIAL. Celtic cross of *c.* 1920. To the w,
ECKFORD HOUSE, the former manse. 1770s, enlarged by *John
Smith*, 1853. Reduced and remodelled after a fire, 1980. KIRK-
BANK HOUSE, N of the church, was built *c.* 1805 as an inn on
the Edinburgh–Newcastle road. By 1836, it had become a villa.
Two storeys, harled and painted, with grey sandstone margins
and overhanging eaves. The centre of the w elevation has a
plain entrance doorway, flanked by full-height shallow bows,
with tripartite windows and narrow sidelights. Mid-to-late C19
N extension with a gable, and, at the other end, a drawing
room, and full-height oriel wrapped around the SE corner.
Courtyard buildings converted.

The VILLAGE proper lies 1 km. S, with a group of Neo-Tudor
cottages in coursed red sandstone. Built 1854 for day labourers on the Buccleuch estate; each had five rooms. At the S end
of the village is LITTLEDENE, a neat, early C20 former police
house in brick and render with a hipped roof and central
cluster of chimneys. Moulded doorway with shallow pointed
arch and wide-arched windows: that to the N lit the cells.

MARLFIELD HOUSE. *See* p. 526.

2040

EDDLESTON

EDDLESTON PARISH CHURCH. 1829, by *James Turnbull*, carpenter, and *Robert Ritchie*, mason. Its predecessor may have
been C16, and the use of old materials was recommended in
the erection of the present church; the N, W and S gables were
to be faced with freestone, the colour to match the existing
church. It is built of coursed sandstone except for the E elevation and the E end of the S side, which are in whinstone rubble.
Strip angle margins. Bellcote at the E end rebuilt with a fish
weathervane by *Thomas Hadden*, 1925; its BELL is Dutch,
inscribed and dated 1507 and decorated with scrollwork and
tracery. It displays three medallions showing the Virgin and
Child, St John the Baptist, and an owl below a scroll. Gothic
doors and mullion windows with moulded copes and Y-shaped
tracery. The latter appears to have escaped the disastrous fire
of 1896, which destroyed the roof and interior. Reconstructed
by *David MacGibbon* who also added an apse at the w end, to
improve interior lighting, and the S vestry. C18 SUNDIAL on
the SW corner; very eroded, but the gnomon survives. The lofty
INTERIOR has a kingpost truss roof. PULPIT, with elders'
chairs, on a raised platform in the apse. Good wrought-iron

standard lights with elaborate sconces down the central aisle.
– FONT, 1904. – ORGAN by *Ingram & Co.*, 1907, made for St
Blane's Church, Dunblane, and rebuilt here in 1980 by *R. C.
Goldsmith Ltd.* – STAINED GLASS. Apse: four windows by *Bal-
lantine & Gardiner*, 1899, dedicated to Rev. A.J. Murray, †1897.
Christ and St Peter in the centre, Moses and David in the side-
lights. Two windows illustrate Faith, Hope and Charity: to John
Somerville, †1911.

GRAVEYARD. A good collection of C18 and C19 TABLE
STONES, mostly with baluster-shaped pedestals, some with
ornamented tops, and panelled ends with emblems of mortality. Most of the C18 HEADSTONES have crude examples of
twisted or plain pilasters. A good example by the entrance gate
has a shaped pediment, the initials of Andrew Wallace and
Marion Neilsone and date of 1703. On the reverse is a cherub's
head and twisted pilasters framing funerary emblems. – Mural
MONUMENTS. On the r. side of the vestry, an illegible early
C18 panel, framed by scrolled foliage. Shields at each corner,
the top ones emblazoned, between them a wreathed helmet
and a boar's head. Skull and thigh bones at the bottom. On
the l. side of the vestry is a monument with Tuscan columns,
entablature and a broken pediment, containing the date 1686,
with heraldic achievement. The re-cut inscription records the
deaths of the Rev. James Smith, †1673, faithful and worthy
minister of Innerleithen and Eddleston, and his son Charles,
†1685. On the E gable an armorial panel bears a shield, which
may show the arms of James Logan, living in Eddleston
1592–1624. Above is a memorial with crude pilasters and capitals; the l. bears the monogram IHM, and a panel contains
heraldry identified as that of Sir John Murray (of Blackbarony), †1617.

EDDLESTON BRIDGE, s end of Station Road. Access from the
toll road (A703) across the Eddleston Water. 1780, by the *Noble*
family and rebuilt by them in 1782 after it had 'tumbled down'
in a flood. Segmental arch, dressed voussoirs and pilaster strips
carried up to the height of the low parapet.

EDDLESTON PRIMARY SCHOOL, Burnside. 1970 by *Borders
Regional Council* (project architect, *Jeremy Snodgrass*). Attractive, single-storey, slightly curved on plan, with the principal
elevation facing SE towards the hills.

DESCRIPTION. STATION ROAD has on each side rows of one-
and two-storey cottages, built 1780 by *James & William Noble*
for Black Barony estate workers. Of harled whinstone from
Newhall quarry, Carlops, with polished dressings. These are
almost in the form of unified terraces, each with two-storey,
three-bay blocks in the centre of each row. These have widely
spaced windows and deep reveals; each block contains two
houses with two narrow sash windows in the middle of the first
floors, one to each house. At the N end of the street, on the l.,
is the STATION HOUSE, built *c.* 1855 on the newly opened
Peebles Railway. Coursed whinstone, bracketed eaves and
gabled porch.

HORSESHOE INN, E side of A703, is the former smithy of 1862,
its original purpose made clear by the picturesque horseshoe-
shaped windows with boarded shutters. Behind the inn

MOREDUN is C18, two-storey with cable-moulded skewputts. Its core is the lower part of a tower house. On the opposite corner, N, the mid-C19 SCHOOLHOUSE.

GEORGE MEIKLE KEMP MEMORIAL, Redscarshead, 3.2 km. S on the W side of the A703. A little-known memorial to the designer of the Scott Monument, Edinburgh, paid for by subscription and erected to designs by *James Grieve* in 1932 (the centenary of Scott's death). The monument is built against the N gable of the cottage of Andrew Noble, whom Kemp served for four years as an indentured apprentice millwright. Crow-stepped and buttressed gable with a Gothic traceried arch, apparently based on one on the Scott Monument; the crow-steps are similar to those at Abbotsford (q.v.). Memorial tablet with a bronze portrait medallion, modelled on the bust of Kemp by A. Handyside Ritchie. Below, four quatrefoils, and some heraldry added at a later date. The memorial overlooks the site of the carpenter's workshop; redesigned by Grieve as a sunken garden, paved with a hundred stones of different colours and surrounded by seating. In the centre is a grind-stone supported on a base of pebbles collected by Grieve from Peeblesshire burns. Gothic gate.

MILKIESTON TOLL HOUSE, 1.4 km. S on the E side of the A703, which was opened as a toll road in 1770. Late C18, single-storey, harled, with a central gabled porch. C20 additions.

OLD HAREHOPE COTTAGE (formerly Harehope House), 6.4 km. SW. Built, according to an inscribed lintel, in 1723 by George Brown, an Edinburgh merchant, and his wife Rachel Selkirk. The lintel is re-set above the central window of the mid-C19 upper storey.

BARONY CASTLE. *See* p. 114.
CRINGLETIE HOUSE. *See* p. 202.
PORTMORE HOUSE. *See* p. 639.

6010   # EDGERSTON

CHURCH. Built as a chapel of ease in 1838. Grey rubble with ashlar dressings; the low-pitched slated roofs oversail the walls creating a pleasingly understated rustic appearance. It lies parallel to the road, the entrance in a gabled salient at the centre of the E front. The rectangular doorway is framed by buttresses below a three-light panel-traceried window and there is a single lancet on each side. A small bellcote rises through the roof over the salient gable. The end walls have triplets of windows, the central one in the N gable having simple tracery, and there is a two-light window at the centre of the W face. In alterations of 1891 the interior was reordered, and a vestry added at the S end of the W face. Internally there is a narrow vestibule below a gallery, the access stair being reached by a doorway in the N wall. The segmental profile ceiling is boarded and ribbed. – STAINED GLASS. W window, Christ the Sower and Christ the Shepherd, 1891. S window, Good Samaritan, 1882, *James Ballantine & Son*. – PULPIT, timber octagon with blind arcading, on slender stem; stairs with barley-sugar balusters, presumably c. 1891. – CHURCHYARD. C19 and C20 memorials, the most striking a bedhead-type memorial to Frederick Scott of Edgerston, with an eagle holding laurel festoons, flanked by a dove. – Former MANSE dated 1853. Gabled dormerheads, and a four-light canted bay.

SCHOOLHOUSE, 1847.

WAR MEMORIAL. *c.* 1920. A tapering pillar, on an octagonal plinth, with a pierced, entwined cloverleaf cross-head.

EDGERSTON MILL, 1 km. SE. Former sawmill. Central gabled bay, the first floor on a continuous corbel, thistle finial. Former wheel house at the rear with a catslide roof. Tall diamond-plan end stacks. Gabled MILL COTTAGE, 1837, with a fanlit doorway.

EDGERSTON HOUSE
0.5 km

The lands of Edgerston were granted to the Rutherford family in 1492 by James IV. Philip Rutherford is reported to have built a new house in 1596: a surviving gunloop in the basement of the present house may support this date, but the rest was probably rebuilt *c.* 1720 when John Rutherford succeeded. The N front is nine bays long, of three storeys and basement, mainly rendered, the rest in rubble. The early C18 part is the centre seven bays, with a three-bay advanced pediment and windows with reeded surrounds; the first-floor windows in the centre bays have lugged architraves, the top windows being tucked under the cavetto-moulded eaves. Splayed steps with scroll detailing lead to a Baroque doorcase with superimposed Tuscan pilasters, the outer ones fluted and corniced. The outer E and W bays are wings added *c.* 1790 by John Rutherford M.P., Sir Walter Scott's 'beau ideal of the character of country gentleman'. They are of equal height but only two storeys above the basement. Each has a tall Venetian window and, on the returns, full-height shallow bows. The garden elevation has at its centre a semicircular bow; the wings have elevations matching their N fronts. At the SW corner on this side is a three-storey 'peel tower', with clasping buttresses and a corbelled and crenellated parapet, which was designed as a bachelors' wing by *John Smith*, 1854. Its hoodmoulded, mullion windows with leaded casements are probably of 1916, inserted during alterations by *John Watherston & Sons* for the writer, F.S. Oliver, who acquired the estate in 1915.

The principal rooms were stylishly refitted in the early C20. Between the vestibule and hall is an Edwardian Baroque pedimented doorcase flanked by Ionic columns. This leads to the stair hall; its cantilevered stone staircase looks mid-C19. A small dining room has imported C18 panelling, and a study is hung with Spanish leather. In the drawing room, the Adam-style chimneypiece with flanking paired Corinthian columns and figurative panel must also be an import. *Guy Dawber* designed Oliver's Library, on the first floor, in 1915.

The ITALIAN GARDENS were created *c.* 1933 by Mrs Oliver. Entered through wrought-iron gates with square red sandstone piers supporting late C17 lions rampant, each holding a child's

head between its paws. Laid out with terraces and ponds. E of
the house an early C20 triangular BIRD POOL has a heron at
each corner. – STABLES. Traditional early C19 quadrangular
block. Harled cottage with overhanging eaves. A dormer pediment has the arms of Thomas Rutherford, †1720, and his wife
Susannah Riddell. – SOUTH LODGE, early C19 with piended
roof and overhanging eaves. – EDGERSTON HOME FARM.
Dated 1839 and 1920. The E front has a three-bay gabled projecting jamb; a datestone inscribed TR 1695 rests on a lintel.
Open cartsheds have solid sandstone columns. – DOVECOT,
probably early C19; re-roofed. Octagonal, in two stages. Sited
on sloping ground, with a door in each stage, an oculus above
the first. – Gabled BARN and piend-roofed ICE HOUSE to
the S.

OVERTON TOWER. See p. 603.

7030   EDNAM

PARISH CHURCH. Ednam, which *c.* 1105 was granted to
Durham Cathedral by its builder Thor Longus, is important
as the earliest known case of a landowner erecting a church
on lands received as part of the feudal settlement of southern
Scotland. The C12 church was presumably a short way NE of
the present church, where the S wall of the Edmonstone burial
enclosure embodies a blocked window embrasure of C12 type,
which was perhaps part of the N wall of the church.

   A new church was built within the village in the mid-C18,
but in 1802 it was decided to return to the old churchyard. The
existing church, by *William Elliot*, was built by 1805. It was a
rectangle of buff-coloured rubble, with block quoins at the
angles of the S front and a birdcage bellcote over the E gable.
Additions were made in 1902–3 by *Hardy & Wight*, including
the E chancel, S porch and N vestry, additions which are
identifiable by the use of more regularly coursed buff rubble.
In its final form the nave has three Y-traceried windows along
the S flank, and a three-light intersecting-traceried W window
(flanked by a pair of blocked window heads from the first
building campaign). The chancel has a single-light window in
each of the S and N walls, and a two-light Geometric-traceried
E window. The interior was reordered in 1903. The choir is
covered by a boarded, pointed barrel ceiling, while the nave
has scissor beams below a boarded ceiling of polygonal profile.
– PULPIT, octagonal with relief-carved symbols on panels,
1903.

   Set in an external arched recess on the E side of the vestry
is a MONUMENT to James Dickson, †1771. Obelisk framed by
an aedicule with pairs of Rococo Gothic triplet shafts on each
side. The detailing is rather like the garden houses at Ednam
House, Dickson's house in Kelso (see p. 464), and therefore
possibly the work of *James Nisbet.* – CARVED STONES, three
panels leaning against the church, with half-figures in relief,
possibly from table tombs. – CHURCHYARD, some C18 stones
with *memento mori,* but mainly C19 headstones.

EDNAM BRIDGE, over Eden Water. Early C19 with three elliptical arches flanked by pilasters. Rounded cutwaters, channelled voussoirs, and mutuled cornice. Inscribed panel to
Henry Francis Lyte †1847, author of 'Abide With Me', born
in Ednam, 1793.

EDNAM PRIMARY SCHOOL, Duns Road. A grand Neoclassical
school with Baroque adornment, provided by Sir Richard
Waldie Griffith, c. 1907. U-plan, in rock-faced rubble with
sandstone margins. Angles with flush-channelled quoins, keystoned doorways, and columned and pilastered porches
for the children. Gabled wings have keystoned roundels,
below mullioned tripartite windows with scrolled cornices.
Columned and domed cupola.

WAR MEMORIAL. Square granite column, c. 1920, embossed
with a cross and wreath; the plinth is a drinking fountain with
lion's mask and bowl. Railings with Art Nouveau ironwork and
stone obelisks.

THOMSON OBELISK, 1.6 km. S. A memorial to James Thomson,
author of *The Seasons*, born in Ednam in 1700. By *John Smith*.

EDRINGTON HOUSE   9050

2.5 km. E of Foulden

The house is classical of two storeys, basement and attic. Probably early-to-mid C18, if not earlier, but later recast and altered.
Stone coped skews, scrolled skewputts and a lintel course
under corniced eaves. The E elevation has a flying stair and
columned doorcase with broken pediment. A two-bay gable
end to the l. is slightly advanced with a decoratively glazed attic
light in the gable-head. The four-bay S elevation has a rather
martial, full-height canted bay with a crenellated parapet and
blind shields in panels. A plaque within a coat-of-arms for John
Sodey, dated 1849. – Former STABLE. Single storey of harl-
pointed rubble. – SUNDIAL. Dial inscribed 'Joseph Douglas of
Edrington 1622'. – WALLED GARDEN, early to mid C19. Ball-
finialled square gatepiers with spearheaded iron gates. –
LODGE, late C19. A stone in the W gatepier is dated 1836 but
set upside-down! Decorative iron gates.

EDROM   8050

PARISH CHURCH. A church here was granted to Durham
Cathedral in the early C12, and the form of the medieval building presumably underlies the rectangular main body of the
present church; a doorway, of the second quarter of the C12,
has been rebuilt as the entrance to the Logan burial vault, W
of the church (*see* Logan Aisle, below). Archbishop Robert
Blackadder of Glasgow, who was of local birth, built c. 1499 a
chantry chapel (Blackadder Aisle) on the S side of the nave,
resulting in an irregular T-shape. Blackadder's work is identifiable in the chamfered plinth of the S wall of the aisle and in
its diagonal buttresses; his arms are below the tabernacle at the

head of its sw buttress. Various post-medieval additions are recorded. Sir John Home of Blackadder remodelled the Blackadder Aisle in 1696 to create a burial vault below a laird's loft, his work identifiable in masonry of diagonally broached blocks. The church itself was extensively remodelled in 1737 when a N aisle, possibly running parallel with much of the church, was added. The greater part of what is now seen, however, is of 1885–6 by *Hardy & Wight* (*George Duns*, clerk of works) when, according to an inscription on the NE buttress of the extended N aisle, the church was 'restored and enlarged'.

The church is of an asymmetrical cross shape which, externally, gives little clue to the internal spaces, and apart from the two-stage birdcage bellcote on the W gable, it is of rather secular appearance. N of the main body is a widely projecting aisle, the unusual salients in the re-entrant angles between aisle and main body possibly representing the remains of the smaller aisle of 1737. Facing that aisle across the church, but to W of centre since it flanked the original nave, is the Blackadder Aisle. The exterior massing is further complicated by projections to house porches and vestries. The work of 1886 is identifiable from its stugged snecked rubble, the earlier masonry being generally left unchanged except where windows – often extending into raised gables – have been inserted.

Internally the church is largely of 1886. Scissor-braced roofs cover the principal spaces, with lattice beams on cast-iron columns defining the areas in the re-entrant angles to each side of the N aisle. The pulpit and communion table are displaced E of centre by the arch of the laird's loft above the Blackadder aisle, which is now closed off by a glazed screen. There is a gallery in the outer part of the N aisle, within which is the organ. – PULPIT, with ogee-arched back-board and cross finial. – PAINTED BOARDS flanking the pulpit with Ten Commandments, Lord's Prayer and Creed. – FONT, 1885. – EFFIGIES in the Blackadder Aisle, of Patrick Home of Broomhouse and his wife Eleanor Wardrop, 1553. The tomb-chest is carved with arms assumed to be of Home and Wardrop and the initials P.H. Confusingly, the chest also bears the date 1668, while the date 1553 on the slab below the effigies appears to be a secondary incision.

LOGAN AISLE, W of the church. A rectangular burial enclosure rising from a well-detailed base course of rather medieval appearance and covered by a pointed barrel vault; the earliest memorial is of 1790. Open archway in the E wall, presumed to be the re-set main doorway of the medieval church. This doorway, of the second quarter of the C12, though now sadly weathered, is one of the finest pieces of Romanesque architectural sculpture in Scotland. It has three orders of arches, the two inner orders with varieties of chevron and the outer one having an embattled moulding. There are two orders of engaged shafts, and there was probably initially a pilaster on each side. Three of the capitals have foliage trails with masks at the angles, the others are cushions or scallops. Leaning against the Logan Aisle are two weathered medieval graveslabs. Within the CHURCHYARD is a notable group of C17–C20 gravestones; especially worthy are James Bruce, †1738, winged angel, trade emblems and *memento mori*; Adam Wait, †1730, simple three-quarter portrait and *memento mori*. The burial enclosure of the Campbell Swintons of Kimmerghame, NW of the church, has a Roman Doric screen; next to that, the memorial of the Fordyce Buchans of Ayton. The low wall N of the church incorporates parts of dismantled table tombs. C20 memorials include: Francis Cowan, †1996, a split boulder with low-relief decoration; John W. Blackadder, †1928, and Anne Wilson, †1946, stylised tree between two arched inscribed tablets. – WATCH HOUSE, at churchyard entrance, now with garage doors in its N wall.

KELLOE BRIDGE. 2.3km. S, over the Blackadder Water. 1872. Three spans; the segmental arches have brick soffits and pilasters above the cutwater buttresses.

MANSE (York House). Rebuilt by *James Stevenson* of Berwick, 1881, probably incorporating the 1825 manse.

Former SCHOOL. Early C19 schoolhouse flanked by a single-storey wing to l. The schoolroom (now Village Hall) to the r. is very likely the sewing school erected in 1866. Hoodmoulded traceried Gothic windows. Attached to the S, the single-storey Weaver's Cottage, and the former Post Office, the gables with exposed rafters and finials.

TODHEUGH BRIDGE. 1.5km. NE, over the Whiteadder Water. Late C19. Three elliptical arches, with rusticated voussoirs and rounded cutwaters terminating as pyramid-capped piers.

WAR MEMORIAL, SE on the A6105. A carved Celtic cross by *J.S. Rhind*, *c.* 1920.

EDROM FARM COTTAGES. Stylish group of five Neo-Jacobean cottages of 1876.

EDROM HOUSE. Perhaps built *c.* 1740, but old-fashioned for that date, since the design derives from the simple classical rectangular piend-roofed houses introduced by Sir William Bruce in the late C17. Thick glazing bars to the first-floor windows, surviving lengths of roof flashing with a scalloped ornament and a number of prominent masons' marks suggest instead an early C18 date. Only the doorpiece with segmental pediment is characteristic of the 1740s, perhaps added during renovation of an existing house. Five bays, two storeys above a basement with a steep piended bellcast roof with later brick chimneystacks and dormers. Coursed sandstone ashlar and raised rusticated quoins; the sandstone is stugged or keyed for harling. Two-storey rear wing added *c.* 1774, linked to mid-C18 outbuildings, with vaulted cellarage. A single-storey and basement dining room (music room), dated 1908, with a square bay window, was added by Major George J.N. Logan Home. The plan is tripartite, divided by transverse walls, with the hall to the rear, an open newel stone stair (treads now encased in wood), and a room on each side. Panelling in a first-floor room is probably *c.* 1740. The early C19 timber and gesso chimneypiece in the music room was brought from Broomhouse (dem. 1971). – The formal LANDSCAPE probably dates from the 1760s when the village manse and offices were moved to their present site. In front of the house a rubble-built BRIDGE, with elliptical panels over the cutwaters, gave access to the parish church. It spans a small canal sourced from the Boatspool Burn to the E.

EDROM NEWTON FARM. Late C18 or early C19 farmhouse with

pavilions with Venetian windows. The large, symmetrical, courtyard STEADING was built in 1874 by Richard Miller of Manderston. Neo-Jacobean. Long s façade with central two-storey tower containing a dovecot above a pend, and end pavilions with striking curvilinear gables.

BLANERNE HOUSE. *See* p. 123.

5030

EILDON HALL
4.9 km. SE of Melrose

Classical villa built for Dr Thomas Mein R.N., 1802–6, but transformed in 1862 into a mansion for the fifth Duke of Buccleuch by *William Burn*, in his neat but rather dull Cotswold Tudor style. The additions were mostly to accommodate visitors and servants, presumably to give the Duke a presence near to the Buccleuch Hunt, then based at St Boswells. The early C19 house was of two storeys, attic and basement with a wide bow flanked by tripartite windows and single-storey and basement pavilions set forward on the N front. Burn raised the roof of the earlier house, added two floors to the pavilions and re-roofed the whole block adding finialled gables and dormer windows. Two-storey canted bays were added to the s fronts of the former pavilions. The w pavilion's basement storey with a balustrade (added in 1866). Segmental-pedimented N portico is also Burn's. Simple interior. – STABLES. Mostly *c.* 1802–6 with small alterations by Burn 1866–7.

3030

ELIBANK CASTLE
3.8 km. SE of Walkerburn

Fragment of a late C16 mansion of unusual design perched above the s bank of the River Tweed. Probably erected by Sir Gideon Murray, founder of the family of Elibank, who acquired the property in 1595. The house was ruinous by 1722.

The L-plan mansion comprised an oblong main block (21.1 m. from NW to SE by 6.9 m. transversely) with a slightly offset wing (about 7.6 m. square) extending NE from its E corner. It appears to have embodied a vaulted cellarage, two main residential floors and a garret. However, the NW end of the main block was vaulted above second-floor level and may have continued upwards as a tower, as at Greenknowe (q.v.). There are no traces of any overt defensive features and the whole fabric appears to be of one build. The main block contained two cellars entered from a doorway (afterwards replaced by another alongside it) in the NE wall. A third cellar at the SE end was entered only from the wing, which presumably had its own external doorway. On the first floor the main block probably contained a sizeable hall with a chamber opening off it to the NW, and a smaller room at the SE end, perhaps a servery, as well as a chamber in the wing. The staircase arrangements are something of a mystery. The principal floor may have been served by a forestair, while the upper floors are said to have been reached from a newel stair of timber commencing above the entrance lobby – i.e. just outside the N corner of the hall. – There are traces of a FORECOURT to the NE, with outbuildings on two sides. The slope below was laid out as a terraced garden.

ELIBANK HOUSE

3 km. SE of Walkerburn

Dated 1912 but appears to be a remodelling in part of a pretty *cottage orné* of 1842. This is shown in a painting as partly thatched with carved bargeboarded gables, Gothic windows and octagonal chimneys. The design is too similar to *John Smith*'s Chiefswood, Melrose (q.v.) to be a coincidence. The r. gable section of the present five-bay W elevation appears to have survived the 1912 remodelling and extension. A single-storey flat-roofed extension along the W front contains some historic items brought here in the early C20 from Ballencrieff House (Lothian).* The pedimented porch comprises a mid-C18 Venetian window with Ionic pilasters and keystoned arch; the centre window adapted as the doorway. Inner door of carved oak panels, each one containing a medallion with a classical head; possibly early C17. A dormer pediment, above a door in a screen wall, is inscribed ED (Elizabeth Dundas) 1625. – Linked to the house by the screen wall is a single-storey building, with a Gothic window and octagonal chimneys; possibly offices and stabling for the earlier house. – LODGES: Early C20, Lorimerian, each with a long stair window and bracketed timber door canopy.

ELLEMFORD   7060

A tiny settlement by the Whiteadder Water.

DESCRIPTION. Of the CHURCH dedicated in 1244 there are only fragmentary remains. ELLEM LODGE, pleasantly situated by the river, is a picturesque two-storey circular house, harled and whitewashed with some painted margins. It dates from *c.* 1800 (cf. The Retreat, p. 646) with later additions and alterations. Flanking single-storey wings, one with a basement to fit the sloping site. A conical roof and round stack to the house, with a three-bay entrance wing and gabled porch; bowed rear projection. Inside is a well-appointed circular room. ELLEM OLD INN probably began as a simple mid-to-late C18 inn by the ford. Gabled wing added *c.* 1841, and a moulded doorcase *c.* 1894. The lintel contains a triangular panel with a thistle cartouche inscribed AS IFL for Andrew Smith and Ida Florence Landale, who altered a forester's cottage in 1894 to create WOODSIDE COTTAGE. Asymmetrical with a crow-stepped wall-head dormer with scrolled beak skewputts, and

*Built in the late C16 and early C17 by John Murray, first Lord Elibank, burnt out in 1868.

architraved and corniced doorway. Two-storey tower with
piend roof and stone-mullioned windows. Cube sundial on the
S corner with carved motifs and metal gnomon.

ELLEMFORD BRIDGE was 'Erected by the Berwickshire Road
Trustees – John Turner – 18[86]' in stugged coursed sandstone
with ashlar voussoirs. Three segmental arches spanning the
Whiteadder Water. Bullet-plan cutwaters, a pair of wide
pilasters at the ends, flat cornice and rounded cope.

ETTLETON

4080

CHURCHYARD. Nothing remains of the medieval church, abandoned for worship c. 1604. Most of the surviving medieval
stones were gathered into a small enclosure at the centre of the
churchyard c. 1900. They include: two parts of a cross shaft with
cable moulding along the edge; a foliate cross-head,
possibly a finial; a number of cross-incised grave-slabs; a
stone with a small arch cut into it, possibly from an early C12
window. Of the post-medieval memorials, the more interesting
are at the E end of the churchyard. Among them are: C18 memorials with angels and other symbols; a tall arched
Italianate aedicule with bronze relief portrait for John Black
by *Charles Bridges*, 1888; a tripartite Neoclassical memorial to
the Armstrong family (first to be commemorated is Agnes,
†1815); William Armstrong of Sorbytrees, †1851, a large obelisk.

MILLHOLM CROSS, on the roadside below. Late medieval cross,
commemorating one of the Armstrongs of Mangerton, traditionally said to have been murdered c. 1320. The shaft has an
incised sword with the initials MA and AA in relief. Across the
short cross arms is the sacred monogram IHS. The top of the
cross is a later stone bearing the family arms.

LIDDELBANK HOUSE. *See* p. 498.

ETTRICK

2010

Small village in the upper reaches of the Ettrick Valley, lying just
off the Edinburgh – Langholm road (B709).

PARISH CHURCH. In an idyllic setting on the N bank of the
Ettrick Water, W of the village. A church, possibly first built by
Melrose Abbey on land granted in 1235–6, was rebuilt in 1619
by Sir Robert Scott of Thirlestane; a stone with the date and
his initials is at the SE angle. The present building, possibly
incorporating parts of its predecessors, is a rebuilding of 1824
(the date on the tower) by *John & Thomas Smith* of Darnick.
A T-plan structure aligned from E to W, it has a N 'aisle' and
W tower with walls of whin rubble and droved buff ashlar dressings. The main S front has four large rectangular windows with
the thin label hoodmoulds characteristic of the Smiths. The
belfry stage of the tower has paired lancets to each face and
an ashlar crenellated parapet above a corbel table. Leading to
the Napier loft, at the E end, is a double perron with cast-iron
balustrade, the main entrance to the church below its landing
being altogether subordinate.

The remarkable unaltered interior, with much grained woodwork, has galleries in all three arms, the fronts panelled and carried on pairs of timber Tuscan columns. The semi-octagonal PULPIT and PRECENTOR'S DESK are at the centre of the S wall, the pulpit surmounted by an ogee-domed tester with a ball finial and dove. – MEMORIALS. Francis Lord Napier and Ettrick, †1898, Gothic red sandstone niche with brass plaques and white marble bust by *Pittendrigh MacGillivray*, 1900. Basil Napier, †1874, white marble oval relief portrait on grey marble surround. Below that, incised brass memorial to Queen Victoria, by *Singer & Sons* of Frome.
CHURCHYARD. A fascinating mixture of headstones, table tombs, obelisks, enclosures and rough grave markers, set amongst mature trees on a site sloping down towards the Ettrick Water. Worthy of note are the headstone of the poet and writer James Hogg, 'The Ettrick Shepherd', †1835, and the obelisk-shaped, reeded Tuscan column on a high plinth for the Rev. Thomas Boston (author of *Human Nature in its Fourfold State*), †1732.

FREE CHURCH, Tushielaw, 5.6km NE. A simple whin rubble cement-rendered box, now semi-derelict. Pointed windows with raised margins and Y-pattern glazing bars. Small gabled bellcote. – The former MANSE (Kirkbrae) is a two-storey, hip-roofed block of harled and limewashed rubble with a three-bay front. Mid-C19 with later alterations.

BOSTON MEMORIAL HALL, 0.5km SE. 1909, refurbished 1947. A cheerful, corrugated-iron hall with a red roof topped by a central ventilator.

BRIDGE over the Ettrick, Tushielaw, 5.5km NE. Rubble, built with two segmental arches of unequal span and a central pier with rounded cutwater. Possibly the bridge for which a site was sought by *John Smith* and Captain Napier in 1819.

MONUMENT to James Hogg, 0.4km SE. 'The Ettrick Shepherd', by *Andrew Heiton*, raised in 1898 by the Edinburgh Border Counties Association to mark the site of the cottage in which Hogg was born in 1779. Obelisk raised on a high plinth and capped by an acroterion; around the base swags are suspended from rams' heads at the angles. Bronze portrait medallion by *W. Hubert Paton*. Behind the obelisk is an exedra with a stone bench.

TUSHIELAW INN, 5.6km NE. Built in 1831 with 'several comfortable apartments'. Originally a plain, two-storey block of harled rubble, it was altered and extended in the late C19, when it was given a porch and dormers with overhanging eaves and finialled gables. A third storey was contrived at the rear

TUSHIELAW TOWER, 5km NE. Adam Scott received a licence to build a tower and fortalice in 1507, but it is impossible to say whether the existing remains belong to this, or to a slightly later, period. The tower (8.8m. by 7.3m.) is now reduced to its lowest storey, and the irregularly shaped barmkin (about 30 m. by 24m.), which lay immediately to the S, is now represented mainly by the E range, part of which was originally at least two storeys in height. Its barrel-vaulted ground floor seems to have been a storeroom, but the upper floor, or floors, could well have contained residential accommodation, as at Smailholm Tower and Whytbank Tower (qq.v.). Footings of other buildings can be seen to the W, while N of the tower are various enclosures, probably associated with stock rearing and horticulture.

3020

ETTRICKBRIDGE

A small village at a crossing point of the Ettrick Water. The village comprises a single main street flanked by houses of mainly C19 date.

KIRKHOPE CHURCH. Designed 1836 by *William Burn* for the fifth Duke of Buccleuch, but not built until 1838–9. Five-bay rectangle of squared snecked rubble with buff droved ashlar dressings and a low-pitched roof; perhaps more *Rundbogenstil* than Romanesque. Around the main body are a low-gabled S annexe, a W porch and a SE vestry; rising above the S annexe a pilaster supports a rectangular arched bellcote. Single-arched windows light the flanks, with a triplet to the N face.

Internally the walls are lined with a boarded dado below masonry-lined strapped plaster, and the ceiling has arched braces. Around the communion table platform at the N end is a timber balustrade. – STAINED GLASS. Central N window, Good Shepherd by *Alexander Ballantine*, 1904. – Timber LYCHGATE at S entrance to churchyard, built as war memorial, *c.* 1920.

Former FREE CHURCH (now VILLAGE HALL). A harled rubble Victorian block with ornamental tiled roof ridge topped by a metal ventilator. Extended 1950s.

ETTRICK BRIDGE crosses the river gorge. A single segmental arch of local rubble with dressed voussoirs. Built in 1780 and widened on the downstream side in 1858. On the upstream face is a panel from an earlier bridge bearing the arms of Sir Walter Scott of Harden and the dates 1628 and 1780.

ETTRICKSHAWS HOTEL, 2.3 km. SW. Built 1889–91 as a shooting lodge for Dr Thomas Scott Anderson by *Kinnear & Peddie* in Old English style. – Contemporary STABLES (Pine Lodge). L-plan with groom's flat, and stables with high rows of semi-circular vents. – The steel lattice-truss BRIDGE over the Ettrick Water, with concrete abutments and timber decking, was cast at Cultha Works, Glasgow, and built by *P. & W. MacLellan*, 1891.

AIKWOOD TOWER. *See* p. 99.
KIRKHOPE TOWER. *See* p. 471.

6050

EVELAW TOWER

4 km. NE of Westruther

The shell of the late C16 L-plan tower house of the Douglases of 'Yvelie' (Evelaw). Repaired and partly re-roofed *c.* 1900, but now again roofless. Random rubble masonry with dressings of red sandstone and rounded external corners. Four storeys in all, the top one a garret within the roof. The main block (10.1 m. by 6.7 m.) was gable-roofed without wall-walks, the corners brought out to the square at wall-head level on a double corbel course of dressed sandstone. The wing (4.4 m. by 3.3 m.) evidently had an open parapet-walk projected on a row of individual double corbels surmounted by a continuous ovolo moulding. Otherwise defence was taken care of by a series of double-splayed rectangular-mouthed gunloops at ground-floor level, probably one in each of the main walls. Some of the windows contained lead-framed glass and all had plain, round-arrised margins. The entrance was probably in the re-entrant angle of main block and wing, opening directly into a wide newel stair occupying the whole of the latter. This stair rose to the first floor only, the upper levels being reached by a smaller newel stair corbelled out in the re-entrant, as at Greenknowe Tower (q.v.); of this a single tread hangs in mid air. The ground floor of the main block, formerly barrel-vaulted, was possibly lit only by its gunloops; a new doorway was inserted in the W wall c. 1900. The first floor contained a well-lit hall with a big fireplace in its S wall and several built-in cupboards; the round-backed recess in the SE corner was probably a latrine of the newly introduced soil-box variety. At second-floor level the main block contained two chambers, each with its own fireplace and latrine; a third chamber in the wing was similarly equipped. Arrangements at third-floor level were probably similar, but the wing was vaulted and one of the chamber windows is formed within the haunch of the vault, as at Dryhope Tower (q.v.).

EYEMOUTH*   9060

Small coastal town at the mouth of the Eye Water, which was   109
made a burgh of barony under the superiority of the Homes of Wedderburn in 1598. It developed as a port for the export of grain from the surrounding countryside from the mid C18 until the mid C19 when most of that trade was transferred to the railways. Fishing then became the principal industry and remained so, together with fish processing, until the late C20 when tourism on a modest scale became of some importance to the town's economy. It is now bordered on the NW by a large caravan park and fringed by extensive late C20 housing developments.

CHURCHES

Former CONGREGATIONAL CHURCH, Church Street. A domestic cement-rendered three-bay two-storeyed block of 1862. Towards the street the lower windows are rectangular and the upper ones round-headed, all having raised margins. The church, at the upper level, is entered through a porch at the head of a flight of steps against the S flank. Over the opening to the steps is a wrought-iron overthrow with a suspended light

---

*The account of Eyemouth's public buildings and the burgh's description is by John Gifford.

Former EAST CHURCH. Converted into a cinema and now disused; the cement-rendered rectangular church of 1842, with two storeys of blocked windows and raised margins, is visible behind a faintly Art Deco frontispiece.

Former EYEMOUTH PARISH CHURCH, Church Street. A museum and tourist centre since 1980. Built 1811–12 by *Alexander Gilkie*, originally a three-bay rectangle with round-headed windows and an axial w tower flanked by a halved pediment. Modified 1836 by *Walter Elliot* of Kelso, who largely rebuilt the tower. Additions to the E and S, and internal reordering, by *George Fortune* in 1902. The tower is of four storeys, the top stage chamfered to an octagon, and capped by an octagonal dome. Internally, the rectangular space became cruciform in its final state, with a small 'chancel' at the E end and 'transeptal' offshoots; the openings into these spaces were framed by three-centred arches carried on fluted pilasters, those into the 'chancel' having Corinthian capitals.

EYEMOUTH PARISH CHURCH, Victoria Road. Built 1878 as St John's Free Church; renovated and remodelled 1902 by *George Fortune*. Designed in the English Decorated style with walls of pink stugged rubble and yellow sandstone dressings. The E entrance front has a salient tower capped by an octagonal spired lantern to its N, and a laterally gabled projection to the S. The E front is given prominence by its traceried windows. A hall block at the w end is now surrounded by modern extensions. The unarticulated rectangular interior has a roof with widely spaced arched braces; a narrow vestibule runs beneath the single E gallery. The reordered communion table area is at the w end. – PULPIT, octagonal with blind traceried panels raised on a bracketed stem. – FONT, 1871, octagonal with arcaded sides.

EYEMOUTH UNITED CONGREGATIONAL CHURCH, corner of Albert Road and Coldingham Road. Originally Eyemouth Primitive Methodist Church, of 1905 by *William J. Gray Jun.* Cruciform and of pink sandstone, with a harled hall at the w end. The Gothic E entrance front is articulated to suggest a basilican space within, having corbelled-out pinnacles to mark the angles of the 'main vessel'; above the doorway is a three-light plate-traceried window. The windows along the flanks are within raised gables.

FREE BAPTIST CHURCH. Harled rectangle of 1987 with distressing crazy-paved entrance front.

ST ANDREW (R.C.). A harled box of the most domestic kind, adapted from a boat building shed in 1961.

ST EBBA (Episcopal), Paxton Road. An unbuttressed two-cell church by *William J. Gray Jun.* of Berwick. The first church on the site, erected in 1883, was of corrugated iron, to which in 1887 the three-bay chancel of snecked buff sandstone rubble was added. The nave, of pink masonry, was built in 1901, together with a vestry and a porch surmounted by a bellcote. The church is lit chiefly by single lancets, with a triplet of lancets behind the altar at the w end. The chancel has a collar-beam and crown-post roof; the nave an arch-braced roof. – PULPIT. With figure of St Ebba, 1905. – STAINED GLASS. E end, formerly in Christ Church Duns, the Transfigured Christ

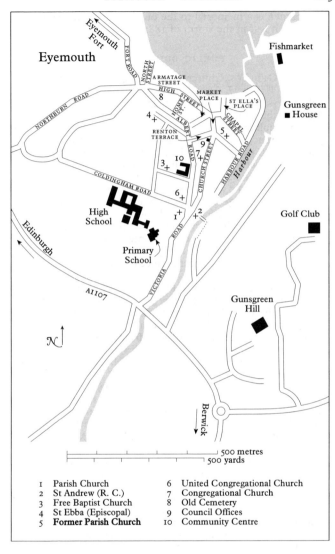

Eyemouth

1 Parish Church
2 St Andrew (R. C.)
3 Free Baptist Church
4 St Ebba (Episcopal)
5 **Former Parish Church**
6 United Congregational Church
7 Congregational Church
8 Old Cemetery
9 Council Offices
10 Community Centre

flanked by St Peter and St Andrew, renewed and enlarged by
Dickson & Walker of Edinburgh; N side nave, St Ebba, by
William Wilson, 1962.

OLD CEMETERY, High Street and Albert Road. The old churchyard may have had a chapel before a separate parish was established in 1618. It is now landscaped as a public garden with
memorials set around the walls. In one corner a folly-like
WATCH HOUSE was constructed in 1849–51. At the centre of

the garden is a memorial to the one hundred and eighty-nine
fishermen lost in the storm of 1881.

PUBLIC BUILDINGS

COUNCIL OFFICES, Church Street. Originally Eyemouth Town
Hall. By *William J. Gray Jun.*, 1874. Flemish-Baronial, of two
tall storeys, the front built of stugged ashlar. Elliptical-headed
lights to the windows, most of which have stiff-leaf capitalled
column-mullions. Stiff-leaf capitals also at the columns of the
main entrance, its round-headed arch decorated with rope
moulding and surmounted by a hoodmould whose label stops
are carved with grotesque heads. Bracketed out above the
entrance, a stone balcony, its parapet pierced with quatrefoils.
It fronts a window whose label stops are carved as bats. Above
this window, a large high relief of the fishing boat, *Supreme*. At
the NE corner, a conical-roofed round tower; in its SE inner
angle with the main block, the carved figure of a griffon pro-
trudes from the wall-head. Canted SE corner with a
crowstep-gabled oriel window projected on continuous corbelling; the ends of the short cornice over its lights bear figures
of grotesque animals.

EYEMOUTH COMMUNITY CENTRE, Albert Road. Originally
Eyemouth School. By *William J. Gray Jun.*, 1876–7, and
extended by *Gray & Boyd* in 1906–7. Constructed of mixed
sandstone and whin rubble, of one tall storey, with a two-storey
centrepiece projecting from the E front. Sparing touches of
Jacobean detail; small ventilators with wrought-iron finials.

Former EYEMOUTH FISHMARKET, Harbour Road. *See*
Description.

EYEMOUTH FISHMARKET, off The Avenue. By *Bain, Swan
Architects*, 2000. Shed-like main block of two storeys, the lower
floor of brick, the upper of wood, under a gently curved metal
roof. At the S end, the taller metal-clad ice plant, its roof, also
curved, at right angles to that of the main block.

EYEMOUTH GOLF CLUB, Gunsgreen Hill, 0.5km. E. By *Bain,
Swan Architects*, 1997. Drydashed and piend-roofed two-storey
pavilion, the upper floor largely glazed. At the S front, an off-
centre balconied portico.

EYEMOUTH HIGH SCHOOL, Coldingham Road. Agglomeration
of buildings, begun in 1923 (by *G.R. Black*) and altered and
extended in 1935–6 (by *Reid & Forbes*), and 1960. The earliest
of the surviving buildings are at the back and quite plain. The
street front, by the Berwickshire County Architect, *D.S. Miller*,
1960, is of two storeys and flat-roofed, the walls faced with a
mixture of brick, glass, render and panels of aggregate and cast
concrete.

EYEMOUTH MUSEUM, Church Street. *See* Former Eyemouth
Parish Church, above.

EYEMOUTH PRIMARY SCHOOL, Coldingham Road. By *Borders
Regional Council, c.* 1970. Postmodern hall, with blockwork walls
and ribbed metal roofs, also by *Borders Regional Council*, 1993.

HARBOUR, Harbour Road. Occupying the mouth of the Eye
Water, the harbour was developed in several stages. The first
was the construction in 1751 of a pier on the W side of the river

and extending partly across its mouth to prevent the growth of a sandbank. An E pier, also at the mouth, was constructed to *John Smeaton*'s design in 1768–73. Both piers were repaired *c*. 1795. In 1843–4 a third pier was constructed to channel the Eye Water, especially when in spate, to the E of the main harbour, while sluice gates controlled entry of the river water to scour the harbour. All these works were reconstructed and extended by *Thomas Meik & Son* in 1885–93. Finally, the harbour entrance was blocked and a new entrance made to its E in *Leitch & Sharpe*'s alterations of 1965. Most of the existing work is of the 1880s and of concrete, but the N end of the W pier and the former head of the E pier (joined to the W pier in 1965) are constructed of large rubble blocks, those on the N side set obliquely.

DESCRIPTION

NORTHBURN ROAD is the steeply sloping W approach to the town centre. At its E end, FORT ROAD leads uphill to Fort Point, a promontory occupied by a caravan park and Eyemouth Fort (*see* below). Between Fort Road and North Street is NORTHBURN HOUSE, a late C19 harled and bargeboarded double house. Elliptical-headed ground-floor windows and doors; first-floor windows rising through the bracketed broad eaves into jerkin-head dormerheads. On NORTH STREET's E side, a SMOKE HOUSE of *c*. 1900, its pantiled roof and ridge ventilator restored in the late C20.

HIGH STREET's N side makes an unpromising start with plain late C19 housing and a car park beside the sea. Opposite, the Old Cemetery (*see* above). Beside it, the HOME ARMS HOTEL of 1867, Georgian survival with a bracketed pediment over the door, but the second-floor windows rise into steeply pedimented dormerheads of Jacobean inspiration. In HOME STREET to the S, late C19 flatted housing with bracketed stone canopies over the doors.

High Street E of Home Street continues with fairly dour C19 fishertown vernacular, mostly of two storeys, some of the fronts covered with render imitating bullnosed masonry. Set back on the S in SPEARS PLACE, the War Memorial of *c*. 1920, a routinely detailed pink granite Celtic cross. The view to the SW up past the steeply rising ARMATAGE STREET's severe late C19 housing is closed by the tall round-headed pend arch of the late Victorian No. 58 ALBERT ROAD on the hill behind. At the end of High Street's N side, Nos. 2–6, pleasant but altered Late Georgian, No. 6 with a pantiled roof. This L-plan block forms an informal little square with another similar block (Nos. 1–9) on the S side of the street. No. 9, with a pantiled piended roof but altered windows, was built as the Eyemouth Parish School in 1819–20 to a design by *Alexander Gilkie*.

MARKET PLACE at High Street's E end begins with the town's roughly triangular former market place. It is bordered by C19 vernacular housing except at the E side where a sizeable block (Nos. 8–10) of *c*. 1930 mixes Art Deco into a traditional general shape. Beside it, the rendered two-storey house at No. 6 has an inserted shopfront, but the small first-floor windows confirm the probability of its date being that on the door lintel, which is inscribed RC MY 1735. In the Market Place, a bronze STATUE (by *David Annand*, 1998) of William Spears, an Eyemouth fisherman who led the mid-C19 revolt against paying tithes on herring catches. He holds a fish in one hand and points imperiously with the other. In CHAPEL STREET E of the market place, more C19 vernacular. Yet more of the same in ST ELLA'S PLACE, but along its N end is the rendered gable of a pantile-roofed late C18 block (No. 12 ST ELLA'S WYND). W front of six bays, the windows grouped 3–3.

In Market Place's short S stretch is the ROYAL BANK OF SCOTLAND of *c.* 1890, its ground floor badly altered but the first-floor windows still set between pilasters. Beside it, RENTON TERRACE climbs up to the W, its N side's tenements remodelled in the late C20. At the top, a tall round-headed pend arch through Nos. 40–56 ALBERT ROAD, a jolly reworking of Eyemouth's late C19 vernacular manner, by *Bain, Swan Architects*, 1995. Opposite the bank, on Market Place's E side, a mid-C19 Georgian survival MASONIC LODGE.

MASONS WYND leads past the N side of the former Eyemouth Parish Church (*see* Churches, above). On the wynd's l. side, another whitewashed and pantile-roofed SMOKE HOUSE of *c.* 1900, the lower part of its walls of rubble, the upper of brick. At the wynd's E end, SALTGREENS, a housing development by *Borders Regional Council*, 1986. Walls of dark red and brown brick, the roofs covered with concrete tiles; low pyramid-roofed tower. It is not unsuccessful in evoking the town's lost warehouses.

CHURCH STREET's W side begins with the Council Offices (*see* Public Buildings, above). After this excitement, Church Street is mostly staid C19 Georgian survival. However, No. 11 (CHESTER HOUSE), set behind a small walled courtyard on the E side, is a well-finished mid-C18 town house. Two-storey rubble front of five bays, the centre door's lugged architrave framed by pilaster strips which end in blocky consoles under a cornice. First-floor lintel course under the eaves cornice. Inside, the entrance hall has touches of stucco decoration at its E end. The walls of the SW ground-floor room (originally the dining room) are panelled, with a dentil cornice and fluted Ionic pilasters framing the fireplace and overmantel. Flying stair to the first floor, whose SW room (originally the drawing room) is similarly treated but with panelled anta-pilasters framing the S fireplace and a shell-headed china recess at the N wall.

A little further S, on Church Street's W side, the former Congregational Church (*see* Churches, above). Near the street's S end, on the E side, CHURCH COURT, by *Bain, Swan Architects*, 2001–2. Colourful pseudo-vernacular, the walls covered with white drydash, the roofs pantiled. It is overlooked by the back of St John's House in Albert Street (*see* below). At the S end of Church Street, on the E, St Andrew's (R.C.) Church (*see* Churches, above). At a higher level on the W, on the gusset corner with Albert Road, CHURCHES HOTEL, a rendered two-storey early C19 piend-roofed villa. The ground floor of its S front has been overlaid by late C20 additions but the first-floor windows are grouped 1-2-1; a pair of wall-head chimneys. In the house's W side, a circular first-floor window.

Further N, in ALBERT ROAD, the piend-roofed and rendered ST JOHN'S HOUSE, built as Eyemouth Free Church manse to a design by *William J. Gray Sen.* in 1848-9. Front of two storeys above a sunk basement, with an advanced centrepiece. At the rear, the basement fully exposed, a bowed centrepiece pierced by a three-light window at each floor, the ground-floor window corniced. For the Eyemouth Community Centre opposite, *see* Public Buildings, above.

COLDINGHAM ROAD sets off W between two opposing churches, the Eyemouth United Congregational Church on the N and Eyemouth Parish Church on the S (*see* Churches, above). Just to the W, on the S side, Eyemouth Primary School, set well back from the road, and Eyemouth High School directly fronting it (*see* Public Buildings, above).

HARBOUR ROAD goes downhill from the foot of Church Street to the harbour (*see* Public Buildings, above). Off the road's S end, beside the Eye Water, is DUNDEE HOUSE of the mid or later C18. Two storeys, rendered, with rusticated quoins and a pantiled roof. E front of seven bays, the ground floor originally aith alternating windows (the r. now a door) and pedimented doors, all with moulded architraves; small corbels under the wall-head cornice. A little to the N, Nos. 31-33 Harbour Road, a three-storey rubble-built warehouse with a two-storey outshot at the E end; it is probably early C19. Otherwise, this end of Harbour Road is a mixed bag of utilitarian and undistinguished buildings of the C19 and C20. On the E side, the mid-C20 former EYEMOUTH FISHMARKET, a long open-sided shelter, the roof carried on concrete pillars. Further N, on the W, the harled SHIP HOTEL. Its S part, presenting a shaped gable with scrolled skewputts to Harbour Road, is early C18, but its windows were altered in the C19. Triple-gabled N part, early C19 in its present form. Beside it, the FISHERMEN'S MISSION, a four-storey pantile-roofed warehouse of the earlier C19. Thinly rendered rubble-built eight-bay front with brick lintels and sills to the windows (one first-floor window originally a hoist opening). N of this, C19 vernacular, not especially picturesque but with several pantiled roofs, and some late C20 pseudo-vernacular. On the E side of the harbour, C20 housing set among trees and, at its N end, Gunsgreen House (*see* below) and the Eyemouth Fishmarket (*see* Public Buildings, above).

EYEMOUTH FORT
off Fort Road

Occupying a coastal promontory *c.* 0.5km. NW of the town centre, this is the best-preserved of the half-dozen or so artillery forts of innovative, bastioned design erected in southern Scotland during Protector Somerset's campaign of 1547-8. Indeed, this is the earliest known example of the *trace italienne* artillery fort in the British Isles. Eyemouth was the first place to be captured as the invading army marched north, and in accordance with the English government's policy of establishing permanent strongpoints in strategic positions, a site for a

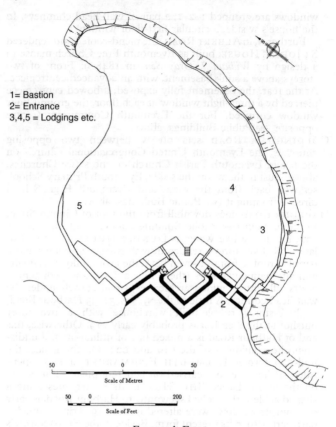

1= Bastion
2= Entrance
3,4,5 = Lodgings etc.

50   0   50
Scale of Metres

50   0   200
Scale of Feet

Eyemouth Fort.
Plan of first phase.

new fort was at once selected. From here a garrison could control traffic on the E coast route and provide early warning of any impending Scottish attack on Berwick. *Sir Richard Lee*, Surveyor of the King's Works, provided the design, and construction was supervised by *William Ridgeway* and his assistant, *Thomas Gower*. Work proceeded rapidly, timber being brought from Coldingham Priory (q.v.) and stone from Dunglass Tower (Lothian). By January 1548, only four months after the commencement of operations, sufficient progress had been made for artillery to be installed, but work continued well into the spring, bringing the total cost up to £1,908 sterling.

As a contemporary drawing shows, the plan comprised a single line of defence drawn across the neck of the promontory. At the centre was a massive bastion having a pointed salient and orillons (ear-like projections) on either side. From the bastion curtain walls ran out to the cliff edge on each side, while in front was a ditch and counterscarp. The sides of the bastion were protected by casemates in the curtain walls, which were themselves flanked by gun emplacements situated behind the orillons. Archaeological excavations undertaken in 1980–8 suggested that the defences were mainly of earth, with stone cladding applied only sparingly, except in the flankers. The internal buildings, shown in the plan of 1549 as single-storeyed, had footings of clay-bonded rubble or, in some cases, of clay alone, but the upper parts of the walls may have been timber-framed.

Eyemouth was surrendered to the Scots and the fort dismantled in 1551, following the Anglo–French treaty concluded at Boulogne a year earlier. Seven years later French forces supporting the Scottish Regent, Mary of Guise, re-garrisoned the fort and reconstituted the defences, adding a second curtain on the landward side, with a huge angular bastion at either end. Artillery was brought from Hume Castle (q.v.), and building materials and provisions were shipped from Leith and other ports in the Forth Estuary. The fort of 1558 had a stone gateway and some, at least, of the internal buildings were of stone and lime. It had an even shorter life than its predecessor, being partially dismantled by the English in 1559 and finally demolished after the Treaty of Edinburgh the following year.

Both lines of defence are readily identifiable today, their most prominent feature being the large central bastion of 1547–8, which retains fragments of masonry cladding evidently dating from the French refurbishment of 1558. The rampart and ditch of 1558 stand a little to the w, where the promontory widens. These have been much reduced by slighting, while the outer extremities of the bastions have been entirely lost through erosion. The excavations of 1980–8 revealed that the base of the N bastion had been clad with masonry, suggesting that the original intention of the builders may have been to face the lower parts of bastions and curtain with stone, leaving the upperworks in turf and clay. Some sections of the internal perimeter are enclosed by a rampart of uncertain date, but there are now no surface traces of the internal buildings of either fort.

GUNSGREEN HOUSE[*]
off The Avenue

An exemplary large villa, Palladian in character, tucked into the steep E bank overlooking the harbour. Built *c.* 1753, most likely designed by *John* and *James Adam* for John Nisbet, an Eyemouth merchant. The attribution is based on a plan and elevation in an architectural notebook associated with James Adam,[†] and the design is almost identical to that illustrated in Isaac Ware's *A Complete Body of Architecture* (1756), for a town house for the fourth Earl of Chesterfield, 1748–9. It sits atop a podium, with a forecourt fronted by an imposing rubble-built later C18 bastion. The house is of three storeys and five bays 109

---

[*]Thanks are due to Professor Alistair Rowan, who carried out a historical assessment of the house in 1998.
[†]In the Clerk of Penicuik collection.

over a basement exposed on the W side, beneath a piend roof
with central platform; the chimney flues in two massive,
square, central stacks. Cream harl with red sandstone for the
V-jointed rustication of the ground floor, window aprons,
band courses and margins. First- and second-floor windows
framed by stone architraves. Those on the first floor have
entablatures, the centre one with a triangular pediment on
console brackets, and balustered aprons; the second-floor
windows are square. The round-arched entrance doorway, with
a dummy fanlight, is approached by stone balustraded steps
bridging the area, attractively splayed at the ends, and joined
to cast-iron area railings, of lattice pattern, perhaps contemporary with the bastion. The other elevations have no significant architectural features, and the symmetrical pattern of
windows on the E side is a restoration of the 1970s.

Much of the simple well-detailed INTERIOR survives, if
obscured, and the plan is clearly discernible. Tripartite, with a
wide central passage, an outer hall at the front, an inner hall
and stair to the rear. The basement floor had a kitchen and
bread oven (surviving), servants' accommodation and stores.
On the ground floor a dining room to the r., with a bedroom
behind, formerly with box beds. To the l. a bedroom with a
dressing room off, and two small rooms, entered from a small
vestibule from the inner hall. A drawing room or salon on the
first floor over the dining room and outer hall, to the rear possibly another small drawing room. A bedroom at the N end
with a dressing room with corner chimneypiece and closet also
entered from a vestibule from the stair landing. The top floor
is dedicated to bedrooms, two with dressing rooms or closets.
The spacious stair rises from the basement to the bedroom
floor; timber treads from the ground floor, stone to the basement, and a Cuban mahogany banister (overpainted) over
barley-sugar balusters. The plastered staircase walls seem to
have been lined out to resemble ashlar, and then painted. The
outer hall cornice has modillions and rosettes, the back hall a
reeded moulding bound with diagonal ribbons, and the main
landing a deep cavetto moulding decorated with shells. The
wainscotted dining room has the best of the original work. The
chimneypiece is flanked by Ionic pilasters, fluted and reeded,
and an entablature, part of which continues round the room
as a cornice. A lugged doorway to the hall, and a jib door (of
unknown date) in the SE corner leading to the room behind.
On the first floor the small drawing room has a lugged, panelled overmantel and a well-proportioned chimneypiece with
a dentilled cornice. The drawing room probably had similar
decoration, mostly now gone. All the ceilings on the bedroom
floor have been covered over, but a small room on the N side
has a deep, moulded late C18 cornice.

A side door in the N elevation gave access to an outside stair,
now removed, which led to a long vaulted cellar set across
the front of the building (not shown on the Adam plan). This
feature is not uncommon in merchants' houses in the Borders,
when built on steeply sloping sites. The cellar now extends in
a dog-leg passage that opens through an archway to the
harbour, with a second large barrel-vaulted chamber parallel

to the bastion. The D-shaped bastion, rubble-built with a battlemented wall-head, has eight pyramidal stone buttresses
alternating with blind oculi.

GATEPIERS and GATE, formerly three rusticated piers with
block cornice and square pyramidal caps. A pedestrian gate at
the w side. The gate and w pier survive, and most of the e pier.
– NISBET TOWER is a square building, battlemented on three
sides. Rubble-built and formerly harled, it has stone cannon
barrels projecting at the upper level. Blind crosslets on E and
N sides. It was probably part of a coachhouse and stables.

GUNSGREENHILL, 0.5 km. SE. Rendered farmhouse of the
earlier C19. To its S, the surviving base of a rubble-built circular and tapering WINDMILL tower of c. 1800.

LINTHILL. *See* p. 501.

NETHERBYRES HOUSE *See* p. 583.

FAIRNILEE HOUSE   4030
4.8 km. SE of Caddonfoot

By *John J. Burnet*, 1904 for A.F. Roberts, a mill owner. Considered by Professor David Walker as Burnet's most fully realised
domestic project, forming an integral concept of house, formal
garden, gardener's lodge, stables and cottages.

The elements of the house are picturesquely grouped in Scottish
Renaissance mode, with a display of Baroque exuberance in
the carved details. Built of whinstone, the harling contrasting
with red sandstone dressings; roofs covered with grey-green
Westmorland slates. Scottish features of crowstepped gables,
circular corbelled-out conical-capped corner towers, canted
bays and wall-head dormers with differently shaped pediments. An entrance forecourt is finished at the E end with a
C17-style ogee-roofed pavilion linked to the house by a screen
wall; a similar pavilion terminates the wall of the office court.
The Baroque Roman Doric aediculed entrance doorway,
flanked by obelisks topped by lions, is linked by curved stone
balustrades with widely spaced balusters to corner plinths with
cast-iron lights; these replaced the original tall stone obelisks.
On the S front the triple-height canted bay window has
Baroque enrichments, and a deep-set panel inscribed AFR ER.
Unusual features are the moulded margins round the top
sashes of many of the principal windows, which terminate in
carved corbels. Crowstepped L-shaped bay added to the w end
of the N elevation by Lord Craigmyle (†1937).

The house is generously planned inside, not palatial
but spacious for entertaining. The plan is almost square with
the principal rooms arranged along the S and E sides, with the
hall and entrance to the N. Attached axially, NE–SW, are the
ground-floor services, cloakrooms, housekeeper's and butler's
rooms and service stair; the porch and vestibule lead diagonally to a wainscotted staircase hall (its decorative scheme
survives unscathed) and from there to an upper hall with an
arched ceiling. A spindle-balustered screen formerly opened
into an inner hall at ground level. At mezzanine level, off the

staircase, a further screen opened into an ante-room over the vestibule; both openings were later wainscotted over. The inner hall and dining room have beamed geometric ceilings, now covered.

The formal E GARDEN has a long terraced walk leading to contemporary GREENHOUSES, probably by *Mackenzie & Moncur*. There are remains of trellising designed by Burnet along the walk. – SUNDIAL with a decorated baluster-shaped support with a copper dial and gnomon dated 1894. – STABLES, 0.8 km. SE, by *Burnet*. An L-shaped range of stable court to the N, the coachman's house to the S, with a half-timbered jettied-out gable over the entrance doorway, and bay window to the W. Semi-detached COTTAGES (Robin's Nest) were remodelled in 1927 by Lord Craigmyle with dormers and bracketed canopies to the doorways. At the E end of a formal approach along a high terrace is a segmental-arched gateway in a screen wall, with a balustraded parapet, and an attached gardener's house, with a deep parapet. Burnet re-roofed the NW end of the old house to serve as a generator house, and linked the two houses together with a high wall pierced by a magnificent set of cast-iron gates, each topped by an enormous urn decorated with grotesque heads.

OLD FAIRNILEE in the garden is an intriguing fragment of a small Renaissance mansion probably erected by Andrew Ker of Linton *c.* 1600. Described in 1649 as one of the principal houses of Selkirkshire, Fairnilee passed to the Rutherfords in 1700 and was roofless by 1882. It was a long, narrow rectangle (25.1 m. by 7.7 m.) of three storeys and an attic, of which the surviving part, repaired and re-roofed *c.* 1904, represents roughly the N (in fact, NW) third. The central portion of the house is much reduced, while of the S portion only footings remain.

Late C19 drawings show that the principal (W) elevation was near-symmetrical, with an off-centre ground-floor entrance and two tiers of tall, regularly spaced windows above. Conical-roofed turrets were corbelled out at either corner at second-floor level, and crowstepped end gables carried square-cut chimneys with moulded copings; a similar mid gable, containing flues from the central and N portions of the house, stood about one third of the way along its length. The masonry is of local whinstone rubble with copious dressings of red and buff-coloured sandstone. Most openings, both inside and out, are wrought with quirked edge-rolls, but a few have plain rounded arrises; some windows were formerly barred. The surviving study projects on a multiple corbel course beneath two courses of scalloped decoration. Its windows have quatrefoil shot-holes (cf. Ferniehirst Castle, q.v.) below their sills, but these may be purely decorative since they seem not to pierce the walls. On one of the chimney copings is chip-carved ornament identical to that on a chimney at Aikwood Tower (q.v.). An illegible coat-of-arms, said to be that of the Rutherfords of Fairnilee and formerly over the front entrance, has been inserted into the E elevation. There was formerly a wing on this side but it is uncertain whether or not this was an original feature.

As at Old Torwoodlee, Torwoodlee House (q.v.), the plan

seems to have hinged on a scale staircase ascending transversely from the entrance lobby to a first-floor landing placed
against the rear wall. On the ground floor the area to the s of
the staircase was probably occupied by a pair of (vaulted?)
cellars and a corridor, while to the N was a vaulted chamber,
perhaps the kitchen, linked by a corridor along its w side to a
well-lit, unvaulted chamber occupying the N end of the house.
This was evidently a living room, perhaps for a steward or
housekeeper, heated by a large, roll-moulded fireplace.
Between this chamber and the kitchen, and partly intruded
into the rear (E) wall of the house, was a secondary stair, evidently of newel type, which apparently served all floors, with
an external doorway at its foot. The first floor seems to have
comprised a good-sized hall to the s of the scale staircase,
together with an outer and inner chamber on the N, the whole
possibly designed as a reception suite, with the secondary stair
providing separate access to the two N rooms. The arrangement of the second floor seems to have echoed that below, but
with the scale stair possibly giving way to a second newel stair;
the chambers at either end of the house communicated with
the angle turrets. If this interpretation is correct, it demonstrates that the planning arrangements at Fairnilee were fully
as advanced as those in grander houses of the period such as
Cowdenknowes and Ferniehirst Castle (qq.v.).

FAIRNINGTON HOUSE

6020

4.km. SE of Maxton

A laird's house, mostly late C17 but incorporating a 'bastell house'
burnt by the garrison of Wark in 1544.* This was acquired
c. 1647 by the Rutherford family; *c.* 1777 it became the property of Robert, 'Baron' Rutherford, a merchant, his title
granted by the Russians for his activities as agent during the
wars against the Turks. The house is L-plan, of three storeys
and attic with crowstepped gables. The long, rectangular w
block is C17, the E wing is partly C16, but remodelled probably in the late C17; slit windows in the lower part indicate the
earliest work. All the other windows have been enlarged or
inserted. In the re-entrant angle is a Late Renaissance doorway
flanked by pilasters and with a moulded cornice and pediment,
now obscured by a porch of *c.* 1968, when a two-storey semicircular bow was added and the interior much altered. In the
E wing survives a vaulted chamber and a late C18 or early C19
geometric stair from the ground to first floor. Also left intact
is a spacious late C17 Scottish Renaissance scale-and-platt pine
stair from the first floor to the attic, identical in detail to the
stair at Lessudden House (q.v.).

BARON'S FOLLY, 1 km. SE, at the summit of Down Law. Ruins
of a whinstone rubble octagon with Gothic windows. Built in
the 1780s by 'Baron' Rutherford as a summerhouse and observatory.

*RCAHMS.

4030

FALDONSIDE HOUSE
4.3 km. SW of Melrose

The house began as a simple, classical three-bay villa with columned porch, built for Nicol Milne *c.* 1800, but recast and enlarged in the late C19 when wings were added and the S front of the villa refaced in matching ashlar blocks. The two-storey pedimented wings are set forward, the W one with a balustraded canted bay. The wide pilasters, replacing corner quoins, must date from the remodelling. Three large pedimented dormers along the roof, a deep band of corbels at the wall-head. The N elevation is mostly *c.* 1800, with a shallow central curved stair-tower. The interior was remodelled in the late C19, with later work. A new staircase and hall fill the centre of the ground floor. The drawing room to the l. has a compartmented ceiling with decorated ribs and a shell cornice. Behind, a well-equipped, top-lit billiard room with a deep coved ceiling with pendants.

STABLES to the rear are part C18 and mid-C19. – WEST LODGE, *c.* 1800, is single-storey and bow-fronted. By the E entrance a former STEADING with some stabling, *c.* 1830. Whinstone with red sandstone margins. Central pediment over the pend with small dovecot entrance. – WALLED GARDEN. Rubble-built with a keystoned Moon gate in the W wall.

8070

FAST CASTLE
8.5 km. E of Cockburnspath

Renowned for its outstanding scenic qualities, this remarkable late medieval castle is also a monument to the ingenuity of its builders. The site, aptly described by Sir Walter Scott as 'an abrupt and inaccessible precipice overhanging the raging ocean', is not only immensely strong but also strategically important, lying close to the main E coast route into Scotland and the vulnerable crossing of the Pease Burn. Not surprisingly, from the time that the castle first comes on record in the early C15, its military history is largely one of alternate occupation by Scottish and English forces. The structure seems to have assumed its present form during the late C15 and early C16, when in the possession of the Home family. It continued to be recognised as a place of some military importance until the middle of the C17, when it was surrendered to Cromwell following the Battle of Dunbar. Abandoned shortly afterwards, the castle was ruinous by 1703.

The rock promontory upon which the buildings stand is quite small (about 80 m. from NE to SW by 27 m. transversely), and a plan of 1549 shows a tightly packed layout comprising two courtyards at different levels, their outer walls following the line of the cliff edge, which is some 50 m. above sea level at its highest point. The outer courtyard contained a hall and chamber block with adjacent kitchen and brewhouse running at right angles to it, while the inner, and lower, court was flanked on its NW side by a single-storey range. The outer courtyard was approached via a timber bridge spanning the gully that traverses the neck of the promontory. This led to the

outer gatehouse, beyond which a second bridge gave access to
an inner gate situated adjacent to the sw gable of the hall and
chamber block. The nw range of the inner courtyard incorporated a postern giving access to the foreshore, while a derrick
at the e corner allowed goods to be unloaded from a boat
landing below. Provision for artillery defence included a gun
platform on the nw side of the upper courtyard. Little now
survives of either gateway, but the adjacent section of the w
curtain wall incorporates part of a splayed gunloop covering
the approach, and the nw gun platform is identifiable. The
walls of the hall and chamber block are fragmentary, apart
from the e corner which rises to a height of about 5 m., at which
level there was evidently a corbelled wall-walk. As elsewhere
in the castle, the masonry is of local greywacke rubble with
dressings of red and white sandstone probably obtained from
the nearby outcrops at Redheuch and Pease Bay. The first-floor
hall, which occupied the ne portion of the block, appears to
have been vaulted, and above the vault there was probably a
garret entered from the wall-walk. The chamber opened off the
upper (sw) end of the hall. The brewhouse and kitchen are
reduced to turf-grown footings and the nw range of the inner
courtyard is in little better shape, except towards the lower
(ne) end, where a fragment of the outer wall rises to a height
of about 5 m.; this shows traces of what seems to have been a
mural stair leading to a wall-walk. The range evidently comprised a series of chambers and storerooms stepped down the
natural slope of the site. The upper chamber was entered from
the outer courtyard, the next from the stair that descended
from the outer to the inner courtyard, and the remaining three
rooms from the lower courtyard itself.

Archaeological excavations undertaken in 1971–81 focused
on the inner courtyard, much of which was shown to have been
quarried, presumably to provide materials for the construction
of the castle. The castle well was also identified on the landward side of the promontory, some 30 m. sw of the entrance.

FATLIPS CASTLE   3020
2 km. ne of Minto

A spirited re-creation of the c16 tower house of the Turnbulls of
Minto. The unlovely name of Fatlips, although not unique among
the castles of southern Scotland, presumably commemorates the
facial characteristics of one of the Turnbull lairds.

The tower was first built about the third quarter of the c16,
following the destruction of an earlier house of 'Mynto Crag' by
an English army in 1545. The Turnbulls lost Minto in the late
c17, and Grose's view of 1789 shows the tower as a ruin less than
two storeys high. By 1838 only the ground floor remained, but c.
1857 the tower was restored as a belvedere and shooting box for
the second Earl of Minto, by *William Anderson* of Galashiels. Pre-
dictably, the style chosen was Scottish Baronial, but while most
of the detail is archaeologically correct, the overall effect is almost
certainly much richer than in the original tower. In 1897–8 the

interior was refurbished by *Robert S. Lorimer* to accommodate a private museum. The building is now derelict.

The castle is prominently sited on the E summit of Minto Craigs, from which it commands a magnificent panorama of Teviotdale, the Eildon Hills and the distant heights of the Anglo-Scottish border. The rock summit is naturally defensible on all except the NW side, where the approach path winds up from the valley below. A secondary approach from the S, via a roughly constructed stone staircase, was probably created during the C19. The original tower was of simple oblong plan (9.8 m. by 8.2 m.), constructed of whinstone rubble with dressings of buff-coloured sandstone quarried locally. An entrance in the S wall opened into a lobby giving access both to a stair in the SE corner and to a barrel-vaulted cellar, which incorporated an entresol floor reached by a ladder. Above this level the fabric appears to be of *c.* 1857 or later.

The Victorian masonry matches well with the original and all the detail is well cut. The upperworks are quite showy, the main elements being continuous, open parapet-walks and angle turrets projected on individual corbels of three members. The stair, completely renewed *c.* 1857, finishes in a conical-roofed caphouse, and the crowstepped gables of the attic rise unusually high above the wall-walks. The attic is lit by distinctive mullion-and-transomed windows capped by triangular pediments. The first-floor chamber mimics the hall of the original tower, being provided with a good-sized fireplace and a series of embrasured windows equipped with bench seats. The decaying coffered and painted ceiling is probably Lorimer's work; the concrete floor bears the incised date 1897. The second floor and attic were rebuilt as single chambers *c.* 1857, and the attic was again refurbished in 1897, when a fancy roll-moulded chimneypiece of red sandstone was installed and the walls lined with simple oak panelling.

6010   FERNIEHIRST CASTLE
                        2.8 km. s of Jedburgh

The best-preserved of a distinctive group of highly prestigious mansions erected by wealthy Border lairds during the closing decades of the C16. Spaciously planned, elegantly detailed and equipped with only token means of defence, it confidently shrugged off generations of frontier warfare in anticipation of better times ahead.

The castle stands high above the E bank of the Jed Water on lands acquired by the Kerrs in or before the second half of the C15. Earlier houses here were destroyed by English armies in 1523 and 1570, and by James VI – following Sir Andrew Kerr's support for the Earl of Bothwell – in 1593. But this last dismantling seems to have been less than total, for the large, courtyard-plan mansion that Sir Andrew began to build *c.* 1598 probably incorporates part of its predecessor of the mid or late 1570s, while a small portion of it may, in fact, be a little older. Whatever its precise age, this early core evidently comprises the lowest storey of an exception-

ally long main block (32.3 m from E to W, by 8.0 m. transversely)
with an attached angle tower at one, if not both, ends. Sir Andrew
reconstructed the original block above the ground floor and
added stubby rectangular wings to the NW and SW corners. The
NW wing, which may replace an earlier angle tower, contained a
new entrance and principal stair with a stack of chambers above,
while the SW wing incorporated a kitchen with a single chamber
above. It was probably also Sir Andrew (†1631) who extended a
wing N from the NE corner of the main block to form the E side
of a courtyard (since demolished). Provision was also made for
a N extension of the stair wing on the opposite side of the courtyard, but all that was built was a low wall containing an entrance
to what seems to have been a service court lying beyond the W
end of the house. The fourth (N) side of the courtyard was presumably enclosed by a wall overlooking the steep-sided gully that
bounds the site in that area, the entrance being at or near the NE
corner.

The mansion was completed by the erection of a chapel,
coachhouse and stable, flanking what seems to have been the
early approach. The chapel was built by Sir Andrew Kerr, while
the coachhouse and stable seem to have been added during the
later C17. At about the same time the main block of the mansion
was heightened and its fenestration improved, while the S side of
the service court was filled by a range built at right angles to the
earlier kitchen wing. For much of the C18 and C19 the castle was
occupied by estate tenants, and in 1826–8 it was fitted up as a
farmhouse to plans by *John Smith*. During this phase new
entrances were formed on either side of the main block and the
E wing was removed. The building was restored in 1984–7
for the twelfth Marquess of Lothian by *James Simpson* and *Mandy
Ketchen* of *Simpson & Brown*.

EXTERIOR. The castle is constructed of random rubble masonry
with dressings of buff-coloured sandstone of local origin. The
main block and SE angle tower incorporate three full storeys,
while the NW wing rises two storeys higher, the top floor being
an attic; all the gables are crowstepped. At first sight the
masonry of the N front looks homogeneous, but on the S side
a change is visible at first-floor level. Also on the S side the
wall-head has evidently been raised *c.* 1.5 m. in height, encasing the lower portions of the chimneys. The first-floor break
probably denotes the level above which the main block was
reconstructed in 1598, while the heightening of the wall-head
marks the conversion of the attic of 1598 into a full storey,
probably towards the end of the C17. The N ELEVATION of the 44
main block and E elevation of the NW wing are designed as a
show-front, with a concentration of ornamental detail around
the principal entrance. The only defensive provision
is a sprinkling of decorative pistol-holes – mostly inverted
keyhole, quatrefoil and circular with *rayonée* surrounds – disposed mainly on the upper floors. The *piano nobile* is articulated by a cavetto-moulded string course at sill level, while
strong vertical accents are provided by a projecting stair-turret
and a massive, stepped chimneystack, as well as by the
continuation of the principal staircase, which rises as a

conical-roofed semicircular turret within the re-entrant angle. The lower parts of the stair-turret and chimneystack are laid against the pre-1598 wall face, obscuring two earlier ground-floor windows. Both projections have bevelled corners up to second-floor level, where the stair-turret breaks forward on faceted corbels to assume a rectangular plan before rising to a crowstepped gablet.

The chimneystack is pierced at base by a doorway, above which is a panel bearing the arms and initials of Robert Kerr, fourth Lord Jedburgh (†1692), one of several, all seemingly of early origin, renewed during a partial restoration of *c.* 1887–98; some of the originals are preserved within the castle. Most of the ground-floor openings in the main block have plain, chamfer-arrised surrounds, while the windows at the upper levels, like those in the 1598 work generally, have round-arrised surrounds. The majority of these windows seem originally to have been half-glazed, with fixed lead frames; many were also barred. The second-floor windows were probably converted from dormers when the wall-head was raised. The big first-floor windows either side of the chimneystack are singled out for special treatment, the E one having spindle-decorated jambs supporting a cable-moulded cornice and its neighbour pilastered jambs with moulded bases and capitals. E of the stair-turret at this level are traces of blocked openings possibly relating to the pre-1598 house. E of these again the abrupt termination of the string course marks the point at which the missing E wing returned N. The communicating door was reopened in 1987 and provided with a porch and forestair.

45   The entrance to the NW WING has an elaborate pilaster-framed surround with claw-foot bases and moulded capitals supporting a cornice enriched with miniature dogtooth ornament. The ogee pediment, which recalls one at Buckholm Tower (q.v.), has pyramidal finials. Above the doorway are three heraldic panels, the central one bearing the arms of the ninth Marquess of Lothian and the date 1898. The flanking panels, replicating earlier ones, commemorate Sir Andrew Kerr and his wife, the dexter (s) one dated 1598. The stair in the re-entrant projects on a corbel course of no fewer than twenty-two members, the uppermost one decorated with a running trefoil pattern. The wing itself sprouts conical-roofed angle-turrets, and its N wall incorporates tusking for the planned extension, now represented only by a screen wall containing a handsome semicircular-headed gateway with rusticated jambs and dogtooth-decorated capitals. The gateway presumably dates from the mid or late 1620s because the (replica) panel above the arch-head bears the arms and initials of Lord Jedburgh, a title conferred upon Sir Andrew Kerr only in 1622.

On the S ELEVATION the ground floor shows two inserted windows. Above this level the masonry is mainly of 1598, but the big roll-and-hollow moulded windows that light the *piano nobile* appear to be late C17 replacements, again altered during the late C19 restoration, when their sills were lowered. The small octagonal window at the same level, also of late C19 date, probably marks the position of a doorway inserted in 1826–8 to give access to this side of the then farmhouse by way of a forestair. The lower part of the SE ANGLE TOWER probably dates from the 1570s or a little earlier; it incorporates two dumb-bell shaped gunloops similar to one of *c*. 1570–85 at Bonshaw Tower (Dumfries and Galloway). At the upper levels, which are mainly of 1598, there are pistol-holes of inverted keyhole and circular shape. A dial-head of late C17 or early C18 date is mounted at first-floor level; beneath, a carving of a sun in splendour for Kerr. The KITCHEN WING (SW) and attached W service range were reconstructed in 1984–7 to form a private residential wing, the existing walls and openings being retained wherever possible and the new masonry matched with the old. The entire wing is covered by a reed-thatched roof, possibly replacing one of locally quarried slabs of red sandstone.

INTERIOR. The GROUND FLOOR of the main block contains six barrel-vaulted cellars. Each except the one at either end has its own external doorway in the N wall, which suggests that the house of the 1570s, like its successor, faced onto a courtyard on the N side. The E cellar has thicker walls than its neighbours and is vaulted in the opposite direction, which may indicate that it and the ground-floor chamber of the adjacent SE angle tower antedate the reconstruction of the 1570s. The kitchen in the SW wing now serves as the entrance hall of the private wing, but retains its big semicircular-headed fireplace in the S wall. The principal entrance in the NW wing opens into a spacious well staircase of stone rising to the first floor. Beneath is a small vaulted chamber, perhaps a strong-room. The staircase was refurbished in 1887–98, the panelled stairwell and lofty gallery evidently having been installed at that time.

As completed *c*. 1598 the FIRST FLOOR or *piano nobile* contained an impressive sequence of reception rooms probably comprising antechamber, hall, outer chamber (or great chamber), inner chamber and closet. These elements are clearly identifiable today, although the removal of the partition between hall and outer chamber, probably during the late C19 restoration, makes the present hall even larger than the original one (*c*. 12.8m. by 5.8m.). From what little remains of their original fittings it is clear that these chambers were richly decorated in the most fashionable style. The ANTE-CHAMBER was formerly a little longer than it is today and communicated with the adjacent chamber and the kitchen staircase via doors in the S wall. Another door in the NW corner opens into a mural stair leading to the cellar below. The painted frieze (*David Wilkinson*, 1987) depicts scenes of Borders history; below are mock corbels showing portraits of the principal craftsmen employed in 1984–7. The chief feature of the HALL is a large joggle-lintelled chimneypiece in the N wall decorated with qua-trefoil paterae, triquetra and fleurs-de-lys; the detail is very similar to that of a chimneypiece of 1597 at Roslin Castle, Lothian. Close to what was formerly the NE corner of the hall a door opens into an extruded stair rising to the second floor. Beyond the stair lies what was originally a separate OUTER CHAMBER; the heavily restored chimneypiece presumably replaces the late C17 one illustrated *c*. 1887 by MacGibbon and Ross, of which there is now no trace. An unusual feature of

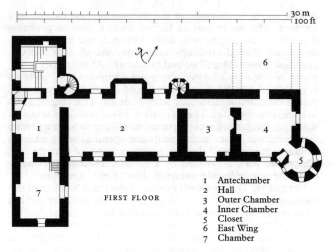

Ferniehirst Castle.
Plan as built, *c.* 1598.

this chamber, as also of the hall and antechamber, is the continuous, scallop-decorated corbel course that supports the
ceiling joists. The INNER CHAMBER, or bedchamber, was converted into a kitchen in 1984–7. The circular closet (now
library) in the SE angle tower is much restored, but drawings
made by MacGibbon and Ross show that the present timber
fittings, which include ornate, bracketed shelves for the display
of books and curiosities, are faithful copies of the originals. The
ribbed and panelled ceiling radiates from a boldly carved
pendant, and a number of the panels contain turned knops,
some evidently original. Off the entry to the closet is a latrine
recess, the only one to survive at this level.

The SECOND FLOOR of the main block was remodelled
some time during the C18 or C19 to form six individual chambers opening off a corridor to the N, with another chamber in
the SE angle tower. The original layout may have been similar
to that below, comprising a secondary, but less extensive suite
for the laird and his family. An account for plasterwork dated
1663 suggests that there may also have been a gallery at this
level, as at the third floor of Traquair House (q.v.). When the
wall-head was raised in the late C17 some of the chambers were
provided with new chimneypieces wrought with roll-and-
hollow mouldings similar to those of the first-floor windows
on the s side.

The NW WING originally contained three floors above the
stair landing, each occupied by an individual chamber opening
off the newel stair in the re-entrant angle. All three chambers
were provided with a latrine, and each probably also contained
a fireplace although only that at third-floor level, a plain, lintelled opening with round-arrised jambs, survives. The second-

floor chamber was replaced by the stair gallery in 1887–98, when the other two chambers were refurbished. The uppermost one is close-boarded and has a mock timber vault; from this chamber access is obtained to the adjacent angle turrets.

The CHAPEL *c.* 25 m. NE of the principal courtyard (refurbished as an information centre and offices in 1984–7), is a particularly stylish member of a small group of private chapels associated with post-Reformation lairds' houses. They are usually described as mortuary chapels, but there is nothing to indicate that the one at Ferniehirst was used for burials. The building is oblong on plan and the steeply pitched gables are crow-stepped. The principal (SE) elevation is highly ornate, the arched entrance at the centre having an elaborately rusticated surround of ovoid projections and imposts decorated with dogtooth ornament; or are these Kerr mullets? Above are the arms and initials – some apparently cast in lead – of Sir Andrew Kerr and his wife before his elevation to the peerage in 1622. Either side of the entrance is a mullion-and-transomed window with a rusticated surround, while the S and E corners of the building have buckle-quoins. The NE part of the interior originally contained a laird's loft approached by a forestair rising against the adjacent gable. The pulpit may have stood against the N wall, while a secondary doorway in the SW gable provided additional congregational access.

Of the COACH HOUSE and STABLE, repaired in 1712, only the SW gable and part of one of the side walls remain. The coach house is said to have occupied the NE portion of the building and the stable the remainder, but to judge from the big first-floor window in the surviving gable the accommodation at this level was residential.

FLEMINGTON TOWER   1040
3 km. S of Romanno Bridge

A superannuated tower house doing duty as a farm store. Apparently erected in the late C16 by a member of the Hay family, the tower seems to have been superseded in 1712 by a new residence (date panel on farmhouse), which in turn gave way to the present farmhouse in the mid C19. Now incorporated within a range of offices, the tower is almost square on plan (7.7 m. by 6.5 m.) and comprises two main storeys of the originally three or four. Local rubble masonry with dressings of red and buff-coloured sandstone from the West Linton area. The ground-floor chamber appears to have been barrel-vaulted, and the original entrance doorway, now blocked, survives in the W wall, together with a slit-window, which seems to have lit a timber bench running along the inner face of the wall. A spiral stair in the SW corner rises to the first-floor chamber, evidently the hall, which has been lit from two sides and heated by means of a large fireplace (subsequently contracted) with round-arrised jambs and lintel; three mural aumbries provided space for the storage of valuables.

7030

FLOORS CASTLE
1.6 km. W of Kelso

The dramatic and romantic silhouette of Floors Castle, sited on a natural gravel terrace overlooking the River Tweed to the S, has magnificent open views as far as the peaks of the Cheviot Hills. The Kers of Cessford, an ancient Border family, acquired Floors after the Reformation when the lands of Kelso Abbey were dispersed. In the early C18 an existing tower house was transformed into a plain Georgian house, in warm cream sandstone, flanked by pavilions, which Groome* described as 'severely plain, not to say heavy looking . . . transformed by Playfair of Edinburgh into a sumptuous Tudor pile – one of the most palatial residences of the Scottish Nobility'.

The first builder of the present castle was John Ker, first Duke of Roxburghe, who in 1711–12 offered it to his mother. The Duke also owned Broxmouth Park (Lothian), and Fryers, SE of Floors, which occupied part of the former Greyfriars convent, and which was to 'be taken down and the materials used in the additions at Floors'. Alterations at Floors were begun by *Alexander McGill*, mason, and the great stair and drawing room were finished by 1717. Building of the Duke's 'palace' in London delayed the start in 1718, however, of a 74 ft (22.54 m.) extension to the E end of Floors. In May 1721 the 'ground stone' was laid of the new building, now to designs by *William Adam*, who may have been introduced to Roxburghe by Sir William Bennet of Marlefield (q.v.).

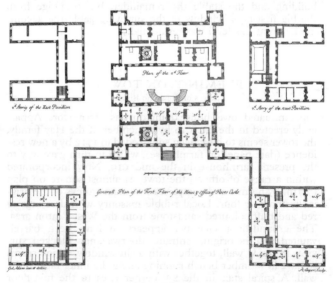

Floors Castle.
Floor plans, *c.* 1721.

---

* Francis H. Groome (ed.), *Ordnance Gazetteer of Scotland*, iii (1883), p. 32.

A plaintive letter★ from Gilbert Ramsay, the Duke's factotum at Floors, to the Duke's mother, written from Floors in April 1721, implies that by this date Roxburghe had gone cold on 'imploying Mr Adams any furdor (sic)'. But as he had more skill in 'getting all the stone in Broxlaw Quarrie than any other', Ramsay pleaded – successfully it seems – that the Countess should tell her son that 'Sir Wm. Bennett as I am sure he will, runs much out in his praise of Mr Adams'. *Adam*'s design for Floors, shown in his *Vitruvius Scoticus*, consisted of a main block of three storeys and basement, of eleven bays on the N front, and eight on the S, with a taller single-bay tower projecting from each corner. On the S front is shown a small stair-turret in the re-entrant angle at each end of the main block. The house fronted a forecourt on the N side, flanked by two-storey, U-plan pavilions, linked to the house by right-angled three-bay quadrants. The windows had lugged architraves. The N front appears to have been based on the S front of Wilton House, Wiltshire, with the top stage of the towers given pedimented windows under a pedimented wall-head. The internal planning had to cope with existing work, the earliest seemingly in the SW tower, and with later alterations by the Duke (not indicated on the published plan). The state apartments are shown enfiladed along the S front, with a library or billiard room in the centre of the first floor. In 1743–7 the second Duke wished to remove a storey from the main block but to retain the turrets. This was considered by experts to be unwise and nothing was done, except repair. Schemes for a classical house, and a castellated envelope, were supplied by *Robert Adam* in the mid 1770s, but again unrealised. However, the house is shown as castellated in a painting of 1809 by William Wilson with oval oculi to the tops of the towers.

p. 58

The present fairytale EXTERIOR is wholly the creation of *W.H. Playfair*, who remodelled the castle in 1837–47 for the sixth Duke by heightening Adam's building while respecting his plan. The model was manifestly the Scottish Renaissance of George Heriot's Hospital, Edinburgh (William Wallace, 1628), which Playfair was restoring from 1829. It shares deep-moulded corbelling to wall-heads, embattled parapets, fluted chimneystacks, some set on gablets, and decorative water-spouts, but with ogee-roofed, square bartizans in place of the round ones at Heriot's, creating a marvellously inventive skyline best described by Marcus Binney as 'double-stepped battlements, sprouting chimneys – in ones, twos and threes – countless square corner turrets with ogee roofs, pedimented brackets in the cornices, and above all rows and rows of gargoyles in the form of cannons of every shape, twisted, fluted, spiralled, knotched and panelled'.[†]

69

To the existing S front Playfair added a central loggia carrying a perron, and Jacobean balustrading to shield the basement. At the E end he extended the façade with a large ballroom, added a bay window to the existing dining room on the W front, and a square bay window each end of the *piano*

★ In the Roxburghe Archives.
† *Country Life* (11/18 May 1978).

nobile on the N side. Adam's right-angled links to the pavilions were also remodelled, giving each a curve and a noble entrance, the E one to the laboratory and billiard room, the W one for the family. He added further courts behind the pavilions, screened from the S by curved crenellated walls. Window margins were changed, hoodmoulds added and some of the facework renewed.

INTERIOR. Much of Playfair's work in refitting Adam's public rooms in the 1840s was swept away in a sumptuous refurbishment of 1927–30 by May Goelet, a New York heiress and wife of the eighth Duke. A bill from the London decorators *Lenygon & Morant*, who specialised in period rooms, describes how they adapted Floors and her London house at Carlton House Terrace to provide an appropriate setting for May's collection of tapestries, furnishings and other works of art brought from America in 1929.

The castle is entered through a PORTE COCHÈRE – note the lion-mask door handles, which Playfair considered 'worthy of the Vatican' – leading to a vestibule and steps up to the ENTRANCE HALL. This retains Playfair's decoration, with a panelled dado and a fretwork ceiling by *Pirie*, a local plasterer. The C17 Revival black marble chimneypiece was made by *David Ness* to Playfair's design. The W end of the house is also Playfair's work, beginning with the principal STAIRCASE. A well stair, with traditional twisted balusters, a panelled ceiling to the cupola, and panelled soffits to stair and landings. Beyond the staircase is the LIBRARY with bookshelves to door height, and a delicately moulded geometric ceiling.

At the W end of the S front Playfair's remodelled DINING ROOM has his large bay window giving extensive views to the W. Bracketed cornice and richly ornamented geometric ceiling, with Ionic-jambed timber chimneypieces and panelled shutters. The furnishings are original to Playfair's room. Further E, in the centre of the S front, is a small ANTE-ROOM with thick walls, possibly within the oldest part of the castle remodelled by *William Adam*, with a high coved ceiling; the fretwork plaster decoration is Playfair's. Then a procession of rooms refitted in the late 1920s in a variety of period styles, beginning with the SITTING ROOM, formerly the drawing room of the C18 state apartment. Convincing Early Georgian-style decoration with panelled walls, originally stripped pine but now painted, and a large recess designed to hold a tapestry. The chimneypiece with Kent-style overmantel was copied from one in Lenygon's London showroom. The DRAWING ROOM was re-fitted to display a set of late C17 Brussels tapestries depicting the 'Triumph of the Gods'. The rather startling Louis XV-style purple marble chimneypiece was no doubt provided to match the French furniture in this room; it replaced one in white marble designed by Playfair with angels carved by *A. Handyside Ritchie* (now owned by the National Museums of Scotland). A geometric ceiling by Playfair has been covered over, but the late C18 window shutters retained. Adjoining is the Louis XVI-style NEEDLE ROOM, formerly the C18 state bedchamber closet, which became an extension to the drawing room in the 1840s. It retains William Adam's coved ceiling, with pretty diamond-coffered decoration added by Playfair.

Through a lobby is the BALLROOM in the E wing, intended by Playfair in 1842 to be a 'New Drawing Room'. Duchess May covered Playfair's ceiling, and the walls were given oak panelling with Grinling Gibbons-type carving by a local craftsman; the E bay window was blocked off to take smaller tapestries. A short corridor leads to a former state bedroom, on the N front, now a BILLIARD ROOM. Remodelled by Playfair, who added the bay window and geometric ceiling. Another corridor to the BIRD ROOM in the NE tower, a rare example of a C19 museum of stuffed birds housed in decorative Gothick mahogany cases. Miraculously, one of William Adam's original marble moulded chimneypieces survives.

A corridor leads to a former spacious passage, now the GALLERY, with stairs to the basement, and access to Playfair's BILLIARD ROOM, first fitted up in 1842 as a temporary dining room; a shallow, ribbed coved ceiling, top-lit by a large cupola. The gallery continues into a room which was designed as the scientist sixth Duke's LABORATORY, fitted up in 1835–6. It was double-height, originally accessible only from the basement, later remodelled to two floors. Both this room and the Gallery have Playfair's picturesque casement windows.

N of the castle are mini Palladian-style KENNELS of 1833. Four-bay centre linked by low walls, formerly railed, to small pedimented wings, with round-arched windows. The N elevation has a three-bay centre, with kennel entrances; the outer wings each have an oculus over the doors. KEEPER'S HOUSE, originally single-storey, with piend-roofed wings, raised in the later C19. Hoodmoulds and gabled dormers. On the opposite side of the road are DAIRY COTTAGES by *W.C. Carnegie*, architect to the Duke of Roxburghe. A two-storey centre in Floors' crenellated style, with tripartite windows, and a hoodmoulded panel above the upper window dated 1875. Flanked by a single-storey house to the r. with overhanging eaves and a timber gabled porch in the re-entrant between the two. A single-storey wing to l. Further E, the HOME FARM, of 1848. E-plan with a symmetrical façade to the road, a remodelling by Carnegie, 1874. High central block flanked by open courts. Ball-finialled gatepiers. Single-storey buildings round the courts, some of which may be *c.* 1848, with finialled gables. Of interest is the sham outside elevation of the W court. Five bays with a deep, moulded cornice and blocking course. In the middle is a finialled gable above a round-arched window. To the S is the STEWARD'S HOUSE. Palladian-style, with three-bay centre linked to two-storey piend-roofed pavilions. Rendered with cream sandstone margins and strip quoins.

WALLED GARDEN, NW of the castle. Brick and stone, 1857, the work supervised by *Mr Rose*. Glasshouses built by *R. & A. Stirling* of Galashiels have gone; one survives in the family's private garden. The GARDENER'S HOUSE is an excellent example of Floors estate building. Two-storey tower with a crenellated parapet. A three-bay S elevation, the centre section advanced, with a corniced doorway, flanked by bipartite windows with decorative hoodmoulds over. A range of bothies, stores etc., were part converted to a tearoom and visitor facilities, *c.* 1978. Most of the lying-pane windows have been preserved. The QUEEN'S HOUSE at the E end is said to have been built in the

mid 1860s for Queen Victoria to view a magnificent range of
hothouses (demolished), known as the 'Tropical Corridor'.
Gabled tripartite window in the E elevation, with narrow sidelights, and a lugged moulded architrave, a segmental pediment
above, and a cartouche in the tympanum. An advanced gabled
entrance on the S side, with a moulded architraved doorway.
Wide depressed arch in the W elevation with glazed door and
panels. A raggle in the wall above indicates the height of the
hothouses. – ICEHOUSE. In woods, W of the kennels. Domed.

EAST LODGES and GATES by *Reginald Fairlie*, 1928, who screened
the C19 avenue from Kelso with a pair of tall square corniced
gatepiers topped by urns supporting an overthrow with a
splendid array of heraldic ironwork; linked by wrought-iron
screens to two-storey lodges in snecked rock-faced rubble, with
bellcast pavilion roofs, and square central stacks. – NORTH
LODGE by *James Hogg*, Superintendent of Works, *c.* 1843. An
elevated two-storey tower with a crenellated parapet in coursed
stugged sandstone. Square porch. Octagonal chimneys. Unfortunate flat-roofed C20 addition. – Picturesque WEST LODGE
with a gabled and finialled porch. By *Playfair* (*James Balmer*,
contractor), *c.* 1840. Steeply pitched roof, and high shouldered
stacks with pairs of octagonal chimneys. Splendid, tall, panelled gatepiers with obelisk finials, and cast-iron gates supplied
by the *Shotts Iron Co*.

FOLLY, *c.* 2.4 km. SW of Kelso on the A699, set on a ridge overlooking the River Tweed. The wall of a sham fort, crenellated
with round corner turrets, reputedly late C18, but most likely
built in 1867 as a stopping point for Queen Victoria to view
the fairytale turrets of the Castle.

LANDSCAPE. Development of the formal landscape began in the
later C17. In 1697 William Jamieson, the fifth Earl of Roxburghe's chamberlain, visited the gardens of James Johnston,
Secretary of State, at Orleans House, Twickenham, for trees
and seeds. John Scougall, the gardener at Chiswick House, also
provided fruit trees – 'all shipped to Scotland'. As late as 1737
fruit trees were still being supplied by Lord Burlington's gardener, Mr Scott. The gardens are shown on William Wyeth's
estate plan of 1736, with the castle set in a very large formal
landscape. During the C18 the banks of the Tweed were
straightened and the islands at Fair Cross Anna were absorbed
into the park. In the later C18 the landscape began to be softened with curving drives and paths, and the sixth Duke undertook a large amount of planting. Today the structure for this
formal landscape has disappeared, but the earlier C18 plantations can still be recognised, with some good C18 specimen oak
trees. A high wall encircles the N and E sides of the park and
fields, and dates mostly from the mid C19.

7040   **FOGO**

A small village of never more than about ten houses, depleted
from the C18 when the leasing of land encouraged large farms
and the removal of the labourers and tradesmen to the towns.

PARISH CHURCH. Largely untouched by either the Ecclesiological revival or by modern trends in worship, Fogo is a splendid illustration of traditional Presbyterian layout and furnishing. A church here was granted to Kelso Abbey around the mid C12, and the rectangular medieval plan governed later development. There was major rebuilding of the upper walls in 1683, when the vaulted burial aisle at the E end (a vestry since 1927) was added; the S 'aisle', which results in a T-plan, is probably of the same vintage. The *c.* 1683 masonry is identifiable in the use of horizontally tooled rubble. Further rebuilding in 1755 provided some new windows. Since a reordering of 1817 little has changed internally apart from the installation of a small organ, but there were further external modifications in 1853.

The two main doorways are on each side of the S aisle, the E one having a block-rusticated surround below an oval window; they have porches, probably of 1853, with raised margins. A doorway into the E burial vault, of similar design to the SE doorway, was blocked when the vault became the vestry, with a new doorway from the church. Another doorway on the S side of the S aisle is also blocked. Lofts at the E and W ends of the church are approached by external forestairs, one against the W wall (leading to a porch) and the other at the E end of the S wall. Most windows along the S flank are round-headed with raised margins, presumably of 1755; the only element breaking the cornice is a dormer lighting the W loft. The N windows are rectangular, and probably of 1853. Rising above the W gable is a square domed bellcote of 1755.

Internally the three arms focus on the pulpit at the centre 22
of the N wall. The Trotter of Charterhall loft at the W end has arms in relief and the date 1671, though the loft largely dates from 1854. The Hog of Harcarse loft at the E end has painted arms and the date 1677, but the loft is later in its present form. There are box pews closest to the pulpit, and open pews further back. – PULPIT, hexagonal with raised and fielded panels; ogee-domed tester carried by backboard with Tuscan pilasters. – BOX PEWS with raised and fielded panels. – W LOFT carried on Tuscan cast-iron piers, with sunk panelled front. – E LOFT carried on a cast-iron column, the front having flush panelling with beaded edges. – WALL MEMORIAL, the Rev. William Home, †1756, erected 1773, swan-neck pedimented frame, to E of pulpit. – Within the burial vault is the lower part of a C13 foliate cross GRAVE-SLAB with lavish stiff-leaf decoration; C18 carving of skull and crossed bones. In the blocked S doorway of the S 'aisle', C17(?) PANEL with three figures and inscribed 'We Three Served God, Lived in His Fear, And Loved Him who bought us Dear'.

The CHURCHYARD has a good group of C18 and C19 gravestones. A series of memorials to ministers and their families runs along the S wall; of note is that of Rev. George Moodie, †1721, fluted Corinthian pilasters and *memento mori*. – LYCHGATE. Memorial to dead of the First World War, *c.* 1920.

FOGO BRIDGE, 0.8 km. NW, over the Blackadder Water. First built in 1641 for Sir James Cockburn of Ryslaw in memory of his parents. Rebuilt 1843, and 1913, at which time it was widened. Single segmental arch of dressed stone with rubble spandrels and a dentilled cornice on the N side.

SCHOOL. Dated 1864, by *David Duns*. Neo-Tudor.

FOGO HOUSE (former Manse) is of 1843 by *James Cunningham*. Two storeys and a piend roof (at the suggestion of the minister) with large chimneystacks. Later additions. Contiguous with the E gable is a contemporary quarter-acre garden with 7 ft (2.13 m.) high walls.

DESCRIPTION: GAMEKEEPER'S COTTAGE, at the E end of the village. 1860, single-storey with a large drip-mould over the doorway, the roof disfigured by a long flat dormer. STUDIO COTTAGE, at the W end of the village, is the late C18 schoolroom and master's house. Single-storey, originally thatched (slated in 1884), with brick chimneys, and two long windows in the W gable, with lying-panes.

CHARTERHALL AIRFIELD, 3 km. SW. Occupied by the R.A.F. during both world wars. Three steel-framed aircraft hangars and brick-built accommodation huts. Now a grain store.

CHARTERHALL HOUSE. *See* p. 163.

9050

FOULDEN

A small Berwickshire village, with church, teind barn and some picturesque cottages.

FOULDEN & MORDINGTON PARISH CHURCH. There was a church here from at least the late C13, and its plan may be perpetuated in the existing rectangular building, though much of the red sandstone rubble fabric dates from a remodelling of 1786. At that time gableted buttresses were added on each flank and Y-traceried windows inserted. The E gable, with an echelon arrangement of three stepped triplets of crenellations and small quatrefoil openings flanking the main windows, was presumably intended to act as an eyecatcher in the view from Foulden House (dem. 1957). More 'correct' detailing was later introduced when a two-light window was cut through the W wall and a bellcote constructed at its gable. A vestry and porch were formed at the W end of the S wall in 1934, possibly incorporating earlier masonry. A doorway at the E end of the S wall opens into the laird's pew. Inside, the communion table is to the W and the pulpit to the NW; the timber-arcaded laird's pew is at the E end. The N and W walls have been stripped of their plaster and the masonry ribbon pointed. The ribbed plaster ceiling is of four-centred profile with tie bars. – FONT. Medieval, brought from Nunlands House *c.* 1871.

CHURCHYARD. C16–C19 memorials. S of the E end of the church, slab with restored inscription to George Ramsay of Foulden Bastle, †1592. Several gravestones show the deceased in prayer: John Sanderson, †1737; Helen Cleghorn, †1751; a member of the Rulle family, †1749, holds a skull to his face.

MANSE (Church House). 1774–6 by *Archibald & Peter Swinie*, masons. Two storeys with an attic, in harl-pointed sandstone rubble. Three-bay S front with a single bay added in 1813. Moulded window pediments, which sit on the parapet, were added in 1841, when the asymmetrical M-gabled N block was built. Gabled porch recessed to the r., sporting a scroll-bracketed stone canopy, a dated wall-head pediment and gables with sawtooth copes and sandstone skews. A curved stone stair with Edinburgh-type balusters is probably of 1841. Alterations and additions by *Hardy & Wight*, 1897.

TEIND (TITHE) BARN, NE of the church. A little building with a more complex architectural history than at first appears. A simple E–W oblong of two storeys and a garret. Local, random rubble masonry with dressings of pink and buff sandstone and a gabled and crowstepped roof, the crowsteps and moulded skewputts evidently being C20.* It appears to have begun as a C17 extension to an existing tower or bastle. To this building belonged the two mural aumbries visible in the barn's E wall, the lower portion of which also embodies a fragment of a barrel vault. Little else survives of this house, which appears to have been rebuilt in the late C17 or early C18 on the evidence of a number of blocked doorways and windows in the surviving wall. The S wall of the barn contains three ground-floor doorways, the W one wrought with an edge-roll moulding of C17 date. Above are two small windows, or ventilators, with others beneath the eaves. The upper floor appears to have been rebuilt in the late C18, and it is likely that the adjacent house was demolished at about this time and the ground floor of the barn converted to domestic use, with a chimney inserted at the E end. Also characteristic of this date is the round-headed window with a dressed and rusticated surround in the W gable. Below this is a first-floor doorway, apparently of C19 date, approached from a stone forestair. In the later part of the C19 the barn served as the granary for the Foulden estate. Inside, the ground-floor dwelling comprised two main rooms, the E one perhaps a kitchen, heated by a big, timber-lintelled fireplace built against the earlier gable-wall. Access to the loft was obtained by means of an internal timber stair. Some of the loft floor joists are supported on stone corbels and others rest in sockets. The roof is largely modern. The building was taken into state care in 1947.

WAR MEMORIAL. A cross with coped octagonal shafts and an embossed sword, *c.* 1920. Pedestal inscribed 'Ye are Bought with a Price'.

DESCRIPTION. The village has a long terrace of late C18 and early C19 estate houses, magnificently sited with a panoramic view of the Cheviot Hills. Single-storey, mostly in sandstone rubble with a surviving cobbled walkway in front. Improved 1850–2 by John Wilkie of Foulden House (dem.), probably with *John Lessels* as architect. Wilkie saw his work on the cottages as 'Flemish' inspired, but the *Ordnance Survey Name Book*'s assessment that 'the houses are ... in imitation of English Cottages' is more convincing, e.g. jettied-out brick bay windows, brick dormers, corbelled brick eaves courses, some with dogtoothed ornament, and mutuled string courses. THISTLE COTTAGE, at the W end of the terrace, was a single-storey smithy but raised and classicised in 1898 by James Bruce

* A corbelled chimney also of this date, which crowns the E gable, is in store.

Wilkie. To the E is an asymmetrical picturesque Gothic range: the former school by *John Lessels*, now housing. In the centre is the former SCHOOLROOM (Drumoyne), dated 1865, with a gabled bay and five-light pointed-arched window; terracotta hoodmould and carved riband. The roof ridge was originally crowned by a spire. THE OLD SCHOOLHOUSE, on the r., may be earlier. It has a row of four small round-arched windows behind a fine projecting three-bay lean-to porch with Corinthian barley-twist columns. BANKHILL to the l. was added in the same style in 1915. To the E is another terrace of two-storey cottages, with dogtoothed corbelled eaves and wall-head windows under broken segmental pediments, with decorative heart and crescent motifs, topped by obelisk finials. MANSEFIELD incorporates a single-storey former school-room, noted as a girls' school in 1885–6. Veranda with slim cast-iron columns; louvred trefoil openings in gabled roof vents. It was originally linked to CHEVIOT VIEW, the former schoolhouse.

NUNLANDS HOUSE, 0.5km. NE. Late C18. A harled, two-storey, five-bay traditional farmhouse. Scrolled skewputts, and a flush, shallow pediment over the doorway.

EDRINGTON HOUSE. *See* p. 255.

FOULSHIELS *see* SELKIRK

FOUNTAINHALL

Small hamlet with a farm, late C18 smithy (derelict) and mid-C19 PRIMARY SCHOOL with Tudor detailing and thistle finials.
BURNHOUSE. *See* p. 146.
CROOKSTON HOUSE. *See* p. 203.

GALASHIELS*

*The introduction, and the accounts of the public buildings, industrial buildings and the burgh's description, are by Sabina Strachan.

INTRODUCTION

The town of Galashiels, aptly known as the 'Lang Toun', stretches SE through the steep-sided valley of the Gala Water towards the broad plain of the River Tweed. This conurbation, the second largest in the Borders, was shaped by C19 industrial endeavour, its linear form being augmented by C20 expansion.

'Galuschel' ('the shieling by the Gala Water') is first recorded in 1337, at which time it was part of Ettrick Forest, which had been granted to Sir James Douglas by Robert I. Devoid of a royal presence or ecclesiastical centre, the medieval settlement appears to have been configured by the towers of 'Hunter's Ha' to the S (dem. 1814–15), the predecessor of Old Gala House to the w (*see* below), and Blindlee Tower to the N (dismantled by the mid C19). A corn mill (dem. 1809) and three waulk (fulling) mills already existed prior to the town's erection into a burgh of barony in 1599, and a tolbooth (dem. 1880) and market cross were shortly afterwards built to the SE of Old Gala House. Galashiels was described in 1722 as 'a market town, having a weekly market on Wednesdays, belonging to Scott of Gala, having a tolbooth in the middle of the town with a clock and bell, also possessing a cross, with a church and burying-ground at the east end'. The parishioners formerly worshipped at Lindean (q.v.) but, as the population of both settlements burgeoned, a church at Boleside (2 km. SE) was also utilised. Both were superseded by the parish church built in Galashiels in 1617.

Topographical constraints hampered the development of Galashiels as a trading centre. Since at least the time the settlement was first documented, a ferry across the Tweed had existed at Boleside, and this continued to operate until 1827. But in 1754 General Roy mapped the road route (A7) from Boleside, northwards to Easter Langlee and on towards Melrose or Stow and southwards to Selkirk; these connections were improved following the 1768 Turnpike Act. Although 'Galashiels Greys' were known by 1733, real progress in the establishment of a local textile industry began only with the foundation of the Manufacturers' Corporation in 1777, which established a cloth hall and warehouse in the heart of the Old Town in 1792 and brought 'a most rapid advancement . . . in the quantity and quality of goods' by 1814. The harnessing of the fast-flowing Gala Water and the freeing of suitable building land on the valley floor between Galashiels and Buckholmside to the NW (following pioneering flood prevention works by George Craig, baron bailie, from 1813) allowed a string of mills to be built. Related industries, such as wool broking and fellmongering, also boomed, most notably through Sanderson & Murray, who operated Buckholmside Skinworks from 1856 (dem. 1983). Industrial expansion was further stimulated by the building in 1849 of the Edinburgh & Hawick Railway, which snaked its way along the narrow cleft-like valley until its closure in 1969. These developments led to a threefold increase in population between 1791 and 1890, and the building not only of workers' housing but also smart Victorian villas.

The population growth halted with the post-war decline of the woollen industry, leading to the 1968 Central Borders plan which promoted major expansion of Galashiels with new housing and

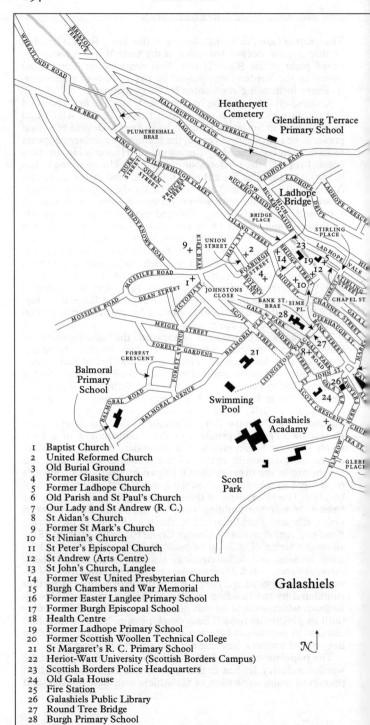

Heatheryett Cemetery

Glendinning Terrace Primary School

Ladhope Bridge

Balmoral Primary School

Swimming Pool

Galashiels Acadamy

Scott Park

Galashiels

1 Baptist Church
2 United Reformed Church
3 Old Burial Ground
4 Former Glasite Church
5 Former Ladhope Church
6 Old Parish and St Paul's Church
7 Our Lady and St Andrew (R. C.)
8 St Aidan's Church
9 Former St Mark's Church
10 St Ninian's Church
11 St Peter's Episcopal Church
12 St Andrew (Arts Centre)
13 St John's Church, Langlee
14 Former West United Presbyterian Church
15 Burgh Chambers and War Memorial
16 Former Easter Langlee Primary School
17 Former Burgh Episcopal School
18 Health Centre
19 Former Ladhope Primary School
20 Former Scottish Woollen Technical College
21 St Margaret's R. C. Primary School
22 Heriot-Watt University (Scottish Borders Campus)
23 Scottish Borders Police Headquarters
24 Old Gala House
25 Fire Station
26 Galashiels Public Library
27 Round Tree Bridge
28 Burgh Primary School

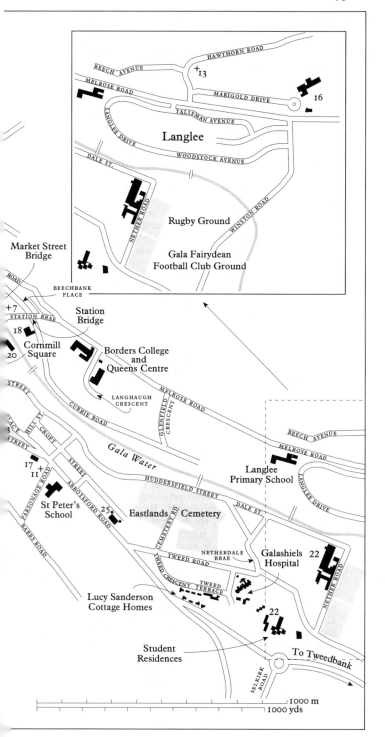

HAWTHORN ROAD

BEECH AVENUE

MELROSE ROAD

+13

MARIGOLD DRIVE

16

TALISMAN AVENUE

LANGLEE DRIVE

Langlee

DALE ST.

WOODSTOCK AVENUE

NETHER ROAD

Market Street
Bridge

Rugby Ground

WINSTON ROAD

Gala Fairydean
Football Club Ground

ROAD

BEECHBANK
PLACE

+7

STATION BRAE

Station
Bridge

18

Cornmill
Square

20

Borders College
and
Queens Centre

MELROSE ROAD

LANGHAUGH
CRESCENT

STREET

CURRIE ROAD

GLENFIELD
CRESCENT

BEECH AVENUE

MELROSE ROAD

STREET

HILL ST.

CROFT

Gala Water

HUDDERSFIELD STREET

Langlee
Primary School

LANGLEE DRIVE

LACE
STREET

17

11

+

PARSONAGE ROAD

STREET

ABBOTSFORD ROAD

St Peter's
School

25

Eastlands Cemetery

DALE ST.

BANKS ROAD

CEMETERY RD.

TWEED ROAD

NETHERDALE
BRAE

Galashiels 22
Hospital

NETHER ROAD

Lucy Sanderson
Cottage Homes

TWEED CRESCENT

TWEED
TERRACE

22

Student
Residences

SELKIRK
ROAD

To Tweedbank

1000 m
1000 yds

industries along the Tweed. Modern Galashiels is characterised
by large municipal housing schemes on either side of the Tweed
at Langlee and Tweedbank to the SE, but the burgh continues to
adapt and expand, eminently suitable for Edinburgh commuters,
by road now rather than by rail.

CHURCHES

BAPTIST CHURCH, Victoria Street. 1883, a rectangle of squared
  whin with buff sandstone dressings, the entrance front facing
  SE. Along the central part of the gabled front a low lean-to
  vestibule has a window on each side of the doorway, itself set
  within a projecting gabled section. Above the vestibule roof is
  a pair of windows, with a smaller window above. The openings
  are mainly shoulder-lintelled. Modern halls to the rear, with
  harled-panel walls.

Former GLASITE CHURCH, Botany Lane. Built 1842 as an elongated block of whinstone rubble, the church to the N and the
  minister's house to the S. The former has tall round-headed
  windows with intersecting glazing; the latter has two storeys of
  rectangular windows and a stair offshoot behind.

Former LADHOPE CHURCH, Ladhope Vale (now a fitness club).
  Built in 1837–8. Rectangular box of squared whinstone with
  ashlar dressings. The tripartite S entrance front, towards the
  Gala Water, has buttresses rising through the shallow gable and
  capped with simple pinnacles. The central square-headed
  doorway is within a crenellated salient, above which is the
  blocked four-centred arch of a window. A bellcote was added
  to the apex of the gable in 1865. The windows along the flanks
  have been insensitively blocked by harled panels.

OLD BURIAL GROUND, Church Street. Site of the former parish
  church, rebuilt in 1617, which was replaced by *John Smith* in
  1812–14, closed in 1931 and demolished in 1960 (*see* also Old
  Parish and St Paul's Church, below). The sole remnant is a
  rectangular family 'aisle' built on its N side for the Scotts of
  Gala in 1636. Walls of whin and sandstone rubble and ashlar
  dressings. The doorway is towards the N end of the W wall,
  below a dated panel with the arms of Hugh Scott and his wife
  Jean Pringle. The N gable-wall has a two-light traceried
  window; a similar window was provided in the new S gable wall
  following demolition of the church. Re-roofed 1992. – MEMO-
  RIALS. Inside the 'aisle', Hugh Scott, †1644; set in inner side
  of E wall, Mark Duncan, minister, †1651. – In the CHURCH-
  YARD, memorials of wide range of dates, including that to
  members of the Young family, dated 1697, with *memento mori*.

OLD PARISH AND ST PAUL'S CHURCH, Scott Crescent. Built
  in 1878–81 by *George Henderson*, with a spire added in 1886;
  halls connected to the church by a glazed cloister were built in
  1927. It became the parish church in 1931 (*see* Old Burial
  Ground, above). An ambitious essay in an English mid-C13
  style, built of red stugged sandstone with polished dressings.
  The main (N) entrance has a barrel-vaulted porch with a relief
  carving of Christ in the tympanum. The nave aisles are below
  a clearstorey in the three N bays, but in the three S bays they
  are higher, with three lateral transept-like gables. There is a
  small organ chamber at the S end, and the tower is set back at

the SW angle. The tower's belfry stage has paired two-light traceried windows, above which is a square base for the spire with
large lucarnes; the spire itself has crenellated bands and smaller
lucarnes, though much detailing has been removed. Throughout, the windows have Geometric tracery: four lights in the
aisles and transepts, three lights in the clearstorey and five
lights in the N gable-wall; above the organ chamber is a rose
with ten quatrefoils around an octofoil.

The internal space is complex, with the taller transept-like
S bays of the aisles subdivided by two-bay arcades. The piers
throughout are polished red granite cylinders, those in the
transepts having shaft-rings; the caps have stiff-leaf foliage. –
COMMUNION TABLE, 1892, ORGAN CASE, 1896, and STALLS,
all on a S platform, in C13 style. – PULPIT, 1917, in subdued
Arts and Crafts Gothic. – LECTERN, brass eagle with evangelist symbols around base. The impact of the interior is
enhanced by fine STAINED GLASS, though the insertion of
plain glass in some windows has detracted from that impact.
Rose in S wall, Good Shepherd. E transept: 1902, memorial for
Queen Victoria, *George Henderson*; Christ Teaching, 1911, *A.
Ballantine & Son* of Edinburgh; Prophets, Adoration of Shepherds and Magi, 1901, *C.E. Kempe*; Supper at Emmaus, 1906,
also Kempe. W transept: SS Peter and Paul by *Douglas
Strachan*, 1911. W nave aisle: Abraham and Moses, *c.* 1906 by
Strachan.

OUR LADY AND ST ANDREW (R.C.), Stirling Street. An
assertive statement of growing Catholic confidence, the church
was first built by Pugin's pupil *William Wardell* in 1856, and
extended by *Goldie & Child* in 1872, both firms favoured by
Scotland's Catholic clergy. It is a massively monolithic rectangular structure in the English Decorated style, of square whinstone with buff ashlar dressings. Low side chapels are slotted
between the wide buttresses in all but the sanctuary bay. The
sense of mass is enhanced by the absence of any tower, a
feature still usually eschewed by Catholics. The S entrance
front has octagonal angle turrets capped by spired ashlar pinnacles. Across the lower level of the front is an engaged five-
arch arcade, with doorways in the outer arches and cusped
single lights between, but the front is dominated by a five-light
window with flowing tracery. The flanks have three-light
windows above the chapels while the N wall has paired three-
light windows and a rose.

The internal unity of space is emphasised by its great width
and height, and confirmed by the high arch-braced roof carried
on shafts rising through the clearstorey. The low chapel spaces
on each side have four inward-arching quadrant ribs rising to
support the roofs in all but the Lady Chapel on the E side. The
only element to encroach on the main space is an organ gallery
on a three-arch arcade in the S bay, which also defines a
vestibule. The internal focus is the N sanctuary bay, with the
altar elevated by seven steps. There is decorative arcading
around the lower sanctuary walls and extensive painted decoration. – HIGH ALTAR and LADY CHAPEL ALTAR, by *Earp* of
London, 1864; the high altar has a tall pinnacle rising above
the tabernacle, between the two N windows. – PULPIT, decorated with scenes of teaching. – FONT, octagon developing

from a square, with evangelist symbols around the bowl. – STAINED GLASS, N windows, earlier panels of Christ and Virgin incorporated in windows of 1886 by *Barnett & Son* of Leith; Lady Chapel, Scenes from the Virgin's life, 1942.

ST AIDAN, Gala Park Road. Formerly South United Presbyterian Church of 1879–80 by *R. Thornton Shiells & Thomson*, in whin rubble and ashlar dressings. The N front is a plastically modelled composition in a C13 idiom owing as much to Normandy as to England. It has a tripartite combination of a central gabled element, flanked by a tower on one side (E) and a lower part on the other. Entrances open through all three parts, but the taller central doorway has a gablet rising across the weathered sill of an arch framing a rose window surrounded by twelve quatrefoils. The upper stages of the four-stage tower are lavishly detailed, with windows at both levels set within arcading; the octagonal spire has square angle pinnacles and lucarnes on the principal faces. The flanks of the church have two levels of windows.

ST ANDREW (Arts Centre), Bridge Street. Former Ladhope Free Church, 1884–5 by *J. McKissack & W. G. Rowan* of Glasgow, replacing a church of 1844 in Island Street (*see* Description). Built of coursed whin rubble with rock-faced dressings, in a mid-C13 English style. The central part of the main S front has a gabled doorway of three orders, one order with foliage carving, below a five-light Geometric-traceried window. Flanking this central section is a lower laterally gabled section to the W, and to the E a tower with plate-traceried belfry windows; the present meagre pyramidal roof of the tower is a poor substitute for what used to be one of the three great spires of Galashiels (along with those of the chuches of Old Parish and St Paul and St Aidan). Aisles flank the church, with two storeys of windows; towards the N end they are wider and higher, and are given prominence by two bays of lateral gables. Halls and offices are to the N and NW. The interior is now much obscured, but still has galleries on three sides, with the pulpit at the N end; cast-iron quatrefoil piers rise in front of the galleries to support the arcades. – PULPIT. Rectangular, with lavishly arcaded front, set slightly intimidatingly below a canopy supporting the organ pipes.

ST JOHN, Hawthorn Road, Langlee. 1970–1 by *Wheeler & Sproson*. This church supersedes one in the burgh of 1874–5 by *John Starforth*. Set against the sloping hillside, the church is a square block, connected by a link building to a hall complex to the W, which includes a small bell tower. Continuing the Nordic modernism of the surrounding housing development (*see* p. 314), the church and halls are flat-roofed and harled above a brick plinth. The main fenestration is a continuous band of clearstorey windows below the overhanging metal-sheathed roof, though the S front also has two columns of five rectangular lights towards the S end, and a low-set row of three rectangular lights to the 'nave'. Internally the walls and principal liturgical fixtures are faced in buff-coloured brick with bands of soldier courses. The band of clearstorey windows is punctuated by the deep, laminated beams supporting the boarded ceiling; the eye is drawn to the vividly coloured abstract designs of STAINED GLASS filling the rectangular openings along the S wall. A raised area along the N side, contained by brick walling, has the organ at its E end. The COMMUNION TABLE and PULPIT are on an E platform, the pulpit a brick-walled ambo. Materials and simple massing of elements create an impressive sense of homogeneity, though not all of its more recent furnishings have been designed in the same spirit.

Former ST MARK, Kirkbrae. Built as a chapel of ease in 1868–70 and enlarged 1887–8; now somewhat brusquely adapted and expanded for housing. The L-shaped group of church and hall, of coursed whin and sandstone dressings, is in simplified Romanesque. The E face of the church has pairs of round-arched windows on each side of a central gabled section with a tightly spaced echelon grouping of five windows; the N and S fronts have triplets of windows. The N and S flanks of the hall reflect the church in their evenly spaced ranks of round-headed windows; the E apse of the hall (containing a stair) has windows framed by shafted arches.

ST NINIAN, High Street. Built 1844, as a United Secession Church. A broad S front was added in 1869–72 by *Robert Aitken* in a manner that would be more at home on a northern English Nonconformist chapel. Restlessly composed with a variety of masonry textures, it also has both buff and red coloured stones in a muted display of polychromy. The central section, with a low pediment-like gable, has three arches embracing three tiers of windows: rectangular at the bottom, then with scalloped round arches, and scalloped oculi above. Slightly recessed sections to each side contain a round-arched doorway with an oculus above. Internally there is a S gallery, and the pulpit and organ are at the N end.

ST PETER (Episcopal), Parsonage Road. The nave was built in 1853–4 by *John Henderson*, and the chancel, S aisle and vestry added by *George Henderson* in 1881; the halls to the W were of 1889 by *Hay & Henderson*. An attractively unassuming exercise in an early C13 idiom, with walls of squared snecked whinstone and droved ashlar dressings. The parallel-roofed nave and S aisle have single lancets along their flanks, with two-light plate-traceried windows in the N chancel flank, the W end of the nave and the aisle ends; the E chancel window has a three-light Geometric-traceried window. Only the N flank of the nave is buttressed. Internally, an arcade with cylindrical piers and waterleaf or crocket caps separated aisle from nave. (The aisle has now been blocked off and a floor inserted to create halls.) The chancel roof has braced collar-beams, and the nave roof arched braces. – ALTAR, stone base with arcaded oak retable by *Robert S. Lorimer*. – PISCINA, shallow trifoliate recess. – SEDILIA, single depressed two-centred arch. – PULPIT, timber blind-arcaded octagon on stone base. – LECTERN, square desk with decorative arcading, 1913. – FONT, octagonal bowl carved with symbols, 1857. – STAINED GLASS: E window, Nativity, Crucifixion and three Maries at the Tomb, *c.* 1873; N side of nave, Transfiguration, 1935; 'many were gathered praying', *c.* 1901; W window, war memorial, 1923.

UNITED REFORMED CHURCH, Union Street. A church here was founded in 1846 (the date in the gable), though the existing simple whin and ashlar building is largely by *Frank Lynes* of 1872 (the date on the E doorway). The broadly gabled main S front is flanked by a more shallowly pitched W section, and an E section rising as a minimal tower with a pyramidal roof. At the centre of the front is a busily detailed round-arched double doorway with a relief carving of the Lamb of God. Above is a triplet of windows, the central one broader than the others. The church has been relocated to an upper floor.

Former WEST UNITED PRESBYTERIAN CHURCH, High Street. Now Hunter's Hall bar and restaurant. By *Carl Ludwig*, 1879–80, but possibly incorporating parts of a church of 1836. The S entrance block is faced in buff ashlar, with rubble flanks. The component parts of the tripartite front are framed by slender buttresses with gablets at mid height and wall-head; the central section is gabled, and the wall-heads emphasised by corbel tables. Above the modern glazed street front, which replaced a gabled central doorway, a three-light window is flanked on each side by a two-light window, all with Geometric tracery.

PUBLIC BUILDINGS

BALMORAL PRIMARY SCHOOL, Balmoral Avenue. *See* Description 2.

BORDERS COLLEGE, Melrose Road. The college occupies two large villas, originally acquired in 1908 by the Galashiels Academy (*see* below) and converted for it by *J. & J. Hall*. Oaklea is of 1860, Neo-Jacobean, the same crenellated vocabulary being used in the extension to the l. Buildings for the Academy's library, hall and primary department were added to its SE and rear in 1939–42 by *J. & J. Hall*; much of it is beige-harled, fairly utilitarian and two-storey, the buttresses of the hall delineating its five bays. Thorniedean House of 1868, on the SE side of Langhaugh Lane, retains its pleasant four-bay bargeboarded main façade, with full-height bay window to the r. and projecting, gabled l. bay with triple lights. Converted for the College in 1964 by *Scott & McIntosh*. NW of Oaklea is the wide shed-like Queen's Leisure Centre recast by *Borders Regional Council*, 1987.

94 BURGH CHAMBERS, Cornmill Square. 1867, by *Robert Hall & Co.* extended in 1923–7 by *Robert S. Lorimer*. The two-storey crowstepped chambers with main façade to Albert Place was built first, at a cost of around £1,600. It has a gabled, slightly advanced centre with round-arched, hoodmoulded traceried window. Lorimer's whinstone extensions to Cornmill Square are Scottish Renaissance in style and provide in the tall clock tower perhaps Galashiels' most picturesque landmark. The upper storey of the rectangular-plan tower is corbelled out and carries the clock, whose Gothic gable breaks the eaves of the bellcast roof. At its base is the War Memorial framed by a segmental arch with Gothic cusping and an inner four-centred pointed arch over a commemorative panel with figure of Peace by *David Sutherland*. Fronting this is *Thomas J. Clapperton*'s accomplished bronze of a mounted Border reiver. Lorimer's range to Paton Street is six bays, of two storeys and basement with shaped dormerheads. Over the Albert Place entrance is an elaborate window with ironwork balcony. The three-storey

five-bay brick block on Paton Street, of 1975–6 by *Aitken & Turnbull*, has a corporate flavour with brown-tinted windows.

Former BURGH EPISCOPAL SCHOOL, Church Street. Now Council offices. 1859, by *George Henderson*. Lightly institutional Jacobean, pleasantly grouped with church and church halls. Single-storey with advanced end bays with steeply pitched roofs and oversailing eaves. Four-bay main NE façade with pointed Gothic windows; three broad bays to the NW side and its two rear wings create a lively SW elevation with half-dormers over the former playground.

BURGH PRIMARY SCHOOL, Gala Park. By *John Starforth*, 1874–5 to serve the late Victorian town's W expansion. Rustic Gothic grey-wacke single storey set on a plateau above the E side of the street. Originally H-plan with symmetrical main façade of five bays, the two gabled end bays and the central bay having three-light pointed-arch windows; the latter is topped by a bellcote. The T-plan E extension of 1881–2, also by Starforth, almost doubled its size. Similarly treated with buttresses and broad octagonal chimney. Hip-ended five-bay hall at the rear of 1934. Sizeable, detached half-hipped SCHOOLHOUSE to W; rear extension by *J. & J. Hall*, 1894–5. Unsympathetic horizontally boarded Scandic-style pre-school block clasped to SSE corner.

Former EASTER LANGLEE PRIMARY SCHOOL. *See* p. 314.

FIRE STATION, Abbotsford Road. 1972–4, by *J. & J. Hall*. An isolated, brick-clad complex with tower.

GALA FAIRYDEAN FOOTBALL CLUB, Nether Road. GRANDSTAND by *Peter Womersley*, 1967 (engineers, *Ove Arup & Partners*). Innovative, sharply defined, origami-like composition in smooth-plastered reinforced concrete. A strong geometry of trapezoidal planes creating thin vertical struts and three broad horizontal bands.

GALASHIELS ACADEMY, Scott Park. 1964 by *Scott & McIntosh*. Roughly quadrangular with courtyard plan. A strong Modernist composition; the main four-storey classroom wing has a butterfly-roofed projection on its flat roof echoed by its canopy entrance. To its r. is the single-storey detached technology department with monopitch roof, and to the NW the games hall (1974) of five broad bays on pilotis faced with interlocking hexagonal brown, pink and white tiles. Parallel with the main block is the concrete-framed school hall, the two buildings linked by a two-storey 1990s entrance. Large L-plan extension by *Campbell & Arnott*, 1969: utilitarian, mainly two storeys.

GALASHIELS HEALTH CENTRE, Currie Road and Station Brae. By the *Common Services Agency Building Division*, 1983. On the site of Galashiels railway station (dem. 1969). A leisurely, pedestrian entrance from Station Brae alongside the riverside walk emphasises the centre's domestic feel; one- and two-storey blocks with stepped, pitched roofs and square windows. Entrance in centre of N elevation in a low link between two parallel wings.

GALASHIELS HOSPITAL, Tweed Road. The former Cottage Hospital. 1892–3 by *John Wallace* of Edinburgh. A single-storey T-plan with two wards either side of a central administrative block. Later extensions including the Nurses' Home, 1930, by *J. & J. Hall* at its NE end, with glass entrance veranda.

GALASHIELS PUBLIC LIBRARY, Lawyers Brae. Built 1873.

Ashlar of three storeys and three bays with a gabled central projection. Round-arched entrance with twin, half-fluted Ionic columns to its porch. Venetian window to the second floor. Double-height reading room with exposed beams, ground-floor librarian's flat and ladies' reading room on the second floor. Two-storey and basement addition to the E gable, of 1889–90 by *George Henderson*, with double-height bay window and crenellated wall-head. The ground floor was remodelled in 1913. Rear whinstone extension of 1936 by *James Watson*, Burgh Architect. Altered internally by *Frank White*, 1965–7.

GALASHIELS SWIMMING POOL, Livingstone Place. 1983–4, by *Duncan Cameron & Associates*. Undistinguished beige brick cladding and low-pitched roof with strip window at the ridge and round windows along the side.

GLENDINNING TERRACE PRIMARY SCHOOL. Mostly by *J. & J. Hall*, 1936. A pleasing Art Deco composition in cream render. Large multi-paned picture windows with red brick sills. T-plan half-dormered two-storey schoolhouse of 1891, and small yellow sandstone single-storey rear wing with exposed rafters survive.

104 HERIOT-WATT UNIVERSITY (Scottish Borders Campus), Nether Road. 1964–6 by *R. Forbes Hutchison* and *George R.M. Kennedy*. Built as the Scottish College of Textiles (*see* former Scottish Woollens Technical College below) on its transfer from Market Street. The campus is composed of several buildings, the last of which was completed in 1973–4 by *Scott & McIntosh* as production workshops and laboratories for the Wool Industries Research Association (superseding C19 premises). The earlier parts, facing SW. are the most satisfying, forming a U-plan around terrace. Mostly two storey with butterfly and monopitched roofs to the upper floors, containing chemistry laboratories and hall, which project over whinstone-clad and glazed ground floors. Squat, long, four-storey SCHOOL OF MANAGEMENT to NE and three-storey workshops with narrow vertical strip windows to N; bright yet uncompromising free-standing single-storey refectory to E corner of the site. Adjacent to the W on Dale Street, the SCHOOL OF TEXTILES & DESIGN occupies the former High Mill (1873) of Netherdale Mill (*see* Industrial Buildings, below), acquired by the College in 1947 for practical training and production. Four storeys in whinstone with a square tower.

Set into the hillside of the rise SW of Tweed Road are strikingly grouped STUDENTS' RESIDENCES of 1968–9 by *Walter Scott*. Of mixed heights, white rendered with inset vertical sections for windows between dark panels, stepping down the hillside and culminating in a low, horizontal dining hall and the vertical accent of a dark whinstone tower.

LADHOPE BRIDGE. *See* Description 1.

Former LADHOPE PRIMARY SCHOOL, Ladhope Vale. 1866. Associated with the former Ladhope Church (*see* Churches, above) until it was taken over by the School Board in 1880. Inconspicuous, two-storey Jacobean, its main façade of squared whinstone with yellow sandstone margins with end chimneys and shaped skewputts. Extended to rear in 1887.

LANGLEE PRIMARY SCHOOL. *See* Description 5.

LUCY SANDERSON COTTAGE HOMES, Tweed Terrace. *See* Description 4.

MARKET STREET BRIDGE. *See* Description 1.

ROUND TREE BRIDGE. *See* Description 1.

SCOTTISH BORDERS POLICE HEADQUARTERS, Bridge Street. 1966–9, by *J. & J. Hall*. Dominant three-storey cube clad in blockwork with square windows. Elevation to street interrupted only by narrow stair light. Single-storey NW wing with the main entrance in a short link.

Former SCOTTISH WOOLLEN TECHNICAL COLLEGE,* Market Street. 1908–9, by *John Hall Jun.* Textile training school founded in 1882 with the support of the Galashiels Manufacterers' Corporation and built at a cost of over £20,000. The main (NE) elevation is Greek Revival, two-storeyed of red sandstone ashlar. Bold, rusticated ground floor, double string course, dentilled cornice and large plain parapet. Symmetrical central D-plan Ionic porch of polished pink granite columns supporting a balustraded balcony. The centre is further enlivened by giant rusticated Doric pilasters in the broken pediment framing the Ionic-pilastered first-floor window. Figure of Industry carved above its entablature. Six-bay flanks and a large two-storey flat-roofed extension to rear of 1922. The college transferred to Nether Road in 1965 (*see* Heriot-Watt University, above).

ST MARGARET'S (R.C.) PRIMARY SCHOOL, Livingstone Place. 1968. An admixture of buildings on a leafy site in the former policies of Gala House. It comprises a main NE–SW oriented two-storey classroom block, with its horizontal frame emphasised, and lower, grey-harled three-storey hall to its E corner, its gable a chequerboard of windows. Entrance canopy in the re-entrant angle. Small single-storey outshots complete the arrangement.

ST PETER'S SCHOOL, Parsonage Road. 1936–8, by *John C. Hall* to succeed the Old Town School of 1806 (*see* p. 310). Z-plan, terraced on the hillside above Abbotsford Road. Two gabled grey-harled classroom blocks sit at right angles to one another with small, flat-roofed utilitarian extensions clasped on to ends and corners. Two-storey extension, by *J. & J. Hall*, 1967–72, joined to the E corner of one of the older blocks, the oversailing second storey perched on slender columns with large windows above.

STATION BRIDGE, Station Brae. *See* Description 1.

TWEEDBANK PRIMARY SCHOOL, Cotgreen Road. *See* Description 5.

OLD GALA HOUSE
Scott Crescent

Formerly a country mansion standing within its own policies but now enveloped by the suburbs. Like many of the neighbouring seats of the older families, it grew accretively over the centuries before being superseded by a new house nearby. Unlike most of

---

* Under threat, 2005.

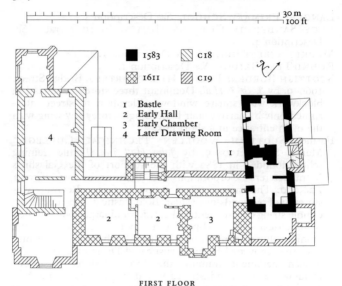

1583   C18
1611   C19

1 Bastle
2 Early Hall
3 Early Chamber
4 Later Drawing Room

FIRST FLOOR

Galashiels, Old Gala House.
Plan of First Floor.

its contemporaries, however, Gala House not only survived the transfer, but also outlived its successor.

The property was originally a stead (tenant's holding) of Ettrick Forest, being leased from the Crown by the Pringles of Smailholm Tower (q.v.). There was a house here by 1544, but the oldest portion of the present building was probably erected by Andrew Pringle in 1583.* This was an unvaulted oblong block of modest size probably best categorised as a bastle. The next laird, Sir James Pringle, decided to make Galashiels his principal residence. In the early C17, probably in 1611, he more than doubled the size of the house by building a second range at right angles to the first to form an L-plan mansion. The English traveller Christopher Lowther, who was entertained there by Sir James in 1629, was particularly impressed by the fine gardens and orchards, while twenty years later 'Galaschiels' was described as one of the principal houses of Selkirkshire. The house passed to the Scotts in 1632 and it was probably John Scott, fifth of Gala (†1785), who added a new suite of public rooms to make the plan a U, open to the NW. Further alterations were made c. 1830 (builders, *Sanderson & Paterson* of Galashiels), and c. 1860 (builders, *Robert Hall & Co.* of Galashiels), but by this time the mansion was becoming engulfed by the rapid expansion of the neighbouring burgh, and in 1872 Hugh Scott, eighth of Gala, commissioned *David Bryce* to design 'New Gala House' to the s (*see* Description 2). Old Gala House is now a museum.

---

*The date is supplied by a panel formerly built into the walls but now preserved at Hollybush Farm, 3 km. to the s.

EXTERIOR. The nucleus of the mansion is evidently the C16 NE WING, a rectangular, two-and-a-half-storeyed block (13.4 m. by 5.6 m.). At present the roof is gabled at one end and hipped at the other, and since all the flues appear to be in the mid wall some such arrangement cannot be ruled out from the beginning. The masonry is of local rubble with dressings of red and buff-coloured sandstone probably quarried in the Melrose–Dryburgh area. The main front evidently faced SW and contained ground- and first-floor doorways, the latter presumably reached from a forestair. Both doorways are framed by quirked edge-rolls, and the same moulding appears on two small ground-floor windows as well as on a larger one on the principal floor. Otherwise the windows are mostly C17 insertions or replacements having round- or chamfer-arrised margins. There may always have been a stair-turret towards the centre of the NE wall, but the present oblong one appears to be of C18 or C19 date. As first built, the house was probably free-standing, but accompanied by outbuildings.

The early C17 SE WING is 20.9 m. long and of three main storeys with a gable-ended roof. The masonry is similar in character to that of the 1583 work, but with freer use of buff-coloured sandstone quoins. The approach at this period was from the NW where there is a rectangular stair-tower which formerly housed the principal entrance. This contains a number of original windows with roll-moulded surrounds, but the remainder of the elevation is masked by C19 corridors. On the SE, or garden, side, however, the original fenestration is better preserved, with two rows of large, regularly spaced openings lighting the *piano nobile* and second floor. Most have chamfer-arrised surrounds, but at least two have quirked edge-rolls like those in the early house. The ground-floor windows, where original, are small chamfer-arrised openings formerly fitted with bars. The C18 WING (14.1 m. in length) forms the central portion of the SW range, the end bays probably additions of the 1830s. It comprises two floors only, the ground floor being a little higher than that of the earlier house; the fenestration appears to have been largely renewed when the end bays were added. The SE end bay contained a new principal entrance overlooking the garden, but this was superseded *c.* 1880 by the present entrance on the SW side. The C19 additions are executed in a mildly castellated style, featuring octagonal and square angle turrets and a variety of window forms, some of the mouldings replicating those in the early house.

The INTERIOR was refurbished by *Page & Park*, 1988. The original layout of the C16 HOUSE is uncertain, but each of the two lower floors seems to have contained two equal-sized rooms, perhaps hall and chamber. The ground-floor hall has a big, corbel-lintelled fireplace, the present stone lintel possibly replacing an earlier one of timber. The side walls incorporate corbels for the runners of the ceiling joists, showing that the rooms were not vaulted. Similar corbels occur on the floor above, where the rooms retain fielded panelling of early C18 date. The addition of the early C17 SE RANGE was designed to create a well-appointed mansion of the front rank. Its entrance opened directly into what was probably a scale-and-platt stair (since renewed) serving the two main upper floors and attic. The ground floor seems to have comprised two cellars and a kitchen, each with its own access to the NW, but none apparently vaulted. At some point during the C19, the kitchen at the NE end was turned into a washhouse and a new kitchen, rising through two floors, was formed at the SW end. There are no obvious traces of the original first-floor layout of the C17 wing. Originally it may have comprised a large hall opening into a chamber to the NE, with mural latrine, these two roms possibly forming the outer rooms of a four-room reception suite which continued with a bedchamber and closet in the C16 house. The hall, originally some 11 m. in length, was lit by three large windows overlooking the garden. A surviving fireplace lintel of very large span (removed to New Gala House in 1876 but recently returned for display) very probably derived from this hall and must have occupied much of its NW wall. It is richly carved with a mixture of Gothic, Renaissance and revived Romanesque motifs, and displays the initials and armorials of Sir James Pringle of Gala and his wife, Jean Kerr, together with various pious mottos and the date 1611. The hall appears to have been subdivided in the early C18, and some of the rooms contain panelling and plaster cornices of that period. The original arrangement on the second floor seems to have been similar to that below and these rooms may have formed a family apartment; a similar process of subdivision also took place in the early C18. The SW room has a tempera-painted ceiling (discovered in 1952), probably one of a series, as at Traquair House (q.v.). The joists have highly coloured geometric and arabesque designs, while the boards display bunches of fruit and winged cherubs' heads. Framed panels contain the date 1635 and the initials of Hugh Scott and his wife, Jean Pringle.

The C18 SW WING provided an additional staircase, together with a good-sized dining room on the ground floor and a drawing room above. Probably c. 1830 an entrance lobby (afterwards morning room) and bedroom were added to the SE end and a smoking room and boudoir to the NW end. The geometric stone stair has a modelled plaster ceiling showing the plum tree and foxes of the Galashiels armorial, perhaps a reference to the fact that the Scotts were superiors of the burgh. The first-floor drawing room has a deeply coved plaster ceiling, the central panel of which contains a modelled figure of Persephone between corner busts of the Four Ages of Woman. The work is similar in character to that of c. 1761 at Ednam House, Kelso (q.v.). The principal rooms were refurnished and redecorated by *William Trotter* of Edinburgh, 1813–19, but the drawing room has a grey marble chimney-piece and moulded plaster frieze and cornice of c. 1860. The morning room has a Jacobean-style chimneypiece of oak said to have been brought from Mary, Queen of Scots' House, Jedburgh (q.v.).

DESCRIPTION

1. Centre

The Burgh Chambers (*see* Public Buildings, above) forms the   94
landmark of the town's C19 centre in CORNMILL SQUARE.
Cleared of its mill after 1903, the square now boasts an extra-
vagant FOUNTAIN designed by *Robert S. Lorimer*, 1912–13.
Dolphins abound, on a central column which rises within a
handsome balustraded enclosure over the former mill lade. On
the S side of the square, marking the foot of Lawyers Brae
opposite the Public Library (*see* Public Buildings, above) is the
BURNS MEMORIAL, a bronze of 1911 by *F.W. Doyle Jones* of
Chelsea.

BANK STREET, leading NW, was laid out as Scotts Place from
1813 by George Craig, baron bailie, as part of expansion on
the haugh of the Gala Water to the N of the medieval burgh.
It was originally built up with houses on one side only with
gardens belonging to the householders on the S side. First, the
elegantly simple, two-storeyed, four-bay ashlar-fronted former
Liberal Club, l. of Store Close, renovated in 1897 and again in
1935–6 by *Dick Peddie, Todd & Jamieson*. The street is dominated, appropriately, by the ROYAL BANK OF SCOTLAND,
built by *J.R. McKay*, 1946, as the National Bank of Scotland
to a pre-war design by *Dick Peddie, Todd & Jamieson*. Impressive advanced pedimented centre with fluted Corinthian cast-
iron columns on raised plinth. Facing are the GARDENS,
preserved for the public in the early 1950s, bordered by the
former Waulkmillhead Mill lade. Bank Street Brae, leading off
S, is carried over the lade by the steeply graded ROUND TREE
BRIDGE, erected in the late C19 to facilitate communication
with the burgh's developing streets to the S (see Description 2).
Red sandstone piers at the NE end were erected in 1907 'to
commemorate Bank Street Improvements'; restored 2000.

Facing Bank Street's NW end are brightly harled façades of
GIBSON'S CLOSE, a housing redevelopment of 1988. Termi-
nating the street, HALDANE'S COURT once housed the Post
Office.

Continuing NW, HIGH STREET begins on the SW side with the
three-storey and attic, red sandstone CLYDESDALE BANK.
Further on, the three-storey REIVERS (No. 69), built as the
Unionist Club in 1897, is beautifully composed with a recessed
entrance with bottle-green tiles, sweeping brackets supporting
a first-floor balconette with lions seated on the piers and a corbelled cornice and bellcote above. Then the half-timbered
LUCKENBOOTH (No. 71). Nearby, a car park marks the site
of the town hall of 1861 (dem. 1969). The former COMMER-
CIAL BANK OF SCOTLAND (now Lauder College Employment & Enterprise) is by *David Rhind*, 1868. Three-storey,
Italianate, its main façades with first-floor Palladian windows
and dentilled cornice above. The well-proportioned red sandstone extension to its r. was added by *A.G. Sydney Mitchell* in
1884. Also red sandstone, but on a grand scale, is the former
Galashiels Co-operative Store at the junction with Roxburgh
Street. French Renaissance by *J. & J. Hall*, 1888–90, extended
1897. Attic storey of pyramidal roofs and cast-iron dormers

and a ten-sided corner turret over chamfered lower floors. Converted to flats and offices in 1984.

N of High Street, on the W corner of BRIDGE PLACE is BRIDGE INN, a former coaching house with corner entrance enlivened by scrolled brackets and pilasters. The solid No. 7, built as the Galashiels Savings Bank by *J. & J. Hall* in 1924, has a rusticated ground floor, three bays and two storeys in ashlar. Next door, the two-storey BALLENCRIEFF, built as Bridge House *c.* 1845 for William Laidlaw of Ladhope Mill. Late Georgian with splayed steps over basement to its classical door surround. From here William could see his factory across the Gala Water. Now only two mid-C19 two-storey weaving sheds survive behind its 1909–19 offices on Low Buckholmside.

Return now along HIGH STREET'S NE side, which begins with the GOLDEN LION BAR, rebuilt in 1923 by *J. & J. Hall* for the Royal Bank of Scotland. Three-storey corner block with round-arched door, squat balustrades to window above, sharply defined keystones and rusticated yellow sandstone ground floor. Visible behind the former West U.P. Church (*see* Churches, above) are rubble-built weaving shops of 1892, occupied by James Noble & Co. from 1896 to 1954. The church is now part of the HUNTER'S HALL pub, which has eclectic Gothic and Scottish Baronial detailing. At Nos. 46–48 the three-storey, five-bay former BRITISH LINEN CO. BANK by *Wardrop & Reid*, 1880, has a solid, Doric-pilastered door surround demarcating the l. bay, and scrolled brackets supporting the entablature on its NW side. Further SE is a pleasant red sandstone ashlar-fronted block with double-height bay window and decorative frieze between the two upper storeys, and the two-storey HARROW INN of 1866. Simply adorned with two flat entablatures on its monochrome façade. The High Street vista terminates with VICTORIA BUILDINGS, a rebuilding after road widening in 1927. Half-timbered, four storeys with a highly decorative attic with pyramidal-capped octagonal corner tower.

Parallel with High Street to the N is BRIDGE STREET. It begins with the former St Andrew's Church (*see* Churches, above), followed by early C19 tenements whose gardens were built over for the police headquarters (*see* Public Buildings, above). Then, beyond Johnstons Close is the former COMMERCIAL HOTEL (now Scottish Enterprise) built *c.* 1850 on the site of a *c.* 1820 tollhouse. Seven-bay French Renaissance façade in coursed greywacke with highly decorative attic storey, extended *c.* 1890. The first LADHOPE BRIDGE, of *c.* 1764, crossed the Gala Water slightly further SE. The present crossing is by *Cunningham, Blyth & Westland*, 1889, widened 1892. Iron girders and steel beams supported by three roughly hewn yellow sandstone and brick piers.

Over the bridge are the former Ladhope Church and Primary School on LADHOPE VALE (*see* Churches and Public Buildings, above). Further on, the street has an industrial flavour, exemplified by a three-storey whinstone mill (Borders Textiles Ltd) of 1872. It now incorporates its neighbour, a two-storey hip-roofed villa. CHAPEL STREET and STIRLING PLACE at its SW end are formed of diminutive mid-C19 whinstone tenements. Some early C19 tannery workers' housing survives in PARK STREET along with a yellow sandstone-fronted former cloth merchant's warehouse of 1880 (now British Legion).

From here a bridge of 1924 crosses back to the pedestrianised CHANNEL STREET. At its corner is a brick-built two-storey range of 1930 with rectangular windows in round-arched recesses. At its NW end, marking the intersection with High Street, are the impressive BANK OF SCOTLAND, 1864, and POST OFFICE, 1894. The former, by *Peddie & Kinnear*, is in squared whinstone with ashlar surrounds and segmental-headed ground-floor openings. The latter, by *H.M. Office of Works* in their usual Free Renaissance, has octagonal corner towers with pointed roofs, an Ionic square-columned porch and Doric pilasters. Extended 1915. The six-bay *c.* 1930 CHANNEL HOUSE (a former hotel) has paired pilasters and plain keystones. Further SE stands the three-and-a-half-storey former DOUGLAS HOTEL, by *J. & J. Hall*; advanced centre and double-height oriels at its end bays. The SE end of the street is characterised by a late C19 and early C20 mix.

Channel Street opens into MARKET SQUARE. The square was occupied by the Subscription School from 1821 to 1862, and for much of the C20 served as a bus station. Re-landscaped in 1968 (and again in 1994) with a sculpture, 'Man With Sheep' by *Ann Henderson*, 1971. In MARKET STREET is the Victorian KING'S HOTEL, with oversailing eaves; the two-storey painted whinstone former RAILWAY INN of *c.* 1849 and PAVILION cinema by *F. E.B. Blanc*, 1919–20; with vestiges of its Italianate frontage still surviving after extension and remodelling in 1995. OVERHAUGH STREET, S (formerly Cowgate), mainly composed of two-storey tenements. Of particular note is the three-storey, C19 former BURNS HALL, with its pair of recessed double-height bay windows adorned with thistles at the High Street end.

Now N, over MARKET STREET BRIDGE, built in the late C19, to replace a narrower road bridge over the Gala Water. Segmental span of yellow sandstone (partly cement-rendered) with square rusticated piers of red sandstone and round-arched niches, carrying lamps. Beyond the bridge is ANDERSON CHAMBERS, built as a tweed merchant's warehouse in 1879, with decorative ironwork above a classical porch, and triple windows to either side. STATION BRAE is over Currie Road by STATION BRIDGE of 1938 by *Blyth & Blyth*, engineers, for Selkirk County Council to replace a bridge erected by the Galashiels Railway Co. in 1878. Flat span supported by three piers with iron cross-bracing. Painted cast-iron blind parapets enlivened by lampposts on yellow sandstone pedestals. From the bridge the view down to the NW to BEECHBANK PLACE is of the mid-C19 BEECHBANK WORKS, partly harled whinstone of eleven bays. One of the two-storey blocks has been converted into flats. Further E, the four-bay, Dutch-gabled Nos. 3–5 MELROSE ROAD was built *c.* 1860 by and for *Adam Stirling*, one of many villas along this principal route.

2. The Old Town, Scott Park and NW

The burgh's Old Town lay uphill to the SE of the C19 centre, focused in the C17 on the historic group of church, tolbooth and pant well. The much-altered MERCAT CROSS survives, now stranded on a traffic island at the junction of Church Street, Scott Crescent and Lawyers Brae. Re-erected in 1864 on a stepped base, its shaft with cubical sundial head is dated 1695 but sports 1930s plaques by *George Hope Tait*. The tolbooth (dem. 1880) and well stood to its NE. Still providing a backdrop to the cross is a significant survival of C18 Galashiels: the harled, four-bay CLOTH HALL on SCOTT CRESCENT (NW), built in 1791–2 as a warehouse and trading centre for the large-scale manufacturers then developing in the town; subsequently it became a public house, then a bank and now flats. E, on CHURCH STREET stood the parish church, rebuilt in 1813 by *John Smith* but demolished in 1960 and replaced by CHURCH SQUARE, a housing development of three-storey whinstone and melamine-clad flats by *Peter Womersley*; opposite are matching blocks by *Duncan Cameron & Associates*, 1963–5. Further down Church Street is the wedge-shaped Old Burial Ground (*see* above) with, opposite, stables and coach house of the parish manse of *c.* 1775. They survived its rebuilding *c.* 1812 by *John Smith* as THE GRANGE.

The ruin of the medieval tower of Hunters Ha' (dem. 1815) and the Old Town School of 1806 (dem. 1937) stood at the SW end of SCHOOL CLOSE. On the site is two-storey housing by *J. & J. Hall*: GLEBE PLACE of 1936 and GLEBE STREET of 1939–40. Only the picturesque C18 whitewashed terrace of TEA STREET was retained and its thatch replaced by slate.

The tour turns l. on to ELM ROW. Behind the former BURGHER MANSE of 1806 is CRAIGPARK, built for Thomas Aimers, engineer *c.* 1860. C19 villas also embellish the old BARRS ROAD further uphill, including GALAHILL built for Henry Brown in the 1840s and extended by his nephew, William; squared red sandstone, advanced entrance bay with single-storey bay window and crenellated parapet, oversailing eaves to gables and dormerheads.

Returning now to the Mercat Cross and SCOTT CRESCENT, driven through the lairdly policies of Old Gala House in 1875–85 by *A. Herbertson & Son* after the Scotts had moved to New Gala House (*see* Scott Park, below). Its landmarks are the contemporary Old Parish and St Paul's Church (*see* Churches, above) and the restored remains of Old Gala House (*see* above) which faces on to the road on the E side; to its immediate l. is the delightful, bargeboarded CLUBHOUSE built in 1883 for GALA BOWLING CLUB (extensions 1930–2 and later). Just behind, on the l. side of GALA TERRACE survives Old Gala House's late C18 laundry (ROSE COTTAGE) and servants' houses (WOODNEUK and BELHENDEN). The red sandstone KIRKLANDS, formerly Moat House, was built as a private school in 1880.

Now into ST JOHN STREET. On the N side is the four-bay, hood-moulded Gothic HAYWARD SCOUT CENTRE and the large Scottish Baronial MASONIC HALL, by *Hall & Murray*, 1876, with rope moulding over the doorway. They create a most pleasant streetscape with the adjacent former VOLUNTEER HALL (now council offices). Built 1874–5 for the Gala Forest Rifles. Yellow sandstone two-storey, five-bay with an advanced centre, under a crowstepped gable – a light Jacobean vocabulary. Single-bay flat-roofed extension to r. Downhill at the foot of St John Street is the SCOTT MEMORIAL, a bronze by *Thomas J. Clapperton*, erected in 1932. On the site of Galashiels Free Church (1875) is CORN MILL COURT, undistinguished three- to four-storey brick-clad sheltered housing. On ALBERT PLACE, note the Ionic-columned, corrugated-iron Sutherland & Sons, sculptors (now disused).

The textile boom in the years after 1870 saw the burgh expand into part of the policies and gardens of Old Gala House (*see* above). NW of St John Street in GALA PARK ROAD is a well-proportioned, loosely Jacobean two-and-a-half-storey building (Council Offices) in roughly hewn sandstone, a cream-harled low-key development (GALA PARK GARDENS) of *c.* 2000 and St Aidan's Church (*see* Churches, above). The street continues NW as GALA PARK. Past the Burgh Primary School (*see* Public Buildings, above) are four-storey flats by *Duncan Cameron & Associates* of 1975–6 in the same genre as their Church Square housing (*see* above). The surrounding streets are characterised by two-storey whinstone and yellow sandstone tenements.

Having developed their policies the Scotts moved W to a new home, New Gala House, in 1876. The house, designed by *David Bryce*, was demolished in 1985 but two yellow sandstone lodges and gatepiers (also by Bryce, 1881–2) survive on SCOTT STREET at the entrance to SCOTT PARK. This formed the policies of the house, gifted to the burgh in 1939. The leafy surroundings now provide the setting for several buildings including Galashiels Academy, St Margaret's (R.C.) Primary School, the Swimming Pool (*see* Public Buildings, above) and the red brick WAVERLEY home for the elderly, of 1983 by *Borders Regional Council*, with steep monopitched roofs and square windows.

NW of Scott Park, housing of the C20 developed first with FOREST GARDENS, 1919–23, by *Elliot Grieve* of Selkirk, then with post-Second World War two-storey burgh council housing around the pleasantly sited BALMORAL PRIMARY SCHOOL by *J. & J. Hall*, 1955 in tree-lined BALMORAL AVENUE. Beige-harled buildings, of one and two storeys with a sensitive disposition of bays divided by square piers; astragalled fenestration. Off-centre entrance under the second storey. Nursery of 1975.

N of this district is a more select area characterised by Victorian villas, e.g. in MOSSILEE ROAD, N side, the two-storey BURN-BRAE, with full-height window at its S corner, built *c.* 1860 for William Sanderson of Buckholmside Skinworks, and in WINDYKNOWE ROAD, the WOODLANDS HOUSE, a two-storey Italianate villa of *c.* 1850 overwhelmed by substantial Neo-Tudor additions of 1884–5 by *George Henderson* for James Sanderson of Comley Bank Mill; contemporary timber-framed conservatory by *Mackenzie & Moncur* and elaborate conical-capped gatepiers and round-arched gateway to the lodge (1896). Less comfortable accommodation was provided in

KIRKBRAE at the Combination Poorhouse at the crossroads
with Gala Park, now GALASHIELS NURSING HOME, by *A.
Herbertson & Son*, 1859–61: a prominent two-storey, eight-bay
L-plan block.

Continuing along KIRKBRAE one turns r. into ROXBURGH
STREET which has Botany Mill on its SE side (*see* Industrial
Buildings, below). Turning l. into UNION STREET is the United
Reformed Church (*see* Churches, above) and the early C20 engineering workshops of Robert Herbert & Son, composed around
an open courtyard with three round-arched openings to the
ground floor (renovated 1994); note the harled elevation of the
late C19 Deanbank Mill on HALL STREET. On ISLAND
STREET, the NW continuation of High Street, is a former warehouse (now HERGES BISTRO) built on the site of the 1844
Ladhope Free Church. Roughly opposite is the three-bay,
hipped ISLAND HOUSE by *Robert Hall & Co.*, *c.* 1865, set back
at Nos. 61–63. The tour can be continued with Description 3.

3. Buckholmside

The former village of BUCKHOLMSIDE, NW of the town, was
also caught up in C19 industrial expansion. LOW BUCK-
HOLMSIDE, visible on the N side of the Gala Water from Island
Street, is now composed of large post-1980 commercial and
industrial units on the site of Sanderson & Murray's 1882 skinworks. A nice latticework bridge spans the footpath N to High
Buckholmside. Large numbers of mills also used to line the
Gala Water's S bank along WILDERHAUGH STREET and
KING STREET, including Wilderbank Mill (1862, dem. 1977)
and Comleybank Mill (1855). Remnants of the associated
workers' housing survive but much was cleared after 1966 and
now replaced by retail parks and industrial estates. Some
industrial activity continues in Wheatlands Road (*see* Industrial Buildings, below).

From King Street, the winding PLUMTREEHALL BRAE crosses
the Gala Water; on the r. of the bridge are interesting, early
C20, L-plan flats with half-timbering and brick chimneystacks.
The 1883 Gala Dyeworks formerly stood further uphill,
towards Bristol Terrace. EDINBURGH ROAD, to the NW, was
developed in the second half of the C19 and includes villas such
as BUCKHOLM BURN, *c.* 1865, built for Henry Brown. Some
properties on MAGDALA TERRACE were demolished by mill-
owner James Sanderson in 1906 and redeveloped from 1937
by *J. & J. Hall*. To its NE is the HALLIBURTON area, terraced
along the hillside and characterised by 1930s housing and some
whinstone tenements but dominated by Glendinning Terrace
Primary School (*see* Public Buildings, above). On the NW side
of HALLIBURTON PLACE is HEATHERYETT CEMETERY with
numerous grand C19 memorials.

High above Ladhope Crescent, the ivy-clad ruins of the C16
APPLETREELEAVES TOWER form part of a store immediately
N of the club house (1912, extended 1960s) of GALASHIELS
GOLF COURSE, laid out in 1884. Of Buckholmside village
there are only a few early buildings including the late C18
shopfront and doorpiece of the former Post Office on HIGH

BUCKHOLMSIDE, which is adorned with engaged Doric columns. Continuing back into the centre along HIGH ROAD are numerous villas, such as LYNWOOD and EASTMOUNT, both *c.* 1870. The tour can now return across Station Bridge towards the town centre.

4. *Abbotsford Road and* SE

ABBOTSFORD ROAD, leading SE, has near the town end many villas funded by the textile industry, including ELMBANK and BYTHORNE, dating from *c.* 1845. *James C. Walker* designed the large, mid-C19 Jacobean NETHERBY (extended *c.* 1875) while the red sandstone FAIRNIEKNOWE, 1862, built for Adam Cochrane at the foot of Parsonage Road (W side), complements St Peter's Church, hall and former school (*see* above). On the N side, THORNBANK HOUSE, *c.* 1845, at the head of Thornbank Street, served as the Baptist Church manse and was occupied by the headmaster of Galashiels Academy from 1870. Villas close to the junction with Tweed Road and beyond belong to the late C19 and early C20. MAPLEHURST is an Arts and Crafts mansion under an expansive hipped roof, its mass and half-timbering evoking a medieval manor house. By *J. & J. Hall* for Andrew Fairgrieve of Huddersfield Mill. Mix of interior styles including Art Nouveau, incorporating many Canadian-inspired motifs due to Fairgrieve's transatlantic marriage. Further out of town to the SE is the large, romantically composed ABBOTSHILL of 1874 by *William Hay* for Archibald Cochrane of Netherdale Mill, with slim, square-plan Baronial corner tower and large apsidal-ended conservatory by *Mackenzie & Moncur*; Jacobean stables converted into ABBOTSKNOWE by *James B. Dunn & Martin* in 1930.

Further on in SELKIRK ROAD to the SE is KINGSKNOWES, built 1868–9 by *William Hay* for millowner Adam Lees Cochrane; expansive red sandstone Scottish Baronial mansion, towers and turrets abound, and fine, unaltered *MacKenzie & Moncur* domed conservatory.

Mill workers' three-storey tenements constitute much of the area to the NE of Abbotsford Road and, further E, TWEED ROAD was predominantly developed by *J. & J. Hall* for the Town Council in the 1920s and 1930s. The EASTLANDS INFECTIOUS DISEASES HOSPITAL, 1872–1921, on CEMETERY ROAD is now renovated into two cottages. Octagonal gatepiers lead to EASTLANDS CEMETERY, with its fine T-plan lodge and memorials.

TWEED TERRACE, to the S, has the pleasant adornment of the model LUCY SANDERSON COTTAGE HOMES, an exemplary scheme of sheltered housing for retired mill workers, made possible by a generous donation from the mill-owning Sanderson family. The scheme, laid out over seven acres in 1930–33 by *Mears & Carus-Wilson*, is based upon a village idyll with its own green. Eight semi-detached single-storey cottages are arranged around a main hall, which also includes the matron's house and rest house wing, washhouse, laundry and gardener's cottage. It was originally intended to finish the buildings in harled brick but local whinstone with yellow sandstone margins was used instead, roofed with green West-morland slates. The gabled HALL, situated midway along Tweed Terrace, has an impressively tall clock tower with ogee roof, and the detailing is enlivened by highly accomplished animal carvings by *Phyllis Bone* and *C. d'O. Pilkington Jackson*. The barrel-vaulted hall is decorated with murals by *W. R. Lawson* and *M. Caird*. Next is Galashiels Hospital on TWEED ROAD, and further E, the flat river bank is dominated by Heriot-Watt University's campus (*see* Public Buildings, above).

5. Langlee and Tweedbank

The expansive housing areas above and below Melrose Road dominate the hillside SE of the town. The first development in this area was for WESTER LANGLEE, begun post-war by the Town Council and advanced enough by 1954 to require LANGLEE PRIMARY SCHOOL, Langlee Drive, completed in 1958 by *Scott & McIntosh*. Several interlocking, predominantly flat-roofed blocks in an H-plan on a sloping site with considerable grounds to its S. Later phases were undertaken by the *Scottish Special Housing Association*. The former site and policies of Langlee House were developed at EASTER LANGLEE from 1967 with Scandinavian-inspired housing designed by *Wheeler & Sproson*, architects too of the landmark St John's church (*see* Churches above). The former PRIMARY SCHOOL, Marigold Drive, 1971, by *Scott & McIntosh* is an uninspiring T-plan with single-storey classroom block and double-height hall at its SW end. Now mainly workshops. Immediately below, on Melrose Road is the COMMUNITY CENTRE, built *c.* 2000 in an inviting domestic vocabulary of pitched roofs, red brick and clay tiles.

The large flat area to the E of the Tweed was identified in the 1968 Central Borders Plan for development by the *SSHA* as TWEEDBANK, intended to expand the burgh's population to 25,000. Two housing clusters in a landscaped setting around the man-made Gun Knowe Loch, which provides a pleasant setting on its N side for the PRIMARY SCHOOL on Cotgreen Road. Built *c.* 1976. Cream rendered single-storey with a courtyard plan. At the E end is an industrial estate, intended to encourage successors to the burgh's declining traditional industries. Linking the scheme to the burgh is a road bridge of 1978.

INDUSTRIAL BUILDINGS

Twenty-eight weaving mills once operated along the Gala Water valley but a major decline of the textiles industries followed the Second World War, and although Galashiels is today a distinguished centre of design, manufacturing no longer provides its economic focus. The majority of mill buildings have been demolished or renovated for multiple occupancy.

BOTANY MILL, Roxburgh Street. 1797. Built by Hugh Sanderson & Son as Weirhaugh Mill; a long eight-bay, three-storey whinstone mill. Large four-storey addition to rear, 1829.

BRISTOL MILL, Bristol Terrace. 1885. Built by Roberts Dobson & Co. as a spinning mill for Victoria Mill at the head of Buckholm Mill Brae. Two storeys, whinstone with yellow sandstone margins and segmental-headed windows. Early 1920s brick-built additions at the N end of the site.

GALA MILL, Huddersfield Street. Originally built 1826 as Wake-field Mill but most of the earlier buildings demolished in the late C20. Impressive whinstone three-storey, five-bay many-gabled late C19 front block with bipartite windows and red sandstone margins. 120

GALABANK MILL (BMR), Huddersfield Street. 1818. Built as a three-storey mill by Richard Lees. Dyehouse added 1919 and other extensions in 1937.

Former HIGH MILL, Paton Road. 1866. The tower of the whin-stone four-storey High Mill (renamed Valley Mill) was removed in 1984. Converted by *Duncan Cameron & Associates* for super-market warehousing; the easternmost sheds survive reused. Two-storey whinstone warehouse and two-storey, seven-bay offices on S side of road, now used by the Territorial Army.

Former NETHER MILL, Huddersfield Street (now Lochcarron and Galashiels Mill Museum). 1804–5 for James Bathgate and Partners. Three-storey and attic whinstone mill with three-storey extension of 1866, contemporary with beam-engine house to N and five bays of weaving sheds parallel to Hudders-field Street.

NETHERDALE MILL, Nether Road. The original 1857 mill, for J. & W. Cochrane of Mid Mill, by *R. & A. Stirling*, was demol-ished 1976. The High Mill survives. Fourteen-bay weaving sheds of 1866; the classical engine house and ten-bay, single-storey office block date to 1893. This was the largest textile mill in Galashiels, employing 650 workers at its peak; now in mul-tiple occupancy.

RIVERSIDE MILL, Wheatlands Road. Two-storey weaving sheds survive in secondary occupation on Mill Park; offices are in converted 1920s flats. Weaving sheds built by Brown Bros. in 1883–4 on the NE bank of the river were associated with the 1846 'Buckholm Mill' (dem. 1975).

TWEED MILL, King Street. 1851–2. Built by *Randolph, Elder & Co.* of Glasgow for Peter & Robert Sanderson. High Mill: prominent two-storey and attic with pair of stair-towers; West Mill: three-storey and ten bays long. High Mill extended in 1949; new offices 1959.

VICTORIA DYEWORKS, Paton Street. Converted by James Brownlee from the Galashiels Gas Co. premises. Two-storey mill of 1833 with full-length roof-lights and louvred ventilator. Three-bay, two-storey office block of 1866.

WAULKRIGG MILL, Duke Street. Built by James Mitchell in 1866 as long two-storey whinstone Tweed Place Mill with weaving sheds. SE block, 1890, for Cochrane Dorward. Two-storey brick building to E end of the mill by 1910, office block and weaving sheds of 1920. Partly converted to flats.

Former WAVERLEY MILL, Huddersfield Street. 1886 for J. & W. Roberts, partly on the site of Thomas Aimers' engineering works (founded 1744). Two-storey and three-storey and attic four-bay offices, single-storey rubble workshops and foundry survive from the later C18.

WHEATLANDS MILL, Paton Street. 1865–6, built by Arthur

Dickson. Ranges of five- and seven-bay whinstone and brick
weaving sheds on the sw bank of the Gala Water, in multiple
occupancy from as early as 1942. se part extended 1960 and
again for a 1970s office block.

FORT and BROCH, Torwoodlee, c. 2 km. NW. The broch is encircled by a ditch and measures 12 m. in diameter within the
stump of a wall over 5 m. in thickness. The checked entrance
is on the ESE, flanked on the s by a guard chamber, and there
is a mural chamber containing a stair on the sw. Excavation
has shown that the broch was built about CI A.D. It overlies a
fort, but quarrying and cultivation have all but obliterated large
sectors of the earlier defences.

BUCKHOLM TOWER. See p. 143.
COLMSLIE TOWER. See p. 191.
GLENMAYNE HOUSE. See p. 330.
HILLSLAP TOWER. See p. 379.
LAIDLAWSTIEL. See p. 479.
TORWOODLEE HOUSE. See p. 726.
WINDYDOORS. See p. 762.

GARVALD HOUSE
1040
7.2 km. sw of West Linton

Now a Rudolph Steiner School and Training Centre. Built soon
after 1827, following purchase of the estate by John Allan
Woddrop of Dalmarnock.

Originally of three bays, two storeys and basement, with single-
storey piend-roofed pavilions. s front of coursed white ashlar,
the rest in red sandstone. Giant corner pilasters and advanced
centre bay with an Ionic portico, windows with framed architraves; those on the ground floor have consoles. In the mid
1860s the e pavilion was raised a storey and extended, and a
large conservatory (dem. c. 1970) inserted behind the façade
of the w one. A late C19 two-storey NW addition in similar style
with a balustraded bay window and two square clusters of
chimneys above. Inside are decorative cornices and marble
chimneypieces; the one in the dining room is Scottish Renaissance of the 1860s. Large and lofty late C19 stair hall, apparently designed to house an organ. The oak staircase, with plain
and twisted balusters, was cut back at the bottom when it was
removed. On the first floor wide semicircular arches with
moulded surrounds, pilasters and keystones.

Small and compact STABLES, NE, probably c. 1860 for
William Allan Woddrop (monogram over the wide pend). –
SYCAMORE HOUSE in the trees to the SE, by Christopher
Butler-Cole of Campbell & Arnott, is for residential and staff
accommodation with space for music and other activities, providing a less monastic atmosphere than Steiner principles
usually afford. A single-storey block (1989) with two-storey
addition (1993), strongly shaped in red brick with wide timber
overhanging eaves and red tile roofs. – HILL COTTAGE, to the
N, was extended in the 1990s. – GARVALD HOME FARM, to
the NE, a courtyard range of c. 1840, was partly converted for
a meeting hall by Morris & Steedman, 1997. Pedimented

archway topped by a bellcote. Inside the court are steadings, a rubble-built farmhouse with a slated timber porch and good spearhead railings to its garden, and four cottages with wall-head pedimented dormers. Opposite the farm a BARN has pigeon holes of unusual design. Twelve open stone pigeon boxes, corbelled out above a door. The barn was adapted to a threshing(?) mill *c.* 1860; the wheel gearing survives. – WALLED GARDEN with a baluster SUNDIAL dated 1832: foliaceous carving, egg-and-dart cornice and scrolled bracket gnomon. – LODGE. Single-storey, *c.* 1840, in white and pink sandstone. Bipartite windows with scrolled consoled cornices and a heraldic pediment. – A GATEWAY,* erected here in 1864, comprised late C16 and C17 fragments possibly from the old house of Ingraston.

GATTONSIDE   5030

Gattonside was originally included in grants of land to Melrose Abbey by David I. Later, holdings were cultivated for orchards, which became celebrated for their fruit. Its plan is still medieval but with a late C18 nucleus and villas scattered among trees in one of the most brilliant landscapes in Scotland. One principal road (B6360) runs through the village from W to E, with narrow and crooked lanes on either side; not a conventional Borders village layout.

DESCRIPTION. Among single- and two-storey cottages, which border the lanes higgledy-piggledy, are HASSENDEAN COTTAGE, W of Hoebridge House (*see* below), probably late C18, harled with sandstone painted margins, and HOLLY-BANK, further W, sited high up and looking S towards the Tweed. Rendered with painted margins. EILDON VIEW and GLENCAIRN, mid-C19 whinstone houses with red sandstone dressings, have their fronts to a small green and backs to the main road. Doorways with stepped pediments and label stops.
The WAR MEMORIAL of 1919, on the E side of the road from the suspension bridge (*see* below) is a red sandstone cross standing on a plinth.
The presence of Sir Walter Scott at Abbotsford inspired the building of summer VILLAS by professional men and their families. At the E end of the village are two good works by Scott's builder, *John Smith*. The classical ABBOTSMEADOW is of 1826   111 for Thomas Scott, lawyer in Melrose. Classical two-storey, of three bays, its front built of small, brick-sized blocks of whinstone, whose darkness is relieved by light sandstone dressings. The red sandstone corner margins on the N side are said to be from Melrose Abbey, which was then being restored by Smith for Sir Walter Scott. Inside, good plasterwork and stone stair, with curving cast-iron balustrade and slim mahogany handrail. Tall arched window flanked by niches. A single-storey WEST LODGE, originally a cottage, is dated 1781.
    ALLERLY, nearby, was built in 1823 by *John Smith* for Dr   110 David Brewster, literary buff, scientist and expert in optics.

*Now owned by the Biggar Museum Trust, Lanarkshire.

Some C20 additions. Comparable in scale and treatment to
Abbotsmeadow, but in buff-coloured coursed ashlar with tripartite windows recessed in tall relieving arches. On the w elevation, three large conservatory-style windows are designed to
catch the setting sun; perhaps inspired by the conservatory at
Abbotsford. Inside, a central vestibule and staircase hall with
a fireplace. To the r., a bow-ended dining room, to the l. the
drawing room, both with simple marbled timber chimneypieces. Single-storey whinstone STABLES to the N, with dressed
margins, and a central high pedimented archway. GARDEN
ROOM in the NE corner of the garden wall, with a small Gothic
window, perhaps Brewster's summer study. At the gate is a
picturesque whinstone LODGE with bargeboarded gables and
overhanging eaves.

FRIAR'S HALL at the E end of village, s of the road, was possibly built to replace the Fryarshall shown on General Roy's
map, c. 1747. This may explain the thick walls in the cellar of
the present house. In the late C18 it is recorded that John and
Thomas Tod, both lawyers, 'resided in a pretty cottage they
built and thatched with heather'. The two-storey shallow
bow on the garden (s) elevation was formerly the principal
entrance. It has a large tripartite window on the first floor
above sash windows on either side of a door. Two-storey w
addition of the 1820s for Thomas Tod of Drygrange, also the
date of the pillared entrance doorway on the otherwise undistinguished N elevation. Mid-C20 E addition. Inside, the oval
entrance hall has remnants of a late C18 painted imitation panelled dado, while the oval room on the first floor has a heavily
decorative, broad chimneypiece in timber and gesso thick with
beading. The stone staircase with cast-iron balusters is of the
1820s.

GATTONSIDE HOUSE, w end of the village, s of the B6360.
Originally a classical villa, built c. 1808–11, which was acquired
by George Cole Bainbridge, a retired Liverpool banker and
keen flyfisher,* who displaced the previous tenants, Sir Walter
Scott's friends Sir Adam and Lady Ferguson. Bainbridge
employed *John Smith*, 1824, to considerably enlarge the house;
a further addition was made c. 1860 and again in 1913–14 by
Robert S. Lorimer for E.B. Ebsworth. The early C19 house is of
five bays, built in whinstone rubble with cream sandstone
dressings, with a central bowed projection to the s front and a
shallow, semicircular Ionic-colonnaded arcaded porch. Set
back are two-storey wings, added by Smith, with straight
passage links. On the N side, the area between the wings is filled
by a three-bay block of c. 1860, with a solid entrance porch
surmounted by a stone balustrade. The central bay is slightly
advanced; the attic projecting above the wall-head contains a
Diocletian window and a stack of ten chimneys across the top.
Lorimer's additions are utilitarian, externally at least. He
extended the w wing and raised both it and the connecting link
by a storey to provide a business room, billiard room and
bedroom. A two-storey canted bay was added on the s front,
and a single-storey one on the w elevation, where an arched

* He published *The Fly Fisher's Guide* in 1816.

loggia (now blocked) was formed by lowering the ground. The N porch leads into an outer hall. On the S side is a double-height, top-lit inner hall; it has an arcaded upper gallery with Ionic columns. Also on the S side is the original oval vestibule of the early C19 house (now an oratory).* The principal staircase to the E, carved out of the link corridor and part of a boudoir, appears to be *c.* 1860. The W dog-legged corridor (by Lorimer with the decorators *Scott Morton & Co.*) to the large billiard room and business room was given a continuous barrel vault with cross-ribs. A double-height schoolroom was 'contrived' in the E wing.

At the E end is a CHAPEL designed and built, from 1921 to 1972, with great dedication by Brother *Columba Farrelly*. A simple rectangular block with a pitched roof. Coursed squared rubble and sandstone dressings, with round-headed windows, and N entrance porch with a circular window above. Unplastered interior with a Norman chancel arch of chevron pattern. – STAINED GLASS. Chancel: three-light window of the Nativity.

The STABLES, 1826, by *John Smith*, were remodelled to take motor vehicles by *Lorimer*, 1913–14. Converted for housing by *Duncan Cameron & Associates*, late C20. – WEST LODGE. Smith, 1826. Gabled cottage with a bay window, and porch with timber columns. Addition of the 1980s in keeping with the rest.

HOEBRIDGE HOUSE (formerly Gattonside Villa) is much altered. Built by Dr Turner, a naval surgeon, who was present at the Battle of Waterloo. His house was of two storeys and three bays, in red sandstone with rusticated quoins at the angles, and the centre bay slightly advanced (the bowed window on the E front may be later). Extended W by two bays and covered by a platform roof. Later canted bay windows, one since adapted as the entrance with an attractive timber porch. A high stone wall, brick-lined on the inner face, surrounds the large front garden, part of the original orchard. Large ornamental cast-iron gates.

THE RIG, E end of village. Of 1956–7 by *Peter Womersley* for himself. He described it as 'a very simple, cheap, traditional load-bearing sand-lime brick structure' on a 3ft (0.91m.) grid with timber-framed windows filled with a mixture of clear and maroon glazing. It has a Miesian open plan; square with rooms arranged in a U-shape round a nearly central cedarwood-clad core containing cupboards, heating plant, and top-lit bathroom. Living room and study occupy the S side, with the living room set slightly lower than the neighbouring spaces. Each 'room' in the living area shares a cupboard unit or seating with its neighbour. The principal entrance is approached from the W by a covered way alongside the S wall of the garage, which later became the drawing office; as the practice grew the accommodation expanded uphill. *p. 320*

ACHNACAIRIDH, on the S side of the village with an open aspect to the Tweed. Of 1967 by *Duncan Cameron* for himself. Cameron worked in Womersley's office and followed his design

---

* Chimneypieces recorded by RCAHMS (1956) have disappeared.

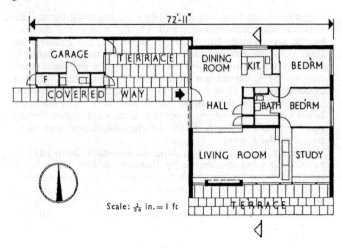

Gattonside, The Rig.
Plan.

philosophy. Brick and glass, planned around a central core of
services linked to the bedrooms and sunken living area.

PAVILION, 1.6 km. w. A low rambling mansion, started by
Benjamin Bell, an Edinburgh surgeon, who sold it *c.* 1805 to
the agriculturist and Lord of the King's Bedchamber, John
Southey, fourteenth Lord Somerville. It seems that the stables
only had been finished, so Somerville adapted them by raising
the walls to form a two-storey house of five bays with a three-
bay centre, defined by flat pilaster strips, beneath a pediment
with a carving of coronet, garlands and an oculus. Three
round-headed windows at ground floor and a plain red sandstone band course. Several additions were made later, including a wing by *John Smith*, 1811, of hollow wall construction;★
possibly the two-storey, one-bay range to the r. Flanking the
house are two blocks, possibly early or mid-C19. The one to
the s (now a separate house) has a raised pediment supported
by consoles, canted bay window and small, columned porch.
To the N are single-storey offices.

88 GATTONSIDE SUSPENSION FOOTBRIDGE, s across the Tweed
to Melrose (q.v.). Until reconstruction in 1991, the only unaltered survivor of the earliest suspension bridge technology, it
was manufactured and erected in 1826 by *Redpath, Brown &
Co.* to designs by *John Smith*. Originally the two castellated
stone pylons with Gothic arches supported four suspending
chains, two on each side, with a flat timber deck hung from
the chains by iron rods. Strengthening by *Borders Regional
Council* altered the character of the bridge by introducing new
chains, hangers and deck. – Single-storey and attic three-bay
TOLLHOUSE at the Melrose end, attributed to John Smith,

★ RIBA *Transactions*, 1837.

1826. Coursed and pinned rubble. Square hoodmoulds over windows, with twelve-pane glazing pattern. Later timber porch and canted attic dormers.

GAVINTON   1050

An estate village built on a regular plan by David Gavin of Langton House, after he purchased the estate in 1758. Feus were offered on easy terms. Most of the housing dates from the late C18, all with mid–late C19 additions or alterations.

Former FREE CHURCH, w end of the village. Now a house. Built in 1843 by the Dowager Marchioness of Breadalbane. Tudor style. The main three-bay s face is of buff snecked rubble with rectangular hoodmoulded windows. Abandoned for worship in 1950. Some way on into the village is Woodside, the former MANSE, also 1843. Traditional, with a pilastered and mutuled doorcase.

LANGTON PARISH CHURCH. Proudly positioned on a sloping site at the w end of the village. Built in 1872 (replacing a church of 1798) for Lady Elizabeth Pringle of Langton House by *J. M. Wardrop* in a not entirely successful attempt to adapt the English mid-C13 style to the needs of a Scottish preaching hall. The s face, overlooking the churchyard, is of buff stugged ashlar; it is divided into two double bays by a central buttress and has two-light windows with Geometric tracery. The rubble N face is unbuttressed, and has only two windows. A timber porch at the w end opens into a vestibule and vestry. The finest feature is a three-storey E tower of rock-faced ashlar, capped by an octagonal stone spire with angle pinnacles and lucarnes. The porch at the base of this tower opened onto the laird's pew.

Inside, an arch-braced roof. The railed enclosure for the communion table and pulpit at the w end are backed by blind arcading framing marble panels with the Lord's Prayer and Ten Commandments. At the opposite end, on the first floor of the tower, is an organ loft opening into the church through an arch with a traceried balustrade.

CHURCHYARD. The continuing Borders tradition of full-length portraits on gravestones is seen in that of Charles Moir, †1832. Carved Celtic cross WAR MEMORIAL, *c.* 1920.

OLD PARISH CHURCH, in the grounds of the demolished Langton House (*see* below); rebuilt 1736. Its site is perpetuated in a derelict burial vault, the main face having an arched window on each side of a blocked doorway, above which is a gable with a skull and crossed bones.

DESCRIPTION

The Parish Church (*see* above) stands close to the start of NORTH STREET at the principal entrance to the village from the w, which is marked on the s side by MYRTLE COTTAGE, with scrolled skewputts and a round-arched window in the w gable with moulded imposts and large keystone. The mid-C19 OLD

SCHOOL HOUSE at the end of this terrace has a plain front
facing the Green. Opposite is the former LANGTON PUBLIC
SCHOOL (School House) of 1874. T-plan, mullioned and transomed windows with shouldered surrounds, and a large corbelled-out bellcote with ball finial. Gabled porches at each end
with carved ribands on the gables, the W one inscribed 'By
Industry we Prosper'. Two diagonally set chimneystacks,
sawtooth copes and gablet-kneelered skewputts. Horizontal-
pane glazing. Further down are JUBILEE COTTAGES, dated
1897, one of a few with their fronts to the street. VICTORIA
COTTAGE, also dated 1897, has rolled skewputts indicating a
refronting of an earlier house; three gabled dormerheads with
obelisk finials. NORWOOD has a Tudor hoodmould over the
doorway, and a mid-C19 high wall with a moulded cope, and
a hoodmoulded Tudor-arched gateway; at the apex is a carved
head, another to the l., which are said to have come from
Langton House (see below). At the foot of North Street is the
former MANSE (Coonanglebah); late C18 with mid-C19 additions and alterations. Two-storey and attic, three bays in harl-
pointed sandstone rubble and polished margins. The street
elevation has a round-arched stair window, the S front a porch
with cornice and parapet, and former stables and steading projecting from the E end.

SOUTH STREET has houses on both sides, those on the S side
facing away from the street. A late C19 cast-iron water PUMP
on the N side has a fluted shaft, lion-head spout and fluted
coping with a bud finial. Two-storey WOODVILLE has blind
windows with painted astragals, and a tall stair window. An
earlier single-storey wing to l. with scrolled skewputts. The
interior is of interest, including a timber chimneypiece with
fluted pilastered jambs and gesso decoration, and a panelled
dado in the dining room. On the N side, GREYSTONE has
wall-head dormers dated 1772–1854. On the S side, to the r. of
EDEN HOUSE, is a moulded stone gateway in a rubble wall,
probably from Langton House.

THE GREEN at the top has GAVINTON HALL at the SE corner,
a mid-C19 former school with a corbelled-out bellcote.
CHEVIOT VIEW, S side, has evidently been a house of some
importance. A steep roof with tall brick chimneystacks and a
strange moulded window margin in the W gable that suggests
an attempted hoodmould or lugged surround. To the r. is a
square gatepier with key-pattern frieze, decorated cornice and
pyramidal cope, the rubble boundary wall finishing in a stable
entry with round gatepiers with ball finials.

LANGTON ESTATE

LANGTON HOUSE, rebuilt in grand Neo-Elizabethan style by
David Bryce, c. 1862(?), for the second Marquess of Breadalbane, was demolished *c.* 1950. Some estate buildings survive.
– TERRACE LODGE. Late C19, L-plan with a three-stage square
conical-roofed tower with weathervane. Decoratively pierced
bargeboards. – GATEWAY. By *D. & J. Bryce, c.* 1877. An extrav-
agant Neo-Jacobean exercise with tall pulvinated piers topped
by obelisks, flanked by corniced pedestrian entrances sur-

mounted by strapwork pediments. Balustraded walls with
carved strapwork, linking to further piers with obelisk finials
and carved urns. Contemporary cast-iron gates, delicately
wrought. – NORTH LODGE. Single-storey Jacobean-style
lodge, monogrammed and dated 1877. – KENNELMAN'S
HOUSE. Late C19. Canted bays corbelled to a square at wall-
head height, ending in large gables with ornate, trefoil-pierced
bargeboards. Plain kennels to the NW. – The WALLED GARDEN
has tall, red brick walls divided into buttressed bays, the
moulded wall cope continuing as a segmental pediment over
each bay.

THE HARDENS FARM. 2.5 km. N of the village. A gabled, single-
storey and attic, three-bay farmhouse with 1860s remodelling,
e.g. bargeboards similar to the Kennelman's House (q.v.), but
also good ranges of earlier C19 (and later) steadings and
cartsheds. Well-built granary, erected during the tenancy of the
Hon. Robert Baillie-Hamilton, 1866–79. Cotswold Tudor-style
farm cottages, possibly c. 1866, with gabled stone porches and
bands of fish-scale grey slates and red tiles.

RAECLEUCHHEAD, 2.5 km. NW. Built by the second Marquess
of Breadalbane, c. 1856, as a farmhouse with a large balconied
dining room for shooting parties. Alpine-style, with deep overhanging eaves with exposed rafters. Two storeys and attic in
red sandstone rubble composed of large stones.

GILSTON PELE   4050
6.2 km. SE of Heriot

The much altered remains of what may have been a small tower
house or pele of late C16 or early C17 date. Oblong on plan
(9.6 m. by 6.7 m.), built of local rubble with sparse use of sandstone dressings, it comprises two storeys (perhaps originally
three) beneath a half-hipped roof. Only two small windows,
one formerly barred, in the SE wall are original survivals. The
interior was probably always unvaulted. Successive alterations
have included the insertion of a timber forestair on one side
and the construction of a single-storey extension at the NW
end. Restored and extended by *Paul Linton c.* 2000.

GLEDSWOOD HOUSE   5030
2.8 km N of Dryburgh

A Regency villa built c. 1805 as a summer retreat for William   73
Sibbald, a Leith merchant. Single-storey and basement.
Entrance (S) front of polished ashlar, framed by paired Doric
columns (on bases) supporting a heavy blocking course; in the
centre are wide circular steps to the semicircular Doric portico
and pilastered doorway. Tripartite windows each side. The W
and E elevations, of coursed rubble, have bowed projections.
On the W elevation, the garden door is framed by fluted
pilasters and a frieze of serpents consuming their tails.
The lower part of the N extension, in whinstone rubble, is

probably early C19; its first floor is 1860s. Identically styled NW
and NE pavilions of 1994 by *Thom Pollock* (of the *Pollock
Hammond Partnership*) for Lord Portarlington. Inside, a tiny oval
vestibule leads to a similarly small hall squeezed between the
drawing room and dining room. Good statuary marble chimneypiece in the drawing room; in the dining room is a buffet
recess flanked by fluted pilasters with acanthus-leaf capitals.

EAST LODGE. Mid-C19, crowned by a cluster of four
octagonal chimneys. Well-designed additions by *Pollock,
Hammond Partnership*, 1994. – WALLED GARDEN, SE, has a semicircular wall open to the S, *c.* 1805. – WEST LODGE, dated 1870.
Broad-eaved with a small gabled porch. A handsome ornamental cast-iron early C19 GATEWAY with square piers of filigree
design topped with gledhawks (red kites). Made (and signed) by
John Anderson of Leith Walk Foundry, who owned the house
from 1817 to 1832. – 0.4 km. W, built on to the wall on the S side
of the road, is a stone rustic ARCH framing a view of the Eildon
Hills, surmounted by five obelisk-shaped finials. It must have
been put here by George Spottiswoode who owned the house in
the mid C19 (cf. Spottiswoode, q.v., for the prototype).

OLD GLEDSWOOD HOUSE, 0.4 km. W, is an unusual architectural hybrid, part late medieval tower house, part C18 domestic residence and part Victorian stables. Probably first built in
the late C16 by John Robson of Gledswood, the tower
was extended and remodelled in 1703. When the present
Gledswood House (*see* above) was built, the older building was
initially adapted as a farmhouse and then, *c.* 1900, merged with
the adjacent steading.

The tower, at the W end, measures *c.* 6.8 m. square externally, but may initially have incorporated a stair wing at the SE
corner, where the quoins are missing; it originally contained at
least three main storeys. The masonry is of random rubble, formerly harled, with red sandstone dressings. The W wall, which
became the W gable of the remodelled house, shows a roughly
constructed plinth, a wide-mouthed gunloop on the ground
floor and blocked windows at first- and second-floor levels.
The windows have round-arrised margins, and the first-floor
one has a dripmould like those at Hillslap Tower and Buckholm Tower (qq.v.). The N wall has a similar, but smaller,
gunloop on the first floor, while the harling of the S wall has
peeled to reveal a blocked first-floor window wrought with a
quirked edge-roll. The early C18 house was formed by extending the tower E to make a symmetrically planned oblong block
of two storeys and an attic *c.* 15.7 m. long. The masonry is
similar to that of the tower, but the windows have chamfer-arrised margins and the gables are crowstepped with
cavetto-moulded skewputts. The five-bay S front has a bolection-moulded central doorway with an entablature bearing the
initials of Patrick Redpath and his wife, Joan Scott, with the
date 1703.

Initially the early C18 house probably had a central scale-
and-platt stair with a single main room on either side at each
level, but subsequently it was subdivided to form two
dwellings, a second entrance being contrived alongside the
original one. A single-storey office wing was also added to the
E gable, and a new first-floor doorway, approached by a

forestair, formed in the N wall. The interior is mainly of *c.* 1900, when the ground floor was fitted out as a stable and bothy and the first floor as a hay loft. Almost the only relic of the tower house is a first-floor latrine in the N wall, which is equipped with a fixed seat and (presumably) a mural discharge chute.

THE GLEN
4 km. SW of Traquair

2030

A commanding Scottish Baronial house built on a plateau above 76 the Quair Water for Charles Tennant of the St Rollox Chemical Works, Glasgow. He purchased the estate in 1853, acquiring a late C18 farmhouse, with classical additions by *W. H. Playfair*, which he demolished. The present house was designed by *David Bryce*, first in 1854, with *Robert Hall* as contractor, in a relaxed almost Scottish Domestic style. In 1874 Bryce added a formidable six-storey tower house in the S angle.

EXTERIOR. The house is approached across a two-span pointed-arch bridge of 1874, with buttressed triangular refuges for pedestrians. A castellated ARCHWAY beckons, fortified by angle bartizans decorated with rope mouldings, the wing walls ornamented with circular gunloops and trefoils. A panel above the arch blazons 'Salve', and on the court side 'Vale'. The entrance courtyard is spacious, with steps and gateway to the garden guarded by two stone lions, their paws resting on stone balls, of 1928. Bryce's first house is an asymmetrical composition mostly of two storeys, attic and exposed basement, built in coursed cream sandstone. Characteristic of Bryce are the crowstepped gables, conical-roofed turrets with fish-scale slates, wall-head dormers with decorative pediments, and canted bays corbelled to the square. A string course between

The Glen.
Perspective by David Bryce, 1874.

ground and first floors meanders attractively round the house up and over windows, and as the top row of corbel courses.

The projecting ENTRANCE TOWER on the NW façade has an ornate version of the oriel at Maybole Castle, Ayrshire, in a slightly corbelled-out crowstepped gable, with a lion sitting on the apex. Behind is a machicolated open-balustraded platform, with an ogee-roofed turret. The Renaissance doorway, which appears to be based on that at Cullen House (Moray), has an aedicular-framed window above with colonnettes, and incorporates a heraldic panel and text: BLISSET BE GOD FOR ALL HIS GIFTIS and THEY AR WELCOME HERE QVHA THE LORD DO FEIR. To the l. a moulded panel with the monogram DB AD 1855, with a Corinthian column.

The family wing is to the r. of the entrance with its principal elevation to the SW, comprising a crowstepped gable with a corner turret to the l., a plain projecting gable in the centre corbelled out from the round, and a full-height conical-roofed canted bay with wall-head pedimented dormers. This was once more prominent before the 'TOWER HOUSE' was built in 1874. This quite spoils the domestic character of the first build. It is square, battlemented, of six storeys and three square pepper-pot turrets (modelled on those at Pinkie House, Musselburgh) to the attic with a sham parapet walk between the SW ones. Its SE front has instead three decorated pedimented dormers rising from the crenellated parapet.

Adjacent to the r. on this side is the garden front of the earlier house, of a nearly symmetrical type often used by Bryce. Here, two-storey canted bays, corbelled out to a square at attic level with crowstepped gables, flank a lower central section with pedimented wall-head dormers. Conical angle tower at the S corner and a small one at the E corner corbelled out from the first floor. In front of this range is a long balustraded balcony with steps at each end to the garden, supported by a Renaissance arcade of segmental arches ornamented with alternate raised voussoirs. It was added by *Robert S. Lorimer c.* 1905, who incorporated an existing balcony of 1854 on this side, as part of a remodelling of the garden terrace. This main block is linked to the kitchen offices, laundry etc. at the NE end. The offices were converted to a private house by *Simpson & Brown*, 2000. Crowstepped and dormered, with a bellcote tucked away at a lower level. Except for Lorimer's work, the exterior is as originally built: the only change was made by Christopher Tennant, second Lord Glenconner, who disliked Baronial architecture and changed all the plate glass windows to Georgian astragals and removed vase finials and stone cresting from the bay window parapets.

The layout of the INTERIOR still conforms to Bryce's plan of a symmetrical suite of rooms along the garden front – dining room, library and drawing room – with further public rooms added in 1874. *Robert S. Lorimer* was called in, however, to reinstate the interior decoration after a fire in 1905. Gothic woodwork and carving executed by *Scott Morton & Co.*, with excellent hand-moulded plasterwork by *Thomas Beattie*. The Bryce HALL, with Jacobean decoration, was mostly reconstructed by Lorimer, who gave the steel ceiling beams a rounded plaster covering enriched with a flowing vine and grape pattern. Bryce's lush Jacobean-style chimneypiece was replaced in the late C20 with a simple marble moulded one. The partition between hall and main stair was removed in the 1930s by the decorator, *Syrie Maugham*, who boxed in the staircase but kept Lorimer's ceiling over the stair with twining stems and leaves and a fleur-de-lys motif in the central dome.

The rooms along the S E front start with the DINING ROOM to the l. Lorimer's fine Scottish Renaissance ceiling – considered too 'Baronial' for the second Lord Glenconner who covered it up – is now revealed as a splendid affair, executed *in situ* by Beattie. A central roundel, a large shell at each end, with fruit and flowers, and guilloche pattern on the flat ribs. The chimneypiece is late C20 but in keeping with Lorimer's decoration. The LIBRARY, next along, is all Lorimer, and in oak, including the Renaissance chimneypiece. The bookcases, supported by brackets with dog-like creatures, are carved with garlands, and the ceiling panel decorated with fruit and flowers. Next are two DRAWING ROOMS. The first (of 1854) is linked to the second (of 1874) by wide doors. Both were redecorated *c.* 1925 by *Lenygon & Co.* in an understated classical manner, similar to that at Floors Castle (q.v.). Quite elegant, but what work by Bryce and Lorimer has been removed? The chimneypiece with a continuous fret frieze and Ionic jambs is probably part of the 1920s furnishings. The remaining rooms along the S W front are entered from the hall. The present LARGE SITTING ROOM is *Syrie Maugham*'s work, made out of three rooms (the 'Walnut Room', billiard room, and small drawing room). She lowered the ceiling, probably obscuring at least one of Lorimer's ceilings. Dummy book runs now decorate some of the walls.

The private 'PELICAN STAIR', in the S corner of the Hall, leading to the bedroom floor and attics, is a pleasant diversion by Lorimer. The central oak newel and balusters have spiral flutings. On top of this 'totem pole' sits a pelican on her nest decorated with grinning masks. Off the bedroom corridor the square GREEN ROOM, with a deeply coved ceiling, domed in the centre, with vine branches climbing up the ribs, and vines everywhere. Further along the ZODIAC ROOM has a coved compartmented ceiling with branches up the corners, and roses decorating the ribs. Carvings of twelve signs of the Zodiac, three on each wall. The HUNTING ROOM, at the top of the entrance tower, survived the fire of 1905. It was very likely originally used as a smoking room. Decorated in Italian style with a game bird theme, by *Purdie* and *Thomas Bonnar Jun.*, who was Purdie's apprentice here in 1893. Red and blue are the dominant colours. The flat, slightly coved ceiling was given a hint of a tent canopy, with game birds in the cove with ribands and sprays. The painting of the family dogs above the oriel window must be mid-to-late C20.

GARDENS. Impressive terraced gardens by Bryce, 1854. Later alterations by Lorimer, *c.* 1905. 1 km. S of the house, at the end of an avenue of Douglas firs, is the TEMPLE, formerly a summerhouse adapted from the portico of Playfair's house of 1822. Rubble work for the rear wall, and a timber ceiling of interlocking circles. In the rear wall, and catching the setting sun, is some engraved glass by *Luke Dickinson*, 1997. Inscribed LIKE BRIGHT SHINING COMETS THEY BURNT OUT SO YOUNG TOUCHING EVERYONE THEY MET. In memory of Charles Tennant, 1957–96, and Henry Tennant, 1960–90.

The STABLES, opposite the entrance tower, have a crow-stepped gabled pend with a balustraded wall-head, rope mouldings, gunloops and a clock. An irregular court behind with coach houses.

ESTATE BUILDINGS. Mostly built by estate masons and joiners, between the late 1850s and 1890. The entrance LODGE is crow-stepped with a corner pepperpot turret. An archway, dated 1858, over the drive ends in a bartizan to the l. A large rope motif over the arch. Good gates with fleur-de-lys motif and a tall central tulip. The road continues up the hill, and on the r. are the KENNELS dated 1888, with braced gables and a gabled stone porch. Four sets of kennels to the rear, with a small off-centre pediment. Next along is FEACHEN VIEW, dated 1889, three superior cottages with timber, columned entrance porches in the W, S and E elevations. THE OLD SCHOOL, of coursed squared rubble with bargeboards, was built *c.* 1869 for the children of estate workers. This was one of the earliest of the estate buildings, and its style and details became the pattern, with variations, for the later buildings. At the top of the hill the CARTSHEDS (*c.* 1854) are all that remain of an extensive steading. Eight segmental arches with gabled dormerheads. To the l., a long single-storey, seven-bay building, built as a communal HALL.

Behind the steading, up the l. side of the Kill Burn, is a row of eight labourers' COTTAGES. Further on are the derelict kennels known as 'Feachen Castle', and on the opposite side of the burn a large derelict walled garden, probably *c.* 1854. NW of the steading is a PIGGERY with two piend-roofed rectangular blocks built across the hillside and a timber dovecot sitting on a shallow corbelled-out gable. On the other side of the farm road, a wrought-iron GATEWAY, decorated with fleurs-de-lys and spirals. To the l. SILO VIEW, dated 1903, has tacked on the back NURSERY COTTAGES, quite palatial bothies.

The WALLED GARDEN appears to date from *c.* 1909. A long, slightly curved buttressed wall with a turreted tower at each end. A timber-lined room in the S tower is used as a summerhouse. A suitable reminder above the door: WHILE THE EARTH REMAINETH SEED TIME AND HARVEST SHALL NOT CEASE. Wrought-iron gateway. This imposing section of the garden wall is probably part of Lorimer's work. – GREENHOUSES by *Mackenzie & Moncur*.

At the end of the farm road is the FARMHOUSE with bracketed overhanging eaves, wide casement windows and fluted octagonal chimneys. The picturesque octagonal DAIRY has a gabled timber porch sheltering two doorways to the preparation room and store.

GLENBURN HALL

6020

1.1 km. SW of Jedburgh

Classical house, built by Thomas Ormiston *c.* 1815. Rusticated pilaster quoins, base and sill courses, with an eaves cornice and prominent ball-finialled balustrade. Piended and platformed roof. The slightly advanced centre bay in the front elevation has a block pediment on the parapet. Wide balustraded steps to a Roman Doric distyle porch with ball finials. The other elevations are similarly detailed. The top-lit hall has some delicate plasterwork, the dining room a Corinthian pilastered and corniced buffet and Doric chimneypiece. – WALLED GARDEN and early C19 stables. – Mid-C19 LODGE, with rusticated angle pilasters and pointed-arched openings.

GLENDOUGLAS

6010

3.3 km. S of Jedburgh

A neat, three-bay classical house, *c.* 1805, probably built for the Douglas estate's factor. Advanced centre with a pilastered doorcase, frieze, cornice and blocking course, approached by a flight of steps with cast-iron railings. A wide band course between basement and ground floor, sandstone dressings and raised angle quoins. The drawing room has a good decorative cornice and marble chimneypiece. – STABLES. Converted. Early C19, U-plan. Projecting pavilions with quatrefoils in their pediments. – LODGE with rustic porch.

GLENHOLM

1030

An upland parish containing only fifty-five inhabited houses and a school at the end of the C18; there was evidently no village at that time and there is none today.

OLD PARISH CHURCH. A chapel dependent on Stobo became parochial by the C13. Remodelled in 1775, it was abandoned in 1794. An overgrown rubble-built fragment of the junction of the E and S walls is all that remains. – CHURCHYARD. Some table tombs, one having balusters at one end and rectangular legs with *memento mori* and foliage trails at the other.

MOSSFENNAN HOUSE, 2 km. SE. Probably erected by Robert Welsh, or his son John, in the late C18, with mid-C19 hip-roofed extensions on either side, the S one incorporating a pair of large bay windows to capture the magnificent views E across the Upper Tweed valley.

QUARTER HOUSE, 0.3 km. NW. Built by Thomas Tweedie in 1762 and enlarged and remodelled *c.* 1860. Tall, conical-roofed entrance porch with a panel bearing the date of erection with the initials of the builder and his wife.

WRAE CASTLE, 1.2 km. E. A fragment of a C16 tower house of the Tweedies of Wrae; only part of the stair tower survives.

GLENMAYNE HOUSE
3.2 km. S of Galashiels

A large Baronial villa on an elevated site overlooking the River Tweed. By *Peddie & Kinnear*, 1866, for John Murray, a wool merchant and fellmonger, who co-partnered one of the largest Colonial wool departments in the world. *Robert S. Lorimer* provided a new library wing in 1913; further interior decoration was undertaken by *Scott Morton & Co.*

A random asymmetrical composition of three storeys and exposed basement, with crowstepped gables and conical-roofed turrets with fish-scale slates. String courses define the basement, ground-floor and first-floor levels, continuing round the corbelled-out turrets, and rising and falling under and round the windows. On the NE elevation a projecting five-storey square entrance tower has a round-arched Renaissance doorway with nailhead decoration, a panel above inscribed 1866 JM (John Murray) IS (Isabella Sanderson). The door itself is protected by sliding timber screens which glide into the wall; the gearing mechanism accessed from inside. Above is a projecting arched window, behind a corbelled-out semicircular balcony, with a canopy supported by colonnettes. At the top of the tower, a heavily machicolated parapet with a conical-roofed stair-turret. To the l. of the entrance door, a circular outshot contains a service stair. Almost symmetrical SE elevation with a three-bay centre with pedimented wall-head dormers and a long balustraded balcony on consoled brackets, the ends rounded and corbelled out in the angles with the flanking bays. The canted bay to the r. is crowstepped and corbelled out to a square; that to the l. is bowed, corbelled out to a canted bay, clasped by two bartizans, and then corbelled out to a square. A smooth cope to the gable, scrolled at the top, the small chimneystack with a Maybole-type cope, similar to Drygrange House (q.v.).

The garden elevation (SW) has pedimented wall-head dormers, the circular-headed windows on the first floor lowered later. A wide projecting bay is curved at the angles, corbelled out to the square and finished with a crowstepped gable with chimneystack. The mullioned and transomed opening recessed in a segmental arch at the ground floor was altered later; the balustraded double perron stair leading to the garden and an alcove seat date from 1867. Lorimer's corbelled-out crenellated oriel built at the N corner was placed on top of a crowstepped single-storey former office building.

The ENTRANCE HALL and stairs to the main hall have ribbed ceilings, a Baronial stone chimneypiece, and a frieze of attached mini-columns with a rope theme. The decoration of the wainscotted staircase HALL is mostly of the 1870s. The doors and dado with decorative detailing, the cornice richly carved with gilded vine leaves and grapes, and the coved and ribbed ceiling with a sprinkling of roses on the ribs. A richly carved oak chimneypiece and overmantel employ a mix of Gothic and Renaissance motifs. Fluted Ionic columns, festoons and bay-leaf decoration, and incorporating a page of musical notation and instruments; above is a Gothic niche supported by angels. The Imperial stair has a cast-iron balustrade, and timber-panelled newel posts. A three-light stained-glass window with central depictive panel and Arts and Crafts motifs, made by *Shrigley & Hunt.*

The principal rooms along the SE front begin with the DINING ROOM with a compartmented ceiling and gilded vine cornice. Its black marble chimneypiece, with free-standing clustered columns, is decorated with antiqued prints depicting cherubs, astrolabes and sphinxes, probably taken from a decorator's catalogue and applied to the panelled frieze, and varnished. The DRAWING ROOM is divided into three by lushly decorated Corinthianesque screens. Two white marble chimneypieces, with panelled jambs, and gilded French overmantel mirrors. A motif of piping cherubs on the late C19 wallpaper on the panelled walls, and a Renaissance ribbed ceiling decorated with a continuous trailing vine, and a deep-coved palmetted frieze. Along the SW front is the MUSIC ROOM, revised from the billiard room, with a low panelled dado, and compartmented ceiling decorated with a stylised flat rose decoration; the paper on the frieze has medallions of musical instruments, and there is a gilded cornice of acanthus leaves. Small decorative cast-iron vents in the ceiling probably extracted cigar smoke. A short corridor leads to the library and is Lorimer's work. Panelled walls, a ribbed ceiling, and a row of small leaded lights. Stained glass by *Alexander Strachan*, 1914.

Lorimer's LIBRARY has a concrete roof for fire protection, with a deep-ribbed ceiling and domed cupola circled by garlands; the theme repeated on the frieze. The library shelves have cupboards below, some having Renaissance carved panels with representations of composers, writers and artists, including the Scottish painter R.S. Lauder (1803–69). They have evidently been reused, and possibly date from the 1870s. The 'Globe-Werniker' glazed fronts to the shelves can be removed by slotting them into the ones above. The ravishing white marble chimneypiece is said to be early Italian Renaissance, but is it mid-C18 English moved here from elsewhere in the house? The flat pilaster jambs are panelled with variegated pink marble, there are heads in the volutes of the capitals, and the classical figurative frieze with a central urn is filled with running small boys, carrying musical instruments and quivers and arrows.

LODGE. Asymmetrical, 1869–70, and likely to be *Peddie & Kinnear.* Overhanging timber eaves, a canted bay and timber porch. – ENTRANCE GATES by Lorimer, 1912. Rusticated piers, formerly topped by carved vases; the wrought-iron double-leaved gates are by *Baylis, Johnes & Baylis*, the railing panels by *Thomas Hadden.* – To the NW, the rubble-built WALLED GARDEN, 1867, faced internally with brick. – CONSERVATORY and VINERY, 1869, by *Peddie & Kinnear* and made by *Beards* of Bury St Edmunds. A central octagonal glasshouse with vineries on each side; the E one demolished *c.* 1990. Cast-iron column supports, and narrow timber strips dividing the glazing. – Also by Peddie & Kinnear, an ICE HOUSE, 1868, with a square chamber, drainage hole and top ventilation, and narrow stone ledge round the walls, and simple STABLES, converted to housing.

On the SE terrace is an Italian marble FOUNTAIN with a circular stone basin. Four shell-shaped basins in the centre with spouting dolphins, boys riding on their backs, and on top a circular basin with four clinging tortoises decorating the rim. Below the fountain stand two venerable marble LIONS on large plinths. On the top of the bank a SUNDIAL with baluster-shaped support.

GLENORMISTON HOUSE

3030

2.4 km. NW of Innerleithen

The former mansion of this name was built *c.* 1805 but demolished 1956. The present house is an early C19 two-storey and harled farmhouse and steading built in its policies. It was remodelled and given tripartite windows with narrow sidelights flanking a central doorway, perhaps by the publisher William Chambers, who acquired the estate in 1849. He erected and improved a number of the estate buildings, e.g. the harled GARDENER'S COTTAGE dated 1870, when it was smartened up and given large shouldered chimneystacks. – U-plan mid-C19 STABLES on the former drive are harled, with wide, bracketed eaves and corner pendants. Arched carriage doors with large decorative cast-iron hinges and a pair of large shouldered stacks. – Mid-C19 gabled LODGE with fine decorative cast-iron gateway and railings.

GLENTERNIE HOUSE

2030

2 km. S of Kirkton Manor

A medium-sized Baronial house by *J.M. Wardrop* of *Brown & Wardrop*, 1867–8, for David Kidd of Leyton, Essex. The house is typical Wardrop with many features derived from Bryce. Two and three storeys in coursed whinstone with sandstone margins. Finialled, crowstepped gables, conical turrets, and a mixture of canted and round bays corbelled out to a square. The main block has a crowstepped-gabled porch and lugged bolection-moulded doorway with panel over. In a re-entrant angle to the l., a three-storey tower with turret. Over and under windows runs an intermittent moulded string course. To the r. of the entrance projects a Scottish Domestic STABLE BLOCK, with wide crowstepped gables and a round corner tower, turreted with crosslets. Similar garden elevation with pedimented wall-head windows. The L-plan interior has public rooms in the Bryce manner, with entrance hall and staircase hall in the re-entrant angle. Timber staircase with twisted balusters and panelled newel posts. Decorative cornices and Renaissance-style chimneypieces.

LODGE by *Brown & Wardrop*, 1863. Large and Baronial of whinstone with some cherry-caulking. Gatepiers and decorative cast-iron gates and railings of 1870.

GOLDIELANDS TOWER   4010
3.2 km. SW of Hawick

The roofless shell of the tower house of the Scotts of Goldielands. It probably belongs to the third quarter of the C16 and is similar in design to Burnhead Tower and Timpendean Tower (qq.v.). Oblong on plan (10.5 m. by 7.3 m.), the tower is prominently sited on the right bank of the River Teviot immediately above its confluence with the Borthwick Water, and formerly contained four storeys and a garret. The upperworks have disappeared, but four projecting corbels on the SW wall-head suggest that there was originally a parapeted wall-walk on one or more sides. Whinstone rubble masonry with sandstone dressings used sparingly. Some of the few original windows display chamfer-arrised margins and some round-arrised margins. On the SE side a round-headed doorway, wrought with a quirked edge-roll, leads into a lobby, off which a newel stair rises in the E corner. At the rear of the lobby another door opens into a vaulted storeroom, which originally incorporated an entresol floor entered directly from the stair. The first floor contains what seems to have been a combined hall and kitchen, together with a small, vaulted chamber, perhaps a prison or strongroom, with its own access from the stair. The hall was heated by a big, corbel-lintelled fireplace and was equipped with two aumbries and a slop-sink, as well as at least one good-sized window with bench seats. The second floor contained one or more chambers.

Nothing remains of the oblong BARMKIN shown in Grose's view (1789). It had a large square tower at one corner and what may be a dovecote at the diagonally opposite corner.

GORDON   6040

Groome described the village in the late C19 as one long street 'containing some good shops and dwelling houses',[*] surrounded by moors and moss. First feued in 1778–91, when the inhabitants built their own houses. Its size hardly changed before council housing first appeared in the late 1930s. Traditional single- and two-storey vernacular housing, mostly in whinstone. Some harled, and others rendered and lined out to simulate ashlar.

PARISH CHURCH, W end of the village. The present church, of 1897, by *Dunn & Findlay* replacing one of 1763, has harled walls and pink sandstone dressings. The main S front is symmetrical, having a doorway in a gabled salient towards each end (that to the W inscribed 'rebuilt 1897'), and with four tall pointed windows between. The W gable has a bellcote, and triplets of windows light both E and W walls; a two-bay twin-gabled aisle runs along the central part of the N flank, with a polygonal enclosure for the gallery stair at its W end and a vestry to its E. Polygonal boarded ceiling supported by arched braces. Aisle arcade of four-centred arches, supported by

---

[*] *The Ordnance Gazetteer of Scotland*, ed. Francis H. Groome, iii (1883), p. 200.

octagonal piers and responds with corbels supporting the gallery. – PULPIT, at SE corner, with linenfold panels. – FONT, stone octagon on quatrefoil alabaster shaft with stiff-leaf cap, 1898. – STAINED GLASS, E window, Faith, Love, Hope; W window 'Come unto Me', both *c.* 1940. – The CHURCHYARD has a good variety of table and altar tombs. Obelisk to the Hogarth family, S of church, *c.* 1793; imposing headstone to George Hogarth †1813. – WATCH HOUSE, N of church. – NE of church, the traditional, harled early C19 MANSE, with canted dormers.

Former FREE CHURCH, E end of the village; now housing. Built in two phases: 1843 and 1893. The original building (dated on an oval tablet) was of whinstone rubble with ashlar dressings. There were perhaps initially four round-arched windows to the S front, the central ones wider than the others. The addition, projecting in front of the E opening, is of pink rubble with buff dressings. The porch has an inscribed round-arched entrance; rounded corners are corbelled out to rectangular quoins above. A round bell-turret with slated conical spirelet is corbelled out between church and porch; circular openings for a clock and six closely spaced arched openings. – The MANSE (Morham), was built in 1849, but probably remodelled and added to in the late C19. Large crowstep-gabled L-plan house with a conical-roofed entrance tower. Rendered.

OLD SCHOOL, S of the church. Early C19 single-storey harled schoolhouse with a tall round-arched window in the W gable. Now a dwelling.

PRIMARY SCHOOL, SE of the church. 1974 by *Berwickshire County Council*. Brick box, the walls lined with tall single windows. Rising from the middle of the N end are the hall and canteen.

PUBLIC HALL. By *T.R. Atkinson* of Galashiels, dated 1911. Rendered with red brick base course, margins and angles. Bargeboards, bracketed eaves and ridge tile cresting.

WAR MEMORIAL at the crossroads. 1920s. A fine Celtic cross, the shaft inscribed with the names of the fallen.

BASSENDEAN HOUSE. *See* p. 116.

GREENKNOWE TOWER. *See* p. 336.

GRANTSHOUSE

Named after the INN owned by Tommy Grant. This is much altered and whitewashed with black-painted margins and a pilastered and corniced doorway. The rest is mostly mid-C19 traditional whinstone housing of two storeys. One or two pantiled cottages are evidence of an earlier village. Late C20 housing at Mansefield at the E end.

Former FREE CHURCH, a house since 1992. Built in 1887–8 by *Chalmers & Robson* of Glasgow, of squared whinstone with ashlar dressings. S front, with a triplet of lancets, capped by diminutive bellcote – MANSE. Late C19 in snecked whinstone rubble. L-plan with a gabled porch in the angle.

DRONE HILL RADAR STATION, 3.8km. NE, set high on Coldingham Moor. Established during the Second World War; now a caravan site. Several brick and concrete buildings remain, including one now adapted as a 'Bunker Bar'. A hip-roofed block of two two-storeyed semi-detached houses, which served as officers' quarters, has tiled roofs and roughcast walls. Octagonal PILLBOXES survive along the perimeter.

RENTON HOUSE, 2 km. E. A classical house built for Sir Robert Home, probably c. 1715 (the date on an inscribed sundial) but possibly later and simply old-fashioned. Whinstone rubble with sandstone margins. Two storeys with half-sunk basement and attic, of five bays with a piended platform roof and chimneystacks on the cross-walls. The central three bays of the main elevations are vertically defined, on the front (N) by very shallow pilasters, on the rear by flush, rusticated pilasters. Windows have shouldered lintels. The entrance is marred by a late C19 two-storey pedimented and balustraded porch. W and E additions have been demolished; only the walls of the E one have been retained as a small court. To the N, a walled forecourt has two early C18 detached pavilions, possibly gatehouses, with slated bellcast roofs. Inside, the only survival is the stone dog-leg stair from basement to attics (cf. Melville House, Fife). Solid newel and moulded steps. In the dining room is a compartmented ceiling with cornice of cabbages, fruit and flowers, and a consoled chimneypiece dating from c. 1900.

GRAY COAT PELE   4000
7 km. E of Teviothead

Probably erected during the late C16 by a tenant of Melrose Abbey, this is an outlying example of a type of small defensible house now found mainly in the upper reaches of the Jed Water valley (cf. Kilnsike Pele, Mervinslaw Pele, Slacks Pele, q.q.v.). It stands on the SE slopes of Gray Coat at a height of about 330 m., overlooking the W bank of the Dod Burn. Oblong on plan (10.8 m. by 6.5 m.) with walls of random rubble masonry laid in clay mortar. The only surviving opening is a ground-floor doorway in the centre of the SE gable, rebated for outer and inner doors, but the principal entrance was probably in one of the side-walls at first-floor level. There is no sign of a vault and internal access to the first floor, if it existed at all, was probably by means of a ladder. Traces of one or more outbuildings can be seen nearby, together with a more recent enclosure.

PALISADED SETTLEMENT. On the N shoulder of the hill is a large prehistoric ring-ditch house c. 15 m. in diameter, enclosed by two concentric palisade trenches, which unite and return on either side of an entrance on the ENE.

GREENKNOWE TOWER

0.9 km. w of Gordon

The shell of a late C16 L-plan tower house of the Setons of Touch occupying the site of an earlier residence. Before the middle of the C17 Greenknowe passed to the Pringles, who appear to have refurbished the tower *c.* 1700. It was derelict by the 1830s, but was extensively repaired *c.* 1937, when the site was taken into state care. The building sequence is more complex than at first appears and the tower seems at one time to have had an integral hall range, as at Traquair House (q.v.).

The main block (10.1 m. by 7.2 m.), aligned N and S, contained a vaulted ground floor and four upper floors, the topmost being a garret within the roof. The lower two floors of the stubby E wing (4.9 m. by 3.3 m.) housed a generously proportioned newel stair rising to the first floor only, above which a smaller newel stair, corbelled out in the re-entrant angle, served the upper levels. Above the stair landing the wing contained another four floors. Local whinstone rubble masonry with dressings of red sandstone probably quarried at Bassendean but finished on site, which would explain why the masons had sandstone to spare for rubble and pinnings by the time they reached the upper parts. The entrance, placed close to the re-entrant angle, has a hoodmoulded lintel carved with the arms and initials of James Seton and his second wife, Jane Edmonston, and the date 1581. The walls are crowned with multi-corbelled angle turrets set at diagonally opposite corners of the main block, with an additional, smaller one at the SE corner of the wing. All this makes the exterior quite showy in a style that was then becoming fashionable in the Borders and the effect is heightened by moulded string courses on wing and stair-turret, a wall-head cornice and crowstepped gables. There was no parapet-walk, the roof falling sheer to the wall-head, and the angle turrets were roofed not open. The original windows were mostly half-glazed and barred, but larger openings for framed glass were substituted on the first and second floors *c.* 1700. Two of the topmost windows have dripmoulds with distinctive pendant stops similar to those at Cowdenknowes (q.v.). Most of the original windows, internal doorways and fireplaces have plain, quarter-round arrises. The gunloops are more carefully sited than often seems to be the case, the main field of fire focusing on the entrance and its immediate approach. They include a double-splayed, oval-mouthed loop on the ground floor of the wing, a dumb-bell-shaped loop high up in the N wall of the wing and canted pistol-holes in the stair-turret and angle turrets.

The N wall displays a confusing array of blocked openings and roof-raggles associated with successive, now vanished, wings. These are best explained by postulating an early, one-and-a-half-storey range (i.e. a low ground floor with a principal floor above) extending 12 m. N, superseded, perhaps *c.* 1700, by a three-storey range of similar dimensions. The absence of quoins at the lower NW and NE corners of the tower suggests that the early range was coeval, but against this is the fact that the communicating doorway with the tower, a handsome, roll-moulded opening midway up the lowest flight of the tower stair, looks like an early C17 insertion. This doorway fixes the principal floor level of this first N range and indicates that it contained a chamber of some importance, probably a hall. The upper roof-raggle and blocked doorways at first- and second-floor levels evidently belong to the later N range, which probably included a first-floor hall with chambers above, the floor levels then corresponding to those in the tower. At this stage, if not before, the N range seems to have been linked to another wing running E from the NE corner of the tower house, of which part of the far end, comprising a cobbled stable floor, was exposed by excavation in 1979.

INTERIOR. The entrance has a well-preserved iron yett with provision for a wooden door outside it; within, a cubbyhole for the doorkeeper with a gunloop to the E. A doorway to the W leads down steps to a combined store-cellar and kitchen, the latter containing a big, segmental-arched fireplace with a slop-sink and cupboard to hand; the hatch in the vault is now blocked. The first-floor chamber has a large, crudely carved chimneypiece, very like one at Torwood Castle (Stirling and Central Scotland), with square-cut pilasters and cubical caps and bases of would-be classical design; in the opposite wall a shelved dresser for plate. As enlarged *c.* 1700 the three windows would have provided ample light. At the N end of the room is a pair of mural cubicles, the W one perhaps a latrine of the soil-box variety and the E one a closet. When the second-phase N range was erected, the rear walls of both cubicles were pierced by communicating doorways. The second floor of the main block contained two chambers of unequal size, each with its own doorway from the stair. Both chambers were heated, the S one by a big, bolection-moulded chimneypiece of *c.* 1700. Arrangements at third-floor level were similar, but the chambers seem to have opened into one another. The fireplaces at this level were richer than those below, being wrought with elegant double-roll and hollow mouldings, and the S chamber had an additional, seemingly superfluous fireplace, which looks like a late insertion. Each chamber opened into one of the adjacent angle turrets, and this must have added to their attractions. The wing contained a single, heated chamber on each floor, the top one again being better equipped than those below (cf. Kirkhope Tower, q.v.).

GREENLAW   7040

Despite its remarkable church and handsome county hall to serve as a visible reminder of its former status as the head burgh and later county town of Berwickshire, Greenlaw was never more than a large village, with few houses of note. The principal street (High Street) runs E–W, taking in the S side of the village green, which has two streets either side, Church Street on the E, and Duns Road on the W. The feuing system is of interest: in the mid C18, the third Earl of Marchmont produced a plan for new housing – houses were to be of two storeys, either rebuilt or raised to that height. Except for a few cottages, which escaped these regulations, the houses conform to this pattern. Most are built in red sandstone, a good few harled.

CHURCHES AND PUBLIC BUILDINGS

Former EAST CHURCH, now a garage. 1855, of red snecked sandstone with buff dressings.

21 PARISH CHURCH, Market Place. The church was granted to Kelso Abbey c. 1159, and the plan of the medieval church was a factor in later building phases. But the existing building, of red sandstone rubble, owes much of its appearance to an unusual series of late C17 and early C18 developments. Structural problems led to major rebuilding in 1675. Then, c. 1700, a court house was built w of it, with a tall E tower containing the jail; c. 1712 the church was itself extended w to meet the tower, resulting in a symmetrical composition with the tower at the centre. The courthouse was demolished in 1830, following construction of the new County Buildings (see below), leaving its tower to serve the church. N 'aisle' added by David Bryce, 1856.

The chief impression is of unusual length. Despite its complex history, the s front is a balanced design with three tall windows at the centre, then a doorway surmounted by a window on each side of those, and at each end of the front are two levels of windows. All openings are round-arched and have rounded arrises, and the windows have intersecting glazing bars; what is striking is the way the arch-heads alternate in height. The crowstepped E gable wall has a single window. The N 'aisle' is flanked by a vestry and offices, and has a single low-level window on its N side, with a gableted w window to the loft. The six-storey tower, with stair-turret at the centre of the E side, has square windows at four levels, and clock faces at the top. The original doorway, now blocked, still has a robust yett. The tower is capped by a widely projecting parapet above two levels of corbels, and an octagonal slated spire with a louvred belfry at its base. Openings to both church and court house at first-floor level are now blocked. The base of the tower is barrel-vaulted.

The interior was reordered by George Duns in 1883. The floors in the E and w arms slope towards the centre, and the polygonal ceilings are plastered. There are galleries on cast-iron columns in all three arms; their fronts in the E and w arms have raised and fielded panels, while that in the N 'aisle' has raised mouldings. The pulpit and communion table are at the middle of the s wall. – PULPIT, semi-octagon with arcaded sides and arcaded back-board, the stair up the E side, 1883. – BOARDS, 23rd psalm on s wall, E of pulpit; Beatitudes and Lord's Prayer on N wall. – GRAFFITI in tower, left by two imprisoned gardeners of Marchmont who had ducked a woman suspected of witchcraft. – CROSS-SLAB, medieval, set against w wall of tower, with simple incised cross, reused, with initials AH IL. – MEMORIAL, on s wall of church, Thomas Broomfield, †1667, erected 1742, renewed 1920. – BURIAL

ENCLOSURES. Hamilton Home enclosure against the E wall of the church; Cockburn enclosure to E of church and Nisbet family enclosure to SE, with cast-iron commemorative plates.

CHURCHYARD. A table tomb to S of the church has the deceased holding book and skull; further S another table tomb has Neoclassical decoration. – Relocated against the W wall of the tower is the MARKET CROSS, with re-set Corinthian cap; said to have been erected 1696 by the future first Earl of Marchmont.

Former COUNTY HALL. Now abandoned. Neo-Grecian by *John Cunningham*, 1829–31, to accommodate the court, sheriff and rooms for county meetings. Paid for by Sir William Hume Campbell of Marchmont. Converted to a community centre in 1960, and a swimming pool in 1973. Buff sandstone from Swinton quarry. A symmetrical S front with a dominant Ionic portico distyle *in antis*, surmounted by a raised dome, and flanked by single-storey pedimented pavilions framed by coupled pilasters, set back with single-bay links. The spacious vestibule housed a marble bust of the donor. A fine room above held the county records. Steps led to a landing flanked by Ionic columns, and the courtroom (8.5 m. high) with at each end a screen of two fluted Corinthian columns.

Outside is the MARKET CROSS of 1829, a replica of the old market cross (*see* Parish Church). Corinthian column on a stepped base, surmounted by a lion holding a shield carrying the Marchmont arms. Immediately in front of the cross is the War Memorial of *c.* 1920, in the form of a classical stone sarcophagus. Angle pilasters, architrave, cornice and blocking course, set within a large alcove on a raised platform finished with capped corner piers. Two marble inset panels.

GOOD TEMPLAR HALL, off Duns Road. Erected 1882. Red sandstone. A blind oculus and a round-arched window in the E gable, the windows with consoled sills.

GREENLAW WESTER BRIDGE over the Blackadder Water. 1829–30 by *John Oliver*. A two-span bridge with flat segmental arches and round cutwaters. Ornamental cast-iron balustrades.

PRIMARY SCHOOL, Duns Road. 1969 by *Berwickshire County Council*. Pinkish brick with timber fascias and trims. Long two-storey glazed W front, with an interesting silhouette of shallow monopitched blocks stretching to the E.

CASTLE INN, S of the green, was built *c.* 1835 (replacing an earlier inn) to designs by *John Cunningham*, architect of the County Hall. Ashlar N elevation facing a forecourt, the rest in coursed red sandstone. Two storey and basement, the five-bay front with advanced pilastered end bays; wide band course and eaves course, cornice and blocking course. Wide-pedimented, pilastered doorcase approached by a flight of steps with a cast-iron balustrade; corniced ground-floor windows. The S elevation was U-shaped, with piend-roofed wings, the gap filled by a later three-storey block in red coursed sandstone, providing a ballroom etc. The stables are probably an addition by *Turnbull & Frater*, 1835. Symmetrical with two arched carriage entrances, a recess in the centre.

DESCRIPTION

Starting at the E end of EAST HIGH STREET, MANSEFIELD
(No. 2) is a harled two-storey and attic former manse of three
bays, by *James Gillespie Graham* and *Robert Wright*, 1817, with
a later flat-roofed porch. Large wide astragalled windows.
Additions in 1829 and C20. Good geometric staircase with
carved timber balusters, and decorative plasterwork cornices.
The attractive single-storey vernacular stables and steading in
red sandstone are probably earlier. Around the village green is
the most attractive group of Parish Church, County Hall and
Castle Inn (*see* above). CHURCH STREET is mostly two-storey,
one block built as a tenement with a yard, 1835. The corner
block with High Street, late C18 or early C19, is more classically detailed with a wide band course and open pedimented
S gable. DUNS ROAD starts with two-storey housing, then
fades away towards the Primary School (*see* above) at the top.
WEST HIGH STREET is visually more interesting, since it curves
slightly and the building line is more haphazard, suggesting
some houses are of an earlier period. Early C19 BANK HOUSE
(No. 5) has a rendered façade with incised lines to simulate
ashlar, and five bays with pilastered doorway, architrave and
cornice. Adapted for the Royal Bank of Scotland in 1882.
CROSS KEYS HOTEL, S side, is of three bays, harled with red
sandstone margins. Canted dormers. Opposite, FAIRBAIRN
COURT partly occupies the site of the West U.F. Church (dem.
1979). Flats for the elderly by the *Bield Housing Association*,
1984. Mostly two storeys, rendered, with some sandstone
detailing.
MILL WYND, S of High Street, has plain two-storey houses on
the l. At the end are rather classy Italianate former stables, now
a Masonic Lodge. Keystoned oval openings at the wall-head
topped by open-pedimented dormers. Back in West High
Street is the BLACKADDER HOTEL. Mid C19 (?). White-
painted render, with black plinth and dressings. Two storeys
with gabled dormers, and a splayed projecting window on the
first floor. Nos. 30 and 32, probably early C19, are framed by
flat pilasters. Red – rather friable – sandstone with cream
margins, band course and dentilled cornice.
EDINBURGH ROAD. No. 2 (THE OLD MANSE) is the former
U.F. manse. 1847. Full-height canted bay and a veranda. Contemporary steading.
CASTLELOAN TOLL BAR. 1.3 km E (A697). Single-storey, pink
sandstone front, with a full-height pedimented stone porch
dated 1831, with deep-set doorway, and flanked by canted bay
windows; central octagonal chimneys.
OLD PURVES HALL. *See* p. 602.
ROWCHESTER HOUSE. *See* p. 650.

THE HAINING *see* SELKIRK

HALLYARDS   2030
1 km. SW of Kirkton Manor

A rambling, two-storey and attic harled house of several periods.
The SE front, with unevenly placed four bays to the l., is probably no earlier than mid-C18, except at the SE corner, where
the lower part of the walls is thicker than the upper part, and
the surviving walls have an obvious batter. This may predate
1666, when a tower house is known to have existed. The prominent bow to the r. providing a drawing room, with a main
bedroom above, was probably added by the tenant Dr Adam
Ferguson, Professor of Moral Philosophy at Edinburgh University, who is known to have carried out work *c.* 1800. The
NE front finishes in a mid-C19 crowstepped gable with a gabled
porch tacked on with a bracketed stone canopy, perhaps the
work of Andrew Clason W.S. (†1850). A two-storey wing to
the E joins the stable block, and a similar one continues from
the W end of the NW front. An inscribed lintel IS (John Scott)
and HG (Helen Geddes) is dated 1647. Of note inside are two
excellent Edinburgh pine and gesso chimneypieces, *c.* 1800.
The drawing room one has a frieze showing the 'shepherd boy'
pattern surrounded by sheep and stunted trees, with sheaves
of corn at the ends, and in a bedroom a 'shell and thistle'
pattern with slim Gothic pilaster jambs.
    WALLED GARDEN. 'Newly walled' in 1811. – SUNDIAL. A
shaft inscribed 'Soli/Posuit/A Ferguson/A.D. 1803', with a
copper dial inscribed '*Miller & Adie*/Edinburgh'. – STATUE of
'The Black Dwarf' carved by *Robert Forrest*; brought here by
Clason from Leith in 1836. – STABLES. Dated 1791. Rendered,
with the advanced three centre bays pedimented and topped
by three urn finials, with a keystoned niche each side of a
doorway, and round-arched loft door above. Wide segmental-
arched carriage opening. – Mid-C19 whinstone LODGE. Gothic
porch, the arch composed of narrow whinstone blocks, with a
blind oculus above.

HANGINGSHAW   3030
7 km. E of Yarrow

A picturesque Jacobethan house by *W.H. Playfair*, 1843. For
James Johnstone of Alva (Stirling and Central Scotland),
whose family owned the estate from the late C18. Its predecessors were a C15 tower house, replaced in the early C18 by a
house for the Murrays of Philiphaugh, which was destroyed by
fire in the late 1760s. The present house is built of sandstone
rubble, squared and snecked, with droved ashlar quoins and
polished margins. Mullioned and hoodmoulded windows
and gables. Inside, the planning of the house runs E–W
with the three principal rooms along the S front and a long,
swept timber staircase with twisted balusters built against the

spine wall. The kitchens are built into the hillside. Modestly decorated. A timber classical chimneypiece in the drawing room is perhaps original, but not what Playfair would normally have supplied. Enriched cornices with much use of an oakleaf motif.

The house stands at the top of a series of terraced HANGING GARDENS cut into the steep N bank above the Yarrow Water in the late C16 or early C17. Some yew and holly trees survive from this period. The N retaining wall against the top terrace is buttressed with two keystoned, round-arched gateways to W and E, perhaps late C18. The revetment at the rear of the top terrace may conceal vaulted cellarage, part of the original tower house. The steps connecting the terraces, now in bad condition, lead down to a rectangular enclosure, to the W the ornamental flower garden, to the E the kitchen garden. Large C19 stone-rimmed BASIN at the foot of the terraces; in the centre a pair of laughing cherubs hold an ornamental vase for a jet of water. At the E end of the second terrace is a colonnaded four-bay LOGGIA with Doric columns and pilasters. It is roofed in concrete, and is said to date from the 1930s. If so the C18 colonnade must have been imported, perhaps from the demolished Alva House (Stirling and Central Scotland). – Late C19 SOUTH LODGE with overhanging eaves and canted bay window. – EAST LODGE. Mid C19 *cottage orné* with tree-trunk columns.

4010   HARDEN HOUSE
                     2 km. E of Roberton

The Scotts acquired Harden early in the C16, but their first house there (described as a fortalice) was ordered to be demolished in 1592, following Walter Scott's involvement in a conspiracy against James VI. The family soon returned to royal favour and acquired large estates in Berwickshire and Selkirkshire, living chiefly at Aikwood Tower and Mertoun House (qq.v.), which last eventually became their principal residence. During the C17 Harden itself was rebuilt and remodelled several times, notably by Scott of Harden's nephew, Walter, Earl of Tarras, c. 1671–91. Then, in 1864, the seventh Lord Polwarth made additions to the N front and remodelled the interior. In 1912 the family sold Mertoun and moved back to Harden. A year later the eighth Lord Polwarth commissioned plans from *J.P. Alison* of Hawick for extensive alterations and additions, but little was done apart from minor changes to the N front.

Unlike many of the historic seats of the principal Border families, Harden is a fairly modest house and retains its original scale and much of its vernacular character. It stands high above the E bank of the Harden Burn in a position which must originally have been selected for its defensive qualities. The approach is from the N, where the building now presents a predominantly mid-Victorian aspect, the additions of 1864 largely obscuring the C17 main block to the rear. On the S SIDE, however, the early house stands open to view, comprising an elongated, oblong block (30.3 m. by 7.0 m.) of two main storeys and an attic. The E portion is narrower than the remainder and roofed at a lower level, but otherwise the building seems at first sight to be homogeneous, all the masonry being of harled rubble with dressings of red and yellow sandstone. The central portion on this side is of four bays with two rows of near-symmetrically placed windows, all but one round-arrised. Most seem to have been enlarged and some were originally barred and half-glazed. Towards the W end is the pre-1864 entrance doorway, with a simple rusticated surround, which probably dates from the first phase of Lord Tarras' alterations (*James Fall*, mason 1671–3). When harling was removed from the vicinity of this doorway in 1968 an earlier doorway, now blocked, was revealed to the E and a vertical masonry joint to the W. This suggests that this portion of the house, perhaps dating from *c.* 1600, was originally freestanding to the W and E, having an overall length of about 13.3 m. Its E extremity is marked by a crowstepped gable separating it from the late C17 E extension (*see* below).

The W EXTENSION of this main block probably dates from about the second quarter of the C17. The ground floor contains two mullioned and transomed windows on the S side, one of eight lights and the other of four; the jambs are chamfered and rebated. Two similar windows, probably originally belonging to the N front, are now incorporated in the 1864 NE wing. Such windows are more characteristic of Cumbria than of central Roxburghshire, and it is possible that the mason came from that region. The first-floor windows are quite different, being single-light openings of late C17 type with chamfered arrises, so it looks as if the upper floors were rebuilt at that time, probably in 1671–3. The attic floor was evidently lit by pedimented dormers, and similar dormers seem to have been provided for the adjacent portion of the main block. Two pediments survive, one built into the NE wing and the other, dated 1671, in the stable court to the NW of the mansion.

The two-bay E EXTENSION of the main block was built in 1690–1 by *Robert Bunzie*, mason in Newstead, incorporating slightly earlier work. Chamfer-arrised windows at ground- and first-floor levels and a crowstepped gable with elaborately carved skewputts. It has its own doorway in the S wall (now blocked), the lintel dated 1680, as well as an alcoved seat from which to view the steep-sided valley below. The keystone of the alcove bears the date 1691 and the initials of Walter, Earl of Tarras, and his second wife Helen Hepburne.

The N additions of 1864 comprise a double-gabled wing to the E containing an entrance porch and principal staircase, and a single-gabled wing to the W containing a secondary staircase, beyond which lies the kitchen. All the work is of the plainest description. The NE and NW wings were originally linked by a corridor laid against the N wall of the early house, but in 1913 the space between the wings was infilled to provide additional accommodation.

The INTERIOR mainly reflects the late C17 layout as modified in 1864, when the introduction of new staircases and the linking corridor on the N side of the house improved circulation. Little can be said about the arrangement of the house of *c*. 1600, except that it probably contained two main rooms on each floor. Behind the lining of the E ground-floor room (now part of the drawing room) can be seen the round-arrised jamb of a N doorway, which probably led to a staircase removed in or before 1864. The building papers indicate that in 1671 the W extension contained a hall with a chamber of dais above. The hall was heated by a large, roll-moulded and lintelled fireplace in the W gable, which was rediscovered in 1936 and subsequently restored. The fireplace incorporates a salt-box. It appears, therefore, that the house that Lord Tarras acquired incorporated three main ground-floor chambers, the central one having an external doorway in the S wall. Tarras retained the hall in the W extension, but remodelled the remainder to form a separate entrance lobby, served by the new front door, with a large dining room to the E. Beyond the dining room, he added a room described as a closet, but probably also serving as his bedchamber. The lobby was paved, *c*. 1684, with black and white marble tiles which survived until at least the 1860s, when the lobby was turned into a business room. At the same time the early C17 hall was subdivided into a servants' hall (W, now sitting room) and pantry (E), later combined with the business room to form a new dining room, which retains a bolection-moulded chimneypiece of the 1680s.

The best-preserved of what was evidently a handsome suite of rooms is the former dining room (now drawing room), which retains a geometric plaster ceiling (*John Scott* and *Thomas Alborn*, 1672) with an enriched central oval incorporating winged cherubs' heads, flower vases and baskets of fruit; most of the modelling is in low relief. The bolection-moulded chimneypiece and entablature were not installed until 1684, and the capitals of the flanking half-columns override the ceiling cornice. The carving, by *Robert Bunzie*, is vigorous but unsophisticated. The E chamber (Lord Tarras's Room) contains another of Bunzie's robustly carved chimneypieces, its lintel incorporating Lord Tarras's initials beneath an earl's coronet.

On the first floor Lord Tarras replaced the chamber of dais in the W extension with two separate chambers. In the central and E parts of the house he seems to have introduced a layout similar to that below, but with a large drawing room opening into the Countess's bedroom/closet in the E extension. The drawing room (now bedroom) has a compartmented ceiling of Jacobean type probably installed in or after 1864 (possibly replacing a genuine Caroline one). The bedchamber contains a bolection-moulded chimneypiece of 1684 incorporating Lady Tarras's monogram initials and coronet. In the NE wing is a notable Neo-Jacobean timber staircase of 1864, with an airy, mock-vaulted plaster ceiling.

SUNDIAL. Early C18, said to have been brought from Dryburgh Abbey House (*see* p. 224). Twisted shaft supporting a plain table head.

HARWOOD HOUSE
4 km. sw of Hobkirk

In possession of the Elliots of Harwood from the early C17. A new house was completed in 1835. Gothic, in coursed red sandstone, with square-headed drip-moulds. Wide entrance doorway, the fanlight with Gothic tracery. On the garden elevation a canted bay, above a hoodmoulded tripartite window, with taller round-arched centre window and pointed sidelights, their heads traceried, mostly blind and painted. Set back to the NW are additions, both Neo-Tudor. Two-storey wing of 1901 for T.R.B. Elliot,[*] who also commissioned *J.P. Alison* to add further servants' accommodation in 1906–7. This part is more interesting: of three storeys, with gables along the wall-head, finished off at the corner with a solid parapet.

HAWICK[†]

INTRODUCTION

The largest of the Border towns, the most remote and the latest to achieve prominence – hence, perhaps, its strong corporate identity and predominantly urban and industrial character. Hawick stands at the confluence of the River Teviot and the Slitrig Water on a site initially chosen for defence, which afterwards proved ideal for the development of a local textile industry. The historic core sits on the flat ground of the Teviot basin, while C18–C20 expansion led to building, for both industry and the industrialists' mansions, on the surrounding slopes, from where impressive views can be enjoyed. Hawick is first recorded in the late C12 as a barony belonging to the Lovel family, who presumably founded the motte castle and nearby parish church on the NW bank of the Slitrig. After the Wars of Independence Hawick passed to the Douglases of Drumlanrig, and land transactions were still being carried out at the 'Moit of

[*] Ambitious plans of 1899 by *Peddie & Washington Browne* were not executed.
[†] The introduction, account of the public buildings, industrial buildings and the burgh's descriptions are by Sabina Strachan.

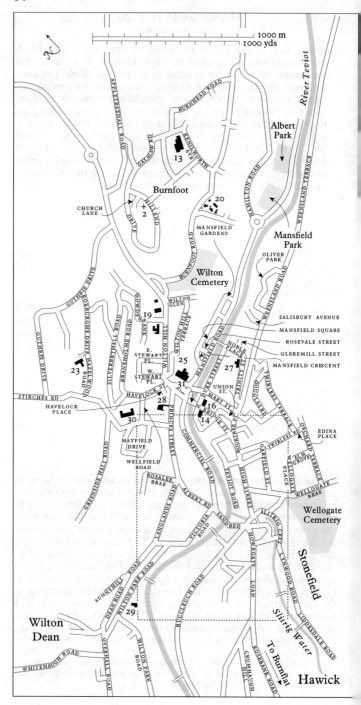

1000 m
1000 yds

River Teviot

Albert Park

Burnfoot

CHURCH LANE

13

KENILWORTH AVE

APPLETREEHALL ROAD

BURNHEAD ROAD

GALALAW RD

20

+2

MANSFIELD GARDENS

Wilton Cemetery

HAMILTON TERRACE

WEENSLAND TERRACE

Mansfield Park

OLIVER PARK

GUTHRIE DRIVE

ROXBURGHE DRIVE

GUTHRIE DRIVE

SILVERBUTHALL ROAD

BRANXHOLME ROAD

HOWDEN BANK

THE LONING

HAZELWOOD

WILTON GLEN

19

WILTON HILL TERRACE

WILTON HILL

E. STEWART PL.

W. STEWART PL.

23

25

SALISBURY AVENUE

MANSFIELD SQUARE

ROSEVALE STREET

NOBLE PLACE

GLEBEMILL STREET

MANSFIELD CRESCENT

MANSFIELD ROAD

RENNIE STREET

TRINITY ST.

STIRCHES RD

HAVELOCK ST.

HAVELOCK PLACE

28

30

31

27

UNION ST.

MART ST.

BRIDGE ST.

16

14

BOURNEE PL.

DOUGLAS RD

TWIRLEES TERRACE

MAYFIELD DRIVE

WELLFIELD ROAD

ROSALEE BRAE

PRINCES STREET

COMMERCIAL ROAD

TEVIOT ROAD

HIGH STREET

GARFIELD ST.

TWIRLEES RD.

ELM GROVE

WELLOGATE

ORCHARD TERRACE

EDINA PLACE

GREENSIDE HALL ROAD

LANGLANDS ROAD

ALBERT RD

VICTORIA ROAD

SANDBED

SLITRIG CRES.

HOWEGATE

LYNWOOD ROAD

WELLOGATE BRAE

Wellogate Cemetery

Stonefield

SUNNYHILL ROAD

DEAN ROAD

OVERHALL ROAD

WILTON PARK ROAD

BUCCLEUCH ROAD

WILTON PARK ROAD

SLITRIG LOAN

LIDDESDALE ROAD

Slitrig Water

29

Wilton Dean

WHITEHAUGH ROAD

CROMBHAUGH HILL

ROSBANK ROAD

To Burnflat

Hawick

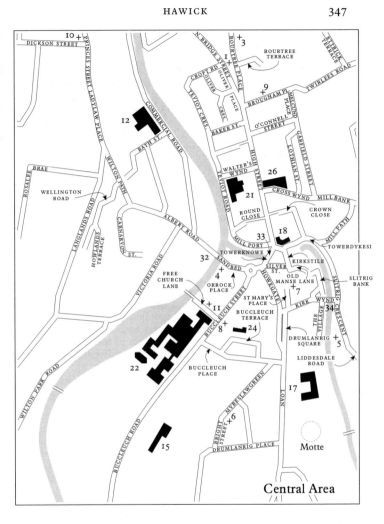

Central Area

1 Baptist Church
2 Burnfoot Parish Church
3 Congregational Church
4 Orrock Place U.P. Church
5 St Cuthbert's Episcopal Church
6 St Margaret's Convent
7 St Mary's Old Parish Church
8 St Mary and St David (R. C.)
9 Trinity Church
10 Wilton Parish Church
11 Teviot Church
12 Borders College
13 Burnfoot Community School
14 Carnegie Public Library
15 Cottage Hospital
16 Crown Buildings
17 Drumlanrig and St Cuthbert's
  Primary School
18 Drumlanrig Tower
19 Emergency Services
20 Former Isolation Hospital
21 Health Centre
22 High School
23 Stirches Primary School
24 St Margaret's R. C. Primary School
25 Teviotdale Leisure Centre
26 Town Hall
27 Trinity Primary School
28 Former Wilton Primary School
29 Wilton Lodge Museum
30 Wilton Primary School
31 North Bridge
32 Albert Bridge
33 Drumlanrig Bridge
34 Slitrig Crescent Bridge

Hawick' in the early C16. The barony then passed to the Scotts of Buccleuch in the late C16 who played a leading role in the C19 development of the burgh.

The first township probably grew up close to the castle and church, but when the Douglases built Drumlanrig Tower in the C16 they chose a site on the opposite bank of the Slitrig, and Pont's map of *c.* 1590 shows the river bridged and the main part of the town on the NE side, along what is now the upper part of High Street. The medieval burgh consisted largely of timber-framed buildings, highly vulnerable to the frequent English raids of the C15 and C16. There were also a number of towers or bastles – three stone towers are said to have been burned in 1548 – and several houses with 'pended' (vaulted) ground floors were still extant in the 1860s; indeed one, at least, still survives.

Hawick became a burgh of barony in or before 1537 and a burgh of regality in 1669. Its burghal status encouraged the holding of weekly markets, initially on the High Street in front of the tolbooth. The market cross was located there, near the weigh house that stood on the site of the present Town Hall, and the town's four ports served a regulatory function, placed as they were at each extremity of the burgh boundary. The Auld Brig, Hawick's only bridge until 1741, was severely damaged in the flash flood of 1767. From the mid C18 onwards Hawick developed as a trading centre for local woollens, its position in the Southern Uplands offering ready access to Edinburgh, Carlisle and Newcastle. Following the introduction of frame knitting in 1771, hosiery manufacture gradually superseded the fledgling carpet and linen trades. C19 industrial expansion was accelerated by the introduction of the railway to Edinburgh (1849) and Carlisle (1862). The ever-increasing number of water- and steam-powered woollen mills first led to the creation of new streets and then to the wholesale rebuilding of old Hawick to house the influx of workers. This was aided by the expansion of the town boundaries in 1861 to include the neighbouring village of Wilton, on the NW side of the Teviot, which had belonged to the Langlands family of Wilton Lodge. Hawick achieved full municipal status in 1861 and became a parliamentary burgh six years later; by 1891 the population had risen to more than 19,000.

Industrial expansion and prosperity in the C18 and C19 led Hawick's wealthy mill-owners to erect large villas, many in close proximity to the mills but set high above the industrial buildings and from where the owner could survey his empire and stroll at leisure in his gardens. Late C19–early C20 villas are situated at the extremities of the burgh, away from the working-class districts and intended to take in views of Scott country.

Hawick is now the largest of the Borders towns, with a population of 15,812, a decline on its C19 peak but sustained by large post-1945 council estates on its periphery.

CHURCHES

BAPTIST CHURCH, North Bridge Street. 1882 by *David A. Crombie*; a rectangle of rock-faced snecked buff rubble. The W front has a projecting central part framed by buttresses, with an arched doorway and two small circular windows below a broad lancet; the recessed hip-roofed outer portions of the front have single lancets. A brick-built hall is at the E end.

BURNFOOT PARISH CHURCH, Hillend Drive. 1953–5 by *J.P. Alison & Hobkirk*, the church extension scheme building, for the new housing estate, on the highest point of the knoll around which the estate was built. At its core a steeply roofed harled rectangle served as both church and hall, with a small chancel at one end (that could be closed off) and offshoots for kitchens and vestry. Faint Arts and Crafts echoes in the alternating triangular and shaped gables rising against the roof along the flanks, and in the tall entrance arch embracing both a doorway and window.

CONGREGATIONAL CHURCH, Bourtree Place. Built 1893–4 on a T-plan, with its main front facing NW, and shallow transept-like projections and an apse at the opposite end. Constructed of coursed and snecked buff rubble with ashlar dressings. The entrance front has a central doorway with arch mouldings emerging from splayed jambs, and a triplet of three cinque-foiled lancets above. Framing the front are slender octagonal turrets capped by open arcaded and spired pinnacles. The SW flank has two tiers of windows: triplets below and paired windows above. The gable-wall of the 'transept' has a central two-light traceried window flanked by lancets. A low apsidal hall continues to the NE across the street front. Inside, beyond a narrow vestibule, are galleries around three sides, and a wagon ceiling; since 1925 the apse has housed an organ.

Former ORROCK PLACE UNITED PRESBYTERIAN CHURCH, Orrock Place, now a mill shop. 1874, replacing a church in Myreslawgreen. Its principal (E) front is tripartite: at the centre a diminutive asymmetrical tower flanking a two-light plate-traceried window rises above the doorway; the two outer portions each have a lancet rising into a gable above a triplet of lancets. On its N flank, which has two major gables, the basement hall is exposed, its walls rising from the Teviot. Converted into halls in 1951, it is now a shop, with a suspended ceiling at gallery level.

ST CUTHBERT'S EPISCOPAL CHURCH, Slitrig Crescent. A small but finely detailed church of 1855, built for the Duke of Buccleuch, and designed on firm ecclesiological principles in the Early Decorated style by *G. Gilbert Scott*. Walls of snecked rubble with buff sandstone dressings. Aligned from NE to SW, the greatest prominence was given to the apsed 'E' chancel. This has two-light bar-traceried windows except on the axis of the apse, where the blocked window arch has a statue of St Cuthbert. On the 'S' side, towards the street, the junction of chancel and apse is marked by a buttress, and there is a wall-head corbel table around both chancel and apse. On the 'N' side of the chancel is a vestry and organ chamber. A double bellcote with miniature crowstepped gable rises above the chancel arch. The four-bay aisled nave is treated more simply than the chancel, apart from the porch in the second bay from the 'W' on its 'S' side and the 'W' front. A single roof sweeps across both nave and aisles, with two-light plate-traceried windows rising into gables. The outer doorway of the porch is of three orders with foliate caps, and has a foliate tympanum. The 'w' front has a pair of tall plate-traceried windows to the nave below a vesica; there are single lancets to the aisles.

Internally chancel and nave are separated by an arch with foliate caps, and a pair of arches opens into the organ chamber and vestry. There is no architectural punctuation between chancel and apse; and the roof has closely spaced arched braces with painted decoration by *Moxon* of London. Nave and aisles are separated by arcades of four arches on cylindrial piers with chalice caps and unmoulded arches; the nave roof has closely spaced arched braces. – ALTARPIECE (blocking E window of apse), 1905, of Caen stone, by *J. Oldrid Scott*, with paintings of Crucifixion and Adoring Angels. – CHANCEL SCREEN, 1908, of five arches with traceried spandrels, by *Robert S. Lorimer*. – FONT, square bowl on five shafts with foliate caps, by *David Kerr* of Edinburgh. – STAINED GLASS, good display, including chancel glass by *Thomas Ward* of London; W window, 1889, memorial to fifth Duke of Buccleuch as donor of the church, together with Bishop of Glasgow and Scottish Saints.

Former ST MARGARET'S DOMINICAN CONVENT, Bright Street. 1912–13 by *Reginald Fairlie*. A striking composition of squared red sandstone rubble; its bow-ended Romanesque chapel is still clearly identifiable. Two-storey E elevation with bold round-headed entrance beneath a statue of Our Lady. Converted to housing in 1987. Opposite is the BUCCLEUCH HOME FOR THE ELDERLY, also by Fairlie, 1934; T-plan, harled and much more subdued.

ST MARY'S OLD PARISH CHURCH, St Mary's Place. Elevated within a churchyard on a steep-sided mound; there has probably been a church here since at least the C12, with a dedication recorded in 1214. The rectangular main body, which may incorporate the walls of its medieval predecessor, is aligned from SW to NE; it was augmented to a T-shaped plan in 1764, with a tower at the extremity of the new NW 'aisle', and stairs within projections in the re-entrant angles between the main body and the 'aisle'. Much now seen dates from a remodelling of 1882–3 by *Wardrop & Reid* following a devastating fire.

The walls are harled, with ashlar margins and dressings (in some cases now cement-rendered). The five-stage tower is slightly intaken above a string course at each stage; the top stage has arched belfry openings and is capped by a slated roof of ogee profile with a tall weathervane. Windows and doorways are mainly rectangular, though the galleries have gableted dormers, and there are steep pediments over the upper windows of the stair projections. Internally the three arms look towards the pulpit and communion table at the centre of the SE wall; ribbed, boarded wagon ceilings of three-centred profile. Galleries with panelled fronts, on pairs of cast-iron columns, are slightly set back within all three arms. A small vestry has been cut off the NE end below the gallery. – COMMUNION TABLE, Ionic arcaded front, memorial to dead of First World War. – PULPIT, panelled bowed front with panelled and balustraded stair, *c.* 1880; modern back-board and tester, the former having a cross with painted symbols of the Evangelists.

CHURCHYARD. Array of mainly C17, C18 and C19 stones around the sloping sides. Several earlier tombstones preserved in Wilton Lodge Museum, together with two foliate capitals said to be from the medieval church.

ST MARY AND ST DAVID (R.C.), Buccleuch Street. A simple building of unusual L-shaped plan. First built in 1844 as a rectangular block with its main N front to the street, and with Y-traceried windows along the flanks. The SW lateral aisle was added in 1879. The entrance front was remodelled in the 1960s, retaining only the lower wall and the central doorway; an echelon of three rectangular windows rises into the gable. – ALTAR, with crucifix and sloping canopy, 1960s. – STAINED GLASS, in S wall of aisle, SS Peter and Andrew.

TEVIOT CHURCH, Free Church Lane. Previously St George's United Free Church. An austere building of 1913–16 by *J.P. Alison*, in an early C13 style; the W front and clearstorey of pink rock-faced snecked rubble and the aisles of whinstone rubble. There are triplets of lancets to the W and E fronts and the aisles, while the clearstorey has paired lancets. The central part of the entrance front is separated by buttresses from asymmetrical lower blocks at the aisle ends, and the main doorway has arch mouldings emerging from splayed jambs.

Internally the four-bay arcades have double-chamfered arches above slender octagonal piers; at the W end is a gallery, partly above a narthex. Roof of widely spaced arched braces. – COMMUNION TABLE, open arcaded base with outer multi-cusped arches. – STAINED GLASS, E window, Good Shepherd, SS Columba and Cuthbert, 1929, by *Lilian J. Pocock*; E bay S aisle, Risen Christ, 1934.

TRINITY CHURCH, Brougham Place. A broad preaching box of whinstone rubble built in 1843, replacing a church for a Burgher congregation of 1780. Probably originally of rectangular plan, it was extended to a compressed T-plan during a remodelling of 1872; it was redecorated in 1892 by *William Jardine*. The main (NW) front has its doorway (dated 1843) in a salient rectangle, above which is a Y-traceried window with a transom; on each side of these is a single lancet. Two tiers of rectangular windows light the flanks, with a more complex arrangement of windows at the head of the T along the SE wall. Internally, panelled galleries on three sides, with the pulpit, communion table and organ at the SE end, the organ now largely blocking the two large central windows. The flat ceiling is divided into three main compartments, each with a large circular vent, with side compartments over the lateral projections at the SE end. – COMMUNION TABLE, Arts and Crafts Gothic. – PULPIT, with blind Gothic arcading to the polygonal central part, and linenfold panels on each side. – HALL to the S, 1896.

WILTON PARISH CHURCH, Dickson Street. Wilton was a separate parish from at least 1170. Its medieval church, rebuilt in 1762, enlarged in 1801 and further modified in 1829, was SE of the present building, where its churchyard is marked by memorials within grassed parkland. A competition of 1858 for a new church was won by *J. T. Emmett* of London; it was built in 1860–2, with carved work by *Farmer & Brindley*, also of

London. It was an aisled rectangle aligned from SE to NW, with a tower at the S corner. Major – but thoughtfully sympathetic – additions were made in 1908–10 by *J.P. Alison* (with carved work by *Joseph Hayes* of Edinburgh), consisting of aisled transepts, a NW shallow chancel, and a small vestry. Built throughout of buff-coloured stugged or polished ashlar (now with extensive cement repairs), the church is an attractive essay in the Early Decorated style. The central, gabled part of the SE entrance front has an echelon of three two-light traceried windows above a doorway of three orders with head corbels; flanking this central gable, at the end of the SE aisle is a three-light traceried window. At the end of the SW aisle is the tower, rising a single storey above the adjacent church roof and capped by a slated pyramidal roof behind a corbelled parapet; it is divided into four squat stages by string courses, with a SW doorway of three orders and two-light windows to the second and fourth stages. The buttressed aisle flanks have Y-traceried windows. The additions of 1908–10 at the NW end continue the idiom of the original building, but are in a slightly more 'correct' manner, albeit with Lorimerian touches to the parapets over the outer parts of the aisles on each side of the transepts. There are traceried windows in the gable-walls of chancel and transepts, of four lights in the former and of 1-3-1 lights in each of the latter.

The interior is an imposing cruciform space. The nave, essentially of 1860–2, is of five aisled bays, with a SE narthex and organ gallery (the latter the only relic of the original galleries removed in 1908). The arcades are carried on quatrefoil piers of Caen stone with dogtooth-decorated caps by *Farmer & Brindley*; the aisles have boarded ceilings and the central vessel a ribbed wagon ceiling. The additions of 1908–10 are seen in the aisled two-bay transepts and a short chancel. The bay left of the chancel is expanded into a baptistery, with a handsomely arcaded dado. The wagon ceilings of transepts and chancel take their lead from that of the nave. Like the baptistery, the chancel also has an arcaded dado, and opens into the transept aisle on each side through an arch with clustered-shaft responds and stiff-leaf caps. The chancel is elevated two steps, with the communion table three steps of Iona marble higher still. Finely detailed CHANCEL FURNISHINGS by *Alison*, 1910. – COMMUNION TABLE, oak, of three open bays in two traceried planes; tabernacles at the corners were intended for images of the Evangelists, oak. – CHOIR STALLS (in fact elders' seats), oak, four on each side, within the arches opening into the transept aisles, behind which rise open screens. – LECTERN, oak, a double desk on four slender piers capped by angels. – FONT, 1910, a square bowl of Caen stone carried on a massive central shaft and four smaller shafts of Iona marble. – PULPIT, oak, 1862, octagonal with a blind arch on each face, raised on a stone plinth. – STAINED GLASS. An extensive scheme; all windows by *Lilian J. Pocock*, 1921–30. – MEMORIALS. SW transept, John James Scott Chisholme, †1899, brass plate with enamelled heraldry in marble frame, by *Cawthorp*. NE transept, Walter Gerald Pringle, †1917, cast bronze tablet with relief portrait bust on green marble base, by *Newbury Abbot Trent*, 1919.

CHURCH HALLS, NW of church. A well-contrived irregular grouping of elements in bright red brick of 1897. The predominant style is Late Gothic/Tudor, with an ogee-capped octagonal cupola as a principal fulcrum.

PUBLIC BUILDINGS

ALBERT BRIDGE. *See* Description 1.

BORDERS COLLEGE, Commercial Road. Henderson Building. By *Bamber, Hall & Partners*, 1970. Three-storey brick, flat-roofed with single-storey wings to N and S and glazed entrance porch to the street. The site was formerly occupied by part of Dangerfield Mill (*see* p. 365) and some of the subsidiary mill buildings have been retained for use by the college.

BRIDGE (A7). Part of the Hawick Traffic Relief Scheme, 2001. Flat with concrete sides. On the site of the 1860 Teviot Viaduct, a six-arched railway bridge (dem. 1982). One of its piers survives on the river bed.

BURNFOOT COMMUNITY SCHOOL, Kenilworth Avenue. Two phases from 1970: harled flat-roofed classrooms and weather-boarded hall, by *Roxburgh County Council*, and a large pale-coloured corrugated-steel-clad block at the rear by *Borders Regional Council*.

CARNEGIE PUBLIC LIBRARY, North Bridge Street. In a   102
deservedly eyecatching position at the corner of the bridge, by *J. N. Scott & A. Lorne Campbell*, 1904, with sculpture by *W. Birnie Rhind*. Funded by a £10,000 donation by Andrew Carnegie. Slim Renaissance ogee-capped octagonal entrance tower of sandstone with an Ionic-pilastered doorpiece, and the three-storey end bays of both the well-proportioned N and E elevations advanced under semicircular pediments. The Laidlaw Terrace façade slopes downhill; the central bay has rusticated giant pilasters under a triangular pediment and a pend to the r. gives access to the rear.

Former COTTAGE HOSPITAL, Buccleuch Road. Built with public subscription by *John McLachlan*, 1885. Appropriately low, many-gabled and picturesque, bargeboarded wall-head gables interspersed with dormers, bay-windowed flanking wings. W wing extended sympathetically in 1924 and a veranda added. Utilitarian X-Ray block, with end pavilions and large windows, built 1933 by *J.P. Alison & Hobkirk* in the grounds to the E. Later additions.

CROWN BUILDINGS, North Bridge Street. By the *Property Services Agency*, 1973–4. Harsh, two-storey flat-roofed government offices with vertical bands of dark glazing and smooth ashlar.

DRUMLANRIG BRIDGE (Tower Knowe Bridge). Built in 1776 by public subscription, to provide an improved route over the Slitrig rather than the narrower Auld Brig upstream (dem. 1851). Its width was doubled in 1828 to extend the Tower-knowe marketplace, and by the same again in 1900 to relieve congestion. At that time its stone parapets were replaced by cast-iron balustrades. The double-span flat segmental-arched bridge was strengthened, footpaths carried on brackets over its triangular cutwaters and its ironwork renewed in 1978.

DRUMLANRIG AND ST CUTHBERT'S PRIMARY SCHOOL, Loan. By *Roxburgh County Council*, 1960. Three-storey harled

SE block with two-storey NW ranges to form a substantial U-plan enclosing the playground. The upper storey of the r. block is supported by slender pilotis on the NE side. Developed from the Hawick and Wilton Industrial School, established *c.* 1855 to make basic education available to working-class children.

EMERGENCY SERVICES, Wilton Hill and Howdenbank, located in a deep valley. – POLICE DIVISIONAL HEADQUARTERS, by *J. & J. Hall*, 1964, is large, flat-roofed, three-storey and concrete-framed, infilled alternately with squared blockwork and render. Vertical screen window to the staircase. – U-plan FIRE STATION of 1970 faced in brick alternating with concrete slabs. The AMBULANCE SERVICE DEPOT is a broad, harled shed.

HAWICK GOLF CLUB, Vertish Hill, S of Burnflat. Clubhouse by *J. P. Alison*, 1894. Tudoresque, with later additions by *Alex Inglis*.

HAWICK HEALTH CENTRE, Teviot Road. 1989 by *Scott & McIntosh*. Low with hipped roof and broad octagonal tower at corner of Walter's Wynd.

HAWICK HOSPITAL, Victoria Road. 2005 by *Aitken & Turnbull*, superseding the Cottage Hospital. Built on the site of Pringle's Victoria Mills.

98 HAWICK HIGH SCHOOL, Buccleuch Street. Originally Buccleuch Higher Grade School (renamed Hawick High School, 1915). By *Joseph Blaikie*, 1908. Largely devastated by fire in 1926, and rebuilt within the original whinstone walls by *J.A. Carfrae*, 1928. This stands at the centre of the long and varied Buccleuch Street façade. Three-storey, six-bay centre block with Renaissance detailing, flanked by three-bay gable-ended wings. A short link connects the two-storey, six-bay annexe to the E, also by *Carfrae*, 1926; the first-floor windows of its penultimate bays are advanced under triangular pediments. Balancing to the W is the former Henderson Technical School (now

100 HENDERSON BUILDING), again by *Carfrae*, 1928. Established separately from the High School but donated to it in 1970. Slightly more ambitious front, cream-rendered with gabled ends, rusticated pilasters and finials. The building was linked to the main block in the 1990s. Numerous post-Second World War additions, including at the corner of Free Church Lane a flat-roofed, two-storey block, 1960, with brightly coloured panels beneath strip windows. Plain rear extensions of the 1970s by *Borders Regional Council*.

Former ISOLATION HOSPITAL, Burnfoot Road. By *Alex Inglis*, 1902, sited outside the burgh to control infection. It primarily consisted of two white-harled, red-tiled blocks (these survive along with two subsidiary buildings to the NW) with a small intermediate building forming an H-plan. *Roxburgh County Council*'s extensive additions and alterations as Burnfoot Primary School Annexe created a cruciform plan. Adapted to mixed use in 1989 with new build uphill.

89 NORTH BRIDGE. By *John & Thomas Smith*, 1832, funded by the Turnpike Trustees. Two of its four arches were later infilled because of new road and house building along the banks of the Teviot. The visible arches are shallow and segmental with a

central panelled pilaster above a curved cutwater. Widened 1882, pedestrianised 2001.

St Margaret's (R.C.) Primary School, Buccleuch Terrace. By *Roxburgh County Council*, 1965. Two-storey N–S oriented block with glazed curtain-walled centre and blockwork ends. Sits behind its associated church and hall, which formerly functioned as the primary school.

Slitrig Crescent Bridge. *See* Description 1.

Stirches Primary School, Roxburghe Drive. *Borders Regional Council*, 1978 (project architects, *James Thornton* and *Ray Licence*). Semi-open-plan school with roof-lights to take advantage of natural daylight to produce interesting, brightly coloured internal spaces.

Teviotdale Leisure Centre, Mansfield Road. 1982, by *Faulkner-Brown, Hendy & Stonor*. Moderately Postmodern. Dominant sheer walls of horizontally banded pink granite and corrugated-steel roofs. A yellow-painted footbridge, with Y-shaped lamps along its length, punctures the E elevation at the entrance. The bowling-rink block is a later extension, distinguished by its cream roof. On the site of Hawick's railway station (1849, closed 1969). A platform survives at the car park entrance. The remainder is laid out as gardens, where a stone plaque marks the site of the Dovemount Toll.

Town Hall, 44 High Street. Designed by *James C. Walker* in 1883 and built in 1884–6 by *John & William Marshall* at a cost of £16,000. Dominant Scottish Baronial sandstone municipal building; its large four-storey square clock tower creates an impressive landmark at the corner with Cross Wynd. The narrow façade is to the High Street; only a single, half-dormered bay, crowned by four corner turrets separated by half-dormers. The pyramidal spire is interrupted midway by a bellcote and topped by a weathervane. Hoodmoulded string courses demarcate the changes in level. The long stepped profile of the SW elevation, however, descends with a sympathetic later addition. A tablet on the façade commemorates the nearby site of the Mercat Cross, first recorded in 1542. It stood in front of the town's tolbooth until 1762 and its base is preserved in Wilton Lodge Museum.

Trinity Primary School, Trinity Street. By *Reid & Forbes*, 1934–5. Hip-roofed two-storey block with set-back end pavilions and large metal-framed windows. Clean lines are created by the ashlar base course, string course and cornice; the remainder is harled. Later, utilitarian flat-roofed nursery at angle along Noble Place.

Former Wilton Primary School, Princes Street. 1847. Built as Wilton Parish School. Two-storey block, set back from the street, with arcaded ground floor and four gables to its main façade. An annexe to the SW is approached by a forestair to the main entrance. The NE range of 1883 is single-storey with hoodmoulded windows to the streetscape.

Wilton Primary School. *See* Description 4.

HAWICK MOTTE
Moat Park

Marooned but instantly recognisable as a medieval castle mound.
This was the *caput* of the Lovels, first Anglo-Norman lords of
the barony of Hawick, who migrated thither from Castle Cary,
Somerset, in about the middle of the C12. The site is protected
on the SE side by the steeply sloping bank of the Slitrig Water,
while to the NE the ground falls gently towards St Mary's
Church, *c.* 0.35 km. distant; the intervening space possibly
marks the position of the earliest town. The well-preserved,
artificial mound rises to a height of about 8 m. and measures
some 12.5 m. across the top. The motte was formerly surrounded by a broad, flat-bottomed ditch, evidence of which
was discovered during archaeological excavations undertaken
in 1912. There may also have been a bailey, presumably on the
NE side.

DRUMLANRIG TOWER
High Street

Hawick's oldest surviving building, transformed into a museum
and public information centre. A tower house built in about the
third quarter of the C16 by the Douglases of Drumlanrig to serve
both as a family residence and as the administrative centre of the
barony of Hawick. Standing on the E bank of the Slitrig Water a
little above its confluence with the River Teviot, the tower originally comprised an L-plan block of three main storeys and a
garret (11.2 m. by 8.0 m. with a W wing 5.8 m. by 5.6 m.); there
may also have been a barmkin. In the late C16 it passed to the
Scotts of Buccleuch and Branxholme, and in 1702–3 Anne Scott,
Duchess of Buccleuch, restored and enlarged the tower, filling in
the re-entrant angle between main block and wing to make the
building oblong on plan, and possibly adding the N wing. This
work (*William Walker*, wright) may have been undertaken with
the advice of *James Smith*, who was then remodelling the
Duchess's principal seat of Dalkeith House (Lothian). In 1769
the Buccleuch family turned the building into an inn, in which
role (latterly as the Tower Hotel) it continued until the early
1980s. In the early C19, probably *c.* 1810, the N wing was extended
and the W front to the High Street remodelled, while in 1835 a
reading room was installed and in 1939 a ballroom (*J.P. Alison &
Hobkirk*). Adapted to its present use in 1990–5 by *Jocelyn M. Cun-
liffe* of *Gray, Marshall & Associates* for Roxburgh District Council
and the Scottish Historic Buildings Trust (Hawick) Ltd.

The symmetrical W FRONT, with its three tiers of windows, displays no hint of the building's medieval origins. Constructed
of local whinstone rubble with dressings of buff sandstone,
mostly renewed in 1990–5. The central entrance of *c.* 1810 has
a pilastered Tuscan doorway and flanking lights framed by
plain pilaster strips which rise to the wall-head. At the rear the
greater part of the main block of the C16 tower house stands
exposed. Harled rubble walls rise to an open parapet-walk
carried on a continuous ovolo-moulded corbel course and a

garret chamber, both largely reconstructed during the 1990s with crowstepped gables. Apart from an oval-mouthed gunloop in the s wall at ground-floor level, which appears to be original, most of the openings, where not renewed in the recent restoration, appear to be of C17 and C18 date. The N wing retains its extruded conical-roofed stair-tower, linked to the tower house by a simple glass-walled extension of 1990–5.

With most of the rooms now refurbished to accommodate museum displays, it is difficult to envisage the early layout of the INTERIOR. The ground floor of the tower house probably contained two barrel-vaulted cellars, the smaller possibly a kitchen, while the principal entrance seems to have been situated at this level, close to the inner angle of the main block and wing. Just inside was a spiral staircase, occupying approximately the same position as the present one, and giving access to all the upper floors. When the re-entrant angle of the tower was infilled in the early C18, a new entrance was formed in the w wall of the addition, and a spacious curvilinear stair (since removed) was inserted in the original wing. At first floor the tower probably originally comprised a hall and chamber, and subsequently a dining room and two chambers. The hall retains an original roll-moulded fireplace similar to one at Timpendean Tower (q.v.). The painted ceiling and panelled doors and ingoes are all of the 1990s, designed to give some indication of changing fashions in interior decoration during the lifetime of the tower. On the second floor the main block retains a latrine closet together with a roll-moulded fireplace similar to the one below. Latterly there were another two chambers to the w, the division now marked by stone slabs set into the floor. In the C18–early C19 N wing there are three main public rooms on the first floor, the middle one being the former commercial room of the inn.

WILTON LODGE MUSEUM
Wilton Park

Early C17 country mansion, enlarged 1859. Now a museum. 115 Originally built, possibly on the site of an earlier stronghold, by the Langlands family who were granted a charter of the barony of Wilton by James II in 1451. The C17 house seems to have formed a U-plan with the principal two-storey, six-bay front facing the river. At some stage the sw wing was rebuilt to lengthen the rooms therein, and the open court gradually filled with additions. The house was acquired in 1805 by James Anderson, whose daughter Mary and her spouse David Pringle, a wealthy mill-owner, undertook major alterations in 1859. *Robert Hall & Co.* of Galashiels added a third storey to all three sides, remodelled the SE façade and added a SW domestic range. Bought by the Town Council in 1890; converted for its present use by *J.P. Alison* in 1910, with later additions.

Wilton Lodge faces SE towards the river with the ground rising steeply behind it. The main front as remodelled in 1859 has an advanced pedimented centre with porch bearing the initials DMP (David and Mary Pringle) and the date 1859 in a shield

above the family coat-of-arms. This addition and the contemporary broad ground-floor bay windows result in a crowded
elevation. The first-floor windows are adorned with broken
segmental pediments while the upper storey is lit by pedimented, finialled half-dormers. The same pattern of fenestration and decoration is carried to the sw wing. Its two Scottish
Renaissance pedimented dormerheads with thistle and rose
decoration, in addition to the four on the principal façade, may
originate from the C17 house. In 1859 the two first-floor
windows on the sw gable were replaced with plaques containing biblical inscriptions, and two broad bay windows were
added to the ground floor. This reconstructed range is considerably wider than its NE partner and slightly advanced from
it. The whinstone coursing of the C17 house was not disguised
on the NE elevation, and windows have been punched through
and subsequently blocked up. The scar of the roofline of the
pre-1859 domestic range is visible on the NW gable of the NE
wing. The rear of the building is dominated by the SCOTT
GALLERY added in 1975 by *Aitken & Turnbull* above part of
the considerable 1859 domestic range. Flat-roofed, harled and
supported by slender piers on its NE side (its windows now
blocked). Access to the covered parking area under the gallery
is via a small pavilion-roofed building to the NE of the museum.
A single-storey monopitch building sits at right angles to the
gallery.

The remodelling in 1859 obliterated all original features of
the C17 INTERIOR. Much altered again in 1910 although mid-
C19 details survive, including cornices and delicate shutters to
the bay windows in the principal rooms to the l. and r. of the
entrance hall. This double-height galleried space serves to
orient the visitor around the series of exhibition rooms on both
floors. The hanging stair, with elliptical-domed ceiling and iron
balustrade, was built in 1910 and replaced a spiral predecessor
at its rear. The area behind the original stair on the ground
floor, which formerly led into the 1859 kitchen and scullery,
was opened out to create a hall and is now used as offices. On
the second floor the long, narrow interior of the Scott Gallery
is sparsely detailed.

WILTON PARK has become one of the burgh's most attractive features. The public amenities include playing fields, tennis
courts, bowling greens and running track (added 1978). – C19
WALLED GARDEN (now nursery), and to its sw, the single-
storey bargeboarded gardener's cottage with projecting eaves.
– The park contains several monuments, including the impressive 1921 War Memorial by *James B. Dunn*; a 6.5m.-high cenotaph as a backdrop to a bronze statue 'Spirit of Youth
Triumphing over Evil' by *Alexander Leslie*. Two tablets have
been built into a low wall to its rear; the coat-of-arms from the
1895 Corn Exchange and a verse of Sir Walter Scott's cut in
1885 from the now demolished Linden Park House. – The
PATRIOTIC MEMORIAL, by *J. N. Scott & A. Lorne Campbell*,
was unveiled in 1903 to commemorate the Boer War; lone
figure of a soldier by *Thomas D. Rhind*. – The FOUNTAIN
was erected in 1896 following a bequest by Gilbert Davidson.
– The 1905 DRINKING FOUNTAIN in granite commemorates

Captain George Fraser Macnee. – The GUTHRIE MEMORIAL, by *Thomas J. Clapperton*, is a life-size bronze statue of James Guthrie, the Hawick-born motorcyclist killed in the 1937 German Grand Prix. Two bridges cross the Teviot from the park to its SE bank – LANGLANDS BRIDGE, to the SW, of 1893, by *Craik & Chisholm*, is a flat-span iron footbridge marking the former burgh boundary. Latticework sides, decorative scrolls and one stone pier at its centre. – LAURIE BRIDGE of 1924 is a shallow segmental arch. Its building was made possible by a bequest from Walter Laurie. – At the entrance from Roadhead Brae grand obelisk GATEPIERS overlooked by the LODGE, one-and-a-half storeys with prominent quoins.

DESCRIPTION

1. The Centre

The historic heart of the town is at the SW end of HIGH STREET, now characterised by sober commercial architecture of the later C19. We begin on the NW side at Mill Port. The BANK OF SCOTLAND was built as the British Linen Co. Bank by *David Cousin* in 1863; a proud three-storey, five-bay Venetian palazzo block beneath a strong entablature. No. 9, the red sandstone BORDER CLUB, is by *J.P. Alison*, 1900, with a broad double-height bay window on the first and second floors; its third floor nestles in the gable. LLOYDS TSB BANK, to its r., was also designed by *Alison*, 1914, as the Hawick Bank for the Savings of Industry, a dignified Italian Renaissance five-bay ashlar façade. Interior by *Scott Morton & Co.* ROUND CLOSE interrupts the row of plain C19 three-storey sandstone tenements. Behind No. 21 is WILLIAM BECK'S STOCKING SHOP, *c.* 1800, a charming whinstone building illustrating the condition of the stocking-makers' trade before industrialisation. Regularly placed small square windows, each of which would have lit the workspace of one stocking-maker. Converted to housing in 1991 by *Denis Rodwell*. Nos. 23–25 by *J.P. Alison*, 1898, has an elaborate yet delicately composed three-storey façade and incorporates a 1683 sundial retrieved from its mid-C18 predecessor. The ROYAL BANK OF SCOTLAND was built as the National Bank of Scotland, by *Archibald Scott*, 1860; its grand stuccoed seven-bay classical front has a mid-C20 marble-faced ground floor. Between Nos. 47 and 49 is the entrance to WALTER'S WYND, the medieval route through North Port to the ford across the Teviot. The vaulted ground floor of the town house of the Scotts of Horseleyhill, now No. 51, survived later rebuilding. Three-storey Nos. 65–67 was built as the Co-operative Society Store by *Michael Brodie*, 1885, with highly decorative French Renaissance façade topped by a part-mansard roof, round-headed dormers and acroteria. In front, THE HORSE, a celebrated bronze statue of a mounted standard bearer by *W.F. & T. Beattie*, 1921, commemorates the capture of an English flag by Hawick youths in 1514. It remains a focal point of the Common Riding ceremonies. Behind the statue, forming a fine terminus to the High Street vista, a Dutch-gabled block of 1894 by *J.P. Alison* with semicircular porch, bowed triple window above and lozenge-shaped window in its attic storey.

Back along the opposite side of the High Street, from the corner of Brougham Place. First, the LIBERAL CLUB of 1894, three and a half storeys with confident Renaissance detailing and balustraded balcony at its rounded corner; by *J.P. Alison*. The site of East Port is marked by a plaque at No. 78. The Town Hall (*see* Public Buildings, above) with its landmark clock tower is situated to the l. of CROSS WYND, which led to the Newcastle road; South Port stood at its foot. At its head is DOUGLAS OF SCOTLAND (hosiery works), an eight-bay mill of 1887 with three-storey square corner block of workshops and a lower, longer range. Nos. 30–32 High Street is the C19 QUEEN'S HEAD pub; with a distinctive bowed corner and balustraded parapet. The mid-C19 former Crown Hotel at Nos. 20–22 (now offices) has a French Renaissance façade topped with a mansard roof. The pend to the r., CROWN CLOSE, led to its stables. No. 12 High Street is the former Royal Bank of Scotland by *John Dick Peddie*, 1857, an Italianate three-storey, five-bay building with a decorative cornice.

Drumlanrig Tower (*see* Public Buildings, above) begins TOWERKNOWE, the continuation of the High Street across Drumlanrig Bridge (*see* Public Buildings, above); now a busy thoroughfare, it served as the marketplace after 1815. The imposing terminus to the High Street axis is the Italianate former COMMERCIAL BANK of 1852, credited to *Alexander Pirnie* but possibly by *David Rhind*; interior by *Scott Morton & Co.*, *c.* 1930. No. 7, at the N end of Drumlanrig Bridge, known as KEDIE'S BUILDING, is a late C19 classical five-bay edifice with a notable projecting parapet. Across the Slitrig Water is SILVER STREET, mainly Victorian apart from No. 5 of *c.* 1710. The street leads to KIRKSTILE where stands what is left of the former CORN EXCHANGE by *J.T. Rochead*, 1865: a fine Scottish Renaissance entrance with a pair of turreted corner towers, and an isolated round-arched gateway across the car park laid out following a fire in 1992. To be renovated in 2005–6 for the Scottish Borders Council archives and family history centre. The bridge upon which Kirkstile stands replaced the medieval Auld Brig in 1851 (the position of its E end is marked by a tablet on No. 2 Towerknowe) and carries above it the bulk of TOWER MILL (*see* Industrial Buildings, below). The rest of Kirkstile is C18 up to the steps leading to ST MARY'S PLACE. The dwellings here are early-to-mid-C19, some single-storeyed, others with forestairs. Skirting now the S boundary of St Mary's Old Parish Church (*see* Churches, above) to OLD MANSE LANE, and the harled two-storey OLD MANSE of 1765, with its pedimented advanced centre; best viewed from Slitrig Crescent. Turn r. at the N end of Kirkstile into TOWERDYKESIDE. Here whinstone buildings were renovated for Scottish Buildings Heritage Trust in the 1990s in conjunction with the restoration of Drumlanrig Tower, successfully conserving the close and retaining its quaint character.

SLITRIG CRESCENT (*c.* 1800), continuing S, one of Hawick's first expansions beyond the medieval burgh, was built up with mills and workers' housing from 1815. These include neat two-storeyed terraced houses, some perhaps originally flatted, now incorporated within Turnbull's Dyeworks (*see* Industrial Buildings, below). Original features such as irregularly spaced windows. The Crescent continues as far as St Cuthbert's Episcopal Church (*see* Churches, above) and the RECTORY at No. 22 by *G. Gilbert Scott, c.* 1858, an irregular L-plan two-storey Jacobean building of coursed whinstone with interesting triangular mouldings and shouldered doorway to porch; now subdivided. SLITRIG CRESCENT BRIDGE, a stone single-span arched road bridge with parapet, replaced the wooden footbridge and ford in 1864. It crosses back to the NW bank and THE VILLAGE. No. 1 (Slitrig Cottage) is an early C19 two-storey, three-bay house with a hipped roof with central dormer and a diminutive front garden. SLITRIG BANK to the r. of the bridge terminates with mid-C19 SLITRIG HALL, originally Hawick's first fire station, a pleasing two-storey harled façade with an engine arch and roundel window. Uphill now to DRUMLANRIG SQUARE, created in 1884 by demolishing the historic Mid Row; in the gardens is an elaborate canopied FOUNTAIN of 1910 by *J.P. Alison:* Ionic columns at its four corners with clock atop. The SE side includes a two-storey *c.* 1930s hosiery works (William Lockie & Co.) with paired windows and oriel on main façade and mill with 1879 date plaque to rear. Renovation and new build of similar scale with sparse detailing by the *Eildon Housing Association* in 1997 amongst C19 survivals. The West Port was located at the junction with the Loan. The NW side of the Square is predominantly C19.

To the NE end two- and three-storey C18 and C19 tenements of HOWEGATE, renovated by *Aitken & Turnbull* from 1978 when its backlands were cleared.

Beyond the crossroads with Buccleuch Street and Towerknowe lies SANDBED, once the focal point of the burgh and its marketplace until 1815. An island block was then built in its midst and stood until 1987. The former UNITED PARISH AND GRAMMAR SCHOOL, by *John & Thomas Smith*, 1825–6, on ORROCK PLACE is a single-storey block with a pedimented centre, the frontage now marred by a garage doorway. Next door is the former Orrock Place United Presbyterian Church (*see* Churches, above). Early C19 BRIDGE HOUSE, two-storey with a pilastered door surround, sits at the S end of ALBERT BRIDGE across the Teviot. The bridge is of 1865, by *A. Wilson.* Three elliptical masonry arches. It replaced Hawick's first bridge over the Teviot of 1741.

2. North and West of High Street

MILL PORT is a narrow lane N off the High Street. The mill succumbed to the great flood of 1767. TEVIOT ROAD continues behind High Street, with C20 redevelopment including the Hawick Health Centre (*see* Public Buildings, above) and, further along, the modern classicism of the *c.* 1930s former Labour Exchange. The brightly painted VICTORIA BRIDGE, across the Teviot, of 1991 (replacing predecessors of 1851 and 1938), has a pair of spherical lamps atop slender posts at its centre. TEVIOT CRESCENT, 1832, is a two-storey terrace in coursed whinstone built as skilled workers' housing. Nos. 1–6 later became part of Teviot Crescent Mill; its CROFT ROAD façade is of two and a half storeys. The cubical-proportioned SALVATION ARMY CITADEL, 1961, at No. 6 replaced the C19 Temperance Hall. To the r. is OLIVER CRESCENT where No. 10, with its chamfered corners, was once St John's Church (1879–80), brutalised into commercial premises *c.* 1960; its 1885 hall survives to the r. The street in front leads to OLIVER PLACE, a continuation of High Street. Nos. 3–4 on the r. are late C19 and display a carved lion atop a decorative dormer.

Oliver Place continues N as NORTH BRIDGE STREET. At the junction with Croft Road is the former POST OFFICE by *J.P. Alison*, 1892, its two-storey main block crowned by a balustraded parapet. Nos. 39–49 are Dutch-inspired Art Nouveau in red sandstone with shaped gables to the street; excellent mosaic work and curvilinear lettering at Nos. 43–45 by *J.P. Alison*, 1900. The Carnegie Public Library and Crown Buildings sit at the N end of the street (*see* Public Buildings, above), while the tenemented LAIDLAW TERRACE, to the l., overlooks the S bank of the Teviot. DOVECOTE STREET is workers' housing interrupted by a converted mill, *c.* 1875, originally four storeys, at No. 13.

In UNION STREET, E of North Bridge Street is another of *J. P. Alison's* designs, the FREEMASONS' HALL of 1893, with distinctive half-dormers. The Congregational Church (*see* Churches, above) lies directly ahead on BOURTREE PLACE. The broad, impressive Hawick Conservative Club (No. 22), again by Alison, 1897, was built on the site of East Toll. No. 2 is East Bank House, gable-ended red sandstone with an elaborate clock and flagstaff. BOURTREE TERRACE is the lane to the E; HAWICK BAPTIST CHURCH HALL with pedimented dormers sits on its r. An 1894 bandstand from Wilton Lodge Park functions as a BUS SHELTER beneath Trinity Church (*see* Churches, above). To the S of High Street BROUGHAM PLACE leads to the 1896 CHURCH HALL and its converted T-plan former school. MELGUND PLACE, on the r., GARFIELD STREET and LOTHIAN STREET to the SW, were originally lined with C19 workers' housing, mostly demolished in the 1960s. MILL BANK, running S, crosses a single-arch railway bridge, with LOCHPARK INDUSTRIAL ESTATE, 1968, to its l., on the site of a drained loch. From here turn uphill along Wellogate Brae.

WELLOGATE BRAE, primarily consisting of large free-standing villas, runs uphill along the N side of Wellogate Cemetery. Smaller villas on ORCHARD TERRACE give way to rows of workers' housing lining the hillside. Note the former Co-operative Society Stables by *Alison*, 1891, at the junction of ELM GROVE and Orchard Terrace, with thistle, star and beehive mouldings. The Hawick Working Men's Building & Investment Company developed the compact WELLOGATE area, predominantly after 1888; it includes a variety of house-types,

89

such as two-storey terraced quarter-houses on ETTRICK TERRACE and three-storey tenements on EDINA PLACE. Workers' housing again predominates in the area immediately N of Wellogate. MART STREET to the W is on the line of the old railway, while to the E is a large supermarket, which incorporates the Post Office. A single brick shed remains of the auction market, 1883, which occupied this site until 1992. On the N side of ESKDAILL TERRACE is DONCASTER BLOODSTOCK SALES LTD, a late C19 sandstone single-storey building of diminutive proportions with a carved bull's head protruding above the entrance. The BUCCLEUCH HOTEL, a two-storey, three-bay building with fretworked bargeboards, sits at the head of TRINITY STREET, while at the foot of the street is Trinity Primary School (*see* Public Buildings, above). The steps at the S end of NOBLE PLACE lead to WEENSLAND ROAD. A village developed E of here after 1835, when the first mill in this area was established. Thereafter the intervening field began to fill with private schemes, such as the elaborate half-timbered villas in SALISBURY AVENUE by *J.P. Alison*, 1897. OLIVER PARK follows and was built in 1922 as Hawick's first council housing. Mostly pairs of two-storey dwellings in English Domestic style; hipped roofs enlivened by gables at the front. Part of Weensland Mills survives to its r. (*see* Industrial Buildings, below), while residential developments cling to the S side of Weensland Road. Amongst these are two villas by *J.T. Rochead*, MANSFIELD HOUSE HOTEL, 1868, with its Italianate tower, and the stunted Grecian HERONHILL, 1865, whose T-plan LODGE is a picturesque interlude on WEENSLAND TERRACE.

3. Buccleuch Street and suburbs to the S

BUCCLEUCH STREET was laid out from 1815 as the 'New Road' W of the medieval burgh boundary, superseding Langbaulk Road as the principal route S, in response to industrial expansion. At the junction with Orrock Place is No. 2, a *c.* 1800 terminal block of three storeys, formerly an inn, restored in 1992. The N side is predominantly early C19 whinstone, interrupted by GRAPES CLOSE, which leads to the converted remains of the Grapes Inn and carrier stables of *c.* 1820. On the S side the former Subscription Rooms, built in 1821 to promote adult and cultural education; the portico of its single-storey Greek-style façade was removed in the C20. Almost opposite on Buccleuch Street's N side is FREE CHURCH LANE, leading to Teviot Church (*see* Churches, above) and the river. Facing the Teviot is ELLABANK, a small, well-proportioned villa, of the second quarter of the C19, in coursed whinstone. Hipped roof with end chimneystacks. Simple entablature above its doorway. Buccleuch Street continues S past the High School as BUC-CLEUCH ROAD, with a mix of housing including the BALCARY HOTEL, a former villa, with elaborate porch, built in 1889 as the residence of Patrick Laing of Wilton Mills by *J. P. Alison*, who also designed the pavilion of the nearby BUC-CLEUCH BOWLING CLUB, 1891 (but much altered) and the well-preserved HAWICK BOWLING CLUB of 1892. Standing behind the greens is the long, two- and three-storey C19 range of the former Green Mill. Dominating the foreground is the Romanesque Church Hall, by *Michael Brodie*, 1885–6, of the Old Parish Church (dem. 1992).

Buccleuch Place gives access to the MYRESLAWGREEN area to the S, which began to be developed from the beginning of the C19, partly with small villas, for example w of Morrison Place, but predominantly with workers' housing. A detour w into BRIGHT STREET leads to the former St Margaret's Dominican Convent (*see* Churches, above) but the SE end of Myreslawgreen opens into the LOAN opposite DRUMLANRIG HOSPITAL (closed 1995), built *c.* 1856 as the Combination Poorhouse and Workhouse. An extenuated block of whinstone with red sandstone dressings; arms from the demolished Buccleuch Memorial adorn its rear pediment. Wester Toll once stood on the site of No. 26, on the r. side of the Loan. Just beyond is Moat Park and Hawick Motte (*see* above).

4. *Wilton and Burnfoot*

The village of Wilton occupied much of the land on the N bank of the Teviot that was integrated into Hawick in 1861. It is reached via North Bridge (*see* Public Buildings, above). To the l. of the river crossing were the former glebe lands of Wilton Parish Church, where mills and workers' housing were built from 1798, including Eastfield Mills (*see* Industrial Buildings, below) on MANSFIELD STREET. The subdivided Jacobean old WILTON PARISH MANSE (by *John & Thomas Smith*, 1847) survives on Mansfield Square, isolated behind whinstone terraces. Large cylindrical gasometers of 1881 are all that remains of The Hawick Gas Light Company's gasworks in this area. Turning w on MANSFIELD ROAD, past the converted Mansfield Mills (*see* Industrial Buildings, below), sits the over-bearing expanse of Teviotdale Leisure Centre (*see* Public Buildings above), which occupies the site of the North British Railway's station (1849; dem. 1969). DOVEMOUNT PLACE includes the STATION HOTEL, 1871, with Doric-columned doorpiece, and the four-storey STATION BUILDINGS, 1947, on either side of LAING TERRACE.

At the foot of Wilton Hill is a well-kept painted whinstone terrace. Semi-detached late Victorian and Edwardian dwellings dominate the lofty WILTON HILL TERRACE on the r., while large C20 private houses line WILTON GLEN, adjacent to Wilton Cemetery (*see* Churches, above). E lies BURNFOOT, a heavily populated suburb developed by the Town Council since 1947; two-storey blocks with brick detailing predominate. Among its maze of streets is the Edwardian former Isolation Hospital on BURNFOOT ROAD (*see* Public Buildings, above). HOWDENBURN, lying in a deep valley to the NW of the cemetery, contains a select number of characterful early C19 residences. The SILVERBUTHALL and HOWDENBANK housing schemes, both developed by *John A. W. Grant* since 1946, rise wilfully to their rear.

Returning SW along WILTON HILL, the butterfly-roofed KATHERINE ELLIOT DAY CARE CENTRE and sheltered housing of 1980 form part of a row of later C20 buildings on the r. side of the road, including the Emergency Services buildings (*see* Public Buildings, above). The l. side consists of moderately sized villas, as does the self-contained STEWART-FIELD area opposite, such as the 1896 pink sandstone STRATHMORE for James Oliver, auctioneer, by *J.P. Alison*, with porch, bay window and Venetian dormer to its principal façade.

HAVELOCK STREET, at the foot of Wilton Hill, is lined with three-storey C19 tenements with the flat-roofed HAWICK YOUTH CENTRE, 1970, at its NW end. HAVELOCK PLACE on the l. consists of a U-plan block of mid-C20 council housing by *John A.W. Grant* and the three-and-a-half-storey rubble former CORN MILL. At the corner of Havelock Street and Wellfield Road are the crowstepped LODGE and gatepiers of Silverbuthall House (dem.). WILTON PRIMARY SCHOOL, on the r. side of WELLFIELD ROAD, was built by *Roxburgh County Council*, 1974 to serve the new housing developments. Flat-roofed, predominantly single-storey, consisting of three blocks with large playing fields to its NE. It stands on the site of Wellfield Villa, whose Gothic Revival LODGE is directly opposite.

Uphill along STIRCHES ROAD the STIRCHES housing development, built since 1973, has overtaken several villas from the later C19, including HAZELWOOD, Hazelwood Road, many gabled and bargeboarded with an advanced four-storey tower in the centre of its SW elevation. Round-arched doorway with balustraded balcony above. BROOMLANDS, of similar date, survives to the SW with its lodge. To the W, the Italianate MAYFIELD HOUSE is also surrounded by modern housing but still commands spectacular views from its square tower. A coach-house survives as MAYFIELD LOUNGE BAR; a T-plan one-and-a-half-storey gate lodge on MAYFIELD DRIVE. Its grounds have been developed with large detached private houses and recent schemes. Now along DICKSON STREET, past Wilton Parish Church (*see* Churches, above), to PRINCES STREET where, set behind a high wall, is a large Georgian mansion (HAIG HOUSE), built for Alexander Laing, co-founder of Wilton Mills.

The industrial heart of Wilton is approached via WILTON LANE, S of here on the other side of the old parish church-yard. Past the understated single-storey MASONIC LODGE, 1922, on the l. at the foot of Wilton Lane. ANDREW ARM-STRONG & SONS is early-to-mid C19, two-storey, rubble-built with timber forestair and short cylindrical brick chimney. The expansive Wilton Mills, and remnants of its neighbours, line much of COMMERCIAL ROAD (*see* Industrial Buildings, below) interrupted on the r. by the Borders College (*see* Public Buildings, above) at the corner with BATH STREET, named for the white-rendered, red-margined former Corporation Baths of 1912. Behind the college survive a few single-storey weaving sheds of DANGERFIELD MILL, whose 1872–3 High Mill and carding shed alas suffered two fires in 2003. The yarn store was converted into a knitwear factory by *Aitken & Turnbull* in 1960. The Bath Street façade of SHORTS OF HAWICK, also once part of Dangerfield, has keystone detailing similar to Eastfield Mills (*see* Industrial Buildings, below). At the SW

end of Commercial Road are the nine-bay late C19 Victoria
Steam Laundry, and the heavily rusticated and towered
former fire station, by *Alex Inglis*, 1913. Rusticated pilasters to
yellow sandstone former foundry, *c.* 1885. Bullnosed corners
demarcate the access to the 'Burgh Yard' opposite TURNBULL
& SCOTT ENGINEERS, early C20, distinguished L-plan
Jacobean two-storey building, shaped gables with arrowslit
motif and high parapet. TEVIOTDALE MILLS is a prominent
but undistinguished two-storey textile mill from the mid-to-
late C19. Finally, at the corner with Albert Bridge (*see* above,
p. 361), the BURNS CLUB, 1928, classical doorpiece with broad
entablature above which is perched a bust of the poet.

5. *Wilton Dean*

W of Commercial Road, extensive redevelopment in the C20
engulfed the Langlands estate around Wilton Lodge (*see*
Wilton Lodge Museum, above, p. 357), including the tiny
village of WILTON DEAN. The T-plan DEAN VILLAGE HALL
is the C19 former school. Its associated spinning mill was
demolished in 1860. Whinstone cottages mark the intersection
with DEAN ROAD which leads W. Large, mainly late C19 villas
adorn the hillside on the W and E branches of SUNNYHILL
ROAD, including WEST LANGLANDS, below which is its elaborate LODGE with ornamental lintel and fretworked bargeboards. Further substantial villas abound above LANGLANDS
ROAD. Nos. 13–19 are a pair of semi-detached houses with
half-dormers and bay windows. To the l. of the intersection
with ROSALEE BRAE is SALTHALL, an interesting thick-
walled, harled two-storey building with a segmental arch and
bow-ended buttresses. The Georgian LADYLAW, 1840, is the
first villa of its kind in the Wilton area, with a one-and-a-
half-storey, mansard-roofed lodge. NORWOOD, *c.* 1910 is an
accomplished Arts and Crafts mansion with mock-Tudor half-
timbering and castellated tower by *J.P. Alison* after 1904.
At the E end of Langlands Road is LAIDLAW PLACE, where part
of the terrace has been converted into commercial premises,
while the former site of Ladylaw Mills and the Hundred Steps
to Bath Street lie beneath to the SE. Underdamside was adjacent, below Wilton Path, which enjoyed rapid industrial expansion from 1826. The former ST ANDREW'S FREE CHURCH
MANSE of 1890 stands on the corner of Langlands Road and
WILTON PATH; it has a gabled advanced centre with a double-
height bay window. Some of the original buildings in the adjacent WELLINGTON area survive amongst the *c.* 1970s housing
estate. These include the small villas of WELLINGTON BANK
and WELLINGTON GROVE and workers' housing in HOW-
LANDS TERRACE and CARNARVON STREET. Here is the
122   impressive and imposing N. PEAL (WHOLESALE LTD.), a
knitwear factory of 1911 by *Alex Inglis*, with a four-storey tower,
red sandstone margins, oversized Mannerist keystone and
white harling in a similar style to Inglis's fire station in
Commercial Road (*see* above).

Scott's View, Dryburgh, showing site of Old Melrose (p. 643) and Eildon
Hills
St Abbs, harbour (p. 655)

Abbey St Bathans, Edinshall, Iron Age Fort and Broch, C1 or C2 A.D.
(p. 90)
Lyne, Antonine fort, C2 A.D. (p. 510)
Kelso Abbey, interior of the NW transept, C12 (p. 442)

6. Melrose Abbey, view looking E. Site of the nave and S nave chapels, C12, C15 and C16 (p. 534)

7. Melrose Abbey, exterior view from SW. S transept and nave, C14 and C15 (p. 534)

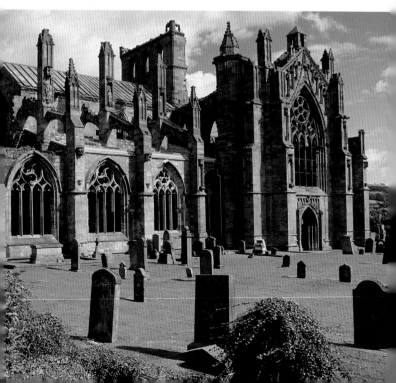

Jedburgh Abbey, exterior view from sw. Nave and central tower, late C12 and early C16 (p. 405)

Dryburgh Abbey, view across the site of the refectory and cloister to the s transept, late C12 and C13 (p. 213)

10	12
11	13
	14

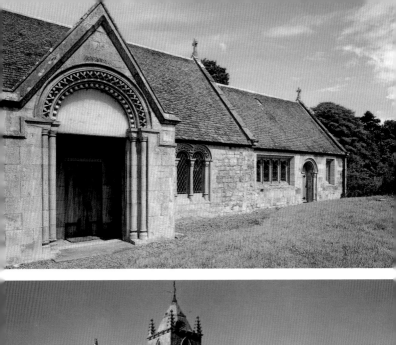

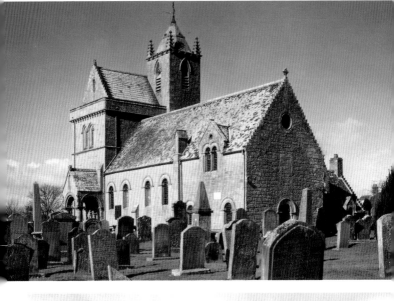

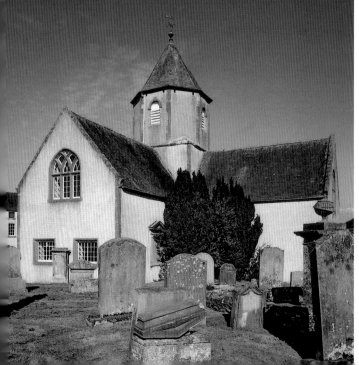

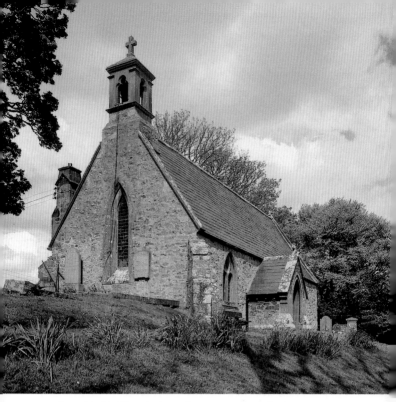

23. Kelso Old Parish Church, exterior, 1771–3 by James Nisbet and John
    Laidlaw; bellcote 1823 by William Elliot (p. 447)
24. Peebles Old Parish Church, exterior, 1885–7 by William Young (p. 616)

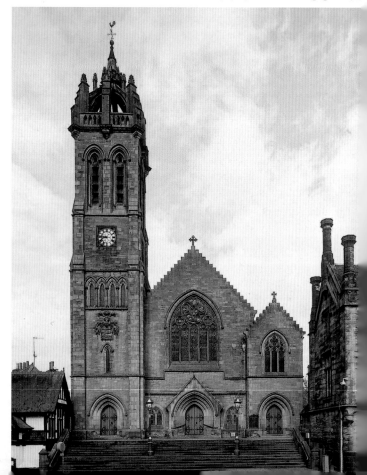

5. Duns Parish Church, interior, 1790, and 1880 by Wardrop & Reid (p. 231)
6. Ayton Parish Church, exterior, 1864–5 by J. M. Wardrop (p. 108)

The Corps of...
of John...
who Depairtit this Liveing th...
of November in the Fyfe Clein
year of his age

As also
The Corps of Grissell Cochrane his
Lady who died the 21 of March 1748
in the 83 year of her age
The Grissell Cochrane here referred to
is she who so heroically succeeded
in saving the life of her father
the Hon Sir John Cochrane of Ochiltree
a son of the 1st Earl of Dundonald
that under sentence of death
at Edinburgh owing to his
connection with the political
troubles of
1685

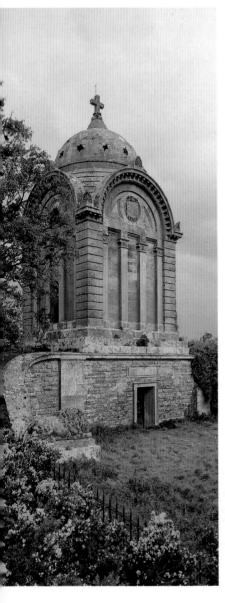

31. Monteath Douglas Monument, Gersit Law (Ancrum), 1864 by Peddie Kinnear (p. 105)
32. Denholm, Leyden Monument, 1861 by Hector H. Orrock and A. Handyside Ritchie (p. 209)

Peebles, Chambers Institution, War Memorial, by B.N.H. Orphoot, 1922
(p. 619)

MUNGO PARK
BORN AT FOULSHIELS
SELKIRKSHIRE
10TH SEPTEMBER 1771.
KILLED AT BOUSSA ON THE
NIGER, AFRICA 1805.

Dryburgh, William Wallace statue, 1814 by John Smith (p. 226)
The Hirsel, monument to Lord Home (†1995) by Bill Scott (p. 381)
Selkirk, High Street, Mungo Park Monument, by Andrew Currie, 1859,
bronze panels and figures by Thomas J. Clapperton, 1906 and 1912
(p. 673)
Neidpath Castle, late C14, upperworks remodelled in mid C17 (p. 577)

34 35
36 | 37

38	40
39	41

4. The Hirsel, west front, *c.* 1706 (right), extended 1739–41 (left).
   Remodelled *c.* 1813 (p. 379)
5. Traquair House, High Drawing Room, chimney overmantel, 1762
   (p. 734)

72. Leadervale House, early C19 (p. 489)
73. Gledswood House, *c.* 1805 (p. 323)

4. Ladykirk, Lion Gateway, by William Elliot, 1799 (p. 479)
5. Carolside, *c.* 1783 with early C19 wings, possibly by Alexander Stevens Jun (p. 152)

86	
87	88

OPENED
26 October
1826

4. Galashiels, Cornmill Square, Burgh Chambers by Robert Hall & Co., 1867, clock tower and war memorial by Robert Lorimer, 1923–7 (p. 300)
5. Kelso, Woodmarket, Corn Exchange, by David Cousin, 1855 (p. 450)
6. Selkirk, Ettrick Terrace, Sheriff Courthouse, by David Rhind, 1868–70 (p. 670)
7. Selkirk, Scotts Place, Victoria Halls, by Hippolyte J. Blanc, 1895–6, bronze statue of 'Fletcher' by Thomas J. Clapperton, 1913 (p. 671)

103. Kelso, High School, 1936, by Reid & Forbes (p. 451)

104. Galashiels, Nether Road, Heriot-Watt University, Scottish Borders Campus, by R. Forbes Hutchison and George R. M. Kennedy, 1964–6 (p. 302)

5. Kelso, High School, music department, by Borders Regional Council, 1994 (p. 451)

6. Kelso, Edenside Health Centre, by Peter Womersley, 1967 (p. 450)

7. Jedburgh, Mary, Queen of Scots' House, *c.* 1600 (p. 425)

8. Kelso, Ednam House, by James Nisbet, 1761 (p. 464)

9. Eyemouth, Gunsgreen House, probably by John and James Adam, *c.* 1753 (p. 271)

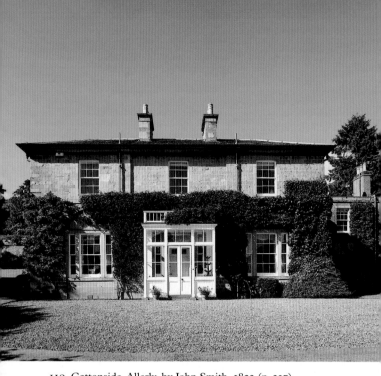

| 110 | 112 |
| 111 | 113 |

114. Walkerburn, Stoneyhill, 1868 by F.T. Pilkington (p. 742)

5. Hawick, Wilton Park, Wilton Lodge Museum, early C17, third storey and bay windows added 1859. War Memorial, by James B. Dunn, 1921 (p. 358)

6. Galashiels, Tweed Terrace, Lucy Sanderson Cottage Homes, by Mears & Carus-Wilson, 1930–33 (p. 313)

117. Kelso, Maxwellheugh Terrace, attributed to Lady Douglas of Springwood, 1863 (p. 464)
118. Selkirk, Bannerfield Estate, by Basil Spence & Partners, 1945–64 (p. 679)
119. Selkirk, Dunsdale Road, Ettrick Mill, 1836, extended by John & James Smith, 1850 (p. 681)
120. Galashiels, Huddersfield Street, Gala Mill, late nineteenth-century (p. 315)

121. Hawick, Commercial Road, Wilton Mills, 1867 (left) and 1877 (right)
    (p. 368)
122. Hawick, Carnarvon Street, Peal knitwear factory, by Alex Inglis, 1911
    (p. 366)

VILLA

LINNWOOD, Liddesdale Road. C19 and early C20. This large white U-plan house on the W bank of the Slitrig appears to have evolved organically; it is sited in front of a wooded backdrop on the steeply sloping river bank. Its principal façade is the E elevation which is two storeys and three bays with a ground-floor bay window and classical door surround. The N range is possibly slightly earlier and has half-dormers and a single-storey wing to its W. The S range is early C20 and has an impressive projecting chimneystack with a roundel in its centre and a short single-storey projection to its W. A private bridge over the Slitrig leads to its driveway, which is preceded by a one-and-a-half-storey lodge with a chamfered gabled projection.

INDUSTRIAL BUILDINGS

EASTFIELD MILLS, Mansfield Road. Opened 1798, one of several water-powered factories established on the glebe lands of Wilton Church for Blenkhorn, Richardson & Co., 1882. Two-storey French Renaissance main block with single-storey wings. Round-headed ground-floor windows with X-incised keystones and a main entrance dominated by its broad entablature with large nailhead mouldings. The end bays are advanced under steeply pitched mansard roofs with balustraded balconettes at first floor.

GLEBE MILLS, Glebemill Street. Established 1815 by Robert Pringle & Son. Rebuilt in the late C19. N façade to the Teviot, the earlier part is of seven bays, flat-roofed and of two storeys, apparently reduced from three given its present disjointed appearance. Crenellated two-storey E projection in coursed sandstone. A single-storey range links W to a large interwar harled block with a steel chimney.

JOHN TURNBULL & SONS, Slitrig Crescent. Built soon after extension of the burgh across the Slitrig, c. 1800. Pringle, Waldie & Wilson had a hosiery business at the Whisky House Mill (now dem.) on the Crescent in 1815–19, and alterations to some of the terrace houses may have begun at this date. The former corn mill on Mill Path dates to c. 1805; three storeys and attic, with a hipped roof, constructed of whinstone with red sandstone dressings. Its associated mill house, on the S corner of Mill Path and Slitrig Crescent, is of three bays and two storeys with a pilastered doorpiece. These buildings and the N part of the Crescent constitute the dyeworks; some of the houses have been demolished, and replaced by a Modernist cubic flat-roofed entrance block of the 1950s and a single-storey range, whilst others have been boarded and modified.

LYLE & SCOTT, Liddesdale Road. An extensive complex developed from the c. 1930s. Flat-roofed entrance with L & S monogram in bordered square and a generous hoodmould over its three windows in a plain, Modern style.

MANSFIELD MILLS, Mansfield Road, 1880–1929. Formerly the mills of James Renwick & Co. Front range converted to housing in 1996. Three-storey and attic block with seven bays

to the W of its three-storey advanced square tower, with a
further two bays to its E on the S elevation. The E bay has a
double-height bay window, and this two-bay appendage is
mansarded. Vestiges of its industrial use include the single-
storey weaving sheds to the rear and the remains of its mill
lade visible below Mansfield footbridge.

PETER SCOTT & CO., No. 9 Buccleuch Street. Peter Scott & Co.
was established in 1872 and moved to existing premises in Buccleuch Street. The central block was erected c. 1816–17 shortly
after the new road was built, and originally functioned as solic-
itors' offices and dwellings. Converted and extended by Scott's
from 1878. This three-and-a-half-storey façade comprises
several phases. From l. to r. these are a long ten-bay block with
four-bay advanced centre and tripartite windows, followed by
a fourteen-bay range with tightly spaced fenestration and,
finally, a broad sandstone gabled end bay with rusticated giant
pilasters. Red-brick octagonal chimney to rear.

TOWER MILL, Towerknowe/Kirkstile. Built by Messrs. Elliot,
hosiery manufacturers. A spinning mill is marked on Wood's
1824 map at the NW end of the Auld Brig, apparently constructed from masonry salvaged from the thinning of Drumlanrig Tower's walls and the demolition of some of the town's
vaulted dwellings. Rebuilt or extended for the Messrs. Elliot
in 1851 when the bridge was renewed and the mill built over
it. This single-span segmental arch carries the larger part of
this mill; three storeys and attic, rubble-built with irregular
pattern of glazing. Angled towards Kirkstile. Its massive waterwheel, housed in a basement to the N, was the first in Hawick
to generate electricity in 1900. To be converted in 2005–6 as
an Arts Centre with a small theatre and learning centre by
Gray, Marshall & Associates.

WEENSLAND MILLS, Weensland Road. Mid-C19. The four-
storey main block is M-gabled, double-roofed with an octagonal ogee-roofed bellcote and open colonnade. Much else
demolished since 1991; its square brick chimney survives.

121   Former WILTON MILLS, Commercial Road. For Dickson &
Laing, established 1811, closed 1908. Their first mill (1815) was
destroyed by fire in 1867, after which a large complex evolved.
Rusticated main block is three storeys and attic, and eight bays
with a long rear parallel wing. The E corner has a four-storey
square clock tower, while a castellated tower clings on to
the N corner of the rear block. To its NE is a two-storey block
of 1877; French Renaissance with diagonally set square
turrets. Largely disused. One- to two-storey buildings and the
former mill house have been converted to l. and r. of the main
block.

STONE CIRCLE, Burgh Hill, 8 km. SSW. Lying just off the crest
of the hill, this oval setting of the second millennium B.C., measuring 16 m. by 13 m., comprises about twenty-five stones.
Many of the stones are now recumbent, but the tallest probably stood on the SW.

BRANXHOLME CASTLE. *See* p. 134.
BURNHEAD TOWER. *See* p. 146.
COLISLINN. *See* p. 191.

HAYSTOUN HOUSE   2030
2.4 km. s of Peebles

A pleasant Scottish Domestic house of several periods concealed behind cream-washed harling after a remodelling from 1920 by *Orphoot, Whiting & Bryce* for Sir Duncan Hay.

The house contains at its sw corner a late C16 or C17 tower house which was first incorporated within an L-plan house *c.* 1660–73 (the dates of two armorials belonging to John Hay). The house was extended e by the addition of a kitchen *c.* 1700. Haystoun ceased to be the family seat after Kingsmeadows House, Peebles (q.v.) was built in 1795, and became a farmhouse in the early C19. Stables and byres, creating the present court-yard plan, were converted from 1920 to form part of the house. Wide gables were added to the e and w fronts of the e range, and also a canted two-storey block at the e end of the original house, with a columned and arched veranda facing s, supported on stone brackets. The C17-type dovecot with eight pigeon holes in the sw re-entrant between the house and w range, and the corbelled-out small turret in the se re-entrant appear to be C20. The interior is all of the C20 except for a late C18 stone geometric stair in the w wing. The principal entrance opens into a hall, formerly the C18 kitchen, which runs the width of the house. w of the hall is the library made from two small rooms. In the drawing room, at the e end, a shallow vault decorated with Scottish Renaissance style plasterwork by *Leonard Grandison,* and a wide stone fireplace from the old kitchen. Also at the e end the dining room with more plasterwork by Grandison. On the e side of the hall a timber stair by *Scott Morton & Co.,* with twisted newels and grotesque finials.

WALLED GARDEN. Dated 1729 over a NW doorway, but this appears too early for the walls. – A former MILL and barn, and the mill lade survive.

HEITON   7030

Small Teviotside hamlet, mostly owned by the Edinburgh Merchant Company.

Former SCHOOL and SCHOOLHOUSE. Rendered with cream sandstone margins and deep overhanging eaves. The schoolroom has a chimneyed gable to the street; two-storey schoolhouse with jerkin-headed gables.

VILLAGE HALL. Mid C20(?). Rectangular, with round-arched

windows along the s side, and a canted bay to the street with
a line of windows round the wall-head.

DESCRIPTION. N of the school are two or three ruinous cottages. They may have been the house and smithy described as
'new' in 1800. Mid-to-late C19 houses line MAIN STREET:
No. 3 has a Baronial canted bay corbelled to a gable, and a
porch with stumpy columns on pedestals; Nos. 17–23, an
asymmetrical Tudor-detailed group, have projecting gables and
clusters of four square brick chimneystacks, and some decorative glazing. At the N end at HEITON MAINS FARM, offices
of c. 1843, with crowstep-gabled ends. Large farmhouse, dated
1883, in rock-faced red sandstone with half-timbered eaves,
and bracketed canopied porch.

HENDERSYDE PARK

7030

2.4 km. NE of Kelso

Classical house of 1938–40 by *Thomas Greenfield* with *E.B. Tyler*
of *John Dickson & Anthony Tyler*, built in polished sandstone,
with timber dentilled eaves, and metal casements. N entrance,
with a wide pedimented Doric doorcase, and an open loggia
on the E side. Excellent chimneypieces, including one of
Carrara marble, from Springwood Park, Kelso (dem. 1954),
with caryatid figures based on the Temple of the Winds, the
centre panel in the frieze alive with cherubs and dancing
females. This house replaced one built 1802–3 for George
Waldie and added to c. 1840 by *John Smith* for John Waldie to
house his extensive picture collection and library. On the long
terrace are urns carved by *William Cockburn*, c. 1840.

STABLES. Most likely by *John Smith*, c. 1830. Pedimented w
front with a rusticated segmentally-arched pend and timber
belfry. E range of the courtyard with a two-bay central pedi-
ment with oculus. – Octagonal SUMMERHOUSE, c. 1830.
Dentilled cornice, and overhanging eaves. – DORIC
GATEWAYS, c. 1840, one in each of the s and E walls of a field.
– WEST LODGE (A698), c. 1830, by Smith. Matching EAST
LODGE (A698) and NORTH LODGE (B6461), by *William
Cockburn*, c. 1840, using stone from the Hendersyde quarry.
Identical square gatepiers and cast-iron railings.

HERIOT

3050

Small village on a high moor, served by the railway from 1849
until 1969.

PARISH CHURCH. Set apart from the village, by *J.M. Wardrop*,
1875, in an English mid-C13 style. Pink rubble structure with
buff dressings (and with a w wall that has been harled). Of
basically rectangular plan, but with gabled transeptal projections close to the W end, a N porch in the angle against the NW
transept, and an irregular grouping of vestry and outbuildings
against the SW transept. A gabled bellcote rises from a broad
turret at the centre of the E wall. Single trifoliate-headed

windows to the nave, pairs of lancets in the s transept and w
wall (the latter with a cinquefoil, above) and a three-light Geometric-traceried window in the N transept. Polygonal ceiling
with arched braces. – Some FURNISHINGS probably retained
from a church of 1804–5. – COMMUNION TABLE, with arcaded
front. – PEWS, some with doors.

Along the exterior of the s wall, three MEMORIALS: at the
centre an arched and gabled composition apparently contemporary with the church. Towards the E end is an imposing mid-
c18 design flanked by volutes and with a winged angel head in
the pediment; the inverted egg-and-dart border suggests mis-
understanding of pattern-book sources.

CHURCHYARD, several good pedimented stones with
memento mori, mainly to s of church. – FIRST WORLD WAR
MEMORIAL of *c.* 1920. Cast-iron decorative gates with a panel
on each pier inscribed with names of the fallen.

Former MANSE (Heriot Water). By *J. M. Wardrop*, 1862–3, in
pinkish red sandstone. Tripartite windows with narrow sidelights flank a consoled and corniced doorway.

MACFIE HALL, 0.6 km. E. Built 1921. Jerkin-headed and gabled
porch. Stained-glass window.

PRIMARY SCHOOL. 1853–4, by *William J. Gray Sen.* of Coldingham. Whinstone with sandstone dressings. Twin-gabled
schoolroom, each gable with a large pointed-arched window.
Carved ball finials. Attached, a two-storey gabled schoolhouse,
the lean-to porch with a Gothic doorway.

HERIOT HOUSE, 3 km. NE. Former late c18 coaching inn with
a bakehouse and brewhouse. Later c19 piend-roofed porch
and canted dormers. Rubble-built stables with segmental-
arched cartshed and brick voussoirs.

RAESHAW LODGE, 3.2 km. W. Shooting lodge by *J.M. Dick
Peddie*, 1910, for T. W. H. McDougal. Eight-bay single-storey
and attic harled house with crowstepped gables, added to an
existing tiny lodge, evidently with a round-capped tower, which
was given an extra storey. E front with a row of eight pedimented wall-head dormers. The ground floor was formerly
fronted by a veranda of tree trunks.

BORTHWICK HALL. *See* p. 125.

GILSTON PELE. *See* p. 323.

HERMITAGE CASTLE   4090
9 km. N of Newcastleton

Bleakest of Border castles, Hermitage stands in a remote upland
valley less than 10 km. from the Anglo-Scottish frontier. This was
one of the most powerful and militarily active fortresses of the
Middle March and its dramatic ruins evoke the comfortless real-
ities of medieval warfare more than most. The existing buildings
belong mainly to the c14 and c15.

The first castle on the present site was probably a massive earthen
ringwork built in the 1240s by Sir Nicholas de Soules, lord of
Liddesdale. By about the beginning of the c14 Hermitage had
replaced Liddel Castle (*see* Castleton) as the principal fortress

of the lordship, and its immense strategic importance ensured the castle a prominent role in the Wars of Independence. In 1355 Hermitage was granted to a Cumberland landowner, Hugh Dacre, who probably erected the core of the present castle, not as one would expect in the form of a major strong-hold but rather as a fortified manor house or hunting lodge of modest size. Its position, however, was precarious, for William, first Earl of Douglas, who eventually obtained the house *c.* 1371, also claimed the lordship. By that date the building (pos-sibly still incomplete) seems to have comprised two blocks flanking a tiny courtyard closed on the other two sides by screen walls, of which that to the N incorporated a staircase and that to the S an entrance.

Shortly thereafter the Douglases began to convert it into an exceptionally well-defended tower house of unusual design, constructed in three distinct phases and only finally completed in the early C15. The lower portion of the manor house was encapsulated within a great, oblong tower house comparable in size (22.9 m. by 13.7 m.) to that of Dundonald Castle (Ayr-shire), its courtyard being covered over and a new first-floor entrance provided on the W side. Before the walls had been carried much above second-floor level, square turrets were added to three corners of the tower. In a third phase of work an oblong chamber block, no doubt for the lord and his imme-diate family, was attached to the remaining, or SW, corner, and the walls were carried to their full height, comprising at least four storeys in the main block and five in the turrets and chamber block. At the same time the entire superstructure was crowned by a semi-permanent timber gallery designed to serve as a fighting platform in times of siege. Since it was impracti-cable to take this platform round the recesses between the corner turrets, massive stone arches were constructed to carry it straight across the W and E sides of the castle. Above the plat-form was a parapeted wall-walk. Hermitage passed out of Douglas ownership in 1491 and was annexed by the Scottish Crown for much of the 1530s and early 1540s, when the castle was adapted for artillery defence. In 1594 it was purchased by Sir Walter Scott of Branxholm, whose descendants are still in possession. Ruinous by the end of the C18, the building was repaired by the fourth Duke of Buccleuch in 1806–10 and, more extensively, by the fifth Duke in 1833–4. Now in the care of Historic Scotland.

EXTERIOR. As recently analysed,* the RINGWORK occupied a roughly square platform bounded on three sides by a ditch and on the third by the Hermitage Water. However, all the ramparts, except that on the W (previously identified as a C16 gun platform), were levelled in the C14 to make way for the manor house. The ditch system surrounding the castle incor-porated part of the flow of two burns draining into the Her-mitage Water, while additional earthworks *c.* 60 m. to the N may have been designed to divert surplus water away from the site. The area of level ground between the two systems of earth-works may originally have contained an outer bailey, but the

* By RCAHMS.

existing surface remains are probably stock enclosures associated with a C18 farmstead lying immediately E of the castle.

The STONE CASTLE is constructed of roughly coursed blocks of coarse, buff-coloured local sandstone, with similar dressings, although the earlier work is of reddish sandstone ashlar probably imported. The most conspicuous exterior features are the flying arches that supported the fighting platform on the W and E sides, and the series of small, rectangular doorways running right round the building at this level, which gave access to the platform from within. Below these openings, which are rebated for external shutters, can be seen the corbels and putlog holes for the supporting timbers. Much of the E wall, including the arch, and almost the entire superstructure, was rebuilt in the 1830s, so it is unclear whether the parapet-walk was used in tandem with the fighting platform or put in place following its final abandonment. Except in the well-lit SW chamber block, there are few windows, most of those at the lower levels being mere slits and many of them refurbishments, but at least one of a pair of round-headed, mullioned and transomed windows at the top of the chamber block appears to be original, a type more usually found on the English side of the Border. The corbelled lintels that span many of the late C14 and early C15 doors and windows are also characteristic of contemporary northern English work. Several windows were converted into gunloops *c.* 1540, some of them large enough to take cannon.

The present entrance is through the S doorway. Although refaced in the 1830s, it was originally the door to the courtyard of the C14 manor house. But the position of the ground-floor entrance has been changed more than once and it was probably blocked in the late C14 when the turrets were built, for the SE turret had a postern doorway, complete with portcullis and slot-machicolation. Subsequently this was blocked up and presumably the S doorway reinstated at that time. The principal entrance to the tower house, however, was by a forebuilding at the SW corner, taking the form of a small rectangular projection, as at Etal Tower, Northumberland. This doorway was blocked *c.* 1540, when the existing wide-mouthed gunloop was inserted in the former opening. After the closure of this entrance, the S doorway became the only means of access to the castle.

The INTERIOR, unsurprisingly, shows traces of extensive alterations and repairs, including several changes in floor levels and staircase arrangements, which makes analysis of layout and function difficult. Apart from the ground floor of the NE turret and the top floors of the NW and SE turrets, which were vaulted, the entire building was floored and roofed in timber. It is evident that the castle was designed with a greater emphasis upon military capability than was usual. The cheerless upper floors, apparently unheated and almost unlit when the fighting platform was in position, could have housed a sizeable garrison. Moreover, there were two wells within the castle walls, together with ample sanitary provision. In contrast, apart from the accommodation in the SW chamber block, there were few chambers equipped for the use of senior members of the

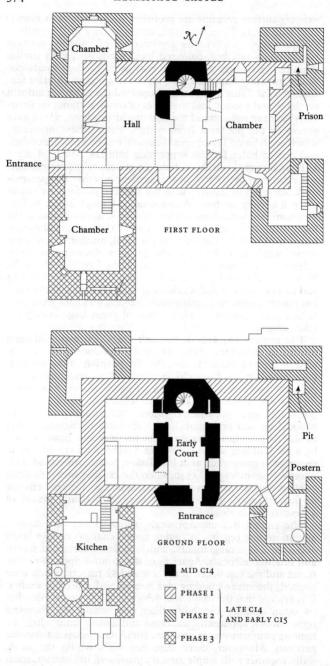

Hermitage Castle.
Plans.

FIRST FLOOR

Chamber

Hall

Chamber

Prison

Entrance

Chamber

GROUND FLOOR

Early
Court

Pit

Postern

Entrance

Kitchen

■ MID C14

PHASE 1

PHASE 2

PHASE 3

LATE C14
AND EARLY C15

30 m
100 ft

household and guests. The s entrance opens directly into what was originally the cobbled courtyard (c. 7.8 m. by 4.4 m.) of the CI4 MANOR HOUSE, whose lower walls display facework of superior quality, many of the stones bearing distinctive masons' marks. Round-headed doorways lead into the flanking blocks, of which that to the E, perhaps originally a cellar with chamber above, retains a two-light window looking into the court, while its neighbour to the W, perhaps originally for kitchen and hall, contains a well. A third doorway on the N gives access, by way of a (much-restored) newel stair, to the first floor, whose joists were supported upon buttressed mid-ribs spanning the rooms below. Little now remains of these upper chambers, but the one to the E evidently had two windows overlooking the court. The stair evidently rose higher, perhaps to give access to a wall-walk. From the late CI4 the ground floor of the main block comprised three unlit cellars. There was no communication at this level between the main block and the corresponding chambers in the NW and NE corner turrets and the SW chamber block. The SE turret, however, communicated directly with the E cellar and contained a well. When the postern doorway into the turret was blocked, a narrow, arched stone staircase was inserted to provide access to the well from the upper floors.

The main SW entrance at first floor led directly into an entrance passage. Only its N side survives, but it can be seen that the entrance was defended by two portcullises, one immediately within the portal and the other at the rear of the passage. The passage led to the outer and larger of two chambers on the first floor. Although poorly lit and now possessing no identifiable fireplace, this was probably a lower hall; it may also have contained a stair rising against the inner face of the W wall to give access to a second floor. When the chamber block was added, the SW corner of the hall was opened up to give access to the adjacent first-floor chamber, which had its own fireplace and latrine. Close by, steps led down to a ground-floor kitchen. The opposite corner of the hall communicated with the NW corner turret, which originally contained a small, but well-lit chamber with a fireplace. Access to the featureless ground floor of the turret was presumably by ladder. The E side of the main block contained a well-lit chamber with a fireplace in its E wall. This may have been the keeper's chamber, and from it access was obtained to the adjacent corner turrets, that to the NE being a prison, with a particularly nasty pit below, and that to the SE housing the service stair already mentioned. Before this stair was inserted, the chamber contained the mechanism for operating the portcullis below, the groove for which can still be seen. The doorway and passage into the NE turret appear to be integral and contemporary with the surrounding masonry, and the same is true of some of the other openings into this and other turrets, suggesting that the addition of corner turrets was anticipated during the construction of the main block.

At second-floor level the main block seems to have contained a single, very large chamber (18.6 m. by 9.1 m.), well furnished with windows and having a sizeable fireplace in its S

wall. This was presumably a great hall, with the adjacent chambers on this and the upper floors of the SW chamber block –
all of them well-appointed – comprising the private quarters
of the lord and his family. Subsequently the hall was subdivided to create an additional chamber at the E end. At this
level the NW turret contained a storeroom and the SE one a
chamber, while the NE turret housed a latrine serving the hall.
Another latrine opened off the service stair in the SE turret, the
chute itself being contained within a prominent corbelled
outshot. The layout at the upper levels is far from clear. The
top floor, or floors, of the main block seem to have served
mainly to give access to the fighting platform and wall-walk,
the general arrangement probably not unlike Threave Castle
(Dumfries and Galloway). The corner turrets and SW chamber
block likewise incorporated doorways to the fighting platform,
but after the platform went out of use many were blocked up
or converted into windows. At the same time vaults were constructed at the tops of the SE and NE turrets, the latter one supporting what seems to have been a lookout stance, approached
by steps from the adjacent wall-walk. The roofing arrangements must have been complicated, for the plan is irregular
and the main block has an exceptionally wide span. It seems
likely, however, that the W and E sides of the building were
covered with pitched roofs and the main block with a flat or
low-pitched roof.

Two well-preserved systems of DEER DYKES, lie on either side of
the castle, enclosing the haugh lands on the N bank of the Hermitage Water. The system to the W also takes in a substantial
area of hill ground from which deer may have been channelled
towards a killing ground c. 0.1 km. W of the castle. c. 0.3 km.
further W is another group of EARTHWORKS, within the E division of which there is a burial ground containing the lowest
courses of a stone-built CHAPEL, excavated in 1900 and 1926.
Constructed of ashlar sandstone blocks, it was a single cell of
five unequal buttressed bays (15.7 m. by 7.4 m.); the floor of
the E bay is raised, presumably to take the altar. The plan and
surviving fragments (some preserved at Hermitage Farm)
suggest a date c. 1300. The older enclosure measures c. 33 m.
square within an embanked dry ditch surrounding it on all
except the S side. Immediately to the W is a second and larger
oblong enclosure containing possible traces of buildings. Both
in size and in their relationship to one another these enclosures
resemble those at Muirhouselaw (*see* Maxton) and it is possible that they mark the site of a seignorial residence of C13 or
C14 date.

HIGH SUNDERLAND
3 km. N of Selkirk

80 An imaginative single-storey house, beautifully situated on the
high shoulder of a hill, making full use of splendid views and sunlight. Built 1956–8 by *Peter Womersley* for Bernat Klein, textile
designer. The Kleins had visited Farnley Hey, near Huddersfield,

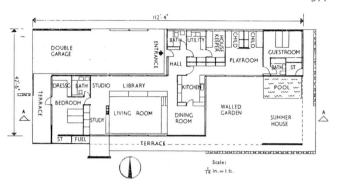

High Sunderland.
Plan.

designed by Womersley for his brother in 1954–5, and liked what they saw.

The house is a flat-roofed rectangle, with a rigidly geometric pattern of white-painted timber frames, faced with vertical boarding, sliding windows and fixed panels of variously coloured glass (green, yellow, black and fawn); all set on a concrete platform. The Miesian open plan comprises two parallel wings, the SW one for living area and principal bedroom, the NE one for children and guests, linked by a central service area. Inside, the central part of the living area is set lower than a raised platform which surrounds it on three sides and serves a variety of functions; the sunken area also has the effect of foreshortening the exterior view, which gets rid of the feeling of exposure through the continuous glass wall. Womersley designed the built-in furniture and fittings, and there is a pleasing pattern of texture and rich colouring from the textiles and wall hangings supplied by *Klein*. Very little alteration has taken place, although the children's recesses, leading off the playroom, have been converted into separate bedrooms, and a study/studio has been fitted into part of the SE courtyard; both carried out by *Bernat Klein*.

DESIGN STUDIO, S of the house in woods. By *Womersley*, 1970. An exceptional composition in concrete, brick and glass, which appears to grow out of the ground and float among the trees. The best approach is from the house, by a wooded path, over a bridge and straight into the first floor. This entrance was not part of the original design, but required as a separate fire escape from the main working area. Reinforced concrete with a base of blue-black bricks. The base carries the central core, and four concrete columns support the first-floor glazed study, sandwiched between horizontal projecting floor beams. The open studio has four zones, the central one for services and exhibitions, the N section for painting, the W one for conferences and the S one – with the comfort of a fireplace – for discussion. Awaiting conversion to a dwelling in 2005.

HILLSLAP TOWER

4 km. NE of Galashiels

42   One of three C16 tower houses standing within about 0.5 km. of one another in the valley of the Allan Water. Hillslap, also known as Calfhill, was erected in 1585 by Nicoll Cairncross, nephew of the laird of Colmslie (q.v.), the nearer of the two neighbouring towers. The Cairncrosses continued to occupy the building until about 1760, and Sir Walter Scott used the tower, then roofless, as the model for Glendearg in *The Monastery* (1820). Hillslap has now resumed its role as a family residence following a sensitive restoration by *Philip Mercer* in 1978–95.

L-plan tower house (main block 9.1 m. by 6.7 m.) of four main storeys constructed of local whinstone rubble with dressings of red and buff-coloured sandstone probably quarried in the Melrose area. A spiral stair commences in the wing (4.9 m. by 3.7 m.) and continues within an extruded turret in the re-entrant angle. The wing rises one storey higher than the remainder, the top storey having its own inner gable. The modern roof follows the original in descending directly to the wall-head, without parapets, and the gables seem always to have been coped rather than crowstepped. The chimney copings partly replicate the decorative chequer treatment of the originals. The windows have been restored mainly with lead-framed glass panes set in the original glazing grooves, some with shutters below. The (renewed) dormers have moulded pediments, one displaying the Cairncross arms, another the Mercer crest. Like the neighbouring towers of Buckholm and Aikwood (qq.v.), the building incorporates an extensive repertoire of mouldings, the variations in this case being so marked as to suggest the presence of masons from at least two separate schools. Thus, the window and doorway dressings include not only plain, rounded arrises, but also bolection, cavetto and roll mouldings, some of unusual profile, as well as a single pilaster-framed surround of the type found at Buckholm Tower. The parallels with Buckholm also include an absence of freestone quoins, despite extensive use of sandstone elsewhere in the fabric, together with certain details of planning, suggesting the probability that both buildings were designed by the same mason. It is difficult to find local parallels for the squinch arch that supports the corbelling of the extruded stair-turret, but a similar feature appeared at the demolished Macbiehill (q.v.) and Luffness House (Lothian). The 'Tudor' label mouldings of the entrance doorway and several windows are also unusual (but cf. Branxholme Castle, q.v.), and suggest possible north of England connections. Even the gunloops eschew uniformity, one of the two survivors (of three, all on the ground floor) showing a conventional oval-mouthed aperture and plain throat and the other a square-cut aperture and faceted throat.

INTERIOR. The entrance in the re-entrant angle is rebated for outer and inner doors and the lintel bears the initials of the builder, his wife Elizabeth Lauder, and the date of erection. Two doors open from the stair lobby to a barrel-vaulted store-room, indicating that this was originally partitioned off at one end, as at Buckholm Tower. On the first floor the well-lit hall, heated by a big, corbel-lintelled fireplace, occupies the whole of the main block; at its lower end a possible service lobby for use with an outside kitchen. The second floor of the main block contains outer and inner chambers for the laird and his wife; both are heated and one formerly had a soil-box latrine. The third-floor arrangements may have been similar, but now comprise three bedrooms. In addition to the accommodation in the main block there are three chambers placed at intermediate levels in the wing, all originally heated and one also provided with a latrine. The uppermost has a corbelled fireplace with shafted jambs wrought with broad fillet, as at Aikwood Tower and Whytbank Tower (q.q.v.).

Traces of a BARMKIN and outbuildings were revealed by excavation in 1983–4. The existing barmkin is of 1982–95, with a two-storeyed gatehouse to N incorporating the roll-moulded jambs of an original gateway, similar to that at Buckholm Tower, found on site during excavation. The two-storeyed NW range occupies the site of the original one, which may have included a kitchen.

THE HIRSEL
1.6 km. NW of Coldstream

8040

Large but unpretentious mansion in wooded parkland. Acquired by Alexander, first Earl of Home in 1611, The Hirsel may already have become the family's principal residence before the destruction of Hume Castle (q.v.) during the Civil War. There are no identifiable remains of the house of that period, however, and the earliest portion of the present building appears to be the U-shaped block at the S end, which was probably erected by the seventh Earl soon after his accession in 1706. In 1739–41 the eighth Earl brought in *William Adam* to extend the house N by means of a two-storey, five-bay wing including services and stables, apparently round a central court. This N extension was in turn enlarged and remodelled for the tenth Earl from c. 1813, by *William Burn*, from sketches supplied by *William Atkinson*, and again remodelled internally by Burn for the eleventh Earl in the early 1850s. Plans were submitted by *Edwin Lutyens* in 1886 for remodelling the entire house in Tudor style, but late C19 additions were made instead by *John Watherston & Sons* including a chapel and music room. They were demolished in 1958–62 by *Ian G. Lindsay*, who also remodelled some of the interior of the N block.

EXTERIOR. Three storeys in creamy-grey harl-pointed sandstone. The W front is U-shaped with a four-bay centre and two projecting two-bay chimney-gabled wings. A three-storey, single-bay tower with a capped roof, topped by a lead ball finial on two steps, projects from the corner of the SW wing. Although once considered to be an earlier tower house, this seems unlikely, as not only are the walls of the U-plan block considerably thicker, but an amateur late C18 drawing shows a similar tower at the NW corner. This was incorporated within William

54

Adam's addition to the N. The wall-head cornice round the projecting wings and tower is very probably of the same date. The present plain elevation of the N BLOCK is as redesigned by *William Burn* with seven single bays but his client demanded one large window at each floor at the N, so here, in place of Burn's proposed two windows, is a single tripartite at each level. The iron veranda under the first floor N window was also recommended by Home. The remaining windows were lengthened and given balconies. Late C19 additions were demolished 1958–62 by *Ian G. Lindsay*, who finished and rendered the N elevation. The E façade of the early C18 S block is a straight façade of nine bays, the centre three of ashlar under an ashlar-faced chimneyed pediment. Late C20 doorcase with a coat-of-arms above.

INTERIOR. The early C18 plan form of the S block survives, only one room deep, with further rooms in the wings. The entrance is straight into the stair hall, which takes up a good third of the main block. The hall panelling is probably late C19. Staircase to the r., and a long room to the l., presently an informal family room. A mural stair (private stair), with the only original sash window, leads from the SW room to the S passage on the first floor. The glory of the STAIR HALL is the grand staircase in pale grey sandstone to the first landing, where it becomes timber. Panelled and ball-finialled newel posts, linked by a heavily moulded cope, supported by chunky silhouette balusters, their stone half-profiles mounted on the inner wall. Above is a deep-coved ceiling with acanthus cornice, the corners decorated with large acanthus, then a deep square void, its corners with rich drops of fruit and flowers falling from carved heads, a decorative plaster ceiling, and an internal wind-vane indicator where the cupola should be.

The staircase serves the former first-floor state apartments, including a great dining room, withdrawing room, state bed-chamber and dressing room. These apartments were unused for many years, but were reorganised in the 1980s. On the l. of the passage from the N end of the first-floor landing is a mid-C18 half-round stair with a mahogany rail, and a stone Tuscan columned newel. It serves all floors, and is described as 'old stair' in 1813. Up steps to the N WING, and a C19 stair hall and central saloon. A door on the l. leads to the former NW tower. Rooms on the E and W in the N block are shown in 1813 as incorporating old corridors with new passages made round Adam's open court, to be covered by a flat lead roof with large skylights. In the mid C19 the roof was remodelled by *William Burn*, who created the grand SALOON as it is today, which became the centre of social life. An oval cupola, and restrained classical decoration, with two borrowed lights, one each side, to give light to the bedroom corridors. The adjoining stair hall has a well stair and a smaller oval cupola. Off the main hall, to the N, a coved dining room with a large bow and rich cornice. On the W side three rooms were opened out by *Ian G. Lindsay* to a spacious drawing room. Of interest at the top of the S block is the early C18 English principal and purlin construction of the roof timbers.

ESTATE BUILDINGS: THE HOMESTEAD and DOVECOT, 0.8 km.

sw. A simple early C19 steading complex. A central square
tower has a modillioned cornice and cap roof; the weathervane
is inscribed EH (Elizabeth Home), Countess of Home,
1798–1837. Two bays each side, and a cottage at the s end. –
WALLED GARDEN, 0.4 km. s of house. Mid-C18, altered *c.*
1800. – GARDEN HOUSE, 0.4 km. w of house. Mid-C19, two-
storey, three-bay house, but indications on the rear elevation
suggest it is a remodelling of an earlier single-storey cottage. –
NW of the house, grand but rather staid crowstepped STABLES,
0.3 km. NW by *John Watherston & Sons*, 1900. In rock-faced red
sandstone with advanced gables, the centre one with a wide
keystoned pend, and a columned domed cupola. Moulded
stone semicircular vents along the tops of the side walls. – THE
LAUNDRY, 0.4 km. NW by *Sydney Mitchell & Wilson*, 1890, is
in the Old English style of Norman Shaw, with some Voyseyesque details, such as the horizontal banding of the bipartite windows along the wall-head. Stone base with a
half-timbered upper floor, the jettied-out end bays with decorative boarding. – DAIRY, 0.5 km. NW of the Laundry, *c.* 1900.
A fine symmetrical dairyman's house in red coursed sandstone, with projecting pedimented wings, and stone-mullioned
windows. A symmetrical dairy to the w similarly detailed.

COLDSTREAM LODGE, 1.6 km. s is late C19 with overhanging
eaves, gabled porch, and a canted bay to the drive. A cluster of
Old English-style square brick chimneys in the estate style. –
COCKBURN LODGE, 1.2 km. w. A simple, well-detailed mid-
C19 single-storey cottage. A cream ashlar front with centre bow,
the windows set in blind arches, flanked by two bays. – CROOKS
LODGE, 1.2 km. w. Mid-C19, T-plan, with piended roof and tall
square brick chimneys. Square rock-faced gatepiers. – MON-
TAGUE LODGE, 1.4 km. NW. L-plan, mid-C19 gabled lodge. A
square bay to the drive with sloping stone canopy, and tall
square brick chimneys. Rusticated gatepiers with ball tops.

LANDSCAPE. During the C18 there was a large formal landscape
around The Hirsel, considerably enlarged by the mid C19. The
lake was made in 1786 from an extensive moss.

OBELISK, 1.3 km. NW at the foot of a wooded bank by the Leet
Water. 6.1 m. high. Erected by the ninth Earl in memory of his
son William, Lord Dunglass, killed at the Battle of Guildford,
North Carolina, 1781.

MONUMENT, 1.6 km. s by Coldstream Lodge, to Lord Home of   35
the Hirsel (Sir Alec Douglas-Home, 1903–95). An elegant
bronze STATUE by *Professor Bill Scott* of Edinburgh College of
Art, on a pedestal decorated with discreet illustrations of
cricket stumps and ball, and a hound. Surrounded by a stone
text wall giving Home's various titles, and sculptured stones
and stone seats which make symbolic reference to his statesmanship and interest in country pursuits.

SITE OF EARLY CHURCH. Excavations *c.* 1980 exposed remains
of high significance for early church architecture in Southern
Scotland. The first element, perhaps of the C9 or C10, was a
small building of roughly square plan with rounded corners.
Probably by the time it was granted to Coldstream Nunnery,
before *c.* 1166, an apse had been added to its e end. A rectangular nave was subsequently added, and by the later Middle

Ages the choir itself may have been rebuilt to a rectangular plan. Following demolition of the chancel, possibly before the Reformation, the nave was evidently converted for use as a barn and was burned down.

5010   HOBKIRK

A small upland village on the Rule Water.

PARISH CHURCH. By *David Rhind*, 1862. Red snecked sand-stone and ashlar dressings, with timber Y-tracery to the windows, in what was probably meant to be a Transitional style. A main body of three bays has a heavy two-storey tower rising over its N (in fact NE) end; a S vestry has the appearance of a small chancel, and there are porches against the N side of the tower (for the laird), and the W side of the S bay. Internally, there is a chancel below the tower, which was the Elliot family aisle until a reordering of 1905. The main body has an arch-braced open-timber roof, and the chancel a polygonal plaster ceiling. – PLAQUES. N wall, Robert Kerr Elliot, †1873, white marble on black base by *Burke & Co.* of London; Sir Walter Elliot, †1887, brass plate within grey and white marble frame, portrait relief in top roundel. S wall, Walter Elliot Elliot, †1958, wood with heraldry in relief. – Several mid-C12 CARVED FRAG-MENTS from the medieval parish church (rebuilt in 1692) are now built into a low rubble wall serving as a font*: a pillar piscina with basin cut into cushion cap; two scallop caps with volute decoration; two nook-shaft caps with foliage trails and masks (cf. the Logan Aisle, Edrom Parish Church, q.v.). Against the N porch is a chevron-decorated voussoir and block with what appears to be an animal head; found during demo-lition of a cottage in 1950.

   CHURCHYARD. The site of the medieval church is identifi-able as a platform NW of the church. Within the churchyard is an attractive mixture of C17, C18 and C19 memorials.

Former MANSE (Nether Swanshiel). Now largely as remodelled and added to, *c.* 1840, with canted bays flanking a pilastered and corniced doorpiece, bipartite windows and a crowstepped central gable. The carcase, however, dates from 1770–1, when it displayed a long front with three widely spaced bays, and a plain chimneyed gable above the door. It was only one room deep with a projecting staircase at the rear. The late C18 roof timbers survive but the graceful Edinburgh-type geometric stair with pretty uprights is of *c.* 1840. Fine range of fully fitted stables and coach house buildings.

Former FREE CHURCH MANSE (Crowntailrigg). 1846. Harled with grey painted margins.

BRAIDHAUGH FARM COTTAGES. 0.5 km. E. In the centre a pro-jecting crowstepped gable, with two tiny pointed windows side by side in the gable-head.

OLD SCHOOL HOUSE. Mid-C19, with wall-head-gabled dorm-ers, and corners corbelled to the wall-head.

---

*They had been removed to Weens House (q.v.).

PRIMARY SCHOOL. By *Reid & Forbes*, 1936. Long, with horizontal-paned windows, and simple detailing at the wall-head of incised lines. Remodelled at rear in the 1970s.

Former SCHOOL (Hartshaugh Mill Cottage). Single storey and attic, 1873.

CLEUGHHEAD FARM, 1 km. SE. Mid-C19, in coursed red sandstone. Two storeys, three bays, the centre one splayed with a projecting crowstepped gable. Piended roof.

HARWOOD HOUSE. *See* p. 345.

HOLYDEAN CASTLE   5030
2 km. SW of Bowden

Fragments of a C16 tower house and barmkin of the Kers of Cessford, probably occupying the site of a former grange of Kelso Abbey. The castle may have been begun by Sir Andrew Ker (†1526) for the tower of 'Halydene' is mentioned in a document of 1524. Further work, probably including the building, or rebuilding, of the barmkin, was evidently undertaken by the next laird, Sir Walter, during the 1580s. Largely demolished in the third quarter of the C18, the castle's appearance is known from a description in *The Statistical Account of Scotland* of 1795, which indicates that it comprised a courtyard, or barmkin, *c.* 0.38 ha. in extent surrounded by loopholed walls 1.2 m. thick and 4.9 m. high. At the front was an arched entrance hung with an iron gate, and within the barmkin were two strong towers, one of three storeys, the other of five, containing eight or ten habitable rooms, 'besides porters lodges, servants hall, vaulted cellars, bakehouses, etc.' There was also a celebrated deer park *c.* 200 ha. in extent, enclosed by a massive drystone wall.

The BARMKIN was probably rectangular on plan with the principal tower occupying the NW part of the enclosure. The semi-circular-arched gateway is constructed of random rubble with round-arrised margins of buff-coloured sandstone; above it a hoodmould with lugged terminals. On one side of the gateway is a double-splayed gunloop with an oval-shaped mouth. The E RANGE has lost its S wall and upper floor, or floors. The ground-floor chamber, originally entered from the barmkin by a doorway in the W wall, seems to have been a kitchen or bakehouse, as evidenced by the large, segmental-arched fireplace in the N wall. Unusually, it is roofed with a pointed, rather than semicircular, vault. The adjacent TOWER, now almost completely obscured by ivy, was roughly square on plan and seems to have projected E from the barmkin wall. It probably contained a single chamber at each level.

N of the tower is HOBY KER'S WELL, probably named after Sir Robert Ker, afterwards first Earl of Roxburghe, who succeeded to the property in 1600. The well-shaft is constructed of excellent ashlar masonry and the mouth of the draw-opening is rebated for a door or shutter. Lord Roxburghe evidently made alterations to the castle in 1621, for a lintel bearing this date is incorporated on the S side of the steading.

Above the entrance to Holydean Farmhouse is an edge-roll

moulded lintel evidently brought from the castle. It bears the arms and initials of Walter Ker, together with a relief inscription in Roman letters: FEIR GOD FLE/ FROM SIN MAK/ [FOR] THE LYFE EVERLESTING/ TO THE END, followed in part Gothic lettering by the name of Walter's wife DEM (Dame) ESBEL (Isobel) KER and the date 15[8-] (read, almost certainly mistakenly, as 1530 by the author of *The Statistical Account*). Like his neighbour, Sir James Home, Ker was a declared Protestant and the pious exhortation of the inscription is almost identical to one at Cowdenknowes (q.v.).

3030

HOLYLEE
3.2 km. E of Walkerburn

Holylee was purchased in 1726 by James Ballantyne, who built Old Holylee (*see* below). His grandson built the present house, 1827, with *John Smith* as architect. A disciplined late Georgian-style mansion in fine polished ashlar without margins. Spacious, with two storeys, basement and attic, its five bays clasped at the corners by large angle pilasters. The S front has an advanced pedimented and chimneyed centre bay, with a well-detailed small Ionic portico and over the entrance a date panel inscribed in Gothic script. Five bays on the W elevation with long fifteen-pane windows, for the sun and view. Imitative two-storey and attic N addition of *c.* 1923 by *R. Carruthers Ballantyne* of *Ballantyne & Taylor* of Inverness, who succeeded to ownership.

Inside, not the usual tripartite plan, but with a T-shaped hall running E–W, the principal stone well stair with decorative cast-iron balusters at the E end, and two principal rooms off the W end. A well-detailed hall ceiling – quite Soanian in its proportions – with pendentived domes at the entries to the main rooms. Drawing room in the NW corner with compartmented ceiling, panelled walls and dado. Good classical cornices and friezes throughout, and timber and gesso chimneypieces with swags, drops and flutings.

WALLED GARDEN, early C19. Crinkle-crankle S wall, the corner angles buttressed for fruit growing. Entrances with tabbed quoins. – LODGE, late C19. Bargeboarded bracketed eaves, the open timber porch with heavy posts and diamond-pattern rails.

OLD HOLYLEE, 0.2 km. NE. Two storeys, built in harled rubble with dressed sandstone margins. The S front, originally of three bays but extended to five in the early C19, has a central doorway with lintel inscribed IB (James Ballantyne) 1734. Original window openings have chamfered arrises. Later gabled porches. Subdivided; a stone chimneypiece with bead moulding is the only survivor internally.

HORSBURGH CASTLE   2030
4 km. SE of Peebles

A prominent landmark on the Peebles–Galashiels road (A72), this little tower house, known also as Over Horsburgh, was probably built *c.* 1600 by one of the Horsburghs of that Ilk. Of the L-plan tower of three or four storeys only a fragment survives, and this was largely rebuilt as a folly in the mid C19. The ground floor of the main block (9.5 m. by 10.1 m.) was evidently vaulted, while the wing (4.4 m. by 2.5 m.) contained a spiral stair, as at the neighbouring Cardrona Tower (q.v.). The N wall incorporates a plaque commemorating the Rt. Hon. Baroness Horsburgh of Horsburgh (†1969).

HOSCOTE HOUSE   3010
4.5 km. SW of Roberton

By *Brown & Wardrop*, 1862, for Archibald Stavert. Two-storey and attic Tudor-style in coursed whinstone with sandstone dressings. Distinctive tall square chimneystacks, singly on corbelled-out plinths on the gable-heads, and in threes and fours on the principal roof. A plethora of hoodmoulded monogrammed panels on finialled dormerheads. Inside, a well stair with barley-sugar balusters, and square newel posts with attached corner pillars and ball finials. Decorative cornices. – Single-storey, harled, mid-C19 LODGE. Jerkin-headed gable to the drive.

HOSELAW CHAPEL *see* LINTON

HOUNDWOOD   8060

Small Berwickshire village.

GRANTSHOUSE AND HOUNDWOOD PARISH CHURCH. 1836. A handsome Italianate building with whinstone walls and red sandstone dressings to the raised margins and the round-arched windows and doorways. The main body is a broad rectangle with a piended platform roof and an axial S tower. On each side of the tower is a pair of windows, the outer ones originally doorways. Above the church wall-head, the belvedere-like belfry stage of the tower has angle pilasters and a round-headed window to each face, with a blind circlet in the panel below the opening; it has a low pyramidal roof with widely spreading eaves. In 1903, a pair of symmetrical off-shoots was added against the flanks of the church, that to the W a porch and that to the E a small chancel, with consequent reordering of the interior.

HOUNDWOOD HOUSE
1.5 km. SE.

The plain Victorian exterior is deceptive, for the house has a
complex building history going back at least to the C16. Originally forming part of the estates of Coldingham Priory,
Houndwood passed at the Reformation to a cadet branch of
the Home family, who continued in possession until 1713, and
for much of the C18 Houndwood belonged to the Turnbulls.
The earliest part appears to be a small, oblong tower house
(9.3 m. by 6.7 m.), at the SE corner of the present mansion,
probably erected not much before 1600. Within a generation
or so a three-storey W wing was placed at right angles to the
tower to form an L-plan, with a S front c. 25 m. in length and
an entrance in the NW re-entrant angle. The first major alteration seems to have been made in the early C19 by Captain
and Mrs Coulson, who inherited from the Turnbulls. They
moved the entrance to the S front but in 1848 Mrs Coulson
enlarged and remodelled the house, adding a three-storey wing
in the NW re-entrant angle and bringing the main entrance
back to the N front. Later alterations included the construction of a two-storey extension to the N front some time after
1875, and of a larger one alongside it, to house a billiard room,
c. 1907. This last masked the N gable of the original tower,
which seems to have been remodelled, and perhaps reduced a
storey in height, c. 1880.

EXTERIOR. As recast during the C19 and early C20 the house
is predominantly Scottish Domestic in character, with harled
walls, crowstepped gables and pedimented dormers. The early
masonry, where it can be seen, appears to be of pink sandstone
rubble, while most of the later dressings are of buff-coloured
sandstone. What little embellishment there is occurs mainly
on the N front. The sizeable, angled entrance porch of 1848
near the NW corner incorporates a bolection-moulded doorway
with a panel above – presumably transferred from the earlier
entrance – bearing the bull's head emblem of the Turnbulls
and their motto I SAVED THE KING. Above is a worn pediment
said to have been brought from a former Coulson family
house at Fulfordlees, near Cockburnspath. As recorded by the
RCAHMS the inscription, now only partly legible, comprises
the initials MTR and the date 1656, together with a Latin
couplet pointing out the vanity of human possessions. The W
wall of the early Victorian wing incorporates an inscribed stone
bearing the initials of George Turnbull and the date 1728.

INTERIOR. The early house survives mainly on the ground
floor. Here the tower retains two barrel-vaulted cellars, their
vaults spanning in opposite directions. The spacious newel stair
in the NW corner, originally entered directly from the exterior,
continues to serve this end of the house. The early C17 W wing,
its walls only slightly thinner than those of the tower (0.8–
1.0 m. as against 1.1–1.2 m.), is also barrel-vaulted at this level.
All the existing partitions seem to be C19 insertions. Towards
the NW corner there is evidence of what may have been a stair
rising to the floor above (and possibly to the second floor). The
principal floor is now approached by a flight of steps leading

up from the porch vestibule to a much-altered hall on the N
side of the house.

The public rooms lie along the S side, with the drawing room
at the W end. Its decoration, all probably of the early C19,
includes a simple classical cornice, panelled dado and shutters.
The shutters in the W bay are very primitive, which may be
explained by the removal in 1919 of a partition that divided off
a very narrow chamber at the W end of the room. The timber
and gesso chimneypiece is a fine example of a type supplied to
the Edinburgh building trade during the first third of the C19.
The jambs have fluted pilasters topped by anchors, and a central
panel shows a female figure leaning on an anchor, with shells
and seaweed fronds at her feet and a tiny, fully rigged sailing
ship in the bottom r. corner. Further E is the dining room,
created *c.* 1848, when the principal entrance was removed from
the S front and its vestibule/hall added to an existing room. Decorative, gilded cornice with bead-and-rail, egg-and-dart and
rinceau enrichments and a gilded sunburst ceiling rose. A sideboard recess in the N wall has reeded pilasters and frieze, and
the white marble Grecian chimneypiece, with reeded jambs and
frieze, is similar to many in Edinburgh's Northern New Town.
The E room on this floor, originally the principal chamber of
the tower, is now a kitchen. Some of the ceiling joists, exposed
during a mid-C20 remodelling, appear to be original. In one of
the S-facing rooms on the top floor is a rare, probably early C19,
band of floor decoration, painted to resemble linoleum, which
was very expensive at that time.

WALLED GARDEN N of the house, probably early C19.
Rubble-built with a curved N wall. – HOUNDWOOD LODGE
(A1). Dated 1849.

HOWNAM

A small upland village with a parish church first recorded in the
C12.

PARISH CHURCH. Formerly cruciform; shortened and remodelled 1752. Renewed in 1844 by *John Smith*, who retained a
round-headed doorway of *c.* 1500. This, along with the walls
and birdcage bellcote, survived rebuilding in 1908 by *J.P.
Alison*. Early English style with Arts and Crafts details,
particularly the battered walls of the S porch, and the vestry
and Roxburghe Aisle on the N side. Sandstone dressings, lancet
windows, hoodmoulds over, with plain label stops. The
medieval doorway with alternating bands of red and pale sandstone is now in the S wall. Inside, a single-arch braced roof. –
Restrained STAINED GLASS with simple borders of coloured
glass and medallions representing the Holy Spirit etc.

GRAVEYARD. Some small headstones with symbols, mostly
framed in Ionic-type pilasters. Margaret Henderson, †1833.
Classical, made up from earlier memorials. Open pediment
with male bust flanked by small urns with foliage and faces at
the corners which looks C18.

GLEBE HOUSE. Former manse. Rendered, two-storey with

octagonal s projection. Basically 1776, added to and repaired
by *John Smith*, 1832, who also built the offices. Some architectural pretension at the E end: rounded corners, stepped back
at the top, triangular kneelers. Of 1866 by *Walter Blaikie*.

DESCRIPTION. The village was developed by Walter Dickson of
Chatto (*see* below) from the 1830s, with two inns to accommodate travellers. Former school (Knowe Cottage) at the N
end. Single-storey cottage with schoolroom, brick chimneys
and tiny swept dormers. Four blocks of sizeable two-storey
houses, of whinstone rubble with sandstone dressings, which
contained the Shepherd's Inn and the Post Office. At the s end
is Kailheugh, formerly Dickson's Inn, the doorway with a solid
fanlight. Single-storey whinstone rubble Tudorish school
(Village Hall), to the s, with a single-storey rectangular well-lit
schoolroom and gabled porch.

CHATTO, 2.5 km. SW. Originally a long single-storey farmhouse,
formerly thatched, with chamfered windows, one dated
17(4?)8. The tall two-storey house at the s end was added
c. 1800, the probable date of the court of vernacular steadings
to the NW.

GREENHILL HOUSE, 2.5 km. SE. Built as a hunting lodge of the
Dukes of Roxburghe, begun in the mid C18. Two-storey N front
of five bays, altered in 1828, e.g. the grand Doric doorpiece,
and again *c.* 1840. Brick chimneys with corbel-like brick detailing below the cope. The SE wing probably began as a single-
storey late C18 house of whinstone rubble with droved ashlar
quoins; also altered in the C19. Inside, the main block is only
one room deep with low ceilings and a good timber staircase
of 1828. Short screen walls enclose the forecourt with entry
through square gatepiers and wrought-iron gates with thistle
finials. Conventional stables and hay lofts of 1834 by *John
Bulmer*.

MAINSIDE, NW, is a traditional two-storey, three-bay harled
farmhouse and steading built in 1775 on the site of a fermtoun
of nine cottages.

FORT, Hownam Law, 3 km. NNE. The whole summit and a
terrace to the N are enclosed by a thick wall, taking in an area
of *c.* 8.8 has. Stances of numerous timber round-houses are
visible within the interior, the E end of which has been incorporated into a later non-defensive enclosure.

FORT, Hownam Rings, 1 km. E. Multivallate fort excavated in
1948, revealing that a palisaded enclosure had been succeeded
first by a complex fort defended by a series of walls and ramparts, and finally by an undefended settlement of stone-walled
round-houses and a small rectilinear homestead.

FORT and LINEAR EARTHWORKS, Woden Law, 6.5 km. S of the
village commanding the upper reaches of the Kale Water. The
defences of this fort are evidently multi-period, comprising at
least four roughly concentric walls and ramparts, and a
complex belt of outlying linear earthworks, once thought to be
Roman investing works. Traces of a row of large timber round-
houses can be seen on the crest of the ridge within the interior.

PALISADED ENCLOSURE, 5 km. S, enclosing the elongated
summit of Stanshiel Hill. It measures *c.* 136 m. from N to S by
52 m. transversely.

HUME

A small village nestling beneath the walls of Hume Castle, a prominent landmark in the lush countryside of the Merse.

CHURCHYARD, 0.75 km. SW of the castle. Mounded earth lines mark the rectangular plan of the parish church granted to Kelso Abbey c. 1159. It fell into ruin after union with Stichill in 1640. Only part of the E wall is still evident. C18–C20 table tombs, headstones and enclosures. The Home enclosure was NW of the church. – WELL, dedicated to St Nicholas, in field to NW.

HUME HALL, 0.7 km. S. A pleasant rambling house built of harled and limewashed rubble. The original oblong hip-roofed block, probably late C18, appears to have been extended into a cross plan by the addition of wings.

HUME CASTLE

Although possibly founded as early as the C13, it was not until the later Middle Ages that the castle began to feature in national affairs as the principal residence of the powerful Lords Home. Partly dismantled by the third Lord Home in 1515, the castle was soon re-fortified by the Regent Albany. During the 1540s it was strengthened with new ramparts and an artillery platform by Franco–Scottish forces before surrendering to an invading English army in 1547. The construction of additional outworks was then begun by *William Ridgeway*, but these may have been unfinished when the Scots recaptured the place in the following year. In 1570 Hume Castle, although 'newe fortified in a great parte, moche stronger than it was' and garrisoned with nearly 200 men, was again captured by the English and held by them for more than three years. Hume made its last appearance as a military stronghold in 1651 when, after a fierce bombardment by Cromwell's forces during which its vaults proved highly resistant to mortar fire, the castle surrendered on terms and was thereafter demolished. Subsequently the property passed to another branch of the family, and some time before 1789 the third Earl of Marchmont rebuilt the outer walls of the castle as a piece of landscape architecture. During the Napoleonic Wars it served as a beacon station. The fabric was consolidated and repaired in 1985–92 by *David Mylne* for the Berwickshire Civic Society.

Now little more than a giant, castellated folly, the castle presents a dramatic silhouette of outsize battlements and mock corner towers. The site is the summit of a rock outcrop from which the ground falls steeply on all sides except the W, while the castle itself comprises an open courtyard, roughly square on plan (*c.* 38.7 m. by 37.5 m. internally), surrounded by a curtain wall. The C18 curtain follows the line of the earlier one, the footings of which can be seen on the W and S sides, indicating an original thickness of *c.* 1.7 m. While the simple, rectangular plan may indicate a C13 origin, the early chronology of the castle remains unresolved. The Georgian masonry is of random rubble, probably quarried from the ruins of the castle, with dressings of pink sandstone. Externally, the parapet level of the curtain is defined by a roll-moulded string course similar to that found in contemporary fortifications, and a similar moulding frames the crenelles and merlons. In their present form the two doorways placed opposite one another in the W and E walls are mainly Georgian, but the W one, which probably marks the site of the medieval entrance, incorporates reused, chamfer-arrised dressings of C16 date. N of this doorway, apparently *in situ*, is a large, dumb-bell-shaped gunloop of the same period, and beyond it a slit window. At the foot of the W curtain can be seen traces of an external cladding of masonry *c.* 1.8 m. thick, perhaps a relic of the refurbishment of the 1540s. There seems always to have been a small, projecting corner tower at the SW angle, while the SE angle is bevelled off to accommodate the edge of the rock summit. The INTERIOR is largely filled with debris, making the ground level seem much higher than it is. The principal buildings seem to have occupied the S side of the courtyard, where a fragment of a vaulted chamber running E and W still stands. A latrine chute at the SE corner of the courtyard indicates the former existence of residential buildings in that area, and there may have been another latrine chute at the NE corner. The well is situated just the inside the W entrance.

Except for a ditch on the E side, there is now little trace of the extensive OUTWORKS mentioned in the C16 documents. Below the castle on the W side can be seen extensive traces of buildings and field systems probably associated with the medieval township of Hume.

6010

HUNDALEE
2.4 km. S of Jedburgh

Built for John, seventh Marquess of Lothian, in 1832. Plans were prepared by Mr *Totnes*, clerk to *Edward Blore*, who seems to have made alterations. Neo-Tudor, with projecting finialled gables, arrowslits in the gable-heads and stone-mullioned and transomed windows, the sashes rising behind the transoms. Sawtooth-coped skews and moulded bracket skewputts. Handsome, well-finished interior. A carved lintel on a service wing, inscribed RKDCH 1667 [Robert Kerr (fourth Lord Jedburgh) and Dame Christian Hamilton], may have been transferred from an earlier tower house.

6010

HUNTHILL HOUSE
2 km. SE of Jedburgh

The lands of Hunthill were acquired by the Rutherfords during the C15 and remained in their hands for some four hundred years. A late medieval panel bearing their arms, with decoration of little paterae and sprays of foliage, survives in the present house, which was described as 'new' in 1800. Three storeys and five bays in sandstone rubble with ashlar dressings; the 'picked out' rubble suggests the house should be harled.

Rusticated quoins and a band course emphasise the *piano nobile* on the E front. The sills of the three drawing-room windows (r.) were lowered later. Late C19 gabled dormers. The original entrance doorway, with a geometric glazed fanlight, was superseded on the W front by a crowstepped porch, added 1955 with a basket-arched doorcase (dated 1850) from *David Bryce's* Hartrigge House, Jedburgh (*see* p. 433). Late C20 S extensions. Altered inside in 1954–8 when the dining room was extended to take in the former front hall.

Square GATEPIERS, crowned with stone lions rampant holding scrolled cartouches, are also from Hartrigge House. – The STABLES were developed in the late C19 to make a traditional court of farm buildings more decorative. U-plan, built in a creamy sandstone rubble with Arts and Crafts-style overhanging eaves and exposed rafters.

HUTTON

PARISH CHURCH. 1835 by *Ignatius Bonomi*. An impressive early essay in Romanesque Revival inspired by Norham Church (Northumberland), where Bonomi also worked, though he had some difficulty in adapting these forms to a large-scale preaching hall. A rectangle of two by six bays with a three-storey NE tower-porch. A second porch, with heating chamber and vestry, was added at the W end in 1879. To S and E the stugged yellow ashlar show façades, of larger-than-life Romanesque, are divided into bays by pilasters rising through a chamfered base course, with nook-shafts and moulded arches to the windows, and with a wall-head corbel table and parapet. The less visible façades are more simply treated. The tower, rather small for so large a church, has two stages of two-light windows within containing arches. The interior is somewhat barn-like because of secondary reorderings; the original arrangement presumably had galleries facing towards a pulpit against one of the side walls. The present communion table and enclosure at the E end were designed by *Reginald Fairlie* in 1918, in memory of David William Milne Home of Wedderburn, and made by *Scott Morton & Co.* New flooring and seating were provided in 1936. The flat ceiling, inserted following major roof repairs in 1961, has not helped the internal proportions. – PULPIT with Evangelist symbol reliefs. – STAINED GLASS in E windows, 'Suffer Little Children' and 'Dorcas', 1917, with grisaille acanthus borders.

CHURCHYARD, to N and W of church, heavily overgrown, with mainly C18 and C19 memorials, but some earlier ones to NE. Worthy of note: James Frisken, †1712, full-length portrait surrounded by angel heads and *memento mori*; John Burn, †1733, full-length portrait with open book. Balusters from table tombs are re-set alongside steps to E. – HUTTON HALL BURIAL VAULT, NW of the church. C17(?), ashlar walls above a chamfered plinth course and barrel vault covered with stone flags.

Former MANSE (Antrim House), N of church. By *John*

Lessels, 1876. Overhanging timber-bracketed eaves, gabled wall-head dormers, and consoled bracketed doorcase.

PRIMARY SCHOOL. Neo-Tudor by *James Cunningham,* 1844 with later extensions.

DESCRIPTION. N of the school is ROYAL TERRACE, of single-storey and attic estate cottages, dated 1901. Red sandstone with brick eaves detail and hoodmoulded doorways. A similar, earlier(?) terrace has two- and three-bay cottages, with flanking gabled ends and overhanging eaves with exposed rafters. SMIDDY COTTAGE, S of the church, is early C19(?). Harled with painted margins, and squat six-pane windows tucked under the eaves. Single-storey SMITHY in sandstone rubble with steeply pitched pantiled roof and slate easing course.

HUTTON MILL BRIDGE, 2.5km. NE, over the Whiteadder Water. A three-span wrought-iron lattice-truss bridge, by *D. & T. Stevenson,* engineers. The ashlar masonry piers were probably built for an iron rod-truss bridge of 1837 by *James Jardine* (cf. Roxburgh Viaduct footbridge, p. 652).

HUTTON HALL
1 km. NW

A late medieval tower with a C16 L-shaped block added to its NW, creating a courtyard open to the SW. This is one of the earliest of a small group of stylish Renaissance mansions built by the greater Border lairds during the last three decades of the C16. Subsequently the house fell on hard times before being given a new lease of life and, in the early C20, a new architectural *persona* as the first home of the Burrell Collection.

During the late C15 and early C16 Hutton Hall belonged to the Kerrs of Samuelstown, one of whom probably erected the tower house which forms the nucleus of the present mansion. In 1532 the property was purchased by the Homes, and in 1544 the tower was besieged and captured by an English army, which then 'burned and spoiled' it. In 1573 Alexander Home, a leading Berwickshire laird and deputy warden of the East March, began to enlarge the house, adding a sizeable L-plan mansion to the N corner of the earlier tower to provide a new entrance and staircase and more spacious public rooms. The new work was carefully detailed in a Renaissance style then becoming fashionable in the Borders. Alexander, or his son John, a prominent figure at the court of James VI, may have intended to extend the house further by completing a fourth (SW) side of the courtyard, but in the event additional chambers were constructed on the upper floors of the NE range.

In or about the middle of the C17 Hutton Hall was sold, and by the mid C19 was tenanted, at one stage being divided into three dwellings. The fabric rapidly deteriorated and by the time Sir Dudley Coutts Marjoribanks purchased the property in 1876 much of the original tower had collapsed. Marjoribanks (created Lord Tweedmouth in 1881) began the rehabilitation of the house by repairing the outer walls of the tower and putting a new roof on (*c.* 1890). His son, the second Baron (†1909), carried out a more extensive building programme in 1896–8 with *George Duns*, making the tower fully habitable, heightening the NE range of the late C16 house and adding a service wing in the outer angle between it and the tower. He also refurbished much of the interior and made extensive improvements to the gardens and policies, including the building of new stables and gate lodges and the construction of new approach roads by *Alexander Ross*, the estate surveyor. The garden works were undertaken by *Messrs Smith and Son*, Derby.

In 1916 Hutton Hall was bought by the wealthy Glasgow shipowner William Burrell, an obsessive collector of pictures, furniture and works of art. Burrell viewed the house primarily as a repository for his collection and was prepared to sacrifice comfort and convenience, as well as the historic integrity of the fabric, to achieve his aims. This attitude, and Burrell's prickly temperament, made for difficult relations with his architects and he fell out, first with *Robert S. Lorimer* (1916–17), who produced various schemes, including one for a new house, retaining only the tower, and then with *Reginald Fairlie* (1926), who took up where Lorimer had left off, but soon gave way to *Frank Surgey* and *Wilfrid Drake*, by whom the interiors were eventually completed in 1927–32. Lorimer had been allowed to do little more than replace Duns's service wing with a larger one in the same position and start remodelling the interior of the late C16 house. Fairlie's main contribution was the enlargement and virtual rebuilding of the NW wing to accommodate a new principal entrance and huge first-floor drawing room. Externally the character of the new work became more uncompromising as it progressed. Lorimer, like Duns, managed to respect the style and scale of the early house, but Fairlie's task could be achieved only by the adoption of a different idiom. In 1944 Sir William (knighted in 1927) donated his collection to the City of Glasgow, and following his death fourteen years later, and protracted negotiations leading up to the establishment of a new art gallery there, the remaining items, including the historic rooms, were removed to Pollok Park (Glasgow). In stripping the house of the bulk of its fittings even less regard was paid to the fabric than at their installation, and, despite the sensitive approach of a new owner, these latest scars will be slow to heal.

EXTERIOR. The house stands at the top of a steep bank overlooking the flood plain of the Whiteadder Water, which flows *c.* 0.25 km. to the NE. The site is potentially strong and its defensive capabilities may originally have been enhanced by the construction, on the other three sides, of a ditch and bank, some traces of which can be seen *c.* 0.05 km. W of the house. This probably predates the stone castle. The TOWER HOUSE, roughly square on plan (9.1 m. by 7.3 m.), is unusual in having a semicircular stair-turret projecting from its N corner. Unsurprisingly, in view of the vicissitudes it has endured, the fabric offers few clues as to its age, but a date during the first third of the C16 seems most probable. A drawing of *c.* 1840 shows that the tower originally comprised three main storeys, above which a pitched-roofed garret rose within a parapeted wall-walk carried on individual stone corbels. The stair-turret rose to the same height as the tower, terminating in a caphouse which gave access to the wall-walk. In the original arrangement the entrance doorway was placed in the NW wall, close to the N corner of the tower, and led directly into the foot of the stair. By 1840, however, this had been replaced by an elevated doorway on the SW side of the stair-turret, approached by a flight of steps. As restored by the first Lord Tweedmouth, the tower is flat-roofed, while the stair-turret (heightened in 1896–8) soars three storeys above it to finish in a look-out platform crowned by a battlemented parapet. Both the early entrance doorways have been blocked. The masonry is of local pink and buff-coloured sandstone with dressings of similar material, and the early walls, as seen e.g. on the NE side, comprise large blocks of rubble roughly brought to courses. A couple of original windows survive in the stair-turret, but elsewhere the fenestration is late C19, comprising tall, oblong openings with roll-moulded margins of C16 character and timber mullions and transoms.

With the addition of the LATE C16 MANSION the house came to occupy three sides of an irregular courtyard, probably with a screen wall on the SW. The mansion itself, in similar sandstone, comprised a NE range (*c.* 15.7 m. by 6.7 m.) placed obliquely to the original tower and abutting it only at its N corner, together with a stepped NW wing (*c.* 13.4 m. by 7.5 m.) set more or less at right angles and joined by a stair-tower in the re-entrant angle, with the principal entrance at its foot and a stack of small chambers behind. As first built, the mansion comprised three main floors and there was neither wall-walk nor parapet, the steeply pitched roof rising directly from an eaves cornice. To judge from the existence of prominent 'straight joints' in the masonry of the side walls, however, the two bays of the NE range lying immediately adjacent to the tower house originally rose to a height of only one, or one and a half, storeys, thus forming a low-roofed link building between mansion and tower. Communication between the two seems at this stage to have been by external means only, a device possibly intended to avoid compromising the defensive strength of the tower. This arrangement, however, was abandoned within a generation or so, when the link building was carried up in greyish green sandstone to the same height as the rest to provide more dwelling space. Communicating doorways were formed between mansion and tower on the two upper floors.

Even in their present mutilated state the courtyard fronts of the mansion show traces of considerable architectural elaboration. The walls rise from a splayed plinth, while between first- and second-floor levels a *cyma reversa* string course runs the full span of the house, stepping up to cross the window heads of the *piano nobile*. The windows themselves, as also the doorway, appear originally to have been framed with roll-and-hollow mouldings and some, at least, of the windows were evidently half-glazed with shutters below. The sills of the first-floor windows seem to have been lowered some time during the late C17 or early C18. Above the former entrance in the stair-tower is an incomplete heraldic panel obviously intended to display the arms of Alexander Home. However, the sculptor has blundered, perhaps working from a tracing viewed back to front, with the result that the executed carving is a mirror image of the correct version. As recorded *c.* 1840, the panel also bore the date 1573, together with the initials of Alexander and his wife Elizabeth [Isobel] Home, but only these last now survive. In the re-entrant angle of the stair-tower and the NW wing can be seen traces of a series of continuous moulded corbel courses that formerly supported an extruded circular turret carrying the upper part of the stair, while the adjacent wall of the wing itself retains the corbelled base of the chimney of the original first-floor hall. The arrangement is similar to that afterwards adopted on a rather grander scale at Ferniehirst Castle (q.v.). Defensive provision seems to have been minimal. Only two gunloops survive, one, possibly quatrefoil-shaped, covering the entrance doorway at the foot of the stair-tower, and the other, oval-mouthed, near the N corner of the NE range. The recent discovery of wall footings just beyond the E corner of this range suggests that it may originally have incorporated an angle tower.

Between them Tweedmouth and Burrell raised the mansion a full storey in height, ironing out the irregular roof line on the courtyard sides by the introduction of a flat roof set behind a corbelled and battlemented parapet matching that of the tower house. Most of the early windows were replaced, those on the third floor of the SW front flanking a giant representation of the arms of the second Lord Tweedmouth and his wife, Lady Fanny Spencer-Churchill. In the NW wing the large size of the new drawing-room and a requirement for an additional storey on the NW side presented Fairlie with considerable problems of scale. He responded with an eclectic design featuring huge mullioned and transomed windows, a recessed oriel and crow-stepped gables, but despite the building's impeccable masonry and detailing the effect is overbearing.

INTERIOR. Successive alterations have made it difficult to chart the development of the house, and the stripping out of most of Burrell's fittings has reduced the interest of the interior. The TOWER remains much as the Tweedmouths left it, with the refurbished interior providing liveable dwelling space. A photograph of *c.* 1880 shows that it originally contained a single chamber at each level, the hall occupying its customary position on the first floor. None of the floors seem to have been vaulted. The ground floor of the NE RANGE seems originally to have comprised kitchen and offices. When David MacGibbon and Thomas Ross surveyed the house *c.* 1892 the whole of this space was vaulted, but the removal of the vaults in 1916–17 exposed traces of corbels in the side walls of the SE compartment, clearly showing that what has been described above as the link building was originally ceiled or roofed in timber. The NE wall incorporates both a slop-sink and a water inlet, the position of the latter suggesting the former existence of a well on this side of the house. The doorway communicating with the adjacent tower at this level appears to have been formed only at the time of the Tweedmouth–Burrell alterations. The adjacent compartment was evidently a kitchen, having a large fireplace and chimney in the NW wall. The first floor contained what had probably always been two good-sized public rooms, of which the SE one was used by both Tweed-mouth and Burrell as a dining room. Tweedmouth refurbished it in Tudor style, complete with panelled walls, arched chim-neypiece (now installed elsewhere in the house) and compart-mented plaster ceiling, but Burrell insisted on doings things his own way, dismantling almost all the interiors in order to install his own medieval fittings, skilfully matched by new carved woodwork designed by Surgey. The plain early C18 pan-elling and pedimented timber chimneypiece in the adjacent chamber to the NW (illustrated by MacGibbon & Ross) must have been removed by Tweedmouth or Burrell. Part of an orig-inal latrine cubicle – the only one now to survive in the house – can be seen within the wall thickness at the N corner of the room. One or two Burrell fittings survive on the upper floors.

The ground floor of the NW WING originally comprised a pair of cellars, which seem to have been vaulted until 1926, when Fairlie formed a new principal entrance at the SW end and created a hall – soon to become the second of Burrell's period rooms. This retains a C16 panelled oak door installed by Burrell, as well as a vestibule paved with glazed tiles of medieval character. The first floor was originally occupied by the late C16 hall. Burrell, wanting much more space to display tapestries and stained glass, extended it both in height and width, with the result that little early work survives. Within the exposed masonry of the SE wall, however, can be seen traces of a massive roll-and-hollow-moulded fireplace with an arched lintel, as well as part of a continuous stone corbel course which must have supported the original ceiling joists. Both these fea-tures are paralleled in the hall at Ferniehirst Castle (q.v.). In the staircase tower in the re-entrant angle between the NE range and the NW wing, Burrell blocked the doorway and replaced the stone newel stair with a much wider newel stair of timber, which serves all the upper floors.

STABLES, S of the house. Mainly C19, the principal part rebuilt c. 1897 by *Duns*. Long gabled block with a tall decorative flèche. Converted to a dwelling-house by *Richard Amos*, 1990–5, when the carriage openings were glazed and given external shutters. Spaciously planned inside, the open timber stair is modelled on one at Packwood House, Warwickshire.

WEST LODGE, c. 1898, by *Duns*. Large, two-storey with crow-steps with a veranda. – The cruciform SOUTH LODGE is probably contemporary but single-storey, in red sandstone rubble. Square corniced gatepiers support bear finials brought from West Lodge.

SUNWICK FARMHOUSE, 1.5km. SW. An attractive late C18 or early C19, two-storey, three-bay farmhouse, with piend-roofed pavilions forming a N court. Constructed in red brick, unusual for Scotland, said to have come from the Netherlands.

3030   INNERLEITHEN

A douce little burgh pleasantly situated on the banks of the Leithen Water a little above its confluence with the River Tweed. Innerleithen was probably a place of some ecclesiastical importance during early Christian times and was certainly the site of a parish church by the C12. Thereafter the village slumbered until the latter part of the C18, when its prospects rapidly started to brighten. The main agents of change were the opening of a turnpike road (now the A72) from Peebles to Selkirk (1775), the establishment of a woollen manufactory (1788) by Alexander Brodie, a Traquair blacksmith who had made a fortune in the English iron industry, and the development of a local mineral spring as a health resort. Of these, the last was initially the most important, with the publication of Scott's novel *St Ronan's Well* (1824) sealing the village's reputation as a fashionable watering place. By 1834 the resident population had risen to about 450, while the number of summer lodgers sometimes exceeded 1,400. Brodie's mill did not enjoy commercial success and it was only in the 1840s, with the assistance of steam power and the introduction of foreign wool, that the textile industry, and the village with it, began its main phase of expansion. Innerleithen achieved burgh status in 1868 and by the end of the C19 had a population of about 2,500, of whom between a third and a quarter worked in the town's six woollen mills. There were still three spinning mills and a hosiery there in the 1960s, but by the early C21 only two small textile operations survived, and Innerleithen now relies for employment mainly on tourism, light industry and the provision of services to an increasingly dormitory population.

CHURCHES

Former CONGREGATIONAL CHAPEL (St Ronan's Lodge), Chapel Street. A whinstone gable to the street is dated 1847, but rebuilt in 1897. Round-headed keystoned windows flanking a corniced doorway, with a pointed window and oculus above.

CONGREGATIONAL CHURCH, Peebles Road. Secularised. Early English by *Frank W. Simon*, c. 1889. In whinstone with margins of Locharbriggs red sandstone. Gabled S front, to the W a circular stair-tower. In the tympanum, a quatrefoiled vesica, a circular cusped window above, with a central cross design.

CRAIGSIDE UNITED PRESBYTERIAN CHURCH, Pirn Road and Buccleuch Street. By *R. Mathison*, 1878. Converted to housing late C20. Gothic, in whinstone with buttressed bays and vermiculated margins, and dark brick detailing.

INNERLEITHEN PARISH CHURCH, Leithen Road. 1865–7, by *F. T. Pilkington* in his unique Ruskinian Gothic. The original plan was an elongated octagon with a square E projection flanked by a session house (SE) and porch (NE). The craggy silhouette of its roof was lost, however, in 1888–9 when *J. Macintyre Henry* made additions to the W end and rebuilt the roof with a pagoda-like flèche in the centre, giving the church a low, dumpy appearance. What survive of Pilkington's work are the hammer-dressed battered base course, the carved wallhead pediments, the lower walls of the N and S elevations and the E gable. This comprises a pointed overarch springing from corner pilasters to frame a recessed screen wall pierced by an exotic assemblage of windows. Three patterned circular lights above a row of Venetian Gothic lancets with delicately carved

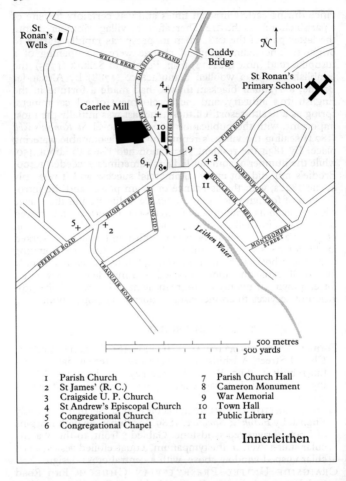

1	Parish Church	7	Parish Church Hall
2	St James' (R. C.)	8	Cameron Monument
3	Craigside U. P. Church	9	War Memorial
4	St Andrew's Episcopal Church	10	Town Hall
5	Congregational Church	11	Public Library
6	Congregational Chapel		

Innerleithen

arabesque heads (repeated in the Session House to the l.). Lush carved capitals and surface decoration. To the r. is a corner tower with Gothic cupola erected *c.* 1920 in place of Pilkington's weirdly roofed NE entrance.

The original arrangement inside was of three galleries, one over the square E end, and one on each long side (N and S) of the octagon. Macintyre Henry reformed this into a nearly rectangular plan, with the addition of a W chancel for the organ, choir and vestry, opening into a long nave with double-roofed N and S transepts. Henry's chancel arch is of red Dumfriesshire sandstone carried on moulded shafts. The galleries appear to have been renewed, but using for the timber fronts a barley-sugar baluster motif favoured by Pilkington. New columns support the galleries; only two original columns survive with carved capitals, one each side at the E end. The open timber roof was almost all renewed. – PULPIT by *Macintyre Henry*.

Octagonal, panelled and carved, resting on a red sandstone base. – ORGAN. *J. Brook & Co.*, Glasgow. Fine display of stencilled pipes. – Eclectic display of STAINED GLASS, including memorials to the two World Wars.

Set against the E wall of the church is the lower part of a C9 or C10 CROSS-SHAFT AND BASE, discovered in the church's foundations in 1871. On all four faces the shaft has loosely organised patterns of pecked cup marks within circles, most of which are linked into vertical linear groupings of two or three cups. – HALL, N of the church. By *Macintyre Henry*, 1887. Early English style.

The GRAVEYARD, and the site of the former parish church, lie to the N on Leithen Road. Good early C18 to early C19 table stones set on pedestals, C19 obelisks in various forms, and traditional C18 stones with carved emblems.

ST ANDREW'S EPISCOPAL CHURCH, Leithen Road. By *C.E. Howse* of London, 1904. A simple Early English style, six-bay rectangular church. Harled with red sandstone dressings. Pointed-arch windows, and entrance doorway with hoodmould and scrolled label stops. Late C20 meeting hall attached. Inside, a carved screen divides off the chancel. A well-painted mural MEMORIAL on the E gable to J.G. Ferguson, by *William K. Blacklock* of Edinburgh School of Art, 1905: 'Virgin and Child' and the 'Adoration of the Magi'. – STAINED GLASS. Single lights on each side of the chancel to Robert Milne Ballantyne, †1917, of St Michael, before and after slaying Satan. Signed by *J.S. Hamilton*, 1920. Inscriptions are stencilled round the window arches. A single light above the altar to members of the Welsh family: 'In my House are Many Mansions', donated by Isabella Milne Ballantyne. S side, a sparkling window, 'All Things Bright and Beautiful' by *Vivienne Haig*, 1998, to Felicity Ballantyne.

ST JAMES' CHURCH (R.C.). High Street and Traquair Road. C14 English Decorated Gothic by *John Biggar*, opened 1881. Erected for Catholics settling in Innerleithen and as a memorial to Charles, eighth Earl of Traquair, and his sister Lady Louisa Stuart. All in snecked rubble with sandstone dressings. Nave with five buttressed bays, transomed and traceried windows, and covered with a steeply pitched roof with cross finials. A tower with a broached spire at the NW corner; stepped angle buttresses, lower cusped window, oculus above, and pointed louvred belfry lights below a corbel table. Two tiers of lucarnes in the spire. The interior has a single-arched brace-trussed roof, otherwise any decoration has been erased and all the stone surfaces painted grey. – STAINED GLASS. Figures of saints commemorating members of the Stuart and Maxwell Stuart families. – MONUMENTS. Memorial on W wall to Charles Stuart, eighth Earl of Traquair, †1861, and a tablet with simple oval wreath and panel on black marble to Mary Langlois, †1878.

PRESBYTERY attached to the E end. Tudor of two storeys, with blind oculi in gables, and shouldered and coped stacks. The single-storey SCHOOL was never used as such, and converted to a dwelling, with a wide projecting gabled bay on the E end, porch at the W end.

PUBLIC BUILDINGS

CAMERON MONUMENT, sw corner of High Street and Leithen
Road. 1906. Obelisk with an incised Celtic cross at the top. A
bronze profile portrait decorates the eulogy on the plinth.

OLD LEITHEN BRIDGE, also known as the Cuddy Bridge, over
the Leithen Water. 1701. A single span of rubble masonry, the
parapets splayed at each end.

PUBLIC LIBRARY, Buccleuch Street. By *Peter L. Henderson*,
1903. Functional and unimpressive. Front of hewn freestone,
sides and back in brick, plastered with cement, and roughcast.

RAILWAY STATION, Traquair Road. Built 1866 on the North
British Railway line to Galashiels. Station master's house and
office survive. Two storeys, whinstone, with bracketed eaves.
Platform canopy decorated with serrated fretted boarding.

ST RONAN'S PRIMARY SCHOOL, Pirn Road. Opened 1957.
Rendered with dark brick dressings. Single-storey entrance
court with Modernist entrance porch. Two-storey blocks on
the s side.

ST RONAN'S WELLS (Interpretation and Fitness Centre), Wells
Brae. The first pavilion was built in 1826 by the seventh Earl
of Traquair to a design by *W. H. Playfair*. A pretty composition
with an open veranda. In 1896 the St Ronan's Well Mineral
Water Co. rebuilt the pavilion to house a pump room, bathrooms, waiting and retiring rooms. Timber-pedimented loggia
facing s, and two round turreted wings with painted thistle
finials set back at each end. The timberwork is blue, the rest
white; all very jolly and you can still taste the waters – if you
want to. Addition to the NW in 1989. – To the E, a lodge with
bracketed eaves and a single-storey range (now the museum)
looks mid-C19 and may be by *John Smith*, who designed ST
RONAN'S LODGE, opposite, *c.* 1824. A classy Regency-style
bungalow with later extensions. The early part has paired,
piended roofs, and oval-plan chimneystacks.

TOWN HALL (Municipal Buildings), Leithen Road. A two-
storey house, with a central buttressed gable, built by the
eighth Earl of Traquair in 1859. Purchased and given to the
town in 1919 by Henry Ballantyne. – On the E side is
the MEMORIAL HALL by *Todd & Miller*, 1922. Classical, rendered with a dentilled cornice. Five-bay front, the centre three
framed by pilasters. Frieze decorated with *paterae*.

TWEED BRIDGE, Traquair Road. Iron bridge of 1886 on stone
piers replacing a timber bridge of *c.* 1830 by *James Jardine*.

WAR MEMORIAL, in front of the Town Hall. Surely a unique
memorial, in the form of a rock garden bisected by a stream
flowing under a replica of the Cuddy Bridge. Monolith set on
a boulder by *Sydney H. Miller*, *c.* 1928, records the names of
the fallen.

DESCRIPTION

House building started in earnest *c.* 1800, principally owing to
the popularity of the spring waters. Starting at the E end of
PIRN ROAD, on the N side are Nos 15–17, a picturesque group
of late C18 harled cottages. No. 15, said to have been an inn,

has a lintel dated 1774 and initialled A.H. Immediately w, a lane leads to HORSBURGH TERRACE, mid-C19 and upmarket, with three two-storey, piend-roofed whinstone villas with sandstone dressings. At the crossroads, over Leithen Bridge (rebuilt 1994), the road becomes High Street (*see* below).

Now up LEITHEN ROAD to the r., where the early village lay. On the l. are the Memorial Hall, Innerleithen Parish and St Andrew's Episcopal churches (*see* above), and the Strand which leads to Wells Brae. Lining the road, between later houses, are early C19 single- and two-storey houses in whinstone, with painted stone margins, some with band courses and corniced doorpieces. Probably built for summer visitors. More sophisticated are LEITHEN HOUSE and BURNSIDE, on the approach to Cuddy Bridge. The first is Regency-style, with ornamental iron trellis window boxes and door surround, the latter single-storey, with small hoodmoulds, canted and straight bay windows, and porch with cast-iron columns and decorative wrought ironwork. On the l. just before the graveyard is THE KIRKLANDS, dated 1831. A farmhouse with prominent quoins, projecting crowsteps, and a central pediment. Past the graveyard is the early C19 MANSE (Mansley Lodge). Traditional, three-bay, rubble-built house, with a central corniced doorway. N addition (Green Gates), 1879, by *Archibald Nicol*. Single-storey stables to the w. DAMSIDE, w of Leithen Road, has some late C18 houses, e.g. Turner Cottage, dated 1783. Further on, mid-C19 HILL HOUSE, with slightly advanced centre bay and corniced doorpiece, followed by two terraced cottages, basically late C18, given later picturesque catslide dormers.

Parts of HIGH STREET are mid-C19 but it now mostly dates from 1881 to 1894, when the building trade was very active. It is of little architectural interest with a few exceptions. The BANK OF SCOTLAND (No. 4) is dated 1882. Two-storey, in red sandstone, many-gabled with decorative bargeboards. No. 9 was ROBERT SMAIL'S PRINTING WORKS. Its late C19 or early C20 shop and office front hides a time capsule (preserved by the National Trust for Scotland) of office, paper store, composing and press rooms, and reconstructed water wheel, using the common lade. ST RONAN'S HOTEL, N side, was built *c.* 1827. Harled and painted. The tiled shopfront of *c.* 1900 at No. 92 is of special interest. Decorated with encaustic tiles by *James Duncan Ltd.*, tile and marble contractors, for the Buttercup Dairy Co. The recessed entrance has a terrazzo floor inscribed BDC, wall tiles with dairymaid and picture tiles in an elliptical Art Nouveau surround. On the NE corner of High Street and Hall Street stands the MASONIC LODGE (Cleikhim Mill), dated 1877. The whinstone symmetrical front gable has vermiculated dressings and narrow-shouldered windows.

TRAQUAIR ROAD (A709), s from the w end of High Street, was opened in 1830. On the l. the TRAQUAIR ARMS HOTEL comprises a mid-C19, three-bay house to the r., with a late C20 top storey, and a porch (1879). To the l. a French-style three-storey and dormer addition, dated 1879, formerly with a cast-iron roof balustrade. The area to the s of the High Street and Pirn Road mainly comprised the Waverley Mills with associated housing. The late C19 housing is mostly traditional single-storey with attic dormers, and two- and three-storey houses, with much use of vermiculated lintels and margins. County Council housing began in 1920, in BUCCLEUCH STREET, by *Dick Peddie & Walker Todd*, and continued in Horsburgh Street, Montgomery Street and Chambers Street. Mostly of two types, rectangular flatted houses, and double, gable-fronted blocks.

VILLAS

BEECHWOOD, N side of Peebles Road. 1870s, by *Robert Mathison* for James Ballantyne. Rather dull Scottish Domestic house, with Tudor detailing, apparently built with material from the demolished Old Parish Church.

BELLENDEN HOUSE (The Pines), St Ronan's Terrace, stands on a high balustraded terrace. By *James B. Dunn* of *Dunn & Findlay*, for Colin Ballantyne, *c.* 1903, with addition to w in the same style *c.* 1913. Swept gables, mullioned windows, and Arts and Crafts detailing, suggest Cotswolds style; the circular Scottish entrance tower to the r. seems out of place.

CAERLEE HOUSE, N of Peebles Road, began as a modest Elizabethan-style house by *David Bryce*, 1865. Plain gables, mullioned windows and a canted bay. Extended w in the same style by *David Robertson*, 1878, and again in 1913, with N and w additions for H. Norman Ballantyne by *W.J. Walker Todd*. – LODGE. Harled and gabled, with bracketed eaves. Gates with Arts and Crafts ironwork.

INDUSTRIAL BULDINGS

CAERLEE MILL, Chapel Street. A plain, T-shaped, harled, five-storey block, begun *c.* 1788 by Alexander Brodie, still survives in the middle of a modern complex.

HOGG & ROBERTSON ENGINEERING WORKS, Morningside. One of a group of mills served by a common lade from the Leithen Water. A remarkable water-powered complex extended and converted from a late C18 farm steading. Probably early C20. Two metal-roofed timber-boarded sheds conceal a 6hp Lister engine in one and a small iron water wheel in the other. Timber-clad pulley chutes across the lade link the works to the power source.

MEIKLE'S SAW MILL, Morningside. Late C18 farm steading and late C19/early C20 timber-clad sawmill with large water wheel, timber-boarded turbine generator house and loom shed. A rubble-built wheel house projects over the common lade.

WAVERLEY MILLS, Morningside. Opened in 1871. Mostly demolished in 1990. The engine shed (with a roof tank by *Thomas Aimers* of Galashiels), a tall octagonal red brick chimney with cream brick dressings and the gatehouse survive.

GLENORMISTON HOUSE. *See* p. 332.
LEITHEN LODGE. *See* p. 492.

JEDBURGH*

INTRODUCTION

The former county town of Roxburghshire, the royal burgh of Jedburgh occupies the flat terraces and lower slopes of a narrow river valley, with Dunion Hill rising to the sw, and, being less than ten miles (16 km.) from the English border, its rich history owes much to its geography. The compact town is dominated by the loftily positioned Victorian Castle Jail at its sw extremity and by the ruined medieval abbey terraced above the nw bank of the Jed Water. The cruciform medieval layout of streets hugs the valley floor, whilst c20 housing and industry snakes along and above the Newcastle–Edinburgh bypass.

The settlement is first documented c. 830, when there is mention of two Gedweardes. The first was probably around the knoll now occupied by the burgh's Castle Jail but the site of the other settlement is uncertain. Most likely at Old Jeddart (6 km. s, where c12 carved fragments have been found, and tombstones were noted in the c19), an alternative location is at Bongate, at the n end of the present burgh, where coin hoards have been found. Military occupation by Romans in the c3 has been suggested and evidence points to the knoll having been fortified in the c10. The settlement would have expanded down the Castlegate ridge and along Canongate as it developed as an important centre of trade between Northumbria and Lothian. There was a church here well before the foundation of the Augustinian monastery c. 1138 (see Jedburgh Abbey, below) and a royal castle and a king's burgh were in existence by the third quarter of the c12, if not before.

The strong position of Jedburgh Castle, second in importance only to Roxburgh, led to frequent English attacks, since control of much of southern Scotland was at stake. The abbey, near completion by 1285, was also vulnerable, given its size and wealth. In 1335–6 the castle consisted of a great tower, lesser tower and pele; the Common Shore gully (which cuts through the ridge and links the Jed and the Skiprunning Burn) may have been artificially deepened, as outworks or a moat. In 1409 the Regent Albany finally ordered the destruction of the castle to prevent yet another episode of enemy occupation. Instead, fortified towers were

*The introduction, public buildings, industrial buildings and the burgh's description are by Sabina Strachan.

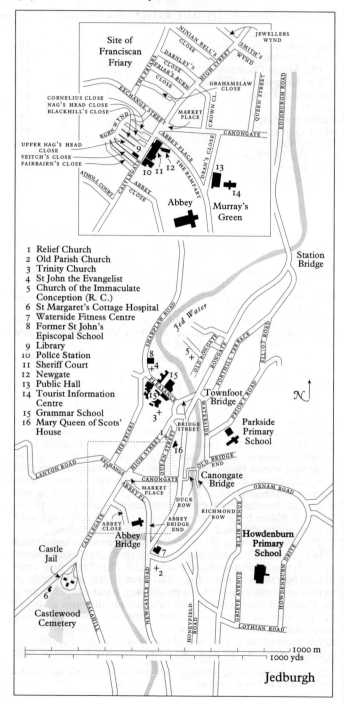

Site of Franciscan Friary

JEWELLERS WYND
NINIAN BELL'S CLOSE
SMITH'S WYND
HIGH STREET
DARNLEY'S CLOSE
FRIAR'S BURN
GRAHAMSLAW CLOSE
THE FRIARS
CLOSE
QUEEN STREET
CORNELIUS CLOSE
NAG'S HEAD CLOSE
BLACKHILL'S CLOSE
EXCHANGE STREET
BURN WYND
MARKET PLACE
CROWN CL.
CANONGATE
ABBEY PLACE
UPPER NAG'S HEAD CLOSE
VEITCH'S CLOSE
FAIRBAIRN'S CLOSE
DEAN'S CLOSE
THE RAMPART
EDINBURGH ROAD
ATHOLL COURT
CASTLEGATE
ABBEY CLOSE
9
10 11 12
13
14
Abbey
Murray's Green
Station Bridge

1 Relief Church
2 Old Parish Church
3 Trinity Church
4 St John the Evangelist
5 Church of the Immaculate Conception (R. C.)
6 St Margaret's Cottage Hospital
7 Waterside Fitness Centre
8 Former St John's Episcopal School
9 Library
10 Police Station
11 Sheriff Court
12 Newgate
13 Public Hall
14 Tourist Information Centre
15 Grammar School
16 Mary Queen of Scots' House

SHARPLAW ROAD
Jed Water
OLD BONGATE
BONGATE
FORTHILL TERRACE
ELLIOT ROAD
8
4
5
15
THE FRIARS
15
EXCHANGE STREET
WATERSIDE
PRIOR'S ROAD
Townfoot Bridge
Parkside Primary School
N
3
BRIDGE STREET
16
HIGH STREET
QUEEN STREET
Old Bridge End
Canongate Bridge
LANTON ROAD
EXCHANGE
CANONGATE
OXNAM ROAD
ABBEY PL.
MARKET PLACE
DUCK ROW
RICHMOND ROW
Abbey Close
BLAIR AVENUE
Howdenburn Primary School
CASTLEGATE
Abbey Bridge
Abbey Bridge End
Castle Jail
6
2
7
GALAHILL
NEWCASTLE ROAD
HONEYFIELD ROAD
GRIEVE AVENUE
HOWDENBURN DRIVE
LOTHIAN ROAD
Castlewood Cemetery

1000 m
1000 yds

Jedburgh

erected at strategic points around the town, three protecting the landward approaches to the abbey. Four ports – Townhead (at the head of Castlegate), Townfoot (at the foot of High Street), Canongate and Burnwynd – controlled access. The tolbooth stood at the Market Place end of the 'Tongue of the Canongate' – so named from a group of buildings running down the centre of the street.

Jedburgh rose in importance following the destruction of Roxburgh Castle (q.v.) in 1460; in 1523 the Earl of Surrey, prior to razing the town, noted that 'there was two times more houses therein than in Berwick, and well builded . . . and six good towers'. The earliest surviving intact structures today are the Canongate Bridge and a *c.* 1600 townhouse in Queen Street. The C13 Maison Dieu survived until after 1696, whereas the early C16 Franciscan friary was sacked in 1544–5 (both at the NE end of the then burgh); the abbey succumbed in 1559. Lands originally belonging to the monastery, and subsequently to the Earls of Lothian, were acquired by the burgh in 1669, by which period the town had a significant brewing and distilling industry. Vestiges of the towers remained until the C18 but burgh improvements from the 1750s onwards swept away the Tongue of the Canongate and the town ports. By the early C19 the Laigh Kirkwynd (the medieval approach to the abbey) had been widened to form Abbey Place, and the Townfoot and Abbey Bridges erected, whilst the Newgate, and then the County Buildings and the Castle Jail, fulfilled the function of the old tolbooth. Likewise, part of the Skiprunning Burn had been culverted to form Friarsgate (now The Friars) and villas built ascending the slope to the w.

The staple trades of Jedburgh was flour and meal grinding, malting and distilling; the burgh had an Abbey, Town and East Mill and numerous malt barns, but they suffered owing to the curbing of the contraband trade with England following the Treaty of Union of 1707. Initially, the woollen industry existed only in a small capacity, with a waulk mill by 1720, though significant developments followed the building of the railway branch line N of Bongate in 1856; the boom financing villa developments on Galahill and along Oxnam Road. The establishment of the North British Rayon Company in 1929 resulted in a doubling of population during the inter-war years as the Bongate and Howdenburn areas were developed. The economy suffered following its closure in 1956 and that of the station in 1964; however, the 1971–6 bypass encouraged new industries. This artery along the w bank of the Jed Water has altered the main N and S approaches to the town, sidelining the three early bridges and adding two more. Nevertheless, Jedburgh remains both a picturesque and a thriving town.

JEDBURGH ABBEY
Abbey Place

Built on a series of terraces above the Jed Water, the ruins of Jedburgh Abbey have always been one of the most impressive sights to confront those travelling N along the road into Scotland. David I's aspirations for the self-sufficiency and modernity of his kingdom's Church find one of their clearest architectural expressions at this remarkable complex. The site is thought to have had a long monastic history. According to Symeon of Durham, c. 830 Bishop Ecgred granted the two Gedweardes to Lindisfarne and built a church at one, to which a community was evidently attached; archaeological finds suggest this was that site.

The later community was founded c. 1138 by King David I and Bishop John of Glasgow for Augustinian Canons; the first colony probably came from St Quentin at Beauvais in the Ile-de-France. The house became a full abbey c. 1154. Construction of the presbytery, choir, crossing, transepts, and perhaps a short abuttal section of the nave, must have started soon after the foundation. On completion of those parts the main building effort was perhaps directed towards providing permanent conventual buildings. The last decades of the C12 and the early years of the C13 witnessed a massive amount of fresh building on the church, probably with different teams working simultaneously on different parts. The presbytery was entirely rebuilt, but to only a slightly extended plan, suggesting that structural problems rather than a wish for more space was the cause. The greatest effort, however, was on the nave, which was started around 1180 on stylistic evidence, and completed in the early C13.

Jedburgh's closeness to the Border made the abbey particularly vulnerable during the wars with England, and attacks in the C15 and C16 necessitated much rebuilding. By 1545 the abbey was governed by commendators of the Home family, for whom the estates of Jedburgh and Coldingham were together eventually made into a temporal lordship in 1606 and 1610. Parts of the damaged abbey church continued in parochial use after the Reformation, with worship conducted initially in the crossing area. That area threatened collapse on more than one occasion (advice was obtained from *John Mylne Jun.*, the King's Master Mason, in 1642) but it was only in 1668–71 that a new church was formed in the five W bays of the nave and N aisle. In 1681 much of the N transept was walled off; it was by then already in use as a burial place. In the final state of the parish church* – which is the only state known in some detail – its roof was at gallery level of the nave, and it had corridors and timber galleries around the W, N and E sides, looking towards a centrally placed pulpit on the S. These insertions were removed in 1875 when a new parish church was built elsewhere (*see* below), largely on the initiative of the ninth Marquess of Lothian. He subsequently undertook repairs to the unencumbered historic fabric under the direction of *R. Rowand Anderson*. There was partial excavation of the E end of the church by *P. Macgregor Chalmers*, 1898. In 1913 the remains were placed in state care, and in 1914–17 an ambitiously engineered campaign of consolidation to the N crossing piers was carried out, in the course of which later buttressing masonry was removed.

The first significant campaign of excavation was in 1935–9, when the remains of the conventual buildings were explored and exposed so far as was possible. Following a road closure and the removal of a number of buildings, major excavations in 1983–6

*Shown on a plan of 1818 by the Rev. John Sime in the National Monuments Record of Scotland.

further elucidated the plan and sequence of construction of the buildings around the cloister. There was limited excavation within the presbytery area of the church in 1990.

THE ABBEY CHURCH

PLAN. The church, on the N side of the site, terminated at its E end in an aisle-less rectangular PRESBYTERY of three and a half narrow bays defined by slender buttresses, of which only fragments remain. In 1898 Macgregor Chalmers claimed that there was archaeological evidence of an earlier E apse but investigations in 1990 suggested that the original presbytery was also square-ended and was only *c.* 3 m. shorter than its successor. The CHOIR is of two bays, with a square-ended aisle along each flank, and there is a CENTRAL CROSSING, surmounted by a tower, with TRANSEPTS on both sides, each originally having an E apsidal chapel. One source for this plan (apart from the rectangular ends of the choir chapels) could have been Southwell Minster (Nottinghamshire), a church of the archbishops of York, whose predatory claims in the C12 were such a source of difficulty for the Scottish Church. The apse of the N transept was suppressed when the transept was rebuilt and extended northwards in the mid C15, and that of the S transept was lost when the transept was truncated as part of C16 stop-gap repairs. The aisled NAVE is of nine bays.

DESCRIPTION: The church provides a fascinating illustration of the range of architectural relationships between Scotland and England in the course of the C12. A tour of the building should begin with the earliest surviving parts, the two bays of the CHOIR, and the inner bays of the transepts where they open into the aisles of the choir and nave. These parts are remarkable for the use of a giant order of cylindrical piers, with the round arcade arch and gallery sub-arches set back on a subordinate plane within the round-headed arch which embraces each bay. This arrangement possibly reached Scotland either by way of Romsey Abbey (Kent), where David I's aunt, Christina, was a nun, or from Reading Abbey (Berkshire), which was another recipient of David's benefactions. This suggests it was the king himself who took the lead on matters of architectural design and who selected the master masons.

The cylindrical pier between the two surviving choir bays on each side is flanked on the E side of the choir by a three-quarter-round respond of similar dimensions, which is separated by a slender shaft from what remains of the aisle-less presbytery wall. At the W end of the choir the two piers on the N side of the crossing (and presumably originally their S counterparts) are each made up of a T-shaped combination of four three-quarter piers, three forming the head of the T, in a line towards the central vessel, and the fourth acting as a respond for the arches into the choir and nave aisles. Within the choir, the arcade arches and the springings of the ribbed vaults over the aisles are carried on impost-like capitals which emerge at the sides and rear of the piers.

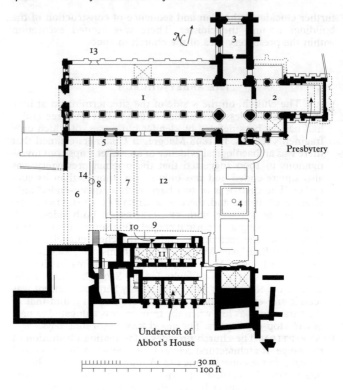

Presbytery

Undercroft of
Abbot's House

||||||||||| | 30 m
                             100 ft

1	Nave	8	Second West Alley
2	Choir	9	First South Alley
3	North Transept	10	Second South Alley
4	Chapter House	11	Refectory over
5	First West Range	12	Cloister
6	Second West Range	13	Position of Parish Door
7	First West Alley	14	Well

Jedburgh Abbey.
Plan.

At gallery level the paired sub-arches are carried on responds
in the form of half-shafts attached to rectangular projections
coursed in with the piers, and there is a monolithic shaft in the
middle of each opening. The only gallery opening which is still
largely as first built is in the E bay on the S side; the W bay
on the S side has been partly rebuilt in the C15 without its
sub-arches, while on the N side the sub-arches have been
rebuilt in pointed form, and an additional skin of arches has
been added behind, supported by chalice caps similar to
another in the S transept clearstorey (see below), and indicating that these changes were of the later C12. All the original
capitals are scalloped; the upper arches, at gallery level, have
chevron decoration, while the orders of the arcade arches are

simply relieved by angle rolls. The relative fluency with which the design appears to have been executed towards the central vessel is less certain when the arcades are viewed from within the aisles, where it can be seen that the inner orders of the arches had to be awkwardly stilted to accommodate them to the junction of pier and vault springing. The clearstorey is discussed below.

Fragmentary stubs on each side of the PRESBYTERY at its junction with the choir hint at its likely first form before the later C12 rebuilding. Beyond the short internal stretch of blank wall corresponding to the E wall of the aisle, a base on each side suggests there was a dado of decorative arcading. At gallery level there is internally a robust half-shaft in front of a section of mural passage. The picture this presents is amplified by the external evidence: on the N side, immediately E of the choir aisle, are slight traces of two window jambs, one above the other, showing that there were windows corresponding to both arcade and gallery levels in the adjacent choir. The internal arcaded dado is thus likely to have been confined to the area below the lower tier of windows.

The REBUILT PRESBYTERY, perhaps of the late 1170s, was only slightly longer than its predecessor and was similarly aisle-less. The form of the external base course makes clear it was a total rebuilding rather than a remodelling, and such a major architectural undertaking with so little spatial gain suggests structural necessity, which could also have been the reason for the doubling-up of the N choir gallery arches. In the rebuilding, significant changes were introduced in the relative proportions of the storeys. At the lower level was again a dado, with a blind pointed-arched arcade, but it probably rose to a greater height than the original dado, and left no space for a lower level of windows immediately above it. At the same time, a considerably greater depth was given to the second storey, which now came down to a level corresponding to the arcade arch springing in the adjacent choir. From a combination of the surviving fabric and the evidence of C18 and C19 views, we know that the new second storey had a continuous arcade of alternating tall and low pointed arches on the inner face of the wall passage, the arches being carried on piers of basically quatrefoil plan. Tall stilted arches corresponded to windows in the outer wall, and the lower arches to blank wall between the windows. The architectural details of the surviving section include crocket and waterleaf capitals. The overall design approach seen in the rebuilt presbytery is essentially comparable to that seen in the aisle-less choir at Coldingham Priory (q.v.), and also in the churches at Nun Monkton and St Bees in England, which could suggest that there was initially no intention to provide a clearstorey.

However, there is considerable uncertainty about the chronology of the CLEARSTOREY along the eastern arm as a whole. The only surviving sections are over the choir. At its NW corner, fragments survive of a clearstorey that is clearly earlier than that now seen, with two string courses that were presumably intended to correspond to sill and arch springing level of the windows. Above these is a short section of arched corbel table representing a wall-head level lower than the present one. There is also a corresponding vertical internal break, presumably relating to an opening. All of this could be the relic of a clearstorey that was part of the same first operation as the giant arcade of the choir; but against this are two main considerations. First, the string courses are different from those elsewhere in the choir in not having a quirk between the vertical and angled lower faces. Instead they are similar to fragments associated with the clearstorey in the s transept, and there the provision for a slender detached nook-shaft to the outer face of the window and the survival of a chalice capital on the respond of the inner arcade suggest the third storey in that part was a later C12 addition. Secondly, as already noted, the strengthened N choir gallery also has later C12 chalice capitals. On balance, it is therefore arguable that the gallery strengthening and first choir clearstorey are contemporary, and that no clearstorey was initially planned for either the original choir or the rebuilt presbytery.

If this is correct, the first clearstorey represented by the fragment at the NW corner cannot have been far advanced before the much higher one now seen replaced it. This change was perhaps made in order to give the choir and presbytery the same overall height as the nave, by then in its final stages of construction. Externally, the clearstorey as built has a single lancet window per bay, each with continuous reveal mouldings. Internally it was designed to a formula very like that of the rebuilt presbytery, with alternating low and tall stilted arches running along the inner side of the wall passage, albeit with an updated architectural vocabulary. While some of the caps to the quatrefoil piers of the arcade are of chalice type, the developed stiff-leaf foliage of some on the s point to an early C13 date of completion.

The s CHOIR AISLE was extensively reconstructed in the second half of the C15. The window in its E wall was blocked, in keeping with the late medieval vogue for blank E walls to accommodate decorated retables; instead, a three-light window was formed in the adjacent s wall, to throw light across the altar. This has tracery inspired by C13 Geometric designs, though with ogee curves that betray the later date. In the w bay of the aisle a doorway with a rectangular window above it was inserted, and externally new buttresses were constructed at the SE angle and between the bays; the diagonal angle buttress appears to have been later modified when a wall was built up to the corner. The arms on the ogee-headed panel of the buttress between the bays are said to have been those of Bishop Turnbull (1447–54). Internally the vault was extensively reconstructed, and the boss of the transverse rib between the bays is inscribed with the monograms of Jesus and Mary and the name of Abbot John Hall (1478–9). The boss of the E bay has the royal arms, while that of the w bay is foliate.

Across the w end of the choir, below the E crossing arch, is part of a wall which may have belonged to the church formed in the crossing area after the attacks of the 1540s.

The s TRANSEPT has undergone many changes, but there is evidence for the elevations having been originally similar to those of the choir, in having a giant order and a suspended gallery. On the E side, the S respond and the arches into the S choir aisle and gallery are partly preserved within the reconstructed masonry. S of the arches into the choir chapel was a short stretch of wall pierced by a narrow window, beyond which was the arch into the E apsidal chapel. The N jamb of this arch is only visible externally. It survived through having had a stair turret set against it when the mid-C16 cross wall was built to cut off the outer part of the transept. Towards the transept the arch had two orders of engaged nook-shafts with cushion capitals, though above these the arch orders were left plain. On the W side, at the junction with the S aisle and gallery of the nave, much of the upper arch survives above blocking, and the S springing of the lower arch is visible above a later arch; the three-quarter respond on the S side of those arches is also well-preserved.

The S transept clearstorey survives only as a fragment on the

Jedburgh Abbey. Elevation of the N wall and section of the Tower, before restoration of the tower piers and wall head.

E side, at its junction with the tower. Its details, similar to the early clearstorey fragment and gallery strengthening on the N side of the choir discussed above, suggest it was a late C12 addition. It was subsequently lost to sight internally when a barrel vault was built over the S transept, springing from immediately above the gallery stage rather than from the wall-head. This vault was presumably contemporary with the reconstruction of the S CROSSING PIERS and the tower, dated by the arms of Abbot Thomas Cranston (1484–1501) on the E side of the SW crossing pier and of Archbishop Robert Blackadder (1483–1508) at the tower head. The SW crossing pier at its lowest level is a lozenge-shaped, biaxially symmetrical cluster of twelve major shafts, filleted on the cardinal axes, with lesser shafts between. The SE pier is similar, but has a flat face towards the central vessel to accommodate choir stalls (?). It must have been built before the SW pier, for on its W side, just below the level of the gallery floor, is a corbel and arch springing, evidently indicating an intention to throw an arch across the S side of the crossing, an idea abandoned by the time the SW pier was built.

The N CROSSING PIERS now appear largely as in their early C12 state. The exception to this is the W part of the NW pier, which was reconstructed along with the nave, and the pier was again worked on in the C15 since it bears the initials of Abbot Cranston. The N crossing arch springs from the high capitals of the piers, while the E and W crossing arches spring from triple corbels.

The N TRANSEPT projects two bays beyond the nave and choir aisles, having been extended and remodelled in the time of Bishop William Turnbull of Glasgow (1447–54) on the evidence of a shield above the N window with arms said to have been his. It is an example of a late medieval vogue at some monastic churches for asymmetrical enlargement of the transept on the side away from the cloister; this was presumably to afford additional space for altars and associated burial places as the number of chantry foundations increased. The E wall was left blank to allow space for altar retables, though externally there are projecting tusks where the C12 apsidal chapel adjoined it. The W wall has a pair of two-light windows to cast light onto the altars, the bays being marked by buttresses, and there are NE and NW angle buttresses. The N gable wall is pierced by a four-light window with a handsome display of flowing tracery, which is of a virtually identical pattern to a window at Melrose Abbey (q.v.) associated with the building operations of Abbot Andrew Hunter (1444–71).

Internally, the northern half of the transept is cut off by a wall dated on a tablet to 1681, by when the transept was used as a burial aisle for the Kerr family, ancestors of the Marquesses of Lothian. The early C12 arches into the N choir aisle and gallery are well preserved, but the gallery opening is now blocked. N of those openings are traces of the rear arches of small windows at two levels which opened between the choir chapel and transept apse (traces of the upper window are also evident externally). There are slight remains of what appears to be arching masonry at the upper level of the E wall next to the tower, suggesting an intention to span the enlarged N transept with a barrel vault, though it is unlikely it was ever built. Below the N window is a tomb recess with a made-up chest on which the arms of Archbishop Blackadder (1483–1508) have been relocated.

The lower part of the TOWER, which rose to less than a single 8 storey above the roofs of nave and E limb, is pierced by large arches in each of its faces: two on the N side and one on the others. These arches must initially have been within the roof area of the nave, choir and transepts, but were left wholly or partly exposed externally when the roofs were lowered in the early C16. Early views suggest some or all were then walled up. At the upper stage, the N and S faces each have a row of three equal-height cusped lancets, which were blocked on the inner plane by a barrel vault running on an E–W axis. The W face also has three lancets, though the sill of the central opening was elevated above the roof ridge. On the E face there was no S lancet because there is a stair at this point, and the central lancet is elevated like that on the W face, with a doorway below it into what was perhaps the space above a wagon ceiling in the choir. Around the tower head is an openwork parapet of square quatrefoils, with a caphouse at the SE corner and square pinnacles at the others. A stone-flagged double-pitched roof on the extrados of the barrel vault, now gone, would have risen behind this. A complex bellcote, possibly of post-Reformation date, used to rise above the N side of the tower.

The NAVE, probably started around 1180, was designed on a 8 more generous scale than the E limb, reflecting both the community's expanding wealth and its enhanced abbatial status. Many influences are discernible in the design, but the basic formula for the internal elevations was probably inspired by the choir of St Andrews Cathedral (Fife), of c. 1160. Internally, the lowest of the three storeys is an arcade of pointed arches carried on octofoil bundled-shaft piers, with a wonderful variety of luxuriant crocket and waterleaf foliage capitals for which there are parallels, amongst others, at Byland Abbey (Yorkshire) and St Mary's Abbey, York. The arcade arches are of three orders; except in the W bay, they have a diagonally set keeled roll to the outer orders and a triplet of keeled rolls on the axial order. As was presumably the case at St Andrew's, the gallery is strikingly tall with round arches containing pairs of pointed sub-arches in all but the second bay from the E on the N; between the sub-arches the tympana are pierced with a variety of small Geometrical shapes. The relatively squat clerestory has a regular succession of four equal-height arches to each bay of the arcade on both the inner side of the wall passage and the outer plane of the wall. Only the central pair of arches in each bay were pierced as windows, however, the others being left blind. The clerestory capitals, although of polygonal form, are of chalice and waterleaf types, suggesting a date not long after 1200.

The interior is strikingly homogeneous, but there are several clues to the building sequence. Most of the nave bases are of early water-holding type, with an arris forming the lip of the hollow between the two rolls, and with a vertical edge to the lower roll. The bases of the two E bays, however, are of a slightly later type, in having a horizontal fillet as the rim to the hollow, and a three-quarter-round bottom roll; this suggests those bays were only built after an early C12 abuttal section for the tower and choir had been removed. At gallery level, the piers of the sub-arches in the five W bays have paired shafts with smaller rolls between, whereas in the four E bays those piers are doubled in size, and are perhaps slightly later. The aisle vault springings also show further modifications down the length of the nave. But the greatest change is at clearstorey level. This stage may have been built after a slight pause in operations, as represented by a change in the manner of constructing the two spiral stairs within the W front turrets, at a level corresponding with the gallery arch springings. (At the lower level there are composite steps supported on a helical vault, but monolithic keyhole-shaped steps at the higher level.) At the W end of the clearstorey, an external arch springing on each side suggests the clearstorey was initially intended to rise higher and be embraced in a single arch.

The W FRONT survives to full height. A pair of stair turrets flanks the high central part,* and lighting each aisle end is a single round-headed window with provision for nook-shafts. In the centre, corresponding to the arcade stage internally, is one of the triumphs of Transitional architectural sculpture in Scotland: a cavernous processional doorway set in a salient section of wall with a low blind arch on each flank. The masonry of the doorway projection is not fully coursed in with the lower wall of the W front, and may represent an addition to the original design. (It may be noted that the internal masonry at this point has a marked slope, and had to be brought back to horizontal courses at a higher level.) The whole projecting doorway section is capped by three gablets above a string course, each gablet containing a trifoliate-headed image recess.† The doorway is of six orders, the five outer orders having been carried on shafts. Between some of the jamb shafts were bands of intersecting chevron, while the inner order of the jamb has fine 'Byzantine blossom' foliage decoration, alternating with heads in quatrefoils comparable with those of the Canterbury Cathedral choir screen. There are Corinthianesque capitals to the doorway and conjoined wyvern-like creatures to the caps of the inner orders; this is a rich repertoire of decoration with many parallels, including the W doorway at Kelso Abbey (q.v.). For the chevron, parallels may be seen at e.g. Selby Abbey (Yorkshire) and St Mary's York.

Parallels with Kelso may also be seen in the design of the upper W front, and particularly in the single round-headed window rising through both gallery and clearstorey levels. The daylight opening of this window has been considerably increased by cutting back the framing mouldings, however,

---

* Reused as a lintel inside the N stair doorway is a Roman altar dedicated to Jupiter by a detachment of Raetian spearmen under the command of Julius Severinus.
† It has been suggested that a fine fragment of a figure with dampfold drapery, now displayed in the visitor centre, may have been housed within one of these recesses.

perhaps at a time when tracery (since removed) was introduced. It is flanked on each side by three blind arches, the
missing shafts of which had two levels of shaft-rings. This was
a slightly later variant on Kelso, where the central window was
flanked by two intersecting blind arches with two levels of rings
to the shafts. The surmounting gable is a C15 reconstruction
with a twelve-petal rose window as its central feature, the only
Scottish parallel for which is in the w gable of the Dryburgh
Abbey refectory (p. 222).

Little of the N AISLE WALL survives above the lower courses,
apart from the stubs of the wall where it adjoined the N
transept and w front. The S AISLE, however, is substantially
complete (though partly reconstructed) up to the roof level of
the N cloister walk. The SE DOORWAY from the cloister into
the s aisle of the church is the most significant survivor of this
part and, like the w doorway, it was set in a salient section of
wall. What has been lost can be partly understood by comparison with a replica inserted on the site of the sw doorway
by *Watts* of *Farmer and Brindley c.* 1875, under the direction of
R. Rowand Anderson. Both jambs and arches have elaborated
interlocking chevron with foliage in the angles, cf. the w
doorway at Selby Abbey, Yorkshire. The central order of the
arch had alternating roundels with figure scenes and 'Byzantine blossom', while the heavily weathered capitals appear to
have had early stiff-leaf foliage.

MONUMENTS. In the S CHOIR AISLE, a partly restored stone
with interlace decoration around its deep flanks, and a cross-
shaft on a stepped base flanked by plaits on the top; this has
been tentatively linked with Bishop John of Glasgow, †1147,
co-founder of the abbey. – N WALL OF PRESBYTERY, imposing ciborium monument of John Rutherfurd of Edgerston,
†1834, erected by subscription. – N TRANSEPT, LOTHIAN
AISLE, N wall, simple tomb-chest within arched recess, on the
front of the chest the re-set arms of Archbishop Robert Blackadder, †1508; added above the arch are pilasters and a cornice
carrying a double-height aedicule with the arms of Kerr and
the initials ALI, possibly for Andrew Lord Jedburgh, †1631. –
At centre of aisle the tomb-chest of the eighth Marquess of
Lothian, †1870, surmounted by full-length effigy by *G. F. Watts*,
dated 1879. Various other monuments to Kerr family.

THE CONVENTUAL BUILDINGS

The remains around the CLOISTER are scanty. As first laid out
the cloister extended along the six E bays of the nave, but it
was subsequently extended westwards with the later outer wall
of the w walk probably on what had been the line of the w wall
of the w range. It was also extended southwards, when it seems
that the s cloister walk was slotted into the lower level of the
refectory range.

The E CONVENTUAL RANGE survives mainly as consolidated
footings at its N end nearest the church, but its walls stand
higher as the ground slopes away to the s. The SLYPE is next
to the footings of the s transept of the church; the foundations
of the earlier chapter house project below its s face, showing

that it must initially have been slightly narrower. The CHAPTER HOUSE has had three forms at various periods, according to excavations carried out in 1984: initially a rectangular chamber projecting a short way beyond the body of the range; it was later extended eastwards, possibly leaving only a vestibule within the range; in its final late C14 or C15 state it was a square chamber entirely within the body of the range, with a central pier to carry the vaulting, as e.g. at Cambuskenneth (Stirling and Central Scotland), Crossraguel (Ayrshire) and Glenluce (Dumfries and Galloway) abbeys. The room S of the chapter house is set at a lower level and is of basically elongated rectangular plan. A broad foundation in its SW corner perhaps supported the day stair from the dormitory. S of this room the ground slopes yet more steeply towards the Jed Water and the next two rooms were on progressively lower levels. Finely worked ashlar walls, with semi-octagonal vaulting shafts rising from chamfered bases, which develop without caps into chamfered wall ribs, point to a C13 date for these outer rooms. The southernmost room was subdivided by a crude cross-wall at some stage, possibly following damage to the outer end of the range during the wars with England, and a mill was built over the lade that had presumably flushed the monastic LATRINE at the outer end of the range.

The S SIDE OF THE CLOISTER has the most extensive remains. Two ranges extend parallel to the S walk. The REFECTORY undercroft, which runs alongside the line of the original S walk, may have been built as early as the C12 and is perhaps the earliest substantial fragment of the conventual buildings. Its unbuttressed S wall was pierced by regularly spaced narrow round-headed windows. When the cloister was extended to the S and W, buttress-like piers of masonry were built inside the S wall, a new inner N wall was built (reducing the undercroft to the dimensions of little more than a corridor) and quadripartite ribbed vaulting was constructed over the modified space, of which some corbels and springings survive. The building was further altered when kitchens and offices that probably served both the refectory and the later Abbot's House in the W range were constructed between the two parts.

The use of the range running parallel to the refectory is uncertain, but the quality of architectural detail shows that it was a prestigious building. It was possibly an early ABBOT'S LODGING, since linkage with the dormitory through the latrine block would have respected the letter – if not the spirit – of the rule that the abbot should live in common with his community, cf. perhaps Iona. Rising from a double-chamfered base course, the S wall has buttresses defining bays that are pierced by doorways or by paired or single lancets, all with chamfered surrounds. The N wall of the range partly revetted the rising ground, and internal buttresses have been added along its length both to withstand the pressure and to provide additional support for the vaulting, of which some wall ribs remain.

The buildings W of the cloister have been frequently altered, and the archaeological evidence has been confused by the construction and demolition of a post-Reformation manse and its outbuildings here. To the SW, traces of two timber buildings

were found in 1984, which were thought to represent temporary structures provided while the more permanent conventual
buildings were being erected. Later, a substantial rectangular
structure was built at the SW angle of the cloister, further
extended to an L-shape by the addition of a wing off the S end
of its W wall. The most prominent part now remaining is its S
wall, revetting the steep bank above the original course of the
Jed Water, which was adapted as a lade when the river was
diverted to a more southerly course. Constructed chiefly of
well-cut ashlar, with two levels of chamfered intakes (and with
latrine outlets at its base), this building was clearly of considerable scale; this, and its location close to the main entrance
to the precinct, suggest it may have replaced or supplemented
the earlier Abbot's Lodging.

Within the VISITOR CENTRE is a fascinating collection of artefacts and of carved and moulded stones associated with the
abbey, most important of which is the 'JEDBURGH SHRINE'.
Either the end gable of a shrine or part of a stone screen, and
dated variously between the early C8 and the early C9, it is
perhaps closer to the latter date if associated with Bishop
Ecgred's foundation. The main field of carving is occupied by
a vine with a central stem and symmetrical scrolls of branches
occupied by birds and mythical beasts. Down the right-hand
side is a border band of interlace.

The GRAVEYARD, N of the abbey church, may be on the site of
the monastic burial ground. It now contains mainly C18 and
C19 monuments.

FRANCISCAN FRIARY
The Friars

The Observant Franciscans were at Jedburgh by 1505; their house
possibly suffered in English raids of 1523, 1544 and 1545. Excavations between 1983 and 1992 revealed the layout of much of
the hitherto unknown claustral complex and parts of the church,
and in 1993 the remains were displayed as the centrepiece of a
public garden. The rectangular church was on a SE to NW axis;
the cloister to its NE had walks on at least three (and presumably
four) sides, with ranges around three sides. A square room at the
centre of the SE range was presumably the chapter house, and an
elongated room on the side facing across to the church was evidently a refectory. The water supply and drainage of the house
required a lade and several stone-lined conduits taken off the
nearby Skiprunning Burn.

CHURCHES

BAPTIST CHURCH. *See* p. 431.
CHURCH OF THE IMMACULATE CONCEPTION (R.C.), Old
Bongate. 1937 by *Reginald Fairlie*. Church and presbytery form
an L-shaped grouping, all with a cream rendering and some
ashlar dressings. The church is an aisle-less rectangle with a
polygonal NW apse and a SW porch on the side towards the
presbytery. Detailing in a simplified Gothic idiom, the main SE

elevation having diagonal buttresses and a four-light loop-traceried window surmounted by a statue of the Virgin below a simple block canopy. The interior is divided into five and a half bays by pilasters carrying segmental arches; ceiling of polygonal section. – ICON, C17 copy of C13 representation of the Virgin.

OLD PARISH CHURCH, Newcastle Road. Built 1872–5 on the S edge of the burgh to house the congregation transplanted from the nave of the abbey church (*see* above). The cost of £11,000 was met by the ninth Marquess of Lothian. Built 1872–5 in a freely interpreted Early English style by *T. H. Wyatt*, using coursed rock-faced dark buff-coloured sandstone with lighter ashlar dressings, much of the stone quarried in the Eildon Hills. It was initially a T-shaped structure with shallow 'transepts' at the E end of an aisled nave, and with a vestry and organ loft in an E apse. That apse was transformed into a polygonal sanctuary in 1888 by *Hippolyte J. Blanc*.

The three-and-a-half bay nave has a deep W narthex the full width of the central vessel; a substantial octagonal bell-turret rises in the angle between the narthex and N aisle, decreasing in scale through a series of intakes, with an arched belfry stage and spirelet. Its lower part has the stair to the W gallery. The cavernous W entrance, dated 1873, is within a gabled projection rising above the sloping narthex roof: two shoulder-lintelled doorways are below a pair of lancets in the tympanum framed by the embracing arch. The upper part of the W gable, set back behind the narthex, has a three-light window with Geometric tracery. Aisle flanks with windows of two lights and a cusped circlet rising into gables, the clearstorey with triplets of lancets. The transepts have stair-turrets in the re-entrant angles between transept and nave, and gable-ends with three tiers of openings: three lancet windows at the lower level, two windows at the gallery level and a plate-traceried rose in the gable. Around the E apse are vestries and an organ chamber.

Internally, the chief impression is of great space, to which the later sanctuary in the remodelled apse is not altogether equal, despite a concentrated display of High Churchmanship. Since 1888 the apse has housed the communion table and choir stalls, and its lower walls have wainscotting, pierced by windows in the diagonal faces, with a further tier of windows at the top. Most striking are the paintings in the middle register: the Angel appearing to the Shepherds, the Transfiguration and the Adoration of the Magi. The Ten Commandments are painted on the straight flanks of the apse, within a field of stencilled decoration. In the nave, E of the W half-bay, are three-bay arcades, with taller arches opening into the transepts. Except for the more complex piers to the transept arches, the piers are cylindrical with caps of waterleaf types. The open-timber roof has scissor-braced trusses, and arched braces to the principal rafters. There are galleries over the W half-bay and set back within the transepts. – PULPIT, to S of arch into apse, ashlar and alabaster polygon with arcaded sides, of the 1888 campaign. – STAINED GLASS. Apse, angels at upper level; NE face, lower level, the Crucifixion; SE face lower level, Christ blessing, *c.* 1905, by *Norman McLeod Macdougall* and

Daniel Cottier & Co. s transept s face, lower level, the True Vine, the Good Shepherd, the Bread of Life, *c.* 1886; upper level, the Light of the World, Christ as the Way, 1899. N transept N face, lower level, Faith, Hope and Charity, *c.* 1876; upper level, Christ and the Children and Christ the Healer, *c.* 1902, signed *EH*; top rose, angels exhorting 'cast thy burden'. Nave s aisle, first from E, SS Andrew and Paul, by *Ballantine*, 1891; w wall, Angel Appearing to Shepherds and Adoration of the Magi, 1883. N aisle, first from E, Holy Family, *c.* 1890, by *Clayton & Bell*; second from E, Lux in Tenebris and Return of Prodigal, *c.* 1914 by *Clayton & Bell*; w wall, Raising of Lazarus, *c.* 1888. w window, Scenes from Life of Moses, *c.* 1870.

Former RELIEF CHURCH, High Street, also known as Boston Church; now British Legion hall. First built 1757 for a seceding congregation, with Thomas Boston as its minister, it was replaced by a new building designed by *William Smail*, mason in Ancrum, in 1818 (both dates on tablet above entrance). There was some remodelling in 1876, and in 1888 a hall and offices were added. Buff stone; stugged ashlar with polished dressings (now painted) to the main front, rubble elsewhere. The five-bay (w) entrance front is of two storeys, the doorways in the central and outer bays framed by Tuscan pilasters and entablatures. Above and between the doorways are round-headed windows with Y-tracery.

ST JOHN THE EVANGELIST (Episcopal), Pleasance. An important monument of the early influence of Tractarian churchmanship on the Episcopal Church, built 1843–4 by *John Hayward* of Exeter. Much of the cost of about £1,800, together with an endowment for the clergyman, was provided by the Marchioness of Lothian. With walls of buff snecked rubble with ashlar dressings, it is a correctly orientated essay in the approved English Decorated style. It consists of a two-bay chancel, a four-bay aisle-less nave, a two-storey s porch in the third nave bay from the E, and a N vestry subsequently extended to accommodate an organ chamber. The bay divisions and angles are marked by buttresses, and a stair-turret on the N side of the porch leads up to what was originally an organ chamber and choir loft. A gabled bellcote surmounts the w gable, and there are cross finials on the bellcote and E gables of nave and chancel. There is curvilinear tracery in the three-light E and W windows, the two-light nave windows and the single-light chancel windows, all of which rest on string courses. Great care was taken in detailing hoodmould corbels and drainage spouts. The Lothian burial vault below the chancel, entered from a timber porch on the N side, was in 1939 adapted as a Lady Chapel.

The church has a full range of ecclesiologically correct furnishings; it is likely *William Butterfield*, at the outset of his career, was involved as at the same time he was building the adjacent school and lychgate (*see* below). The chancel has a panelled pointed-barrel ceiling, the beams painted, and the panels filled with porcelain tiles decorated with stars and sacred symbols by *Minton*. Arch-braced nave roof originally enriched with painted decoration by *D.R. Hay*, but now painted an inappropriate blue. The finely detailed rood screen

has a prominent pulpit to the N. There are Minton tiles to the
floors and to the chancel walls, decorated with heraldry, evangelist symbols and other imagery after designs by *A. W. N.
Pugin*. – ALTAR, of Caen stone with quatrefoil decoration, by
Rowe of Exeter, and later timber-arcaded retable. – SEDILIA
and PISCINA, painted stone and lavishly arched and canopied,
by *Rowe* of Exeter. – CREDENCE SHELF, with angel corbel. –
SCREEN, oak, two narrower bays to each side of wider central
bay, all with curvilinear tracery, with later painted rood and
figures of the Virgin and St John. – PULPIT, given by Dowager
Queen Adelaide, a stone polygon with traceried faces, built
into NE angle of nave, and reached by a mural stair from the
vestry through an angled doorway. – FONT, painted stone with
alternating evangelist symbols and quatrefoils. – ALMS BOX,
with scrolled ironwork, by *William Dyce*. – STATIONS OF THE
CROSS, 1993, modern icons. – STAINED GLASS. E window,
Agony in Garden, Christ Bearing Cross, Ascension; chancel N
window, Miracle of Loaves and Fishes; S side, Raising of
Lazarus, Suffer Little Children, all by *Ward & Nixon*; W
window, entombment of Christ, 1853; nave N flank, 3rd bay
from E, arms of dioceses of Glasgow and Durham, by *Ballantine*. Other windows mainly mosaic patterns.

LYCHGATE, 1844, timber framed with tiled roof, by *William
Butterfield*.

TRINITY CHURCH, High Street. Previously known as Blackfriars
and Boston Blackfriars Church, the present building of 1818 is
set further back from the road than predecessors of 1746 and
1801. It is a square building of buff sandstone; polished or
stugged ashlar with polished dressings to the main front, and
rubble elsewhere. The main (SE) front is a chastely secular classical design of two storeys and five bays, the two end bays projecting as pavilions, between which runs a Tuscan colonnaded
loggia to the lower storey. The central doorway and the two tiers
of windows are round-arched and without margins. A simple
base course is reflected in an equally plain string course below
the upper windows, while the wall-head cornice supports a
blocking course with a central raised tablet to each section, that
above the central window inscribed 1818. The two-storey side
elevations have three bays of windows, while the NW face has a
pair of tall windows flanking the location of the pulpit, and
blocked doorways towards each end. The low-pitched piended
roofs are slated, with a central flat to the main roof.

Within the entrance is a vestibule; gallery stairs can be
reached from both the vestibule and the loggia. The gallery,
carried on square timber piers, runs around three sides of the
interior, looking NW towards the two-stage pulpit and organ.
The flat plastered ceiling has a simple central rose and traceried ventilator holes. There was an internal reordering by *J. P.
Alison* in 1896. – PULPIT and PLATFORM, with barley-sugar
balusters, perhaps by *Alison*. – COMMUNION TABLE, 1930. –
FONT, marble on wooden stand, 1888, from the former Relief
Church (q.v.). – STAINED GLASS, central window of SW flank,
Adoration of Shepherds and Magi, 1902, by *Kemp, Benson &
Co.* of Glasgow; otherwise mosaic patterns. – MEMORIAL, in
vestibule, the Rev. Alexander Shanks, †1799, and Rev. Peter

Young, †1824, tablet capped by urn against obelisk, by *J. Thin* of Edinburgh. – OFFICES, 1899, by *Alison*.

PUBLIC BUILDINGS

ABBEY BRIDGE. *See* p. 432.
CANONGATE BRIDGE. *See* p. 432.
HOWDENBURN PRIMARY SCHOOL. *See* Description 2, The Suburbs.
JEDBURGH CASTLE JAIL, Castlegate. Now a museum. 1820–3 by *Archibald Elliot*. Scotland's only surviving example of a prison modelled on the principles set out in the late C18 by the reformer John Howard. It makes an imposing landmark, dominating the SW end of old Jedburgh on Galahill. This was the site of the royal Jedburgh Castle (dem. 1409), and the castellated design of the jail pays homage to the site's provenance and its 'fortress' associations.

Prior to construction of Elliot's prison and Bridewell the convicted, or those awaiting trial or sentencing, were detained in Newgate (*see* below) while vagrants, prostitutes and petty criminals were held in the county's House of Correction (dem., 1789) next to Abbey Bridge. Elliot accommodated these separate functions in a T-plan layout of three two-storey detention blocks, with vaulted ground-floor arcades open to exercise yards, and a central jailer's house connected to the upper floors of the detention blocks by a series of wooden bridges. The prisoners were segregated: debtors and female prisoners in the vertically divided N range; male prisoners in the W range (which included two cells for the condemned); Bridewell at the S, and even a separate treason room in the gaoler's house. Within each block the ground floor was for communal day activities with individual sleeping cells in the

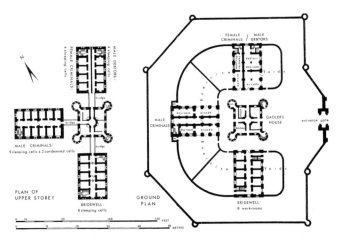

Jedburgh Castle Jail.
Plan in 1823.

upper floors: an arrangement central to Howard's ideas. Few of the rooms were heated: two of the debtors' cells had fireplaces for those who could afford coal; pipes heated the day-rooms (where debtors cooked their food), one workroom and one cell of the Bridewell for sick inmates, and the condemned cells.

Facing down Castlegate is the gatehouse, slightly advanced between square towers, within which is a false portcullis, and there are projecting round towers at the corners of the high, secure D-shaped outer wall. Inside, the crenellated gaoler's house mimics the pattern, with round towers at each angle and a central belltower. The main door has a moulded architrave and fanlight and is flanked by round-headed windows; the upper storeys delineated by string courses. The whole is reminiscent of the symmetrical, delicately castellated classicism of Robert Adam. The cell blocks have paired round-headed windows at first floor and round-headed recesses at ground floor, originally for the open arcades. These were enclosed during major alterations by *Thomas Brown Jun.* in 1847–8. This followed the 1839 Prisons Act, which introduced the 'separate' system with its emphasis on solitude for inmates. The communal work and recreation areas of Elliot's prison were subdivided as cells or converted for other purposes. Only the Bridewell block, with its individual cells, remained unaltered. Closed in 1886, the jail was converted for a museum in 1964. Refurbishment during the 1990s has restored the general internal arrangement of the early c19.

JEDBURGH GRAMMAR SCHOOL, Pleasance. 1884 by *Hardy & Wight* with extensive c20 additions. The Grammar School was founded before 1556 and first housed in the Abbey where it may have originated from a 'sang schule'. The school had several locations before it was acquired by the burgh after 1872 and rebuilt near the site of the medieval Maison Dieu.

The main building faces High Street. Neo-Jacobean, two-storey with pointed-arch windows in triplets at ground floor, mullioned segmental-headed windows above and central louvred bellcote. Houses for the rector and janitor were built at the same time, the former is on The Friars. Apsidal-ended single-storey NW extension of 1926 by *Reid & Forbes* with picturesque tiered belltower to the l. with a pointed-arch doorway at its foot. Contemporary single-storey infants' department (now concert room) built behind the rector's house with a semi-hexagonal chimneyed projection between the girls' and boys' entrances on its SE façade.

Across the road on Priors Meadow is an Art Deco E-plan block of 1935 by *Reid & Forbes*, with white-harled, hipped two-storey wings with square and flat entablatures over doorways and a gabled hall to the NE with narrow clearstorey windows. The Games Hall of 1974, consists of two interlocking blocks clad in pink brick and grey harl with horizontal boarding immediately beneath its flat roofs.

To the NW of the site, at the junction of Pleasance and The Friars, rebuilding in 1997–2000 by the *Scottish Borders Council Technical Services* produced an uninspiring block in yellow sandstone and white harl with triangular-headed windows in gablets, broad oriel windows and blue-painted railings.

JEDBURGH LIBRARY, Castlegate. 1900, by *George Washington Browne* and beautifully composed in his favoured Arts and Crafts/Scottish Renaissance style in yellow sandstone. On a sloping site, the entrance, to the l., is reached via steps under a round-arched opening with a decorative panel, containing 'LET THERE BE LIGHT' and a sunburst, and a tripartite mullioned window above. The main part of the street façade projects to the r. with a chamfered corner and a plain ground floor with square-headed pend to Upper Nag's Head Close. At the r. resting on a first-floor string course is the large, semicircular reading room window. At the top a segmental-pedimented window, its tympanum covered with the town motto STRENUE ET PROSPERE and a figure of a mounted knight. The librarian's flat (now Registrar's Office) has a three-storey rear elevation with chamfered corner and gabled, two-storey rear extension.

JEDBURGH POLICE STATION, Castlegate. 1870. Built as the County Constabulary Buildings close to the County Buildings (*see* Sheriff Court). Stark Jacobean façade with a rusticated ground floor, grey sandstone above and crowstepped gables. Scroll moulding around a datestone above the central round-arched doorway. Two-storey extension to rear.

NEWGATE, Market Place. Built in 1755–6, possibly on the site of the main gateway into the abbey precinct. It replaced the county prison as the medieval jail in the Tongue of the Canongate. Newgate remanded those awaiting trial by the High Court, petty criminals who were tried in the adjacent Council House (*see* Sheriff Court), and debtors.

The well-proportioned Market Place elevation is simple, a small harled block, but the completion in 1761 of its magnificent central 36m.-high ashlar tower, topped by a broach spire and weathervane, lends it landmark status. Round-arched openings to the bell-chamber (dated 1761 beneath the s opening), which contains three bells: one of pre-Reformation date from the abbey, a 1692 bell from the Old Parish Church and a third of 1780 by *Mines Royal Company* of London. In the upper stage, the clock of 1881, its faces set beneath shaped and pointed pediments. At the foot of the tower, an arched pend, originally gated, gave access to the crossing over the Jed Water prior to the building of Abbey Bridge (*see* Description 1, below). Above the arch, a panel inscribed NEW GATE 1755. A second plaque, carved with the burgh arms and dated 1720, originates from Jedburgh's first public well in the Market Place and was built into a blocked window in the early C19. Doorways within the pend open into windowless vaulted cells on either side. Condemned prisoners were detained in a first floor cell reached by a forestair against the E side.

Newgate was superseded in 1823 by construction of the model Jedburgh Castle Jail (*see* above) and annexed to the County Buildings (*see* Sheriff Court). The w cell block appears to have been heightened at that date, when the chambers on the upper floor were converted for a jury room. Major renovation in 2003.

PARKSIDE PRIMARY SCHOOL, Priors Road. Built for infants and juniors previously at Jedburgh Grammar School (*see* above). Brusquely composed. Originally two utilitarian, single-storey, pink-harled classroom blocks, with large windows in projecting surrounds. L-plan nursery wing to Priors Road. Enlarged 1971 with a large square, single-storey, flat-roofed grey-harled block with slim windows and a two-storey block in similar style.

PUBLIC HALL, Abbey Place. 1900–1, by *J.P. Alison* to replace the Corn Exchange burned down in 1898. French Renaissance red sandstone ashlar façade of two storeys with pyramidal-roofed towers clasping each corner. Advanced centre topped with decorative ironwork and a central round-arched entrance with broken pediment beneath a Venetian window with deep entablature. A single bay to the N probably dates to the 1930s with Art Deco lettering over the door leading to the public gallery; the curvilinear glazing bars of the main block seem to be contemporary. The s façade sits back from the line of the corner tower. Venetian window with giant Doric pilasters at either side supporting a triangular pediment. In the centre, giant Doric pilasters rising to a triangular pediment over a Venetian window and balustraded bow. Rusticated quoins and blocking to the windows. Inside, beneath the main hall, two vaulted rooms of an early malt barn were retained and used as the burgh armoury. The barrel-vaulted main hall has a gallery supported on cast-iron columns. There is also a small hall and a drill hall.

SHERIFF COURT, Market Place/Castlegate. Greek Revival of 1812, extended in 1861–2 by *David Rhind*. Originally the County Buildings, built on the site of the Council House (1664, superseding the *c.* 1504 tolbooth). The stone was quarried from the abbey church. The building originally faced Castlegate; nine bays wide, with the central three behind a large arcaded porch with cast-iron railings between the piers and a balustraded balcony above. Doric pilasters and round-arched windows on the first floor demarcate the court room, which was subdivided when the new principal court room was built by Rhind over the site of the neighbouring fleshmarket. This three-bay extension is in keeping, also adorned with Doric pilasters. The three-bay elevation towards Market Place now dominates with an advanced centre and segmental-headed windows at either side. The original court room is marked by tall, round-arched windows divided by paired Doric pilasters beneath a broad frieze and entablature. Sculptured panel by *Alexander Carrick*, commemorating Sir Walter Scott, erected in 1932. From the first floor is a connecting door to the former jailhouse in the Newgate (*see* above).

Former ST JOHN'S EPISCOPAL SCHOOL, Pleasance. Now Community Centre. 1844 by *William Butterfield*, his first work in Scotland. Gothic, square-plan, two-storey gabled block with pointed-arch doorway in central shaped projection, pointed triple windows to N façade. Trefoil in attic of w gable between bellcote and first-floor triple window. Matching rear extension of 1854, repeating triple window motif on w elevation with four-light first-floor window in s gable. Extensions after 1918 by the *Roxburghshire County Education Authority*. Two-storey hip-ended extension at re-entrant angle on w side and later single-storey flat-roofed addition clasping the NW corner of the original block.

ST MARGARET'S COTTAGE HOSPITAL, Castlegate. 1894, on a site granted to the Scotts of Langlee by the Marquess of Lothian for the building of a convalescent home for the county. Classical L-plan two-storey ashlar 'villa', with single-storey flat-roofed grey and cream harled extensions of after 1948.

STATION BRIDGE. *See* p. 433.

TOURIST INFORMATION CENTRE, Abbey Place. 1975 by *Morris & Steedman*. Highly visible from the Abbey Bridge or Canongate approaches into the town centre, but uninspiring. Stone-clad frame with strip windows on its S and E sides and forestair to entrance. There is a second, D-shaped, projecting entrance to the office from Abbey Place, which is level with the first floor.

TOWNFOOT BRIDGE. *See* p. 431.

WATERSIDE FITNESS CENTRE, Oxnam Road. The former Laidlaw Memorial Baths of 1922, presented by James Laidlaw of Allars Mill. Main five-bay pedimented and pilastered ashlar façade and white-harled side elevation. Unsympathetically re-roofed in 1974, the date of the brick-clad swimming pool to its SE, built on the site of the 1843 Old Abbey Church.

MARY QUEEN OF SCOTS' HOUSE
Queen Street

Now a museum. This fine building owes its survival to a local tradition which associates it with Mary Queen of Scots' four-week stay in Jedburgh in 1566. But contemporary record is silent as to the whereabouts of the queen's lodging on that occasion and, to judge from its appearance, the existing house is unlikely to have been erected much before *c*. 1600. Although often classified as a bastle, the building is more appropriately described as a town house, since it has few, if any, defensive features and cannot be identified with any of the towers that are known to have existed in Jedburgh in the C16. Before coming into possession of the burgh of Jedburgh in 1929, the house belonged to a succession of local mercantile and landowning families, but the identity of its builder is unknown. Restored under the supervision of *H.M. Office of Works* and opened as a museum in 1930. The present layout and display are by *Page & Park*, 1987.

EXTERIOR. The house is T-plan, with an oblong main block (16.0 m. by 6.8 m.) and a rectangular stair-tower (5.2 m. by 4.3 m.) – thought by some to be an addition – projecting about midway along its E side. Two storeys and a garret, the tower rising a storey higher and the two upper floors reached by a newel stair corbelled out in the SE re-entrant angle. Random rubble masonry with dressings of buff and red sandstone of local origin. The roof is known to have been thatched *c*. 1880; it was subsequently tiled and is now slated. The gables are crowstepped with cavetto-moulded skewputts. Most of the original openings have plain, round-arrised margins and some of the windows were formerly barred. At the S end of the main

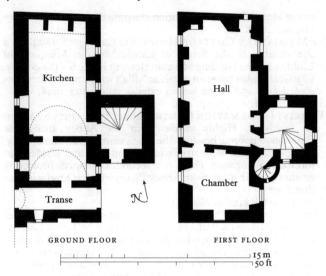

Kitchen

Hall

Chamber

Transe

GROUND FLOOR

FIRST FLOOR

15 m
50 ft

Jedburgh, Mary Queen of Scots' House.
Plan.

block are traces of a single-storey extension. Two blocked doorways in the N gable show that there was also an outshot at that
end, possibly a pair of timber galleries serving the two upper
floors. There was formerly a courtyard on the S side, as well as
a large garden and orchard to the E, which extended as far as
the bank of the River Jed. The original access from the street
was by way of a transe running beneath the S end of the main
block to the principal entrance at the foot of the stair-tower.
The transe was subsequently blocked and a new doorway
formed midway along the W front. The original arrangement
was restored in the late C19, and in 1929–30 the transe was
vaulted, probably for the first time. Above its outer entrance is
a (renewed) armorial panel, which still awaits satisfactory iden-
tification.

INTERIOR. The ground floor is now entered via a doorway
in the N wall of the transe. It comprises two barrel-vaulted
chambers, the larger one to the N being a cobble-floored
kitchen with a corbel-lintelled fireplace of late C17 date. The
first floor, reached by a wide newel staircase carried on vaults,
contains a spacious hall (8.5 m. in length) to the N and a
chamber to the S. The well-lit hall contains a buffet recess on
the W side and a large, corbel-lintelled chimneypiece in the wall
opposite, its back at one time pierced by a window. To the S is
a doorway to a former service lobby perched over the lowest
flight of the stair. A smaller fireplace in the N wall was probably inserted when the hall was temporarily subdivided in the
late C17 or early C18. The ceiling joists are carried on a continuous, moulded corbel course running along the side walls,
a feature found also at the neighbouring Ferniehirst Castle

(q.v.). The adjacent chamber, which opened off the lower end of the hall, is lined with panelling of *c.* 1700 and has a bolection-moulded chimneypiece of the same period. The W wall incorporates an original latrine, said to be equipped with a mural discharge-chute. The stair in the re-entrant gives access to the garret of the main block and to two chambers placed at intermediate levels in the wing. The arrangement of the main block is similar to that below. Both rooms are lined with tongue-and-groove panelling of c19 date, and the hall has an original double-leaved door of oak (formerly on the first floor), and a big corbel-lintelled fireplace. The upper of the two chambers in the wing is vaulted and each contains a fireplace with plain, round-arrised jambs.

Within the grounds is the tapered base of a C9 CROSS. Found on Old Bongate in 1834, and later moved to the Market Square, it was in the policies of Hartrigge House (q.v.) by 1903. The fragmentary tenon on its upper surface would have slotted into a mortice at the base of a cross shaft. Traces of carvings of beasts, with pairs of facing or opposing beasts on three sides and a single beast on the fourth; interlace decoration.

DESCRIPTION

1. The Old Town

The heart of the Old Town is MARKET PLACE. The Tongue of the Canongate with its tolbooth stood here until 1759, the Kirkwynd Tower was demolished in 1787 and the mercat cross was removed in 1866. This opened up this busy intersection and allowed Newgate, and later also the Sheriff Court (*see* Public Buildings, above), to dominate and form an appropriate municipal focus. Marking its centre is a Gothic pink granite and red sandstone JUBILEE FOUNTAIN by *George Bell II* of 1889, with triumphant unicorn (replaced in 2000) atop a clustered shaft.

From this hub radiate five streets. HIGH STREET leads downhill to the NE. From the junction with Canongate we begin on the r. with Nos. 1–7, a plain, broad two-storey block with a bowed r. corner. The street then widens as No. 9 is set back, the first of a group of c19 three-storey tenements. Nos. 15–17 is earlier and has a painted façade whilst No. 19 dates to 1897 and has a pilastered Victorian shopfront, with first-floor windows under scroll-bracketed entablatures beneath a dentilled cornice. Nos. 21–23 is five bays and three storeys with its central pend giving access to CROWN CLOSE. Here, set back on the r. is CROWN CLOSE HOUSE, a small Regency villa with narrow lights either side of its doorway. The segmental-headed archway of the former coach house is visible opposite, but the remainder of the close consists of two- and three-storey tenements.

Returning to High Street, Nos. 25–27 is an interesting pink-painted early c19 two-storey building, with pedimented doorpiece and two vertically aligned roundels. A stepped string course marks the first-floor level and the ground-floor windows have flat entablatures. The SE side of the street is set back once more from No. 33, the former offices of the *Jedburgh Gazette* of 1886, which has a pilastered doorway. Next door the former Jedburgh Public Library, built in 1884 as a narrow two-bay block with dentilled cornice, quickly superseded by the new building in Castlegate (*see* Public Buildings, above). The plain, single-storey POST OFFICE, by *H.M. Office of Works*, 1926, is remarkably unspoilt, with doors at either side of a central stone-mullioned window (the astragals of one of the upper lights are arranged to allow easy viewing of the wall clock inside). Three-storey C19 blocks to No. 49, which has a chamfer to first-floor level at the corner with SMITH'S WYND. Further on the former Relief Church (*see* Churches, above) is set back from its neighbours; the harled, thick-walled vernacular building on its l. sits snugly between church and THE PHEASANT pub. Squared red sandstone rubble Jacobean with shaped dormerheads and decorative door surround. Nos. 63–71 were demolished for a link to the bypass, now a rather over-generous gap for its purpose, which foreshortened the High Street and has the unfortunate effect of disowning the remnants of the Townfoot and its bridge (*see* Bridge Street, below).

Returning uphill, Trinity Church (*see* Churches, above) is on the NW side of the High Street and TRINITY MANSE, by *John Thomson*, 1870–1, with a hoodmoulded triple window and double-height bay window. The BANK OF SCOTLAND was built as a Georgian hip-roofed villa with ridge stacks, set within its own grounds; it has a proud Tuscan pilastered porch and a single-storey range of the same date. Next is JEWELLERS WYND, where the cream-harled CO-OP, 1992, dominates the vista. Next is the three-storey ROYAL BANK OF SCOTLAND with a marble-faced ground floor. No. 38 has an engaged columned doorpiece. Two four-bay tenements stand adjacent to NINIAN BELL'S CLOSE, entered via a pend at No. 30. This varied lane has two- and three-storey tenements, and on the l. are one-and-a-half-storey housing of 1990s at Nos. 3–11 with two early C19 coachhouses behind. The L-plan FRIARS COTTAGE sits in front of a delightful two-storey corrugated-iron building which faces SE, enlivened by bargeboarded gables and decorative roof ridge. Back on the High Street is the SCOTTISH BUILDING SOCIETY with Ionic columns and Doric pilasters demarcating the entrance on the r. and pedimented dormerheads over the attic windows. No. 24, *c.* 1883, has an impressive first-floor recessed balcony with central supporting column, a 1–3–1 second floor and a two-light dormer with scrolled skews above. A square pend under No. 22 leads to DARNLEY'S CLOSE, which is composed of pink-painted flats on the r. with tenements opposite; these then give way to lower rubble-built ranges towards The Friars.

The biggest event on the High Street is the imposing early C19 SPREAD EAGLE HOTEL with its gilded double-headed eagle presiding over the Doric-columned entrance. Painted window surrounds and smaller attic windows complete the frontage with a lower three-storey infill extension to the l. FRIAR'S BURN CLOSE at No. 16 marks the site of Moscrope's

Tower, one of the medieval town's defences. Return to High
Street via GRAHAMSLAW CLOSE. The street narrows at No.
6, which is advanced and has a bowed r. corner with scrolled
top. The tall No. 2, with No. 12 Market Place, is a Scottish
Renaissance block built in 1866; of four wide bays with decorative dormerheads, it forms a pleasant terminal to the High
Street.

ABBEY PLACE affords splendid views from Market Place of the
abbey ruins at the foot of its descent. This street was created
in 1825 by the levelling and widening of Rampart Brae and
Laigh Kirkwynd. The four-bay Nos. 1–2 has an oversized sill
beneath the r. ground-floor window and an oriel on the second
floor. The JEDBURGH ARMS is two storeys and four bays with
extensions down the lane to the E. The picturesque No. 5 has
a bowed front facing W with sloped roof and dormer above its
three storeys, while No. 6 is early C19 in narrow-coursed red
sandstone with round-arched recesses and pilasters on the
shopfront. CARTERS REST was built in 1771 as Jedburgh
Grammar School (*see* Public Buildings, above), a single-storey
hipped L-plan with chamfered SW corner. Next, the delicately
Francophile Public Hall (*see* Public Buildings, above).
MURRAY'S GREEN, formerly the site of the horse market,
covers part of the abbey's graveyard. THE RAMPART, originally the *c.* 2.4m.-high boundary to the graveyard and part of
the abbey's E defences, became a fashionable promenade in the
C19. Midway along is the sensitive, pink sandstone, octagonal-
based WAR MEMORIAL by *James B. Dunn*, 1921, the focus of
the burgh's annual Callants Festival.

Heading SW from Market Place, begin the steep ascent up
CASTLEGATE, the earliest part of the burgh to be developed.
The junction is marked by the quaint and colourful crowstepped Nos. 7–10 Market Place. C17, with C18 alterations
and renovation in the 1970s by the *Scottish Special Housing
Association*. Castlegate itself begins with CORNELIUS CLOSE
on the r., which may have been in existence from as early as
1425 as stabling for Melrose Abbey. Backland clearance here
and at NAG'S HEAD CLOSE formed part of the SSHA's redevelopment. Nos. 1–7 BLACKHILL'S CLOSE includes a
moulded Renaissance doorway. Nos. 7–11 Castlegate is a
delightful late C17 rendered tenement with elaborate sundial
and the arms of the Blackhill family. Further on is the picturesque Jedburgh Library (*see* Public Buildings, above) and
pends lead off Castlegate to small-scale housing of the 1990s
in UPPER NAG'S HEAD CLOSE and VEITCH'S CLOSE.
Castlegate continues to ascend steeply towards the staggered,
flat-roofed ATHOLL COURT by the *Scottish Special Housing
Association* (*Harold Buteux*, Chief Technical Officer), 1972,
which was built on the site of the Sessional School of 1851.
The early C19 vernacular Nos. 47–55 and mid-C18 Nos. 61–89
form a crescent divided by the gatepiers of the Georgian
GLENBANK HOTEL, with Doric pilastered doorpiece, and
GLENCAIRN, a villa behind No. 77. Ahead, the former jail
(*see* Public Buildings, above) crowns the Townhead, where
once Jedburgh Castle dominated the vista. Castlegate con-

tinues to the r. but to the l. are a number of fine large villas along GALAHILL, with Castlewood Cemetery as their back-drop.

Return downhill on the SE side of Castlegate. Nos. 76–52 were rebuilt in the C19; No. 74 is the site of the Townhead toll-house; the Antiburghers' Meeting House of 1765 stood at Nos. 58a–56c. The two gables of No. 48, C17, project into the street as an eyecatching vernacular interlude. The distinctive brown-harled Scottish Revival Nos. 44 and 34 (as at No. 66) date to 1935. ABBEY CLOSE is a pretty lane that includes the crow-stepped ABBEY HOUSE, 1877; next is No. 6 in uncharacteris-tic black whinstone. Abbot's Hall stood at the junction with THE BOW alongside the impressive W end of the abbey church. Overlooking the Jed is the early C18 Scottish Renaissance THE NEST; its seven-bay red sandstone principal façade has swept stairs to its entrance. At one time it housed Jedburgh Academy and bears the 1862 marriage stone of its headmaster Dr George Fyfe. Back on Castlegate, at No. 16 is the red sandstone, stone-mullioned MASONIC LODGE with double entrance and Jacobean wall-head gable; by *J.P. Alison*, 1903. Marking the return to Market Place are Jedburgh Police Station and Sheriff Court (*see* Public Buildings, above), occu-pying the site of the covered fleshmarket.

EXCHANGE STREET, formerly the route down from the W con-trolled by the Burn Wynd Port, builds impressively with Nos. 3–5, built as the Commercial Bank in lively Italian Renaissance style by *David Rhind* in 1868. Corinthian-columned central doorpiece and twin opening, topped by a balconette. Together with the shallow double-height oriel composed within Nos. 7–9 and No. 11, an early iron-framed building, its façade pri-marily glass, by *J.P. Alison* of 1899–1900 for the Co-operative Society on the site of the Corn Exchange. On the SW side demolition, rehabilitation and new build created BURN WYND, *c.* 1980, a mix of housing and commercial premises. C19 GLENVOHR and the brightly harled C18 LARKHALL BURN LODGE can be found towards its SW end. Return to Exchange Street via the white-rendered BALFOUR COURT, an Eildon Housing Association scheme of the 1990s.

Uphill on LANTON ROAD, SPRINGFIELD HOUSE, uncomfort-ably re-roofed, was built as the Combination Poorhouse by *John Smith*, in 1850–1 as a long three-storey plain ashlar block. Below lies CAIRNMOUNT, a row of stout and traditional *c.* 1936 flatted houses by *Wilson & Tait* for the Burgh Council.

Turn NE along THE FRIARS (formerly Friarsgate), with the Skiprunning Burn culverted beneath it and villas nestling along the NW bank. The SE side is the rear of High Street: only the Jacobean HOME MISSION HALL, 1887, provides an interesting digression on the l. side of Grahamslaw Close. KILMUIR COURT is an early C19 three-storey, L-plan villa built on the site of the Franciscan Friary church (*see* above) – nicely shaped nepus gable and narrow square-plan full-height tower, with weathervane atop. The quadrant-walled gateway survives at the SW corner at Ninian Bell's Close. GLENFRIARS HOUSE is a delightful tall three-storey rambling house with two double-height bay windows. Further NE, the

Grecian BRAE HOUSE, of c. 1835, built as the rectory of St John's Episcopal Church (see Churches, above), is one-storey and basement with steps up to the centrally placed entrance, its doorway flanked by fluted Doric columns supporting a flat pediment.

SHARPLAW ROAD was formerly known as 'Sickman's Path' in reference to the medieval Maison Dieu which stood here; its site is now occupied by Jedburgh Grammar School (see Public Buildings, above) along PLEASANCE to the E. Nearby, a single yellow sandstone shed is a remnant of the 1834 gas works; the site of the contemporary Barass Tannery is now occupied by the FIRE STATION of c. 1977 at the junction with BRIDGE STREET. The medieval Townfoot Port stood between the BAPTIST CHURCH, a truncated three-storey house with single-storey shop block, and the bow-cornered MAITLAND HOUSE on the r. Pyle's Walls Tower was situated in front of TOWNFOOT BRIDGE, which crosses Goose Pool on the Jed Water. One of five identical bridges (including Station Bridge, see below) erected over the Jed in the 1920s by J. & A. Leslie & Reid, engineers, to replace existing crossings.* Single-span shallow segmental arch of reinforced concrete with squat parapets with simple, square-plan balustrades and pyramidal-topped piers at either side of parapet. The present bridge replaced one of 1803. Before then the crossing was made by the ford at the foot of Old Bongate, although there is evidence of a bridge here in the 1680s.

Turning S back to the centre via the N end of QUEEN STREET, whose N end was obliterated in 1971 to make way for the bypass. Nos. 1–10 Queen Street were retained as QUEEN MARY'S BUILDINGS, a pleasant, two-storey bay-dormered terrace with lion's head door knockers; next is Mary Queen of Scots' House (see above). The large, unexceptional JEDBURGH HEALTH CENTRE of 1979 and QUEEN'S COURT, three colourful, and somewhat overpowering, blocks by Duncan Cameron & Associates, 1985, for Hanover (Scotland) Housing Association mark the junction with CANONGATE. The medieval Ladfield's House and Canongate Port have long disappeared. Thankfully fine C17 and C18 buildings survive at its E end. Nos. 12–16 have rendered façades; the last dates to 1729 with an elaborate doorway and a pend to the l. to Crown Lane. No. 10 is a tightly spaced five bays with dentilled cornice incorporating a bull's head from a coaching inn on this site, and No. 6 has two vertically positioned roundels. The three-storey Nos. 1–5, 1893, on the S side has its gable to Market Place. Descending westwards is the austere five-bay grey sandstone ROYAL HOTEL. An early C19 Georgian villa languishes, uncomfortably, amongst heavy extensions for MILFIELD GARDENS DAY CENTRE, a collection of vivid white-harled single-storey ranges. The one-and-a-half-storey coachhouse survives (Council Offices).

DUCK ROW, continuing the line of Canongate E of the bypass, is reached via an underpass. First is the PIPER'S HOUSE of 1604, remodelled in 1896, which formerly had a forestair to the first

*The other three lie outside Jedburgh.

floor. It bears a carved skewputt of a bagpiper. Immediately E is the fine C16 CANONGATE BRIDGE across the Jed. It was built slightly downstream of a ford and once provided the main route into the town, but is now superseded and used as a foot-bridge. A shallow hump-back crossing of three segmental arches. For defensive purposes it is sharply approached from both its E and W ends; the latter approach has been significantly altered but formerly Canongate met the bridge via a dog-leg. Repaired in 1677, the gateway at its centre was removed in the late C18. Bold triangular cutwaters support semi-hexagonal refuges; built into the two E refuges are several chamfered rybats, possibly from the friary. The former mill lade at its SW end has been covered and a footpath built under the W arch; visible under the soffit are ribs.

Following the RIVERSIDE WALK S is ABBEY BRIDGE. Built after 1785, when the turnpike road to Newcastle was constructed, contemporary with burgh improvements. Three segmental ashlar arches crossing the water. Wide central span, triangular cutwaters and plain parapets. Medieval fragments are incorporated into the bridge; possibly quarried from the friary, abbey, or perhaps the Abbot's House, which was demolished in the mid C18. The route into town at that time was more laboured, over stepping stones to The Bow and through the kirkyard to Newgate to enter into the narrow Kirkwynd and thence into the Market Place.

ABBEY MILL HOUSE, at ABBEY BRIDGE END, is two-storeys with oversailing eaves. It sits to the r. of gatepiers commemorating employees, killed in the Second World War, of the North British Rayon Company, which occupied the Canongate Mills (dem.) from 1929 to 1956. Nearby is the site of the 1789 House of Correction which was superseded by the Jedburgh Castle Jail (*see* Public Buildings, above).

On Abbey Bridge End's W side was the S approach to Jedburgh Abbey. Nos. 5–11 Abbey Bridge End is a renovated three-storey tenement.

2. *The Suburbs*

Jedburgh's expansion in the C19 and C20 took place on the opposite side of the Jed Water from the Old Town. The building of Abbey Bridge (*see* above) encouraged expansion S along the NEWCASTLE ROAD. The C19 two-storey OLD PARISH MANSE with notched bargeboards stands next to its associated church (*see* Churches, above). LOTHIAN PARK, opposite, formerly part of glebe lands, was originally held for a nominal rent from the Marquess of Lothian. Above Newcastle Road is ALLERLEY WELL PARK, gifted to the town in 1891 by Mr John Tinline and opened in 1898. On its E side the Arts and Crafts Highcroft nestles amongst traditional 1930s council housing on HONEYFIELD ROAD. The OLD ABBEY MANSE of 1850, adorned with shaped skewputts and finialled gables, survives in OXNAM ROAD. Further uphill picturesque villas include KENMORE BANK HOTEL, a hipped Georgian villa, and THE FIRS, a w-facing double-pile M-gabled house. Also taking advantage of the lofty position, the late C19, lightly Baronialised ALLERTON HOUSE (now a nursing home), the upper storey of the advanced centre corbelled out over the entrance.

The extensive HOWDENBURN housing area was laid out to the E, *c.* 1970, on rising ground. It consists of grey-rendered pitch-roofed flatted council dwellings placed around streets and courtyards. At its heart in Howdenburn Drive is HOWDEN-BURN PRIMARY SCHOOL of 1974–6 by *Borders Regional Council* (project architect, *James Thornton*). Two groups of conjoined buildings around two internal courtyards. Harled brick, flat-roofed single-storey ranges, with long monopitch roof-lights over corridors.

Returning to the riverside, RICHMOND ROW, on the E side of Canongate Bridge (*see* above), consists of colourful SHELTERED HOUSING of 1975 by *Borders Regional Council* (project architect, *James Thornton*). They respect the scale of the original buildings of 'Reakman's Row' but lack character. On WATERSIDE is the large, picturesque, L-plan THE WELL HOUSE of 1936, a cream-harled tenement, and the long, buttressed WATERSIDE COTTAGE, with small square windows. In PRIORS ROAD is Parkside Primary School (*see* Public Buildings, above). The school takes little advantage of its pleasant wooded site in HARTRIGGE PARK, the former policies of HARTRIGGE. Extensive Scottish Baronial additions were made in 1854 by *David Bryce*, for the first Lord Campbell. Demolished *c.* 1950; fragments were salvaged and taken to Hunthill House (q.v.). Surviving are its rubble-built coach-house, head keeper's cottage (now WILDCAT GATE) with red fish-scale tiles, *Bryce*'s stables of 1853–4 (converted to housing), walled garden and gate lodge. The Burgh Council built housing on part of the estate, including FORTHILL and HEAD RIGG in 1937 and 1935 by *Wilson & Tait* and *John Innes* respectively. Crowning the steep ascent is HARTRIGGE INDUSTRIAL ESTATE, principally consisting of the metallic and light-grey shed for STARRETTS, engineers, who have developed at Annfield since 1959, and the 1975 MAINETTI leather manufactory – their lofty position means they now dominate this aspect of the town.

The town grew alongside the flat bank of the Jed, around the old village of BONGATE; its superiority was acquired from the Earl of Lothian in the C17. Bongate is now a busy thoroughfare, part of the bypass N from the Townfoot Bridge. Some early houses survive e.g No. 45, which preserves evidence of much rebuilding. Otherwise, a mix of C19 cottages, houses and *c.* 1935 tenements such as those at BONGATE VIEW. A remnant of Bongate Mill survives next to the R.C. Church of the Immaculate Conception (*see* Churches, above), but the more substantial New Bongate Mill is further NE (*see* Industrial Buildings, below). EDINBURGH ROAD, now dominated by BANKEND SOUTH and NORTH INDUSTRIAL ESTATES, once led to the railway station (1856; dem. 1965). STATION BRIDGE, replaced the Flour Mill Bridge over the Jed in the 1920s. It identical to the same engineer's Townfoot Bridge (*see* above). Returning to the town centre via the Riverside Walk, Anna

Scour cliff provides a dramatic landscape feature looking across to the steep side of Sharplaw Road.

INDUSTRIAL BUILDINGS

Former ALLARS MILL, Newcastle Road, 1806. The oldest surviving example of a spinning mill in Jedburgh, served by a lade taken from the cauld at Inchbonny, and linked to Newcastle Road by a bridge over the Jed. The main building with bellcote was demolished in the early 1970s, but three single-storey weaving sheds survive, two of which are brick-built.

Former BONGATE MILL (William Young Knitwear), Old Bongate. Mid C19. One of only a small number of woollen mills; its lade was drawn off the Jed Water at the adjacent cauld. The tweed mill thrived under the Hilsons, who had also acquired Canongate Mill. Closed 1963, and the fine three-storey and attic, eight-bay main building with bellcote demolished in 1986. The sole survivor is a broad, mansarded single-storey squared rubble block.

NEW BONGATE MILL (Upper Bongate Mill), Bongate. Late C19. Built on the site of 'Bongate Mill', which milled corn, and was served by the same lade as powered its namesake (*see* above). The two-storey corn mill house with rear wing survives as No. 101 Bongate. A two-storey 1878 block was reduced to one storey after 1976. It formerly had a central gable and bellcote, but now reads as a projection with chamfered corner and square-plan porch, with dentilled cornices. The long, squared yellow sandstone rubble block, with rounded corner, sits behind. The weaving sheds are to the r., originally an L-plan block, with rubble façade and shaped gable. The sw end of the main block was demolished in 1956 and replaced with a narrower, modern gabled addition for Lyle & Scott of Hawick. Weaving ceased in 1982.

BONJEDWARD HOUSE. *See* p. 125.
FERNIEHIRST CASTLE. *See* p. 278.
GLENBURN HALL. *See* p. 329.
GLENDOUGLAS. *See* p. 329.
HUNDALEE. *See* p. 390.
HUNTHILL HOUSE. *See* p. 390.
JEDWATER HOUSE. *See* below.
KERSHEUGH. *See* p. 467.
LANGLEE PARK. *See* p. 481.
LINTALEE HOUSE. *See* p. 500.
MOSSBURNFORD HOUSE. *See* p. 576.
MOUNT ULSTON. *See* p. 576.
TIMPENDEAN TOWER. *See* p. 723.

6020

JEDWATER HOUSE
1.2 km. s of Jedburgh

Small Baronial mansion house, built 1861 by the Rev. William Lee, against the backdrop of the Scaurs. Asymmetrical, in sandstone rubble with sandstone dressings. Crowstepped gables, some on continuous corbel courses, and stone, coped gabled wall-head dormers. Three-stage circular conical-roofed tower, with fish-scale slating and weathervane.

KAILZIE HOUSE   2030
1 km. w of Kirkburn

Built 1803 for Robert Nutter Campbell, a Glasgow merchant; demolished in 1962.

The STABLES (now a restaurant) are a courtyard range of c. 1811. The N front has projecting crenellated screens at each end of the four-bay central section; some Gothic detailing. Classical E elevation, with a central entrance framed by tall, rusticated piers, with fluted friezes and ball finials; each side are keystoned niches. – DOVECOT, NE, dated 1698. Lectern type, with crowstepped gables with ogival skewputts, and three ball finials across the wall-head. To its E, a single-storey, piend-roofed building of four bays housed two game larders. Hoodmoulds and crude fluted friezes. – The WALLED GARDEN, SE of the stables, was formed in 1811. It has a SUNDIAL, with gnomon, by *Alexander Adie* on a baluster support and octagonal base. Acanthus leaf and egg-and-dart decoration, and carved roses and lozenges round the top. – Late C19 GREENHOUSES by *Mackenzie & Moncur*, with a projecting gabled plant house. – Twin LODGES at the entrance to the W drive, c. 1803, formerly single-storey, but reconstructed in quite a sophisticated Classical style by *J.M. Dick Peddie*, 1920. W elevations have large recessed panels, with corniced windows, corbels along the top and, either side, dummy windows. Octagonal capped gatepiers with decorated friezes.

HOME FARM, 0.6 km. s, is an expensive steading built c. 1802 by Campbell. Apparently extended and heightened to its present form in 1827. The farmhouse's three-bay N front has a canted centre bay and square hoodmoulds over the windows, which have lintels and jambs of whinstone 'bricks' and distinctive horizontal glazing. On the s side are three piend-roofed byres, with the dairy in the centre, its roof swept out at the rear over pigsties. A sawmill, formerly a threshing mill, is attached at the NW corner, with granary above. Overshot waterwheel.

SCOTSMILL, 1 km. NW, now a dwelling, has an inscribed panel: RNC 1802 MM. L-plan, with a large pyramidal-roofed kiln forming one arm. At the W end, a two-storey granary. A waterwheel, from elsewhere, has been placed against the W gable and a Venetian window inserted above, c. 1990. Across the road a Gothic *cottage orné* dated 1812.

KAMES HOUSE   7040
1 km. NW of Leitholm

A moderately sized laird's house owned by the Dicksons until the C17, when it passed to a younger son of the Homes of Cowdenknowes. Henry Home, Lord Kames, Lord of Session, philosopher and agriculturist, began his pioneering agricultural pursuits here during the late 1740s. The house was reconstructed by *H. Ramsay Taylor* for Colonel John Menzies, *c.* 1913.

The principal part is U-plan, with later additions to the E and N. Two-storey and attics, harled all over, with red sandstone dressings painted a pale grey. The earliest part is the main rectangular block, aligned E–W with crowstepped gable-ends. Perhaps mid-C17. Two wings, projecting S to flank a small court, must be later as they abut the main block in an awkward manner, inside and out. They have conical-roofed circular towers on the outer angles, with small closet windows, but the inner angles have large square classical shafts resembling triumphal columns with high pedestals, entablatures and urn finials. These must have been added by Lord Kames, who undertook some work to classicise the house before 1759, perhaps for the visit of Dr Benjamin Franklin in that year. Kames also regularised the windows, all of which have sharp arrises, recut in 1913. Two windows at the W end are taller than the rest, the upper one cutting into earlier corbels, perhaps the base of an angle turret. The wall-head dormers with curly gablets are *c.* 1913. The S front's entrance door is slightly off-centre, and suggests that the re-cut moulded frame (1913) was placed in an original opening. The two-bay W elevation has a crowstepped gable with central chimney; the cope of the r. gable is curved at the wall-head as if to avoid an earlier feature, perhaps another angle turret. Single-storey crowstepped N addition: C20. The two-storey piend-roofed addition to the E wing may be late C18; reconstructed 1913, when the thistle-finialled square shaft was added at the SE corner. The N elevation has lost some integrity with the addition of attic dormers of different dates.

The interior was recast by Taylor in Scottish Renaissance style. At the W end deep window and door embrasures suggest this part may incorporate an earlier tower house. The low ceilings were retained by Taylor. The grand staircase has twisted balusters, panelled newel posts and large ball finials. Coved ceiling with acanthus leaves and rosettes on the cornice. Roses and pomegranates, with grinning faces at the corners, decorate the frame for a painting; it is dark but looks C18.

LANDSCAPE. Well-wooded policies, the view to the Cheviot hills enhanced, 1990–1, by a lake and tree planting by *Robin Lane Fox*. – Pretty U-plan classically detailed mid-C18 STABLES to the W. Harled with red sandstone bands and quoins. Symmetrical E elevation, the projecting wings each having two segmental-arched and keystoned stable entrances; incised panels each side of the doors. – A C18 whinstone rubble BARN is all that remains of Kames's farm buildings. Wide stone copes on the gables meet at the apex with a square stone set diagonally. In the W gable a semicircular-headed opening, in the E a similar opening cut out of the centre of a large stone.

KELSO

4030

INTRODUCTION

Kelso lies in the centre of the broad valley of the Lower Tweed, bordered on all sides by lush countryside, and occupying one of the most attractive situations of any Borders town. Its early history was overshadowed by that of the royal castle and burgh of Roxburgh (pp. 653–4), lying only about 1 km. distant, on the opposite (s) bank of the Tweed. Kelso itself grew up under the protection of the abbey founded by David I and first comes on record as an ecclesiastical burgh in 1237. By the time of Robert I there were two towns, of which the older, known as Wester Kelso, may have antedated the abbey. Easter Kelso, in the immediate vicinity of the abbey, is first mentioned in the early C14. During the following century Roxburgh declined, a victim of the Anglo–Scottish wars, and many of its inhabitants crossed the river to settle in Kelso, which soon became the first town of the district.

Kelso.
Engraving by J. Storer, early nineteenth century.

But Kelso's enhanced status, bolstered by the great wealth of the abbey, increasingly attracted the attention of English armies, who laid waste the town on several occasions, most severely in 1523 and 1545. There were further setbacks in the C17, when the town – presumably still mainly timber-built – was twice accidentally burned. Following the second conflagration in 1686, Wester Kelso was not rebuilt, and future development became concentrated upon the area immediately N of the former abbey. Meanwhile Kelso had passed into the possession of the Kerrs of Cessford, ancestors of the Dukes of Roxburghe, a family still closely associated with the town, and in 1614 it became a burgh of barony. Not until the C18, however, did the town begin to assume the appearance that it bears today, as prosperity grew and the population increased – from a little over 2,000 in the mid C18 to c. 3,500 in 1792 and 4,800 in 1851, following which it gradually declined until the 1920s.

The increase after 1750 stemmed largely from the migration of small farmers and labourers from the surrounding villages, following the establishment of fewer and larger farms. Kelso also developed as a halt on one of the principal roads from Edinburgh to London, a route recommended by Defoe, when he visited the 'handsome Market Town' during the 1720s. The lack of a bridge over the Tweed, which Defoe had remarked upon, was remedied in 1754. The railway arrived 1.6 km. s of the town in 1850 (closed 1968), bringing business and supplies; before then Northumberland was the nearest supplier.

Kelso never became a major manufacturing centre, being protected, in the mid C19, from too much industrialisation by the Duke of Roxburghe. By the mid C19 most people were employed in the retail trade, the town becoming well-known for coach building and the supply of agricultural machinery. Fishing tackle was made and a cabinet and upholstery works supplied furniture, even over the border to Northumberland. Other products included leatherwork, woollen cloth and blue bonnets. Salmon fishing and horse racing helped to make the town a centre for field sports, and tourism developed steadily to become what is now a thriving trade.

By the end of the C18, Kelso consisted of a spacious market place with four principal streets leading from the corners, and narrow wynds, mostly leading to the river. The architecture of the present town dates basically from the late C18 and C19, and is little touched by major C20 industrial development. Thatched houses and gabled tenements were rebuilt or remodelled, and architects and builders purchased and developed villa plots from nurseries, orchards, and the large gardens of existing houses. In the later C19 a few large Victorian merchants' villas were built on vacant feus in Edenside Road. Light industry is hidden away on the station site, established firms still thrive, and successful small businesses have been established. Kelso remains a peaceful town to live in.

KELSO ABBEY

No more than a fragment survives, although a highly impressive one, of the Tironensian abbey, which was the successor of

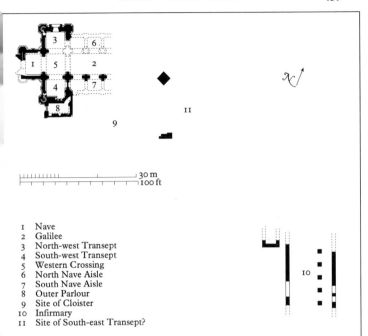

Kelso Abbey.
Plan.

1 Nave
2 Galilee
3 North-west Transept
4 South-west Transept
5 Western Crossing
6 North Nave Aisle
7 South Nave Aisle
8 Outer Parlour
9 Site of Cloister
10 Infirmary
11 Site of South-east Transept?

possibly the first foundation for any of the reformed Benedictine
orders anywhere in Britain. The community was first established
at Selkirk *c.* 1113 by David I, before his succession to the throne
in 1124. In 1128 he moved it to its present site, on the E bank of
the Tweed, thus placing it closer to his favoured burgh and castle
of Roxburgh. Work was presumably begun at once with the
(destroyed) E parts of the church, housing the presbytery and
monastic choir, but the nave arcades and the lowest storey of the
W transepts and vestibule must also have been built as part of
that first campaign. Enough of the church was complete for the
king's son, Henry, Earl of Northumberland, to be buried within
it in 1152. The architectural evidence suggests that the upper
levels of the W parts of the church were completed layer after
layer, not bay after bay; the nave clearstorey was not complete
until the later C12 and the W tower until the early C13. Dedication of the abbey church took place in 1243.

The abbey suffered badly in the wars with England in the
C14–C16. After the final attack in 1545 a proposal to turn it into
a fortress was abandoned, but it was stripped of its lead 'and all
put to royen, howsses and towres and stypeles'. The abbey church
was probably 'cleansed' by the reforming party in 1559, in the
prelude to the Reformation, and in 1607 the abbey estates were
erected into a temporal lordship for the future Earl of Roxburghe,
whose descendants still hold it.

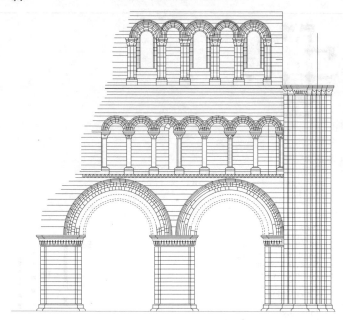

Kelso Abbey.
Elevation of the Nave South wall.

The nave of the abbey church was probably parochial from the start and continued to house the parish church until a new one was built to the NE in 1771–3 (*see* p. 447). Considering the damage suffered in the 1540s, it is unlikely the post-Reformation church occupied more than a small part of the nave. But, in about 1648, an even more compact vaulted structure was formed within the W transepts, with a stone-vaulted gaol set above the vault of the church itself. These insertions were removed in 1805–16. Major repairs to the historic fabric were carried out in 1823 and 1866. Other repairs probably postdate a survey of 1869 by *R. Rowand Anderson*, who had designed the nearby Episcopalian church in 1867 (*see* p. 448). In 1919 the abbey was placed in state care, and there was some subsequent clearance excavation.

The church was set out to a DOUBLE-CROSS PLAN that is unique in Scotland. The surviving fabric comprises the greater part of the two W bays of the three-storeyed S arcade wall of the aisled nave; a pair of full-height aisle-less W transepts, each of square plan; the S and W faces of the W crossing tower; the N half of an axial W vestibule of square plan and of the same width and height as the main space of the nave. The church E of those parts has entirely disappeared, but an invaluable description of the abbey* in 1517 by a priest, John Duncan, makes clear that there was a second pair of transepts to the E, and pyramidal-roofed

* In the Vatican archives.

towers over each crossing. Excavations in 1971–2 located what was thought to be the site of the SW pier of the E crossing, suggesting the nave was of six bays. Further S were located what may have been the foundations of the SW corner of the SE transept, indicating that the E transepts projected further beyond the nave aisles than the W transepts. The layout E of the E transepts is unknown. Such a plan invites comparison with the double-ended churches of Ottonian and Romanesque Germany and the Netherlands. But the use of the W projection as a high vestibule, rather than as a second choir, shows more direct similarities with the double-transept East Anglian cathedral of Ely (Cambridgeshire) in its final form.

DESCRIPTION OF THE ABBEY

NAVE. The earliest surviving remains are the two bays of the S ARCADE, presumably built in the first phase after 1128. These are carried on squat, basically cylindrical piers, with three engaged pilasters bearing single semicircular shafts to carry the inner orders of the arcade arches and the springings of the aisle vaults. This arrangement is similar to piers at Ely Cathedral (Cambridgeshire), Peterborough Cathedral (Northamptonshire) and Thorney Abbey (Cambridgeshire). The arcade capitals are scalloped, and the semicircular arches have three (extensively renewed) chamfered orders. Little remains of the outer aisle wall, but its stub projecting from the E wall of the SW transept embodies the W jamb of a doorway from the cloister. The jamb of this simple doorway also served as the N jamb of the doorway from the outer parlour, which is now blocked. The S AISLE had rib vaults of pointed profile, which were probably only set in place in the later C12 on the evidence of the rib profile, which has a keeled roll flanked by cavettos. The steep curvature of the vaulting left exposed an unusually large expanse of crudely faced wall between arch and vault, while the threshold of the opening into the aisle roof space from triforium level is well below the vault crowns.

p. 440

The bay system established by the arcade arches was ignored when eventually the TRIFORIUM was added; Kelso is the only major Scottish church known to have had such independent treatment of the storeys. The triforium rests on a chevron-decorated string course directly above the arcade arch heads, and it takes the form of a continuous arcade of small arches. Its arches are carried by single circular or octagonal shafts, with capitals that are either scalloped or decorated with waterleaf foliage, details which suggest that this stage was not completed before the third quarter of the C12. (The earliest datable waterleaf capitals in Scotland are likely to be at St Andrews Cathedral (Fife), begun by Bishop Arnold (1160–2), who had earlier been abbot of Kelso.) Above the second pier from the W is a section of solid wall, which is evidently part of the C19 strengthening and unlikely to perpetuate the original arrangement. Access to the roof space over the aisles was through openings above the arcade piers; the aisle roofs evidently swept down steeply, with no outer wall to the roof space.

Like the triforium, the CLEARSTOREY has a continuous arcade

in front of a mural passage. On the outer face are two round-headed windows to each bay of the arcade, with a shallow pilaster between each of the windows which rises up to the wall-head corbel table. Internally this spacing of the windows is reflected in an alternating pattern of arches, with semicircular heads corresponding to the windows and narrower stilted arches between. The small piers supporting the clearstorey arches have triplets of keeled shafts towards the central space, attached to rectangular tails. The capitals are decorated with waterleaf foliage or crockets. The arches are similar to those of the triforium, having an angle roll to the inner order and a cavetto to the outer order, though the clearstorey arches do not have a quirk at the outer edge of the cavetto. The flat wall-head and continuous clearstorey arcading make clear that there was no intention to have high vaulting; the 1517 description confirms that the roof was wooden, and says it was sheathed in lead.

There are no surviving closely comparable elevations in Scotland or England. Comparisons might be made with St John's Church in Chester, where the triforium and clearstorey are also significantly later than the arcade, and similarly take the form of two layers of continuous arcading. But there the bay divisions, as established by the rhythm of the arcades, were clearly marked by wall shafts rising through the two upper storeys. That other buildings must once have shown something closer to Kelso's independence of rhythm between the three storeys, however, is supported by comparisons with the English-inspired work in the s transept of Trondheim Cathedral in Norway, where each stage also sets its own independent pace.

5 The W TRANSEPTS and W VESTIBULE have a lowest dado level decorated with intersecting arcading both internally and externally, except for the sections flanking the N doorway (*see* below), where there are single arches. The caps are scalloped or foliate with some pellet decoration. Internally there are beakhead-like spurs to the arcading in the SW transept and along the flanks of the vestibule, whereas there is chevron or embattled decoration in the N transept. At the E end of the s wall of the s transept the arcading is interrupted by a low arched recess, within which are an arched piscina and two aumbries to serve an adjacent altar.

The two most important surviving doorways into the church are through the W front and the N face of the NW transept. The N DOORWAY, the main lay entrance to the church, is a round-headed opening of four orders with scalloped or foliate capitals; the disengaged shafts of three of the orders are now lost. The arch has mouldings with nutmeg, billet and nailhead decoration. This doorway is set within a salient section of wall capped by a superstructure having intersecting arcading below a triangular gable with diaper decoration. The arcaded superstructure (but not the gable) is paralleled at Dunfermline Abbey (Fife) and Dalmeny Church (Lothian). Within this superstructure is a small mural chamber, reached by steps down from the triforium passage, and lit by five narrow windows set within the arcading. This could have been a watching chamber, or it may have been provided for a choir, cf. Salisbury and Wells Cathedrals. Only the N jamb and arch springing survive of the magnificent W DOORWAY, set in a projecting section of wall capped by a gable. Its jambs had five shafted orders, of which only the outermost engaged shaft survives, and the arches were decorated with varieties of chevron, ringed rolls, cable and beakhead.

Where not adjoined by other structures, each face of the W transepts and W vestibule was pierced by two windows at the three levels corresponding to arcade, triforium and clearstorey in the nave. The chief exception to this is the vestibule's W front, the main frontispiece to the church, where, above the great doorway, was a single window rising through both upper storeys, and flanked by blind intersecting arcading. Along the two lower storeys of the surviving parts of the N transept, the vestibule and the W side of the SW transept, the windows have nook-shafts to carry the plain outer arch order, with scalloped or waterleaf capitals to the shafts. The wall passages at arcade and triforium levels pass through the window embrasures. Along the E and S sides of the SW transept, however, where there could be no windows, there is an inner triforium arcade at the middle level. More widely spaced arcades run throughout the clearstorey in the western parts. These arcades are similar to those of the nave clearstorey and therefore probably late C12; the several scalloped capitals interspersed with waterleaf or crocket capitals in this later arcading had presumably been cut at an earlier phase.

Externally the W transepts and W vestibule have pilaster buttresses at the angles, with rolls in the re-entrant angles; single narrower pilasters subdivide the W faces of the transepts and the flanks of the vestibule. There are spiral stairways at the two W outer angles of the transepts. The angles of the transepts are surmounted by circular turrets, and those of the vestibule by octagonal turrets. The W gable evidently had a stepped profile with deep weathered coping, and was pierced by a central circlet. The S transept gable also has part of a circlet, evidently almost entirely C19 restoration as now seen. The N transept gable similarly has a circular window, evidently a late modification since there are traces of a slightly higher circlet both internally and externally. The N gable rises up to a horizontal string course running above the roof apex. Above this string is a three-arched bellcote, with a circlet in its pediment-like gable, and a date of 16?? (probably 1648) carved on a stone tablet above. Its details, however, partly correspond with those in the later work of the nave, suggesting that some earlier masonry was reused.

The W TOWER, of which only the S and W faces survive, rose one and a half storeys above the surrounding roofs, and can hardly have been completed before the early C13. Flanking the roof creases are quatrefoiled circlets, and above this the belfry stage has three lancets to each face, with three orders of chamfers in the arches emerging from a single broad chamfer in the jambs. This tower is perhaps the earliest example of what was to become an enduring medieval Scottish taste for towers with rows of equal-height windows at belfry stage. Internally, the

tower was supported on pointed arches springing from the
base level of the clearstorey; the scalloped capitals of some of
their responds had most likely been cut in an earlier campaign.
Above the arch apices and looking down into the crossing is a
mural passage. Its details are similar to those of the clearstoreys
in the nave and w transepts, with an arcade of four round
arches carried on keeled triplet shafts, though with chalice capitals. Behind this passage a single opening in each face looked
into the roof spaces. The tower was floored above this level. At
the level corresponding to the quatrefoils on the outer faces,
two round arches opened onto a mural passage. At the belfry
stage the three lancets were internally of the simplest character. Corbels in the angles presumably supported the pyramidal roof menioned in 1517.

MEMORIALS. SW transept. Grave of the seventh Duke and
Duchess of Roxburghe, †1892 and †1923, a recumbent Celtic
cross within a kerb.

Of the MONASTIC BUILDINGS nothing remains except the outer
parlour next to the SW transept, but where it abutted that
transept the w range was evidently of two low storeys. The
OUTER PARLOUR, on its ground floor, is a rectangular
chamber covered by a barrel vault. Along its N, S and E walls,
above a bench, are the remains of intersecting arcading carried
on scalloped or volute capitals, and with beakhead decoration
to the arches. The w entrance has been rebuilt. A doorway from
the parlour led into the adjoining w range chamber; access to
the cloister was by a dog-legged passage within the SE corner
of the SW transept. Both doorways are now blocked.

SE of the cloister, excavation in 1975–6 located part of the
INFIRMARY. A rectangular structure on a N–S axis, with an E
aisle of at least six bays separated from the main hall by an
arcade of alternating round and octagonal piers, suggesting a
late C12 date. Running parallel with the Infirmary towards the
N end of its w flank was a smaller chamber, possibly either a
misericord or a kitchen. Part of the ABBEY MILL has been tentatively identified 0.25km. NW of the abbey church at the
mouth of the lade which conducted water from the River
Tweed to the abbey. It consists of a much rebuilt wall carried
across the lade on an inserted segmental arch, above which are
traces of earlier arches.

ROXBURGHE MEMORIAL CLOISTER. 1933–4, by *Reginald
Fairlie*, over the site of the w claustral range. Pink rock-faced
coursed masonry with polished dressings. L-shaped with two
bays to the N walk and four bays to the E walk. The round-
arched arcades are carried on cylindrical piers with interlace-
decorated caps; the walks are covered by domical quadripartite
vaults with ridge ribs. At the w end of the N walk is a rebuilt
mid-C13 doorway with dogtooth decoration and waterholding
bases; it has a cusped inner order, and an outer order with a
filleted roll originally flanked by shafts in the jambs. In the
window at the s end of the E walk is a panel of medieval
STAINED GLASS depicting the Deposition from the Cross.
Within the blind arches of the back wall of the E walk are
memorials to the eighth Duke of Roxburghe, †1932, his widow,
†1937, and the ninth Duke, †1974. Within the cloister garth
are memorials to members of the ducal family.

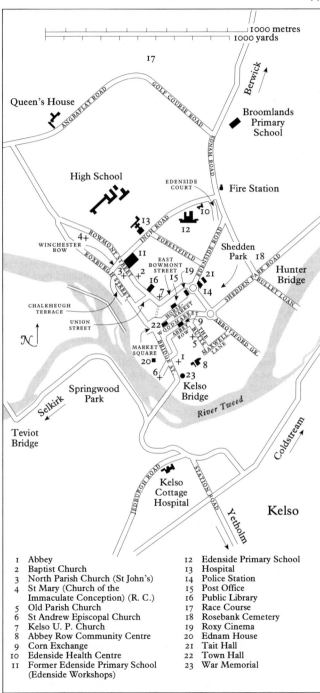

1000 metres
1000 yards

17

Queen's House

ANGRAFLAT ROAD

GOLF COURSE ROAD

Berwick

Broomlands
Primary
School

EDNAM ROAD

High School

EDENSIDE
COURT

Fire Station

BOWMONT STREET

13

INCH ROAD

FORESTFIELD

10

12

WINCHESTER
ROW

4

ROXBURGHE STREET

11

3

2

EAST
BOWMONT
STREET

EDENSIDE ROAD

Shedden
Park

18

Hunter
Bridge

16

15

19

21

SHEDDEN PARK ROAD

BULLET LOAN

ABBEY

7

14

CHALKHEUGH
TERRACE

HORSE
MARKET

9

ABBOTSFORD GR.

UNION
STREET

22

WOODMARKET

ABBEY
ROW

THE BUTTS

N

BRIDGE ST.

5

MAXWELL-
HEUGH
LANE

8

MARKET
SQUARE

20

1

6

23

Kelso
Bridge

Springwood
Park

River Tweed

Coldstream

Selkirk

Teviot
Bridge

JEDBURGH ROAD

Kelso
Cottage
Hospital

STATION ROAD

Yetholm

Kelso

1	Abbey	12	Edenside Primary School
2	Baptist Church	13	Hospital
3	North Parish Church (St John's)	14	Police Station
4	St Mary (Church of the Immaculate Conception) (R. C.)	15	Post Office
		16	Public Library
5	Old Parish Church	17	Race Course
6	St Andrew Episcopal Church	18	Rosebank Cemetery
7	Kelso U. P. Church	19	Roxy Cinema
8	Abbey Row Community Centre	20	Ednam House
9	Corn Exchange	21	Tait Hall
10	Edenside Health Centre	22	Town Hall
11	Former Edenside Primary School (Edenside Workshops)	23	War Memorial

GRAVEYARD. The small graveyard within the site of part of the abbey nave and cloister has mainly C19 memorials, although there are C17 and C18 memorials against the s boundary wall.

CHURCHES

BAPTIST CHURCH, Bowmont Street. 1878. Bright red sandstone with buff dressings. Entrance block with central gabled section projecting minimally and framed by buttresses; decorated with incised texts. The arched doorway is framed by a square label, and above is a three-light panel-traceried window. The laterally gabled side sections of the front each have a two-light window.

CHURCH OF THE IMMACULATE CONCEPTION. *See* St Mary, (R.C.), below.

Former KELSO UNITED PRESBYTERIAN CHURCH, East Bowmont Street. 1885–6, by *John Starforth*. A fine example of his adaptation of correct Gothic forms to unconventional combinations of elements and massing (cf. Greyfriars Church, Dumfries, and Nairn Old Parish Church, Highland and Islands). Its Early English style is afforded added robustness by the use of rock-faced buff ashlar. It is dominated by a four-storey tower at the SE end, with a gabled doorway at its base, a flat crenellated parapet, and a salient stair-turret at the S angle. Symmetrical circular offshoots contain stairs to the galleries, beyond which are canted gabled bays with side entrances at the lower levels and triplets of windows above. NW of these is more orthodox massing with a lower two-storey section leading on to transept-like gabled projections at the far end of the church itself. Beyond the church is a smaller-scale hall complex.

NORTH PARISH CHURCH, Roxburgh Street. Originally North Free Church. A characteristically creative development of Gothic by *F.T. Pilkington*, to which he brought experience gained in designing churches at Edinburgh, Irvine (Ayrshire) and Penicuik (Lothian). It was built in 1865–7, when its minister was Dr Horatio Bonar, the hymn writer. Pilkington was constrained by the site being hemmed in on three sides, and the SW entrance front could give little hint of the complex volumes behind, other than through tantalising glimpses of the roof-scape. It walls are a mixture of buff, grey and pink ashlar and rubble, all rising from a high, battered rock-faced plinth. The entrance front is a splendidly complex composition, giving full expression to the architect's love of the interplay of planes and textures: NW of the central gabled section is a tall spired tower, while to the SE is a lower gabled section, these elements being articulated by broad buttressing with recessed tabernacles. The cavernous axial entrance is emphasised by a projecting gable on cylindrical piers, above which is a pair of two-light plate-traceried windows framed by outer arches with dropped cusping, with a heavily cusped vesica in the gable. At its head the tower has two-tiered open pinnacles (with fish-scale slated spirelets) flanking traceried windows with tall gablets, through which rises the octagonal spire. The architect's taste for foliage decoration is manifest throughout, though here it is more clearly inspired by medieval prototypes than at some of his other churches.

The central entrance archway gives onto a shallow open narthex, with stairs on each side up to the two doorways, within which is a deep vestibule below a gallery. The main space of the church is initially rather difficult to grasp, but is essentially cruciform, with polygonal apsidal terminations to three arms, and a gallery stretching back over the vestibule to the windows of the SW front. The pews are arranged in a polygonal formation, and the floor is stepped down towards the communion table platform in the NE arm. Flanking the platform is a characteristically Pilkingtonian touch, where higher intakes in the wall are carried on slender cylindrical piers and corbels with foliate crocket caps, behind which run narrow angled 'corridors'. It is perhaps slightly anti-climactic that the light oak furnishings on the NE platform, largely of 1934, are a little over-couth for such an interior. The open-timber roof is, of course, a notable feature. It is basically of hammerbeam construction, with barley-sugar hammerposts (reflected on a smaller scale in the divisions of the gallery front), but with a complex sequence of intersections over the arms and window gables; a heavy central pendant is supported from iron tie bars and timber braces. – PULPIT, COMMUNION TABLE and ORGAN, all of 1934. There was earlier a massive pipe organ and pulpit in this area. – FONT, c. 1926, brought from the former Kelso United Presbyterian Church. – STAINED GLASS, in apse behind communion table. 1870s, the Good Shepherd, Angels and foliage, all in an Arts and Crafts idiom. – ENGRAVED GLASS, in gallery, Snow White and the Seven Dwarfs, to commemorate a children's performance that paid for the re-glazing.

OLD PARISH CHURCH, Abbey Row. By 1770, when part of its 23 roof collapsed, it was clear the church within the W parts of the abbey (*see* above) was beyond repair, and plans for a new building were sought. The chosen design, built 1771–3, was by the masons *James Nisbet* and *John Laidlaw* and the wright *John Purves*. Its octagonal plan is an important attempt to create a centralised space appropriate for Reformed worship, and is one of the first of a series of octagons built in the later C18, cf. Glasite Church Dundee, Dreghorn Parish Church (Ayrshire) and St George's Episcopal Chapel Edinburgh. The walls are of buff sandstone, with droved ashlar dressings to quoins and windows, and polished ashlar to the plinth, string courses, cornice and doorways. The lower windows are rectangular while the upper ones are arched, all having mildly Gothic hoodmoulds. The principal entrances were through pedimented vestibules on the N and S faces, but there were also arched and pedimented doorways (now blocked) through the E and W walls. The octagon has a slated roof capped by a cupola, now with open arcaded sides, but originally glazed. A substantial wooden bellcote was added over the N vestibule by *William Elliot* in 1823; it has paired consoles below the piers framing the arched and louvred openings on all sides, and a bracketed cornice. Vestries flanking the S vestibule were added c. 1833.

Initially galleries ran around all eight sides; heavy Tuscan columns (with a marked entasis) supported them, while lighter Tuscan columns carried the ceiling, which was originally open to the cupola. But in 1823 William Elliot introduced a flat ceiling, remodelled the galleries into a horseshoe formation directed towards a pulpit relocated towards the S end, and introduced a cross-wall behind the pulpit. On the panelled front of the W gallery are the arms of Douglas of Springwood, and on the E gallery is a clock. There was further remodelling in 1894, when *Francis Usher Holme* of Liverpool formed a triumphal arch in the S wall, framing a gargantuan pulpit; there were further changes in 1904 when the pipe towers of a new organ were built around the pulpit. – COMMUNION TABLE, 1952, and rather understated for its situation. – PULPIT, 1894 by *Usher Holme*. An elevated construction with a baldacchino supported by piers and with flanking balustraded platforms. – ORGAN, 1904, rising above and behind the pulpit and slightly stealing its intended thunder. – TRADE GUILD PANELS, of the shoemakers and hammerers, dated 1757.

CHURCHYARD. A charming grassed and wooded area at the heart of the burgh, with a random spread of headstones, obelisks and table tombs, chiefly of the C18 and C19.

Former RELIEF CHURCH, Horsemarket. *See* Roxy Cinema, below.

ST ANDREW (Episcopal), Abbey Court. 1867–9, by *R. Rowand Anderson*, replacing a church of 1764. Anderson was to become the favoured architect of the Episcopal Church, and in his early work at Kelso it is easy to see why his restrained but scholarly designs endeared him to increasingly Anglican-orientated congregations. His earlier, unexecuted, design included an ambitious tower with a broached spire in the angle between the south nave aisle and chancel, but the final design is equally satisfying. Of red coursed rock-faced masonry with buff dressings, it consists of a four-bay aisled nave and a two-bay aisle-less rectangular chancel with an organ chamber and sacristy on its W (liturgical N) side. A tall steepled circular bellcote is corbelled out from buttresses at the junction of nave and choir on the E side, the inverse cone of the corbelling reflecting the conical spirelet, which has miniature lucarnes. The aisles and chancel have two-light Geometric-traceried windows, and there is a three-light window to the chancel gable and a four-light window to the nave gable; pairs of foiled circular windows pierce each bay of the clearstorey. A vaulted porch was added against the E flank of the nave in 1895, and the sacristy has been extended.

The arcades have cylindrical and quatrefoil piers with moulded caps, above which the paired clearstorey windows are set within rear arches. The nave has closely spaced but slender scissor-braced trusses, while the chancel has a panelled wagon ceiling. The latter has stencilled decoration, part of a rich scheme which originally covered the walls, its impact enhanced by *Anderson*'s excellent FURNISHINGS. – ALTAR, oak, with inset paintings of the Agnus Dei, four Evangelists and SS Paul, Peter, James and Jude. – REREDOS, marble tripartite composition with gabled and pinnacled centrepiece, carved with scenes of Moses striking the rock, the Agony in the Garden, and Manna from Heaven. – PULPIT, stone, circular with integral lectern, arcaded perimeter with inset paintings of the Good Shepherd, Prophets and Saints. – FONT, stone and marble, of quatrefoil plan with foliage trail decoration to bowl, carried on five marble shafts. – LECTERN, brass eagle, donated 1869. – ROBERTSON TOMB, designed by *Anderson* and carved by *Farmer & Brindley*, 1872. Sicilian marble sarcophagus elevated on four groups of four coloured marble shafts, the sides having roundels depicting the acts of mercy. Surrounded by marble inlaid floor. – MEMORIALS. Two heraldic timber panels in memory of members of Balfour family, †1921 and 1939.

STAINED GLASS. 'E' window, designed by *Anderson*, Christ in Majesty, the Crucifixion, Transfiguration, Ascension, and other Scenes from Life of Christ. Chancel 's' side, Acts of Mercy, designed by Anderson and made by *Stephen Adam*(?). – 's' aisle, 'E' end, St Andrew. 's' aisle, 'E' bay, SS Michael and Gabriel, *c.* 1942, *Douglas Strachan*. – 'E' bay of 'N' aisle, war memorial, Douglas Strachan. – Baptistery window, Christ with Children and Noah's Ark, designed by Anderson. – 'W' window, *Nunc Dimittis*, 1880, by *Henry Holiday*, made by *Powell & Sons*. – PANELLING in the inner porch, from the chapel at the Hirsel, demolished 1958–9. – Some MEMORIALS are reset from the old church along the outer face of the 'N' nave aisle. The most significant is a marble relief plaque to John Paterson, †1842, a matron weeping over books, beneath a Gothic canopy, by *Henry Weekes*.

ST MARY (R.C.), Bowmont Street. Started in 1857, by Pugin's pupil *W.W. Wardell* of London, after cottages adapted for worship were burned in riots the previous year. The nave was built first, an understated design of buff squared rubble aligned from NE to SW, with a porch off the SE flank. The NE gable-wall, surmounted by a gabled twin-arched bellcote, has a pair of two-light plate-traceried windows; the flanks have paired lancets. A chancel, added possibly *c.* 1914, is lit by an echelon triplet of lancets in its SE flank and a traceried vesica high in the SW gable. Both nave and chancel have scissor-braced roofs. The church is connected to the presbytery of 1933 by a low sacristy block. – ALTAR RETABLE, 1916, by *Archibald Macpherson* of Edinburgh, figures of the Annunciation. – STAINED GLASS, SE window of chancel, the Holy Family, 1914 by *Hardman*; in vesica behind retable, Angels and Sacrament.

ROSEBANK CEMETERY
Shedden Park Road

Gifted to the town in 1863 by the sixth Duke of Roxburghe. Single-storey gabled and bracketed lodge with columned porch, at the SW corner.

PUBLIC BUILDINGS

ABBEY ROW COMMUNITY CENTRE, Abbey Row. Former public school by *A. Herbertson & Son*, dated 1878. Converted to its present use by *Borders Regional Council* (project architect, *Mike Davidson*), 1979–80. Red sandstone. Two storeys with crowstepped gables, and mullioned and transomed windows; square stair tower with a tall pointed turret.

BROOMLANDS PRIMARY SCHOOL, Ednam Road. 1980 by *Borders Regional Council* (project architect, *Glen McMurray*). A striking metal and glass structure. A lightweight steel frame clad with a double skin of cement sheeting, given prominent turned-down eaves of profiled metal. Open-plan classrooms face s, with a deep overhang providing shelter from rain and sun.

95 CORN EXCHANGE, Woodmarket. An aggressively Cotswold Tudor conception by *David Cousin*, 1855. Built by public subscription for a weekly corn market, but used also for social occasions. Gabled three-bay street frontage, with a four-centred arched entrance and a square hoodmould over. Mullioned tripartite windows on the ground floor, a five-light mullioned and transomed one on the first floor, flanked by crenellated oriels. Latticed panes in the attic gables. A large wide gable on to Abbey Row with centre-arched door, and a five-light mullioned and transomed window to light the broad hammerbeam roof inside. A musicians' gallery at the N end.

106 EDENSIDE HEALTH CENTRE, Inch Road. 1967 by *Peter Womersley*. An innovative design in traditional materials mixed with white render, glass and slate. Womersley, fascinated by basic geometry, began here to explore 'additive' architecture, which he described as a collection of similar closed volumes. The centre has pairs of drum-shaped consulting rooms, linked round a circulation area and held in position by the domed, top-lit sunken waiting room. A detached two-storey caretaker's house. Sensitively enlarged in 1980 by *Aitken & Turnbull* to Womersley's plans.

Former EDENSIDE PRIMARY SCHOOL, Inch Road. A late C19 Board School. Gabled and gableted T-shaped block with mullioned windows, and buttressed entrance porch. Good, tall ventilator with conical fish-scale slated roof and louvres. Additional classrooms at the E end *c.* 1960. The present EDENSIDE PRIMARY SCHOOL, at the E end of Inch Road, is glass, render and timber by *Borders Regional Council*, 1972. U-plan, the well-designed row of eleven classrooms, divided by rendered projecting piers, faces s, backed by a central butterfly-roofed school hall. Wings to the N with offices and reception. Good landscaping with low walls, mounds and planting.

FIRE STATION, Ednam Road. Completed 1980 by *Borders Regional Council* (project architect, *Dennis Fortune*). Sensitively sited. Boldly rounded corners.

HUNTER BRIDGE. A by-pass bridge, quite simple and unpretentious, curving over the River Tweed. Opened 1999, by *Blyth & Blyth*, engineers. Piers of high-quality finished concrete with aluminium parapets. Exterior faces of the outside beams finished in hammered red aggregate.

86 KELSO BRIDGE, over the River Tweed. One of *John Rennie's* finest bridges. Designed in 1799 for the local road trustees, to

replace a six-arch bridge built *c.* 1755 a short distance upstream. Contracted by *Murray & Lees* between 1801 and 1804, with *John Duncan* as resident engineer. The foundations of the new bridge were sunk into bedrock in coffer dams, pumped dry by the power of a waterwheel set in a mill race on the s bank of the river. Level carriageway carried by five elliptical arches with V-jointed voussoirs. Rusticated semicircular cutwaters carrying pairs of engaged Doric columns which support shallow refuges for pedestrians; projecting dentilled cornice (similar to Teviot Bridge, *see* below). Blank parapets. The design is very similar to Rennie's later Waterloo Bridge (London) and bears cast-iron lamps salvaged at its demolition in 1936. The TOLL HOUSE (Bridgend Cottage), NE end, is also by *Rennie*. Single storey of polished sandstone to the carriageway, three storeys and coursed squared rubble to the river. Three bays with central Tuscan doorway; Tuscan pilasters at the angles. Also at this end is a Second World War PILLBOX with loopholes cut through the parapet to cover the bridge and approach road.

KELSO COTTAGE HOSPITAL, Jedburgh Road. By *Sydney Mitchell & Wilson*, opened 1909; plain and appropriately cottagey, but with many additions, including an out-patient department in 1968, and a day-room extension in 1978.

KELSO HIGH SCHOOL, Bowmont Street. 1936, by *Reid &* 103 *Forbes* in their typically accomplished Art Deco style with distinctive carved motifs of South American derivation. Harled brick with sandstone dressings. The SE entrance façade, a symmetrical range of two flat-roofed blocks, has a dominant square tower at the centre, and single-storey blocks at the ends. Entrance slightly advanced, beneath an open canopied porch with an architraved doorway with decorative two-leaved panelled doors and, in the face of the tower, a small canopied bell-louvre and clock (cf. Chirnside Primary School, Chirnside, q.v.). Inside, the foyer has glazed doors with Art Deco fittings; geometric polished granite floor with decorative corner details. Adjoining to the r. the contemporary SCIENCE BLOCK, U-plan with an entrance tower. Separate is the MUSIC DEPARTMENT by *Borders Regional Council*, 1994. A high glazed 105 corridor cuts through the building between two fin-like classroom blocks – very dramatic when seen from the school entrance. – GAMES HALL, by *Borders Regional Council* (project architect, *Dennis Fortune*), 1978. Simple and straightforward utilising the industrial character of its dark grey metal cladding.

KELSO HOSPITAL, Inch Road. The centre section, with seven bays and slightly advanced three-bay pediment, dated 1854 in the tympanum, was the former Kelso Union Poorhouse built by *John Smith*. Converted to hospital use and extended at the E end by *J.P Alison*, 1911. After a fire in 1934 *Tarbolton & Ochterlony* reconstructed the building, and made further extensions in 1936–7.

KELSO RACECOURSE, Golf Course Road. Kelso Races were established by Sir Alexander Don and others at Caverton, s of Kelso, in 1751, but were moved to the present site by the fifth

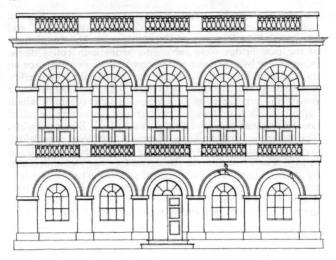

Kelso.
Racecourse Grandstand, Elevation, 1778.

Duke of Roxburghe in 1818, bringing greater financial rewards and benefit to the town.

The handsome, stone GRANDSTAND was built 1822–3, to a design supplied by *John Carr* of York in 1778 to the first Earl of Minto, who wrote on one of the drawings, 'Got by me at the desire of the gentlemen of the County'. This was Carr's second design, simpler and cheaper than the first but comparable to his designs for Doncaster and York. Two storeys, with an observation platform on the roof, and additional accommodation at the rear and sides; comparatively unaltered except for the inelegant bits and pieces required for C21 racing. The ground-floor changing rooms, weighing room etc. for staff and jockeys, are fronted by a rusticated arcade. Now blocked, these arches continue to the E elevation where the Duke's private entrance is framed by a large stone porch, which leads to a wide stone stair. The entrance to the first-floor public room is through a small Doric-columned portico at the W end, giving access to a hanging stone stair in a square corner tower; brick newel added late C20. The first floor has five spacious windows divided by pilasters, repeating the arcaded form below. Set back with a balcony in front, and a very fine decorative cast-iron rail, the intermediate panelled stone piers decorated with rosettes. A simpler rail fronts the rooftop platform.

The interior is, unexpectedly, almost complete. The public room has a fruity, foliaceous cornice, the timber chimneypiece decorated with columned jambs. The adjacent Duke's Room also has a carved frieze, and simple white marble chimneypiece. The stand was always considered too close to the course. Late C20 stand adjoining to the W – not stylish.

Former POLICE STATION, Edenside Road/Rose Lane. Now offices. By *J.P. Alison & Hobkirk*. A rock-faced corner block, with a Baroque frontage. A set-back crenellated corner tower draws the differently detailed elevations together.

Former POST OFFICE, Horsemarket. Now offices. *W. T. Oldrieve* of *H.M. Office of Works*, 1910. Elegant and neat Neo-Georgian. Two storeys, five bays, in polished ashlar with a bold modillion cornice and shallow bellcast roof. Segmental pediment over the entrance doorway.

PUBLIC LIBRARY, Bowmont Street, set back behind a small forecourt. By *Peddie & Washington Browne*, dated 1905. Scottish Renaissance. Single storey, attic and of three bays. Large four-light mullioned and transomed window on the ground floor to light the reading room. Wall-head dormers with decorated gablets to the librarian's flat. Pilastered entrance doorway with a sculptured panel over, displaying the burgh arms between panels with inscription, 'Let there be Light' and corresponding pendant of the rising sun. Small forecourt with square, panelled and cornieed gatepiers, topped by iron obelisks and overthrow. Inside, a vaulted vestibule, and lofty reading room with the burgh arms in the cornice.

QUEEN'S HOUSE, Angraflat Road. Former infectious diseases hospital by *Sydney Mitchell & Wilson*, 1903. Single-storey, rock-faced sandstone, with canted bays at each end, and recessed centre bays. Later additions. Separate two-storey administrative block with a first-floor timber oriel window, and a rather strange, deep-set, mullioned and transomed window over a canopied entrance. Housing at the rear, 2001.

ROXY CINEMA, Horsemarket. Former Relief Church of *c.* 1792, altered 1877, but remodelled as a cinema by *J.P. Alison & Hobkirk*, 1931. The front and rear walls were extended and rebuilt; original lancet windows were retained, blocked, in the side elevations. Two-storey white granite-chip frontage with an advanced three-bay arcaded entrance, with well-detailed Art Deco entrance doors.

TAIT HALL, Edenside Road. 1934 by *J. P. Alison & Hobkirk*. White rendered walls on a stone base course, and well lit by large windows. Five-bay front, with wide entrance canopy below red ashlar walling set between two advanced wings. Square stair-towers set back each side. Geometric glazing. Inside, a shallow barrel vault and large stage.

TEVIOT BRIDGE, across the River Teviot, SW of the town. *Alexander Stevens Sen.* submitted designs and estimates in 1784 and 1788. The builder, however, was *William Elliot* in 1794–5, although the style suggests Stevens' hand. Curved and pointed cutwaters (cf. Drygrange Old Bridge, Leaderfoot, q.v.) supporting coupled engaged Doric columns to each pier, which continue to rectangular pedestrian refuges. This motif, derived it seems from Robert Mylne's Blackfriars Bridge, London (1760–9), was repeated by Rennie, although critical of the design of the Teviot Bridge, at Kelso Bridge (*see* above).

TOWN HALL, Market Square. Erected 1816, replacing an earlier 92 tolbooth, the greater part of the cost being met by James, fifth Duke of Roxburghe. Classical with substantial Edwardian Baroque remodelling by *J.D. Swanston & Syme*, 1904–6. Two-storey, with a piended platformed roof, and octagonal cupola. Five bays face the square, the centre three slightly advanced, with a pedimented Ionic portico at first-floor level. The ground floor is rusticated, originally with an open arcade, but infilled with glazing and a central Baroque pedimented doorpiece in 1906, when the portico was balustraded and the windows given pedimented Gibbs surrounds. At the same time the clock cupola was given its lead, bellcast roof and Gibbs surrounds to the bellcote openings.

WAR MEMORIAL, Bridge Street. Within a peaceful railed garden. By *Robert S. Lorimer*, 1921. A square shaft rises from a balustraded octagonal platform, surmounted by a cross standing on a pedestal with a niche containing a statue of St George sculpted by *C. d'O. Pilkington Jackson*.

SHEDDEN PARK
Shedden Park Road

Presented to the town in 1851, by Mrs Robertson of Ednam House in memory of her nephew, Robert Shedden, who died searching for Sir John Franklin's expedition in 1849. The triumphal arched entrance GATEWAY on the S side of the park was erected in 1852. Tall keystoned archway between paired Tuscan pilasters; in the spandrels carved armorials. Pedestrian archways each side. – KEEPER'S LODGE, Rose Lane, on the W side of the park. Single-storey classical lodge of three bays, the central canted bay containing the entrance. Armorial panel in the parapet.

DESCRIPTION

1. The Centre and Suburbs North of the River Tweed

1a. Market Square to Kelso Bridge

92   Start in the irregularly shaped, granite-setted MARKET SQUARE, called Market Place until 1797. From the end of the C18 the square was transformed, the housing rebuilt or remodelled, and given the appearance of Edinburgh-type town houses, but with shops integrated into the ground floors. Mostly three-storey and attic, the buildings are usually rendered and painted, with brick chimneys. Numerous good examples of late C19 pilastraded shopfronts face the square on all sides. In the centre of the square is the BULL RING, for tethering bulls during the cattle markets, but dominating the E side is the Town Hall (*see* Public Buildings, above). In the middle of the N side the Cross Keys Hotel (*see* below), flanked by houses and shops. Houses and shops on the W side have their backs towards the river; the principal closes, Mill Wynd and Peat Wynd, have been mostly cleared of buildings over the years, making way for the growth of Kelso Mill (*see* below), and room for heavy transport.

Description should begin in the SE corner where Nos. 1–4 are set back from the square. No. 1 is mid-C18, and has all the interest on its six-bay symmetrical front to Abbey Row, accessed by Wester Kirk Stile. Altered but recognisable, a steep pediment over the centre two bays; the square frontage altered

mid C19. Nos. 3–4 basically mid C18, extended and refronted
c. 1890, losing a Venetian window in the process. Banks are
prominent on the S side, beginning with the ROYAL BANK OF
SCOTLAND, dated 1934 but a Neo-Georgian re-fronting of an
earlier building, regrettably in red brick above a granite marble
ground floor. The BANK OF SCOTLAND began as the British
Linen Co. Bank by *Walter Elliot*, 1839, little more than a four-
bay house, altered by *Kinnear & Peddie* in 1885 and in 1935 by
Dick Peddie & Walker Todd, who added the black granite plinth,
banded rustication, and a wide entrance doorway, in place of
a balustraded first-floor balcony.

First along the W side are Nos. 10–11, a block of five bays
with angle quoins. Probably late C18, but refronted in the mid
C19. Late C19 shopfront at No. 11. Nos. 12–20 originated as a
symmetrical terrace with a narrow three-bay centre, the
windows closely spaced, with narrower ones in the outer bays
on the top floors and flanked by giant pilasters, rusticated at
ground floor. The entry to Mill Wynd, next, leads to KELSO
MILL (Hogarth's Mill), built on the site of the medieval mill.
Three-storey mill buildings still operate, producing animal
feedstuffs, in a much-reduced complex. Mid-C19 three-storey
office building with classical doorway. Remnants of the monastic mill (*see* Kelso Abbey, above) can be seen from the river
bank.

Return to Market Square's N side (Innes Place), which starts
with a late C18/early C19 block at Nos. 30–32, of six bays, with
the windows grouped together in pairs. Fine catslide dormers.
Plain early C19 shopfronts. The CROSS KEYS HOTEL was
built, *c*. 1760 by James Dickson of Ednam House (*see* Villas,
below). Three storeys and seven bays originally with a central
pend to extensive stabling at the rear. Given an Italianate
frontage in 1879, when a fourth storey was added, corniced
architraves introduced at first-floor level, and shouldered
lugged ones at the second. The rusticated quoins continue up
to a dentilled cornice, and the balustraded parapet, with interval piers, is topped by ball and spike finials. The central attic
pavilion, topped by cross-keys, has a similar balustrade and
gave access to a roof promenade. Stables demolished and the
pend filled in the later C20. On the r. of the hotel, set forward,
the six-bay theme continues, tied together with a band course
acting as sills between first and second floors. No. 46 has a late
C19 Tuscan pilastraded shopfront. Filling in on the E side, Nos.
47–49 turn the corner to Horsemarket. Bellcast piended platform roof, banded quoins, and a band course.

BRIDGE STREET, from the SW corner of the square, was formed ⁹¹
into a principal street after Rennie's Kelso Bridge (*see* above)
was finished in 1804. OVEN WYND is first on the r. Some two-
and three-storey early-to-mid-C19 houses remain. No. 15, part
of a six-bay block of *c*. 1820, became Kelso New Library
(founded 1778). At the end, on the r., the late C18 or early C19
RAMSAY LODGE sports a large Venetian window over a
corniced and bracketed doorway. On the l. is the front of the
two-storey U-plan EDNAM HOUSE STABLES, by *James Nisbet*,
and probably contemporary with the house (*see* Villas, below).

Coursed rubble with rusticated angle quoins and sandstone
margins; moulded eaves course. Derelict, but restoration is
contemplated.

In Bridge Street itself, No. 3, an intrusion of 1911 with
corner turret and balcony. Nos. 5–7 looks like a classical town
house of three storeys and seven bays, with a long wing extending down a close (Havannah Court). The core appears to be a
two-storey house, built for the Ormistons of Hendersyde,
which was erected over a large late C17 or early C18 vaulted
cellar. The present façade seems to be early C19 when it was
rendered, given rusticated quoins, and the central window
altered to one of Venetian form. Broad C19 shopfront along
the ground floor with oversailing bracketed cornice. Inside the
shop, cast-iron columns with decorative capitals of c. 1898,
very likely by *R.J. Charters* of Jedburgh. Façade conserved and
restored by *Simpson & Brown*, the rest remodelled by *Roger G.
Dodd & Co.*, 1997. As part of the restoration, and to add a
touch of unnecessary 'class', a small wall-head pediment was
added centre front. Interesting room at the N end of the second
floor, with a coved stencilled ceiling, said to have been a
Catholic chapel, which seems unlikely if this part of the building is early C19. Next along (Nos. 9–11), an early C19 five-bay
house, with inserted shopfront, in 1822 evidently the first
house in Scotland to be lit by gas. The gates to Ednam House
(*see* Villas, below) follow. Next is the OLD WEIGH HOUSE
INN, a Tudor extravaganza of c. 1900, probably a remodelling:
symmetrical frontage with gables, canted oriels and mullioned
windows. Tudor detailed bar.

On Bridge Street's opposite side Nos. 4–8, dated 1870, and
Gothic, with contemporary shopfronts flanking a central
gabled door. Next, the diminutive former office of the *Kelso
Mail* (Nos. 10–12), the newspaper founded by James
Ballantyne in 1797. A slightly advanced pediment is framed by
rudimentary pilaster strips. No. 20 is mid-C18 and the best-
preserved of the remaining houses of this type. Three storeys,
four widely spaced bays, and harled with rusticated quoins. A
corniced wall-head and open central pediment over two round-
headed windows. The QUEEN'S HEAD HOTEL follows. Late
C18, with early C19 additions; rusticated ashlar quoins, chamfered and moulded window margins. The early C19 former
Spread Eagle Hotel (Nos. 30–32) was converted to flats in
1999. A pilastraded shopfront each side of the central doorway.
Abbey Row elevation dated 1809. No. 46 Bridge Street and
No. 1 Abbey Row is a remodelling of 1873 (dated) of an earlier
building. A rounded, angled corner with Abbey Row, with a
massive central corbelled stack. The ground floor (including
No. 44) is fronted by excellent cast-iron pilastraded
shopfronts. Opposite, Nos. 21–25 inscribed RR and dated
1872, with a cast-iron shopfront, the doorways flanked by
Ionic pilasters, beneath a continuous cast-iron fascia with
balustraded parapet. Nos. 29 and 31, also remodelled in 1872,
is a curved corner block with Abbey Court. Continuous
shop façade with cast-iron Ionic pilastered doorways, and
unorthodox Tuscan pilasters. These curved corners act as
important portals to Bridge Street.

ABBEY COURT, to the r., was the route to the pre-C19 Kelso Bridge. Facing is a late C19 irregular polygonal-ended block, with a shop, filling in an awkward space, then a row of late C18 and early C19 traditional three-bay houses (Nos. 2–7) making a pleasant group with original cobbles in front. These are followed by a former entrance to Ednam House, and the neatly placed St Andrew's Episcopal Church (*see* Churches, above), with its small, tranquil graveyard. By the river a mid-C19, L-plan terrace, BELMONT PLACE. Housing of 1998–9, by *Cameron Associates*, has taken over most of the area between Bridge Street and Kelso Bridge. On the s side the much-altered TURRET HOUSE, two storeys, four bays and crow-stepped, with a large round stair-tower corbelled out to a square at attic level, with a crowstepped gable. The lintel of a chamfered doorway, within the tower, is inscribed IMP 1678, evidently for John Palmer, a boatman, for whom the house appears to have been built. The RCAHMS casts doubt on the authenticity of the C17 date for the tower, which is probably C19. On the corner with the continuation of Bridge Street is ABBEY HOUSE, a neat early C19 villa remodelled in 1998–9. The principal w front looks down Bridge Street. Square gatepiers with cornices and shallow pyramidal caps. Continuing along Bridge Street the new housing, RENNIE'S COURT (1999), curves gently round the corner to the bridge. On the E side lie the Abbey, Abbey Row Community Centre and the War Memorial (*see* Kelso Abbey and Public Buildings, above). The entrance to the MANSE in Abbey Road follows. Built *c.* 1801, but extensively repaired in 1832. A five-bay s front to the River Tweed.

1b. Town Centre

WOODMARKET leads from the SE corner of Market Square. This was the principal road to Berwick and the main port for medieval Kelso. On the s side, Nos. 3–6; mid-C18 with a mid-C19 continuous pilastraded shopfront flanking a central doorway. Four storeys, three bays, and harled with rusticated quoins, moulded eaves course and bellcast piended roof; first-floor Venetian windows. The central window and those on the second floor have margins with swept lugged sills. Nos. 7 and 9–11 were evidently built in the early–mid C19 as a six-bay block. Shallow bow to Nos. 9–11 as the street narrows; pilastraded shopfront at No. 7. Another Kelso-type mid-C19 block at Nos. 13–19 with pilastraded shopfronts, followed by the Italianate BARCLAYS BANK (Nos. 21–23), former offices built for Stuart & Mein, seed merchants, by *James W. Smith*, 1865. A modest palazzo of two storeys and three bays, the r. one slightly recessed. Rusticated pilaster strips. Round-headed, key-blocked windows on the ground floor carved with goddesses' heads, the fruits of the earth woven into their hair. Roundels in the spandrels have putti engaged in gardening activities, the windows on the first floor have panelled aprons and key blocks carved with birds, flowers and fruits. A large two-storey GRANARY at the rear to Abbey Row was closed *c.* 1990. Well adapted to housing in 1999 by *Roger G. Dodd & Co*. The former BANK OF SCOTLAND follows at No. 25. Also

Italianate, by *John Burnet*, 1860. A square plan of two storeys,
five bays, with a single-storey projecting porch, flanked by cast-
iron tripod lamps. Lower pedimented block to r., with a round-
arched rusticated gateway, gave access to Abbey Row and the
agent's house at the back; the elevation here with round-arched
windows and doorway. Then the Corn Exchange (*see* Public
Buildings, above). Nos. 33–35 is early C19, the doorpiece with
a moulded architrave and triglyph frieze, and No. 41 a diminutive survival of the late C18, with a pantiled roof and easing
courses.

Redevelopment of the N side of Woodmarket was proposed
as part of a plan to improve housing contiguous with the s side
of Horsemarket (*see* below). At first, wholesale demolition was
considered, but sense prevailed, and a scheme of restoration and
new build, in matching style, by *J. & F. Johnston & Partners*, was
substituted in the mid 1970s. The housing which survives is standard Kelso-type. The mid-C19 BORDER HOTEL at Nos. 12–14
has four storeys, five bays and a channelled ground floor with
alternate windows and blind openings; a large lamp over the
door on a wrought-iron bracket. Nos. 22–24 is probably late C18
(cf. No. 20 Bridge Street), altered mid C19, when a pilastraded
shopfront was inserted. Centre wall-head gable with open pediment, a mid-C19 balustraded parapet each side. At the E end
on the r. is SIMON SQUARE, where much has gone. No. 3, a
former school, early C19, with a harled gable to Abbey Row, and
segmental-headed Venetian window above a coach house.

Continue round to ABBEY ROW and the Old Parish Church (see
Churches, above) on the l. After the rear elevations of properties along Woodmarket and Bridge Street is the mid-C19
MASONIC LODGE, set back within a forecourt. E of the graveyard is THE BUTTS, where ROXBURGH HALL, about halfway
along, was opened in 1817 as a school for children of the
deserving poor. It became a police house and jail *c.* 1872; now
the parish hall. At the s end in THE KNOWES are three large
villas. ABBEY BANK, a former rectory, was built by Dr James
Douglas in 1815; three bays with piended roof and central
stacks. Picturesque WALTON GROVE was built *c.* 1840 with a
two-bay advanced wing in the centre with square hoodmoulds
over ground-floor windows. Mid-C19 WAVERLEY COTTAGE
occupies the site of a cottage where Sir Walter Scott stayed in
spring 1783. s front of two storeys, the centre bay advanced
with a curvilinear gable over; square bays added in the late C19.
Plaster bust of Scott on a bracket between the windows, a
painted plaster model of his dog Maida over the side gate.

Now E along MAXWELL LANE, where on the N side was the gas
works, now housing and light industrial units. Of the villas, the
most interesting are MAXWELL PLACE and BELLACHROY, a
curious concept built in 1806 by Robert Nichol, a wine merchant, and described in 1836 as 'three modern and substantial
houses in wings attached thereto'. Two storeys, with a five-bay
s front, and lower two-storey, single-bay wings to E and W,
the window pattern 1–2–1–2–1. Six full-height rusticated
pilasters, and channelled pilaster strips at the angles. Slightly
recessed pedimented centre bay, the doorpiece with a fluted
pilaster frame. The N elevation has a broad segmental bow at

the ground floor, the lower floor masked by a projecting single-storey corridor linking the wings. Later additions in the N court. At the end of the street ST LEONARD'S, the early C19 former Relief Church manse.

ABBOTSFORD GROVE is lined by mostly mid- to late-C19 villas and terraced houses, except for KOREA HOUSE on the r. towards the river, of *c.* 1830 with a Tuscan doorcase with cavetto reveals and lying-pane glazing. Down by the river mid-C19 picturesque HEMPFORD COTTAGE. Two storeys, gables, bracketed eaves, a canted bay and an oriel.

At the top of Abbotsford Grove, SHEDDEN PARK ROAD (Bullet Loan) leads E. On the l. is Shedden Park (*see* p. 449). On the r., a mixture of terraced and single houses, similar to the rest of central Kelso, dating from late C18 to mid C19. Narrow HERMITAGE LANE leads down to the river. At the bottom POINTFELD, early C19, its N front with a pilastered doorway, the S with an attractive wide segmental bow. On the same side returning up the lane is PRIOR BANK, a late C19 gabled house, with hoodmoulds, bracketed eaves and octagonal chimneys. Further along is TWEEDBANK, built *c.* 1806 by Thomas Nisbet of Mersington. N front of three bays, divided by rusticated pilasters supporting a dentilled eaves course, and with a dentilled corniced doorway. S elevation with a centre advanced pedimented bay, and mid-C19 wing addition to the W. A single-storey and attic wing to the E by *Dick Peddie, Todd & Jamieson, c.* 1946, in concrete, replacing flanking screen walls with arched pedimented doorways, one of which was relocated to the garden. Good plasterwork in the oval drawing room. Single-storey gabled STABLE block, with coachman's house.

Now back to Horsemarket via COALMARKET: mostly new building except for the WAGGON INN. Really good Edwardian, with crowsteps, and lots of horizontal rustication, horribly ruined by a flat-roofed single-storey addition stuck to the front. Then Cross Street with RUTHERFORD COURT, sheltered housing by *J. & F. Johnston & Partners*, 1980, set round a paved court and enlivened by coloured render and the planting of trees.

HORSEMARKET follows. On the N side the Roxy Cinema (*see* Public Buildings, above), sitting back from the street, No. 50 with a good shopfront, and Nos. 46–48 with late C18 catslide dormers. The SW corner angle of No. 22 is curved, with a shop entrance, the windows framed by pilaster strips, above a dentilled cornice composed of brick headers. Up to the side is ELLIOT'S CLOSE, which led to the premises of William Elliot, architect, builder and developer in early C19 Kelso. The S side of Horsemarket was part of the renewal scheme of the N side of Woodmarket, so there are few survivors. Nos. 1–5 date from the mid C18; rendered, with four bays and a late C19 continuous pilastraded shopfront. A central chimney gable over an open pediment. Reaching Market Square turn r. through THE DARDANELLES. On the corner of Crawford Street the Edwardian RED LION INN, rebuilt and dated 1905. Crowstepped and turreted, with rusticated arches infilled with Art Nouveau timberwork. On the NW corner with Bowmont Street is BRISBANE PLACE, housing by the *Eildon Housing Association* curving satisfyingly round the corner. Attached to Nos. 1–3, a

terrace of three houses restored at the same time. The deep
cavetto reveals of the doorways and giant pilaster strips suggest
the hand of *William Elliot*, who made a plan for this property
in 1833.

Continue into EAST BOWMONT STREET, where there has been
a lot of demolition. Past the former Kelso United Presbyterian Church (*see* Churches, above) on the l., marooned in a car
park is No. 4 (Coldale House) an attractive early C19 villa with
single-storey wings, a former United Secession manse restored
in the 1990s. The other side of the road has GEORGE HEN-
DERSON'S Office and Agricultural and Engineering Works,*
c. 1900. Strident red brick, the office with Baroque detailing.

At the end turn l. into EDENSIDE ROAD, past the former Police
Station and Tait Hall (*see* Public Buildings, above). The road
is mostly expensive C19 villadom, the houses built mainly by
merchants, taking advantage of the fine view over the Tweed.
On the l. is EDENSIDE HOUSE, *c.* 1796, a classical villa on the
site of an earlier house called Essex Hall. s elevation of three
bays under a wide pediment, containing an oval oculus. Tuscan
doorpiece with cavetto reveals. Straight screen walls flank the
main block, each with round-headed blind arches, and an
advanced centre pedimented bay, containing a blind Venetian
window. Two-storey addition (1932) to rear with a bow at the
w end. Contemporary STABLE range with courtyard behind.
Octagonal GATEPIERS linked by serpentine walls to rectangular terminal piers. Late C20 housing occupies the extensive
grounds. On the E side: Baronial SHELBURN, dated 1881 over
the gateway, and mid C19 KERFIELD, delightful with shallow
bows flanking a corniced doorway; at the end is OAKLANDS,
late C19, large and rather pretentious. Across Ednam Road lies
WOODSIDE HOUSE. A classical house built *c.* 1800 for Miss
Jean Scott of Harden. Alterations 1931 and 1936 by *Leadbetter
& Fairley* and *J. McLeod & Reid*. The s front, in coursed
squared ashlar with sandstone angle quoins, and band courses,
has three bays with an advanced centre pediment, and a
pilastered doorcase. Tripartite windows at basement level,
overarched Venetian windows at ground floor. Attached to the
w end, a mid-C19, single-storey rectangular piend-roofed
SUMMER HOUSE. Converted to housing 2000, with much late
C20 housing in the grounds.

1c. North towards Floors Castle

ROXBURGH STREET, N of the square, has DUNS WYND on the
l., leading down to THE COBBY, a riverside walk; the retaining wall was built *c.* 1810. The street continues with three-
storey housing and shops, mostly of four or five bays, and
dating from the mid C19. Some blocks have been conserved,
minus their moulded and dentilled cornices, others replaced
by *Forgan & Stewart* in 1987. Some of the usual Kelso-type
details survive – giant pilaster strips, pilastered doorways, and
pilastraded shopfronts. SAFEWAY on the l. by *Comprehensive
Design*, 1984, tries its best to integrate in height, but not in
materials – concrete blockwork. On the E side, after Nos.

* Under threat 2005.

37–43, built by *John D. Oliver* of Eccles, 1835, with giant order pilaster strips, is mid-C19 UNION STREET. No. 1 has a Tuscan doorpiece, Nos. 9–15 a terrace of four houses with paired doorways and a good shopfront, attributed to *Dods & Cockburn*, 1848.

Back to Roxburgh Street and the mid-C18 RAGGED SCHOOL (No. 51). Gable to the street on the r., and a cobbled path to a small narrow court. A forge on the l. was the original schoolroom. The headmaster's house, *c.* 1850 overlooking Union Street, is a typical Kelso villa with a corniced doorway, front garden, and a cast-iron overthrow above the entrance gate. The next section of Roxburgh Street is disappointing; empty sites replaced by an unattractive bus station and unlandscaped car parking. Better on the opposite side, starting with ROXBURGH HOUSE (No. 48) dating from the late C18, with gatepiers, and a stable block onto the street. Two-storey and basement, with a piended and platformed roof, and a cluster of chimneys in the centre. A central single-bay pediment, corniced windows on the ground floor, and a Doric pilastered doorcase with sidelights. Two early C19 traditional villas at Nos. 50 and 60, the latter dignified by cast-iron railings between rectangular corniced angle piers.

It is more rewarding now to take CHALKHEUGH TERRACE, a high walk with a superb prospect over the river towards the castles of Floors and Roxburgh (qq.v.). Notable villas are the two-storey and attic, three-bay DUNCAN HOUSE, on the l., a school for young ladies, built *c.* 1837 by *Gray & Ker* with access to a subterranean apartment under the terrace path, leading to a garden above The Cobby. N and W (river) fronts of droved ashlar, with a deep-moulded eaves course, channelled angle quoins, and pilastered and corniced doorway. Next along is the ROYAL BRITISH LEGION CLUB. Kelso's first library (opened 1750), was established here in 1795, with the librarian's house in the lower level. Single-storey on a raised basement, rendered and lined out as ashlar. Five bays, with a splendid unorthodox columned doorpiece; the front mutilated by its present use. Before rejoining Roxburgh Street, walk S a few yards to No. 66, built *c.* 1834 as the museum of the Tweedside Physical and Antiquarian Society. Classical, two storeys and three bays, and deep projecting dentilled cornice. The first floor has blind windows to l. and r.; unhappily a central pedimented niche has been removed.

On the E side of Roxburgh Street is the North Parish Church (*see* Churches, above), followed by WINCHESTER ROW, which links to Bowmont Street. *John Winchester*, mason, built Nos. 3–6, *c.* 1833. An interestingly designed terrace of three two-storey houses, formerly with advanced three-bay end blocks; only the E one, No. 6, survives. Giant pilaster strips, rusticated on the ground floor, define the two-bay houses. From here little remains of note on the E side of Roxburgh Street. On the W, No. 106 was built as the KELSO DISPENSARY, founded in 1777. Additions of 1818 (Ormiston Cottage) for hot- and cold-water baths. Three-bay villa with a nice Tuscan columned and pedimented porch, in front of a moulded doorcase. Closed 1906 when Kelso Cottage Hospital was built. A three-bay villa,

FALCON HALL (No. 108), is perhaps late C18, with an open pediment over the centre bay, a bellcast roof and single-storey gabled wings.

Roxburgh Street widens out towards the entrance to Floors Castle (*see* p. 284), with on the l. a high wall guarding Walton Hall (*see* Villas, below), followed by a terrace of mostly late C18 or early C19 two-storey, two- and three-bay houses, some with later alterations. No. 144 still has its original twelve-pane glazing, and rectangular cavetto-corniced stacks. On the corner of Roxburgh Street and Bowmont Street, also hidden by a wall, is THE ELMS (formerly Seven Elms), a *cottage orné* by *William Elliot*, 1820, for Alexander (Sandy) Ballantyne, brother of John Ballantyne of Walton Hall and father of the author R.M. Ballantyne. A two-storey bow to the l., with a single window. Set back to the r., an entrance doorway with cavetto reveals, and a tripartite window in the outer bay; in front a veranda with a leaded bellcast roof, supported by slim, reeded cast-iron columns. A cast-iron finial atop the bow, and a fine set of octagonal chimneys. Sympathetic mid-C19 two-storey addition to the N, by the Roxburghe estates. The Floors Castle estate is bounded by the imposing high wall known as the Duke's Dyke.

Return SE via BOWMONT STREET, the old Back Way between the castle gates and the town centre; renamed in 1892. The E side of the street developed from the mid 1820s, except for a couple of villas. On the l. ORCHARD HOUSE, probably built *c.* 1820, as an estate house, by the fifth Duke of Roxburghe, who is given as the owner on John Wood's 1823 map. A classical town villa, originally set in orchards, the centre bay slightly advanced with a garlanded parapet, the entrance doorway framed by panelled pilasters. Surprisingly complete inside, with well-detailed doors and shutters, one or two with small cupboards behind, and classical cornices. A graceful geometric stair reaches the coved attic bedrooms, squeezed in between floor and roof; box beds survived until recently. ORCHARD COTTAGE is its single-storey former lodge, with an E wing. Early C19 square-plan and gabled DOVECOT, the only one in Kelso. Next of interest is Kelso High School on the l., and opposite St Mary's R.C. Church (*see* Churches and Public Buildings, above).

A detour next up INCH ROAD, important in Kelso for its dedication to education, health and social housing. On the SW corner the former Edenside Primary School, on the l. Kelso Hospital (*see* Public Buildings, above) and 1930s burgh housing which continues to Ednam Road. On the r. FOREST-FIELD is a pleasant lane running through to Edenside Road, composed of mid-to-late-C19 well-built villas, of interest in their different styles, detached, semi-detached, and imposing flatted houses, with their entrances and gardens well out of view of each other. Continuing up Inch Road following one another are the drab Swimming Pool, opened 1973, Edenside Primary School, and the exquisite Edenside Health Centre (*see* Public Buildings, above). At the end EDENSIDE COURT, well-integrated sheltered housing by *Aitken & Turnbull*, 1988, in facing brick sympathetic to its important neighbour.

Return to the end of Bowmont Street, opposite which is
INCH HOUSE (No. 48) with angle pilasters, and a small Tuscan
porch. Further down is the North Church Hall. Opposite, the
stark red sandstone of the Baptist Church (*see* Churches,
above), followed by a cul-de-sac with ALBERT TERRACE on
the l., 1874, built by the Working Men's Building Society; two-
storey flatted houses entered by steps to the first floors at the
rear. Then VICTORIA PLACE, on the r., grander, artisan
housing, with a pair of canted bays in the centre. PRINGLE-
BANK HOUSE (No. 25) next in a large garden. The s part of a
late C18 villa; the N part was rebuilt in the late C19. A three-
bay front, a centre pediment, channelled angle pilasters, the
entrance doorway with an incised Soanic architrave. No. 29 is
a late C18 single-storey and basement lodge, with a pair of
central stacks. The welcoming Public Library (*see* Public Buildings, above) follows. Opposite, on the NW corner of Union
Street is BOWMONT HOUSE (No. 22) *c.* 1800. Three storeys,
three bays, and a corniced doorway, the dentilled eaves breaking forward over giant angle pilasters. On the other corner, No.
20, another villa of *c.* 1830s, followed by Brisbane Place (*see*
above).

2. *Springwood Park and Maxwellheugh*

SPRINGWOOD PARK lies on the other side of the Tweed from
the town centre. The mansion house was built in 1756 by
Captain James Douglas (later Sir James Douglas of Springwood). Altered in the 1820s by *James Gillespie Graham*, and
enlarged to the designs of *Brown & Wardrop* in 1850–3, it was
demolished in 1954. Some estate buildings remain, notably the
GATEWAY, on the axis of Kelso Bridge, by *Gillespie Graham*,
1822. Classical triumphal archway with moulded keystone and
coffered soffit. Coupled engaged Doric columns on pedestals,
with triglyph frieze, a mutuled cornice, and raised centre
armorial panel. Flanking screen walls, with square pyramidal-
capped terminal piers. Graham's contemporary Neoclassical
MAUSOLEUM for the Scott Douglas family has unfluted
Roman Doric pilasters, an entablature with triglyphs and
guttae, and a mutuled cornice. Pedimented each end, the E
front with niches, above which are blind panels, the W elevation has a semicircular headed window flanked by niches.
Much vandalised. To the s is the HOME FARM, a mid-C19 picturesque courtyard steading and farmhouse with alterations
and additions by *Brown & Wardrop*, 1870–1. Single-storey
entrance front with central two-storey crowstepped tower
roofed with decorative clay tiles in alternate horizontal bands,
a segmental-arched pend below, and segmental openings in the
flanking wings. Decorative brick pepperpot turrets with polychrome fish-scale slated caps and decorative ridge tiles. Farmhouse at the NE angle with a bothy and L-plan dairy with more
use of decorative and plain clay tiles, pierced tile cresting and
English brick ridge-stacks. The early C19 WALLED GARDEN,
extended late C19, just survives but filled with caravans.
Continuing uphill, BRIDGEND PARK on the l. was created in
1954. At the top on the l. the former ENGLISH SCHOOL by

John Smith, 1847–8. Two-storey, sandstone with angle quoins, and a bipartite round-headed keystoned window with heraldic panel above. On the s side the sad remains of the STABLES of Pinnaclehill House, which was built for Mr Elliot by *John Smith*, *c.* 1822 and demolished *c.* 1956. Down SPROUSTON ROAD on the l. the Picturesque PINNACLEHILL LODGE, also by *John Smith*, *c.* 1822. Asymmetrical plan with canted angles, the flanks carried up as gablets. Wide pilastered pedimented porch. At the foot of Station Road is MAXWELLHEUGH TERRACE (Nos. 1–8), built in 1863, on high ground. Picturesque double cottages in red sandstone rubble with bands of cream sandstone. Practically symmetrical, each group differently detailed, but all with broad-eaved roofs, bargeboards and finials. The architect for the terrace is thought to be *Lady Douglas of Springwood*. At the start of Jedburgh Road, on the r., is MAXWELLHEUGH COTTAGE, a late C18 house of two storeys and attic, and three bays. A single-storey wing to l., with a tall round-headed window, probably added when it became a hotel. Further along the road is the Kelso Cottage Hospital (*see* Public Buildings, above).

117

VILLAS AND MANSIONS

BROOMLANDS HOUSE, Ednam Road. Marooned amidst late C20 housing in its once finely wooded grounds. Built for John Don of Attonburn. Two-storey, basement and attic in coursed squared rubble with polished margins, and piended platform roof, the basement treated as a plinth, rusticated quoins at ground and first floors and a banded eaves course and cornice. Dated 1719 on one of the lower quoins (now concealed). Attributed to *William Adam*, for it was published in *Vitruvius Scoticus*, though unclaimed by Adam and not built exactly to the design shown, i.e. without pavilions and linking walls. The house became the property of the Dukes of Roxburghe in the mid C18 and its simple elegance is marred by mid-C19 additions by the Roxburghe estates, particularly on the w front, by a pedimented doorcase and two-storey canted bay windows. The house was deepened from two to five bays at the same time. Now flats.

108 EDNAM HOUSE, Bridge Street. A neat Georgian Palladian mansion; now a hotel. Designed and built by *James Nisbet*, 1761, for James Dickson, a saddler's apprentice in Kelso, who eventually made his fortune in London. Built on the site of Ker of Chatto's Lodging. Originally called Havannah House after the siege of Havana, Cuba, in which Dickson's nephew and heir, William Dickson, served. Renamed after James Dickson purchased the Ednam estate, NE of Kelso, in 1765.

Ednam House is Nisbet's first recorded work, and amongst his most elegant. The scheme is based on designs from Isaac Ware's *Complete Body of Architecture* (1756), a source familiar to Nisbet from his work at Paxton House (q.v.). Two storeys, attic and sunk basement. Band course incorporating the ground floor (*piano nobile*) sills. Deep projecting eaves and a piended and platformed roof. Quite a severe E front. The standard of the masonry is high; an undroved projecting base course, deep horizontal droving below the sill band, and above, broached work. No window margins except lugged ones over the entrance doorway. This has a consoled cornice and round-headed doorway, which looks early C19, as do the widely splayed steps with curved stone balustrade, square piers and lamps. A dentilled three-bay pediment contains foliaceous carving framing James Dickson's coat-of-arms. A stone balustrade extends to the S with a central pedimented key-stoned archway; that to the N incorporates a 1937 addition, its archway becoming an entrance door. Plain ashlar W elevation, which has a balustraded, perhaps later, semi-octagonal bay in the centre, corniced windows with moulded margins on the ground floor, with triangular and curved pediments to those on the bay, and lugged margins to the top ones. The ground-floor windows have been lowered through the sill course, perhaps in the early C19.

Several extensions for the hotel. The S wing, 1932, of two storeys with pediment, is discreetly linked to the main block, while the N extension, 1937, extends from the N wall of the house, and c. 1962 incorporated the former Playhouse Cinema in Havannah Court, off Bridge Street. In 1956 a dining room was added to the W façade.

INTERIOR. A sketch plan of the ground floor is recorded in Robert Mylne's diary for 1776 and shows the principal entrance and hall with the main stair through a door to the r.; beyond is a dressing room and charter room in the NE corner. Along the W front were the principal rooms, in the centre the drawing room, library to the N, a parlour on the S. A door from the hall leads to a secondary stair, and former breakfast room (reception). The plan is unaltered except for a corridor to the N extension. Mahogany woodwork throughout, with carved entablatures, doors and shutters in the principal rooms. Some good examples of fretted door furniture. The decoration is Rococo and outstanding. In the square HALL, the ceiling has birds, fruit and flowers twining round a central rose. A magnificent marble chimneypiece and overmantel decorated with foliage and profile heads, a full-face head in the frieze. The overmantel surround has heads and trailing ivy and foliage.

A Baroque broken pedimented doorcase leads W to the DRAWING ROOM, the glory of which is a magnificent ceiling. Apollo in his chariot chases Aurora – a garland in her hand – into the window bay, with cherubs floating in the sky and lots of billowing clouds; foliage and scrolls surround small medallions, each containing a lively representation of a motif from *Aesop's Fables*. A marble chimneypiece flanked by caryatids, the frieze with garlands and panel displaying a sunburst head. The DINING ROOM (S, former parlour) has a central ceiling rose outlined by a garland of vine leaves and fruits. Green, yellow and white marble chimneypiece with garlands and urns. Above, a delicate relief of Europa and the Bull in a Rococo frame. The LIBRARY (Blue Room) ceiling has an oval centre-piece displaying music, sculpture and painting, the winged cherubs floating on clouds surrounded by garlands of fruit and flowers. The decorative plasterwork in the principal rooms is perhaps by *George Morison*, who worked at Paxton c. 1760. Red and white marble classical chimneypiece. A timber STAIR with alternating twisted and straight balusters at the N end on the E side. Decorative cornice and foliaceous ceiling rose.

At the top of the stairs is the grand square UPPER HALL, with deeply coved cupola supported by two Ionic columns and with Ionic pilasters on the walls. Round the cupola winged cherubs hold garlands suspended from bows, and there are profile male and female heads on each side, which appear to represent the seasons.

GARDEN. Of two late C18 Gothick SUMMERHOUSES, the smaller one was swept away by floods in 1948 and the survivor converted to a house. Five bays, with slim full-height Gothic clustered shafts with acanthus capitals and quatrefoil panels between the ground-floor and first-floor windows. The principal entrance was from Abbey Court to the E. Cast-iron GATEWAY dated 1845, and square channelled-corniced gatepiers with lion supporters as finials. A similar entrance was made from Bridge Street in 1928–9, on the site of the Tron (public weigh beam). – STABLES. See Description, p. 455–6.

ROSEBANK, Shedden Park Road. The home of Captain Robert Scott, uncle of Sir Walter Scott, who briefly resided here. The main block, a two-storey classical villa, described as 'lately built' in 1804, was added to an existing mid-C18, three-storey house, its top-floor windows tucked neatly under the eaves. The later house is in coursed squared rubble, with a block eaves course and piended roof. Three-bay W front with a later canted porch, and the N and S elevations have full-height shallow segmental bows with tripartite windows. Later C19 additions to the E. Inside, dining room to the l., a good timber and gesso chimneypiece decorated with the swags and fruits of autumn. A simple cornice, and round the edge of the ceiling, a flat rib of plaster roses. In the drawing room to the r., the same cornice and ceiling plasterwork, and a version of the 'Lady with Anchor' pattern chimneypiece, with shells. – Extensive STABLES to the N with a large court; much altered. – Late C19 LODGE (Tweedsyde Lodge). Single storey with canted ends and open-timber gabled porch. – Rectangular GATEPIERS linked by quadrant walls to terminal piers. – In the WALLED GARDEN a house by *Forgan & Stewart*, 1985. Brick with a pyramid roof.

WALTON HALL, Roxburgh Street. An attractive Regency-style bungalow, with a Veneto villa plan. Building in 1820 as a summer retreat for John Ballantyne, friend and publisher of Sir Walter Scott, but he died early in 1821 before he could enjoy the delights of his new house. Possibly by *William Elliot*, designer of The Elms (*see* Description, above), across the road, for Ballantyne's brother, Alexander, who succeeded to ownership of Walton Hall. Restoration in 1978–9, by *Lorne Brown & Partners*, removed the kitchen wing and poor C19 additions.

The house is shielded from the street by a high rendered rubble wall, formerly the fronts of two cottages but now displaying two arched pedestrian gates and a triumphal-arched vehicular entrance with Tuscan pilasters at the angles; cornice and blocking course. Splendid cast-iron 'blue poppy' gates by *Denys Mitchell*, c. 1990. The single-storey, almost square-plan villa has harled rubble walls with moulded sandstone margins, eaves course and shallow, piended roof. Three bays on the E front, the central entrance bay *in antis* with Ionic columns. Raised quoins and a cornice blocking course complete the classical front. The W front has a central semi-octagonal bay. At the N end a dwarf wall with cast-iron railing, ironwork by Mitchell, 1979, attaches to a rubble, single-storey and loft stable range, with a handsome octagonal timber lantern topped by a fish weathervane; restored 2001.

Inside, a vestibule leads into an inner hall lit by a high-domed cupola supported by four Ionic columns. The house is planned round the hall, with public rooms on the W side, all with bold modillion cornices, and bedrooms tucked round the rest. The drawing room, in the centre, has a white and grey marble chimneypiece, fluted pilaster jambs, and acanthus consoles; ribbed frieze and panel with a reclining lion. The dining room to the S has an Ionic screen at the E end, and a plain buffet recess. The N room, probably the library, was altered in the 1920s. The martial stone chimneypiece and overmantel, probably Edwardian, was imported from the demolished Blackadder House (q.v.). Mahogany panelling probably from the same source. A recent discovery behind the hall door to the dining room is shutters which fold into the wall and open out into double doors.

FLOORS CASTLE. *See* p. 284.
HENDERSYDE PARK. *See* p. 370.
NEWTON DON. *See* p. 593.

KERSHEUGH   6010
3.8 km. S of Jedburgh

A well-mannered classical farmhouse by *J.P. Alison*, 1912, in squared and snecked cream sandstone with long and short pink dressings. The S front has a doorcase with deep concave jambs. A canted bay on the W front breaks the overhanging eaves to form a balcony; the E elevation has a tripartite stair window with a decorative, shaped transom.

KILBUCHO   0030

OLD CHURCH probably existed by the C13 but was abandoned after 1810. The most complete surviving parts are the gable walls.

OLD MANSE, to the SE, is mid-C18 and a particularly fine example of its kind. Two main storeys, part basement and attic, with a semicircular stair-tower projecting from the rear (N) elevation. Gable-ended with cavetto-moulded skewputts. The S front has windows regularly placed and a central doorway beneath a semicircular-headed niche and chimneyed gablet. A bolection-moulded doorway on the N side bears the initials of John Douglas, minister of Kilbucho, 1614–60, and his wife, Margaret; it evidently derives from an earlier manse. (The

well-preserved interior has an axial entrance flanked by the
parlour (l.) and study and kitchen (r.). The elegant timber stair
rises to a longitudinal passage connecting three chambers. The
central, and largest, is pine-panelled and has an integral box
bed, also seen in the E room. A pair of pyramidal-roofed garden
pavilions flanks the house.)

HARTREE HOUSE, 3 km. NW. Built *c.* 1790 by Alexander
Dickson, a plain, gable-ended Georgian block of five bays and
two storeys with a basement, still recognisable on the rear (SW)
elevation. The rest was remodelled and partly overlaid from
1880 by Professor Alexander Dickson, who extended the house
in an eclectic mixture of styles, mainly Baronial and Scottish
Domestic; the architect was probably *John Lamb Murray* of
Biggar. Its principal front (NW, dated 1880) has a three-storey
entrance tower with battlemented parapet and corbelled angle
turret, flanked by lower bays. Inside, an impressive three-bay
axial corridor, punctuated by elaborate Gothic archways of
crisply worked sandstone and marble (the floor also in part of
inlaid marble), leads from the main entrance to the dining
room, drawing room and staircase.

KILBUCHO PLACE, 3.3 km. NE. A skilful remodelling of a large,
multi-phase house by *Robert J. Naismith* of *Sir Frank Mears &
Partners*, 1961–3. L-plan, the oldest portion is the S range, a
narrow rectangular block which may have been erected by John
Dickson, who acquired Kilbucho in 1628. The house was
extended during the early C18 and again in the C19, when it
became a farmhouse. Refurbishment successfully drew the
various elements of the house together and gave it a new focus
in the form of a conical-roofed entrance tower in the re-entrant
angle. Several ornamental dormer pediments have re-cut classical inscriptions. The entrance gateway incorporates rusticated piers with acorn finials, all probably C18.

6010   KILNSIKE PELE
                      2.6 km. NE of Chesters

Remains of one of a distinctive local group of late C16 pele
houses. Oblong on plan (11.6 m. by 7.6 m.), it probably comprised two storeys and a garret. Although less well-preserved
than its neighbouring peles at Mervinslaw and Slacks (qq.v.),
the building is of interest for its cyclopean masonry, some of
the larger blocks being rebated to facilitate bonding. The
mortar is mainly of clay, but lime was used in the construction
of the very massive NE wall, which contained the ground-floor
entrance. This was unusual in having no fewer than three
doors, two opening outwards and one inwards. The first floor
had its own entrance, formerly approached from a forestair,
and its floor joists rested on runners supported on scarcements
in the side walls. The chamber within was well equipped with
aumbries.

KIMMERGHAME HOUSE

8050

3.8 km. SE of Duns

Scottish Baronial mansion in squared and snecked sandstone by *David Bryce*, 1851, for John Campbell Swinton.* Severely damaged by fire in 1938, and much reduced before remodelling *c.* 1947–8 but retaining two-storey service wings and the four-storey entrance block. This has crowstepped gables, dormers with semicircular pediments, and corbelled conical-capped angle turrets. Finials carved with crescent, fleuron, fleur-de-lys etc, and good heraldic panels. The entrance front has a round-arched doorway, roll-moulded surround and rope-moulded hoodmould with knot label stops, and an aedicule window in a crowstepped chimneyed gable. A gable-head to the l. is carved with a relief of a boar chained to a tree and motto '*J'espere*'. The garden wing has steeply pedimented dormerheads and a rounded corner corbelled to a square, with paired gable-heads. Entrance court defined by low walls with decorative cast-iron urns and panelled piers surmounted by seated Florentine boars.

STABLES. *Bryce*, 1853. Baronial, U-plan, with a pyramidal-roofed birdcage bellcote. The carriage range has a circular tower with lead ball finial. – SUNDIAL. Mid-C19 cubical dial. A baluster-shaft with carved floral ornament, gnomon and ball finial. – ICE HOUSE. Early C19, circular, brick-domed. – WALLED GARDEN. Mid-C19 brick-lined sandstone rubble walls, curved at intervals and urn-finialled. – The early C19 gabled and bargeboarded GARDENER'S COTTAGE has a Tudor-arched porch, with stone seats inside. – Segmental-arched riveted iron FOOTBRIDGE. Late C19(?) with scissor-braced panels with *paterae* bosses. – WATER TOWER. Mid-C19 Gothic, with carved animal waterspouts. – NORTH LODGE by *George Smith*, 1835. L-plan, Tudor-style, with a stone gabled porch with four-centred arched lintel. Impressive octagonal gatepiers with quatrefoil panelled friezes. Long quadrant dwarf walls with continuous Tudor-arched stone balustrades. – SOUTH LODGE. Three-bay cottage, *c.* 1830. Rustic gabled porch.

KIMMERGHAME BRIDGE. Dated 1822. Classical, segmental arch over the Blackadder Water, with polygonal outer piers, dentil cornices and balustrades.

KIMMERGHAME MILL. Early C19 Scottish Domestic complex of corn mill, steadings and housing. Crowstepped, with some crosslet loops and stone gabled dormerheads. Oriel window to Mill Cottage. T-plan Mill House in the same style.

THE OLD SCHOOLHOUSE, *c.* 1825, has tripartite hoodmoulded windows, and a row of octagonal chimneys. A rustic dentilled pedimented porch, with paired tree-trunk columns, was later given a tall gable decorated with applied branches. The mid-C19 Tudor-detailed former SCHOOL has tripartite windows, a shouldered wall-head stack, and a four-centre arched doorway.

---

*The estate belonged to the Swintons from 1760 but was purchased in 1818 by Andrew Bonar, an Edinburgh banker. He, *c.* 1825, commissioned *William Burn* to design an Elizabethan-style house but died soon after.

SINCLAIRSHILL. Two rows of early C19 estate cottages, added to and romanticised in the mid C19. Cotswold Tudor style, with busy façades of gables and bay windows variously treated, and chunky-columned porches. The centre gable of the N row has a stylised monogrammed hoodmould and a full-size stork finial. The S row has projecting ends, the W decorated with a stone riband announcing 'Sinclairshill', and a large horseshoe in the E gable-head for the blacksmith.

5020   KIPPILAW
                        5.6 km. W of St Boswells

A large, rather gaunt, composite house, of which the earliest part is said to be the three-storey block on the S side. The quoins at the SW corner look C16; during alterations in 1946, a blocked pointed window was also revealed in what was a NE gable.* These small details may indicate a former tower house on the site. Mostly rubble-built with grey sandstone margins. In 1818 *John Smith*, for John Seton Kerr, added a classical block to the E end of this early part, extending to the N. Three storeys and five bays with a pediment over the centre three. Single bay added in 1886; the large porch probably dates from the same time. The three-storey, three-bay S elevation incorporates the earlier work but must have been partly remodelled. The S end of Smith's block was given a two-storey bay window, and extending from the SW corner is a billiard room, built after 1894. In the middle is a veranda, the canopy with flat decorated iron columns. The N elevation's W end has a high canted gable with a prominent large keystoned window on the top floor and a conical-capped stair-tower. Interior remodelled, rather indiscriminately, in the late C19, but much of the fittings and decoration survives.

    STABLES, N of the house. An extensive late C19 two-storey, U-plan gabled range. Square, corniced and capped GATEPIERS, with fluted friezes.

KIPPILAW MAINS, N of the house. U-plan whinstone range of a farmhouse on the N side, and two steadings enclosing the W and E sides. Pink sandstone margins. Two-storey, three-bay house, its small pediment with a panel dated 1770. The wings each have basket-arched cartshed openings. Wall-head dormers added by *Peddie & Kinnear*, 1871. On the r., cottages by *John Dick Peddie*, 1856.

2030   KIRKBURN

A tiny group of buildings at the N edge of Cardrona Forest.

Former KIRKBURN CHURCH. Now a dwelling. Simple and dignified former community hall built in 1921, when the walls of two early C19 whinstone rubble cottages were retained and

*RCAHMS.

remodelled by *J.M. Dick Peddie* in the style of Voysey. Dedicated as a memorial chapel to William Cree of Kailzie in 1926. Overhanging bellcast eaves, the side elevations with a row of windows with Tudor glazing, nestling under the eaves. The roof ridge is carried out over a scroll-bracketed timber and slated canopy, with bell, over an entrance porch with round-headed windows. A panel is inscribed W & I C (Cree) 1921. Inside, a reused lintel is inscribed HOUSE FOR PRAYER 1614. Single-light STAINED GLASS window of the Crucifixion, by *Douglas Strachan*, 1929.

BURIAL ENCLOSURE, immediately to S. Kailzie church passed into the possession of Kelso Abbey soon after the middle of the C12. A new parish church was built in 1614. The dimensions of the enclosure, formed in 1724, suggest it incorporates parts of this building. The N doorway has a quirked edge roll, and its dated lintel bears an inscription from Juvenal's *Satires*. The lintel over the S doorway bears a reversed illegible monogram.

Nearby is a group of FORESTRY COMMISSION HOUSES: a standard Swedish design adapted by *Robert H. Matthew* in the 1960s, with horizontal timbers and sloping roof dormers. They have worn well.

CARDRONA HOUSE. *See* p. 149.

KAILZIE HOUSE. *See* p. 435.

KIRKHOPE TOWER

3020

2 km. N of Ettrickbridge

A late C16 tower house of the Cranstouns, occupying a dramatic upland setting overlooking an ancient river crossing in the Ettrick Valley. Described in 1649 as one of the principal houses in Selkirkshire, it afterwards became a farmhouse and then stood empty for more than a century before being restored in 1996–7 by *France Smoor*.

Oblong on plan (8.5m. by 7.0m.), the tower comprises four storeys and an attic below a gabled roof. There is an open parapet-walk on three sides and gable-roofed caphouses at diagonally opposite corners, as at Whytbank Tower and the more prestigious Aikwood Tower (qq.v.). The masonry is mainly local whinstone, with buff-coloured sandstone dressings used very sparingly; only the larger openings have dressed margins and these are chamfered. The ground-floor entrance in the S wall leads into a barrel-vaulted cellar with a mural stone stair opening E off the lobby. Above first-floor level the stair may always have been of timber and situated, like the present one, in the SE corner. Surprisingly, in a tower of this date (but cf. Windydoors and Old Gala House at Galashiels (qq.v.)), there is a first-floor entrance as well, reached from a timber forestair rising against the S wall and leading straight into what may originally have been the hall (now kitchen). Each of the upper floors seems originally to have contained a single room. The third-floor one, perhaps the laird's private chamber, is better lit than its neighbours; the S window is furnished with bench seats in the ingoes, while the W one, for some unexplained reason, is placed horizontally rather than vertically. The garret must always have been lit mainly by dormers.

Immediately to the S are the turf-covered remains of the oblong BARMKIN (27.4m. by 13.7m.), through which the tower was evidently approached. It had ranges of buildings to W and S and an entrance at the NE corner.

6020   KIRKLANDS HOUSE
1 km. W of Ancrum

A small Tudor-style mansion house of the early 1830s by *Edward Blore* for John Richardson, a parliamentary solicitor. Two storeys and attic in stugged ashlar, with tall octagonal chimneys in groups of two or three. Mullioned and transomed windows with hoodmoulds, and an oriel window on the principal front. Gabled porch, each jamb of its four-centred arch decorated with a carved hound's head. Large alterations and additions were planned for Lord George Scott by *Robert S. Lorimer*, but all that was done, 1907–8, was to raise the gable to the l. of the entrance, insert bay windows, and to enlarge a window to a hoodmoulded bipartite. Additions were made to the offices, W, and some rooms remodelled. – LODGE. Mid-C19 Tudor, with latticed windows.

5010   KIRKTON

PARISH CHURCH. Built 1841. The core is a small whin-built rectangle with margins and dressings of droved ashlar. Three pointed windows along each flank have timber two-light panelled tracery; over a similar window in the entrance front rises a birdcage bellcote. In 1906 a pinnacled porch was added, and a short chancel and vestry at the opposite end, the chancel gable having a triplet of trifoliate-headed windows within a containing arch. The 1906 openings are framed by chunky roll mouldings. – CHURCHYARD, mainly C18 and C19 headstones and obelisks, some with trade symbols.

2030   KIRKTON MANOR

A large, sparsely populated parish occupying the valley of the Manor Water. There is no village, but Kirkton Manor, at the lower end of the valley, with its church, hall and cluster of houses, provides a focus for the community.

PARISH CHURCH. 1872–4, by *Brown & Wardrop*. It is an unbuttressed rectangle with an E (in fact SE) apse, a N porch and a W bellcote, constructed of pink coursed rock-faced masonry with stugged ashlar dressings. The S face has, from E to W, three two-light windows, a single lancet and a small blocked doorway in a salient; the N face has two two-light windows E of the porch and a single lancet to its W.

The surprise on entering is that it is a rectangular space with no evidence of the apse: to reconcile ecclesiological correctness with Protestant sensibilities the apse housed the vestry. The interior is covered by a ceiled arch-braced roof, and the main focus is the communion table enclosure at the E end, while at the W end is a narrow laird's pew. – PULPIT, octagonal with linenfold panels. – COMMUNION TABLE, donated 1940. – STAINED GLASS. E wall, N of communion table, Works of Charity, *c.* 1862; to S, Gathering the Tares; S wall, E window, SS Francis and Margaret by *Margaret Chilton*, 1931; third from E, two Maries and Angel at Tomb by *A. Ballantine & Gardiner*, 1893.

CHURCHYARD, SE of the church, a fragment of the E wall of its predecessor of 1697. C18 stones with *memento mori* and burial enclosures of Forresters of Barns and Burnets of Barns. – NW of the church is the memorial to David Ritchie, †1811 (the inspiration for Scott's 'Black Dwarf'), erected 1845.

Immediately NE of the church is the former MANSE of *c.* 1800, a mainly two-storey, gable-roofed block of buff, harled rubble with dressed sandstone quoins and margins. Three-bay front with slightly advanced centre rising to an attic gablet; single-storeyed range of offices to SW.

MANOR BRIDGE, 2 km. NE, by *Blyth & Cunningham*, 1883. A wide, graceful bridge built to replace a ford across the River Tweed. Five flat segmental arches with rounded cutwaters.

OLD MANOR BRIDGE, SE of Manor Bridge, crosses Manor Water. A single-arched hump-back, of random rubble with dressed voussoirs, its origin is recorded on the NW face: WILLIAM. DUKE/OF QUEENSBERRY/ DESIGNED THIS WORK/ AND WILLIAM/ EARLE OF MARCH/ HIS SECOND SONE/ BUILT THE SAME/ ANNO 1702.

NEIDPATH VIADUCT, 2.5 km. NE. Opened 1864, closed 1954. Built in a magnificent setting to take the Caledonian Railway across the River Tweed, leading dramatically into South Park tunnel. Eight sandstone arches incorporating skew arches on springing courses. Decorative piers and cast-iron parapet railings.

DESCRIPTION. At the rear of Kirkton Manor Farm stands a large, three-storey former WATER MILL, of late C18 and C19 date, which retained a breast-shot wheel into the late C20. Another interesting relic of rural industry is the nearby SMITHY, now disused. Of similar date to the mill, it is single-storey, with two prominent chimneys, each of which served its own forge. It stands behind the Community Hall of *c.* 1920

BLACK DWARF'S COTTAGE, 1.5 km. SW at Woodhouse Farm. Provided by Sir James Naesmyth of Posso for David Ritchie, who inspired Sir Walter Scott's *The Black Dwarf*. Ritchie lived here from *c.* 1762 until his death in 1811 (*see* churchyard, above). The cottage, originally built of alternate layers of stone and turf, was reconstructed in 1802 as a pair of one-room dwellings for Ritchie and his sister. The façade is of whinstone rubble with red sandstone margins and asymmetrical façade, with a very small doorway and tiny window to the l. (above an inscription DR 1802). The full-size central doorway and window to its r. appear to be of after 1836, when Alexander Archer 'sketched the cottage on site' and also showed it to be thatched. The changes must have been made when a new cottage with a projecting gabled porch was added to the l. and the cottage given a continuous slate roof. There used to be a small bust of Ritchie in the porch gable, supported by the surviving frame.

CROSS BASE, near Posso Craig, Newholm Hope Burn, 7.8 km. SW. Possibly brought from Kirkton Manor churchyard c.1874, when this was believed to be the original site of St Gordian's Chapel.

FORTS, Cademuir, 1 km. SE. Two contrasting Iron Age forts set about 0.45 km. apart. The larger, on the summit, encloses about 2.25 ha. within two stone ramparts, and contains traces of numerous stances for timber round-houses. The other, to the SW, takes in only 0.25 ha. but has a massive inner wall, in places over 5 m. in thickness and now largely reduced to a mass of rubble. Other walls enclose several outlying terraces, that on the W embracing the entrance, but the most striking feature of the outer defences is a *chevaulx de frise* of upright stones in a shallow gully flanking the E side of the fort.

BARNS HOUSE. *See* p. 112.

CASTLEHILL TOWER. *See* p. 155.

GLENTERNIE HOUSE. *See* p. 332.

HALLYARDS. *See* p. 341.

1040   # KIRKURD

Small Peeblesshire parish.

OLD PARISH CHURCH. *See* Castlecraig House p. 153.

Former PARISH CHURCH. Relocated here from the policies of Castlecraig (q.v.) in 1766 by John Carmichael of Skirling, fourth Earl of Hyndford from 1767 (date and arms over N doorway). Harled T-plan structure with red sandstone margins to the windows, doorways and gable skews; the main body runs from E to W, the N aisle facing the churchyard entrance. A square birdcage bellcote with ogee cap on the W gable was renewed by *Alexander Noble* and *James Proudfoot*; chimney on E gable, and cross finial on N gable. The S front has four lancet windows, while the N side has a single lancet on each side of the aisle; the N aisle itself has a central doorway between a pair of lancets. W porch added 1869 (date on rainwater head). There was a major reordering in 1893, though the interior is now largely stripped out. – STAINED GLASS. Armorial in windows of N front of main body; Geometric designs in window to E of N doorway. – MEMORIALS along exterior S wall to ministers and their families, the earliest to Thomas Gibson, †1787.

CHURCHYARD. Some handsome gravestones, including John Swan, mason, †1792, with urn finial and masonic symbols, and John Baillie, gardener, †1811, with gardening tools. – Square WATCH HOUSE with walls of red coursed rubble and block quoins, dated 1828 in oval plaque. – GIBSON CARMICHAEL BURIAL ENCLOSURE, NW of church, remodelled by *James & William Noble* in 1814 (date above entrance). Red droved ashlar masonry to front and sides, with chamfered block quoins and classical cornice; rubble to rear. *Memento mori* each side of central E doorway. On S side, central salient with re-set memorial flanked by symbolic plaques.

MANSE (Kirkurd House), SW of the church. Harled with painted margins. The two-storey, three-bay E block was built by *James & William Noble* in 1788–9. Extended by *John Lessels* in 1856. Gabled with decorative thistle finials. Later porch on the N side.

Former SCHOOL, now a dwelling. Single-storey schoolroom of *c.* 1870, replacing one of 1773. Tall pointed windows, and two gables with windows between canted projections. To the E, a two-storey rubble-built schoolhouse, 1836 by *John Noble*, with wall-head dormers and hoodmoulded windows.

WAR MEMORIAL, 0.6 km. N of the church on the E side of the A701. A distinctive cone of red sandstone with a cross finial, 1919; steps provided after 1945.

WEST MAINS FARM. Two-storey late C18(?) harled farmhouse with small single-storey straight wings. The single-storey pedimented stables of red sandstone rubble are by *James & Alexander Noble*, 1809. Converted to a dwelling 1997.

CASTLECRAIG HOUSE. *See* p. 153.

NETHERURD HOUSE. *See* p. 584.

KNOWESOUTH

0.8 km. W of Lanton

A medium-sized mansion house built for William O. Rutherford and described as 'newly erected' in 1836. Two storeys in coursed sandstone, with deep overhanging gables dressed up with heavily carved bargeboards weighed down each end with pendant bosses, the same design repeated over the wall-head dormer windows, which have timber canopies resting on the roof slates. The conventional house sheltering beneath has a stone porch and single- and two-storey canted bays. Plain and carved terracotta chimneypots. The three S bays were added later, seamlessly. Replanned internally but a mid-C19 well stair has finely wrought cast-iron uprights.

E LODGE matches the house, with carved bargeboards and a corbelled-out oriel over a four-light window. – At the W gate, hidden from view, a C18 double-chambered, rubble, crow-stepped DOVECOT with dormered entries. – ICEHOUSES built into banks E and W of the house. Probably early C19, square and stone-built.

LADYKIRK

A small village on the N bank of the River Tweed. The parish was formed soon after the Reformation by the union of Horndean and Upsettlington, whose names are still in use.

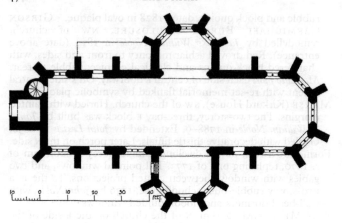

Ladykirk Church.
Plan.

16 PARISH CHURCH. Also known as Kirk of Steill, this is a key building for Scottish late medieval church architecture. Set on the N edge of the village, it replaced a church that had served the community of Easter Upsettlington from at least the C13. It was built under the patronage of James IV; traditionally it is said this was in thanksgiving for his being saved from drowning in the Tweed. References in the royal accounts show that *Nicholas Jackson* was master mason up to 1507; in that year *Thomas Peebles* was fitting glazing, suggesting work was nearing completion. The only structural element left unfinished was the upper part of the tower.

The church is cruciform, with an aisle-less rectangular main body terminating in a three-sided E apse, and full-height transeptal apses halfway down the main body; the small W tower has a circular stair-turret in the N angle between tower and nave. E apses had become relatively common since the building of St Salvator's Chapel at St Andrews in about 1450, and laterally-apsed side chapels were to be built at Arbuthnott (before 1506) and the Dominican friary at St Andrews (after 1516), perhaps reflecting a wider European vogue. But the combination of these elements in a symmetrical design at Ladykirk is unique in Scotland. All parts have pointed barrel vaulting covered by stone-flagged roofing. Barrel vaulting, which was characteristic of many of the more ambitious Scottish late Gothic churches, has several implications for the overall design. Externally, since the vaults spring from below the wall-head, the windows have to be set rather low in the walls (and internally the arches into the transept chapels also have their apices at a relatively low level). But the most striking external consequence is the rather ear-like appearance that results from the vaults of the transeptal chapels stopping against gable-walls rising from the walls of the main body.

The pink sandstone ashlar walls rise from a deep base course, with a string course below the windows. The buttresses have a single intake at about mid-height and are capped by minimal pinnacles a little above the wall-head cornice. The window tracery is of the simplest kinds, and in most cases all lights reach up to the window arch. In the apses the windows have equilateral arches with Y-tracery, or with three-light intersecting tracery in the case of the E window. Along the S flank, however, the three-light windows have flattened three-centred arches, perhaps partly in response to the horizontal springing line of the vault. There are doorways for the laity on both sides of the nave, that on the N now opening into a heating chamber and vestry. A priests' doorway was provided through the S chancel wall, above which is a C18(?) inscribed tablet recording in Latin the construction of the church.

Internally the architectural forms are markedly austere. The 17 pointed barrel vaulting, which runs straight through into the E apse, has widely spaced parallel ribs over the main space, and radial ribs above the apses. The ribs spring from corbels, and the heavily restored responds and arches into the transeptal chapels are simply chamfered. The lower storey of the tower does not communicate with the church; the two upper storeys appear to have been habitable.

In 1741–3 repairs were carried out for local landowners, William Robertson of Hillhousefield and Thomas Coutts, and the former had the tower completed by the addition of a top storey with a round-arched opening to each face and a square dome capped by a lantern. This addition is said to have been designed by *William Adam*. The completion of the tower was commemorated by a tablet inside the W wall. In 1793 the church was subdivided to house the parish school in the W bays, entered through a (blocked) doorway in the W wall of the S transept. These partitions were removed during a restoration of 1861 by *James Cunningham*, and the pulpit was placed by the arch into the S transeptal chapel, with pews facing towards it on three sides. A reordering of 1987 relocated the pulpit in the chancel. – PEWS, brought from Berwick, St Andrew, 1987. – DOLE CHEST, from Liverpool, St Nicholas, donated 1885. – STAINED GLASS. Apse, E window, 23rd Psalm, N window, Resurrection and Ascension; S window, Ascension; S transept window, Sacrifice of Isaac, Christ and the Samaritan woman, 1887; N transept N window, Christ Teaching, *c.* 1894. – SUNDIAL, on SW pinnacle. – CLOCK FACE, dated 1882.

MANSE by *John Lessels*, 1875. Two storeys in coursed sandstone. Finialled and bracketed gables, a full-height canted bay on the S front, and finialled timber-canopied doorway.

LADYKIRK & NORHAM BRIDGE.* A powerful stone bridge by *Thomas Codrington* and *Cuthbert Brereton*, 1885–7, constructed by *Meakon & Deans*, to replace a timber bridge on stone piers by *John Blackmore*, 1838–9. Four segmental arches, dressed stone voussoirs, coursed rubble spandrels and corbelled string courses at the parapet base. The central cutwater is rounded

*This is a revision, with new information, of the entry in *The Buildings of England: Northumberland*, p. 524.

and carried up to form a retreat; the others are pointed. At the Ladykirk end is a late C19 TOLLHOUSE with hoodmoulds and central chimney.

Former SCHOOL, W end of the village. Dated 1859, by *James Cunningham*. T-plan with carved bargeboarded gables. S projecting classroom with a large tripartite window, flanked by porches with pointed windows, the tops with intersecting tracery, and stone slab hoods over the windows and doors. Opposite, a mid-C19 two-storey schoolmaster's house, somewhat mutilated.

WAR MEMORIAL, W of the church. Celtic cross, *c.* 1920.

HEMMEL (cattle shed), E of the church. By *Smith & Stirling, c.* 1845. In red sandstone with a pantiled roof, formerly thatched.

FOUNTAIN COTTAGE, 0.3 km. S on the B6470, is a mid-C19 tollhouse. L-shaped and gabled, with a porch and bay window. Opposite, the classical JUBILEE FOUNTAIN was erected in 1887 by Lady Marjoribanks of Ladykirk House (*see* below). Square with angle columns supporting a frieze and cornice, with some Jacobean strapwork, and an open crown; decorated with coronets and shields.

OLD LADYKIRK FARM, E end of the village. By *James Cunningham, c.* 1840.

LADYKIRK HOUSE

2.1 km. S

The estate was bought by William Robertson of Hillhousefield, Edinburgh, and a mansion by *William Elliot* finished in 1799; it copied the front elevation of William Chambers's Dundas House, Edinburgh (1771). Added to and altered in 1843–4 by *Burn & Bryce*, the mansion was gradually demolished from the late 1930s and replaced by the present house, built in the walled garden, by *J.D. Cairns & Ford*, 1965–6 for Major J. Askew. This has Lorimer-type bellcast gables in Dutch colonial style, and a long staircase window. Some fittings were reused from the previous house, including the library woodwork.

LADYKIRK STABLES AND RIDING SCHOOL. A Victorian essay in Palladianism, built on a vast scale at a cost of £11,836, a U-plan complex of two-storey stables with a large rectangular riding school attached to the E. Designed in 1845 by *George Tattersall*, specialist in equestrian architecture, and complete by the mid-1850s. *H. S. Ridley* was paid for plans for the riding school and seems to have been working as executant architect after Tattersall's death in 1849.

The stables have a thirteen-bay centre block with nine-bay S projecting wings ending in open-pedimented gabled façades. Bold smooth rustication emphasises the angles of the building and the tall archway in the centre of the main range, which has above it a domed octagon with arched openings, pilasters and ribs, rising from a square base. Copper weathervane and conductor supplied by *R. & E. Kepp*, London, under the direction of Tattersall; its spindle was painted and gilded. A water tank in the dome was linked to the house water supply. Blind arches with raised margins and keystones contain the ground-floor windows and doors, and a string course round the courtyard façade links the sills of the first-floor windows. The entrance, tall enough for a rider and horse, leads to a lobby through a great iron gate with a coat-of-arms and artfully detailed handles and lock (the *Shotts Iron Co.* carried out the ironwork in the stables in 1847). The fittings in the harness room are mostly intact. The riding school is a two-storey shed of vast size with a shallow overhanging roof. The exterior has blind arches on the ground floor with glazed fanlights in the semicircular heads; above are eighteen circular glazed windows. A large entrance porch projecting from the s elevation is emphasised by smooth rustication and a deep blocking course. Inside is an immense empty space with a queenpost roof. Tiny w gallery for the family to view the activities.

EAST LODGE, 1875, with bracketed eaves and bipartite windows. Capped stone gatepiers and pedestrian cast-iron gates of 1850; moved here in the 1990s. Classical NORTH LODGE by *John Dobson*, 1850, with a Tuscan pedimented porch. Gatepiers and decorative cast-iron gates moved here from the East Lodge, but the ball-finialled corniced piers are 1850.

The LION GATEWAY and PORTER'S LODGE by *William* 74 *Elliot*, inscribed WR 1799, is based on the entrance screen (1773) by Robert Adam for the Duke of Northumberland at Syon House. A high arch surmounted by a *Coade* stone Percy lion, linked by five-bay colonnades to single-storey, piend-roofed, four-bay lodges; each with a niche on its principal front. The arch has decorative pilasters, the acanthus-leaf capitals repeated on the colonnades. Original cast-iron gates and railings.

By the entrance to the new house, through the garden wall, is a mid-to-late C19 two-storey house (BUTLER'S HOUSE) with wall-head dormers. The entrance looks original, *c.* 1799, the tall square piers with garlanded urns on top. – GARDENER'S COTTAGE by *John Oliver* and *Adam Young*, *c.* 1846. Tudor-style, the pedimented wall-head dormers with triangular-shaped kneelers. – To the s a MAUSOLEUM. Stone slab roof, pointed-arched doorway, and traceried opening in the s elevation. Said to have been built *c.* 1900 for the first Lord Tweedmouth but never used. – ICEHOUSE, SE of the present house. Egg-shaped with passage entrance.

LADYKIRK HOME FARM. 1.3 km. sw. Mid-C19 farmhouse, offices and cottages, the latter flanking a prominent two-storey square DOVECOT with classical detailing, tall bellcast roof and fine cock weathervane.

NEW LADYKIRK FARM, 1.3 km. NE, built by *James Cunningham*, *c.* 1854. Solid farmhouse with a well-finished interior and large complex of traditional farm offices, also by Cunningham, *c.* 1840. Mostly single-storey farm buildings tucked in low, away from the elements. One court later infilled with sheds with interesting boat-shaped roofs.

MILNE GRADEN HOUSE. *See* p. 567.

LAIDLAWSTIEL 4030
8 km. w of Galashiels

Dated 1870. A crowstepped Scottish Domestic country house, transformed from a nucleus of traditional farmhouse and steadings as a summer residence for Eneas, tenth Lord Reay. The buildings occupy four sides of a court, the principal block on the s side, with wings to the N; the E one a two-bay billiard room. Harled with red sandstone margins. The principal E addition to the farmhouse has a two-storey canted bay, and a three-storey conical-roofed octagonal tower at the sw angle. The N front of the two-storey farmhouse was dressed up with crowstepped gables and wall-head windows, with a plain porch fronted by a red sandstone door surround which may be of earlier date and imported. Some of the farm buildings have been reconstructed, and others adapted for domestic use. Spacious hall with a columned screen and rather thinly detailed timber staircase. Decorative cornices and French-style marble chimneypieces.

LAMANCHA
5 km. E of West Linton

A slimmed-down version of a much larger house that stood here during the C19. The oldest part may be the 'little house' erected by Robert Hamilton of Grange in 1663. In 1726 the estate was purchased by Thomas Cochrane (afterwards eighth Earl of Dundonald) and renamed Lamancha. Cochrane refurbished the house and 'considerably extended (it) in point of length', but it was left to James Mackintosh, c. 1832, to bring the mansion up to its maximum size by the addition of a second range to the rear. In 1926–7 the house was reduced to its present dimensions by J. Drummond Beaton, who also remodelled the interior.

An early C20 photograph of the principal (SE) front shows a three-storey and basement block, gabled at the sw end and hip-roofed at the NE end. Harled rubble masonry with exposed dressings and rusticated quoins. Ten bays of regularly placed windows, the ground-floor ones large round-headed openings with prominent keystones; the principal entrance, slightly off-centre, approached through a porte cochère. Beaton evidently rebuilt the house above the ground floor, removing the second floor altogether and reducing the first floor to seven bays of crowstepped dormers placed rather higher than the earlier first-floor windows. He also demolished the porte cochère and raised the ground level at the front, leaving the basement to be approached only from the rear, where the greater part of the mid-C19 range was also demolished. As it now stands, then, the house dates mainly from the 1730s and 1920s, part of the vaulted basement possibly being earlier. The keystone of the entrance doorway bears the Cochrane crest and the date 1736.

Handsome stone SUNDIAL with canted dial of c. 1700 in front of the house. Entrance GATEWAY to policies with rusticated piers and urn finials.

MADRISA, 0.8 km. E. This very stylish mid-C18 farmhouse and associated steading originally formed part of the Lamancha estate. The house, hip-roofed, with a central chimney, has a four-bay front; the centre and ends are slightly advanced and the windows in the end bays have semicircular arch-heads. A circular stair-tower, now truncated, projects from the centre of the rear elevation. – LOWER GRANGE, 0.3 km. SW, is another former estate farm. The farmhouse of 1825 is a plain two-storey gable-ended block with a three-bay front and a single-storey outshot. An inscription on the steading commemorates the Duke of Cumberland's ('Liberty and Property's Defender') victory at Culloden in 1746.

Former LAMANCHA SCHOOL, SE side of A702. An attractive mid-C19 group comprising schoolmaster's house and schoolroom.

LAMBDEN HOUSE 7040

3 km. NW of Eccles

Dated 1839 and built for Nisbet of Lambden, with additions and alterations by *T. Bowhill Gibson* from *c.* 1920. An elegant two-storey house in the best Borders villa tradition, with shallow bows flanking a central tripartite window, with narrow side-lights, above a C20(?) Doric portico, formerly fronted by a columned screen. Piended and platformed roof, and groups of three octagonal chimneystacks. Single-storey wings are set far back with balustraded links to the main block. Single-storey crowstepped former offices at the rear, dated 1840, the central part built up, by Gibson, to a four-storey Italianate water tower, with flat angle pilasters and tripartite mullioned openings in the top tier. – STABLES. A red-tiled U-shaped range by *Gibson* in red brick, with pebble-dashed walls and brick detailing. Splendid lantern ventilator with timber louvres and bell-cast lead roof with weathervane. – WALLED GARDEN, dated 1840. – LODGE. By *Gibson*. Classical but inelegant, in concrete lined out as ashlar.

LAMBERTON 9050

A hamlet close to the English Border.

CHURCH. A church at Lamberton was granted to Durham shortly before 1200. This forlorn site was an important rendezvous on the Border with England: here in 1503 Princess Margaret Tudor was met by the representatives of James IV, her espoused husband, and in 1633 Charles I met delegates of his northern kingdom on his 'homecoming'. Abandoned after union with Mordington in 1650, the church is now divided between the derelict burial enclosures of the Rentons of Lamberton and the Logans of Lintlaw and Burnhouses. – CHURCHYARD, scattering of C18 and C19 gravestones.

LANGLEE PARK 6010

3.2 km. SW of Jedburgh

Scottish Baronial mansion of 1868 by *David Bryce* for Charles Scott, incorporating an earlier house built by James Fair W.S. (†1796).

Stugged cream ashlar, with extended service ranges forming a U-plan. A moulded stringcourse between ground and first floors meanders up and over windows and panels. Crow-stepped gables and pedimented dormerheads and finials. The entrance elevation has a three-storey square entrance tower to the l., topped by machicolations, balustraded parapet and waterspouts, with a round turret corbelled out in an angle, taking a stair from the first floor to a viewing platform, and ending with an ogee cap. The detailing, e.g. round-arched doorway with rope hoodmould and first-floor aedicule window, was used in Bryce's earlier Kimmerghame House (q.v.). Garden front with a five-light canted bay, the first floor corbelled to a square. The other elevations have been altered and the interior was subdivided in 1981. Spacious timber staircase with barley-twist balusters, panelled newel posts and carved finials.

6020   LANTON

A straggling village of medieval origin with a mix of C18 and C19 houses supplemented by newly built bungalows.

DESCRIPTION. The former SCHOOL, at the NE end, comprises a late Victorian schoolmaster's house and an attached single-storey classroom, topped by a pair of prominent louvres (now village hall). The older houses stand mainly at the SW end of the village, towards Lanton Tower (see below). They include the OLD MANOR INN, a two-storey gable-roofed block of mid-C18 date; heavily restored in 1980–1. Harled rubble walls with sandstone dressings, and a five-bay front showing two rows of narrow-chamfered windows flanking a lug-moulded entrance doorway. Immediately SW is the mid-C19 BEESWING COTTAGE, a two-storey, three-bay house of pink sandstone, with an earlier wing to N. LANTON PLACE COTTAGE, next again to the SW, may be late C18. It has an ashlar eaves course and cavetto-moulded skewputts.

LANTON TOWER. One of three tower houses that formerly stood hereabouts. Probably late C16, with a plain C17 NE wing (extended towards the end of the C18) and a sizeable early Victorian NW wing, which probably replaces an earlier stair wing. In 1989–90 the house was reduced in size and restored by *Philip Mercer*. The tower is a simple oblong (8.3 m. by 7.0 m.) of three storeys and an attic, built of local sandstone rubble with dressings mainly of buff-coloured sandstone. The original windows have rounded arrises and some were evidently barred and glazed; many were renewed in 1989–90, to which period belong also the upperworks, with their crowstepped gables and dormer windows. Two original oval-mouthed gun-loops pierce the SW wall at ground-floor level, while a similar pair of loops was placed, or replaced, in the NE wall during restoration. A new entrance doorway of red sandstone was formed in the SE wall of the C17 wing. Its semicircular-headed surround is seemingly modelled on the cloister doorway at Dryburgh Abbey (q.v.). The tower retains a barrel-vaulted cellar equipped with a ceiling hatch, while the first-floor chamber, probably the hall, has a big, corbel-lintelled fireplace, the lintel renewed in 1989–90.

KNOWESOUTH. *See* p. 475.

LAUDER

A good example of an C18 Scottish burgh. An early royal burgh, its charter renewed in 1502 by King James IV, Lauder still retains the alignment of the long main street, with rigs which run N and S down to back lanes, Castle Wynd (formerly North Backside), and Crofts Road (formerly South Backside). The only industry was agriculture, and Lauder never became more than a centre for the local farming community, and a stop, at a number of inns, on the journey between Edinburgh and Jedburgh. Described as 'plain and dull with a few neat villas and well-built houses' as late as 1901, it remained that way until well into the C20. Now expanding fast to the S and W, its appearance remains neat, no longer dull, but still lacking a little personality.

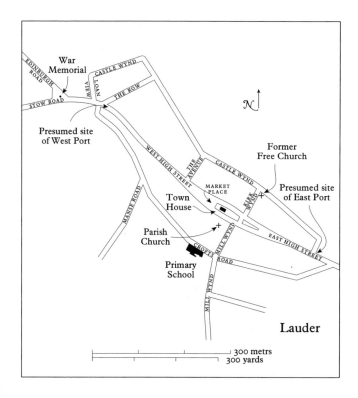

CHURCHES

Former BURGHER CHURCH, The Row. 1795; now a house.

Former FREE CHURCH, Kirk Wynd. 1843. Harled rectangle. Now in industrial use.

18 PARISH CHURCH, Mid Row. First built as a chapel of Chan-nelkirk on a site close to Thirlestane Castle (q.v.).* Permission was given to relocate in 1617, but it was only in 1673 that the Duke of Lauderdale gave orders for this, instructing that the new building should be 'decent and large enough, with a handsom litle steeple'. The architect was *Sir William Bruce*, then working on the castle; the mason was *Alexander Mein* of Newstead, the wright *John Young* and the slater *Gilbert Ander-son*. Work started in 1673 (date inscribed on N gable) and it was largely complete by the end of 1674. Major additions and re-furnishing were made in 1820 by *John Smith*, and *David Bryce* was consulted on further works in 1860. Wooden floors were extended throughout in 1864. There was a general restoration in 1973 by *Neil Jack* of *Miller & Black*.

The plan is a Greek cross, with a central tower carried on four engaged piers at the junction of the arms. Churches laid out to such a plan had been partly foreshadowed before the Reformation, as at Tullibardine (Perth and Kinross) of *c.* 1500, and became more common as laird's aisles were added around rectangular churches with increasing regard to symmetry, as at Thurso (Highland and Islands) and Glencorse (Lothian). Some churches had already been planned from the start with such a plan, as at Fenwick (Ayrshire) and Kirkintilloch (Stir-ling and Central Scotland). But nowhere before Lauder had the spatial equality of the four arms been so clearly expressed, and with such concentrated focus on the central space. Exter-nally, each arm was lit by two tiers of windows in the gable-wall, reflecting the intended provision of lofts within all (but only two may have been initially built). A pair of rectangular windows light the lower level of each of the four gables, while the upper level has a pointed three-light window with inter-secting tracery and a transom, demonstrating that windows of 'ecclesiastical' character were still considered seemly for churches. The skewputts at the base of the N gable have minia-ture obelisk finials, and the other gables may have been simi-larly treated. The tower is square up to the roof ridges, but is then intaken to an octagon, with broaches at the angles and round-headed windows to the cardinal faces; it is capped by a pyramidal roof with a ball finial. In 1820 *John Smith* added porches with crenellated wall-heads in the NW and SE re-entrant angles; as well as covering the ground-floor entrances, these house stairs to the lofts. Since the 1973 restoration the walls have been re-harled, leaving the red sandstone margins and dressings exposed.

Internally there are plastered walls above a boarded dado, and all four arms have plastered ceilings of polygonal profile, while there is a flat ceiling with a central circular opening

* Remains can still be seen 0.8 km NE of Old Thirlestane Castle (p. 723).

within the tower. In the original arrangement, and in keeping with the patron's High Church views, it seems the E arm contained the communion table, though by 1746 that arm was said to have been reduced to use as a joiner's workshop.

Much of the internal furnishing dates from Smith's work of 1820, including the pews, the loft fronts and the pulpit. – BOX PEWS. To a uniform pattern at lower level of all four arms, of 1820. – LOFTS. Fronts of 1820 with panelling, and with armorial achievements of 1973. The Lauderdale Loft in the w arm extends up to the tower piers; the Tweeddale Loft in the E arm also reaches close to the tower piers; the Burgess Loft in the N arm is set back a little; and the Trabrown Loft in the s arm is set well back. – PULPIT. Against the E pier, an elevated octagon with raised and fielded panels, beneath a tester with fretted cornice and concave-sided pyramidal cap. – BAPTISMAL BASIN. On bracket off pulpit steps, dated 1821. – HAT PEGS. Running along sides of all four arms. – COMMUNION TABLE. Post-1944, reduced Gothic. – STAINED GLASS. At upper level N arm, Supper at Emmaus, dedicated 1901, *A. Ballantine and Gardiner*, Edinburgh. – BELL. 1681, recast 1751 and 1834. – MEMORIALS. Around w arm, various memorials to members of the Lauderdale family; N aisle, tablet to Adam Fairholme, white marble scroll by *G. Maile*, London.

CHURCHYARD. Entered through channel-rusticated piers with obelisk pinnacles. HEARSE HOUSE AND VESTRY, by *Thomas Hislop*, 1831, now church hall. Memorials mainly of C19 and C20. Murray of Woodlaw enclosure to s of church, wall with Tuscan pilasters, incorporating earlier gravestone.

Former RELIEF CHURCH, Crofts Road. Built in 1834; now divided into houses. A whinstone rectangle with a slated piend roof.

UNITED ASSOCIATE CHURCH, West High Street. 1841 by *Robert Hall*. Largely demolished.

LAUDER PRIMARY SCHOOL, Croft's Road. By *Berwickshire County Council*, 1960s, incorporating parts of an earlier school by *John Smith*, 1835.

PUBLIC BUILDINGS

TOWN HOUSE, Market Place. A tolbooth has been on this site   93
since at least 1543. Repaired in 1729 by the sixth Earl of Lauderdale, but evidence suggests that it was largely rebuilt *c.* 1773, presumably to the original plan, and incorporating earlier work. Harled rubble of three storeys and pyramidal capped clock tower. The straight forestair has cast-iron railings, a late C19 replacement for a solid stone balustrade. Entrance doorway with a Gibbsian surround; above are two blind oculi. The clock, made by *R. & R. Murray* in 1859, replaced one of 1735 by *John Kirkwood* which was removed to Mellerstain House (q.v.). Two barrel-vaulted prison cells on the ground floor, the court room and council chamber on the first floor.

WAR MEMORIAL, Edinburgh Road. 1923. An octagonal granite shaft on a stepped base surmounted by a lion rampant holding a shield, with cross and dates, 1914–18.

DESCRIPTION

The houses mainly date from the late C18 and C19, and are mostly built to a symmetrical design of two storeys and three bays, with byres to the rear. Some single-storey cottages survive. Most houses were built of sandstone or whinstone rubble and harled; many were formerly thatched. Some villa-style ones in rubble and coursed whinstone exhibit good examples of cherry-caulking.

EDINBURGH ROAD and STOW ROAD lead in from the N and W. At their junction is the War Memorial (*see* above). On the l., LAUDERDALE HOTEL, a late C19 temperance establishment. Gabled, in red sandstone, with some timid Tudor detailing. The interior, remarkably, retains an oakleaf and fruit cornice in the bar, and stained-glass stair window. In THE LOAN, at the top, LEA PARK, a mid-C19 villa in coursed whinstone rubble with long and short quoins. Nos. 8 and 9 have rock-faced margins and angles to the front, but cheaper brick ones at the back and sides; behind is No. 12, a pair of single-storey cottages, probably late C18, the S one an example of a single-cell cottage. At the bottom of the hill the former United Associate Church Manse, *c.* 1841, in coursed whinstone, with a classical doorcase. All that remains of its associated church is a boundary wall. On the N side of the road, LOAN VIEW and No. 68 West High Street is an attractive curved terrace of three cottages. Coming in from the N is THE ROW (Rotten Row), an entrance to Thirlestane Castle (q.v.) prior to 1823. No. 3, late C18 and later, was once single-storey and thatched. The added upper storey overlaid an inglenook fireplace, some traces of which remain inside.

WEST HIGH STREET proper now starts. At No. 61, good cherry-caulked whinstone. No. 43, a six-bay cottage formed from two late C18 single-storey cottages is of particular interest for the survival of a box bed, complete with its top and bottom tracks to take timber sliding doors; a fitted panelled dresser dates from the same period. The byre to the rear has a cobbled floor and drainage channel. Nos. 31–33 and No. 13 were repaired and improved through the National Trust for Scotland's Little Houses Improvement Scheme for Borders Regional Council, *c.* 1986. On the S side, Nos. 22–26, a two-storey and attic terrace, was restored by the Scottish Historic Buildings Trust (*Ben Tindall*, architect), 1989. No. 22 began as a single-bay, two-storey cottage, given a two-storey polygonal-roofed oriel in the late C19. This was removed in an earlier botched repair, and re-created from early photographs. No. 24 has a contemporary shopfront with a shallow bracketed canopy.

MARKET PLACE is Lauder's centre, with on the N side THE AVENUE, the principal approach to Thirlestane Castle from the 1670s until the C19. Some mid-C19 villas on the l. The EAGLE HOTEL, No. 1 Market Place, is a historic inn probably formed from two early C19 houses. Harled with painted margins, it retains some early whinstone rubble stabling on the E side of a rear courtyard. A small pediment with a pointed-arched window adds a hint of architecture. Nos. 3–5 were built in the mid C19 as shops with dwellings above. Coursed cherry-caulked whinstone, and long and short margins to the windows. Inside, the ground floor of No. 3 retains a pair of fluted columns with stylised capitals, and a dog-leg stair with a cast-iron balustrade. Unexpected is a late C19 stained-glass window which portrays Napoleon on horseback within a floral design, and a coat-of-arms and motto HOC SECURIOR, signed *William Gardner*, St Helens. The shop at No. 5 retains its fluted columns. Next, the BLACK BULL HOTEL facing the Town House (*see* Public Buildings, above). Late C18, extended in the C19, and much altered. The two-storey and attic six-bay coaching inn has later wall-head dormers, to the l. an early C19 additional bay with a Palladian window on the ground floor with Gothick astragals in the round head, and a tripartite window with narrow sidelights above. The whole rendered with incised lines to resemble ashlar, and painted sandstone margins. Inside, only the ballroom, with Adamesque plasterwork, survives unaltered. On the s side of Market Place, Nos. 20–24, an unaltered late C18 terrace of two-storey and attic cottages.

MID ROW, extending E from the Town House, mostly dates from the mid C19. One or two examples of gable-ended houses survive, but gone are the forestairs which were a feature of this part of the burgh in the late C18. Opening out of Mid Row to the s is MILL WYND. On the l., the former East United Free Church Manse, built by *John Smith* for Mr Robson, a seceding minister, 1836. Two-storey, and rendered with Tudor detailing. A canted bay to the W may be later; fine stacks of brick chimneys. No. 6 is a good mid-C19 classical villa in coursed cherry-caulked sandstone, with a porch having a large tripartite window with narrow sidelights, and side entrance door. Above, a wide window, and a bracketed pediment framing a lunette. Cast-iron railings with stylised finials front the garden.

Return to EAST HIGH STREET. On the l. KIRK WYND leads to Castle Wynd. At the bottom the former Free Church (*see* Churches, above). Back to the High Street and No. 1, BANK HOUSE. Early C19, doorway with a canopy on ornamental brackets, and flanking tripartite windows with narrow sidelights. On the opposite side of the road, No. 10 is a mid-C19 two-storey, three-bay classical villa. A projecting pilastered entrance bay and moulded cornice, flanked by tripartite windows with narrow sidelights. At the corner with Factor's Park, was the mid-C19 house (Nos. 32 and 34) for the Lauderdale Estate's factor, with a bellcast-roofed square tower in the re-entrant; built into sloping ground with a side gable to the High Street, in which a doorway leads to steps up to its forecourt. The keystone of the doorway is decorated with a tiny cast-iron crest of the Earls of Lauderdale. To Factor's Park, a terrace wall with good cast-iron railing and floral finials. A pilastered and corniced entrance doorway, and an eaves course continuing across both gables. At the bottom of the High Street on the s side, WYNDHEAD FARM may have been the home farm for Thirlestane Castle. The farmhouse (No. 38) has canted tripartite windows, deep overhanging eaves, and horizontal sliding windows in the upper floor of the front elevation. Entrance doorway with a decorative panel set within an elaborate canopy on decorative consoles. Coped square gatepiers. No. 40 was the farm grieve's house. A mid-C19 single-storey and attic cottage, with a half-storey entrance porch with crowstepped gable. Single-storey wing, formerly bothies. Barns to the NE date from early-to-mid C19. Two-storey, seven-bay, and five-bay cartsheds with tall segmental-headed openings and three lower ones.

Return to FACTOR'S PARK, and continue round to CROFTS ROAD and LORD LAUDERDALE SCHOOL (Nos. 7 and 9). Picturesque mid-C19 single-storey school and teacher's house, in coursed whinstone with red sandstone margins, built by the Lauderdale family. Overhanging eaves with exposed rafters. Gabled porches, and mullioned and transomed windows with leaded diamond-paned glazing. Converted to dwelling houses. On the l., Lauder Primary School (*see* above). In Manse Road, THE GLEBE, built in 1812. Two storeys, five bays, and harled white. Slightly advanced end bays with block pediments, and band course incorporating the sills of the first-floor windows. Contemporary steading at the back. Opposite, ALLANBANK HOUSE, early C19 two-storey and attic piend-roofed villa with contemporary(?) single-storey wings on either side. Three-bay S front of buff sandstone with central bay rising to a triangular pediment above a columned porch and tripartite first-floor window. Single-storey LODGE with open canted porch supported on four Tuscan columns. Cast-iron railings with some crocketed finials.

HARRYBURN, Edinburgh Road. Typical three-bay villa, in local dark whinstone. By *John Smith*, 1827, for John Romanes, banker and town clerk of Lauder. Regency-style balconies supported on slim columns added by Smith, 1851. Each side, recessed to the rear, are screen walls surmounted by large classical urns, hiding the single-storey stables, now housing. Formerly detached, the two-storey piend-roofed bachelor wing linked house and stable in the later C19.

    CHUCKIE LODGE, by *John Smith*, 1854, is remarkable. Single-storey, with walls of coursed (river?) pebbles framed in slim sandstone margins. Pierced cast-iron gatepiers with pyramidal caps and finials. Iron gates with anthemion details, the railings having fleur-de-lys heads. – Another LODGE, red sandstone, dated 1894 and monogrammed HB at the entrance from Edinburgh Road.

NORTON, 1.5 km. NE, prominently situated on the W side of the A697. The shell of the former farmhouse, a two-storeyed gable-roofed block of probably late C18 date with a symmetrical three-bay front.

STONE CIRCLE and CAIRNS, Borrowston Rig, 5 km. NE. Situated in open moorland this circle of the second millennium B.C. comprises in excess of thirty small stones no more than 0.6 m. in height, and is laid out in an egg-shaped arrangement measuring 41 m. from ESE to WNW by 36 m. transversely. Lying immediately to the NNW, there is a cairn 14 m. in diameter by 0.6 m. in height, while a second to the S is some 10.5 m. in diameter and has two upright stones of a megalithic setting protruding from its cairn material.

FORT and SETTLEMENT, Haerfaulds. 4.5 km. ENE. At the top of a steep slope above the Blythe Water, this fort measures about 115 m. by 70 m. internally, its wall reduced to a mound of rubble *c.* 5 m. thick. A later settlement of stone-walled round-houses is visible immediately within the interior.

THIRLESTANE CASTLE. *See* p. 716.

WHITSLAID TOWER. *See* p. 760.

LEADERFOOT
5030

An Act of Parliament of 1768 provided for the construction of a road from Lauder to Carter Bar (A68), following the general route of the Roman and medieval roads. The crossing over the Tweed has collected its fair share of impressive bridges and a railway viaduct.

The earliest surviving crossing is DRYGRANGE OLD BRIDGE: by *Alexander Stevens Sen.*, 1778–80. A three-arched stone bridge whose pier foundations are of large hewn stones, joined by cramps, laid directly on the rock. Cutwaters are curved and pointed like the prows of boats, as preferred by French engineers but new to Britain (cf. Hyndford Bridge, Lanarkshire). Parapets are on a rising corbel course and the triangular buttresses terminate in pedestrian refuges. Decorative quatrefoil medallions on the faces of the buttresses, and large recessed circular panels in each spandrel containing classical urns of yellow sandstone. Conical finials at the approaches. Piers strengthened below the water with mass concrete in the 1920s.

Road traffic is now taken by DRYGRANGE BRIDGE, E, of 1971–3 by *Sir Alexander Gibb & Partners*. Built by *Miller Construction (Northern) Ltd*; steelwork by *Clarke Chapman Ltd* (*Sir William Arrol Branch*). A composite structure of reinforced concrete and steel box girders, prefabricated and assembled on site. The slight longitudinal curve was obtained by providing skew ends to the prefabricated units. W is the LEADERFOOT VIADUCT by *Charles Jopp*, *Wylie & Peddie*, 1865, for the Berwickshire Railway (closed 1948). A striking structure of nineteen arches of 13.1 m. (42.9 ft) span, built of brick with abutments, piers and walls of rustic-faced sandstone. The height from the river to the soffit of the arches is 35.5 m. (116.5 ft). Several tiers and buttresses have been added to the valley sides. Repaired by *Church Conservation Ltd*, 1994, and opened as a walkway.

LEADERFOOT BRIDGE. 0.4 km. E across the Leader Water. Mid-C19. Narrow, slightly hump-backed, of two arches. Central V-splayed cutwater, dressed stone rings and rubble spandrels.

LEADERVALE HOUSE
5030
1.7 km. NW of Earlston

A delightful Regency villa on the W bank of the Leader Water. A 72 piend-roofed square on a raised basement, of harled rubble lined out to resemble ashlar, with sandstone margins and quoins. Wall-head balustrade replaced in iron in the 1940s. Three bays on the s elevation and the bowed E and W elevations; the recessed service courtyard on the N side was sensitively filled in with a bowed addition by *William Grime*, 1999.

The s façade has a wide band course between basement and ground floor, the pilaster strips at the angles above the band course continued below as rusticated quoins. Bowed Ionic portico approached by a wide fan-shaped flight of steps with cast-iron balustrades. The flanking bays each have a tripartite window with stone mullions treated as columns; below is a blind balustrade with fluted side panels. This detail is similar to the wings of Carolside (q.v.), on whose estate the house stood, suggesting the same architect. Similar too is the oval hall with a Corinthian screen at its N end; four niches, a ceiling rose and enriched cornice. The dining room and drawing room both have bowed ends and simple enriched cornices. Two good chimneypieces, one of white marble with fluted Ionic columns topped by a figure holding a musical instrument, and central panel of huntress and her dog, the other timber and gesso, the panel with 'Lady with Anchor' pattern surrounded by seashells and seaweed fronds. – WALLED GARDEN. Early C19(?). – Mid-C19 LODGE with projecting finialled gable.

THE LEES

0.8 km. SW of Coldstream

The excellent classical house built here *c.* 1770 for Edward Marjoribanks in a beautiful wooded park bordering the River Tweed was demolished 1980. The central bow of its E front, ornamented with Ionic pilasters, was ingeniously adapted by *Nicholas Groves-Raines* as half of a circular house; perfect in such an idyllic setting. The new parts are rendered brick with sandstone margins. The original Doric portico was also reused. Two pavilions added in 1988 by the same architect.

Late C18 estate buildings also survive, including a subterranean domed ICE HOUSE with a curved approach to the entrance door. Rustic bracketed cornice. – Elegant octagonal Doric TEMPLE, with columns on panelled pedestals linked by an entablature and bellcast roof with finial. – STABLES. Converted to housing. Courtyard range in rubble with sandstone dressings. The principal elevation is surmounted by a four-stage battlemented tower, the third stage with blind quatrefoils, the later top stage with oculi and a pyramidal roof. – LODGE, Kelso Road. Single-storey, the doorpiece with coupled Ionic half-columns and entablature. Piended roof with dentilled eaves course. Gatepiers with oval panels.

LEGERWOOD

A small village with church and manse, and 1.2 km. W a farm, school and several small cottages.

PARISH CHURCH. After Stobo (q.v.), this is the most complete Romanesque parish church in the Borders. A priest is on record in 1127, and on stylistic evidence, the church must have been built around the second quarter of the C12. It had a two-compartment plan, a square chancel and rectangular nave, to which no later medieval additions were made. After the Reformation the chancel was walled off and reduced in height for use as a burial enclosure. There were repairs to the nave in 1717 (inscription on w wall) and 1804 (inscription on s wall). A lateral 'aisle' was added N of the nave, creating a T-plan, and with a vestry at its outer end; this aisle is said to date from 1880, though it may be basically of the C18. In 1898–9 the chancel was restored for W. van Vlack Lidgerwood (commemorated on wall plaque) by *Hardy & Wight*, and a s porch was added.

Built throughout of red sandstone, the widely occuring cubical blocks indicate that much of the masonry is still of the C12. But much reconstruction has taken place, particularly at the quoins, where there are raised margins to both the nave and N aisle, and around the window openings. The chancel has narrow arched windows to E, S and N that are essentially C12, and an oculus in the E gable of 1899; the nave has C19 single or paired arched windows along the s wall and a wheel window in the w wall. The s and N chancel wall-heads have corbel tables of 1898–9. The w gable has a rectangular birdcage belfry.

Internally, the finest feature is the chancel arch; the responds have a half-round engaged shaft to the axial order, flanked by engaged nook-shafts. The caps of the s respond are cushions; those of the N respond are cushions, scallops and volutes. There is chip carving to the abaci, to the string course that extends across the wall from the abaci, and to some of the capitals. Within the chancel the widely splayed rear arches of the narrow windows have been restored. The most intriguing feature of the chancel is the single shaft in each corner, now carrying restored capitals – is it possible vaulting was contemplated? There is an aumbry in the N wall. The nave and aisle have boarded ceilings of polygonal section.

COMMUNION TABLE, within chancel, 1899. – Polygonal PULPIT. Re-set against nave s wall, Romanesque Revival. – STAINED GLASS. E gable, roundel of Light of the World by *A. Ballantine & Gardiner*; nave s wall, E window, the Good Shepherd, *c.* 1899. – PAINTED DECORATION. Slight traces in the chancel, especially at the back of the aumbry in the N wall. – CARVED FRAGMENTS, built into the N wall of the chancel, one with interlaced ornament, another with part of a Corinthian cap(?). – STANDING MONUMENT. Chancel E wall, dating from when the chancel was used as burial aisle. Imposing Baroque aedicule with fluted Ionic columns and substantial entablature and pediment. In memory of John Ker of Moristoun, †1691, and his wife Grissell, †1748. (Grissell's successful effort to save her father, Sir John Cochrane, from execution by robbing the carrier who bore her father's death warrant is briefly referred to.) – SUNDIAL, embodied at sw angle nave, dated 1689. – STONE BENCH, against w wall, handsomely carved back on a massive Romanesque-style base, in memory of W. Selby Tulloch, †1988.

CHURCHYARD. Mainly C18 and C19 memorials. One table tomb commemorates the Rev. William Calderwood, †1709, periodically minister during the troubled times between 1655 and his death.

Former MANSE (The Glebe House). Built 1750, repaired 1812. Court of contemporary steadings.

SCHOOL. Converted to dwelling. Two-storey schoolhouse, early C19(?), with a mid-C19 T-plan schoolroom; moulded margins, kneelers, and some lying-pane glazing.

LEGERWOOD HOUSE. The farm was laid out c. 1805, the house built c. 1808. Two storeys, three bays, in red sandstone with cream dressings. Advanced centre bay with pediment and oculus. Later attic dormers and addition. Good steadings and barns.

CORSBIE TOWER. *See* p. 193.

CORSBIE TOWER. *See* p. 193.

3040

LEITHEN LODGE
6.4 km. N of Innerleithen

A splendid house set deep in the Moorfoot hills. The early C19 Leithenhopes was bought in 1852 by the civil engineer *John Miller* (of *Grainger & Miller*) who considerably extended the house S. In 1885–7 George Miller Cunningham employed *A.G. Sydney Mitchell* to design a new SE wing, for guest accommodation, billiard room, gun room etc., and remodel the house in the style of a mid-to-late C17 laird's house, appropriate to its site and use. *Robert Mathison* was the contractor. Restored in the early 1990s, after many years of neglect, by *Hugh Ross* for David Lumsden.

Mitchell's house is harled and painted yellow, contrasting with Corsehill red sandstone dressings and red Brosely tiles. U-plan symmetrical S front, with a recessed centre section, a rubble-built conical roofed stair-tower to the r., on the l. an asymmetrical gable. The remainder is filled with a first-floor conservatory veranda with good cast-iron brattishing; the only straight link between the family part of the house and the billiard room in Mitchell's SE wing. Below is an open-pedimented timber porch on Jacobean columns. The entrance doorway to the l., at the other end is a door into the wing for shooters and fishers with dirty boots. Each side of the court a crowstepped gable contains a two-storey canted bay, the first floors corbelled out; a neat way of adding to the existing W bay. Two irregular gabled bays on the W elevation, that to r. recessed with tall stair windows, to the S a projecting timber-balustraded balcony with lean-to tiled roof, formerly with a timber garden stair. Offices at the N end with an ogival-roofed bellcote on the gable end.

The long E elevation has a tall narrow slightly projecting gable, incorporating a classical Serlian ARCHWAY dated 1684. This was moved here in 1992 from the site of Lochend House (Lothian), and looks rather incongruous. Set on a high plinth, the lower parts of the jambs have niches flanked by pedestalled fluted pilasters. Slightly advanced pedimented portico, with carved ornament in the spandrels, and a dated cartouche in the tympanum. A Doric architrave ties the parts together. The arch links to the mostly mid-C19 L-plan stable and hay loft range, given a new look by Mitchell, including a large ogee-capped ventilator. In the NW corner of the courtyard is the original piend-roofed two-storey, four-bay house, as remodelled in the mid C19. Swept eaves, central chimney and harled porch.

INTERIOR. Completely redecorated in Scottish Renaissance style with Arts and Crafts detailing, much of it designed by Mitchell, but with some later 'antique' enhancements by Hugh Ross. The plasterwork, by *L. Grandison & Son*, was carried out in a range of styles to reflect the various functions of the rooms. The hall with wainscot panelling, and an arcaded balcony landing, the balustrade with twisted balusters, kept aloft by carved Jacobean balusters. Canopied red sandstone chimneypiece. A well stair, on the W side, has ornate twisted balusters and Jacobean newel posts; the ribbed barrel-vaulted ceiling dates from the 1990s. Classical Scottish C17 dining room; the coved ceiling and columns at the N end added in the 1990s. The billiard room, latterly music room, has an inglenook fireplace in a segmentally arched recess with marble chimneypiece. Arcaded plasterwork frieze, and a high barrel-vaulted ceiling with decorated plaster ribs, ornamented with a continuous thistle design. Mural paintings of stylised views, mostly of the estate, in the manner of Robert Adam, by *Alastair Macleod*, 1991. The drawing room has Adamesque decoration with interesting canopied wall recesses flanked by glazed cupboards. On the S side access to the conservatory, with encaustic tiles and cast-iron plant stands.

BRIDGE over the Leithen Water. Picturesque mid-C19 hump-back crossing with cutwater buttresses to centre piers. A course of vertical masonry below the upper coping apparently hides pipes carrying water to the house from a reservoir. – Late-C17 or early C18 SUNDIAL. Lectern shape with a copper gnomon and irregularly shaped cup dials to sides. – Crowstepgabled POWER HOUSE with swept dormerheads.

LEITHOLM

7040

A small village on the former turnpike road from Kelso to Swinton. Only a church, an inn, and a single street of unpretentious late C18–C20 cottages.

LEITHOLM CHURCH, Church Lane. A piend-roofed preaching box built in 1835 for an Original Secession Congregation. Two bays, with a SW gabled entrance porch (1872), surmounted by a bellcote (1874). Coursed rubble with whinstone dressings. An inscribed memorial panel on the bellcote. The U-plan galleried interior was installed in 1877. The pulpit, communion table and organ came from the Rodger Memorial Church, Coldstream, in 1950, and the pews from St Cuthbert's Church, Coldstream, in 1968.

WAR MEMORIAL. Celtic cross on a two-tier boulder base. *c.* 1918.

WEST LEITHOLM BRIDGE over the Lambden Burn. Single-arch, hump-backed with rubble walls, dressed voussoirs with raised keystones inscribed AD 1783(?). Corbelled parapets and splayed approaches ending in squat circular-plan piers.

DESCRIPTION. At the E end of the village is the picturesque mid-C19 BUCHTRIG COTTAGE (former private school) and in the centre the PLOUGH HOTEL of c. 1800, with a two-storey central block and single-storey wings. Harled white with black-painted margins. Gabled wings at the rear form a courtyard. The VILLAGE HALL, N side of the street, built c. 1910, is well detailed in red brick.

ANTON'S HILL. See p. 105.

BELCHESTER HOUSE. See p. 118.

BUGHTRIG HOUSE. See p. 144.

KAMES HOUSE. See p. 435.

STAINRIGG HOUSE. See p. 696.

7030

LEMPITLAW

CHURCHYARD. HOGBACK STONE, probably C12, excavated in 1969, tegulation down one side. – Several attractive C17, C18 and C19 memorials, one with a relief carving of Pegasus.

8040

LENNEL

A former village on the N bank of the River Tweed, destroyed by the English on their predatory incursions. Some C18 cottages, mostly altered.

OLD PARISH CHURCH, 0.6km. E. Granted to Coldstream Nunnery in the 1160s, abandoned when the parish was relocated to Coldstream in 1705. It appears to have been a two-cell structure, and references to repairs in 1704 suggest it was partly vaulted. The heavily overgrown W gable has two levels of rectangular windows presumably to light the areas above and below a post-Reformation loft; the rebuilt N and S walls survive chiefly where monuments have been built against them. Within the W end a mort-house of 1821. – CHURCH-YARD, some C18 memorials and table tombs, but mainly C19 headstones. – MORT-SAFES, sunk into ground to NE of church, iron-plated and coffin-shaped, decaying rapidly.

LAINDENN was originally at least two cottages. Mid-C18, with its original thackstane but now pantiled and harled with brownish-red sandstone margins. Late C19 porch with tree trunk supports, and a picturesque bracketed oriel window in the S gable. A large arched stone fireplace inside.

LENNEL HOUSE

Designed c. 1820 by *John Paterson*, one-time clerk to the Adam brothers, for the eighth Earl of Haddington. A classical villa, built of creamy yellow ashlar, mostly with diagonal droving. The composition was ingenious; V-shaped E part with a domed bow at the apex. Filling the open centre of the V, a triangular block, its long w front of seven bays. Across the outer ends of the two-bay wings of the V and the w block, three bay N and s wings, which projected one bay to the w. No embellishment except for a band course under the first floor and a Doric portico at the centre of the w front. An addition on the N side, set back from the e front, was built *c.* 1855.

In 1904–5 *Peddie & Washington Browne* were employed by the estate's new owner, Captain Walter Waring, to remodel and extend the house, the stonework of the additions impeccably matched to the existing. They added a bow to each wing of the V and lengthened the N and s wings by one bay to the w, erecting a porch (the new principal entrance) at the centre of the s wing. At the same time they rebuilt the w block's front further w and removed its portico. Further alterations were made *c.* 1955 by *Claud Phillimore & Aubrey Jenkins* who reinstated Paterson's portico at the centre of the w front, removed the Edwardian s porch and in its place inserted a trio of French windows, the centre one with a dummy fanlight.

The original plan of the principal floor showed Paterson's predilection for oval and circular rooms. Each side of the entrance lobby was a small apsidal-ended room, and tightly curved geometric stairs, one either side of the principal rooms. This inconveniently planned interior was seemingly a bit too cosy to suit Waring who had married the eldest daughter of the tenth Marquess of Tweeddale and anticipated a grander lifestyle. Washington Browne's s entrance opened instead into a long entrance hall, with a longitudinal corridor passing through a staircase hall with a T-plan stair of imperial size with a strapwork Jacobean balustrade. All that remained of Paterson's work were the rectangular dining and drawing rooms with a circular room in between, on the e front.

The approach to the house is through a forecourt. On the N side are STABLES, now accommodation, of five bays with slightly advanced ends. Pedimented doorpiece. On the s side of the courts an L-plan LODGE, *c.* 1820, with a pedimented porch. Droved ashlar, moulded cornice. Well-detailed late-C20 extension. Double gates from the road (centre capped piers set back probably in the early C20). – NW of the house are further STABLES by *Peddie & Washington Browne,* 1904–5. Red-tiled roof and overhanging eaves with exposed rafters. Pedimented pend, and a long road elevation with a row of pedimented dormers.

LESSUDDEN HOUSE

0.5 km. NE of St. Boswells

5030

Possibly built by a member of the Plummer family *c.* 1600, Lessudden was acquired *c.* 1664 by Walter Scott of Raeburn. Between them Walter (†*c.* 1693) and his son, William (†1699) considerably remodelled the house, which was again enlarged during the following century. Further improvements were made during the C19, and in 1967–9 *Schomberg Scott & R. McInver* completed yet another scheme of alteration. All these changes have left their mark on the fabric without altogether extinguishing its original character as a semi-defensive house of modest size.

The early house seems to have been an L-plan block of three storeys and a garret measuring 11.4m. from W to E by 5.0m. transversely with an oblong stair wing (3.3 by 2.0m.) at the SE corner and a smaller, semicircular stair-turret on the N side. To this core was added in the late C17 a three-storey E wing which was itself subsequently extended N, possibly by *John & Thomas Smith* in 1814 or 1837. During the C18 the main block was also extended W by the addition of a two-storey wing. This, too, was subsequently extended further W and S by the erection of a kitchen and other offices. The masonry is of harled rubble with dressings mainly of red and buff-coloured sandstone quarried locally. Most of the windows have quirked edge-rolls or some other variety of roll moulding, those of the C18 being noticeably thinner than the earlier ones. Looking rather out of place in the gable of the W wing is a circular window with blind Gothic tracery of *roue tournante* form, perhaps a trophy from the nearby ruins of Dryburgh Abbey (q.v.). Most of the gables are crowstepped with moulded skewputts, and two of the chimneys have moulded copings.

The N FRONT is dominated by the massive, stepped chimney of the hall and its adjacent stair-turret, both projecting well forward of the main wall face. The grouping recalls that at Ferniehirst Castle (q.v.), but here stack and stair are designed as a single unit. The turret gable is shaped to the curve of the wall below, as in the neighbouring tower house of Littledean (q.v.). The wall-head is crowned by an ovolo-moulded eaves cornice from which the roof rises sheer to the ridge. The principal entrance, formerly on the S, was replaced in 1967–9 by a new N doorway, approached by a stair. Bolection-moulded surround, wrought-iron handrail and heraldry commemorating Sir Tresham and Lady Lever.

The S FRONT and SE STAIR WING have seen even more radical changes. Prior to 1967–9 the wall-head was surmounted by a corbelled parapet, apparently added in the C19 in a misguided attempt to baronialise the house. Either then, or perhaps earlier, most of the second floor of the main block on this side was rebuilt above a splayed inset course. The second floor of the stair wing seems to have been offset on individual stone corbels from the beginning, although the buttresses below appear to be C19 additions. There has probably always been an entrance at the foot of the wing, but the present lug-moulded doorcase presumably dates from the late C17 rebuilding of the staircase. The obliquely aligned figure-of-eight-shaped gun loop in the re-entrant angle appears to be a relic of the original security arrangements, while the adjacent roll-moulded doorway in the main block (reopened 1967–9) is probably a contemporary entrance to the cellarage. The door has a wrought-iron knocker (previously on the stair door?) dated 1685 with the initials of William Scott, second of Raeburn, and his wife, Anna. Between the two big first-floor windows is a worn panel, said to be dated 1666, displaying the arms of the Scotts of Raeburn.

INTERIOR. The early house evidently had a vaulted cellarage with two main residential floors above, each probably containing a hall and chamber. At second-floor level there would also have been a smaller chamber in the SE wing, which probably housed a scale stair ascending to the first floor only, access to the upper levels being obtained from the newel stair on the N side, the lowest flight of which would have functioned as a service stair. The late C17 alterations seem to have involved the replanning of both residential floors to provide four main chambers at each level, the principal ones on the first floor. The main outlines of this arrangement persisted until 1967–9, when a family dining room and breakfast room were formed on the ground floor. A key element in the late C17 remodelling was the insertion of a stylish new staircase in the SE wing to serve all floors. The present N entrance opens into a hall; to the r. the dining room, with a bolection-moulded chimneypiece of 1967–9 probably replacing a late C18 kitchen fireplace. Traces can be seen of the original barrel vault, while the vault of the late C17 E wing remains intact. The STAIRCASE of c. 1685 is of open-well construction, with a massive carved balustrade and handrail and moulded treads. This is a type usually found only in the grandest houses – the model may have been the great stair of c. 1675 at Holyroodhouse, Edinburgh – but here the stair is wedged into a space only 2.6 m. square, making the access distinctly cramped. Even more unexpected, and giving the construction a perhaps unintended Dutch flavour, is the screen of Tuscan columns which supports the first-floor landing. Here the stair changes from stone to timber, the upper flights being of oak; a similar staircase at the nearby Fairnington House (q.v.) is built entirely of timber.

As remodelled in the late C17, the FIRST FLOOR of the main block probably comprised a dining room, bedchamber and closet, with a parlour in the E wing. The subsequent enlargement of the E wing and the addition of a W wing enabled a more spacious layout to be introduced, which in 1842 comprised a large drawing room (E wing), with en-suite book room, followed by a dining room, bedroom (all in the main block) and dressing room (W wing). The drawing room was again remodelled in the late C19 or early C20, when the plaster ceiling cornice, decorated with the bearings of the Scotts of Raeburn, was probably inserted. The late C17 bolection-moulded chimneypiece was presumably moved to its present position when the room was enlarged. The former dining room (now sitting room) and bedroom in the main block are handsome rooms which retain their late C17 panelling and bolection-moulded chimneypieces flanked by pilasters – Corinthian in the dining room and Ionic in the bedroom – and moulded ceiling cornices. The rather rustic joinery details are similar to those in the state rooms at Traquair House (q.v.), as refurbished c. 1700. Some C17 work also survives on the second floor. The garret is part open to the roof, which appears to preserve part of its original collar and tie-beam framework.

MAUSOLEUM of the Scotts of Raeburn, c. 50 m. N. Rubble-built rectangular structure with raised margins at the angles. Arched SW entrance with moulded stones alternating with block rustication and a keystone dated 1684, though it seems unlikely that the building in its present form dates from before the later C18. The interior has plastered walls and a plaster ceiling of four-centred profile, all with masonry lining. Memorials around the walls. – Nearby is an attractive circular DOVECOT of c. 1800 with a hoodmoulded doorway and quatrefoil entry port; the roof was renewed in 1845.

LIDDEL CASTLE see CASTLETON

4070

LIDDELBANK HOUSE
6.2 km. S of Ettleton

Built by Sheriff William Oliver of Dinlabyre in the early C19 in wooded policies high above the Liddel Water. Two and three storeys in squared and coursed rubble with polished margins, the sides in snecked rubble. Piend roof framed by tall chimneystacks; overhanging eaves and cavetto cornice. A double-bowed, three-bay centre block, with a wide pilastered and pedimented doorcase. Lower two-bay wings. Partially built into the hillside at the rear, with a projecting full-height semi-circular stair tower. One room deep with a central hall corridor running from the front to the staircase.

5020

LILLIESLEAF

A picturesquely sited village on the spine of a ridge. Chiefly one long, straggling narrow street, with houses on both sides. Considered in the mid C19 to be 'of poor description', with the exception of the manse, public houses, joiner's workshop and smithy.

PARISH CHURCH, E of the village amid open fields. The church belonged to the bishops of Glasgow by 1170. Fragments of the medieval building may survive in a burial enclosure in the churchyard, S of its successor. The earliest part of the church is of 1771, and now forms the NE and SW 'transepts' of a cruciform structure. The 'nave', projecting to the NW, was part of a major enlargement of 1882–3 by *James C. Walker* of Edinburgh. At the same time a three-storey crenellated tower-porch and a vestibule were added between the new nave and what had become the SW transept, and a second porch, vestibule and vestry were added on the opposite side, between the nave and NE transept. A final addition of 1909–10, by *J. P. Alison* of Hawick, was an apse with small lateral offshoots on the SE side of the C18 church, creating a cruciform plan. The 1771 building is of squared rubble, some possibly reused from its medieval predecessor, with roughly droved quoins. Its round-arched windows set the theme for all later fenestration; one of the sills has the re-cut date 1771. It has a bellcote on one gable and a ball finial on the other. The 1882–3 additions are of whinstone rubble with ashlar dressings. The apse, in stripped-down Romanesque, is of squared rubble with ashlar dressings.

Internally the nave floor slopes to the SE, towards the triple arches of the apse and flanking offshoots; these three arches reflect the smaller triple windows in the NW wall. – COMMUNION TABLE, PULPIT and CHAIRS, all 1910 in subdued Arts and Crafts idiom. – FONT, medieval, a roughly cut cylinder. – STAINED GLASS. In apse: Good Samaritan, Good Shepherd, Christ in House of his Parents, 1910, *William Wilson*. – MONUMENTS. In SW transept several monuments to ministers; in NW transept, memorial to Charles Russell Currie, †1855, a mourning maiden places a branch over the plaque. – SUNDIAL, reset in SE wall, dated 1642.

CHURCHYARD. Three substantial walled burial enclosures; that for the Riddell family containing some C17 memorials, may incorporate fragments of the medieval church. The churchyard itself has mainly C18 and C19 memorials.

Former UNITED PRESBYTERIAN CHURCH. Now a store. 1891. A small rectangle of squared red sandstone rubble with buff-coloured ashlar dressings; low S vestry block. The N front has buttresses set in from the edges while the outer parts of the roof are hipped on each side of the central gable. Above a central pointed doorway is a three-light rectilinear-traceried window; on each side of the doorway is a cinquefoil lancet.

DESCRIPTION. Starting at the E end of the village, on the r. is the former MANSE (Lilliesleaf House) in a large walled garden, by *John Smith*, 1819. Harled, with a pilastered doorway and entablature, and two canted dormers. Entrance porch on the N side, c. 1970s. Later addition. Some former steadings and stables. A carved stone over a doorway is inscribed MWW (Mr William Wilkie) MIC (Mr John Chisholme) over RK, EW, presumably their respective wives, 1642, 1686. Built into a coachhouse is the remains of a sundial inscribed MMC (Mr Matthew Couper), minister 1691–4. Opposite, a pair of Tudor farm cottages, c. 1864. Next on the S side, a picturesque harled range of buildings (EASTER COTTAGE, BARNLEE and ELWIN), said to be weavers' cottages; the cores probably late C18, with mid-C19 alterations. Easter Cottage is least altered, with three charming diminutive wall-head dormers with pointed windows in deep openings; ball finials top the outer ones, an obelisk in the centre. The WAR MEMORIAL follows, c. 1920. A Celtic cross incorporating a sword, and a heraldic shield in the cross-head.

Further on is WESTWOOD, originally the Black Bull Inn, the earliest of the village pubs. Late C18 with later alterations. The former entrance remains, marooned at first-floor level with a decorative frieze, carved with a garland, and cornice, still *in situ*. Then the early-to-mid-C19 PLOUGH INN, harled with sandstone margins. Although much altered it still has a cast-iron gas lamp standard at the front door. On the N side, a complex including the CURRIE MEMORIAL HALL, built 1891, in memory of William Currie (†1889). Slightly

Tudorish, in coursed sandstone with rough sandstone margins. Good ironwork finials. To the W, the OLD SCHOOL HOUSE, two-storey with bargeboarded gables, c. 1860. The undistinguished PRIMARY SCHOOL, 1962, replaced the 1860 Currie Female School using only parts of the original building.

ALEWATER HOUSE 1.2 km. N. Built and endowed in 1881 for destitute and deserving widows or daughters of ministers and farmers, and aged servants. Six houses each with two rooms, scullery and garden. Converted to a single dwelling c. 1971. A picturesque symmetrical W front, the gabled centre flanked by lower gabled wings. Panels in each gable are inscribed with Biblical texts mindful of the foundation's intentions. Decorative E porch, the canopy supported by heavily carved brackets.

ALERIGG. *See* p. 100.

BEWLIE HOUSE. *See* p. 121.

CAVERS CARRE. *See* p. 158.

LINTHILL HOUSE. *See* p. 501.

RAWFLAT. *See* p. 645.

RIDDELL. *See* p. 647.

4030

LINDEAN

Lindean was perhaps the site of the Tironensian Abbey of Selkirk, before its move to Kelso; the parish was annexed to Kelso in the C12. The CHURCH was abandoned for worship in 1586. The much-rebuilt lower walls of the rectangular building stand to about 1 m., revetting the ramped surrounding ground. A shallow tomb(?) recess on the N side of the chancel holds a C17 LEDGER SLAB to a member of the Ker family. Evidence of a doorway towards the W end of the S wall.

6010

LINTALEE HOUSE

2.5 km. S of Jedburgh

A Classical villa, of *c.* 1815 for Major Archibald Oliver, of the East India Company, built by the proprietor the Marquess of Lothian. Two-storey and basement, in pale cream sandstone with a piended and platformed roof. Full-height shallow bows. Extended 1903 by *Peddie & Washington Browne*, who altered the interior in simple Edwardian Baroque style. – Unusual polygonal plan WALLED GARDEN.

The house occupies the site of a FORT. This was the encampment, or 'fayr maner', constructed by Sir James Douglas in 1317 to guard the Border against English incursions. It comprises a quadrilateral area *c.* 1.8 ha. in extent, bounded by a massive ditch drawn across the neck of a natural promontory, which falls steeply to the Jed Water and one of its tributary burns on the other three sides. The ditch has an average width of about 7.5 m. and a present depth of 1.0 m., while the outer rampart has a maximum height of 1.5 m. and the inner one of 5.5 m. Crowned with palisades and equipped with fortified gateways, these defences would have presented a formidable obstacle.

LINTHILL   9060
1.5 km. SW of Eyemouth

A C17 laird's residence of the Home family. William Home of
Linthill is on record in the 1630s and either he, or his son Alexander, sheriff depute of Berwickshire, probably built the present
house.

A plain, L-plan block of three storeys and a garret with a square
stair-tower in the re-entrant angle. Harled rubble masonry
with dressed sandstone margins, most of the early openings
having rounded arrises; the fenestration of the two principal
floors is near-symmetrical. Crowstepped gables with cavetto-
moulded skewputts. The main entrance was probably at the
foot of the stair-tower, where there is now a later doorway carrying an inscription commemorating the restoration of the
house in 1969. Well before this, however, a new first-floor
entrance approached by a stone forestair had been formed near
the centre of the principal (SE) front. As first built the house
probably comprised an unvaulted cellarage with a kitchen at
the SW end of the main block, two main dwelling floors and
an attic. The stone, scale-and-platt stair evidently served all
floors, as it still does today. – Early C19 OFFICES with an
arched and pedimented central bay.

LINTHILL HOUSE   9060
2 km. NE of Lilliesleaf

Built before the end of the C18, by descendants of the Rev.
William Hunter (†1736), succeeding a house called Union Hall
on the S side of the Ale Water. Three bays, Classical, with two
flanking wings set back; the E wing is early C19 and extends to
the N, the W one is later with a bay window. Harled with red
sandstone dressings. Venetian windows each side of the S
entrance, which is masked by a later pedimented Tuscan porch,
perhaps c. 1864, which may also be the date of the balustraded
parapet. Much-altered N side, but still retaining a mid-C19
wide archway to a court. Extensively altered inside by *John
Watherston & Sons*, 1924. They provided the spacious panelled
hall and staircase. Louis XV-style decoration in a drawing
room in the W wing.

STABLES, S of the house. Mid-C19 courtyard range in whinstone rubble with red sandstone margins. Nine-bay N front,
the centre with a high, wide carriage pend, over which is a pediment. On each side an oculus, the one to the l. is boarded and
painted with an eye outlined in white; it opens to allow pigeons
into nest boxes. – Octagonal corniced GATEPIERS, c. 1835. The
frieze of one has vertical droving like fine fluting, a carved
bearded head on the N side.

WALLED GARDEN. Harl-pointed rubble walls, probably late
C18 with extensions. Late C19 *Mackenzie & Moncur* conservatory and greenhouse. On the N side of the N wall are a series
of circular projections with coped tops, some of which are
removeable. Were these used for primitive heating? A decorative cast-iron gate in the W wall with a Tuscan columned and
pedimented portico from the demolished W lodge. – Mid-C19

GARDENER'S HOUSE. – BRIDGE across the Ale Water. Single-span, rubble with sandstone cope. Probably *John Smith*, c. 1835.

LINTHILL BRIDGE, SW of the house, c. 1864. An ornamental iron suspension bridge. Classically detailed balustrades with scrolls.

9020   LINTON

The village situated by Linton Loch has largely disappeared and little remains of Linton Tower, a medieval residence of the Somervilles.

12 PARISH CHURCH. C12, and along with Stobo, Legerwood and Old Cambus, one of the most significant Romanesque churches in the Borders. Although low in profile, it is a prominent landmark, occupying the summit of a mounded churchyard. It was probably set out from the start with two rectangular compartments; stretches of chamfered base course extend around the E and N walls of the chancel and at the E and W ends of the N nave wall. It has been argued there was originally an E apse, though the Romanesque character of the E wall base course suggests this is unlikely. There are extensive areas of cubical masonry, some of which is probably reused. Two animal-head corbels, one in the porch, the other (heavily restored) in the chancel, were presumably part of a wall-head corbel table. The most important survivor of the C12 building is a carved tympanum, presumably cut for the S doorway. This tympanum (reset in the S porch in 1858, and now almost invisible beneath Perspex), with its spirited depiction of St George slaying the Dragon (?), and with further carvings along the lower border, is unique in Scotland. However, related iconography is found on tympana elsewhere, as in south-western England (e.g. Brinsop, Herefordshire) and western France (as at Parthenay-le-Vieux), and it may be suspected that one of the Somerville patrons of the parish brought masons up to Scotland from the family's estates in the English Midlands. A later patron, Thomas, Lord Somerville, carried out works on the chancel in 1424 or 1426, possibly including the addition of a sacristy, since the doorway into the present vestry incorporates two late medieval double-chamfered jamb stones.

There were major post-Reformation repairs in 1616, and in 1754 (by when it had probably been adapted as a laird's 'aisle') the chancel was shortened. Following the collapse of the W gable in 1774, the nave was in turn truncated by about 1.5 m., and the birdcage bellcote from that gable was reconstructed on the E gable. There were further works in 1784, by *Andrew Ker*, mason, and *John Fox*, wright, and yet more in 1813, when the S wall was demolished and rebuilt by *James Hay*. In 1857–8, in a more medievalist spirit, *John Smith* inserted new windows and added the S porch, relocating the Romanesque tympanum within its outer arch. A more scholarly restoration was undertaken by *P. Macgregor Chalmers* in 1910–12, when the E arm was restored to its original length, apparently on the original base course, and re-furnished as a chancel. At the same time a chancel arch in a Scottish late Gothic idiom was constructed, a N vestry was added, possibly on the site of a late medieval sacristy, and the bellcote was moved back to the W gable, but the nave was not extended to its pre-1774 length.

The N wall is windowless. On the S side yellow masonry paint covers the aggressively Romanesque detailing of the S porch, the two paired windows in the nave and the chancel doorway, all of 1857–8. The 1910–12 work in the chancel inserted flat-headed windows, of one light E of the doorway, and of four lights to its W. The pointed-arched three-light traceried E window has a pair of quatrefoils at its head. Internally the chancel has a ribbed barrel ceiling, and the nave an arch-braced open-timber roof.

FURNISHINGS. – COMMUNION TABLE, 1912. – CHOIR STALLS, with reused C18 timber panelling from the Clifton Hall Loft originally in the chancel. On each side are stall fronts with raised and fielded panels; on the N side the back panelling has Ionic pilasters at each end of four raised and fielded panels. – FONT. Romanesque, returned to the church in 1868 and re-set on modern base at the NE corner of the nave, circular with scalloped pattern around bowl. – POOR BOX and IRON-BOUND CHEST, on S side chancel. – STAINED GLASS. E wall, Resurrection, *A.L. Russell*, 1915. Chancel, S side, E: Simeon, *Douglas Strachan*, post-1898; W: St Christopher, loaves and fishes, Good Samaritan, Washing of Feet, *Douglas Strachan*, 1936. – GRAVE SLAB, at NE corner chancel, with what appears to be a raised cross-shaft flanked by chevron decoration, C12? – CARVED TYMPANUM, reset above vestry entrance, with arms of Walter Douglas, minister 1698–1727. – MEMORIALS. Chancel S side, Robert Kerr Elliot, †1873, Romanesque aedicule. Nave N wall, reset C18 gravestone with three-quarter portrait of man reading book, above memorial plaque to Major-General David Walker, †1840, and other members of that family. – MONUMENTS. Several re-set in external walls of the church. Chancel N side, small medieval(?) stone with incised dagger. Nave S wall, W of porch, Andrew Davidson, †1787: Ionic aedicule with winged angel heads and *memento mori* in segmental pediment. Porch N side, large C18 tablet with swan-necked pediment supported by Ionic pilasters for members of the Read family. – SUNDIAL, reset at SW angle of nave, dated 1699.

CHURCHYARD. Several good C18 memorials. Memorial to sixteenth Lord Trimlestown, disc-headed cross by *Peddie & Kinnear*, 1879, within Gothic balustraded enclosure.

Former MANSE (Linton Lee). T-shaped; the early part of 1781, originally thatched, lies to the rear. *John Smith* added bay windows and projecting centre gabled entrance in 1857. A circle of light-coloured slates set in the roof celebrates the completion of alterations *c.* 1805. Court of single-storey stables and steading by *Smith*.

Former SCHOOL 1.2 km. N. Single-storey schoolroom to the S, *c.* 1800, harled and heightened by *Adam Young*, mason, 1842, the coved ceiling still visible in the roof space. Two low rooms (N) one above the other, comprised the schoolmaster's house.

Altered and added to *c.* 1912, when it was converted to a dwelling.

To the w is the former PAUPERS' HOUSE, by *John Bulman,* 1856. Rectangular with a piended roof, which extends down over a dry closet. The w door led into the 'hospital'; the framing of its box beds is still visible on the walls. Behind the E door was stabling for the schoolmaster's horse. Behind, the T-plan SCHOOL (Community Hall) of 1881 by *Herbertson & Son.* Coursed ashlar with overhanging bracketed eaves. One large room with separate entrances for boys and girls.

WAR MEMORIAL. Celtic cross, *c.* 1920.

CLIFTON PARK, 0.8 km. N. Neo-Tudor. Dated 1849, with additions of 1873 by *Peddie & Kinnear,* and 1894. Only the walls remain after demolition *c.* 1950. Mosaic floor and adjoining fernery survive. – Large Neo-Tudor LODGE by *Peddie & Kinnear,* 1879–80, with tall clustered red brick chimneys. – Mid-C19 STABLES with Tudor detailing. Detached two-bay coach house, *c.* 1879 by *Peddie & Kinnear.*

HOSELAW CHAPEL, 6.5 km. NE. by Hoselaw Loch. By *P. Macgregor Chalmers,* 1906, in memory of the minister, Dr Thomas Leishman. Modest but dignified with a coursed white freestone front, rubble elsewhere. Rectangular, with an E apse and belfry topped by a simple cross. Narrow round-headed windows. Unplastered interior with an open timber roof. – STAINED GLASS. A tiny apse window of Our Lord holding the Sacramental Cup by *S. V. Willis,* copied from one at Weobly, Herefordshire. At the w end Christ in Majesty, the Four Evangelists and the Nativity. – The apse is decorated with a FRESCO of Angels standing on clouds in front of a blue background. The banner they hold carries the words 'Alleluia for the Lord God Omnipotent reigneth'. Border of grapes and vine leaves entwined. By *Jessie Rintoul MacGibbon.*

6030

LITTLEDEAN TOWER
2 km. NE of Maxton

An extraordinary little building looking at first sight more like an artillery bastion than the C16 residence of the Kerrs of Littledean. The oldest portion is probably the 'stone house' that escaped destruction when the hall and stables of Littledean were burnt by the English in 1544. Towards the end of the century the house was extended and strongly fortified for firearm defence, probably by Walter Kerr, whose descendants continued to live there until about the middle of the C18, when they moved to Nenthorn (q.v.); the house was ruinous by 1772.

The early house seems to have been an oblong block of three main storeys with its long axis running W and E. To judge from Moses Griffith's drawing of *c.* 1772, the building is unlikely to have exceeded 13 m. or 14 m. in length, while transversely it measured 8.0 m. over walls some 1.1 m. thick. Random rubble masonry with chamfer-arrised dressings of white sandstone, all probably from the quarry at Ploughlands (1 km. s). All that can be said about the internal arrangements is that an entrance doorway in the s wall opened into a vaulted cellarage above which there were at least two residential floors. The late C16 extension takes the form of a D-plan tower wrapped round the w end of the early house, a shape evidently chosen for defensive reasons, for the tower walls are some 1.8 m. in thickness and contain a formidable array of gunloops. The concept is similar to that employed on a much grander scale in the Half Moon Battery of 1572–8 at Edinburgh Castle, whence Kerr and his master-mason may have derived their inspiration. At Littledean, however, the tower, of four storeys and a garret, also provided additional accommodation linked to the earlier house. Local red and white sandstone masonry, mostly comprising coursed rubble blocks, the s e corner, however, of ashlar, probably obtained second-hand from the nearby abbeys of Melrose or Dryburgh (qq.v.). Above a chamfered base course two tiers of double-splayed gunloops, six in each tier, provide an all-round sweep of fire, the upper ones specifically designed to take account of the high ground to the w. There is a roll-moulded string course at second-floor level, and the walls are crowned by a corbelled parapet-walk, now ruinous. Within the wall-walk rise the crowstepped gables of the two upper storeys, the w gable shaped to the curve of the wall below. The windows are mainly confined to the upper levels; most have been wrought with a quirked edge-roll and some have been barred. Close to the s e corner is an empty panel frame which seems to have had a drip-moulded lintel and shafted jambs like those at Greenknowe Tower and Buckholm Tower (qq.v.).

The entrance doorway in the s e re-entrant angle is protected by a gunloop contrived within the blocked doorway of the early C16 house and leads into a newel stair which served all the upper floors. The ground floor of the extension contains two irregular-shaped, vaulted cellars, the smaller one now inaccessible. On the first floor was a kitchen, which probably communicated with a hall formed within the earlier house. Above the entrance lobby was a small vaulted chamber opening directly off the stair. The second floor contained two heated chambers, each with its own latrine, as well as a smaller vaulted chamber like that below. The arrangement on the third floor was similar, while the garret seems to have contained a single heated chamber.

LONGFORMACUS

A former estate village, improved by a number of 'neat cottages' in the mid C19, and not much else, until some late C20 housing.

PARISH CHURCH, s e of the village. The medieval church, dependent on Mordington, was granted to Dalkeith Collegiate Church in 1477; parts of that church survived extensive rebuilding in 1730 and further repairs *c.* 1830. But much of what is now seen dates from restoration by *George Fortune* in 1892–4 for Andrew Smith of Whitchester. Around the rectangular medieval plan were added a semicircular e apse with round-arched windows, for the relocated communion table, a narrow rectangular w extension, and a n laird's aisle (on the site of an earlier 'aisle') flanked by lean-to vestry and porches. The walls throughout are of whin and buff sandstone rubble, the later parts having ashlar dressings, with buttresses to the w extension. A birdcage bellcote surmounts the original w gable. The s flank of the main body has three c19 Y-traceried windows and a pointed single light to the original chancel area, while the w extension has a Y-traceried window to each flank and a three-light intersecting-traceried w window. There is delicate foliage decoration to the two-light n windows flanking the gable of the laird's 'aisle'.

Internally, there are pointed barrel ceilings, through which project false hammerbeams and collars, the braces of the former carried on corbels with stiff-leaf decoration. At the junctions of the main body of the church with the apse, the laird's aisle and w extension are arches with heavy semicylindrical responds. – PULPIT. Octagonal with blind traceried panels. – STAINED GLASS. e window, Crucifixion, post-1891. Nave s wall, from e to w: Good Shepherd, post-1892; St Francis, post-1943 by *Marjorie Kemp*; the Church and Light of the World, post-1896. w extension, s wall, SS Andrew and James the Great, *G.J. Baguley* of Newcastle, 1894. w window, Judas, Ascension, Doubting Thomas, post-1885. – ARMORIAL PANEL towards e end s wall, arms of Sinclair with initials IS. – CROSS-INCISED GRAVE-SLAB, against wall in NE porch, simple c13(?) design. – MEMORIAL BRASS, in laird's aisle, to Andrew Smith of Whitchester and Cranshaws, †1914, by *J. Wippell & Co.* – SUNDIAL, on corbel at sw angle of original church. – JOUGS, below the sundial.

CHURCHYARD, s of the church. Some table tombs, but mainly headstones. Good lettering and detail on headstone of George Sherritt, schoolmaster, †1821(?). Massively Romanesque w wall to burial enclosure of Brown family in SE corner of churchyard.

Former FREE CHURCH, now a store. By *James Cunningham* of Greenlaw, 1848. A small rubble-built rectangular box, extended 1869 by the addition of an e aisle and a small s vestry. Four round-arched windows along main front, the central two replaced by a garage door. s gable has the base of a bellcote.

MANSE (Craigie Lodge), 1.2 km. NE. Traditional, *c.* 1818, with a two-storey gabled porch added by *John Smith*, 1849. Scrolled skewputts to chimneyed gable-head. Inside a geometric stair, and bow-ended drawing room.

PRESTON BRIDGE. A single, segmental arch spanning the Dye Water. Rubble walls and voussoirs. Two much-weathered panels: the coat-of-arms in the outer face of the e wall is reputedly dated 1820; the other panel, dated 1851 with a decorative motif flanked by carved figureheads, was formerly the panel of a well (dem.) at the N end of the bridge.

VILLAGE HALL. Dated 1913. Rubble-built with sandstone margins. Later additions at the N end.

DESCRIPTION. Beginning at the s end of the village, on the l. is the attractive mid-c19 ASH COTTAGE in harl-pointed rubble. Overhanging timber-bracketed eaves and a full-height canted bay. On the r., before Preston Bridge (*see* above), is a long path to the Parish Church. Over the river, on the l., is RIVERSIDE COTTAGE, a former inn, possibly mid-to-late C18. Two storeys, three bays in whitewashed rubble sandstone and painted margins. A chamfered surround to the entrance doorway, its weathered lintel inscribed 1751 (or 57). Later gabled dormerheads. Opposite, THE ROW leads to the walled garden of Longformacus House (*see* below) with square rusticated ball-finialled gatepiers. An irregular mid-C19 terrace of two-storey cottages faces the Dye Water. No. 1 is L-plan, with a gabled porch and a stork finial on the principal gable. Two cottages with stone-gabled dormers have a centre corbelled-out gabled dormer, with two narrow lights, over two entrance doors. No. 12, with deeply set small windows under the eaves, may be late C18. No. 13 (Gardener's House) terminates the terrace. It has overhanging eaves, a slightly advanced gabled bay with a tripartite window, and a small porch in a re-entrant angle.

Back to the main street, and continuing up the hill, is the former Free Church (*see* above) on the r. DYEBANK HOUSE, its former manse, is of 1870, in coursed dark whinstone, with a piended roof and brick chimneys. THE MILL HOUSE is a mid-to-late C19 Picturesque former miller's house in harl-pointed whin rubble, with sandstone margins and overhanging timber-bracketed eaves. Three-bay s front with a bracketed stone pentice canopy over the former entrance, and gabled wall-head dormers. The last house at the N end of the village is the former SCHOOLHOUSE. Mid-C19 with Tudor detailing. Across the rear an earlier rectangular schoolhouse dressed up by *John Smith*, 1849, with a gable, shouldered margins, bracketed skew-putts and ball finials.

CAIRNS, Dirrington Great Law, 2 km. s. Crowning the summit of this prominent hill, there is a row of three cairns. Two of them stand 1.8 m. in height, the E cairn measuring 15.5 m. in diameter, and the W cairn 17 m. within a ditch 2.5 m. in breadth, but the third, which lies midway between them, is only 7.5 m. in diameter and 0.5 m. in height.

CAIRN, Dirrington Little Law, 4 km. s. A large cairn measuring some 20 m. in diameter by 2 m. in height.

LONG CAIRN, Mutiny Stones, in open moorland 7 km. WNW. This cairn measures 82 m. in length and tapers from 27.5 m. in breadth at the ENE end to 9.8 m. at the WSW end, and stands 2.5 m. in maximum height. Parts of the mound have been reconstructed since excavations of 1871 and 1924, probably including the stretches of drystone masonry visible at the E end and along the s side.

WHITCHESTER HOUSE. *See* p. 758.

LONGFORMACUS HOUSE
0.3 km. E

A moderately sized early C18 classical house built for Sir Robert Sinclair *c.* 1727; its design is illustrated in William Adam's *Vitruvius Scoticus*, which shows a two-storey, seven-bay house on a low basement plinth, the raised entrance with a lugged architrave and segmental pediment approached by splayed steps. Rusticated quoins and a piended and platformed roof. This is still largely recognisable today, except for the addition, probably *c.* 1847 by *John Smith*, of an advanced three-bay pedimented centrepiece with carved palmette framing an oculus and three urn finials. Doric portico. In 1884 *R. Rowand Anderson* enlarged the house, by adding a pyramidal-roofed attic with pedimented wall-head dormers to the centre of the w front. Anderson's N wing has been demolished but a kitchen court survives with ball-finialled gatepiers. Much is altered inside. In the basement two stone chimneypieces, one with bolection moulding, the other with a lugged architrave.

Early C19 WALLED GARDEN with harl-pointed rubble walls, and crowstepped buttresses. Brick-columned pavilion, and late C19 GREENHOUSE with a central projecting polygonal bay. – SUNDIALS, probably mid-to-late C19, one with an engraved baluster base, square table and gnomon, the other with urn-shaped drum and circular table. – LODGE. Single-storey, with advanced full-height gabled entrance with blind oculus, moulded skewputts and decorative finial. – Early C18 cylindrical DOVECOT. in harled red rubble sandstone. Bracketed eaves, bellcast roof topped by a louvre, with pigeon openings, its bellcast cap with ball finial and weathervane.

5030   LOWOOD HOUSE
                    2.5 km. NW of Melrose

A beautifully situated house on the s bank of the River Tweed, developed from a small early C19 villa purchased *c.* 1829 for his country seat by *Robert Reid*, Master of Works and Architect to the King. The original villa, two storeys, three bays, with a slightly advanced centre bay, faced s. Reid seems to have added a simple two-storey kitchen office range to the w, and a Regency-style veranda across the ground floor which incorporated a projecting porch. The villa mostly disappeared when the house was extended by Henry Kidd in the late C19, when the w end was remodelled and added to. An L-shaped addition was built across the s front, and a billiard room with a bedroom above, at the E end. Mutule blocks were added to the roof line. The interior was completely recast in the late C19 mostly in a classical style.

The large STABLES date from the mid-to-late C19. Gateway framed by square-capped piers, its cast-iron overthrow supporting a clock. Gabled fronts on each side of the court.

BRIDGEND HOUSE, w, of *c.* 1800, but altered. The LODGE was perhaps adapted, in the late C19, from a cottage built by the bar across Melrose Bridge's s end, when the new picturesque drive was made to the house. Whinstone rubble with red dressings. Two round-headed windows in the E gable.

LYNE

A small parish on the N bank of the Lyne Water immediately above its confluence with the River Tweed.

PARISH CHURCH. 0.9 km. SW. Delightfully situated within a 19 mounded churchyard that betokens long occupation of the site. A chapel here, dependent on Stobo by the late C12, became parochial in the later Middle Ages, and that medieval church probably underlies the present largely C17 structure. Repairs are recorded in 1603, but much now seen dates from rebuilding for John, Lord Hay of Yester, later first Earl of Tweeddale, in 1640–5. There were further repairs in 1830, and in 1888–9 there was a major restoration and reordering for the Earl of Wemyss.

The church is a rectangular structure with diagonal buttresses to the W angles, and is of rubble with sandstone dressings. Above the W gable a bellcote has trifoliate-headed openings to all faces and an inscription recording that it is an 1888 rebuilding of a predecessor of 1708. The E gable has a replacement rosette finial of 1888, the original propped against the wall; there are two other finials along the ridge. The round-arched S doorway, in the second bay from the W, has a roll moulding and raised margins; it is now covered by a small porch of 1888, said to be on the foundations of a predecessor. The other three bays of the S flank have two-light windows with a vesica at their head, all with raised margins; that in the W bay is of 1888 and replaces an earlier rectangular window. Also of the late C19 is the lancet in the W gable. The E gable has a three-light window with intersecting tracery. The N flank appears to have been originally unwindowed until an opening was cut in 1888 to light the vestry in the W bay.

The plastered ceiling is largely of 1888; it is of polygonal profile with exposed timbers of the lower rafters and collars. Also late C19 is the partition enclosing the W bay as a vestry, against which two halves of a laird's pew are now set. Since the late C19 reordering the pulpit has been in the SE corner. – MURAL AUMBRY, towards E end of N wall, possibly a retained Sacrament House. – PULPIT, 1640s, oak, circular with blind arcading and Tuscan pilasters. – FONT, medieval, upward-tapering octagonal stone bowl on modern base. – LAIRD'S PEWS, oak, divided and re-set on each side of the central doorway of the vestry partition, now forming two small enclosures with modillioned cornices and Tuscan piers. They bear the initials of Lord John and Margaret, Lady Hay of Yester, and the ghosting of the date 1644. – STAINED GLASS, first window from E on S, Sower and Good Shepherd, c. 1860.

CHURCHYARD. Against E wall of church, Robert Wales, †1793, pedimented aedicule; Paterson family, aedicule with swan-necked pediment (1809). In churchyard, Janet Veitch, †1712, with early depiction of temptation of Adam and Eve.

Former MANSE (Hallyne House), immediately E of the church, was completed 'in a substantial and tradesmanlike manner' in 1830 to a design of Mr *Turnbull*, architect, Peebles; repaired by *David Rhind*, 1872. Two-storeyed, hip-roofed block of exposed whinstone rubble with grey sandstone dressings; side and rear elevations clad with pink harling. Three-bay front with advanced centre rising to a blocking course; prominent porch. Later wings at rear and detached range of offices. In the E wing a reused stone, presumably from the church, inscribed: HOLINES BECVMS THY HOVS O LORD.

BRIDGES over Lyne Water. FIVE MILE BRIDGE, 0.7 km. W, built *c.* 1775 to carry the Peebles–Biggar road. A single segmental arch of whinstone rubble with sandstone dressings; now bypassed. – BEGGAR'S PATH BRIDGE, 1 km. E. *c.* 1825, is a substantial four-span bridge carrying the Peebles–Stobo road. Mainly of rubble, but two segmental arches have pink sandstone voussoirs; central rounded cutwater also of sandstone, repaired with brick. – LYNE TOLL BRIDGE, 1.8 km. SE. 1718, carrying Lyne Station Road. Two segmental arches and a central cutwater. The E side shows coursed blocks and voussoirs of buff-coloured sandstone, while the W side has been renewed (widened?) in rubble with red sandstone voussoirs. The VIADUCT at Lyne Station, 1.9 km. SE, formerly carried the Peebles–Biggar railway and is now a public footpath. A handsome three-span bridge with a subsidiary steel girder span across the adjoining roadway. Three skewed arches of rock-faced buff sandstone with rounded cutwaters carrying piers decorated with dummy arrowslits; grid-pattern, cast-iron parapet rails.

MELDONFOOT, 1.8 km. E. Attractive, L-plan house built for Capt. George Wolfe Murray, formerly of Cringletie, in 1924. Two storeys, with gabled roofs. Brick-built, harled and lime-washed, with black-painted sills and label moulds to the principal windows, which have lattice glazing.

FORT, White Meldon, 2.6 km. NE. Crowning the summit of the easterly of the Meldons, this fort is defended by at least three ramparts. Within the interior, which extends to about 3.6 ha., stances of numerous large timber round-houses are visible, and there is also a large Bronze Age cairn upon the summit.

PALISADED SETTLEMENT, South Hill Head, 1.9 km. NE. This settlement lies on a low rise E of the summit, and comprises a single ring-ditch house some 13 m. in overall diameter, with an entrance facing ENE towards the entrance into the surrounding enclosure. The latter is defined by two palisade trenches, which probably represent separate periods of construction.

4 ROMAN FORT, on the broad gravel terrace to the W of the church. Substantial portions of the defences of this small late CI A.D. Antonine fort, which measures *c.* 2.2 ha. internally, are still visible. These include sectors of the inner turf rampart at the NE corner and along the W side, and the accompanying ditch system on the E and S. It probably housed a detachment of cavalry guarding the road between Newstead (q.v.) and Castledykes.

STANDING STONES, Sherriffmuir, 0.9 km. S, on a gravel plateau in the angle formed by the confluence of the River Tweed and the Lyne Water. Standing 1.1 m. and 1.25 m. in height some 2 m. apart, these are now the sole visible elements of a concentration of Neolithic and Early Bronze Age ceremonial and funerary monuments recorded in antiquarian accounts and from aerial photographs.

UNENCLOSED PLATFORM SETTLEMENT, Green Knowe, 2.7
km. NE. This settlement comprises at least nine circular platforms strung out along a slope of the Meldon Valley above a
small field system. The platforms range from 10 m. to 17 m. in
diameter, and excavation has shown that they are the stances
of timber round-houses dating from the Bronze Age.
DROCHIL CASTLE. *See* p. 210.

MACBIEHILL   1050
4 km. E of West Linton

An eye-catching tower house by *Crichton Wood*, 1998–2000.
Strictly contemporary design, relying for its effect upon form
and massing rather than the replication of medieval detail.
Three main storeys and a stepped L-plan, each element slightly
angled to make the simple juxtaposition of boxes more
dynamic. A circular stair-turret in the main (W) re-entrant
angle, with the principal entrance alongside it, and a low W
wing. Rendered breeze block and brick, with gabled slate-
covered roofs. The stair-turret rises to a glazed caphouse, and
two of the salient angles of the main tower sprout metal-framed
glass turrets to capture the magnificent views to S and E.

Behind the site of the former house (of *c.* 1600, remodelled,
1835 and dem. *c.* 1950), 0.2 km. SE is the STEADING, now
adapted for residential use. Single-storey courtyard plan, of
C19 and earlier date; local rubble masonry with slate roofs. –
The outlet from Macbiehill Loch is crossed by a single-arched
stone BRIDGE dated 1838. – At the entrance to the drive
leading to the tower house is an early C19 Gothic LODGE with
earlier gatepiers. Across the road a wooded knoll with a MAU-
SOLEUM (*Robert Somerville*, mason, 1769) on its summit.
Square on plan with pyramidal, vaulted roof covered with
stone slabs. Excellent masonry of dressed sandstone rising to
an ogee-moulded eaves cornice. Plinths for stone urns at the
corners and apex, but the urns themselves are now stacked
below. A pointed-arch window in the S wall. Within are the
memorials of the Montgomery and Beresford families, the earliest a recumbent slab commemorating William Montgomery,
second of Macbiehill (†1768). Beside the entrance gates a
panel inscribed: THE VAULTS OF/ MACBIEHILL/ BUILT 1769/
RESTORED 1974/.

MAKERSTOUN   6030

PARISH CHURCH, 0.5 km. N of the village. Rebuilt here in
1807–8 for Sir Henry Hay Makdougall. Of rectangular plan,
with a two-storeyed entrance block added at the E end. The
main S front is of red stugged masonry with raised margins at
the quoins, the other walls of harled rubble. At the centre of
the S wall is a small square turret (dated 1808) topped by an
arched bellcote with a spirelet cap and cross finial. Two pointed
windows on each side of the turret; that at the W end of the

front had a doorway beneath it (now blocked), and its sill is higher than the others. The w wall has two pointed windows, and the N wall is blank. The interior, covered by a flat plaster ceiling, has good FURNISHINGS, despite unfortunate changes in the 1960s. The pulpit and precentor's desk are at the centre of the w wall. The kirk session and manse pews used to be on each side of the pulpit, while the laird's pew is in the gallery, with a retiring room in the entrance block. – PULPIT. Semi-hexagonal with panelled faces; backboard framed by fluted Tuscan pilasters, capped by a tester with hexagonal concave-sided canopy. Rectangular precentor's desk in front.

CHURCHYARD, C19 monuments to S of church. – SUNDIAL. Tall stone baluster on S axis of church.

BURIAL ENCLOSURE, NW of Makerstoun House (*see* below). The likely location of the parish church granted to Kelso Abbey *c*. 1159. A rubble-built rectangle incorporating work of several periods. The N wall and N part of the E wall are of buff rubble, with a raised margin at the NE angle. The E and W walls incorporate work of two or more phases, the later work being of red sandstone rubble; the S wall is of a single build. The first phase work, along the N and E walls, incorporates a C18(?) burial aisle, possibly created within the chancel of the medieval church. Perhaps in anticipation of the removal of the rest of the church in 1808, its W side was rebuilt, and in the later C19 the enclosure was extended to the S, and a new S front formed. Arched recesses contain marble tablets, that on the w commemorating Isabella, Lady Hay Makdougall, †1796. At the centre of the N wall is a memorial to General Sir Thomas Makdougall-Brisbane (Governor of New South Wales), †1860. The S front, of red snecked sandstone with buff dressings, is Gothic: an arched doorway with continuous mouldings has a hoodmould carried on head corbels, on each side of which is a decorative quatrefoil.

CHURCHYARD, a number of C17 and C18 memorials, some with unusual incised decoration. Headstone of Thomas Hill, †1747, has three-quarter profile portrait reading book.

MANSE (Kirklee House). Traditional, harled with sandstone margins, 1808. Late C19 stone porch and two-storey N addition. Contemporary single-storey steading.

MAKERSTOUN PRIMARY SCHOOL (Girl Guide Centre). Erected by Henrietta Makdougall in 1862. Red sandstone with cream dressings. High, ridge-roofed schoolroom, with twenty-pane windows in the N and S elevations. Double chimneys mounted on large stone blocks on each gable whose copes have triangular steps.

Former SCHOOL of 1810. Now a dwelling. Two storeys, three bays, harled with painted margins.

MAKERSTOUN HOUSE
1.6 km. s

A moderately-sized classical house, reconstructed after a fire by *John H. Reid* and *Crichton Lang* of *Ian G. Lindsay & Partners*, 1973–4. They removed early C19 additions to give the house the appearance shown in a scheme of 1725 by *William Adam*, itself based on one by *Alexander McGill*, who reported in 1714 that the NW end of the existing house of the Makdougalls 'being very Crazy is to be taken down'. As reconstructed, the house is harled, of three storeys with a seven-bay N front, the centre three slightly advanced, with a curved pediment, and five-bay S elevation with a triangular pediment over the advanced central three.

The carcase of the pre-1725 house, built on the site of a house destroyed in Hertford's invasion of 1545, was incorporated in the new building. Details found during demolition in 1973 have been reused in the walls at the W end; including a gunloop in the N wall, moulded fragments and a blocked fireplace. The E end of the house appears to be earliest, attributed (by the RCAHMS) to the C16; two vaulted rooms on the ground floor, the E with a segmental-arched kitchen fireplace. A two-storey servants' wing to the W was remodelled in 1973–4. Projecting from its SW corner is a cubical SUNDIAL with three dial faces, the centre one with initials HM (Henry Makdougall) and BM (Barbara Makdougall), and the date 1684. – Large WALLED GARDEN, NE, with red sandstone walls. C18 (?). – In 1826 Sir Thomas Makdougall-Brisbane (†1860), a keen astronomer, built an OBSERVATORY. Of two domed buildings one survives in part.

MANORHILL FARM. 0.2 km. W. A model farm of *c.* 1890. A red sandstone gabled farmhouse, with a canted bay and advanced gable feature with gunloops. A fine range of large cattlesheds in coursed red sandstone, the end gables with round-headed ventilation openings. Internally, rows of back-to-back fitted feeding troughs are still in use, but the truck on bogie rails to fill the feeders has gone. – Nos. 1–8 MANORHILL. Late C19 cottages, with wall-head ball-finialled pedimented dormers.

MANDERSTON HOUSE★

2.9 km. E of Duns

Manderston House, together with its park, gardens and estate buildings, illustrates to perfection the swansong of the great Classical country house; its order and refinement are Georgian, but the equipment for comfort, convenience and pleasure is Edwardian.

Dalhousie Watherston bought the Manderston estate in 1789–90, and built a new house, possibly by *Alexander Gilkie*, who produced plans in 1789, similar in design and details to the one built. Its N front, of nine bays, had a slightly advanced three-bay pediment fronted by giant engaged Ionic columns, Ionic pilasters at the angles, a Venetian window with a plain window above, framed in a recessed arch in each of the end bays, and a Diocletian window in the basement.

Watherston died in 1803 and the house was sold by his widow's heirs to Richard Miller in 1859. Five years later,

★ This account is indebted to C. McWilliam, 'Notes on the Architecture of Manderston', in *Prospects for Manderston* (Borders Regional Council, 1977).

Manderston House.
Ground Floor Plan.

Ballroom

Drawing Room

Library/
Billiard Room

Ante Room

Vestibule

Corridor

Hall

Corridor

Morning Room

Tea Room/
Writing
Room

Dining Room

Green
Room/
Business
Room

Entrance Hall/
Gunroom

Smoking Room

Wash Room

Courtyard

30 m
100 ft

Earlier House

Miller's elder brother William purchased the estate from his trustees after amassing a fortune in the Baltic and Russia. During his time Manderston was enlarged by *James Simpson* with the addition of inappropriate French Renaissance style mansard roofs; a porte cochère was added to the centre three bays, and carving inserted in the pediment. The outer single bays were extended forward, as short flanking two-bay wings, with classical windows with curved pediments on the ground floor and plain above. Sir James Miller inherited in 1887, and set about its transformation to provide a suitable setting in which to live 'in grand style', and one which would provide his wife, the Hon. Eveline Curzon, with accommodation to match that of her childhood home at Kedleston Hall, Derbyshire. First, Miller commissioned *John Kinross* to improve the estate buildings 1894–7, before he returned home in 1901 to reconstruct the existing house, add a new wing (the Bachelors' Wing) and servants' court to the w, and completely refurbish the interior. Kinross was primarily known for his careful restoration work, particularly for the third Marquess of Bute, e.g. Greyfriars Church, Elgin, Moray, and Falkland Palace, Fife. He was not therefore the most obvious choice but he had reconstructed Thurston House, East Lothian (dem.), for Miller's brother-in law, Richard Hunter. From this Miller must have judged his competence in aggrandising his mansion of Manderston.

In 1902 *The Building News* reported that the work was just beginning at a contract price of £70,000 – 'the original s front, of eleven bays, being retained as far as possible', and 'the new entrance front to be built on similar lines'. Work was completed in 1905 at a final cost of £221,000. Kinross removed the 1860s roofs, and remodelled the flanking wings and provided an entablature with a balustraded parapet, urn finials at the angles and Ionic angle pilasters with fluted necks, defining the end bays.

The N and E fronts of the house were reconstructed in warm sandstone from Whitsome Newton Quarry (Swinton stone), but adopted details from the C18 house, notably the band course between the basement and ground floor, and a Vitruvian scroll band between the upper floors, which continues across the bachelor wing. The principal alteration on the N FRONT was the removal of the pediment over the three centre bays, which Kinross extended forward in line with the flanking wings of the 1860s, and in front of which he placed a giant tetrastyle portico – the fluted necks of the columns and pilasters, the portico frieze enriched with paterae and husk-garlands, and the fluted carving on a panel above the centre bay are the only decorative elements – which achieved a severely classical style considered by Colin McWilliam as reminiscent of the stern Neoclassical spirit of Bonomi's Rosneath, Dunbartonshire, 1803 (dem.). The columns stand on corniced pedestals on which are mounted bronze scrolls with lions' heads, each with a bell-pull in its mouth; two for pulling by hand, and two by the rider's boot. An architraved and console-cornived entrance doorway with a carved swagged armorial above.

The E ELEVATION is seven bays, the centre three slightly advanced, with a pilastered and pedimented aedicule in the centre with a semicircular pedimented glazed doorway. The eleven-bay S FRONT to the garden is all late C18, with a full-height bow to the centre (reflected in the centre of the bachelors' wing to the l.); its balustrade is probably C18, and its outer two bays slightly advanced and framed by Ionic pilasters. A decorative cast-iron balcony on iron posts encircles the bow, with steps to the garden. A corniced ashlar wall shields the basement.

Although the smaller-scale BACHELORS' WING reflects the form and detail of the main house, its treatment is plainer, i.e. of two storeys with a blocking course instead of a balustraded parapet. It shares a similar N entrance, with an appropriate swagged medallion of Diana (the goddess of hunting), above. Its seven-bay W elevation, partly concealed by the SERVICE COURT, contains the crucial luggage door and mounting block (with steps). The service court is of two storeys and quite plain and understated, as it should be, with an entrance pend in the W side. The S façade is decorated with a round-arched recess containing a bronze statue and a carved panel above. Its W range contains the motor house, still with its machinery, which has a tall pedimented round-arched entrance and keystoned oculus above. Fully fitted inside with glazed enamel tiles. The laundry range is similarly tiled.

INTERIOR. The late C18 sequence of rooms along the S front was retained by Kinross, but the rest entirely reconstructed with the principal space in the centre of the plan taken by an immense rectangular hall. C18 chimneypieces and decoration survive in part, and for the remainder Kinross employed an Adamesque decorative scheme derived from Kedleston Hall and elsewhere, but frequently overlapping with a more luxurious Edwardian fashion, e.g. opulent Louis XVI styles in the ballroom and drawing room. The exceptional woodwork is largely by *Scott Morton & Co.*, the plasterwork by *Leonard Grandison* of Peebles. The layout is spacious and lavish, and the open budget enabled Kinross to create an Edwardian house without compare in Scotland.

Inside the main entrance is an oval VESTIBULE, lined in sandstone ashlar walls of superb quality, with a classical stone chimneypiece, niched recesses, a Vitruvian scrolled dado band, and a coved ceiling over bowed steps leading to the rectangular HALL beyond. In the centre of the plan, four fluted Roman Doric columns support a panelled dome on pendentives, decorated with classical oval plaster reliefs; the rest of the surface filled with plaster reliefs in the Adam manner, but as Colin McWilliam suggested, 'in too much profusion to be truly Adam'. To the r. a white marble chimneypiece, with a carved panel of Galatea and two female figures above supporting a painted roundel, is modelled on that in the hall at Kedleston. Venetian openings (white marble with figured black columns) in each corner. The circular MORNING ROOM, lying straight ahead, appears to have its original late C18 decoration, e.g. the ceiling with central fan and delicate plasterwork, but the Ionic pilastered chimneypiece is evidently imported. Swagged niches, the one to the r. with a curved jib door to the tea room (*see* below). In the E wall a rich Corinthian pilastered doorway leads through an ante-room to the drawing room. This was narrowed when organ works (*see* below) were inserted; the part showing of the delicate plaster ceiling surely dates from the C18. The SE ANTE-ROOM off the hall contains the oak display front of the ORGAN, closely modelled on Adam's design for one at Wynn House, St James's Square, London.* Female figures support a circular pipe-lined opening below a heraldic cartouche (the console is now in the SE corner of the hall). The decoration of the ante-room is also Adam-inspired, with pilasters and a geometric patterned ceiling.

The ensuing great rooms, the DRAWING ROOM (S) and BALLROOM (N), run the depth of the house's E end and are interconnected. The Louis XVI decoration is very probably by *Charles Mellier & Co.*, London, who decorated Miller's London house at Grosvenor Square in 1897, and provided furnishing plans for these rooms. Damask velvet walls with gilded filigree margins; smooth velvet in the drawing room, and figured velvet in the ballroom, on white and gold walls. The drawing room ceiling, pink and green with blue ovals in the corners, has a goddess and harp in the central octagon, and panels of dancing ladies in the end panels; the ladies on the chimneypiece panel have garlands. The Adamesque ceiling in the ballroom is based on the one in the dining room at Kedleston and has paintings by *Robert Hope*, signed and dated 1905, not as good as Kauffmann or Zucchi, but very passable. Apollo in the centre with Venus and Mars on one side, and Adonis on the other, with cupids in the corner roundels fishing, playing instruments, making wine and playing with fire. The Judgment of Paris is carved on the centre panel of the chimneypiece. En suite with the ballroom is the LIBRARY, which opens directly off the hall. It doubles as a billiard room, but was originally intended for a writing room with the billiard table in the ballroom. Possibly the best Adam-style ceiling in the house, with a central star within a square, and shield-shaped panels enclosed in the rectangles at each end. A white and gold marble chimneypiece with fluted columns and centre panel of female figures and a tripod. The bookcases with marble busts on top must be derived from those at Kedleston.

The DINING ROOM is preceded by an ante-room, designed as a gallery in which guests congregated before dinner. On the r. a two-bay arcade with ornate grilles, and a translucent Derbyshire alabaster parapet screens the lower cloakroom. On the l. a plaster relief of Diana. The ceiling pattern of diagonal ribs is repeated in the inlaid floor. The DINING ROOM was the last room to be completed. The ceiling with Mars in the centre has muses and vases crowding the surrounding lozenges.† Richly ornamented, pilaster-framed buffet recess with a superb plaster panel dominated by an urn and cupids. Consoled chimneypiece. S of the staircase, the TEA ROOM (formerly writing room),

---

*Now in the National Museum of Wales, Cardiff.
†John Gifford suggests that it was based on an unexecuted design by Adam for the Japanned Room in the Queen's House.

has an Adam-style ceiling with a pattern of four concave curves within a circle. On the chimneypiece panel are Father Time and a young girl. Adjoining to the W the GREEN ROOM (former business room) has a ceiling with octagonal coffers and tiny rosettes in the corners.

77   On the W side of the hall, the main 'SILVER' STAIRCASE is top-lit and modelled on the design of the staircase in the Petit Trianon at Versailles. A cantilevered marble well stair with a silvered balustrade and brass handrail. The bedroom floor corridor has screens of fluted columns at the ends and round-arched doorways; most of the bedrooms have Adam-style chimneypieces, although the principal bowed bedroom has, surprisingly, a timber-ribbed ceiling, Neo-Jacobean decoration and a canopied chimneypiece. The marble-lined bathroom has a silver-plated bath set in a Doric-columned recess.

In the BACHELORS' WING, a marble-lined octagonal entrance hall with glass-fronted gun cabinets. Through a mahogany door on the r. is a magnificently appointed wash-room. In the bow-ended room on the S front was the SMOKING ROOM. The BASEMENT, lined with enamel glazed bricks supplied by *Craig & Co.*, has all the rooms and equipment necessary for the impeccable running of an Edwardian country house.

ESTATE BUILDINGS

Reconstruction of the house was preceded by rebuilding of the estate buildings by *Kinross* from 1895 onwards. Of this date the sandstone rubble STABLES. Two-storey seven-bay show front, the central pedimented pend fronted by coupled Roman Doric columns. Inside the comfort for the horses is as good as that for house guests; teak stalls with solid brass finials to the posts. Adjoining to the N, a U-plan paddock and sick bays, the twin-gabled GROOM'S HOUSE in the NE corner; in its S elevation a wall-mounted lead sundial, dated 1663, is inscribed VIVAT CAROLUS SECUNDUS ('Long Live Charles II').

BUXLEY FARM (Home Farm and Dairy). An extraordinary group, functional in layout but picturesque in their Scottish Baronial and Renaissance treatment. Added to and rebuilt from 1897 by *Kinross*. In the centre is the DAIRY COURT (dated 1900). Adjoining, the CLOISTER GARTH, a covered walkway, startling in its whiteness, the timber arcade supporting a lean-to roof, the decorative lead frieze embossed with *paterae*. At the SE corner a miniature two-stage DAIRY TOWER with a deep corbelled parapet, waterspouts and a caphouse, its upper floor reached by a forestair, with a squat-columned loggia beneath, having a carved cornucopia in the central spandrel. Within the tower the high Gothic MILK HOUSE, square on plan, has a sumptuous marble and alabaster floor, green marble shelves, and wall-shafts of the same supporting an octagonal ribbed vault, the central boss carved with a milkmaid milking a cow. The upper storey contains a TEA ROOM lined in Tudor-style oak panelling using Spanish oak, carefully made without nails. Ribbed geometric ceiling, and traceried display alcoves for blue and white china. The tower's S terrace is approached from the garden by the UNICORN STAIR, modelled after the Lion and Unicorn stair at Glasgow University of 1690; here there are two unicorns. The single storey and attic L-plan DAIRYMAN'S HOUSE, dated 1900, crowstepped gables and roll-moulded surrounds to doorways and multipaned windows.

The estate cottages are equally eclectic; Scottish Renaissance GARDENER'S HOUSE, dated 1897, with ornately carved dormerheads and circular capped stair-tower. Good interior. In its garden a FOUNTAIN by *Kinross*, based on an early C17 design with a gadrooned basin, and tumbling dolphins. Excellent garden walls with fleuron finials, and fine wrought-iron gates with climbing rose decoration. ENGINEER'S HOUSE, dated 1897, but C17 in style with an ogee-roofed polygonal tower. Of the same date E of the main steading, a splendid Scottish Baronial group of former ENGINE HOUSE and FIRE HOUSE. The engine house with distinctive gables, each different, and ogee-roofed lantern ventilators. Crowstepped-gabled fire house, with a large pedimented doorway, and blue tiled interior. BUXLEY GATE, *c.* 1840. U-plan court with cottages, the pend beneath an ogee-roofed tower and belfry.

WALLED GARDEN. Designed by *Kinross*, 1898–1901. In two sections. The N incorporates a late C18 brick-lined wall, the S part a formal garden divided into four quarters. In the S wall tripartite gilded gates with channelled piers surmounted by marble cherubs representing the four seasons. Inside, two lions survey the garden towards a pedimented Ionic gateway. On the E side a Roman-style portico gate with channelled piers, their cornices continuing across the arch, with modillions, and another, swagged with fruit-filled urns on square piers, with an armorial overthrow. An Italianate FOUNTAIN, the gadrooned basin supported by four consoled busts, and an upper basin with two jolly cherubs carrying a fluted spout.*

NE of the house, the CRICKET PAVILION, *c.* 1903, with veranda, timber posts and lattice railings, the pentice roof with segmental bargeboards. Added to in the same style by *Bain, Swan Architects*, 1988–9. – BOAT HOUSE, NW bank of the lake, reached through a wrought-iron gateway with guilloche decoration. *John Kinross*, 1894. A picturesque Swiss chalet in Edwardian dress, harled with rusticated quoins, shingle roofed, bracketed overhanging eaves and elaborate red-painted woodwork. Well-appointed interior with an Ionic pilastered chimneypiece and coombed ceiling ornamented with vine plasterwork with birds. – CHINESE BRIDGE of *c.* 1800, rising in the centre, with lattice balustrade, renewed late C19.

Four large TERRACES to S and E of the house were designed by *John Kinross* as a suitable setting. Enclosed within balustraded walls with banded pilasters, and all linked together by ornamental steps and gates. Three terraces laid out with lawns, decorated with statuary and urns, in one a wall summerhouse with Tudor detailing and pyramidal-roofed dovecot like a

* Supplied by the art dealer, Joseph Duveen, who provided most of the formal statuary in the house and garden, and marble seats, urns and garden ornaments too numerous to mention individually.

minuscule pele-tower. The s terrace was laid out as a parterre, with a splendid horseshoe stair, an alcove below the platt.

SOUTH LODGE. Mid-C19 with round-arched windows and projecting porch. Pyramidal-capped rusticated gatepiers with crimped coping. Ornate cast-iron railings. Early–mid-C19 WEST LODGE. Wide canted bay with a Doric-columned doorpiece. Later additions. Late C19 double ornamental cast-iron gates with curvilinear tops and gilded shaft-heads, the iron gatepiers topped by urns with gilded cherubs clambering round the sides.

LANDSCAPE. The basic structure of the designed landscape is shown on General Roy's map of c. 1750. The parklands had been laid out by the mid C19.

7040

MARCHMONT HOUSE
2 km. s of Polwarth

67 An impressive mid-C18 Palladian mansion built for the third Earl of Marchmont. Altered by Burn, 1834–42 and recast for the advocate, R. F. McEwen, in 1914–17 by *Robert S. Lorimer*.

Hugh, third Earl of Marchmont, in 1750 laid the foundation stone of a new house a little to the NW of the old Redbraes Castle (*see* below), his family's former seat. The architect, *Thomas Gibson*, also acted as draughtsman and clerk of works, receiving advice from his client, and also from the Earl's friends, Alexander Pope, and the third Earl of Burlington. Marchmont House's internal plan and elevations seem to have been borrowed from Houghton Hall, Norfolk, the choice perhaps influenced by the published view of Houghton in Vol. III of *Vitruvius Britannicus* (1725) to which the second Earl had subscribed, perhaps leading to the tradition that Marchmont House was planned by both father and son.*

The mansion built in 1750–7 consisted of a piend-roofed H-plan main block of two storeys and a basement linked by balustraded screen walls (concave on the E side, straight and set well back on the W) to single-storey pavilions; the walling was all of brick construction, faced with ashlar at the basement and rubble above. The main block's E and W faces were almost identical, each of nine bays, the ends advanced and with rusticated quoins. Lugged architraves to the windows of the two main floors, the ground floor's tall to denote the *piano nobile*, the first floor (bedroom) openings small and flanked by swags at the end bays. On the E front the end bays also had Venetian windows with balustraded aprons. Urns along the wallhead. The E (entrance) front's pedimented door was reached by a double stair, the W (garden) front elevation's door by a perron with hammered-iron panel of the arms of the second Earl, reused from Redbraes. The screen walls extending from the ends enclosed service courts whose end pavilions (the N stables,

* James Macaulay, *The Classical Country House in Scotland 1660–1800*, 1987.

the s kitchen accommodation) were boldly advanced to the E and set well back to the W). In the fronts of each pavilion, a round-headed niche flanked by dummy windows, all with Gibbsian surrounds. Astride the centre of the roof of each, a broad chimney pierced by a round-headed arch; ball finials on the outer corners of the wallhead's moulded cornice.

Lorimer's remodelling of 1914–17 was thorough-going, giving the house more than a touch of pomposity. Most dramatic in its effect was his heightening of the roof, the steep pitches studded with dormer windows to light the new attic and surmounted by a flat platform on which stands the rather skimpy ogee-roofed square cupola. C18 urns were replaced on the wallheads. Below, the C18 first-floor windows were heightened, those of the end bays provided with new swags, and the basement windows deepened. At the E front, the piano nobile's Venetian end windows had already been replaced by *Burn* with tripartites whose heavy cornices carry swan-neck pediments over the straight-lintelled centre lights. This front's external stair was replaced by a broad three-bay balustraded porch, with round-headed openings piercing its rusticated ashlar masonry. This fronted the new principal entrance at C18 basement level, the original front door above, becoming a French window opening onto the porch's flat roof, stripped of its pediment and surmounted by a swagged cartouche carved by *Alexander Carrick*. On the garden front the perron ascends to a French window with two flanking windows.

At each end of the main block was added a full-height one bay projection (the s incorporating an extension by *Burn*, provided to take delivery of trolleys which crossed the yard from the kitchen through a tunnel). These are set well back from the main elevations. Less tactful was the erection of new blocks on the W side of the service courts, their outer fronts on the line of the C18 screen walls but considerably higher, the N range's face pierced by four large round-headed ground floor windows, the s by three widely spaced rectangular openings. Lorimer also rebuilt the end pavilions, heightening them by an additional storey and setting back their E ends from the building line of the C18 pavilions whose front walls were however, retained as screens but remodelled, with their central niches placed at a higher level. On the E wallhead of the new pavilions were rebuilt or replicated the central chimneys of the C18 pavilions. At the W front of each pavilion, three close-set large windows in Gibbsian surrounds.

The INTERIOR is one of the most exciting in any Scottish country house; a seamless mixture of periods from the C18 to the C20, all outstandingly well crafted. The low ENTRANCE HALL was created by Lorimer out of basement rooms. Simply decorated with Ionic pilasters. The floor, paved in Hoptonwood marble, with black marble dots, is carried to the r. through to the foot of Lorimer's principal STAIRCASE, a spacious well stair constructed of reinforced concrete, rising through two storeys to a domed cupola with pendant. It replaced several rooms and a cramped private stair at this end

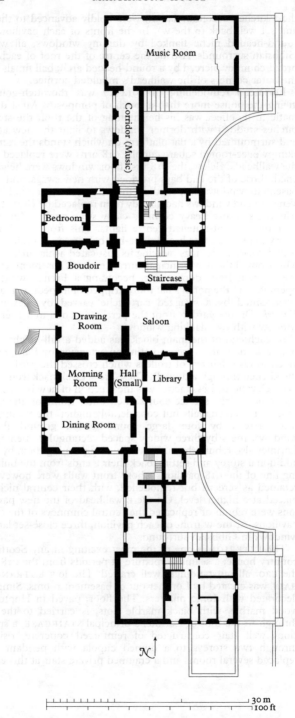

Marchmont House.
First Floor Plan.

of the C18 house. Fine wrought-iron balustrade by *Thomas Hadden*, with panels of sinuous curves, decorated with pecking birds, roses and sprays of cherries. The high dado rail has a Vitruvian scroll and egg-and-dart decorates the wall panels, based on C18 ornament in the Saloon and Drawing Room. At the first floor, a pair of arches in the w wall with plasterwork palm fronds in the spandrels, and a central armorial trophy, resembling authentic C18 work but in fact by *Thomas Beattie*, who undertook most of the early C20 plasterwork in the house. Above the trophy, the date 1916 in memory of James McEwen, killed in the First World War. To the l., above the door to the saloon is a panel of pipes and cutlasses, with long panels of twining leaves and roses. On the second landing two panels, one of musical instruments; the other celebrates the hunt, music and shooting. On the w wall a flower basket in typical C18 style. The weighty enriched C17-style ceiling, the central dome with carved pendant, is mostly by *James Annan, c.* 1834, with 'fresh' flowers and fruit added to the wreath by Beattie.

On the first floor, the former *piano nobile* of the third Earl's house, the Palladian planning was largely unaltered by Lorimer. At the front of the house in the centre is the SALOON, previously the entrance hall. Decorated in 1753–7 by *Thomas Clayton* (*Samuel Bryson, William Cunningham* and *Thomas Blackwell*, craftsmen) with some of the most spectacular plasterwork in the Borders. The walls and ceiling are awash with Neoclassical military trophies and shields in high relief, in the corners are the heraldry of the Marchmont family. An egg-and-dart cornice, a metope and triglyph frieze with sparsely spaced shields and rosettes matching that on the chimneypiece (moved to the s wall by Lorimer to make way for the doorway from the staircase). This is of pale grey veined marble with dark grey jambs. Above, on a console, is a bust of the third Earl in classical dress; a copy of the original,* now at Mellerstain House (q.v.). Above the doors, coroneted monograms of the third Earl and his second wife Elizabeth.

Niches each side of the Saloon's pilastered and corniced w door which leads to the DRAWING ROOM, a splendid room decorated by Clayton with Rococo plasterwork in honour of the heat and light of the sun. In the centre of the ceiling, the sun surrounded by baskets of fruit and flowers. Its rays penetrate the four corners, which have panels of sinuous palm fronds. Heads crowned with bows and sprays of leaves and fruit, representing the Seasons. A frieze of foliage, with a pineapple in the centre of each spray. Mahogany doors with lugged surrounds, those to the s and e with consoled cornices. A Vitruvian scroll round the dado and acanthus ornament round the skirtings. The chimneypiece is the most remarkable in the house, with a sunburst surround and integral Rococo mirror, within which is a painting of the first Earl by *William Aikman, c.* 1720. s of the drawing room is a MORNING ROOM. Fine classical timber chimneypiece with a swagged frieze and caryatid piers, their heads topped by baskets. e of this room is a small HALL, created by Lorimer from the former principal stair com-

*The original was reputedly bought at the Stowe sale in 1848.

partment. (The C18 stair was replaced by *Burn* in the 1830s.) The plaster decoration here is mostly by *Samuel Wilson* and in C17 style. Moulded panels and corniced doorways are divided by garlanded fluted Ionic pilasters. Ingeniously lit by a richly plastered oval opening to the floor above, surrounded by a low balustrade and four screens of Ionic columns, which support an oval glass lantern with thickly enriched plaster surround.

At the SE corner of this floor is the DINING ROOM (former Library, remodelled by Burn). On the ceiling a wide circle of fruit and flowers in the centre, at each end panels with guil-loched decoration contain the Marchmont(?) arms – perhaps a mix of C18 and 1830s work. Frieze copied from the C18 one in the drawing room by *James Annan* (1834). The room was remodelled by Lorimer in a restrained Neo-Georgian style. The Hoptonwood chimneypiece with green inlay has a circu-lar cartouche showing Orpheus, surrounded by birds and beasts, modelled by *Louis Deuchars*, carved by *Allan & Sons*. The present LIBRARY, E of the Hall, was formed from the former dining room and smoking room. Wainscotted in veneered mahogany, excellently finished by *Nathaniel Grieve*. Recessed shelving and a Hoptonwood stone chimneypiece.

To the N of the drawing room is a BOUDOIR. All Lorimer, with a coved ceiling, wall panels and a chimneypiece of Hoptonwood stone; in the frieze another circular cartouche of goats, putti and grapes modelled by Deuchars. Next, the prin-cipal BEDROOM, with a high coved ceiling; remodelled except for a C18 Kent-style chimneypiece with drop ornament jambs, foliage and flowers in the frieze with a sunburst head in the centre, and a sarcophagus-shaped support with a pineapple-finialled urn on top.

W of the staircase is a CORRIDOR which descends to the N pavilion. Groin vaults on decorative corbelling. On the E side at high level, four circular consoled niches with consoled brackets facing four round-headed windows to a sunken garden designed by Lorimer. The door to the MUSIC ROOM, in the N pavilion, has carving on an appropriate theme by *Alexander Carrick*. Inside, a lofty space with a deep coved ceiling and shallow central dome decorated in C17 style, the ribs richly decorated with acanthus and roses. Oak wainscot-ting (much of it originally intended for Lorimer's Rowallan House, Ayrshire), arranged in large panels framed by gar-landed fluted Ionic columns; each with a frieze of putti mod-elled by *Louis Deuchars* and carved by *W. & A. Clow*. Across the E end a full-sized ORGAN by *Norman & Beard* of Norwich, 1914, with richly decorated pipes flanked by pairs of panels pierced with arabesques. Along the top are six little figures of a faun and children, also by Deuchars, and a central group of four celestial musicians, the outer two by *C. d'O Pilkington Jackson*. Below the music room is a small ROMAN CATHOLIC CHAPEL, sparingly decorated and furnished, created in 1936. The formal gardens W of the house were replanned by *Lorimer*, with new entrances with cushioned piers topped by pineap-ples, walls and balustrades.

REDBRAES CASTLE, *c.* 0.3km. SE. Fragmentary remains of the castle of the Humes of Polwarth (Earls of Marchmont from

1697) which was razed by an English army in 1545 but subsequently rebuilt and enlarged by successive lairds. Pulled down during the 1750s to provide materials for the new Marchmont House. It seems to have included a five-storey central block, possibly a tower house, together with flanking wings added in about the second quarter of the C17. The character of the surviving carved detail (not all of it *in situ*) suggests that these wings were stylishly built in the Scottish Mannerist style. The angles are emphasised by distinctive buckle quoins, and some of the doors and windows have boldly channelled margins.

Close by are the STABLES, a courtyard range, partly reconstructed by *Lorimer* (who matched details from the earlier stable buildings, and incorporated a fragment of the castle; chamfered openings are particularly prominent). He added a circular battlemented Gothic tower at the s end and at the other a crowstepped Scottish Renaissance power house. The two-storey former granary(?) became a squash court, stabling and hay loft (now cottages), with a bellcote at the N end. Filling the SE side, the CHAUFFEUR'S HOUSE (Old Coach House) in Lorimer's Arts and Crafts manner, with low, sweeping bellcast roofs. – GARAGES with reinforced concrete canopy and original roller shutters. Similar LAUNDRY HOUSE, to the E. – To the NW a pair of single-storey and attic late C19 red sandstone, three-bay ESTATE COTTAGES. Gabled and bracketed dormers, and bracketed pentice porches.

WALLED GARDEN. Laid out from the mid C18. Three carved stone panels, said to come from Redbraes Castle, are placed over the doorways. Of the two that are still legible, one, now considerably worn, is a reused lintel bearing the monogram initials of Sir Patrick Hume, second Baronet, the date 1677 and a pious three-line inscription, the other has the well-cut arms of Sir Patrick and his wife following his creation as Earl of Marchmont in 1697. Fine, large range of GREENHOUSES by *Mackenzie & Moncur*, 1915.

LANDSCAPE. Mostly laid out and planted from 1726, it was planned around *William Adam*'s unexecuted design for a new house. From that time the long avenue (1.5 km.) remains, originally planted first with Dutch elms but replanted with beech in the 1880s. At the NE end of the avenue is a circular-plan DOVECOT, built by *James Williamson* in 1749 as a terminal vista. A domed roof surmounted by a tapering cupola with flightholes. Shouldered architrave to the doorway, and blank panel above; to the r. are two rows of flight-holes with tiered stone ledges. – ADAM BRIDGE, over the Swarden Burn. Attributed to *George Paterson*, 1759. – ICE HOUSE. W of the mansion in the undergrowth. Dated 1828 in a segmental-arched pediment over a round-arched entrance to a vaulted passage. – LODGE (Rowieston Cottage), 2.25 km. s on the A697. Probably built *c.* 1816 by *John Cunningham*, when a new drive was constructed. Gothic, octagonal with a central chimney and dentilled cornice.

MARLEFIELD HOUSE
3 km. E of Eckford

An intriguing and little-known house built for Captain William Bennet of Grubet *c.* 1695–1717. Repaired and altered by *George Paterson* in 1754–7 for William Nisbet of Dirleton who had acquired the estate by marriage. Further changes in the 1890s by *Kinnear & Peddie* for Athole Stanhope Hay and his wife Caroline Margaret, daughter of Sir Edward Cunard.

The late C17-early C18 house consists of a three-storey and attic M-roofed double-pile block (the valley mostly covered over in the 1890s), with square three-storey towers projecting at the corners. Walling of rubble, its harling unfortunately removed in the mid C20. Chamfered margins to the windows (the first floor openings lowered in the mid C18); the eaves cornice appears to be a replacement. The main block's long E and W elevations are each of five bays. In the centre of the E front, the principal door, with a lugged architrave, its pediment and sidelights added in 1891–2 by Kinnear & Peddie who also formed the tripartite window in a red sandstone surround to the r. Between the first and second floor windows of the centre, the coat of arms of the Bennets of Grubet. The W elevation's Venetian central doorway, formerly with steps to the garden, is an insertion, probably by Paterson in the 1750s. The dormer windows on this side were added in 1891–2 when Kinnear & Peddie also built a two-storey rectangular bay window at the S side. In the S side's walling, the fragment of a stone carved with the head and torso of a cherub holding foliage, and a panel bearing a classical scene.

L-plan, two-storey pavilions, their first floor windows tucked neatly under the eaves, are linked to the house by three-bay quadrant walls, with central round-headed doorways, the S one still surmounted by a stone lion. The pavilions were not harled, and appear to have been built or rebuilt by Paterson, *c.* 1754. The survival of an early C17 bolection-moulded chimney-piece in the S pavilion may be evidence of an earlier house on the site.

INTERIOR. A survey of 1890 by Kinnear & Peddie shows the double-pile plan with a longitudinal spine, four rooms on each floor and closets in the towers. Many of the closets have small bolection-moulded stone chimneypieces, perhaps surviving from the early years of the C18. The stair, centrally placed on the W side, continues from ground level to the attic floor, with moulded stone treads to the first floor, and timber ones from there on. The mahogany balusters are alternately straight and twisted, and finish in a fluted newel post; the way they fit into the treads suggests they are no earlier than the mid-C18. In the NE corner a former kitchen, now study, probably had a shallow vault, of which remnants remain. The window shutters have fielded panels. The NE closet appears to have some early C18 details. Unlike the other closets, there are an angle fireplace, pine panelling, and a coved ceiling with a circular painting. The other details are of 1891–2.

The HALL is now lined with panelling, said to have been retrieved from Cunard liners. An inscription plate identifies the frontdoor lock as having come from Robert Adam's Calton Jail, Edinburgh. The DINING ROOM, to the r., was restyled in 1891 and lined with panelling, given a large buffet recess, and timber chimneypiece with fluted Corinthian pilasters. The chimneypiece in the former SMOKING ROOM, to the l., has stone jambs with large consoles, supporting a timber overmantel, and imported Renaissance-style doors, one inscribed 'H L H fecit MDCCCXCI ROMA', with the coat-of-arms of the Hays. A lobby was created from the first-floor landing to serve the two E rooms, the southernmost two combined to make a new drawing room with a lowered ceiling and classical decoration. The N bedroom is higher and gives the impression of originally being a much grander room.

GARDEN. Nothing remains of the considerable landscaping planted in the early C18. On a modern support is a C17 red sandstone bowl, decorated with four grotesque heads, upside down, their hands pulling at their moustaches.

STABLES. Mid-C18 five-bay elevation, in coursed red sandstone, with later alterations. A central piend-roofed three-bay block with a Gibbsian surround to the doorway, repeated on the round-arched outer bays, and quoins at the angles. Wall-head frieze fronted by rows of balusters. Converted for domestic use by *Bain, Swan Architects*, 1990.

MAXPOFFLE HOUSE
5030

1 km. SE of Bowden

Built for Sir John Boyd, Lord Provost of Edinburgh, 1865. Asymmetrical, Scottish Domestic with a Baronial tower, in which there is little harmony between the various parts. Coursed whinstone with red sandstone dressings. A continuous string course takes in lintels, corbel courses and hoodmoulds. The three-storey tower has a crenellated parapet with angle bartizans and crowstepped caphouse. At its foot, curiously, is a Tuscan-columned porch with architrave, cornice and blocking course. Are this and the three bays to the l. part of the previous house (built by *John Smith, c.* 1810) on the site? Inside, the vestibule has a Gothic ceiling, and the timber well stair carved piers and uprights. Oakleaf and acorn cornice, compartmented ceiling and Gothic doors in the dining room.

STABLES. Probably former steadings, converted in 1904 to stabling and garages with some Arts and Crafts detailing. A panel in a wall of an early(?) C19 farmhouse is inscribed AD MR 1622. – Small circular rubble-built DOVECOT, said to be C17, has a narrow timber perching ledge round the wall-head, and a conical roof, formerly with a central conical capped pigeon entry. – LODGE. Mid-C19, gabled, with overhanging eaves.

6030   MAXTON

A small agricultural village on the s bank of the Tweed.

PARISH CHURCH. Set in isolation across a field N of the village,
the church is of T-plan, the rectangular main body probably
perpetuating a medieval church first recorded in the later C12.
The SE and SW doorways, with round arch and moulded
imposts, and of a type similar to one at Stow (q.v.), presumably point to C17 alterations. Remodelled by *Alexander King-
horne*, 1812, the date of the pair of windows (now with late C19
glazing) on each side of a centrally placed oculus, and the birdcage bellcote with ogee-profile dome on the W gable. The N
aisle, creating the T-plan, was added in 1866, possibly by *David
Duns*, who was consulted around that time; against its W wall
are traces of a blocked arch of uncertain significance. The
vestry at the NE corner was added in 1962.
   The interior, which has plastered coomb ceilings, is of great
charm because of the fine painted FURNISHINGS, most presumably dating from 1812. The pulpit is at the centre of the S
wall, while galleries at the E and W ends now have enclosed
vestibules below. – BAPTISMAL BOWL, brass, 1897. – PEW
FRONTS, raised and fielded panels. – PULPIT, rectangular with
projecting desk, set against an arched exedra framed by pilasters,
and with an oculus behind the arch. – STAINED GLASS. N wall
of N aisle, Jesus Healing and Suffer Little Children, 1914, *James
Henry Coram*(?), with a carved timber aedicule. – CARVED
TABLETS. Towards E end of S wall, Hebrew text from Psalms 89
and 95, 1724. Towards E end N wall, grey oval tablet with white
inset armorial commemorating the burial place of Kerrs of Littledean. Towards W end S wall, memorial to members of Brown
family, last of whom †1816, by *James Dalziel* of Edinburgh.
Above N window, and partly eclipsed by timber aedicule, 'Jesus
solus est nobis salus'. – SUNDIAL, SW corner.
   CHURCHYARD. Several enclosures, including that of
Cunninghams of Muirhouselaw in NW corner.
MANSE (Glebe House). Built 1804–6 in roughly coursed sandstone with pilastered doorway. A contemporary U-plan range
of steading and stables, each wing with an oculus.
MAXTON CROSS. Only the lower part of the shaft is original,
perhaps late C16; its capital, with a recumbent lion holding a
lamb in its paws, is lost, but was replaced by a simple cross in
1881 by Sir William Ramsay Fairfax.
VILLAGE HALL. Former Carnegie library and reading room, by
George MacNiven of Edinburgh, opened 1908. Red sandstone
Tudor-detailed hall with mullion and transom windows. Over
the door is inscribed 'Let There be Light'.
DESCRIPTION. The village consists of much-altered early C19
red sandstone vernacular houses built for agricultural workers.
At the E end, a red sandstone Tudor-detailed block, BYFIELD,
of *c.* 1900 designed by the mason-builder *Robert Grieve* as his
own house, office and workshop.
MOATED SITE, Muirhouselaw, 2 km. SE. Well-preserved earthwork remains of a probable medieval manorial residence,
possibly associated with the Rutherford family, and the meeting place in 1367 of Scottish and English commissioners for
peace negotiations. The earthworks comprise two contiguous,

ditched enclosures. On the NW side of the larger one (*c.* 67 m. square with rounded corners) a broad, flat-bottomed ditch is partially replaced by a pond, perhaps originally intended for keeping fish, which is fed by a channel running within the NE ditch. Most of the internal buildings were probably of timber, but within the E corner of the enclosure can be seen turf-grown footings of stone-built structures. The entrance probably stood hereabouts. The adjacent enclosure to the NW, which is less well preserved, is about half the size of its neighbour.

FAIRNINGTON HOUSE. *See* p. 275.

LITTLEDEAN TOWER. *See* p. 504.

MELLERSTAIN HOUSE
4 km. NW of Nenthorn

6030

A complete and little altered ensemble – building, interior decoration and contents – in a perfect, beautifully wooded landscape setting on a S-facing slope of the Eden Water valley. The house is of two periods: a classically proportioned main block with minimal castellated Gothic embellishments by *Robert Adam*, *c.* 1770–8 linked to the pavilions of an uncompleted house designed by *William Adam* in 1725–9.

60

The Mellerstain estate had been bought from Andrew Edmonston of Ednam by George Baillie, first of Jerviswood, in 1643. In 1700 George Home of Kimmerghame visited the Baillies and noted that 'they have ane old tower wt but one room off a floor about 5 storey high but it looks vert ruinous'. Even in the early 1720s, when the Baillies were contemplating a new house, the tower was being repointed and the windows reglazed. William Adam was working for George Baillie's brother-in-law, the second Earl of Marchmont in 1724, so what could have been more natural than to employ him to Mellerstain?

The new house designed in 1725 by Adam for George Baillie of Jerviswood (and Mellerstain) would have consisted of a main block in an Anglo-Dutch style of at least twenty years earlier and two pavilions. Only the pavilions, built round courtyards and resembling small classical country houses in their own right, were erected in the 1720s. These are rubble-walled oblongs of seven bays by four, the long sides facing each other across the mansion's forecourt. Gibbsian surrounds to the ground-floor windows, and entrance doorways to the court; the small square windows above have moulded margins. Platformed and piended roofs with central octagonal domed cupolas, each with a single ball finial, originally gilded.

Robert Adam's main block, built for George Baillie's grandson, George Hamilton (later Baillie) is linked to the pavilions' inner S corners. Faced with beautifully worked yellow sandstone, its shape is that of a pair of back-to-back Es, the piend-roofed transverse blocks of three storeys above a basement (the centre block taller than the end ones), the rest of two storeys and basement. Carried round is a band course between the basement and ground floor piano nobile, and string courses under the upper floor. Tudor hoodmoulds over the rectangular windows, the second-floor openings of the end transverse

sections small. The wall-heads are all finished with battlements, mostly carried on corbels, those of the transverse blocks
on machicolation. The ends of the transverse blocks, three bay
at the centre and two bay at the ends, project only slightly at
the seventeen-bay S elevation but boldly at the otherwise
almost identical N (entrance) front whose elaborate doorway
is early C20.

The modern visitor enters the house via the E wing (*see*
below) but this description begins with the main block, which
contains a series of stunning INTERIORS by Robert Adam.
These were executed progressively, the ceilings in particular
being designed as work continued, mostly in answer to George
Baillie's particular requests. The drawings were often returned
to Mellerstain by clerks of works on their way back from
London to Adam's other projects in Scotland. *John Bonnar*
carried out the painting, working 1771–8. *James Adamson*,
carver, who received payment of £500 in January 1777, undertook the carving. Mahogany, specially finished, was supplied
by *Mr W. Hamilton*, Edinburgh, for rails, astragals and panels;
his account was discharged in 1773. An otherwise unknown
plasterer called *Powell* was working at Mellerstain in 1777.

The plan form of the interior is in the shape of an E and strikingly shallow, merely one room deep with the rooms set in
enfilade along the S front with corridors on their N side. As
Mark Girouard has noted,* Mellerstain is almost unique in
Adam's *oeuvre* for the use of rectangular spaces. The exception
is the ENTRANCE HALL, which is contained within the projecting centre of the N front. This has a typical Adam plan with
apsidal ends, round-headed niches, and a good Doric frieze;
the metopes contain shields with crossed swords and daggers.
Richly embellished ceiling. Adam also designed the curved
marble chimneypiece, like most of the chimneypieces on the
principal floor. The double stair is squeezed in along the N wall
and meets in the middle, with a single flight over a bridge to
the bedroom corridor. Beneath the stair, a door in the N wall
to the corridors, one of the few Gothic interludes in an otherwise strictly Neoclassical interior. The W corridor is groin-
vaulted, the E corridor is tunnel-vaulted, divided into four
sections and decorated with some inventive Gothic plaster
detailing, cleverly arranged to give a diminishing spatial effect
towards the cosiness of the breakfast room (sitting room) at
the far end. The use of the Gothic is unusual for Adam, but
it bears similarity to a design (now in the Soane Museum)
for the library at Alnwick Castle, Northumberland. There is
more Gothic work on the E back staircase. The ceiling of the
BREAKFAST ROOM also has delicate Gothic decoration of interlocking circles, and Gothic-style decoration on the friezes above
the doors. The chimneypiece has coupled columns on the
jambs.

The remaining rooms from E to W begin with the beautifully
proportioned LIBRARY, one of Robert Adam's most impressive interiors. The scale is intimate, helped by the four groups
of low bookshelves sunk into the wall and divided by Ionic
pilasters, which also frame the doorcases. The sequence of
Ionic pilasters is continued on the window wall, where they

61

Country Life 28 August and 4 September, 1958.

frame oval mirrors. A deep decorative palmette frieze along the tops, fluted with paterae over the doors. Above the bookcases low-relief plaster panels of subjects taken from antique models, white against a dark background. The panel at the w end, showing Priam entreating Achilles for the body of Hector, has been identified* as deriving from an illustration from Pietro Bartoli's *Gli antiche sepolchri overo mausolei romani ed etruschi* (1727, pl. 82), a copy of which was purchased by George Baillie. Above the doors are six circular recesses fitted with a single bust: all but two are by *Scheemakers* and *Roubiliac* and date from the 1740s. The best and most appealing is surely Lady Grizell Baillie, aged 81, with exceptionally fine drapery. Anthemion and palmette frieze round the wall-head, for which there is a drawing by Adam. The ceiling drawing, dated 1770, seems to be the earliest one for Mellerstain. In strong pinks and greens, with a painting of Minerva in the centre, surrounded by panels of musical trophies and medallion heads. The design for the centre of the ceiling is taken from Adam's unexecuted design for the library at Luton Hoo, Bedfordshire.[†] White marble chimneypiece with black marble backgrounds to the fluting, and patera ornament.

The DINING ROOM (Music Room) at the centre of the s front is modest after such richness. Pretty compartmented ceiling of light blues and greens, with a central medallion showing the sacrifice of an ox, encircled by a band of grapes and vine leaves, within an octagon with rinceau and fan ornament, and eagles holding up four medallion panels of dancing girls; griffin plaques in the end rectangles. The chimneypiece is an 1820s replacement, signed by the apparently unknown *J. Marshall*. Marble with figures of War and Peace on pedestals and a centre panel of oxen ploughing. The DRAWING ROOM ceiling has delicate patterns of circles linking panels of vases and supporting griffins. White marble chimneypiece with insets of brown marble simulating fluting, and a centre panel of cherubs. The frieze of thistle-filled vases is used elsewhere on this floor.

STATE BEDCHAMBER (Small Drawing Room). A white marble chimneypiece with a panel of Apollo and lion. At the w end, a BEDCHAMBER and DRESSING ROOM, now combined into a small library. The ceiling in the corner dressing room is delicate, with a centre oval and stylised Etruscan vases in lozenge-shaped medallions. Later timber chimneypieces. On the floor above, the bedrooms are simple with plain cornices, some improved by imported chimneypieces.

The largest room is the GALLERY, at the top of the house in the centre tower, with long vistas to the Cheviot Hills to the s and Mellerstain Hill to the N. It is approached through a square, domed anteroom with a dummy Gothic window in each wall. The, gallery has screens of Ionic columns supporting a barrel vault: a drawing for an ornamented ceiling is dated 1775, but was never carried out. The idea seems to have come from George Baillie, but in a letter written in spring 1778 Robert Adam suggests that the ceiling should remain 'plain and elegant and not expensive', and the ornament be restricted

---

*by Mark Girouard.
[†]E. Harris, *The Genius of Robert Adam*, 2001.

to the end 'upright walls' (tympana), which are decorated with tripods and vases, griffins and enchanting cherubs. Similar frieze. One other room must be mentioned: the so-called ADAM BATHROOM in the centre of the basement's N side. This has a Gothic chimneypiece, fan-shaped shells over the windows and spouting dolphins decorating the arch to the bath. Is this a fantasy by Robert Adam, or something whimsical by a craftsman?

Before the construction of the main house, the family lived in the 1720s E WING. Of William Adam's interior, a survival is a particularly fine wrought-iron birdcage newel at the head of the spiral stair. E of this wing is a service court with a two-storey crowstepped cottage, now a tearoom. Probably remodelled c. 1859. Its W gable has a clock dated 1735, made by *John Kirkwood* of Ridpath for Lauder Tolbooth (q.v.). On the gable apex a square bellcote. The W WING contained the stables, completed by *James Runciman*, c. 1729–38. Converted to domestic use in 1971–3 by *W. Schomberg Scott*, who removed all the original fittings.

MAUSOLEUM. In an enclosure N of the house, approached by a short avenue of trees. Classical temple, in yellow Coldstream sandstone and rubble. 1736, by *James Runciman*. Three-bay pedimented façade with a cartouche in the tympanum and three parapet urns. Gibbsian surrounds to the doorways and blank arches, which contain marble memorial plaques. The l. one, to George Baillie (†1738) has a Latin text by Dr William King, Principal of St Mary Hall, Oxford.

THE OLD COTTAGE, N of the house, is thought to have been two former cottages, their present form dating from the mid-to-late C19. Harled walls, punch-dressed quoins, and pyramidal thatched roofs. – Mid-C19 rustic SUMMERHOUSE with walls of vertical split logs and ceiling of pine-cones. – LODGES date from the early-to-mid C19, when a minor road, N of the house, was curved and sunk, so that it could not be seen from the house. EAST and WEST LODGES built in the earlier C19. Two ruinous C18 lodges; one, on the old drive, is single storey with a two-bay façade divided by engaged Doric columns supporting a wide semicircular pediment, the other, by the walled garden, pedimented, with oculus, and hood-moulded porter's window. – THE ROW, opposite the E lodge. Mid-C19, single-storey cottages, the roofs raised and dormers added in 189[8], and given a screen wall, with oculus, across the W end, flanked by a ball-finialled N gateway and s pier.

LANDSCAPE and GARDENS. Developed over a long period from the late C17 to the early C20. The mid-C18 landscape, contemporary with the formation of the landscape at Marchmont (q.v.), was already complete by 1738 and can be seen on General Roy's map of c. 1750. It began with the formation of enclosures, the planting of formal avenues and the creation of ponds and waterworks. *William Adam* had a hand in designing the landscape, when he planned his house on a N–S axis with a wide avenue to Mellerstain Hill. The E–W axis was marked by a double avenue of trees over 3 km. long, reduced to a single avenue, planted with beech and lime c. 1800. A canal was made c. 1727 by widening the Eden Water, its s end dammed in 1748 by Mr *Craw* to create a series of cascades.

On the skyline 2 km. SW of the house, the vista is closed by an eyecatcher, the HUNDY MUNDY. A tall Gothic archway with square, turreted towers. Begun 1726, credibly with advice from *William Adam*, possibly using rubble from the old tower (*see* above). In 1909–11 *Sir Reginald Blomfield* redesigned the park on the S side of the house as GARDEN TERRACES with a wide lawn, bordered by clipped beech hedges, running down to the canal, emphasising the view to the Hundy Mundy and the distant Cheviot Hills. Imposing, formal Italianate terraces are linked by an impressive flight of steps forming an arch over a loggia on the lower terrace. In the centre of the lawn is a circular fountain. Blomfield also redesigned the canal and renovated the cascade. Wisely, only half of the formal scheme was completed. A boathouse dates from this period. – WALLED GARDEN. E of the house on a steep slope running down to the river, with a high N wall, *c.* 1756. Cottage and conservatory, *c.* 1900.

WHITESIDE TOWER. *See* p. 689.

MELROSE

INTRODUCTION

The medieval and early modern town of Melrose grew up at the gates of the abbey. All the inhabitants were tenants of the abbey and subject to the jurisdiction of the Abbot's court. After the Reformation these rights of superiority passed to a succession of temporal lords, for much of the C17 the Earls of Haddington and subsequently the Dukes of Buccleuch. Melrose became a burgh of barony in 1609 and a burgh of regality in 1621. The town developed to the S, with Market Square, and had its own gates; the narrow East Port survives, but the West Port disappeared when the High Street was extended to the W in the middle of the C19. The principal C18 industry was the production of Melroseland linen. This trade declined in the late C18 when water-driven woollen mills were developed in Galashiels and Selkirk. There was no industry in Melrose in the C19, but the renewed interest in Gothic architecture through the writings of Sir Walter Scott, and his presence at Abbotsford (q.v.), combined to put new life into the town. It became a tourist centre, heightened by the coming of the railway in 1849, and a place for professional people to holiday in the summer months, especially enjoying their favourite pastime of fishing in the River Tweed. To accommodate this influx of professionals and summer visitors, a brisk trade in villa building began. From *c.* 1830 building continued W from the High Street, until *c.* 1855, at which time the building trade went into the doldrums, but began again in 1867, when large Baronial-style villas began to be built at High Cross.

MELROSE ABBEY

6, 7 Melrose, the eventual successor to the c7 community at Old Melrose (*see* p. 643), is probably Scotland's best-known abbey, and is of supreme importance both for its architecture and for its place in the history of the nation's monasticism. It was the first house for the Cistercian order in Scotland, with monks brought from Rievaulx in Yorkshire by David I, and all but three of the order's ten other Scottish foundations were descended from it. Its early history is outlined in the *Melrose Chronicle*, which

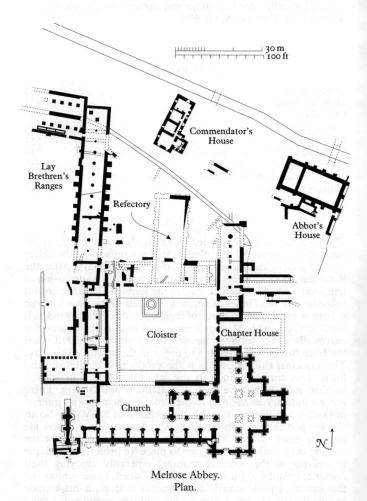

Melrose Abbey.
Plan.

was compiled at the abbey between its foundation in 1136 and 1266. The abbey prospered, becoming amongst other things Scotland's greatest producer and exporter of wool, already by the 1180s enjoying a special relationship with Flanders, where the main markets for its wool lay. Little survives of the first stone church, which was badly damaged by English armies in 1385. Rebuilding on a magnificent scale was initiated soon after then, the main phases of that process providing what is arguably the most valuable expression of developing architectural attitudes in later medieval Scotland.

Since at least the C18 the abbey ruins have been a major source of artistic and architectural inspiration, not least to Sir Walter Scott, in whose own house at Abbotsford (q.v.) and in Kemp's Monument to Scott in Edinburgh, the abbey's architecture finds its modern reflection.

CHRONOLOGY

In accordance with Cistercian custom, work on site may have begun with construction of the monastic buildings and a temporary oratory. The *Melrose Chronicle* records the dedication of the church as early as 28 July 1146, however, and a Galilee porch was added at the W end of the church in the late C12. The abbey's Border location assumed new significance with the outbreak of the Wars of Independence in the 1290s, and as early as 1307 Edward I of England was asked for timber to carry out repairs. Further major damage was caused by his son's armies in 1322, and Robert I made provision for grants totalling £2,000 in 1326, suggesting extensive rebuilding was contemplated.

The greatest turning point in the abbey's architectural history was the assault on the church in 1385 by English troops, after which total rebuilding was commenced, though possibly with the earlier church being only progressively demolished as the work advanced. It is unlikely that the late medieval church was ever more than two-thirds finished; the structural history of what was built can be divided into three main phases.

The FIRST PHASE (*c.* 1385–1400) established the new church on a magnificent scale, employing superbly worked ashlar masonry and with stone vaulting over all parts. This phase embraced much of the presbytery and S transept, the E side of the N transept, and the arcade level of the monks' choir in the three E bays of the nave. But not all of the vaults over those parts were then constructed, and several of the windows only received their tracery later. Richard II of England made a brief contribution to the work through reductions in customs dues in 1389, and it is possible that he provided the first designing mason. The essentially English character of the work is especially evident in the rectilinear window tracery.

The SECOND PHASE of the church is associated with the Paris-born mason *John Morow* and represents a particularly important phase in the opening up of Scottish architectural thought to Continental influences, at a time when the wars with England had resulted in a reaction against English ideas. Morow inserted in the S transept two inscriptions relating to his work, listing other buildings on which he had worked, which together suggest he was active around the first decades of the C15. His contribution to Melrose is best seen in the introduction of a new type of window tracery, characterised by a careful balance between restrained flowing forms and 'spherical' figures.

The THIRD PHASE of rebuilding is particularly associated with the long abbacy of Andrew Hunter (1444–71), but was probably started before his term of office. Thereafter progress was slow, and was almost certainly incomplete when work was largely abandoned after English attacks in the 1540s.

The REFORMATION in 1560 brought an end to conventual life, and in 1609 the abbey's estates were erected into a temporal lordship for John Ramsay, Viscount Haddington, who took the additional title Lord Melrose. Parochial worship in the abbey continued, however, and since the nave seems never to have been completed, it is possible that it took place in a surviving portion of the earlier church. c. 1621, on the instigation of Thomas Hamilton, Earl of Melrose, a new church was formed within the monastic choir, in the E bays of the nave. Massive piers of masonry were inserted on the N side, a pointed barrel vault constructed, the N clearstorey was blocked and major modifications made to the S clearstorey. A simple bell-cote was placed on the S transept gable, suggesting the parochial entrance was by way of the doorway there.

By 1808 it was decided a new church should be built elsewhere (p. 548), and the Duke of Buccleuch, successor to the Earls of Haddington, then assumed responsibility for the old church. The E and W walls of the post-Reformation church were removed to re-open the vista through the church, though its N piers and pointed barrel vault were retained. Periodic repairs were carried out, and the abbey transferred to the State in 1919. Between 1921 and 1936 most of the complex was excavated.

DESCRIPTION OF THE CHURCH

The church is described broadly chronologically following the main phases of its construction.

The PLAN OF THE FIRST CHURCH (begun c. 1136) was established through excavation in 1923 and shows that it belongs within a seminal phase in the development of Cistercian architectural ideas. It was a variant of the so-called 'Bernardine' plan employed at St Bernard's abbey of Clairvaux in Burgundy in the 1130s, and then favoured throughout the order for its extreme simplicity. Its hallmarks are a short rectangular presbytery, transepts with chapels on their E face for additional altars, and a relatively long aisled nave to house the two choirs, of monks and of lay brethren. At Melrose, the three chapels on each transept were arranged in echelon, with that flanking the presbytery on each side stepped slightly eastwards, an arrangement used at Rievaulx after 1147, but perhaps also in an earlier church of the 1130s, and at Fountains Abbey after c. 1133. This stepping was possibly to accommodate more easily the higher processional entrance to the presbytery.

The only upstanding part of the original church is the lower part of its W WALL, which is of rubble with ashlar dressings. Its extreme simplicity, devoid of all mouldings, is an eloquent indicator of the stark austerity of the first building, the masonry of which would have been simply rendered over. There is a single central doorway with simple rectangular rebates, and the plane of the front is broken only by shallow pilaster buttresses on the line of the nave arcades. The Cistercians' processional requirements encouraged construction of a GALILEE over the W entrance. It usually extended across both nave and aisles, and was one bay deep. At Melrose the only Galilee of which evidence remains was a secondary addition, and unusual in being wider than the central nave but not as wide as the aisles; it was also two bays deep, with arcades carried on four piers of quatrefoil plan. A single surviving base of early water holding type suggests a late C12 date.

The E parts of the LATER CHURCH are relatively well preserved, 6 including most of the walls of the presbytery, the transepts, the three E bays of the nave and eight of the chapels against the S side of the planned ten-bay nave. The seven W bays of the nave itself and the two W chapels along the S side of the nave were probably never completed, possibly leaving the western bays of the earlier church in place. The greatest post-Reformation structural losses resulted from the collapse of the E, N and S faces of the central tower, and the construction and subsequent partial removal of the post-Reformation parish church in the E bays of the nave.

The PLAN of the later church is essentially a larger version *p. 534* of its predecessor, including the echelon arrangement of the inner transept chapels. Elsewhere, the need for more altars had already led to the general adoption by the Cistercians of more complex plans, e.g. at Newbattle Abbey (Lothian) and Kinloss Abbey (Moray), though the 'Bernardine' plan was still chosen for the order's final Scottish foundation at Sweetheart Abbey (Dumfries and Galloway) in the 1270s. Its revival at Melrose is therefore not altogether surprising. Existing foundations were used as far as possible, though a little extra width may have been gained for the central spaces by setting the walls and piers towards the outer edges of those foundations. This, and the location of the cloister, meant that the new N nave aisle was possibly even narrower than its predecessor. The chief scope for enlargement was by lengthening to E and W. The continuity of the base course indicates that much of the church was set out in the early stages, though on the S side of the nave it must have been moved outwards when chapels were added. But above that level, as work moved from E to W, there were changes of detail within the limits of an overarching homogeneity of approach.

In the FIRST PHASE of rebuilding these changes are most evident in the INTERIOR. At first it seems there were to be no wall-shafts in the presbytery, and when they were introduced after a few courses they were given no bases. But subsequently there are telling changes of base and capital types to the piers, responds and wall-shafts. The earliest two base types, to the E responds of the presbytery arcades and the wall-shafts in the

inner transept chapels, are of revived waterholding profile. A
third base type also has a form of waterholding hollow, but of
late medieval form with an ogee moulding rather than a lower
roll. This third type is used throughout the arcades of the presbytery and transepts, and in the three bays of the monks' choir
at the E end of the nave. There are three main types of arcade
pier capital. In the presbytery and inner bay of each transept
they have multiple mouldings separated by bands of square
flower. Elsewhere there are two types of foliate capitals to the
arcade piers: in the S transept the foliage is relatively freely
composed, whereas in the N transept and monks' choir the delicately finished two-dimensional foliage follows a tight convex
profile. The more freely composed foliage type is presumably
the earlier, since something similar was used for the E responds
of the presbytery arcades. Despite changes in the capitals, the
piers throughout are of modified octofoil plan with keeled
diagonal shafts, but with a twin-shafted element towards the
central vessel. The way these twin shafts are corbelled out in
stages, until triplet vaulting shafts develop above the level of
the arcade capitals, is a particularly attractive feature. In the
presbytery they are further enriched with a tabernacle.

The aisled sections are two-storeyed throughout, and the
elevations of presbytery and transepts suggest an origin for the
master mason of the first phase of rebuilding in the lodges of
p. 539 E Yorkshire. The rear arch with traceried balustrade to the
clearstorey windows of these parts points to an awareness of
the approach that developed through the choirs of Selby Abbey
and Howden Collegiate Church. But Melrose's clearstorey has
an inner screen of arches within the rear arch, with differences
of detailing between the single surviving aisled presbytery bay
and the narrower transept bays. The rather plastically modelled
octofoil form of the piers may also owe something to E
Yorkshire, e.g. Beverley Minster, while the shafts towards the
central vessel and the tabernacles could have taken a lead from
the eastern parts of York Minster.

The surviving VAULTING over the E bay of the presbytery
has a tunnel-like profile partly comparable to roughly contemporary work in the aisles of St Giles', Edinburgh, and over
the upper hall of the royal castle of Dundonald (Ayrshire). Yet
it has more elaborate ribbing, set out to a basically tierceron
arrangement, but with pairs of ribs branching out either side
of the transverse ridge rib, and others intended to cross into
the next bay. This decorative pattern of ribs, in which the structural sense has been largely forfeited, shows awareness of the
net vaults that had been developing in western England in the
C14, e.g. Tewkesbury Abbey (Gloucestershire) and Gloucester
Cathedral. However, Melrose's vault is less accomplished, and
the way its ribs and bosses appear to be simply set against the
vault surface is rather unusual. English West Country developments could also have influenced the design of the vault of
the chapel on the N side of the presbytery, which must
have been almost flat; it may have been completed in timber.
The vaulting over the other transept chapels and the high
spaces of the transepts was probably only completed later on
the evidence of the rejection of more complex forms in favour

of a tierceron pattern seen in the middle chapel of the N transept.

On the EXTERIOR the chief foci of this first phase are the E wall of the presbytery and the S wall of the S transept. They are closely related compositions, though the latter was only completed later. The E WALL is framed by angle buttresses, which have tabernacles in rectangular recesses at the intermediate level and blind tracery to the upper sections, from which square pinnacles develop. The gable of this wall has a panelled arrangement of tabernacles, through which an ogee hood-mould is struck. Such enrichment of the gable is partly reminiscent of work in eastern England of the first half of the C14, e.g. the Lady Chapel at Ely Cathedral (Cambridgeshire) or the

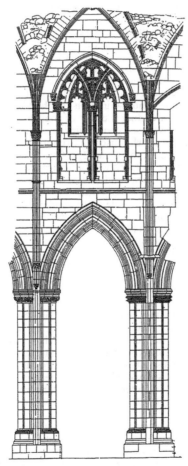

Melrose Abbey.
Elevation of one bay of the North Transept.

E face at Howden Church (Yorkshire). The tabernacles have figurative sculpture; at the apex is a pair of figures usually identified as the Coronation of the Virgin, but possibly an incomplete Trinity, and partly comparable in style with the late C14 kings above the w door of Lincoln Cathedral. The E window is of unique angularity, with mullions that rise unbroken to the arch, triangular light-heads and lozenge-shaped forms, all showing some parallels with Yorkshire work, e.g. St Mary's, Beverley. Tracery of more common English rectilinear types is found in the s flank of the unaisled section of the presbytery, the clearstorey of the aisled section, and in the chapels s of the presbytery, as well as in the E clearstoreys of both transepts. Apart from examples at Corstorphine (Edinburgh) and Carnwath (Lanarkshire), such rectilinear tracery was to be seldom employed in Scotland.

6

The s TRANSEPT FAÇADE was no doubt designed and mostly built by the master mason who built the presbytery. However, the overall effect is very different, as a result of a change of window design and the insertion of a doorway.

The SECOND PHASE, of the early C15, was probably not of long duration, but was of great significance in reflecting a radical shift of architectural attitudes in Scotland. It possibly embraced little more than the completion of the s transept, the insertion of some windows in parts that had already been built, and the start of building the row of chapels against the s wall of the nave. This phase can be linked with the arrival of the mason *John Morow*, who inserted two inscriptions on the inner face of the w wall of the s transept. One of these, on a framed stone tablet (now replaced with a replica) records that Morow had been born in Paris, and that he had already been responsible for mason work at St Andrews (Fife), Glasgow, Paisley (Renfrewshire), Nithsdale (Lincluden?) and Galloway (Whithorn?; Dumfries and Galloway). At a time when extended warfare had created a deep antipathy against England, this suggests the abbey had now chosen to look to France for architectural guidance.

7

Instead of the hard angularity of the E window, the five-light s transept window has sinuously flowing forms within two subarches and a large circlet with a grouping of 'spherical' triangles and cusped circlets at the head of the composition. Flowing tracery was also introduced in the N flank of the unaisled section of the presbytery and at the upper level on the w side of the s transept. The subtle balance between flowing and 'spherical' forms seen in the s transept window is paralleled, albeit on a smaller scale, in the two easternmost chapels against the nave s flank. The window design in the E chapel is also found at Lincluden Collegiate Church (Dumfries and Galloway) and at Paisley Abbey (Renfrewshire), and this allows Morow's work to be firmly identified at those buildings. He may also have inserted the crouching figure corbels bearing inscribed scrolls below a number of the s transept buttress tabernacles, which are of a type related to examples at Lincluden College and Glasgow Cathedral (ex situ, but probably from the w towers).

The idea for the ROW OF CHAPELS against the S flank of the nave could also have been Morow's. This was a way of gaining the additional altar space required for the monks in priest's orders that was adopted at several European Cistercian churches, e.g. Fontfroide in southern France. The vault of the first chapel also has a French flavour, with ghosting of a ring of lierne ribs around the central intersection, and remains of suspended cusping from the ridge ribs. The addition of the chapel aisle was marked by the introduction of a new base type to its responds and vaulting shafts, with a fully Late Gothic vertically flattened ogee form. Related bases were also inserted, probably around the same time, for the S respond of the S transept arcade, and for the wall-shafts at the outer corners of the transept chapels.

Of the DOORWAYS constructed as part of this second phase, the S transept doorway, which must have served as the chief lay entrance, is the most important. It is flanked by miniature pinnacles, and has four continuous orders of filleted rolls separated by hollows rising from a deep base. The arch has an ogee-flipped hoodmould, and running behind it is blind arcading; a partial parallel for this might be traced in the panelled decoration behind the arch of Princess Margaret's tomb at Lincluden (Dumfries and Galloway), presumably also a work of Morow's. At the apex of the hoodmould is a crouching figure of St John the Baptist holding a scroll, rather like the crouching figure corbels of the S transept tabernacles. The arcading embraces secondarily inserted Apostle figures, some being set uncomfortably off-centre; their heavy drapery is analogous to that of figures of SS Peter and Paul on the W wall of the S transept. Three other doorways of this phase have semicircular arches, and are among the earliest examples of the renewed fashion for such arches in late medieval Scotland. Those in the N transept, at the head of the night stair and into the sacristy, have simple continuous mouldings. The third is the processional entrance from the cloister into the N aisle, and is more elaborate, with three filleted shafts to each jamb and drilled foliage carving to the capitals and hoodmould.

The THIRD PHASE, c. 1430–c. 1470, included the completion of the N transept, the clearstorey of the monks' choir, the continuation of work on the S nave chapels, and possibly the insertion of some windows in the N transept chapels. It also involved the construction of vaults throughout the high spaces of the transepts and monks' choir, together with some of those of the transept chapels. One of those chiefly involved in this campaign was Abbot Andrew Hunter (1444–71), whose arms are on the S transept vault, on the buttress between the fifth and sixth of the nave chapels, and are said to have been on the intermediate buttress above the first nave chapel. This phase of works is of particular interest for showing how, after English and French masons had been at work, an essentially Scottish architectural synthesis was emerging. In this synthesis ideas were being assimilated from both of those sources and also from Scotland's own architectural traditions.

Externally the changes introduced at this stage are most

obvious in the use of paired single-light windows at the upper
levels, in preference to larger traceried windows. These are seen
first on the W side of the N transept, and then in the monks'
choir clearstorey (i.e. the first three bays of the nave). Another
change at this phase is seen in a slight thinning of the N nave
aisle wall after the first bay, which coincides with a change in
the design of the decorative blind arcading on the side of the
wall towards the cloister. Internally, the change from traceried
clearstorey windows at the E end to paired single lights further
W is eased by the continued use of openwork balustrades to
the clearstorey passage. The construction of tierceron vaulting
over both the transepts and monks' choir must also have
increased the sense of architectural unity. (The existing
pointed barrel vault over the monks' choir was constructed in
the early C17, and the rear arches of the S clearstorey were then
reconstructed to a segmental form.) The second of the S nave
chapels was completed and much of the work on the next
four chapels executed during this phase. Windows in three of
these chapels have identical tracery, with spiralling daggers in
a circlet as their main motif, and all three have the same reveal
mouldings. The other chapel of this group, the fifth from the
E, has slightly different reveal mouldings, and triplets of
daggers within the sub-arches and at the window head. This
window, the same as one of the mid C15 in the N transept at
Jedburgh Abbey (q.v.), has the arms of Abbot Hunter
(1444–71) on the buttress to its W.

The STATUARY carved during this phase (now replaced by
replicas) is particularly distinguished. Within the N transept,
between the paired windows at the upper level of the W wall,
are badly weathered figures of SS Peter and Paul, their heavily
draped clothing, if nor their facial characterisation, showing
something of the same spirit as the figures carved by John
Thirsk in the 1430s and 1440s for the chapel of Henry V in
Westminster Abbey. By a different hand are statues of St
Andrew and the Virgin and Child in buttress tabernacles rising
between the two levels of flyers abutting the high vault on the
S side of the nave. The latter, with its swaying pose and elegantly disposed patterns of thin drapery, is the finest thing of
its kind in Scotland. It shelters within a highly enriched tabernacle flanked by vertical bands of miniature tabernacles. The
architectural decoration of this part of the building varies in
quality, however, and many of the head corbels to the window
hoodmoulds are more stereotyped than those further E. More
individualised is the famous bagpipe-playing pig on the clearstorey cornice.

Only two further bays of the chapel aisle were completed in the
FINAL PHASES of work after 1470, and it is doubtful how much
further W the main body of the nave was taken than the pulpitum at the end of the monks' choir. The moulded details of
the last chapels took their lead from those in the earlier
chapels, and the window of the seventh chapel had spiralling
daggers based on the earlier type. A piscina in the sixth chapel
has initials assumed to refer to Abbot William Turnbull
(1503–7), while a panel of the royal arms on the buttress on
the W side of the eighth chapel is dated 1505. N of this but-

tress, within the nave, are the lower courses of the w front of the first church, indicating that reconstruction of the main body of the nave can never have progressed so far, and supporting the idea that parts of the first church remained in use to the end.

Only the w side of the crossing tower survives, rising a low single storey above the surrounding roofs and presumably originally surmounted by a timber spire. In keeping with Scottish preferences – perhaps first expressed at Kelso in the C13 (q.v.) – its face has three equal-height lights. Like the s transept stair-turret, the angles of the tower have recessed three-quarter shafts, here carrying miniature bartizans. The wall-head balustrade is of square quatrefoils, like the internal clearstorey passages, but evidently punctuated by short shafts carried on corbels between the window heads.

FIXTURES AND FURNISHINGS. PRESBYTERY. Two aumbries (relic lockers?), behind the site of the high altar. In the N and s walls, a symmetrical pair of segmental-arched tomb recesses. w of that in the s wall are two finely detailed small ogee-arched recesses, one presumably serving as a credence, and the other containing two piscina bowls. Facing these on the N is a rectangular recess, possibly associated with an Easter Sepulchre. In the MONKS' CHOIR, in the three E bays of the nave, are stumps of a low wall running along the inner side of the piers. Against this would have been placed the stalls.* The PULPITUM, at the w end of the monks' choir, is a relatively plain structure, albeit with foliage enrichment of the cornice and doorway hoodmould on the w side. The passage through the pulpitum has a miniature tierceron vault, and off its N side a stairway led up to the loft. In the s CHAPELS several good piscinae.

MONUMENTS. PRESBYTERY, a number of relocated coped gravestones. N NAVE AISLE, w of door to cloister, a mural tablet to 'ye race of ye hous of Zair', with arms of Ker and *memento mori*. s CHAPELS, first chapel from E, a lectern-shaped stone in the floor has an inscription requesting prayers for Brother Peter the Cellarer; third chapel from E, on w wall, tablet with strapwork for Master David Fletcher, †1665; fourth chapel from E, on E wall, three-arched Gothic Revival tablet for Scott of Gala family, first recorded death 1877; panel for Sir James Pringle of Galashiels, †1635; on floor, small effigy of Andrew Pringle of Galashiels, †1585; fifth chapel from E, three-arched Gothic Revival memorial for Pringle of Whytbank family; against w wall, C17 memorial for same family; sixth chapel from E, slab with incised representation of George Haliburton, †1538.

THE CONVENTUAL BUILDINGS AND PRECINCT

The church and main conventual buildings were at the centre of a PRECINCT of about 16 ha.; little, if any, of its enclosing wall survives except possibly at Greenyards (*see* Description,

---

* Stalls were ordered from *Cornelius de Aeltre* of Bruges, and when the abbey eventually went to law over their non-delivery in 1441 it was said they had been ordered many years before.

below). The precinct was entered through three or four gateways; the main (s) one, facing towards the later market place,
is known to have had a chapel on its upper floor. Water was
brought in by a lade from the River Tweed, N of the abbey, and
from there was conducted around the buildings through stone-
lined channels and lead pipes. It was presumably the water
supply which dictated that the CONVENTUAL BUILDINGS
were N, rather than S, of the church, but otherwise the layout
of the main core is orthodox in its arrangement around three
sides of a cloister against the nave flank. The site was excavated
in the 1920s and 1930s, excluding those areas beneath the
roads overlying the N parts of the three claustral ranges and
parts of the lay brethrens' quarters W of the cloister.

Little is known about the CLOISTER WALKS, though C12 double
capitals likely to be from the cloister, of both scalloped and
waterleaf type, survive in the Commendator's House museum
(*see* below). The walls of the church towards the cloister as
rebuilt from the later C14 onwards suggest the latter was itself
to have been lavishly rebuilt. Towards the cloister, along the N
transept and the first bay of the N nave aisle, stone benches
support wide two-centred arches, framed by crocketed ogee
hoodmoulds and with miniature pinnacles between. These
arches would presumably have been reflected in openings
along the outer walls of the walks. W of the first nave bay, the
arcading is more two-dimensional, though still more ambitious
than anything else surviving in Scotland. The probable seat of
the abbot for the daily reading from the *Collations* of Cassian
is given particular emphasis.

Enough of the E CLAUSTRAL RANGE survives as consolidated
lower walls to understand its basic planning. N from the
church, the sequence was: sacristy, chapter house, day stair,
parlour, and an extended chamber (probably the novices' day
room) with a central row of cylindrical piers to carry vaulting.
The latrine projected at right angles, E from the range, above
the great drain. It would have been approached through the
DORMITORY, which must have occupied the whole of the
upper floor. The dormitory roof was hipped at the junction
with the S transept to clear the traceried circular window below
the apex of the transept vault.

The E range incorporates work of a variety of dates. The only
part to survive complete is the barrel-vaulted SACRISTY, which
is entered from the N transept of the church. The cubical
masonry of the wall it shares with the chapter house, together
with the vault, are evidently mid-C12, though much of the rest
is late medieval. Much of the E range was remodelled around
the second quarter of the C13. References in the *Melrose Chronicle* to the re-burial of abbots at the E end of the CHAPTER
HOUSE in 1240 suggest it had recently been rebuilt, and the
surviving details of the entrance front would accord with such
a date, the jambs having shafts with waterholding bases. The
tomb of St Waltheof (†1159) was immediately within the
entrance. The main body of the chamber has been lost, but
four phases of its plan were identified in excavations in 1996.
As first built it was probably entirely within the body of the
range, and possibly stretched further N, but in the *c.* 1240

works, and again after the damage of 1385, it was considerably extended to the E. In its most extended form it was square-ended and probably vaulted in three aisles. Areas of a complex tile pavement have been found within, including some fine inlaid tiles, and with parts set out in interlocking wheel patterns. Some of these remain *in situ*, while others are displayed in the Commendator's House. At a late stage the part of the chamber beyond the range may have been demolished.

The N CLAUSTRAL RANGE, which survives only as fragmentary footings, was initially largely given over to the REFECTORY. First set E–W alongside the cloister walk, as part of mid-C13 rebuilding it was realigned to project at right angles to the cloister. The refectory itself was presumably on the first floor, above a vaulted undercroft of three by eight bays. There were kitchens on its W side, where they could serve the refectories of both monks and lay brethren. The warming house and day stair were probably relocated to the E. Projecting into the cloister was a square lavatory pavilion, with the foundations of a circular basin.

The foundations and lower walls of the LAY BRETHREN'S QUARTERS, W of the cloister, extend further to the N than the buildings on the other sides of the cloister. Excavation suggested there was initially a lane between the lay brethren's range and cloister (as at Byland Abbey, Yorkshire), which was later absorbed into the cloister. The earliest part of the range, probably of the mid C12, would have contained a ground-floor refectory and a dormitory above. Like the E range, much of the ground floor was presumably vaulted in two aisles carried on the cylindrical columns which partly survive, though this may have been a later insertion. A shorter block projected W from its S end, apparently in the form of an open N-facing loggia. Its upper floor or roof was carried by a stone arcade of alternating cylindrical and octagonal piers on its outer (N) face, and by timber posts in sockets along the central E–W axis. The pre-waterholding form of the bases is of late C12 type. Its S wall was blank, presumably to shield the processional W entrance to the church from the mundane activities within the lay brethren's courtyard.

Overlying the N end of the earlier range is a major C13 addition, which was vaulted in two aisles. Differences in the surviving pier fragments suggest that they and the vaulting were inserted in more than one operation, and buttresses were added along its outer walls for support. Projecting W from the N end of the range, and straddling the drain, are the lower walls of a large aisled hall; nothing survives of its piers apart from the square sub-bases. Its W parts are now overlain by the road, and its original extent is unknown. Parallels with the Cistercian houses of Fountains and Jervaulx (Yorkshire) suggest it was the LAY BRETHREN'S INFIRMARY. The survival of tanks shows the building was later put to some industrial use, such as leather tanning.

Foundations assumed to be of the ABBOT'S HALL have been excavated NE of the cloister on the lade bank. This was presumably the 'magna camera abbatis' for which Abbot Matthew (1246–61) was given credit in the *Melrose Chronicle*. It was a substantial structure with a rectangular hall of four bays and what was probably a chamber of one bay at its W end; it also seems to have extended E beyond the boundary wall of the adjoining property. Traces were found of a porch and other structures on its S side. The principal rooms were perhaps at first floor, above a vaulted basement.

W of the Abbot's Hall is the presumed COMMENDATOR'S HOUSE. Its date of construction is unknown, though *James Richardson*, who restored it in the 1930s, argued that it was first built for Abbot Hunter in the mid C15. As now seen, however, it largely dates from reconstruction in 1590 by the post-Reformation commendator James Douglas (his initials and the date are on a replica lintel over the entrance), and from Richardson's restoration. Of two storeys, with four compartments connected by a corridor at the lower level, and three compartments above; a square offshoot on the E side contains the entrance and the stair. It houses an important collection of worked masonry and artefacts from the abbey, including fragments thought to be from the shrine of St Waltheof.

A short way E of the cloister, within a later brewery complex, is a vaulted chamber that possibly formed part of the MONKS' INFIRMARY.

GRAVEYARD. S and E of the abbey church. Some C17, but mainly C18, C19 and C20 memorials. One of the earliest, some 20m. S of the S transept, is an incised slab for Andrew Mein (†1624), mason in Newstead. Several show a local taste for chests with open arcaded bases. Opposite the eighth bay of the S chapel aisle, burial enclosure of the Smith of Darnick dynasty of masons and architects, with memorial to Andrew Smith, †1695, and two later obelisks; S of the presbytery, a second enclosure with monuments of the Smith of Darnick family, including a Tuscan column surmounted by an urn for John Smith, †1815, flanked by later obelisks commemorating other family members. E of the presbytery, Andrew Pringle, †17?0, high-relief three-quarter portrait to rear and capped by angel pediment. Also E of the presbytery, two Neoclassical monuments with panelled bases and urn finials, to James Fisher of Sorrowlessfields, †1820, and to George Thomson, †1835. S of the S transept, a fine (late C18?) stone with crossed violin and flute, and with portrait profile, but no inscription.

CHURCHES

CONGREGATIONAL CHAPEL, Buccleuch Street. Dated 1843. Two-storey, with a round-headed doorway under an inscribed panel.

CONGREGATIONAL CHURCH, Weirhill. Built 1878. Secularised. Steeply pitched roof, corner buttresses, pinnacles and lancet windows.

HIGH CROSS CHURCH (R.C.), High Cross Avenue. Originally the United Presbyterian Church by *Peddie & Kinnear*, 1866, with monogram and date on the N front. A Romanesque hall church of four bays. A broad gabled front to the N, with gabled doors to l. and r., and a shallow projecting narthex between.

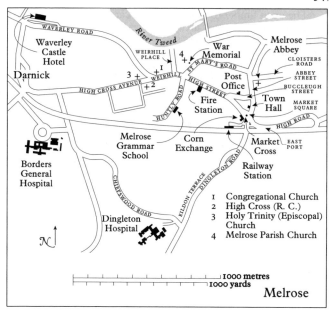

This has a dwarf arcade with five single-light windows, sculptured capitals and alternate red and yellow voussoirs. A large plate-traceried rose window over. The massive NE tower was completed 1872. Of three stages; a clock in the second stage, a belfry in the third stage with triple round-headed louvred openings in each face. Corbelled octagonal buttresses at the angles, with conical spirelets; on top the main broad octagonal spire. The front and tower are of snecked rock-faced rubble, with stugged and polished dressings. Each side elevation has three round-headed windows divided by large buttresses. The addition to the s is C20. A simple interior. White walls, and coved flat timber-boarded ceiling arranged in large squares with diagonal and horizontal ribs.

HOLY TRINITY (Episcopal), High Cross Avenue. *Benjamin Ferrey* prepared the first set of plans for the Duchess of Buccleuch in 1846, in which year the site of the church was staked out. Enlarged to the E in 1900 by *Hay & Henderson*. Ferrey's aisleless church is E.E., of creamy-white sandstone with a green slate roof. Four bays long with stepped buttresses at the angles and between the nave windows. A two-storey porch on the s side has an octagonal staircase turret on the E side. At the w end are paired lancets, with a trefoil opening above, and a bellcote on the gable. The later chancel and two transepts, provided to give more interest and dignity, have a broad chamfered plinth and the stepped buttresses of the nave. Projecting window gablets light the chancel; delicate flèche to the crossing.

The open timber roof of the nave is carried on mask corbels; alternate trusses have arched braces. The pierced-traceried balcony at the w end of the s side fronts the room over the porch, accessed by the outside turreted stair. It was originally designed to hold an organ and choir. At the crossing (1900), the principals are in pairs, and from the angles of the four walls, the horizontal beams form a great cross. Each transept is divided from the nave by two high traceried arches springing from slender shafts. The central column in the s transept has a capital of carved heads and incised names of the four saints chiefly associated with Old Melrose, Eata, Aidan, Boisil and Cuthbert. Richly sculptured corbels on each side bear the names of the two dioceses of Glasgow, 1849, and Edinburgh, 1900.

The woodwork is mainly pine, stained brown; the choir stalls are oak. The ALTAR, with delicate green riddels with gilded angels, and the COMMUNION RAIL, were renewed in 1945. – PULPIT of Caen stone, by *Winsland & Holland* to *Ferrey*'s design. – FONT (Caen stone), also by Ferrey? – The chancel floor is paved with *Rust*'s mosaic work; steps and platform of Sicilian marble. – ORGAN, N transept, 1931. – STAINED GLASS. In the chancel a three-light window (the Adoration of the Risen Christ by Angels and Saints), by *James Powell & Sons*, 1913; N wall, composite window by *William Wailes* (Calvary, the Annunciation, Nativity and Gethsemane) formed in 1900 out of three earlier windows; crude colours; s wall, three-light window of the Annunciation, dedicated in 1891; in the s transept, a three-light window by *C.E. Kempe* (the Blessed Virgin with SS Agnes and Cecilia), *c.* 1895; nave N side, SS Peter and John, *c.* 1890; to the l., the Good Shepherd by *Mayer*, *c.* 1882; the designer's mark on one of the sheep; nave s side, the Blessed Virgin and St Elizabeth, *c.* 1885 (by Kempe?); at the w end (SS David and Gregory), two lights by *William Wilson*, executed by *John Blyth*, signed and dated 1963. Some Geometrical glass by *James Powell* in the rest of the windows.

GRAVEYARD. w of the church, the Middleton headstone, *c.* 1928, lettering by *Eric Gill*, the male figure presumably also by him; to the N, a headstone to James Walker Fairholme R.N., who 'Perished in the Arctic Region with (Sir) John Franklin in HM Ship Erebus – with the Tergon 1845/6'. A well-detailed plaque with angels, in the background a ship on rough seas – splendidly evocative. In the NW corner the DUNDAS CROSS, modelled on the Kildalton Cross (Islay), to Sir Philip Dundas of Arniston, †1952, and Sir Henry Dundas, †1963.

MELROSE PARISH CHURCH, Weirhill. The removal of the congregation from the dismal parish church within the Abbey ruins left the fifth Duke of Buccleuch free to preserve the 'Gothick Fabrick' of the Abbey at his own expense, and the heritors free to build a new church. The first church on this exposed site was an early work by *John Smith*, 1808–10, who, together with his brother Thomas, also acted as contractor. Built of Quarry Hill stone. Nearly destroyed by fire in 1908, but the steeple survived. *Thomas Ross* and *J.P. Alison* were asked to submit drawings for a new church, but another invitee, *J.M. Dick Peddie*, who declined to participate in the first round, won the second one. Smith's tower is of four stages with round-headed openings. The third stage, set back, contains the clock, while above is an octagonal belfry and spire; the fine weathervane was supplied in 1809 by *William Muir*. The earlier church was square on plan, entered from the tower, with a three-tier pulpit, and galleries on three sides. In the new arrangement the tower remains in the centre of the s side, with no communication with the interior. Peddie's block is Georgian Revival, built of coursed squared rubble with polished ashlar dressings. On the N and s elevations are tall round-headed windows between buttresses, and a moulded cornice and wall-head balustrade. The nave roof is pitched, and the aisles have flat roofs. At the E end the gable is supported by huge consoles; a Venetian window almost fills the wall space.

The interior is spacious and monumental. A five-bay nave with Doric columns on high octagonal bases, two aisles, and a chancel at the w end. It is vaulted throughout. The chancel is panelled with African mahogany, the four pilasters decorated with carvings of fruit and flowers. At the E end, a small chapel, 1984, by *Duncan Cameron & Associates*, the screen by *Martin & Frost*. – STAINED GLASS. Three-light chancel window (King David, St Margaret and St Cuthbert attired as a bishop) by *Christopher Whall*, *c.* 1908. – At the w end, a memorial to Hyndman Rutherford Crawford, 1911. In the vestry, a fragment from the Free Church, demolished in the 1950s, is all that is left of a memorial window to Anne Ross Cousin, †1906, hymn writer, showing her portrait bust with an hourglass above, and the text 'I'll bless the hand that Guided/I'll bless the heart that Played', signed by *James Benson*, Glasgow.

CHURCH HALL; 1950s in matching style. Later, another pitch-roofed single-storey block was added along the N elevation; the steps and pedimented entrance door are of 1997.

PUBLIC BUILDINGS

BORDERS GENERAL HOSPITAL, 0.8 km. sw. By *Reiach & Hall*, 1976–87. On an open site at the foot of the Eildon Hills. Three storeys, built of load-bearing white concrete blockwork, with contrasting pink bands specially manufactured to relate to local earth colours. Flat asphalt roofs; these should have been pitched but cost cutting defeated common sense. Entrance canopies, like Middle Eastern tents, are fun, but cannot disguise the impression of entering the hospital through the loading doors. – To the r. of the entrance is the CHAPLAINCY CENTRE by *Reiach & Hall*, 1993. A semicircular chapel, clearstorey-lit, with the roof soaring upwards. Glazed rear wall; behind it is a cross in a tranquil pool, and another small chapel. Nurses' housing to the E, also by *Reiach & Hall*, designed to become general housing if required. Excellent landscaping by *David Skinner* with grassy knolls successfully hiding the cars and access roads.

CORN EXCHANGE, Market Square. By *David Cousin*, 1863. A Scottish Jacobean three-storey, five-bay symmetrical street frontage. Coursed, squared, rock-faced rubble with polished sandstone dressings. Doors and windows with carved crestings and strapwork-pedimented heads, the outer ones on the first floor with tabernacle frames. The centre three windows are grouped together behind an enriched cast-iron balcony, and the crowstepped gable above is corbelled out on three blank arches. The interior of the rear hall has a timber roof (concealed) with hammerbeams and semicircular ties in the centre.

DINGLETON HOSPITAL, Dingleton Road. Built as the Melrose District Asylum, begun in 1869 by *Brown & Wardrop*. An Italianate E-plan block was first, the SW elevation with two advanced wings housing the infirmaries, the recreation hall projecting in the centre, with the chapel above, both with large windows. Two tall ventilation towers rise from the roof, ornamental as well as practical. Later ADDITIONS 1895–1904 by *Sydney Mitchell & Wilson* included a new female hospital, laundry, and wings added to the NE front of the main hospital. – NURSES' HOME by *Tarbolton & Octerlony*, 1936, and HOUSING by *J. & J. Hall*, 1931 and 1936. Now utilitarian, but a brief respite is the BOILER HOUSE on the NE side of the site by *Peter Womersley*, 1977. A concrete wall, visible from the town, hides three low extensions with long sloping roofs. *Brown & Wardrop* were also responsible for the DOCTOR'S HOUSE (Kiloran), SW of the hospital, dated 1869, an asymmetrical, two-storey Italianate house with timber-bracketed eaves, and for the two LODGES of the same date, both single-storey and attic, with bracketed eaves.

Former FIRE STATION, 1901, in the NW corner of Gibson Park. A small coursed and squared, rubble building with red sandstone dressings, and piended roof with timber dentilled cornices. Classical N elevation with double timber doors. Above, a small semicircular dummy window contained in a heavy ogee-moulded surround which is continued across the lintel.

90 MARKET CROSS, Market Square. Dated 1645 on a square capital bearing the initials IEH for John, Earl of Haddington. It replaced an earlier cross in a similar position. Restored shaft rising from a mid-C19 octagonal stepped base. The eroded unicorn, with mell (mallet) and rose for Melrose, replaced in 1991.

MELROSE BRIDGE, 1.5 km. NW, over the Tweed. Much reworked bridge of 1762, narrow with two arches, centre cutwaters and square, recessed pedestrian refuges; buttressed approaches. – TOLL HOUSE at the N end. LOWOOD LODGE at the S end may incorporate the small square house for the keeper of the bar.

MELROSE GRAMMAR SCHOOL, Huntly Road. 1990, by *Borders Regional Council* (project architect, *Glen McMurray*). Wide horizontal panels of coloured brick, curtain-walled with blue panels. Over the doorway an inserted lintel dated 1670 from an earlier school erected from funds bequeathed by David Fletcher, a former minister of Melrose. The grammar school previously occupied the Board School to the N (now Resources Centre) of 1874 by *A. Herbertson & Son*. Tudor, single-storey, in red sandstone, the skyline broken by projecting gables and a belfry.

POST OFFICE, Buccleuch Street. By *H.M. Office of Works*, 1902. Renaissance, single-storey, snecked rubble with sandstone dressings. An off-centre door with oculus and semicircular pediment over, which breaks into the wall-head balustrade. Mullioned tripartite window in an advanced bay, with single windows either side.

Former RAILWAY STATION, Palma Place. Converted to a restaurant and offices by *Dennis Rodwell*, 1986. Opened 1849 on the Waverley line of the North British Railway Co., and partly demolished for the by-pass along the line of the old track. By *John Miller*, consulting engineer, *Hall & Co.*, contractors. Closed 1969. The station was built into the side of an embankment, entered from street level, with the two platforms at first-floor level. Its Scottish-Jacobean offices were suitably impressive for visitors to Scott country, and provided a good vantage point for a first view of Melrose Abbey. Built of coursed, squared rubble with sandstone dressings, with rendered sides and rear. Curvilinear gable with Jacobean cresting and octagonal chimneys. Surviving platform awning, made by *Blackie & Sons*, with a sloping roof springing from curved wooden brackets, supported by cast-iron columns with lotus capitals. A superb prefabricated cast-iron urinal made by *George Smith & Co.'s Sun Foundry*, Glasgow, has been moved to the Severn Valley Railway.

SUSPENSION BRIDGE *see* GATTONSIDE

TOWN HALL, Abbey Street. By *John & Thomas Smith*, 1822, reconstructed *c.* 1896, when the sixth Duke of Buccleuch gifted the building to the burgh. Two storeys, four bays, with doors in the outer bays. On the N gable a double chimneystack with a belfry (with bell). A carved panel from the abbey, built into the centre window at first-floor level, bears the arms of Abbot William Turnbull (1503–7).

WAR MEMORIAL, Weirhill. By *Robert S. Lorimer*, 1921, in the form of a Greek cross. Three bronze panels.

WAVERLEY CASTLE HOTEL, Waverley Road. 1871, by *James C. Walker* for the Waverley Hydropathic Co. Extended 1876. Four-storey, built in technically innovative mass concrete, probably the earliest use in Scotland, originally lined out to resemble ashlar but now of bland lumpy appearance. The people it accommodated were there to receive curative treatment, to enjoy 'the beautiful scenery, and the historical and classical associations of the site'. Further additions were made to the N in the late C19, and a recreation room added by *J.M. Dick Peddie* in 1912. The string courses between the floors, the raised long and short quoins, and raised window margins on moulded console brackets, are all mock-ashlar details. The principal elevation is composed of two linked blocks. The W block of 1871 has an advanced centre bay containing the main entrance, now at ground-floor but originally at first-floor level, approached by a broad flight of steps, with a flat-roofed porch and decorative cast-iron railing along the wall-head. Full-height canted bay at the W end. The E block (1876), slightly projecting, has three-storey canted bays, another one on the E gable, with a polygonal five-storey turreted tower at the NE corner; a slim six-storey, square-parapeted, originally balustraded tower rises in the re-entrant angle. The upper-floor windows have bead-and-reel-moulded timber window frames. The loss of wall-head gablet chimneys has resulted in a bald appearance. Inside, the dining room (former drawing room), has a deep, compartmented ceiling with decorated ribs.

In the grounds is a STATUE of Sir Walter Scott seated with his dog Maida at his feet, presented by Mrs Merryweather of Clapham Common and Long Acre, London; presumably contemporary with the hotel. Some original cast-iron GAS LAMPS survive. To the E is the former PUMP KEEPER'S HOUSE, also built of concrete. Altered.

DESCRIPTION

1. The High Road, Market Square and High Street

The HIGH ROAD is the entry from the E. On the N side is PRIORWOOD HOUSE. Built as Priorbank for Major Gowdie, c. 1815. The square, three-bay villa was raised and extended and given dull bargeboarded gables and dormers by *Peddie & Kinnear*, 1875. PRIORWOOD COTTAGE (Abbey Street) was the gardener's cottage at the S end of the WALLED GARDEN whose early C19 rubble wall steps up the E side of Abbey Street. It was raised in 1905 and given large semicircular scallops along the top, containing decorative wrought-iron work of grapes and vine leaves, and a square-headed gateway with the same, dated JC 1905 BC. Two-storey cottage with gable to Abbey Street, a canted bay window, and three bays to the S with a forestair to the first floor.

Following on High Road is PRIORWOOD COURT, sheltered housing by the *Bield Housing Association*, 1980. On the opposite side of the road THE WALL (1988), the massive concrete retaining structure of the Melrose by-pass, relieved with a pattern of pink concrete strips. It was designed to be ornamented with references to the Waverley Novels, but audacity ran out. Continuing to EAST PORT, with a bow-ended corner building of c. 1830. Rubble with sandstone dressings. Three bays on the N side, and a tripartite window with dummy outer lights at first floor. Restored by *Aitken & Turnbull*, 1981. To the corner with the Market Square (*see* below) a mid-C19 remodelling of a thatch-roofed cottage. Inserted in the middle of the first floor, a lintel dated 1635, and a vaulting boss from the abbey. On the N side, mid-C18 housing. A terrace of three, then the SHIP INN, formerly a pair of houses, with their gables to the street, altered mid C19, both blocks retaining their chamfered window margins.

90 The triangular MARKET SQUARE, with the Market Cross (*see* above), has three main streets branching out from its corners. Dingleton Road (S), High Street (W) and Abbey Street (N).

First up DINGLETON ROAD, whose corner block with East Port was reconstructed in the late C19, and turned to front the Square. The remainder of the mid-C19 terrace along Dingleton Road includes the STATION HOTEL. Formerly thatched, mostly of two storeys, three bays, and with dormer windows. Opposite, PALMA PLACE leads to the former station (*see* above). The by-pass bridge cuts off the rest of the town to the S, and blights EILDON HOUSE, immediately on the S side, a villa built by *John Smith*, 1814, for James Curle, Sir Walter

Scott's local lawyer and financial adviser. Coursed and squared
rubble with sandstone dressings. Two-storey, three-bay with
advanced centre, cornice, blocking course and block pediment.
The doorway has a cornice, architrave and fanlight. Additions
by *Eildon Housing Association*, 1996. Opposite is MAVISBANK,
a late C18 two-storey, three-bay harled house with later
pilastered doorcase, fanlight, and twelve-pane glazing. Later
gabled dormers. Uphill, late C19 housing towards Dingleton
Hospital (*see* Public Buildings, above).

Returning to MARKET SQUARE, on the S side is the LIBRARY,
a mid-C19 Georgian survival house of two storeys and three
bays, with ground-floor shops. A typical example of its kind,
repeated with varied details throughout the town. Next the
CORN EXCHANGE (*see* Public Buildings, above), followed by
the ORMISTON INSTITUTE, erected by the Trustees of
Charles Waller Ormiston in the late C19. In red stugged ashlar
with round-headed windows. Projecting from the front, a cast-
iron clock dated 1892, on an ornamental bracket; in memory
of John Meikle, physician and surgeon. Across a lane is BURT'S
HOTEL, originally two separate buildings. The E part mid-C18,
the W later C18. Both two-storey, three-bay, harled houses, with
painted margins and quoins. The W block has a key-blocked
Venetian window on the first floor with Gothick glazing in the
centre window; above is a wall-head gable, formerly surmounted by urns.

Now westwards into HIGH STREET and an entry to PEND-
STEAD, the former United Secession Church of 1823. A two-
storey, six-bay block of coursed, squared rubble with sandstone
dressings, with a segmental-headed pend in the centre of
the ground floor. A stone forestair leads to the upper floor.
Well-detailed C20 catslide dormers in the roof. Further down,
Melrose's premier hotel, the GEORGE & ABBOTSFORD
HOTEL, was built as the George Inn in the early C19. Originally a six-bay block, the l. bay advanced with a pilastered
doorcase with sidelights, and a tripartite window over. In the

Melrose, Market Square.
Watercolour by Sir David Erskine, 1821.

late C19 a second floor and mansarded attic were added, with a bold cornice at the wall-head and pilastered and pedimented dormers to the attic. Recessed to the r., a two-storey addition containing the main entrance; porch with paired Tuscan columns, and a balustrade over continued as a balcony round a canted bay which rises from the ground floor. Further W is the simpler and more austere KING'S ARMS HOTEL. Three-storey and attic, four bays. Coursed, squared rubble. The main entrance through a Tuscan-columned doorpiece. Original twelve-pane glazing on the first floor. A long single-storey stable range to the S. Further on, a mid-C19 four-bay house and shop or office, with a timber oriel window on the first floor. Next, BIRCH HOUSE, set back from the street, with a centre advanced bay and pediment. Beyond is the ROYAL BANK OF SCOTLAND, former Commercial Bank of 1887, rather feeble compared to its Renaissance rival in the Square (see below). A tall red sandstone, three-storey building, with curved central gable. The ground floor has a long dentilled cornice across the front which rises over small blank arches above the banking hall entrance. Three villas follow: the former ST DUNSTAN'S (Borders Regional Council) is by John Smith, c. 1835. The doorway in the centre bay has cavetto reveals and bracketed cornice, with a blocking course. Later extension to the E. Also attributed to Smith are two other villas: WEST END HOUSE, which has a centre window with dummy sidelights, and a mini semicircular blind window in the pediment. Across the ground floor a projecting late C19 glazed shopfront. The last villa has a round-headed doorcase with cornice and blocking course, a tripartite window above, with the centre block pediment carried on corbels. A large late C20 car showroom extends from the NW corner. On the l. of High Street is VICTORIA PARK and THE GREENYARDS on the r., originally common land, part of whose S boundary overlies the footings of a WALL which may have formed part of the medieval precinct of the abbey.

E of The Greenyards, at the corner of High Street and Buccleuch Street is ABBEY PARK (St Mary's School), built for Captain Stedman, a retired army major, c. 1820. Typical classical house of coursed squared rubble with sandstone dressings, with a segmental bow in the centre of the S front and wide Tuscan pilastered doorway with side lights and armorial panel above. Added to in the late C19, and in 1960–4 by Cowie & Seaton, for the school. The W front has an advanced pedimented bay. Contemporary classical stables (Hugh Fraser Buildings) to the NE, converted to housing, 1975. Single-storey LODGE, c. 1820, with piended roof and windows with sloping hoods.

The tour returns E along the N side of the High Street, with part of a terrace of mid-to-late C19 housing and shops as far as the N side of MARKET SQUARE. First is the plain MASONIC LODGE, rebuilt in 1861, with craft symbols displayed at first-floor level. Inside, built into the wall of the first-floor hall, is a stone window surround brought from the masons' lodge at Newstead (dem. 1892). Decorated surround with guilloche and dogtooth ornament and jambs rising from foliaceous stops; above the lintel is a hoodmould with label stops carved as miniature classical capitals. To the E, the BON ACCORD

HOTEL. Formerly two separate buildings, the w part is early
C19, two storeys and two bays, with a tripartite window on each
floor. A pilastered doorcase to the l. Mid-C19 three-bay house
to the E. Both fronts rendered and lined out as ashlar. The
BANK OF SCOTLAND follows. Built as the British Linen Co. 101
Bank by *George Washington Browne*, 1897, in his free Renaissance style. A tall red sandstone building of two storeys and
attic, behind a high shaped gable topped by obelisks. Three
bays wide, the bays divided by panelled pilasters at each floor.
Entrance in the E bay and a large segmental-headed window
lighting the telling hall to the l. On the first floor two bipartite
mullioned and transomed windows, another lights the attic.
Two-storey E wing, also mullioned and transomed, for the
offices and shops. The mid-C19 two-storey CLINKSCALES has
a recessed curved corner with a crowstepped gable over. It continues down the w side of Abbey Street, as a four-bay block,
formerly two houses, linked to the Town Hall (*see* above) by a
recessed single bay. The well-built and detailed houses and
shops on the E side of the Market Square are probably those
built in 1868 by Adam Black of Priorbank (*see* Priorwood
House, above), when he cleared away a number of thatched
houses. An eroded small cube SUNDIAL projects from the SE
corner of the block on the N side of East Port.
After the Town Hall (*see* above), the w side of ABBEY STREET
continues with a *c.* 1900 Renaissance block in red sandstone.
Behind this intruder is LITTLE FORDEL, a two-storey mid-
C19 house, formerly the stables of Priorwood House (*see*
above). Much altered but retaining the cartshed openings as a
screen to the garden of the house. Following on is MOROW
GARDENS, which continues into Buccleuch Street. Tenements
by *Roxburgh County Council*, *c.* 1960, rendered with sandstone
margins and a high base course. Gabled and dormered with a
turret at the corner.

2. The Abbey's environs

The clearing of buildings from the site in front of the Abbey
began in 1919, but was not completed until *c.* 1950. On the E
side of Abbey Street is Priorwood Cottage and walled garden
(*see* Priorwood House, above). In CLOISTERS ROAD, E of
Abbey Street, the Commendator's House (*see* Melrose Abbey,
above) on the l. To its NW, an early C18 DOVECOT, formerly
associated with Priory Farm. Rectangular, lean-to, with crowstepped gables; those on the E gable renewed when it became
part of the farm steading. Tall central dormer in the S roof,
containing tiers of flight-holes. Past the abbey on the r. is THE
CLOISTERS, formerly the parish manse, by *John Smith*, 1815;
built after Melrose Parish Church had been erected on Weirhill
(*see* Churches, above). Symmetrical, the doorway with corniced architrave and fanlight. Later two-storey canted bay to
w. At the end of the road on the r. is a remnant of the
BREWERY established in the early C19. The late C19 N range
of a courtyard complex remains. Two storeys and loft. A wide
central pend with moulded impost blocks and segmental arch;

the inscription, 'Simson and McPherson Ltd Brewers and Maltsters', is fast fading away. Ahead, the panelled and ball-finialled gatepiers to ABBEY PLACE. Built *c.* 1835 in whinstone rubble, extended to form an L-plan in the late C19, when the entrance was moved to the E front. N along ABBEY STREET stands the early C19 ABBEY MILL. A former two-storey corn mill, four bays wide, with the kiln at the N end. Now a woollen mill showroom.

Return S past the junction with ST MARY'S ROAD. On the r. is the entrance to HARMONY HALL, built for Robert Waugh, *c.* 1818, and probably by *John Smith.* Waugh originally trained as a joiner, but made his fortune in Jamaica, returning to Melrose to build his large house, surrounded by a garden and high precinct wall, from which he seldom emerged except to join the Abbotsford Hunt. Sir Walter Scott always referred to him as 'Melancholy Jacques'. Two storeys, basement and attic. Three-bay S front, in black whinstone blocks with warm cream-coloured sandstone dressings and quoins, the back and flanks of coursed red and cream sandstone. The centre bay advanced with a pediment. Wide flight of steps, with decently curved cast-iron balustrades, and a small Ionic porch, with blocking course. The doorway has sidelights and a segmental-arched fanlight. On the N elevation the central bay is bowed and contains the stair. Early C20 two-storey NW addition, and one to the NE, built in two stages during the C19, with a castel-lated parapet.

The entrance opens into a square vestibule, treated archi-tecturally with free-standing columns at the corners support-ing a coved plaster ceiling. A geometric staircase rises from the basement to the attics. The dining room and drawing room are 'large and very lofty and finished in the first style'.* The dining room to the W has doorways with pilasters and enriched over-doors, and matching enriched friezes above the windows. In the N wall a buffet recess, framed by composite columns. Dado panelling round the walls. To the E is the drawing room, bowed at the N end; the very well-detailed cedarwood finishings, described by Scott as 'quite beautiful' and 'the prettiest apart-ment with it that I have ever seen'.† STABLES, on the opposite side of St Mary's Road, were probably built before the house, when Waugh acquired the ground in 1807. In the style of *John & Thomas Smith.* A classical symmetrical range with an advanced centre bay with pediment, and segmental-arched coachhouse doorway, and blind oculus in the pediment.

Back in ABBEY STREET, the late C18 ABBEY HOUSE is a harled two-storey and attic, three-bay house. The windows have chamfered margins. Tuscan pilastraded entrance doorway (cf. St Helen's, Waverley Road, *see* Villas, below), probably added at the same time as the two-storey W addition, *c.* 1810. Inside, one room on the upper floor retains dado panelling and an enriched chimneypiece. Good garden, with a range of green-houses, but the setting of the house is severely compromised by a public car park.

---

* *Kelso Mail,* 14 January 1833.
† *Kelso Chronicle,* 30 December 1842.

BUCCLEUCH STREET was cut through between the Abbey and the High Street *c.* 1840. Contemporary villas, mostly altered, but also the POST OFFICE (*see* above) and BUCCLEUCH HOUSE, large with a five-bay symmetrical front and a tripartite window above the entrance door, which has a consoled hood. Additions to the l. by *Morton J. Cowie*, 1962, and an earlier one to the r. On the s side some villas retain their twelve-pane glazing. THE WYND through to the High Street has a two-storey, three-bay house said to have been a smithy, with carved pieces from the abbey built into it and adjacent buildings. Back in Buccleuch Street, the former CONGREGATIONAL CHAPEL (*see* Churches, above).

3. The West End: Weirhill and High Cross Avenue

The tour starts in CHURCH PLACE, at the w end of Victoria Park, with the former FREE CHURCH SCHOOL, added to an earlier schoolroom in 1844. Symmetrical, with Tudor detailing, in coursed, squared rubble with sandstone margins. A gabled centre bay contains a pair of doorways, one each for boys and girls. Narrow windows on the first floor have wall-head gablets. Next, WESTHILL, *c.* 1830, with a stugged ashlar front, and corniced doorway with sidelights. The roof pitch was raised when two segmental roof dormers were inserted. The late C19 ELLIOTLEA and BOOKLAWS have a mutual crowstepped gabled porch. DOUGLAS COTTAGE, *c.* 1830, has an advanced centre bay, the doorway with deep cavetto reveals. Later piended canted bay windows.

WEIRHILL was developed to the w of the Parish Church (*see* Churches, above) by *John Smith* from *c.* 1840. Weirhill and No. 1 WEIRHILL PLACE were finished in 1851 for Miss Rodger. Semi-detached villas, three-bay and four-bay, neatly arranged round a corner. A canted-bay centre front to Weirhill, the window glazing with margin panes, two canted dormer windows to Weirhill Place. To the e is EILDON BANK, given a later pilastered doorpiece, and canted-bay addition by Smith. The best villas in Weirhill Place are: No. 8, two-storey and three-bay, the centre door with a bracketed hood; ELMWOOD, one of a two-storey pair of villas, with a typical Smith full-height bay window; WEIRKNOWE, single-storey and basement, five-bay front (w), steps and railed balustrade to entrance door, and half-octagon centre projection bay to e; WEIRHILL COTTAGE and ELLWOOD, both single-storey and attic, the first with twelve-pane glazing, and the other with tripartite windows. At the n end, TWEED HOUSE, with bracketed eaves and hoodmoulds over the lower windows. WAVERLEY, opposite, has a bargeboarded canopy, with small carved heads on the frieze, and a contemporary cast-iron flower balcony.

TWEEDMOUNT ROAD, off the n side of WAVERLEY ROAD to the w, has two distinctive buildings, TWEEDMOUNT and TWEEDKNOWE, a pair of large semi-detached picturesque villas dated 1877, with bargeboarded gablets and bracketed cornices. Tweedknowe, to the rear, has a large domical lead piended roof with top light, Tweedmount has a tall French roof with a gabled dormer to the E. At the end on the l., ST CUTH-BERT'S MANSE, by *Andrew G. Heiton*, 1901. The gabled E front has a central projecting lean-to porch, above an inscription and the date.

In the gusset of Waverley Road and HIGH CROSS AVENUE is HOLY TRINITY RECTORY by *Benjamin Ferrey*, 1847–8. A large asymmetrical Jacobean house with a gabled Gothic entrance porch at the E, projecting to the l. of the symmetrical main house block. To the r. the service wing breaks forward, from a recessed link, a large stepped chimney to S and gable to E. Now subdivided. The former STABLES, entered from Waverley Road, are L-plan, single-storey and gabled. Nice entrance with ashlar gatepiers with cornices and shallow pyramidal caps. Next along the N side of High Cross Avenue is Ferrey's Holy Trinity (Episcopal) Church (*see* Churches, above). Note also on this side WEIRDLAW, a mid-C19 two-storey, three-bay villa, the centre bay gabled with a Tuscan, columned porch; above is a canted bay with mullioned tripartite window. EAST and WEST FORDEL comprised the U.P. manse; mid-C19, originally a three-bay block with advanced gabled two-storey centre canted bay. Now with a screen linking to a later wing. On the S side of the road, EILDONSIDE is a house of *c.* 1830 much altered by *Peddie & Kinnear*, and again later. Further along, ASHBY (Miller House) by *Peddie & Kinnear*, 1867, an asymmetrical picturesque villa built in coursed squared rubble, with elaborate flatwork bargeboarded gables, with ornamental ridges. Cusped Gothic heads on the first-floor windows, segmental below. To the rear a brick-built extension for a nursing home, 1998. Finally THE ANCHOR-AGE and KOTOGIRI, an asymmetrical Scottish Baronial villa by *Peddie & Kinnear*, *c.* 1867. Off-centre projecting gabled entrance bay.

MANSIONS AND VILLAS

CHIEFSWOOD, off Chiefswood Road, 1.6 km. S. Originally Burn-foot Cottage on Toftfield Farm. Bought, with adjacent land, in 1820 by Sir Walter Scott for his daughter Sophia and son-in law J.G. Lockhart. *John Smith* designed an addition for Lockhart and sent it to Scott who 'wanted it less'. Smith immediately modified the plans, which were approved. The result is a pretty *cottage orné* built of Quarry Hill stone. The SE block must be the original gabled farm cottage, with a low-pitched slated roof, probably thatched originally. Dormer windows were pushed through the wall-head, some hoodmoulds placed over the windows, a bay window added, and another on the SW gable. Two small cottage-style blocks were added to the W, with gable-ends to the garden. A new entrance was made through a rustic porch, copied from that at Abbotsford (q.v.), with timber columns, cornice and lead roof to take Scott's beloved creepers and climbers. Above the porch a small Gothic window lights a dressing room for Sir Walter to use as a study when in residence. All the parts are bound together by cream sandstone dressings, there are overhanging eaves with small timber blocks, and the windows have horizontal panes. Very simple inside, originally there were two grey marble chimneypieces, one removed; in the hall a niche for a stove. – Across the burn the MONK'S WELL is decorated with sections of C15 carved tracery from Melrose Abbey, now well protected by moss. It was used by Scott as a wine cooler. – WALLED GARDEN, NE, the lower E wall with cast-iron railings with decorative baluster heads.

DARNLEE, Waverley Road, W towards Darnick. Two-storey, three-bay villa with piend roof and gable chimneys. 1816, by *John Smith* for himself; two-storey canted bay added by *Brown & Wardrop*, 1872, using the original pilastered doorway. Anthemion frieze balcony to first floor, pierced balustrade and fluted parapet with four urns. The SW façade is ruined by a large flat-roofed extension.

HARLEYBURN HOUSE, Chiefswood Road. Symmetrical two-storey Italianate villa by *Brown & Wardrop*, 1872, for James Curle of Evelaw. Coursed red sandstone with cream dressings. Lower two-storey N service block. In the centre of the W front a projecting Ionic porch with balustraded balcony and, above, a tripartite round-headed window. Advanced outer bays with rusticated quoins and bipartite windows. Single-storey billiard room to the E by *J.R. McKay*, 1939. Renaissance, with a large semicircular pediment supported by consoles. Unaltered interior with classical decoration, except for the Neo-Georgian staircase. – STABLES, E of the house, are a contemporary U-shaped range of red sandstone with cream sandstone dressings. Reconstructed as a dwelling in 1989, with the addition of piended wall-head dormers. – LODGE, dated 1876, by *Brown & Wardrop*. Asymmetrical with overhanging timber bracketed eaves. Gabled timber porch.

HUNTLYBURN HOUSE, 1.8km. SW. Sir Walter Scott purchased the lands of Toftfield in 1817, on which 'there had recently been erected a substantial mansion house' which he renamed. The W end is the earlier house. Built of Quarry Hill stone, of two storeys with a piended roof; the chimneys frame the roof. The front's centre is advanced with a tall crowstepped gabled pediment, with a tripartite window. The wall-head has an ashlar cornice continued round the projection as a moulded string course; the simple doorcase with a projecting cornice is now a window. At the N corner, a two-storey addition in coursed ashlar with whinstone pinnings and pretty cast-iron balconies, by *John Smith*, 1824, for Scott's school friend Captain Adam Ferguson, provided a new drawing room and dining room. In 1854 Smith extended the SE front with another two-storey addition, and a new flat-roofed stair-tower built into the re-entrant angle with his earlier work. The staircase is lit by a tall window. In the centre of the S front is a wide entrance door with sidelights and decorative fanlight; the lights embellished with cast-iron screens representing the sun's rays. Plain frieze and blocking course, the roof-line interrupted by a small crow-stepped gablet to match that on the original house.

Single-storey servants' accommodation added to the NW. – STABLES and small farm buildings have been adapted to office accommodation. Single-storey brick U-shaped block added in

1988 by *Reiach & Hall*. – WALLED GARDEN, open to the SE, with a two-storey building with piended roof built into the SW wall. Honey-coloured sandstone with relieving arches over the two centre doors. These probably date from the early house and appear to have been two bothies.

ST HELEN'S, Waverley Road, W towards Darnick. A pretty villa built in 1806 for Isaac Haig, brother of the laird of Bemersyde, and who made his money from the wine trade in Bordeaux. Extended by *John Smith*, 1835. Built of coursed squared rubble with polished ashlar dressings and angle quoins. Single-storey above a raised basement and attic. Piended roof with two rows of six octagonal chimneys on the transverse walls, each group tied together by a string course. Three-bay S front, the centre advanced in a segmental bow, which is carried up to form the attic storey, with a tripartite window. A wrought-iron balcony is carried across the width of the bow. Tuscan pilastered entrance doorway, with sidelights and decorative fanlight. Steps with Grecian balustrades. The N elevation, also of three bays, has a central three-storey bow, with tripartite windows on each floor. Smith's two-storey, harled addition is to the W. Refurbished by *Laurie Nisbet Associates*, 1995. Early C19 rubble STEADING to the W, an excellent conversion to a house, by *Thom Pollock* of *The Pollock Hammond Partnership*, 1999. W extension in sympathetic materials and sensitive to the vernacular.

FORT. The northern of the Eildon Hills, overlooking the town from the SE, is the site of a major fort enclosing *c.* 15.8 ha. and upwards of five hundred house-platforms. Excavation of several platforms has revealed occupation dating from the Late Bronze Age and the Roman Iron Age. It is usually identified as the main tribal *oppidum* of the Selgovae, the tribe encountered by the Romans in this part of the Tweed basin.

ABBOTSFORD. *See* p. 91.
DRYGRANGE HOUSE. *See* p. 226.
EILDON HALL *see* p. 258.
LOWOOD HOUSE. *See* p. 508.
RAVENSWOOD. *See* p. 643.

6030   MERTOUN

The village of Mertoun (Myreton) was cleared away when the policies round Mertoun House (*see* below) were extended in the mid C18, and the villagers moved to Clintmains farm (*see* p. 565).

MERTOUN PARISH CHURCH. One of the few churches built in the South of Scotland during the Cromwellian period. The principal part of the whinstone rubble T-plan kirk was built in 1658 by *Robert Mein*. The columned and stone-capped birdcage bellcote extended up from the W gable on a high shouldered plinth, and the sundial on the SE corner carved by *Alexander Mein*, appear to be the only visible surviving mid-C17 details. Both Meins were members of an important C17 family of masons based in Newstead. The four-bay S elevation has deep-set Gothic windows with square hoodmoulds over,

repeated on the vestry extension at the W end; an inscription
REP 1820 over the W door implies that this was the date for
these Gothic alterations. The N aisle was extended by *Hardy
& Wight* in 1897–8, who also provided a new roof with bracketed eaves, over the whole church. Above a door in the W elevation of the aisle is the original datestone IVLIE 1658, put
here in 1898, and on the E side a short length of stone carved
with an interlaced pattern has been inserted. Penitential jougs
hang on the S wall. The interior is all 1898 and very simple.
Galleries were removed, and a new kingpost roof was 'formed
open to give more cubic space'. A W rose window dates from
1899, and the octagonal pulpit and communion table from
1908.

GRAVEYARD, 0.85km. E. The parish burial ground remained
round the Old Parish Church of St Ninian, probably founded
in the C12 and belonging to Dryburgh Abbey. Only a rectangular vault remains, made into a MAUSOLEUM for the Scotts
of Harden in the late C18, with the addition of an outer skin
of droved ashlar and a classical pedimented porch at the W end,
inscribed with the names of family members formerly buried
here. In bad repair. Some good C18 GRAVESTONES. Two with
angels' heads and double portrait heads below; one to Thomas
Locky, †1741, the heads in niches. A jolly one to William
Sanderson, †1744, sports billowing clouds above an angel's
head.

OLD MERTOUN BRIDGE, 0.6km. NW. A wide single-span late
C18 bridge across to an island. Further W is a SUSPENSION
BRIDGE, by *John M. Henderson & Co.*, Aberdeen, 1880.

NEW MERTOUN BRIDGE, 0.6km. NW carries the B6404 over
the River Tweed. Built by *James Slight*, 1839–41. Constructed
with arches of laminated rib-beams formed of five thicknesses
of half-logs of timber, although the stone piers and abutments
were built strong enough to take the superstructure of five segmental masonry arches in 1887. TOLLHOUSE in coursed
ashlar, with a central chimneystack and canted-bay window.

MERTOUN HOUSE
0.2 km. E

Formerly known as Harden House or Kingsdale. Charming,
moderately sized Classical house, begun 1703 for Sir William
Scott of Harden. The design of the elevation and plan in
William Adam's *Vitruvius Scoticus* is specifically attributed to
Sir William Bruce, an attribution supported by Bruce's second
marriage in 1700 to Magdalene Scott, a second cousin of Sir
William Scott, and by the similarity of the published plan to
that of Bruce's own Kinross House. Mertoun shows a similar
double-pile plan to Kinross, and an arrangement of mezzanine
levels at each end of the principal floor. After the shell was
completed *c.* 1707 the house seems not to have been fully
habitable since it was recommended in 1710 that windows
should be boarded up to preserve the fabric. According to
William Adam, *Tobias Bachop* was master mason and payments
for work done under the contract of 1703 were still being made

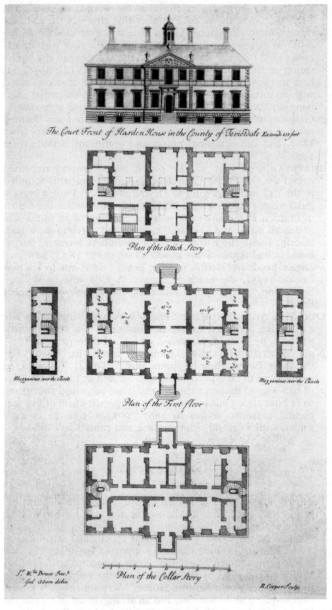

The Court Front of Harden House in the County of Teviotdale Extends 105 feet

Plan of the Attick Story

Mezzanines over the Closets

Mezzanines over the Closets

Plan of the First floor

Plan of the Cellar Story

S.ʳ W.ᵐ Bruce Inv.ᵗ
Gul. Adam delin.

R. Cooper Sculp.

Mertoun House.
Plans and elevation, c. 1703.

to his son, Charles, in the late 1730s. Sir Walter Scott of Whitefield (†1746) succeeded to the property in 1734, and only then
does it seem that a serious attempt was made to complete the
house and fit it out for occupation. Flanking pavilions, not
shown in the Adam engraving, were probably constructed *p. 562*
later. In view of their similarity to those at Marchmont House
(*see* above), the home of Walter Scott's wife, it may well be that
these were commissioned from *Thomas Gibson*, who received
payment for unspecified plans in 1760 and 1762. N and s additions by *Burn & Bryce*, 1841–3, and *Gibson, Skipwith & Gordon*,
1913–16, for John Egerton, later fourth Earl of Ellesmere, were
removed in a skilful scheme of reconstruction by *Ian G.
Lindsay* in 1953–61, for the fifth Earl, later sixth Duke of
Sutherland. This reduced the house to its C18 dimensions.

The HOUSE, built in old red sandstone which has weathered
to an attractive pink, comprises an oblong block of two storeys
on a raised basement, linked by straight (the reduced walls of
the C19 and C20 additions) and concave walls to the single-
storey pavilions (*see* below). The ground was cut away from the
basement in 1913–16, to expose the rubble base, and the
windows lowered. The w (front) and E (garden) elevations are
identical. They have channelled rusticated masonry throughout, which contrasts very successfully with the wide band
courses between the principal and upper floors. Both fronts
are of nine bays, with centre three advanced under pediments
with pineapple finials, and containing carvings of the family
coats-of-arms. The entrance doorways have segmental pediments and pilasters, but the carving is surprisingly coarse. No
evidence for the appearance of the early C18 N and s elevations
survived, and these were rebuilt by Lindsay using stone from
the demolished wings, excellently re-cut to match the horizontal rustication and band courses on the other fronts. An
Ellesmere coat-of-arms, removed from the 1913 addition, was
added to the s end, and a projecting garden entrance made
with a reused pediment. A coronet and the date 1961 at the N
end record the completion of the massive reconstruction.
Bullseye windows light the surviving mezzanine floor, and a
porch gives access from a court made behind the retained C20
basement walls. The six-bay classical office block in the NE
corner of the court appears to be a remodelling of a mid-C18
building. The early C18 roof was removed as part of the
Ellesmere work, and no attempt made to reinstate its form.
The cupola shown on the *Vitruvius Scoticus* engraving was
probably never built.

The Gibbsian, rectangular gabled PAVILIONS are fronted by
tall pedimented centrepieces, each with a blind-arched recess,
flanked by small horizontally proportioned windows. There is
much use of rustication, and ball finials on the corners. The N
pavilion survives intact. The s one was used by Burn & Bryce
to provide a conservatory; the w front had glazing inserted; the
roof was also glazed. Lindsay restored the w elevation, and
redesigned the rest of the conservatory in the style of Bryce.

Of the INTERIOR created between the late 1740s and early
1770s nothing remains of its layout and decoration, except
the N mezzanine, and two mid-C18 marble chimneypieces,

probably those supplied by Gibson in 1761 and 1765. Much
was changed in the mid C19 and early C20, and in reducing
the house Lindsay could start again with a special brief. His
interior is simply decorated, using mostly modillioned cornices. The walls have been left plain to accent the display of
the notable collection of pictures formed by the last Duke of
Bridgewater and first Earl of Ellesmere. The saloon and hall
had been thrown together in the early C20 alterations, leaving
a shallow hall separated by a glazed screen. This large room
was redivided by Lindsay, but the screen was retained. The
present sitting room to the r. of the entrance hall has a fine
yellow-streaked Carrara marble chimneypiece with beautiful
classical detailing said to have come from Sir Henry Raeburn's
house in Edinburgh. The library decoration is Edwardian,
removed from the demolished Worsley Hall, Lancashire, the
Ellesmere family home. In the drawing room is a splendid mid-
C18 chimneypiece, with a jolly Bacchic scene along the frieze.
The dining room ceiling is based on one at Hampton Court,
and the mid-C18 marble chimneypiece is Baroque, with
flowers, fruit and mask cornucopiae, and festooned caryatid
jambs.

SUNDIAL. From Sketchworth House, Newmarket, opposite
the W front along with two small carved foxes on the E front steps.

STABLES, NE of the house. Once extensive, a semi-
octagonal court is all that survives. Reconstructed c. 1912, and
given flat-topped wall-head dormers.; a laundry and associated
buildings, with wide-bracketed eaves, were added at the NE
corner. Some mid-C18 rubble work remains in the centre of
the S elevation, and on the W side an infilled keystoned arch
remains from the 1750s work when the old house of Mertoun
(1680) was vandalised to make stables, and a N courtyard and
more stabling built. To the E a late C18 ICE HOUSE. The egg-
shaped interior has been concreted over, but what survives is
the long loading shute, narrow steps at the sides and cobbled
loading area at the top. The excess water from the drain outlet
fell through a pipe into a stone basin in the wooded bank
below, covered by a small stone GROTTO.

Within the walled garden stands OLD MERTOUN HOUSE, a
small, late C17 building, usually identified as the old mansion
house, but more probably designed as offices. An oblong block
(15.5 m. by 6.6 m.) of two storeys and an attic, of harled rubble
masonry (the harling renewed during refurbishment in
1992–4) with sandstone dressings; most of the original
windows have chamfer-arrised margins and some were originally barred. The roof is gabled, with crowsteps and cavetto-
moulded skewputts, and the chimneys are coped. Dormer
windows were added to the W side of the house in 1925, one
with the initials of the fourth Earl of Ellesmere. The interior
must have been altered on several occasions and at present
comprises ground-floor storage with living accommodation
above. One of the two doorways in the E wall, dated 1677
on the lintel, opens into the foot of a straight stair rising against
the E wall, but this was probably not the original arrangement. The first-floor doorway in the N wall was inserted in
1992–4. The oak roof, largely original, is of collar-rafter type

but, unusually, the common rafters are joined at the apex by saddles.

Just outside the SE corner of the walled garden stands a well-preserved beehive DOVECOT. Built of red sandstone rubble, it is divided into four diminishing stages by string courses and has a C20 pavilion-roofed pigeon-port at the top. Buttresses have been added to support the fabric, concealing some of the nest boxes. The entrance is rebated for an outward-opening door dated 1576 on the lintel. 82

BROOMHALL FARMHOUSE, 0.6 km. S. Originally Mains Farm. Straw-packed partitions supporting the wide stair inside suggest a mid-C18 date.

THE BUNGALOW, by *J.P. Alison* for the Countess of Ellesmere, *c.* 1915, housed the family while the additions to Mertoun House were underway. Harled with red sandstone dressings. H-plan with bipartite and tripartite windows protected by external shutters.

CLINTMAINS, 1.2 km. N, is an estate village with the former SCHOOL of 1838 with a large addition of 1874. Whinstone rubble with droved red sandstone dressings. To the S, the early C19 SCHOOLMASTER'S HOUSE. Rendered with red sandstone dressings. Projecting bracketed eaves added 1838, and Venetian windows probably *c.* 1915. The N elevation of the former MANSE (Mertoun Glebe) is dated 1769 in a gable over the former entrance, and seems to have been added to an earlier manse. It makes a court with the steadings and stabling on each side. S elevation with a two-storey gabled porch by *John Lockie*, wright, 1861. Four LABOURERS' COTTAGES survive, with piended dormer windows, probably from the 1840s. Two cottages have moulded door surrounds, the side bays with Venetian windows, C20.

MERVINSLAW PELE

5.0 km. E of Chesters 6010

The best-preserved of a group of fortified farmhouses situated in the upper reaches of the Jed and Rule waters, close to the Anglo–Scottish border. Probably built in the late C16 by one of the numerous families of Oliver who then dominated the area.

Oblong on plan (7.8 m. by 6.4 m.), the building is perched on steeply sloping ground overlooking the Peel Burn. Local sandstone rubble masonry laid in clay mortar, with sparse dressings of the same stone. Roofless, but otherwise almost entire, comprising two storeys and a garret beneath a gabled roof probably originally covered with turf. Separate doorways to ground and first floors, the former centrally placed in the S gable and the latter, which must have been approached by a ladder or timber forestair, towards the lower end of the W wall. Each was equipped with an outward- and an inward-opening door, the inner doors strengthened by draw-bars. No other external openings at ground level, apart from a gunloop or spyhole beside the doorway. The first floor was lit by a crudely formed slit in the S gable, together with a small, but carefully formed, window in the w wall. This has roll-moulded margins, but those of the garret window in the s gable are round-arrised. No internal access, other than by ladder, between ground and first floors. The first-floor chamber was equipped with no less than six aumbries, some with additional cupboards above their lintels. No obvious trace of a fireplace, but two socket-holes in the N gable could have carried supports for a canopied chimney of clay and timber. The garret must have been reached from a ladder. Turf-covered footings of outbuildings of the farmstead can be seen on the sloping ground immediately s of the pele house.

5020   MIDLEM

A small village on a sloping site.

DESCRIPTION. The houses, grouped round a large rectangular green, probably of some antiquity, were 'improved' in the late C19 and C20. At the top of the green is the Victorian OLD SCHOOLHOUSE. To the N, the mid-C19 OLD MANSE, the former Original Secession manse, is harled with bipartite windows. Close to the centre of the green is a late C19 cast-iron PUMP by *Glenfield & Kennedy* with fluted column and iron mask spout. On the E side of the green is the OLD SMITHY, mid-C18 of whitewashed rubble built into the sloping ground and whose skylights have painted glazing. Inside, a double hearth and round bellows. The PALL HOUSE, also white-washed, was built in 1796 by the Midlem Pall Association, to house two-wheeled, hand-propelled biers, required to reach the parish graveyard at Bowden Church (q.v.).

5010   MIDSHIELS
                            4.8 km. NE of Hawick

Laird's house perhaps dating from the mid C18, extended late C18 by John Douglas of Cavers (†1786), who bought Midshiels from the Scotts of Crumhaugh. Extended again in the early to mid C19. Evidence of the building history is obscured by harling, but tantalising details remain. Two storeys and attic with a five-bay E front, and two parallel wings to the rear; the N is aligned with the N gable, the shorter s wing steps back from the s gable. The earliest part seems to be at the NE corner, where the lower floor has small C18 windows with wide glazing bars, four bays on the N side, three on the E front, one obscured by a later flat-roofed porch; a shallow stair tower, probably C18, in the s elevation of the N wing, contains a timber newel stair. The tripartite windows with narrow sidelights in the extended N wing are C19. Some upper windows with horizontal-paned glazing were lengthened at this time. The two bays at the s end of the E front were perhaps added by John Douglas, and the s wing may be of either C18 or C19 date. At the rear of the court-yard there are vaulted cellars in a retaining wall. Interior replanned in the C19 with spacious, well detailed timber well stair.

MILNE GRADEN HOUSE

8040

5.8 km. SW of Ladykirk

Classical house on the high S bank of the River Tweed. Built for Admiral Sir David Milne, by *James Gillespie Graham*, 1822. In 1852–3 *John Lessels* made alterations for David Milne Home which included the provision of small dormer windows, but most of these were removed, except for those on the W and E elevations, c. 1960.

Two-storey, basement and attic, seven by three bays in polished white sandstone. The windows have architraved surrounds, the deeper ones on the *piano nobile* dignified by cornices. A wide band course between the basement and ground floor, a moulded string incorporating the sills of the first-floor windows, and a bold overhanging wall-head cornice and blocking course, run round the whole building. The N (principal) front has advanced ends and a slightly advanced and pedimented centre with Doric portico, a tripartite window with narrow sidelights, and ball finials on the pediment. Heraldry in the pediment, and above the entrance door. The S elevation also has an advanced centre pediment with ball finials, flanked by gently swelling three-bay bows, giving magnificent views over the river. A pedimented doorcase with console brackets fronts the garden entrance. A large, almost underground, court of kitchen offices at the W end probably dates from the 1850s.

The interior is not lavish, but spacious. The square entrance hall has tall round-arched doorways with glazed tops by Lessels, who made an opening in the S wall to the drawing room behind. The walls are lined out as ashlar blocks, repeated on the walls of the principal stair through to the l. On the original drawings this is shown as a well stair in the entrance hall, which would have been less convenient and impressive than the geometric stone stair supplied. It rises two storeys with tall ornate cast-iron balusters, a coffered arch above the landing, a decorative cornice and key pattern round the ceiling. Anthemion and palmette, egg-and-dart and guilloche motifs decorate the friezes and cornices in the rooms on the ground floor.

The processional route starts at the E end with the DRAWING ROOM, curved at both ends with three tall niches at the N end, leaving a space behind useful only for cupboards. A meritorious white marble chimneypiece celebrates the relief of Algiers by Admiral Sir David Milne on 27 August 1816, with a three-dimensional battle scene of Algiers in the background and fortifications ranged in front. Above the l. jamb a prisoner drops his chains, on the r. a pirate loses his cutlass. Fluted Ionic columns on the jambs. Next along is the library, and in the centre the ROUND ROOM with four tall niches. The two N niches were given doors by Lessels, one to a cupboard, the other communicating with the hall. Green marble chimneypiece. Next a parlour, then the DINING ROOM at the W end, its sideboard recess treated architecturally, with flanking pilasters and coffered arch. Black marble chimneypiece.

The STABLE COURT to the E may also be the work of Gillespie Graham. The W front of polished ashlar, the rest of coursed ashlar. Three windows in blank arches each side of a deep pedimented pend. The court is cobbled, and practically unaltered, with keystoned segmental arches to the stables. – WALLED GARDEN across the Graden Burn, with a gardener's house. – A mid-C19 IRON BRIDGE over the gorge is now inaccessible.

SOUTH LODGE (Parkend), c. 1853. Single-storey with a central chimney and bracketed eaves. Tripartite windows, and timber porch. The classical WEST LODGE is focally placed at the end of a long drive from West Mains. Wide Doric portico and elaborate mid-to-late C19 cast-iron gateway with square cast-iron piers.

EAST MAINS FARM, 1.5 km. NE. A model farm built by *James Cunningham*, c. 1843. Traditional farmhouse with raised window surrounds and wide pilaster bands at the angles. Late C19 addition. Well-detailed plain steadings and cartsheds. The wall fronting the main drive has a wide gable with a pedimented pigeon house in the wall, above a half-height entrance with wooden doors – presumably designed to look decorative for visitors approaching the house.

5020

MINTO

A pleasant informal village with church, school, and early-to-mid C19 estate workers' housing. Mostly of three bays in sandstone rubble, in two basic designs but unusually laid out with large gardens, placed to catch the sun and an open view.

PARISH CHURCH. The church was relocated from the vicinity of Minto House (*see* below) to a site at the S end of the newly laid out village in 1830–1; its ambitious scale and spacious churchyard proclaim the interest of a great landholder. By *W. H. Playfair*, it is of grey snecked rubble with droved ashlar dressings, in a mixed English medieval style. The three-storey tower, straddling the E wall, has a flat crenellated parapet carried on widely projecting corbel courses; its doorway opens onto a stair to the Minto gallery, and there are two levels of windows above, the belfry stage having pairs of lancets to each face. W of the basically cruciform main body is a vestry, beyond which is the apsidal-ended Minto burial vault, approached down a stair in its W wall. The main church entrance is towards the E end of the N nave wall, and there are two levels of windows on each side of this part, with a three-light intersecting-traceried window to the area below the loft, and two pairs of lancets above. The gable-walls of the transeptal aisles have four-light windows, the lights grouped in two pairs, and there is a three-light window to each flank of the 'chancel' W of the transepts. The entrance opens into a vestibule below the gallery and, since reordering in 1934, the internal focus has been the communion table at the w end, with the pulpit to its s. The plastered ceiling is of polygonal profile. – MEDIEVAL FRAGMENTS, from the old church, at the base of the tower, include a voussoir with chevron decoration, a child's coffin, and a small tapered grave-slab with an incised foliate cross.

BURIAL ENCLOSURE, 0.5 km. E. Heavily overgrown. Formed in 1831 on the site of the old church, which is mentioned in Bagimond's Roll of the 1270s. Surviving mid-C12 fragments in the enclosure's E wall include a scalloped nook-shaft capital, a stone with a diaper-pattern design, several stones with sawtooth chevron, a nook-shaft base with angle spurs, and a number of broadly chamfered stones. Within the enclosure are several memorials, including a medieval grave-slab with an incised foliate-headed cross and sword, and a coped medieval gravestone.

Former PRIMARY SCHOOL. A Tudor gabled schoolroom, with hoodmoulds, and porch dated 1889. Early C19 schoolhouse attached.

WAR MEMORIAL, by *Thomas J. Clapperton*, 1925. A memorable figure of a soldier standing guard, set on a high boulder base, and surrounded by a memorial garden.

MINTO HOUSE. Demolished 1992–3 after long neglect. Developed from a V-planned house for Gilbert Eliot, Lord Minto by *William Adam c.* 1738–43, with numerous C19 alterations. *Robert S. Lorimer* created the GARDEN TERRACES 1897–1906. – WEST LODGE. Mid-C19 in stugged sandstone. Decorative bargeboards and octagonal chimneystalks. Decorative cast-iron gates with the Minto monogram and coronet date from 1921. – SOUTH LODGE. Mid-C19, picturesque, with broad eaves. Single-arched rubble BRIDGE, built 1900 by *Robert S. Lorimer*. Formerly with supporters of the Minto arms at each end of the parapet.

FATLIPS CASTLE. *See* p. 277

6020

MONTEVIOT HOUSE
2 km. E of Ancrum

The present rambling house stands on high terraced gardens, the ground falling steeply away to the River Teviot. Monteviot was developed by the Kerrs of Ferniehirst from a mid-C18 farmhouse. Acquired by the third Marquess of Lothian, *c.* 1740 and apparently used for fishing and shooting, the building was altered and added to in 1743, 1754 and 1815 (by *William Elliot*). Between 1830 and 1832 it was substantially enlarged by the seventh Marquess to designs by *Edward Blore*. Of his ambitious Neo-Tudor scheme, rambling and irregular in character, only the E wing was completed. The earlier farmhouse was retained and the two were not properly joined together until the 1960s, when *W. Schomberg Scott* remodelled the farmhouse, added a long entrance wing and family accommodation to the w and adapted the C19 wing, which he drastically cut back. The work was completed in 1963.

The two-storey, three-bay, piend-roofed farmhouse has s-facing, single-storey, three-bay pavilions, linked to the main block by short concave quadrants. The U-shape encloses a formal garden. The centre light of the s canted bay window of the w pavilion was raised, and given a round-headed arch, by *Ian G. Lindsay* in 1957; the canted bay on the E drawing room pavilion was given the same treatment in the 1960s. A blocking course with some stone balls on the parapet was added to the centre block. Schomberg Scott's entrance wing to the w, connecting to two-storey gabled family accommodation, is flat-roofed with a wall-head balustrade, and six tall vertical astragalled windows with slightly segmental heads. Placed over a traditional C17-style entrance doorway is a copy of a carved armorial stone, inscribed 'Robert Ker and Isobel Home/ Foundar and /Compleitar/Anno 1558'. The original, now in the E garden, was previously at Ancrum House (dem.), from which also came C18 stone urns on the front steps.

On the l. side of the entrance court some two-storey buildings with wall-head dormers have been retained: one window pediment is dated 1877. The balustraded walls and gateways connecting these buildings were demolished, as well as some single-storey extensions. Blore's E wing, looking over the E garden, has suffered much truncation, and the removal of Tudor detailing. The two-storey block projecting to the E was largely rebuilt by Schomberg Scott, in a very bland Scottish Georgian style, and the range of office buildings running to the N was shorn of its top storey, except for a high central gable. This wing terminates in a three-storey square balustraded tower with square pepperpot turrets. These are similar to ones at Drumlanrig Castle (Dumfries and Galloway), home of Victoria, wife of the ninth Marquess, so probably date from the 1870s. This building housed a reservoir for a water-driven organ by *August Gern*, provided for the neighbouring chapel, *c.* 1882.

The interior was completely remodelled by Schomberg Scott with, wrought-iron work by *Thomas Hadden*, and plasterwork by *L. Grandison & Son*. The well-lit entrance hall is high, and has painted heraldic shields (plywood pinned to plaster) by *Don Pottinger* on the barrel-vaulted ceiling. The two-storey Great Hall has a shallow vaulted ceiling, compartmented with timber ribs, and a staircase and gallery with an elegant wrought-iron balustrade, with a pattern of birds and acanthus leaves. The room was designed to take some of the largest pictures in the Lothian collection, mostly brought here from their seats of Newbattle Abbey (Lothian) and Blickling Hall (Norfolk). The DINING ROOM to the E is long and narrow, and has a plaster panelled ceiling decorated with stars from the Lothian arms, and a plain classical chimneypiece. The LIBRARY, in the oldest part of the house, was reconstructed from the former front two rooms and entrance hall. The DRAWING ROOM in the E wing has a high coved ceiling, and chimneypiece with fluted columns and frieze.

STABLES, NW. Now housing. Mostly dating from the late 1870s, but the w and E ranges of the court seem to have earlier work incorporated. A conical-roofed circular tower is recessed

at each end of the N and S ranges, the NW one dated 1879. The
N range has pentice-roofed wall-head dormers repeated elsewhere on the stables, and on estate cottages.

SW of the house is a COTTAGE, a former curling or tea house.
Probably mid-C19 with a central chimney. Timber-lined room
with a coved ceiling and chimneypiece. – CRICKET PAVILION,
c. 1900 but timeless, with a deep canted veranda, its roof supported on timber posts, and timber balustrade. Large timber-
lined room to the rear. – BELL-TOWER opposite the house
entrance. Late C19. A square stone column with slightly battered walls and timber bellcote.

HOME FARM (Harestanes Countryside Visitor Centre). Parts
converted to craft workshops, with visitor centre in the W
range, by *Alistair M. Smith*, 1992. A mid-to-late C19 complex,
built in coursed red sandstone, with bargeboarded gables, deep
overhanging timber-lined eaves and canted bay windows, in
the domestic parts. A two-storey conical-roofed square tower
with buttressed angles is dated 1877. Detached farmhouse on
the S side with a gambrel roof, and timber porch with decorative bargeboards.

JEDFOOT LODGE on the corner of the A68 and B6400. Mid-C19
asymmetrical gabled cottage with blind slits and octagonal
chimneys. The gabled WEST LODGE (A68) is probably mid-
C19, with a fine set of late C19(?) timber gatepiers and carriage
and pedestrian gates, decorated with cast-iron detailing; apparently moved here in the late C20. At the N entrance (B6400),
four stone piers each topped with an obelisk and decorated
with Lothian heraldry. – WALLED GARDEN, further N, c. 1830;
brick walls.

MONTEVIOT BRIDGE over the Teviot. First erected in 1858, but
rebuilt in 1999. A long suspension bridge with concrete pylons,
and timber decking and rails. E of the bridge a large circular
battlemented DOVECOT built of grey rubble sandstone.
C16/C17 base, the top probably late C19.

LANDSCAPE. The structure of the present parkland was laid out
between 1829 and 1860. The present grass terraces are a
remodelling of a formal Victorian terraced garden. By 1897 the
impressive wall-walk and bastion W of the house had been
formed, probably in the time of *John Page*, a Chelsea gardener,
who worked here in the late C19. From 1961–8 *Percy Cane*
made many plans and planting designs, but only a few were
carried out, including the paved rose garden, and the
rearrangement of the long grassy slope to the river's edge.

MORDINGTON   9050

A moorland parish, the only centre is the small village known as
Clappers.

MORDINGTON PARISH CHURCH. Of the church possibly here
by the end of the C11 there are fragmentary footings within an
overgrown churchyard. The chief upstanding remains are of a
BURIAL VAULT, which evidently adjoined the E gable. It has
ashlar gables to E and W, and an ashlar barrel vault. Rebuilt in

the E gable wall, which contains the entrance, are stones with the initials of Anne, Lady Mordingtoun, and her son William, second Lord Mordingtoun, said to have been dated 1662. Set into the internal W wall is a late medieval carving of the Crucifixion, flanked by doll-like figures of the Virgin and St John. The GRAVEYARD contains table tombs and stones carved with *memento mori*.

After it was destroyed by fire in 1757, a second church was built some distance to the S; its fragmentary remains are in the NE corner of a churchyard perpetuating the site, but this church was itself replaced by a third church, built on a site between its two predecessors in 1867 by *John Lessels*; largely demolished in 1989 except for the lower courses of part of its S wall, into which a number of memorials are built.

Former MANSE. W of the old graveyard. Mid-C19, of three bays, in harl-pointed rubble and red sandstone margins. Single-storey extension across the front, late C20.

MORDINGTON SCHOOL, Clappers. A two-storey, three-bay former schoolhouse built to a plan by *Mr Murray*, schoolmaster, *c.* 1819, the five-bay schoolroom altered and extended to a T-plan. Gabled porch, and large S gable with a three-light window inscribed 'Mordington Public School 1909'.

DESCRIPTION. The small village of CLAPPERS has, apart from the school (*see* above), a blacksmith's house and shop (THE OLD SMITHY HOUSE and SMITHY). Perhaps late C18 or early C19, but altered and adapted over the years. Formerly a three-bay cottage, raised 1975, and given a centre gabled wallhead dormer to match those on the mid-C19 building (No. 1 Clappers) to its N. This was originally two cottages, each of two bays with stone slab pentices. The single-storey pantiled working smithy, at the S end, is a remarkable survival, with a square-headed forge, work benches and tools – nothing has been thrown away. In the cobbled area outside is an iron wheel-pattern in working order.

MORDINGTON HOUSE. Unexciting, of *c.* 1975. Mid-C19 GATE LODGE, with projecting bipartite windows in W and E gables, and early C19 WALLED GARDEN with rounded corners.

MORDINGTON MAINS FARMHOUSE (Century House). By *Swan & Whitlie*, 1840. An improved farmhouse in harl-pointed sandstone rubble with droved sandstone margins and long and short quoins.

MOREBATTLE

On the S bank of the Kale Water. Although of medieval origin, the present village developed only after the mid-C18, when small upland farms were merged and tenant farmers and their labourers lost their holdings and were settled in Morebattle.

PARISH CHURCH. The medieval church was a possession of the Bishops of Glasgow by *c.* 1116. Its only recognisable relic is a short stretch of base course at the SE corner of the present church, though parts of the S wall have been found further E, and are shown on a plan of 1915 in the porch. Substantial foundations were also found running W from the nave, perhaps for a tower. The rectangular core of the existing church was built in 1757–9, by *John Laidlaw*, mason, and *John Purves*, wright, both of Kelso. New windows were apparently inserted in 1807. Major remodelling was carried out in 1898–9, when *Hardy & Wight* added an E chancel over the Pringle of Clifton Aisle, which was possibly itself on the site of a medieval chancel. In doing this the burial vault was retained, its raised margins still evident at the lower level. A vestry was added at the W end of the N wall, with access to a new W gallery. In 1902–3 a porch was added at the W end of the S wall. Most recently, in 1999, the birdcage bellcote on the W gable was rebuilt, with channel-rusticated piers and lintels, and a cap of ogee profile.

The church of 1757 was of red sandstone rubble, and three of its original four arched windows survive along the S flank; within those windows timber tracery of two arched lights and a circlet has been inserted. At the W end two arched windows light the area below the gallery, and one arched window the area above. At the E end the Pringle Vault has a blocked entrance on its S side, and the vault's purpose is explained by an inscription and a re-set heraldic plaque in the E wall; its S wall is of red rubble, and the same type of masonry was adopted for the S wall of the 1898 chancel above it, but without the raised margins. However, the E and N chancel walls are mainly of whin rubble. The 1902 porch is of buff rock-faced masonry with polished dressings. Internally the nave has an arch-braced roof, and the chancel a boarded ceiling of polygonal profile. The W gallery is supported by two cast-iron columns. – LECTERN, brass eagle, 1919. – FONT, octagonal, Sicilian and Rouge Royal marble, 1899. – PAINTED TEXTS along N wall, Words of Comfort, Creed, Lord's Prayer. – STAINED GLASS. Chancel: E, supper at Emmaus, N, Sower, S, Good Shepherd, all *A. Ballantine & Gardiner*; S side nave, three Maries at Sepulchre, 1910, *A. Ballantine & Son*. – SOUTH AFRICAN WAR MEMORIAL, W end, a Celtic cross by *P. Macgregor Chalmers*, 1919; surprisingly late. – PLAQUES, chancel, to various members of the Pringle family.

CHURCHYARD. The memorial stone for Janet Kedzie, †1729, has a three-quarter portrait contemplating a skull.

Former MANSE (Wellgate), Toongate St. Built in 1828–9 by *John Winchester*, mason, and *William Clark*, joiner. A simple, two-storey and basement, harled house with piend roof and central pilastered doorway. Low rooms with simple cornices, and a pretty, tightly curved geometric stair, supported by a contemporary iron column. Two-storey dark whinstone bay windows, to the garden front, of 1852. The classically detailed U-plan court of offices by *David Thomson* of Glasgow, 1856, housed the minister's gig.

MOREBATTLE UNITED PRESBYTERIAN CHURCH, Main Street. Now a garage, the entrance blasted through the E end of the main front, and a concrete lintel placed across the top. By *F. T. Pilkington*, 1865–6. There is typical Pilkingtonian decoration, but not lavish. A simple chapel with a rectangular plan. The W and E elevations are pierced with square-headed three-light windows. The principal elevation (N) has three gabled divisions, the centre taller with a deeply cut tracery rose window (the rose window in the s elevation has a Geometric pattern of trefoils); the other two divisions contain the deep entrance porch (w) and the vestry. The string course below the rose window is broken by two diamond-shaped lozenges which rise from the spandrels of two sets of paired lights, between which is a central roundel with a florette. The corners of the N front have stretched-out pilasters of polychrome stones, the leafy tops curved over. The interior is completely mutilated, but still has its simple scissor-truss roof supported by columns; the capitals Ionic, with curved leaves.

Former MOREBATTLE FREE CHURCH (Village Hall), Main Street. 1845. Pointed windows and a C20 vestibule.

MOREBATTLE BRIDGE, 1.1 km. NE on the B6401. Wide, mid-C19, with a single segmental arch and a dry arch to the E. Narrow voussoirs and rubble spandrels.

MOREBATTLE TOFTS BRIDGE, over the Kale Water. 1857. Single span with a dressed stone segmental arch and regular coursed spandrels.

PRIMARY SCHOOL. By *J.S. Forbes* of *Reid & Forbes*, 1931. Long single-storey block, with a brick base course, tile roof and rendering. Projecting piend-roofed ends and an arched brick entrance beneath a central projecting gable. The classrooms each side have glazed walls, open to a veranda with a glazed awning on cast-iron columns. Clearstorey of small, opening windows; airy for the health of the pupils. Later additions.

VILLAGE INSTITUTE. Former school. Early C19. Built by *Richard & John Balman*, contractors, apparently to sketches of the local joiner, *Robert Fox*, but based on a plan provided by *John & Thomas Smith*. Neo-Tudor, broad-eaved gables, stone mullions to the tall windows, and sloping stone hoodmoulds over windows and porch.

WAR MEMORIAL, *c.* 1920. Rugged standing stone with incised cross.

DESCRIPTION. The houses of the village were described in 1793 as mostly of one storey and covered with thatch; by 1839 the majority were two storeys, roofed in slate. At the E end TEMPLE HALL HOTEL, an L-shaped range, is two storeys, the six sash windows with black painted surrounds suggesting that it was formed from two C18 houses. THE JOINERY, on a narrow site between the manse garden and Main Street, is early-to-mid C19. A two-storey building housing a workshop, rubble with flat brick arches over the windows and doors, and a large Palladian window to the E. On the angle of the gable, a sundial comprising a square block of stone, three of its faces with numbered dials and gnomons. Adjacent to the workshop, a two-bay house with similar detailing, presumably built by the Fox family, who were joiners of some standing in Morebattle from the end of the C18. Further E, mid-C19 ST AIDAN'S (former Free Church manse). T-shaped of two storeys and three bays, in rendered rubble with sandstone dressings, and a simple doorcase with a heavy cornice. A date-stone of 1780 indicates that the steading and stabling, to the NW, may have been part of the offices for the 1780 Antiburgher Church (*see* above) near this site. To the N, a similar house, GLENDALE, its projecting centre bay containing the doorway with hoodmould over.

Along MAINSFIELD AVENUE are three houses, two storeys with tall wall-head pediments, dated SWM 1899. Built by William Moscrip in anticipation of the railway proposed to run from the Jedburgh–Roxburgh line to Wooler via Morebattle and Yetholm; but lack of subscribers scuppered both the scheme and Mr Moscrip. Built of whinstone rubble with red brick detailing. Flat brick bay windows on two houses, and one with an open gabled porch, with a balustrade of short uprights.

TEAPOT STREET, laid out 1767, leads N to the ford over the Kale Water – where some of the causeway timbers still survive – now crossed (0.3 km. E) by the JUBILEE BRIDGE, an iron girder pedestrian bridge built in 1887.

CESSFORD HOUSE, 3.7 km. SW. U-plan farmhouse. Its front (E) block is mid-C19, of three bays, with full-height canted bays in cream ashlar flanking the entrance. The SW wing contains an earlier farmhouse, however, with an addition of the 1820s, superintended by *William Elliot*, of two storeys and attic with a long service wing to the N. Inside, a tightly curved geometric stair with a cast-iron balustrade. The matching NW wing is later. It has a timber stair with carved balusters and rooms with rich decorative cornices.

GATESHAW FARMHOUSE, 2.5 km. S. Built c. 1860. Two storeys with three bays to the S and E, whinstone, and sandstone dressings with a broached finish. A solid corniced stone porch on the S front. Several dummy windows with well-detailed painted glazing bars, probably provided to preserve the symmetry of the elevations seen by visitors to Gateshaw House (*see* below). GATESHAW COTTAGES, N, a row of three, are probably late C18 but improved c. 1860, the date of NEW GATESHAW COTTAGES, 0.3 km. N, whose porches have overhanging and barge-boarded gable-ends.

GATESHAW HOUSE. 3.3 km. SE. It appears to date from three different periods. First the late C18, visible on the E elevation, where there is a Venetian window on the ground floor at the N end – was there another to balance it? The S front is of three bays; the first-floor windows have been given casements but the spacing suggests the openings date from the C18, as does the piend roof with a central platform, although it has been extended to the N. The three first-floor windows on the W front seem to match those on the S elevation, which suggests a square-plan house. The ground floor of the S elevation was altered c. 1860. A wide band course across the front incorporates the consoled sills of tripartite windows, between which is a central cornieed porch. On the W gable, a two-storey canted bay, rising from basement to ground floor, c. 1860. – The STABLES on the N side, of rubble with sandstone dressings, are probably late C18, with later alterations. The N wall of the garden contains a small pointed window, with Gothic glazing, lighting the potting sheds behind.

EARLY SETTLEMENTS, Crock Cleugh, deep into the hills 9 km. SE. Two settlements, excavated in 1939. Each comprises a small enclosure measuring some 30 by 20 m. internally, with a stone-walled round-house standing to the rear of a sunken yard immediately within the entrance. They were probably occupied in the early centuries AD, but a C5 brooch was recovered from the E settlement.

FORT, Kip Knowe, 8 km. ESE. Early Iron Age. The easiest lines of approach are barred by three ramparts, but the steep slope falling away into the valley of the Sourhope Burn is apparently undefended. Several well-defined timber round-house stances are visible within the interior.

CESSFORD CASTLE. See p. 159.

CORBET HOUSE. See p. 192.

CORBET TOWER. See p. 192.

WHITTON TOWER. See p. 761.

6010   MOSSBURNFORD HOUSE
                       4.8 km. SE of Jedburgh

A superior farmhouse built c. 1825, replacing, or perhaps incorporating, an earlier house. Three storeys and a deep basement. Coursed cream sandstone with ashlar margins and quoins. Three-bay S front with a later porch, spanning the area, with a pair of Tuscan columns *in antis*. Ground-floor Venetian windows with Y-glazing, set in blind arches, and a shallow bowed bay on the N elevation with tripartite windows on the lower floors. Broad wall-head stacks on the side elevations.

6020   MOUNT ULSTON
                        2 km. NE of Jedburgh

Good but modest early C19 farmhouse with later additions. Three bays, with lower single-bay wings, all in limewashed sandstone rubble. Steeply pitched piended roofs. S elevation with a classically detailed timber-columned porch, frieze and cornice, and the W elevation with a projecting canted bay. Rubble stables with two-storey carriage block. Corniced gatepiers linked to the house by a carved coped rubble wall. – The WALLED GARDEN has a weatherboarded summerhouse, one corner sits on the wall, the others supported by three timber poles. Pointed-arched windows with diamond panes and Y-tracery glazing.

MOW CHURCH *see* YETHOLM

MUIRHOUSELAW *see* MAXTON

2040   NEIDPATH CASTLE
                        1.5 km. W of Peebles

37   Widely celebrated for its picturesque appearance and literary associations, Neidpath's architectural importance is often overlooked. Yet it is probably the earliest, and certainly the grandest, of the region's tower houses.

Probably erected towards the end of the C14 by Sir William Hay of Locherworth, sheriff of Peebles, or his son Thomas, the castle stands on the N bank of the Tweed, close to the route leading W from Peebles to Upper Tweeddale and Clydesdale. Sir William's castle was an L-plan tower house massively constructed in three tiers, each ceiled with a stone barrel vault; there was probably a barmkin on the E side from the beginning. Neidpath never became the Hays' principal residence and the castle seems to have been little altered until about the second quarter of the C17, when the upper floors of the main block were remodelled, the vault being replaced by a timber roof and new wall-walks constructed, with corbelled turrets at the NE and SE corners (*Robert Murray*, wright). Following the Civil War, during which the castle was garrisoned on two occasions, surrendering to Cromwell's army upon terms in 1651, building work resumed in the late 1660s, continuing until *c.* 1686 (*James Bain*, wright, *James & John Nichol*, masons), when John Hay, second Earl of Tweeddale, sold the estate to the Douglases, Dukes of Queensberry. However, the building ceased to be a family residence *c.* 1731, and in 1795 the fourth Duke had the surrounding timber felled, an action for which he was later castigated by Wordsworth ('*Degenerate Douglas! Oh the unworthy Lord*'). Two years later Francis Grose reported that the building was 'now in ruin, part of it' (evidently the upper portion of the wing) 'having fallen down'. A further collapse of the wing, including the middle vault, seems to have occurred not long afterwards. In 1810 Neidpath passed to the Earls of Wemyss and March, who, probably in the mid C19, roofed the stump of the wing and adapted parts of the castle for occupation by estate workers. During the second half of the C20 the twelfth Earl repaired the surviving fabric of the tower and developed it as a visitor attraction.

The defensive nature of the site is most obvious to W and S, 37 where the ground slopes steeply towards the river. The tower itself (main block 18.9 m. by 11.9 m., wing 9.1 by 5.5 m.) is set obliquely upon a rocky knoll, its walls, *c.* 3 m. in thickness, rising to a height of 18.3 m. at parapet level. The middle tier of the main block, being designed to accommodate what was evidently a great hall, was left undivided, but the other two contained entresol floors of timber, making five storeys in all. The bottom tier of the wing was subdivided by an additional vault, while the two others contained entresol floors, making six storeys in all. The uppermost vaults of both main block and p. 44 wing probably carried stone slab roofs within open wall-walks. In addition to the principal chambers, there were a considerable number of smaller mural chambers disposed at various levels. Surprisingly, in a tower house of so early a date, the principal entrance seems always to have been on the ground floor. From this entrance, placed on the S side at the junction of main block and wing, a spiral stair rises to the full height of the building. There were two subsidiary wheel stairs, one (now blocked) in the SE corner of the main block connecting the two lower floors with the hall, and the other in the diagonally opposite corner of the main block leading from the hall to the two upper floors. During the late C17 alterations a new entrance was cut through the E wall of the tower to give direct access to the entresol floor of the lowest tier and to a new scale stair formed in the SE corner of the main block. The masonry is of local whinstone sparsely relieved by sandstone dressings, a yellow stone generally being employed for the original dressings and a dark red stone for the later work. Both probably emanate from quarries in the West Linton area, *c.* 16 km. to the NW. The absence of freestone in the immediate vicinity may account for the fact that the external angles of the tower are rounded off in rubble masonry rather than brought to the square with freestone dressings as is usual. Few of the C14 dressings exhibit mouldings, but several bear masons' marks. Most of the doors and windows are lintelled, but some have pointed or segmental arch-heads; the larger windows have been mullioned and transomed.

The original entrance in the S wall may formerly have been approached by way of a moveable timber bridge spanning a cleft in the rock below, a device also employed at Craigmillar Castle (Edinburgh). The doorway, somewhat altered in the C17, enters a lobby opening r. into a porter's lodge and l. into the main turnpike stair. At the rear of the lobby a third opening leads into the ground floor of the main block. This was originally a combined store-cellar and well-house, but it was partitioned during the C17 to form three separate chambers. The rock-cut well has a depth of 7 m. The existing windows, which light both this floor and the one above, are of C17 date, but the one in the W wall probably replaces an original postern. The present window frames, equipped with leaded lights above and shutters below, are based on a C17 frame discovered in the W window in 1955. Close to the SE corner of the largest chamber can be seen the lowermost treads of the original service stair, the remainder of which was blocked when the scale stair was inserted above. The wing contains a windowless prison, referred to in 1594 as the 'pitt' of the place of Neidpath and originally accessible only by means of a hatch in the vault above; it contains a latrine.

The tower is now entered from the upper level of the courtyard through the bolection-moulded doorway of *c.* 1670 cut through the E wall. This opens into a large entrance hall (the Laigh Hall), created in the C17 from a storeroom and ceiled with a (C14) segmental vault bearing the imprint of the centering boards used in its construction. In the wing at this level is a chamber, conveniently placed to observe comings and goings, and probably occupied by the constable, or keeper, of the castle. It is well lit and equipped with its own latrine and built-in cupboard, as well as a fireplace, which in its present form sports an elegant, roll-moulded surround decorated with a fleur-de-lys centrepiece, all evidently of early C17 date.

The scale stair leads to the first floor. It is difficult now to appreciate the original layout, but the great hall was evidently a noble chamber, for it occupied almost the full length of the middle tier of the main block and was ceiled with a pointed vault *c.* 8 m. in height. At the upper end was a dais lit by a pair of large windows, of which the one on the W seems to have been provided with bench seats and a built-in cupboard in the

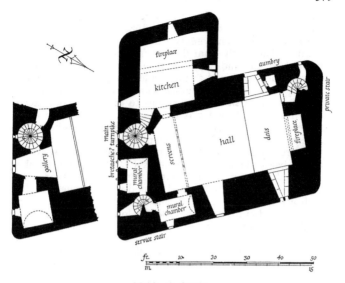

Neidpath Castle.
Reconstruction of First Floor Plan.

embrasure. The segmental-headed fireplace in the N wall, restored in 1957, is of impressive size, but surprisingly plain. Beside it a door gives access to the private stair in the NW corner. At the lower end of the hall there was probably a service area communicating with the adjacent kitchen in the wing, as well as with the main stair and the service stair, this last also giving access to a pair of mural chambers. These chambers were probably residential, but the one in the S wall may also have given access to a corbelled bretasche defending the entrance below. Above the service area there was probably a gallery formed partly within the embrasure of a high-level window. This also gave access to yet another mural chamber, the general arrangement being similar to that found in the great hall at Borthwick Castle (Lothian). The damaged kitchen, cleared of debris only in 1993, can be viewed through a glass-panelled screen; in the W wall are traces of the original, very large fireplace, as also of two later ones. The present arrangement at this level dates from the 1670s or '80s, when the hall was divided by a timber partition into a large and small chamber; both are lined with bolection-moulded pine panelling. An entresol floor also contrived within the hall vault at this time contains two chambers of equal size (the S known as Queen Mary's Room), with plainer panelling. Possibly the first-floor rooms were intended to serve as a principal apartment and the entresol rooms as a lesser one, with the small chamber over the kitchen providing an additional room for either suite as required. The temporary removal of panelling in Queen Mary's Room has revealed what appear to be design drawings for a balustraded staircase scratched into the plaster surface of the N wall. These may be associated with the construction of garden terraces in the 1680s (*see* below).

The existing arrangements at the upper levels of the tower seem to date partly from the second quarter of the C17 and partly from the mid C19. Originally, however, this upper tier was probably designed as the residential quarters of the lord and his family. The main block seems originally to have contained a hall of similar dimensions to the one below, except that the ceiling height was curtailed by the existence of an entresol floor. This hall, of which little survives, was heated by a segmental-arched fireplace in the N wall, of which some traces remain. Opening off the private stair in the NW corner a little below the level of the hall is a vaulted mural chamber equipped with two built-in cupboards perhaps intended for valuables. The wing contained a good-sized private chamber with a smaller one in its N wall, while a third chamber was incorporated in the S wall at a slightly lower level. The accommodation on this floor can best be interpreted as lord's hall and chamber with one or more associated closets, and the entresol may have been organised along similar lines for the lord's wife. At the lower level the C17 alterations created what was probably a three-room family apartment comprising two chambers in the main block – formed by subdividing the hall – and a third in the wing. At the S end of the main block is a lobby entered from the principal stair through a doorway whose lintel is a reused medieval tombstone. The rooms at this level show traces of tempera painting, but they were further refurbished in the C19, when the C17 chambers above were similarly treated. The single-rafter timber roof of the main block is probably of C17 date, but it looks as if the original tie-beams have been cut back and tenoned into wall-pieces.

The C17 alterations also included the construction of new wall-walks and associated caphouses on three sides of the main block. The W and E walks are open, while the N one is enclosed, being lit by a row of small windows interspersed with pistol-holes, the latter all now blocked. The existence of what seems to have been a small window looking onto an earlier wall-walk suggests that on the N side, at least, the original walk was set at about the same level as the C17 one. Elsewhere, however, it may have been higher, corresponding with the level of the wing walk, of which a fragment survives. This would have enabled the original lord's hall to have been lit by large windows piercing the full thickness of the walls.

OUTBUILDINGS. The early barmkin on the E side of the tower was extended N on made-up ground and provided with a handsome new gateway and approach avenue *c.* 1670 (*James & John Nichol*, masons). The arch is framed by a rectangular hoodmould with carved stops, and the keystone is carved with the crest of the Earls of Tweeddale (a goat's head erased upon a coronet of five points). Among the buildings mentioned in the late C17 accounts are a kitchen, brewhouse, stables and coachhouse, all of which were presumably situated within the barmkin. The kitchen and brewhouse may have occupied the S part of the E range, the lowest floor of which probably originated during the C16. The existing fireplaces and ovens,

p. 44

however, are more likely to date from the early C18, when the upper floors were rebuilt. The N part of this range was erected *c.* 1670, but it, too, was remodelled during the C18. By *c.* 1860 the E range, like the other offices, was ruinous, but the ground floor of the N portion has since been re-roofed, while the shell of the S portion was consolidated and restored in 1950. The S range, perhaps originally fitted out as stables, was remodelled for occupation *c.* 1900.

The GARDEN of Neidpath is on record in 1581, but the existing remains probably date from 1682–6, when *Robert Inglis* and *Thomas Boyd* were employed to construct terraced walks linked by steps, together with a summerhouse. In 1715, when the garden was still in its prime, Pennecuik described it as 'a sloping Parterre in good order, and three or four pretty Terraces betwixt the house and water', but a century later it was turned over to sheep. The head of a late C17 or early C18 sundial that formerly stood in the garden is preserved in the Laigh Hall, and the footings of the summerhouse can be seen on the knoll overlooking the barmkin gateway.

NEIDPATH VIADUCT *see* KIRKTON MANOR

NENTHORN

6030

There is evidence of an early medieval settlement at Nenthorn, and until the late C18 there was also a small village in the vicinity of the old parish church. The present village, which straddles the main road, is a C19 creation.

Former FREE CHURCH, now derelict. Built in a subdued Romanesque manner to house a congregation formed at the 1843 Disruption. The main W front is of squared whinstone rubble with droved ashlar dressings. The central round-headed doorway, set in a salient, is flanked on each side by an arched window; above the doorway the salient narrows and is pierced by an arched window before rising up to the wall-head, where it presumably once carried a bellcote. The flanks are of harled rubble pierced by three arched windows.

Plain two-storey gabled manse was built 1846–7 by *John Bulman*.

OLD PARISH CHURCH. 0.5km. SSW of the village. Originally a chapel in the parish of Ednam, it was granted to Durham *c.* 1105. Little more than fragmentary and overgrown footings survive. Within the churchyard a variety of mainly C17, C18 and C19 headstones, table tombs and obelisks raise their heads above the vegetation.

Former PARISH CHURCH, now a dwelling. A small T-plan structure of whinstone rubble, built in 1802 and remodelled in the mid C19. Gabled bellcote on the SW gable. A session house and ashlar-fronted porch project at the NE end. The SE flank has two three-light windows, while the gable walls each have a circular window and an asymmetrically set round-headed Y-traceried window.

Former SCHOOL, N of the Parish Church. A rectangular plan with central projecting porch. Erected by Lady Eleanor Balfour of Newton Don, 1859.

WAR MEMORIAL, at the junction with the A6089. By *A.C. Anderson*, 1920. Octagonal shaft on a square base topped by a shield incised with a Saltire Cross.

NENTHORN HOUSE, 0.8 km. W. By *George Beattie & Son*. Dated 1894. Largely Baronial, with some Cotswold Tudor detailing. Built of local stone with hammer-dressed facings of Dumfriesshire red sandstone. Mullioned and transomed windows throughout, and curvilinear pediments to wall-head dormers. The E (entrance) front has gabled advanced ends with square bay windows and a parapeted stone porch, and the S elevation two-storey canted bays in the flanking gables. Single-storey extension to the NW corner, of the 1990s, and an enclosed service court at the N end. Inside, a staircase hall and timber stair with carved balusters, and a sparsely ribbed ceiling. The principal rooms have deep decorative friezes and marble chimneypieces. Panelled drawing room. – Along the S front, a TERRACE with well-detailed Scottish Renaissance balustrade and steps. – To the W, a KITCHEN GARDEN with a fine range of greenhouses.

OLD NENTHORN HOUSE, 0.5 km. SE, probably incorporates part of a house built by the Kerrs of Littledean before *c*. 1680. Largely rebuilt in about the second quarter of the C18, and enlarged by the addition of an E wing about half a century later, the house remained the principal residence of the Nenthorn estate until 1894. Refurbished *c*. 1911, but unroofed in the late 1940s, the building is now ruinous.

Early C20 photographs show that the principal (N) front comprised three distinct units. In the centre stood the early-to-mid C18 main block, of five bays and two storeys, unusual in that the central bay rose a storey higher to a crowstepped gable, while the flanks had flat roofs with balustraded parapets. To the rear (S) the main block comprised three full storeys, as did a linked W service block, which was set back from the principal front. The late C18 E wing, of three bays and hip-ended, was single-storeyed to the N, but seemingly higher on the S side. The principal entrance, centrally placed in the main block, has a lug-moulded doorway with pulvinated frieze and triangular pediment; above is an elegant Gibbsian oculus. Internally the main block seems to have been two rooms in depth, perhaps with a central stair opening off the entrance. One of the first-floor rooms retains a handsome bolection-moulded chimneypiece, and another has a lug-moulded chimneypiece with egg-and-dart decoration. The W service block incorporates a barrel-vaulted undercroft probably belonging to the earlier house.

STABLES. Possibly late C18. Symmetrical S elevation, with a centrepiece of projecting two-storey gable containing a round-arched opening and door to a hay store above. On each side, three-bay stable blocks with central doors flanked by Diocletian windows, their keystones linked to blank panels above. On the N side a deep pend, leading to a small court, is surmounted by a square dovecot, with a tall pointed slated roof, in poor condition, topped by a foxhound weathervane. The interior is wholly devoted to horses; some well-detailed stalls remain.

MELLERSTAIN HOUSE. *See* p. 529.

NETHER HORSBURGH CASTLE
5.7 km. E of Peebles

3030

The fragmentary remains of a tower house and barmkin. The plan is unusual in that the tower seems to have been erected as an integral feature of a longer and lower range, as at Traquair House and Greenknowe Tower (qq.v.). Probably built during the second half of the C16 by the Horsburghs of that Ilk, who moved to the nearby Horsburgh Castle (q.v.) *c.* 1617.

Oblong on plan (9.8 m. by 8.0 m.), the tower rose to the height of four main storeys. Local whinstone rubble masonry, with quoins of the same material, but the other margins were evidently of freestone and have all been robbed. On the ground floor was a barrel-vaulted cellar entered from the barmkin on the N. The first floor was probably reached by a now vanished stair in the E wall leading to a vaulted lobby at the SE corner of the hall. This last was a spacious and well-lit chamber equipped with several mural aumbries, a large fireplace and what seems to have been a latrine in the S wall. The upper floors were reached via a spiral stair in the NE angle. The second floor seems to have contained a single chamber, almost identical to the one below, and the third floor at least two chambers. From the E wall of the tower a contemporary two-storey range, now almost entirely demolished, ran E for a distance of *c.* 14 m. A second range of buildings, of which only a fragment now survives, ran N to form the E side of the barmkin, which may have contained the principal entrance, while further ranges, or enclosing walls, probably returned W and S to complete an oblong courtyard on the N side of the tower house.

NETHERBYRES HOUSE
0.8 km. S of Eyemouth

9060

1834–5 by *George Angus*, in a Tudor Jacobean style, for Captain (later Sir) Samuel Brown, businessman, engineer and patentee of chain cables for the Royal Navy. Remodelled in the 1860s by John Ramsay L'Amy, and in the 1930s by Sir Christopher Furness.

A picturesque two-storey, basement and attic house built in cream sandstone. The S entrance front is of five bays. The three E bays (of the 1830s) have unusual decorative sandstone barge-boards, with rows of rosettes and scalloped edges; massive gable finials. Hoodmoulds over the windows, stepped up over the entrance door, which has a heraldic panel with the arms of Ramsay L'Amy. Gables flank the centre bay, which has a projecting oriel at first floor. The carved pediment, containing Brown's arms, is set in a wide, curvilinear and finialled gable-head. In the gablehead of the w two bays, dull and plain but formerly so picturesque, is the armorial of Sir Christopher Furness. On the N elevation the ground falls away to garden level. The centre bay has a projecting pedimented first-floor window in a curvilinear gable-head, flanked by gabled bays, over two-storey canted bays with strapwork parapets. Set back to the r. is a tall, ogee-roofed tower.

The interior has compartmented ceilings, decorative cornices and black marble chimneypieces. Of most interest is the stair hall or saloon, with rooms opening off this central space and a first-floor gallery around three sides, supported on ornamental consoled brackets. The T-plan stair rises at the N end, each side arriving at the continuous gallery, curved at the s end. Its s window embrasure has Gothic recesses on each side, the detailing continued over the window arch. In the centre of the high ceiling is a large rectangular cupola, and a hammerbeam-type roof of unusual construction, with arched braces each side linked by Jacobean pendant bosses.

COACHHOUSE and STABLES, W of the house. Perhaps late C18, but mostly mid-C19. U-shaped court with centre two-storey, two-bay coachhouse, with segmental-arched openings. A large circular ridge vent, possibly a former dovecot, is topped by a weathervane.

The estate was owned in the C18 by *William Crow*, mathematician, engineer and horticulturist, who devised and built the fine and unusual elliptical WALLED GARDEN, 1720–51. The tall coped walls have an outer skin of stone, and an inner one of brick, completed and heightened by Samuel Brown at least by 1850.

NETHERBYRES MILL, N of house. Two- and three-storey rubble building with pantiled roof; two cast-iron overshot wheels, wooden hoppers and machinery.

1040

NETHERURD HOUSE
0.5 km. w of Kirkurd

Palladian-derived mansion of 1791–4 for William Lawson of Cairnmuir, who took a personal interest in the design but with much advice from his neighbours. Documents suggest that Lawson took account of designs previously prepared by *Alexander Stevens Jun.*, for John Loch of Rachan and by *Robert Adam* for James Cunison of Jerviston (Lanarkshire). The house was extended NW in 1856–7 and altered, after two damaging fires, in 1925 and 1968.

The house is of three storeys and built of random rubble from Deepsykehead quarry near Carlops, with dressings of buff sandstone. At the entrance (s) front, a base plinth, plain band at first-floor level, and another at the wall-head, a dentilled cornice, and quoins at the outer angles; the margins are offset as if to receive harling. The centre bay of this front is slightly advanced; the entrance doorway is flanked by Tuscan pilasters, but is now fonted by a heavy Doric portico, with entablature and a coarse strapwork balustrade, probably of the 1850s.

Above is an over-arched Venetian window (strongly reminiscent of one at Jerviston) and at the second floor a three-light window. At the main block's w elevation, a two-storey bay window with a balustrade like that of the s portico and probably also of the 1850s. Plain full-height NW wing of 1856–7, its lower two storeys' stonework with cherry-caulking; at its NW corner, a battlemented low tower. The Venetian window in the centre of the main block's E elevation seems to have been moved here in 1925. At the NE corner, a range of single-storey offices built into the bank to the N must date from the late C18.

The inside was partially rebuilt in 1925. All the principal rooms have been remodelled, the original hanging stair replaced by a large central scale-and-platt stair of oak with nicely twisted balusters. Two chimneypieces survive from 1791: that in the drawing room (Scotland Room) is marble with a centre panel illustrating a harvest theme; the one in the outer drawing room (Edinburgh Room) is pine with fluted frieze and urns.

STABLES to the E by *James & Alexander Noble*, with sandstone dressings and quoins. A tall pend, slightly advanced, with an elegant timber cupola. – Adjacent WALLED GARDEN. Incorporated in an outbuilding on the E side is a fragment of a small C17 dormer pediment, a shield with the arms of Mark Hamilton, and above, a carving representing a human mask, perhaps from an earlier house.

LODGES. On the E drive, lodge with hoodmoulded windows and diagonally set chimneys, c. 1835. Overhanging timber eaves added 1856–7, the date of the w drive's lodge with stone-mullioned windows and central projecting gable, the top corbelled out above the doorway. Decorative iron gates with a distinctive rose motif.

WHALEBONE ARCH (A721). Here by 1808 and rebuilt in the 1960s. Square stone piers, with strange stunted birdcage and obelisk tops, support two whalebones.

NEWARK CASTLE
5 km. w of Selkirk

Well-preserved shell of a major late medieval tower house with barmkin. Founded by the Black Douglases c. 1424 with the construction of 'the New Werk' to distinguish it from its predecessor. The castle was forfeited to the Crown in 1455 and became one of only two major royal castles in the Middle March, serving both as an estate centre for Ettrick Forest and a hunting retreat. The existing tower was probably commenced in 1465–8 (*Thomas Joffrey*, master of the fabric) and completed by the 1490s. Damaged by English attack in 1548, it was fortified against civil unrest by the Scotts of Buccleuch (the castle's keepers from the early C16) in 1638–9, when substantial repairs were made to the upperworks of the tower (*Andrew Mein*, master mason, *William Storey*, master wright). Gutted and unroofed in the second half of the C16, it was preserved from further decay by the fifth Duke of Buccleuch (†1884) and his descendants.

Oblong on plan, the TOWER is solidly built, measuring 19.8 m. from W to E by 12.2 m. transversely over walls up to 2.7 m. thick. There were seven storeys in all, comprising a ground floor and entresol ceiled by a barrel vault, together with four main upper floors and an attic, all of timber. At the wall-head an open parapet-walk, set slightly forward upon a series of rough stone corbels, ran round all four sides of the building and communicated with rectangular caphouses at the NW and SE corners. These were gable-roofed N and S, while the steeply pitched roof of the tower itself was gabled W and E. The RCAHMS has suggested that the lower floors of the tower belong to the Douglas occupation, but the structural evidence, like the documentary, suggests a late C15 date for the whole, while the closest parallels for the planning arrangements are to be found at Elphinstone (dem., Lothian) and Comlongon Castle (Dumfries and Galloway), both attributable to the turn of the C15 and C16. The walls show traces of extensive stone robbing and subsequent repair. The masonry is of roughly coursed whinstone rubble of local origin with dressings of pink and buff-coloured sandstone, but all the lower quoins and most of the other original dressings have either disappeared or been replaced in whinstone. The original windows, where they survive, have broadly chamfered margins, while the later ones have narrow chamfers or quirked edge-rolls. The most notable external feature is the carved stone panel at first-floor level in the W wall, which displays the royal coat of arms beneath a winged angel's head. The ground-floor doorway in the N wall, with its lugged and bolection-moulded surround, is of late C17 date, but occupies the position of an original entrance. Above it can be seen the patched-up remains of an original round-headed first-floor doorway which must have been approached from a timber forestair.

INTERIOR. The tower is skilfully and compactly planned to achieve good security, efficient circulation and at least the partial separation of public and private areas, with generous provision within the latter of heating, sanitation and personal space. Having no fewer than six residential floors, the building was able to accommodate important guests or senior members of the royal household, as well as the king. At first-floor level and above the interior is now a roofless shell. The lower entrance leads via a lobby to the ground-floor chamber, a dimly lit storeroom whose only means of communication with the entresol floor above was a hatch or timber stair. The entresol chamber, most likely a hall for the household, had a timber floor supported on rough stone corbels and was lit by large windows to N and W, both equipped with bench seats, and heated, somewhat inadequately, by a fireplace in the E wall. A door at the SE corner opens into a newel stair descending from the first floor, while a hatch in the diagonally opposite corner communicated with the principal stair, which began as a straight flight in the thickness of the N wall and continued as a broad newel stair in the NW corner, rising to the full height of the building. The existing stair is a C19 replacement.

At FIRST FLOOR the planning seems to have been similar to that at Elphinstone Tower and Comlongon Castle, with an upper entrance lobby leading into what was presumably the king's hall, and also by means of a separate doorway into a kitchen at the hall's w end. The hall was of a respectable size (*c.* 11.3 m. by 7.0 m.), lit from the s by two large windows, both provided with seats, while to the N was a smaller window and alongside it a mural chamber in the NE corner. The large canopied fireplace, now entirely rebuilt, stood at the centre of the E wall. Halfway down the stair connecting the hall with the entresol chamber below there was a rather makeshift latrine, the only such provision for either floor. The rather cramped kitchen was screened from the hall by a timber partition and lit from a high-level window in the N wall. The fireplace, rebuilt in the C19, seems to have had a window in the back wall, as at Neidpath Castle (q.v.), another to the s and a cupboard in the N jamb. The s wall of the kitchen incorporated a mural chamber, possibly entered from the adjacent corner of the hall, and below this there was a second chamber, now inaccessible, within the haunch of the entresol vault. This lower chamber, probably a prison, was lit by a small window in the s wall, the whole arrangement greatly resembling that at Comlongon Castle.

The SECOND FLOOR contained two main rooms of unequal size. The larger, probably the king's outer chamber, lay to the E and was approached from the upper end of the king's hall via the SE stair. It was heated by an elaborately moulded chimneypiece in the N wall (one of the late Gothic bases survives) and had windows to N and s, the latter equipped with seats. Additional private space was provided by a mural chamber in the NE corner, and there was a latrine in the s wall. All these facilities were replicated on a smaller scale in the w room, or inner chamber, where, however, the mural chamber, or closet, lay to the s and the latrine occupied the SW corner. A doorway at the NW corner of the inner chamber communicates with the principal stair, the threshold now being 1.2 m. above floor level. This arrangement looks distinctly awkward, and since both doorway and stair have been rebuilt in the C19 it is possible that there was originally a serving hatch only in this position. The layout of the THIRD FLOOR, probably designed for occupation by the queen or, in her absence, by the keeper, was broadly similar to that below.

The FOURTH FLOOR, lit by dormers, communicated with the parapet-walk as well as with both stairs. It contained a single fireplace in the E gable, but it is not clear whether the space was undivided, as at Hermitage Castle (q.v.), or partitioned to form two or three chambers. Certainly accommodation in the tower was at a premium, for the existence of a fireplace in one of the ATTIC gables shows that even that level was regarded as habitable space. The caphouses, too, were floored, presumably to create extra storage space. The arrangements at parapet level in general resemble those at Comlongon. The main elements appear to be original, but later modifications have been made, including the construction, or reconstruction, of the caphouses in the late 1630s.

The tower stands near the centre of a roughly quadrangular BARMKIN (*c.* 62 m. by 50 m.) of the mid or late C16, which probably replaces an earlier one containing various ancillary buildings, including a great hall mentioned in 1447. A fragment of an earlier building can be seen within the NE corner. The C16 barmkin was designed for firearm defence, the walls (1.3 m. thick and 3.3 m. high) on all sides except the N, where the steepness of the ground made attack unlikely and guns useless, being equipped with a single tier of gunloops a little above ground level. The S and E walls each incorporate a single projecting tower of rectangular plan equipped with loops for flanking fire. Both towers were two-storeyed, the S one containing a latrine on each floor, and its neighbour, which was larger, having upper and lower chambers extending some distance W into the barmkin; the lower chamber may have been a kitchen. Little now remains of the entrance gateway, which seems to have been contained within a rectangular tower at the S end of the W wall. All the gunloops are double-splayed, but while those in the S wall have oval mouths and circular muzzle-holes, those on the other two sides and in the towers are more varied, some having square-cut mouths and/or keyhole-shaped muzzle-holes.

4080   NEWCASTLETON

A planned village on the l. bank of the Liddel Water, SW of the ancient settlement of Castleton (q.v.). Laid out from 1793 by Henry, third Duke of Buccleuch, to his own plan 'for the accommodation of labourers and encouragement of manufacturers', in this case handloom weaving. But was it also to rival his English neighbour, Dr Robert Graham of Netherby Hall, Cumberland, who in the late C18 planned a town at Longtown (c. 14 km. SW), of four streets with a square? The layout is a simple gridiron bounded by Hermitage Street, the main street, on the W, and Liddel Street on the E, with cross streets at right angles. Hermitage Street widens out about halfway along its length into Douglas Square, for a market place, and two smaller squares to N and S, which give vital character to the plan. The tenants built their own houses, and held their property on 99-year leases. Plots were provided for single-storey houses with two acres, the two-storey houses with four acres being concentrated in and around Douglas Square. Mostly rubble-built, some harled, of three bays, and many with bipartite windows to light the looms.

Former BURGHER CHURCH, at far S end of village. Liddesdale Heritage Centre since 1994. Built in 1804, as a rectangle with walls of rendered rubble, with two tiers of rectangular windows at each end of the long S front, and two taller windows at the centre. In 1838–45 an ambitious slender five-stage steeple capped by an octagonal spire was built at the centre of the S front by *James* or *William Scott*. Despite the classical design of this steeple, in 1874–5 the windows on each side were converted to lancets, and in 1890 an E chancel was added in a simplified Romanesque style. The upper parts of the steeple were demolished in 1976, and an inadequate bellcote with a pyramidal roof placed over its stump in 1986.

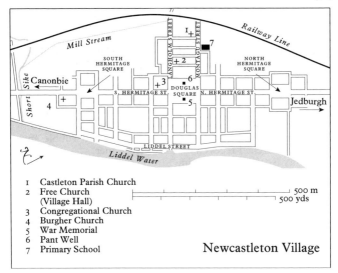

1 Castleton Parish Church
2 Free Church
  (Village Hall)
3 Congregational Church
4 Burgher Church
5 War Memorial
6 Pant Well
7 Primary School

500 m
500 yds

Newcastleton Village

CASTLETON PARISH CHURCH, Montague Street. Built 1888–9
(the former date above the entrance) as St John's Mission
Church, renamed after union with Castleton Church (*see* p. 156)
in 1946. Of grey snecked rock-faced rubble with ashlar dressings, the buttressed main body runs from N to S (in fact NE to
SW), with offshoots on the W side for a porch, a library, a tall
gabled transeptal aisle, and a vestry; a shallow chancel projects
to the S. The N entrance front has five lancets within a single
arch, the gable being capped by a coped bellcote, and W of the
front is the gabled and buttressed porch. Along the E flank are
paired lancets within containing arches. The W transept could
be screened off by a falling shutter when not required, but
since 1998 has been subdivided by an inserted floor. The nave
has a scissor- and collar-beam roof of meagre scantling, and
the chancel a diagonally boarded ceiling of polygonal profile.
Former CONGREGATIONAL CHURCH, South Hermitage Street,
now a dwelling. Built in 1850, it was originally single-storey
and of roughly coursed rubble. In 1889 the original church was
made into the manse, and the church moved to an added upper
floor with walls of snecked rubble. In its remodelled form the
main E front has two doorways alternating with two paired
windows to the lower floor, while the upper floor has four
paired windows with segmental heads.
Former NEWCASTLETON FREE CHURCH, Langholm Street.
Now village hall. Dated 1853. By the *Rev. James B. Johnstone*.
Rectangle of grey snecked rubble with stugged and droved
ashlar dressings. The SW flank has two lancets on each side of
the central doorway, and there are triplets of lancets to the
gable walls. The base of a truncated bellcote is at the apex of
the SE gable. A cement-faced rectangular doorway has been

formed at the centre of the front (dated 1956), and a hall and offices have been added to the rear.

MECHANICS HALL (Royal British Legion Scotland), North Hermitage Street. Built in 1898. A stepped and finialled gable in the centre of the three-bay front, a hoodmoulded Venetian window in the first floor, above a corbelled round-arched pilastered panel inscribed 'In God is Our Trust' 'TUC', a pair of compasses and 'Mechanics Hall 1898'.

NEWCASTLETON BRIDGE, s of the village. Probably c. 1790. A graceful two-span bridge over the Liddel Water, with two flat segmental arches, dressed stone voussoirs and rubble spandrels. An arched recess above the centre pier.

PRIMARY SCHOOL, Montague Street. 1858. H-plan school with stepped gables. s front with stone-mullioned windows and, set back at each end, crowstepped gabled pupils' entrances. Single-storey extension, with surprisingly ornate lead rainwater hoppers inscribed VGR 1935.

DESCRIPTION. Begin in DOUGLAS SQUARE, which has on its w side the small late C19 domed PANT WELL, with a cast-iron lion's-head spout, and on its e side the WAR MEMORIAL of 1920. Figure of a soldier with fixed bayonet, on a granite support. At the square's sw corner (with Langholm Street) is the Italianate former Free Church Manse. By *James Burnet* of Langholm, 1891–2, but remodelled 1892 after a fire. Tripartite windows flank a wide corniced doorway with round-headed bipartite windows above. On the s side of the square, and e side of South Hermitage Street, is the BANK OF SCOTLAND, a former British Linen Co. Bank by *Kinnear & Peddie*, 1895. Curvilinear gables and a corbelled-out oriel overlooking the square. Down SOUTH HERMITAGE STREET, the former Congregational Church. On the opposite corner with Union Street, a former CLUB HOUSE, built in 1896 by the Duke of Buccleuch's architect (presumably *James Burnet*), with a wide pilastered and corniced doorway. No. 21, one of the earliest houses, is single-storey, the lintel inscribed 1793 RM (Robert Murray).

MONTAGUE STREET opens out of the NW corner of Douglas Square. At the foot on the r. is the Primary School (*see* above), but closing the vista from the square is housing for the British Legion Housing Association by *Cairn Housing Association,* built on the site of part of the former station. Opened 1989. A U-plan block of single-storey cottages; in the centre is a stone-fronted double-arched pend in a ball-finialled gable. A low-key development, well planned, which complements the earlier single-storey housing.

In NORTH HERMITAGE STREET on the r., the former Mechanics Hall (*see* above). No. 44 is evidently the first house to have been finished in the town, dated 1793 and inscribed FB (Frances Ballantine).

STONE CIRCLE, Ninestone Rig. 10 km. NNE. In trees on the crest of a ridge, this oval setting measures 7 by 6.3 m. and now comprises only eight stones. The two largest stones stand eccentrically to the axis of the setting on the sw arc and measure up to 1.8 m. in height

HERMITAGE CASTLE. *See* p. 371.

NEWLANDS

A village close to the Lyne Water.

OLD CHURCH. The first known reference to this now roofless church was in 1317, and there was a donation to the roof in 1390. Of rectangular plan, the rubble-built walls are essentially medieval. The E wall, with a double-chamfered string course and a wide window arch of three orders both internally and externally, may be the earliest part. The set-back wall face of the W gable and the roll moulding of the (possibly relocated) round-arched doorway towards the W end of the S wall are probably late C15. There was perhaps a porch towards the W end of the S wall on the evidence of roof chases above a window formed within an earlier doorway; a blocked doorway with rounded arrises on the N side of the chancel suggests there was a sacristy.

There was extensive post-Reformation remodelling, one phase dated 1725(?) by a doorway towards the E end of the S wall; it was perhaps also then that a loft stair was inserted in the E window, the lower steps of which survive. Two rectangular windows with raised margins near the middle of the S wall are probably later C18. Two burial enclosures were built against the church. That against the W wall for John Murray is of the C17, and has a crowstepped W gable; a later enclosure against the N chancel flank was possibly on the site of the sacristy. After passing out of use, the church was divided into burial enclosures, with a small watch house in the SE corner.

CHURCHYARD. The entrance is dominated by the Mackay of Scotston enclosure of post-1798. It has Tuscan pilasters to the axial doorway, and also to the pediment which caps the façade. A number of carved stones of late medieval date have been reused in the churchyard wall. There are several interesting memorials and table tombs; worthy of note is the headstone of Andrew Borrouman, †1710, depicting a soul accompanied by two spirits.

PARISH CHURCH. *James Currie*, 1838, retaining a largely unmodified interior. Of pink coursed rubble with buff droved ashlar dressings, it is of T-shape, with the main body running from NW to SE, and the 'aisle' extending from the middle of the NE flank. There are entrances through the gable wall of the NE aisle and at each end of the SW front, the latter within pointed-arched recesses that continue the form of the windows; the windows themselves have lattice glazing. A substantial octagonal bellcote above the NE gable has gone.

The interior is covered by plaster ceilings of depressed parabolic profile with ridge ribs. The galleries in all three arms have panelled fronts, and are carried on slender cast-iron Tuscan columns. The imposing semi-octagonal PULPIT at the centre of the SW side is capped by a domed tester of ogee profile, and in front of it is a square precentor's desk; a symmetrical pair of stairs with cast-iron balusters leads up to the pulpit itself, only one giving access to the pulpit door. – COMMUNION TABLE. 1925, replacing an earlier removable trestle table. – STAINED GLASS. Heraldry and grisaille, *c.* 1869.

A hall block was added in 1969 towards the end of the sw front, blocking a door; its historicist detailing is because it was built of stone from the demolished Bordlands House. Further halls have since been added at its rear.

NEWSTEAD

There was a settlement here in Roman times (*see* p. 15), and Newstead's importance as a centre of the mason trade probably goes back to the Middle Ages. But it is not until the late C16 and C17 that evidence survives to reveal a community dominated by long-continuing families of operative masons – notably the Meins and Bunzies – who had established themselves as portioners (feuars) of small parcels of land formerly belonging to Melrose Abbey, and who practised their trade throughout the Borders and beyond. Newstead was also the meeting place of the Melrose lodge of masons until its transfer thither in 1741. The village comprises a long straggling street curving attractively downhill to the w. C20 infill housing and some small housing schemes.

Former MELROSE INFECTIOUS DISEASES HOSPITAL (Borders Primary Care). By *G. Monteith*, 1903. Red sandstone with red brick dressings. Oversailing eaves and decorative bargeboarded gables throughout. The former wards have tall gabled porches and gableted wall-head windows.

VILLAGE HALL (former School). Mid-C19. Plain red sandstone four-bay schoolroom with small roof ventilators.

WAR MEMORIAL. *c.* 1920. In rock-faced sandstone. A simple Celtic cross with small incised cross in the centre.

DESCRIPTION. At the e end of the village is RUSHBANK, by *Borders Regional Council* (project architect, *James Thornton*), 1975. A prefabricated development with one- and two-storey houses of standard type, which conform to the character of the village. Most of the late C18–early C19 surviving houses of two storeys, formerly with small gable attic windows, can be easily identified. On the s side, TOWNHEAD FARM, at the e end, preserves one of the best of Newstead's once prolific array of sundials; dated 1659 and inscribed in both Hebrew and Latin. Halfway down the hill is THE AULD HOOSE; the w gable window has been altered to a round-headed one, while mounted lower down is a small red sandstone carved head, possibly of medieval date. Finishing the s side of the street, a mainly two-storey development for the Eildon Housing Association by *Walter Wood Associates*, 2002. Mostly flatted, and mainly harled white, but some with a welcome colour wash, and quite skilfully built into the steep slope. Traditional features including timber canopies over the doorways.

On the opposite side of the road a pair of red sandstone harled cottages. Three bays each, the w one (ROSEDALE), with a triangular pediment over the doorway, the e one (WEST END COTTAGE), with a doorway with a moulded and lugged architrave, and segmental pediment, dated 1764. Further up the n side, the garden of No. 23 contains fragments of three sundials, one dated 1683, while No. 25 has an angular sundial, dated

1751. Following on the l. is St John's Wynd, which leads to the site of the former Masonic Lodge (dem. 1892), of which carved fragments are now preserved in the Lodge at Melrose (p. 554). This is marked by a small octagonal marble plaque, in a private garden, incised with crossed compasses and text.

MONUMENT, 0.5km. E. An inscribed stone in the form of a Roman altar, erected in 1928 by the Edinburgh Border Counties Association to commemorate the site of the Roman fort of Trimontium, which once occupied the plateau immediately to the E of the village and whose defences and surrounding annexes and camps are only known through excavation and aerial photography. Renovated and relettered in 1997. A second monument, comprising a column of pink marble, was set up at the E entry to the village in 2000.

NEWTON DON

7030

3.3 km. NW of Kelso

An austere Neoclassical house of 1817–20 by *Robert Smirke* for Sir Alexander Don, a Tory politician, whose family owned the estate from the late C17 until 1847, when it was sold to Charles Balfour of Balgonie, Fife.

The house is in a softened version of Smirke's 'New Square Style'. Bare of ornament, the emphasis is on horizontal lines. Two and three storeys over a sunk basement in an almost yellow stone over a grey stone base course. Symmetrical s elevation of nine bays, the central three-storey block of three defined by wide flat pilasters and tripartite windows on the ground and first floors, flanked by two-storey, bow-fronted wings at the ends. The principal entrance is in the recessed centre bay of the w façade, and the three-bay E elevation has a recessed centre and overarched tripartite window. The N elevation and office court have been reorganised at various times, principally late C19 and again late C20. Moulded eaves course and blocking course, but no balustrade. A rather tight round-arched porte cochère was added to the w front, probably in 1862 by *Brown & Wardrop*, who appear to have carried out some work on the principal floor at that time.

The plan of the INTERIOR of the early C19 house was no doubt compromised by an existing mid-C18 house, suggested by an earlier wall in the cellar, with door and window openings. It is not known what plan-form Smirke provided, though the entrance in the w elevation suggests that a long axial corridor was considered, and it is possible that the interior was not fully finished when Sir Alexander Don died, in debt, in 1826. The trustees of his heir, William Don, sold the furnishings *c.* 1828. The entrance leads up a flight of steps into a small hall; more steps up to a staircase hall and an inner hall. The dining room, billiard room and drawing room are the principal rooms along the s front, and a library and boudoir in the NE corner.

The interior is now largely as redecorated *c.* 1892 in spare

Scottish Renaissance style, although a Doric frieze in the hall remains from Smirke's time. The staircase hall and inner hall were restored *c.* 1950, when amazing timber Egyptian decoration of 1889–90 was removed from the staircase and first-floor landing, where *McArthy & Watson* had installed timber fronts from Cairo houses – creating a place of much delight to later generations of children. In the restoration *Thomas Hadden* made a new cast-iron stair balustrade, with a mix of plain and decorative wrought-iron uprights. The hall chimneypiece, marble with anthemion panel and urns, is said to have come from Ladykirk House (q.v.) and the former billiard room, now Chinese Room, has a timber and gesso chimneypiece from Ednam House, Kelso (q.v.). A new entrance hall was made from the N side of the office court in the late C20, reusing panelling from a former business room.

STABLES. Possibly late C18. The W front of nine bays, the centre and two-storey flanking bays slightly advanced. A pedimented pend surmounted by an octagonal two-tiered clock tower with a high domed roof.

SUNDIAL. On the S lawn. The pedestal, in the form of a stone lion rampant, was restored *c.* 1893, and given a bronze dial bearing the name of Richard Carre 1665, found in a joiner's shop on the estate. A shield on the lion's breast impales the arms of Sir Alexander Don and May Murray of Philiphaugh, who married in 1750. – NE of the house is a charming late C19 SHELTER with large rustic canopied seat made from patterned panels of bamboo and wood. Lead canopy roof with log columns to the front. Decorated eaves cornice and a bell and palm tree motif below the finial. The GARDEN GATE from the entrance court, an ornamental arch topped by a unicorn, inscribed DB AB and dated 1779, was brought from Balgonie Castle (Fife).

Early–late C19 WALLED GARDEN N of the stables. Rubble with mostly brick-lined inner walls. Two ornate cast-iron gates by *Thomas Hadden*, with tall, square, stone piers and ball finials; one dated 1907, the other 1888–1913 (commemorating a silver wedding). Late-C19 GENERATING HOUSE by the Stichel Linn. Castellated upper storey, and a crow-stepped porch with a round-headed moulded doorway with label stops.

EAST LODGE (B6364). Based on a 'Greek-Doric' design by *Robert Smirke*, built *c.* 1820. Smirke's drawing shows two single-bay lodges either side of a wide flat arch supported by four columns with a deep wall-head metope frieze continued across the arch. A simpler design was built. Single-storey, but the centre filled with a canted entrance bay, with the same detailing. Angle pilasters clasp the corners, and sparsely spaced paterae decorate the eaves course. Square-capped gate piers and cast-iron gates with acorn finials, supported by curved screen walls. – LODGE (A6089). 1892. Gabled.

HOME FARM, 0.7 km. SW. The mid-C19 rubble-built STEADING has a central two-bay pedimented section and large sundial covering an oculus at the apex. HARRIETFIELD, a farmhouse, lies to the S. Two storeys and harled with dressed margins. The original farmhouse was probably built after the marriage of Sir Alexander Don to Lady Harriet Cunningham in 1778. Central s-facing block of four bays, with a chimneyed pedimented gable and tiny oculus in the apex. On the N front, flanking lower piended wings have Palladian-style windows; the E one is a dummy. Two-storey C19 extension from the centre of this front. The interior was remodelled, presumably when the wings were added, and a palatial Neoclassical room pushed up into the first floor, perhaps designed as a dining room – was the house used as a banqueting house? A deep classical cornice, a ceiling rose, and a screen of timber Ionic columns along the W wall. Splendid white marble chimneypiece, in which the centre panel has an urn; circular medallions, a head in each, top the jambs. These are decorated with inlaid yellow marble flutings, repeated across the frieze.

NEWTOWN ST BOSWELLS   5030

Formerly Newtown of Eildon, which owed its origins to the monks of Melrose, who established a grange and corn mill here. It remained a small settlement until the railway arrived *c.* 1849, which led to expansion and some prosperity. From the 1870s the building trade was described as brisk. It became known as Newtown, then Newtown St Boswells, probably after it became a burgh in 1901. Newtown produces more industry than its neighbours, from a large auction mart and an oil distribution centre and depot, as well as agricultural engineers in the later C20. Scottish Borders Council has its headquarters here, which led to a large expansion in local authority housing on the W side of the village. By-passed 1990.

NEWTOWN PARISH CHURCH, at the SE end of the town. 1866–7 by *John Paterson,* for a United Presbyterian congregation, with walls of pink stugged ashlar (to the main front) and rubble (to the flanks and back), and buff-coloured dressings. The main SW front has a busily gabled three-sided apse; it is flanked to the W by a squat two-storeyed tower-porch capped by a splayed-foot spire, and to the E by a pyramidal-roofed porch, both with fish-scale slating. This front gains added prominence from superior masonry, deep sloping plinths, pilaster-like down-pipes at the angles of the apse, and a plethora of iron finials to gables and roofs. The leading face of the apse has a two-light Y-traceried window, unlike the single lancets of the rest of the building. At the NE end is a lower vestry block, with a plate-traceried rose window to the church gable above.

Internally the SW apse has no liturgical significance, attention instead being directed towards the pulpit and communion table at the NE end. Beyond the vestibules at the aisle ends are slender three-bay cast-iron arcades, with cylindrical piers and traceried spandrels. Over the central space is a ceiled scissor-braced roof. – COMMUNION TABLE. Simplified Gothic, *c.* 1926. – PULPIT. Set within arched recess below rose window. – STAINED GLASS. Aisles: Agnus Dei and Evangelist symbols, 1963. Apse: Chalice and Cross, arms of SS Ninian, Kentigern, Cuthbert and Columba, and XP monogram, 1965.

AUCTION MART. Built in 1872. The original sale ring of that

date survives. Octagonal, rendered, with a flattish octagonal ventilator, topped by a weathervane decorated with a vigilant cow.

Former BAILLIE HALL. By *Hardy & Wight*, opened 1890. Neo-Tudor gabled hall, a memorial to the Hon. Robert Baillie, with a frontage of coursed red sandstone. Bargeboarded gables, and pedestalled finials. Three-light and four-light mullioned windows, a clock and panegyrical panel. A louvred flèche with bellcast top. Inside, a statuary marble memorial tablet to Lady Grizell Baillie, 1894, by *William Fraser* of Edinburgh.

NEWTOWN PRIMARY SCHOOL, Sergeants Park. Late 1990s by *Borders Regional Council* (project architect, *Glen McMurray*). A large hangar with a shallow, vaulted glazed roof over a wide longitudinal communal corridor, flanked by lower open class-rooms with some wall glazing. An attractive exterior in grey walling with white band courses.

SCOTTISH BORDERS COUNCIL SOCIAL WORKS DEPART-MENT, Sprouston Road. Designed as offices for Roxburghshire Education Committee by *Reid & Forbes*, 1928, and apparently adapted *c.* 1930 as a large extension to the late C19 Newtown School. The SCHOOL is in rock-faced sandstone, with over-hanging eaves and exposed rafters. Contemporary two-storey, late C19 gabled schoolmaster's house to S. The C20 part is two-storey and rendered, with sandstone margins and end gables, each with a shaped apex. Long S front with a central Lorimer-style entrance tower with ogee roof, long stair window and moulded doorpiece. Gablets at each end and cusped dormer-heads in Lorimer's Colinton cottage style. Venetian windows each side of the entrance.

SCOTTISH BORDERS COUNCIL HEADQUARTERS. Built as Roxburgh County Offices. Won in a competition in 1961 by *Peter Womersley* but only half completed. It never realised Wom-ersley's ambition, but was seen by Colin McWilliam as the 'most encouraging of Scotland's local authority buildings'. The first phase, for a square block of offices and an almost free-standing service tower, providing a focus for distant views within the surrounding landscape, was only completed in 1968. This was due to a late start after, in Womersley's words, 'outcries from local ratepayers'. The design is only mildly Bru-talist; the building is too sculptural and carefully designed and detailed. The four floors of offices, in grey, shuttered concrete have bands of horizontal glazing, and originally had an open court in the centre – later filled in. Further phases were to include a high-level concourse to a Council Chamber and Committee Rooms on the S end of the site, and a link extended to the earlier, single-storey, red brick County Buildings to the W of *c.* 1930. These are now linked to a S extension, 1989, designed by *Ron Russell* of *Borders Regional Council*. L-shaped with a bowed corner with curtain-wall glazing round two floors, the windows shaded by projecting canopies. The design is hardly consistent with the unforgiving concrete monumen-tality of the original, but pleasanter.

WAR MEMORIAL, in front of the Council buildings. Celtic Cross with interlace decoration, *c.* 1920.

DESCRIPTION. Coming from the N on the old A68, first on the

l. is LANGLANDS MILL, Langlands Place, a former spinning mill built 1889 and later for A. Hall & Sons. Six-bay block of single-storey N-light weaving sheds with a two-storey, six-bay front office block. Late C19 mill-workers' housing in two blocks S of the mill and, opposite, SPROUSTON COTTAGES, red sandstone workers' housing. SPROUSTON ROAD off to the r. leads to the Primary School (see above). Continuing, and immediately on the r., the earlier School and Council Offices, and the Auction Mart on the l. (see above). In MELBOURNE PLACE the mid-C19 RAILWAY HOTEL, which comprised a booking office, post office, refreshment room and stabling for eight to ten horses, is all that remains of a large junction on the North British Railway (closed 1969). U-plan in red sandstone, Baronial with corbelled-out chimneystacks and decorative bargeboards to three large, canted, bracketed and gabled dormer windows. A pend leads to the former railway concourse, where there is now housing. A terrace of houses in the same Baronial style was built to the S, dated 1878, with shops on the ground floor. Downhill on the corner of Tweedside Road on the l., the mid-C19 BANK OF SCOTLAND, a former British Linen Co. Bank. Crowstep-gabled, with a full-height canted bay on the S elevation, and a flat-roofed, bow-ended banking hall added in 1904–5. Opposite is the ROYAL BANK OF SCOTLAND, 1871. Single-storey in red sandstone with a canted entrance bay.

The early-to-mid C19 settlement extends each side of TWEEDSIDE ROAD, the villas on the r. here with their backs to the road, the Classical fronts to the S much altered. The villas and their gardens on the l. are much better preserved; the best is NEWTOWN HOUSE, two storeys and three bays in red sandstone rubble with pink dressings, corniced doorway and canted dormer. At the end THE OLD MANSE. A former United Presbyterian manse, 1881. Two storeys and three bays with two canted bays flanking the round-arched moulded doorway.

NISBET HOUSE
3 km. SE of Duns

Not, as it looks at first sight, a medieval tower house with a Renaissance mansion tacked on, but a C17 house to which a vast Georgian tower has been added. The mansion, traditionally ascribed to the reign of Charles I but looking a generation earlier, was built by Alexander Nisbet of that Ilk – perhaps soon after his accession c. 1609 – to replace an earlier castle. Nisbet bankrupted himself in support of the royalist cause, and in 1649 the 'Palace of West Nisbet', as it was described by a late C17 writer, passed to the Kers. About the middle of the C18 the mansion was refurbished and a new entrance formed on the S side, while in 1774 a large tower was added to the W end to provide additional public rooms. A sensitive restoration for the present owner was completed in 2001–3 by *William Grime*.

The C17 HOUSE comprises an oblong main block (21.3 m. by 8.5 m.) of four storeys and a garret running W and E, having two square stair towers extruded from the N front, together with boldly projecting circular towers at the SW and SE angles. The walls of the E portion are thicker than the remainder and there is a disparity of levels on the third floor, suggesting that part of the earlier castle is incorporated at this end of the house. Harled rubble masonry with dressings of buff-coloured sandstone and crowstepped gables. Many of the windows appear to have been renewed in the C18. The stair-towers on the N FRONT are corbelled out at third-floor level to make space for chambers within, the stairs themselves continuing upwards within semicircular turrets corbelled out in the adjacent re-entrant angles. There is another turret at the NE corner, its eaves cornice continuous with that of the main block. Here, and on the main block itself, the cornice is of two members, the lower comprising individual corbels, whereas the corbelling of the stair-towers and of the other turrets comprises four continuous courses of ovolo mouldings. The early entrance is centrally placed between the two stair-towers, with a secondary entrance at the foot of the E stair-tower. The principal doorway has a bolection-moulded surround surmounted by a segmental-headed moulding with label stops, above which is a re-cut panel with the arms and initials of John Ker of West Nisbet and his wife, Jean. Possibly this entrance was formed by Ker, for there seems to have been an older doorway at the foot of the W stair-tower. Above the Ker panel is another bearing the Nisbet armorial, with the initials of Sir Alexander Nisbet and his wife Dame Katherine Swinton. This was installed, or reinstalled, during the 1980s, having lain for many years within the nearby family burial place (*see* below), to which it is said to have been removed by Ker. Whatever its original position, the panel can hardly be earlier than *c.* 1633, when Sir Alexander was knighted. The windows are more or less regularly disposed, the three upper tiers arranged in diminishing order of size; the original openings are round-arrised.

On the S FRONT, which is plainer than the N one, the fenestration is similar and the walls rise to a simple eaves band, which continues round the conical-roofed angle towers. These towers, the only ones in the Borders apart from those at Thirlestane Castle (q.v.), recall those of twin-towered houses of a generation earlier, such as Ardmillan (Ayrshire), and Cortachy Castle (Angus). At the foot of the SW angle tower is a handsome Doric doorway with pilastered jambs and full entablature, evidently inserted during the mid-C18 refurbishment to supplement the earlier N entrance, which at some point was blocked up and remained so until the late C20. The SE angle tower has a first-floor doorway reached from a stone forestair and balcony, the latter supported on cast-iron columns; all probably early C19. The most remarkable feature of the exterior as a whole is the proliferation of splayed GUNLOOPS, some two dozen in all. They occur in all parts of the building, from ground floor to wall-head, and are of two main types, some being oval-mouthed while others incorporate an additional downward splay at the centre, making the external aperture T-shaped, as at Murroes House, Angus. Such an array of military capability is unparalleled in the Borders and a little unexpected in a house of this date. History does not record whether the gunloops were brought into play when Sir Alexander garrisoned the house against his creditors in the 1640s.

The LATE C18 TOWER is built of exposed random rubble masonry with dressed quoins and margins, the contrast in surface treatment emphasising the disparity of scale in relation to the earlier house. The tower is of four storeys, the crenellated parapet set out on a prominent corbel course and each of the three upper storeys defined by a plain ashlar band. The windows to N and S are plain, but those facing W have Gibbsian surrounds, the one lighting the first floor being a Venetian. Within the pediment of the third-floor W window are carved the date 1774 and the initials I (or A) L, possibly for an unidentified tenant of the Ker proprietor.

INTERIOR. The internal planning of the C17 HOUSE was similar to that at Cowdenknowes (q.v.), the residential accommodation, stacked above a ground-floor cellarage, being served by separate public and private stairs. At Nisbet, however, the entrance led into a corridor which linked the cellars and the two newel stairs; on the upper floors the principal rooms opened directly into one another. In the original arrangement the W, or public, stair rose to a first-floor hall (c. 12.2 m. by 6.4 m.) beyond which were an outer and inner chamber, the latter contained within the SE angle tower. The E, or private, stair provided separate access to the two inner rooms of the suite and may also have been used to bring food from the kitchen to the upper end of the hall. The first floor was probably designed mainly as a reception suite, with the family occupying the two upper floors, where the arrangements seem to have been similar. Some of the rooms were provided with mural latrines.

Since the mid C18 the house has been entered mainly via the door in the SW angle tower, leading into an inner hall formed out of an earlier cellar. The remaining rooms at this level are barrel-vaulted, the far (E) one being the original kitchen, complete with massive flue and oven in the gable wall. The FIRST FLOOR remains much as it was in the mid C18, when the original hall was partitioned to form a dining room and ante-room, together with a N corridor leading to what were probably a bedchamber and dressing room. The dining room is lined with simple framed panels, and the bead-moulded marble(?) chimneypiece has a timber entablature. There is a homely, but ornate, Doric plaster frieze and cornice, similar in conception to the more sophisticated versions at Marchmont House and Mellerstain House (qq.v.). The plain plaster ceiling covers what seems to have been an early C17, open-joisted and boarded one with painted graining (fragments recovered in 2001). The Doric frieze reappears in the corridor, while the arabesque ceiling frieze in the ante-room is similar in character. Opening off the S end of the ante-room is a small plain chamber in the SW angle tower, possibly a servants' room. The bedchamber (now nursery) has plain walls above a dado, and a timber chimneypiece with pilastered overmantel – perhaps C18 in origin but partly renewed. The dressing room (now office) in the SE angle tower is panelled throughout in pine, and the ceiling incorporates a high oval centre.

The SECOND FLOOR, too, largely preserves its mid-C18 character, the rooms at that time probably comprising parlour, family bedchamber, dressing room and closet. Some have panelled doors and window ingoes and simple plaster ceiling cornices, while the parlour (Matilda's Room) retains a stone bead-moulded fireplace. Less remains of the C18 arrangements on the THIRD FLOOR, where some of the partitions and fittings appear to date from the following century. During the mid-C18 refurbishment the E division of the main block – still probably a single chamber at that time – may have been fitted out as a study or library, for one of the s window embrasures incorporates a neatly fitted, if homely, writing desk with folding lid. The landing at the top of the W newel stair has cut-out balusters of C17 character similar to one at Traquair House (q.v.). The collar-rafter ROOF, probably not earlier than the C18, has subsequently been strengthened by braces, purlins and kingposts with angle struts.

By incorporating the new reception rooms within a lofty w TOWER the designer of the 1774 additions dramatised the external appearance of the mansion, but made internal planning difficult. The new accommodation, arranged vertically, comprised a servants' hall etc. on the ground floor, with a spacious drawing room above, reached from the SW newel stair. From the first floor a new geometric stair, elegant but cramped, rose to the two upper storeys, comprising a guest apartment and library. These rooms were floored at different levels from the corresponding chambers in the old house and direct communication was possible only at first-floor level. The new rooms are notable for their fine interior decoration, distinct from the work in the main block although probably less than a generation later in date. The staircase has a delicate wrought-iron rail of network punctuated with ball finials echoing that at Paxton House (q.v.). Paxton may also have provided the inspiration for the ornamental plaster ceilings of the staircase and principal rooms – some perhaps by *George Morison* – for these show a similar dualism of style, part Rococo, part Adamesque. The drawing room is boarded in pine above a dado, but the damask(?) linings have disappeared; low-relief plaster ceiling with petalled centrepiece. The second-floor apartment, comprising parlour, bedchamber and closet, is similarly treated, but with a plain ceiling. In the library the upper walls have rectangular plaster panels framed with vases of flowers in low relief. The main tower rooms formerly had white marble chimneypieces with coloured slips and cast-iron hob grates, probably by *Carron*. The second-floor ones survive, the remainder now restored with near replicas.

The COURT OF OFFICES appears to be of mid-C18 date. Two-storey U-plan facing an open courtyard to s; grooms' house to w, stables to N and coachhouse to E. Random rubble masonry with dressed sandstone margins and rusticated quoins. – BURIAL VAULT, 50 m. NW, contains several recumbent slabs of the Kers of Cavers and West Nisbet, including one to John Ker (Carre), (†1667), the probable builder of the vault. In the E wall, a stone panel carved with the full armorial achievement of the family. – WALLED GARDEN, 0.2 km. E, has a segmental-arched entrance on the W side; beyond it there is said to be an ICE HOUSE.

Almost nothing now remains of the extensive PARK of Nisbet, first recorded on Pont's map *c.* 1590 and much improved in the C17 and C18. The handsome, late C18 DOVECOT, 0.7 km. S, is probably by the same architect as the W tower. Pentagonal on plan, with a modillioned eaves cornice and crenellated parapet; the stone-flagged, domed roof is topped by a ball finial.

NORTH SYNTON

1 km. NE of Ashkirk

A tower house converted firstly into a manse and then into a farmhouse. The tower house was probably built during the latter part of the C16 by one of the Veitches of North Synton, a cadet branch of the Veitches of Dawyck, who had been in possession of the property since the end of the previous century. In 1641 North Synton 'with its tower' passed to Francis Scott of South Synton and thence, probably by marriage, to Robert Cunningham, minister of the parish of Ashkirk. The house probably became a farmhouse sometime during the late C18 or early C19.

The building is T-shaped on plan, comprising an oblong main block of three storeys and a two-storey N wing, together with various single-storey outshots. The masonry is of harled rubble with sandstone dressings, most of the older windows having rounded or chamfered arrises. The early C19 chimneystacks are of brick with corbelled copings. Only the lowermost storey of the tower seems to survive and this takes the form of a barrel-vaulted cellar occupying the basement of the main block; the internal dimensions suggest that the tower was of simple oblong plan measuring *c.* 11.0 m. by 6.5 m. externally. The S wall contains an original semicircular-arched entrance rebated for outer and inner doors and formerly equipped with a draw-bar. There were windows on three sides, as well as an aumbry and what may have been a gunloop. A hatch in the vault formerly gave access to the floor above, but there is no obvious sign of a stair, so it is possible that there was a second entrance at first-floor level, as at Windydoors and Kirkhope (qq.v.).

Robert Cunningham evidently remodelled the house at the end of the C17, refurbishing the upper floors and raising the ground level on the N side, where he also built a new entrance wing. The new doorway has a bolection-moulded surround surmounted by an entablature, of which the frieze bears the initials of the owner and his wife, possibly Isobel Scott, together with the date 1699. One of the rooms on the top floor has a stone bolection-moulded chimneypiece of similar date. Subsequent alterations to the house included the construction of a terrace on the S side, thus encasing the ground floor of the original tower on this side also.

OLD CAMBUS *see* COCKBURNSPATH

OLD JEDDART *see* JEDBURGH

OLD MELROSE *see* RAVENSWOOD

7040

OLD PURVES HALL
5 km. SE of Greenlaw

Probably begun in the early C17, when the property, then known as Nether Tofts, belonged to the Belsches family. In 1673 the estate was bought by Sir William Purves, Solicitor General for Scotland, who reconstructed the house. His great-grandson, another William (fourth baronet), remodelled and extended the house, while the next laird, Sir Alexander, added a wing in 1790. After the family moved to Marchmont House (q.v.) in 1812 the house was neglected and a sizeable portion of it demolished when the present Purves Hall (*see* below) was erected. The surviving fragment is currently being restored for occupation.

Close scrutiny suggests that the existing fragment comprises the W half of a rectangular main block (*c.* 21 m. from W to E by 7.6 m. transversely), together with a N wing having a projection of 6.3 m. and a width roughly corresponding to the reduced length of the main block (10.5 m.). So what was formerly a large, L-plan house with the long axis running W and E has become a smaller, oblong house with the long axis running N and S.

The reduced main block, of three storeys and an attic, is of harled rubble masonry with dressings of red and buff-coloured sandstone; crowstepped gables. The W gable provides a clue to the building sequence – an attic window bearing the date 1738 and the initials of Sir William Purves and his wife, Ann Hume Campbell, daughter of the second Earl of Marchmont. But while the upper part of the block is evidently of this date, the chamfer-arrised and bolection-moulded windows seen on the ground and first floors are probably relics of the C17 house. At first-floor level the present SE corner incorporates the left-hand (W) side of a moulded doorway, formerly reached from an external stair. This probably marks the midpoint of a seven-bay S front formed when the house was enlarged in 1738. The N front of that date seems to have had a central staircase bow, visible internally. The N wing of 1790 (dated on N gable) is similar in character to the remainder, except that the dressings are all of buff-coloured sandstone and the gables are coped. The W elevation incorporates a big Venetian window on the first floor.

The house has entrance doorways on all four sides, none of them earlier than 1790. On the ground floor the main block contains a single room originally used as a kitchen. The big, segmental-arched fireplace in the W gable has been partially blocked and a smaller, roll-moulded one inserted in the opposite wall. A second kitchen, again with a large fireplace, occupies much of the adjacent area of the N wing. On the first floor the E of the two rooms occupying the main block has a moulded ceiling-cornice and panelling of *c.* 1738; the egg-and-dart moulded chimneypiece of this date also survives behind a later columned surround. At this level the N wing may originally have contained a large dining room.

PURVES HALL, 0.1 km. SE, is mid-to-late C19, with a service wing of 1908, and another wing dated 1938. Of most interest is the late C17 classically detailed double-arched opening in the W elevation, perhaps from Old Purves Hall. Georgian-style interior. – Weathered SUNDIAL, in the grounds, with circular cup hollows in a polyhedral head. – WALLED GARDEN. L-plan, possibly late C18, with coped rubble walls.

OLD TORWOODLEE *see* TORWOODLEE HOUSE

ORCHARD HOUSE   3010
2.5 km. E of Hawick

Built *c.* 1800 for an Elliot of Borthwickbrae (q.v.), probably by his relative, *William Elliot.* Classical, in whinstone rubble with rusticated angle quoins. Two storeys, basement and platformed bellcast roof. Three bays, with a later full-height porch and canted bay to the r. Inside, a tripartite plan, the hall with an Ionic pilastered archway to a graceful geometric staircase. Decorative friezes. – STABLES. Pedimented.

OVERTON TOWER   6010
1.5 km. N of Edgerston

The ruined shell of a cross between a tower house and a pele house, which was the subject of a complaint by the English Warden of the Middle Marches in 1596, shortly after it was erected. Oblong on plan (11.1 m. by 7.2 m.), it contained two main storeys, together with a garret formed within the gabled roof. As at Mervinslaw Pele and Slacks Pele (qq.v.) there was a ground-floor doorway in one of the end walls and a separate first-floor doorway in one of the side walls, but here the masonry was laid in lime mortar. The building was unvaulted and internal communication was probably by means of a timber stair. Single chamber to each floor, the two lower ones with stone fireplaces and mural chimneys.

OXNAM   7010

A village strung out along the banks of the Oxnam Water.

PARISH CHURCH, 0.7 km. N. Largely rebuilt 1738 (dated on one of the S windows) and an unusually unspoilt example of a rural, early Georgian church. Relatively sympathetic additions and remodelling were carried out in 1878–9 by *A. Herbertson & Son* of Galashiels. The main body is of harled rubble with exposed margins and a birdcage bellcote on the w gable. Four large arched windows along the s wall, and an oculus in each of the gable walls; the placing of the windows away from the ends of the s wall, and the height of the oculi, suggest there were galleries at the E and W ends. In 1878–9 a T-plan resulted from the addition of a lateral 'aisle' off the centre of the N flank; the additions also included a lean-to porch at the W end and a transversely roofed vestry at the E end. The 'aisle' has a window with two lights and a circlet in its N wall and arched windows in its flanks; there are shoulder-lintelled windows and doorways to the porch and vestry.

Internally, the three arms are directed towards the pulpit and communion table at the centre of the s wall, and have plaster ceilings of polygonal section. Thoughtful reordering and redecoration in 1954, since when the pews and pulpit (of 1879) have had a limed finish. – COMMUNION TABLE AND CHAIRS, minimal Gothic detailing, 1933. – PULPIT, with a bracket on its side for a baptismal basin. – PLAQUE, N aisle, commemorating Charles Philip de Ainslie of Dolphinston. – MEMORIAL, against s external wall, to a member of the Elliot family, †17–, swan-necked pediment framing portrait bust above winged angel head. – CROSS-INCISED GRAVE-SLAB, medieval, set against s wall of vestry. – SUNDIAL BRACKET, at SW corner. – JOUGS attached to s wall.

CHURCHYARD, several interesting C17, C18 and C19 memorials. Rev. Alexander Colder, †1736, Corinthian aedicular monument, at E end of churchyard. Mary Rutherford, †1749, a pair of death's-heads below winged angel head, to SE of church. Fine lettering on headstone of Robert Thomason, †1796, with egg-and-dart border. WATCH HOUSE, small rectangular structure at NW corner, probably early C19.

MANSE (Kirkstyle House). Stylish, harled house with broad eaves and piended and platformed roof. By *John Smith*, *c.* 1830; stables and steading may be earlier. In the garden is a medieval grave-slab (propped against the stables) bearing a cross, the shaft rising from a stepped mount. Inscribed 'O.R. 1853'.

ROMAN TEMPORARY CAMPS, Pennymuir, 7 km. SE. Two well-preserved temporary camps standing on the W side of Dere Street as it climbs NNW from Tow Ford, across the Kale Water. The main camp, which overlies an earlier linear earthwork, encloses 17 ha., and has six entrances, each guarded externally by a traverse comprising a short length of rampart and ditch. The second camp is smaller and occupies the SE corner of the interior. This was a regular staging post for the Roman army; traces of several other camps have been recorded in the vicinity.

4050   OXTON

A village comprising mostly late C18 and C19 houses of two storeys; thatched single-storey houses were formerly the standard pattern.

CHANNELKIRK PARISH CHURCH. 2.4 km. NW. A handsome
structure of 1817 by *James Gillespie Graham*, set on the hillside
at Kirktonhill within an attractively irregular churchyard overlooking the Leader Valley.*

With harled walls and ashlar dressings, the main body of the
church is a broad rectangle, N of which a substantial offshoot
with chamfered angles houses the gallery stair. E and W walls
have shallow-pitched crowstepped gables, the former with a
cross finial, and the latter a square bellcote (repaired 1857) with
gabled faces and a crocketed spirelet. The four-centred-arched
main entrance, with a broadly chamfered surround, is in the E
wall; above is a three-light window with rectilinear tracery. The
W gable window is set lower. Along the S face are four two-
light Y-traceried and transomed windows, with a sundial on
the central axis. Two similar windows flank the N offshoot, with
a third, central window for the stair. Inside, a flat ceiling with
a simple cornice. The pews and galleries range around the E,
N and W sides. Panelled fronts to the galleries carried on cast-
iron reeded columns; small vestry beneath the E gallery. –
PULPIT, semi-octagonal, approached by an E stair with turned
balusters and newel; above a deep niche for the minister's seat
is a tester capped by a concave-sided pyramid. – COMMUNION
TABLE, *c.* 1923.

CHURCHYARD. Many memorials now in poor repair.
Against W wall of church, family of James Waterston, 1781:
rustic Neoclassicism, with portrait bust against a pyramidal
superstructure. In NW corner of churchyard, Marion Brock,
†1721, with what appears to be a female cadaver.

CHANNELKIRK HOUSE. Former manse, built 1784 by *Charles
Sanderson* and *Andrew Thomson*. Addition at the W end of the
N elevation by *Thomas Brown*, 1815, making an L-shaped plan.
Further N addition of 1863, perhaps the date of the porch in
the re-entrant angle.

CHANNELKIRK PRIMARY SCHOOL. Mid-1850s schoolroom
with an extension across its S end of 1910 by *T.R. Atkinson*;
bracketed eaves and bipartite windows. Extended 1992, with
long rendered wings whose gable ends have two semicircular-
headed windows from the earlier schoolroom.

MEMORIAL HALL. 1924. An inscribed panel with a scrolled
pediment and St Andrew's Cross.

TOWER HOTEL. Originally a C18 thatched cottage, which later
became a pub. Remodelled in 1903 according to a panel on
the S elevation. Two storeys, defined by an octagonal corner
tower with turret covered with rosemary tiles. Harled, with
decorative timbering to first floor. Original Edwardian panelled bar fittings, with painted glass in two windows.

JUSTICE HALL, NE of the village. A long narrow laird's house
built by James Justice, advocate, botanist and horticulturist,
who bought the lands of Luckenhaugh in 1739. It seems first
to have been built with the principal front to the N but was
probably turned back-to-front by James Justice Jun., a leading
light in Edinburgh's theatrical circles, who succeeded in 1799

---

* The site is traditionally linked with St Cuthbert, but the first certain reference is
c. 1150, when it was granted to Dryburgh Abbey.

and occupied the house until he was bankrupted in 1816. He appears to have classicised the house a little, providing the new entrance door (S), above which is an apology for a pediment with a central oculus. Inside, a new curved stair was provided from ground to first floor, with cast-iron decorative balusters, continuing as a scale-and-platt stair to the attics. – A courtyard STEADING to the W. The E range appears to be the earliest, *c.* 1740, probably used for horticultural purposes by James Justice Sen.

9050

PAXTON

A small, scattered village whose villagers in the mid C19 were employed on the land and in salmon fishing on the River Tweed.

PARISH CHURCH. Built as Mordington and Paxton United Free Church, probably by *William J. Gray Jun.* of Berwick; opened 1908. Compressed T-plan, extended to a cross by a vestry at the head. Entrance front of pink snecked rubble with ashlar dressings, with axial porch flanked by lancets; a two-light window with Geometric tracery stretches up into the gable, which is surmounted by a bellcote. The roof has laminated timber arched braces, crossing at the junction of the arms.

CROSS INN. Mid-C19, rendered and pantiled, with late C19 square glazed bays.

OBELISK. 'A replica of a Jacobean Mercat Cross . . . Rebuilt 1999'.

WAR MEMORIAL. Celtic cross in pink sandstone, *c.* 1920.

SCHOOLS. Four former schools have been converted to dwellings. THE SCHOOLHOUSE, late C19 Italianate T-plan with overhanging timber-bracketed eaves, round-headed windows, and a lean-to gabled porch. SOUTHERNWOOD, at the E end, was the first school, *c.* 1814. Rubble-built, the school on the lower floor, schoolmaster's residence above. From 1846 to the mid C20, it was used as the Library and Reading Room. THE OLD SCHOOL was the Board School, by *William J. Gray Jun.*, 1873. Picturesque, gabled with red tiles, grey slates and decoratively carved bargeboards. Spired bellcote with trefoil-headed openings. The Italianate THORN COTTAGE, dated 1846, founded by William Forman Home, also by *Gray*.

PAXTON BRICK & TILE WORKS, E of the village. Ruinous remains of a former kiln block of *c.* 1830. New kilns were installed in the mid 1880s, designed by *James Stevenson*, but by 1900 the works were disused. Sandstone rubble walls with red brick-lined barrel-vaulted chambers ('Newcastle' kilns) inside. Three round-arched openings, with polychrome margins, between lean-to buttresses.

SPITAL HOUSE. *See* p. 692.

TWEEDHILL HOUSE. *See* p. 736.

UNION CHAIN BRIDGE. *See* p. 739.

PAXTON HOUSE
0.8 km. s

The dramatic site of this dignified C18 mansion forms part of the lands belonging to the Home family since the C15. It became the property of Patrick Home of Billie when he succeeded to the Paxton and Wedderburn estates on the death of his mother in 1754. The Palladian plan of a villa linked by corridors to pavilions was adopted by Patrick in the hope that it would be impressive enough to become the home of a member of the Prussian court, Sophie de Brandt, whom Patrick believed to be a natural daughter of Frederick the Great. This personal ambition was never realised. Designed by *John Adam*, who was paid £26 6s. for plans in January 1758, with *James Nisbet* as principal mason and superintendent of works. The source for the design of the principal elevation seems to be Isaac Ware's *A Complete Body of Architecture* (1756, pl. 57). The principal change at Paxton was the use of a prominent Doric free-standing portico, instead of the engaged Ionic portico in Ware's engraving. Building began in 1758, but the house was unfinished by the mid 1760s, by which time Patrick had succeeded to Wedderburn Castle (q.v.) and turned to a new building enterprise. He sold Paxton to his nephew Ninian Home in 1773. Ninian was often in his estates in the West Indies, but appears to have finished Paxton before his brother George succeeded him.

Paxton House is built in warm pink sandstone quarried locally, given a smooth ashlar N front with diagonal broaching; the S front is of coursed rubble possibly intended to be harled. The central block is of two storeys, with a raised basement and a piended platform roof, slightly bellcast.

The striking N FRONT of the central block has seven bays, 57 the centre three recessed and fronted by a free-standing giant Doric columned portico, given prominence by a wide flight of steps flanked by impressive pedestals – described by Nisbet as 'very massy'. Behind the portico, a corniced door flanked by pedimented ground floor windows. At the outer bays, corniced ground floor windows. Small square windows to the basement and first floor. Wall-head entablature with bold triglyphs and metopes, and an overhanging cornice which extends round the whole building. The three advanced centre bays on the S 56 FRONT carry a pediment with oculus. Corniced and pedimented windows as on the N front, but the first floor windows are full height. The four-bay side elevations are unadorned.

Single-storey, three-bay quadrant screen passage walls, with central round-arched doorways and balustraded parapets, link the centre to four-bay U-plan PAVILIONS. They have side elevations of five bays, with consoled and pedimented doorcases, fronting the N forecourt. More screen walls, with ball-finialled gateways to service courts, link the pavilions to two-bay pedimented outbuildings, possibly those being planned by Nisbet in 1768. The E pavilion and outbuildings were formerly used as stables, while kitchen and services were in the W one. The stables were adapted to tearooms and shops etc., and the service accommodation was altered and extended for family

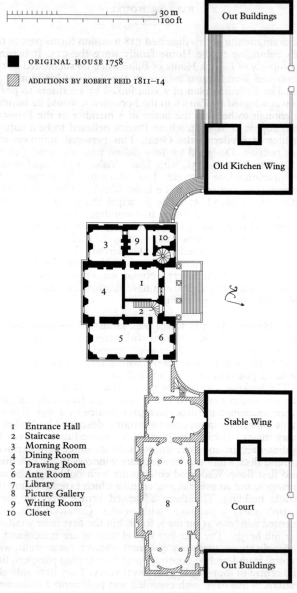

├──────────────────────────────┤ 30 m
├──────────────────────────────┤ 100 ft

■ ORIGINAL HOUSE 1758
▨ ADDITIONS BY ROBERT REID 1811–14

Out Buildings

Old Kitchen Wing

Stable Wing

Court

Out Buildings

1   Entrance Hall
2   Staircase
3   Morning Room
4   Dining Room
5   Drawing Room
6   Ante Room
7   Library
8   Picture Gallery
9   Writing Room
10 Closet

Paxton House.
Ground-floor plan.

use in the 1990s by *Ian Begg* for the Paxton Trust and *Donald Chapman* for John Home Robertson.

Adjoining the s front of the house is a severe, two-storey, eleven-bay range containing the LIBRARY AND PICTURE GALLERY. This comes as a shock after the rusticity of the s elevation of the house. Designed by *Robert Reid*, King's Architect and Surveyor in Scotland, and built for George Home between 1811 and 1814 in matching pink sandstone from Nabdean Quarry. A two-bay library block, and nine bays for the picture gallery. The centre five bays are slightly advanced as a parapeted centrepiece, with round-arched niches at first-floor in further advanced end bays; otherwise plain square-headed windows throughout. Painted dummy windows at gallery level.

A compact arrangement of rooms inside; services in the basement, a *piano nobile*, and bedrooms on the first floor (always referred to as the top floor). The spacious HALL has walls decorated with shouldered plasterwork panels decorated with egg-and-dart moulding, and a continuous moulded dado rail. The splendid, delicate but robust Rococo plasterwork is by *George Morison*. Over the chimneypiece, arabesques frame delicate fronds of leaves and fruit, all collected together by a basket of fruit and flowers with contents spilling out each side in garlands. Similar arabesques in the corner of the ceiling. To the l., through a doorway, is the STAIRCASE with similar plasterwork by Morison, the curved walls and ceiling cove awash with Rococo arabesques; in the centre a graphic eagle hangs on to a chain carrying a central light. The dog-leg timber stair, with an attractive net-patterned balustrade of curvilinear iron bars and ball finials, was probably made by the *Berwick Foundry*, Tweedmouth, who supplied matching ornamental net-work for the stair window in 1814. These were the only principal rooms finished with plasterwork in Patrick Home's day.

The three rooms along the s side of the *piano nobile* had to wait until the mid 1770s for Ninian Home to commence furnishing them with Adam-style decoration, and furniture ordered from *Chippendale, Haig & Co.*, most of which is still in the house. At the w end is a morning room, simply decorated with an Edinburgh-style white marble chimneypiece with roundels. The DINING ROOM occupies the centre front, the decoration dating from *c.* 1775, but by whom is not known. Plaster-panelled walls decorated with strips of oak leaves and acorns. Over the chimneypiece a large, scuptural vertical oval of the Rape of Europa, framed by Neoclassical arabesques. The overdoors have dark cameo heads of Roman Emperors dangling from more filigree plasterwork. The Adam-style ceiling is composed of concentric circles with a long rectangle of geometric patterns at each end. The DRAWING ROOM at the E end has a frieze of garlanded vases, linked by honeysuckle and bay-leaf sprigs. Geometrical patterns round the ceiling frame a circular centrepiece set with plaques of dancing ladies. A complete scheme of decoration, *c.* 1789, made use of French wallpaper strips and overdoors made by *Reveillon,* and chosen for Paxton by Thomas Chippendale, but much was painted out when Patrick Home's picture collection first came into

59

the house from Wedderburn Castle. Twelve arabesque strips between the panels, and three overdoors with arabesques framing Pompeian plaques against black backgrounds are all that are left.

The attic floor is all bedrooms, simply decorated, mostly with modillion and rosette cornices, and a mixture of marble and Edinburgh-type timber and gesso chimneypieces. At the W end is Mr Home's suite of bedroom, dressing room and closet, served by a corridor from the upper landing, and a newel service stair tucked in beside the portico. The closet was fitted up (1761) as a Charter Room, with a high-domed ceiling, clay floor tiles, and strengthened door.

In the early C19 E extension, the LIBRARY is similar to a well-proportioned drawing room of Edinburgh's Northern New Town. A bow end to the N, and bookcases supplied by *David Chartres* of Berwick in 1814. The niche in the W wall is said to be a later insertion, and the grey and white marble chimneypiece with a central urn, swags and drapes, was moved here from the morning room. Beyond is the majestic, rectangular, 58 PICTURE GALLERY, designed by Reid for the collection of paintings acquired on the Grand Tour by George Home's uncle, Patrick Home of Wedderburn. Completed the same year as Soane's public Dulwich Picture Gallery, this was the first private gallery in a Scottish country house to have been designed around its paintings, which are top-lit through a central cross vault with a domed, circular roof-light and cupola. Apsidal ends, marked off by screens of ochre-marbled Ionic columns, are also top-lit. Redecorated by *Bonnar & Carfrae* in 1871, when Reid's Neoclassical painted scheme of imitation ashlar decoration disappeared. During the Second World War the E apse was converted to a chapel, but in 1993 the gallery was restored to its original dimensions and opened as an outstation of the National Galleries of Scotland. Surviving plasterwork of 1812, by *Anderson & Ramage*, was replicated and the room redecorated to the 1871 scheme.

The POLICIES of this exposed and treeless site were planted to an improvement scheme by *Robert Robinson*, who was paid £6 6s. in 1758 for drawing a plan. Much of the tree planting along the steep banks of the Linn Burn and the strips along the straight avenue to the bridge date from this time. More planting took place at the end of the C19. Impressive tall pink sandstone rubble BOUNDARY WALLS front the road and River Tweed.

At the main entrance the SOUTH and EAST LODGES, in Palladian-style, are linked by a classical screen, c. 1789. Venetian windows with painted imitation glazing to upper and side lights. The screen is connected to the lodges by engaged pilasters, and has central columns topped by urns, with draped festoons and cherubs' heads, by *Coade*, and paired pilastered inner gatepiers surmounted by recumbent lions inscribed 'Coade London 1789'. The screen was truncated in the 1990s. Opposite, the NORTH and WEST LODGES. Simple early-to-mid-C19 two-by-one-bay cottages.

Down the long avenue, the WALLED GARDEN on the r. was laid out in 1761, extended 1780. Mostly in pink rubble

sandstone. Then the BRIDGE of 1759 by *James Nisbet*. Pink
sandstone with three round arches and plain voussoirs. Four
polished keystones, and two ornamented carved heads added
in 1765. Under the bridge, an oval late C18 domed ICEHOUSE.
– BOAT HOUSE. SE of the house, beside the River Tweed. Pantiled, with wide-arched entrance, used for commercial fishing.
Reconstructed by *Bain, Swan Architects* in 1995. A fish store is
built into the bank.

FINCHY SHIEL, 1.4 km. E of the house. Mid-C19 two-bay
rectangular fishing shiel. A solid bulge in the W elevation protected the gable from floods. A fishstore is built into the bank.

Set deep in the trees *c.* 0.8 km. NW are three estate houses.
DENE HOUSE, possibly mid-C19, orginally two cottages. The
S elevation has rustic porches with tree-trunk columns. A
chimneystack sports a sculptured dog. – DOWER HOUSE (formerly The Cottage), by *William J. Gray Jun.*, 1881. Swiss-style,
of pink sandstone rubble and decorative half-timbering. Decorative string course with zigzag frieze of stencils of circles and
quatrefoils, embossed with the words REMEMBER TRUE TO
THE END. – GARDEN COTTAGE is in the same style; its S-
facing balcony has a cut-out balustrade, fretted to read CON-
SIDER THE LILIES HOW THEY GROW BELOW.

FISHWICK MAINS FARMHOUSE, 3.3 km. SW. Early to mid-C19
and traditional in coursed pink sandstone and squared rubble.
The well-planned irregular courtyard STEADING, probably
contemporary with the house, has segmental-arched cartsheds,
granary and gabled hay loft.

FISHWICK FISHING SHIEL, 3.7 km. S. Early C19(?), rebuilt *c.*
2000 after a fire. Single storey, two bays, with a separate fish
house built into the hillside. A bulge in the gable end protects
the shiel from floods.

PEEBLES

INTRODUCTION

A small burgh set in a secluded valley enclosed by sheltering hills,
Peebles Old Town occupies a low ridge N of Eddleston Water,
the New Town a peninsula between Eddleston Water and the
River Tweed. The Old Town probably originated as an early
Christian ecclesiastical centre, and the parish church of Peebles
was situated here until the late C18. The New Town – a rather

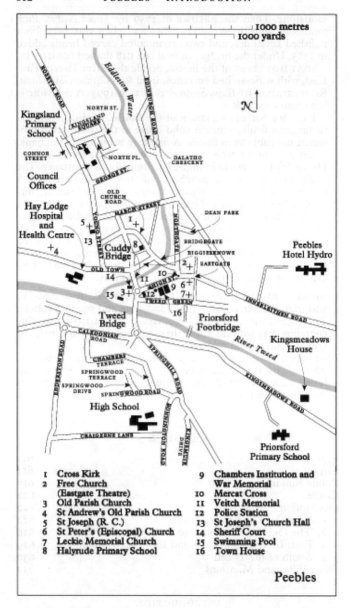

1000 metres
1000 yards

1	Cross Kirk	9	Chambers Institution and
2	Free Church		War Memorial
	(Eastgate Theatre)	10	Mercat Cross
3	Old Parish Church	11	Veitch Memorial
4	St Andrew's Old Parish Church	12	Police Station
5	St Joseph (R. C.)	13	St Joseph's Church Hall
6	St Peter's (Episcopal) Church	14	Sheriff Court
7	Leckie Memorial Church	15	Swimming Pool
8	Halyrude Primary School	16	Town House

Peebles

misleading title – seems to have been founded as a royal burgh
during the reign of David I (1124–53). By the early 1150s there
was also a royal castle here, perched on a steep-sided mound at
the confluence of the two rivers. Initially, the castle enjoyed some
eminence as a royal centre, but it appears to have been abandoned by about the middle of the C14, while the medieval burgh

never became a place of much political or economic importance. From time to time, however, Peebles was the target of damaging raids from English armies, and in 1570 a defensive town wall (*see* below) was built.

Any prosperity that the burgh once possessed had evaporated by the late C17, when a report on the condition of Scottish burghs (1692) revealed that Peebles had no foreign trade and that her inland trade was 'verrie mean and inconsiderable'. Daniel Defoe, in his *Tour thro' the Whole Island of Great Britain* (1724–6), considered it small 'and but indifferently built or inhabited, yet the High Street has some good houses on it'. There was some expansion, during the latter part of the C18, when a distillery was established at Kerfield and new and larger houses were built, especially for handloom weavers. In the mid-1840s great improvements were made. The High Street was lowered two or three feet, projecting buildings were removed, and two-storey slate-roofed houses filled in spaces on the straightened street line. Change was on the way.

The economic roots of expansion lay in the mid- to late C19 development of the textile industry by entrepreneurs from Galashiels and Hawick, the catalyst for prosperity being the opening of the North British Railway between Peebles and Edinburgh (1855), and the Caledonian Railway, from Glasgow, via Symington (1864). Following the establishment of the first large-scale mill in 1858, woollen manufactories dominated the local economy for more than a century, continuing at a reduced level today. Tourism became increasingly important from the late C19 onwards and the the town soon became a popular centre for walking, fishing and scenic excursions along the Tweed valley. A vast hydropathic hotel was opened in 1881, the railways began to attract commuters as well as visitors, and house building advanced on all sides, especially on the hitherto undeveloped slopes above the S bank of the Tweed. Lord Cockburn's quip, 'As quiet as the grave – or Peebles', may still apply to this gentle rural burgh on each bank of the silvery Tweed, but for how long? Ease of access by motor-car and an insatiable demand for new housing now threaten to turn Peebles into a rural suburb of Edinburgh.

CHURCHES

CROSS KIRK, Old Church Road. A chapel is said to have been built here *c.* 1260 when a cross, a memorial stone associated with 'St Nicholas the Bishop' and an urn (a Bronze-Age burial?) are said to have been discovered. Later it was believed the cross was a relic of the true cross. By *c.* 1448 a small community of Trinitarians had been established here and in 1473–4 the house became fully conventual. After the Reformation in 1560 the monastic church was given to the parish, the parish church having been burnt by the English in 1548; this was formalised in 1612, and the church remained in parochial use until a new church on the High Street was built in 1784. Following excavation of the conventual buildings by the *Office of Works* in 1923, the remains were taken into state care in 1925.

The CHURCH as built *c.* 1260 was a basically rectangular structure of whinstone with buff sandstone dressings, and with a sacristy projecting near the E end of the N wall. Running around the exterior was a chamfered base course, with a string course below the windows, and some of the windows along the S flank appear to have been traceried. The W doorway has waterholding bases and bell capitals. The greatest decorative emphasis was probably on a small feretory towards the E end of the S wall of the nave. A description of 1790 refers to a tomb-like arch above it, which presumably allowed sight of a reliquary from both outside and within the church; this wall, however, has been completely rebuilt and no traces remain. Inside the church at this point spreads of masonry have been found which may represent altar platforms. This suggests that the screen dividing nave from choir was on the same line as the post-Reformation wall which truncated the E end of the church, and that these were platforms for nave altars in front of it. At the angles of the sacristy sub-bases of shafts suggest it was vaulted.

A five-storeyed TOWER-PORCH with a barrel-vaulted lowest storey was added at the W end of the nave, over the existing entrance, possibly around the time the church became conventual in 1473–4. It had a spiral stair at the SW angle from the first floor upwards, and is known from early views to have been capped with a corbel table and parapet. Some of the upper storeys have fireplaces and were habitable, perhaps by the obedientiary responsible for the relics. At the SW angle a stone is carved with the arms of Peebles and an unidentifiable charge.

In 1656 (date on doorway lintel) the E end of the nave was cut off by a wall, its masonry evidently taken from the demolished choir, and a medieval window was re-sited in its upper part. Galleries were inserted within the church, for which several joist pockets survive.

The CONVENTUAL BUILDINGS, on the N side of the church, were presumably of c. 1473–4; they survive as little more than fragmentary consolidated lower walls or are marked as lines of parallel kerbstones. The CLOISTER was approximately square, and the three ranges around it defined a larger rectangle. The only feature to break that rectangular outline is a pair of roughly parallel walls on the E side of the E range which may represent the chapter house. The W range had a barrel-vaulted PARLOUR or SLYPE, adjoining the W front of the church. In the corresponding situation in the E range was the SACRISTY, probably built along with the church before the rest of the conventual buildings. The only access from church to cloister was by a doorway aligned on the W walk.

At least three post-Reformation BURIAL AISLES were added against the flanks of the church. Against the E end of the S wall were the aisles of the Hay and Erskine of Venlaw families, though only the decaying shell of the latter, possibly built c. 1804, survives. Near the middle of the N wall, and still entered from the church, is the aisle of the Douglas Earls of March of c. 1705.

The GRAVEYARD, S of the church, is dominated by the grey granite memorial to the Hay of Haystoune family, a rectangular pedimented base capped by a draped urn.

Fragments of an INCISED SLAB are preserved within the Chambers Institution (*see* below). This evidently had a depiction of an ecclesiastic in a processional cope with the date 1268. Although probably of late medieval date, this may commemorate the completion of the church and its dedication to the St Nicholas whose memorial stone had been found *c.* 1260.

Former FREE CHURCH, Eastgate. Now EASTGATE THEATRE AND ARTS CENTRE. 1871–2, by *John Starforth* in an early Gothic style, its prominent spire marking the turning of High Street towards its E end. With walls of whinstone with ashlar dressings, the S front follows the familiar formula of gabled central section flanked asymmetrically by a tall tower on one side and a lofty porch rising to a similar height as the central section on the other. Doorways in all three sections. The central doorway is bipartite, within a gabled salient flanked on each side by three tightly spaced lancets; above is a lofty triplet of two-light plate-traceried windows, with a cusped triangle in the gable. The SE tower has paired lights at the belfry stage, above which is a squat octagonal stage with spirelet pinnacles at the angles; the tall stone spire has triangular lucarnes to the cardinal faces. The porch, corresponding to the tower at the W side of the front, is capped by a pyramidal roof. At the N end, below a triplet of lancets, was a low hall and vestry block. Imaginatively adapted in 2003–4 by *Richard Murphy Architects* as a theatre and arts centre, a glazed E screen acting as the frontispiece to the new studio and auditorium.

LECKIE MEMORIAL CHURCH. Of the close concentration of three churches at the E end of High Street, this – the most recent – turns its back on the street, instead contributing splendidly to the view of the burgh from across the river. (Its name is taken from the Rev. Thomas Leckie who served its Associate Burgher (later United Presbyterian) congregation from 1794.) Designs for the church, on this new site and in a mid-C13 English idiom, were drawn up by *Peddie & Kinnear* in 1875, and it was opened in 1877, having cost nearly £8,000 to build. The materials are whinstone with rock-faced dressings of orange-coloured stone.

The church is an aisle-less hall with a N apse; the main emphasis is on the S front, elevated above an extended flight of steps. The entrance is framed by four orders of mouldings, with a pair of lancets on each side. Above the doorway is a closely set pair of two-light Geometric traceried windows, with an oculus containing three smaller circlets embraced by a relieving arch at their head. The tower, which continues the line of the S front, has a belfry stage with a pair of wide but deeply set two-light windows to each face. The stone broached spire, with lucarnes to the main faces, soars to 43 m. The church's W flank is divided by buttresses into five bays, with a traceried window in each bay. Framing the apse, and extending northwards from it, a low block houses lobby, vestry and session room, with a later hall to the N.

Within the S doorway, an entrance vestibule is screened off, with a gallery above which is accessed by stairs within the tower. The church roof has widely spaced arched braces. Since a reordering which followed union with St Andrew's Church in 1976, the pews have been replaced by stacking chairs and the organ has been removed from the apse, resulting in a slightly bleak appearance. – COMMUNION TABLE, stripped Gothic, donated 1962. – PULPIT, from St Andrew's Church, on E side of communion table platform; Gothic arcading and a relief carving of a dove on the panels, carried on a base with eight shafts around an octagonal stem. – STAINED GLASS, mostly mosaic designs; grisaille with texts in S window. – MEMORIALS, in vestibule, to members of Leckie family, within Gothic frames.

24   OLD PARISH CHURCH. A fine piece of urban scenery terminating the vista at the W end of High Street, and a bold statement of civic pride, the church was built at a cost of £9,500 to the Scottish Late Gothic designs of *William Young*, in 1885–7. Its ashlar E entrance front, approached up a broad flight of steps, is tripartite. The central part, corresponding to the main vessel, has an axial gabled doorway flanked by two Y-traceried windows and surmounted by an ambitious five-light window with spiralling mouchette tracery, below a crowstepped gable. Fronting the N aisle is a slightly projecting two-storeyed gabled porch, with a three-light window to the upper floor. On the S side is the dominant element of the front, a four-storeyed tower-porch capped by a crown steeple, with the arms of Peebles prominently displayed at the second storey. It must be conceded that the tower is perhaps too slender and the central gable too wide for complete comfort, but it is an imposing essay. The N flank has two distinct storeys of windows corresponding to aisle and gallery internally; the originally more prominent S flank has its two central bays capped by crowstepped gables with transomed windows rising through both levels.

The nave of four and a half bays has arcades with cylindrical piers of Early English form, but no clearstorey. Galleries with blind-arcaded fronts run along the upper level of the aisles and also above the E one and a half bays of the central space. Over the nave is an arch-braced roof. The rectangular chancel, with its floor elevated three steps above the nave, dates from remodelling in 1937 by *J.D. Cairns*; it has a collar-beam roof. It was reordered in 1987. – COMMUNION TABLE, 1937. – LECTERN, brass eagle, 1897. – PULPIT, polygonal, designed by *P. Macgregor Chalmers*, made by *J. Grant* and carved by *John Crawford*, 1913. – FONT, white marble, 1898, with sacred monogram. – N AISLE CHAPEL SCREEN, oak, 1972. – ENTRANCE SCREEN, oak, wrought iron, bronze and engraved glass, 1965, by *Scott Morton, Charles Henshaw & Sons* and *Helen Turner*. – STAINED GLASS, to a unified scheme by *Cottier*. W window, behind communion table, Scenes from Life of Christ, *c.* 1887. Rose window above chancel arch, Cherubim. S aisle, Prophets, Saints and Virtues. Galleries, Apostles, 1893. – WAR MEMORIAL TABLETS, First World War, on each side of the chancel arch, 1921; Second World War, on arcade piers, 1954, by *Charles Henshaw & Sons*.

CHURCH CENTRE, added at the W end in 1981–2 by *Smiths Gore*.

St Andrew's Old Parish Church, Old Town. There was a parish church by *c.* 1120, and in 1541 a collegiate establishment was founded within it by the baillies and councillors of the burgh, together with John Hay of Yester. In 1548–9 the church was damaged by the English, and after 1560 the parishioners decanted to the recently abandoned Cross Kirk (q.v.).

The church probably consisted of a chancel and nave, with a N aisle alongside both, a W tower, and a small N chapel. The last of these was probably the Lady Chapel founded by John Geddes *c.* 1427. There were at least eleven other altars. The only upstanding features are the W tower, and an ivy-clad stretch of N wall containing a robbed doorway. The tower had lost most of its dressed stone by the time of a restoration of 1883 by *George Henderson*, paid for by William Chambers, and much of what is now seen does not reflect the medieval design. Of whinstone rubble with red sandstone dressings, it rises through three unbuttressed storeys, and is entered by a doorway of 1883 where the tower arch would have been. Each face at belfry level has a paired opening with a mid-wall shaft, embraced by a segmental arch with a circlet piercing the tympanum. Above a corbel table and parapet is a double-pitched roof with crowstepped gables to E and W.

The CHURCHYARD contains a wide range of memorials, some of high interest. Several C18 stones demonstrate a local taste for barley-sugar columns framing winged angel heads and *memento mori*. Worthy of note: table tomb of Thomas Hope, †1704, coped lid with full-length figures of man and wife on each side of central scroll; table tomb of Tweedie family, end legs with caryatid-like figures, central support with baroque cartouche, merchant's mark and date 1708, coped top with rich Baroque border of fruit and acanthus; coped top of table tomb of Tweedie family, set against S wall tower, inscriptions on elaborate scrolls along each side, heraldic cartouche at end, cherubs blowing last trump, and seating for lost inscription plate on top; Smibert family headstone (1842) with naïvely represented female in costume more appropriate for about a century earlier (is it reused?). Above W doorway of tower, memorial plaque to William Chambers, †1883, who restored the tower.

St Joseph (R.C.), Rosetta Road. The church, built in 1858 and remodelled in 1913, groups with the detached hall to the N (*see* below), and the presbytery to the S, with which a link was made in 1899. Walls of whinstone with ashlar dressings, except for the rendered W front. The nave is of five aisle-less bays marked by buttresses, with a Lady Chapel and porch on the N side. The W front has two two-light windows with spherical trefoils at their heads, and there are two oculi on the central axis; the gable is capped by a truncated bellcote. The single-bay chancel, which is narrower than the nave, has a four-light E window with uncusped loop tracery. Internally, there is a W gallery; the nave has an arch-braced roof and the chancel an arched plaster ceiling. – RETABLE, marble veneers with a central crucifix above the tabernacle (possibly by *Reginald Fairlie*, who worked at the church on several occasions). –

FONT, octagonal, with crocket cap to pier. – STAINED GLASS.
E window, Virgin and Child and St Joseph; Lady Chapel, Holy
Family; Nave N side, first from E, St John Ogilvie, second from
E, St Margaret; S side, third bay from E, the Virgin (War Memo-
rial), fourth bay from E, St Michael, by *Nina Miller Davidson*;
W front, lower oculus, Baptism of Christ.

The CHURCH HALL was converted from a former school of
1865 and its schoolhouse, formerly a pair of cottages.

ST PETER (Episcopal), Eastgate. A broad aisle-less rectangle of
three bays built in 1830–3 by *William Burn*, to which a more
ritualistically disposed Gothic chancel and W porch were
added by *Hay & Henderson* in 1882–4. The N front, of polished
ashlar, is tripartite. Four pinnacle-capped buttresses separate
outer sections beneath half-gables from a central section with
a parapet that is flat apart from a small triangle supporting a
cross finial. The central section is emphasised by a Y-traceried
and transomed window above a doorway that was covered by
the porch of 1882. The unbuttressed flanks are of whinstone
with cream sandstone dressings.

The interior has a slightly domestic boarded dado and
strapped upper walls, below a ribbed ceiling of triangular
section; it originally had a W gallery. The change of spirit that
had entered the Episcopal Church of Scotland between building the nave in the 1830s and adding the chancel in the 1880s
is obvious in the exposed ashlar of the wall between nave and
chancel, pierced by a broad chancel arch with mouldings
carried on corbels with stiff-leaf foliage. Off the E side of the
chancel is a two-bay organ and vestry aisle, the arcade carried
on a polished granite cylindrical pier with stiff-leaf foliate cap.
The parts of the chancel floor exposed between the choir stalls
have a mosaic pavement. – ALTAR, given 1926, simple mosaic
panels to the retable. – PULPIT, stone semi-octagon with shafts
at angles and crosses set in vesicae on faces. – FONT, Caen
stone, octagonal basin carved with sacred monogram and with
stiff-leaf foliage to pier. – STAINED GLASS. Behind altar,
Calling of Disciples, 'Feed my Sheep', Baptism of Ethiopian
Eunuch, *c.* 186-; chancel, W side, Light of the World, *c.* 1884;
nave W side, S bay, St Columba and Virgin and Child *c.* 1927;
E side, S bay, St Catherine and St Christopher, by *Joyce Mered-
ith*. – MEMORIAL, E wall nave, painted wood Renaissance
plaque with prominent heraldry to Dugald Charles Bremner,
†1922.

PUBLIC BUILDINGS

CHAMBERS INSTITUTION, High Street. A large, Baronial-style
building mainly of mid-Victorian and early C20 date, but incorporating fragments of the early C17 lodging of the Queensberry
family. Following its presentation to the town by Dr William
Chambers, the Peebles-born encyclopaedist, the building was
remodelled in 1857–9 as a reading room, library and museum
by *John Paris*; he also added a public meeting hall, opening off
a courtyard to the rear. The principal (N) façade fronts the
High Street. To the E the remodelled lodging, an irregular four-
storey block with a plausible clutter of gables and dormers, a

corbelled turret and a prominent corner tower with an ogival roof. The w extension, its design evidently indebted to Mussel-burgh Tolbooth of 1590 (Lothian), is of three storeys, the top one rising within a corbelled parapet; library windows below and shops on the ground floor. A single-storey and attic museum extension on the w side of the courtyard replaces earlier stables. On the s side, the five-bay hall, entered from a porch at the sw corner; lush heraldry above the entrance. Other decorative panels are dotted about the exterior. The masonry is mainly of harled rubble with dressings of Caen stone.

On the top floor the PICTURE GALLERY has a coved and ribbed ceiling and central skylights. The CHAMBERS ROOM (former museum) on the first floor of the w courtyard range has a braced panelled ceiling. Most of its cast collection was destroyed when this became a library store in the late 1950s. Happily, two wall-mounted friezes survive: an 18.9 m. section of a cast of the Parthenon Frieze, probably commissioned by Chambers for the museum; and a rare survival of a complete facsimile of the 'Triumph of Alexander' frieze executed by *Bertel Thorwaldsen* in 1812 for the Palazzo del Quirinale, Rome. A memorial chimneypiece, dated 1858, to William Chambers's dog is marooned in a partitioned-off section at the s end, but the life-size sculpture of 'Fiddy' weighing down the frieze deserves to be seen. There is a further galleried exhibition room with timber panelling.

In the courtyard is the WAR MEMORIAL by *B.N.H. Orphoot* of *Orphoot & Whiting*, 1922. An unexpectedly fine hexagonal shrine of white stone, surmounted by a dome with a tall cupola and pineapple finial; it shelters a Celtic cross of Sicilian lime-stone decorated with inlaid mosaics based on the C12 mosaics at Monreale, Sicily. The cross is by *Professor G. Malranga* of Palermo, *Thomas Beattie* did the carving, and the *Bromsgrove Guild* the large bronze panels inscribed with the names of the fallen.

COUNCIL OFFICES, Rosetta Road. A pleasing building, almost rural. On the site of, and partly incorporating, a quadrangular poorhouse by *W. L. Moffat*, 1856. The Neo-Baroque w front range was added by *Dick Peddie & Walker Todd* in 1932. Harled with cream sandstone margins and quoins. Two storeys with a five-bay piend-roofed central block flanked by single-storey wings and topped by an octagonal cupola placed on a balustraded platform. The remodelled e front of the poorhouse resembles a villa, a central block with curving walls linked to single-storey pavilions. Refurbished inside by *Scott Morton & Co.*, c. 1935. Much survives, including the top-lit council chamber with a raised dais, and Lorimer-type fur-niture.

EASTGATE THEATRE AND ARTS CENTRE. *See* Free Church, above.

HALYRUDE PRIMARY SCHOOL (R.C.), Old Church Road. A late C19, single-storey and gabled infant school. Enlarged in the early C20.

HAY LODGE HOSPITAL AND HEALTH CENTRE. *See* Hay Lodge, p. 633.

KINGSLAND PRIMARY SCHOOL, Rosetta Road. *Robert Wilson*, supervised by *J. A. Carfrae*, opened in 1900. Two-storey gabled English Renaissance block topped by a square domed cupola bellcote. Squared and snecked rock-faced sandstone with polished margins. Single-storey N addition of 1965. Interior reconstructed in 1973, by flooring over the huge two-storey galleried hall for open-plan classrooms, reflecting then current trends in education. – JANITOR'S HOUSE. Gabled, two storeys, 1900.

MERCAT CROSS, High Street. The cross originally stood at the intersection of High Street, Northgate and Eastgate. Dismantled in 1807, returned to its original site in 1895 and, finally, moved a few metres to the E in 1965, when the shaft was placed on an octagonal plinth and small octagonal pedestal, designed by *W. Schomberg Scott*. The C15 shaft has plain shields to alternate faces, while the contemporary octagonal capital incorporates shields bearing fish (salmon) and cinquefoils (strawberries), from the burgh arms and those of the Frasers of Oliver and Neidpath. On top is a faceted cubic sundial dated 1699, surmounted by a weathervane, dated 1662.

PEEBLES HIGH SCHOOL, Springwood Road. A shapeless collection of buildings, built around the Bonnington Park Academy from the late C19. Greatly extended to designs by *Robert Wilson*, 1902 as the High School. A spreading gabled building. Additions *c.* 1920 by *J.D. Cairns*. Reconstructed by *Reid & Forbes c.* 1936, to form a technical building and a new post-primary building, with a round brick observatory tower for the use of pupils and interested members of the public. Large extensions by *Stanley P. Ross-Smith* in the 1960s for Peebles County Council, including the 'Tower Block'.

PEEBLES HOTEL HYDRO, Innerleithen Road. By *James Miller*, 1905–7. Georgian-style, with Queen Anne Revival detail, on a massive scale. It replaced a large French Renaissance-style hotel by *John Starforth*, of 1878–81, which was mostly destroyed by fire in 1905. Miller retained the foundations and its NE wing. The design is similar to one Miller supplied for Turnberry Hotel, Ayrshire, in 1904 – especially the glazing of the two-storey canted bays, and the balconied entrance bay. The bright cream harling and steeply pitched rosemary-tiled piended and platformed roof supposedly helped the cheerful outlook on life expected from the clients taking a hydropathic cure – it still preserves this tradition.

A symmetrical main block faces S, of eleven bays, three storeys with deep attics and two tiers of dormers, flanked by three-bay pavilion wings with two-storey canted bays, each with decorative glazing incorporating Venetian windows divided by embossed bronze aprons. In the centre, a gabled entrance bay, with a large porte cochère and semicircular glazed dome. Above, open verandas along the main front have misguidedly been enclosed by large windows (1952) to form a sun lounge. At the E end a late C20 two-storey five-bay dining room with tall wrought-iron windows, and a mediocre extension at the W end, *c.* 1970, replaced a superb conservatory – a serious loss. The three-storey red sandstone block at the NE corner is all that remains of the earlier hotel.

Surprisingly, much of the Victorian and Edwardian interior

survives. Impressive steps lead from the entrance vestibule to the first-floor corridor and the Ionic-columned reception area, repeated at the entrance to the BALLROOM to the r. This has Ionic pilasters, a proscenium arch and decorative plasterwork by *Leonard Grandison*. The full-length elliptical ceiling of lattice design is quite splendid. The Baronial BANNOCKBURN ROOM from the late C19 hotel has a panelled dado, a ceiling with pendants and suitably Baronial chimneypieces. The walls are covered with an enormous panorama of Robert the Bruce at the Battle of Bannockburn, 1314. Painted in Munich by *Ernst Philipp Fleischer, c.* 1888, it was shipped to Glasgow for exhibition, and then bought by the hotel manager, cut up, and displayed in the former billiard room.

The terraced GARDEN layout also survives. Splendid wide steps, decorated with urns, descend to lawns. At the top, a fountain with a large basin, in which a boy supports another basin on his head. At the E entrance, a single-storey picturesque T-plan LODGE with decorative bargeboards, by *John Starforth*, 1888.

POLICE STATION, West Port. Dated 1881. A six-bay building on an elongated site falling away towards the river. In the centre, a pedimented aedicule date panel above a tripartite window, topped by a consoled wall-head stack. Roll-moulded, round-arched doorway with keystone, and elaborate consoled pediment.

PRIORSFORD FOOTBRIDGE, over the River Tweed. By *James Bell*, 1905, replacing an earlier one built in 1817 by *John Stevenson Brown* of *Redpath, Brown & Co.* A graceful single-span segmental-arched steel cable bridge with red brick piers and sandstone copings; latticed and finialled steel pylons, and latticed parapets with curved ribs. [87]

PRIORSFORD PRIMARY SCHOOL, Marmion Road. By *G.R.M. Kennedy & Partners*, 1972. The distinctive open-plan design drew visits from educationalists from all over the world. Basically a single storey with load-bearing brick walls with lead cladding and steel and timber roof. Teaching areas linked with communal areas around a central core ensured a domestic-scale environment.

SHERIFF COURT, High Street (former Court House and Prison). By *Thomas Brown Jun.*, 1848. Neat Jacobean composition of two storeys and attic in cream sandstone, built against the former jail of *c.* 1780 on the W side. Four storeys, rendered whinstone rubble. Some blocked Gothic windows indicate the style of the previous building, in which mullioned and transomed windows were later inserted. Interior remodelled by *Kinnear & Peddie* in 1892.

SWIMMING POOL, Greenside. *Morris & Steedman*, 1983. Simple but effective; yellow steelwork supporting a blue-slated and piended roof, oversailing a balcony walkway round the building.

TOWN HOUSE, High Street. Built 1752–3 to accommodate meetings of the town council. Symmetrical three-bay Classical front surmounted by a triangular pediment containing the burgh arms and date of erection. The ground floor is pierced by two pends; the r. one now glazed, the l. leads down Schoolbrae to

Tweed Green. The interior is much altered, except for the council room on the first floor, which retains a high coved ceiling, and a moulded stone chimneypiece. The former Corn Exchange by *John Lessels*, 1860, extends from the rear.

TWEED BRIDGE. Probably C15, much repaired. In 1793 additional arches were built by *John Hislop* at the S end, but these were replaced by a railway bridge, *c.* 1865. Widened in 1834 by *John & Thomas Smith*, and again in 1897–1900 by *McTaggart, Cowan and Barker*, engineers. The bridge now consists of five segmental arches, rusticated piers and a dentilled parapet. There is a ramp to Tweed Green at the NE end on five round-headed arches. Cast-iron lamps of entwined dolphins decorate the piers. Underneath, the original arch soffits are clearly seen, of random rubble with dressed voussoirs.

VEITCH MEMORIAL, High Street, in front of the Tontine Hotel. A pink and grey granite drinking fountain to the poet, John Veitch, designed by *Sydney Mitchell & Wilson* in 1898. Decorative modelling and granite work by *Kerr Bros.* of Edinburgh. The fountain has panels round the base; above, a bulbous Roman Doric column stands on a plinth decorated with a bronze profile portrait by *George Webster.*

CASTLE
Castlehill

Founded by David I, the castle was probably destroyed during the Wars of Independence and the site afterwards passed to the burgh. Some time during the C18 the W part of Castlehill was laid out as a bowling green, while since *c.* 1780 the E part has been occupied by the Parish Church. All that now remains of the castle is the mound (40 m. by 22 m. at the summit), which is probably of natural origin but trimmed to form a motte. Excavations in 1977 revealed traces of two C12 timber buildings on the summit. The short section of rubble wall visible on the SW flank of the mound is probably of post-medieval date.

DESCRIPTION

I. New Town and the riverside

HIGH STREET was the principal street of the medieval burgh, continuing to the Mercat Cross (*see* above) and continuing beyond it for a short distance on a slightly different alignment (Eastgate). At the W end of the N side is BANK HOUSE (Nos. 88–90), remodelled for the Union Bank by *William Railton*, *c.* 1860. Altered and added to in 1871 by *David Rhind* for the Commercial Bank. Two-storey gabled Italianate to the r., with a slightly recessed two-bay wing to the l. Partly demolished in 1984 when the Cuddy Bridge was widened (*see* Description 2, below). Further along, the BANK OF SCOTLAND (Nos. 70–74) by *J.D. Cairns*, 1934–5, displays a stripped Art Deco classical front with polished black and grey granite on the ground floor, and channelled cream sandstone on the first. Full-height glazing on the ground floor. The Art Deco frontage of the former PLAYHOUSE CINEMA by the cinema specialist, *Alister MacDonald*, 1932, is a lucky survival; the auditorium has been demolished. Shallow paired pilasters with channelled bases and volute capitals. The three bays on the first floor have recessed aprons divided by stylised moulded pilasters breaking the eaves, and a conventional block keystone rises stylishly to cross the eaves in the centre. A recent shopfront is the only change. Next the early-to-mid-C19 CROWN HOTEL. Five bays with a pilastered and corniced doorway and a thackstone on the l. gable. Gabled extensions to the rear.

Nos. 50–52 High Street have Baronial detailing. The second floor jettied out on a moulded and crenellated course with mock cannon spouts. Dormer windows with scrolled and finialled pediments. Wall-mounted sundial on second floor is inscribed 'Greenwich Solar Time' and dated 1877. Nos. 26–28 are dated 1790 on the rear (N) elevation, but may be earlier. A three-storey, three-bay house with a rectangular stair tower to the back. Probably whinstone to the street, now rendered with pebbledash. Square brick chimneys. A vault below No. 28 was briefly used as a prison in the C18. Nos. 22–24 are known as the 'House of the Turnbull family'. An inscribed stone tells all: 'God provides a rich inheritance – WT 1724'. Early to mid-C18 with later additions. On the first floor, a carved panel shows a pair of baker's peels (shovels) crossed in saltire with a scuffle (mop) between them. The pitch of the roof suggests the house was formerly thatched. Further down High Street is the MEDICAL HALL (Nos. 18–20). Late C19 with a shopfront by *J.D. Cairns & Ford*, *c.* 1933. Three storeys, three bays, in stugged cream ashlar with polished margins. Good interior plasterwork by *L. Grandison & Son*. A substantial building at Nos. 2–6, which returns round the corner into Nos. 1–3 Northgate. A good townscape block built as a commercial development by Robert Veitch. Dated 1885 and 1886. Mildly Baronial, with prominent dormer windows and conical-roofed turrets corbelled out at the corners.

Down NORTHGATE, on the l. is BRIDGEGATE which leads down to Eddleston Water, known locally as the Cuddy. On the r., on a sloping site fronting the river, is PROVOST WALKER'S COURT, 1990, a well-detailed development of 26 flats by the Eildon Housing Association. Two and three storeys with tiers of triangular bay windows. Built on the site of the medieval tolbooth, excavated in the 1980s. On the l., BRIDGEGATE COURT, equally good, completed in 1994. Back to Northgate passing Nos. 5–7, a mid-to-late C18 house of two storeys with widely spaced windows, rendered and lined out as ashlar. A Greek Doric doorpiece. The MASONIC HALL at No. 9 has the recut date 1716, but the building looks late C18, with later alterations. Scrolled skewputts with a rope motif. Rusticated ashlar on the ground floor, concrete rendered and lined out as V-jointed masonry at first-floor level, *c.* 1900(?). A well-detailed Gibbsian doorway with a broken pediment on scrolled brackets and armorial shield in the tympanum. Adam-style interior plasterwork by *Leonard Grandison*, *c.* 1900.

Opposite is the late C17 CROSS KEYS INN, formerly the town house of the Williamsons of Cardrona, the initials WW just discernible in the decorative roof slates. Much added to and altered, gutted and reconstructed in 1994. Now an irregular three-storey Z-plan forming two sides of a courtyard. White harling with black margins. A number of houses in Northgate, mostly two-storey with three bays, date from the early to mid C19, but with C18 origins, recognisable by chimneystacks with thackstones. Some good shopfronts: e.g. No. 27, dated 1893, which has an excellent classical double shopfront with fluted pilasters and dentilled cornice; Nos. 43–47 with a moulded surround, panelled doors and a continuous fascia with console brackets and fleurs-de-lys gablets. No. 85 is the best survival of a mid-C18 two-storey house, set below street level at the front, with basement at the back. The lined-out rendered front is late C19. Interesting for the good N apex chimneystack with thackstones. NORTHGATE HOUSE (Nos. 32–34), is a well-detailed classical villa, c. 1840, set back from the street. Flanking the entrance steps, two stone lions on pedestals; one asleep, the other awake. At Nos. 40–48 a row of single-storey shops, c. 1900, erected by *Thomas Tod*, builder. No. 46 has a fine Classical doorway with Arts and Crafts detailing, a stained-glass fanlight and decorative door handle and plate. Continue N to where DEAN PARK (Station Road) comes in from the E. The street takes a sharp bend N, past a tenement on the corner, and continues almost parallel with Northgate. An interesting late C19 terrace of single-storey and attic houses, each built with different motifs, including oculi and blind arrowslits.

EASTGATE starts on the N side at Nos. 3–9, a three-storey corner block, dating from the late C19. A corbelled-out turret with pepperpot roof and ball finial in the r. bay, a canted bay window corbelled from a pier at ground-floor level, with a truncated pyramidal roof and decorative lead flashing. A row of two-storey late C19 houses follows, all with shops on the ground floor. Eastgate Theatre and Arts Centre (*see* former Free Church, above) is next on the corner of VENLAW ROAD, a pedestrian route; Nos. 1 and 2 by *Robert Mathison*, 1890, is a good example of a single-storey and attic double cottage, distinguished by vermiculated quoins and a continuous rounded eaves band. At the end, on the l., is a section of the TOWN WALL (*Thomas Lauder*, mason, 1570–4). It enclosed the New Town only, apparently forming a continuous barrier linking the earlier gateways of West Port, Bridgegate, North Port and East Port. Maintained in good repair until the early C18, most of the wall had disappeared by 1800. All that now survives is the NE corner, part of which forms the W boundary wall of Eastgate Car Park. Two short sections running at right angles to one another with a projecting tower, or 'blokhous', at their intersection. The wall, originally specified as 4½ ells (4.2 m.) high and 3½ ft (1.1 m.) thick, is considerably reduced in height. The circular blockhouse incorporates two wide-mouthed gunports aligned to provide flanking fire along the adjacent sections of wall.

On the SE corner of Venlaw Road stands the GREEN TREE INN. Much altered and added to from the early C19 to the

present day. White render and green cement mouldings. The
s block is early C19. Two storeys and five bays with large
windows on the w façade. The late C19 N block has a part
balustraded, part decorative cast-iron parapet, a swan-necked
pediment in the centre, and a row of urns on pedestals. A
rounded corner at the s end with a pepperpot roof and ball
finial, behind the shaped parapet. Double Venetian window to
Venlaw Road. A lower entrance block to the s, 1924.

The s part of EASTGATE starts with St Peter's Episcopal
Church, and set back from the road, Leckie Memorial Church
(*see* Churches, above). At No. 10. Eastgate (EASTWARK
HOUSE) an Art Nouveau shopfront by *J.D. Cairns*, 1931.

The s side of HIGH STREET begins with Nos. 5–11. Dated
1878–88. A three-storey and attic irregular six-bay building
with classical ornament and two two-storey canted bays, one
blocked by the Corinthian pilastered shopfront in the centre.
The site of the African explorer Dr Mungo Park's surgery is
recorded on an inscription. Next along, the Chambers Institution and the Town House (*see* Public Buildings, above). Nos.
27 and 29 show a late C19 front but a pend leads to the C18
work on the N side. A three-storey, three-bay house given classical ornament. A good pair of timber shopfronts, divided and
framed by stone panelled and fluted pilasters; the outer ones
have segmental cornices with garland cresting. In the pend, an
entrance doorway embellished with homespun classical detail
beneath a 1672 datestone. The COUNTY HOTEL (former
Harrow Inn) follows. The present street façade with entrance
porch and central chimney gablet appears to date from the mid
C18, but the existence of a barrel-vaulted room within suggests
that part of the structure originated as a late C16 or early C17
bastle. Remodelled *c.* 1939 by *B.N.H. Orphoot*. No. 37, imposing Italianate, was designed as the British Linen Co. Bank by
Wardrop & Reid, in 1882 but the work was carried out in 1887
by *Wardrop & Anderson*. Coursed stugged cream sandstone. A
deep band course incorporates the aprons of the first-floor
windows, and there is an eaves frieze and cornice. On the principal front, an arched doorway to the bank, with pilasters and
keystone. Three bays on the w elevation, one the doorway to
the manager's house above.

Next is the TONTINE HOTEL. Erected by private subscription, in the form of an annuity, from which the last of the subscribers to survive inherits the property. Advertised as 'nearly
finished in 1808', it comprised fourteen bedrooms, several par-
lours, ballroom and supper room, and offices. Set back from
the street with a court in front. Two-storey and basement to
the s. Five bays. Squared and snecked whinstone rubble,
whitewashed on the street (N) frontage. A slightly advanced
centre bay, the doorpiece with narrow sidelights framed by
shallow paired pilasters. Above, a tripartite window with
narrow blank sidelights. The s elevation has a central full-
height bow window, with tall round-arched windows to light
the ballroom. An unsympathetic 1960s bedroom addition built
in front of the basement. The ballroom (now dining room) has
its original plasterwork, a coved ceiling, a gallery at the N end

with ornamental iron railings and slender balusters, and a timber and gesso chimneypiece, with a 'shepherd boy' motif in the centre panel, flanked by eagles.

Nos. 41 and 43 High Street are dated 1897. A four-bay tenement with corner turrets and Scottish C17 detailing; two good timber shopfronts. No. 49, a three-storey tenement with shop and flats above, is dated 1873. Nos. 63–67 High Street, mid-C18 but much altered, has a chimneyed, wide central gable with an ogee lintel above a window dated 1759, and a late C19–early C20 shopfront.

A pend leads to PARLIAMENT SQUARE. In the square a moulded doorway and dated lintel inscribed RS HM 1743. The square was improved in 1999. Nos. 69–73, formerly the Caledonian Railway Hotel, is dated 1886, but its rear section, entered from a roll-moulded doorway of C17 character, is said to be built over a vaulted chamber.

WEST PORT leads down to Tweed Bridge (*see* above). On the l., the Police Station (*see* above); opposite, on a curved sloping site, is the BRIDGE INN, rebuilt in 1900, when the bridge was widened. Arts and Crafts with half-timbered gables and bracketed eaves. Decorative terracotta roof tiles and rainwater hoppers. Across the w end of the High Street is the Old Parish Church and the Sheriff Court (*see* above).

Port's Brae turns towards TWEED GREEN, formerly the town's common land. About halfway along at the foot of Schoolbrae, a former school dating from 1766, heightened by a storey and altered in 1878. Symmetrical, five bays, in whinstone with cream dressings. On the opposite corner the former GRAMMAR SCHOOL, built in 1812 and heightened a storey in 1861. A symmetrical two-storey, three-bay block. A framed panel in a gable-head shows St Andrew. Next along is the late C18 CABBAGE HALL, once used as the schoolmaster's house. Extended and remodelled in the mid C19. In the garden, a SUNDIAL on a concrete pedestal, inscribed *James Tollis* of York, 1673. At the end, the OLD RECTORY and TWEEDBRAE. Subdivided. Late C18, altered and heightened by *David MacGibbon* of *MacGibbon & Ross*, in 1888. A two-storey and attic three-bay house with small wings. Along the E side of the green is the PEEBLES NURSING HOME, which began as two separate late C19 villas. Added to, and linked with a third villa of three bays, and opened in 1922 as the War Memorial Hospital. At the s end, by Priorsford Footbridge (*see* above), is PRIORSFORD HOUSE, a late C19 two-storey, two-bay gabled villa built for James 'Paraffin' Young, pioneer of the shale oil industry. In Tweed Avenue is its entrance with two single-storey and attic, three-bay lodges. Gatepiers with fluted friezes and ball finials.

2. The Old Town and area to its north

CUDDY BRIDGE links the New and the Old Towns. It was widened and rebuilt in 1984 in the same form as the mid-C19 bridge. Concrete and whinstone. On the l., on the NW corner of Greenside and Old Town, is the prominently sited BRIDGE HOUSE, built in 1878 for the Peeblesshire Co-operative

Society; a dominant high pavilion roof with fish-scale slates Late C20 shopfronts. An E elevation of four bays, with an angled bay to the r., and a date panel in the gable-head. The main street of OLD TOWN retains some early C19 single-storey and attic cottages on the r., despite extensive demolition. An imaginative scheme of renewal by *Aitken & Turnbull*, 1989, on the N side of the street for the Eildon Housing Association, has resulted in some good urban work. Best on the S side are No. 51, a late-C18 four-bay terraced house with window lintels tight up against the eaves and a steeply pitched roof, and No. 53, an early C19 tenement in whinstone. No. 84, although much altered, retains its doorway with consoled cornice and date-stone, now inscribed 1775/1990. On the S side at the end of Old Town is Hay Lodge (*see* Villas, below) and HAY LODGE PARK, purchased by the town from the Earl of Wemyss in 1919 for public use. In the park, an ICE HOUSE built into the S bank of the Tweed has a low doorway into two chambers, presumably storage for the day's catches. The GATEPIERS and GATES date from *c.* 1930. Square rusticated piers with fluted friezes, cornices and large ball finials.

Returning to the Cuddy Bridge turn along BIGGIESKNOWE, which in the C18 was the centre of the handloom weaving industry in Peebles. The cottages on the N side were probably all single-storey and basement, but on the S, where the ground falls to the Eddleston Water, they have two storeys and gardens. Most have been altered. Nos. 1–6 were rebuilt as a tenement block by William Chambers in 1872. A two-storey and attic terrace, with access balconies on cast-iron columns overlooking the river. No. 14, the birthplace of John Veitch (1829–94), poet and historian of the Borders, is a typical late C18 single-storey and basement whinstone rubble three-bay weaver's cottage. Two steps down to the deep-set entrance doorway, the flanking windows hard up under the eaves. No. 18, the birthplace of William and Robert Chambers, was built by their father James, a weaver, in 1796. At the E end is No. 36 (RED LION HOUSE), single-storey to the street with a single window, but aggrandised, probably in the mid C19, with the principal entrance given a central classical doorway with fluted columns and entablature supporting a stone lion.

Turn l. along the continuation of Bridgegate, which leads into OLD CHURCH ROAD. On the r., the site of the Cross Kirk (*see* Churches, above). The KEEPER'S LODGE (No. 8 Cross Road) is a mid-C19 picturesque single-storey cottage in whinstone, with overhanging eaves and simply decorated barge-boards.

The following area, bounded roughly by March Street, Young Street and Old Town, was developed in the 1880s and 1890s for housing of a superior kind. A mixture of single- and two-storey housing, and some tenements, mostly in cream sandstone with polished margins on the fronts, and whinstone on the other elevations. Different architects and builders repeated their individual house types. The overall informal plan appears to have been provided by *George Wilkie*, builder, later Provost of Peebles. No. 26 ELCHO STREET (Graham Cottage), *c.* 1890, has long and short vermiculated quoins, a fish-scale banded roof and gable skews inset with blind trefoils. A two-storey, three-bay L-plan house at No. 7 CROSSLAND CRESCENT (Edrom Villa), dated 1880, has bargeboarded gables, cross-bracing and finials, and No. 13, c. 1882, is similar, with some interesting carved detail. A neat suburban cottage at No. 10 (1882) has rock-faced margins, overhanging eaves and basket-arched windows. In a gable-head, a triangular oriel window with fluted and strapwork cresting. A four-bay veranda with a catslide roof completes the picture. Both Nos. 3 and 5 DAMDALE ROAD have excellent timber detailing, some scrolled, and vine-leaf bargeboarding. No. 4 MURRAY PLACE (ALLENBANK), dated 1883, single-storey and attic, with wide dormers. On the l., one of the two centre windows canted out as a triangular oriel, the r. one with a bracketed piended gable. The timber-slated porch is kept up by clusters of chamfered columns. No. 17 MARCH STREET (ROSEBERY COTTAGE), dated 1880. Another well-detailed cottage, the margins with buckle-type quoins, bracketed sills and carved lintels. Bands of fish-scale slates across the roof.

On the N side of March Street is the entrance gateway, dated 1884, to the MARCH STREET MILLS (Robert Noble), established by D. Ballantyne & Co., the last survival of the town's once renowned textile mills. The mill buildings visible from the road are C20. At the back of the site is a large complex of late C19 single-storey whinstone weaving sheds, with cream sandstone dressings. The complex was larger but fire destroyed about a third. Large, wide round-arched sash windows, the glazing comprising four upper panes and three lower. To the rear, the engine house, and a water tank by *Turnbull, Grant & Jack*, engineers, Glasgow, dated 1884. The base of an octagonal brick chimney survives.

The HOUSING in the Rosetta Road area is the result of an enterprising programme of local authority house building undertaken following the Housing Acts (Scotland) 1919 and 1932; unfortunately the architecture is not distinguished. Initially two-storey flatted houses, by *Samuel Cowan*, Burgh Surveyor, were built on the E side of GEORGE PLACE, finished 1914. The w side appears to be by *J.D. Cairns*, c. 1928. On the E side of the Eddleston Water, DALATHO CRESCENT and EDINBURGH ROAD were built by *A.H. Swanson*, Burgh Surveyor, 1924–8. Across the corners of the streets are later(?) blocks of two-storey cottages, probably by *J.D. Cairns*, since they have his 'thistle' device (*see* Arnsheen, Bonnington Road) in the centre of the front elevations; now coloured and more interesting, with the side roofs sloping down over internal stairs. NORTH STREET and NORTH PLACE were developed c. 1934, to relieve overcrowding in the burgh, still using the same dreary design. On the W side of the site, on steeply rising ground, interest quickens, as here the 'garden suburb' mixture of cottages and flatted houses has made an appearance. Even before that, in 1919–22, at ELLIOT'S PARK, garden suburb principles seem to have been adopted by *J.D. Cairns* for the Scottish Veterans Garden City Association. Blocks of two-storey cottages, locally referred to as 'Corporation Cottages', planned round a large grassed area, with E-facing views to the hills. Two designs: in one, the blocks have two gabled projections, while the others have sloping roofs over internal stairs. Very costly at £1,200 per block. For CONNOR STREET, *Mears & Carus-Wilson* produced a plan on behalf of the Association for the Preservation of Rural Scotland, *c.* 1934, for two blocks of six houses with double cottages between, later rearranged as mixed houses and cottages around an irregular square.

3. East: Innerleithen Road and Edinburgh Road

INNERLEITHEN ROAD has on the N side mostly solid Victorian villas beginning with the imposing MANSE, *c.* 1888, by *David MacGibbon* of *MacGibbon & Ross*. Three storeys, three bays, with C17 detailing. Next come the first of three pairs of identical double villas starting with KENMORE and finishing with THE ROWANS, dated in order, 1894, 1895 and 1896, by *Robert Murray*. Distinctive central chimneystacks with shaped shoulders over pairs of entrance doorways. Then come VENBRAE and RAVENSMEADE (formerly Wemyss Villa). A double villa by *J. Hall*, 1898. Two storeys and three bays with some Arts and Crafts detailing. It is followed by ASHLEIGH and ROSEMOUNT, dated 1896, the fourth of the double villas by *Murray*. Before the entrance to Peebles Hotel Hydro (*see* above) is GLENTRESS, designed by the hotel's architect, *James Miller*, in 1904. A stylish two-storey, three-bay piend-roofed Neo-Georgian villa.

Returning along the S side, first is Kerfield House (*see* Villas below), then WHITESTONE PARK, once part of the Kerfield estate. The entrance gates dated 1934, with square stone gatepiers and good cast-iron gates decorated with the Peebles crest. Set in the N wall, on the roadside, is the WHITE STONE, a large quartz rock *c.* 1 m. in diameter said to have been carried here during the Ice Age. Used as a boundary mark for the burgh from at least 1462. Two late C19 villas follow. WHITESTONE, built in whinstone with red sandstone dressings, and a pilastered and corniced doorpiece. WHITEKNOWE faces away from the road. Strapwork pediment to the entrance door, finials and rosettes and a sunburst fanlight. The PARK HOTEL, formerly Minden House, started as an early C19 three-bay villa, extended by *David MacGibbon* for Henry Ballantyne in 1865 to form an asymmetrical Baronial villa. Extensively remodelled by *Cooper & Taylor* in 1901–2. Further later C20 additions are not particularly distinguished. Finally on the N side, close to Eastgate, is THE CORNICE, the Scottish Museum of Ornamental Plasterwork, which exhibits examples of the art and craft of the architectural master plasterers, *L. Grandison & Son*, established in 1886 and still in operation today.

When EDINBURGH ROAD, leading N, was reformed it obliterated the North British Railway station and goods yard (opened 1855; closed 1962). On the l., in the NW corner of the depressing Eastgate Car Park, the early C20 former GOODS OFFICE remains. Brick and vertical-boarding with overhanging eaves. On the N side of the car park is the remarkable HOLLAND & SHERRY'S WAREHOUSE, built for Lowe Donald & Co., formed in 1860 by Walter Thorburn, who had earlier developed selling tweed and cloth in his shop outlet in the High Street. The office and warehouse complex is dated 1885 with extensions of 1897 and 1910. The office block has an impressive E front to Edinburgh Road and the former railway station; a suitable introduction for intending clients. Inside, the earliest part has timber floors and cast-iron columns with acanthus capitals. The walls are vertically boarded throughout and originally were decorated with stencilling, now painted over; a sample survives in a cupboard. Each floor has a dedicated use – offices, ordering, cutting, examining, selling, and shipping.

VENLAW HIGH ROAD goes off to the r. The first villas date from the mid-to-late C19, taking advantage of a glorious view. Gabled REDBRAES (formerly Summerfield) by *John Lessels*, 1857, has overhanging eaves and bargeboards. HYNDLEA and RATHACRAIG are Queen Anne with C17 Scottish detailing.

4. South of the Tweed

Late C19 building on the S side of the river developed especially after the arrival of the Caledonian Railway in 1864. This line connected Peebles with Glasgow, terminating at the SW side of Tweed Bridge with a connection to the Edinburgh–Galashiels line across the river. The roads that wind up the hill to the S of the former station still show a rich assortment of Late Victorian and Edwardian villas. KINGSMEADOWS ROAD begins with a few of the early C19 houses on the S side, e.g. Nos. 8 and 9, altered to their detriment. No. 10 (Woodbine Cottage) was a schoolmaster's house, remodelled and extended in the mid C19, with a single-storey schoolroom. Diamond-paned latticed windows, probably later. The late C19 ST PETER'S OLD RECTORY (No. 14) is robust, of whinstone with red sandstone dressings. Stone-mullioned and transomed windows and gabled dormerheads to the first-floor windows. Wide canted bays on the S elevation overlook Victoria Park (*see* below). Four-pane upper sash windows; surprisingly, the lower sashes open by sliding up behind the stone transoms. Further on, past the park, is Nos. 1–7 TALISMAN PLACE, the former stables belonging to Kingsmeadows House (*see* Villas, below). Tucked behind the stables is the early C19 picturesque T-plan WHITE COTTAGE. Whitewashed rubble with overhanging eaves, and a three-window shallow bow on the S elevation. To the S is Priorsford Primary School (*see* Public Buildings, above).

SPRINGHILL ROAD ascends uphill to VICTORIA PARK, gifted to the town by Sir John Hay of Haystoun to mark Queen Victoria's Golden Jubilee. Square chamfered-corniced gatepiers, with acroteria and ball finials, inscribed '1887 – VR'. At the upper end of the park on the l., two blocks of semi-detached single-storey and attic houses with single bays at the outer ends, the parapets decorated with a row of blind roundels. Past several good late C19 villas, some classical with solid pilastered porches.

At the top of the hill on the r. are Kingsmuir Drive and KINGSWOOD HOUSE, inscribed RLDC – DLE 1883 on the entrance (E) elevation. U-plan villa, with Jacobean detailing. W elevation with later additions for the Rev. Professor Charteris, *c*. 1902, for a projecting three-storey crenellated tower and conservatory with a canted end. Inside, leaded windows decorated with small panels depicting historic figures, flowers and animals. The drawing room has two fluted columns decorated at their base with carved animal heads, fluted columns also on the chimneypiece. Stained glass in the dining room.

To the w, BONNINGTON ROAD. Late C19 KINGSMUIR HALL is gabled with canted windows and cast-iron balconies. Late C19 single-storey, three-bay L-plan whinstone LODGE. Next, Kingswood's former COACHMAN'S HOUSE, *c*. 1883. Three-bay crowstepped lodge with gabled dormerheads. Carriage arches blocked and glazed. Whinstone rubble. KINGSVILLE, No. 2, is a small two-storey, three-bay villa, with gabled dormerheads and crowstepped gables. Nos. 4–6, late C19 or early C20, semi-detached two-storey and attic houses with interesting Voyseyesque Arts and Crafts detailing. U-plan with projecting gables at each end with tripartite windows and decorative bargeboards. ELMSWOOD (No. 8) dates from 1890. CRUACHAN (No. 10) and HAYSTOUN COTTAGE (No. 12) are early C19. They were evidently thatched, and probably part of the Haystoun House estate (q.v.).

At the top of Bonnington Road and almost in the country, a diverse group of villas. On the E side at the very top is REIVERSLAW by *A. Hunter Crawford*. Dated 1904 on a sundial on the s elevation. Two-storey and attic five-bay Arts and Crafts house. Gabled dormerheads, overhanging eaves, terracotta tiles, and mullioned windows, their leaded casements surprisingly covered with heavy arrow-headed wrought-iron grilles, said to be later additions. A Tudor-arched pilastered doorway with cartouche, and strapwork cresting framing an oculus. Single-storey LODGE with an extension to the w elevation, 1974. The E elevation continues the boundary wall, with scrolled consoles abutting the lodge. Corniced GATEPIERS with ball finials on cushions. Elaborate wrought-iron gates; some uprights decorated with knots.

Opposite is the Free Style ARNSHEEN by *J. D. Cairns* for himself, dated 1914 above the bolection-moulded entrance doorway, a carved thistle in the centre. Impeccably sited overlooking a panorama of Peeblesshire hills and the Tweed. The W elevation has grouped windows, a corbelled-out turret with bellcast roof and finial at the sw corner, and a tall stair window. The s elevation is blank, like a tower house, the turret to the l., a wall-head stack, and a wall-mounted sundial with copper gnomon. The garden side is Scottish Domestic in character with canted bays and gabled dormerheads. Drum gatepiers with domed caps and wrought-iron gates. The garden layout survives; a yew hedge surrounds a paved rock garden; in the centre a pedestal sundial.

N of Reiverslaw is TORWOOD. Early C20, probably built for George Pringle, Rector of the High School, who acquired the site in 1904. It became a boarding-house for the High School, *c*. 1920; the attic a dormitory. Harled with projecting eaves, and dormer windows. Next along is CRAIGMOUNT, built *c.* 1905 for F. Plew, a German–South African engineer. Large, with a square entrance tower in the centre, a pyramidal roof and swept eaves, fish-scale slates and a weathervane.

At the foot of Bonnington Road is SPRINGWOOD DRIVE, which leads to SPRINGWOOD HOUSE. Dated 1869. Gabled square villa in stugged and coursed cream sandstone. The s front with an open projecting gabled timber porch with elaborate bracing and square columns. The picturesque LODGE, 1869, just survives on the corner of Springwood Drive and Terrace. Along Springwood Terrace into CHAMBERS TERRACE on the r. is DILKUSHA, a large villa erected for Master Mariner John Gordon Spence in 1897. Built on sloping ground and prominently sited to be seen from the Tweed Bridge. Whinstone with buff sandstone dressings. From the s, a three-bay villa with a gable, and projecting single-storey piend-roofed ballroom to the r. N elevation of six bays, with a broad gabled bay in the centre, and a corbelled and piend-roofed canted window at first-floor level. A round corner tower with a conical roof and finial. Inside, at the end of the oak-panelled hall, an open timber stair returned as a bowed gallery front at the end of the upper landing; a rope motif decorates the balusters. The impressive dining room, probably designed as a billiard room, is panelled in Indian laurel, exhibited at the British Empire Exhibition in London in 1924, when the house was occupied by Mr Roger of Garland & Roger, Timber Importers of Edinburgh. Renaissance plasterwork, a large black and white marble chimneypiece, and decorative light switches.

Along Chambers Terrace and down Frankscroft is CALEDONIA ROAD with some fine villas, including LINDENLEE and NEIDPATH VIEW by *Fryers & Penman, c.* 1901, for George Hamilton, a Glasgow builder, and NETHERCROFT, 1898, with a corner ogee-roofed turret, and KENDALMERE, 1905, both by *Robert Murray.*

OTHER VILLAS AND MANSIONS

CRAIGERNE HOUSE, Edderston Road. Baronial villa by *Peddie & Kinnear,* 1869. Small with bargeboarded gables and canted bay windows. Now flats. Single-storey STABLES with bracketed eaves, and a central pend topped by a weathervane. Converted to domestic use. A single-storey LODGE, bracketed eaves and porch. Corniced and ball-topped gatepiers.

GREYBIELD, Edderston Road. A compact two-storey T-plan Arts and Crafts villa set in a sea of late C20 housing; built in 1928 by *Orphoot, Whiting & Bryce.* A small addition by *Cameron Associates* fits in well.

HAY LODGE, Old Town. Now offices for Hay Lodge Hospital and Health Centre (*see* below). Built by Captain Adam Hay of Soonhope on ground falling away to the River Tweed. Described as 'lately built' in 1777, but added to and remodelled in the C19, with early C20 mansard roof and attics, to form a three-storey L-plan villa – two-storey and basement at the N end. Harled with cream sandstone margins and quoin strips. A wide eaves band and deep moulded cornice, and segmental-headed dormers in the roof. The W entrance front has

five bays; the C18 house is to the r., with three bays; its S elevation has a three-bay full-height bow. Windows with late C18
glazing bars, six panes over three, survive on the first floor and
the basement. Inside, a narrow hall leads to a cantilevered stair
(mostly boxed in) at the rear. On the r., a bow-ended drawing
room with dado panelling, the chair rail with a robust Vitruvian scroll, and elaborate dentilled cornice. The Neoclassical
chimneypiece has slender flanking consoles, while an elaborate
doorway sports acanthus-leaf consoles with carved fruit, a classical frieze of urns, swags and flowers, and a swan-necked pediment enclosing a basket of fruit and flowers.

Single-storey, harled LODGE with a centre gabled projection
with a pigeon loft. Long runs of the high C18 garden wall with
ashlar coping survive. At the NE corner is a blocked keystoned
arch with a blind oculus above; further along the E wall is a
keystoned archway, which must have been the entrance into
the courtyard of the C18 house. – STABLES on the N side of
Old Town. Much-altered late C18 rectangular range of seven
bays with a pediment in the centre.

HAY LODGE HOSPITAL and HEALTH CENTRE was built
in part of the policies in 1983. Low U-plan with services block
at the W end, a single-storey health centre and two-storey hospital block. Cream-coloured brick, with a deep parapet tying
the various parts together. Some classical pretensions are
reserved for the S façade of the hospital block, divided into
three bays by brick buttresses.

KERFIELD HOUSE, Innerleithen Road. A small neat Georgian
villa probably built c. 1800 for William Ker, who established a
brewery here towards the end of the C18. When the brewery
moved to Edinburgh, the estate developed as a small, Classical country seat. The garden was built over in the late C20 as
Peebles crept E, and the house has been added to over the
years, principally by a two-storey extension to the E. The principal block has piended roofs and tall octagonal chimneys on
the transverse walls. Pilasters at the angles and dividing the
three bays of the W front. Widely spaced bays on the N and S
sides with two-storey canted bays. Tuscan-columned doorway.
Inside, a tripartite plan, with circular entrance hall, and
morning room to the S. The dog-leg stair, with turned pine
balusters, fits very awkwardly. Two rooms to E and W of the
hall. The principal rooms contain fine black and white marble
chimneypieces, two embellished with delicately carved
figurines.

Carrying the drive over the Soonhope Burn is a BRIDGE
with a latticed iron balustrade. – WEST LODGE. Built c. 1840.
Picturesque and gabled. Lattice windows in sliding timber
sashes. Square gatepiers. Similar East Lodge.

N of the house a picturesque group of whinstone buildings
incorporates the remains of the C18 brewery. KERFIELD
COTTAGE may be the house built by Ker in 1781. Two-storey
and attic with a corniced entrance doorway placed to the l.,
set in a small walled garden with its own entrance. A former
COACH HOUSE, W, has corbelled-out corner turrets, decorated
with roundels and crosslets. On the N side is a two-storey
former BARN and, opposite, STABLES built over the Soonhope

Burn, which runs under a culvert arch in the S gable. –
WALLED GARDEN c. 1840.

KINGSMEADOWS HOUSE, Kingsmeadows Road. A substantial
classical mansion now almost swallowed up by Peebles' E
suburbs. Reported as 'lately built' in 1795 for Sir John Hay of
Smithfield and Haystoun, a banker, it began to assume its
present form c. 1811, with an addition to the W front. Sir Adam
Hay enlarged the house again c. 1855 with an addition to the
NE corner of the C18 house. From 1890 extensions were added
to the N and S gables of the (just) surviving villa, with small
turrets linking the top floors, and a large two-storey block was
added to the NE corner. This disparate group now comprises
the nine-bay W front of 1811, an octagonal bay in the centre
fronted by a large pilastered porch (c. 1855); its N and S elevations with three tiers of three-light windows with narrow sidelights. The NE block (c. 1855) with two bay windows, one
square, the other canted. A terrace wall with ball finials runs
along the forecourt's N side. Inside, surviving from c. 1811, is
an oval hall with a coved ceiling and curved doors, which leads
through to a curved stone stair with elegant balusters and rosewood rail. A new suite of rooms was created along the N front
in the late C19 with suitable cornices and grand marble
chimneypieces.

The STABLES (Nos. 1–7 Talisman Place; a late C20 conversion to cottages) comprise a quadrangular court with a secondary E court. Segmental carriage arch in the centre of the
W range with the Hay crest on the keystone of the outer face;
the inner face is inscribed JAH (Sir John Hay) 1890, and has
a timber dovecot above.

ROSETTA HOUSE, Rosetta Road. A small late Georgian villa,
built c. 1806 for Thomas Young, a military surgeon, who took
part in Sir Ralph Abercromby's expedition to secure the
Rosetta Stone for Britain, after the capture of Alexandria in
1801. Principal (E) three-bay front of coursed snecked whinstone rubble with sandstone margins and quoins; the centre
bay slightly advanced and pedimented, with a blind oculus.
Splayed steps with curved ends and plain cast-iron railings to
a pilastered doorcase with a decorated entablature of flutes and
rosettes. A crenellated circular bay, projecting from the centre
of the W front, contains inside an oval-plan room. Usual tripartite plan with a central entrance lobby. Unusually, the
handsome stone geometric stair rises from the far end, unseen
from the front door. Good marble chimneypieces, that in the
drawing room with fluted columns topped by dancing figures.

WALLED GARDEN, SW of the house. Rubble walls with a
wide stone cope. A C17 or C18 carved stone head is built into
the W wall. – STABLES. Square court 'lately built' in 1805. The
S and E elevations have whimsical Gothic façades with crenellated corner features, decorated with quatrefoils, hoodmoulds
and crosslets. – Early C19 single-storey LODGE with bell-
shaped roof and bracketed eaves.

TANTAH, Edderston Road. Free Style Baronial villa built by the
Inglis family and dated 1884. Divided in 1949. – STABLES similarly treated, and a LODGE dated 1884; canted bay with a
sloping roof and a rear addition by *Robert Murray*, 1898. Just

s is the well-cared-for survival of the contemporary(?), corrugated-iron TANTAH COTTAGE with timber bargeboarded gables with finials, and a central brick chimney.

VENLAW CASTLE (Castle Venlaw Hotel), Edinburgh Road, occupies a commanding position on the W slope of Venlaw Hill overlooking the town, the view now partly obscured by mature trees. The earliest part, a small Georgian Gothic villa, was described by Sheriff Alexander Stevenson in 1780 as 'lately built' on the site of Smithfield Castle, the seat of the Hays of Smithfield in the C16 or C17. It passed to the Erskine family in 1798, and in 1892 a large Baronial tower house, designed by *David MacGibbon* of *MacGibbon & Ross*, was added to the S for Admiral Sir James Elphinstone Erskine.

The original villa, of two storeys and basement, has a five-bay E front with the centre three bays advanced. Deeply splayed Gothic windows but without their original glazing pattern. Simple rectangular E porch, with dated lintel – JE (John Erskine) *fecit* 1854. Above, within a former window opening, a lengthy inscription of 1892(?) records the early history of the house. The Victorian tower house is rectangular, with a large, round turreted tower at the SE corner, complete with corner bartizans, a cap house and crowstepped gables; tall chimneystacks to the N and S. To link the old with the new, a deep wall-head was added to the entrance elevation of the earlier house, with a central pedimented window.

Inside, the C18 house was replanned; the SW room became part of a new drawing room, with a scheme of rather insipid classical decoration. The present dining room, formerly the drawing room, has an authentic-looking C18 chimneypiece and overmantel, but the whole thing looks contrived and must be two classical chimneypieces superimposed. The late C19 smoking room and library to the SE is well detailed, with large timber Baronial chimneypiece and overmantel.

The WALLED GARDEN, E, has a small circular SW tower with a crenellated wall-head, a feature seen from the house. Now in separate ownership, with a house erected in the 1990s. – NORTH LODGE, gabled with overhanging eaves *c.* 1880. – SOUTH LODGE, *c.* 1893; picturesque Tudor.

HAYSTOUN HOUSE. *See* p. 369.
HORSBURGH CASTLE. *See* p. 385.
NEIDPATH CASTLE. *See* p. 576.
NETHER HORSBURGH CASTLE. *See* p. 583.
WINKSTON. *See* p. 763.

PEEL HOUSE

4030

3 km. W of Caddonfoot

A Baronial house by *John Kinross*, 1899–1905, for William Roberts Ovens, a seed and grain merchant in Leith. The house is notable for its superb craftsmanship. The contractor was *Arnott McLeod*, the builders *Beattie & Son*. Built in coursed dark whinstone, much of it from a specially opened quarry at Caddonfoot, with cream dressings. Kinross appears to have referred to R.W. Billings's *The Baronial and Ecclesiastical*

Antiquities of Scotland (1848–52) for many of the external details. The house is mostly two-storey with an almost symmetrical entrance (s) elevation, with turreted projecting wings flanking a five-bay centre block with an advanced gabled entrance bay, the first floor jettied on corbel courses. At the E end are the offices and a kitchen court. Symmetrical four-bay W elevation with angle turrets, and N elevation dominated by a four-storey crenellated D-plan tower of Midmar Castle type, with a bellcast turret. Gabled wall-head dormers, some with triangular heads, others carved with rosettes. Set into the walls in various places are moulded panels with different carved motifs, including vases of flowers. Grotesque animals and thistle motifs finish off short string courses.

The plan of the house is most suitable for its use as a shooting or fishing lodge, each part serving its function, as at Manderston House (q.v.) but on a much smaller scale. The source used for much of the interior decoration appears to have been *Later Renaissance Architecture in England* (1901, eds. John Belcher and Mervyn E. Macartney), and the opulent mix of classical and late C17-style decoration mostly remains intact. *Scott Morton* carried out the woodwork; most if not all of the plasterwork is by *Leonard Grandison* of Peebles. The provenance of the sumptuous chimneypieces is unknown. Entrance is into a vestibule and up two steps to a hall, partitioned by a central column into four vaulted ceilings. From the hall double doors lead to an arched corridor, and opposite, arches leading to the ballroom have Corinthian columns with recessed alcoves. At the E end of the corridor the STAIRCASE HALL, with the well stair to the first-floor gallery landing, with a richly carved balustrade, very similar to the late C17 one at Kinross House. A finely decorated ribbed ceiling with runs of guilloche ornament, and a large cupola with an arched window each side, giving a generous amount of light. To the s, a DINING ROOM, accessed from the hall and kitchen, on the N side the DRAWING ROOM with access from the staircase hall and BALLROOM, with richly decorated ceiling with fruits etc., panelled walls and cherubs' heads above the window pelmets. From the ballroom a short passage, with a door to the garden, leads to a bow-ended BOUDOIR, also with a door from the transverse corridor. A lushly ornamented overmantel of two lively cherubs clinging to fruity drops and festoons adds to the charm. At the W end is the suite of study, gun room (acting as a vestibule from the garden) and billiard room.

PEELWALLS HOUSE
1 km. SW of Ayton

Built *c.* 1830 for John Dickson. Classical two-storey, five-bay house of Cullalo stone which fronts a small farmhouse of earlier date. The S entrance elevation has a rusticated ground floor below a plain band course and a moulded eaves course. Doorway with detached fluted Doric columns and decorative frieze of triglyphs, guttae and metopes. The first-floor windows with panelled aprons. Later canted bays to the side elevations

and N addition of between 1860 and 1900, the date of the interior's redecoration by *P. R. McLaren*. He inserted a new staircase in a central hall with an oval cupola on concave spandrels.
Pretty shell cornice in the morning room; much use of
Tynecastle paper friezes in the public rooms.

WALLED GARDEN with brick-lined and stone-coped walls. –
Appealing rustic SUMMERHOUSE with a slate roof and walls
covered with a decorative pattern of branches. Tiny windows
with stained glass. – Much-altered STABLES with kennels and
other offices to the E. – Of the two LODGES, the S one (*c.* 1830)
is the more sophisticated. Classically detailed, in cream-
coloured finely droved ashlar with a niche in each side elevation. Rusticated V-jointed gatepiers with pyramidal caps, and
ball-finialled caps flanking the vehicle entrance. Decorative
cast-iron gates.

PENCHRISE PEEL   4000
8 km. S of Hawick

A C17-style tower house, tucked among Scots pines with an open
view to the S, by *J. P. Alison* for W. Macfarlane-Grieve, 1908.
Extended 1912. A rectangular block with corbelled parapet,
corner bartizan and a corbelled-out ogee-capped angle tower.
Low two-storey wing, crowstepped with a conical-roofed
turret, and triangular and curved wall-head dormers.

PHILIPHAUGH HOUSE   4020
1.5 km. SW of Selkirk

Neo-Georgian by *William H. Kininmonth*, 1964, replacing an
earlier house. – WEST LODGE, 1877, by *J. M. Wardrop*. Jacobean,
with curvilinear gables.

ESTATE SAWMILL. *c.* 1858. Water-powered with a cast-iron
undershot wheel in a wheelhouse.

COVENANTERS' MONUMENT. Rustic, pyramidal-shaped cairn,
erected by Sir John Murray (1817–82), in honour of the
Covenanters' defeat of the Marquess of Montrose, 1645.

POLWARTH

Just the church, manse and a scattering of once thatched cottages
by a village green. All that remains of the flourishing settlement
of over three hundred people recorded in 1811, principally
weavers, blacksmiths, and souters (shoemakers), who served the
farm tenants on the Marchmont estate (q.v.).

PARISH CHURCH. A delightful and rewarding rural church in
open countryside S of the village. An existing building was dedicated in 1242, and inscriptions record extensive rebuilding in
1378. But most of what is now seen was built by Patrick Hume,
first Earl of Marchmont, in 1703, probably using the walls of
the earlier church.

The building is T-plan, with a w tower and a lateral N 'aisle'; harled walls with exposed red sandstone margins and dressings. There were four entrances, one at the tower base (round-headed), and the others along the s flank (with rounded shoulders and an ogee), all with bolection-type mouldings. There are heraldic panels on the w and s sides of the tower and carved shields below the volute skewputts at the four angles of the church itself. Prominent framed Latin inscriptions with biblical texts and accounts of the church's history are interspersed with the pointed windows along the s flank and on the sides of the tower. The four-storey tower has a minister's room on the first floor; it is capped by a slated splay-foot spire with a chimney emerging through the E side. At the E end of the church, below the Marchmont pew, is a burial vault; if this is the vault where Patrick Hume took refuge after being implicated in the Rye House plot of 1683, it confirms that the shell of the church pre-dates the 1703 remodelling.

Internally the three arms have collar-beam roofs of the standard type, albeit more roughly finished than might be expected in a church of such quality; were they intended to be ceiled over? The furnishings were reordered in 1928 for R.F. McEwen of Marchmont by *Robert S. Lorimer*, when the communion table was removed from the centre of the s wall to the E end. The rails of the Marchmont pew, with its gate, were reused as a communion rail, an unusual feature in a Presbyterian church. – COMMUNION RAIL, closely spaced turned balusters. – PEWS, framed and panelled construction, some with raised and fielded panels. – PULPIT VALANCE, worked by *Lady Grizell Baillie*, 1703. – FONT, simple cylindrical medieval bowl, re-sited in base of tower. – WALL MEMORIALS. Anna Western, Countess of Marchmont, †1747; Robert McLean Calder, poet, †1896, by *J. W. Dods* of Dumfries, lyre cartouche with thistles. – SUNDIAL, at SW angle of tower. – BURIAL ENCLOSURE, to N of tower, for Rev. George Howell, †1742.

CHURCHYARD, memorials of Hume Campbells of Marchmont, and of McEwens of Marchmont, to NE of church; wide range of C17, C18 and C19 memorials to s. Several late C17 and early C18 gravestones showing shared motifs that may be the work of a single family of masons.

MANSE, Packman's Brae. By *James Cunningham*, *c.* 1836. An elegant two-storey symmetrical ashlar building with lower wings. Moulded stone eaves and piended roof. Five-bay s elevation with full-height shallow bows. Tripartite windows with panelled aprons in the wings. U-plan red-rubble steading, NW, and SW walled garden.

OLD SCHOOLHOUSE, Packman's Brae. Mid-C19. Built for girls. Panelled doorway with narrow sidelights.

THATCHED COTTAGE, Packman's Brae. Early to mid-C19 double cottage, in red sandstone rubble with roughly squared quoins. Brick chimneystack in the centre of the ridge. Wheat-straw thatch on thin purlins and couples survives below a corrugated iron covering. Distinctively piended at each end with overhanging eaves.

MARCHMONT HOUSE. *See* p. 520.

PORTMORE HOUSE

2040

2.4 km. NE of Eddleston

A moderately sized red sandstone Scottish Jacobean mansion house. Built in two stages, it was begun in 1850 by *David Bryce* for William Forbes Mackenzie M.P., who had obtained preliminary drawings for a new house on this site from *William Burn* in 1833. In 1883 *John Bryce* added a family wing to the N end and remodelled the interior after a fire. Restored in the 1980s, after long neglect, by *Duncan Cameron* of *Cameron & Gibbs* but damaged again by fire in 1986 and subsequently remodelled.

Principally two storeys on a raised basement. The W elevation contains the principal entrance, with a three-storey square tower at the N end, of the type at Winton House (Lothian), with a balustraded viewing roof accessed by an ogee-roofed round turret. A shallow Jacobean projecting porch is surmounted by an ornamental strapwork pediment and corner obelisks; strapwork pediments over the windows above. Three recessed bays to the S have finialled wall-head dormers. The two tall octagonal chimneys between each dormer also appear to be based on similar details at Winton. Projecting from the S end is the crowstepped gable of the S block, in front of which was a conservatory by David Bryce (dem. 1920s). A four-storey octagonal ogee-roofed tower, in the re-entrant with the gable, formerly contained a private stair. The symmetrical E façade is of five bays, the three bays to the r. belonging to John Bryce's 1883 addition. A large crowstepped projection to the E has the same detailing as the earlier work. At the N end, the stables of 1850. A crowstepped block projecting from the end of the W front was formerly a separate building, but was linked to the house by John Bryce, with an ogee-roofed entrance tower in the re-entrant.

The INTERIOR of the E wing was entirely gutted by fire in 1986, and replanned. The rest of the house was heavily damaged and new plasterwork undertaken by *Grandisons* of Peebles, who had retained the original moulds from work carried out by *Leonard Grandison* in 1883, resulting in a seamless mix of old and new. The public rooms are arranged along the E and S sides. The entrance is into a vestibule and through to the staircase hall, whose Jacobean stair probably dates from *c.* 1900, as it bears the monogram of the then owner, John Moncur Somerville. A large wyvern terminal at the foot of the stair holds a shield displaying the Somerville crest and motto. To the r. is the hall, which probably originally held the billiard table, but now has an organ by *Harrison & Dummer*, *c.* 1883, overhauled by *Rushworth & Dreaper* in 1980. The Jacobean ceiling with small pendants, and the oak wainscotting and Ionic pilastered timber chimneypiece are of 1883, as is the frieze of fruit and flowers with intermittent stumpy composite pilasters – all by Grandison. Along the E front is the dining room, with foliaceous cornice and a red marble chimneypiece with clustered columns brought here *c.* 1990. To the S, the library, with some surviving shelving, perhaps by David Bryce.

Along the S front the drawing room has another foliaceous

frieze, but recent strapwork decoration in the corner of the ceiling. The master bedroom above the drawing room has the business and/or smoking room to the E; an L-shaped room, with a deep cove covered in gilded Tynecastle-type canvas or paper.

WALLED GARDEN. 1850. A range of greenhouses and conservatory along the N wall, the centre part erected by *Mackenzie & Moncur* in 1898. Opening out of the N wall of the conservatory is a delightful GROTTO, made after 1911, when it was given a glazed lean-to roof, and the walls decorated with clinker or tufa, and planted with ferns and other appropriate plants by Mrs Morton Robertson, an Italian, who found the heated space a refuge from the damp Peeblesshire climate.

LODGE. Probably 1850. T-plan. Crowstepped with scrolled skews and hoodmoulds, A crenellated balustrade to the porch. Commanding tall square, panelled GATEPIERS with dentilled cornice, topped by stone balls.

HARCUS HOUSE, 0.7km. SW. The first place of residence on the estate after it was acquired in 1798 by Alexander Mackenzie, W.S. Probably built as a farmhouse and used by the estate factors or tenants. A courtyard range of whinstone rubble steadings; some cartshed openings have round whinstone columns.

9050
PRENDERGUEST HOUSE
1.5km. S of Ayton

Built as a mansion house, 1834, but later became a farmhouse. Two-storey, piend-roofed and classically detailed with a sandstone ashlar front. Prominent rusticated quoins. The advanced centre of its SE elevation has a wide round-arched recessed doorway with sidelights, the corniced doorpiece with engaged columns topped by carved busts, a frieze of flutes and rosettes, and decorative fanlight. A Venetian window ornaments the floor above. Canted bays in the SW elevation, and a contemporary lower wing set back to the r. – Five-sided WALLED GARDEN.

8060
PRESS CASTLE
3km. W of Coldingham

A mid-C19 house, of two storeys with a raised basement. Castellated Gothic detailing of a crenellated parapet with cannon poised for action in each embrasure. All the interest is on the W (principal) front, formerly of three bays, extended c. 1900 to the S by a single window and a full-height canted bay. Solid porch with a Tudor-arched doorway, the fanlight and side windows with intersecting tracery. This has a solid parapet with side embrasures with more cannon, corner turrets with small figures and a central pediment surmounted by a bust. Prominent chimneystacks with linked flues on the gables. Later additions, the NE one attached to two-storey former stables. Much

altered inside, but in the hall is a Jacobean-style chimneypiece
and overmantel, *c.* 1900, either resited or brought from elsewhere.

DOVECOT. SE of house. Dated 1607, but worked over. Two-
stage, rectangular, and harled with red sandstone margins and
corbelled eaves with crenellated parapets, formerly with metal
cannons. The S door has a moulded panel above with coat-of-
arms and inscription TA 1607. – WALLED GARDEN. S of house.
Early-to-mid C19. Rubble walls. – LODGE. Mid-C19, Neo-
Tudor. Square, ball-finialled gatepiers with horizontal bands
carved with fleurs-de-lys to the l., lions to the r.

PRESTON

A small village, the centre of Bunkle and Preston parish.

OLD PARISH CHURCH. An outlying enclave of the diocese of
Dunkeld, and a possession of its bishops by 1275. Abandoned
in 1718 in favour of Bunkle, and now a decaying and overgrown
ruin subdivided into burial enclosures. An elongated rectangle
in plan, with a buttressed W wall and traces of a sacristy offshoot on the N. The E wall has a pair of narrow windows with
widely splayed rear arches, possibly of the C12–C13, and there
was a related single window in the W wall. The only other
medieval window is a later small pointed opening with a lintelled rear arch on the S side of the chancel, above the piscina.
The main lay entrance was a rectangular doorway with chamfered surrounds of late medieval date, above which are re-set
carved and moulded fragments, including some with double
chevron. The priest's doorway in the chancel has rounded
arrises. A third doorway is evidently a C17 insertion. –
PISCINA. A massive triangular basin below a round-arched
recess. – MONUMENTS. S wall of nave, James Johnston, mason
in Preston, †1779, Tuscan pedimented aedicule.

CHURCHYARD, to S of church, some C17–C18 monuments
with *memento mori*.

LINTLAW SCHOOL, 5.5km. NE. The former Bunkle school.
Dated 1860. Single-storey and attic with Tudor detailing. Sawtooth coped stone skews, gableted skewputts. Lying-pane
glazing. On the other side of the road is an earlier two-storey
schoolhouse.

MARKET CROSS. Opposite Preston Farm. Probably early C17.
Square plan shaft and broken cross.

NEL LOGAN'S BRIDGE (B6355). Dated 1793. A single segmen-
tal-arch bridge over Preston Burn. Rubble voussoirs with keystones. The arch was later enclosed to form a cell below and
is said to have been used as a jail. One doorway, a small S
window, and narrow N slit.

PRESTON BRIDGE (A6112) spanning the Whiteadder Water.
Dated 1770. Three segmental arches in red sandstone rubble.
Flush voussoirs, each outlined by a raised band incorporating
a keystone, with a panel above. Round recesses in the spandrels, with carved floral decoration in the S ones. Dentilled
cornices and coped parapets.

VILLAGE HALL. Erected 1911 as Preston Recreation Rooms. Rectangular, in brick, with a flèche ventilator.

WAR MEMORIAL. N side of road. A carved Celtic cross, c. 1920.

BONKYL LODGE. At the E end of the village. Solid classical house, built by the twelfth Earl of Home, c. 1890. Additions by *Leadbetter, Fairley & Reid*, 1938. – LODGE (B6438). Picturesque English Domestic suggesting the hand of *Sydney Mitchell & Wilson*, who were working at Bonkyl c. 1890, and designed the laundry at The Hirsel (q.v.) in similar style.

PRESTON FARM COTTAGES. Nos. 1–5. A late C19 U-plan range of nine cottages (now four). Rendered mullions to bipartite windows and bracketed skewputts. Entrances in narrow full-height gabled porches extending above the wall-head. A cobbled walkway in front. – Nos. 6–7 (Tom Brockie's Cottage) is a picturesque mid-C19 pair built end-on to the road. Blind armorial shields in the gable-heads and casements with diamond-paned glazing. – To the E, Nos. 8–9, a similar pair. Possibly by *Robert Bell*, Edinburgh, who built new steadings at Preston Farm in 1855, using similar features.

BASTIE MONUMENT, 4 km. SE. Early C19. Square plinth and pedestal embossed with crosses and classical cornice, topped by a stylised urn. Erected by General James Home (†1849), in honour of Antoine d'Arces, Seigneur de la Basti, who had been appointed a Warden of the Marches, instead of Lord Home, and was slain in a battle with Home's clan near Langton in 1517. Re-erected here in 1975.

CRUXFIELD HOUSE, 2 km. E. Former farmhouse, built c. 1800 and described as 'a neat house of two storeys and excellent steading'. Now a small mansion with a number of significant early-to-mid-C19 additions. Two storeys and attic. The S entrance block, likely to be mid-C19, of three bays, rendered and lined out to resemble ashlar, with shaped gables with decorative steps to the ends and centre, the latter with a tall finial. Pilastered and corniced doorpiece. Shallow bow set back to the r. linked by a screen wall to a projecting single-storey similarly gabled pavilion. To the N, another shallow bow, facing W, with added crenellations, then a crenellated block with hoodmoulded windows. The last is probably the earlier farmhouse, the bowed fronts added later, though not symmetrically. A curved screen wall fronting the stables, to the N, ends in another shaped gable, with painted diamond-paned windows. Inside a dog-legged stair with decorative cast-iron balusters and a timber-panelled hall, the upper part with decorative arcading between pilasters. Extensive farm offices.

PURVES HALL *see* OLD PURVES HALL

RACHAN MILL

Some good cottages including mid-C19 MILLSIDE, an old mill cottage with lying panes in casement windows, and the single-storey and attic SAWMILL COTTAGE, whose rear elevation preserves a derelict water turbine. Small 1811 datestone, probably referring to the erection of the cornmill from which the sawmill was adapted.

RACHAN MILL FARM. *c.* 1850. Farmhouse and steading, distinguished by crowstepped-patterned eaves, large round-arched cartshed doors, and prominent square finials.

RACHAN MILL HALL, known as the 'Recycled House'. By *Jim Abbot*, 2000 for himself, remodelling a recreation hall built in 1922 for Broughton estate workers. This is of whinstone with red sandstone dressings and ornamental tiled roof ridge, connected to an open-plan studio with a timber-framed extension for services and a bedroom. Heather turf-covered flat roof and fully glazed wall-head. A drystone wall acts as a rain screen, harmoniously integrated against the grey-stained pine of the walling on the N side. Extensive use of reclaimed materials. A slate and cedar-clad garage and workshop, designed for future extension, steps down a slope to a pond.

RAVENSWOOD
3.3 km. E of Melrose

5030

The mansion of the historic estate of Old Melrose, where there seems to have been a house as early as the 1570s (*see* summerhouse, below). The present building was begun in 1824 by *John Smith* for Major John Scott of the East India Co., who named it Ravenswood. This Neo-Tudor asymmetrical castellated mansion of two storeys and basement with crowstepped gables, turreted towers, mullioned windows and hoodmoulds, was extended and remodelled at the W end in similar style by Admiral Sir Henry Fairfax in 1864. He moved the entrance from s to N, building the crenellated porch. The W elevation has a crowstepped gable feature set behind the parapet, repeated on the s front, and a panel with a carved lion flanked by griffin(?) spouts. In the centre of Smith's s elevation is a castellated tower, with small corner square towers with slit windows. The former entrance door has narrow sidelights and pointed-arched tops. Fairfax added a single-storey and basement library at the E end, raised by a storey for William Younger, 1900, and given a veranda with three octagonal-columned, pointed arches with a stone balustrade. Sundial in the gable initialled WYK (William and Katherine Younger). Modernised internally in 1961–3. Only the library retains a compartmented ceiling, decorated frieze and some shelving.

STABLES. U-plan. Dated 1883, with fittings by *Musgrave & Co.* of Belfast. To the rear is a fitted harness room. The court was given a fully glazed canopy on cast-iron columns in the motor age.

OLD MELROSE HOUSE, 0.8 km. SE. A large quadrangular courtyard with a reconstructed steading and a late-C19 two-storey symmetrical house, with a projecting gabled entrance bay, bipartite windows, and overhanging eaves. Two houses have been formed from the original stables. No. 2 has wall-head gabled dormers and between them, a small (reused?) panel contains a glazed quatrefoil. The central segmental-headed red sandstone pend must date from *c.* 1800. – WALLED GARDEN. Probably *c.* 1800. Large, with immensely high coped rubble walls. In the SW corner, a small window from the gardener's cottage (derelict), allowed some surveillance.

OLD MELROSE FARM (Dairy Cottage). Probably *c.* 1800 but with dormers and porch in the late-C19 style of Ravenswood. U-plan steading with cobbled court.

The POLICIES of Old Melrose were laid out with walks and plantations along the Tweed in 1809 by *Thomas White Jun.* for Colonel Lockhart. White's plan shows the SUMMERHOUSE set on the promontory N of Old Melrose House. Three bays, canted at the rear, the centre round-arched window giving splendid views over the Tweed. The doorway lintel comprises a damaged, reused stone inscribed with the sacred monogram IHS, the date 1575 and the initials RO, probably commemorating the erection of a house by Robert Ormiston of Old Melrose in that year. Above is a moulded pediment with a ball finial. The window and door margins have distinctive moulded margins. After 1885 the windows were changed to plate glass casements with stained glass in the heads, and the roof (now fallen in), was altered and given two chimneys *c.* 1892 by *John Starforth.* Inside, a good Late Victorian interior with a timber coved ceiling, tiled floor, glazed tiles on the walls, and a Lorimer-style canopied chimneypiece.

NORTH LODGE. Gabled. Decorative bargeboards and cast-iron thistle finials suggest late C19 additions, but the hood-moulds and bay window look 1820s. Splendid cast-iron decorative gates and railings. Banded cast-iron uprights with finials, and some decorative Arts and Crafts wrought ironwork. – SOUTH LODGE (A68) to old drive. Early C19 crowstepped-gable, with crenellated porch. – OLD MELROSE LODGE. (A68). Mid-C19, with wall-head dormers, finialled timber porch and fish-scale banded roof.

MONASTERY SITE, Chapel Knoll, 1 km. SE. On a promontory formed by a tight loop of the Tweed, is the likely location for the monastery founded, according to Bede, by St Aidan (presumably as a satellite of Iona) probably *c.* 635–51. St Cuthbert joined the community at the latter date, in the time of Abbot Eata and Prior Boisil. The only visible remains are of a vallum across the neck at the W end of the promontory. It was burned by Kenneth MacAlpin before his death in 858, though monastic life appears to have continued for a while. In 1074 an attempt to re-colonise it from Jarrow was thwarted by Malcolm III. There must, however, have been a chapel here by the second quarter of the C12, when David I made arrangements for its possession to be transferred to his new Cistercian abbey of Melrose. A grotesque head corbel assumed to be from this chapel is preserved at Melrose Abbey, and foundations and graves are recorded as having been found SE of the house, at the centre of the promontory.

RAWFLAT

4 km. SE of Lilliesleaf

Former late C18 laird's house; only its single storey S elevation, with recessed centre bays and pilastered doorway, was retained in the rebuilding of 1975 by *W. Schomberg Scott* for the Hon. James Galbraith. The new house is two full storeys with an entrance front of five bays, minimally detailed. – Late C18 WALLED GARDEN with splendid steel GATES of the 1990s, with the heads of a bear and lion.

REDBRAES CASTLE *see* MARCHMONT HOUSE

REDPATH

A small village, described in the mid 1860s as wearing 'a quiet and decayed look'.

VILLAGE HALL. Former school. Dated 1837 inside. Curvilinear gables with moulded stone copes, and a corbelled-out octagonal chimney at the E gable, the corbels decorated with a carved face. The lintel above the former entrance is inscribed 'Misericordia et Pax'. Surprising survival of the contemporary schoolmaster's desk and other equipment.

DESCRIPTION. An E–W main street, with a farm at each end: of the two, REDPATH WEST is probably *c*. 1800. Two storeys and attic, with four widely spaced windows and a steeply pitched roof. Harling covers clay-bonded walling. A carved head built into the front wall sports a periwig. In the remaining outbuildings there are elements of moulded doorways *in situ*, which may suggest an earlier structure on the site. REDPATH EAST END, an early C19 farmhouse, has a good set of contemporary steading buildings. SUNDIAL COTTAGE at the E end of Main Street has a dial mounted on the front wall, inscribed WB MR 1675.

RENTON HOUSE *see* GRANTSHOUSE

RESTON

A small straggling village on the S bank of the Eye Water. At one time a railway junction for Duns and St Boswells, its principal interest since the mid C19 has been the auction mart for the sale of stock and agricultural implements, which has kept Reston a lively place. In the mid C19 the inhabitants were mainly mechanics and agricultural labourers.

PARISH CHURCH. Built 1879–80 as a Free Church, a rectangular block of coursed rubble with sandstone dressings, having a low vestry at the S end and the main entrance to the N. The doorway is within a gabled salient, flanked by two-light plate-traceried windows; above the doorway is an ogee-arched tablet dated 1879, and at the gable apex is a bellcote. The angles of the N front have absorbed buttresses. Along each flank are four spaced lancets and a central two-light plate-traceried window rising into a gablet; on the S wall truncated plate-traceried windows rise above the vestry and flank the pulpit. All windows now unfortunately double-glazed. Ceiling of polygonal profile with expressed principal rafters and collars. – COMMUNION TABLE and PULPIT within enclosure at S end, the former originally in Langton Free Church.

PRIMARY SCHOOL. Board School, dated 1897, in coursed rock-faced cream sandstone. Three large round-headed windows, a circular window above, and a bellcote at the apex. Polygonal, single-storey SE block. To the W is the harled and whitewashed Old Schoolhouse. Early-to-mid C19.

RESTON AUCTION MART. Early C20, on the site of the earlier mart. A single-storey octagonal-shaped timber sheep ring, with triangular-shaped ventilators, and additions to the S and E. Four-stage tiered seating survives inside.

DESCRIPTION. MAIN STREET has, on its N side, mid-to-late C19 villas (among them might be noted EDGEBANK, MARCH HOUSE, ST MARY'S VILLA and CULBLEAN) with large gardens and fine front railings, mostly with fleur-de-lys finials, and square pyramidal-capped gatepiers. Some have contemporary stabling and hay lofts to the rear. RESTON HOUSE is mid-C19 Classical, of three bays, in squared and snecked red sandstone. Round-arched doorway with paired pilasters. The core of CRUACHAN, originally a pair of two-storey cottages, is probably late C18 – suggested by an exterior stair to the first floor to the l. – with a mid-C19 addition. To the r., a four-bay block, mid-C19, with classical detailing, has a projecting late C19 gabled shopfront, with panelled pilasters and a corniced fascia, of a type which appears elsewhere in the village. At the foot of Main Street is BERRYHAUGHS FARM, a crowstepped C18 farmhouse with carved skewputts. Harled with painted margins. Deep reveals to the windows on the S side, with red pantiles also on this side, slates to the N. A small inscribed date panel, A[D] [M]H 1706 has been built into the N elevation. Contemporary red pantiled C18 farm buildings survive.

STONESHIEL HALL. See p. 706.

THE RETREAT
0.5 km. SE of Abbey St Bathans

A fascinating circular house built in 1778–80 as a hunting lodge for Francis Charteris, titular Earl of Wemyss. The masons were *William & James Craise* but payments were made to *James Brown* of Haddington, wright, and *Alexander Russell*, plasterer. The design is possibly by *John Henderson*, for whom the Craises and Brown worked at Charteris's home, Amisfield House (Lothian).

The main body is circular, with ochre-washed harled walls and a conical slated roof through which rises a central circular chimneystack. Pointed Gothick windows with intersecting tracery light the two main storeys, and there are small leaded box dormers to the attic. To each side are independent T-shaped pavilions, originally of one storey, for kitchens and offices (SE), and stables and kennels (NW); their stems extended in 1793 by *Adam & Thomas Russell*. In the early C19(?) the SE pavilion was linked to the house by a corridor, in which a new principal entrance framed by a four-centred arch was formed. The NW pavilion has a range running parallel to the head of the T that is evidently original; more recently part of the main body of that pavilion has been heightened by a half storey.

The plan suggests the builder may have been aware of Belle Isle, *John Plaw*'s circular house of 1774 on an island in Lake Windermere. The main axis through the house runs SW, towards gardens stretching down to the Whiteadder, and the original entrance (now a window) was from the NE. The drawing room on the SW side is a rectangle with exedras at each end, as at Belle Isle, where the stair, as here, is also contained within an extended apsidal space, though here it is pushed to one side of the entrance axis, and rises around a spine wall. Particularly intriguing are the ceilings undulating around the joists not only of the corridors running across the principal axis of the two main floors but also in some lesser rooms. The contrast between the cool Neoclassicism of the drawing room and the artful rusticity of these corrugated ceilings is a delight.

RIDDELL   5020

2.8 km. W of Lilliesleaf

A possession of the Riddell family, who originally occupied the nearby motte (*see* below) and, in the C19, of the Sprots. The house, burnt in 1943 and now a crumbling shell, is composed of two parts: the six bays to the W are partly C16 or C17, probably extended in the C18; the other three bays and the three crowstepped gables on the E elevation were probably added *c.* 1830 for Mark Sprot. A weathered C16 dormer pediment is built into the outside of the NW wall and shows three sheaves of rye, and initials, probably John Riddell, and the date 15[6?]7. Inside, two *in situ* C16 or C17 door-ways.

RIDDELL (former Estate Office and Mains Farm). 'Built by Mark Sprot Esq. 1826. Extended, improved and repaired by Lt. General Sprot 1898.' Originally single-storey, with pedimented two-storey centre, its design similar to one by J.C. Loudon* for a cottage villa with 'ample sized windows'. In 1898 the single-storey parts were raised and provided with gablets and broad overhanging eaves. The end bays of the N façade are slightly advanced with open pediments. Entrance doorway with pretty fanlight. Two storey harled additions of the 1920s to the NE.

---

* *An Encyclopaedia of Cottage, Farm and Villa Architecture* (1833), 107, pl. 30.

648   RIDDELL · ROBERTON

HOME FARM, much altered c. 1823; the cartsheds have circular columns, but the roofs have been renewed, and given overhanging eaves and timber brackets. – STABLES. Central high-arched pend, formerly with a timber cupola, and pigeon loft. – Octagonal DEER LARDER, W of the old house, dated 1836 MS, and formerly with a domed lead roof. Pedimented porch. Around the wall-head stone blocks alternate to allow a draught of air. MAUSOLEUM by *John Smith* for Mark Sprot; dated 1858. A screen front with a crenellated gable, topped by a Celtic cross. Brick-lined vault. LODGES. At the entrance to the S drive. Single-storey, both harled with slate roofs but perhaps of different dates. The W lodge was extended in 1909 and given overhanging, bracketed eaves; the E lodge acquired a rustic timber porch at this time.

Sir John Buchanan Riddell improved the farms and roads on his estate in 1794, and built the castellated public bridge (B6400) and the humpbacked SOUTH DRIVE BRIDGE, crudely carved square balusters, and chunky round pillars with conical caps. Cement-rendered and lined out as ashlar in the C19. Unfortunate repairs on the NE side c. 1996. – PARK BRIDGE, SW of the old house, provides a picturesque front to a culvert where the burn issues from a small ravine into a sloping field. Dated MS 1851, designed by *John Smith*.

RIDDELL MOTTE, 0.5km. NE, overlooking the Ale Water. Probably erected by Walter of Rydale, a Yorkshire baron who was granted lands here in the mid C12 and founded the Scottish family of Riddell. The motte (c. 29 m. by 12 m. on top) was formed by trimming a natural ridge and stands almost at the centre of a small oblong bailey (52 m. by 35 m.) defended on three sides by a ditch lying between two ramparts and on the fourth by a natural scarp. Rising from the middle of the site is the GENERAL'S TOWER, by *A. Herbertson & Son*, 1885; built by Lt. General John Sprot. A tall square tower of rubble with sandstone dressings, with a corbelled-out wall-walk and pitch-roofed crowstepped caphouse containing a panelled garret chamber. This has a stone chimneypiece sporting carved herons on the jambs.

4010   ROBERTON

Church, school and village hall comprise the only village in Roberton parish.

Former FREE CHURCH, 1.2km. SW of the village. 1844, a simple limewashed rubble rectangle; it was remodelled in 1906 and given slight Arts and Crafts nuances (both dates inscribed on a tablet over the doorway). Ultimately it had a NW porch, a SE apsidal vestry and a lead-sheathed flèche rising from the roof. Along each flank pairs of windows rise into arched slated dormers. Closed for worship in 1927, it became a Youth Hostel (the association's badge still over the entrance), and is now a house.

PARISH CHURCH. 1863–4, by *David Rhind*, an orientated rectangle of stugged buff ashlar, with a W porch balancing a larger E vestry. There are buttresses at the angles, a gabled bellcote on the W gable, a chimney on the E gable, and the wall-head is enlivened by a corbel table of simple blocks. Five windows along each flank, the end ones single lancets and those between with timber Y-tracery. On the W gable, above the porch, a relief carving of the Burning Bush. The roof, of arch-braced and collar construction, is slated with alternating horizontal and fish-scale bands. The communion table platform is at the E end with an oak COMMUNION TABLE of Jacobean design. Both this and the FONT, an oak octagon with volute brackets, are from the demolished St Andrew, Drumsheugh Gardens, Edinburgh. – STAINED GLASS, E lancets, Christ Teaching and the risen Christ, c. 1864. – MEMORIAL PLAQUE, eighth Baron Polwarth, †1920. – BELL, 1649, from Melrose Tolbooth, given 1721 by Countess of Haddington.

OLD CEMETERY, 0.5 km. N of the church. A separate parish was established here in the C17, the only relic of the church being a stone dated 1659, built into the memorial of Rev. Robert Scott, †1727.

Former MANSE (Easter House). By the old parish graveyard. Large, Victorian, of two storeys with piended and platformed roof and canted and square bays.

FORMAN MEMORIAL HALL. Presented by Mrs Maria Forman and designed by *J.P. Alison*, 1923. He added the gabled rectangular hall, and loggia (now glazed), to two single-storey cottages, dated G.P. 1854 (George Pott). The W end became the hall keeper's cottage, the E end was given gables and Venetian window for a small hall. Large Baroque entrance porch. The hall has a scissor-truss rafter roof.

OLD SCHOOLHOUSE. 1790. Two storeys, harled, with steep piended roof. Sandstone margins painted black. Single-storey schoolroom attached.

ROBERTON PRIMARY SCHOOL. Mid-C19(?). Two-storey schoolhouse, with schoolroom addition. Further alterations in 1884 (dated).

BORTHWICKBRAE HOUSE. *See* p. 126.
BORTHWICKSHIELS HOUSE. *See* p. 126.
CHISHOLME HOUSE. *See* p. 170.
HARDEN HOUSE. *See* p. 342.
HOSCOTE HOUSE. *See* p. 385.

ROMANNO BRIDGE

A small village, mostly built about the beginning of the C19 by Peter and William Sanderson at the crossing of the Lyne Water by the Edinburgh–Moffat road (A701); the neighbouring mansion of Romanno House was demolished c. 1950.

NEWLANDS SCHOOL. 0.2 km. SW. Built by *Thomas Lawson*, it seems originally to have incorporated a schoolmaster's two-storey house and single-storey classroom under the same roof; now all given over to classrooms. Twin-gabled front overlooking the road, dated 1876; arch-pointed window with central blind quatrefoil to the house.

OLD BRIDGE. Built by *James & Alexander Noble*, masons,

1773–4, a handsome segmental-arched structure with two subsidiary arches, constructed of rubble masonry with local red
sandstone dressings and parapet set out on a corbelled string
course.

DESCRIPTION. At the N approach to the Old Bridge (*see* above)
a mid-C19, three-bay TOLL HOUSE of red sandstone, harled at
the sides and extended to the rear. On the W side of the Peebles
road, which leaves the A701 just N of the bridge, is a red harled
two-storey block of eight bays with a three-bay dwelling house
at one end. Originally a woollen manufactory, this served for
many years as the incubator house of a celebrated poultry farm
established here *c.* 1913; now mainly residential. The farm
offices were opposite, in the mid-C19 former ROMANNO INN,
a tall, gable-roofed building of red sandstone neatly laid to
courses in brick-sized blocks with quoins and dressings of
white sandstone, probably from Deepsykehead. Further N, an
L-plan block of two-storey houses, some originally flatted, with
forestairs.

HALMYRE HOUSE, 2.2 km. NE. Restrained Scottish Baronial
style of 1856, probably incorporating part of a house of *c.* 1600.
Only the ground floor of the three-storey main block facing E
seems to survive from the early house. Above the principal
entrance, a commemorative panel with the arms of Richard
Gordon and his wife Catherine Ferrier. An earlier carved
panel, re-set in the court of offices, bears the initials of Wilkin
Johnstone († *c.* 1653) and his wife Margaret Joussie. – To the
N, a brick-lined WALLED GARDEN, with a square two-storey
pavilion (or dovecot?) on the W side and a bolection-moulded
doorway, possibly a relic of the early house, near the SE corner.

FLEMINGTON TOWER. *See* p. 283.
SPITALHAUGH. *See* West Linton.

ROWCHESTER HOUSE

4.5 km. SE of Greenlaw

A castellated Gothic house built *c.* 1830 for John Castell Hopkins,
in the style of James Gillespie Graham. A symmetrical composition with narrow square-plan angle towers rising above the
battlemented parapet, and square-headed hoodmoulds with
label stops over mullioned and transomed windows. Flat buttresses flank the gabled Gothic entrance doorway; above is a
traceried window. On the garden front buttresses enclose a
full-height canted bay. In 1913–14 *Peddie & Forbes Smith*,
added a kind of vernacular Scottish-Jacobean storey with plain
gables, hoodmoulded bipartite windows, and gabled wall-head
dormers with kneelers and finials. Inside, the hall was remodelled, given linenfold panelling and a stone chimneypiece. The
drawing room appears to retain its earlier decoration with a
Gothic arch to the bay window, and an attractive swirling
ribbed ceiling with pendants, and modillioned cornice. White
marble chimneypiece. – Balustraded garden TERRACES by
Peddie & Forbes Smith.

STABLES. Mid C19(?) with later additions. U-plan in red
snecked rubble with red sandstone margins. Centre gable with

weathervane, dated 1877, R.H.B. (Robert H. Broughton). Segmental-arched opening, flanked by carriage entrances. Long whinstone barn with steps at the W end to a store; entry for pigeons above in a pointed arch. – WEST LODGE, mid-C19, with some carved bargeboards. Ball-finialled circular gatepiers. – EAST LODGE, mid-C19, with three-bay ashlar front. Doric-columned porch *in antis*, supporting a deep cornice. Decorative cast-iron gates, 1914.

ROXBURGH   6030

A tranquil Teviotside village.

PARISH CHURCH. Built 1752 (date on tablet at centre of S front), of buff and pink rubble with ashlar dressings. The church is an orientated rectangle likely to be at least partly on the site of its medieval predecessor, and to its SE is the burial vault of the Kers of Chatto, which perhaps originated as an aisle off the S side of the earlier church. Remodelling in 1828 created a symmetrical S front with four tall arched windows at the centre, and lower windows towards each end below the inserted galleries (reached by external forestairs). The windows have keystones and imposts, and a similar window is set high in each gable wall. The W gable has a birdcage bellcote, with a ball finial at the apex of a square dome of ogee profile.

In 1878 major extensions by *W. C. Carnegie*, including a lateral 'aisle', a vestibule and a vestry, were added to the N, together with a N gallery; the E and W gallery forestairs were removed, though the blocked E stair doorway remains visible in the N wall. The new N 'aisle' has a broad entrance within a salient, with a window on each side; above the entrance is a triplet of lights within a containing arch, all of the openings on this front being of depressed two-centred form. The vestry is within the re-entrant between the N 'aisle' and the nave, its roof parallel to the latter. Within a gable on the E side of the N 'aisle' is a tablet with the arms of James IV.

From a vestibule below the N gallery, stairs lead up to the lofts in all three arms. The fronts of the lofts have raised and fielded panels, and there is a semicircular projection at the centre of the N loft, and quadrant projections at the N ends of the other lofts, where the doorways are located. Supporting the E and W lofts are cast-iron columns. Plaster ceilings of polygonal profile. – COMMUNION TABLE, timber-framed marble slab, with four rectangular corner legs and an octagonal pier at centre, 1923, designed by the *Rev. Henry Mathers*. – PULPIT also by *Mathers*. – STAINED GLASS, S wall, from E to W: Sower, *William Wilson*, 1946; Good Shepherd, 1929; King of Kings, 1934. – PLAQUES, on N gallery: arms of James IV and of Edinburgh Merchant Company. – CROSS SLAB, medieval, near N doorway. – SUNDIAL CORBELS, at SW and SE corners.

MEMORIALS. Several set into the exterior walls. E of entrance, Thomas Douglas, two arched panels with *memento mori*, below pediment. On W side N aisle, stone with three-quarter frontal relief portrait. Against the vestry, William

Weymes, minister, †1658, swan-neck pediment supported by Ionic pilasters and flanked by winged angel heads. E end, S wall, Hogg family, pilasters and pediment. W end, S wall, Rev. Robert Hogg, †1781, capped by shallow pediment.

CHURCHYARD. Of a number of enclosures, that of the Robertons, NE of the church, is the most impressive; first recorded death, 1830. KER OF CHATTO VAULT, SE of church, rectangular and originally covered by a barrel vault with a stone slab roof; an arch opened to the N, presumably into the earlier church.

Former RAILWAY STATION. Built for the North British Railway, 1850. Two-storeyed office, now a dwelling.

ROXBURGH VIADUCT, 0.5 km. E. By *G. Glennie*, 1850 (and closed 1964), it carried the St Boswells–Kelso–Berwick branch line over the Teviot. A splendid, curved viaduct of dressed sandstone incorporating six main skew arches of ashlar, together with shorter runs of subsidiary arches on either side. The river piers on the downstream side are extended to accommodate a low-level footbridge carried on lenticular wrought-iron trusses.

WAR MEMORIAL, SW of the church, comprising a granite cross on a stepped base.

DESCRIPTION. The former SCHOOL, to the rear of the church, is Late Victorian with label-moulded windows and an entrance porch topped by a miniature bellcote. The former MANSE (mainly 1820) on the SE side of the main street, has a three-bay front with an advanced centre rising to a triangular pediment; offices and later extensions to the rear. The remainder of the village comprises a mix of HOUSING, including a pair of late C18 cottages with corrugated-iron (formerly thatched?) roofs, a row of solidly built Victorian estate cottages with spreading eaves and dormer windows, a few post-war council houses and an increasing number of newly built villas and bungalows.

WALLACE'S TOWER, 0.2 km. S. Probably the 'towre of Rockesborough' razed by the English in 1545. The present remains are likely to represent a slightly later rebuild.

KERSMAINS, 1.1 km. N. Began as two single-storey cottages. In 1834 a storey was added, together with a two-storey, bow-fronted connecting wing providing dining and drawing rooms. Harled with black-painted margins. Traditional farm offices to the rear. A range of seven segmental-arched cartsheds attached to a large walled garden contiguous with the house. A single-storey and attic farm cottage with bracketed stone canopies to door and windows, and wall-head dormers, 1834.

ROXBURGH BARNS, 2.4 km. N. A prominent two-storey and basement harled farmhouse, *c.* 1840. Brick chimneys frame the piended roof. Steps to a consoled corniced doorway. Simple farm offices, including a good range of segmental-arched cartsheds.

ROXBURGH MAINS, 1.8 km. SW. 1835. A superior two-storey farmhouse of three bays with an advanced centre bay and block pediment. Doorway with cavetto reveals, architrave and cornice. Coursed fine sandstone, the rest harl-pointed rubble. Piended roof and brick chimneys on the transverse walls. Simple cornices and a bracketed archway to the good geometric stair with Edinburgh-type balusters. The only change is an access from the stair to the first floor of the servants' quarters. An excellent large range of contemporary farm offices, shown as existing on an 1835 survey, and incorporating an earlier farmhouse. Re-roofed and mostly slated, the original walls retained. Used as cattle courts and pens. Good range of basket-arched cartsheds with stores above, ventilated by timber-louvred openings. A threshing mill, added later, is still operating for farm use, but only the base remains of the brick chimney.

ROXBURGH MILL, 0.6 km. NE. A plain two-storey, three-bay farmhouse, c. 1830, fronts an early C19 two-storey cottage, with a single storey wing to the r. The four bays of cartsheds, with stores above and a lantern, were remodelled and extended later.

SUNLAWS HOUSE. *See* p. 711.

ROXBURGH CASTLE

6030

3.3 km. NE of Roxburgh

The impressive, but sadly wasted, remains of what was once the most powerful fortress in the Scottish Borders. Founded in the early C12, the castle, originally known as Marchmount, had already seen two prolonged periods of English occupation when recaptured by the Scots and 'pulled down to the ground' in 1314. Following the castle's return to English control in 1334, Edward III began a major programme of reconstruction, which continued during the following reign, when *John Lewyn*, the celebrated English mason, built a new line of defence and strengthened the existing walls at a cost of £1,910. A survey of 1416 paints a picture of a powerful, if poorly maintained, fortress equipped with well-defended gateways, battlemented curtain walls, a large hall and no fewer than eight towers, including a donjon called Douglas Tower. The castle was recaptured by the Scots in 1460, the besiegers' success being overshadowed by the death of James II through the bursting of one of his own cannon. Again demolished, the castle remained derelict until 1547–8, when an English army adapted part of the site as an artillery fort, designed by *Sir Richard Lee*, Surveyor of the King's Works, and built by *William Ridgeway*. The fort had an uneventful life, being surrendered to the Scots in 1551 and immediately razed.

The castle stands on a prominent steep-sided ridge rising to c. 25 m. at its summit, a short distance above the confluence of the Rivers Tweed and Teviot, and overlooking the site of the former burgh. Its inherent defensibility was enhanced by cutting a ditch on each side except the SE, where the Teviot skirts the base of the ridge. The ditch, re-cut c. 1400, is best-preserved on the SW side, where it measures up to 12 m. wide and 4 m. deep. These formidable defences must date, at least in part, from the EARLY CASTLE, which is also known to have included a church and a great tower. The LATE MEDIEVAL CASTLE, mentioned in the survey of 1416, seems to have comprised a roughly oblong inner bailey (c. 90 m. by 60 m.)

occupying the central portion of the ridge, with an outer bailey at either end, each provided with its own external gateway. Both gates can be identified today, the NE one, which stands near the apex of the ridge, retaining part of a D-shaped tower, vaulted on the ground floor, which probably flanked an entrance passage. From the tower a short length of curtain wall runs SE to cut off the remainder of the ridge. The masonry is of well-coursed sandstone blocks. Of the inner bailey there remain substantial portions of the SE curtain and a few fragments of the NW curtain. These are probably the old walls that *John Lewyn* contracted to raise to a height of 30ft (9.1m.) in 1378; he also agreed to provide each with a mid-turret and to build a new wall, with a gatehouse, across the ridge, linking the NW and SE curtains. As it now stands the SE curtain, constructed in random rubble masonry, is *c.* 5m. high and 1.8m. thick. There is no sign of the turret, but traces can be seen of two posterns overlooking the Teviot, mentioned in the survey of 1416.

It was evidently the inner bailey alone that the English remodelled as an ARTILLERY FORT when they reoccupied the ruined castle in 1547. On the NW and SE sides the medieval curtain walls were incorporated in the new defences, the NW wall being provided with two flankers to deter frontal assault. To SW and NE, however, where the extremities of the ridge remained outside the new fort, more substantial defences were required. Accordingly, turf-built ramparts *c.* 20ft (6.1m.) broad and high, with outer ditches of similar breadth and depth, were constructed across the ridge to join the medieval curtains on either side. Both ramparts had provision for mounting guns and each was equipped with a stone-built flanker. In addition, gun platforms were built at the N and W corners of the fort. These ramparts and gun platforms are readily identifiable today and the NW ditch is also well preserved. The ramparts probably follow the line of the earlier curtains of the inner bailey and may embody medieval masonry. Likewise, the W gun platform known as Bell Mount, which stands on the highest part of the ridge, may occupy the site both of the early great tower and of the late medieval donjon. The fort accommodated about 450 men, and a plan of *c.* 1547 shows the captain's lodging, brewhouse and bakehouse ranged along the SE side of the interior. The NE side was occupied by a storehouse, and the NW side by lodgings for the men. The entrance was placed at the S corner, where one of the medieval gateways had probably been situated.

The castle overlooks a level piece of ground, 0.5 km NE, at the confluence of the Rivers Tweed and Teviot. This was the site of the MEDIEVAL BURGH of Roxburgh, founded in the C12 and second in importance only to Berwick among the burghs of the region before being eclipsed by Kelso in the C15. It is known to have been enclosed by a defensive wall with gates, one evidently leading to a bridge across the Tweed. Within were schools, two churches and numerous houses, while immediately outside the S wall stood a convent of Grey Friars. It was abandoned in favour of the neighbouring burgh of Kelso in the C16–C17.

ST ABBS

A picturesque fishing village and harbour at Coldingham Shore, established in the early C19 to provide housing for fishermen, who formerly resided in Coldingham.

PARISH CHURCH. Originally a Free Church. 1892 by *J.L. Murray* of Biggar, and paid for by Andrew Usher of Northfield (*see* below); it became the parish church in 1929. Prominently set on the main approach to the village, its design is in a simplified unbuttressed Romanesque style, having pink rock-faced ashlar walls with polished dressings and a red-tiled roof. Arched windows along each flank. A three-storeyed E tower-porch, flanked by vestibules, terminates in a flat corbelled parapet. Above a transverse W vestry block is a small rose window. Interior reordered in 1947. – FONT, 1941.

ST EBBA'S CHAPEL, 2.4km. NW. A puzzling site traditionally identified as the Northumbrian double monastery of Urbs Coludi (*see also* Coldingham), founded by St Aebbe in the C7. A cliff-girt promontory is cut off from the mainland by a broad ditch with fragments of a lime-mortared stone wall on its inner lip. Upon the summit (*c.* 1 ha. in area) are one or two possible building platforms and the lime-mortared stone footings of an oblong building. Towards the end of the promontory, aligned from SW to NE, is a basically rectangular structure, *c.* 21.1m. by 6.6m. internally. Usually described as a chapel, it has more recently been suggested that it was a medieval ground-floor hall, and that the existing remains may be entirely secular in character. If so, the early monastery may have stood on KIRK HILL, some 0.8km. to the SE, where excavations were carried out in 1980. These suggested the palisaded defences of a burh or fort had been replaced by a turf and clay bank around the earlier C7. Several structures were traced within the enclosed area.

HARBOUR. The oldest part is the inner harbour (SW basin), by *Mitchell & Wilson,* 1831, providing a refuge for fishing boats. Improved 1848–99, and extended 1883–6 by *D. & T. Stevenson,* to the E and NW of the original basin. C20 additions. The original harbour has an L-shaped pier of well-dressed scabbled blocks (unfinished stone from a quarry), rusticated on the seaward faces. The harbour to the E is rectangular, and the NW extension runs as a straight pier from the shore. Coursed cream sandstone.

LIGHTHOUSE, St Abbs Head, 2km. NW. By *D. & T. Stevenson,* 1862. A small, but important, circular-plan lighthouse on a low base, with a triangular-paned lantern and finialled hemispherical cap. The FOGHORN sits on a semicircular-plan block to the N. LIGHTKEEPERS' COTTAGES, also by the Stevensons. Traditional one- and two-storey cottages in whitewashed brick with painted margins. M-gabled roofs.

VISITOR CENTRE (St Abbs and Eyemouth Voluntary Marine Reserve). Former Board School of 1886, with Tudor detailing.

DESCRIPTION. By the harbour are two mid-C19 houses: the harled and whitewashed CYRUS HOUSE of two storeys and attic was built as a fisherman's cottage, the family housed above with gear below. Remodelled 1972. ROCK HOUSE, of the same type, incorporates the natural rock in its base. On the cliff above the harbour, of most interest are SEAVIEW TERRACE and MURRAYFIELD, probably mid-C19, two streets of single-storey and attic fishermen's cottages, with decorative timber canopies and finialled and bargeboarded dormers. A fine row of almost unaltered fishermen's gear huts in front of Seaview Terrace was removed in the late C20, leaving only concrete bases. Those behind Murrayfield have been mostly adapted for other use. CASTLE ROCK at the S end of Seaview Terrace is a symmetrical three-bay gabled house, c. 1895. Whitewashed harl and painted band courses. Overhanging timber-bracketed eaves and mostly decorative bargeboards.

NORTHFIELD, 0.5 km. w. The lands and farm of Northfield were acquired by Andrew Usher in 1885. Prominently sited, the house is dated 1888–92. Two storeys with a three-storey, square, pyramidal-roofed entrance tower to the l., with a rope-moulded eaves course and some decorative brattishing. A two-storey octagonal tower with an octagonal spire is tucked between gables to the r. Coursed and rock-faced pink sandstone. Overhanging timber-bracketed eaves and decorative finialled bargeboards. A stone, pointed-arched GATEWAY with rock-faced voussoirs and quoins. Apex decorated with a carved head backed by a halo, probably St Ebba. Cast-iron gates.

ST BOSWELLS

A small village known as Lessudden until the late C19.

CHURCHES

Former PARISH CHURCH, Benrig, 1 km. S. Built in 1652, a short distance to the W of the medieval church, and lengthened by *Thomas Laidlaw* and *John Smith*, masons, and *Thomas Cochrane* and *James Paton*, wrights in 1789–91. Unroofed in 1951, and now reduced to footings. A T-shaped structure, with a porch at each end of the main body, and an offshoot in the NW re-entrant angle between main body and 'aisle'; there was a chamfered plinth course along the S side. Carved fragments, including some beast corbels, are said to have been built into the walls, but are now lost.

The older part of the CHURCHYARD, S of the church, has mainly C19 headstones, obelisks, pier memorials and some enclosures. There is what appears to be a medieval cross-incised grave-slab; a number of C18 ledger slabs and some headstones against the church wall.

By the church is MANSFIELD, the former manse built 1791, but extensively worked on by *John Smith*, 1828. Rear extension by *A. Herbertson & Son* of Galashiels, 1865.

ST MODAN'S PARISH CHURCH. Built 1844 as a Free Church, it became the parish church in 1940. A vestry was added in 1862, and there were further modifications in 1909, with major works of repair and reordering undertaken in 1957. Initially a short rectangle of snecked pink and buff rubble, with an axial

W porch, and with raised ashlar margins to the windows and quoins, it was lit by three pointed windows along each flank, and one on each side of the porch, all with intersecting timber tracery. In the course of the later modifications, identifiable in a change to stugged snecked masonry, the W gable was rebuilt, and a tower was erected above the porch. This tower steps inwards through its upper storeys, being capped by a squat belfry stage with three pointed arches to each face and a low pyramidal roof. Also as part of these later works the W window on each flank was extended up into a stilted gable, perhaps to accommodate a gallery that has since been removed. At the E end a chancel (with a S vestry) now dates largely from 1957. The interior is covered by a segmental plaster ceiling, with groined intersections over the W window on each side. – STAINED GLASS. E window, Christ the Vine, 1959; over chancel arch, Dove, 1985 by *Liz Rowley*(?).

CHURCH HALL, opposite, built as a mission hall by the former Parish Church congregation and dedicated 1911. Red sandstone with pointed-arch windows and gabled porch.

BURIAL GROUND, Birselees, 3.9 km SW. A platform at the N end indicates the likely site of a chapel granted to Dryburgh Abbey in the mid C12; it was abandoned in 1684. Several HEADSTONES with three-quarter portraits. Towards the NE corner a pedimented wall with the headstone of John Blakie, mason, †1772 (presumably the mason who worked at Ancrum church in 1761). Tuscan pilasters support a swan-neck pediment enclosing masonic symbols; on each side arched recesses contain other memorials, one housing a re-set headstone with double relief portrait for James Blakie and wife, †1739(?). 29

MAJOR BUILDINGS

CENTRE FOR SUSTAINABLE TECHNOLOGY, 1.5 km. W. Built as St Columba's College by the White Fathers Society, 1934, the design entrusted to *D. Chisholm Cameron* who is said to have followed the general plan of Dryburgh Abbey (q.v.), which nestles in the trees below. *Charles W. Gray* designed substantial additions, including a chapel, after a fire in the early 1950s. Gray worked with Reginald Fairlie in the late 1940s, which perhaps explains the simple lines of the building. Unfinished, and never great architecturally, but today an attractive landscape feature set like a beacon on the hilltop, reminiscent of an Italian monastery.

Scottish Vernacular in style, harled and cream-painted, mostly two storeys, with dormitory blocks along the S front, and a central tower with turret roof and a long astragalled vertical stair window; three small windows at the top. The block to the W was raised a storey and the E side rebuilt in 1947. The N range, with another tower, seems to have been built in the late 1930s. – At the E end is Gray's CHAPEL, of red sandstone mortared rubble, with long narrow circular-headed windows, and octagonal chancel surmounted by a cross. A central cloister with open corridors on the E, S and W, now glazed, and open loggia on the N. Converted to a conference centre by *Cameron Associates* from 1994, who added the monstrous glazed porch to the entrance.

PUBLIC HALL, Main Street. 1896. Red sandstone, Neo-Tudor, gabled with exposed rafters and large stone-mullioned windows each side. A bargeboarded gable to the front with hoodmoulded mullioned windows; clock and bellcast-roofed belfry added in 1897 for Queen Victoria's Jubilee. Flanking conical-roofed entrances; in front, cast-iron bracketed lights inscribed 'Coronation of Edward VII 1902'.

ST BOSWELLS PRIMARY SCHOOL. Late 1950s. Single-storey with much horizontal glazing, marred by later additions.

WAR MEMORIAL, w side of the A68. Celtic cross on a boulder-cairn base, *c.* 1920.

THE KENNELS, West Green. A large complex built for the Duke of Buccleuch's fox-hunting pack. Converted to housing by *Simpson & Brown*, 2002–3. Two ranges face SE across the Green. The earlier part is the single-storey six-bay block at the S end, quickly and cheaply provided in the early C19, in pink ashlar (badly weathered). Centre pediment and circular-headed window breaking the base of the pediment. To the rear there were kennels with a large court. Next along was the contemporary huntsman's house (dem.). A smart stable block of white ashlar completes the range. This must be the large improvement made in 1843, to provide more stabling for family and guests when a change of horse was required. In the centre, an archway of rusticated stone flanked by pedimented wings with oval openings in the pediments. Ranged round the courtyard behind, simple two-storey blocks with some C20 additions. To the NW a late C19, large and airy barn-store, with tall cast-iron columns, the horizontal timber slats sliding into slots in the columns. New housing to the rear.

DESCRIPTION

Beginning at the E end of the N side of MAIN STREET is a house, either remodelled or rebuilt, by *David Patterson*, dated 1724 above the door, with mason's tools and initials. On the opposite side WEIRGATE BRAE runs S, with two pleasant villas on the r.: WEIRGATE HOUSE, *c.* 1832, harled with tripartite windows on the ground floor, and MEADOW HOUSE, early C19, in red sandstone with small pediment. Continuing along Main Street, up a lane to the N are the former BRAEHEAD STABLES, converted for a veterinary practice. Simple U-plan range with ogee-topped flèche ventilators, the stalls well adapted for business use. On a wall, a mounted sundial, inscribed TM 1851, was presumably brought from elsewhere.

On the S side THE MANSE (originally a Free Church manse) of 1854. Two storeys, three bays with corniced doorpiece, in coursed red sandstone. At the corner of Jean Lawrie Court is a Gothic, gableted and pinnacled WELL-HEAD, with a decorated niche. Erected by the eighth Lord Polwarth, 1870s, to celebrate the first piped water supply to the village. Next along, SANDSFIELD HOUSE, a stylish mid-C19 single-storey ashlar street elevation, dropping to two storeys in red sandstone at the rear. The central entrance is set *in antis* behind a square-columned pedimented screen, flanked by tripartite windows with narrow sidelights. Attributable to *John Smith*, the entrance very similar to his Harryburn, Lauder (q.v.), and possibly his design (1844) of a house for Mrs Dunlop.

Continuing on the N side is THE CRESCENT, building in 1834 by *James Hunter*, mason, who was providing seven dwelling-houses, probably thatched, with gardens; all are now slated and some have been rebuilt or remodelled. This is followed by the entrance to The House of Narrow Gates (*see* below). A mid-C19 single-storey LODGE on the r., STABLE COTTAGE opposite, both altered. MORAY HOUSE, further on in Main Street, is an attractive mid-C19 two-storey villa with corniced door-piece and quoins. Next of note is EDENSYDE, the W part of two two-storey cottages; the door lintel is dated 1730, and a sundial mounted at an angle is inscribed J.A. 1731. Chamfered openings on the ground floor suggest these were two single-storey cottages, the walls raised later.

Beyond St Modan's Parish Church and the Public Hall (*see* Churches and Public Buildings, above), Main Street opens out to THE GREEN. On the N side, the former SCHOOL (Old Schoolhouse), by *John Smith, c.* 1836. Two storeys, three bays, in coursed red rubble with a corniced doorway and attached single-storey schoolroom with large windows. A late C20 octagonal library built in front spoils the setting. Then WEST CROFT, which has two-storey villas, most with canted bays and round-arched keystoned doorways. On the S side of The Green is GREENSIDE PARK, a group restored (1983) by *Dennis Rodwell* through the National Trust for Scotland's Little Houses Improvement Scheme. Two-storey, three-bay rubble house with three-bay, single-storey wing, formerly a shop. An extension to the front dated 1882 in a panel decorated with cable moulding and a riband. At the W end the SMITHY HOUSE. Early C19 single-storey with stone-gabled wall-head windows; a centre pilastered doorway with a small glazed quatrefoil above. L-shaped with smithy to the rear, still in use.

BUCCLEUCH ARMS HOTEL, across the A68, was built in the mid C19 by the Duke of Buccleuch to accommodate his hunting friends. Two storeys in red sandstone, gabled with exposed rafters. Much altered.

BRAEHEADS HOUSE, Main Street. Massed on a ridge above the village, a boldly individual house taking full advantage of its site. Designed in 1905–6 by *F. W. Deas*, a close friend of Robert S. Lorimer, who persuaded Deas to take up the study of architecture rather than follow a career in interior decoration. The client was John Cuthbert Spencer, whose family had iron and steel works at Newburn, Newcastle-upon-Tyne, but he died before work was complete.

Braeheads is Scottish Domestic in character, based on a Z-plan with much use of slated roofs and crowstepped gables, creating a picturesque skyline in the Lorimer tradition. The crowding together of elements and detail is rather wilful, being an assemblage of parts rather than a coherent design. The entrance to the house is contained within a crowstepped NW block, of gatehouse form, with double corbel course and a recessed two-storey doorpiece. On the NE elevation is a tall shouldered chimneystack – the shoulders unmatching – and, in the re-entrant angle with the SE wing, a turret with bell-shaped roof corbelled out above an arched squinch, like the stair-tower at Pilmuir House (Lothian), but here containing curved passages on each floor between the wings. Along the ground floor portholes light the servants' passage. Braehead's SE elevation is similar to the garden front of R. Rowand Anderson's house of Allermuir, Colinton (Edinburgh), but with an open loggia whose design Deas repeated at his home, The Murrel (Fife). The SW court elevation has a high terrace with access from the dining room corridor, with offices below. Along the SW boundary a high wall – like a fortification – protects the house from the country lane below.

The INTERIOR work was by *Scott Morton & Co*. One enters up a wide circular flight of steps through the porch, then up steps and through a screen wall into the 'Great Hall' with barrel vault and timber panelling (originally painted white). Yellow marble columned chimneypiece, an insertion that seems to have come from Minto Manse (by *W. H. Playfair*, 1827; burnt in the 1950s). The drawing room has a deep bay with wide windows to soak up the sun. The decoration is typical of the Lorimer style but has sadly lost a plaster frieze designed by *J.S. Rhind*. To the E, via a short curved passage, is the smoking room (now study), with a private stair leading down to the housekeeper's room. From the W end of the hall the corridor leads to a spacious timber scale-and-platt stair, with Renaissance-style balusters. At the end of the corridor, the charming octagonal dining room has a shallow-domed ceiling, the ribs outlined with tendrils of leaves and summer flowers – hollyhocks, lilies etc. Large windows give grand views; the N one appears to have been punched through the wall but is original.

The curving drive is entered from Main Street under a simple archway, and is flanked by a LODGE with Scottish Domestic detailing. The compact STABLES, designed for horses and motor cars, have square gatepiers with obelisk finials screening the courtyard; Scottish Vernacular with lots of crowsteps, skewputts and a turret to the NW. A screen wall links the stables to the house and obscures the servants' yard.

THE HOUSE OF NARROW GATES, Braeheads. The original house on this site (Tweedmount) forms the E end – two storeys, three bays, the front harled, with red sandstone dressings – to which a large C17-style Baronial addition was made in the early C20. This has prominent crowsteps, a turreted tower entrance with ogee-moulded door surround and a large battlemented corner tower, with conical cap, corbelled out from the first floor; elements which suggest *J.P. Alison* as the architect. – SUNDIAL, dated 1739. Carved face decorating the side of the dial, with gnomons.

THE HOLMES, 1.2 km. W. 1894, by *Thomas Leadbetter* of *Leadbetter & Fairley*, for Daniel Norman Ritchie. Red sandstone in a classical style with some Baroque theatricality of Gibbsian door and window surrounds, rightly described by a contemporary as 'chaste and elegant'. Rectangular plan with an octagonal entrance porch in the angle with a projecting wing to the SW. On the symmetrical river front, full-height canted bay windows flank an Ionic-pilastered and pedimented centrepiece. Service quarters continue to the NW, terminating in a dairy with an excellently detailed louvre.

Inside, the principal rooms are ranged along the SE and NE fronts with a corridor and staircase along the rear and billiards room (now library) in the SW wing. Excellent plasterwork by *Leonard Grandison*, including enriched cornices and ceilings with moulded ribs. Mantelpieces have broken architraves and ogee friezes; some incorporate shelving. The inner hall, lit by a large Venetian window, has a coved ceiling and frieze of Tynecastle canvas paper with seahorses and sea urchins. The stair, with two large panelled mahogany pedestals at the bottom, and a screen of Ionic columns across the top corridor, is lit by a large roof-light with a deep coved ceiling.

STABLES, 1902–8, probably designed by *R. & J. Grieve*, builders. A traditional court of offices in red sandstone with much use of crowstepped gables. The coachman's house, loose boxes and stables – still with their fittings – are approached through a miniature entrance with a low pointed turret and gilded weathervane; a pigeon loft with a row of entry holes from the court completes the picture. – WALLED GARDEN, *c.* 1902. High brick walls with stone coping. Contemporary greenhouse by *Mackenzie & Moncur*.

Former CHARLESFIELD MUNITIONS FACTORY, 1.5km. SW, within an expanding industrial estate. Opened by ICI in 1943, principally to make incendiary bombs. Several small factories lie scattered over a wide area, together with remains of ancillary buildings and a loopholed observation post. The factories are brick with concrete roofs, partly earth covered, supported on steel joists. Curved entrance passages and surrounding earth walls were designed to minimise the effects of an explosion. The principal buildings were linked to a railway system (dismantled) which connected with the main line at Newtown St Boswells.

KIPPILAW. *See* p. 470.

LESSUDDEN HOUSE. *See* p. 495.

SAUGHTREE   5090

CHURCH. Built 1872 for the Duke of Buccleuch. A modest unbuttressed two-cell building of buff snecked rubble. Early English style, with a porch towards the road; what appears to be a chancel is in fact a vestry. Paired lancets light the 'nave', with a triplet in the S gable wall, above which rises a gabled bellcote. – Grisaille STAINED GLASS, 1875. – MEMORIAL to Charles Jardine, †1886, with portrait.

SCOTSTON HOUSE   1040
1.2 km. E of Blyth Bridge

A delightful Georgian house of unusual design. It evidently dates from the 1750s or 1760s and was presumably built by Alexander Telfer, who acquired the estate in 1749.

The house comprises a N-facing, three-storey block of villa proportions with full-height panelled pilasters at the corners and
a pedimented Ionic porch; rising above the eaves cornice is a
central triangular pediment set out on moulded consoles. This
part, containing modest-sized family rooms, is flanked by substantial two-storey, three-bay wings housing large public rooms
on the first floor. They have two tiers of windows, the upper
ones round-headed with prominent imposts and keystones.
These wings may be slightly later than the centre part, for their
roofs partly encroach upon blocked second-floor windows in
the gable walls of the main block. The plan is essentially linear,
the whole house being one room deep except for the central
part of the main block, which projects at the rear as a semi-
octagonal bay.

The central entrance hall contains an elegant timber hanging
stair with alternating plain and twisted balusters. The layout
on the two main floors was originally the same. Short corridors ran E and W from the staircase along the N side of the
house, while behind the stair a doorway opened into the projecting bay on the S side, which at ground floor contains a
charming little morning room overlooking the garden;
enriched architraves to door and windows and a marble chimneypiece with carved entablature. The E room in the main
block, now united with the corridor, may always have been the
family dining room, while the adjacent wing houses the
kitchen, formerly connected by a service stair to the principal
dining room above. The rooms to the W were probably mostly
bedrooms, as today. On the first floor lateral corridors open
off the stairhead through Ionic-pilastered arches; another
handsomely fitted out chamber in the central bay. The main
block was probably always occupied by family bedrooms,
leaving the wings free for the very large dining room (now
library) and drawing room. Both have good modelled plaster
ceilings with covings above a modillioned cornice, that in the
library incorporating a centrepiece depicting Harvest. The
work is similar to that at Old Gala House, Galashiels, and
Ednam House, Kelso (qq.v.). In the drawing room is a handsome marble chimneypiece, possibly of Edwardian date.

STABLES, 0.1 km. SE. A courtyard square with a pedimented
entrance topped by a belfry; dated 1770 and refurbished 1909.
Behind, a WALLED GARDEN with an C18 copper sundial on a
later shaft. – Mid-C19 NORTH LODGE to A701, of red sandstone rubble with spreading eaves and a pair of octagonal
chimneys.

SELKIRK*

INTRODUCTION

The royal burgh of Selkirk sprawls over the steep gradient on the SE side of the Ettrick Water. Despite its long history its present urban form can be attributed to the C19 textile boom, though at the heart of modern Selkirk is a triangular medieval layout of streets set on a high plateau.

Some time during the reign of Alexander I, and probably by 1113, David, Earl of Huntingdon (later David I) founded a castle at Selkirk, subsequently making it the centre of an extensive hunting reserve known as Ettrick Forest. Also in 1113 David brought Tironensian monks to Selkirk, probably to a site at Lindean (q.v.), 3 km. NE of the castle. The monks moved to Kelso in 1128, but the castle survived into the C14, long enough to influence the topographical development of the early burgh. There was already an 'old town' at Selkirk when the castle was founded, and this may have been situated at Lauriston, close to the present Ettrick Road. The new town – probably established as a burgh by David I although not recorded as such until c. 1300 – is likely to have grown up on the ridge N of the castle, along what are now Castle Street and Back Row. There may have been a market place at the junction of Back Row and Kirk Wynd, where the road to Hawick forks E. As the burgh expanded, however, a larger market place seems to have developed on flatter ground N of the church, with a High Street continuing NE to intersect Back Row at the apex of the triangle.

   Following Robert I's grant of the Forest of Ettrick to the Douglases in the 1320s the castle was abandoned. Selkirk declined in importance and English raids further hampered its struggling economy during the C15 and early C16. However, a series of royal charters in 1536–40 confirmed Selkirk's status as a royal burgh, established a second annual fair and made the burgh an independent sheriffdom. At this time the burgh would primarily have contained timber-framed buildings; stone structures such as the Auld Kirk and a tower house in High Street were rarities. The tolbooth and market cross stood in the market place, the E, W and S ports were located at the burgh's extremities and the town walls were constructed of earth surmounted by a palisade.

---

* The introduction, account of the public buildings, mills and the burgh's description are by Sabina Strachan.

1   Heatherlie Church
2   Old Parish Church
3   Our Lady and St Joseph (R. C.)
4   Parish Church
5   Philiphaugh Congregational Church
6   St John's Episcopal Church
7   St Mary's West U. P. Church
8   United Reformed Church
9   West U. P. Church
10 Municipal Buildings
11 Sheriff Courthouse
12 Former Employment Exchange
13 Town House
14 Selkirk Health Centre
15 St Joseph's R. C. Primary School
16 Halliwell's House Museum
    and Tourist Information Centre
17 Victoria Halls

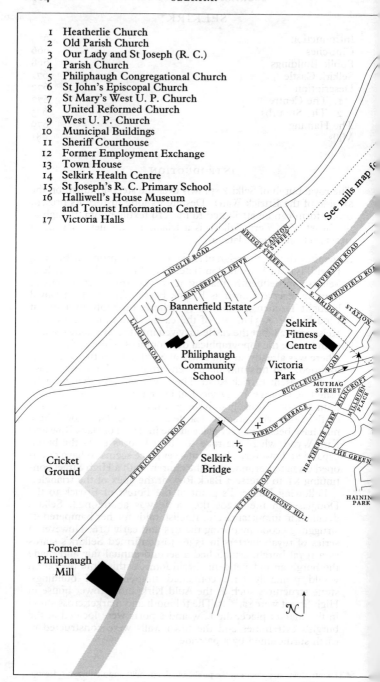

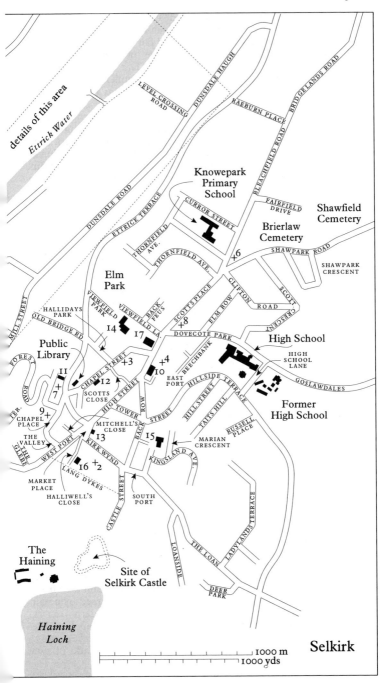

details of this area

Ettrick Water

LEVEL CROSSING ROAD

DUNSDALE HAUGH

RAEBURN PLACE

BLEACHFIELD ROAD

BRIDGELANDS ROAD

Knowepark
Primary
School

FAIRFIELD DRIVE

Shawfield
Cemetery

DUNSDALE ROAD

ETTRICK TERRACE

CURROR STREET

+6

Brierlaw
Cemetery

SHAWPARK ROAD

SHAWPARK CRESCENT

THORNFIELD AVE.

THORNFIELD AVE.

Elm
Park

CLIFTON

SCOTT CRESCENT

ROAD

MILL STREET

HALLIDAYS PARK

OLD BRIDGE RD

VIEWFIELD PARK

VIEWFIELD LA.

BACK FEUS

SCOTTS PLACE

ELM ROW

High School

14

17

+8

DOVECOTE PARK

HIGH SCHOOL LANE

Public
Library

FOREST ROAD

11

+7

CHAPEL STREET

+3

12

SCOTTS CLOSE

+4

10

BEECHBANK

EAST PORT

HILLSIDE TERRACE

GOSLAWDALES

Former
High School

TER.

9 +

CHAPEL PLACE

HIGH STREET

BACK ROW

HILL STREET

TAIT'S HILL

RUSSELL PLACE

THE VALLEY

THE GLEBE

WEST PORT

TOWER STREET

MITCHELL'S CLOSE

13

15

MARIAN CRESCENT

KIRK WYND

16

+2

LANG DYKES

CASTLE STREET

KINGSLAND AVE.

MARKET PLACE

HALLIWELL'S CLOSE

SOUTH PORT

LADYLANDS TERRACE

The
Haining

Site of
Selkirk Castle

THE LOAN

LOANSIDE

DEER PARK

*Haining
Loch*

1000 m
1000 yds

Selkirk

Shoemaking was the staple trade of the burgh in the late C16 and C17, and although the craft began to subside after the 1745 Jacobite rising, Selkirk's markets and fairs were sustained. Poor communications and the power of the town guilds hampered the growth of the textile industry in the late C18 and early C19. Despite the tentative establishment of a waulk mill and an incle (linen tape) manufactory, substantial progress became possible only with the passing of the 1833 Municipal Reform Act, which demoted the guilds. The opening of a turnpike road (Ettrick Terrace) to Galashiels in the same year revolutionised the town's fortunes, and mills were constructed on the NE bank of the river from 1837, a process accelerated by the building of the Galashiels–Selkirk branch railway line in 1855–6. The influx of textile workers more than trebled the burgh's population in the second half of the C19 century to *c.* 6,000. During the same period the town spilled out beyond its medieval bounds, with the erection of rows of workers' housing and terraces for managers. Public and private housing continued to creep up the steep hillside to the E and along Bleachfield Road to the N. The mid-C20 renewal around Back Row, South Port and Kirk Wynd and the building of the Bannerfield estate to the NW have had significant impact upon the townscape. Today, the ongoing rehabilitation of the mill area along Dunsdale Road is doing much to bolster Selkirk's economy, following widespread decline of the textile industry.

CHURCHES

Former HEATHERLIE CHURCH, Yarrow Terrace. *See* p. 677.

OLD PARISH CHURCH, Kirk Wynd. Abandoned in 1863; now a burial enclosure.* The parish originated in the early C12, but the rubble-built shell, now roofless and ivy-swathed, results largely from a rebuilding of 1748. Rectangular plan with lateral S laird's 'aisle'. Open arch in E wall, surmounted by crow-stepped gable and bellcote. Built into the W wall is a weathered C17 incised slab thought to depict one of the Scotts of Harden and Oakwood. Within the S aisle, arched recesses in a red sandstone skin frame memorials to the Murrays of Falahill and Philiphaugh. Memorials in a variety of styles inside the main body of the church, including Neo-Baroque monuments to the Brown family. Around the CHURCHYARD an attractively random spread of mainly C17, C18 and C19 memorials, including several obelisks. A number of the earlier stones have full- or three-quarter-length portraits of the deceased.

OUR LADY AND ST JOSEPH (R.C.), High Street. 1886, by *George Goldie* of London. An understated five bay aisleless rectangular structure, set well back from the street. The main (SE) front is of whinstone rubble with ashlar dressings, pierced by a pair of lancets; suspended between the lancets is a modern STATUE of the Virgin Annunciate. A vestibule and Chapel of the Resurrection were added to the E by *Kathleen Veitch*, *c.* 1965. Scissor-braced roof. – ALTAR, carried on an arcade of two

---

* Its replacement in Ettrick Terrace, 1861–3 by *Brown & Wardrop*, was demolished in 2005.

reused trifoliate arches. – STAINED GLASS. The Virgin and St John, in side walls flanking the altar; roundel behind altar, Virgin and Child.

PARISH CHURCH, High Street. Originally Selkirk First United Presbyterian Church, it became the parish church in 1986. An imposing, if slightly mechanical, Early English composition by *Robert Baldie*, 1878–80. The main (NW) front is of buff stugged ashlar with polished dressings. The central gabled section houses the main entrance, flanked by steeply pointed lancets, above which is a four-light traceried window, and to its S the laterally roofed end bay of the aisle has paired lancets. The front is dominated by the three-storey tower, with lancets to each stage, capped by a tall stone spire with elongated broaches. The flanks are of coursed whinstone rubble, with lancets separated by buttresses. Beyond the SE end of the church is a hall complex.

Inside, five-bay arcades are carried on slender cylindrical cast-iron columns, with mid-height caps supporting the horse-shoe gallery. The entrance end is now cut off by a glazed screen. The pulpit, communion table and organ are at the SE end, where there were reorderings in 1900 (when the organ was installed) and 1952–5. A boarded ceiling of triangular profile was inserted in 1955. – FONT. Grey marble, cruciform base and circular bowl, in memory of the Rev. John Lawson (1850–98). – STAINED GLASS. SE windows, Moses, Samuel and Isaiah.

Former PHILIPHAUGH CONGREGATIONAL CHURCH, Yarrow Terrace. Now flats. 1853, built as Christ Church Episcopalian Church, but after a quarrel the patron offered it to the Congregationalists. Squared rubble with red sandstone dressings. Textbook Early English, a structure of two cells with a porch off the NW flank and a bellcote on the SW gable. A triplet of lancets survives in the chancel gable.

ST JOHN'S EPISCOPAL CHURCH, Bleachfield Road. 1867–9, by *J.M. Wardrop* of *Brown & Wardrop*. An effectively grouped small-scale building of whinstone rubble with red sandstone dressings, in the English Decorated style. An aisle-less two-compartment core with a porch off the S flank, and an organ chamber and vestry off the N side of the chancel. An octagonal spired bellcote, carried on squinch arches, develops out of the buttressing at the SW angle of the nave (caps and corbels blocked out). Cross finials to the E walls of both nave and chancel. The W wall has a four-light traceried window; the E wall has three single lights, with trefoils above trifoliate arches at their heads. The nave flanks have two-light windows with either trefoils or spherical triangles. Doors carved with angels holding scrolls inscribed PAX INTRANTIBUS.

Inside, the church has a scissor-braced roof carried on corbelled wall-posts; much of the overall impression is created by FURNISHINGS by *Robert S. Lorimer* of 1908–12, including the RETABLE, a plain tripartite composition with foliate border and cresting; the SCREEN with a linenfold dado, foliate cusping to the openings, surmounted by a plain cross with Evangelist symbols at the extremities, and rectangular PULPIT with linen-fold panels and an angel in relief at the angle. – STAINED

GLASS. E window: Virgin, Good Shepherd, St Mary Magdalene. Chancel, N side: Noli Me Tangere and Annunciation; S
side: Gethsemane and road to Calvary, *c.* 1880; Crucifixion.
Nave, S side, Noli Me Tangere, by *Wailes*, of Newcastle, 1869;
Salvator Mundi (German?); N side: SS John and Christopher,
and W window: Noah, Moses, St Stephen and St Paul, both by
Herbert Hendrie, 1933.

UNITED REFORMED CHURCH, Scotts Place. Rectangle of
whinstone rubble with red sandstone dressings. Porch against
the SW wall and a low vestry block at the SE end. The NW front
has clasping buttresses capped by square, gabled pinnacles and
is pierced by three lancets.

Former WEST UNITED PRESBYTERIAN CHURCH, Chapel
Place. Derelict. *c.* 1850, rectangular with lower vestry block at
SW end. Minimally Gothic entrance front of snecked whinstone with droved ashlar dressings, the doorway framed by
three Y-traceried windows.

PUBLIC BUILDINGS

Former EMPLOYMENT EXCHANGE, Chapel Street. Now Social
Work Department Local Office. 1938, by *J. Wilson Paterson* of
H.M. Office of Works. Single-storey, Neo-Georgian with subtly
modern overtones. The five-bay elevation overlooking Ettrick
Terrace has three central windows slightly recessed with keystones. Main entrance on Scotts Close with flat entablature
with scrolled brackets. Flat-roofed outshot to r., *c.* 1980s.

HALLIWELL'S HOUSE MUSEUM, Halliwell's Close. *See*
Description 1.

KNOWEPARK PRIMARY SCHOOL, Curror Street. Public school
of 1872. Lightly Jacobean single-storey and basement in red
sandstone with yellow sandstone surrounds and quoins, slate
roof with exposed rafters and two decorative bellcotes. The
front elevation has a central, slightly advanced gable with two
end gables (that to the r. forms the NE end of the small SE
wing), its composition marred by unsympathetic additions of
c. 1960. Next door is a large two-storey whinstone building
built for secondary education in *c.* 1918, four bays of its main
elevations crowned by two gables projecting from the ends of
the double-hipped roof. Along Anderson Road, later ranges of
the late 1950s to the 1980s.

MUNICIPAL BUILDINGS, High Street. A classical villa built in
1836 for Dr Thomas Anderson, taken over by burgh in the late
C19. Symmetrical, of five bays and two storeys in yellow sandstone with a Doric-pilastered doorcase beneath a simple entablature. Projecting quoins, string course, bold cornice and
surrounds of ashlar. The four-bay harled coach house to the l.
served as the town's fire station until 1978. NE wing converted
to residential use as part of the East Port scheme (*see* p. 673).

PHILIPHAUGH COMMUNITY SCHOOL, Linglie Road. 1875,
built by *A. Herbertson & Son* as the Selkirk Landward School.
Single-storey, whinstone with bargeboarded gables. Small
gabled extension of 1890 to centre of the main front. The
development of the Bannerfield Estate (*see* p. 679) from 1949
necessitated major additions and remodelling, notably an

L-plan arrangement of three, harled two-storey steel-framed classroom blocks by *J. & J. Hall*, 1954–7, and a flat-roofed entrance. At the s corner a COMMUNITY CENTRE, 1985. Convergent monopitch corrugated steel roofs and high-level and corner windows create varied elevations.

PUBLIC LIBRARY, Ettrick Terrace. The former jailhouse, built in 1803–4 to replace the tolbooth prison after the building of the new Town House (*see* below). Extended in 1865–6 by *A. Herbertson & Son* and converted for library and reading room in 1884 at the behest of Thomas Craig-Brown, a local historian, who donated it to the burgh in 1888. A dominant, two-storey, four-bay, gabled block with small segmental-arched windows for the cells above Ettrick Terrace is bound by string and eaves courses; crowstepped roof with single steeply pitched dormer and end chimneystack. This was extended NE in the early C20 by a single bay with turret; three square openings and an oriel were inserted at ground floor. The jail was originally surrounded by a high wall with rounded corners (remnants survive), entered via a gatehouse (replaced in the late C19 by a house with advanced, pedimented nepus gable) on Back Road (now Chapel Street); Ettrick Terrace was only laid out in 1833. Herbertson's extension was built at right angles to the jailhouse and consists of the harled square-plan tower with projecting round turret. An underground passage was created to the basement of the Sheriff Courthouse (*see* below), which was built on the other side of Ettrick Terrace in 1868–70. The crowstepped arched gateway on Ettrick Terrace, with burgh seal, is probably of 1888. A small blockwork stair-tower dates to *c.* 1990. Inside, the first-floor barrel-vaulted reading room has a marble memorial panel with a bronze medallion portrait of the Selkirk writer and scholar, Andrew Lang (†1912) by *Percy Portsmouth*, 1915.

SELKIRK BRIDGE, over the Ettrick Water. 1980. Steel parapets and two shallow segmental arches centrally supported upon a single lozenge-shaped reinforced-concrete pier. Yellow sandstone returns belong to its 1778 predecessor. An earlier five-arch bridge, of 1739–40, stood downstream; a single stone remains *in situ*. Both C18 bridges succumbed to flooding.

SELKIRK FITNESS CENTRE, Victoria Park. By *Borders Regional Council*, *c.* 1980. Expansive but undistinguished steel-framed structure faced with pink brick and corrugated steel; large windows along the SW façade light the pool; small additions include a canopied entrance to the SE.

SELKIRK HEALTH CENTRE, Viewfield Lane. Developed around Viewfield, an early C19 classical villa. Ashlar-fronted, five-bay, single-storey and basement with shallow-hipped roof and steps to the pedimented Doric doorpiece. Wings l. and r., slightly set back, added by 1858; hipped roofs and end chimneystacks. Broad octagonal corner towers added to the rear. The villa (Andrew Lang Unit) became the Cottage Hospital in 1920, with later grey-harled and clumsy additions much disguising its impressive form. Set at right angles is the low, flat-roofed 1970s MEDICAL PRACTICE, rendered in vertical bands. Large abstract mosaic next to the recessed entrance.

Former SELKIRK HIGH SCHOOL (now Argus Centre),

Goslawdales. 1896–7. Built of coursed whinstone enlivened by red sandstone margins, stone-mullioned windows and red clay ridge tiles. Originally cruciform plan with a two-bay advanced centre on the NE side between single-bay wings with a central bellcote. Relieving arches picked out in red masonry add to the pleasing aesthetic. The W re-entrant angle was infilled c. 1918 to create a near-symmetrical NW composition using the same materials and Jacobean language. Small shallow-hipped extension to the S corner.

SELKIRK HIGH SCHOOL, Hillside Terrace. Begun 1959 to succeed the earlier High School (*see* above), extended 1973 to form an L-plan. The N arm is the early part; pink-harled flat-roofed one- and two-storey block with large windows separated by projecting margins, mullions picked out in brick as is the recessed entrance. The main entrance is through a three-storey blockwork block. The functionalist four-storey W arm of 1973 has narrow bands of windows with the shallow-pitched hall at the pivot between the main ranges. Detached steel-framed HALL of c. 2000 with a segmental-arched roof, five slim windows at one end and low aisles along its sides.

SHERIFF COURTHOUSE, Ettrick Terrace, 1868–70. One of the most conspicuous features of the town, built as the County Buildings by *David Rhind* at a cost of £10,152. Opulent Scottish Baronial style, set on a steep downhill slope opposite the jailhouse (*see* Public Library, above), with which it is linked underground. The yellow sandstone front has three broad bays with a central rope-moulded round-arched doorway and double-height oriel above. A walkway from the street is carried on five round arches to a subsidiary entrance into the SW wing, but dominating all is a massive five-storey round donjon with pierced parapet. The Forest Road façade is of four storeys, the upper stage defined by a stepped string course. Resplendent courtroom with open-timber roof.

ST JOSEPH'S R.C. PRIMARY SCHOOL, Back Row. The C19 former Burgh School. Whinstone with yellow sandstone margins, slate roof and projecting rafters. The gable of the N wing has cusped bargeboards with a mullioned double window below and single window beneath the string course to the basement. Small gabled outshots for the girls' and boys' entrances. Small, though conspicuous, additions to the S wing of c. 1960.

Former TOWN HOUSE, Market Place. Built 1803–4 as the Town Hall and Sheriff Courthouse, where Sir Walter Scott dispensed justice until 1832; the building has been converted into Sir Walter Scott's Courtroom Museum by *Douglas Hogg* of *Borders Regional Council*. Designed by a *Mr Lees*, following a competition to replace the early C16 tolbooth, whose materials were reused; the total cost amounted to £1,292. Classical, square plan of three bays and two storeys with a hipped roof and 33 m.-high five-stage and spired clock tower advanced in the centre, whose octagonal bell-chamber contains the 1757 bell from the old tolbooth. The spire has three blind oculi to each plane. To l. and r. of the tower's base are shopfronts inserted c. 1870 when the courthouse was removed to Ettrick Terrace (*see* above). The entrance is via Fleshmarket Street and through antechambers via a forestair up to one of two C19 outshots to the rear. It is likely that the ground floor housed cells, while the main entrance led to a flight of steps to the courtroom, which has replica furnishings. The tower has a STAINED GLASS window by *J. Milroy & Son* of Galashiels, inserted in 1891 to commemorate those who fell at Flodden.

VICTORIA HALLS, Scotts Place. Fine red sandstone French 97 Renaissance edifice of 1895–6 by *Hippolyte J. Blanc*. Three-bay main façade with a central triangular pediment, with an oculus, supported by Ionic pilasters which frame at first floor a Venetian window and flanking double windows. Central porch with an open pediment on Ionic columns. The side elevations have a Venetian window beneath end stacks, but on the Chapel Street elevation this is accompanied by a round, ogee-capped three-storey stair-tower. Harled hall at the rear with three round-arched windows; further additions of 1960s–70s. Inside, the main hall has a vaulted roof and stage; the design of its square panelling reflected on the balcony opposite. A lesser hall is placed across the front of the upper storey; both halls retain their lavish original features.

The grounds include a large FOUNTAIN of uncertain date with a female figure as its centrepiece, formerly on the Philiphaugh estate (q.v.). Incorporated into the boundary wall is a memorial plaque to James Brown, poet and man of letters (†1904) by *Thomas J. Clapperton*, 1931. Also by *Clapperton* is the bronze figure of 'Fletcher', traditionally the only survivor of eighty townspeople who fought at Flodden Field, commissioned by the burgh to commemorate the 400th anniversary of the battle in 1913; he is depicted wearily returning with halberd in one hand and bearing an English banner in the other.

SELKIRK CASTLE
off Castle Street.

Originally part of the demesne lands of the kings of Scots. The existing remains of the castle founded *c.* 1113 by Earl David, now largely tree-covered, comprise an irregular-shaped mound (73 m. by 56 m.) of mainly natural origin having a roughly circular summit at its N end. A surrounding ditch can be seen on the N and E sides, while to the S the mound falls steeply to Haining Loch; the entrance was probably on the W side, where the ditch has been lost. The C12 castle was evidently of motte-and-bailey type, the mound summit (12 m. in diameter) constituting the motte and the remainder the bailey. In 1302 the castle was refurbished as a pele for Edward I, being provided with a timber tower and palisade and a stone gateway (*Reginald the engineer* and *Stephen of Northampton*, master carpenters). The original configuration was preserved, for the building accounts indicate that the palisade was to have a total length of 57 perches (*c.* 285 m.), a figure that corresponds closely to the circumference of the surviving bailey, inclusive of the motte. In this phase of occupation the tower presumably occupied the summit of the motte, while the principal gateway is likely to have stood, as before, on the W side of the bailey.

DESCRIPTION

1. The Centre

The fledgling burgh developed around the crossroads to the immediate N of the royal castle (*see* above), but the focus of trade soon shifted to a larger market place at the NW end of Kirk Wynd, which with High Street and Back Row forms a triangle of streets at the heart of the town.

The description begins with the triangular MARKET PLACE, on whose E side the tolbooth was built in C16. This was replaced in 1803 by the loftily spired former Town House and Sheriff Courthouse (*see* above), in front of which is the appropriately placed but badly overpainted SIR WALTER SCOTT MEMOR-IAL of 1839 by *A. Handyside Ritchie*. Scott, robed in his guise as Selkirk's Sheriff, stands on a pedestal decorated with the Selkirk and Scott arms. Base replaced in 1932 by *Dick Peddie & Walker Todd* (similar to the original). The Mercat Cross was removed in 1766, its site marked by a cobbled octagon. The tron stood immediately behind the PANT WELL, set further W on a second island which was built in 1706 as the first munic-ipal water supply. Rebuilt in 1898 by *Peddie & Washington Browne*, who replicated its original box-like form with pilastered corners and dentilled cornice but extended it sky-wards with a parapet surmounted by pairs of obelisk finials at its corners and a triumphal lion atop a central crocket-capitalled shaft (originally three times higher).

The NW and E sides of Market Place read as a continuation of High Street. Beginning at the W corner of the NW side, the TOWN ARMS INN of 1876 has a rope-moulded string course above the ground floor, and an arched pend to C18 buildings in BOGIE'S CLOSE on the l., with a re-set late medieval carved animal head. The whinstone, classically proportioned No. 2 was the original Freemasons' Hall. Beyond is the elegant two-storey and attic, yellow sandstone BANK OF SCOTLAND, *c.* 1860s, with balustraded first-floor balcony in front of a Corinthian-pilastered three-light window. Then the colourful FLEECE HOTEL, whose elaborate third storey has ogee dormerheads. Ettrick Road, laid out as a turnpike road in 1833, interrupts the NW streetscape, while Nos. 8–10 to its r. has a fine Victorian shopfront.

The street narrows as it joins HIGH STREET, which begins with the early C19 COUNTY HOTEL, whose main façade (Nos. 3–11) has a Tuscan Doric columned doorpiece and a platform-roofed third storey of *c.* 1950. A fine C18 Assembly Room and coaching stables to the rear have been demolished. A memor-ial plaque with bust of the artist Tom Scott (1854–1927) adorns the second floor of the SELKIRK INSTITUTE reading room, 1883, at No. 51. The adjacent crowstepped, gable-fronted SOUTHERN REPORTER building of 1885 provides a light, Baronial interlude. Further on is SCOTTS CLOSE, which has in its midst delightful vernacular ranges with forestairs and a former Telephone Exchange of 1938 by *J. Wilson Paterson* of *H.M. Office of Works*, now a SALVATION ARMY CITADEL. Back in the High Street is THE HERMITAGE, a charming two-

storey three-bay whinstone hipped Georgian villa of *c.* 1810 set
back from the street with a corniced doorpiece, advanced
centre and tablet above. This was the extent of the medieval
town marked by its East Port until 1765. To its r. is Our Lady
and St Joseph Church (*see* Churches, above) and slightly
further on at the corner with Chapel Street is the two-storey
canted and bowed E corner of the former CO-OPERATIVE
STORE with shaped gables on its N side; four-bay block to the
rear by *J. & J. Hall*, 1897, now flats.

Returning down the SE side of HIGH STREET are the Parish
Church and Municipal Buildings (*see* Churches and Public
Buildings, above), behind which are cream-harled three-storey
flats and semi-detached houses built in 2001 by the Eildon
Housing Association as part of their EAST PORT scheme; the
U-plan MUNGO PARK COURT for sheltered housing is of the
1990s. Standing at High Street's junction with Back Row is
a MONUMENT to Selkirkshire-born explorer Mungo Park   36
(1771–1806), who led major expeditions to map the River
Niger and tragically drowned in that same great river.
His statue was erected in 1859 by public subscription in
front of the home (*see* Municipal Buildings, above) of Dr
Thomas Anderson, the surgeon to whom Park served his
apprenticeship. The proud tall figure by *Andrew Currie* of
Darnick stands atop a square base with diagonally set corner
pilasters, elaborate lion heads and tapered pedestal. Badly
overpainted, but adorning the base are beautifully executed
life-size bronze figures and pictorial panels recording Park's
expeditions in West Africa by *Thomas J. Clapperton*, 1906 and
1912.

Behind is the UNION HALL, 1876; its two-storey façade
has a 1–1–3–1–1 arrangement of bays, the outermost
bowed. Further r. is the former British Linen Co. Bank by
David Cousin, 1863, its fine Victorian façade topped by a
pair of square dormers behind balustrades with a central
nepus gable. Nos. 40–42, on the site of the Black Swan
Inn (marked by a panel depicting a swan) has encaustic
tiles of *c.* 1900 on the door jambs by *James Duncan Ltd.* of
Glasgow, recalling its former use as butcher's shop and dairy.
To its r. the pink sandstone ABBEYFIELD HOUSE with a
heavily rusticated ground floor and dentilled cornice. No. 26
stands on the site of the incle manufactory of 1771–3, which
represented one of Selkirk's first steps into the weaving industry. Tower Street was broken through in the early C19, when
the road level was raised and a ruinous tower house at No. 18
demolished.

The SE side of MARKET PLACE begins with No. 20, which projects forward of its neighbours in High Street. Close to the
Town House (*see* above), the monochrome CROSS KEYS INN
has a late C20 platform-roofed third storey, which mars its
appearance. Beyond Fleshmarket Street, which formerly led to
the Secession meeting house of 1759 but now provides access
to council housing (*see* below), is a white-rendered POST
OFFICE which replaced C18 tenements. Finally, a three-storey
whinstone tenement of 1820 at No. 33 with ashlar-fronted
ground floor.

Behind the s arm that encloses Market Place, at Nos. 38–39, is a group of renovated vernacular buildings in HALLIWELL'S CLOSE. HALLIWELL'S HOUSE MUSEUM is Selkirk's oldest surviving domestic property, dating from *c.* 1800 but on the site of earlier ranges. Walter Halywall of Duns owned most of the buildings in the close by 1768. Over time dwellings behind the shops on Market Place became stores and in the 1950s these were converted, by the owner Fred Robson, to house 'Halliwell's House Museum of Old Ironmongery'. Originally, the low, two-storey whinstone rubble range included a byre at the sw end. Converted into a local history museum in 1983–4 by *Borders Regional Council*; one of its two doorways was blocked and a steel stair to the new upper floor was installed.

The early C19 buildings to either side of the round-arched gateway to the graveyard of the Old Parish Church (*see* Churches above) on KIRK WYND were cleared in 1910 for road widening. CASTLE STREET leads to The Haining (*see* p. 679); its EAST LODGE disguised behind heavy *c.* 1960s extensions. All of the C19 terraces that formed Castle Street, Kirk Wynd, South Port, upper Back Row and the sw side of lower Tower Street (and the last two C18 houses in Market Place) were cleared and replaced from the mid 1960s by *Sir Frank Mears & Partners* for the Town Council's OLD TOWN RENEWAL scheme. While motifs such as forestairs and the general scale of the development relate to the vernacular, the planning reflects contemporary design with façades stepped back from the street and groupings of dwellings around courts and terraces accessed off the main streets. The port marking the s boundary of the town stood at the junction of SOUTH PORT and Kingslands Avenue until 1767. Notable features within the modern development include a large re-set carving of a 'souter' (shoemaker) at No. 72 BACK ROW, and between No. 64 and No. 66 there is a re-set marriage lintel dated 1700. In the lower half of the street C19 buildings are retained, including a steeply pitched-roofed COTTAGE at No. 28 and the broad, pale grey whinstone VOLUNTEER HALL of 1867 with rusticated ashlar pilasters beneath the projecting entablature carried on scrolls. Adjacent is the MASONIC HALL, 1887, by *Hippolyte J. Blanc*, with square pend and turret to its r. bay. At Nos. 17–19 TOWER STREET is the Classical GUIDE HOUSE, 1829, with oversailing stair, to the rear of which is a vernacular courtyard.

Behind the NW side of High Street is CHAPEL STREET (formerly Back Road), which marked the W extent of the medieval burgh. Approaching from the NE end, the principal buildings of interest are the hipped, two-storey, whinstone mid-C19 ETTRICKBRAE set behind a high wall on Hallidays Park, and RAEBANK, to its SW, built as the Second United Secession Church (converted to residential use, *c.* 1920s). Nos. 3–17 Chapel Street are C19 basemented tenements, opposite which are the backlands of the High Street across which the old Grammar School was built (dem.), though in general represented by C19 vernacular buildings like CHAPEL STREET STORE. Late C20 infill includes the Eildon Housing Association's SOUTER COURT set back from the street.

Back Road once continued along Backsides (Chapel Place) until
it was bisected in 1833 by ETTRICK TERRACE, the main N
approach into the town. Following this route is the single-
storey late C19 CONSERVATIVE CLUB, opposite the former
jailhouse (*see* Public Library, above), with crenellated parapet
and hoodmouldings. The street was dominated until 2005 by
St Mary's Church of 1861–3 by *Brown & Wardrop* (dem.), but
the principal accent is now provided by the Scottish Baronial
flourish of the Sheriff Courthouse (*see* above) and Ettrick   96
Lodge and Ettrickdene. This prominent ensemble in yellow
sandstone and harling comprises the resplendent ETTRICK
LODGE to the N (1853, remodelled for T. Craig Brown by
David Rhind, 1870), ETTRICKDENE, *c*. 1870s, to the S and the
intervening COACH HOUSE. The E façade of Ettrick Lodge is
of three storeys with a four-storey tower to its NE corner. The
gabled advanced centre bay has a rope moulding over the
arched doorway; above, a shield with the initials TCB. A six-
bay loggia links the Coach House, which reads as part of
Ettrickdene – one and a half storeys, advanced centre with
prominent conical-roofed corner turrets.

Returning S, the fine two-storey, yellow sandstone KIRK-
BRAE sits aloft with double-height bay window facing the tiered
WAR MEMORIAL, 1922, by *Robert S. Lorimer* on the corner of
CHAPEL PLACE (formerly Backsides). A high base supported
by a column topped by a foliated cross, and in a round-arched
niche on the base is a bronze figure of Victory holding a wreath
and sword, by *Thomas J. Clapperton*. To the r. of the derelict
West U.P. church (*see* Churches, above) is BEMERSYDE CRES-
CENT, 1967, built on the site of the parish manse of 1806.
FLETCHER COURT, on the W corner of THE VALLEY, was built
on the site of Selkirk's brewery; to its r. is the white-harled
QUEEN'S HEAD INN, with an oriel above its chamfered corner
to WEST PORT. The port was removed in 1771. The Forest Inn
is commemorated in a plaque to the SW of its original site while,
further uphill, a 1622 marriage lintel has been inserted into
Nos. 16–18. MITCHELL'S CLOSE opposite incorporates C17
fragments behind its C19 façades. HALLIWELL'S RESTAU-
RANT at Nos. 31–33 is a distinctive early C20 three-storey, gable-
fronted half-timbered affair. Nos. 37–47, descending towards
The Green, are early C19. LANG DYKES, on the r., marks the
old burgh boundary and provides a path to Castle Street.

2. The Suburbs

During the second half of the C19 there was significant expansion around Selkirk's medieval core to house the influx of workers
attracted by industrial development along the Ettrick Water. By
the end of the century development had spread along the lower
part of the Hawick Road (now Hillside Terrace) to the E, Scotts
Place and Bleachfield Road stretching out to the N, and descending from the old town around Heatherlie to the w. Major development on the W bank of the Ettrick Water came in the C20 in
the form of the Bannerfield Estate.

SCOTTS PLACE is the NE continuation of High Street. On the l.
is the splendid Victoria Halls (*see* Public Buildings, above) and

to its r. VICTORIA LODGE, a single-storey and bow-ended lodge of 1824 framing the gateway to Viewfield House (*see* Selkirk Health Centre, above). Its square-plan STABLES are visible to the NW of BACK FEUS, a mid to late C19 row of cottages, at the NE end of which is the COACH HOUSE of HAWTHORN BANK; its M-gabled LODGE is on Scotts Place next to a short early C19 range. Beyond is ELM PARK, sheltered housing of 1963–5, which leads to council housing of 1939 around THORNFIELD AVENUE (*Thomas Beattie*, Burgh Architect), with THORNFIELD HOUSE at its centre. A characteristically Italianate villa by *Peddie & Kinnear*, 1871, for James Brown, mill-owner and poet, with three-storey rectangular-plan tower and round-arched openings. Now a home for the elderly. Its well-articulated LODGE and STABLES survive at the E foot of the avenue. On the r. side of Scotts Place is the prominent THORNCROFT, a former villa, by *Peddie & Kinnear*, 1873, now a petrol station. Further N, early C19 dwellings opposite the United Reformed Church (*see* Churches, above) on DOVECOTE PARK have been raised to two storeys. ELM ROW is a pleasant row of cottages with the rear of the POLICE STATION on its NW side, an understated and domestic design by *Scott & McIntosh*, c. 1975.

Scotts Place forks N and E; the N arm is BLEACHFIELD ROAD (the site of the burgh's linen bleachfield in the C18); where the corrugated-iron EPISCOPAL CHURCH HALL sits inconspicuously behind St John's Church (*see* Churches, above). Workers' cottages and tenements line CURROR STREET to the NE, amongst which is the expansive Knowepark Primary School (*see* Public Buildings, above). To the N is more municipal housing of 1927–37 by *Thomas Beattie*, and low-rise blocks of 1968 in the RAEBURN area behind terraced tenements and semi-detached cottages on Bleachfield Road. RAEBURN PLACE is a delightful mix of housing with C19 cottages set back behind the Shaw Burn, which runs through the front gardens. Further N the early C19 pink-painted TANNAGE survives on the r. side of BRIDGELANDS ROAD.

The E fork from the N end of Scotts Place is SHAWPARK ROAD; on the corner of CLIFTON ROAD is the expansive brick TELEPHONE EXCHANGE of 1975, built on the site of a villa, Annieston, and behind which is the town's first municipal housing, of 1924 by *Thomas Beattie*, which continues as far as SCOTT CRESCENT. Further W is the FAIRFIELD estate of 1966, on the site of a villa by *Wardrop & Reid*. The broad-eaved BRIERLAW CEMETERY LODGE, 1872, is next to DANDSWALL, c. 1879, a large villa built for George Roberts, provost, mill-owner and chairman of the Selkirk–Galashiels Railway Co. Characterised by oversailing roofs, many gables, bargeboards and projecting rafters. Unusual five-light bayed first-floor window to the centre of the N façade under a large gable and Z-plan one-and-a-half-storey lodge with quadrant walls. The FIRE STATION, by *Scott & McIntosh*, 1978, sits amongst the small private housing scheme of SHAWPARK CRESCENT. Utilitarian and inoffensive with cream-rendered walls and wedge-shaped projection above engine door.

TOWER STREET, E of its junction with Back Row, continues uphill as HILLSIDE TERRACE. On the S side is a mix of late C19-early C20 cottages, houses and terraces around HILL STREET, TAITS HILL and RUSSELL PLACE and the ANTIBURGHER CHURCH of *c*. 1810 at No. 32, which later served as a manse. On the N, the former and present buildings of the High School (*see* Public Buildings, above) flank HIGH SCHOOL LANE. The upper reaches of the terrace consist of early C20 and post-war detached dwellings with open vistas to Pot Loch.

Further SE, continuing the line of Kirk Wynd and South Port uphill, is The LOAN, with on the l. KINGSLAND AVENUE, developed with municipal housing in 1968 and served by St Joseph's R.C. School (*see* Public Buildings, above), above which is the late C19 MARIAN CRESCENT. An interesting diversion at the end of the avenue is a low, four-bay whinstone Victorian RESERVOIR with slit windows and shuttered doors. No. 15 The Loan is a diminutive rubble-whinstone early-C18 dwelling with a steeply pitched roof. Further E, the pink-harled, two-storey ROSEBANK of a similar date has hipped pavilions and is set back from the street. Late C20 private schemes and individual houses cling to the hillside in LOANSIDE, DEER PARK and LADYLANDS.

THE GREEN is the continuation of West Port SW of the town centre; THE GLEBE on the r. was developed from the 1880s for owner-occupation, mainly with small houses, at the head of which is the yellow sandstone MANSE of 1901 by *Adam Grieve*. The TOWN GATE of The Haining (*see* p. 679) opens off The Green. By *John Smith* c. 1825. Impressive Classical arch flanked by paired pilasters, with entablature, delicately dentilled frieze and blocking course. Heraldic panel over the arch. A mirror image on the S side. Quadrant walls terminate in coped square piers. The lodge with a four-columned pedimented porch was demolished in the 1960s. Beneath The Green is the 1990s HAINING PARK development, while opposite, tenements descend steeply into the HEATHERLIE area. Part of the late C19 Currie's hosiery firm survives at No. 19. Large Victorian villas such as WOODBURN (1869) and HEATHERLIE HOUSE (*Peddie & Kinnear*, 1875) line HEATHERLIE PARK to the E.

ETTRICK ROAD is opposite the park to the l. of THE MAPLES (1860), whose tenements were renovated in 1974–6. FOREST LODGE (former Free Church manse) of 1848 sits among extensive gardens adjacent to the MUIRSONS HILL scheme of the 1990s. Opposite is the PRIORY HOUSE HOTEL, built as a large two-storey and basement red sandstone villa by *Wardrop & Reid*, 1879. Slim, three-storey octagonal tower at one corner of the bargeboarded, half-dormered elevations. Its one-and-a-half-storey, L-plan COACH HOUSE with unusual dormers was converted in 1978 by *Jean Laing* of *Borders Regional Council*, as an annexe to its former function as a children's home (now Ettrick Family Resource Centre).

YARROW TERRACE, 1873, with basemented terraces along its N side, winds downwards to the Ettrick Water at the NE end of Ettrick Road. HEATHERLIE CHURCH, built 1874 as a chapel of ease by *Brown & Wardrop*, in Early English style, has been largely demolished except for a few fragments retained in a house, *c.* 2004. To its r. is the former manse in a plain Scottish C17 style by *R. Rowand Anderson*, 1888–97. Opposite, overlooking Selkirk Bridge, is THE GLEN HOTEL (formerly Mauldsheugh), built in 1856 as the parsonage of the Episcopalian church of 1853 to its NE, reconstructed and enlarged in 1888 by *Wardrop & Reid*. Expansive, almost square-plan, two-storey and attic former villa in dark whinstone with red sandstone margins. Small, astragalled windows, broad slated roofs and dark bargeboards combine to emphasise its mass. Elaborate tenements frame the opening to KILNCROFT; those to the r. date to 1878 and 1886. MILLBURN PLACE, MILL STREET and GLEBE TERRACE are a mix of late C19 workers' housing, while older dwellings to the SW of GREEN TERRACE have made way for a park. At the foot of Forest Road at MILL STREET is a fine red sandstone Scottish Renaissance block; two-storey tenements wind uphill to Ettrick Terrace.

On MUTHAG STREET to the W of Mill Street is the remnant of the town's gasworks of 1835 (now a garage), and heightened tenements here and on BUCCLEUCH ROAD, at the N end of which is the yellow sandstone BUCCLEUCH BUILDINGS, 1875. The railway station of 1849 (dem. 1964) once stood on South Bridge Street, but the French Renaissance STATION HOTEL with shaped dormerheads survives on STATION ROAD. At the corner with MILL STREET over the lade bridge is the WATER WORKS, 1903, with Jacobean gables and elaborate doorpiece. On the site of the corn mill of *c.* 1830; to its rear stood a waulk mill of 1718. Unfolding out from here on the broad, flat river bank on the NW side of Mill Street, Dunsdale Road and Dunsdale Haugh, the main industrial artery of the town, are the majority of Selkirk's surviving mill buildings (*see* Mills below). Amongst these on RIVERSIDE ROAD is the Georgian WHINFIELD HOUSE between Heather and Whinfield Mills. On WHINFIELD ROAD are remnants of an early C19 sawmill (now part of Travis Perkins) and the 1877 engine and boiler house of YARROW MILLS (established 1866), which survived demolition in 1995. Some of the early C19 DUNSDALE COTTAGES have been converted to industrial use and straddle the gap between Ettrick and Tweed Mills on DUNSDALE ROAD where there is also a pocket of 1930s and 1960s housing at the junction with LEVEL CROSSING ROAD. Here, the RAILWAY COTTAGE and the T-plan ST MARY'S LODGE, 1894, stand to the r. of the old trackway to the SE of St Mary's Mills.

Above, on ETTRICK TERRACE, heading N out of town past the Sheriff Courthouse (*see* Public Buildings, above), No. 32 sits on the red sandstone base of the town's second U.P. Church (1889, dem. 1983). On the l. next to Ettrick Lodge and Ettrickdene (*see* p. 675), OLD BRIDGE ROAD consists of a double row of C20 houses on one side. The pink-harled COMELY BANK, *c.* 1830s–40s, is on the corner while the Georgian whinstone BRAESIDE opposite is of lesser proportions. VIEWFIELD PARK was laid out in *c.* 1910 with substantial houses, while large C19 villas, such as RESTHARROW and WELLWOOD, line the NW hillside overlooking the Ettrick Water. Considerably further N, at the end of the terrace, is SLOETHORNBANK: a short range of early C19 whinstone tenements associated with the mills on Dunsdale Haugh below.

The NW bank of Ettrick Water was first developed in the late C19 with BANNERFIELD MILL (alternatively Ettrickhaugh Mills), 1881; its remnants are retained as an arcaded boundary to the public park. Workers' tenements to the NW and on CANNON STREET were renovated in 1974–6. The innovative BANNERFIELD estate, 1945–64 by *Basil Spence & Partners*, 118 unfurls to the SW in a rather regimented layout of terraced housing and three-storey flatted blocks arranged round grass squares and linked by a broad tree-lined street. An important landmark in the development of post-Second World War council housing and the first use in Scotland of Radburn planning principles for segregation of traffic with pathways and open front gardens created by banishing parking to inner courts – a feature still apparent today.

In LINGLIE ROAD is the former schoolhouse of Philiphaugh Community School (*see* Public Buildings, above) with cast-iron gatepiers. Two whinstone sheds which survived a fire in 1916 at the former BURN MILL, built for Johnstone & Johnstone in 1871, sit behind the park between Long Philip Burn and Selkirk Bridge (*see* Public Buildings, above). Finally, beyond a long row of one-and-a-half-storey cottages and the 1872 CRICKET PAVILION along ETTRICKHAUGH ROAD is Philiphaugh Mill (*see* Mills, below).

THE HAINING
Off Castle Street and The Green

A simple Classical villa, begun by Mark Pringle in 1795 and attributed to *William Elliot*, who built The Yair (q.v.) to a similar design and for the same family. Pringle's son John returned home to his inheritance in 1810, imbued with a love of the Classical world, and *c.* 1820 commissioned *Archibald Elliot* to transform the house into a Roman villa. *John Smith*, already it seems at work on the design of new stables and office buildings, appears to have served as contractor.

The C18 house was built in local whinstone, seven bays wide, of three storeys and attic with a piended platform roof. The centre three bays in the S elevation had a full-height canted entrance bay, balustraded and with a pedimented doorcase. Archibald Elliot's scheme proposed the addition of set-back, two-storey wings. These were not carried out but the N and S elevations were faced with thin slabs of ashlar in a greyish-yellow crumbly sandstone; the ashlar is carried round to the rubble-built W and E elevations as prominent quoins, otherwise they remain as built. Windows were lengthened and given casements, with louvred shutters on the N front. Moulded surrounds and architraved cornices were added to the first-floor windows, and the parapets were given balustrades front and back. Importantly, the main entrance was transferred to the N front, where was added an impressive three-bay arcaded porte cochère supporting a prostyle, pedimented Ionic portico with fluted columns. The spandrels of the arcade and the pilastered doorway have single paterae and husk garlands; a motif seen elsewhere on the house and stables, perhaps Smith's contribution. On the S elevation the canted bay was remodelled to a wide bow, fronted on the ground floor by a splendid Ionic loggia, the necks of the columns carved with anthemion and palmette ornament, which supports a balustraded balcony. Above the centre window, an oval panel (inserted) contains a slab inscribed CONDITA 1795. It was discovered at the base of the N front.

The INTERIOR originally had a tripartite plan, with the entrance from the S and the staircase on the N side. After 1820 a large rectangular vestibule was created on the N side, with a black and white marble floor, continued through to the stair hall; four oval medallions containing bust-reliefs of Roman emperors decorate the vestibule walls. An elegant geometric stair, transversely placed, rises to an oval cupola, the frieze decorated with plasterwork. A well-detailed balustrade, the cast-iron balusters linked together in pairs, with a net pattern. On the S side is a dining room with a black marble chimneypiece; grey marble chimneypiece in the drawing room on the floor above.

In 1818–19 discussions were under way with *John Smith* concerning office buildings and hunting stables. The STABLES, W of the house, are two ranges built in rubble whinstone with sandstone margins, planned round a rectangular court. The imposing, attractively crescent-shaped two-storey, nine-bay S range, converted to domestic use by *Fergus Lenaghan*, 1983, has an arcaded S elevation with a panel in the centre carved with husk garlands and paterae. A door leads into a pend, with stair access for grooms on the l., and a semicircular arch (now blocked) to the court. In the centre of the N elevation of the L-plan N block a monumental square-headed sandstone arch fronts the pend, supported by Tuscan columns flanked by niches, formerly holding busts, with moulded panels above, a blocking course and block pediment. Flanking the centre, three rubble-filled semicircular-headed arches. Small voussoirs over the pend arch, the keystone carved with a horse's skull.

W of the stables is the mid-C19 DAIRY COTTAGE. Two storeys, with segmental-headed casement windows and a single-storey wing with iron ventilators. To the E, two cast-iron railed cages, one with high, curved railings, designed for wolves and bears brought home from St Petersburg. – DEER LARDER, NW of the house, *c.* 1830. Sandstone octagon built into a bank, formerly domed with pairs of narrow openings and pedimented porch. A ventilated store below. – Square ICE PIT, NW of house, formerly covered with slabs. The ice was lowered and raised by lifting gear, recently removed. Now infilled. – Ruinous mid-C18 DOVECOT W of the house. Rubble-built lectern type; wide projecting rat course. – WEST LODGE. Mid-C19, gabled, with bracketed eaves. Square urn-finialled gatepiers. East Lodge and Town Gate, *see* Description, p. 677.

LANDSCAPE. The parkland was laid out in the late C18 and early C19. In the late 1820s a formal cast-iron SCREEN, with square stone piers bearing stone busts and urns, was placed in front of the N court, and a TERRACE was constructed on the S side, enhanced with a row of Canova-style marble STATUES pensively gazing out over Haining Loch. An artificial outlet in the loch's N bank is ornamented with two OBELISKS, formerly with busts on top.

MILLS

The development of Selkirk's textile mills along Dunsdale Haugh on the W side of the Ettrick Water began in 1837 with Dunsdale Mill, which gave its name to Dunsdale Road, and it was soon followed by other spinning and carding mills. In spite of their number by the end of the C19, few of the buildings now serve their original function.

BRIDGEHAUGH MILL, South Bridge Street. Built 1865 by Dobie & Richardson as a spinning and weaving mill but mostly cleared in the early C20 and now in other use. Only the single-storey five-bay SE front of 1871 survives with central porch and wall-head gable.

DUNSDALE MILL, Dunsdale Road. The mill built by the Town Council in 1837, as one of the first attempts to encourage the industry, survives in the midst of a much larger complex. It is T-plan with seventeen bays and three storeys. Waddell & Turnbull took over the lease in 1863 and began an ambitious building programme. A mill house was added to the rear and a new double-pile spinning mill to the SW of the site. An elaborate L-plan engine/boiler house was built between the two mills. Its square-plan tower has a round-arched window and corbelled parapet. The 1837 mill is framed by two-storey shops and sheds and a c. 1960 dyehouse. Spinning ceased in 1984.

ETTRICK MILL, Dunsdale Road. An imposing, whinstone, four-storey and double attic U-plan spinning mill begun in 1836 for J. & H. Brown, with a ten-bay range, extended to the r. in 1850 by eleven bays and given gabled wings at either end to the designs of *John & Thomas Smith*. The central three bays are pedimented, with clock and Palladian window within the double attic. A pyramidal-roofed square-plan machicolated water tower is clasped to the S corner of the weaving mill built to the NW by *Thomas Aimers* of Galashiels in 1874. Other ranges date from 1858 onwards, amongst which is a c. 45 m. high octagonal brick chimney. The late C19 sheds to the NW were conjoined by a large building in 1968. Renovations by *Gray, Marshall & Associates* since the closure of Ettrick & Yarrow Spinners in 1998. 119

FOREST MILL, Station Road. The four-storey High Mill and the long three-storey block to its r. were built in 1838 along the NW and NE sides of the mill pond; good details include the hipped stair-tower with bellcote at the E corner of the High Mill. The two-storey wheelhouse was built in 1868 along the SE side of the pond, while remnants of Hogg's Hosiery Works of 1807 may survive to its l. An unusual, single-storey, early C20 extension to the NE façade of the NE block has a Doric-columned aedicule. The three-storey dyehouse wing was

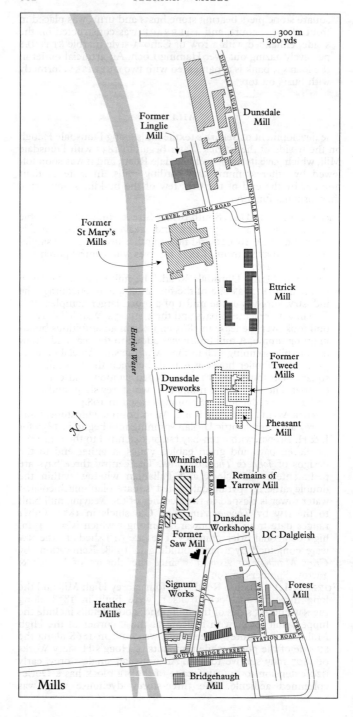

300 m
300 yds

Former
Linglie
Mill

DUNSDALE HAUGH

Dunsdale
Mill

DUNSDALE ROAD

LEVEL CROSSING ROAD

Former
St Mary's
Mills

Ettrick
Mill

Ettrick Water

Former
Tweed
Mills

Dunsdale
Dyeworks

Pheasant
Mill

Whinfield
Mill

ROGERS ROAD

Remains of
Yarrow Mill

Dunsdale
Workshops

DC Dalgleish

RIVERSIDE ROAD

Former
Saw Mill

Signum
Works

WEAVERS COURT

MILL STREET

Forest
Mill

Heather
Mills

WHINFIELD ROAD

STATION ROAD

SOUTH BRIDGE STREET

Bridgehaugh
Mill

Mills

added to the r. in 1927 by George Roberts & Co. Weaving sheds to the NW have been converted into retail units and, consequently, large portions of the complex have been demolished.

HEATHER MILLS, South Bridge Street. 1864. Built for J. & J. Bathgate as Cheviot Mills. The courtyard is framed by the one-and-a-half-storey, whinstone, ten-bay block at the W corner and the S block, which has eleven bays to Whinfield Road. Two ranges of mid-to-late C19 single-storey weaving sheds stand to the NE. Additions and reconstructions in brick around the interior of the courtyard date to the first half of the C20.

Former LINGLIE MILL, Level Crossing Road. 1894. A small weaving and finishing mill established by Eoin & Sanderson. The weaving sheds survive as two parallel ranges. Their combined single-storey SE elevation is of exposed whinstone with red sandstone margins and a wall-head gable with a louvred oculus; the six bays to the NW comprise the former engine and boiler house. Converted to industrial units in 1978 by *Derek Turner* of *Borders Regional Council.*

Former PHILIPHAUGH MILL, Ettrickhaugh Road. Built by Thomas Walker upon ground feued from Sir John Murray of Philiphaugh (q.v.), 1856. Single-storey and attic, well-proportioned spinning mill of whinstone with yellow sandstone margins; its SE bay is topped by a wall-head gable and bellcote. The double-pile plan is disguised by a shaped gable. Eleven-bay addition to the SW for George Roberts & Co. in 1876, with a tall engine house with round-headed windows amongst auxiliary buildings to the SW of the distinctive mill lade. The large SE block dates to *c.* 1929.

Former ST MARY'S MILLS, Level Crossing Road, 1894. Single-storey weaving mill built for Gibson & Lumgair. The E corner, opposite St Mary's Lodge (*see* p. 678), contains the most elaborate architecture since it defines the original entrance. Squared whinstone with red sandstone margins and round-arched openings; four-light rounded bay at corner. The entrance is slightly advanced within a nepus gable. Extended NW in the 1950s. Weaving ceased in 1964, and much of the site was cleared before the remainder was converted by *Jeremy Snodgrass* of *Borders Regional Council* as library headquarters.

Former TWEED MILLS, Dunsdale Road. Weaving mill built by William Brown & Son in 1883 and acquired by Gardiners of Selkirk in 1895. Ten-bay, two-storey whinstone SE façade with lower two storeys of three bays to the l.; the SW bay has an elaborate entablature over the doorway. Four bays of single-storey sheds to the NE. The sheds to the SW have a three-light turret at the E corner; now occupied as Pheasant Mill. Expansion to the N took place after 1958, and older weaving sheds to the NW were linked to the reconstructed 1875 Dunsdale Dye-works, *c.* 1971.

WHINFIELD MILL, Riverside Road, 1875. Built as the Riverside spinning mill for Gordon & Brydone. Of the original complex there survives a two-storey, four-bay whinstone building at the SW, with two bays of one- and two-storey sheds at either side. Fires of *c.* 1909 and 1926 destroyed much of the remainder,

which was thereafter rebuilt in brick upon a similar plan by the
Heather Mills Co.

MUNGO PARK'S COTTAGE, Foulshiels, 5 km. W. The roofless
shell of a small, dark whinstone farmhouse; birthplace of the
African explorer Mungo Park (1771–1806). Walls renovated c.
1960 by the Selkirk Antiquarian Society.

BRIDGELANDS HOUSE. *See* p. 137.
BROOMHILL HOUSE. *See* p. 138.
HIGH SUNDERLAND. *See* p. 376.
NEWARK CASTLE. *See* p. 585.
PHILIPHAUGH HOUSE. *See* p. 637.
SUNDERLAND HALL. *See* p. 710.

5000   SHANKEND

SHANKEND RAILWAY VIADUCT, 8.5 km. SW. By *Charles Jopp*,
built for the Border Union Railway, 1862, and fiercely impressive in the landscape. 1,200 m. long with fifteen tall semicircular-headed arches built of random rubble with rock-faced
quoins. Marred by later, hasty repairs in blue-grey glazed engineering bricks, including all the voussoirs. 0.1 km. SE is the
STATION HOUSE in rock-faced rubble. Two-storey, twin-
gabled, with timber porches at each end and a piended roof to
the station. Further SE, a SIGNAL BOX, the lower part in brick,
with timber superstructure.

8040   SIMPRIM

An ancient parish, united with Swinton (q.v.) in 1761.

OLD PARISH CHURCH. Abandoned after union, and now a ruin.
It was a tiny two-cell structure of pink rubble, the walls incorporating many squared stones that point to a C12 or C13 origin
for much of the structure. The only part to stand to near full
height is the E gable, which has a blocked round-headed
window likely to be of later medieval date, as are the gable's
skews. The N wall of the chancel stands to nearly 2 m., and
there appear to be traces of a window rear arch towards the W
end of its internal face. – CHURCHYARD. Some good C18
stones with *memento mori*, many fallen over or simply propped
against the church walls; also some table tombs.

SIMPRIM FARM, 0.2 km. W. Largely obscured from view by later
accretions, a huge GIRNEL (granary), one of the most remarkable early farm buildings in Scotland. Erected in 1686 by Sir
Archibald Cockburn of Langton, a pioneering agricultural
improver. Sandstone rubble masonry with dressed quoins and
chamfered margins; crowstepped gables with cavetto-moulded
skewputts. The arrangement of windows in the S gable suggests
that there were originally four floors, the top one probably
removed during the C18, when the roof is said to have been
lowered. The building is an elongated rectangle (64.3 m. from
N to S by 7.6 m. transversely), and the original design allowed
for a pair of oblong stair-towers, one at each end of the E wall.

Only the N tower seems to have been completed, however, its entrance doorway bearing the initials AC and the date 1686; inside, a scale-and-platt staircase of stone. The elevations of the main block were symmetrical, each of the side walls originally containing five segmental-arched doorways placed opposite one another with windows directly above; additional ventilation was provided by slits. The lowest storey was probably originally used as a threshing floor and the upper levels as granaries.

SKIRLING

0030

An attractive village with buildings clustered round a spacious green, shaded by lime trees. The site of a late medieval castle, now represented by a rectangular mound and ditch, lies in an open field 300 m. W of the parish church. Skirling was erected into a burgh of barony by James VI, with power to hold a weekly market and an annual fair.

SKIRLING PARISH CHURCH. Built in 1720 but much altered in 1891–3 except for the four walls, the attractive ogee-roofed bellcote on arched openings (bell dated 1748), and the sundial on the SW angle of the tower. Sandstone rubble covered with a thick render. Five-bay S elevation with intersecting glazing bars in the tops of the round-arched windows, and a red sandstone buttressed porch with foliated label stops, dated 1893, at the W end. A vestry and boiler house (1910) against the N wall. The interior was completely renewed following the removal of a gallery and stairs. – An oak-panelled PULPIT, situated in the NE corner, has a large red velvet padded back board and seat cushions. – The COMMUNION TABLE, together with the Minister's and Elders' CHAIRS with carved details, were designed and gifted by *D. Y. Cameron*, brother-in-law of the minister. – STAINED GLASS. Double-light window at the E end, a floral medallion in each light, dedicated to the Rev. Matthew Armstrong, 1888.

GRAVEYARD. Surrounded by a circular stone wall, the site protected by pine trees. Wrought-iron GATES and pier finials at the entrance, also the minister's gate in the W wall with a cheeky bird sitting on the crossbar. This decorative ironwork was by *Thomas Hadden*, 1907 (*see* Skirling House, below), mixing flower forms derived from the gates at Traquair House (q.v.) with tightly branched spirals. – Against the NW wall is the CARMICHAEL BURIAL GROUND, designed by *Robert S. Lorimer*, 1905. Two grave-faced angels act as portals, their praying hands resting on tablets. – Some simple C18 GRAVESTONES with symbols of mortality, and table tombs with shapely baluster supports. At the E end of the church, James Howe, artist, erected *c.* 1836 by his artist friends and decorated with a painter's palette.

DESCRIPTION. Clockwise from the Parish Church (*see* above). First, a school. Two-storey, three-bay schoolmaster's house, with a single-storey schoolroom attached. At the N end of the green, some cottages including PIPER'S COTTAGE, with a coloured figure of a piper, dated 1810, built into the wall. From the NW corner up the A72 is the former FREE CHURCH (1843, now a dwelling). Harled rectangle with a pleasant stone bellcote and pointed windows with intersecting astragals. Up a lane behind is the former FREE CHURCH MANSE (Hanna House), 1846. Two-storey L-plan, the S elevation comprising three gables with bracketed eaves, the E one set back with the entrance in the angle. Offices attached to the N, the original effect spoilt by an early C20 addition. On the other side of the A72 is the VILLAGE HALL. Rectangular with buttresses for decoration, and at the S end an addition in rock-faced ashlar, dated 1903. To the N is the WAR MEMORIAL by *Robert S. Lorimer*, 1920, and *R. Gray* of Dolphinton. A square shaft crowned by a cross, set on a high red sandstone plinth bearing Lorimer's monogram of a heart crossed by an L.

The E side of the green has a farm and row of single-storey cottages. Finally, 0.5km. from the S end, the former parish church MANSE. Core *c.* 1803, remodelled in 1837. Two-storey, three-bay, piend-roofed. Cream-washed harling with sandstone margins and quoins. An arched stone porch set forward to the r. is linked to an imposing high concave garden wall. A two-storey range at the rear is probably later. Mid-C19 stables and steading survive on the l. of the entrance court.

SKIRLING HOUSE
s end of the green

The highly personal and unique result of collaboration between Sir Thomas Gibson-Carmichael (afterwards Lord Carmichael of Skirling) and his architect *Ramsay Traquair*, 1908–12. Traquair worked in the office of *Robert S. Lorimer*, from whom in 1906 Carmichael had acquired a design for a large Baronial house, to be set on a hillside N of Skirling. This project was cancelled when Carmichael lost money from the failure of Hailes Quarry, Edinburgh, one of his principal sources of income. He turned instead to remodelling a farmhouse and barn by wrapping round them the present, mostly timber, structure; the result described by May, Lady Carmichael as 'most comfortable though a most unconventional house'. The style probably evolved as it was built, but can best be described as in the English Domestic tradition, with Arts and Crafts details, and strongly influenced by Lorimer, e.g. the differently shaped roofs, swept down low over the eaves, and the prominent square bays (cf. Whiteholm at Gullane (Lothian)). Z-plan and harled, except for brick-lined horizontal weatherboarding on the N and W fronts and to the square bay windows and dormers on the remainder.

What distinguishes the house is the use of decorative wrought IRONWORK, an important, and mostly humorous collection designed by Carmichael and Traquair but executed by *Thomas Hadden*. Carmichael learnt practical ironwork at Hadden's Edinburgh forge, providing a plethora of ideas to incorporate in his house. A low iron rail along the W side of the house is decorated with a selection of creeping and writhing creatures, comical monkeys and hens, and impish people, including a top-hatted gentleman.

Inside, ironwork is everywhere employed, from doors and windows to handles, light fittings and radiator covers. Sculptured stones are used in floors in various parts of the house. The majority of rooms are simple and domestic in character, relieved by the witty use of ironwork, and some with classical chimneypieces. Plasterwork by *Isaac Whitefield*. The only stately room is the DRAWING ROOM created from the earlier barn. Into this Carmichael fitted a C16 Italian ceiling, removed from Castlecraig House (q.v.) after its sale in 1905, together with carved and inlaid Italian furniture. Each compartment of the ceiling contains a single carved rose; painting was touched up by *Moxon & Carfrae*, who also provided the classical decoration of sphinxes on the ceiling in the square bay window. A built-in full-length wall cabinet by *Scarselle* of Florence (1900), with *trompe l'oeil* decoration, remains *in situ*. Timber chimneypiece with fluted Ionic pilasters and acanthus capitals, and architrave over the doorway, carved by *H. W. Palliser*. Panelling, by *David Macdonald* of Melrose, was removed to London in 1920. The dining room has a beamed ceiling and stone chimneys.

GARDENER'S HOUSE, originally a single-storey rubble-built cottage, with alterations dated 1821. Porch and rear extension added *c.* 1908. Converted by the *Appleton Partnership*, 1997. – Early C19 stone BARN. – The SUMMERHOUSE, presumably by Carmichael and Traquair, has horizontal timber boarding and a central door flanked by sixteen-pane astragalled windows. Also surviving are terraced steps with decorative arrangements of stones and pebbles, a well and stone garden seat, and ironwork decorated with birds, leaves and seeds and particularly lily motifs. Two former totem poles with toucans on top are near at hand, one in the house, the other in a village garden. – SUNDIALS. The supports of both are by *Traquair*. One dial is said to have come from Chiefswood, Melrose (q.v.). A cluster of four Ionic columns supports a capital, dated 17[9]3, with a marble dial. The other C18 octagonal dial and gnomon, possibly from Castlecraig House, has an octagonal panelled base supporting a panelled baluster shaft. – CARVED STONES. Built into the SE wall of the house, symbols of SS John and Mark, said to have been brought back from Italy. At the end of a dyke on the E side of the house is a C17 or C18 carved head, which may have been part of a churchyard monument.

Opposite Skirling House, on the green, is a red sandstone PILLAR with a pelican feeding her young. A wrought-iron bracket supports a lantern held in the mouth of a crocodile, a 'loupin-on-stane' abuts one side, with another crocodile on a short rail.

SLACKS PELE

6000

2.2 km. SE of Chesters

The roofless shell of a late C16 pele house belonging to the same group as Mervinslaw Pele (q.v.). Oblong plan (11.8 by 7.4 m.), originally comprising two storeys and a garret. Constructed of local red sandstone rubble laid in clay mortar. The gabled roof was no doubt turf-covered. There were probably separate ground- and first-floor doorways, but only the former survives, a lintelled opening beneath a relieving arch at the centre of the NE gable; the doorway is rebated for outer and inner doors, the latter provided with a draw-bar. Above the doorway a row of socket-holes at second-floor level, perhaps flight-holes for pigeons, like those at Hole (Northumberland). The ground-floor chamber had no openings other than the doorway. A pair of corbels flanking may have carried the framework of a hatch, but otherwise there seems to have been no direct communication with the first floor. The first-floor chamber contained several mural aumbries; a crudely-carved corbel at the centre of the SW gable could have supported the hearth of a clay-canopied fire-place. The garret must have been reached from a ladder.

6030   SMAILHOLM

A small settlement with a church, manse, and former school. A few single-storey early C19 labourers' whinstone cottages survive, presumably built to serve the farm in the centre of the village, the rest added to or remodelled in the late C19 and C20.

PARISH CHURCH. The Romanesque two-compartment building that forms the basis for this attractive church was dependent on Earlston in the 1170s, but soon afterwards achieved parochial status. The C12 fabric is best seen in the chancel and the E end of the nave, where there are narrow chamfered base courses and extensive areas of cubical masonry; there are also (restored?) blocked narrow round-headed windows in the E and N walls of the chancel. Significant works took place in the C17 (most notably in 1632) when a birdcage bellcote was added to the W gable, a porch built for the W loft, and new doorways formed in the S flank of both nave and chancel (the latter now blocked). In works by *William Elliot* in 1820, the S windows were enlarged, some capped by pediments rising above the wall-head, and the apsidal N aisle is also likely to be largely of this date. In 1895 *Hardy & Wight* re-medievalised the church. The N aisle was opened up towards the church, with a vestry within the apse itself; plaster ceilings were replaced by boarded and ribbed barrel ceilings; the chancel again became a chancel (with a new arch carried on foliate corbels); and the S windows were lowered and their pediments removed. Nevertheless, much of the Georgian character was retained, as seen in the round-arched S windows and the intersecting glazing bars of the W window. – COMMUNION TABLE, two planes of Romanesque arcading. – PULPIT, relief carvings of Evangelist symbols, from Jedburgh Trinity Church. – STAINED GLASS, E window, SS Giles and Cuthbert, 1907. – CARVED FRAGMENT, C13 with bands of dogtooth and interlace. – SUNDIAL, at SW corner of nave, said to have been dated 1622.

Former MANSE (Smailholm Lodge), E of church. Built *c.* 1800, but remodelled in the mid C19. Tall corniced doorway with rectangular fanlight, flanked by bipartite windows. High rubble-built garden walls.

VILLAGE HALL. Former school of 1862. Converted in 1973. Single-storey with a three-bay centre block, and flanking, slightly recessed, lower two-bay wings. Well-lit schoolroom, with twenty-four-pane glazing.

SMAILHOLM FARMHOUSE. At the junction of the B6361 and B6397. A most attractive harled, L-shaped range of a two storey farmhouse with wallhead dormers, and a lower two storey stable wing. Probably early C19 with later alterations. – 0.7 km. W (B6361), is a group of late C18 buildings, partly reconstructed in the mid C19, including a granary, barn and cottage, unhappily cement-harled in 1992.

SMAILHOLM HOUSE 0.6 km. NE. In 1663 James Don, clerk of Kelso, was granted a charter to the twenty-merk lands of 'Smalhome' formerly belonging to William, Earl of Roxburghe. Andrew Don, his second son, succeeded to the property after his elder brother Alexander had been declared 'fatuous', and remodelled it to its present appearance in 1707. The house is an L-plan, with N and S blocks. Crowstepped gables, the skewputts carved with grotesque heads, the chimneystacks rebuilt in brick. N extension of 1864. Recent repair work (2004) has revealed traces of early work suggesting that the N block originally comprised a C16 tower house, built by Cranston of Smailholm, with a kitchen and hall extension to the E. To this was added the S block, perhaps in the early C17 (indicated by window lintels discovered at the lower level of this block), which was linked to the N block by a turnpike stair, remains of which have also been exposed. The S block was heightened by Andrew Don in 1707 and given sash and case windows. The entrance doorway within the re-entrant angle has a bolection-moulded lugged architrave which sweeps upwards at the lintel in an ogival curve; below are the initials and date AD (Andrew Don) 1707. There are small niches each side, the r. one now glazed. What was their function? The window to the S has an inscribed marriage lintel JD (James Don) and EK (Elizabeth Ker) and the date 1663.

The house is compactly planned. The entrance opens into a staircase hall which occupies the full width of the S wing, and contains a fine open-well oak stair of 1707 rising from the ground floor to the attic. There is a solid panelled balustrade, while ball-shaped finials cap the panelled newel posts and hang as pendants from the corners. On the ground floor the S room has deal panelling; the present marble chimneypiece is imported (the original is still behind the panelling). Within the N wing is the former kitchen, and to the E is a vaulted cellar, which has traces of a newel stair to the first floor. The kitchen is entered from the 1864 extension through a door (originally external), dated July 21 AD 1717, with a simple chamfered surround. There are three panelled rooms on the first floor with bolection-moulded chimneypieces, the painted panelling in the NE room has been finely grained, and the chimneypiece marbled. Could this be mid-C18 work?

WHITESIDE TOWER, 1.9 km. N. Now a ruin. Probably the structure indicated on Pont's late C16 map of the Merse.

Unusually elongated proportions (16.1 m. by 7.6 m. externally), which suggest that it may have been a bastle. Rubble masonry; its ground-floor chamber was originally barrel-vaulted.

6030   SMAILHOLM TOWER
                        2 km. sw of Smailholm

A tower house dramatically sited on one of the exposed rock ridges of Sandyknowes Craigs. The irregular-shaped barmkin follows the contour of the summit to form two courts, the larger one to the w and smaller to the e, with the tower between them.
The Pringles held part of the barony of Smailholm by the mid c15, but the appearance of the existing tower suggests it was erected half a century later. Smailholm was particularly hard hit by a series of English raids during the 1540s, and the upperworks of the tower were remodelled later in the century. The tower's last recorded military activity was in 1640, when a group of Covenanters successfully resisted siege by a detachment of Royalist musketeers. In c. 1650 Sir William Scott of Harden erected a substantial dwelling-house in the barmkin, which seems to have been occupied until the early c18, when the family took up residence at the nearby house of Sandyknowe, where Walter Scott spent his formative childhood years. He published the earliest historical and archaeological account of the tower in his *Border Antiquities* (1814), paying homage to his early memories of the place in the introduction to *Marmion* (1808). Now in the care of Historic Scotland.

41   The TOWER HOUSE, of simple, oblong plan (12.1 m. by 9.7 m. over walls 2.1 m. thick), comprises a ground floor and vaulted entresol, a first-floor hall and two more floors above that, the top one also vaulted. The masonry is mostly of random rubble with dressings of bright red sandstone, which contrasts sharply with the local black dolerite of the main wall surfaces, its preponderance in the top storey probably reflecting the utilisation of offcuts from dressings. At this level the windows have round-arrised margins whereas those below are chamfered, suggesting substantial reconstruction in the late c16 (the internal openings show a similar distinction). The larger windows were originally barred. The wall-walks on the two long (N and s) sides of the tower, with a parapet projecting marginally from the wall face beneath, look late c16 (cf. Bemersyde House, q.v.), but the plain, square-cut drip-course is unusual. Greig's engraving of 1815 shows that the parapets and the crowstepped gables of the main roof have been extensively repaired.
      The gunloops are a puzzle. There are only two, an inverted keyhole loop placed high above the ground-floor entrance looking s, and an oval-mouthed loop, now blocked, on the top floor looking w. The latter, evidently inserted during the late c16 alterations, might have been useful for covering the barmkin entrance, but the s loop has such a poor field of fire as to be quite ineffective for firearm defence. Could it be a slit-window with its lower half enlarged to admit more light? The round-arched s doorway admits to a lobby with a newel stair

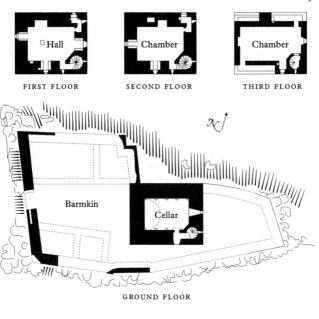

FIRST FLOOR   SECOND FLOOR   THIRD FLOOR

GROUND FLOOR

Smailholm Tower.
Plans.

to the E, serving all floors, and a cellar doorway to the N. The entrance has an inner iron yett and an outer door of timber, the former apparently original, the latter new. A tall, transomed E window lights both the ground-floor and entresol chambers; a new stair to the entresol replaces the original ladder access. Timber floor on corbelled runners restored, with others throughout the tower, c. 1980. The first-floor hall is lit by three large windows, all with bench seats and one also with a mural cupboard. Big corbel-lintelled fireplace with stop-chamfered jambs, one carved with a bearded human head, the other perhaps with a heart (the Pringle crest). Latrine with mural shaft in NE corner. The second floor, probably the laird's private chamber, is similar to that below but with fewer and smaller windows and a plain lintelled fireplace. On the top floor another quite lofty chamber with no entresol beneath the crudely built late C16 vault. Doors to N and S wall-walks, the former having a watchman's seat with a lamp recess cosily built into one side of the chimney, perhaps a response to the Act of Council of 1587 directing lieges to 'keip watch nyght and day, and burn baillis (beacon fires) according to the accoustomat ordour observit at sic tymes upoun the borderis'. Only an athletic watchman could have done the job, because the chimney bars access to the W end of walk other than by scrambling over the roof.

The BARMKIN wall, 1 m. or more in thickness, skirts the edge of
the rock outcrop, bridging a natural cleft towards the centre of
its S side. Remains of barmkin buildings, bonded mainly in clay
mortar, were laid out and consolidated following archaeological excavations in 1979–81. These showed that the W court
contained a ground-floor hall and chamber on the N side, possibly contemporary with the tower, but replaced c. 1650 by a
two-storey dwelling-house with attached storehouse abutting
the W wall of the tower. Its ground floor had a central kitchen
with a parlour (E) and stair (W); part of a big inglenook fireplace survives. The S side of the W court was occupied by a
service range which, in the first phase at least, probably
included a kitchen. The barmkin entrance lay between the two
W ranges and comprised a round-arched gateway with corbelled wall-walk above (cf. Buckholm Tower, q.v.); only jambs
and bar hole remain. The E court may have been a garden.

c. 0.1 km. SE is an enigmatic earthen RINGWORK, perhaps
the site of an early medieval residence.

SOUTHDEAN see CHESTERS

SOUTRA

4050

HOSPITAL. A hospital dedicated to the Holy Trinity was founded
here by King Malcolm IV before 1164, the brethren following
the rule of St Augustine. By the mid C15 it was in decay, and
its endowments were diverted elsewhere. The only upstanding
structure is a rectangular rubble-built barrel-vaulted BURIAL
CHAMBER built in 1686 for David and Agnes Pringle (initials
and date over W doorway). It was presumably formed from
medieval fabric, and reused details are seen in the small paired
lancets in the W gable, and the roll moulding and nailhead decoration of the W doorway jambs. Excavations carried out from
1986 revealed extensive traces of ranges of buildings to the N,
now consolidated and displayed. – MEMORIAL, ogee-headed
tablet in E wall, John Pringle, †1777.
DUN LAW HILL WINDFARM, 2 km. SE, gives interest and movement to an otherwise featureless expanse of high moorland.
Commissioned by Scottish Power from *Renewable Energy
Systems*, and opened in 2000, the site comprises twenty-six
giant wind-driven turbines with propellers mounted on tubular
steel towers 40 m. high.

SPITAL HOUSE

9050

1 km. W of Paxton

An early-to-mid-C19 traditional three-bay house, with a large
two-storey and attic Tudor-detailed extension of 1859, for
the Rev. W.C. Lundie, in cream sandstone with ashlar dressings; rusticated quoins and tabbed surrounds, ball finials to
gable-heads. – WALLED GARDEN, NW, dated 1859. – ROSE

COTTAGE, 1838. Originally two single-storey and attic pic-
turesque cottages with lattice-paned windows. – Square pyra-
midal cusped outer GATEPIERS, inner corniced ones.
Decorative iron gates. – RUSTIC BRIDGE over the Netherlough
Burn. A single arch, hump-backed with pointed arch openings.
Square blocks resembling crenellations.

SPITAL MAINS. 0.5 km. SE. Farmhouse with Tudor detailing,
rendered and lined out as ashlar. Panel inscribed W.C.L. 1856.
Remains of a range of contemporary steadings, mostly pantiled, and an octagonal threshing mill with an open-timber
roof.

SPITAL TOWER   5010
2 km. SE of Denholm

A shooting lodge designed by *Thomas Leadbetter* for himself,
1913. Scottish Domestic style with Baronial detailing of crowstepped gables and spare use of conical-roofed turrets. Curved
and triangular pedimented wall-head dormers and tiny catslide
attic windows, enlarged into full-size dormers in 1956 when
the interior was drastically cut about for conversion to flats by
Ian G. Lindsay & Partners. Leadbetter had a dining room,
smoking room, drawing room and billiard room with a large
sitting recess, arranged in an L-plan round the stair hall and
central full-height galleried hall. At the NE corner, a towered
wing linked to the house by courtyard walls; the two-storey
conical-roofed tower at the E end has a secure top-floor gun
room accessed by an outside stair.

SPOTTISWOODE   6040
3.3 km. W of Westruther

The large Jacobethan house built in 1832 by *William Burn* for
John Spottiswoode was demolished in 1928.

On the site of the old house is EAGLE HALL, designed by *Andrew
Lester*, 1997–8, with some Scottish Domestic character.

The STABLES (now Spottiswoode House, converted 1996 by
Lester) to the N are by *Thomas Grieve*, begun 1770. The date
1796 over a doorway at the E end of the N block must relate to
the later improvements, which gave the building its S-facing
Palladian aspect. A U-plan courtyard with centre two-storey
harled groom's house, formerly crowned by an ogee-roofed
cupola, the gables with rolled skews. Three widely spaced bays;
the windows all have prominent red sandstone Gibbsian surrounds. A central Palladian window on the first floor with a
Gibbsian surround; pedimented doorway below. Single-storey
flanking blocks. The cartshed entrances have inserted, attached
Doric columns. In the late C20 the openings were filled in and
given matching Gibbsian surrounds. Two whinstone rubble
wings project S, the gable ends with loading doors for hay in
the form of wide Gothic lancets. Below each are circular blind
windows, which have triple-blocked keystones similar to those

in the screen wall at Chatelherault (Lanarkshire). Painted Gothic rose tracery fills the circular spaces. The seven-bay W elevation of the E wing has a circular niche with a Gibbsian surround in the centre. To the W, the KENNELS, dated 1798. A three-bay symmetrical block with an advanced centre, a plaque with the Spottiswoode eagle in the pediment.

ESE of the stables is a ruinous cylindrical DOVECOT formerly with an ogee-shaped roof. A rubble-built lower stage, and brick upper one. Five doors opened into the base, which has been divided into wedged-shaped compartments. – WALLED GARDEN, SE of the stables, has the vestigial remains of Lady John Scott's rustic shelters.

WEST LODGE. Late C19, harled with sandstone margins and scalloped bargeboarded gable. A pedimented window surround in the centre of the gable is inscribed MIHI VIVERE CHRISTUS ET MORI LUCRUM 1596 ('For me to live is Christ and to die is gain'), with the initials MIS and shield; on a chevron between three oak trees a boar's head couped. Said to originate from the house of Archbishop Spottiswoode in Glasgow (to which see, however, he was not provided until 1603). Some Arts and Crafts detailing on the N elevation.

EAGLE LODGE (Clock Lodges) on the A697. An amusing pair of single-storey three-bay lodges with bowed ends. The centre doorways (the E one dated 1796) are flanked by plaques with sandstone-moulded surrounds, holding timber panels giving mileage to London, Edinburgh, Perth and points N and S. The outer E and W ends terminate in battlemented Gothick pylons decorated with blind intersecting tracery in the centre, with flanking arrowslits, and above, quatrefoil niches – similar to Gothick detailing found on the stables. The large stone cyclopean quoins at the ends are quite Vanbrughian. On the inner face of each screen wall is a circular opening with painted clock faces, recording, as tradition has it, the times of passing stagecoaches. Semicircular and corniced gatepiers with urn finials. A pair of stone eagles found near the lodge are now kept at Choicelee Farm.

A pair of primitive rustic ARCHWAYS spans the estate road, presumably mid C19. At PYATSHAW, on the N side of the A697, is a Gothic arch of mortared rubble crowned with five obelisks. Further on at BRUNTABURN, another arch with inscription plaques, now overgrown. Through the arch on the l., a STANDING STONE. 0.6 km. N at the side of the road is a MONOLITH known as the 'Popping Stone', where, it is said, Lady John Scott and her husband plighted their troth. Monograms on two faces and the date (of their marriage) 1836. Opposite the West Lodge is the HOUSE OF BRUNTA. Picturesque additions were made in the late C19 to a thatched cottage.

7030   SPRINGHILL HOUSE
                         0.5 km S of Birgham

Built c. 1816 by *William Leitch*, factor of the Hirsel estate. A U-plan two-storey extension to the N was added in 1906 and 1912. Two-storey and basement in cream sandstone with raised quoins. The three-bay s front has a pedimented doorpiece with engaged columns, flanked by keystoned Venetian windows with pilaster mullions.

STABLES, NW of the house. U-plan range in red sandstone rubble. Arched carriage entrance with a pointed-arched pigeon hole above and four-bay cottage in the NE section. – Roofless rubble lectern DOVECOT, W of the house. with a continuous rat course. – SW of the house is a roofless rectangular rubble structure, inscribed 'St Anne's Well, Spring Found 6th June 1859'.

SPROUSTON   7030

Large green bordered by the church, school, and some C19 estate cottages.

PARISH CHURCH. Built 1781, a broad harled box, originally with four round-arched windows along each flank, a doorway towards the W end of the s wall, and a birdcage bellcote on the W gable. Alterations in 1822 included the enclosure of the area under the W gallery as a vestibule, with the blocking of the W window on the s side. A major reordering by P. Macgregor Chalmers in 1911 created a chancel at the E end, on the site of the vestry, with a new vestry at the W end of the N flank. The plaster coomb ceiling over the main body of the church was retained, but a ribbed barrel ceiling was provided over the new chancel, with a chamfered chancel arch reflecting the curve of that ceiling; despite Chalmers' efforts, the contrast between 'nave' and chancel is marked. A medieval carved stone of uncertain function, with a recessed arch and head keystone (found when digging the chancel foundations) was set in the s chancel wall to hint at a piscina. – COMMUNION TABLE, open arcaded front with Ionic pilasters. – PULPIT AND TESTER, in NE corner of nave, polygonal with panelled faces. – FONT, stone octagon with symbols on four faces. – STAINED GLASS. E window, St Michael, Douglas Strachan, 1922; s side nave, the Sower, 1948.

CHURCHYARD. Some C17 and C18 stones with memento mori and trade emblems. – TRUNCATED CROSS SHAFT AND SOCKET STONE, to s of church, reused as a memorial.

Former MANSE (Stone House). By John Bulman, c. 1846–7. In coursed red sandstone and cream dressings, with a piended and platformed roof. Wide doorway with concave jambs, consoled cornice and blocking course. Elegant Geometric stair inside. Contemporary stabling.

SMITHY. Dated 1876. A block with a cart entrance and store above; adjacent, a single-storey workshop with vertical-paned glazing.

SPROUSTON PRIMARY SCHOOL. Series of monopitch-roofed blocks with groups of tall narrow windows. 1960s.

WAR MEMORIAL. By J.S. Rhind, c. 1920. Tall cairn built of roughly cut sandstone blocks, in layers, tapering to a rock topped by a striding lion.

DESCRIPTION. At the SE corner of the green, BELLEVUE, a

classy mid-C19 former schoolmaster's house and schoolroom. Piended roof with central chimneys. Centre bay advanced with block pediment and a corniced doorway. School to the l., accessed by capped gatepiers. Two blocks of mid-C19 estate COTTAGES on the S side of the green, each with a gabled centrepiece with obelisk finial. A late C19 HOUSE at the W end, with plain and jerkin-headed gables, and bipartite and tripartite mullioned windows. At the E end, two mid-C19 houses with Tudor detailing: BOWDEN COTTAGE with overhanging eaves, and a window dated 1904, and TWEED VIEW with horizontal-paned glazing.

7040
STAINRIGG HOUSE
0.5 km. W of Leitholm

1880, by *C. G. H. Kinnear* of *Peddie & Kinnear* for General Cockburn Hood. A typical Scottish Baronial remodelling and extension of an early C19 Classical house, which itself appears to have incorporated earlier work dating from 1631. Asymmetrical, with a NW two-storey Renaissance-detailed wing, and NE wing with stables and groom's cottage. Squared and snecked cream and red sandstone rubble with cream sandstone dressings. In the re-entrant angle of the L-plan S block, a circular capped tower and pilastered porch, with ball-finialled balustraded parapet and a round-arched pedimented shell-shaped heraldic panel. The NW wing has an ogee-roofed square tower and a segmental-arched loggia. Inside, a timber panelled vestibule, decorative cornices, and contemporary chimneypieces. Dog-leg stair, with twisted balusters and panelled, ball-finialled newel posts.

STABLES with a crowstepped S façade to the garden, a U-plan N range and fully equipped stalls. – L-plan KENNELS with a railed exercise yard, and pigeon loft whose entries have stone slab perches. – Early C19 horseshoe-plan WALLED GARDEN and late C19 GARDENER'S HOUSE. – A classically-detailed circular domed WELL-HEAD has a Latin inscription, largely illegible, appearing to record its erection by John Hood of Stoneridge in 1827.

7030
STICHILL

Small village of mostly mid-to-late C19 estate housing associated with the Bairds of Stichill House.

PARISH CHURCH, at SW end of the village. With its elongated rectangular main body, of whinstone rubble and ashlar dressings, the E–W axis of the present church suggests the plan was partly conditioned by a medieval predecessor, though as now seen it is substantially of *c.* 1770. A small W chancel and N vestry were added in 1905 by *J. P. Alison*, when the interior was also reordered. At the E end is the burial enclosure of the Pringles of Stichill, with the date 1783 on the entrance pediment. A forestair to the loft runs up the side to a porch at the

E end of the N wall, though the original door appears to have been in the E wall. The church's S flank has four evenly spaced round-headed windows with impost and keystone blocks, and the entrance at the E end of that wall; the N flank has only two windows, a reminder of the earlier location of the pulpit. Above the W gable is a small ogee-capped birdcage bellcote. The added chancel has a Venetian W window.

Internally there is a marked spatial contrast between the main body and the more compressed space of the chancel; what unifies those spaces is the high-quality fixtures and furnishings of 1905 by *Alison* in a carefully detailed classical Arts and Crafts idiom. The main roof has two levels of collars connected by king- and queenposts treated as Tuscan piers and surmounted by arches, with pendants below; the chancel roof has a ciborium-like barrel ceiling. Both are stained dark brown, but elsewhere the woodwork is of a bright limed finish, applied not only to the 1905 fixtures, but to the existing ones as well, including the raised and fielded panelling of the E gallery and the boarded dado around the walls. The quality of work is best seen in the chancel, where the throne-like MINISTER'S CHAIR and the ELDERS' SEATS along the flanks are built in with the wainscotting. The COMMUNION TABLE is particularly attractively detailed, with quadrant brackets projecting from the pier supports. In the nave the pew ends, which are also part of this scheme, are panelled and have shallowly pedimented tops. One discordant note is the brown-coloured lectern of *c.* 1948. – STAINED GLASS, W window, Emmanuel, the Sower, the Reaper, *c.* 1927. – MEMORIAL PLAQUES, within church, mainly to members of the Pringle family. – ARMORIAL PLAQUE, on E wall, within Pringle enclosure, arms of Pringle with Baroque mantling, *c.* 1700?

CHURCHYARD, one C18 headstone with relief portrait of deceased holding book; some stones with *memento mori*; some table tombs. A C18 mural memorial SE of the church is set against a section of wall that may perpetuate an enclosure associated with the earlier church. To NE of the church, two opulent enclosures in polished granite to the Baird and Deuchar families, later owners of the Stichill estate. – GATE, NE, dated 1869.

Former CAIRNS MEMORIAL CHURCH, now Cairns House. 1877–8 by *James Stevenson* of Berwick. Whinstone rubble with ashlar dressings. The main (NW) front is articulated into a tripartite composition by buttresses, the intermediate buttresses rising through the gable to be capped by pinnacles. Above a central cusped entrance doorway, flanked by small cusped lights, is a four-light Geometric-traceried window; the flanking sections have quatrefoil windows below cusped lights. Hall and offices to S.

WAR MEMORIAL. *c.* 1920. Centre block with flanking pilasters and open pediment. A granite inscribed panel with a lion-mask faucet below (cf. War Memorial of Ednam, q.v.).

BAIRD MEMORIAL COTTAGES. Erected for Mrs Baird of Stichill by *Thomas Leadbetter*, 1894, in the English cottage style of Norman Shaw. A fine, harled U-plan row, with projecting bracketed half-timbered gables at each end, and centre gable flanked by Venetian windows with bracketed sills.

STICHILL HOUSE (dem.) was built by *J.M. Wardrop* for George
Baird of Gartsherrie, ironmaster, in 1866. Its GATEWAY survives: tall obelisk-topped, square, heavily rusticated gatepiers
flanked by architraved pedestrian gates and square ball-
finialled banded piers. Neo-Tudor former LODGE (Eildon
View).

DESCRIPTION. HAWTHORN COTTAGE is 1890s, English cottage
style of harling with a rosemary-tiled gambrel roof
and basket-arched openings. Entrance doorway with sidelights
under a bracketed pedimented gablet. Opposite, THE OLD
SCHOOLHOUSE is mid-C19 with a hoodmoulded tripartite
window with narrow sidelights, and blocked sandstone round-
arched doorway with sidelights. Later schoolroom with tall
gableted windows to the E (Whinstone). DUNS ROAD has a
terrace of mid-to-late C19 cottages with stone pentice canopies,
the bottom of the stone gable-heads with quirky M-shaped
mouldings. In EDNAM ROAD the SMITHY HOUSE is early
C19. A single-storey and attic rubble cottage with sloping stone
canopies. Workshop attached. Opposite is STICHILL MAINS
FARMHOUSE, Arts and Crafts of *c.* 1900 with a rendered
ground floor and half-timbered gables, each treated differently.
The former mid-C19 harled Free Church Manse is of three
bays, the flanking tripartite windows on each floor with narrow
sidelights.

STIRCHES HOUSE
4010
1.6 km. NW of Hawick

A seat of the Chisholme family, remodelled for John F. Blenkhorn
at the beginning of the C20. Now a care home.

Perhaps originally a square tower house of late medieval date; the
upper storeys were demolished in 1686 and the house given a
new front by Walter Chisholme. Gilbert Chisholme greatly
improved the house *c.* 1864, but *J.P. Alison* made Tudor-style
additions and renewed most of the interior in 1900–4. As
remodelled the house is of local whinstone, rendered, with
sandstone dressings and red Ruabon tiles on the roof. Each of
the three centre bays of the S front has a gablet, and two-storey
canted bays flank a pointed-arched Tudor doorway with
Gothic-topped niches and carved arcading in the spandrels.
Four-storey tower to the l., crenellated and bartizaned, with an
octagonal angle tower corbelled out from the first floor, and
four-light windows to each floor. The two-storey and attic
crowstepped gable at the E end is mid-C19 but given small
capped crenellated turrets and a corbelled-out crenellated oriel
window. Large red brick chimneystacks whose tall linked flues
are advanced and recessed, giving a serpentine effect to the
surfaces. Between the gables are roof valleys, drained through
arched openings flanked by jambs, enclosing lead chutes to the
down-pipes. A late C20 gabled two-storey accommodation
block to the r., and chapel to the l.

The interior, except for the dining room, is Edwardian with
oak panelling and ceilings with enriched fibrous plaster. The

library has dark mahogany shelving. In front of the house, a high balustraded terrace, with flights of steps to the former garden, has weighty ball finials at each corner of the platts.

STABLES. U-plan, rendered with red tiled roofs. The s elevation has curvilinear gabled wings each side of the court, with blind windows and lunettes above. The N front, manifestly with Beaux Arts influence, has two-storey corner towers, each with an ogee-roofed tourelle at the corners, linked by stone arcades set back from the parapet of the high pyramid roof. Large ogee-roofed louvres on top. A tile-hung cupola in the centre with clock and ogee-shaped leaded roof. – LODGE to stables. Rendered base and tile-hung gables, square brick chimneys set diagonally. – GATEPIERS. Square channelled piers with curved walls to finialled piers. Grand cast-iron gates and railings with decorative panels.

STOBO 1030

The village, strung out along the B712 for 1.6 km., began to take shape in the early C19 when housing was erected for labourers on the estate of Stobo Castle (q.v.), and expanded after the Caledonian Railway arrived in 1864.

PARISH CHURCH. The most complete and the most impressive 14 Romanesque parish church in the Borders. Although possibly an ecclesiastical site of greater antiquity, there was a parish church here belonging to Glasgow Cathedral by c. 1120, with the same dedication to St Mungo as the cathedral itself. Much of the building must date from not long after 1120. It has a rectangular chancel, a larger rectangular nave, and a slightly skewed W tower which could be later. The only other additions were a S porch and a laterally projecting aisle towards the E end of the N wall, both of which are barrel-vaulted, and both of which appear to be late medieval.

The leading architectural features of the Romanesque church are a pair of round-headed windows with widely splayed rear arches in the N chancel wall, and the two nave doorways. The s doorway is of two orders: framing a plain continuous inner order is an outer order with an equally plain arch, but octagonal nook-shafts and scalloped caps to the jambs. The simpler N doorway has been converted to a window. Thick harling obscures the extent to which the rest of the walls are C12. The nave's s wall has two Y-traceried windows E of the porch, and a lancet to its w, none of which appear authentic. The chancel's s wall has, from w to E, a small rectangular window, a simply moulded priest's doorway, and a unique four-light window of intersecting tracery with a circlet breaking the arch apex. The upper parts of the tower, with its double-pitched roof and arched bellcote to the w gable, have evidently been rebuilt on more than one occasion, with works recorded in 1657 and 1765.

After the Reformation the chancel and N chapel were cut off from the rest, and the latter was allowed to collapse. Restoration in 1863 by *John Lessels*, for Sir Graham Graham-

Montgomery of Stanhope, brought the chancel back into use and reopened the N chancel windows; less happily, it replaced the original chancel arch with a wider one, and removed an arched tomb recess from between the chancel windows to the W end of the N wall. Arch-braced roofs, with four dormers along the N side, and the W gallery were also of this campaign. Further restoration by *James Grieve* in 1928 rebuilt the outer walls and vault of the N aisle on the mistaken assumption that they were a hermitage, with uncomfortably pebbly masonry externally and a curious wave profile to the extrados of the vault. CARVED FRAGMENTS, found during restoration, include a scalloped nook-shaft, a fragment of tegulation from the upper part of a hogback stone, and a socket stone (for a gable finial?).

Inside, behind the COMMUNION TABLE, a three-arched masonry blind arcade with painted texts of the Lord's Prayer and Beatitudes, *c.* 1871. – PULPIT, S side of chancel arch, restrained timber polygon with interlace decoration to cornice, donated 1936. – PISCINA(?), restored, in N chapel. – STAINED GLASS. Chancel, W window S wall, 'the Resurrection and the Life', *c.* 1894. Nave, W window N side, Christ and Children, *c.* 1923, *Jasper Brett.* Most other chancel and nave windows have Geometric patterns and foliage. N aisle, E face, Burning Bush; W face, St Kentigern and Merlin. – ARCHED TOMB RECESS, relocated to W end of N chancel wall, with defaced heraldry at apex of round arch, probably intended to serve as both tomb and Easter Sepulchre. – MONUMENTS in N aisle. N wall, to E of window, Master Robert Vessy, vicar, †1473, with incised chalice and sacred monogram; to W of window, incised slab with delightfully naïve depiction of man in armour, C16.

The CHURCHYARD has several good table tombs and gravestones. Notable amongst these are: S of tower, Martin Crawford, †169-, with *memento mori*; W of S porch, John Noble, †1723, figure holding gun; NE of chancel, three daughters of Thomas Thomson, †1723, a movingly detailed portrayal beneath Baroque swags of drapery; member of Cunningham family(?), †1730, standing figure holding inscribed scroll; E gable of church, James Russell, †1692, Tuscan aedicule with swan-neck pediment. Also against E wall of church, burial enclosure of family of the Rev. Alex Ker, first recorded death 1812.

MANSE (Glebe House). L-shaped. Harled and limewashed N part of 1791, with a raised attic gable in the centre. Extended 1842–3 by *Robert Hall* with a piend-roofed S wing; the rear (S) wall of the earlier house remodelled to match. Stables courtyard, built of coursed whinstone and using old material, probably from the previous manse, including chamfered window rybats and a carved stone, dated 1645.

DESCRIPTION. At the NE end are EAST LODGE COTTAGES, built by *Robert Lawrie*, mason, *c.* 1804. Originally a pair of whinstone cottages in the centre, with two widely spaced dormers, and a low flanking cottage each side. E of the church is the former STOBO SCHOOL. Gothic, dated 1887, now a workshop. A mid-C20 rear addition dates from its use as a library. Attached two-storey house with wall-head dormers, probably that enlarged for the schoolmaster in 1860. Returning towards the SW, on the S side of the road is the VILLAGE HALL. Coursed whinstone with vermiculated red sandstone dressings, a timber porch at the E end, and a small room to balance at the W end. Dated 1906 on a central gablet. On the l., in the manicured garden of a private house, is a restored TRAIN SHED in whinstone, with bracketed eaves and round-arched openings; the RAILWAY STATION of *c.* 1864 survives as a house – sandstone and bracketed eaves. Of the early C19 smithy, mostly destroyed to make way for the railway in 1864, there remains the whinstone OLD SMITHY and WORKSHOP. On the N side of the road are NEWHOUSES, labourers' cottages built 1812–13, and given this name when the railway arrived. Single-storey and attic, they originally had Yorkshire-type sliding sash windows, with lattice glazing, and wide entrance doorways under rough porches made of knobbly tree trunks.

CROWNHEAD BRIDGE, 1.3 km. S, over the River Tweed. 1986, by *R.I. Hill*, Director of Roads and Transportation, Borders Regional Council, with *Edmund Nuttall Ltd.*, contractors.

DAWYCK HOUSE. *See* p. 207.

STOBO CASTLE
1.3 km. SW of Stobo

A symmetrical castellated mansion, set in a mature landscape on the broad shoulder of Quarry Hill, on the W bank of the River Tweed. 1804–5, by *Archibald & James Elliot* for James Montgomery, whose father, Sir James Montgomery, Chief Baron of Exchequer, had purchased the estate in 1767. It became a health spa in 1975.

Built of random whinstone, with red sandstone used for dressings and central tower, the design derives from Inveraray Castle (Argyll and Bute). The battlemented main block is generally a rectangular-windowed three-storey oblong of nine bays by five, with four storey round corner towers, their tops ornamented with crosslets. However, the oblong's centre is crossed by a four-storey block whose ends project slightly to form the three-bay centrepieces of the long N and S fronts. Over the centre of this transverse block, a yet higher tower whose turrets carry the chimney flues (cf. Inveraray Castle). The original entrance in the S front at *piano nobile* level was approached by a wide ramped perron, supported by battered walls that extended across the basement. The tall central doorway was flanked by two round-headed sidelights, all under a hoodmould. An armorial panel was incongruously set between the top of the door and the decorative fanlight above. All this was obliterated when the military-style projecting porte cochère was added by *John Lessels* in 1849 for Sir Graham Graham-Montgomery. At the centrepiece's second floor, above the porte cochère a round headed central window and, at its third floor, a trio of round-headed openings. On the W elevation a double stone stair leads to a terrace supported by arcades, which was added by *Peddie & Washington*

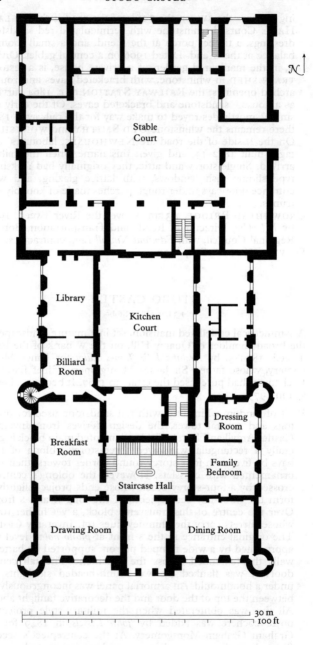

Stobo Castle.
Principal Floor Plan, *c.* 1805.

Browne, *c.* 1907, for Hylton Philipson who had bought the estate in 1905. The three breakfast room windows to the r. have decorative cast-iron balconies which appear to be early C19, and may have taken the place of a long balcony proposed in a preliminary scheme.

From the approach the castle appears to be a free-standing structure, but extending back from the N elevation is a two-storey kitchen court and behind it, at a higher level because of the rise in the ground, the stables court, its ground level lining through with the first-floor level of the kitchen court and the castle. The wall-heads are battlemented and the stables block incorporates turrets at the angles; the E entrances to the kitchen and stables courts are designed in the form of gate-houses.

The INTERIOR has been much modernised and embellished in the C20, supposedly in matching style but tending more towards Rococo than the classical character of the original decoration. The plan, quite different from the unorthodox one used for Inveraray, is classical, and as Mary Cosh has shown, owes something to James Playfair's Melville Castle (Lothian), with rooms on each floor ranged round a rectangular hall containing a cantilevered, top-lit double-return stair-case. The Elliots' plans show the dining and drawing rooms to the E and W of the entrance hall. N of the dining room was the family bedroom and dressing room. To the N of the drawing room, the breakfast room, then the billiard room and library (gutted by fire, 1950) extending along on the W side of the kitchen court.

Originally, entry was straight into the ENTRANCE HALL, but the mid-C19 changes lowered the principal entrance almost to basement level with steps up to the hall; the late C17-type timber balusters must date from the early C20. The entrance hall decoration seems to be a mixture of early C19 and early C20. The walls are divided by pilasters into three bays with round-headed niches, each bay with a groined plaster vault, and flowers at the intersections; the vaulting, flowers and niches are most likely Elliot work. The black marble chimney-piece was provided by *W. Pistell* of London in 1811 for £20. A short flight of steps leads to the central STAIRCASE HALL. This rises through the height of the building to a glazed and cof-fered dome carried on shallow pendentives between segmental arches which have panelled soffits and oculi – those on the side walls to admit some light into the attic floor. The handsome stair with stone treads has an elegant cast-iron balustrade; a niche faces the entrance and there are also niches at the top of each return of the stair.

The DINING ROOM (SE) was redecorated *c.* 1907, given timber panelling on the lower walls, a vine cornice and a stone bolection-moulded chimneypiece. The FAMILY BEDROOM (now dining room) has panelled walls, and the doorpieces have high broken-pedimented consoled tops; a deep frieze is carved with musical instruments. The decoration is repeated in the former DRESSING ROOM (bedroom). The DRAWING ROOM (SW, conference room) apparently retains its simple early C19 decoration, with an anthemion and palmette frieze, and a good white marble chimneypiece, which may be that supplied by *Charles Gowan, c.* 1810. The BREAKFAST ROOM (drawing room) received some sumptuous Rococo decoration, *c.* 1907. In the friezes of the six-panelled early C19 doors are small panels with bows and swags; the doors are trimmed with classical ornament, and flowers and foliage drip from the ceiling. Fluted Ionic pilasters flank the white marble chimneypiece, and carvings of fruit and flowers surround the overmantel mirror. The bedrooms on the first floor are quite plain, several having well-proportioned black and white Kilkenny marble chimneypieces supplied by *W. Pistell, c.* 1811.

The stable and kitchen courts were converted for spa use in 1997–8 by *R.D. Cameron Associates.* Over the stable court, a glass roof supported on a steel frame, over which the frameless glazed panes seem to float like a lierne vault. Large, well-designed glazed N extension by *Ron Cameron,* 2003–4.

LANDSCAPE. The planting of the policies was begun by the first Sir James Montgomery and was continued with woodland planting, *c.* 1804–11, by his son. *Hylton Philipson* designed and created the WATER GARDEN between 1905 and 1913 to produce electricity by harnessing water power. Three large lakes were made, the highest one towards the source of the Weston Burn, the lower two to the E of the castle. The dam across the lower end of the middle lake is 6.1 m. (20 ft) high and is faced with dressed stone. *Edward White* produced a plan for the WILD GARDEN in 1911. Although apparently unexecuted, the present layout is fairly similar. White also supplied a drawing for the timber 'Japanese' bridge.

LODGES and ESTATE BUILDINGS. WEST LODGE, to NW. Built *c.* 1820 on a former approach road. Picturesque, in whinstone, on a sloping site. Bay window to N with sliding sashes and lattice glazing. Mid-C19 KENNELS at Coshbog. Bracketed eaves, wedge-shaped voussoirs over tripartite windows with decorative glazing. To the NE, the GAMEKEEPER'S HOUSE. Mid-to-late C19. Wide bracketed eaves with steep piended red slated roof and decorative tiled ridge. Returning S to the estate entrance, the drive crosses the late C18 segmental-arched GARDEN BRIDGE. Much repaired. On the l. is STOBO MILL, *c.* 1804. Gutted by fire in the early C20 and rebuilt as a granary, retaining a picturesque front façade, with crosslets.– HOME FARM to the N. Square court of offices and farmhouse built for the overseer of the estate, *c.* 1804 and later. Vernacular steading with some good cartshed openings. A mid-to-late C19 block, with a turreted tower in the angle, was added to the early C19 farmhouse. At the foot of the drive is GARDEN LODGE, *c.* 1812, square-plan, piend-roofed, in whinstone with an acute-angled porch. Central red sandstone Tudor stacks. The ornamental gates and screen railings are probably early C20. On the opposite side of the road, the WALLED GARDEN, probably late C18, and disused. The mid-C19 gabled EAST LODGE 1.6 km. NE has overhanging eaves, and gabled porch. Diagonally set square chimneys, and some decorative glazing. Square gatepiers and ornamental gates.

STOBS CASTLE
4.8 km. s of Hawick

Standing like a toy fort in a tight bend of the Slitrig Water, Stobs
Castle, the last of *R. & J. Adam*'s Castle style houses, was
designed just before Robert Adam's death in March 1792, and
completed with modifications by *William Elliot* in 1794. The
Adam design was for a two-storey and basement battlemented
and piend-roofed main block of three bays by one, the outer
corners clasped by square turrets with slit and crosslet openings;
conical-roofed and smaller round turrets rising within the s
turrets' battlements. Principal fronts to the w (entrance) and e
(garden), each with a slightly advanced and crowstep-gabled
centre bay of two storeys, basement and attic, also clasped by
turrets but taller than those of the outer corners, the conception
reminiscent of the centrepiece of Adam's slightly earlier Seton
Castle (Lothian).

This was modified in execution, the basement being omitted, the
outer bays of the fronts raised to three storeys and deprived of
battlements, and the outer corner towers also heightened, all
the masonry of rubble. Nevertheless, the w and e fronts' centrepiece (above their altered ground floors) are stylish, their
pedimented gables with dummy oculi and topped by Latin
crosses. At the w, a simple tripartite first floor window , the
second floor (Adam's attic) window also of three lights but the
openings small, rectangular and horizontally proportioned.
The e centrepiece is the same but its first floor window is a
simple tripartite. Unfortunately, the ground floor of each centrepiece was overlaid in the mid C19, the e with a battlemented
conservatory of porte cochère appearance. To the w front was
added a deep porch and a single-storey corridor across the
outer bays, all this work also battlemented; above the new
entrance, a reused heraldic panel dated 1793, probably from
above the original entrance. Also mid-C19 is the canted bay
window on the main block's n elevation.

Adam designed parapeted single-storey links joining the
main block's w corners to castellated pyramid-roofed pavilions. What were built were piend-roofed L-plan wings (the n
originally stables, the s kitchens), with jambs projecting to the
w and turrets at the e outer corners. The wings were balanced
to the w by similar blocks (the n more stabling, the s a coach
house, its arched carriage entrances now converted to
windows) and joined to them by turreted gateways into the
courtyard in front of the house. Closing this courtyard's w side,
a turreted screen, probably also of the 1790s. This hides a vernacular barn, perhaps of the later C18, its w corners joined to
the courtyard's w stable and coach house blocks by curved
walls pierced by tripartite windows.

INTERIOR. The plan is a basic villa one, and follows Adam's
layout for the principal floors quite closely, but the detail is
presumably Elliot's who agreed to finish the house 'agreeable
to the most approved taste of finishing modern houses in Edinburgh'. The graceful hanging stair of two flights, with stone
platts, combined with the entrance hall, with niches on the w
wall, creates a grand space. The interior ornamentation is

simple with decorative friezes at the ground floor. There are two excellent chimneypieces dating from *c.* 1760 which possibly came from London. The white marble one in the sitting room, to the S (former dining room) has medallion portraits, and a central plaque showing a seated gentleman, a sphinx in the background, and musical instruments, pan-pipes, and archery, indicating a portrait of life's pleasures. The other one in the dining room (former drawing room), is of white marble with mustard yellow inserts, and has a Greek key pattern frieze. There is a billiard room in the N pavilion, *c.* 1865.

NORTH LODGE. The N gate has a red sandstone rustic screen similar to Adam's Moor Park (1763), but likely to be the work of *William Elliot*, *c.* 1817. Doric entrance arch set between flanking screen walls, the one to the E masking a one-roomed porter's lodge. – BLACK LODGE, at the E entrance, a gabled house of *c.* 1865. Close by, two good mid-C18 square rustic gatepiers with vermiculated rustication, deep friezes with triglyphs and paterae, and a cornice topped with square-shaped urns. – GOTHIC BRIDGE crossing the Slitrig Water, NE of the house. Mostly *c.* 1817, but the arch may be earlier.

STOBS CAMP, 1 km. NW. Opened 1903 for military training; it became a prisoner of war camp in the First and Second World Wars. Closed in 1959. The main features are the grid-plan of the main hutted camp. 0.2 km. W of Barns Farm, to the NE, remains of the associated sewage works, one of the most advanced systems of its day, and 2 km SW a practice trench system.

STOBS VIADUCT. 0.3 km SW. 1862 for the Border Union Railway. Four tall arches.

8060

STONESHIEL HALL
2.8 km. SW of Reston

An incoherent small mansion apparently of several stages of development, the building history hidden under its mid-C19 clothing of coursed red sandstone decorated with battlements on the wallheads and Tudor hoodmoulds over the windows. The earliest part seems to be at the back, a pyramidal-roofed three-storey square tower, its W side now with a (blocked) C19 door and octagonal second floor window. This may have begun as a small C16 or C17 tower house (the W wall has a thick upper part, thinned below). To this was added a two-storey S range, probably in the C18, its E part of three bays, now with pilastered and corniced doorpiece at the l., its lower W part of two bays. Inside, the house is spacious at the E end; only a geometric stair with straight timber uprights, a large room on the ground floor, with a room above. The other rooms appear to have been remodelled.

Mid-C19 single-storey LODGE with round-arched windows with lying-panes and intersecting tracery tops. Good gatepiers with carved rosettes and fluted hemispherical caps.

A two-storey rectangular lectern DOVECOT, at the SE corner of a steading, is perhaps mid-C18. Rounded angles and pointed-arched windows in the upper storey. Possibly remodelled in the mid C19, to resemble a gazebo. Converted to a dwelling by *Bain, Swan Architects*, 1995. The gable-head at the NE corner of the steading has a small panel of red sandstone inscribed W.H. (William Home), who owned the estate from 1799 to 1828.

STOW*   4040

Stow in Old English means place – usually a holy or consecrated place. The ancient church of St Mary of Wedale (valley of sorrow – the old name for the Gala Water) was famous throughout the Middle Ages for its privilege of sanctuary and for the fragments of an image of the Virgin supposedly brought from Jerusalem by King Arthur. The parish belonged to the bishops of St Andrews, whose church and manor on the E bank of the river formed the nucleus of the early village. Until 1818, however, the main N–S road from Edinburgh to Galashiels followed the w bank, being linked to Stow by a bridge on the s outskirts of the village. A textile industry was established as early as 1778 and continued on a modest scale until the late C20. The village now comprises a core of plain, single- and two-storeyed houses, mostly C19 (one in Earlston Road sports a C17 sundial), with a sprinkling of solid late Victorian villas and some late C20 infill.

OLD PARISH CHURCH. Roofless. Medieval fabric is evident in the western parts of the N and s walls, which have large extents of Romanesque cubical red sandstone masonry, and there are relics of possible pilaster buttresses at the SW and NE corners of the nave. The blocked round-arched N nave doorway (now with the date 1714 at its head) may also be medieval. The church represented by these fragments was evidently of two compartments, and Cardinal Beaton of St Andrews re-roofed its chancel in 1541.
   Ultimately a T-plan structure, with an orientated main body, and a laird's 'aisle' off the s side; the wall between nave and chancel was rebuilt in 1655. Those earlier post-Reformation modifications were consciously medievalising in their details; the two-light upper w window with uncusped loop tracery, and the round-arched s nave doorway with moulded imposts, could be assumed to be *c.* 1500 if not for their raised margins. Dates of 1660, 1771 and 1794 are provided for some later works by recorded inscriptions on a blocked elevated N doorway, a window in the s wall and the square belfry corbelled out above the w gable respectively (there are also records of earlier work on the belfry in 1627 and 1770, and it is known the chancel was truncated in 1771). There were galleries in the laird's aisle (warmed by a fireplace), and at the w and E ends of the main body (the latter approached by a forestair and porch). An upper doorway on the N side is perhaps more likely to have given access to the pulpit than to a loft.
   CHURCHYARD. Interesting group of memorials and enclosures, including several table tombs to s of church. Against s

---

* The account of the village, but not the churches, is based on that by Colin McWilliam, *The Buildings of Scotland: Lothian* (1978)

wall, Tait of Pirn enclosure, with engaged Tuscan columns, 1851, by *Archibald Ritchie*. Handsome pier memorial capped by urn to William Lees, †1792, sw of church.

St Mary of Wedale Parish Church, at the s end of the village on a terrace above the A7. 1873–6, by *Wardrop & Reid*. An impressive church with walls of pink coursed rock-faced stone and buff ashlar dressings; its planning and detailing show many similarities with the same architects' earlier church at Ayton (q.v.) in the attempt to reconcile mid-C13 style with Presbyterian needs. It is a subtly contrived T-plan structure, with an apsidal 'chancel' at the s end, a 'transept' on the w side, to which a gable and lower vestry block correspond on the E; to the N is the 'nave' with a single w aisle and an imposing N steeple. The three-storey tower is capped by a broached spire with pinnacles and gargoyles at the angles, and lucarnes on the cardinal faces; the second floor of the tower and the N gallery are reached by a circular stair-turret on its w side. The tower has a vestibule at its base, and there are further porches against the w side of the nave, the E side of the chancel, and in the angle between chancel and w transept, the last with an angled face. Further incidental interest is provided by gabled windows at the N end of the nave to light the gallery. Fine displays of Geometric tracery in the chancel, transept and tower, and a rose window in the E gable.

The pulpit and communion table (and later the organ) were initially all against the E gable, with the three arms directed towards them, and with pews for the major families in the s apse and the w nave aisle. The pulpit and organ are still against the E gable, but the communion table has been relocated to a platform below the 'crossing' to face down into the nave, and the chancel is largely empty. Ceilings of polygonal section with arched braces. The two arches of the w nave aisle are carried on a cylindrical pier and responds with highly enriched crocket caps. – COMMUNION TABLE by *John Taylor & Son*, 1912. – PULPIT, octagonal with linenfold panels, originally approached from vestry. – ORGAN, installed 1905, and still a major element in the internal appearance. – STAINED GLASS. w transept: w wall, Scenes from Life of Christ; s wall, Stoning of St Stephen; N wall, St Paul Preaching, by *James Ballantine II*, 1912. s gable: N of pulpit, the Sower; s of pulpit, Ruth Gleaning. Apse s window, SS Luke and Margaret of Scotland by *William Wilson*, 1967. s side of nave, Good Shepherd, *c.* 1965.

Bishop's House (se of the Old Parish Church). This probably originated as part of the estate centre established here by the bishops of St Andrews in or before the C13. The existing building is unlikely to be older than the C16, when no arch-bishop appears to have resided at Stow, and may instead have served as a courthouse. Burnt out before the mid-C19. The building is oblong on plan (15.2 m. by 6.2 m.). The side walls were reduced to their lowest courses in 1979, but the gables stand to a height of three storeys, terminating in massive chim-neystacks. Random rubble masonry, but the rybats of a cen-trally placed doorway in the s wall are of buff-coloured sandstone wrought with shallow cavetto and ovolo mouldings of late C16 or C17 character. Investigations in 1984–5 suggested

that the earlier (w) portion of the building, possibly c16, originally contained a heated chamber over an undercroft. Later
in the c16 the undercroft became a heated living room and the
house was extended E to include a ground-floor kitchen.
Further alterations were made during the c18 and c19. Excavations also revealed that church and house were formerly
enclosed by a shallow ditch, possibly representing the boundary of the bishop's manor.

PRIMARY SCHOOL. *c.* 2002. Cheerful. A low, elongated range
clad with pink blockwork heightened with red sandstone, with
a swept monopitch roof extending as a veranda to classrooms
overlooking the river.

Former SCHOOL, on the E side of the main road. Attractive
Scottish Victorian of 1878 with conspicuous pyramidal-roofed
ventilators.

TOWN HALL. Formidably Baronial for such a small village. Style
is a long way ahead of function. Three-bay balustraded
entrance porch beneath a heavily corbelled parapet, with a
carved panel dated 1855 above an intricate monogram design
probably commemorating Captain Alexander Mitchell-Innes
of Stow (†1873). The accommodation originally included a
library and reading room.

Former MANORHEAD HOTEL, originally the Torsonce Inn. Built
at the expense of the local heritors in 1818–19 to serve
travellers on the new Galashiels road; the designer appears to
have been *John Smith*. Described not long afterwards as
'perhaps unequalled by any country inn in Scotland', it comprises a substantial, two-storey and attic main block of squared
whinstone with buff sandstone dressings, together with a W
wing and N service court. The principal elevation, facing the
main road, has an advanced three-bay centre topped by a
blocking course.

Former WOOLLEN MILL, 0.4km. NW. Probably mid-c19. Plain
three-storey, gable-ended block of whinstone rubble with pink
sandstone dressings. Now residential.

BRIDGES. The PACK BRIDGE (or Old Bridge), at the S extremity of the village, was thrown across the Gala Water in 1654–5
(*Alexander Mein*). Now a picturesque ruin, it comprises three
rubble arches of diminishing span from E to S supporting a
narrow roadway. – LUGATE BRIDGE, 1.7km. SW, is a handsome three-arch structure of local rubble with dressed voussoirs of pink sandstone and rounded cutwaters. Built *c.* 1790
to carry the Edinburgh–Selkirk road across the Lugate Burn.
– FERNIEHIRST BRIDGE, 3.3km. SW, is a single-span built
across the Gala Water in 1829 to connect the roads running
along each bank of the river.

BOWLAND HOUSE. *See* p. 134
TORQUHAN HOUSE. *See* p. 725
TORSONCE HOUSE. *See* p. 726
WOOPLAW HOUSE. *See* p. 763

SUNDERLAND HALL
3.2 km. N of Selkirk

A modest-sized Scottish Baronial house, by *David Bryce* for
Charles Scott Plummer, 1850, incorporating a mid-C18 laird's
house. Bryce retained the C18 house's two-storey, basement
and attic main block but remodelled it and wrapped additions
of the same height round its N side and E end, facing the whole
building in red Denholm sandstone. The C18 four-bay s front
survives but with the addition of a crowstepped gable over the
two E bays, a gabled dormer window between the two W bays,
and conical-roofed round angle turrets, the E of two storeys,
the W of one. At this house's W gable, crowsteps renewed or
added in 1850 together with a gabled square bartizan at the N
corner. N of this, full-height extensions of 1850, the entrance
(now with a late C19 pedimented porch) in an advanced crowstepped gable whose N re-entrant angle contains a conical-
roofed round stair tower abutting the W end of the N range.
Built into this end, a panel carved with the weathered coat of
arms of the Kers of Yair who owned the estate from 1647. In
front of this was a single-storey service block ending in a
conical-roofed round tower, both the service block (now containing a billiard room) and the tower heightened by *Kinnear
& Peddie* in 1885. Bryce's E elevation is symmetrical with
canted bays corbelled out to a square and topped by crowstepped gables, flanking a two-storey, three-bay centre with
gabled wall-head dormers, and a stone balustraded balcony
with wide steps to the garden – a favourite Bryce feature. A
conical-roofed bartizan at each end completes the picture. The
twin-gabled s end of this range, slightly recessed from the s
front of the house, has a wide, two-storey canted bay window
with a battlemented parapet.

INTERIOR. A flight of timber-balustraded steps leads from
a vestibule, with some late C19 painted ceiling decoration and
a stained-glass window, to the inner hall, where the well stair
has carved balusters. A shouldered arched screen divides the
hall from public rooms ranged along the E front. The drawing
room at the s end has decorative cornice and yellow marble
C17-style chimneypiece. In the centre is the library, equipped
with good contemporary bookshelves, with ascetic-looking
carved heads along the top and twisted balusters at the bottom.
The dining room (now kitchen), at the N end, has a thistle
cornice. One mid-C18 panelled room survives in the older part
of the house. Mutuled cornice and fluted pilasters flanking the
chimneypiece (not original). Inserted into the panelling, probably in the late C19, are leather wall coverings said to be Italian.

STABLES (The Square). W of the house. U-plan range of different dates, mostly coursed whinstone with red sandstone
margins. Mid-C19 three-bay cottages (Nos. 1 and 2) with
pentice-roofed porches, and wall-head dormers with catslide
roofs. – Picturesque EAST LODGE, probably by *John Smith*, c.
1830, who designed the adjacent bridge (*see* below). Crowstepped with prominent octagonal chimneys. – NORTH and
WEST LODGES (A707), 1870s.

GARDENS. The terraced gardens N of the house may date

from the mid C18, but were developed in the C19 and C20 down the steeply sloping site. High coped rubble walls. A terrace wall divides the garden, the top one accessed by stone steps with solid balustrades and ball finials and with stone urns along the terrace wall. Decorative wrought-iron gates at the bottom, with flowers and leaves in the manner of the Bear gates at Traquair House (q.v.).

ETTRICK BRIDGE, 0.6 km. SE and TWEED BRIDGE, 0.9 km. NE. Founded in April 1831, designed and built by *John Smith*. Both are handsome triple spans with sandstone voussoirs, rubble spandrels and wing walls. The two principal spans have elliptical arches, the small flood arches are semicircular. The grander Tweed Bridge, with a corbelled parapet over the two main arches with flat pilasters between and blank shield-shaped panels decorating the spandrels, was founded by Sir Walter Scott. He described the occasion as 'of good humour, though without parade, extremely interesting'. The Ettrick Bridge was founded by Charles Scott of Woll.

SUNLAWS HOUSE   7020
1 km. SE of Roxburgh

Now Roxburghe Hotel and Golf Course. A large asymmetrical Scottish Jacobean mansion, incorporating several phases of work, set in a superbly treed park whose planting dates from the early-to-mid C19.

A C18 cottage was enlarged *c.* 1817 by *William Elliot*, with further additions by *John & Thomas Smith, c.* 1820. Major extensions were made for William Scott Kerr of Chatto and Sunlaws by *David Rhind* in 1840–3, but the house was damaged by fire and reconstructed in 1885–6 by *John Watherston & Sons*. The house is mostly three storeys, in stugged coursed sandstone, taken from Sunlaws Quarry. The principal part of the entrance (N) elevation, with central Tudor-arched doorway with hoodmoulded heraldic panel, is probably mostly the Smiths' work. Flanking l. and r. are square bay windows, that to the l. of two-storeys, lighting the extension at this end of 1853 by Rhind for a billiard room; its gabled E facade has a decorative oriel window to the upper floor. At the corresponding W end of the house is a three-stage octagonal tower of *c.* 1820, linking the main block to the kitchen offices. The lancets of the tall, top stage, and its open parapet, formerly with tall decorative finials, are doubtless additions by Rhind. From the tower a lower office wing projects to the N with two courts behind. On the S elevation, where the fire damage was most severe, Watherston rebuilt and extended the main block by five bays, taking in part of the kitchen court. The wallhead was raised and provided with pedimented dormers, and a projecting gable was built at the W end to match an existing one at the E end.

The interior was reconstructed. The saloon became the stair hall, with a T-plan timber staircase and a dark oak chimneypiece with elaborate Gothic ornament, and figures in niches. This was found in the stable offices and 'used again'. The

entrance hall was widened, and the billiard room became the
library, with well-detailed bookcases. Late C19 decoration with
decorative ceilings, deep ornamented cornices, and carved
chimneypieces.

   STABLES, now converted for hotel use. Tudor Gothic by
   David Rhind, 1840–1. The pend topped by a crenellated three-
   stage square tower, a clock face in a diamond panel in the top
   stage. Mullioned windows. – WEST LODGE. Built by *Dods &*
   Cockburn, c. 1836. Asymmetrical with decorative bargeboards,
   a projecting porch and lying-pane windows. Square-capped
   gatepiers. Square stone GATEPIERS at the E entrance, the
   cast-iron inner piers fluted with cone finials.
SUNLAWS MILL, by the River Teviot. Rebuilt 1846–7.

SWINTON

A pleasant late C18 village with a large rectangular green,
improved and enlarged by Lord Swinton in 1799, by granting
perpetual feus and long leases. The cottages were described in
the mid C19 as 'mostly one storey and thatched' and 'occupied
by farm labourers and carters'. Many of the cottages were
remodelled in the late C19, some given another storey, others have
wallhead dormers, and all were reroofed with slate.

Former FREE CHURCH (now village hall). Dominating the
   green. 1859–60, to replace the church of 1843 (*see* below). Buff-
   coloured snecked sandstone and ashlar dressings; five-bay basically rectangular main body. The main S front has a five-light
   window (now bricked up) with tracery of late C13 type rising
   into the gable, above a row of seven cusped lights. A steeple,
   on the W side of the front, tapers inwards above the second
   storey, and had a slender spire (now largely removed) rising
   through the gables of the belfry stage. N of the tower is a porch,
   with the vestry against the N front.
Former FREE CHURCH (now Hope House). Dated 1843.
   Church at lower level and manse above; essentially domestic
   in character.
PARISH CHURCH. Self-effacingly set back within its churchyard
   at the E end of the village, the church is an attractive aggrega-
   tion of elements around a much-rebuilt medieval rectangular
   core. It was in existence by the early C12, when it was granted
   to Durham Cathedral. The principal post-medieval augmentations were two porches and a forestair on the S front; along
   the N side are a burial enclosure, an extended 'aisle', a vestry
   and a small boiler-house. The earliest post-Reformation work
   is perhaps commemorated on an *ex situ* stone within the SW
   porch inscribed 'Mak no delay to turn to the Lord. Anno 1593'.
   But the first significant addition was probably the C17 Swinton
   family burial vault, N of the chancel, later converted into an
   unroofed enclosure. In 1782 a T-plan resulted from the addition of a lateral 'aisle' by the feuars of Swinton, at the centre
   of the N flank. Works involving modifications to windows are
   dated 1796 and 1800 by inscribed gablets, and in 1837 the N

'aisle' was extended westwards. In 1910–11 there was a major restoration by *Robert S. Lorimer*, with the involvement of *Thomas P. Marwick*.

Apart from the Swinton enclosure, the church is rubble-built. The main S front is a pleasingly free composition, with no attempt at symmetry in the placing of the porches (each with a W doorway) and three irregularly spaced windows rise into gabled dormers, two dated 1796 and 1800. A smaller window lights the space below the Swinton loft, in the original chancel area; that loft has a forestair with a C17 moulded doorway at its head, capped by a steep pediment containing the family's arms. The E wall, with a medieval chamfered plinth, has a window to the loft with an ogee-shaped moulding below its lintel; over the window is an armorial tablet with the arms of Swinton, the initials of Alexander Swinton and Margaret Home and the date 1635, the year of their marriage. The W wall, surmounted by a bellcote on a stepped base, has a three-light simply traceried window of *c.* 1913. The N front is the most complex. At the E end is the ashlar-built Swinton burial enclosure, evidently originally covered by a barrel vault. An armorial panel built into the refaced N wall of the church has initials of Alexander Swinton and Margaret Home, pointing to a C17 date for the enclosure's construction. The window looking from the church into the enclosure has the date 1910 in its gablet. The rest of the N front is dominated by the gables of the Feuars' Aisle of 1782 and its W extension of 1837; in front of the former is a widely gabled C19 vestry with a two-light window, and in front of the extension is the boiler-house with a modern relief cross-head in its W wall.

Internally, there is the traditional arrangement of the pulpit and communion table at the middle of the S wall, with the local great family's loft within what had been the chancel. But much now seen dates from 1910–11, when the wall-heads of the N aisle were raised and the ceilings re-formed. The Tuscan columns carrying the roof junction between the main body and N aisle are evidently of 1837, but were elevated on plinths in 1910. – AUMBRY/SACRAMENT HOUSE, N wall of chancel, rectangular but with modern lintel; shelf at mid-height. – COMMUNION TABLE ENCLOSURE and PULPIT, given by Swinton family *c.* 1910, made by *Kensington School of Art*; pulpit with linenfold panels. – FONTS. Pewter basin on wooden stand; a second stone font originally made for the Free Church in 1917. – STAINED GLASS. W window, commemorating members of the Swinton family who re-acquired family estates in 1913. – EFFIGY. In arched recess at middle of S wall, to E of pulpit, knight with inscription HIC IACET ALANUS SVINTONIUS MILES DE EODEM, possibly post-medieval and crudely carved to suggest greater antiquity. – MEMORIAL TABLETS. N wall of N aisle, William Baird, †1872, by *Gaffin & Co.* London. Various memorials to members of Swinton family and to ministers. – SUNDIALS. Old sundial at SW corner. Fine modern sundial on S wall of SW porch, open inscribed book capped by pediment.

SWINTON CROSS. A much-worn classical column in the middle of the green, dated 1769. On top a square block, three faces with sundials, each with gnomons, the fourth with a carving representing a boar under a tree (the Swinton family crest).

SWINTON PRIMARY SCHOOL, Coldstream Road. A mid-C19 gabled schoolhouse and school, dated 1876, just visible behind additions of 1988.

WAR MEMORIAL, at the corner of Coldstream and Main Streets, *c.* 1920. In the form of a Border Cairn, with a granite panel containing the names of the fallen.

DESCRIPTION. Houses border the green on three sides, enclosed on the N side by Main Street. Worthy of attention around the green are the former cart openings in a number of houses, infilled or utilised as garages. The W side is mostly single-storey. On the S side MARYHOLM (No. 20) is late C18, remodelled and refronted, with a corniced doorpiece and panelled pilasters, after 1888 by the trustees of Alan Swinton, who left the house to the village for use as a library and reading room. Converted to flats late C20. Nos. 21–24 have steeply pitched roofs and low wall-heads, No. 24 improved with crowstepped dormerheads and decorative finials. On the E side, No. 27 is dated 1774, and No. 30 was formerly rubble-fronted with an outside stair to the upper floor, but in the late C19 was improved with harling, and gabled wall-head dormers.

At the E end of MAIN STREET, Nos. 46 and 48 with steeply-pitched roofs are single-storey with two-bay wings, formerly housing coaches or workshops. Further on is MARYFIELD, a traditional Free Church MANSE, *c.* 1860. A piended roof with transverse wall chimneystacks, and imposing square, mutule-corniced and finialled gatepiers, with decorative iron gates and spearheaded railings. On the N side, No. 43 is dated 1826 and sports a cubical sundial on a sandstone support, with dials and gnomons. No. 35 a two-storey classical-style house; to the l., a glazed, pilastered and corniced shopfront, a late C19 infill of a former vennel. The WHEATSHEAF INN, the site of an inn since the late C18, is early C19 with mid-C19 bipartite windows with shallow segmental heads. At the foot of Main Street, No. 1 (BEECH HOUSE) is a late C19 former police station. The house with a kingpost and tie-beam gable-head. The single-storey, two-bay station has an architraved surround to a panel over the door and boarded and studded cell door with original fittings *in situ*. Well protected by a railed boundary wall and an iron gate with fleur-de-lys finials.

SWINTON HOUSE
1.8 km. w

Rebuilt in 1800 after a fire, the N block added mid-C19. A two-storey, basement and attic Classical house in mostly coursed sandstone ashlar, band courses dividing the floors, mutuled corniced eaves. A lower mid-C19 two-storey wing to the W. Six bay asymmetrical N elevation. The entrance doorway, with flanking pilasters, is set within a Tuscan Doric porch surmounted by a pediment, with a projecting full-height pedimented bay to the r. The five-by-three-bay S block has a full-height shallow bow. The interior is mostly C19, with a top-lit inner hall, a compartmented ceiling, and a landing balustrade with Chinese-Chippendale style balusters. A bowed sitting room has a decorative cornice, and broken pediment overdoors.

STABLES, NE of the house. Built 1830–40. Large court of stables and coach houses with grooms' and tackmen's rooms over, with later additions to E and N elevations comprising sawmill and covered courts. Coursed rubble with sandstone dressings. A U-plan S elevation, the coach house in the centre two bays. Gabled end pavilions fronted by plain pilasters. – DOVECOT. Cylindrical building of dark red sandstone and dark whinstone. Dividing 'rat course', and an inscribed slab over the entrance dated 1746. Re-roofed in the late C20 and given an upper drum with arched flight-holes. – WALLED GARDEN. Rubble coped walls, with steps to an upper terrace. Square rusticated gatepiers with corniced finialled caps, another pair with finialled pyramidal caps and decorative wrought-iron gates. – GARDENER'S HOUSE. Prominent castellated gable-heads, and pointed-arched windows in side elevations. A byre also has the same detailing. Panel with Swinton coat-of-arms. – EAST LODGE. Mid-C19, gabled, in red sandstone rubble. Corbelled eaves, and depressed-arched openings. Four-light canted window. Square gatepiers with strapworked ball finials.

TEVIOT BANK   5010
2 km. w of Denholm

The estate was purchased c. 1804 by John Scott, son of William Scott of Woll (q.v.). The present mansion is Cotswold Tudor-style, in honey-coloured sandstone, dated 1833. By *William Burn*, replacing an elegant house by his father *Robert Burn*, built c. 1791. Full-height exposed chimney-breasts to the principal kneelered gables, deep chamfered surrounds to the windows, and ball finials to the gables and dormerheads. – Mid-C19 STABLES, incorporating late C18 work.

TEVIOTHEAD   4000

Small village in a predominantly pastoral landscape.

OLD CHURCH, 0.3 km. N. The shell of a church built c. 1790 was incorporated into the school after its replacement in 1856, but is still identifiable on its NW side.

PARISH CHURCH. Built in 1855–6 (1855 inscribed over vestry doorway), by *Mr Cowan*, clerk of works to the Duke of Buccleuch. In mid-C13 English style, and built of squared snecked whin with buff droved ashlar dressings. Buttressed at the angles and along the flanks; gabled S porch, and N vestry. Two-light windows with Geometric tracery, and groupings of lancets with an upper foiled figure in the E and W walls. Gabled bellcote. Ceiling of polygonal section, following the profile of the lower rafters and collars, with arched braces marking the bays.

– COMMUNION TABLE, E end, with openwork traceried front, 1923. – STAINED GLASS. Grisaille E lancets.

GRAVEYARD. Interesting MEMORIALS including a relief carving of an angel and one of a couple standing arm-in-arm: Adam Robson, †1760 and Jean Beatie, †1760. The headstone of John Renwick, †1625, has a curious arrangement of *memento mori*, symbols and animals in a raised arched border around the inscription. In the E boundary wall is a memorial of 1897 to John Armstrong of Gilnockie, the notorious Border Reiver executed by James V in 1530.

COLTERSCLEUCH MONUMENT, 1.25 km. NE. A large cairn, *c.* 1874, to the memory of the poet Rev. Henry Scott Riddell (1798–1870). It overlooks his home, Teviothead Cottage.

TEVIOTHEAD PRIMARY SCHOOL. A mid-C19 T-plan gabled school with overhanging eaves and exposed rafters. A large mullioned tripartite window in the E gable.

VILLAGE HALL. Built in 1907 as a hall and reading room. Corrugated iron, with half-timbered bargeboarded gables, and a hoodmoulded window above the porch.

WAR MEMORIAL, *c.* 1920. A square plinth, supporting an octagonal shaft topped by a cube with shields, and a cross.

DESCRIPTION. THE OLD SCHOOLHOUSE. Mid-C19 former schoolmaster's house, of two storeys, in coursed whinstone, with overhanging eaves and sloping roofed porch. BEADLE'S COTTAGE is an early C19 single-storey former school and schoolhouse, dignified with flush quoins to windows and doors. Stable at the N end. BOWANHILL COTTAGE is possibly early C19, two cottages with a smithy in the middle, raised to two storeys *c.* 1870. The smithy has lattice-glazed windows and the hearth and presses survive. A cobbled area in front has the jig for wheelmaking and an anvil base.

GRAY COAT PELE. *See* p. 335.

5040   THIRLESTANE CASTLE
                    0.8 km. E of Lauder

49 One's first impression of Thirlestane's splendid Scottish Baronial exterior is spectacular but misleading, for this is only the final chapter in a very long story that encompasses castle, fort, Renaissance house and Early Victorian mansion. The site is a long low hillock overlooking the right bank of the Leader Water. The De Morvilles erected what seems to have been a motte-and-bailey castle here in the C12, but little trace of it can now be seen. This was followed by an artillery fort of Italianate design, erected by the English government in 1548 (*Thomas Petit*, surveyor), dismantled by the Scots only two years later and now represented mainly by the remains of earthen bastions. The Maitland family were landowners in Lauderdale from the C13, and in 1587 Sir John Maitland, secretary and acting chancellor of Scotland, purchased the Castlehill of Lauder and began to erect a splendid new house there, which he named Thirlestane after the earlier family residence of that name (*see* p. 723). This forms the nucleus of the present mansion and was probably largely complete by 1590, when Maitland was created Lord Maitland of Thirlestane.

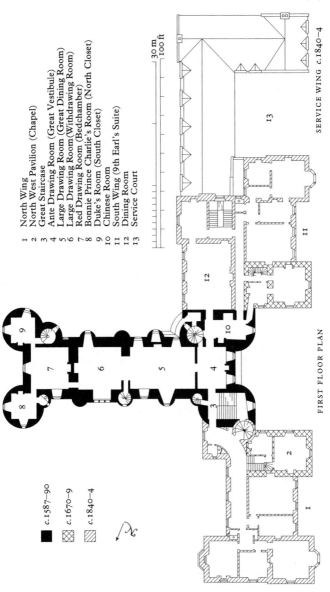

1 North Wing
2 North West Pavilion (Chapel)
3 Great Staircase
4 Ante Drawing Room (Great Vestibule)
5 Large Drawing Room (Great Dining Room)
6 Large Drawing Room (Withdrawing Room)
7 Red Drawing Room (Bedchamber)
8 Bonnie Prince Charlie's Room (North Closet)
9 Duke's Room (South Closet)
10 Chinese Room
11 South Wing (9th Earl's Suite)
12 Dining Room
13 Service Court

c.1587–90
c.1670–9
c.1840–4

30 m
100 ft

SERVICE WING c.1840–4

FIRST FLOOR PLAN

Thirlestane Castle.
Plan.

p. 717

The late C16 was a time of innovation and experiment in Scottish domestic architecture and Thirlestane stands at the forefront of these developments. Indeed, the PLAN was unique: an exceptionally long main block (*c.* 36 m.) aligned W–E, four-and-a-half-storeys in height with a large drum tower at each corner and no fewer than five pairs of semicircular turrets regularly spaced along the flanks. The tops of the corner towers were corbelled out to the square to form caphouses with gabled roofs, while the intermediate turrets rose like massive buttresses to support unusually wide wall-walks on all sides. Thirlestane was conceived more as a house than a castle, and the only overtly defensive features were the iron window grilles, yett (removed *c.* 1670–8) and a sprinkling of gunloops. The clustered towers and oversailing wall-walks that give the building such a striking appearance would have been seen by contemporaries not as aids to security but as appropriate expressions of the baronial status of the builder, one of the most powerful men in Scotland.

Although the original design is much altered, its salient features are still apparent. The plan skilfully achieved spaciousness, privacy and efficient circulation. Above what was almost certainly a vaulted ground floor the main block contained, from W to E, a large hall, outer chamber and bedchamber, with a pair of cabinets in the E corner towers. Possibly this was a reception suite, while the household resided mainly on the second floor, where there seem to have been two principal apartments, with numerous suites and chambers on the floors above. These were served on the S side by turnpike stairs in the re-entrant angles of the two corner towers, and on the N by a third turnpike in the central turret and by a wide circular stair in the NW corner tower, which gave direct access to the hall from the principal entrance in the re-entrant angle between the tower and main block.

The house was little altered until 1670–9, when John Maitland, first and only Duke of Lauderdale, an even more formidable figure than his grandfather and for many years the virtual ruler of Scotland, remodelled Thirlestane as part of a concerted programme of new building at his several Scottish and English residences, including Ham House, Surrey, a property of his second wife, Elizabeth, Countess of Dysart, whom he married in 1672. At Thirlestane, the Duke's principal Scottish residence, *Sir William Bruce*, architect, and *Robert Mylne*, master mason, concentrated on increasing accommodation while at the same time creating a new and more digni-

p. 54

fied W approach. The entrance was switched to the W gable, which was rebuilt with a pedimented centrepiece between circular-topped towers. In front, the sharply sloping ground was terraced to create a paved courtyard, flanked on each side by new four-storey pavilion wings with ogee roofs, descending via a balustraded stair to the first of three outer courts. The central one incorporated the main gate and a pair of two-storey outer pavilions, the lateral ones contained stables and kitchens. Additional service accommodation created beneath the terrace allowed Bruce to dispense with the vaulted cellarage of the old house, which he now converted into a spacious apartment for the Duke and Duchess. This, in turn, freed the second floor for use by other members of the family and by guests. But the main effort was directed at the first floor *piano nobile*, where the state apartment was completely refurbished, the hall being partitioned to create an additional vestibule at the W end, unless there was always an anteroom here, as at Ferniehirst (q.v.). A new scale stair was constructed in the NW corner tower to give access to the vestibule, beyond which lay a sequence of five rooms, all provided with new windows and lavishly fitted out in the latest style by Dutch and English craftsmen recruited by the Lauderdales from Ham House and elsewhere in the London area. An avenue was planted along the new line of approach from the burgh of Lauder and gardens were laid out, probably to the design of *John Slezer*, p. 54 the Duke's surveyor, working under Bruce's direction. Plans were also drawn up for an extension to the E end of the house, including matching wings, but little progress had been made with this before work was halted following the Duke's death in 1682. The total cost, including a new church in Lauder (q.v.), was about £10,000.

Two proposals for remodelling Thirlestane were drawn up during the C18, one by *Robert Adam*, but neither was implemented. However, the seventh Earl (†1789) pulled down the walls of the outer courts, together with the outer pavilions, while his successor closed the W avenue and formed a new approach from Lauder some distance to the N. The ninth Earl, succeeding to the property in 1839 and finding the house greatly dilapidated, decided upon more fundamental changes and lost no time in calling in *William Burn*, who, from 1840 to 1844, provided a new suite of private rooms at the SW corner of the old house, with separate access via the main entrance hall. The old corner tower and adjacent pavilion were incorporated in this new wing, with rooms for the Earl on the second floor, staff quarters below and a new kitchen court extending S. Balancing this was a similar N wing with numerous bedrooms for guests, for whose entertainment the Duke's apartment on the ground floor of the main block was now remodelled to provide a suite of handsome public rooms. Burn also renewed much of the external detail and remodelled the upperworks in a mixed Jacobean and Scottish Baronial style sympathetic to the earlier work. Burn planned and supervised the work himself, but it is possible that *David Bryce*, whom Burn took into partnership in 1841, may have had some part in the final design. The work was completed at a cost of over £25,000. Further repairs and alterations were carried out by *D. & J. Bryce* for the eleventh Earl (†1878), who also extended the N wing to provide a conservatory and other outbuildings (dem.). In 1978–82 a major programme of conservation was undertaken under the direction of *Crichton W. Lang* and further repairs were completed by *David Willis* in 1990–3. Work continues on the restoration of the interior.

EXTERIOR. The visitor normally approaches Thirlestane by way of the W FRONT, and it is here that the piecemeal development of the castle is most clearly apparent. Little can now be seen of Chancellor Maitland's house on this side, and 49 although much of Bruce's front remains in place, the whole composition has been brilliantly dramatised by Burn, to whom are due the contrasting roof forms, soaring turrets and eye-catching, ogee-roofed central tower. In remodelling the w corner towers Burn went some way towards restoring them to their original form, corbelling the tops out to the square. Initially he also proposed to cap them with crowstepped gables, but in the event substituted flat roofs and balustraded parapets that echo those of the terrace below. The successive building periods are reflected by variations in the character of the masonry. The C16 and C17 facework is composed of small stones bonded with generous quantities of mortar, while the N and S wings of the early 1840s are built of fair-sized blocks of dark greywacke. A similar stone, laid with wider joints, appears in the NW corner tower, largely reconstructed, it seems, for the eleventh Earl. Pink Bassendean sandstone dressings are used throughout. Much of the superficial detail, including the terrace staircase, was renewed or created by Burn, but Mylne's classical doorpiece survives intact. It is cut from a superior sandstone brought from Dalgety (Fife) and the design appears to be derived from plates in Alessandro Francini's *Book of Architecture* (published in English in 1669). The frieze incorporates the monogram initials and crests of the Duke and Duchess, while the date of their marriage is carved in the pediment along with the Duke's armorial achievement. The Duke considered placing a balcony over the doorway, but the existing balcony is Burn's. The flanking windows have rusticated surrounds – a favourite device of Bruce – and the pavilions originally had rusticated quoins. The N and S wings, of five bays and three main storeys, have prominent oriel windows on the principal floor, and the adjacent service court to the S has unusual arcaded galleries at two levels to give all-weather cover to servants.

The N and S ELEVATIONS reveal the structure of the early house, with its intermediate turrets and oversailing wall-walks behind balustraded parapets. On the S side the walk is carried on arches springing from turret to turret, while on the N, where the spans are wider, it is in part supported by intermediate corbels; this method is also used to carry similar walks between the corner towers on each gable (the W one renewed by Burn). This construction is without parallel in Scottish architecture and it has usually been assumed that the walks were contrived by Bruce. But what purpose do the intermediate turrets serve – only one originally contained a stair – if not to support the walks, and the balustrades are described in 1677–8 as 'ye old ballasters in ye top of ye house'? Bruce, in fact, seems to have done no more than repair the wall-walks, while Burn restored them, added caphouses over the mid-turrets and renewed the dormer windows. Quite apart from the upperworks, the elevations of the early house were originally more showy. Traces can still be seen of the decorative triangular- and semicircular-headed pediments formerly over the upper-floor windows (two of them clipped by the arches of the wall-walk). The corbelling of the two re-entrant N turrets is carved with nailhead ornament, while the original entrance doorway beside the W turret, although renewed by Burn, retains a blocked panel frame probably intended for a coat of arms. The existing windows are mainly of the 1670s and 1840s, but a number of earlier openings survive, together with an assortment of gunloops – those on the ground floor look more businesslike than those above. Their redented ingoes, perhaps designed as much for effect as for deflection, echo those at Drochil Castle (q.v.).

The E FRONT of the castle, with its attached corner towers, retains much of its original late C16 character, providing a yardstick against which the successive alterations to the W end can be unravelled. The parapet of the E walk incorporates square shafts instead of balusters and it is possible that these are survivors from the original scheme. The square caphouses are set within the diameter of the corner towers, as at Drochil Castle.

The spectacular INTERIORS are a mixture of Caroline and Victorian, the two styles marrying surprisingly well. The principal doorway opens into the lower entrance hall. Beyond is the suite of PUBLIC ROOMS created by Burn in the early 1840s. The original sequence comprised breakfast room, billiard room and library, with the books overflowing into the adjacent corner towers, but the positions of the billiard room and library have been reversed, perhaps by the 11th Earl. In converting the cellarage of the early house into a family apartment in the 1670s Bruce lined most of these rooms with bolection-moulded oak panelling and Burn saved what he could, cannibalising the linings of the (present) billiard room and adjacent tower rooms to make up deficiencies in the breakfast room and library. The hall panelling, together with all doors and shutters, is of the 1840s by *Francis Farquharson*, of Haddington. In the four main rooms chunky, proto-classical chimneypieces of polished red granite and compartmented ceilings of Jacobean type by *James Annan & Sons*, of Perth, with a thin sprinkling of pendants and floral ornaments. The STATE APARTMENT is now approached by the SE turnpike stair, which leads directly into the most intimate chambers, but as designed by Bruce, access was via the stair in the NW corner tower. As on the ground floor, Burn's renovations were thorough, but one or two state rooms survive more or less intact and all preserve their magnificent ceilings by the English plasterers *George Dunsterfield* and *John Hulbert*, who were also employed at Holyroodhouse, Edinburgh. Their work is remarkable not only for 50 its technical competence and richness of invention, but also for the marked individuality of treatment accorded the various rooms.

The C19 Jacobean-style timber GREAT STAIRCASE (replacing the C17 stone one) has bolection-moulded oak panelling of the 1670s, rearranged by Burn. The lofty ceiling is given even greater depth by a coved frame containing boldly modelled eagles (a reference to the Duke's coat-of-arms) and cartouches displaying the Maitland lion beneath a ducal coronet. The ANTE DRAWING ROOM (former Great Vestibule) has another richly ornamented ceiling with broad ribs decorated with leaf sprays and bunches of fruit. Most remarkable are the three columned doorpieces with broken pediments and distinctive panelled doors, which closely resemble those of the late 1630s at Ham House. One may be the pillars and door-case shipped to Scotland, with two doors and other items from Ham and Lauderdale House, Highgate, London, in 1673. The others were perhaps matched by the Dutch joiners, *Mathias Jansen*, *Heinderich Meinners* and *John Ulrich*, who presumably installed the rest of the panelling. The doorcases were heightened in the early 1840s, when the doors were renewed, but retain the original mouldings. They were painted and gilded by *Francis Chalmers* in 1842–3. Yellow marble chimneypiece of the 1840s.

Beyond was a sequence of great dining room, withdrawing room and bedchamber, together with a pair of closets in the E corner towers. Burn created a single LARGE DRAWING ROOM from the first two rooms, renewing the doors, windows and shutters. Enough remains of the upholstery and curtains, supplied by *Thomas Dowbiggin & Co.*, London, to demonstrate the very lush effect that he sought. The original dining room ceiling has an elaborate double border filled with leaves, fruits and coronets, and an eagle at each corner, but the central panel was reworked in 1844 by *Annan* for a chandelier. Over the former withdrawing room the ceiling is more restrained; a plain central panel bordered with musical instruments.

Chimneypieces of yellow Siena marble, modelled in the French manner, were from *David Ness*, Edinburgh; he presumably also supplied the similar one in the Ante Drawing Room and a plainer one in the RED DRAWING ROOM (former bedchamber). Its ceiling is different again, with hanging garlands spilling out of the coves of the central compartment and cornice, while the closet ceilings, apart from an inserted(?) Maitland crest in the DUKE'S ROOM (S), have plain central panels perhaps intended for paintings. In BONNIE PRINCE CHARLIE'S ROOM (N) the corners of the ceiling contain garlands with central rosettes from which fully modelled miniature lions emerge, a device employed also at Holyroodhouse. The NW PAVILION (burnt out in 1822) contained a richly furnished chapel created by Bruce, with a private gallery entered from the landing of the adjacent staircase. The SW corner tower (now the Chinese Room) and its adjacent pavilion contained a separate small apartment.

The UPPER FLOORS of the early house may not have been fitted out until the beginning of the C17. Two rooms on the third floor have bolection-moulded fireplaces with false keystones, and on the second floor survives an exceptionally fine ceiling, with floral patterned ribs and compartments containing medallion heads of four of the Nine Worthies (Alexander, David, Hector and Joshua) after engravings by *Nicholas de Bruyn*. This must date from before 1616 (it bears the initials of Sir John Maitland, son of Chancellor Maitland, created Viscount Lauderdale in that year) and is therefore amongst the earliest of a group, also seen at Balcarres and Kellie Castle (Fife) and Muchalls Castle (Kincardineshire). The armorial of the Earl of Lauderdale, created 1624, must have been added later. In the S WING the ninth Earl's dining room has a good Jacobean-style ceiling with strapworked panels and pendants by *Annan*, 1841–2, and a contemporary chimneypiece of red

granite. Other rooms have plain marble chimneypieces supplied by Ness. The SERVICE QUARTERS have a first-floor
kitchen and a huge groin-vaulted coal house below.

POLICIES. The park and gardens in their present form seem
to have been laid out mainly by the eighth, ninth and eleventh
Earls, although the enclosure wall is probably earlier. A
plan by *Slezer* shows the elaborate formal garden designed
for the Lauderdales and incorporating features similar to
those also proposed for Ham House (Surrey) and Lethington
(Lennoxlove, Lothian); the terraced slope towards the S
extremity of the site may be a relic of this. The 9th Earl formed
a new W approach on the S outskirts of Lauder with a COURT
OF OFFICES by *Burn* just inside the entrance. Compact layout
at two levels with the stables and coach house approached
directly from the avenue and the cartsheds less visibly from
below. The adjacent W LODGE is also by Burn. The S
ENTRANCE, now the usual approach for visitors, was probably
created by the 13th Earl (†1924); the swept screen walls terminate in rusticated piers with eagle finials and ornamental
cast-iron gates.

OLD THIRLESTANE CASTLE, 3.3 km. E. The ruins of a C16 tower
house on the W bank of the Boondreigh Water, possibly the
site of an early Maitland residence. The tower itself is probably associated with a branch of the Cranstoun family, near rel-
atives, and possibly tenants, of the Maitlands. The tower seems
originally to have been oblong on plan (*c.* 10.1 m. by 7.3 m.)
and at least three storeys high. It was probably built shortly
before 1572, when it was attacked and burnt by Alexander
Home of Crosbie. Thereafter the castle seems to have been
rebuilt and it may have been during the course of this reconstruction that a stair-turret was added to the W wall to convert
the building into a T-plan.

TIMPENDEAN TOWER
2.6 km. NW of Jedburgh

6020

The incomplete shell of a C16 tower house standing beside the
well-preserved earthwork remains of an earlier residence. Timpendean belonged to the Douglases from the early C14 to the
early C19, and the earthwork probably incorporated the house,
or tower, destroyed by Hertford's army in 1545. The present
tower must have been constructed soon afterwards. It was superseded in the C18 by a new residence, 1.2 km. N, and was ruinous
by 1834.

The TOWER HOUSE is almost square on plan (8.8 m. by 7.3 m.)
and originally contained four storeys. Buff-coloured sandstone
rubble with similar dressings and windows with chamfer-
arrised margins. The roof was gabled and parapet-walks, if
they existed, must have been confined to the side walls. In the
original arrangement each wall probably contained a single,
wide-mouthed gunloop at ground-floor level, but one of
these was subsequently replaced by a doorway and another
by a window. The original entrance in the NW wall has a

semicircular-arched opening rebated for outer and inner doors. The SW wall shows the scar of a wing possibly added in the C17. A newel stair contrived partly within the wall thickness of the tower served the first and second floors of the wing but, curiously, there was direct access between tower and wing only at third-floor level, where the wing did not communicate with the staircase below. Inside, a lobby to a barrel-vaulted ground-floor chamber and broad newel stair in the N corner of the building. The chamber, perhaps initially a storeroom and subsequently a kitchen, has a large fireplace in the SW wall. A little below the level of the first floor a stone laver, or slop-sink, opens directly off the staircase. The greater part of the first floor was occupied by what was perhaps originally a combined hall and kitchen. This was lit by generous windows in the side walls and heated by a big, lintelled fireplace with a quirked edge-roll surround; immediately beside it, two mural aumbries. Off the lower end of the hall is a small, unheated, vaulted chamber possibly designed as a prison or strongroom (cf. Goldielands Tower and Burnhead Tower (qq. v.)). The second floor may have contained a single chamber only; all the upper floors were of timber.

The EARTHWORK, measuring 82 m. by 58 m. internally, was enclosed on three sides by two ramparts and a medial ditch, with an additional rampart on the more vulnerable SW side. The entrance lay close to the S corner.

1030

TINNIS CASTLE
1 km. E of Drumelzier

The enigmatic remains of a late medieval castle of the Tweedies of Drumelzier, who had a deserved reputation as one of the most lawless families in the Borders. Its lofty, but comfortless perch, high on a rocky knoll overlooking the valley of the Upper Tweed, may have been chosen to impress. Probably erected not long before its first appearance in record as the 'place of Tynnes' in 1525, the castle's shattered appearance may corroborate a late C17 account of Tweeddale which states that it was blown up by Malcolm, third Lord Fleming (†1547), in retribution for his father's murder by the Tweedies.

The castle stands within the outer ramparts of an Iron Age hill fort (*see* below), some portions of which may have been robbed to provide building materials. The masonry is of random rubble so tenaciously bound with lime mortar that several large fragments of walls survive scattered across the site; some show traces of barrel vaulting. Only the lowest courses of the walls remain *in situ*, but the castle seems to have comprised a quadrangular barmkin (*c.* 27 m. by 22.7 m.) with a residential block, perhaps a tower house, on the E side. At the NW and SW corners of the barmkin there were projecting circular towers *c.* 5.7 m. in diameter with walls only 1.1 m. thick, an uncommon feature in late medieval Borders castles. Where they occur elsewhere, e.g. at Boghall Castle and Cadzow Castle (Lanarkshire), they usually incorporate gunloops, but here the surviving openings were deeply splayed slits unsuitable for firearm defence.

The remains of the FORT comprise an elongated enclosure taking in the summit, and at least two additional lines of defence barring the NE and SW approaches. An exposure of vitrefaction on the SW shows that the innermost rampart was timber-laced.

TODRIG

5 km. SW of Ashkirk

4010

An enlarged and much-modified tower house of the Scott family. A charter of 1553 mentions the mansion or manor place of Todrig, with its 'houses, biggings (buildings) and pertinents', but to judge from its appearance the present tower was not erected until the late C16, while the plain three-storeyed W extension probably belongs to the late C18 or early C19.

Oblong on plan (9.7 m. by 7.2 m.), the tower house rises to a height of three storeys and a garret. The masonry, formerly harled, is of local random rubble with quoins of the same material and dressings of pink- and buff-coloured sandstone. The margins of the original windows are mostly round-arrised (one is chamfer-arrised), while the semicircular-headed entrance, placed towards one end of the S wall, is wrought with a continuous, quirked edge-roll. The doorway is rebated for outer and inner doors, the inner one originally equipped with a draw-bar. Gabled roof. The interior has been much altered. The ground-floor chamber, probably originally vaulted, has been re-ceiled at a higher level, while the first-floor chamber appears to have been subdivided c. 1750, when a bead-moulded chimneypiece was inserted in the E room. The second floor, also subdivided, contains a bolection-moulded chimneypiece of c. 1700. Unusually, the original oak and ash roof frame appears to survive. This is of simple, collar-rafter construction with pegged joints and incised assembly marks. Access to the upper levels is by means of a timber stair in the W extension, which may replace an earlier one of stone situated in the SW corner of the tower.

The STEADING incorporates a carved panel bearing the inscription 1698/GP [George Pott] REBUILT /1833.

TORQUHAN HOUSE*

3 km. NW of Stow

4040

Built 1823 for William Colvin of Mitchelson. In the style of *John Smith* (cf. Burnhouse). Two storeys, five bays, the front in dark brick-sized whinstone blocks with sandstone dressings, the rest in coursed whinstone. The pedimented centre has a Roman Doric doorpiece. Single-storey wings, set back, each with a

---

* Account adapted from that by Colin McWilliam, *The Buildings of Scotland: Lothian* (1978)

Venetian window. In 1850 a circular bay was added to the s
end of the ground floor. *Kinnear & Peddie* did work here in
1885 and may have been responsible for the pretty interior.

TORSONCE HOUSE*
0.5 km. s of Stow

The former house, by *David Bryce Jun.*, 1864, was tall and hard
with braced gables and iron balconies. Rebuilt after a fire in
1992–4 by *Simpson & Brown* (architect-in-charge, *Andrew
Davey*), using the original sturdy dark whinstone foundations;
the new work is rendered. The gable pattern was repeated, producing a dramatic composition which would not be out of
place in the Bavarian Alps. Single-storey entrance front (E) on
to a large flat terrace; two-storey where it drops down the hill.
Savings from the previous house include mullioned windows
(added to Bryce's house *c.* 1900) and iron balustrades,
superbly matched with new work. The drawing room chimneypiece and overmantel were formerly in the dining room,
and elsewhere Jacobean panelling of *c.* 1900 has been repro-
duced. Pretty shell niche in the principal bedroom. The large
terraced garden of 1864 heightens the dramatic aspect.
TORSONCE MAINS, 0.4 km. s. Late C19. An impressive three-
storey block (animal shed downhill, stable uphill and lofts on
top).

TORWOODLEE HOUSE
3 km. NW of Galashiels

Classical house built for James Pringle of Bowland *c.* 1783, probably by *William Elliot* who later built the similarly detailed The
Yair (q.v.) for the same family. The design looks to the Palladian
villa, and has the feel of the young Elliot searching for a style.

Main block of two storeys above a high basement; piended platform roof. At each end and set well back from the s elevation of the main block, a small court (offices at the E, stabling
at the W) with N and s screen walls originally topped by decorative urns. These link to pavilions, all built of whinstone
with red sandstone dressings for the window margins and
rusticated quoins; the margins on the basement (s) have
Gibbs surrounds which are continued across the screen walls.
s front of five bays, the centre slightly advanced and surmounted by a triangular pediment with three decorative urn
finials, and a central oculus. An excellent pedimented
doorway is approached by a graceful flight of steps, with decorative balusters; above is a Venetian window set on prominent trusses. The small attic windows recessed in the roof
appear to be original.
    The N elevation was similar but extensively altered in 1864

* Account adapted from that by Colin McWilliam, *The Buildings of Scotland: Lothian*
(1978)

by *Peddie & Kinnear*, who made a new principal entrance here, rebuilding the central bay. It now rises 60ft (18.29m.) to a large pediment, under which three small oblong windows light the cistern and closets. The new entrance is reached through a large solid porch with cushioned quoins and wall-head balustrade. Above is a Venetian window supported by stone brackets. Also in 1864, the pavilions were given extra floors, with pedimented gables to N and S.

Inside the N entrance, stairs rise to an inner hall. Two flights of the original curved stair were removed in 1864, and a large timber stair inserted in the adjacent rooms to the W, rising to the bedroom floor. The late C18 entrance hall to the S was incorporated into the existing drawing room, and both this and the dining room were redecorated – the opulent window pelmets must date from this period. Late C18 carved pine chimneypiece with Ionic pilasters, fluted frieze and centre panel with an urn – similar to one at The Yair. Preserved in the present hall are two carved stone panels from Old Torwoodlee (*see* below) and Buckholm Tower (q.v.).

STEADING, NE. Late C18. – Semicircular WALLED GARDEN approached over a burn by a bridge with ornamental iron balustrade of *c.* 1864. – Bow-fronted LODGE, *c.* 1810.

OLD TORWOODLEE, 0.7km. SW, is the ruin of a very smart house erected by George Pringle of Torwoodlee in 1601. The sloping site has been terraced to accommodate a roughly square courtyard with the dwelling-house to the W, a linked range of offices to the N and (presumably) screen walls on the other two sides. Little now survives apart from the shell of the three-storeyed house (21.9m. by 7.9m.), parts of which stand almost to their full height. Local whinstone rubble masonry with dressings of red and buff-coloured sandstone; some of the windows were barred and all seem to have had plain round-arrised margins. As at Old Fairnilee (Fairnilee House), there was a near-central entrance in the principal (W) front giving access to a scale stair rising to the first floor. At Old Torwoodlee, however, the entrance is contained within an extruded semicircular tower, which also housed the spiral upper flights of the stair. Above the bolection-moulded doorway, an empty panel frame beneath a drip-mould. The missing date panel (now at Torwoodlee House, above) bears the arms and initials of Pringle and his second wife, Mary Stewart (whom, however, he did not marry until 1605). The tower is corbelled out to the square at second-floor level, and the uppermost member of corbelling is decorated with a band of miniature dogtooth ornament. It rose a storey higher than the remainder to a gabled caphouse lit by a hoodmoulded window. This, and the other decorative details of the tower, link Old Torwoodlee to a number of neighbouring buildings, including the towers of Aikwood, Hillslap and Greenknowe (qq.v.).

On the ground floor two barrel-vaulted cellars and a vaulted passage S of the stair and another vaulted room to the N, perhaps a kitchen. On the first floor there seems to have been a three-roomed suite comprising a hall to the N of the stair and an outer and inner chamber to the S; the arrangement on the second floor probably similar. Apart from window bars, there is no surviving evidence of any defensive provision, but the courtyard wall is said to have incorporated a loopholed parapet.

BURIAL ENCLOSURE, I.I km. sw. Small rectangular rubble-built enclosure with red sandstone dressings to the doorways. The date 4.8.09 on the sw doorway presumably refers to repairs.

3030

TRAQUAIR

A small village which for much of its history functioned mainly as a satellite of Traquair House.

PARISH CHURCH. There was probably a church on this site from at least the C17, and there are references to work on the w gable by *William Hislop* in 1694. Much of the building dates from a remodelling of 1778 by *John Haldane*, with further works in 1821, 1840 (by *W. H. Playfair*), 1863 and 1897. At its fullest extent the church was of T-shaped plan, with the Stuart of Traquair 'aisle' forming the N arm. In 1913–14 a vestry was added in the NW re-entrant between 'aisle' and main body, and new furnishings were installed. Harled rubble masonry with ashlar dressings. The main (s) front was originally a symmetrical composition having two round-arched windows with keystones and impost blocks at the centre, the keystone of the w window dated 1778. Following internal reordering (in 1897?), a third round-headed window was added in the w part of the wall to light a chancel area. A squat two-light rectangular window towards the E end lights the space below the gallery, and there was probably once an upper window lighting the gallery itself; any evidence of similar windows at the w end of the wall has been lost below two C19 memorials. The w wall has two round-headed windows with shutters, and there is a birdcage bellcote to its gable. Against the E wall is the gallery stair, beneath which is the main entrance to the church; was there originally a similar arrangement at the w end? The N wall had a single rectangular window with chamfered surrounds on each side of the aisle, but that to the w is now blocked by the vestry.

The N AISLE, which is unroofed, has a pointed window above a memorial to the Earls of Traquair. Beneath the flaking harling of its E face is a blocked doorway with round-arrised dressings of red and buff sandstone, similar to those of a window of 1599 at Traquair House (*see* below). Investigations *c.* 1997 revealed traces of burials but no vault below the aisle.

The church has a coomb ceiling with simple mouldings. The surviving E gallery, carried on cast-iron columns and with a raised and fielded panelled front, has been enclosed. The pulpit and communion table are on a platform between the two w windows. – PULPIT and FONT, 1914. The former semi-octagonal with simple Gothic detailing. – MONUMENTS. Towards w end N wall, Janet Tennant of the Glen, †1866, by *John Steell*, 1877–8, white marble angel in high relief holding cross and pointing expressively heavenwards (the inscription records the

restoration of the church by Sir Charles Tennant). Towards E
end N wall, Edward Wyndham Tennant, †1916, by *Allan G.
Wyon* (1920), Jacobethan strapwork in coloured marbles.
Bronze tablet to Douglas Oliphant Constable, †1916, by *G.
Maile & Son*, London. – EXTERNAL MONUMENTS. N wall of
N aisle, aedicular memorial to Earls of Traquair, containing
tablet to Lady Louisa Stuart, †1875; towards W end S wall,
Alexander Brodie, ironmaster, †1811, marble tablet in simple
classical frame.

CHURCHYARD. Good group of C17–C19 memorials, upright
slabs, obelisks and table tombs, with usual range of *memento
mori* and some trade emblems. David Bel, †1691, has emblems
of a tailor; Andrew Hay, †1736(?) has spade and rake. Against
N boundary wall, burial enclosures for Williamson of Cardrona
and Tennant of the Glen families.

KNOWE BRIDGE, 0.3 km. W, over the Quair Water. Peebles Town
Council voted six guineas towards the cost in 1769. Single segmental arch with a high parapet. Whinstone rubble and
dressed voussoirs. Splayed approaches end in rudimentary circular piers.

MANSE (Kirkbride House). Built first in 1694 by *William Hislop*,
mason, and *John Paterson*, wright, but added to and remodelled, 1793, and enlarged *c.* 1814. Harling covers all the
changes but windows with chamfered arrises on the N and E
elevations look C17. The three-bay S façade is probably late C18,
with later porch topped by a finial. Interior refurbished in the
mid C19. A bedroom has a delightful timber and gesso chimneypiece with centre panel of a linden or lemon tree, a church
at each end of the ornamented frieze, and tulips topping the
jambs. Range of small offices, including a barn, probably late
C18.

TRAQUAIR PRIMARY SCHOOL. Dated 1828. Single storey, L-
plan containing two classrooms. Whinstone rubble with sandstone margins, and flush angle quoins. Wide astragalled
windows with top opening lights. In the centre of the W elevation, a pedimented entrance porch, with central doorway and
sidelights. Mid C20 E addition.

WAR MEMORIAL, *c.* 1920. Celtic cross standing on a large
roughly sculpted boulder.

HOWFORD FARM, 2 km. NW. Built 1839–40, by *Robert Lochie*
and *Robert Hall* of Galashiels and *Robert Ritchie* of Reston,
masons. Stylish two-storey farmhouse with a long wing projecting from the W elevation, by tradition built for farm servants. Polished ashlar front, the rest harled. The main block
has a deep stone plinth, giant corner pilasters, projecting
cornice and parapet. The E front's centre bay projects, with a
block pediment and Tuscan Doric columned doorpiece; its
windows have polished jambs, the side windows alternate
blocks of stone.

TRAQUAIR MILL, 0.5 km. WSW. Dated 1778. Built by *John
Haldane*, who at the same time repaired an existing kiln, which
probably survives from an earlier building. Rubble-built corn
mill built into the high ground on the E side. Kiln at the S end
linked to the mill and wheelhouse by a range of cartsheds.
MILL HOUSE. Dated 1779 on a stone at ground level. Central

door with rectangular fanlight. A mid-C19(?) two-storey N addition, with wall-head dormers that have sandstone margins, bargeboarded gables and slate cheeks, but the irregular arrangement of windows suggests it may have been an earlier single-storey cottage. Single-storey bothy on the l. converted to accommodation and studio by *Ben Tindall*, *c.* 1995.

THE GLEN. *See* p. 325.

3030

TRAQUAIR HOUSE
0.5 km. N of Traquair

The epitome of traditional Scottish Domestic architecture, Traquair's great charm stems from the fact that, unlike many other historic Border seats, it has been neither classicised nor Baronialised. Indeed the exterior has hardly changed since the Treaty of Union (1707), although the well-preserved interior contains some exceptional decorative schemes of mid-and late Georgian date.

The Kings of Scots had a residence here during the C12 and C13, quite likely on the present site, a low gravel mound at the confluence of the River Tweed and the Quair Water. Subsequently the property was held by various owners before passing, in 1491, to James Stewart, a son of the Earl of Buchan and founder of a long line of Stewart (Stuart) lairds and Earls of Traquair. When the present house was founded and how it first developed are hard to say, for inspection is hampered not only by the harling, but also by the palimpsest nature of much of the interior. The present appearance is largely that arrived at by *c.* 1700 of one long four-storeyed range aligned N–S with two low wings projecting forward, either side of the entrance forecourt. The earliest portion appears to be at the E range's N end, where evidence has been found of the thick-walled base of a tower house, probably the 'tower and fortalice of Traquair' mentioned in a charter of 1512 (but possibly erected a little earlier), which also licensed its extension and fortification. By 1541, when a 'new tower' is mentioned, the upper floors of the tower seem to have been rebuilt and a lower wing added to the S. This wing was itself rebuilt *c.* 1550 to a height of three main storeys with a projecting stair-tower at the SW corner containing the entrance. The N tower retained its identity, however, rising a storey higher than the remainder, as at Greenknowe Tower (q.v.).

Two further phases of work, the second dated 1599 on the W front, saw the main block extended S to its present length, its W face aligned with the stair-tower and thus standing forward of the earlier house. This new work, as also the stair tower, was carried to a height of four storeys, with prominent angle turrets at eaves level. Further S still was a two-storeyed kitchen extension. The top-floor gap between the 1599 work and the tower house was filled *c.* 1642 by John, first Earl of Traquair, who also regularised the fenestration. The last significant work was that of 1695–9, when *James Smith* added the offices at the N and S sides of the courtyard. However, Smith's scheme for regularis-

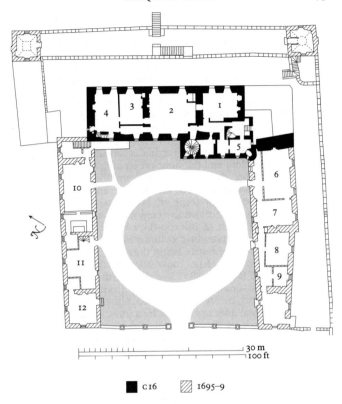

■ C16   ▨ 1695–9

1 Lord Traquair's Room (Dining Room)
2 High Drawing Room
3 Dressing Room (Bedroom)
4 King's Room (Closet)
5 Tailor's Room
6 Low Dining Room
7 Low Drawing Room
8 Bedroom
9 Dressing Room
10 Chapel
11 Malt Loft
12 Ticket Office (Carpenter's Shop)

Traquair House.
Plans of ground (N and S wings) and first (E range) floors.

ing the main block's W front and adding a new central doorway
was not implemented. Subsequently, successive Stuarts, principally the fourth Earl (†1741), fifth Earl (†1764), and eighth
Earl (†1861), restricted themselves to alterations, albeit major,
to the interior of the house, its gardens and policies, while since
the mid C20 the Maxwell Stuarts have undertaken an extensive
programme of repair and conservation to adapt the complex as
a family home and tourist attraction.

52 EXTERIOR. The original approach to the house reflects the intention of the fourth and fifth Earls to introduce an axial layout focused on a symmetrical w front. The house is first glimpsed through the celebrated Bear Gates (*see* below) and then held in view as the main avenue, broad and tree-lined, descends gently towards the forecourt. Here the grand design falters for, although Smith's forecourt provides a symmetrical frame, his intended regular centrepiece is absent and the existing aspect of the house is manifestly Scottish vernacular. All the ELEVATIONS of the E range show an overwhelming preponderance of wall surface to void and this gives the building an appearance of solidity and repose that is further accentuated by the broad expanses of harling and the long sweep of the tall, slated roofs (the older slates derive from the family's own quarry at Grieston). Windows have red and yellow sandstone dressings. Few are moulded, but some of 1599 have rounded arrises, while the majority of those inserted in the 1640s have chamfered margins. Most of the top-floor windows of the w and E elevations have triangular pediments with finials, those in the N portion of the house being dormers. One incorporates a pediment dated 1642 (now illegible but recorded by MacGibbon & Ross in 1887) and another the Traquair mullet. The wider first-floor window in the w front, with a moulded surround of C17 character, was probably enlarged *c.* 1642 to form an external doorway served by a forestair. The most conspicuous feature of the elevations is the varied array of angle turrets. The most decorative of these, crowning the sw corner, is corbelled out on two courses, carved with chequer and dogtooth ornament. Its neighbour at the NW corner of the stair-tower is carried on two rows of individual corbels, while a third, at the SE corner of the main block, now lacking its upperworks, is likewise carried on individual corbels, but rises from a lower level. All these turrets are circular on plan and probably date from 1599, but that at the NW corner of the main block was added *c.* 1642, when the top floor of the tower house seems to have been rebuilt. Square with rounded corners; there may originally have been a similar study at the NE corner. Some, at least, of the turrets were equipped for firearm defence. The NW one incorporates three spectacle-shaped pistol-loops, while the sw turret has a pair of smaller apertures perhaps designed as a combined peephole and pistol-hole. Another loop has recently been rediscovered beneath the sill of one of the ground-floor windows on the w front, so the C17 house may have been better defended than at first appears. The late C16 entrance doorway in the w front probably replaces a slightly earlier one in the adjacent re-entrant angle, while the porch was added in the mid C19. The doorway, with lug-moulded surround, sports a wrought-iron knocker dated 1705, together with a coronet and the initials of the 4th Earl and his wife. Above the doorway is a stone armorial now almost obliterated by the porch roof.

Smith went to considerable trouble to give the FORECOURT an appearance of symmetry, successfully disguising the differing sizes of the flanking wings. These are of one and a half storeys, the N one (built by *John Mein*) also incorporating a basement, constructed of the same materials as the main block and similar in character. In addition to their moulded eaves courses, the gables have angle sundials at their outer corners (one with a re-set 1664 datestone) and crow-shaped lead finials – the Stuart crest. The stylish SCREEN WALL across the court-yard's w side has a wrought-iron rail punctuated by rusticated piers topped with urns, grander at the central gateway, whose overthrow of tulips and roses bears the full armorial achieve-ment of the Earls of Traquair. All of excellent workmanship, perhaps by the same hand as the gates now at Castle Gogar (Edinburgh).

INTERIOR OF E RANGE. The N side of the entrance lobby opens onto the principal STAIR. The arrangement of the treads is awkward and it looks as if the original access was from an external door on the far (N) side, giving direct communication to the cellar corridor to the E. At the foot of the stair, an oak door from Terregles House (Dumfries and Galloway), a former residence of the Maxwells, dated 1601, with a vigorous carving of a lion and unicorn locked in combat upon the back of an elephant carrying a howdah. Opposite the stair is a vaulted cubbyhole presumably intended for the doorkeeper, but sub-sequently used as a charter room. This is equipped with a gunloop and a mysterious stone conduit – perhaps a speaking-tube – formerly communicating with the floor above. In the inner lobby, a set of servants' bells installed by *James Cameron & Son* of Selkirk in 1809, and beneath it an oak panel with the royal arms of Scotland and initials of Mary, Queen of Scots. Opening E off the inner lobby is the STILL ROOM, which served as a family parlour or dining room during the c18. Bolection-moulded pine panelling and buffet apparently installed by the fourth Earl; the painted fireplace overmantel may be a little later. The buffet retains its original folding table flap, the only known example in Scotland. A door on the s side of the lobby gives access to a number of small rooms and passages mostly carved out of the old kitchen, but including what may origi-nally have been a small prison or strongroom, as well as the entrance to the service stair. Beyond are the present kitchen premises, largely rebuilt *c.* 1800. A door opens N from the lobby into the CELLARAGE of the mid-c16 house, which com-prises a range of four barrel-vaulted chambers linked by a cor-ridor. Each is lit by a single E window, but these are set at different levels and two are awkwardly placed in relation to the vault, which suggests that the first three cellars were built against a pre-existing E wall. The fourth (N) cellar probably belongs to the original tower house (9.5 m. by 7.3 m.), which initially seems to have been entered via the door in its w wall.

The upper floors of the main block housed the principal accommodation until about the third quarter of the c18; the family probably lived mainly on the second floor, using the grander rooms below on special occasions and as a guest suite. All three floors were remodelled during the c18. The mid-c16 house had three main FIRST FLOOR rooms, comprising a hall and two chambers, but the addition of a room to the s in 1599 enabled the apartment to be replanned as what seems to have been a sequence of dining room, drawing room, bedchamber and closet. Their existing appearance reflects the major refurbishment by the fourth Earl *c.* 1700 and a lesser one by his son *c.* 1762. LORD TRAQUAIR'S ROOM (dining room), conveniently placed near the service stair, has simple moulded doorcases of *c.* 1700, but a marble chimneypiece and painted overmantel of the 1760s. The HIGH DRAWING ROOM was panelled *c.* 1700 in a rather rustic classical style with Corinthian pilasters and Corinthian caps, some renewed or added in 1762 by the fifth Earl's decorators, *Charles Robertson & Co.* of Edinburgh, who also executed the gilded *trompe l'oeil* overdoors (one incorporating the arms of the Earl and his wife, Theresa Conyers) and 55 painted Rococo overmantel. This contains a remarkable seascape centrepiece of a chiaroscuro wood engraving, probably by *John Baptist Jackson*; marble chimneypiece. The panelling extends into the embrasures, showing that the w doorway inserted by the first Earl to provide access to the great apartment had reverted to a window by that date. The plain C18 plaster ceiling largely conceals an earlier open beam ceiling, rediscovered in 1954. Only the beams survive, but boards found elsewhere in the house have been incorporated to form two specimen panels showing much-restored tempera-painted decoration, including biblical texts running along the beams. Similar ceilings, all probably of early C17 date, have been discovered elsewhere. The TAILOR'S ROOM, s of the main staircase, has a *trompe l'oeil* composition of clouds and heavenly bodies in red, blue, gold and black similar to one at Cullen House, Banff. The DRESSING ROOM N of the high drawing room was the principal bedchamber *c.* 1700. It is panelled throughout, with Ionic pilasters flanking the chimneypiece and painted overmantel. The similarly panelled KING'S ROOM (closet) contains a handsome C17 bed from Terregles House. The stair in the w wall and the latrine in the NW corner are relics of the early tower.

The main rooms of the SECOND FLOOR were bedchambers by 1783. The CHINTZ ROOM, refurbished *c.* 1700, retains traces of a mid-C17 ribbed plaster ceiling in a cupboard, and two of the small chambers at this (s) end of the house have similar ceilings. The MUSEUM ROOM at the N end was originally two chambers. Its N half is contained within the C16 tower, whose external SW and SE corners were revealed in 1993. The position of the s wall of the tower, removed *c.* 1642, is marked by a change of wall thickness. The most interesting feature of the room is the painting covering the upper part of the s wall, discovered *c.* 1880. Of tempera on plaster, the principal colours being red, yellow and black, it shows birds and animals disporting themselves in the branches of a vine, including a squirrel, a camel and a dog, some probably copied from illustrations in Conrad Gesner's *Icones Animalium* of 1560. The scene is bordered at top and bottom with biblical texts (Acts I: 14–17) apparently unrelated.

At the s end of the THIRD FLOOR, a long L-shaped room, possibly a gallery of *c.* 1599, but now subdivided, opens off the head of the principal staircase, which terminates in a distinctive cut-out balustrade of C17 character. In the centre of this

floor is the principal LIBRARY, apparently fitted out in the mid 53
C18 to hold the collections of the fourth and fifth Earls, which
are catalogued by reference to portrait busts of classical
authors painted in grisaille at regular intervals around the
ceiling cove. The lush imitation marble and graining by the
Edinburgh painter *James West*, 1823, probably replicates the
original scheme. Immediately to the N is the SECOND
LIBRARY, decorated in a much plainer style, and beyond it lie
the ARCHIVE ROOM and PRIEST'S ROOM (Chapel Room),
first mentioned in 1774. In all probability, however, a clandes-
tine oratory was established here by 1688, when a large quantity of 'Popish Trinkets' were seized by anti-Catholic zealots.
Most of the Priest's Room's existing fittings, including the cupboard in the SW corner, with its concealed opening to the tower
stair, date from 1823–4, when the chapel was refurbished by
Thomas Sanderson and *James West*.

The family apartment on the ground floor of the S WING
was probably created by the fifth Earl, and in 1783 comprised
a large dining room, a drawing room, two large bedrooms and
a smaller one. In its present form the LOW DINING ROOM,
with its cheerful French wallpaper, reflects the taste of the
eighth Earl (†1861), although the panelled dado and Adam-
style chimneypiece with applied white metal ornament are a
little earlier. The adjacent LOW DRAWING ROOM is similar in
character, apart from the marble chimneypiece, which looks
mid-C18. Beyond lie the principal bedchamber and a dressing
room. In the attic one bedroom has a mid-C18 chimneypiece
with a painted Italianate overmantel. Access was presumably
by means of a wheel stair of which traces can be seen in the
corridor outside the Low Dining Room.

The N WING originally comprised a coach house, stables and
'furniterhouse' (harness room?), all presumably at the lowest
level, together with a 'laich hall' (servants' hall?) and other
unnamed rooms on the two upper floors. The lowest floor now
contains the BREWHOUSE, first mentioned in 1727, revived in
the 1960s and extended in 1993. Some of the apparatus in the
E compartment (the former coach house) is of C19 or earlier
date. At courtyard level there was a billiard room, a combined
meal and malt loft and a carpenter's shop, while the attic contained a laundry and two servants' bedrooms. The eighth Earl
turned the billiard room into a CHAPEL. Unusually, its altar is
at the W end; richly modelled marble by the Italian sculptor
Brumidi, said to have been brought from Genoa in 1870. The
family pew (now sacristy) fills the opposite wall. Two sets of
carved oak panels, which furnished the earlier chapel, were
acquired by the fifth Earl from a church in Leith (Edinburgh).
They portray scenes from the Nativity and the Passion and
look like C16 Flemish work.

GARDENS and POLICIES. *James Smith* undertook extensive
garden works, including the provision of a piped water supply
and fountains, c. 1700, but all that remain are the terraced
walks and ogee-roofed PAVILIONS behind the house. The
pavilions are characteristic of Smith's work (cf. Melville
House, Fife). The S one has a ceiling whose centrepiece bears

a homespun version of the *Toilet of Venus* painted on boards; in the N pavilion, a similar ceiling painting of *Venus and Adonis* and bolection-moulded panelling. A garden doorway near the SW corner of the forecourt is surmounted by two displaced stone bears carrying the family crest (a crow upon a garb), while 0.1 km. S of the house is a pretty wattle-and-heather SUMMERHOUSE of 1834, the interior lined with hazel rods.

The fifth Earl improved the gardens and policies and laid out the great W avenue. Near its foot a pair of single-storeyed cottages, one bearing the date 1745, all that remain of the court of offices erected by the fifth Earl, who also built the WALLED GARDEN, its doorway dated 1749. At the head of the avenue are the BEAR GATES (closed until another Stuart monarch ascends the throne), flanked by curved screens leading to alcoved seats, with L-plan lodges beyond. The ensemble, possibly designed by *John Douglas*,* took surprisingly long to complete. The lodges seem to have been roofed by 1733, but the rusticated gatepiers and seats (*John Burns*, mason) with their associated ironwork (*David Aitken* and *Charles Braidie*, smiths) were not finished until 1737–8. The piers were heightened in 1745–6 to receive the splendid stone bears with heraldic cartouches carved by *George Jameson*. The E avenue, with its castellated bridge and barge-boarded GATE LODGE, remains much as laid out by *Buchanan* in 1880–1.

TUSHIELAW *see* ETTRICK

9050

TWEEDHILL HOUSE
2 km. S of Paxton

A small mansion, probably replacing a late C18 house. The three-bay E elevation with slightly advanced centre is probably the original mid-C19 front. Four-bay W extension of the late C19, creating a T-plan, with the entrance in the re-entrant angle of the S front with an Ionic-columned porch. Consoled cornices to the lower windows, margins and segmental heads to the upper ones. – The STABLES, SW, are late C18–early C19. Converted to residential use. Symmetrical E front with a high round-arched pend breaking the eaves, and tall round-arched recesses with blank openings. The WALLED GARDEN closing the W side of the stable court is probably of the same date.

0020

TWEEDSMUIR

A small upland settlement in one of the most remote parts of the region. Although a church was built here in the mid C17, its minister, writing in 1834, had to acknowledge that 'in the parish there

---

* Douglas produced unexecuted designs for classicising the house *c.* 1744.

is no village of any description', and even today the community is sparse and widely scattered.

PARISH CHURCH. By *John Lessels*, 1874–5, of whinstone rubble with red sandstone dressings, replacing a church of 1648 (probably altered or repaired in 1662, the date on a stone). The E end expands into narrow transeptal projections, and an axial tower-porch and spire straddles the W wall, with a polygonal N stair-turret (dated 1874). Designed in a version of early Gothic that is perhaps a little over-precious for such a small building. Windows are single round-headed openings along the nave flanks, and paired plate-traceried openings in the tower and transepts (with an oculus above each of the latter), while the E window has plate tracery. The tower has two levels of corbel tables below an ashlar splay-foot spire with pinnacles and lucarnes. Braced collar roof with a diagonal crossing of rafters at the E end. – COMMUNION TABLE, open arcaded ends, 1903. – PULPIT, re-set on the N side of the communion table platform, with arcaded faces, c. 1874(?). – FONT STAND, four legs rise from a cruciform base to support an octagonal top, Arts and Crafts Gothic, 1920. – STAINED GLASS. E window, St Paul and angels, *A. Ballantine & Gardiner*, 1903. N transept, 'Feed my Sheep', Dove. S transept, 'Be Thou Faithful', 1914, Burning Bush. Nave, N side, Harvester, c. 1919; S side, Sower. – Triptych FIRST WORLD WAR MEMORIAL, in porch, made from oak planted at Abbotsford by Sir Walter Scott.

CHURCHYARD. C18 and C19 table tombs interspersed with other gravestones on the top of the mound and the area to the N, some with *memento mori*. To SW of church, tall memorial of 1837 to John Hunter, Covenanter martyr (†1685); his gravestone below the mound erected 1726 and badly re-cut 1910.

CARLOW'S BRIDGE, 0.4km. SW of the church. By *James & Alexander Noble*, 1783 and much repaired later. Spanning the Tweed as it passes through a rocky gorge, a single segmental arch of local whinstone rubble with a 9.2 m. span; dated on the S face.

MANSE (Glebe House). Two gable-roofed blocks of harled rubble forming an L-plan, with a later, smaller one in the re-entrant angle between them, the whole now limewashed, with black painted dressings. The E block, with a first-floor Venetian window, is probably the manse of 1798, while the N block (although displaying a 1902 datestone) looks like a mid-C19 addition.

SCHOOL, 0.2km. SW. Now an Outdoor Centre. Single-storey, gable-roofed with spreading eaves, built of harled rubble with red sandstone dressings. Schoolmaster's house, dated 1898.

BIELD, 0.5km. NE. An attractive vernacular group comprising three sides of a small courtyard facing the A701, was occupied as an inn in 1715. Enlarged and remodelled in 1726 (*John Hislope*, mason, Peebles) and again extended in the early C19, when part of it was used as a post office. Harled, limewashed rubble, some parts heightened with black-painted dressings. The four-bay rear (W) block is probably of 1726, but the associated datestone bearing the initials of James Tweedie of Oliver and his wife, Margaret Ewart, now surmounts a doorway in the more substantial three-bay s block of 1821.

CROOK INN, 2.4 km. NE. Rebuilt, early C19, remodelled 1935 by *James Taylor*. Three-bay, hip-roofed block facing the A701, the front originally of rubble with sandstone dressings. To the s, looking slightly out of place in rural Tweeddale, is the smart 1930s extension, with curved metal-framed windows, flat roof and balcony. Inside Art Deco cloakrooms with colour coded tiles. Across the road a delightful wrought-iron garden GATE displays shepherds' crooks, gambolling lambs and initials CH.

OLIVER, 0.4 km. N. Late C18 date, a substantial, two-storey block of exposed rubble with rusticated quoins and moulded eaves cornice. Three-bay E front with central doorway with moulded architrave and bracketed cornice; later bay windows top and bottom on either side. Two-storey wings to N and S, the latter incorporating a Tweedie armorial, dated 1739, presumably brought from the previous house, part of which survives within the steading at the rear. A symmetrically planned three-bay block, probably of two main storeys, with a central entrance; the lintel bears the date 1734 and the same initials as at Bield (*see* above).

POLMOOD, 3.1 km. NE, was built by Houston Mitchell *c.* 1872 to replace an earlier residence of the Hunter family. A solidly built U-plan block of two main storeys with a three-bay W front, the end bays slightly advanced and gable-roofed; central doorway with angled head and corbelled canopy. The walls originally of exposed rubble with sandstone dressings, but harled and limewashed some time after 1910, when the crow-steps were presumably added. On the E elevation a re-set inscription: RH 1638, for Robert Hunter of Polmood (†1689). – Rectangular lectern-roofed DOVECOT, 50 m. E, possibly of C17 origin but extensively rebuilt in Victorian times. – The C19 COURT OF OFFICES is entered through attractive wrought-iron gates hung from cast-iron piers; the stables retain many original fittings, including part-tiled walls. – The approach to Polmood is by way of a liberally detailed Scottish Domestic LODGE of 1887 and a steel girder BRIDGE of similar date (reputedly by *Tancred, Arrol & Co.*) spanning the Tweed.

TALLA WATER WORKS, 1.7 km. S. A scheme to augment Edinburgh's water supply by harnessing the Talla Water and Gameshope Burn was approved by Parliament in 1895 and implemented in 1897–1905, by *J. & A. Leslie & Reid*. An earth DAM was built at the mouth of Talla Glen, a tunnel for pipes and draw-off valves bored through the adjacent hillside, and an aqueduct, mainly of concrete but with cast-iron pipes at crossings, was carried for 36 miles (56.6 km.) to Edinburgh. The aqueduct, still in use, is clearly visible at various points e.g. in Broughton village and near Carlops (q.v.), while traces can also be seen of the temporary light railway laid between Broughton and Tweedsmuir to transport men and materials. The system was extended in 1950–5, when the waters of the adjacent valleys of Fruid and Menzion were partially impounded.

The architectural highlight is VICTORIA LODGE, 0.2 km. N of the dam, a striking Scottish Jacobean composition perched on the valley slope just beyond the E end of the dam. Harled and limewashed rubble with red sandstone dressings. The main (s and w) elevations incorporate bay windows, shaped dormer pediments, prominent chimneystacks, crowstepped gables and green slate roofs. Inside, the Edinburgh and District Water Trustees spared no expense, providing not only well-appointed working accommodation, but also a very grand panelled Board Room, with lavishly tiled and fitted washrooms and lavatories, all happily still intact.

UNION CHAIN BRIDGE*   9050
2.1 km. s of Paxton

Linking Scotland and England, and erected 1819–20 to the design of *Captain* (later *Sir*) *Samuel Brown,* R.N., patentee and manufacturer of iron chains to the Royal Navy, who later designed the chain piers at Newhaven and Brighton, as well as other chain bridges (*see* also Eckford). *John Rennie* advised on the design of the masonry abutments and N tower. This was the first public suspension bridge in Europe to be built for vehicular traffic. The iron chains were made to conform with Brown's 1817 patent for bridge parts, including chains, and similar methods were adopted contemporaneously by Telford for the Menai Straits bridge, not completed until 1826. The earliest comparable bridges in the Western world were designed by James Finley, in the United States, from 1801 onwards. In the Union Bridge the link bars are no more than 5 cm. (2 in.) in diameter, and so from a distance are almost invisible against the darker waters of the Tweed. The Scottish support tower is a free-standing structure, whose sides have a marked batter (suggested by Rennie) and a large round-headed vehicle arch. The tower on the English side is built into the vertical face of the rock, with the anchorages of the chains embedded deeper in the rock. The chains are 7–8 m. (23–26 ft) above the roadway. A small toll-collector's lodge was then incorporated in the face of the tower. The span of the suspension chains is 133 m. (437 ft) – approaching twice the length of span of any existing chain bridge in Scotland (or Europe), which allows the roadway running parallel to the river to turn onto the bridge. The entire bridge cost only £7,700, about one-third the cost of an equivalent masonry bridge, and took only eleven months to complete. The original suspension hangers were replaced in 1870–1, and in 1902 additional wire suspension ropes and suspension hangars were provided. General refurbishment continued in the C20.

WALKERBURN   3030

Nothing but a farmhouse and steading until 1855 when Henry Ballantyne of Galashiels founded the Tweedvale Mill for the pro-

---

*This is a revised account of the entry in *The Buildings of England: Northumberland* (J. Grundy *et al.* 1992), with new information kindly supplied by Dr E.C. Ruddock.

duction of woollen cloth. Tweedholm Mill established by Robert
Frier, also of Galashiels, followed in 1859, together with housing
for the mill workers, and the village soon became a thriving, self-
contained industrial community, one of the last to be created in
Scotland. Walkerburn acquired a school, a railway station and a
church – in that order – and by 1901 the population had risen to
1200. The mills combined in 1918 under the name of Tweedvale
Mill. With the decline of the textile trade, the village now looks
to tourism and light industry for its livelihood.

CHURCHES AND PUBLIC BUILDINGS

WALKERBURN PARISH CHURCH. On an elevated site at the E
end of the village. Built 1875, possibly by *Robert Mathison*, who
extended it in 1891. It began as a five-bay buttressed church
with a high base course. Whinstone with sandstone margins.
A gabled porch at the W end of the S front, and an octagonal
capped stair-tower tucked into the l. angle. A simple bellcote
with a weathervane at the W end. Two small saddle-roofed circular windows in the front and rear elevations. A chancel was
added to the E end to accommodate additional sittings, and an
organ.
   The interior was converted in 1982 by partitioning off the
W gallery. Scissor-braced roof on stone corbels, otherwise
rather bleak, with the loss of the gallery and the bright stained-
glass windows. – ORGAN, E end, by *Ingram & Co.* of Edinburgh, with stencilled pipes. – COMMUNION TABLE with
Gothic detailing, *c.* 1945, and an octagonal Gothic PULPIT. –
On the N wall, classical pedimented marble PLAQUE to the
Rev. James S. Goldie, †1908. – STAINED GLASS. Each side of
the organ, two windows by *A. Ballantine & Gardiner*, the one
to the l. Christ the Sower to Henry Ballantyne, †1865. On the
S side a single-light window St Agnes and the Lamb by *Percy
Bacon & Bros*, 1905, to Agnes Ballantyne, †1902, and on the
N side The Good Shepherd to Robert Milne Ballantyne, †1892.
In the upper hall three lights in vibrant colours, formerly at the
back of the gallery, to David Ballantyne, †1912 and Isabella
Milne, †1907.
CONGREGATIONAL CHURCH, E end of Galashiels Road. 1890.
Disused. A long harled rectangle.
BALLANTYNE MEMORIAL INSTITUTE, Caberston Road. 1903,
by *James B. Dunn* for library, reading room, billiard room and
other character-forming public rooms – and still performing
its purpose. Scottish Domestic style of crowstepped gables,
mullioned and transomed windows and harled walls with a
decorative red sandstone gable.
RAILWAY BRIDGE, Jubilee Road. Rebuilt 1914. A four-span
bridge with bowed steel trusses on masonry piers.
Former RAILWAY STATION. 1866. Converted to a dwelling house
in the 1980s; the platform and canopy removed. Harled with
painted dressings, overhanging bracketed eaves and vermiculated quoins.
SCHOOL, Caberston Road. 1861–2, by *Robert Hall & Co.* of
Galashiels. Single-storey with further classroom and a schoolmaster's house by the same architect, 1866–7.

WALKERBURN PUBLIC HALL, Galashiels Road and Hall Street. Built as the Good Templar Hall in 1877, and converted to a Public Hall *c.* 1908. Harled, single-storey and gabled.

WAR MEMORIAL, Galashiels Road. By *James B. Dunn*, *c.* 1920. A three-sided enclosure of concrete and white granite, with bronze inscription panels. The large fibreglass statue of a great-coated soldier, with his hands resting on his reversed rifle, is a copy of the bronze original, by *Alexander Carrick*, which was resited in 2000 in a Memorial Garden opposite the remains of Tweedvale Mill.

DESCRIPTION

CABERSTON FARMHOUSE is a surprising survival in the centre of the village. 1850 by *James Brown*, wright of Innerleithen. The farmhouse, in whinstone with sandstone margins, is set on a terrace with a good, large steading in whin rubble below by the road. Semicircular piers at the two court entrances, and on the s side, four segmental-headed cartshed openings, with lofts above. At the SE corner of the steading is a classic, cast-iron URINAL, *c.* 1897, prefabricated by the *Saracen Foundry*, Glasgow.

The original parts of the 1850s TWEEDVALE MILL were demolished in 1986, much of the remainder in 1999, although a range of weaving sheds at the E end of the site was converted into an industrial unit in the late C20. So the village's architectural interest lies instead in its workers' HOUSING, initially concentrated around the mills on a steep site on the s side of the Peebles–Galashiels Road (A72). Three blocks of houses were built in 1855, the first block w of Tweedvale Mill between it and the Walker Burn, the others E of the mill; four dwellings upstairs, four at ground level entered from the s side. They are plain, built in sandstone and quite substantial; most have been added to on the road side for kitchens etc. More of the same were added in the later C19, including some tenement blocks. The housing for artisans and managerial staff was mostly concentrated on the N side of Galashiels Road, at its w end. HIGH COTTAGES, CABERSTON AVENUE, were the first, *c.* 1860; a traditional single-storey and dormered terrace. Similar houses were built *c.* 1866 in CABERSTON ROAD, each side of the mill entry.

The final investment in workers' housing began in 1919 in PARK AVENUE along the riverbank. Sir Henry Ballantyne of Monkrigg and Walkerburn was chairman of the Royal Commission on the housing of the industrial population in Scotland, which produced the Ballantyne Report in 1917. Its recommendations for low-density cottage housing were put to good effect here, and the contemporary Tudor Walters Report (on working-class housing in England and Wales) also proved influential, providing not only ideas for planning on Unwinian Garden City principles but also as a source for elevations of individual cottages. The first blocks, for double cottages, were built in 1921–5 and were followed in 1934 by flatted houses with bipartite windows and central doorways, all by *Dick Peddie & Walker Todd*. Responsibility for housing passed in 1937 to the County Council, who commissioned *Dick Peddie, Todd &*

Jamieson with further additions after the Second World War by *Dick Peddie & McKay*. This has contributed to the uniformity of the layout and design, respected by later housing. Three-storey 1960s(?) tenements with two-storey gabled wings close the vista at the E end of the street, with central access balconies to each flat.

VILLAS

BELLENDEN HOUSE, Caberston Avenue. A prefabricated house for Jeremy Ballantyne, greatly improved during building by *Duncan Cameron*, 1991. Rendered, Scottish Domestic L-shape with a round entrance tower in the angle.

THE KIRNA, 1.25 km. W. 1867, by *Pilkington & Bell* for George Ballantyne and sited in a terraced garden enjoying a superb view over the River Tweed. Ruskinian Gothic, except for a strong, perverse and, perhaps, roguish element in the detailing, which Ruskin would have considered vulgar. The villa is asymmetrical in rock-faced whin rubble with patterned sandstone dressings and a mixture of square, round-headed and shouldered windows with roll-and-rope mouldings, bands and ornament. The polygonal entrance bay has an arcaded loggia, the shafts with hybrid leafy capitals supporting rope-moulded arches, chequered banding above, and a turret with two bold pedimented and finialled dormers rising from the wall-head. Flanking canted and gabled bays with stone-mullioned ground-floor windows. The detailing is very similar to Pilkington's Craigend Park (Edinburgh), built at the same time for William Christie, an Edinburgh tailor, who presumably obtained his cloth from the Ballantyne mills. Inside the decoration is not startling. A scale-and-platt timber stair with twisted columned newels with elaborate finials, and an arcaded gallery on the first floor. In the drawing room, an ornate cornice and plaster ceiling incorporating Ballantyne's initials.

114   STONEYHILL. A strikingly eccentric house by *F.T. Pilkington*, 1868, for John Ballantyne. The design tries hard for asymmetry, with elaborate and often witty detail. Canted and bowed windows, and characteristically varied roof shapes, all in French Gothic mode. Octagonal shafted chimneys in a mixture of styles, and barley-twist rainwater pipes with grotesque spouts. Beast-like crockets to chimney flues, architectural plant life decorating the chimney cornices, and elaborately detailed flashings. Large, deep, W entrance porch, its stilted segmental arches with slim shafts and waterleaf-type capitals, the parapet decorated with moustachioed heads between rinceaus, a cavetto floral cornice and rosettes in the spandrels. Ballroom to the l., added 1890 by *James B. Dunn*, with a four-light oriel above, topped by a blocked parapet with decorative balusters. At the SE angle a large bowed bay has the first floor set back, and the ground-floor section given a stone roof with the illusion of rolled lead. To the E, a three-storey square pyramid-capped tower. Plain N and E elevations, facing a cobbled court with a stable block.

The interior has classically derived plaster cornices and centre roses and oak stair balustrade, whose newels have lion finials. The ballroom has a deep coved and panelled ceiling, the top light with coloured leaded glass and central decorated cast-iron vent. Oak-panelled dado with acanthus-moulded balusters supporting round sills for glasses.

The GATE LODGES are a theatrical pair by *Pilkington*. Lozenge-plan with apsidal ends. Squared and textured whin rubble and sandstone. Sunk diamond-panel detailing with spiky botanised carvings. Triple gableted porches, whose roof flashings rise into a pair of decorative finials. – STABLES in the same style and materials, with quatrefoil cusped gunloops.

SUNNYBRAE HOUSE. Built for David Ballantyne, 1857, with a large harled addition set forward on the r., possibly early C20. Advanced gable on the s front with round bay to the l. At an angle at the E end is a porch, with shouldered arches decorated with laurel wreaths. Two-storey, round bays clasp a tall chimneystack on the E elevation. – Remains of a ROCK GARDEN with grotto, and pools fed by a rill.

TWEEDVALE. Simple, harled, traditonal villa for Henry Ballantyne, 1859. – The small LODGE is by *F.T. Pilkington*, 1868, with low-key Pilkingtonian decoration of crowstepped and arcaded porch, with a stilted arch on dwarf columns. Unsympathetic late C20 addition.

TWEED VALLEY HOTEL, Galashiels Road. Former Nether Caberston House, built for J.K. Ballantyne by his relative, *James B. Dunn* of *Dunn & Findlay*, 1906. Neatly built but unexciting Scottish Domestic villa, with some Arts and Crafts detailing. A pleasant mix of coloured whinstone rubble from local quarries. Symmetrical s front with a central loggia (unsuitably filled in) flanked by advanced gables with canted oriels. At the E end a flat-roofed octagonal entrance tower, with moulded doorway, the panel above inscribed JKB [John K. Ballantyne] 1906 HM [Hilda Moritz]. Fine craftsmanship inside in an eclectic mix of Scottish Renaissance, Adam and Arts and Crafts styles. Plasterwork by *Leonard Grandison*, masonry, joinery and panelling by *Robert Hall & Co.*, and *Allan & Sons* did the marble and tile work. Vestibule with a shallow domed ceiling decorated with vine leaves and grapes. The oak-panelled hall has a frieze of vine leaves, grapes and birds, and leafy cornerpieces. A Hopton stone medieval-style chimneypiece. The oak staircase has panels with a floral design, and the finials on the first-floor rail comprise birds' heads back to back. The dining room and drawing room are now one room. Oak-panelled with a fitted dresser by *James B. Dunn* in the dining room; at the other end, an Adam ceiling from Grandison's catalogue, and an inglenook with a *vert-antique* marble chimneypiece.

ELIBANK CASTLE. *See* p. 258.
ELIBANK HOUSE. *See* p. 259.
HOLYLEE. *See* p. 384.

WATERLOO MONUMENT

Peniel Heugh, 3 km. NE of Ancrum

6020

Erected by William Kerr, sixth Marquess of Lothian and his tenantry. Dedicated June 30th, 1815, but conceived before the

Battle of Waterloo; it commemorates instead a chain of earlier victories by Wellington. The first design, by *William Burn*, which fell with a resounding crash in 1816, was succeeded by the present design by *Archibald Elliot*, tapering sandstone column, built 1817–24 with Greek Doric detailing on a square plinth, soaring 150 ft (45.7 m.) to a platform, reached by an internal cantilevered spiral stair, which affords magnificent views over the surrounding countryside. Sir David Brewster, scientist and expert in optics, advised on the lightning conductor; some of his thunder rods, which connected with a central conductor, still project from their openings. A mighty superstructure was added in 1867 (designed by *J.H. Pollen* of London, assembled by *A. Herbertson & Son* in Galashiels); it comprises a timber balustrade, lead roof, spire and a weathervane, making the monument 187 ft (56 m.) tall.

8050

WEDDERBURN CASTLE
3.3 km. SE of Duns

Castellated mansion built in 1770–6 for Patrick Home of Billie, who had inherited the estate in 1766, and erected during his absence on the Grand Tour. The principal (w) range was designed by *R. & J. Adam*, most of the rest is in the same manner by *James Nisbet* who acted as executant architect for all the external work.

62 The house is quadrangular, built round an inner courtyard. Projecting from each of the four outer corners, a four-storey octagonal tower. The N, W and S ranges are all of three storeys but with a four-storey centrepiece marking the W's principal entrance, the E range single-storey and containing the service entry to the courtyard. Masonry from Putton Hill to the W, all of ashlar, rusticated at the main range's ground floor, droved above. Tying together the main ranges and the corner towers are string courses to delineate each floor and with an additional sill course linking the taller windows of the first floor piano nobile. Hoodmoulds over the upper floor's windows. All wall-heads are finished with battlements, those of the corner towers carried on modillion cornices. The first floor windows of the towers' principal faces are round-headed, as are all their second floor openings. Otherwise all the windows are Georgian rectangles except at the centrepiece of the W range. This is derived from the E gate of Diocletian's palace at Spalatro (illustrated in Robert Adam's *Ruins of the Palace of the Emperor Diocletian at Spalatro*, published in 1764). Narrow rectangular turrets with tall battlements and round-arched second floor windows grip the broad centre. Here, above the entrance's early C19 castellated porte-cochère, a tripartite first floor window under a segmental-arched dummy fanlight containing a *Coade* stone heraldic achievement. Three round-headed windows at the second floor and a trio of rectangular lights at the third.

At the N elevation, a slightly advanced three-bay centrepiece, its battlement rising a little higher than those over the outer three bays each side. The upper part of the E third of this elevation is really a screen wall to the courtyard. At the S elevation, a broad central bow. Another three-storey bow at the S end of the E elevation but the remainder of this range is single-storey with a slightly taller and advanced tower-like centre containing the round-headed entrance to the courtyard. Much of the rubble walling on the courtyard's W side and at the W end of its S side (i.e. the back walls of the Georgian W and S ranges) represents surviving work of the previous house on the site but the only early detail is found in the blocked openings and a panel bearing a recut Latin inscription ('George Home, lord of Wedderburn, caused me to be made'), a reminder that that house had been built by 'George Home of Wedderburn (†1497) who fortified it with three towers and ditches'.

The Adams appear to have had no hand in the design of the INTERIOR. A plan of the principal floor by Nisbet, *c.* 1770, shows the intended sequence of rooms as follows: on the W side, and linked by a corridor overlooking the courtyard, drawing room (N), dining room (centre), and bedroom, with a dressing room in the SW tower; on the S side, Mr Home's study and the library, with a charter room in the SE tower. The principal staircase at the N end of the corridor would have served all floors. Work on the interior proceeded slowly. Chimney-pieces were ordered in 1774, but not installed until two years later, while some bedrooms were not papered until 1791. The decorative plasterwork throughout was carried out by *George Morison* and his labourer *R. Heatly.* Mostly Classical cornices and friezes of anthemion and palmette, and waterleaf and guilloche decoration are prominent. Ceiling roses are quite coarse in their boldness. Most of the very fine chimneypieces came from Italy, ordered by the sculptor Francis Harwood, one of the principal dealers to aristocrats visiting Florence. Simple panelled doorcases with architraves and cornices made by *Alexander Cairns,* who supplied doors and windows between 1771 and 1776. Cairns also supplied superb mahogany six-panelled doors and doorcases, modelled on one supplied to Adam's design by *Henry Wishart,* 'carpenter of Oxford's Chapel Court, London'. The panels were to be of tulipwood, mouldings of ebony and borders of rosewood; a difficult commission as special woods were hard to obtain in Scotland.

The present interior arrangements were probably introduced in the early C19. These alterations created the large, high, STAIRCASE HALL, incorporating the original hall and dining room above. This has an impressive short stone cantilevered staircase, designed as two geometric stairs, one against each wall, with a simple decorative cast-iron balustrade; it leads to a slightly bowed platform, in front of a screen with Ionic columns *in antis,* carrying an entablature and segmental arch above. This opens into a long groin-vaulted corridor leading to the *piano nobile.* The E (rear) wall incorporates some earlier work. At the N end of the corridor is the earlier PRINCIPAL STAIRCASE – apparently occupying part of the previous house. A spacious well stair with a pretty net-patterned wrought-iron balustrade, probably made by the *Berwick Foundry* at Tweedmouth, Northumberland (cf. Paxton

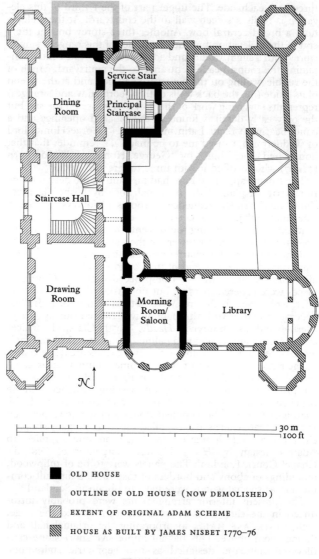

Dining Room

Service Stair

Principal Staircase

Staircase Hall

Drawing Room

Morning Room/ Saloon

Library

N

30 m
100 ft

⬛ OLD HOUSE

▨ OUTLINE OF OLD HOUSE (NOW DEMOLISHED)

▨ EXTENT OF ORIGINAL ADAM SCHEME

▨ HOUSE AS BUILT BY JAMES NISBET 1770–76

Wedderburn Castle.
Plan

House and Nisbet House, qq.v.). The lower flight of stairs to the ground floor was removed in the early C19. Formerly the walls were panelled, and the mouldings over the windows were enriched with fruit and flowers. The D-shaped service stair to the N looks early C19. All the principal rooms and bedrooms are large and high, getting progressively lower towards the top.

Along the W front from the N end is the DINING ROOM. The chimneypiece is described in the agreement with Francis Harwood as with 'Bas reliefs in the tablet and frieze'. Cleverly, the enfilade along the front of the house is preserved by a balcony which links through the early C19 staircase hall to the DRAWING ROOM. Its glory is a Neoclassical marble chimneypiece made by *G.B. Piranesi*, and purchased in Rome in 1774 by Patrick Home, who acquired it before the Earl of Arundel could buy it for Wardour House; beautifully worked with cameos, and amethyst and *rosso antico* reliefs. E across the corridor is the MORNING ROOM (saloon) in the E wing. This is bowed at both ends, the bow of the N wall cutting into earlier work. Then straight into the LIBRARY, a vast room, the bowed recess at the E end set behind an arcaded Ionic screen with timber columns painted to resemble marble; two tall niches in the N wall flank bookcases. The SE tower was Patrick Home's charter room, not finished until 1781.

At the second floor, bedrooms have the usual classical cornices, and all have well-designed marble chimneypieces. The arrangement of the bedrooms along the front is quite interesting. To the r. at the top of the stairs a vestibule serves two rooms, in the centre another vestibule gives access to a third bedroom, with a closet below a timber stair from the vestibule to a third floor room lit by a trio of windows with a superb view to the W.

STABLES, NW of castle. *c.* 1790, with many changes and additions. Two quadrangular courts. E elevation of three bays with an advanced pedimented centre bay and segmental-arched pend, pilastered and pedimented on the court side, and a thermal window in each flanking bay. Partly adapted to housing.

LION GATE. Designed by *John Plaw*, 1790, completed 1794. A splendid Neoclassical archway with a martial presence. Round-arched pedimented entrance with corniced panelled piers, and round-arched pedimented niches which break the cornices. On top a *Coade*-stone couchant lion. Quadrant walls link the archway to sentry-box pavilions, each with slightly advanced panels containing recesses. Ornamental wrought-iron gates. Behind the screen wall at the W side is a delightful Palladian front to a simple cottage.

WEST GATE (East and West Lodges). Late C18 or early C19 single-storey with diagonally set chimneys and round-arched recesses. Linked by quadrant walls to a round-arched carriage entrance flanked by square pedimented piers with round-arched panels (cf. The Lion Gate). Simple cast-iron gates with a cast-iron popinjay in the centre.

A tall, harl-pointed BOUNDARY WALL of immense grandeur undulates round the estate for *c.* 5.6 km., occasionally dipping down to allow views from the house. Built *c.* 1780 when George Home complained that too many carts were being used for transporting material and, unless Patrick sent money, the work could not continue.

6050

WEDDERLIE HOUSE

2 km. NE of Westruther

An unassuming house of vernacular character built by the Edgars of Wedderlie. The oldest portion, probably of late C16 date, comprises a tiny T-plan tower house (main block 6.9 m. by 5.5 m., wing 4.1 m. by 3.8 m.) of three storeys, with the wing projecting from near the W end of the S side. To the E end of the tower there was added in 1680 a much larger L-plan block of three storeys and an attic, its broad wing projecting N, thus converting the house into an irregular U. In 1734 the estate passed to the Stewarts of Blantyre, but because the property was not their main residence the house escaped improvement, the only significant alterations made during the next two centuries being the addition of a corridor on the N c. 1800 and the erection of a single-storey service outshot on the E in the early C20. A sensitive restoration was completed 1960–3 by *R. A. C. Simpson* of *Oldfield, Simpson & Saul.*

The original entry was from the N, where the tree-lined avenue still stands, and where the house most clearly reveals its anatomy. To the W is the early tower house, its top floor corbelled out on individual corbels of three members, whose large size and unusually low height above ground gives the building a distinctly top-heavy appearance. The masonry, fully exposed since 1963, is a mixture of whin and red sandstone rubble with dressings of red sandstone probably quarried at Bassendean. The wing is gabled and crowstepped, but the roof of the main body of the tower house is hipped to conform with that of the late C17 house. Although small in size, the tower house seems originally to have been free-standing. As remodelled in the late C17, the N front presents an axial layout focused on a central doorway, now concealed by the corridor of c. 1800. Twin stair-turrets with catslide roofs rise in the re-entrant angles, while the crowstepped and chimneyed gable of the E wing reflects its neighbour to the W but on a much larger scale; the skewputts are carved with rosettes. The masonry of the E wing's gable was left exposed in 1963, matching that of the early tower house, but elsewhere the walls are harled. The windows (one dated 1680) have plain, chamfer-arrised dressings of red sandstone, apart from two in the E gable, perhaps reused from the E wall of the tower house, which have a double edge-roll and fillet. The S elevation is dominated by three massive chimneystacks placed at regular intervals along the wall-head.

INTERIOR. As first built the tower seems to have incorporated an unvaulted ground-floor kitchen with a barrel-vaulted cellar in the wing, a first-floor hall and chamber and another pair of chambers above; there may also have been an extruded stair. The enlarged house provided family rooms and a new kitchen on the ground floor, a first-floor suite probably intended to function as a state apartment when required, and another series of chambers on the floor above. The two newel stairs were well placed to provide convenient access to all floors, but their lower flights were subsequently altered to communicate directly with the N corridor. The C17 entrance, rediscovered in 1960–3, has a heavily rusticated surround possibly modelled on the slightly earlier one at Thirlestane Castle (q.v.), with detail comprising a mixture of Classical and Gothic Revival ornament, including egg-and-dart and nailhead. Above, the rather battered armorial achievement of John Edgar of Wedderlie, with the date 1694. Ground-floor hall and parlour in late C17 main block with contemporary panelling and ceiling cornices, the hall subsequently subdivided and panelling rearranged. The chamber in the tower has a big, corbel-lintelled fireplace, two aumbries and a latrine which discharges into a mural chute. In the E wing the late C17 kitchen, with semicircular-headed fireplace and massive, stepped chimney. On the first floor, a dining room in the E wing, a drawing room and two bedchambers in the main block, and another bedchamber and closet in the tower. Some of these rooms have late C17 panelling and chimneypieces, while the tower chamber retains its C16 fittings, including a window embrasure equipped with stone bench seats and a corbel-lintelled fireplace of dressed stone. The arrangement of the second floor is similar. The two stairs terminate at this level, the landings being furnished with simple, cut-out balustrades like those at Traquair House (q.v.). The attic formerly contained servants' bedrooms, but is now open to the collar-rafter roof of 1680.

COURT OF OFFICES to the NE of the house dated 1775, its W range incorporating a C17 sundial.

WEENS HOUSE 5010
1 km. N of Bonchester Bridge

Built in the late C18 by William Oliver of Dinlabyre, in place of an earlier house. The centre block is three storeys and five bays, in coursed red sandstone, with mutuled eaves along the S front and steeply piended roof. Two-storey, single-bay gabled wings, each with a Venetian window and Gothic window above, were added later – the S wing heightened and added to in 1889 by George Tancred of Weens. He continued his alterations in 1901 by adding a square bay to the S elevation and a massive gable, curved up from the wall-head to tall, shouldered, paired chimneystacks. The tall, paired stacks with carved urns on the house are perhaps of this date too. Tancred added the plain two-storey extension to the N wing. Well-detailed single-storey extension of the 1980s. Mid-C19 geometric staircase inside. – GATEPIERS. Rusticated, with stugged pattern of stars and obelisk finials.

WEST LINTON 1050

Known as Linton Roderick in the C12, the village was erected into a burgh of regality in 1631, eventually enjoying a modest level of prosperity as a sheep market and cotton-weaving centre, before the coming of the railway in 1864 and improved road transport gave it a new role as a summer resort for Edinburgh professionals. A further phase of expansion, which began after the Second World War, today threatens to engulf the village with commuter housing estates, but the historic core retains both charm and character. West Linton had a reputation as a centre for masons and sculptors, and much of the stonework is of exceptionally high quality. During the middle decades of the C19 brick, used mainly for outbuildings, was available from the nearby brick and tile works at Upper Whitfield and Lamancha, although it is likely that later supplies were brought in mainly by rail. Early roofing materials, probably thatch, Stobo slate and pantile, subsequently gave way to more durable Welsh and West Highland slate.

PARISH CHURCH. Built in 1781–2, reusing stonework from its medieval predecessor. It was initially a hipped-roof rectangle aligned E–W, with a low tower capped by an ogee-roofed belfry at the centre of the N flank. Extensively remodelled 1871, when gables were built over the E and W walls and at the centre of the S wall, and an upper storey and spire were added to the tower. At the same time a S vestry and porches were added, and some windows were enlarged and traceried. The rectangular core and the lower part of the tower are harled with ashlar margins; the rest is of coursed rubble with ashlar dressings. The S side has a rose in the central gable and four round-headed windows: the inner single-light pair (one dated 1781) are raised above the porches, the outer two-light windows have transoms at mid-height. In the upper part of the W and E walls are three-light round-headed traceried windows, each with a transom and a circlet above the central light-head. The upper storey of the tower has chamfered angles and a single round-headed window in each face; the stone splay-foot spire has two levels of string courses. Flanking the tower are pairs of superimposed round-headed windows.

There is a collar-beam roof with steel ties. The polygonal arrangement of galleries, reached from a stair in the tower, is carried on slender cast-iron Corinthian columns: the gallery fronts have texts and panels of naturalistic foliage carving, executed *c.* 1871 by *Jane Fergusson* of Spitalhaugh. Her work is also seen around the windows and the boarded dado. – The PULPIT and COMMUNION TABLE are at the centre of the S wall, the former decorated with carving by *Harriette Woddrop*, wife of the laird of Garvald. – FONT, re-assembled from late C12/early C13 fragments found in 1929, though the result is surprisingly small; arcaded sides above a cable moulding – STAINED GLASS. Flanking the pulpit, 'Her Children Shall Arise Up', 'The Lord Reigneth', 1871. E window, Good Shepherd, SS Peter and John, *c.* 1892. Lower N windows, Sacrifice and Peace, *Sadie McLellan*, 1967–8.

CHURCHYARD. A particularly interesting group of memorials, including table tombs, headstones and obelisks. Worthy of note: table tomb of John and Richard Alexander, with two full-length recumbent figures and *memento mori*, early C18; gravestone of Archibald Wilson, †1705, a cloaked figure below an ogee arch; memorial to Robert Sanderson, poet, erected 1929, with bronze portrait medallion by *C. d'O. Pilkington Jackson*. Double burial enclosure to NE of church, for Lawson of Cairnmuir and Douglas of Garvald families, incorporating part of earlier manse garden wall. – BURIAL ENCLOSURE of Fergusson of Spitalhaugh at N end of churchyard, near site of church. Gatepiers to NW of church (opening now blocked), both dated 1601, and one bearing the arms of Lawson of Cairnmuir.

ST MUNGO (Episcopal). Former school of 1851–2, with a truncated chimney at the middle of the SW flank; adapted as a church by *Hay & Henderson* later in the C19. A rectangular core of grey coursed rubble with ashlar dressings projects out from the slope of the hillside over an undercroft. Slight changes in coursing show that the small square chancel with a slated flèche at the middle of the NE flank (resulting in a T-shaped plan unusual for an Episcopal church), and the porch at the W corner, were amongst the additions. Along the SW flank are two pairs of cusped single lights, while the SE gable wall has five single lights with quatrefoils between their heads. Two-light Geometric-traceried window to the chancel. Collar-beam and arch-braced roof to nave and a scissor-braced roof to chancel. – CHANCEL SCREEN, simple intersecting tracery. – STAINED GLASS by *C.E. Kempe*. Chancel, Moses and the Serpent; Crucifixion. SE window, Supper at Emmaus, Melchizedek and St Thomas Aquinas, 1893. NW of chancel, Virgin and Child.

Former TRINITY UNITED PRESBYTERIAN CHURCH, *see* Church House, below.

CROSS WELL, Main Street. Erected 1666 by the local sculptor, *James Gifford*, at his own expense to serve not only as a well house and market cross, but also as a memorial to Gifford's wife and children, whose statues originally adorned the pedestal. This was replaced in 1861 and heightened in 1894 to form a clock tower, when the surviving statue of 'Lady Gifford', a costumed figure on a decorated base, was relegated to a less prominent position directly above the well. The statue was replaced by a cast by *Graciela Ainsworth Associates*, Edinburgh, in 2001. The original is now in the Graham Institute.

GRAHAM INSTITUTE, off Main Street. Built as a Working Men's club in 1882. About as plain as a village hall can be, apart from the crowstepped gable overlooking the Lower Green, erected when the building was extended in 1905.

PRIMARY SCHOOL, School Brae. 1907, replacing the earlier parish school (*see* below). Reconstructed 1938 by *Reid & Forbes* and further enlarged after 1945. Originally with a T-plan main block and Italianate belfry. Coursed sandstone rubble, gabled roofs with rusticated oculus in N gable.

'ROMAN BRIDGE', 1.3 km. W, over the West Water. A single-arched structure of rubble with ashlar dressings, built in 1620 and restored in 1899. Follows line of former Roman road.

DESCRIPTION

Much of West Linton's character stems from its random and manifestly unplanned layout, perhaps a consequence of the village's former status as a regality, under which land was feued out to a large number of very small – but by all accounts fiercely independent – proprietors, known as portioners. The older houses flank the sinuous MAIN STREET, some facing the highway, others gable-fronted or set well back, others again lining the numerous closes and tiny squares that run off on either side. Their building materials illustrate the varied products of the local quarrying industry, including red sandstone from Broomlee and Kaimes, a superior white freestone from Deepsykehead at Carlops, and a buff-coloured sandstone possibly from Marlfield.

Immediately s of the Parish Church (*see* above) at the SE end stands a plain, pink sandstone WAR MEMORIAL, and beyond it the early C19 OLD TOLL HOUSE (now tearoom), on the former Edinburgh–Moffat road. Gable-roofed with overhanging eaves. Prominent stone weather shields above main windows; ticket window beside entrance. On the opposite corner a cast-iron LAMP STANDARD and beside it a splendid HORSE TROUGH with hooved feet, both erected (originally in Raemartin Square) to commemorate Queen Victoria's Diamond Jubilee in 1897. Across the Lyne Water is the OLD MANSE (1780), an oblong two-storey block of two main storeys with modillioned eaves. Three-bay front with later porch. Later gabled wing to rear. Contemporary U-plan offices, now converted to housing. At the start of BOGSBANK ROAD two pairs of semi-detached two-storey villas. Projecting eaves above entrance doorways with flanking bow windows; dormers with pretty bargeboards. Probably the 'small villas in cottage style' for which designs by *J.N Scott* and *A.Lorne Campbell* were exhibited in 1902.

Running N from the church MAIN STREET contains a mixture of solid, two-storey houses and cottage rows. On the l., BANK HOUSE incorporates two carved stones in reuse, one a 1737 datestone, the other a somewhat earlier portrait head possibly sculpted by *James Gifford*. On the r. is RIVENDELL, the former parish school. Early C19, originally single-storey with bellcote; heightened 1864. Carved figure of St Andrew on the porch. Beyond the Cross Well and on the N side of the close which runs off to the l. stands the LARGE CHURCH HALL, former Somervail School, built 1851–2 for the children of the United Presbyterian congregation by *John Dick Peddie*. Gothic, with three-light, gabled centrepiece, formerly with bellcote. Interior now a single chamber open to the arch-braced collar-rafter roof. A little further up the street on the r. is GIFFORD STONE COTTAGE, adjacent to the site of *James Gifford*'s house (dem. *c.* 1864), from which a number of carvings survive. The most interesting of these, built into the w gable of the cottage, incorporates a central panel containing portrait busts of Gifford and his wife, Euphemia Veitch, along with their coats of arms. To the l. is another panel divided into four frames, each containing two full-length costumed male figures identified in an accompanying inscription as Gifford's six immediate forebears ('progenetors'), together with the sculptor himself and his eldest son. A third panel to the r. depicts Gifford and his wife standing beneath an apple tree. A worn inscription on the lower margin of the l. panel reads: WROUGHT BY ME JAMES GEFERD ARCHITECTOR YE 7TH MAY 1660. The cubical sundial may be another specimen of his work.

Directly opposite, ALDERSYDE, on the W side of RAE-
MARTIN SQUARE, was the former Somervail schoolmaster's
house by *John Dick Peddie*, 1851, with a fine two-storey front
of dressed coursed rubble. On the N side the RAEMARTIN
HOTEL (1789, extended 1879), a substantial, gable-roofed
building of two main storeys with roll-moulded skewputts and
moulded eaves cornice. Off the NW corner, CHURCH HOUSE
(formerly Trinity Church), first built in 1739 for a Secession
congregation. Rebuilt in 1784. A regular succession of round-
headed windows along each flank. Remodelled 1869, when the
windows along the SE flank were made pointed and furnished
with Y-tracery; the two central bays were projected forward
and capped by a gable decorated with a traceried spherical triangle, and a bellcote was set at the gable apex. Nearby, the
former manse and stables of *c.* 1812, also improved *c.* 1869.

N of Raemartin Square the houses in Main Street display a
sprinkling of carved stones, all now apparently in reuse, but
illustrative of earlier building activity – late C17 datestones at
CAMERON SQUARE and LYNEBANK, C19 medallion head at
Cameron Square. The mid-to-late C19 OLD BAKEHOUSE to
r. (now a restaurant) retains two brick ovens and various
baking implements. At the top of the street on the r., the OLD
MANOR HOUSE, seemingly the oldest house in the village,
although probably not earlier than *c.* 1600. Originally L-plan
(main block 8.0 m. by 5.8 m., wing 3.9 by 3.1 m.) of two main
storeys, perhaps formerly three. C18 extension to E. Rubble
masonry with dressed sandstone margins, the older openings
with rounded arrises, the later ones chamfered. The S wing may
originally have housed a spiral stair.

Immediately N of the old village runs the Edinburgh–Biggar road
(A702), brought to its present alignment *c.* 1830 to replace the
earlier turnpike road some 0.9 km. to the NW. Single-arched
BRIDGE over Lyne Water dated 1831 on parapet; widened
1965. On either side of the main road are late Victorian and
Edwardian villas.

West Linton is fortunate in its two spacious village greens, situated on the l. bank of the Lyne Water immediately W of Main
Street. Overlooking the LOWER GREEN, at one time the stance
for sheep markets, is a row of cottages incorporating the former
school for females and infants (now ST ANDREW'S NEW
CHURCH HALL), a mildly Gothic, gable-fronted building
(1863) with the schoolmaster's house alongside it. On the
opposite side of the Lyne Water, at the foot of Chapel Brae,
yet another C19 SCHOOL (now a dwelling), this time for children of the Episcopalian congregation of St Mungo's.

In THE LOAN is SRON GARBH of 1935 by *Leslie Grahame Thomson* 79
for himself. Dutch Colonial style, with no concessions to the
local climate and altitude (nearly 300 m.), other than the stone
slate roof. Harled brick walls painted white, with reconstituted
stone dressings. Forecourt with flanking garages focused on
entrance front; screen walls with busy wrought-iron rail by
Charles Henshaw. Doorway with full armorial achievement. To
the rear, an arcade of big, astragalled windows overlooking a
terraced garden, pool and summerhouse. The clever, if whimsical, plan makes the house look a good deal bigger than it really

is. Many original fittings, all well detailed. SORAIDH, near the foot of The Loan, was built for Thomson's chauffeur. Rather surprisingly, it is a mass-produced log house imported from Norway – the maker's name, *Bernt Paulson* of Oslo, is recorded on a metal plate. Set on a brick base, the walls comprised logs with notched joints and projecting ends. The roof, originally felted, is now covered with concrete tiles.

BADDINSGILL HOUSE, 3.7 km. NW. A former shooting lodge probably built *c.* 1892 for Charles Ferrier Gordon. C17 Scottish Domestic style, complete with crowstepped gables and pedimented dormers; pedimented entrance to S with bolection-moulded surround. Excellent coursed rubble masonry of buff-coloured sandstone with pink sandstone dressings. Altered 1948–50 by *Lindsay Auldjo Jamieson* of *Dick Peddie, Todd & Jamieson*. The interior is mainly of this date; spacious and attractive entrance hall with open-well pine staircase.

LYNEDALE, 1.1 km. NW. Delightfully situated on the Lyne Water, mainly early C19, but with an early C20 double bow front over-looking the river; harled and limewashed rubble with sand-stone dressings.

MEDWYN HOUSE, Medwyn Road, 0.7 km. NW. The former Bridgehouse Inn, remodelled after 1858 by William Forbes as the centre of a substantial estate. Scots Domestic, enlarged by accretion, its most conspicuous feature the tower-like block of three storeys with prominent bay windows, pedimented dormers and crowstepped gables; sumptuous panelled entrance hall and staircase.

SPITALHAUGH, 3 km. SE, was commenced by Richard Murray, brother of Sir Alexander Murray of Blackbarony, in the late 1670s. The C17 house probably survives as the core of the present mansion, an attractively rambling composition of mainly Baronial and Scottish Domestic elements dominated by a four-storey tower house erected *c.* 1860 by Sir William Fergusson, surgeon to Queen Victoria. High up on the S face of the tower, a statue of St Andrew (?) by *James Lawson*, with a 1677 datestone commemorating the earlier house. Inside, two of the public rooms have good compartmented ceilings with decorated ribs, one of them also containing an imported oak Jacobean chimneypiece. Other antique fragments collected by the Fergussons include a remarkable stone fireplace of 1658 by the sculptor *James Gifford*, formerly in his house at West Linton; figure sculpture and armorials. Sir William's daughter *Jane Fergusson* also contributed to the decoration of the inte-rior by carving the very handsome pine balustrade of the stair-case hall.

Pretty, vaguely Gothic LODGE on the West Linton road dated 1866. Metal lattice-glazed windows and hipped roofs with spreading eaves. Glazed tile with crest and initials WF mounted as external panel.

CAIRNS, North Muir, 4 km. WSW. Two cairns standing 700 m. apart. The Upper Cairn (NE) has been extensively quarried, but it still forms a substantial mound of stones over 4 m. in height. The Nether Cairn is undisturbed, displaying a conical profile 3.5 m. high and a low platform of cairn material encircling its base. Numerous smaller cairns can be seen in the vicinity, the majority probably the result of Bronze Age field clearance.

GARVALD HOUSE. *See* p. 316.

LAMANCHA. *See* p. 480.

MACBIEHILL. *See* p. 511.

THE WHIM. *See* p. 756.

WESTRUTHER   6050

The village was evidently of some local importance by 1649, when the parish church was erected. Houses, each with a small garden, were built during the late c18 and many cottages improved in the late c19 by the Scotts of Spottiswoode (q.v.).

Former FREE CHURCH, N of the village, now a house. 1854, apparently designed by *Alexander Shillinglaw*. S entrance front with central arched doorway framed by buttresses and flanked by lancets; blind quatrefoil in the gable, capped by a gabled bellcote.

OLD PARISH CHURCH. 1649, following the creation of a new parish. Superseded in 1840, except as a burial place for the Spottiswoode family, it was unroofed in 1969. At its fullest extent it was of T-plan, with the Wedderlie Aisle to the N, but that 'aisle' was removed in works of 1752 and there was further remodelling in 1807. The surviving rubble-built structure is complete to the wall-head, though now in a precarious state. The 1649 work has chamfered surrounds to the openings, except for the two principal openings through the S wall (one rectangular; the other round-arched), which have angle rolls. Later openings have squared arrises or narrow chamfers, with a preference for Gothick pointed arches. Forestairs to loft doorways in the E and W walls. Covering a later doorway, E of centre in the S wall, is the skeleton of an iron-framed porch.

CHURCHYARD. Tiny aedicular headstone of 1674. Notable table tomb to George Edgar, †1716. Some handsome tall Neoclassical headstones, including those to Helen Pringle, †1812 and Alexander Trotter, †1824.

PARISH CHURCH. 1840, by *John Smith*. An austere box of whin rubble with droved ashlar dressings and raised margins, and with a corbelled cornice along the flanks. There were finials at the bases of the E and W gables, and a corbelled-out bellcote at the apex of the W gable (dem. *c.* 1994). The rectangular entrance is in a salient at the centre of the W wall, above which is a triplet of pointed windows, and there is a similar triplet in the E wall. The flanks have four evenly spaced pointed windows, but in addition the S flank has a second doorway, and a smaller window to the W loft. There is a vestibule below the W loft. Boarded ceiling of flattened polygonal profile. Much of the internal arrangement, with the communion table at the E end, is of a reordering of 1896. – COMMUNION TABLE, open-arcaded front, 1911. – PULPIT and CHAIRS, minimal Gothic, post-1951. – FONT. Octagonal timber base of 1908 incorpo-rating a hollowed stone from Bassendean; more likely to be a domestic mortar than a font. – STAINED GLASS. E window, Good Shepherd, post-1900. E end S wall, Melchizedek, fine Arts and Crafts detail, post-1896. E end, N wall, Valley of the Shadow of Death, post-1966. – MONUMENT, S internal wall, handsomely detailed plaque to Cecil Grace, lost at sea, 1910.

WAR MEMORIAL, inside the church gate. 1919. Celtic cross with a central boss and interlacing on the shaft.

Former MANSE (Kelmscot), 0.1 km. S. Much altered. Basically by *William Lamb*, 1818–19. Two-storey, three-bay S front with single-storey wings, that to the W incorporated in a flat-roofed extension.

Former FREE CHURCH MANSE. 1840, enlarged 1872 and extended 1890s. Over the doorway a red sandstone slab commemorates John Veitch, minister, 1649–1703.

PRIMARY SCHOOL. School Board Tudor by *George Duns*, c. 1896, with bargeboarded gables and a hoodmould over the door. Linked to the two-storey schoolmaster's house by *T.R. Atkinson*, c. 1907. Bull-nosed dressings.

DESCRIPTION. In the centre of the village is the OLD THISTLE INN. Harled, two-storey house with rolled skews dated 1721. Single-storey coach house wing. – SMITHY on the approach from the E. Formerly the schoolhouse of 1810. In whinstone rubble with red sandstone dressings and broad timber-bracketed eaves.

EVELAW TOWER. *See* p. 262.
SPOTTISWOODE. *See* p. 693.
WEDDERLIE HOUSE. *See* p. 748.

EVELAW TOWER. *See* p. 262.
SPOTTISWOODE. *See* p. 693.
WEDDERLIE HOUSE. *See* p. 748.

2050

THE WHIM
6 km. NE of West Linton

Medium-sized C18 mansion house developed in two principal stages. The name commemorates the 'comical' challenge undertaken by Archibald, Earl of Ilay (later third Duke of Argyll) to make 'a blade of grass grow' where none had grown before on the estate of Blair-Bog, which he acquired in 1730.

The first phase was undertaken by Ilay in 1732–41. His Edinburgh 'man of affairs', the judge *Andrew Fletcher, Lord Milton*, appears to have been primarily responsible for the design, with advice from *Alexander McGill* and with *William Adam* as architectural supervisor. This house was unpretentious, a main block of two storeys above a sunk basement, with single-storey and basement end pavilions, their one-bay gables projecting slightly from the three-bay principal elevations to W and E, all built of rubble, now rendered. The moulded string course above the first floor of the W front's centre three bays is probably the eaves course of the 1730s house.

In 1763 the estate was bought by Sir James Montgomery, Chief Baron of Exchequer, who probably employed *David Henderson* in 1775 to heighten both the main block and pavilions to a uniform three storeys and basement, the new work faced in ashlar (now rendered) with a continuous frieze of fluting and paterae below the dentilled cornice under the hipped roofs. The upper windows of the E and W elevations' end bays (i.e. the 1730s pavilions' gables) are contained in giant overarches.

In 1883 the house was sold to J. Maitland Thomson who probably added the W front's unadventurous classical porch, its frieze and cornice quoting the 1770s wall-head design, dormer windows and, at the centre of the E elevation, a full-height staircase wing which was extended by a lower addition in the later C20. In 1996 the Tweed Wing with pedimented end gables and overarches was added at the S end. The building is now a nursing home.

The interior plan has been considerably altered, especially when the new staircase was added to the rear, and the former stairs removed. Nothing survives of interest except for the spacious late C19 oak well stair with carved balusters and newel posts, and, surprisingly the attic floor (1775). The 'Rooms in the Roof', remain remarkably intact and are approached from the second floor by enclosed C18 stairs with swept strings. Two large rooms each end, furnished with partitions for beds. Six-panelled doors have been retained or reused. Most unexpected is the use of terracotta tiles as the floor covering in this location. Was this a form of fire protection?

STABLES (Whim Square). A splendid W façade by *David Henderson*, 1775, screens a courtyard with ranges of farm buildings and cottages on the N and S sides, which may partly date from the late 1730s. The well-detailed and articulated ashlar seven-bay pedimented front to the drive has a central segmental-arched pend, with a moulded panel over, fronted by a shallow twin-columned portico. Composite capitals of acanthus and flutes, and a plain architrave, except for a patera above each capital. Elegant, slightly projecting, corniced niches on panelled bases decorate the links to pedimented pavilions framed by pilasters. In the pavilions round-arched windows, with intersecting tracery at the top, break through the moulded eaves course, acting as the base of each pediment. The end bays contained coach houses with grooms' quarters above. The other elevations are in rubble, with round-headed overarches, similar to the house, each end of the N elevation, but only at the W end of the S front. In the courtyard the farm buildings have been converted to housing, except for a barn at the E end of the S side, which looks older than the late C18 work.

ICE HOUSE, *c*. 0.25 km. W of the stables. Mid C18. An ovoid chamber lined in ashlar, a moulded architrave to the doorway. DOVECOT. *c*. 0.25 km. SE of the stables. Lower courses remain of a circular dovecot, probably the one supplied in 1738–40. – COWDEN LODGE. Late C18, possibly by *David Henderson*. The front has a central niche flanked by tripartite windows. – CISTERN. In the garden of Cowden Lodge. A pedimented Gothic arch.

LANDSCAPE. Some policy woodland survives, and probably contains trees planted by Sir James Montgomery, who also laid out a new walled garden to the E of the house in 1776, with advice from *James Robertson*. The walls have mostly gone but three cylinder-shaped canals remain. A large ornamental lake, formerly with three small islands, is about half its former size.

7050   WHITCHESTER HOUSE
                        3.3 km. NE of Longformacus

Described in the late 1850s as a 'substantial two-storey farmhouse with outbuildings and hinds' houses'. Bought in 1878
by Andrew Smith, an Edinburgh brewer, for the pursuit of
shooting, fishing and arboriculture. He added to, and remodelled, the farmhouse and cottages, planted trees and shelter
belts, and created a notable garden. The two-storey, three-bay
farmhouse was given a large stone porch and bipartite
windows on the S (entrance) elevation and full-height canted
bays on the E side. The inside was gutted to provide a staircase hall, business room to the l., dining room to the r., billiard room on the N side. A two-storey brick-built and rendered
square tower was added to the N, with a two-storey, four-bay
bachelor wing extending from its E side. In 1897 the cottages
were linked to the W end of the house by a pedimented
archway, remodelled, and given crowstepped gables and pediments with ball finials, resting on the parapet. In 1894 a mock-
Baronial tower appeared, attached to the NW corner of the
house, with a moulded doorpiece, inscribed on the lintel
'Blissit Be God in all his giftis'. All the embellishments, decorative pediments, curvilinear gables and the balustrading
round the top of the canted bays were added in 1897.
   The STABLE BLOCK along the N side of the court dates from
the earlier period, but the well-appointed interior must date
from the 1890s. A well-designed lean-to glazed and slated
passage along the front by *Richard Amos*, 1990s. Gatepiers at
the W end of the court, by the N one a square tower, with a
dovecot at the top, slated with small louvred openings.
   The house developed in a haphazard way, and the INTE-
RIOR decoration reflects the various activities. Each part is
decorated accordingly, in a different range of styles and materials, and suggests the hand of *Scott Morton & Co*. A timber-
lined hall, the business room with a compartmented ceiling,
thick with decorative plasterwork, including coats-of-arms.
The walls are covered in 'Cordoba' paper. Compartmented
ceiling in the dining room with a classical frieze and cornice.
The billiard room half-panelled with wood veneer, and top lit
by a rectangular cupola, the sides decorated with excellent
plasterwork – cherubs, lyres, vases – and a continuous frieze
of oakleaves and acorns. The drawing room on the first floor,
more relaxing, with low-key Adam decoration, and classical
chimneypiece with pilaster jambs, and centre panel displaying
a chariot drawn by lions, the driver blows a horn. The corridor to the square tower has painted leaded glass initialled AS
FL (Andrew Smith and Florence Landale); one panel illustrates a hooded woman carrying logs.
   The entrance forecourt, perhaps by *John Kinross* (*see* below),
with octagonal gatepiers, tiered caps and ball finials, linked to
outer wrought-iron octagonal ball-finialled piers. Much use of
decorative wrought-iron railings. SW of the house a rubble-
built, square-plan late C19 WALLED GARDEN, the principal
entrance by *John Kinross*. Up steps with squat balusters to

square ball-finialled gatepiers, decorative wrought-iron gates with overthrow. Greenhouse by *Mackenzie & Moncur.*

WEST LODGE. Originally a small two-storey castellated lodge with corbelled parapets and bartizans, 1897. Remodelled *c.* 1910–20, with Scots-Renaissance details. The lintel above a deep-set entrance doorway inscribed 'AL My Hoip Is In Ye Lord'. Square-plan panelled gatepiers, cavetto cornices, and pineappled bellcast caps. Wrought-iron gateway, 1897, with heraldic motifs and fleur-de-lys finials. – Two KENNELS, NW of the lodge, with scalloped bargeboarding.

WHITEHALL HOUSE
1.7 km. s of Chirnside

8050

An unexciting, plain mansion house of several dates, almost impossible to pick apart. Sir James Hall of Dunglass bought the estate for his son William in the early C18. The earliest part appears to date from the mid 1730s or early '40s but the house was extensively remodelled in the mid and late C19. Harl-pointed cream sandstone rubble, with rubble quoins on the W part, and tooled sandstone quoins on the E end. On the S front the entrance doorway is offset to the r. with three bays beyond that. To the l. of the entrance, at ground level, is a segmental-arched niche with rubble voussoirs – was this formerly a doorway? Two small keystoned windows in the next two bays, and a Venetian window above with the centre light blocked, still with their original glazing bars, must date from the mid C18 or earlier. The next three bays have single windows, in the last bay a keystoned segmental-arched one in the ground floor, and two widely spaced windows above, perhaps added after 1837 when the house was sold to William Mitchell-Innes of Ayton Castle. Piend-roofed dormers and brick chimneys date from the late C19.

Inside is a mid-C18 panelled room on the ground floor at the E end, remnants of a stone stair in the present entrance hall and a large kitchen fireplace and bread oven in the western-most room. Staircase with good iron uprights, perhaps 1840s, and first-floor 'Music Room' with exquisite decorative mural plasterwork depicting musical instruments, and naturalistic flowers, foliage and seeds, set off by a fluted dado rail and mutuled cornice. Above the chimneypiece, with a lugged archi-trave which matches the doors, an eagle plucks up a frame of festoons and swags. The freedom of expression suggests a date *c.* 1740.

STABLES are dated 1896, but probably incorporate earlier work. – Late C19 NORTH LODGE, gabled with timber-braced porch and decorative ridge tiles. – DOVECOT, NW of house, a C18 two-chambered lectern with very thick (0.91 m.) rubble walls. Projecting rat course and beak skewputts with carved faces, and bracketed water trays. Tiered rows of flight-holes, and inside, sandstone nesting boxes; some timber climbing poles survive.

WHITEHAUGH HOUSE

4010

4 km. W of Hawick

A charming small classical mansion in coursed pinkish sandstone, for Walter Scott of Whitehaugh to a design by *R. & R. Dickson*, with their father *John Dickson* as builder. An essay in neat asymmetry of two storeys with a square three-storey, piend-roofed tower, a Gothic-detailed tripartite window at the top. To the l., an advanced narrow gable with Tudor hood-moulded doorway, and shield above inscribed W.S. 1822. At the E end, a projecting piend-roofed canted bay; at the W end, a single bay with a tall Tudor-detailed tripartite window. Later extensions are in whinstone rubble.

WHITESIDE TOWER *see* SMAILHOLM

5040

WHITSLAID TOWER

4 km. SE of Lauder

The ruins of a late C15 or early C16 tower house of the Lauder family, probably occupying the site of an earlier residence. Oblong on plan (9.7 m. by 7.3 m. over walls 2 m. thick) and constructed of local rubble masonry with dressings of buff-coloured sandstone. The N end has collapsed, but the S end survives in part to a height of three storeys. From a doorway in the E wall access was obtained both to the ground-floor chamber, which was barrel-vaulted, and to a straight stair rising in the thickness of the E wall to a first-floor hall. Plans (1912) show this was heated by a fireplace in the N wall and provided with two windows, as well as a latrine served by a mural discharge chute. The stair continued to the second floor as a straight flight within the S wall.

8050

WHITSOME

PARISH CHURCH. 1803, initially a rectangle augmented by a small bell turret with a spired bellcote at the centre of the S wall, and N vestry; the entrances through the two end walls. S face of pink stugged ashlar, and other faces of rubble with raised block quoins, the windows pointed. Originally a horseshoe arrangement of galleries faced the S pulpit. But in 1912 it was rendered more ecclesiologically 'correct' when an E chancel was added, with a vestry to its S; the original vestry was adapted as a lateral N 'aisle' and the galleries suppressed. – FONT, 1910 by *Robert S. Lorimer*, octagonal with concave sides and carving of descending dove.

OLD CHURCHYARD, 0.2 km. N. A church is on record from the later C13, but only fragmentary footings survived demolition in 1803. – Simple rectangular WATCH HOUSE of red sandstone, dated 1820. Amongst earlier stones: Alison Edington, †1732, rustic full-length depiction holding book. Prominent memorial to David Hogarth of Hilton on pedimented Tuscan screen wall.

DESCRIPTION. The village comprises a short street of C19, mostly single-storey, cottages. At the W end WHITSOME LEA, a former manse, with a pilastered doorcase and canted bay. Contemporary stables and steading. In MAIN STREET, past the Parish Church (*see* above), is the mid-to-late C19 OLD SCHOOLHOUSE, with kneelered skewputts and stone-mullioned bipartite windows. U-shaped, gabled schoolroom (now dwelling), with gableted skewputts and diagonally set brick stacks. Nos. 1–2 is a double cottage of *c.* 1840, the paired doors centred under a pediment; Nos. 3–4 (dated 1840) are also paired, the flanking bays with pedimented dormers. BOURRIOT HOUSE has a pilastered doorcase, with shallow pediment and crudish acroterion. EWART HOUSE, dated 1845 with deep-set doorway and shouldered doorcase, was formerly the Crown Inn. A group on the N side includes GLAMIS HOUSE, classically fronted with columned doorcase. At the E end, mid-C19 VULCAN COTTAGE is the former blacksmith's house, the garden wall in front with intersecting wrought-iron hooped railings, and similarly detailed gateway. Behind is a smithy with small-paned fixed glazing.

JARDINEFIELD FARMHOUSE, 2 km. SE. Early C19, classically detailed, in coursed red sandstone.

THE LAWS, 4.8 km. NW. Late C19 Tudor-Jacobean gabled mansion house for Alexander Low, Lord Low, a judge. LAWS COTTAGE is late C19, with projecting five-light windows and a catslide-roofed arcaded veranda.

LEETSIDE FARMHOUSE, 2 km. N. Dignified mid-C19 gabled Tudor-Jacobean.

WHITTON TOWER   7020
3 km. SW of Morebattle

The ruins of a four-storey tower house of the Riddells of that Ilk, possibly built, or rebuilt, following the 'throwing down' of an earlier tower by an English army in 1523. Of simple, oblong plan (10.9 m. by 7.8 m. over walls 1.5 m. thick), only the W and S walls remain above the level of the lowest floor. Local random rubble masonry with quoins and dressings of dark red sandstone. The ground floor contained a barrel-vaulted cellar lit by slit windows; above was a single chamber, presumably the hall, with a large fireplace in the S end wall. The second floor also seemingly a single chamber.

WHYTBANK TOWER   4030
1.5 km. N of Clovenfords

A late C20 tower house incorporating the ground floor and one complete corner of an earlier one, probably erected by James Pringle of Whytbank during the last quarter of the C16. Ruinous

until 1988–92, when the tower was reconstructed and the associated barmkin walls consolidated and partly rebuilt for the Sir
Harold Mitchell Foundation by *John H. Reid.*

The original TOWER HOUSE seems to have been a four-storey
oblong block (10.9 m. by 7.5 m) with distinctive upperworks
featuring a pair of gable-roofed caphouses set at diagonally
opposite corners, as at Kirkhope (q.v.). Local whinstone
rubble masonry with dressings of red and buff-coloured sandstone and rubble quoins. A massive buttress was constructed
to support the E corner of the tower some time during the C17
or C18. On the ground floor a vaulted cellar equipped with no
fewer than five mural cupboards, as well as an entresol floor
beneath the vault. The entrance in the SE wall opened both
into the cellar and into a mural stair rising to the first floor.
The ground floor was restored in 1988–92, but the remainder
of the interior was left open to the roof. The W caphouse was
also rebuilt and prominent gable chimneys were reared at each
end of the tower, following the evidence of a drawing of 1828.

The BARMKIN, one of the few to survive in the Borders, is
irregular on plan (33 m. by 30 m.), with the tower occupying
the NW side, ranges of outbuildings on the W, S and E sides and
a small gap to the N, where the entrance probably lay. There
is evidence of four main phases of construction, all probably
of the second half of the C16. The two-storey E range contained
a barrel-vaulted kitchen at one end and a first-floor hall and
chamber at the other; fragments of a handsome chimneypiece
similar to one at Aikwood Tower (q.v.) were recovered during
site clearance. The W range, occupying the driest part of the
site, may have contained a granary, and the S range, which still
awaits excavation, a barn and brewhouse. In the SW corner of
the barmkin a well, approached by steps. Fragments of a possible bakehouse 30 m. N. Apart from the kitchen, where the
masonry is laid in lime mortar, all the buildings appear to be
bonded with clay, as in the barmkin at Smailholm Tower (q.v.).
On the sloping ground below the barmkin is a terraced
GARDEN, partially reconstituted in 1992–4; one of the lower
terraces has a pair of bee-boles built into the retaining wall.

4030   WINDYDOORS
                      7.2 km. NW of Galashiels

The shell of this small defensible house, perhaps best classified
as a bastle, now forms part of the N range of Windydoors Farm,
high up in the valley of the Caddon Water. Probably erected in
the late C16 by a tenant of the Kerrs of Cessford.

An elongated rectangle (14.8 m. by 7.5 m.) of two main storeys
built of rubble masonry with sandstone dressings. On the
ground floor a barrel-vaulted cellar lit by slits, the only communication with the floor above a hatch in the crown of the
vault. An original entrance in the S wall, but the handsome roll-
moulded surround looks too grand for a cellar and may originally have framed the missing first-floor entrance, presumably
approached from a forestair. There were evidently two first-

floor rooms, perhaps hall and chamber, each with its own fire-place, and probably also an upper floor reached by an internal stair.

WINKSTON

2.8 km. NW of Peebles

A much-altered C16 tower house, but important in providing a firm date for the appearance of certain architectural details – notably the horizontal gunloop and the edge-roll moulding – in late medieval Borders castles and houses. Erected by William Dickson, a Peebles burgess, in 1545, the tower was subsequently converted first into a Georgian box and then into a farm storehouse. Oblong on plan (10.7 m. by 7.6 m. over walls 1.3 m. thick), it comprised at least three storeys. Local whinstone rubble masonry with sandstone margins, some wrought with edge-roll mouldings. In the NE gable-wall a single-splayed, oval-mouthed gunloop at ground-floor level and traces of similar loops in the NW and SW walls. An original lintel, inscribed ANNO DOM 1545, is reused above an C18 doorway in the SE wall.

The original internal arrangements probably comprised a vaulted cellar with a hall and additional chambers above. The C18 remodelling is commemorated by a window lintel in the SE wall bearing the initials of John Little and his wife and the date 1734. At that time the building was reduced to a height of two storeys and an attic and equipped with new chimneystacks. The SE front was regularised, two tiers of large, chamfer-arrised windows being grouped round a central doorway. Inside, the vault was removed and new partitions inserted on either side of a central stair. On the ground floor the NE room became the kitchen, equipped with a big, timber-lintelled fireplace, while the SW room was probably a parlour. Two more chambers on the first floor with others in the attic; the principal rooms retain handsome, bead-moulded fire-places. The final phase, c. 1850, saw the blocking up of many of the external openings and the remodelling of the interior.

THE WOLL

0.7 km. SW of Ashkirk

Victorian Georgian survival of 1874. By *John Lessels* for William S. Bell, apparently incorporating a two-storey piend-roofed late Georgian house on the W side. In coursed cream sand-stone, with lugged surrounds, bracketed sills and consoled cornices, some with a little ornamentation. Bold cornice at eaves level surmounted by a parapet over the E two-thirds of the house. S front of four bays, the centre two advanced under an open pediment; bipartite ground floor windows in the outer bays. An oval panel with Hebrew text decorates the parapet over the r. bay. Similarly detailed E elevation but with pedimented dormers breaking the parapet, a full-height canted bay window in the centre and a pedimented gable at the N end. At the N front, a tall lugged doorway, with a window in the centre; another panel with Hebrew text. W elevation of four bays, with shouldered stacks framing the roof.

LODGE. Mid-C19 and rendered, with gabled porch and overhanging eaves. Chamfered and shouldered surrounds. – STABLES (Garden House and Coach House). 1831, for Charles Balfour Scott W.S. of Woll. The design can be safely attributed to *John Smith*, who was working at the time for Charles Scott and Sir Walter Scott on bridges for the road trustees (*see* Sunderland Hall). Stables by Smith at The Haining and Dryburgh Abbey House also have many similarities.

Splendid, assertively crenellated, in cream stugged ashlar, the rest in whinstone rubble. A symmetrical S block of five bays, the centre with a segmental-arched pend, a circular quoined opening above, a stepped hoodmould, and raised centre panel with the Scott of Woll coat-of-arms and prominently carved crest. Embossed across the front is 'C.B.S. 1831', with the motto *Pacem Amo*. Single-bay links to gabled pavilions, each with a stepped hoodmoulded window. From the E end, a long nine-bay curved block links to a coachman's house. Three segmental-arched carriage houses, flanked by stores, to a court on the concave W side, a pavilion at the S end of the E elevation, and the coachman's house to the N. Similarly detailed S elevation, with the rear of each carriage house pierced by an oversized gunloop. Partially converted to two houses in the late 1990s, and finished by *Andrew Davey* of *Simpson & Brown* in 2003–4.

WOOPLAW HOUSE

4040

5.2 km. SE of Stow

An asymmetrical gabled house described in 1844 as 'an excellent and newly built (never occupied) house' but a C17 door discovered during renovations in 1980 is evidence that it incorporates an earlier house, probably represented by the recessed end of the W elevation. Built of whinstone rubble, with irregular fenestration, the upper windows with later dormerheads.

The work of *c.* 1840 is of two storeys, built in droved pink sandstone, with finely tooled margins. Deep chamfered arrises and Tudor hoodmoulds to all the windows and doors. The E entrance elevation with wallhead dormers and a projecting square bay window. On the S elevation is a full-height canted bay window with a shaped parapet; gable behind with a corbelled finial. The lower block to the l. was the attached stable, altered *c.* 1910 for use as a library and bedroom above. The most interesting feature of Wooplaw is in the display of groups of very tall diamond-plan chimney flues, set on plinths. On the N elevation a bold stack, partly corbelled, rises to a cluster of four, dated 1841 on a panel. The interior is simply detailed, and much has been sympathetically renewed. A screen with Gothic detailing defines the vestibule from the hall, and the curved stone staircase has a good Edinburgh-style decorative cast-iron balustrade.

THE YAIR

4.8 km. NW of Selkirk

A stylish, classical house, sitting on low ground in an idyllic 70 setting, by a gentle curve of the River Tweed. James Pringle of Whytbank acquired the estate in the mid C17. It went out of Pringle ownership for short periods, but was repurchased *c.* 1784 by Alexander Pringle, who amassed a fortune in India, then built the present house to the design of *William Elliot* in 1788. There was evidently an 'old house' on the site in which the family lived while the new house was under construction. The family considered the house an 'excellent one, vastly well-contrived'.

Three-storey and attics, in coursed rubble work with sandstone margins, raised quoins, corniced eaves, and a piended roof with chimneystacks on the transverse walls. The E front of seven bays, with a full-height centre bow with corniced balustrade, fronted by a well-detailed Doric-columned doorpiece, with triglyphs and metopes in the frieze and mutuled pediment. The side elevations have three bays. U-plan court to the W, with a three-storey extension on the N side (formerly a much lower office building of two-storeys and contemporary with the main block, but extended and with a third storey added in the late C19/early C20, when the earlier kitchen block was probably remodelled.) On the court's S side, a single-storey extension to the house, with a balustraded S wall of three bays linked to an ogee-roofed C17-style pavilion. Probably early C20 and similar to a feature at nearby Fairnilee House (q.v.). On the keystone of the round-headed staircase window in the W elevation is inscribed: AP (Alexander Pringle) 1788. Above a rubble-built archway to the courtyard is a SUNDIAL with an ogival top. Three faces have dials, the fourth some heraldry; what can be read suggests it belongs to Pringle of Whytbank.

Internally is a strict C18 tripartite plan. The entrance opens *p. 767* straight into a circular hall, doors l. to the dining room, and r. is a morning room, with a room to its rear, now a gun room. In the hall there are niches each side of a basket-arched opening with a view, through a similar arch, to the staircase hall. Behind the walls between the two arches is a stair to a cellar and a cupboard (l.). A spacious well stair fills the space at the rear of the house. Simple classical decoration, the stair with plain cast-iron uprights. Above two doorways on the upper landing are carved plaster panels, one showing Europa and the Bull, the other a Bacchic ritual. The dining room has a Doric columned archway at the W end, to a small anteroom, and a timber chimneypiece with a dentilled cornice and a sphinx in the centre panel. In the same position on the first floor, the drawing room has a composite columned archway to a similar room; what purpose did these rooms serve? White marble chimneypiece flanked by fluted pilasters. Centre front is a bow-ended library, the timber and gesso chimneypiece carved with a centre swag, urns and flutes.

STABLES, S of the house. Built 1788. A much altered two-storey whinstone courtyard range with a screen wall, flanked by gables to l. and r., the entrance through whinstone rubble

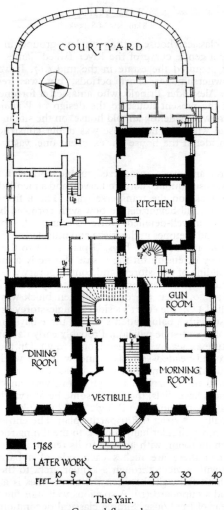

The Yair.
Ground-floor plan.

corniced piers topped by ornamental urn finials. The stables appear to have been remodelled, at least partly, in the early-to-mid C19. Harled and gabled LODGE dated 1820. The entrance in a sloping roofed extension built over the Yair Burn. GATEPIERS. Probably 1820. Square piers with fluted architraves and capped tops. ICE HOUSE NW of house. Cone-shaped with a domed roof. – WALLED GARDEN on a steeply sloping site across the Yair Burn, reached by a timber dry bridge with an ornamental iron balustrade. A cast-iron gate in a whinstone arch into the garden has a circular opening at the top; below are conventional spearheaded uprights. Divided across the top by two curved fruit walls, fronted by terraces, their copes decorated with stone balls. Built into the upper terrace is preserved a stone dated 1661, and inscribed 'All is vanity one thing is needful'; formerly at Whytbank Tower (q.v.). – GARDENER'S HOUSE, dated 1820, in whinstone with red sandstone margins. Bipartite windows.

YAIR BRIDGE. Designed by *William Mylne*, 1759, but probably not built until 1764 when the Act for the road was passed. Three-span rubble bridge with segmental arches, and triangular cutwaters extending upwards to form pedestrian refuges. Much repaired over the years.

YARROW 3020

A large and scattered upland parish with villages only at Cappercleuch (q.v.) and Yarrowford.

PARISH CHURCH. Built 1640, and probably T-shaped from the start, with the main body extending from E to W and the 'aisle' off the N side. During major works in 1771–2 the walls were heightened and lofts inserted; there were further works in 1826 by *John Smith*, and in 1876 by *Mr Hood*, the Duke of Buccleuch's clerk of works. The architectural character was greatly modified in 1906 by *A.N. Paterson*, who added a polygonal apse at the centre of the S front, removed the galleries, and provided timber-screened vestibules at the ends of all three aisles. Doorways, some of the windows, and the ceilings were modified, and the bellcote was re-positioned from the W gable to behind the new apse. The church was burned out on Easter Sunday 1922, but was carefully rebuilt the following year, with the addition of a porch and session house in the NE re-entrant.

The three arms of the church are harled, with pink or buff ashlar dressings, and with crowsteps and cross finials to the gables. The round-arched moulded doorway at the E end of the S wall is presumably of 1640, and was symmetrically replicated by another towards the W end of that wall. The four windows along the S wall, with thin label hoodmouldings, date from the work of 1826, although modified in 1923. By contrast, the apse windows are round-arched with lugged surrounds, the central one dated 1906 and with the initials of Robert Borland (minister) and A.N. Paterson (architect). The slightly busy pinnacles at the angles of the apse build up to the square bellcote rising from the wall behind, with its pyramidal spirelet.

The interior is a delight. The three arms have segmental plaster ceilings, but there is a ribbed 'vault' over the apse. Exposed stonework to the window surrounds, cornice, string course, apse arch and arcaded apse dado. Some fine Arts and Crafts detailing: flanking the apse arch angels bear scrolls with sacred symbols, the apse ribs have winged angel corbels, and there are foliate terminals to the deep continuous mouldings of the chancel arch. All of these help to concentrate attention on the communion table in the apse, the pulpit to the E of the apse arch, and the font below the crossing. – COMMUNION TABLE, oak, rectangular with pilasters at the angles and relief carving of chalice and vine. – LECTERN, oak, desk on spiral column, 1924. – PULPIT, on stone base, oak octagon with lofty tester, incorporating C17 carved panel from St Mary's Chapel (crypt of St Nicholas Church) Aberdeen. – FONT, stone, bowl with carved panels, and with shafts capped by Evangelist symbols at corners. – Jacobethan VESTIBULE SCREENS, oak, at E and W ends of the main body and to the enclosed pew at the end of the N aisle. – STAINED GLASS, in apse, Nativity flanked by Adoration of Magi and Shepherds, *Douglas Strachan*, 1927. – PLAQUES: Internal, to W of apse arch, James Lorimer, †1775; external, on N side towards E end, John Rutherford, †1710, aedicule framing renewed tablet; on SW and S sides of apse, lists of ministers. – BELL, 1657. – SUNDIAL, 1640.

CHURCHYARD, mixture of C17, C18 and C19 table tombs, headstones and obelisks, some with *memento mori*, and one with depiction of deceased.

MANSE. Probably built in 1811 as a plain, two-storeyed, gable-roofed block with a three-bay front. Subsequently enlarged by the addition of an attic storey contrived within a hipped platform roof, and a semi-octagonal entrance bay at the centre of the original front. Further alterations in the late C19.

DEUCHAR BRIDGE, 0.4km. downstream. Fragment of a two-arch bridge over the River Yarrow, possibly dating from 1748 but replacing an earlier one commissioned by the Duchess of Buccleuch (†1732). Only the N arch and central pier and cutwater remain.

YARROW BRIDGE, opposite the church, by *John Smith*, 1833. A fine single-span bridge of local whinstone with a long elliptical arch and corbelled parapet with red sandstone coping.

YARROW STONE. 1km. WSW, in an enclosure by the track leading up to Whitefield. Thought to have been found in the course of ploughing in 1803. It is a roughly worked piece with a C5 or C6 inscription in Roman capitals which can be roughly translated 'In this place [is] the everlasting memorial of the most famous princes Nudus and Dumnogenus'. The form of the inscription suggests those commemorated were Christian.

PUBLIC HALL, Yarrowford, 5.8km. NE. Of red-painted corrugated iron topped by two ridge ventilators.

SCHOOL, Yarrowford, 5.8km. NE. *c.* 1872. Single storey of dressed whinstone rubble with yellow sandstone dressings and a gable-ended roof with overhanging eaves. Schoolmaster's house at one end and classroom at the other, each with an arch-pointed doorway and canopied porch.

YARROW HALL, Yarrowfeus, 2.1km. SW. A handsome village institute with integral custodian's house by *A. N. Paterson*, 1908. One and a half storeys high, of harled rubble with buff sandstone dressings; gabled roofs with overhanging eaves and swept skewputts. An H-plan block with the hall to the N, amply lit by a Venetian window overlooking the road, a Diocletian one at the rear and a big three-light dormer to the N; ridge ventilator. The house, elaborated by a circular window bay at one corner, adjoins to the S.

HANGINGSHAW. *See* p. 341.

YETHOLM

Yetholm stands on the Bowmont Water, at the gate or passage to a narrow open valley between England and Scotland. During border warfare this access afforded an easy entrance either way for raiding purposes. A village in two parts, consisting of the older Kirk Yetholm occupying the E bank of the river, while Town Yetholm stands on the W one, both governed by baron bailies appointed by the Marquess of Tweeddale, and Wardrop of Niddrie, respectively. In the later C18 the population of both settlements grew, as a consequence of changing patterns of agriculture. By the early 1850s Kirk Yetholm was composed mostly of single-storey thatched houses, occupied by farm workers on the Tweeddale estate. In the mid-to-late C19 many of the cottages were improved, becoming two-storey, harled houses. Town Yetholm, regularly laid out and prosperous, improved with the building of two-storey slated houses by the Wauchope estate from *c.* 1800. It was populated by tradesmen, cottars, and long-leased feuars with a portion of land.

CHURCHES

EVANGELISTIC GOSPEL MISSION, Grafton Road, Town Yetholm. 1931, a small corrugated-iron mission hall. It has a N porch, shaped bargeboards and a roof-top louvre; there are rectangular windows along the flanks. Now an increasingly rare survival.

KIRK YETHOLM PARISH CHURCH. By *Robert Brown Jun.*, 1836–7. A rectangle with walls of squared dark grey andesite, and buff ashlar dressings from the Coldstream quarry; it is aligned from E to W (in fact NE to SW), with a W tower, and a vestry added on the N side of the tower. The flanks of the church have broad lancets, with a pair of two-light loop-traceried windows at the E end, while the tower has a loop-traceried window at the lower level and Y-traceried windows to the belfry stage. There are polygonal buttresses at the angles. With its plethora of buttresses and pinnacles, and the gables around the tower head, it has something of the same make-believe Gothick quality as Cavers Parish Church (q.v.). The doorway in the S face of the tower opens onto the gallery stair, while that on the S side of the nave gives onto a vestibule below the gallery.

Internally there is a flat plastered ceiling with a rose that was originally central; the W gallery is carried on three cast-iron fluted columns. Major remodelling in 1934 by *A. Lorne Campbell*, when two galleries were removed and a chancel formed within the E end: the communion table became the focus of liturgical attention, and the truncated pulpit was moved to the N. The chancel itself is flanked by recesses, the S recess housing the organ, and the N recess being walled off; all are framed by moulded segmental arches. In 1973 the W gallery was enclosed as a utility room by *Duncan Cameron & Associates*. – STAINED GLASS. Chancel: Good Shepherd, Light of World, Christ and Children, *James Ballantine II*, *c.* 1935. Nave, S. side: 'I will sing unto the Lord', *c.* 1933. – MEDIEVAL GRAVE-SLAB, in base of tower, with incised foliate-headed cross and sword. Built into the vestibule walls, STONES bearing the dates 1610 and 1763, evidence of repairs and rebuilding of the church's predecessor.

CHURCHYARD. Mainly C19 memorials, many of slate with excellent lettering and relief decoration, e.g. Walter Scott, †1850. BOYD OF CHERRYTREES BURIAL VAULT. Andesite walls with ashlar doorway and crowsteps; plaster masonry-lined walls and segmental ceiling. Built for Adam Boyd, †1831, possibly by *Robert Brown Jun.*

Former ST JAMES CHURCH, Dow Brae, Town Yetholm. Now in other use. Built 1882; closed in 1940. Squared whin with buff sandstone dressings (the lower part of the w front harled), it has single or grouped lancets along each flank and high in each gable wall. Stump of a bellcote on the w gable.

PUBLIC BUILDINGS

VIRTUE WELL, *c.* 0.3 km. N of the junction of B6352 with the road to Cherrytrees. Late C18. Set in a rubble whinstone retaining wall, a segmental-arched panel inscribed '1887 AW FW' Wauchope(?); spout missing.

WAR MEMORIAL, Kirk Yetholm. *c.* 1920. White granite with a Celtic cross. Panelled base and inscribed shaft to the dead, set within a railed enclosure

WAUCHOPE HALL, former Border View Church, Bowmont Terrace, Town Yetholm. 1818, with gallery added 1820; redundant following a union of 1914. Built of whin, and of rather domestic appearance, the main E front having a wide segmental-arched central doorway with raised margins, fluted impost blocks and a keystone, and at its head is a fanlight. Rectangular windows flank the doorway, and there are three arched windows at the upper level.

WAUCHOPE MONUMENT, Main Street, Town Yetholm. A Boer War Memorial by *Thomas P. Marwick*, executed by *Waldie & Son*, Edinburgh, 1902. Tall obelisk of Aberdeen grey granite, 'Erected by the inhabitants of Yetholm and other friends to the memory of Major General Wauchope, CB CMC, of Yetholm, who fell in battle while leading his troops at Magersfontein, 11th December 1899'.

YETHOLM BRIDGE between Kirk and Town Yetholm over the Bowmont Water. By *John Smith*, dated 1834. Three segmental arches with channelled stugged sandstone cutwaters and quadrant abutments. Corbelled string course and whinstone voussoirs. Unsympathetic later steel railings.

YETHOLM PRIMARY SCHOOL. Beautifully sited at the N end of Town Yetholm. *c.* 1825, designed by *William Elliot.* Single-storey in whinstone rubble. The w front of six bays with gabled doorway, and tripartite windows; every alternate one with sloping stone canopies, the rest break the eaves. S elevation with tall wallhead windows. A seamless, rendered addition for classrooms, to the SE, by *Thomas P. Marwick*, 1901. A further extension, late 1980s, with piended roof and wide, splayed eaves. Well-glazed, with large tripartite windows. In the playground, piend-roofed playsheds, probably by Marwick, 1901.

DESCRIPTION

Kirk Yetholm

KIRK YETHOLM's chief interest was as the principal settlement of Scottish gypsies, the Faas apparently being the first to settle here before *c.* 1700. Approaching the village from the s the War Memorial (*see* above) on the r., and YETHOLM MILL on the l. A former barley, wheat and oat mill mostly built in 1812; also a three-storey miller's house, with cartshed, cattle court and stables. Harled. As the road bears l. into Main Street the parish church is on the l. On the r. the MANSE, built in 1786–8 (*James Hope*, mason, and *Robert Fox*, wright). Improvements were carried out by *George Angus*, *c.* 1830, providing a kitchen, with a drawing room above. Two-storey, crowstepped L-plan house, harled, with raised sandstone margins. A three-bay s front with crowstepped gabled porch, and four bays on the w side with advanced gabled bays. T-plan range of harled, single-storey outhouses. In the garden carved stone fragments of mid-C12 date from the former Parish Church (dem. 1836). They include a Romanesque cushion cap with decorated lunettes, two chevron-decorated voussoirs, a later capital decorated with foliage and mythical beasts, and some nook-shaft bases.

MAIN STREET is wide and lined with a mixture of single and two-storey harled whinstone houses; mostly late C18 and C19, but demolition and time have taken their toll. On the e side is CHURCH VIEW, a restored late C18 house, the top windows close to the eaves; timber lintels. ROWANTREE COTTAGE is late C18, single-storey, harled and thatched. On the rear elevation an attractive wall-head attic window set well into the thatched roof. On the w side of Main Street early C19 TYNE-HOLM, of two storeys, pebbledashed. Three bays with centre gabled pediment and attic window. CROSS KEYS HOUSE, formerly a late C18 inn with remodelled stabling extending down the N side. Curly skews, that on the l. with cube sundial; some gnomons just survive. The street widens into the large, open green. At the sw corner a late C19 cast-iron WATER PUMP by *Glenfield & Kennedy*. Fluted column with lion spout, topped by a fluted cap with foliate finials; others at the apex of the green, and w side of Main Street. On the w side only THE GREEN asks to be noticed: dated 1902 in the shouldered gable over the centre bay. Urns on the skews. On the N side the BORDER HOTEL, a hostelry formerly for drovers, and today a haven for walkers. The original inn is still thatched, with its former stabling extending e from the NE corner. Its w section has a roof of rosemary tiles and jettied upper floor from the 1920s, when the rest was remodelled. *c.* 1932 half-timbering was applied to the original inn and stables extension, the interior of which was recast in Tudor style with beamed ceilings, and panelling. Mural paintings depict hunting scenes, including the hunt leaving the refurbished inn, and a panorama of the Grand National of 1967.

HIGH STREET is narrow with the earliest housing on the w side. At the top, set back from the road, is THE PALACE. Originally a small single-storey cottage with crowstepped porch and round-headed window, harled and washed pink. It was the home of Esther Faa Blythe, the last 'Queen of the Gypsies' (†1883). Downhill from here High Street is known as Tinkers' Row. Two-storey, three-bay houses have replaced single-storey thatched cottages, inhabited by tinkers selling horn spoons and coarse earthenware. From the SW corner of the green, Mill Drive leads to BLUNTY'S MILL, a former water-powered woollen mill built by the Marquess of Tweeddale. A large early C19 two-storey, L-plan whinstone group in poor condition. WAULKFORD BRIDGE is a single-span segmental-arched whinstone pack-horse bridge over the now dry mill lade. Close to, Nos. 1 and 2 WAULKFORD. Mid-C19, two-storey, three-bay houses, harled with painted margins and quoin strips; corniced doorways. Adjacent is the former SCHOOL, adapted and added to as a youth hostel. Rebuilt 1841; a single-storey whinstone classroom with a schoolmaster's house at the S end.

Town Yetholm

TOWN YETHOLM has a long street running N to S. Wide at the N end with a sloping green on the W side, and a very wide dusty pavement, formerly cobbled, on the E. It narrows to High Street at the S end. Improvements began on the S side c. 1800. In the C20 some good vernacular late C18 and early C19 houses were removed.

Starting at the N end, and opposite the school, the former United Presbyterian Manse, of five bays, with a two-bay house at the E end. The E gable to the road. Harled with raised painted margins. A panel from the former Border View Church (*see* Wauchope Hall, above), records the Rev. Walter Home, †1861, first minister, and the Rev. Ebenezer Erskine Wight, second minister, †1863. Down Kelso Road is YETHOLM HALL, an early C19, three-bay T-plan villa. Ashlar fronted, the rest whinstone with cream dressings. Giant pilasters flank the advanced central bay, pilastered quoins at the angles. Stacks of five polygonal chimneys. A mixture of late C18-to-late C19 houses in BOWMONT TERRACE on the W side of MAIN STREET. Refinements at No. 3, with a full-height canted bay, and at No. 5, with a canted oriel on the first floor. PINFARTHINGS looks to be a late C18 survival with timber lintels. At the end is Wauchope Hall (*see* above), before THE CRESCENT follows on to the S and curves slightly behind the High Street. Again a mixture of housing, late C18 to-late C19, mostly remodellings, the late C18 houses identified by their widely spaced bays and timber lintels. Mostly substantial houses with stables and byres to the rear, some of which survive almost unaltered. All two-storey except CRAIGLEA, single-storey with gableted block skewputts. TWIZEL HOUSE was remodelled in the mid-C19 for the British Linen Co. Bank.

MAIN STREET, E side, has little architectural incident. Mid-to-late C18 GREYSTONE has widely spaced windows, steeply pitched roof and a thackstane (the weathering device used for thatched roofs). RUTHERFORD has a bracketed three-light oriel, and PARAMOUNT is dated 1875, when it was remodelled to form a shop with pilastered shopfront. PLOUGH HOTEL. probably c. 1800. Formerly a two-storey, three-bay inn with a bracketed canopied doorway. Remodelled and extended to match to the S, and all harled with painted margins. Decorative iron and glass canopy above a lugged entrance doorway.

Where the road narrows it becomes HIGH STREET. Note MYRTLE COTTAGE at the corner of Yew Tree Road. A reconstructed mid-to-late-C18 two-storey cottage, formerly two cottages, with widely spaced bays. Harled with slightly battered walls and steeply pitched thatched roof. GRAFTON HOUSE faces S, its W gable to the street. Entrance doorway with bracketed timber pediment. Much demolition of earlier housing here for access to GRAFTON COURT and sheltered housing by Roxburgh County Council, c. 1970, and the Evangelistic Gospel Mission, see Churches, above. Opposite is ROSE COTTAGE. Late C18 and thatched. Heavily remodelled mid C20 and given tripartite windows, those on the first floor breaking the eaves in thatched hoods. MERTOUN COTTAGE, late C18, is correctly thatched and rendered with black painted timber lintels. Three bays grouped together in the centre, with a bracketed and canopied doorpiece. Late-C19 *Glenfield & Kennedy* WATER PUMP in front. At the S end of the street two villas. COPESWOOD was the late C19 Free Church Manse. Whinstone rubble, formerly harled, with grey rock-faced sandstone dressings. Overhanging timber eaves. Finally, ROMANY HOUSE is a two-storey asymmetrical Italianate villa with attached stables, c. 1900. Built of rock-faced sandstone with polished dressings on the principal elevations, the rest are squared and snecked whinstone rubble. Heavily bracketed eaves cornice. Shallow segmental-arched windows and two-storey pedimented bays, with a Venetian stair window in the W elevation. Decorative classical chimneypiece in the encaustic-tiled hall, a vestibule door with etched glass, and a pair of glass panels set in leaded glass in the stair window.

ATTONBURN, 6.4 km. S. Two-storey harled farmhouse, the main block rectangular, perhaps dating from c. 1800. Mid-C19 addition to the W for a new drawing room, stair and bedrooms, and a porch placed in the NW re-entrant angle, the doorpiece with pilasters and cornice and blocking course, characteristic of the Roxburghe Estates office. Late C19 addition on the E side with brick dressings. To the N the STABLES and STEADING. Symmetrical W front with central segmental-arched pend, and a round-arched upper opening with keystone detailing and consoled sill; the opening has five rows of timber pigeon entries. Wide overhanging timber-bracketed eaves. Segmental-arched cartsheds, with haylofts above. To the N four mid-C19 two-storey farm workers' cottages. Whinstone rubble with sandstone dressings, stone chimneys and later wall-head dormers.

BELFORD ON BOWMONT, 7.8 km. S. A fashionable two-storey and attic five-bay laird's house, with piended roof and gable chimneys. Built 1794. Harled with painted stone dressings. The S front has a large mid-C19 slated porch, the original tall late C18 doorpiece has deep cavetto reveals and fanlight. A simple interior with a curving staircase, decorative cast-iron balusters and mahogany rail. Six-panelled doors and a classical chimneypiece in the drawing room.

OLD BELFORD HOUSE, vacated when the new house was built, is now part of the farm. Exposed rubble, formerly harled, with surviving crowstepped gable. Late C18 or early C19, two-storey outshot for a new kitchen. The window openings are either chamfered or have rounded arrises. There are two rooms remaining on the ground floor; that at the W end appears to have been the original kitchen. Whinstone rubble threshing BARN with water-powered threshing machine; part of the machinery is still in position, the enclosed waterwheel was housed in an extension with an external stair. Its 14 ft (4.2 m.) diameter iron overshot wheel with forty metal buckets remains. The site of the mill pond, with the dam wall and the masonry supports for an aqueduct, completes this interesting survival.

The MILLER'S HOUSE to the S, dated 1875 on an inscribed panel with the initials GHSD [Sir George Henry Scott Douglas] and JRS [James Robertson Scott]. Single-storey with a jerkin-headed slate roof and central brick chimney.

MOWHAUGH, 7.7 km S on the E bank of the Bowmont Water. Early C19 traditional FARMHOUSE in harled rubble. Reconstructed and given a new pedimented doorway dated 1914. Two whinstone rubble COTTAGES c. 1864, with pedimented wall-head windows, and a good drying BARN of six bays, possibly the same date; the roof supported by timber columns, rubble ends with sandstone quoins. Three slated louvres along the roof ridge.

CHURCH SITE 0.5 km. N of Mowhaugh in a field. The parish church of Mow or Molle was granted to Kelso Abbey before 1152, the terms of the grant suggesting there was already a mother church or minister there. It was abandoned after union with Morebattle in 1635. The sole remains are linear mounds marking the walls of a possible two-cell structure, around which are fallen headstones and table-tomb slabs. One stone may have a worn incised foliate-headed cross.

CHERRYTREES. *See* p. 163.

FURTHER READING

General

A good starting point is *The Borders Book* (1995; ed. D. Omand), which also contains a useful bibliography. There is no modern history of the Borders, but much valuable information is to be found in the earlier topographical histories, notably R.B. Armstrong's *The History of Liddesdale* (1883), J.W. Buchan and H. Paton's *A History of Peeblesshire* (1925–7), W. Chambers' *A History of Peeblesshire* (1864), T. Craig-Brown's *The History of Selkirkshire* (1886), A. Jeffrey's *The History and Antiquities of Roxburghshire* (1857–64), J.R. Oliver's *Upper Teviotdale and the Scotts of Buccleuch* (1887) and A. Thomson's *Coldingham: Parish and Priory* (1908). Although published as long ago as 1851, the first volume of Cosmo Innes's *Origines Parochiales Scotiae* is still the most convenient source of information on the medieval history and topography of the region (but excluding Berwickshire), while many aspects of pre-c18 Borders history are illuminated by the excellent maps contained in the *Atlas of Scottish History to 1707* (1996), edited by P.G.B. McNeill and H.L. McQueen. *The Annals of a Border Club* (1903), by G. Tancred, is strong on family history and the succession of estates.

Periodical sources are also helpful, especially the long running *Proceedings of the Berwickshire Naturalists' Club* (1831–) and *Transactions of the Hawick Archaeological Society* (1863–). The wide ranging surveys published on a parish arrangement in *The Statistical Account of Scotland* (OSA; 1791–9), the *New Statistical Account* (NSA; 1845) and the *Third Statistical Account* (TSA; *c.* 1950–1992) are essential points of reference and the county volumes of the second editions of the *General View of Agriculture* (*c.* 1796–1816) contain useful sections on industry and communications as well as farms and houses. Much relevant topographical information is also to be found in Francis Groome's *Ordnance Gazetteer of Scotland* (various editions *c.* 1880–1900).

For both archaeology and architecture additional material can often be found in the invaluable county inventories published by the Royal Commission on the Ancient and Historical Monuments of Scotland (RCAHMS), namely *Berwickshire* (1915), *Roxburghshire* (1956), *Selkirkshire* (1957) and *Peeblesshire* (1967). These have little to say about c19 and c20 buildings, however, for which reference should be made to the descriptive Lists of Buildings of Architectural and Historic Interest prepared by Historic Scotland, currently being reissued in updated form. Recent published surveys include Charles Strang's *Borders and Berwickshire: An Illustrated Guide* (1994), John Baldwin's *Exploring Scotland's Heritage: Lothian and the Borders* (1996) and John Dent and

Rory McDonald's *Heritage Sites in the Borders* (Scottish Borders Council, 2001). Two of the most useful general surveys are *Scotland: An Oxford Archaeological Guide* (1998) by A. and G. Ritchie and *A History of Scottish Architecture* by M. Glendinning, R. MacInnes and A. MacKechnie (1996). The latter includes a select list of Scottish architects, many of whom are more fully treated in Howard Colvin's *A Bibliographical Dictionary of British Architects* 1660–1840 (3rd ed., 1995) and D. M. Walker's *Dictionary of Scottish Architects* 1840–1940 (www.scottisharchitects.org.uk).

Readers living within convenient reach of Edinburgh will find that many of the books and other items mentioned here are available for public reference in the library of the National Monuments Record of Scotland (NMRS), a branch of RCAHMS (John Sinclair House, 16 Bernard Terrace, Edinburgh, EH8 9NX; www.rcahms.gov.uk). In particular, the NMRS houses the *Buildings of Scotland* archive for the present volume. This incorporates more detailed, referenced versions of many of the gazetteer entries, as well as authors' research notes and a large amount of relevant information extracted over the years by John Gifford, Head of the Buildings of Scotland Research Unit, and others, from C19 and C20 architectural periodicals (*The Builder, The Building News, The Architect* etc.), local histories and guidebooks. Also available in NMRS are Ordnance Survey maps and microfilm copies of the Ordnance Survey Name Books (OSNB) containing brief, but often valuable, notes on mid-C19 site visits to many of the buildings described in this volume.

Geology and Topography

Scottish Borders Geology – An Excursion Guide (1992), edited by A.D. McAdam, E.N.K. Clarkson and P. Stone, includes a chapter on the building stones of the Borders abbeys. D.C. Greig's *British Regional Geology* (3rd ed., 1971) is currently being revised. Both volumes contain useful bibliographies and further information can be found on the British Geological Survey website: www.bgs.ac.uk.

Churches

Of the standard works on church architecture in Scotland that have useful things to say about the churches in this area, particular mention must be made of David MacGibbon and Thomas Ross, *The Ecclesiastical Architecture of Scotland* (1896–7), George Hay, *The Architecture of Scottish post-Reformation Churches* (1957) and Peter Anson's, 'Catholic Church Building in Scotland, 1560–1914' (*Innes Review*, 6, 1954). Much valuable material is also to be found in the relevant chapters of *Scottish Architecture from the Accession of the Stewarts to the Reformation 1371–1560* (1994), by Richard Fawcett, and in the same author's *Scottish Medieval Churches: Architecture and Furnishings* (2002). An attractively presented overview of the physical evidence for the church in the area that should be mentioned is John Dent and Rory Macdonald's *Christian Heritage in the Borders* (Scottish Borders

Council, 1998). So far as the documentation associated with the medieval parishes and religious houses is concerned, much of the information is carefully summarised in Ian B. Cowan's *The Parishes of Medieval Scotland* (Scottish Record Society, 93, 1967) and Ian B. Cowan and David E. Easson's *Medieval Religious Houses, Scotland* (1976).

The Scottish Borders has been particularly fortunate in attracting the attentions of G.A.C. Binnie, who has published two detailed volumes on the churches in two of the old county areas, and these are altogether invaluable for the history of those churches. They are: *The Churches and Graveyards of Berwickshire* (2001) and *The Churches and Graveyards of Roxburghshire* (2001). Also still of value are two late c19 books by James Robson on the churches and churchyards of these same two areas. Histories are available for a number of parishes, as are guidebooks or leaflets to individual churches, and although they vary greatly in quality they are often worth consulting for information that would be difficult to obtain from other sources.

Some of the churches of Jedburgh have attracted more attention than almost any others, and reference must be made to a number of the resulting books and papers. James Watson's *Jedburgh Abbey and the Abbeys of Teviotdale* (2nd edn, 1894) is still of great value. However, it has been superseded in many aspects by J.H. Lewis and G.J. Ewart's *Jedburgh Abbey, the Archaeology and Architecture of a Border Abbey* (Society of Antiquaries of Scotland monograph, 10, 1995). Another important excavation was that carried out at the Franciscan Friary in Jedburgh, which has now been published in *Archaeological Excavations at Jedburgh Friary, 1983–1992*, by Piers Dixon, Jerry O'Sullivan and Ian Rogers (2000). Unfortunately, post-Reformation churches have seldom been published as fully as their medieval predecessors, though mention must be made of an exemplary study by Tristram Clarke, 'A display of Tractarian energy: St John's Episcopal Church, Jedburgh' (*Records of the Scottish Church History Society*, 27, 1997). An excellent account of the history and architecture of the neighbouring abbey of Melrose is now available in Richard Fawcett and Richard Oram's *Melrose Abbey* (2004).

Castles etc.

So far as castles and other defensible buildings are concerned, the five volumes of David MacGibbon and Thomas Ross's *Castellated and Domestic Architecture of Scotland* (1887–92) and the six county volumes of the RCAHMS *Inventories*, as detailed above, remain indispensable. The considerable volume of building activity undertaken by English occupying forces during the Anglo-Scottish wars is meticulously chronicled in H.M. Colvin (ed.), *The History of the Royal Works* (1963–82). Volume IV of this work contains an account of the Henricean fortresses in Scotland by Marcus Merriman, who has recently elaborated this theme in *The Rough Wooings, Mary Queen of Scots 1542–1551* (2000). Joachim Zeune's *The Last Scottish Castles* (1992) contains much detailed information about the late medieval castles and tower houses of the region, while Iain MacIvor's *A Fortified Frontier* (2001) offers a perspective that takes in both sides of the Anglo-Scottish border. A good deal of information is usefully summarised in Mike Slater's *The Castles of Lothian and the Borders* (1994), while John Dent and Rory McDonald's *Warfare and Fortifications in the Borders* (Scottish Borders Council, 2000) provides an excellent introduction to the subject as well as a list of sites to visit. The social and economic background to late medieval castle building in lowland Scotland is illuminated in the publications of Margaret H.B. Sanderson, notably *Scottish Rural Society in the 16th century* (1982) and *A Kindly Place?: Living in Sixteenth-Century Scotland* (2002).

Much of the research on more specific aspects of the subject has been published in guidebooks or as papers in national and local journals and these are best tracked down in specialised bibliographies, notably the invaluable *Castles, town defences, and artillery fortifications in Britain and Ireland: a bibliography* by John Kenyon (three volumes to date (Council for British Archaeology, 1978–90)). Among the most valuable of those consulted in the preparation of this volume are Alastair Maxwell-Irving's 'Early Firearms and their influence on the Military and Domestic Architecture of the Borders (*Proceedings of the Society of Antiquaries of Scotland*, 103, 1970–1) and three papers by Philip Dixon: 'Hillslap Tower, Masons and Regional Traditions' (*Proceedings of the Berwickshire Naturalists' Club*, 40, 1975); 'Towerhouses, pelehouses and border society' (*Archaeological Journal*, 136, 1979) and '*Mota, Aula et Turris: the manor-houses of the Anglo-Scottish border*' (G. Meirion-Jones and M. Jones, *Manorial Domestic Buildings in England and Northern France*, Society of Antiquaries of London, 1993). A copy of Dixon's thesis 'The Fortified House on the Anglo-Scottish Border in the Social and Economic Context' (University of Oxford, 1976) is available for reference in the NMRS. RCAHMS' *Southdean, Borders: An Archaeological Survey* (1995) includes new information on pele houses.

Country Houses

The literature on the earlier country houses overlaps to a considerable extent with that relating to later castles and tower houses. In addition, Deborah Howard's *The Architectural History of Scotland 1560–1660* (1995) outlines the wider cultural context against which local architectural developments need to be considered, while Charles McKean's *The Scottish Chateau* (2001) offers new interpretations of some of the great Renaissance mansions of the region. Among individual studies mention should be made of D.B. Adam's thesis 'Scottish Architectural Decoration 1560–1620' (1977, copy available in NMRS) and Maureen Meikle's *A British Frontier? Lairds and Gentlemen in the Eastern Borders, 1540–1603* (2004) and 'The C16 Border Lairds: A Study of the Links between Wealth and House Building' (*Proceedings of the Berwickshire Naturalists' Club*, 40, 1993).

Useful sources for later houses include James Macaulay's *The Gothic Revival 1745–1845* (1975) and *The Classical Country House in Scotland 1660–1800* (1987); also *The Journal of Sir Walter Scott*, edited by W.E.K. Anderson (1998) and 'Extracts from the diary, and copy letter book, of John Smith (of Darnick), 1812–1854' (copy available in NMRS). A.A. Tait's indispensable *The Land-scape Garden in Scotland, 1735–1835* (1980) is supplemented by the *Inventory of gardens and designed landscapes, Borders*, surveyed for Historic Scotland during the 1980s. The extensive series of illustrated articles on country houses published in *Country Life* can be consulted via its cumulative index.

For the definitive account of Abbotsford see Clive Wainwright, '*The Romantic Interior, The British Collector at Home, 1750–1850*' (1989). This should be read in conjunction with Iain Gordon Brown (ed.), '*Abbotsford and Sir Walter Scott*' 2003. Clive Wainwright did not have access to the architects' designs and tradesmen's accounts for building Abbotsford which were bound up for preservation with Scott's Library. For a Catalogue of Sir Walter Scott's Collection of architectural fragments at Abbotsford see *Inventory of the Ancient and Historical Monuments of Roxburghshire*, Vol. II, 1956. *The Catalogue of Armour and Antiquities at Abbotsford* by the Hon. Mrs Maxwell-Scott, 1925, contains much information not readily available elsewhere.

Burghs

The numerous guidebooks and histories published over the last century and a half vary greatly in quality. Among those that have been found most useful during the preparation of the present volume are: Adam S. Grant (ed.), *Galashiels, A Modern History* (1983); Robert Hall, *The History of Galashiels* (1898); W.S. Robson, *The Story of Hawick. An Introduction to the History of the Town* (revised ed. 1947); R.E. Scott, *Companion to Hawick* (Hawick Archaeological Society, revised ed. 1998); Tom Dobson (ed.), *A Historical Guide of Jedburgh* (revised ed. 2000); J.L. Brown and I.C. Lawson, *History of Peebles 1850–1990* (1990); John M. Gilbert (ed.), *Flower of the Forest: Selkirk, a new history* (1985). RCAHMS's *Tolbooths and Town Houses: Civic Architecture in Scotland to 1833* (1996) offers a valuable assessment of Borders tolbooths in a wider context. *Town Trails*, published by Scottish Borders Council and the Scottish Tourist Board, are available for most of the larger burghs and provide an excellent introduction to their streets and buildings. Many burghs also feature in the series of *Scottish Burgh Surveys*, initiated in 1976 and currently published by Historic Scotland. Although focused on the archaeological implications of urban development, these reports also contain valuable material on burgh history and morphology.

Industry and Communications

The best introduction to the impact of the industrial revolution on the region is *Farm and Factory: Revolution in the Borders* by John Dent and Rory McDonald (Scottish Borders Council, 2001). The relevant chapters of David Bremner's classic *The Industries of Scotland* (1869) can still be read with profit. Clifford Gulvin's *The Border Hosiery and Knitwear Industry, 1770–1970* (1997) is a handy regional summary of a dominant part of the textile trade, dealt with in greater depth in his *The Scottish Hosiery and Knitwear Industry 1689–1980* (1984). John R. Hume's invaluable gazetteer of industrial buildings – including farms, bridges and harbours – published in *The Industrial Archaeology of Scotland* vol. I (1976), provides a yardstick against which to measure the changes of the last thirty years.

Recent research on Borders bridges has been made available in *Heritage of Bridges between Edinburgh, Kelso and Berwick*, by Roland Paxton and Ted Ruddock (n.d.) and *Arch Bridges and their Builders 1735–1835*, by Ted Ruddock (1980). Many of the smaller road bridges constructed in Tweeddale in the late c18 and early c19 were the work of the Noble family of masons and are documented in *The Diary of James and Alexander Noble 1762–1827*, edited by Meredyth Somerville (Biggar Museum Trust, 1984). The rise and fall of the Berwickshire fishing industry, with particular reference to Eyemouth and its harbour, is charted in Peter Aitchison's *Children of the Sea: The Story of the Eyemouth Disaster* (2001).

Rural Buildings

Dent and McDonald's *Farm and Factory*, mentioned in the previous section, again provides a useful introduction, while recent research on pre-improvement buildings is summarised by Piers Dixon in *Puir Labourers and Busy Husbandmen: The Countryside of Lowland Scotland in the Middle Ages* (2003) and 'Champagne Country: A review of medieval settlement in Lowland Scotland', in Sarah Govan (ed.), *Medieval or Later Rural Settlement in Scotland: 10 Years On* (Historic Scotland, 2003). Dixon's paper 'A Rural Settlement in Roxburghshire; excavations at Springwood Park, Kelso, 1985–6' (*Proceedings of the Society of Antiquaries of Scotland*, 128, 1998), describes one of the few investigations so far undertaken into the physical remains of pre-improvement houses in the Borders. Many kinds of small rural building, including dwellings and work places, are discussed in *Scotland's Buildings*, edited by G. Stell, J. Shaw and S. Storrier (*Scottish Life and Society: A Compendium of Scottish Ethnology*, vol. 3, 2003), which also contains a valuable bibliography.

GLOSSARY

Numbers and letters refer to the illustrations (by John Sambrook) on pp. 792–9.

ABACUS: flat slab forming the top of a capital (3a).

ACANTHUS: classical formalized leaf ornament (3b).

ACCUMULATOR TOWER: see Hydraulic power.

ACHIEVEMENT: a complete display of armorial bearings (i.e. coat of arms, crest, supporters and motto).

ACROTERION: plinth for a statue or ornament on the apex or ends of a pediment; more usually, both the plinth and what stands on it (4a).

ADDORSED: descriptive of two figures placed back to back.

AEDICULE (*lit.* little building): architectural surround, consisting usually of two columns or pilasters supporting a pediment.

AFFRONTED: descriptive of two figures placed face to face.

AGGREGATE: see Concrete, Harling.

AISLE: subsidiary space alongside the body of a building, separated from it by columns, piers or posts. Also (Scots) projecting wing of a church, often for special use, e.g. by a guild or by a landed family whose burial place it may contain.

AMBULATORY (*lit.* walkway): aisle around the sanctuary (q.v.).

ANGLE ROLL: roll moulding in the angle between two planes (1a).

ANSE DE PANIER: see Arch.

ANTAE: simplified pilasters (4a), usually applied to the ends of the enclosing walls of a portico (q.v.) *in antis*.

ANTEFIXAE: ornaments projecting at regular intervals above a Greek cornice, originally to conceal the ends of roof tiles (4a).

ANTHEMION: classical ornament like a honeysuckle flower (4b).

APRON: panel below a window or wall monument or tablet.

APSE: semicircular or polygonal end of an apartment, especially of a chancel or chapel. In classical architecture sometimes called an *exedra*.

ARABESQUE: non-figurative surface decoration consisting of flowing lines, foliage scrolls etc., based on geometrical patterns. Cf. Grotesque.

ARCADE: series of arches supported by piers or columns. *Blind arcade* or *arcading*: the same applied to the wall surface. *Wall arcade*: in medieval churches, a blind arcade forming a dado below windows. Also a covered shopping street.

ARCH: Shapes see 5c. *Basket arch* or *anse de panier* (basket handle): three-centred and depressed, or with a flat centre. *Nodding*: ogee arch curving forward from the wall face. *Parabolic*: shaped like a chain suspended from two level points, but inverted.

Special purposes. *Chancel*: dividing chancel from nave or crossing. *Crossing*: spanning piers at a crossing (q.v.). *Relieving* or *discharging*: incorporated in a wall to relieve superimposed weight (5c). *Skew*: spanning responds not diametrically opposed. *Strainer*: inserted in an opening to resist inward pressure. *Transverse*: spanning a main axis (e.g. of a vaulted space). *See also* Jack arch, Overarch, Triumphal arch.

ARCHITRAVE: formalized lintel, the lowest member of the classical entablature (3a). Also the moulded frame of a door or window (often borrowing the profile of a classical architrave). For *lugged* and *shouldered* architraves *see* 4b.

ARCUATED: dependent structurally on the arch principle. Cf. Trabeated.

ARK: chest or cupboard housing the tables of Jewish law in a synagogue.

ARRIS: sharp edge where two surfaces meet at an angle (3a).

ASHLAR: masonry of large blocks wrought to even faces and square edges (6d). *Broached ashlar* (Scots): scored with parallel lines made by a narrow-pointed chisel (broach). *Droved ashlar*: similar but with lines made by a broad chisel.

ASTRAGAL: classical moulding of semicircular section (3f). Also (Scots) glazing-bar between window panes.

ASTYLAR: with no columns or similar vertical features.

ATLANTES: *see* Caryatids.

ATRIUM (plural: atria): inner court of a Roman or C20 house; in a multi-storey building, a toplit covered court rising through all storeys. Also an open court in front of a church.

ATTACHED COLUMN: *see* Engaged column.

ATTIC: small top storey within a roof. Also the storey above the main entablature of a classical façade.

AUMBRY: recess or cupboard, especially one in a church, to hold sacred vessels used for the Mass.

BAILEY: *see* Motte-and-bailey.

BALANCE BEAM: *see* Canals.

BALDACCHINO: freestanding canopy, originally fabric, over an altar. Cf. Ciborium.

BALLFLOWER: globular flower of three petals enclosing a ball (1a). Typical of the Decorated style.

BALUSTER: pillar or pedestal of bellied form. *Balusters*: vertical supports of this or any other form, for a handrail or coping, the whole being called a *balustrade* (6c). *Blind balustrade*: the same applied to the wall surface.

BARBICAN: outwork defending the entrance to a castle.

BARGEBOARDS (corruption of 'vergeboards'): boards, often carved or fretted, fixed beneath the eaves of a gable to cover and protect the rafters.

BARMKIN (Scots): wall enclosing courtyard attached to a tower house.

BARONY: *see* Burgh.

BAROQUE: style originating in Rome

c. 1600 and current in England *c.*1680–1720, characterized by dramatic massing and silhouette and the use of the giant order.

BARROW: burial mound.

BARTIZAN: corbelled turret, square or round, frequently at an angle (8a).

BASCULE: hinged part of a lifting (or bascule) bridge.

BASE: moulded foot of a column or pilaster. For *Attic* base *see* 3b. For *Elided* base *see* Elided.

BASEMENT: lowest, subordinate storey; hence the lowest part of a classical elevation, below the piano nobile (q.v.).

BASILICA: a Roman public hall; hence an aisled building with a clerestory.

BASTION: one of a series of defensive semicircular or polygonal projections from the main wall of a fortress or city.

BATTER: intentional inward inclination of a wall face.

BATTLEMENT: defensive parapet, composed of *merlons* (solid) and *crenelles* (embrasures) through which archers could shoot (8a); sometimes called *crenellation*. Also used decoratively.

BAY: division of an elevation or interior space as defined by regular vertical features such as arches, columns, windows etc.

BAY LEAF: classical ornament of overlapping bay leaves (3f).

BAY WINDOW: window of one or more storeys projecting from the face of a building. *Canted*: with a straight front and angled sides. *Bow window*: curved. *Oriel*: rests on corbels or brackets and starts above ground level; also the bay window at the dais end of a medieval great hall.

BEAD-AND-REEL: *see* Enrichments.

BEAKHEAD: Norman ornament with a row of beaked bird or beast heads usually biting into a roll moulding (1a).

BEE-BOLL: wall recess to contain a beehive.

BELFRY: chamber or stage in a tower where bells are hung. Also belltower in a general sense.

BELL CAPITAL: *see* 1b.

BELLCAST: *see* Roof.

BELLCOTE: bell-turret set on a roof or gable. *Birdcage bellcote*: framed structure, usually of stone.

BERM: level area separating a ditch from a bank on a hillfort or barrow.

BILLET: Norman ornament of small half-cylindrical or rectangular blocks (1a).

BIVALLATE: of a hillfort: defended by two concentric banks and ditches.

BLIND: see Arcade, Baluster, Portico.

BLOCK CAPITAL: see 1a.

BLOCKED: columns etc. interrupted by regular projecting blocks (*blocking*), as on a Gibbs surround (4b).

BLOCKING COURSE: course of stones, or equivalent, on top of a cornice and crowning the wall.

BÖD: see Bü.

BOLECTION MOULDING: covering the joint between two different planes (6b).

BOND: the pattern of long sides (*stretchers*) and short ends (*headers*) produced on the face of a wall by laying bricks in a particular way (6e).

BOSS: knob or projection, e.g. at the intersection of ribs in a vault (2c).

BOW WINDOW: see Bay window.

BOX FRAME: timber-framed construction in which vertical and horizontal wall members support the roof. Also concrete construction where the loads are taken on cross walls; also called *cross-wall construction*.

BRACE: subsidiary member of a structural frame, curved or straight. *Bracing* is often arranged decoratively, e.g. quatrefoil, herringbone. *See also* Roofs.

BRATTISHING: ornamental crest, usually formed of leaves, Tudor flowers or miniature battlements.

BRESSUMER (*lit.* breast-beam): big horizontal beam supporting the wall above, especially in a jettied building.

BRETASCHE (*lit.* battlement): defensive wooden gallery on a wall.

BRICK: see Bond, Cogging, Engineering, Gauged, Tumbling.

BRIDGE: *Bowstring*: with arches rising above the roadway which is suspended from them. *Clapper*: one long stone forms the roadway. *Roving*: see Canal. *Suspension*: roadway suspended from cables or chains slung between towers or pylons. *Stay-suspension* or *stay-cantilever*: supported by diagonal

stays from towers or pylons. *See also* Bascule.

BRISES-SOLEIL: projecting fins or canopies which deflect direct sunlight from windows.

BROACH: see Spire and 1c.

BROCH (Scots): circular tower-like structure, open in the middle, the double wall of dry-stone masonry linked by slabs forming internal galleries at varying levels; found in W and N Scotland and mostly dating from between 100 B.C. and A.D. 100.

BÜ or BÖD (Scots, esp. Shetland; *lit.* booth): combined house and store.

BUCRANIUM: ox skull used decoratively in classical friezes.

BULLSEYE WINDOW: small oval window, set horizontally (cf. Oculus). Also called *oeil de boeuf*.

BURGH: formally constituted town with trading privileges. *Royal Burghs*: monopolized foreign trade till the C17 and paid duty to the Crown. *Burghs of Barony*: founded by secular or ecclesiastical barons to whom they paid duty on their local trade. *Police Burghs*: instituted after 1850 for the administration of new centres of population and abolished in 1975. They controlled planning, building etc.

BUT-AND-BEN (Scots, *lit.* outer and inner rooms): two-room cottage.

BUTTRESS: vertical member projecting from a wall to stabilize it or to resist the lateral thrust of an arch, roof or vault (1c, 2c). A *flying buttress* transmits the thrust to a heavy abutment by means of an arch or half-arch (1c).

CABLE or ROPE MOULDING: originally Norman, like twisted strands of a rope.

CAMES: see Quarries.

CAMPANILE: freestanding bell-tower.

CANALS: *Flash lock*: removable weir or similar device through which boats pass on a flush of water. Predecessor of the *pound lock*: chamber with gates at each end allowing boats to float from one level to another. *Tidal gates*: single pair of lock gates allowing vessels to pass when the tide makes a level. *Balance beam*: beam projecting horizontally for opening and closing lock gates. *Roving bridge*: carrying a towing path from one bank to the other.

CANDLE-SNUFFER ROOF: conical roof of a turret (8a).

CANNON SPOUT: *see* 8a.

CANTILEVER: horizontal projection (e.g. step, canopy) supported by a downward force behind the fulcrum.

CAPHOUSE (Scots): small chamber at the head of a turnpike stair, opening onto the parapet walk (8a). Also a chamber rising from within the parapet walk.

CAPITAL: head or crowning feature of a column or pilaster; for classical types *see* 3a; for medieval types *see* 1b.

CARREL: compartment designed for individual work or study, e.g. in a library.

CARTOUCHE: classical tablet with ornate frame (4b).

CARYATIDS: female figures supporting an entablature; their male counterparts are *Atlantes* (*lit.* Atlas figures).

CASEMATE: vaulted chamber, with embrasures for defence, within a castle wall or projecting from it.

CASEMENT: side-hinged window. Also a concave Gothic moulding framing a window.

CASTELLATED: with battlements (q.v.).

CAST IRON: iron containing at least 2.2 per cent of carbon, strong in compression but brittle in tension; cast in a mould to required shape, e.g. for columns or repetitive ornaments. *Wrought iron* is a purer form of iron, with no more than 0.3 per cent of carbon, ductile and strong in tension, forged and rolled into e.g. bars, joists, boiler plates; *mild steel* is its modern equivalent, similar but stronger.

CATSLIDE: *see* 7.

CAVETTO: concave classical moulding of quarter-round section (3f).

CELURE or CEILURE: enriched area of roof above rood or altar.

CEMENT: *see* Concrete.

CENOTAPH (*lit.* empty tomb): funerary monument which is not a burying place.

CENTRING: wooden support for the building of an arch or vault, removed after completion.

CHAMBERED TOMB: Neolithic burial mound with a stone-built chamber and entrance passage covered by an earthen barrow or stone cairn.

CHAMFER (*lit.* corner-break): surface formed by cutting off a square edge or corner. For types of chamfers and *chamfer stops see* 6a. *See also* Double chamfer.

CHANCEL: E end of the church containing the sanctuary; often used to include the choir.

CHANTRY CHAPEL: often attached to or within a church, endowed for the celebration of Masses principally for the soul of the founder.

CHECK (Scots): rebate.

CHERRY-CAULKING or CHERRY-COCKING (Scots): decorative masonry technique using lines of tiny stones (*pins* or *pinning*) in the mortar joints.

CHEVET (*lit.* head): French term for chancel with ambulatory and radiating chapels.

CHEVRON: V-shape used in series or double series (later) on a Norman moulding (1a). Also (especially when on a single plane) called *zigzag*.

CHOIR: the part of a church E of the nave, intended for the stalls of choir monks, choristers and clergy.

CIBORIUM: a fixed canopy over an altar, usually vaulted and supported on four columns; cf. Baldacchino.

CINQUEFOIL: *see* Foil.

CIST: stone-lined or slab-built grave.

CLACHAN (Scots): a hamlet or small village; also, a village inn.

CLADDING: external covering or skin applied to a structure, especially a framed one.

CLEARSTOREY: uppermost storey of the nave of a church, pierced by windows. Also high-level windows in secular buildings.

CLOSE (Scots): courtyard or passage giving access to a number of buildings.

CLOSER: a brick cut to complete a bond (6e).

CLUSTER BLOCK: *see* Multi-storey.

COADE STONE: ceramic artificial stone made in Lambeth 1769–c.1840 by Eleanor Coade (†1821) and her associates.

COB: walling material of clay mixed with straw.

COFFERING: arrangement of sunken panels (coffers), square or polygonal, decorating a ceiling, vault or arch.

COGGING: a decorative course of bricks laid diagonally (6e). Cf. Dentilation.

COLLAR: see Roofs and 7.

COLLEGIATE CHURCH: endowed for the support of a college of priests, especially for the saying of masses for the soul(s) of the founder(s).

COLONNADE: range of columns supporting an entablature. Cf. Arcade.

COLONNETTE: small column or shaft.

COLOSSAL ORDER: see Giant order.

COLUMBARIUM: shelved, niched structure to house multiple burials.

COLUMN: a classical, upright structural member of round section with a shaft, a capital and usually a base (3a, 4a).

COLUMN FIGURE: carved figure attached to a medieval column or shaft, usually flanking a doorway.

COMMENDATOR: receives the revenues of an abbey in commendam ('in trust') when the position of abbot is vacant.

COMMUNION TABLE: table used in Protestant churches for the celebration of Holy Communion.

COMPOSITE: see Orders.

COMPOUND PIER: grouped shafts (q.v.), or a solid core surrounded by shafts.

CONCRETE: composition of cement (calcined lime and clay), aggregate (small stones or rock chippings), sand and water. It can be poured into formwork or shuttering (temporary frame of timber or metal) on site (in-situ concrete), or pre-cast as components before construction. Reinforced: incorporating steel rods to take the tensile force. Prestressed: with tensioned steel rods. Finishes include the impression of boards left by formwork (board-marked or shuttered), and texturing with steel brushes (brushed) or hammers (hammer-dressed). See also Shell.

CONDUCTOR (Scots): down-pipe for rainwater; see also Rhone.

CONSOLE: bracket of curved outline (4b).

COPING: protective course of masonry or brickwork capping a wall (6d).

COOMB or COMB CEILING (Scots): with sloping sides corresponding to the roof pitch up to a flat centre.

CORBEL: projecting block supporting something above. Corbel course: continuous course of projecting stones or bricks fulfilling the same function. Corbel table: series of corbels to carry a parapet or a wall-plate or wall-post (7). Corbelling: brick or masonry courses built out beyond one another to support a chimneystack, window etc. For continuous and chequer-set corbelling see 8a.

CORINTHIAN: see Orders and 3d.

CORNICE: flat-topped ledge with moulded underside, projecting along the top of a building or feature, especially as the highest member of the classical entablature (3a). Also the decorative moulding in the angle between wall and ceiling.

CORPS-DE-LOGIS: the main building(s) as distinct from the wings or pavilions.

COTTAGE ORNÉ: an artfully rustic small house associated with the Picturesque movement.

COUNTERSCARP BANK: low bank on the downhill or outer side of a hillfort ditch.

COUR D'HONNEUR: formal entrance court before a house in the French manner, usually with flanking wings and a screen wall or gates.

COURSE: continuous layer of stones etc. in a wall (6e).

COVE: a broad concave moulding, e.g. to mask the eaves of a roof. Coved ceiling: with a pronounced cove joining the walls to a flat central panel smaller than the whole area of the ceiling.

CRADLE ROOF: see Wagon roof.

CREDENCE: shelved niche or table, usually beside a piscina (q.v.), for the sacramental elements and vessels.

CRENELLATION: parapet with crenelles (see Battlement).

CRINKLE-CRANKLE WALL: garden wall undulating in a series of serpentine curves.

CROCKETS: leafy hooks. Crocketing decorates the edges of Gothic features, such as pinnacles, canopies etc. Crocket capital: see 1b.

CROSSING: central space at the junction of the nave, chancel and transepts. *Crossing tower*: above a crossing.

CROSS-WINDOW: with one mullion and one transom (qq.v.).

CROWN-POST: *see* Roofs and 7.

CROWSTEPS: squared stones set like steps, especially on a crowstepped gable (7, 8a).

CRUCKS (*lit.* crooked): pairs of inclined timbers (*blades*), usually curved, set at bay-lengths; they support the roof timbers and, in timber buildings, also support the walls. *Base*: blades rise from ground level to a tie-or collar-beam which supports the roof timbers. *Full*: blades rise from ground level to the apex of the roof, serving as the main members of a roof truss. *Jointed:* blades formed from more than one timber; the lower member may act as a wall-post; it is usually elbowed at wall-plate level and jointed just above. *Middle*: blades rise from halfway up the walls to a tie-or collar-beam. *Raised*: blades rise from halfway up the walls to the apex. *Upper*: blades supported on a tie-beam and rising to the apex.

CRYPT: underground or half-underground area, usually below the E end of a church. *Ring crypt*: corridor crypt surrounding the apse of an early medieval church, often associated with chambers for relics. Cf. Undercroft.

CUPOLA (*lit.* dome): especially a small dome on a circular or polygonal base crowning a larger dome, roof or turret. Also (Scots) small dome or skylight as an internal feature, especially over a stairwell.

CURSUS: a long avenue defined by two parallel earthen banks with ditches outside.

CURTAIN WALL: a connecting wall between the towers of a castle. Also a non-load-bearing external wall applied to a C20 framed structure.

CUSP: *see* Tracery and 2b.

CYCLOPEAN MASONRY: large irregular polygonal stones, smooth and finely jointed.

CYMA RECTA and CYMA REVERSA: classical mouldings with double curves (3f). Cf. Ogee.

DADO: the finishing (often with panelling) of the lower part of a wall in a classical interior; in origin a formalized continuous pedestal. *Dado rail*: the moulding along the top of the dado.

DAGGER: *see* Tracery and 2b.

DEC (DECORATED): English Gothic architecture *c.* 1290 to *c.* 1350. The name is derived from the type of window tracery (q.v.) used during the period.

DEMI- or HALF-COLUMNS: engaged columns (q.v.) half of whose circumference projects from the wall.

DENTIL: small square block used in series in classical cornices (3c). *Dentilation* is produced by the projection of alternating headers along cornices or string-courses.

DIAPER: repetitive surface decoration of lozenges or squares flat or in relief. Achieved in brickwork with bricks of two colours.

DIOCLETIAN or THERMAL WINDOW: semicircular with two mullions, as used in the Baths of Diocletian, Rome (4b).

DISTYLE: having two columns (4a).

DOGTOOTH: E.E. ornament, consisting of a series of small pyramids formed by four stylized canine teeth meeting at a point (1a).

DOOCOT (Scots): dovecot. When freestanding, usually *Lectern* (rectangular with single-pitch roof) or *Beehive* (circular, diminishing towards the top).

DORIC: *see* Orders and 3a, 3b.

DORMER: window projecting from the slope of a roof (7). *Dormer head*: gable above a dormer, often formed as a pediment (8a).

DOUBLE CHAMFER: a chamfer applied to each of two recessed arches (1a).

DOUBLE PILE: *see* Pile.

DRAGON BEAM: *see* Jetty.

DRESSINGS: the stone or brickwork worked to a finished face about an angle, opening or other feature.

DRIPSTONE: moulded stone projecting from a wall to protect the lower parts from water. Cf. Hood-mould, Weathering.

DRUM: circular or polygonal stage supporting a dome or cupola. Also one of the stones forming the shaft of a column (3a).

DRY-STONE: stone construction without mortar.

DUN (Scots): small stone-walled fort.

DUTCH or FLEMISH GABLE: *see* 7.

EASTER SEPULCHRE: tomb-chest, usually within or against the N wall of a chancel, used in Holy Week ceremonies for reservation (entombment) of the sacrament after the mass of Maundy Thursday.

EAVES: overhanging edge of a roof; hence *eaves cornice* in this position.

ECHINUS: ovolo moulding (q.v.) below the abacus of a Greek Doric capital (3a).

EDGE RAIL: *see* Railways.

EDGE-ROLL: moulding of semicircular section or more at the edge of an opening.

E.E. (EARLY ENGLISH): English Gothic architecture *c.* 1190–1250.

EGG-AND-DART: *see* Enrichments and 3f.

ELEVATION: any face of a building or side of a room. In a drawing, the same or any part of it, represented in two dimensions.

ELIDED: used to describe a compound feature, e.g. an entablature, with some parts omitted. Also, parts of, e.g., a base or capital, combined to form a larger one.

EMBATTLED: with battlements.

EMBRASURE: splayed opening in a wall or battlement (q.v.).

ENCAUSTIC TILES: earthenware tiles fired with a pattern and glaze.

EN DELIT: stone laid against the bed.

ENFILADE: reception rooms in a formal series, usually with all doorways on axis.

ENGAGED or ATTACHED COLUMN: one that partly merges into a wall or pier.

ENGINEERING BRICKS: dense bricks, originally used mostly for railway viaducts etc.

ENRICHMENTS: the carved decoration of certain classical mouldings, e.g. the ovolo with *egg-and-dart*, the cyma reversa with *waterleaf*, the astragal with *bead-and-reel* (3f).

ENTABLATURE: in classical architecture, collective name for the three horizontal members (architrave, frieze and cornice) carried by a wall or a column (3a).

ENTASIS: very slight convex deviation from a straight line, used to prevent an optical illusion of concavity.

ENTRESOL: mezzanine floor subdividing what is constructionally a single storey, e.g. a vault.

EPITAPH: inscription on a tomb or monument.

EXEDRA: *see* Apse.

EXTRADOS: outer curved face of an arch or vault.

EYECATCHER: decorative building terminating a vista.

FASCIA: plain horizontal band, e.g. in an architrave (3c, 3d) or on a shopfront.

FENESTRATION: the arrangement of windows in a façade.

FERETORY: site of the chief shrine of a church, behind the high altar.

FESTOON: ornamental garland, suspended from both ends. Cf. Swag.

FEU (Scots): land granted, e.g. by sale, by the *feudal superior* to the *vassal* or *feuar*, on conditions that usually include the annual payment of a fixed sum of *feu duty*. Any subsequent proprietor of the land becomes the feuar and is subject to the same obligations.

FIBREGLASS (or glass-reinforced polyester (GRP)): synthetic resin reinforced with glass fibre. GRC: glass-reinforced concrete.

FIELD: *see* Panelling and 6b.

FILLET: a narrow flat band running down a medieval shaft or along a roll moulding (1a). It separates larger curved mouldings in classical cornices, fluting or bases (3c).

FLAMBOYANT: the latest phase of French Gothic architecture, with flowing tracery.

FLASH LOCK: *see* Canals.

FLATTED: divided into apartments. Also with a colloquial (Scots) meaning: 'He stays on the first flat' means that he lives on the first floor.

FLÈCHE or SPIRELET (*lit.* arrow): slender spire on the centre of a roof.

FLEURON: medieval carved flower or leaf, often rectilinear (1a).

FLUSHWORK: knapped flint used with dressed stone to form patterns.

FLUTING: series of concave grooves (flutes), their common edges sharp (arris) or blunt (fillet) (3).

FOIL (*lit.* leaf): lobe formed by the cusping of a circular or other shape in tracery (2b). *Trefoil* (three), *quatrefoil* (four), *cinquefoil* (five) and *multifoil* express the number of lobes in a shape.

FOLIATE: decorated with leaves.

FORE-BUILDING: structure protecting an entrance.

FORESTAIR: external stair, usually unenclosed.

FORMWORK: *see* Concrete.

FRAMED BUILDING: where the structure is carried by a framework - e.g. of steel, reinforced concrete, timber - instead of by load-bearing walls.

FREESTONE: stone that is cut, or can be cut, in all directions.

FRESCO: *al fresco*: painting on wet plaster. *Fresco secco*: painting on dry plaster.

FRIEZE: the middle member of the classical entablature, sometimes ornamented (3a). *Pulvinated frieze* (*lit.* cushioned): of bold convex profile (3c). Also a horizontal band of ornament.

FRONTISPIECE: in C16 and C17 buildings the central feature of doorway and windows above linked in one composition.

GABLE: peaked external wall at end of double-pitch roof. For types *see* 7. Also (Scots): whole end wall of whatever shape. *Pedimental gable*: treated like a pediment.

GADROONING: classical ribbed ornament like inverted fluting that flows into a lobed edge.

GAIT or GATE (Scots): street, usually with a prefix indicating use, direction or destination.

GALILEE: chapel or vestibule usually at the W end of a church enclosing the main portal(s).

GALLERY: a long room or passage; an upper storey above the aisle of a church, looking through arches to the nave; a balcony or mezzanine overlooking the main interior space of a building; or an external walkway.

GALLETING: small stones set in a mortar course.

GAMBREL ROOF: *see* 7.

GARDEROBE: medieval privy.

GARGOYLE: projecting water spout, often carved into human or animal shape. For cannon spout *see* 8.

GAUGED or RUBBED BRICKWORK: soft brick sawn roughly, then rubbed to a precise (gauged) surface. Mostly used for door or window openings (5c).

GAZEBO (jocular Latin, 'I shall gaze'): ornamental lookout tower or raised summer house.

GEOMETRIC: English Gothic architecture *c.* 1250-1310. *See also* Tracery. For another meaning, *see* Stairs.

GIANT or COLOSSAL ORDER: classical order (q.v.) whose height is that of two or more storeys of the building to which it is applied.

GIBBS SURROUND: C18 treatment of an opening (4b), seen particularly in the work of James Gibbs (1682-1754).

GIRDER: a large beam. *Box*: of hollow-box section. *Bowed*: with its top rising in a curve. *Plate*: of I-section, made from iron or steel plates. *Lattice*: with braced framework.

GLACIS: artificial slope extending out and downwards from the parapet of a fort.

GLAZING-BARS: wooden or sometimes metal bars separating and supporting window panes.

GLAZING GROOVE: groove in a window surround into which the glass is fitted.

GNOMON: vane or indicator casting a shadow onto a sundial.

GRAFFITI: *see* Sgraffito.

GRANGE: farm owned and run by a religious order.

GRC: *see* Fibreglass.

GRISAILLE: monochrome painting on walls or glass.

GROIN: sharp edge at the meeting of two cells of a cross-vault; *see* Vault and 2b.

GROTESQUE (*lit.* grotto-esque): wall decoration adopted from Roman examples in the Renaissance. Its foliage scrolls incorporate figurative elements. Cf. Arabesque.

GROTTO: artificial cavern.

GRP: *see* Fibreglass.

GUILLOCHE: classical ornament of interlaced bands (4b).

GUNLOOP: opening for a firearm (8a).

GUSHET (Scots): a triangular or wedge-shaped piece of land or the corner building on such a site.

GUTTAE: stylized drops (3b).

HALF-TIMBERING: archaic term for timber-framing (q.v.). Sometimes used for non-structural decorative timberwork.

HALL CHURCH: medieval church with nave and aisles of approximately equal height. Also (Scots C20) building for use as both hall and church, the double function usually intended to be temporary until a separate church is built.

HAMMERBEAM: see Roofs and 7.

HARLING (Scots, *lit.* hurling): wet dash, i.e. a form of roughcasting in which the mixture of aggregate and binding material (e.g. lime) is dashed onto a wall.

HEADER: see Bond and 6e.

HEADSTOP: stop (q.v.) carved with a head (5b).

HELM ROOF: see IC.

HENGE: ritual earthwork with a surrounding ditch and outer bank.

HERM (*lit.* the god Hermes): male head or bust on a pedestal.

HERRINGBONE WORK: see 6e (for brick bond). Cf. Pitched masonry.

HEXASTYLE: see Portico.

HILLFORT: Iron Age earthwork enclosed by a ditch and bank system.

HIPPED ROOF: see 7.

HOODMOULD: projecting moulding above an arch or lintel to throw off water (2b, 5b). When horizontal often called a *label*. For label stop see Stop.

HORIZONTAL GLAZING: with panes of horizontal proportions.

HORSEMILL: circular or polygonal farm building with a central shaft turned by a horse to drive agricultural machinery.

HUNGRY-JOINTED: see Pointing.

HUSK GARLAND: festoon of stylized nutshells (4b).

HYDRAULIC POWER: use of water under high pressure to work machinery. *Accumulator tower*: houses a hydraulic accumulator which accommodates fluctuations in the flow through hydraulic mains.

HYPOCAUST (*lit.* underburning): Roman underfloor heating system.

IMPOST: horizontal moulding at the springing of an arch (5c).

IMPOST BLOCK: block between abacus and capital (1b).

IN ANTIS: see Antae, Portico and 4a.

INDENT: shape chiselled out of a stone to receive a brass. Also, in restoration, new stone inserted as a patch.

INDUSTRIALIZED or SYSTEM BUILDING: system of manufactured units assembled on site.

INGLENOOK (*lit.* fire-corner): recess for a hearth with provision for seating.

INGO (Scots): the reveal of a door or window opening where the stone is at right angles to the wall.

INTERCOLUMNATION: interval between columns.

INTERLACE: decoration in relief simulating woven or entwined stems or bands.

INTRADOS: see Soffit.

IONIC: see Orders and 3c.

JACK ARCH: shallow segmental vault springing from beams, used for fireproof floors, bridge decks etc.

JAMB (*lit.* leg): one of the vertical sides of an opening. Also (Scots) wing or extension adjoining one side of a rectangular plan making it into an L-, T- or Z-plan.

JETTY: the projection of an upper storey beyond the storey below. In a stone building this is achieved by corbelling. In a timber-framed building it is made by the beams and joists of the lower storey oversailing the wall; on their outer ends is placed the sill of the walling for the storey above.

JOGGLE: the joining of two stones to prevent them slipping by a notch in one and a projection in the other.

KEEL MOULDING: moulding used from the late C12, in section like the keel of a ship (1a).

KEEP: principal tower of a castle.

KENTISH CUSP: see Tracery.

KEY PATTERN: see 4b.

KEYSTONE: central stone in an arch or vault (4b, 5c).

KINGPOST: see Roofs and 7.

KNEELER: horizontal projecting stone at the base of each side of a gable to support the inclined coping stones (7).

LABEL: see Hoodmould and 5b.

LABEL STOP: see Stop and 5b.

LACED BRICKWORK: vertical strips of brickwork, often in a contrasting colour, linking openings on different floors.

LACING COURSE: horizontal reinforcement in timber or brick to walls of flint, cobble etc.

LADE (Scots): channel formed to bring water to a mill; mill-race.

LADY CHAPEL: dedicated to the Virgin Mary (Our Lady).

LAIGH or LAICH (Scots): low.

LAIR (Scots): a burial space reserved in a graveyard.

LAIRD (Scots): landowner.

LANCET: slender single-light, pointed-arched window (2a).

LANTERN: circular or polygonal windowed turret crowning a roof or a dome. Also the windowed stage of a crossing tower lighting the church interior.

LANTERN CROSS: churchyard cross with lantern-shaped top.

LAVATORIUM: in a religious house, a washing place adjacent to the refectory.

LEAN-TO: see Roofs.

LESENE (lit. a mean thing): pilaster without base or capital. Also called pilaster strip.

LIERNE: see Vault and 2c.

LIGHT: compartment of a window defined by the mullions.

LINENFOLD: Tudor panelling carved with simulations of folded linen.

LINTEL: horizontal beam or stone bridging an opening.

LOFT: gallery in a church. Organ loft: in which the organ, or sometimes only the console (keyboard), is placed. Laird's loft, Trades loft etc. (Scots): reserved for an individual or special group. See also Rood (loft).

LOGGIA: gallery, usually arcaded or colonnaded along one side; sometimes freestanding.

LONG-AND-SHORT WORK: quoins consisting of stones placed with the long side alternately upright and horizontal, especially in Saxon building.

LOUVRE: roof opening, often protected by a raised timber structure, to allow the smoke from a central hearth to escape. Louvres: overlapping boards to allow ventilation but keep the rain out.

LOWSIDE WINDOW: set lower than the others in a chancel side wall, usually towards its w end.

L-PLAN: see Tower house and 8b.

LUCARNE (lit. dormer): small gabled opening in a roof or spire.

LUCKENBOOTH (Scots): lock-up booth or shop.

LUGGED ARCHITRAVE: see 4b.

LUNETTE: semicircular window or blind panel.

LYCHGATE (lit. corpse-gate): roofed gateway entrance to a churchyard for the reception of a coffin.

LYNCHET: long terraced strip of soil on the downward side of prehistoric and medieval fields, accumulated because of continual ploughing along the contours.

MACHICOLATIONS (lit. mashing devices): series of openings between the corbels that support a projecting parapet through which missiles can be dropped (8a). Used decoratively in post-medieval buildings.

MAINS (Scots): home farm on an estate.

MANOMETER or STANDPIPE TOWER: containing a column of water to regulate pressure in water mains.

MANSARD: see 7.

MANSE: house of a minister of religion, especially in Scotland.

MARGINS (Scots): dressed stones at the edges of an opening. 'Back-set margins' (RCAHMS) are actually set forward from a rubble wall to act as a stop for harling (q.v.). Also called rybats.

MARRIAGE LINTEL (Scots): door or window lintel carved with the initials of the owner and his wife and the date of building work, only coincidentally of their marriage.

MATHEMATICAL TILES: facing tiles with the appearance of brick, most often applied to timber-framed walls.

MAUSOLEUM: monumental building or chamber usually intended for the burial of members of one family.

MEGALITHIC: the use of large stones, singly or together.

MEGALITHIC TOMB: massive stonebuilt Neolithic burial chamber covered by an earth or stone mound.

MERCAT (Scots): market. The Mercat Cross of a Scottish burgh was the focus of market activity and local ceremonial. Most examples are post-Reformation with heraldic or other finials (not crosses).

MERLON: see Battlement.

MESOLITHIC: Middle Stone Age, in Britain *c.* 5000 to *c.* 3500 B.C.

METOPES: spaces between the triglyphs in a Doric frieze (3b).

MEZZANINE: low storey between two higher ones or within the height of a high one, not extending over its whole area.

MILD STEEL: see Cast iron.

MISERICORD (*lit.* mercy): shelf on a carved bracket placed on the underside of a hinged choir stall seat to support an occupant when standing.

MIXER-COURTS: forecourts to groups of houses shared by vehicles and pedestrians.

MODILLIONS: small consoles (q.v.) along the underside of a Corinthian or Composite cornice (3d). Often used along an eaves cornice.

MODULE: a predetermined standard size for co-ordinating the dimensions of components of a building.

MORT-SAFE (Scots): device to secure corpse(s): either an iron frame over a grave or a building where bodies were kept during decomposition.

MOTTE-AND-BAILEY: C11 and C12 type of castle consisting of an earthen mound (motte) topped by a wooden tower within or adjoining a bailey, an enclosure defended by a ditch and palisade, and also, sometimes, by an inner bank.

MOUCHETTE: see Tracery and 2b.

MOULDING: shaped ornamental strip of continuous section; see Cavetto, Cyma, Ovolo, Roll.

MULLION: vertical member between window lights (2b).

MULTI-STOREY: five or more storeys. Multi-storey flats may form a *cluster block*, with individual blocks of flats grouped round a service core; a *point block*, with flats fanning out from a service core; or a *slab block*, with flats approached by corridors or galleries from service cores at intervals or towers at the ends (plan also used for offices, hotels etc.). *Tower block* is a generic term for a high multi-storey building.

MULTIVALLATE: of a hillfort: defended by three or more concentric banks and ditches.

MUNTIN: see Panelling and 6b.

MUTULE: square block under the corona of a Doric cornice.

NAILHEAD: E.E. ornament consisting of small pyramids regularly repeated (1a).

NARTHEX: enclosed vestibule or covered porch at the main entrance to a church.

NAVE: the body of a church W of the crossing or chancel, often flanked by aisles (q.v.).

NEOLITHIC: New Stone Age in Britain, *c.* 3500 B.C. until the Bronze Age.

NEWEL: central or corner post of a staircase (6c). For Newel stair see Stairs.

NIGHT STAIR: stair by which religious entered the transept of their church from their dormitory to celebrate night offices.

NOGGING: see Timber-framing.

NOOK-SHAFT: shaft set in the angle of a wall or opening (1a).

NORMAN: see Romanesque.

NOSING: projection of the tread of a step (6c). *Bottle nosing*: half round in section.

NUTMEG: medieval ornament with a chain of tiny triangles placed obliquely.

OCULUS: circular opening.

OEIL DE BOEUF: see Bullseye window.

OGEE: double curve, bending first one way and then the other, as in an *ogee* or *ogival arch* (5c). Cf. Cyma recta and Cyma reversa.

OPUS SECTILE: decorative mosaic-like facing.

OPUS SIGNINUM: composition flooring of Roman origin.

ORATORY: a private chapel in a church or a house. Also a church of the Oratorian Order.

ORDER: one of a series of recessed arches and jambs forming a splayed medieval opening, e.g. a doorway or arcade arch (1a).

ORDERS: the formalized versions of the post-and-lintel system in classical architecture. The main orders are *Doric, Ionic* and *Corinthian*. They are Greek in origin

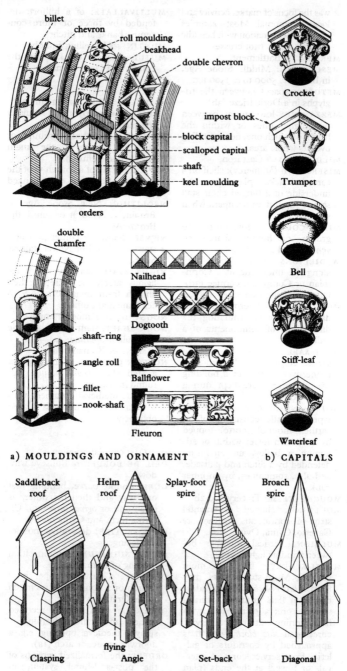

billet
chevron
roll moulding
beakhead
double chevron

impost block
block capital
scalloped capital
shaft
keel moulding

orders

double chamfer

shaft-ring
angle roll
fillet
nook-shaft

Nailhead
Dogtooth
Ballflower
Fleuron

Crocket
Trumpet
Bell
Stiff-leaf
Waterleaf

a) MOULDINGS AND ORNAMENT

b) CAPITALS

Saddleback roof
Helm roof
Splay-foot spire
Broach spire

Clasping
Angle
flying
Set-back
Diagonal

c) BUTTRESSES, ROOFS AND SPIRES

FIGURE 1: MEDIEVAL

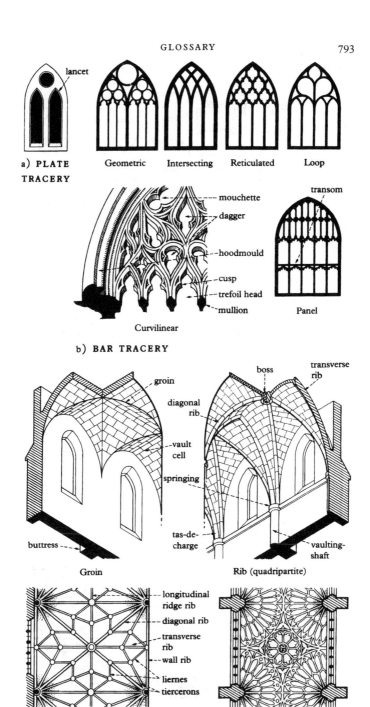

a) PLATE TRACERY

lancet

Geometric Intersecting Reticulated Loop

mouchette
dagger
hoodmould
cusp
trefoil head
mullion

Curvilinear

transom

Panel

b) BAR TRACERY

groin
diagonal rib
vault cell
springing
buttress

Groin

boss
transverse rib
tas-de-charge
vaulting-shaft

Rib (quadripartite)

longitudinal ridge rib
diagonal rib
transverse rib
wall rib
liernes
tiercerons

Lierne

Fan

c) VAULTS

FIGURE 2: MEDIEVAL

ORDERS

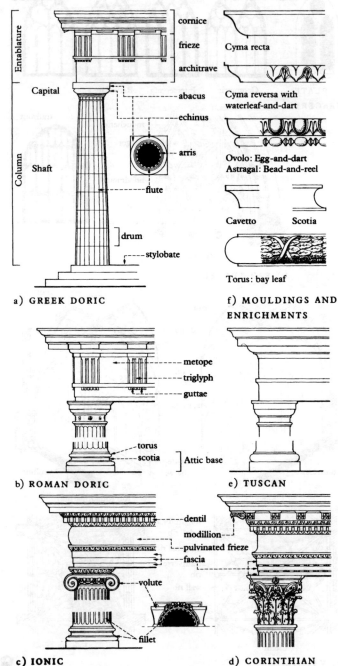

a) GREEK DORIC

f) MOULDINGS AND ENRICHMENTS

Cyma recta

Cyma reversa with waterleaf-and-dart

Ovolo: Egg-and-dart
Astragal: Bead-and-reel

Cavetto　　　Scotia

Torus: bay leaf

b) ROMAN DORIC

e) TUSCAN

c) IONIC

d) CORINTHIAN

FIGURE 3: CLASSICAL

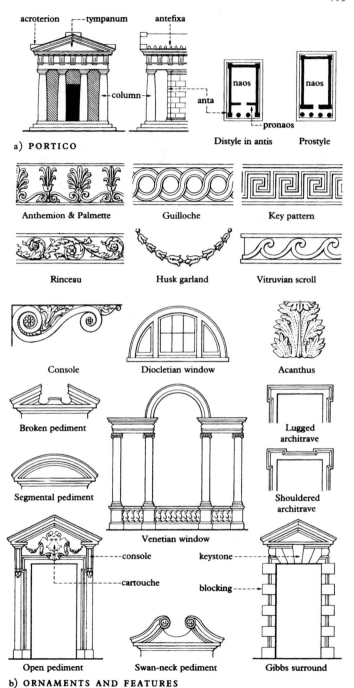

a) PORTICO

Distyle in antis   Prostyle

Anthemion & Palmette   Guilloche   Key pattern

Rinceau   Husk garland   Vitruvian scroll

Console   Diocletian window   Acanthus

Broken pediment   Lugged architrave

Segmental pediment   Shouldered architrave

Venetian window

Open pediment   Swan-neck pediment   Gibbs surround

b) ORNAMENTS AND FEATURES

FIGURE 4: CLASSICAL

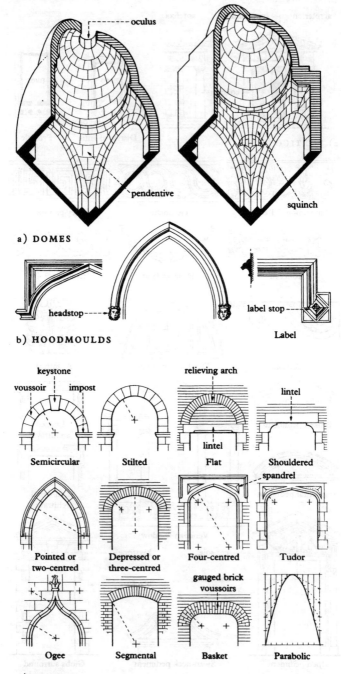

a) DOMES

oculus

pendentive

squinch

b) HOODMOULDS

headstop

label stop

Label

c) ARCHES

keystone

voussoir · impost

Semicircular

Stilted

relieving arch

lintel

Flat

lintel

Shouldered

Pointed or two-centred

Depressed or three-centred

Four-centred

spandrel

Tudor

Ogee

Segmental

gauged brick voussoirs

Basket

Parabolic

FIGURE 5: CONSTRUCTION

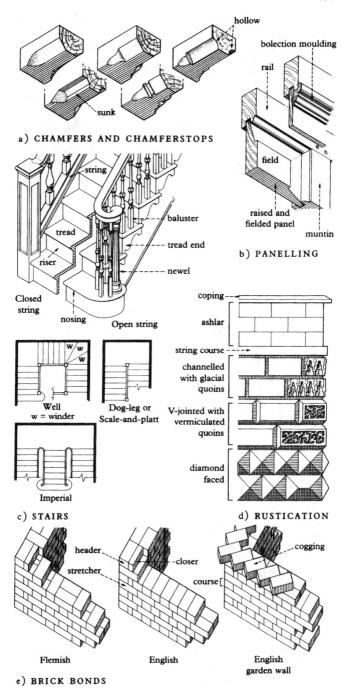

a) CHAMFERS AND CHAMFERSTOPS

b) PANELLING

c) STAIRS

d) RUSTICATION

e) BRICK BONDS

FIGURE 6: CONSTRUCTION

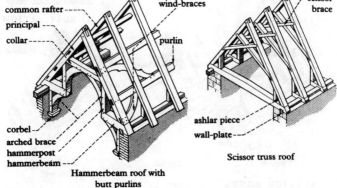

FIGURE 7: ROOFS AND GABLES

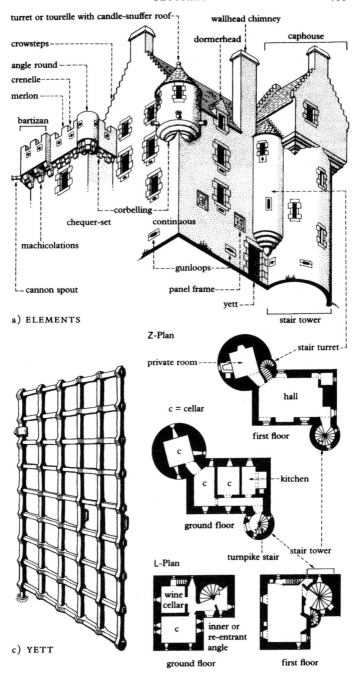

a) ELEMENTS

turret or tourelle with candle-snuffer roof
crowsteps
angle round
crenelle
merlon
bartizan
machicolations
cannon spout
chequer-set
corbelling
continuous
gunloops
panel frame
yett
wallhead chimney
dormerhead
caphouse
stair tower

c) YETT

Z-Plan
stair turret
private room
hall
first floor
c = cellar
c
c   c
kitchen
ground floor
turnpike stair
stair tower

L-Plan
wine cellar
c
inner or re-entrant angle
ground floor
first floor

b) FORMS

FIGURE 8: THE TOWER HOUSE

but occur in Roman versions. *Tuscan* is a simple version of Roman Doric. Though each order has its own conventions (3), there are many minor variations. The *Composite* capital combines Ionic volutes with Corinthian foliage. *Superimposed orders*: orders on successive levels, usually in the upward sequence of Tuscan, Doric, Ionic, Corinthian, Composite.

ORIEL: *see* Bay window.

OVERARCH: framing a wall which has an opening, e.g. a window or door.

OVERDOOR: painting or relief above an internal door. Also called a *sopraporta*.

OVERTHROW: decorative fixed arch between two gatepiers or above a wrought-iron gate.

OVOLO: wide convex moulding (3f).

PALIMPSEST: of a brass: where a metal plate has been reused by engraving on the back; of a wall painting: where one overlaps and partly obscures an earlier one.

PALLADIAN: following the examples and principles of Andrea Palladio (1508–80).

PALMETTE: classical ornament like a palm shoot (4b).

PANEL FRAME: moulded stone frame round an armorial panel, often placed over the entrance to a tower house (8a).

PANELLING: wooden lining to interior walls, made up of vertical members (*muntins*) and horizontals (*rails*) framing panels: also called *wainscot*. *Raised-and-fielded*: with the central area of the panel (*field*) raised up (6b).

PANTILE: roof tile of S section.

PARAPET: wall for protection at any sudden drop, e.g. at the wallhead of a castle where it protects the *parapet walk* or wall-walk. Also used to conceal a roof.

PARCLOSE: *see* Screen.

PARGETING (*lit.* plastering): exterior plaster decoration, either in relief or incised.

PARLOUR: in a religious house, a room where the religious could talk to visitors; in a medieval house, the semi-private living room below the solar (q.v.).

PARTERRE: level space in a garden laid out with low, formal beds.

PATERA (*lit.* plate): round or oval ornament in shallow relief.

PAVILION: ornamental building for occasional use; or projecting subdivision of a larger building, often at an angle or terminating a wing.

PEBBLEDASHING: *see* Rendering.

PEDESTAL: a tall block carrying a classical order, statue, vase etc.

PEDIMENT: a formalized gable derived from that of a classical temple; also used over doors, windows etc. For variations *see* 4b.

PEEL (*lit.* palisade): stone tower, e.g. near the Scottish-English border.

PEND (Scots): open-ended ground-level passage through a building.

PENDENTIVE: spandrel between adjacent arches, supporting a drum, dome or vault and consequently formed as part of a hemisphere (5a).

PENTHOUSE: subsidiary structure with a lean-to roof. Also a separately roofed structure on top of a C20 multi-storey block.

PEPPERPOT TURRET: bartizan with conical or pyramidal roof.

PERIPTERAL: *see* Peristyle.

PERISTYLE: a colonnade all round the exterior of a classical building, as in a temple which is then said to be *peripteral*.

PERP (PERPENDICULAR): English Gothic architecture c. 1335–50 to c. 1530. The name is derived from the upright tracery panels then used (*see* Tracery and 2a).

PERRON: external stair to a doorway, usually of double-curved plan.

PEW: loosely, seating for the laity outside the chancel; strictly, an enclosed seat. *Box pew*: with equal high sides and a door.

PIANO NOBILE: principal floor of a classical building above a ground floor or basement and with a lesser storey overhead.

PIAZZA: formal urban open space surrounded by buildings.

PIEND AND PIENDED PLATFORM ROOF: *see* 7.

PIER: large masonry or brick support, often for an arch. *See also* Compound pier.

PILASTER: flat representation of a classical column in shallow relief. *Pilastrade*: series of pilasters, equivalent to a colonnade.

PILE: row of rooms. *Double pile*: two rows thick.

PILLAR: freestanding upright member of any section, not conforming to one of the orders (q.v.).

PILLAR PISCINA: *see* Piscina.

PILOTIS: C20 French term for pillars or stilts that support a building above an open ground floor.

PINS OR PINNINGS (Scots): *see* Cherry-caulking.

PISCINA: basin for washing Mass vessels, provided with a drain; set in or against wall to S of an altar or freestanding (*pillar piscina*).

PITCHED MASONRY: laid on the diagonal, often alternately with opposing courses (*pitched and counterpitched* or herringbone).

PIT PRISON: sunk chamber with access from above through a hatch.

PLATE RAIL: *see* Railways.

PLATEWAY: *see* Railways.

PLATT (Scots): platform, doorstep or landing. *Scale-and-platt stair*: *see* Stairs and 6c.

PLEASANCE (Scots): close or walled garden.

PLINTH: projecting courses at the foot of a wall or column, generally chamfered or moulded at the top.

PODIUM: a continuous raised platform supporting a building; or a large block of two or three storeys beneath a multi-storey block of smaller area.

POINT BLOCK: *see* Multi-storey.

POINTING: exposed mortar jointing of masonry or brickwork. Types include *flush*, *recessed* and *tuck* (with a narrow channel filled with finer, whiter mortar). *Bag-rubbed*: flush at the edges and gently recessed in the middle. *Ribbon*: joints formed with a trowel so that they stand out. *Hungry-jointed*: either with no pointing or deeply recessed to show the outline of each stone.

POPPYHEAD: carved ornament of leaves and flowers as a finial for a bench end or stall.

PORTAL FRAME: C20 frame comprising two uprights rigidly connected to a beam or pair of rafters.

PORTCULLIS: gate constructed to rise and fall in vertical gooves at the entry to a castle.

PORTE COCHÈRE: porch large enough to admit wheeled vehicles.

PORTICO: a porch with the roof and frequently a pediment supported by a row of columns (4a). A portico *in antis* has columns on the same plane as the front of the building. A *prostyle* porch has columns standing free. Porticoes are described by the number of front columns, e.g. tetrastyle (four), hexastyle (six). The space within the temple is the *naos*, that within the portico the *pronaos*. *Blind portico*: the front features of a portico applied to a wall.

PORTICUS (plural: porticūs): subsidiary cell opening from the main body of a pre-Conquest church.

POST: upright support in a structure.

POSTERN: small gateway at the back of a building or to the side of a larger entrance door or gate.

POTENCE (Scots): rotating ladder for access to doocot nesting boxes.

POUND LOCK: *see* Canals.

PREDELLA: in an altarpiece, the horizontal strip below the main representation, often used for subsidiary representations.

PRESBYTERY: the part of a church lying E of the choir where the main altar is placed. Also a priest's residence.

PRESS (Scots): cupboard.

PRINCIPAL: *see* Roofs and 7.

PRONAOS: *see* Portico and 4a.

PROSTYLE: *see* Portico and 4a.

PULPIT: raised and enclosed platform for the preaching of sermons. *Three-decker*: with reading desk below and clerk's desk below that. *Two-decker*: as above, minus the clerk's desk.

PULPITUM: stone screen in a major church dividing choir from nave.

PULVINATED: *see* Frieze and 3c.

PURLIN: *see* Roofs and 7.

PUTHOLES or PUTLOG HOLES: in wall to receive putlogs, the horizontal timbers which support scaffolding boards; not always filled after construction is complete.

PUTTO (plural: putti): small naked boy.

QUARRIES: square (or diamond) panes of glass supported by lead strips (*cames*); square floor-slabs or tiles.

QUATREFOIL: *see* Foil.

QUEEN-STRUT: *see* Roofs and 7.

QUILLONS: the arms forming the cross-guard of a sword.

QUIRK: sharp groove to one side of a convex medieval moulding.

QUOINS: dressed stones at the angles of a building (6d).

RADBURN SYSTEM: pedestrian and vehicle segregation in residential developments, based on that used at Radburn, New Jersey, U.S.A., by Wright and Stein, 1928–30.

RADIATING CHAPELS: projecting radially from an ambulatory or an apse (see Chevet).

RAFTER: see Roofs and 7.

RAGGLE: groove cut in masonry, especially to receive the edge of a roof-covering.

RAIL: see Panelling and 6b.

RAILWAYS: Edge rail: on which flanged wheels can run. Plate rail: L-section rail for plain unflanged wheels. Plateway: early railway using plate rails.

RAISED AND FIELDED: see Panelling and 6b.

RAKE: slope or pitch.

RAMPART: defensive outer wall of stone or earth. Rampart walk: path along the inner face.

RATCOURSE: projecting string-course on a doocot to deter rats from climbing to the flight holes.

REBATE: rectangular section cut out of a masonry edge to receive a shutter, door, window etc.

REBUS: a heraldic pun, e.g. a fiery cock for Cockburn.

REEDING: series of convex mouldings, the reverse of fluting (q.v.). Cf. Gadrooning.

RENDERING: the covering of outside walls with a uniform surface or skin for protection from the weather. Lime-washing: thin layer of lime plaster. Pebble-dashing: where aggregate is thrown at the wet plastered wall for a textured effect. Roughcast: plaster mixed with a coarse aggregate such as gravel. Stucco: fine lime plaster worked to a smooth surface. Cement rendering: a cheaper substitute for stucco, usually with a grainy texture.

REPOUSSÉ: relief designs in metalwork, formed by beating it from the back.

REREDORTER (lit. behind the dormitory): latrines in a medieval religious house.

REREDOS: painted and/or sculptured screen behind and above an altar. Cf. Retable.

RESPOND: half-pier or half-column bonded into a wall and carrying one end of an arch. It usually terminates an arcade.

RETABLE: painted or carved panel standing on or at the back of an altar, usually attached to it.

RETROCHOIR: in a major church, the area between the high altar and E chapel.

REVEAL: the plane of a jamb, between the wall and the frame of a door or window.

RHONE (Scots): gutter along the eaves for rainwater: see also Conductor.

RIB-VAULT: see Vault and 2c.

RIG (Scots): a strip of ploughed land raised in the middle and sloped to a furrow on each side; early cultivation method (runrig) usually surrounded by untilled grazing land.

RINCEAU: classical ornament of leafy scrolls (4b).

RISER: vertical face of a step (6c).

ROCK-FACED: masonry cleft to produce a rugged appearance.

ROCOCO: style current between c. 1720 and c. 1760, characterized by a serpentine line and playful, scrolled decoration.

ROLL MOULDING: medieval moulding of part-circular section (1a).

ROMANESQUE: style current in the C11 and C12. In England often called Norman. See also Saxo-Norman.

ROOD: crucifix flanked by representations of the Virgin and St John, usually over the entry into the chancel, painted on the wall, on a beam (rood beam) or on top of a rood screen or pulpitum (q.v.) which often had a walkway (rood loft) along the top, reached by a rood stair in the side wall. Hanging rood: cross or crucifix suspended from roof.

ROOFS: For the main external shapes (hipped, gambrel etc.) see 7. Helm and Saddleback: see 1c. Lean-to: single sloping roof built against a vertical wall; also applied to the part of the building beneath. Bellcast: sloping roof slightly swept out over the eaves.
Construction. See 7.
Single-framed roof: with no main trusses. The rafters may be fixed

to the wall-plate or ridge, or longitudinal timbers may be absent altogether.

Double-framed roof: with longitudinal members, such as purlins, and usually divided into bays by principals and principal rafters. Other types are named after their main structural components, e.g. *hammerbeam*, *crown-post* (see Elements below and 7).

Elements. *See* 7.

Ashlar piece: a short vertical timber connecting an inner wall-plate or timber pad to a rafter.

Braces: subsidiary timbers set diagonally to strengthen the frame. *Arched braces*: curved pair forming an arch, connecting wall or post below with a tie- or collar-beam above. *Passing braces*: long straight braces passing across other members of the truss. *Scissor braces*: pair crossing diagonally between pairs of rafters or principals. *Wind-braces*: short, usually curved braces connecting side purlins with principals; sometimes decorated with cusping.

Collar or *collar-beam*: horizontal transverse timber connecting a pair of rafter or cruck blades (q.v.), set between apex and the wall-plate.

Crown-post: a vertical timber set centrally on a tie-beam and supporting a collar purlin braced to it longitudinally. In an open truss lateral braces may rise to the collar-beam; in a closed truss they may descend to the tie-beam.

Hammerbeams: horizontal brackets projecting at wall-plate level like an interrupted tie-beam; the inner ends carry *hammerposts*, vertical timbers which support a purlin and are braced to a collar-beam above.

Kingpost: vertical timber set centrally on a tie-or collar-beam, rising to the apex of the roof to support a ridge piece (cf. Strut).

Plate: longitudinal timber set square to the ground. *Wall-plate*: along the top of a wall to receive the ends of rafters; cf. Purlin.

Principals: pair of inclined lateral timbers of a truss. Usually they support side purlins and mark the main bay divisions.

Purlin: horizontal longitudinal timber. *Collar purlin* or *crown plate*: central timber which carries

collar-beams and is supported by crown-posts. *Side purlins*: pairs of timbers placed some way up the slope of the roof, which carry common rafters. *Butt* or *tenoned purlins* are tenoned into either side of the principals. *Through purlins* pass through or past the principal; they include *clasped purlins*, which rest on queenposts or are carried in the angle between principals and collar, and *trenched purlins* trenched into the backs of principals.

Queen-strut: paired vertical, or near-vertical, timbers placed symmetrically on a tie-beam to support side purlins.

Rafters: inclined lateral timbers supporting the roof covering. *Common rafters*: regularly spaced uniform rafters placed along the length of a roof or between principals. *Principal rafters*: rafters which also act as principals.

Ridge, ridge piece: horizontal longitudinal timber at the apex supporting the ends of the rafters.

Sprocket: short timber placed on the back and at the foot of a rafter to form projecting eaves.

Strut: vertical or oblique timber between two members of a truss, not directly supporting longitudinal timbers.

Tie-beam: main horizontal transverse timber which carries the feet of the principals at wall level.

Truss: rigid framework of timbers at bay intervals, carrying the longitudinal roof timbers which support the common rafters. *Closed truss*: with the spaces between the timbers filled, to form an internal partition.

See also Cruck, Wagon roof.

ROPE MOULDING: *see* Cable moulding.

ROSE WINDOW: circular window with tracery radiating from the centre. Cf. Wheel window.

ROTUNDA: building or room circular in plan.

ROUGHCAST: *see* Rendering.

ROUND (Scots): bartizan, usually roofless.

ROVING BRIDGE: *see* Canals.

RUBBED BRICKWORK: *see* Gauged brickwork.

RUBBLE: masonry whose stones are wholly or partly in a rough state. *Coursed*: coursed stones with rough faces. *Random*: uncoursed stones in a random pattern. *Snecked*: with courses broken by smaller stones (snecks).

RUSTICATION: *see* 6d. Exaggerated treatment of masonry to give an effect of strength. The joints are usually recessed by V-section chamfering or square-section channelling (*channelled rustication*). *Banded rustication* has only the horizontal joints emphasized. The faces may be flat, but can be *diamond-faced*, like shallow pyramids, *vermiculated*, with a stylized texture like worm-casts, and *glacial* (frost-work), like icicles or stalactites.

RYBATS (Scots): *see* Margins.

SACRAMENT HOUSE: safe cupboard in a side wall of the chancel of a church and not directly associated with an altar, for reservation of the sacrament.

SACRISTY: room in a church for sacred vessels and vestments.

SADDLEBACK ROOF: *see* 1c.

SALTIRE CROSS: with diagonal limbs.

SANCTUARY: part of church at E end containing high altar. Cf. Presbytery.

SANGHA: residence of Buddhist monks or nuns.

SARCOPHAGUS: coffin of stone or other durable material.

SARKING (Scots): boards laid on the rafters to support the roof covering.

SAXO-NORMAN: transitional Romanesque style combining Anglo-Saxon and Norman features, current *c.* 1060–1100.

SCAGLIOLA: composition imitating marble.

SCALE-AND-PLATT (*lit.* stair and landing): *see* Stair and 6c.

SCALLOPED CAPITAL: *see* 1a.

SCARCEMENT: extra thickness of the lower part of a wall, e.g. to carry a floor.

SCARP: artificial cutting away of the ground to form a steep slope.

SCOTIA: a hollow classical moulding, especially between tori (q.v.) on a column base (3b, 3f).

SCREEN: in a medieval church, usually at the entry to the chancel; *see* Rood (screen) and Pulpitum. A *parclose screen* separates a chapel from the rest of the church.

SCREENS or SCREENS PASSAGE: screened-off entrance passage between great hall and service rooms or between the hall of a tower house and the stair.

SCRIBE (Scots): to cut and mark timber against an irregular stone or plaster surface.

SCUNTION (Scots): reveal.

SECTION: two-dimensional representation of a building, moulding etc., revealed by cutting across it.

SEDILIA (singular: sedile): seats for clergy (usually for a priest, deacon and sub-deacon) on the S side of the chancel.

SEPTUM: dwarf wall between the nave and choir.

SESSION HOUSE (Scots): a room or separate building for meetings of the minister and elders who form a kirk session. Also a shelter by the church or churchyard entrance for an elder collecting for poor relief, built at expense of kirk session.

SET-OFF: *see* Weathering.

SGRAFFITO: decoration scratched, often in plaster, to reveal a pattern in another colour beneath. *Graffiti*: scratched drawing or writing.

SHAFT: vertical member of round or polygonal section (1a, 3a). *Shaft-ring*: at the junction of shafts set *en délit* (q.v.) or attached to a pier or wall (1a).

SHEILA-NA-GIG: female fertility figure, usually with legs apart.

SHELL: thin, self-supporting roofing membrane of timber or concrete.

SHEUGH (Scots): a trench or open drain; a street gutter.

SHOULDERED ARCH: *see* 5a.

SHOULDERED ARCHITRAVE: *see* 4b.

SHUTTERING: *see* Concrete.

SILL: horizontal member at the bottom of a window-or door-frame; or at the base of a timber-framed wall into which posts and studs are tenoned.

SKEW (Scots): sloping or shaped stones finishing a gable upstanding from the roof. *Skewputt*: bracket at the bottom end of a skew. *See* 7.

SLAB BLOCK: *see* Multi-storey.

SLATE-HANGING: covering of overlapping slates on a wall. *Tile-hanging* is similar.

SLYPE: covered way or passage leading E from the cloisters between transept and chapter house.

SNECKED: *see* Rubble.

SOFFIT (*lit.* ceiling): underside of an arch (also called *intrados*), lintel etc. *Soffit roll*: medieval roll moulding on a soffit.

SOLAR: private upper chamber in a medieval house, accessible from the high end of the great hall.

SOPRAPORTA: *see* Overdoor.

SOUNDING-BOARD: *see* Tester.

SOUTERRAIN: underground stone-lined passage and chamber.

SPANDRELS: roughly triangular spaces between an arch and its containing rectangle, or between adjacent arches (5c). Also non-structural panels under the windows in a curtain-walled building.

SPERE: a fixed structure screening the lower end of the great hall from the screens passage. *Spere-truss*: roof truss incorporated in the spere.

SPIRE: tall pyramidal or conical feature crowning a tower or turret. *Broach*: starting from a square base, then carried into an octagonal section by means of triangular faces; *splayed-foot*: a variation of the broach form, found principally in the south-east of England, in which the four cardinal faces are splayed out near their base, to cover the corners, while oblique (or intermediate) faces taper away to a point (1c). *Needle spire*: thin spire rising from the centre of a tower roof, well inside the parapet: when of timber and lead often called a *spike*.

SPIRELET: *see* Flèche.

SPLAY: of an opening when it is wider on one face of a wall than the other.

SPRING OR SPRINGING: level at which an arch or vault rises from its supports. *Springers*: the first stones of an arch or vaulting-rib above the spring (2c).

SQUINCH: arch or series of arches thrown across an interior angle of a square or rectangular structure to support a circular or polygonal superstructure, especially a dome or spire (5a).

SQUINT: an aperture in a wall or through a pier, usually to allow a view of an altar.

STAIRS: *see* 6c. *Dog-leg stair* or (Scots) *Scale-and-platt stair*: parallel flights rising alternately in opposite directions, without an open well. *Flying stair*: cantilevered from the walls of a stairwell, without newels; sometimes called a *geometric* stair when the inner edge describes a curve. *Turnpike* or *newel stair*: ascending round a central supporting newel (8b); also called a *spiral stair* or *vice* when in a circular shaft, a *winder* when in a rectangular compartment. (Winder also applies to the steps on the turn.) *Well stair*: with flights round a square open well framed by newel posts. *See also* Perron.

STAIR TOWER: full-height projection from a main block (especially of a tower house) containing the principal stair from the ground floor (8a).

STAIR TURRET: turret corbelled out from above ground level and containing a stair from one of the upper floors of a building, especially a tower house (8a).

STALL: fixed seat in the choir or chancel for the clergy or choir (cf. Pew). Usually with arm rests, and often framed together.

STANCHION: upright structural member, of iron, steel or reinforced concrete.

STANDPIPE TOWER: *see* Manometer.

STEADING (Scots): farm building or buildings; generally used for the principal group of buildings on a farm.

STEAM ENGINES: *Atmospheric*: worked by the vacuum created when low-pressure steam is condensed in the cylinder, as developed by Thomas Newcomen. *Beam engine*: with a large pivoted beam moved in an oscillating fashion by the piston. It may drive a flywheel or be *non-rotative*. *Watt* and *Cornish*: single-cylinder; *compound*: two cylinders; *triple expansion*: three cylinders.

STEEPLE: tower together with a spire, lantern or belfry.

STIFFLEAF: type of E.E. foliage decoration. *Stiffleaf capital: see* 1b.

STOP: plain or decorated terminal to mouldings or chamfers, or at the end of hoodmoulds and labels (*label stop*), or stringcourses (5b, 6a); *see also* Headstop.

STOUP: vessel for holy water, usually near a door.

STRAINER: see Arch.

STRAPWORK: decoration like inter-laced leather straps, late C16 and C17 in origin.

STRETCHER: see Bond and 6e.

STRING: see 6c. Sloping member holding the ends of the treads and risers of a staircase. *Closed string*: a broad string covering the ends of the treads and risers. *Open string*: cut into the shape of the treads and risers.

STRINGCOURSE: horizontal course or moulding projecting from the surface of a wall (6d).

STUCCO: decorative plasterwork. *See also* Rendering.

STUDS: subsidiary vertical timbers of a timber-framed wall or par-tition.

STUGGED (Scots): of masonry hacked or picked as a key for ren-dering; used as a surface finish in the C19.

STUPA: Buddhist shrine, circular in plan.

STYLOBATE: top of the solid plat-form on which a colonnade stands (3a).

SUSPENSION BRIDGE: see Bridge.

SWAG: like a festoon (q.v.), but rep-resenting cloth.

SYSTEM BUILDING: see Industri-alized building.

TABERNACLE: safe cupboard above an altar to contain the reserved sacrament or a relic; or architec-tural frame for an image or statue.

TABLE STONE or TABLE TOMB: memorial slab raised on free-standing legs.

TAS-DE-CHARGE: the lower courses of a vault or arch which are laid horizontally (2c).

TENEMENT: holding of land, but also applied to a purpose-built flatted block.

TERM: pedestal or pilaster tapering downward, usually with the upper part of a human figure growing out of it.

TERRACOTTA: moulded and fired clay ornament or cladding.

TERREPLEIN: in a fort the level sur-face of a rampart behind a parapet for mounting guns.

TESSELLATED PAVEMENT: mosaic flooring, particularly Roman, made of *tesserae*, i.e. cubes of glass, stone or brick.

TESTER: flat canopy over a tomb or pulpit, where it is also called a *sounding-board*.

TESTER TOMB: tomb-chest with effigies beneath a tester, either freestanding (tester with four or more columns), or attached to a wall (*half-tester*) with columns on one side only.

TETRASTYLE: see Portico.

THERMAL WINDOW: see Diocletian window.

THREE-DECKER PULPIT: see Pulpit.

TIDAL GATES: see Canals.

TIE-BEAM: see Roofs and 7.

TIERCERON: see Vault and 2c.

TIFTING (Scots): mortar bed for verge slates laid over gable skew.

TILE-HANGING: see Slate-hanging.

TIMBER-FRAMING: method of con-struction where the structural frame is built of interlocking timbers. The spaces are filled with non-structural material, e.g. *infill* of wattle and daub, lath and plaster, brickwork (known as *nogging*) etc., and may be covered by plaster, weatherboarding (q.v.) or tiles.

TOLBOOTH (Scots; *lit.* tax booth): burgh council building containing council chamber and prison.

TOMB-CHEST: chest-shaped tomb, usually of stone. Cf. Table tomb, Tester tomb.

TORUS (plural: tori): large convex moulding, usually used on a column base (3b, 3f).

TOUCH: soft black marble quarried near Tournai.

TOURELLE: turret corbelled out from the wall (8a).

TOWER BLOCK: see Multi-storey.

TOWER HOUSE (Scots): for elements and forms *see* 8a, 8b. Compact fortified house with the main hall raised above the ground and at least one more storey above it. A medieval Scots type continuing well into the C17 in its modified forms: *L-plan* with a jamb at one corner; *Z-plan* with a jamb at each diagonally opposite corner.

TRABEATED: dependent structurally on the use of the post and lintel. Cf. Arcuated.

TRACERY: openwork pattern of masonry or timber in the upper part of an opening. *Blind* tracery is tracery applied to a solid wall. *Plate tracery*, introduced c. 1200, is the earliest form, in which shapes are cut through solid masonry (2a).

Bar tracery was introduced into England *c.* 1250. The pattern is formed by intersecting moulded ribwork continued from the mullions. It was especially elaborate during the Decorated period (q.v.). Tracery shapes can include circles, *daggers* (elongated ogee-ended lozenges), *mouchettes* (like daggers but with curved sides) and upright rectangular *panels*. They often have *cusps*, projecting points defining lobes or *foils* (q.v.) within the main shape: *Kentish* or *split-cusps* are forked.

Types of bar tracery (*see* 2b) include *geometric(al)*: *c.* 1250–1310, chiefly circles, often foiled; *Y-tracery*: *c.* 1300, with mullions branching into a Y-shape; *intersecting*: *c.* 1300, formed by interlocking mullions; *reticulated*: early C14, net-like pattern of ogee-ended lozenges; *curvilinear*: C14, with uninterrupted flowing curves; *loop*: *c.* 1500–45, with large uncusped loop-like forms; *panel*: Perp, with straight-sided panels, often cusped at the top and bottom.

TRANSE (Scots): passage.

TRANSEPT: transverse portion of a cruciform church.

TRANSITIONAL: generally used for the phase between Romanesque and Early English (*c.* 1175–*c.* 1200).

TRANSOM: horizontal member separating window lights (2b).

TREAD: horizontal part of a step. The *tread end* may be carved on a staircase (6c).

TREFOIL: *see* Foil.

TRIFORIUM: middle storey of a church treated as an arcaded wall passage or blind arcade, its height corresponding to that of the aisle roof.

TRIGLYPHS (*lit.* three-grooved tablets): stylized beam-ends in the Doric frieze, with metopes between (3b).

TRIUMPHAL ARCH: influential type of Imperial Roman monument.

TROPHY: sculptured or painted group of arms or armour.

TRUMEAU: central stone mullion supporting the tympanum of a wide doorway. *Trumeau figure*: carved figure attached to it (cf. Column figure).

TRUMPET CAPITAL: *see* 1b.

TRUSS: braced framework, spanning between supports. *See also* Roofs.

TUMBLING or TUMBLING-IN: courses of brickwork laid at right angles to a slope, e.g. of a gable, forming triangles by tapering into horizontal courses.

TURNPIKE: *see* Stairs.

TUSCAN: *see* Orders and 3e.

TUSKING STONES (Scots): projecting end stones for bonding with an adjoining wall.

TWO-DECKER PULPIT: *see* Pulpit.

TYMPANUM: the surface between a lintel and the arch above it or within a pediment (4a).

UNDERCROFT: usually describes the vaulted room(s) beneath the main room(s) of a medieval house. Cf. Crypt.

UNIVALLATE: of a hillfort: defended by a single bank and ditch.

VAULT: arched stone roof (sometimes imitated in timber or plaster). For types *see* 2c.

Tunnel or *barrel vault*: continuous semicircular or pointed arch, often of rubble masonry.

Groin vault: tunnel vaults intersecting at right angles. *Groins* are the curved lines of the intersections.

Rib vault: masonry framework of intersecting arches (ribs) supporting *vault cells*, used in Gothic architecture. *Wall rib* or *wall arch*: between wall and vault cell. *Transverse rib*: spans between two walls to divide a vault into bays. *Quadripartite* rib vault: each bay has two pairs of diagonal ribs dividing the vault into four triangular cells. *Sexpartite* rib vault: most often used over paired bays, has an extra pair of ribs springing from between the bays. More elaborate vaults may include *ridge-ribs* along the crown of a vault or bisecting the bays; *tiercerons*: extra decorative ribs springing from the corners of a bay; and *liernes*: short decorative ribs in the crown of a vault, not linked to any springing point. A *stellar* or *star* vault has liernes in star formation.

Fan vault: form of barrel vault used in the Perp period, made up of halved concave masonry cones decorated with blind tracery.

VAULTING-SHAFT: shaft leading up to the spring or springing (q.v.) of a vault (2c).

VENETIAN or SERLIAN WINDOW: derived from Serlio (4b). The motif is used for other openings.

VERMICULATION: see Rustication and 6d.

VESICA: oval with pointed ends.

VICE: see Stair.

VILLA: originally a Roman country house or farm. The term was revived in England in the C18 under the influence of Palladio and used especially for smaller, compact country houses. In the later C19 it was debased to describe any suburban house.

VITRIFIED: bricks or tiles fired to a darkened glassy surface. *Vitrified fort*: built of timber-laced masonry, the timber having later been set on fire with consequent vitrification of the stonework.

VITRUVIAN SCROLL: classical running ornament of curly waves (4b).

VOLUTES: spiral scrolls. They occur on Ionic capitals (3c). *Angle volute*: pair of volutes, turned outwards to meet at the corner of a capital.

VOUSSOIRS: wedge-shaped stones forming an arch (5c).

WAGON ROOF: with the appearance of the inside of a wagon tilt; often ceiled. Also called *cradle roof*.

WAINSCOT: see Panelling.

WALLED GARDEN: in C18 and C19 Scotland, combined vegetable and flower garden, sometimes well away from the house.

WALLHEAD: straight top of a wall. *Wallhead chimney*: chimney rising from a wallhead (8a). *Wallhead gable*: gable rising from a wallhead.

WALL MONUMENT: attached to the wall and often standing on the floor. *Wall tablets* are smaller with the inscription as the major element.

WALL-PLATE: see Roofs and 7.

WALL-WALK: see Parapet.

WARMING ROOM: room in a religious house where a fire burned for comfort.

WATERHOLDING BASE: early Gothic base with upper and lower mouldings separated by a deep hollow.

WATERLEAF: see Enrichments and 3f.

WATERLEAF CAPITAL: Late Romanesque and Transitional type of capital (1b).

WATER WHEELS: described by the way water is fed on to the wheel. *Breastshot*: mid-height, falling and passing beneath. *Overshot*: over the top. *Pitchback*: on the top but falling backwards. *Undershot*: turned by the momentum of the water passing beneath. In a *water turbine*, water is fed under pressure through a vaned wheel within a casing.

WEALDEN HOUSE: type of medieval timber-framed house with a central open hall flanked by bays of two storeys, roofed in line; the end bays are jettied to the front, but the eaves are continuous.

WEATHERBOARDING: wall cladding of overlapping horizontal boards.

WEATHERING: or SET-OFF: inclined, projecting surface to keep water away from the wall below.

WEEPERS: figures in niches along the sides of some medieval tombs. Also called *mourners*.

WHEEL HOUSE: Late Iron Age circular stone dwelling; inside, partition walls radiating from the central hearth like wheel spokes.

WHEEL WINDOW: circular, with radiating shafts like spokes. Cf. Rose window.

WROUGHT IRON: see Cast iron.

WYND (Scots): subsidiary street or lane, often running into a main street or gait (q.v.).

YETT (Scots, *lit.* gate): hinged openwork gate at a main doorway, made of iron bars alternately penetrating and penetrated (8c).

Z-PLAN: see Tower house and 8b.

INDEX OF ARTISTS

Peebles, Thomas (glazier) 26, 476
Petit, Thomas (surveyor) 716
Philipson, Hylton (landscape architect) 704
Phillimore (Claud) & Aubrey Jenkins (Claud Stephen Phillimore, b. 1911; Aubrey Jenkins) 495
Pilkington & Bell (Frederick Thomas Pilkington, q.v.; J. Murray Bell, 1839–77) 742
Pilkington, Frederick Thomas (1832–98) 33, 80, 397–8, 446, 573, 742–3, Pl. 114
Piranesi, Giovanni Battista (sculptor, 1720–78) 747
Pirie (plasterer) 286
Pirnie, Alexander 360
Pistell, W. (marble-cutter) 703, 704
Plaw, John (c. 1745–1820) 747
Playfair, William Henry (1790–1857) 31, 59, 285–7, 288, 325, 328, 341, 400, 568, 660, 728, Pl. 69
Pocock, Lilian Josephine (glass-stainer) 158, 351, 352
Pollen, John Hungerford (1820–1902) 744
Pollock Hammond Partnership, The (Thomas A.J. Pollock, q.v.; Malcolm T. Hammond, q.v.) 113, 324, 560
Pollock, Thomas A.J. 324, 560; see also Cadell (William A.) Architects
Portsmouth, Percy (sculptor, 1874–1953) 669
Pottinger, Don (painter) 570
Potts, G.H. (tile-maker) 126
Povall, Worthington 164
Powell (plasterer) 530
Powell (James) & Sons (glass-stainers: Arthur Powell; James Cotton Powell; Nathaniel Powell; James Hagan) 34, 449, 548
Pringle, James (builder) 119
Property Services Agency 353
Proudfoot, James (builder) 474
Pugin, Augustus Welby Northmore (1812–52) 420
Purdie (decorator) 327
Purves, John (wright-architect) 447, 573
Pyemont, Tom 189

Rae, Alexander (builder) 110
Railton, William A. (1820–1902) 75, 622
Randolph, Elder & Co. 315
Rasmussen, Michael 190
Reavell, George, Jun. (1865–1947) 185
Redpath, Brown & Co. (engineers: John Brown, 1772–1846; John Stevenson Brown, q.v.) 67, 320, 621, Pl. 88

Reginald the engineer (master carpenter) 671
Reiach (Alan) Eric Hall & Partners see Reiach & Hall
Reiach & Hall (Alan Reiach, 1910–92; Eric Hall; George McNab; James Stuart Renton; W. Alistair Miller; Leslie Mitchell; Jack Oberlander; John Spencely, b. 1939; Tom Bostock; Neil Gillespie) 74, 549, 560
Reid & Forbes (G. Reid; J. Smith Forbes, q.v.) 73, 140, 168, 187, 266, 355, 383, 422, 451, 596, 620, 751, Pl. 103
Reid, John Herdman (d.2004) 512, 762; see also Lindsay (Ian G.) & Partners
Reid, Robert (of Haddington, fl. c. 1740–66) 66, 186
Reid, Robert (of Edinburgh, 1774–1856) 60, 508, 609–10, Pl. 58
Reid, William (sculptor) 221
Renewable Energy Systems 692
Rennie, John (engineer, 1761–1821) 66, 450–1, 739, Pl. 86
Reveillon (wallpaper manufacturer) 609
Rhind, David (1808–83) 32, 70, 75, 76, 147, 245, 307, 360, 382, 424, 430, 509, 622, 648, 670, 675, 711–2, Pl. 96
Rhind, John Stevenson (sculptor, 1859–1937) 40, 257, 660, 695
Rhind, Sir Thomas Duncan (sculptor, 1871–1927) 39, 358
Rhind, William Birnie (sculptor, 1853–1933) 353
Richardson, James Smith (1883–1970) 546
Richardson (W.) & Co. (founders) 123
Ridgeway, William 270, 389, 653
Ridley, H.S. 65, 478
Ritchie, Alexander Handyside (sculptor, 1804–70) 38, 39, 187, 209, 286, 672, Pl. 32
Ritchie, Archibald (sculptor) 708
Ritchie, Robert (mason) 250, 729
Robertson (Charles) & Co. (decorators) 734
Robertson, David (1835–1925) 402
Robertson, James (landscape architect) 757
Robertson, John (builder) 129
Robinson, Robert (landscape architect, b. 1734) 64, 610
Robinson, Robert (sculptor, fl. 1895) 38, 210
Rochead, John Thomas (1814–78) 75, 360, 363
Rodwell, Dennis 129, 359, 551, 659
Roos, Alexander (c. 1810–81) 114, 115
Rose (overseer) 287

Ross, Alexander (surveyor) 393
Ross, Hugh 492–3
Ross, Thomas (1839–1930) 548;
  see also MacGibbon & Ross
Ross-Smith, Stanley Patrick 620
Roubiliac, Louis François (sculptor,
  1702–62) 531
Rowe, Simon (sculptor) 420
Rowley, Liz (glass-stainer) 657
Roxburgh County Council 353, 354,
  355, 365, 555
Roxburghshire County Education
  Authority 424
Roytell, John (master mason) 54
Runciman, James (builder) 58, 532
Rushworth & Dreaper (organ
  builders) 639
Russell, Adam & Thomas (builders)
  647
Russell, Alexander (plasterer) 646
Russell, Alexander L. (glass-stainer,
  fl.1915–56) 503
Russell, Ronald J.J. 596
Rust (mosaicist) 548

Sanderson, Charles (mason) 605
Sanderson & Paterson (builders) 92,
  304
Sanderson, Thomas (joiner) 735
Saracen Foundry (founders) 741
Scarselle (cabinet-maker) 687
Scheemakers, Peter Gaspar (c. 1691–
  1781) 531
Scott, Archibald (c. 1798–1871) 359
Scott, Bill (sculptor, b. 1935) 39, 381,
  Pl. 35
Scott, Sir George Gilbert (1811–78)
  32, 349, 361
Scott (J.N.) & A. Lorne Campbell
  (John Nichol Scott, b. 1863;
  Alexander Lorne Campbell, q.v.)
  39, 72, 353, 358, 752, Pl. 102
Scott, James (builder) 588
Scott, Joanna (glass-stainer) 180
Scott, John (plasterer) 344
Scott, John Oldrid (1841–1913)
  350
Scott & McIntosh (Walter Scott,
  q.v.; John Malcolm McIntosh) 73,
  300, 302, 314, 354, 676
Scott Morton & Co. (decorators and
  cabinet-makers) 62, 63, 197, 319,
  326, 330, 359, 360, 369, 391, 516,
  616, 619, 636, 660, 758
Scott (Schomberg) & R. McInver
  (Walter Schomberg Scott, q.v.;
  R. McInver)
Scott, Walter, 74, 302, 495
Scott, Walter Schomberg (1910–98)
  532, 569–70, 620, 645
Scott, William (builder) 588
Scottish Borders Council 422

Scottish Special Housing Association
  (chief technical officer: Harold
  Ernest Buteux, q.v.) 79, 429
Seitschler, F.D. (sculptor) 39, 231
Selkirkshire County Education
  Department 300
Sherriff, William (sculptor) 154
Shiells (R. Thornton) & Thomson
  (R. Thornton Shiells, 1833–1902;
  James M. Thomson) 298
Shillinglaw, Alexander 755
Shillinglaw, Joseph (joiner) 94, 96
Shotts Iron Co. (founders) 288, 479
Shrigley & Hunt (glass-stainers:
  Arthur William Hunt, 1848–1917;
  Carl Almquist, 1848–1924) 331
Sim 89
Simon, Frank Worthington
  (1863–1933) 397
Simpson & Brown (James Walter
  Thorburn Simpson, q.v.; Andrew
  Stewart Brown, b. 1945; Andrew
  Davey; John Sanders; Elizabeth
  Hurst) 195, 202, 279, 326, 456,
  658, 726, 764
Simpson, James (1831–1934) 515
Simpson, James Walter Thorburn
  (b. 1944) 279
Simpson, Robert Alison Crichton
  (1903–62) 188, 748
Simson, Adam (mason) 224
Singer & Sons (smiths) 261
Skinner, David Neave (landscape
  architect, 1928–89) 549
Slezer, John (surveyor, c. 1645–1717)
  719, 723
Slight, James (c. 1785–1854) 67, 561
Smail, William (mason-architect) 419
Small, David (glass-stainer,
  1846–1927) 34, 231
Smeaton, John (engineer, 1724–92)
  66, 68, 186, 267
Smeaton, William (sculptor) 232
Smirke, Sir Robert (1780–1867) 60,
  593–4
Smith, Alistair M. 571
Smith, George (1793–1877) 469
Smith (George) & Co. (founders) 551
Smith, James (c. 1645–1731) 56, 356,
  730–2, 735, Pl. 52
Smith, James (c. 1779–1862) 238
Smith, James W. 76, 457
Smith, John (mason, c. 1748–1815) 656
Smith, John (architect, sculptor and
  builder, 1782–1864) 38, 60, 65, 67,
  74, 80, 98, 103, 106, 107, 121, 126,
  127, 129, 131, 133, 134, 135, 137,
  138, 163–4, 166, 196, 197, 205,
  206, 224, 225, 226, 249, 250, 253,
  255, 259, 261, 279, 296, 310, 317,
  318, 319, 320, 370, 384, 387, 388,
  400, 430, 451, 464, 470, 484, 485,

INDEX OF PATRONS AND RESIDENTS

Indexed here are families and individuals (not bodies or commercial firms) recorded in this volume as having owned or lived in property and/or commissioned architectural work in Borders. The index includes monuments to members of such families and other individuals where they are of particular interest.

Haig, William, 13th of Bemersyde 119
Haig of Bemersyde, Field Marshal
    Douglas Haig, Earl 120, 218
Haliburton, George 543
Haliburton, John 218
Haliburton of Mertoun, George 224
Haliburton of Newmains family 214
Hall, Lady Helen 172
Hall, Abbot John 410
Hall, Sir John 194
Hall of Dunglass family 193, 759
Hall of Dunglass, Sir James (3rd
    Baronet) 759
Halywall of Duns, Walter 674
Hamilton, George 632
Hamilton, Sir John 184
Hamilton of Grange, Robert 480
Hay family 527
Hay, Sir Adam 634
Hay, Athole Stanhope, and Caroline
    Margaret (Cunard) 526
Hay, Lady Jean 172
Hay of Drumelzier family 213
Hay of Drumelzier, William 239
Hay of Duns Castle family 231, 232,
    241, 243
Hay of Duns Castle, William, 4th of
    Duns Castle 59, 64, 229, 239–40, 244
Hay of Duns Castle, William James,
    5th of Duns Castle 243
Hay of Flemington family 283
Hay of Haystoun(e) family see Hay
    of Smithfield and Haystoun family
Hay of Haystoun, Sir Duncan 369
Hay of Haystoun, John 369
Hay of Locherworth, Thomas 577
Hay of Locherworth, Sir William 577
Hay of Smithfield and Haystoun
    family 369, 614, 635
Hay of Smithfield and Haystoun, Sir
    John (5th Baronet) 634
Hay of Smithfield and Haystoun, Sir
    John (9th Baronet) 630
Hay of Soonhope, Capt. Adam 632
Hay of Yester, John, 8th Lord see
    Tweeddale, 1st Earl of
Hay of Yester, John (C16) 25, 617
Heiton family 205, 206
Hog of Harcase family 289
Hogarth family 334
Hogarth of Hilton, David 761
Hogg family 652
Hogg, James ('Ettrick Shepherd')
    38–9, 149, 261
Home family (Coldingham and
    Jedburgh) 182, 406
Home family (Fast Castle) 276
Home family (Houndwood House)
    386
Home family (Lords Home; Home
    Castle) 389
Home family (Paxton House) 607

Home, Alexander and Elizabeth
    (Hutton Hall) 392, 394–5
Home, Alexander Home, 3rd Lord
    (Hume Castle) 389
Home, Elizabeth Douglas-Scott,
    Countess of (wife of 10th Earl) 381
Home, David Milne 567
Home, Dorothea see Veitch,
    Dorothea
Home, Alexander Home, 1st Earl of
    177, 379
Home, Alexander Home, 7th Earl of
    56, 379
Home, William Home, 8th Earl of 379
Home, Alexander Home, 9th Earl of
    39, 381
Home, Alexander Home, 10th Earl
    of 379–80
Home, Cospatrick Alexander, 11th
    Earl of 379
Home, Charles Alexander Douglas-
    Home, 12th Earl of 642
Home, Major George J.N. Logan 257
Home, Henry see Kames, Lord
Home, General James 642
Home, John, and Margaret Virtue 175
Home, John (son of Alexander) 392
Home Lords 389
Home, Mungo 194
Home, Ninian 607, 609
Home, Patrick see Home of
    Broomhouse, Patrick; Home of
    Wedderburn, Patrick
Home, Rev. Robert 82
Home, Sir Robert 335
Home, William (Stoneshiel Hall) 707
Home, William Forman (Paxton) 606
Home of Ayton, George and John 239
Home of Bassendean family 117
Home of Bassendean, William 116
Home of Billie family 145
Home of Billie, Patrick see Home of
    Wedderburn, Patrick
Home of Blackadder family 196, 256
Home of Blackadder, Sir John 256
Home of Broomhouse, Patrick, and
    Eleanor Wardrop 27, 256
Home of Cowdenknowes family 51,
    194, 246, 435
Home of Cowdenknowes, Sir James
    194, 196, 384
Home of Cowdenknowes, Sir John,
    and Margaret Kerr 196
Home of Crosbie, Alexander 723
Home of the Hirsel, Lord (Sir Alec
    Douglas-Home) 39, 381
Home of Hutton Hall family 51, 392,
    394–5
Home of Linthill, Alexander 501
Home of Linthill, William 501
Home of Wedderburn family 231,
    263, 609

INDEX OF PLACES

Principal references are in **bold** type; demolished buildings are shown in *italic*.

Laidlawstiel **479–80**
Lamancha **480–1**
Lambden House **481**
Lamberton **481**
Langlee Park 62, **481–2**
Langton *see* Gavinton
Lanton **482–3**
Lauder *41*, **483–9**, *716*
  church 29, **484–5**, Pl. 18
  fort and settlement (Haerfaulds)
    489
  stone circle and cairns
    (Borrowston Rig) 11, **488**
  streets and houses 76, 78, 483,
    486–8, 659
  Town House (tolbooth) 69, **485**,
    532, Pl. 93
Lauderdale *11*
Leaderfoot 66, 67, 68, **489**
Leadervale House 60, 153, **489–90**,
  Pl. 72
Lees, The 187, **490**
Legerwood 24, 28, 30, 33, 36, **490–2**,
  Pls. 15, 30
Leithen Lodge 62, 63, **492–3**
Leitholm 29, **493–4**
Lempitlaw 18, **494**
Lennel 7, **494**
Lennel House 191, **494–5**
Lessudden *see* St Boswells
Lessudden House 47, 57, 275, **495–8**
Liddel Castle *see* Castleton
Liddelbank House **498**
Lilliesleaf 26, 35, *82*, **498–500**
Lindean 293, **500**
  Tironensian Abbey 19, 20, 500, 663
Lintalee House **500**
Linthill *10*, 55, **501**
Linthill House **501–2**
Linton **502–4**
  church 24, 25, 26, 33, 35, 36,
    502–3, Pls. 12, 27
  Hoselaw Chapel **504**
Linton Roderick *see* West Linton
Littledean Tower 49, 205, **504–5**
Longformacus 24, 34, 35, **505–7**
  cairns (Dirrington Little Law and
    Dirrington Great Law) 12, 507
  long cairn (Mutiny Stones) 10, **507**
Longformacus House 58, **507–8**
Lowood House **508**
Lyne **509–11**
  Antonine fort 7, 16, 510, Pl. 4
  church 26, 29, 30, **509**, Pl. 19
  fort (White Meldon) 13, **510**
  Meldon Bridge 11, 12, **510**
  palisaded settlement (South Hill
    Head) 13–14, **510**
  platform settlement (Green
    Knowe) 12, **511**
  standing stones (Sherriffmuir) 11,
    510

Macbiehill 38, *378*, **511**
Makerstoun 30, 37, **511–13**
Makerstoun House 84, **512–13**
Manderston House 63, 65, 84,
  513–20, Pl. 77
Marchmont House 58, 63, 65, **520–5**,
  532, 563, 599, Pl. 67
  Redbraes Castle 52, 55, 520, **524–5**
Marlefield House 56, 57, 91n., **526–7**
Maxpoffle House **527**
Maxton 30, **528–9**
  moated site (Muirhouselaw) 41,
    376, **528–9**
Meldon Bridge *see* Lyne
Mellerstain House 38, 58, 59, 64,
  485, 523, **529–33**, 599, Pls. 60–1
  Hundy Mundy 64, **533**
Melrose 9, 26, **533–60**
  Abbey 7, 9, 20, 206, 227, 317,
    505, 533, **534–46**, 559, 644;
    church 20–1, 22, 25, 26, 27, 28,
    412, **535–43**, Pls. 6–7; conven-
    tual buildings and precinct 9,
    22–4, 26, 37, **543–6**, 555
  Bank of Scotland 75, **555**, Pl. 101
  churches 35, 37, **546–9**
  fort (Eildon Hills) 13, 15, **560**
  mansions and villas 81, 259,
    533–4, **558–60**, 687
  Old Melrose *see* Ravenswood
  Ploughlands 7
  public buildings 7, 39, 68, 74, 75,
    77, **549–52**, 649; Market Cross
    69, **550**, Pl. 90
  streets and houses 85, 87, 533–4,
    552–60
Mertoun 67, **560–1**, Pl. 82
Mertoun House 57, 65, 342, **561–5**
Mervinslaw Pele 49, 335, **565–6**, 603
Midlem 84, **566**
Midshiels **566–7**
Milne Graden House 60, **567–8**
Minto 24, 30, 31, 40, 107, *277*,
  568–9, *660*
  Minto House 58, 197, 568, 569
Monteviot House **569–71**
Mordington 84, **571–2**
Morebattle 69, 73, **572–6**
  churches and manse 33, 82,
    572–4, Pl. 112
  fort (Kip Knowe) 14, **576**
  settlements (Crock Cleugh) 17, **575**
Mossburnford House **576**
Mount Ulston **576**
Mow *see* Yetholm
Muirhouselaw *see* Maxton
Mutiny Stones *see* Longformacus

Neidpath Castle 43–4, 56, 160, **576–81**,
  587, Pl. 37
Neidpath Viaduct *see* Kirkton Manor
Nenthorn **581–3**